America's Top-Rated Cities

In-Depth Statistics & Comparative Rankings of the Best Big Cities in America

2025
Thirty-second Edition

America's Top-Rated Cities

In-Depth Statistics & Comparative Rankings
of the Best Big Cities in America

Volume 1: Southern Region

Grey House Publishing

Cover images: Savannah, Georgia

PUBLISHER: Leslie Mackenzie
EDITORIAL DIRECTOR: Stuart Paterson
SENIOR EDITOR: David Garoogian

RESEARCHER & WRITER: Jael Bridgemahon; Laura Mars
MARKETING DIRECTOR: Jessica Moody

Grey House Publishing, Inc.
4919 Route 22
Amenia, NY 12501
518.789.8700 • Fax 845.373.6390
www.greyhouse.com
books@greyhouse.com

While every effort has been made to ensure the reliability of the information presented in this publication, Grey House Publishing neither guarantees the accuracy of the data contained herein nor assumes any responsibility for errors, omissions or discrepancies. Grey House accepts no payment for listing; inclusion in the publication of any organization, agency, institution, publication, service or individual does not imply endorsement of the editors or publisher.

Errors brought to the attention of the publisher and verified to the satisfaction of the publisher will be corrected in future editions.

Except by express prior written permission of the Copyright Proprietor no part of this work may be copied by any means of publication or communication now known or developed hereafter including, but not limited to, use in any directory or compilation or other print publication, in any information storage and retrieval system, in any other electronic device, or in any visual or audio-visual device or product.

This publication is an original and creative work, copyrighted by Grey House Publishing, Inc. and is fully protected by all applicable copyright laws, as well as by laws covering misappropriation, trade secrets and unfair competition.

Grey House has added value to the underlying factual material through one or more of the following efforts: unique and original selection; expression; arrangement; coordination; and classification.

Grey House Publishing, Inc. will defend its rights in this publication.

Copyright © 2025 Grey House Publishing, Inc.
All rights reserved

Thirty-second Edition
Printed in the U.S.A.

Publisher's Cataloging-in-Publication Data
(Prepared by The Donohue Group, Inc.)

America's top-rated cities. Vol. 1, Southern region : in-depth statistics & comparative rankings of the best big cities in america. — 1992-

v. : ill. ; cm.
Annual, 1995-
Irregular, 1992-1993
ISSN: 1082-7102

1. Cities and towns—Ratings—Southern States—Statistics—Periodicals. 2. Cities and towns—Southern States—Statistics—Periodicals. 3. Social indicators—Southern States—Periodicals. 4. Quality of life—Southern States—Statistics—Periodicals. 5. Southern States—Social conditions—Statistics—Periodicals. I. Title: America's top rated cities. II. Title: Southern region

HT123.5.S6 A44
307.76/0973/05 95644648

4-Volume Set	ISBN: 979-8-89179-096-4
Volume 1	**ISBN: 979-8-89179-098-8**
Volume 2	ISBN: 979-8-89179-099-5
Volume 3	ISBN: 979-8-89179-100-8
Volume 4	ISBN: 979-8-89179-101-5

Athens, Georgia

Background	1
Rankings	2
Business Environment	3
Demographics	3
Economy	5
Income	5
Employment	6
City Finances	8
Taxes	8
Transportation	9
Businesses	10
Living Environment	11
Cost of Living	11
Housing	11
Health	12
Education	14
Employers	16
Public Safety	16
Politics	16
Sports	17
Climate	17
Hazardous Waste	17
Air Quality	17

Atlanta, Georgia

Background	19
Rankings	20
Business Environment	23
Demographics	23
Economy	25
Income	25
Employment	26
City Finances	28
Taxes	28
Transportation	29
Businesses	30
Living Environment	32
Cost of Living	32
Housing	32
Health	33
Education	36
Employers	37
Public Safety	38
Politics	39
Sports	39
Climate	39
Hazardous Waste	39
Air Quality	40

Austin, Texas

Background	43
Rankings	44
Business Environment	47
Demographics	47
Economy	49
Income	49
Employment	50
City Finances	52
Taxes	52
Transportation	53
Businesses	54
Living Environment	56
Cost of Living	56
Housing	56
Health	57
Education	60
Employers	61
Public Safety	62
Politics	62
Sports	63
Climate	63
Hazardous Waste	63
Air Quality	63

Cape Coral, Florida

Background	65
Rankings	66
Business Environment	68
Demographics	68
Economy	70
Income	70
Employment	71
City Finances	73
Taxes	73
Transportation	74
Businesses	75
Living Environment	76
Cost of Living	76
Housing	76
Health	77
Education	79
Employers	80
Public Safety	80
Politics	81
Sports	81
Climate	81
Hazardous Waste	82
Air Quality	82

Charleston, South Carolina

- **Background** 85
- **Rankings** 86
- **Business Environment** 88
  - Demographics 88
  - Economy 90
  - Income 90
  - Employment 91
  - City Finances 93
  - Taxes 93
  - Transportation 94
  - Businesses 95
- **Living Environment** 96
  - Cost of Living 96
  - Housing 96
  - Health 97
  - Education 100
  - Employers 101
  - Public Safety 101
  - Politics 102
  - Sports 102
  - Climate 102
  - Hazardous Waste 102
  - Air Quality 103

Clarksville, Tennessee

- **Background** 105
- **Rankings** 106
- **Business Environment** 107
  - Demographics 107
  - Economy 109
  - Income 109
  - Employment 110
  - City Finances 112
  - Taxes 112
  - Transportation 113
  - Businesses 114
- **Living Environment** 115
  - Cost of Living 115
  - Housing 115
  - Health 116
  - Education 118
  - Employers 119
  - Public Safety 119
  - Politics 120
  - Sports 120
  - Climate 120
  - Hazardous Waste 121
  - Air Quality 121

College Station, Texas

- **Background** 123
- **Rankings** 124
- **Business Environment** 125
  - Demographics 125
  - Economy 127
  - Income 127
  - Employment 128
  - City Finances 130
  - Taxes 130
  - Transportation 131
  - Businesses 132
- **Living Environment** 133
  - Cost of Living 133
  - Housing 133
  - Health 134
  - Education 136
  - Employers 138
  - Public Safety 138
  - Politics 138
  - Sports 139
  - Climate 139
  - Hazardous Waste 139
  - Air Quality 139

Columbia, South Carolina

- **Background** 141
- **Rankings** 142
- **Business Environment** 144
  - Demographics 144
  - Economy 146
  - Income 146
  - Employment 147
  - City Finances 149
  - Taxes 149
  - Transportation 150
  - Businesses 151
- **Living Environment** 152
  - Cost of Living 152
  - Housing 152
  - Health 153
  - Education 155
  - Employers 157
  - Public Safety 157
  - Politics 157
  - Sports 158
  - Climate 158
  - Hazardous Waste 158
  - Air Quality 158

Dallas, Texas

Background	161
Rankings	162
Business Environment	165
Demographics	165
Economy	167
Income	167
Employment	168
City Finances	170
Taxes	170
Transportation	171
Businesses	172
Living Environment	174
Cost of Living	174
Housing	174
Health	175
Education	178
Employers	180
Public Safety	180
Politics	181
Sports	181
Climate	181
Hazardous Waste	182
Air Quality	182

El Paso, Texas

Background	185
Rankings	186
Business Environment	188
Demographics	188
Economy	190
Income	190
Employment	191
City Finances	193
Taxes	193
Transportation	194
Businesses	195
Living Environment	196
Cost of Living	196
Housing	196
Health	197
Education	199
Employers	200
Public Safety	201
Politics	201
Sports	201
Climate	201
Hazardous Waste	202
Air Quality	202

Fort Worth, Texas

Background	205
Rankings	206
Business Environment	209
Demographics	209
Economy	211
Income	211
Employment	212
City Finances	214
Taxes	214
Transportation	215
Businesses	216
Living Environment	217
Cost of Living	217
Housing	217
Health	218
Education	221
Employers	223
Public Safety	223
Politics	224
Sports	224
Climate	224
Hazardous Waste	224
Air Quality	225

Gainesville, Florida

Background	227
Rankings	228
Business Environment	229
Demographics	229
Economy	231
Income	231
Employment	232
City Finances	234
Taxes	234
Transportation	235
Businesses	236
Living Environment	237
Cost of Living	237
Housing	237
Health	238
Education	241
Employers	242
Public Safety	242
Politics	243
Sports	243
Climate	243
Hazardous Waste	243
Air Quality	244

Houston, Texas

Background	247
Rankings	248
Business Environment	251
Demographics	251
Economy	253
Income	253
Employment	254
City Finances	256
Taxes	256
Transportation	257
Businesses	258
Living Environment	260
Cost of Living	260
Housing	260
Health	261
Education	264
Employers	266
Public Safety	267
Politics	267
Sports	267
Climate	267
Hazardous Waste	268
Air Quality	268

Jacksonville, Florida

Background	291
Rankings	292
Business Environment	294
Demographics	294
Economy	296
Income	296
Employment	297
City Finances	299
Taxes	299
Transportation	300
Businesses	301
Living Environment	302
Cost of Living	302
Housing	302
Health	303
Education	306
Employers	307
Public Safety	307
Politics	308
Sports	308
Climate	308
Hazardous Waste	309
Air Quality	309

Huntsville, Alabama

Background	271
Rankings	272
Business Environment	274
Demographics	274
Economy	276
Income	276
Employment	277
City Finances	279
Taxes	279
Transportation	280
Businesses	281
Living Environment	282
Cost of Living	282
Housing	282
Health	283
Education	285
Employers	286
Public Safety	287
Politics	287
Sports	287
Climate	287
Hazardous Waste	288
Air Quality	288

Lafayette, Louisiana

Background	311
Rankings	312
Business Environment	313
Demographics	313
Economy	315
Income	315
Employment	316
City Finances	318
Taxes	318
Transportation	319
Businesses	320
Living Environment	321
Cost of Living	321
Housing	321
Health	322
Education	324
Employers	325
Public Safety	325
Politics	326
Sports	326
Climate	326
Hazardous Waste	327
Air Quality	327

McAllen, Texas

Background	329
Rankings	330
Business Environment	331
Demographics	331
Economy	333
Income	333
Employment	334
City Finances	336
Taxes	336
Transportation	337
Businesses	338
Living Environment	339
Cost of Living	339
Housing	339
Health	340
Education	342
Employers	343
Public Safety	344
Politics	344
Sports	344
Climate	344
Hazardous Waste	345
Air Quality	345

Memphis, Tennessee

Background	347
Rankings	348
Business Environment	350
Demographics	350
Economy	352
Income	352
Employment	353
City Finances	355
Taxes	355
Transportation	356
Businesses	357
Living Environment	358
Cost of Living	358
Housing	358
Health	359
Education	361
Employers	363
Public Safety	363
Politics	364
Sports	364
Climate	364
Hazardous Waste	364
Air Quality	364

Miami, Florida

Background	367
Rankings	368
Business Environment	371
Demographics	371
Economy	373
Income	373
Employment	374
City Finances	376
Taxes	376
Transportation	377
Businesses	378
Living Environment	380
Cost of Living	380
Housing	380
Health	381
Education	384
Employers	385
Public Safety	386
Politics	386
Sports	386
Climate	387
Hazardous Waste	387
Air Quality	387

Midland, Texas

Background	389
Rankings	390
Business Environment	391
Demographics	391
Economy	393
Income	393
Employment	394
City Finances	396
Taxes	396
Transportation	397
Businesses	398
Living Environment	399
Cost of Living	399
Housing	399
Health	400
Education	402
Employers	403
Public Safety	404
Politics	404
Sports	404
Climate	404
Hazardous Waste	405
Air Quality	405

Table of Contents

Nashville, Tennessee

Background ... 407
Rankings ... 408
Business Environment ... 411
    Demographics ... 411
    Economy ... 413
    Income ... 413
    Employment ... 414
    City Finances ... 416
    Taxes ... 416
    Transportation ... 417
    Businesses ... 418
Living Environment ... 419
    Cost of Living ... 419
    Housing ... 419
    Health ... 420
    Education ... 423
    Employers ... 424
    Public Safety ... 425
    Politics ... 425
    Sports ... 426
    Climate ... 426
    Hazardous Waste ... 426
    Air Quality ... 426

Orlando, Florida

Background ... 451
Rankings ... 452
Business Environment ... 455
    Demographics ... 455
    Economy ... 457
    Income ... 457
    Employment ... 458
    City Finances ... 460
    Taxes ... 460
    Transportation ... 461
    Businesses ... 462
Living Environment ... 463
    Cost of Living ... 463
    Housing ... 463
    Health ... 464
    Education ... 467
    Employers ... 468
    Public Safety ... 468
    Politics ... 469
    Sports ... 469
    Climate ... 469
    Hazardous Waste ... 469
    Air Quality ... 470

New Orleans, Louisiana

Background ... 429
Rankings ... 430
Business Environment ... 433
    Demographics ... 433
    Economy ... 435
    Income ... 435
    Employment ... 436
    City Finances ... 438
    Taxes ... 438
    Transportation ... 439
    Businesses ... 440
Living Environment ... 441
    Cost of Living ... 441
    Housing ... 441
    Health ... 442
    Education ... 445
    Employers ... 446
    Public Safety ... 446
    Politics ... 447
    Sports ... 447
    Climate ... 447
    Hazardous Waste ... 447
    Air Quality ... 448

San Antonio, Texas

Background ... 473
Rankings ... 474
Business Environment ... 477
    Demographics ... 477
    Economy ... 479
    Income ... 479
    Employment ... 480
    City Finances ... 482
    Taxes ... 482
    Transportation ... 483
    Businesses ... 484
Living Environment ... 485
    Cost of Living ... 485
    Housing ... 485
    Health ... 486
    Education ... 489
    Employers ... 491
    Public Safety ... 491
    Politics ... 492
    Sports ... 492
    Climate ... 492
    Hazardous Waste ... 492
    Air Quality ... 493

Savannah, Georgia

Background.. 495
Rankings.. 496
Business Environment............................. 497
   Demographics..................................... 497
   Economy... 499
   Income.. 499
   Employment...................................... 500
   City Finances................................... 502
   Taxes... 502
   Transportation.................................. 503
   Businesses...................................... 504
Living Environment............................... 505
   Cost of Living.................................. 505
   Housing... 505
   Health.. 506
   Education....................................... 508
   Employers....................................... 509
   Public Safety................................... 510
   Politics.. 510
   Sports.. 510
   Climate... 510
   Hazardous Waste................................. 511
   Air Quality..................................... 511

Tampa, Florida

Background.. 513
Rankings.. 514
Business Environment............................. 517
   Demographics.................................... 517
   Economy... 519
   Income.. 519
   Employment...................................... 520
   City Finances................................... 522
   Taxes... 522
   Transportation.................................. 523
   Businesses...................................... 524
Living Environment............................... 525
   Cost of Living.................................. 525
   Housing... 525
   Health.. 526
   Education....................................... 529
   Employers....................................... 530
   Public Safety................................... 531
   Politics.. 531
   Sports.. 531
   Climate... 532
   Hazardous Waste................................. 532
   Air Quality..................................... 532

Appendixes

Appendix A: Comparative Statistics A-3
Appendix B: Metropolitan Area Definitions A-171
Appendix C: Government Type & Primary County .. A-175
Appendix D: Chambers of Commerce............. A-177
Appendix E: State Departments of Labor A-183

Introduction

This thirty-second edition of *America's Top-Rated Cities* is a concise, statistical, 4-volume work identifying America's top-rated cities with estimated populations of 100,000 or more. It profiles 97 cities that have received high marks for business and living based on our unique weighting system.

Each volume covers a different region of the country—Southern, Western, Central, Eastern—and includes a detailed Table of Contents, City Chapters, Appendices, and Maps. Each city chapter incorporates information from hundreds of resources to create the following major sections:

- **Background**—lively narrative of significant, up-to-date news for both businesses and residents. These combine historical facts with current developments, "known-for" annual events, and climate data.
- **Rankings**—fun-to-read, bulleted survey results from over 100 books, magazines, and online articles, ranging from general (Great Places to Live), to specific (Friendliest Cities), and everything in between.
- **Statistical Tables**—88 tables and detailed topics that offer an unparalleled view of each city's Business and Living Environments. They are carefully organized with data that is easy to read and understand.
- **Appendices**—five in all, appear at the end of each volume. These range from listings of Metropolitan Statistical Areas to Comparative Statistics for all 97 cities.

This new edition of *America's Top-Rated Cities* includes cities that not only surveyed well, but ranked highest using the following criteria: population growth, crime, household income, poverty, housing affordability, educational attainment, and unemployment. Part of the criteria, in most cases, is that it be the "primary" city in a given metropolitan area. For example, if the metro area is Raleigh-Cary, North Carolina, we would consider Raleigh, not Cary. This allows for a more equitable core city comparison. In general, the core city of a metro area is defined as having substantial influence on neighboring cities. A final consideration is location—we strive to include as many states in the country as possible.

You'll find that we have included several American cities despite having lower rankings in some categories. New York, Los Angeles, and Miami remain world-class cities despite challenges faced by many large urban centers. We also decided to include all major cities with historic or cultural significance. For example, Detroit, Michigan, the birthplace of the American automotive industry.

New to this edition are:
Volume 1: Midland, TX
Volume 2: Salem, OR
Volume 3: Green Bay, WI; St. Paul, MN

Praise for previous editions:

> "... [ATRC] has...proven its worth to a wide audience...from businesspeople and corporations planning to launch, relocate, or expand their operations to market researchers, real estate professionals, urban planners, job-seekers, students...interested in...reliable, attractively presented statistical information about larger U.S. cities."
> —ARBA

> "... For individuals or businesses looking to relocate, this resource conveniently reports rankings from more than 300 sources for the top 100 U.S. cities. Recommended..."
> —Choice

> "... While patrons are becoming increasingly comfortable locating statistical data online, there is still something to be said for the ease associated with such a compendium of otherwise scattered data. A well-organized and appropriate update..."
> —Library Journal

BACKGROUND
Each city begins with an informative Background that combines history with current events. These narratives often reflect changes that have occurred during the past year, and touch on the city's environment, politics, employment, cultural offerings, and climate, and include interesting trivia. For example: Tampa, Florida was known as the Cigar Capital of the World in the early 1900s; Wilmington, North Carolina was the site of one of the first rebellions in the United States'

revolt against British rule; and the first mail-order business, Montgomery Ward, was established in Chicago in 1872. Current events include: the most devastating fires recorded in the city of Los Angeles destroyed entire neighborhoods, including Pacific Palisades in January 2025; MARTA (Metropolitan Atlanta Rapid Transit Authority) unveiled its first state-of-the-art CQ400 railcar in early 2025; and Jaialdi, a large Basque festival held once every five years, is being held in Boise City in July 2025.

RANKINGS

This section has rankings from over 100 articles and reports. For easy reference, these Rankings are categorized into 16 topics including Business/Finance, Dating/Romance, and Health/Fitness.

The Rankings are presented in an easy-to-read, bulleted format and include results from both annual surveys and one-shot studies. **Fastest Job Growth** . . . **Best Drivers** . . . **Most Well-Read** . . . **Most Wired** . . . **Healthiest for Women** . . . **Best for Minority Entrepreneurs** . . . **Safest** . . . **Best to Retire** . . . **Most Polite** . . . **Best for Moviemakers** . . . **Most Frugal** . . . **Best for Bikes** . . . **Most Cultured** . . . **Least Stressful** . . . **Best for Families** . . . **Most Romantic** . . . **Most Charitable** . . . **Best for Telecommuters** . . . **Best for Singles** . . . **Nerdiest** . . . **Fittest** . . . **Best for Dogs** . . . **Most Tattooed** . . . **Best for Veterans** . . . **Best for Wheelchair Users**, and more.

Sources for these Rankings include both well-known magazines and other organizations, including *The Advocate*, *Condé Nast Traveler*, *Forbes*, *Kiplinger*, and *National Geographic*, as well as American Lung Association, Asthma & Allergy Foundation of America, National Civic League, People for the Ethical Treatment of Animals, and *Site Selection*.

Rankings cover a variety of geographic areas; see Appendix B for full geographic definitions.

STATISTICAL TABLES

Each city chapter includes 88 tables and detailed topics—45 in Business and 43 in Living. Over 90% of statistical data has been updated. This edition also includes new data on the economy from the U.S. Bureau of Economic Analysis and mortality rates from accidental poisonings and exposure to noxious substances.

Business Environment includes hard facts and figures on 8 major categories, including Demographics, Income, Economy, Employment, and Taxes. *Living Environment* includes 11 major categories, such as Cost of Living, Housing, Health, Education, Safety, and Climate.

To compile the Statistical Tables, editors have again turned to a wide range of sources, some well known, such as the Bureau of Labor Statistics, Centers for Disease Control and Prevention, Federal Bureau of Investigation, U.S. Census Bureau, and U.S. Environmental Protection Agency, plus others like The Council for Community and Economic Research, Federal Housing Finance Agency, and Texas A&M Transportation Institute.

APPENDIXES: Data for all cities appear in all volumes.
- **Appendix A**—*Comparative Statistics*
- **Appendix B**—*Metropolitan Area Definitions*
- **Appendix C**—*Government Type and County*
- **Appendix D**—*Chambers of Commerce and Economic Development Organizations*
- **Appendix E**—*State Departments of Labor and Employment*

Material provided by public and private agencies and organizations was supplemented by original research, numerous library sources and Internet sites. *America's Top-Rated Cities* is designed for a wide range of readers: private individuals considering relocating a residence or business; professionals considering expanding their businesses or changing careers; corporations considering relocating, opening up additional offices or creating new divisions; government agencies; general and market researchers; real estate consultants; human resource personnel; urban planners; investors; and urban government students.

Customers who purchase the four-volume set receive free online access to *America's Top-Rated Cities* allowing them to download city reports and sort and rank these cities by 50-plus data points.

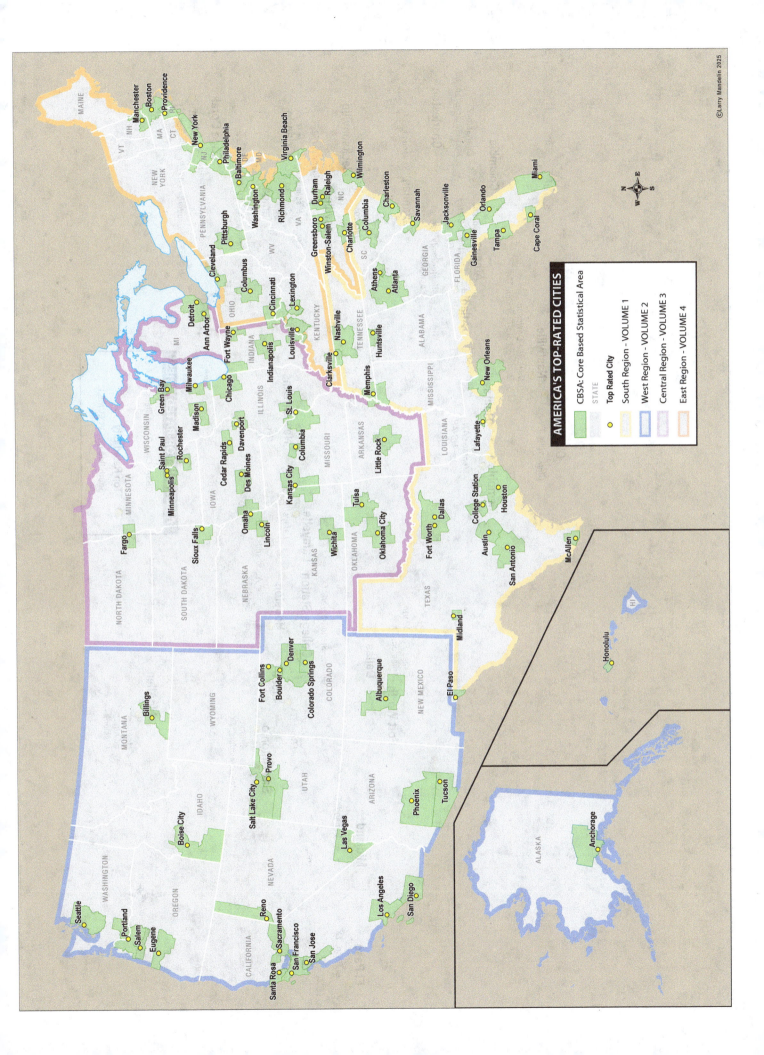

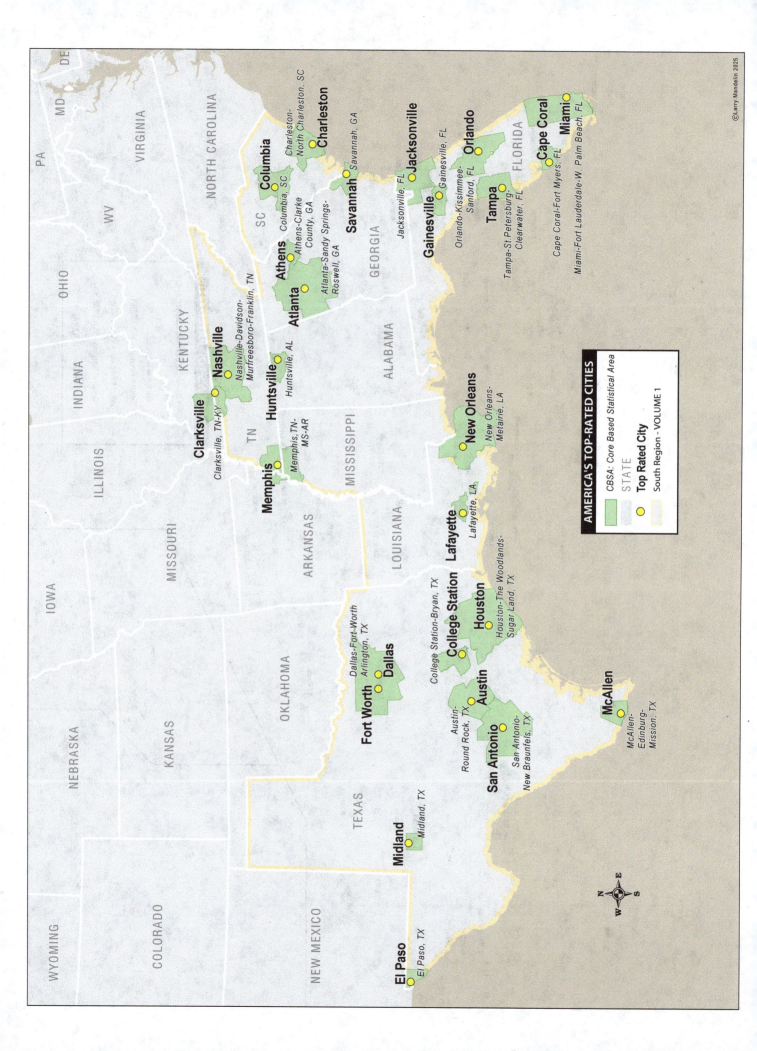

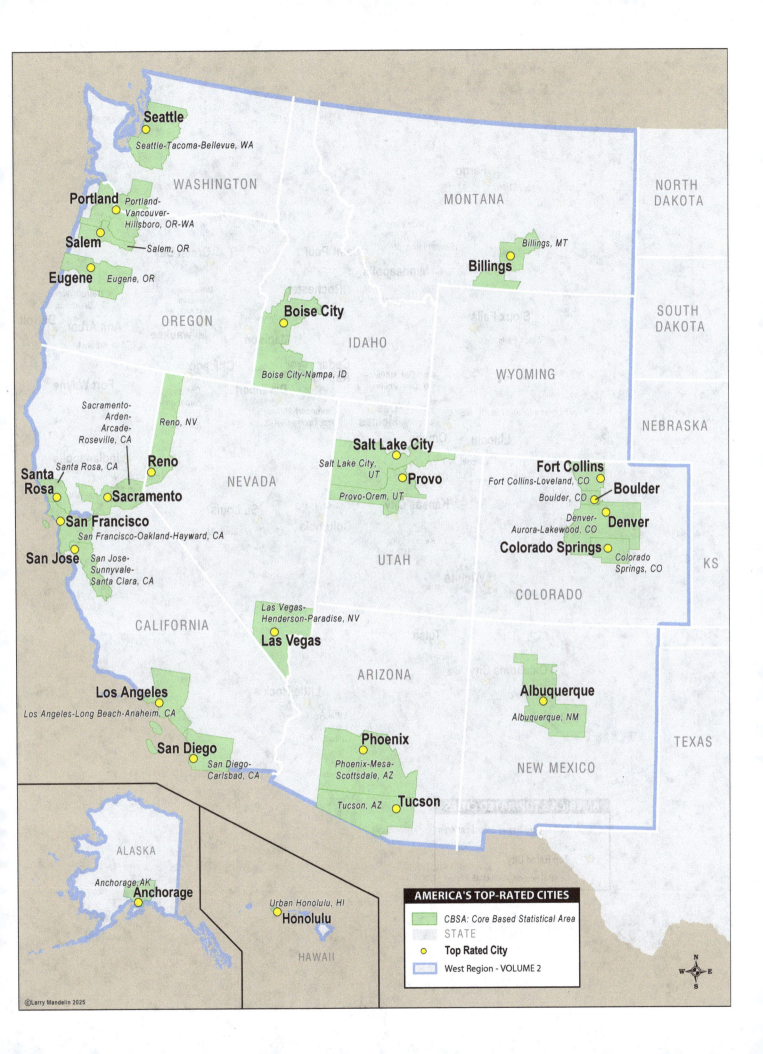

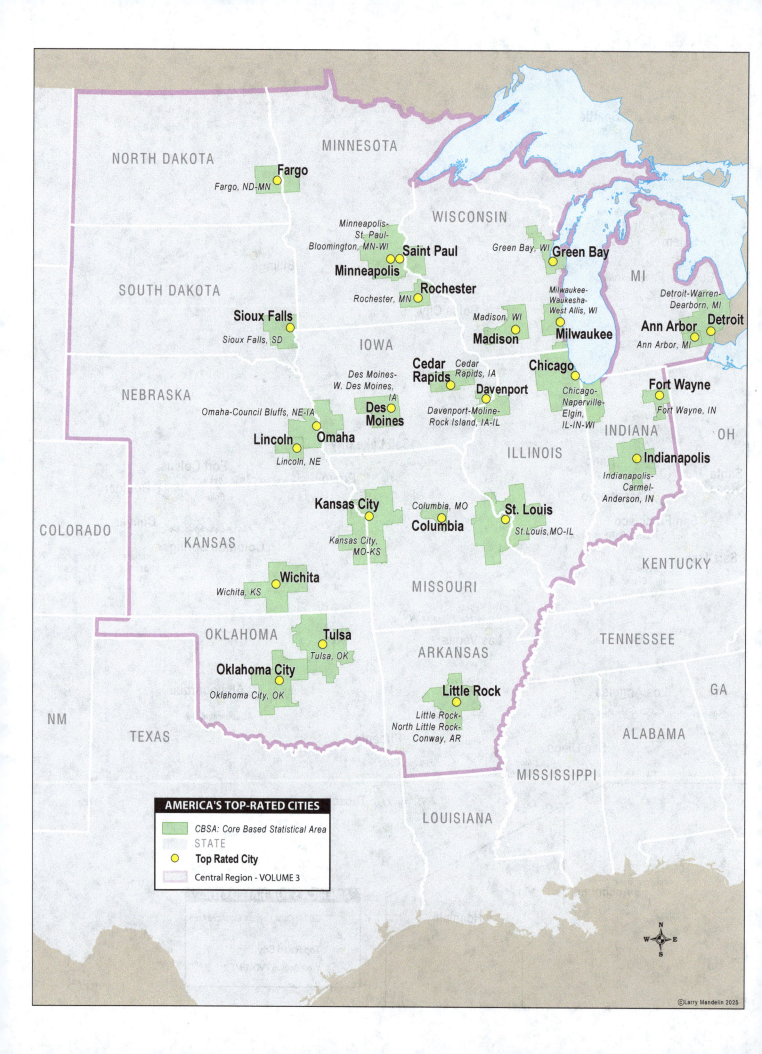

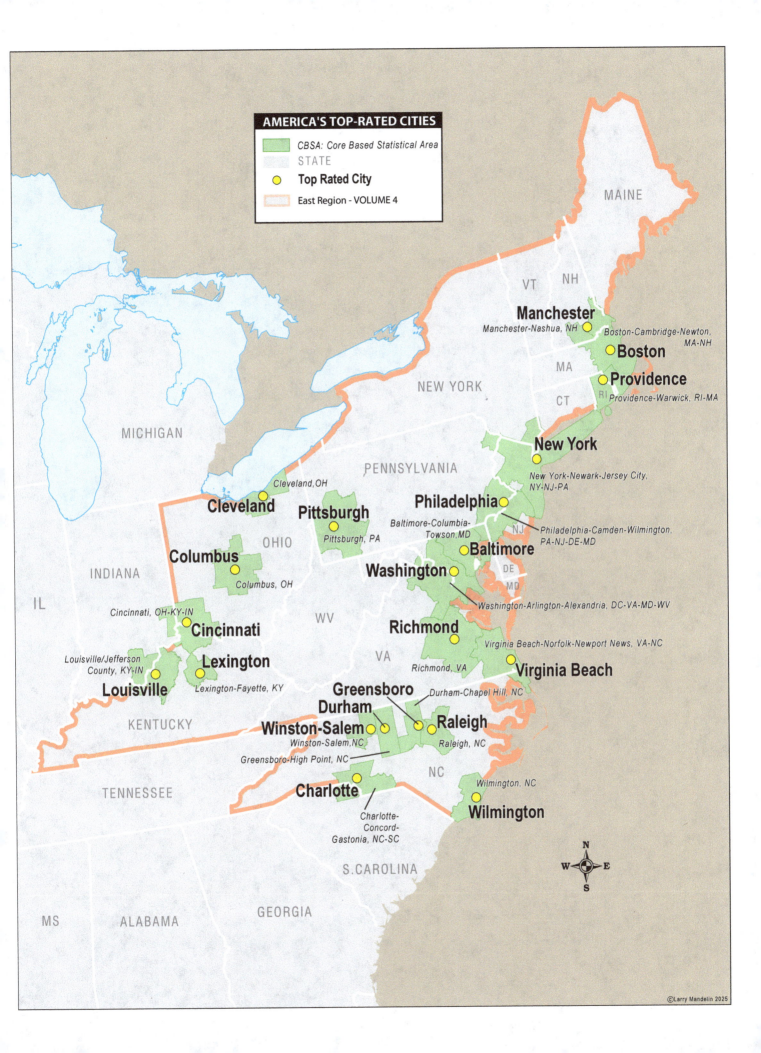

Athens, Georgia

Background

Athens, home to the University of Georgia, retains its old charm while cultivating new ideas. Antebellum homes that grace the city still stand because Gen. William Tecumseh Sherman's March to the Sea took a route that left this northeast Georgia town intact (while burning Atlanta, about 60 miles to the southwest). The Athens Music History Walking Tour, available through the local convention and visitors' bureau, stops at Weaver D's soul food restaurant with the slogan, "Automatic for the People," that went national as the name of locally grown R.E.M.'s 1992 album. In September 2020, the city launched the Athens Music Walk of Fame. The public art walk spans a two-city block loop around West Washington and Clayton Streets connected by North Lumpkin Street. Guitar pick plaques are located on the sidewalk in front of significant music venues like the Georgia Theatre, the 40 Watt Club, and the Morton Theatre. The first round of inductees included The B-52s, Danger Mouse, and R.E.M.

Present-day Athens started as a small settlement where an old Cherokee trail crossed the Oconee River. In 1785 the state's General Assembly chartered the university, which established a campus here in 1801. Three years later, the school held its first graduation ceremony. The city was named for the ancient Greece's center of learning.

A major influence in the city and surrounding Clarke County is the University of Georgia, which is also the area's largest employer. The comprehensive land- and sea-grant institution offers all levels of degree programs in numerous disciplines. Other educational institutions in Athens are the Navy Supply School, Athens Technical College, and branches of Piedmont College and Old Dominion University.

Other major employers focus on health care, government, and manufacturing and include Athens Regional Medical Center and St. Mary's Health Care System, which specialize in oncology, pediatrics, heart disease, and other areas. Manufacturing continues to be a major employment sector, and Athens is home to young tech companies Docebo, RoundSphere, and Cogent Education. Tweed Recording made an already vibrant music scene more so with a new (2018) downtown recording studio, academy and community space.

With its shops, boutiques and restaurants, Athens offers plenty to do. The Georgia State Museum of Art, Museum of Natural History, and the State Botanical Garden are affiliated with the university. The restored 1910 Morton Theater once hosted Cab Calloway, Duke Ellington, and Louis Armstrong, and now hosts dramatic and musical performances. With a strong presence of young people, Athens also has a burgeoning artistic scene. The city center is home to bars, galleries, cafes, and music venues that cater to its creative climate. The annual AthFest is an outdoor celebration of Athen's creative scene in the downtown area. Athens is repeatedly named one of the best places for small business, the best college town for retirees, and the best place to recapture your youth. The city also boasts a bicycle-friendly culture and hosts several annual bicycle races.

The climate is mild, with average temperatures about 20 degrees warmer than the U.S. average. Snowfall is next to nothing, but precipitation is at its highest from January-March. Spring is lovely, with three to four inches of rain, sunshine up to 70 percent of the time starting in April, and temperatures averaging in the 70s.

Rankings

General Rankings

- In their annual survey, Livability.com looked at data for more than 2,000 mid-sized U.S. cities to assign a "Livability Score" for each. The top 100 scoring cities make up Livability's "Top 100 Best Places to Live in the U.S." in 2025. Athens was placed among the top 100 of the customizable list. Criteria: housing and economy; cost of living; environment; education; health care options; transportation; safety; and community amenities. *Livability.com, "Top 100 Best Places to Live in the U.S. in 2025" April 15, 2025*

Business/Finance Rankings

- The Athens metro area appeared on the Milken Institute "2025 Best Performing Cities" list. Rank: #128 out of 203 small metro areas (based on performance category). Criteria: job growth; wage growth; high-tech growth and impact; community resilience; housing affordability; household broadband access. *Milken Institute, "Best-Performing Cities 2025," January 14, 2025*

Seniors/Retirement Rankings

- Athens made the 2024 *Forbes* list of "25 Best Places to Retire." Criteria, focused on overall affordability as well as quality of life indicators, include: housing/living costs compared to the national average and taxes; air quality; crime rates; median home prices; risk associated with climate-change/natural hazards; availability of medical care; bikeability; walkability; healthy living. *Forbes.com, "The Best Places to Retire in 2024: Las Cruces and Other Unexpected Hot Spots," May 10, 2024*

Business Environment

DEMOGRAPHICS

Population Growth

Area	1990 Census	2000 Census	2010 Census	2020 Census	2023 Estimate[2]	Population Growth 1990-2023 (%)
City	86,561	100,266	115,452	127,315	126,987	46.7
MSA[1]	136,025	166,079	192,541	215,415	218,190	60.4
U.S.	248,709,873	281,421,906	308,745,538	331,449,281	332,387,540	33.6

Note: (1) Figures cover the Athens-Clarke County, GA Metropolitan Statistical Area; (2) 2019-2023 5-year ACS population estimate
Source: U.S. Census Bureau, 1990 Census, 2000 Census, 2010 Census, 2020 Census, 2019-2023 American Community Survey 5-Year Estimates

Race

Area	White Alone[2] (%)	Black Alone[2] (%)	Asian Alone[2] (%)	AIAN[3] Alone[2] (%)	NHOPI[4] Alone[2] (%)	Other Race Alone[2] (%)	Two or More Races (%)
City	57.6	26.2	4.3	0.4	0.0	3.4	8.1
MSA[1]	67.1	18.6	3.7	0.4	0.2	3.0	7.1
U.S.	63.4	12.4	5.8	0.9	0.2	6.6	10.7

Note: (1) Figures cover the Athens-Clarke County, GA Metropolitan Statistical Area; (2) Alone is defined as not being in combination with one or more other races; (3) American Indian and Alaska Native; (4) Native Hawaiian and Other Pacific Islander
Source: U.S. Census Bureau, 2019-2023 American Community Survey 5-Year Estimates

Hispanic or Latino Origin

Area	Total (%)	Mexican (%)	Puerto Rican (%)	Cuban (%)	Other (%)
City	11.5	6.1	0.4	0.7	4.2
MSA[1]	9.3	5.1	0.4	0.5	3.3
U.S.	19.0	11.3	1.8	0.7	5.2

Note: Persons of Hispanic or Latino origin can be of any race; (1) Figures cover the Athens-Clarke County, GA Metropolitan Statistical Area
Source: U.S. Census Bureau, 2019-2023 American Community Survey 5-Year Estimates

Age

Area	Under Age 5	Age 5–19	Age 20–34	Age 35–44	Age 45–54	Age 55–64	Age 65–74	Age 75–84	Age 85+	Median Age
City	4.8	19.9	33.9	11.5	9.1	8.9	7.4	3.5	1.1	29.2
MSA[1]	5.0	20.7	26.4	12.2	11.0	10.6	8.8	4.1	1.3	33.2
U.S.	5.7	19.1	20.2	13.1	12.3	12.8	10.0	4.9	1.9	38.7

Note: (1) Figures cover the Athens-Clarke County, GA Metropolitan Statistical Area
Source: U.S. Census Bureau, 2019-2023 American Community Survey 5-Year Estimates

Disability by Age

Area	All Ages	Under 18 Years Old	18 to 64 Years Old	65 Years and Over
City	12.2	5.9	10.1	34.0
MSA[1]	12.8	4.9	11.0	32.7
U.S.	13.0	4.7	10.7	32.9

Note: Figures show percent of the civilian noninstitutionalized population that reported having a disability. Disability status is determined from six types of difficulty: vision, hearing, cognitive, ambulatory, self-care, and independent living. For children under 5 years old, hearing and vision difficulty are used to determine disability status. For children between the ages of 5 and 14, disability status is determined from hearing, vision, cognitive, ambulatory, and self-care difficulties. For people aged 15 years and older, they are considered to have a disability if they have difficulty with any one of the six difficulty types; Note: (1) Figures cover the Athens-Clarke County, GA Metropolitan Statistical Area
Source: U.S. Census Bureau, 2019-2023 American Community Survey 5-Year Estimates

Ancestry

Area	German	Irish	English	American	Italian	Polish	French[2]	European	Scottish
City	9.0	8.9	12.2	3.9	3.1	1.8	1.6	2.7	2.7
MSA[1]	8.8	10.4	13.5	6.1	2.8	1.4	1.5	2.4	2.5
U.S.	12.6	9.4	9.1	5.5	4.9	2.6	2.0	1.6	1.6

Note: Figures are the percentage of the total population reporting a particular ancestry. The nine most commonly reported ancestries in the U.S. are shown. Figures include multiple ancestries (e.g. if a person reported being Irish and Italian, they were included in both columns); (1) Figures cover the Athens-Clarke County, GA Metropolitan Statistical Area; (2) Excludes Basque
Source: U.S. Census Bureau, 2019-2023 American Community Survey 5-Year Estimates

Foreign-born Population

Area	Percent of Population Born in								
	Any Foreign Country	Asia	Mexico	Europe	Caribbean	Central America[2]	South America	Africa	Canada
City	9.8	3.2	2.3	0.9	0.4	1.3	0.8	0.7	0.2
MSA[1]	8.0	2.7	1.7	0.7	0.2	1.1	0.5	0.7	0.2
U.S.	13.9	4.3	3.3	1.4	1.4	1.2	1.2	0.8	0.2

Note: (1) Figures cover the Athens-Clarke County, GA Metropolitan Statistical Area; (2) Excludes Mexico.
Source: U.S. Census Bureau, 2019-2023 American Community Survey 5-Year Estimates

Household Size

Area	Persons in Household (%)							Average Household Size
	One	Two	Three	Four	Five	Six	Seven or More	
City	33.6	35.1	15.3	10.6	4.0	0.9	0.6	2.18
MSA[1]	28.1	35.1	16.5	12.8	5.1	1.7	0.7	2.43
U.S.	28.5	33.8	15.4	12.7	5.9	2.3	1.4	2.54

Note: (1) Figures cover the Athens-Clarke County, GA Metropolitan Statistical Area
Source: U.S. Census Bureau, 2019-2023 American Community Survey 5-Year Estimates

Household Relationships

Area	House-holder	Opposite-sex Spouse	Same-sex Spouse	Opposite-sex Unmarried Partner	Same-sex Unmarried Partner	Child[2]	Grand-child	Other Relatives	Non-relatives
City	40.1	11.6	0.2	2.7	0.2	20.8	2.0	3.7	10.7
MSA[1]	38.6	15.6	0.2	2.3	0.2	25.1	2.3	3.7	7.3
U.S.	38.3	17.5	0.2	2.5	0.2	28.3	2.4	4.8	3.4

Note: Figures are percent of the total population; (1) Figures cover the Athens-Clarke County, GA Metropolitan Statistical Area; (2) Includes biological, adopted, and stepchildren of the householder
Source: U.S. Census Bureau, 2020 Census

Gender

Area	Males	Females	Males per 100 Females
City	60,237	66,750	90.2
MSA[1]	105,119	113,071	93.0
U.S.	164,545,087	167,842,453	98.0

Note: (1) Figures cover the Athens-Clarke County, GA Metropolitan Statistical Area
Source: U.S. Census Bureau, 2019-2023 American Community Survey 5-Year Estimates

Marital Status

Area	Never Married	Now Married[2]	Separated	Widowed	Divorced
City	53.9	31.2	1.3	4.3	9.3
MSA[1]	43.0	41.4	1.3	4.7	9.5
U.S.	34.1	47.9	1.7	5.6	10.7

Note: Figures are percentages and cover the population 15 years of age and older; (1) Figures cover the Athens-Clarke County, GA Metropolitan Statistical Area; (2) Excludes separated
Source: U.S. Census Bureau, 2019-2023 American Community Survey 5-Year Estimates

Religious Groups by Family

Area	Catholic	Baptist	Methodist	LDS[2]	Pentecostal	Lutheran	Islam	Adventist	Other
MSA[1]	6.4	12.8	5.7	1.0	2.4	0.3	0.2	1.3	7.9
U.S.	18.7	7.3	3.0	2.0	1.8	1.7	1.3	1.3	11.6

Note: Figures are the number of adherents as a percentage of the total population and cover the eight largest religious groups in the U.S; (1) Figures cover the Athens-Clarke County, GA Metropolitan Statistical Area; (2) Church of Jesus Christ of Latter-day Saints
Sources: 2020 U.S. Religion Census, Association of Statisticians of American Religious Bodies; The Association of Religion Data Archives (ARDA)

Religious Groups by Tradition

Area	Catholic	Evangelical Protestant	Mainline Protestant	Black Protestant	Islam	Judaism	Hinduism	Orthodox	Buddhism
MSA[1]	6.4	19.1	7.2	2.6	0.2	0.2	0.2	0.1	<0.1
U.S.	18.7	16.5	5.2	2.3	1.3	0.6	0.4	0.4	0.3

Note: Figures are the number of adherents as a percentage of the total population; (1) Figures cover the Athens-Clarke County, GA Metropolitan Statistical Area
Sources: 2020 U.S. Religion Census, Association of Statisticians of American Religious Bodies; The Association of Religion Data Archives (ARDA)

ECONOMY

Real Gross Domestic Product (GDP)

Area	2017	2018	2019	2020	2021	2022	2023	Rank[3]
MSA[1]	10.0	10.3	10.3	9.8	10.4	10.8	11.0	211
U.S.[2]	17,619.1	18,160.7	18,642.5	18,238.9	19,387.6	19,896.6	20,436.3	—

Note: Figures are in billions of chained 2017 dollars; (1) Figures cover the Athens-Clarke County, GA Metropolitan Statistical Area; (2) Figures cover real GDP within metropolitan areas; (3) Rank is based on 2023 data and ranges from 1 to 384
Source: U.S. Bureau of Economic Analysis

Economic Growth

Area	2014	2015	2016	2017	2018	2019	2020	2021	2022	2023
MSA[1]	2.4	4.3	2.2	5.7	3.5	-0.7	-4.3	5.7	4.5	1.5
U.S.[2]	2.6	3.2	2.0	2.7	3.1	2.7	-2.2	6.3	2.6	2.7

Note: Figures are real gross domestic product growth rates and represent percent change from preceding period; (1) Figures cover the Athens-Clarke County, GA Metropolitan Statistical Area; (2) Figures are the average growth rates within metropolitan areas
Source: U.S. Bureau of Economic Analysis

Metropolitan Area Exports

Area	2018	2019	2020	2021	2022	2023	Rank[2]
MSA[1]	378.1	442.1	338.7	448.1	489.9	533.9	217
U.S.	1,664,056.1	1,645,173.7	1,431,406.6	1,753,941.4	2,062,937.4	2,019,160.5	—

Note: Figures are in millions of dollars; (1) Figures cover the Athens-Clarke County, GA Metropolitan Statistical Area; (2) Rank is based on 2023 data and ranges from 1 to 386
Source: U.S. Department of Commerce, International Trade Administration, Office of Trade and Economic Analysis, Industry and Analysis, Exports by Metropolitan Area, data extracted April 2, 2025

Building Permits

Area	Single-Family			Multi-Family			Total		
	2023	2024	Pct. Chg.	2023	2024	Pct. Chg.	2023	2024	Pct. Chg.
City	168	212	26.2	238	960	303.4	406	1,172	188.7
MSA[1]	776	863	11.2	250	972	288.8	1,026	1,835	78.8
U.S.	920,000	981,900	6.7	591,100	496,100	-16.1	1,511,100	1,478,000	-2.2

Note: (1) Figures cover the Athens-Clarke County, GA Metropolitan Statistical Area; Figures represent new, privately-owned housing units authorized (unadjusted data)
Source: U.S. Census Bureau, Building Permits Survey (BPS), 2023, 2024

Bankruptcy Filings

Area	Business Filings			Nonbusiness Filings		
	2023	2024	% Chg.	2023	2024	% Chg.
Clarke County	2	5	150.0	176	189	7.4
U.S.	18,926	23,107	22.1	434,064	494,201	13.9

Note: Business filings include Chapter 7, Chapter 9, Chapter 11, Chapter 12, Chapter 13, Chapter 15, and Section 304; Nonbusiness filings include Chapter 7, Chapter 11, and Chapter 13
Source: Administrative Office of the U.S. Courts, Business and Nonbusiness Bankruptcy, County Cases Commenced by Chapter of the Bankruptcy Code, During the 12-Month Period Ending December 31, 2023 and Business and Nonbusiness Bankruptcy, County Cases Commenced by Chapter of the Bankruptcy Code, During the 12-Month Period Ending December 31, 2024

Housing Vacancy Rates

Area	Gross Vacancy Rate[3] (%)			Year-Round Vacancy Rate[4] (%)			Rental Vacancy Rate[5] (%)			Homeowner Vacancy Rate[6] (%)		
	2022	2023	2024	2022	2023	2024	2022	2023	2024	2022	2023	2024
MSA[1]	n/a	n/a	n/a	n/a	n/a	n/a	n/a	n/a	n/a	n/a	n/a	n/a
U.S.[2]	9.1	9.0	9.1	7.5	7.5	7.6	5.7	6.5	6.8	0.8	0.8	1.0

Note: (1) Figures cover the Athens-Clarke County, GA Metropolitan Statistical Area; (2) Figures cover the 75 largest Metropolitan Statistical Areas; (3) The percentage of the total housing inventory that is vacant; (4) The percentage of the housing inventory (excluding seasonal units) that is year-round vacant; (5) The percentage of rental inventory that is vacant for rent; (6) The percentage of homeowner inventory that is vacant for sale; n/a not available
Source: U.S. Census Bureau, Housing Vacancies and Homeownership Annual Statistics: 2022, 2023, 2024

INCOME

Income

Area	Per Capita ($)	Median Household ($)	Average Household ($)
City	31,836	51,655	76,375
MSA[1]	36,105	62,897	91,841
U.S.	43,289	78,538	110,491

Note: (1) Figures cover the Athens-Clarke County, GA Metropolitan Statistical Area
Source: U.S. Census Bureau, 2019-2023 American Community Survey 5-Year Estimates

Household Income Distribution

Area	Percent of Households Earning							
	Under $15,000	$15,000 -$24,999	$25,000 -$34,999	$35,000 -$49,999	$50,000 -$74,999	$75,000 -$99,999	$100,000 -$149,999	$150,000 and up
City	15.5	10.4	10.3	12.4	16.1	10.9	12.9	11.6
MSA[1]	12.6	8.5	9.0	11.3	15.5	12.1	14.8	16.2
U.S.	8.5	6.6	6.8	10.4	15.7	12.7	17.4	21.9

Note: (1) Figures cover the Athens-Clarke County, GA Metropolitan Statistical Area
Source: U.S. Census Bureau, 2019-2023 American Community Survey 5-Year Estimates

Poverty Rate

Area	All Ages	Under 18 Years Old	18 to 64 Years Old	65 Years and Over
City	26.3	24.3	29.5	11.7
MSA[1]	19.7	19.0	22.1	10.1
U.S.	12.4	16.3	11.6	10.4

Note: Figures are percentage of people whose income during the past 12 months was below the poverty level; (1) Figures cover the Athens-Clarke County, GA Metropolitan Statistical Area
Source: U.S. Census Bureau, 2019-2023 American Community Survey 5-Year Estimates

EMPLOYMENT

Labor Force and Employment

Area	Civilian Labor Force			Workers Employed		
	Dec. 2023	Dec. 2024	% Chg.	Dec. 2023	Dec. 2024	% Chg.
City	61,309	61,837	0.9	59,338	59,852	0.9
MSA[1]	103,836	104,775	0.9	100,776	101,698	0.9
U.S.	166,661,000	167,746,000	0.7	160,754,000	161,294,000	0.3

Note: Data is not seasonally adjusted and covers workers 16 years of age and older; (1) Figures cover the Athens-Clarke County, GA Metropolitan Statistical Area
Source: Bureau of Labor Statistics, Local Area Unemployment Statistics

Unemployment Rate

Area	2024											
	Jan.	Feb.	Mar.	Apr.	May	Jun.	Jul.	Aug.	Sep.	Oct.	Nov.	Dec.
City	3.7	3.5	3.6	2.8	3.7	4.6	4.5	4.5	3.8	4.0	3.3	3.2
MSA[1]	3.4	3.2	3.3	2.6	3.4	4.1	4.0	4.1	3.4	3.6	3.1	2.9
U.S.	4.1	4.2	3.9	3.5	3.7	4.3	4.5	4.4	3.9	3.9	4.0	3.8

Note: Data is not seasonally adjusted and covers workers 16 years of age and older; (1) Figures cover the Athens-Clarke County, GA Metropolitan Statistical Area
Source: Bureau of Labor Statistics, Local Area Unemployment Statistics

Average Wages

Occupation	$/Hr.	Occupation	$/Hr.
Accountants and Auditors	39.24	Maintenance and Repair Workers	20.51
Automotive Mechanics	25.81	Marketing Managers	72.47
Bookkeepers	21.79	Network and Computer Systems Admin.	40.57
Carpenters	22.39	Nurses, Licensed Practical	27.62
Cashiers	12.95	Nurses, Registered	40.42
Computer Programmers	36.03	Nursing Assistants	17.28
Computer Systems Analysts	36.11	Office Clerks, General	20.80
Computer User Support Specialists	24.25	Physical Therapists	45.86
Construction Laborers	19.20	Physicians	148.79
Cooks, Restaurant	15.36	Plumbers, Pipefitters and Steamfitters	26.20
Customer Service Representatives	17.62	Police and Sheriff's Patrol Officers	28.56
Dentists	86.37	Postal Service Mail Carriers	28.08
Electricians	28.38	Real Estate Sales Agents	27.38
Engineers, Electrical	52.45	Retail Salespersons	14.88
Fast Food and Counter Workers	12.25	Sales Representatives, Technical/Scientific	n/a
Financial Managers	70.43	Secretaries, Exc. Legal/Medical/Executive	17.77
First-Line Supervisors of Office Workers	29.73	Security Guards	21.83
General and Operations Managers	48.33	Surgeons	n/a
Hairdressers/Cosmetologists	20.63	Teacher Assistants, Exc. Postsecondary[1]	12.66
Home Health and Personal Care Aides	13.58	Teachers, Secondary School, Exc. Sp. Ed.[1]	31.86
Janitors and Cleaners	14.96	Telemarketers	n/a
Landscaping/Groundskeeping Workers	17.53	Truck Drivers, Heavy/Tractor-Trailer	26.99
Lawyers	49.61	Truck Drivers, Light/Delivery Services	22.11
Maids and Housekeeping Cleaners	13.10	Waiters and Waitresses	12.40

Note: Wage data covers the Athens-Clarke County, GA Metropolitan Statistical Area; (1) Hourly wages were calculated from annual wage data based on a 40 hour work week
Source: Bureau of Labor Statistics, Metro Area Occupational Employment & Wage Estimates, May 2024

Employment by Industry

Sector	MSA[1] Number of Employees	MSA[1] Percent of Total	U.S. Percent of Total
Construction, Mining, and Logging	4,200	3.9	5.5
Financial Activities	3,500	3.3	5.8
Government	30,700	28.7	14.9
Information	700	0.7	1.9
Leisure and Hospitality	12,200	11.4	10.4
Manufacturing	7,200	6.7	8.0
Other Services	3,800	3.6	3.7
Private Education and Health Services	17,100	16.0	16.9
Professional and Business Services	9,400	8.8	14.2
Retail Trade	11,900	11.1	10.0
Transportation, Warehousing, and Utilities	1,900	1.8	4.8
Wholesale Trade	4,300	4.0	3.9

Note: Figures are non-farm employment as of December 2024. Figures are not seasonally adjusted and include workers 16 years of age and older; (1) Figures cover the Athens-Clarke County, GA Metropolitan Statistical Area
Source: Bureau of Labor Statistics, Current Employment Statistics, Employment, Hours, and Earnings

Employment by Occupation

Occupation Classification	City (%)	MSA[1] (%)	U.S. (%)
Management, Business, Science, and Arts	46.0	44.8	42.0
Natural Resources, Construction, and Maintenance	5.5	7.0	8.6
Production, Transportation, and Material Moving	12.3	12.4	13.0
Sales and Office	16.8	18.5	19.9
Service	19.4	17.3	16.5

Note: Figures cover employed civilians 16 years of age and older; (1) Figures cover the Athens-Clarke County, GA Metropolitan Statistical Area
Source: U.S. Census Bureau, 2019-2023 American Community Survey 5-Year Estimates

Occupations with Greatest Projected Employment Growth: 2022 – 2032

Occupation[1]	2022 Employment	2032 Projected Employment	Numeric Employment Change	Percent Employment Change
Fast Food and Counter Workers	116,400	132,810	16,410	14.1
Laborers and Freight, Stock, and Material Movers, Hand	122,550	138,390	15,840	12.9
Stockers and Order Fillers	87,050	101,950	14,900	17.1
Cooks, Restaurant	41,200	56,070	14,870	36.1
Software Developers	46,900	60,700	13,800	29.4
General and Operations Managers	101,650	115,240	13,590	13.4
Retail Salespersons	137,730	150,700	12,970	9.4
Registered Nurses	81,800	94,310	12,510	15.3
Heavy and Tractor-Trailer Truck Drivers	78,240	90,230	11,990	15.3
Home Health and Personal Care Aides	36,890	46,020	9,130	24.7

Note: Projections cover Georgia; (1) Sorted by numeric employment change
Source: www.projectionscentral.org, State Occupational Projections, 2022–2032 Long-Term Projections

Fastest-Growing Occupations: 2022 – 2032

Occupation[1]	2022 Employment	2032 Projected Employment	Numeric Employment Change	Percent Employment Change
Nurse Practitioners	7,900	12,500	4,600	58.2
Data Scientists	5,340	7,680	2,340	43.8
Statisticians	520	720	200	38.5
Cooks, Restaurant	41,200	56,070	14,870	36.1
Recreational Vehicle Service Technicians	310	420	110	35.5
Medical and Health Services Managers	8,760	11,860	3,100	35.4
Entertainment Attendants and Related Workers, All Other	600	810	210	35.0
Rail Yard Engineers, Dinkey Operators, and Hostlers	230	310	80	34.8
Information Security Analysts (SOC 2018)	4,990	6,710	1,720	34.5
Actuaries	350	470	120	34.3

Note: Projections cover Georgia; (1) Sorted by percent employment change and excludes occupations with numeric employment change less than 50
Source: www.projectionscentral.org, State Occupational Projections, 2022–2032 Long-Term Projections

CITY FINANCES

City Government Finances

Component	2022 ($000)	2022 ($ per capita)
Total Revenues	360,272	2,819
Total Expenditures	316,018	2,473
Debt Outstanding	424,288	3,320

Source: U.S. Census Bureau, State & Local Government Finances 2022

City Government Revenue by Source

Source	2022 ($000)	2022 ($ per capita)	2022 (%)
General Revenue			
From Federal Government	31,019	243	8.6
From State Government	5,177	41	1.4
From Local Governments	100,188	784	27.8
Taxes			
Property	80,771	632	22.4
Sales and Gross Receipts	26,435	207	7.3
Personal Income	0	0	0.0
Corporate Income	0	0	0.0
Motor Vehicle License	0	0	0.0
Other Taxes	5,784	45	1.6
Current Charges	84,025	657	23.3
Liquor Store	0	0	0.0
Utility	18,670	146	5.2

Source: U.S. Census Bureau, State & Local Government Finances 2022

City Government Expenditures by Function

Function	2022 ($000)	2022 ($ per capita)	2022 (%)
General Direct Expenditures			
Air Transportation	3,760	29	1.2
Corrections	15,523	121	4.9
Education	0	0	0.0
Employment Security Administration	0	0	0.0
Financial Administration	10,546	82	3.3
Fire Protection	16,217	126	5.1
General Public Buildings	8,067	63	2.6
Governmental Administration, Other	25,021	195	7.9
Health	2,626	20	0.8
Highways	24,300	190	7.7
Hospitals	0	0	0.0
Housing and Community Development	0	0	0.0
Interest on General Debt	19,525	152	6.2
Judicial and Legal	14,493	113	4.6
Libraries	7,108	55	2.2
Parking	0	0	0.0
Parks and Recreation	27,450	214	8.7
Police Protection	31,303	244	9.9
Public Welfare	765	6	0.2
Sewerage	18,302	143	5.8
Solid Waste Management	17,022	133	5.4
Veterans' Services	0	0	0.0
Liquor Store	0	0	0.0
Utility	21,995	172	7.0

Source: U.S. Census Bureau, State & Local Government Finances 2022

TAXES

State Corporate Income Tax Rates

State	Tax Rate (%)	Income Brackets ($)	Num. of Brackets	Financial Institution Tax Rate (%)[a]	Federal Income Tax Ded.
Georgia	5.75 - 6.0	Flat rate	1	5.75	No

Note: Tax rates for tax year 2024; (a) Rates listed are the corporate income tax rate applied to financial institutions or excise taxes based on income. Some states have other taxes based upon the value of deposits or shares.
Source: Federation of Tax Administrators, State Corporate Income Tax Rates, January 1, 2025

State Individual Income Tax Rates

State	Tax Rate (%)	Income Brackets ($)	Personal Exemptions ($)			Standard Ded. ($)	
			Single	Married	Depend.	Single	Married
Georgia	5.5	Flat rate	–	–	–	12,000	18,500 (i)

Note: Tax rates for tax year 2024; Local- and county-level taxes are not included; Federal income tax is not deductible on state income tax returns; (i) GA moves to a flat tax rate regime, eliminates the personal exemption and increases the standard deduction amounts for single, HOH and married jointly filers.
Source: Federation of Tax Administrators, State Individual Income Tax Rates, January 1, 2025

Various State Sales and Excise Tax Rates

State	State Sales Tax (%)	Gasoline[1] ($/gal.)	Cigarette[2] ($/pack)	Spirits[3] ($/gal.)	Wine[4] ($/gal.)	Beer[5] ($/gal.)	Recreational Marijuana (%)
Georgia	4	0.34	0.37	3.79	1.51	0.48	Not legal

Note: All tax rates as of January 1, 2025; (1) The American Petroleum Institute has developed a methodology for determining the average tax rate on a gallon of fuel. Rates may include any of the following: excise taxes, environmental fees, storage tank fees, other fees or taxes, general sales tax, and local taxes; (2) The federal excise tax of $1.0066 per pack and local taxes are not included; (3) Rates are those applicable to off-premise sales of 40% alcohol by volume (a.b.v.) distilled spirits in 750ml containers. Local excise taxes are excluded; (4) Rates are those applicable to off-premise sales of 11% a.b.v. non-carbonated wine in 750ml containers; (5) Rates are those applicable to off-premise sales of 4.7% a.b.v. beer in 12 ounce containers.
Source: Tax Foundation, 2025 Facts & Figures: How Does Your State Compare?

State Tax Competitiveness Index

State	Overall Rank	Corporate Tax Rank	Individual Income Tax Rank	Sales Tax Rank	Property Tax Rank	Unemployment Insurance Tax Rank
Georgia	26	12	31	23	34	24

Note: The Tax Foundation's State Tax Competitiveness Index enables policymakers, taxpayers, and business leaders to gauge how their states' tax systems compare. A rank of 1 is best, 50 is worst. Rankings do not average to the total. States without a tax rank equally as 1. DC's scores and rankings do not affect other states. The report shows tax systems as of July 1, 2024 (the beginning of Fiscal Year 2025).
Source: Tax Foundation, State Tax Competitiveness Index 2025

TRANSPORTATION

Means of Transportation to Work

Area	Car/Truck/Van		Public Transportation			Bicycle	Walked	Other Means	Worked at Home
	Drove Alone	Car-pooled	Bus	Subway	Railroad				
City	72.0	7.8	2.1	0.0	0.0	0.9	4.5	0.8	11.9
MSA[1]	74.7	7.3	1.3	0.0	0.0	0.6	3.3	0.9	12.1
U.S.	70.2	8.5	1.7	1.3	0.4	0.4	2.4	1.6	13.5

Note: Figures are percentages and cover workers 16 years of age and older; (1) Figures cover the Athens-Clarke County, GA Metropolitan Statistical Area
Source: U.S. Census Bureau, 2019-2023 American Community Survey 5-Year Estimates

Travel Time to Work

Area	Less Than 10 Minutes	10 to 19 Minutes	20 to 29 Minutes	30 to 44 Minutes	45 to 59 Minutes	60 to 89 Minutes	90 Minutes or More
City	17.2	45.0	17.6	10.5	3.8	3.6	2.3
MSA[1]	13.4	38.2	22.3	13.7	5.2	4.1	3.0
U.S.	12.6	28.6	21.2	20.8	8.1	6.0	2.8

Note: Note: Figures are percentages and include workers 16 years old and over; (1) Figures cover the Athens-Clarke County, GA Metropolitan Statistical Area
Source: U.S. Census Bureau, 2019-2023 American Community Survey 5-Year Estimates

Key Congestion Measures

Measure	2000	2010	2015	2020	2022
Annual Hours of Delay, Total (000)	n/a	n/a	3,417	1,707	4,154
Annual Hours of Delay, Per Auto Commuter	n/a	n/a	24	12	29
Annual Congestion Cost, Per Auto Commuter ($)	n/a	n/a	555	286	658

Note: n/a not available
Source: Texas A&M Transportation Institute, 2023 Urban Mobility Report

Freeway Travel Time Index

Measure	1985	1990	1995	2000	2005	2010	2015	2020	2022
Urban Area Index[1]	n/a	n/a	n/a	n/a	n/a	n/a	1.09	1.05	1.12
Urban Area Rank[1,2]	n/a	n/a	n/a	n/a	n/a	n/a	n/a	n/a	n/a

Note: Freeway Travel Time Index—the ratio of travel time in the peak period to the travel time at free-flow conditions. For example, a value of 1.30 indicates a 20-minute free-flow trip takes 26 minutes in the peak (20 minutes x 1.30 = 26 minutes). (1) Covers the Athens-Clarke County GA urban area; (2) Rank is based on 101 larger urban areas (#1 = highest travel time index); n/a not available
Source: Texas A&M Transportation Institute, 2023 Urban Mobility Report

Public Transportation

Agency Name / Mode of Transportation	Vehicles Operated in Maximum Service[1]	Annual Unlinked Passenger Trips[2] (in thous.)	Annual Passenger Miles[3] (in thous.)
Athens Transit System			
Bus (directly operated)	18	1,183.2	4,180.5
Demand Response (directly operated)	2	3.6	16.8

Note: (1) Number of revenue vehicles operated by the given mode and type of service to meet the annual maximum service requirement. This is the revenue vehicle count during the peak season of the year; on the week and day that maximum service is provided. Vehicles operated in maximum service (VOMS) exclude atypical days and one-time special events; (2) Number of passengers who boarded public transportation vehicles. Passengers are counted each time they board a vehicle no matter how many vehicles they use to travel from their origin to their destination. (3) Sum of the distances ridden by all passengers during the entire fiscal year.
Source: Federal Transit Administration, National Transit Database, 2023

Air Transportation

Airport Name and Code / Type of Service	Passenger Airlines[1]	Passenger Enplanements	Freight Carriers[2]	Freight (lbs)
Athens Municipal (AHN)				
Domestic service (U.S. carriers only)	6	1,935	0	0
International service (U.S. carriers only)	0	0	0	0

Note: (1) Includes all U.S.-based major, minor and commuter airlines that carried at least one passenger during the year; (2) Includes all U.S.-based airlines and freight carriers that transported at least one pound of freight during the year.
Source: Bureau of Transportation Statistics, The Intermodal Transportation Database, Air Carriers: T-100 Domestic Market (U.S. carriers only), 2024; Bureau of Transportation Statistics, The Intermodal Transportation Database, Air Carriers: T-100 International Market (U.S. carriers only), 2024

BUSINESSES

Major Business Headquarters

Company Name	Industry	Rankings	
		Fortune[1]	Forbes[2]
No companies listed	-	-	-

Note: (1) Companies that produce a 10-K are ranked 1 to 500 based on 2023 revenue; (2) All private companies with at least $2 billion in annual revenue through the end of their most current fiscal year are ranked 1 to 275; companies listed are headquartered in the city; dashes indicate no ranking
Source: Fortune, "Fortune 500," 2024; Forbes, "America's Largest Private Companies," 2024

Living Environment

COST OF LIVING

Cost of Living Index

Composite Index	Groceries	Housing	Utilities	Transportation	Health Care	Misc. Goods/Services
98.9	100.4	97.3	99.4	95.0	96.7	100.8

Note: The Cost of Living Index measures regional differences in the cost of consumer goods and services, excluding taxes and non-consumer expenditures, for professional and managerial households in the top income quintile. It is based on more than 50,000 prices covering almost 60 different items for which prices are collected three times a year by chambers of commerce, economic development organizations or university applied economic centers in each participating urban area. The numbers shown should be read as a percentage above or below the national average of 100. For example, a value of 115.4 in the groceries column indicates that grocery prices are 15.4% higher than the national average. Small differences in the index numbers should not be interpreted as significant; Figures cover the Athens GA urban area.
Source: The Council for Community and Economic Research, Cost of Living Index, 2024

Grocery Prices

Area[1]	T-Bone Steak ($/pound)	Frying Chicken ($/pound)	Whole Milk ($/half gal.)	Eggs ($/dozen)	Orange Juice ($/64 oz.)	Coffee ($/11.5 oz.)
City[2]	15.55	1.45	4.70	3.57	4.49	5.28
Avg.	15.42	1.55	4.69	3.25	4.41	5.46
Min.	14.50	1.16	4.43	2.75	4.00	4.85
Max.	17.56	2.89	5.49	4.78	5.54	7.89

Note: (1) Values for the local area are compared with the average, minimum and maximum values for all 276 areas in the Cost of Living Index; (2) Figures cover the Athens GA urban area; **T-Bone Steak** (price per pound); **Frying Chicken** (price per pound, whole fryer); **Whole Milk** (half gallon carton); **Eggs** (price per dozen, Grade A, large); **Orange Juice** (64 oz. Tropicana or Florida Natural); **Coffee** (11.5 oz. can, vacuum-packed, Maxwell House, Hills Bros, or Folgers).
Source: The Council for Community and Economic Research, Cost of Living Index, 2024

Housing and Utility Costs

Area[1]	New Home Price ($)	Apartment Rent ($/month)	All Electric ($/month)	Part Electric ($/month)	Other Energy ($/month)	Telephone ($/month)
City[2]	483,427	1,622	-	113.87	91.54	192.87
Avg.	515,975	1,550	210.99	123.07	82.07	194.99
Min.	265,375	692	104.33	53.68	36.26	179.42
Max.	2,775,821	5,719	529.02	397.28	361.63	223.33

Note: (1) Values for the local area are compared with the average, minimum and maximum values for all 276 areas in the Cost of Living Index; (2) Figures cover the Athens GA urban area; **New Home Price** (2,400 sf living area, 8,000 sf lot, in urban area with full utilities); **Apartment Rent** (950 sf 2 bedroom/1.5 or 2 bath, unfurnished, excluding all utilities except water); **All Electric** (average monthly cost for an all-electric home); **Part Electric** (average monthly cost for a part-electric home); **Other Energy** (average monthly cost for natural gas, fuel oil, coal, wood, and any other forms of energy except electricity); **Telephone** (price includes the base monthly rate plus taxes and fees for three lines of mobile phone service).
Source: The Council for Community and Economic Research, Cost of Living Index, 2024

Health Care, Transportation, and Other Costs

Area[1]	Doctor ($/visit)	Dentist ($/visit)	Optometrist ($/visit)	Gasoline ($/gallon)	Beauty Salon ($/visit)	Men's Shirt ($)
City[2]	123.75	128.33	97.63	3.12	56.40	40.51
Avg.	143.77	117.51	129.23	3.32	48.57	38.14
Min.	36.74	58.67	67.33	2.80	24.00	13.41
Max.	270.44	216.82	307.33	5.28	94.00	63.89

Note: (1) Values for the local area are compared with the average, minimum and maximum values for all 276 areas in the Cost of Living Index; (2) Figures cover the Athens GA urban area; **Doctor** (general practitioners routine exam of an established patient); **Dentist** (adult teeth cleaning and periodic oral examination); **Optometrist** (full vision eye exam for established adult patient); **Gasoline** (one gallon regular unleaded, national brand, including all taxes, cash price at self-service pump if available); **Beauty Salon** (woman's shampoo, trim, and blow-dry); **Men's Shirt** (cotton/polyester dress shirt, pinpoint weave, long sleeves).
Source: The Council for Community and Economic Research, Cost of Living Index, 2024

HOUSING

Homeownership Rate

Area	2017 (%)	2018 (%)	2019 (%)	2020 (%)	2021 (%)	2022 (%)	2023 (%)	2024 (%)
MSA[1]	n/a	n/a	n/a	n/a	n/a	n/a	n/a	n/a
U.S.	63.9	64.4	64.6	66.6	65.5	65.8	65.9	65.6

Note: (1) Figures cover the Athens-Clarke County, GA Metropolitan Statistical Area; n/a not available
Source: U.S. Census Bureau, Housing Vacancies and Homeownership Annual Statistics: 2017-2024

House Price Index (HPI)

Area	National Ranking[2]	Quarterly Change (%)	One-Year Change (%)	Five-Year Change (%)	Since 1991Q1 (%)
MSA[1]	145	0.95	4.82	77.54	363.29
U.S.[3]	—	1.43	4.51	57.13	327.82

Note: The HPI is a weighted repeat sales index. It measures average price changes in repeat sales or refinancings on the same properties. This information is obtained by reviewing repeat mortgage transactions on single-family properties whose mortgages have been purchased or securitized by Fannie Mae or Freddie Mac since January 1975; (1) Figures cover the Athens-Clarke County, GA Metropolitan Statistical Area; (2) Rankings are based on annual percentage change for all metro areas containing at least 15,000 transactions over the last 10 years and ranges from 1 to 241; (3) figures based on a weighted average of Census Division estimates using a seasonally adjusted, purchase-only index; all figures are for the period ending December 31, 2024
Source: Federal Housing Finance Agency, Change in FHFA Metropolitan Area House Price Indexes, All Transactions Index, 2024Q4

Home Value

Area	Under $100,000	$100,000 -$199,999	$200,000 -$299,999	$300,000 -$399,999	$400,000 -$499,999	$500,000 -$999,999	$1,000,000 or more	Median ($)
City	8.3	18.2	31.4	20.3	9.1	11.0	1.8	271,800
MSA[1]	10.5	18.0	26.3	18.0	10.1	14.3	2.8	280,900
U.S.	12.1	17.8	19.5	14.4	10.5	19.1	6.5	303,400

Note: Figures are percentages except for median and cover owner-occupied housing units; (1) Figures cover the Athens-Clarke County, GA Metropolitan Statistical Area
Source: U.S. Census Bureau, 2019-2023 American Community Survey 5-Year Estimates

Year Housing Structure Built

Area	2020 or Later	2010 -2019	2000 -2009	1990 -1999	1980 -1989	1970 -1979	1960 -1969	1950 -1959	1940 -1949	Before 1940	Median Year
City	1.6	8.9	19.0	16.3	14.5	14.3	12.0	5.8	2.7	4.9	1987
MSA[1]	1.8	10.2	19.4	18.1	15.0	14.1	9.5	4.6	2.2	5.1	1990
U.S.	1.2	8.9	13.6	12.8	13.0	14.4	10.0	9.7	4.5	11.9	1980

Note: Figures are percentages except for Median Year; Note: (1) Figures cover the Athens-Clarke County, GA Metropolitan Statistical Area
Source: U.S. Census Bureau, 2019-2023 American Community Survey 5-Year Estimates

Gross Monthly Rent

Area	Under $500	$500 -$999	$1,000 -$1,499	$1,500 -$1,999	$2,000 -$2,499	$2,500 -$2,999	$3,000 and up	Median ($)
City	3.8	33.4	37.8	17.1	5.0	1.5	1.3	1,162
MSA[1]	4.0	34.6	36.7	16.4	4.9	2.0	1.4	1,144
U.S.	6.5	22.3	29.5	20.2	10.8	4.8	5.9	1,348

Note: Figures are percentages except for median; Gross rent is the contract rent plus the estimated average monthly cost of utilities (electricity, gas, and water and sewer) and fuels (oil, coal, kerosene, wood, etc.) if these are paid by the renter (or paid for the renter by someone else); (1) Figures cover the Athens-Clarke County, GA Metropolitan Statistical Area
Source: U.S. Census Bureau, 2019-2023 American Community Survey 5-Year Estimates

HEALTH

Health Risk Factors

Category	MSA[1] (%)	U.S. (%)
Adults aged 18–64 who have any kind of health care coverage	n/a	90.8
Adults who reported being in good or better health	n/a	81.8
Adults who have been told they have high blood cholesterol	n/a	36.9
Adults who have been told they have high blood pressure	n/a	34.0
Adults who are current smokers	n/a	12.1
Adults who currently use e-cigarettes	n/a	7.7
Adults who currently use chewing tobacco, snuff, or snus	n/a	3.2
Adults who are heavy drinkers[2]	n/a	6.1
Adults who are binge drinkers[3]	n/a	15.2
Adults who are overweight (BMI 25.0 - 29.9)	n/a	34.4
Adults who are obese (BMI 30.0 - 99.8)	n/a	34.3
Adults who participated in any physical activities in the past month	n/a	75.8

Note: All figures are crude prevalence; (1) Figures for the Athens-Clarke County, GA Metropolitan Statistical Area were not available.
(2) Heavy drinkers are classified as adult men having more than 14 drinks per week and adult women having more than 7 drinks per week; (3) Binge drinkers are classified as males having five or more drinks on one occasion or females having four or more drinks on one occasion
Source: Centers for Disease Control and Prevention, Behaviorial Risk Factor Surveillance System, SMART: Selected Metropolitan Area Risk Trends, 2023

Acute and Chronic Health Conditions

Category	MSA[1] (%)	U.S. (%)
Adults who have ever been told they had a heart attack	n/a	4.2
Adults who have ever been told they have angina or coronary heart disease	n/a	4.0
Adults who have ever been told they had a stroke	n/a	3.3
Adults who have ever been told they have asthma	n/a	15.7
Adults who have ever been told they have arthritis	n/a	26.3
Adults who have ever been told they have diabetes[2]	n/a	11.5
Adults who have ever been told they had skin cancer	n/a	5.6
Adults who have ever been told they had any other types of cancer	n/a	8.4
Adults who have ever been told they have COPD	n/a	6.4
Adults who have ever been told they have kidney disease	n/a	3.7
Adults who have ever been told they have a form of depression	n/a	22.0

Note: All figures are crude prevalence; (1) Figures for the Athens-Clarke County, GA Metropolitan Statistical Area were not available.
(2) Figures do not include pregnancy-related, borderline, or pre-diabetes
Source: Centers for Disease Control and Prevention, Behavioral Risk Factor Surveillance System, SMART: Selected Metropolitan Area Risk Trends, 2023

Health Screening and Vaccination Rates

Category	MSA[1] (%)	U.S. (%)
Adults who have ever been tested for HIV	n/a	37.5
Adults who have had their blood cholesterol checked within the last five years	n/a	87.0
Adults aged 65+ who have had flu shot within the past year	n/a	63.4
Adults aged 65+ who have ever had a pneumonia vaccination	n/a	71.9

Note: All figures are crude prevalence; (1) Figures for the Athens-Clarke County, GA Metropolitan Statistical Area were not available.
Source: Centers for Disease Control and Prevention, Behavioral Risk Factor Surveillance System, SMART: Selected Metropolitan Area Risk Trends, 2023

Disability Status

Category	MSA[1] (%)	U.S. (%)
Adults who reported being deaf	n/a	7.4
Are you blind or have serious difficulty seeing, even when wearing glasses?	n/a	4.9
Do you have difficulty doing errands alone?	n/a	7.8
Do you have difficulty dressing or bathing?	n/a	3.6
Do you have serious difficulty concentrating/remembering/making decisions?	n/a	13.7
Do you have serious difficulty walking or climbing stairs?	n/a	13.2

Note: All figures are crude prevalence; (1) Figures for the Athens-Clarke County, GA Metropolitan Statistical Area were not available.
Source: Centers for Disease Control and Prevention, Behavioral Risk Factor Surveillance System, SMART: Selected Metropolitan Area Risk Trends, 2023

Mortality Rates for the Top 10 Causes of Death in the U.S.

ICD-10[a] Sub-Chapter	ICD-10[a] Code	Crude Mortality Rate[2] per 100,000 population	
		County[3]	U.S.
Malignant neoplasms	C00-C97	122.5	182.7
Ischaemic heart diseases	I20-I25	48.6	109.6
Provisional assignment of new diseases of uncertain etiology[1]	U00-U49	34.7	65.3
Other forms of heart disease	I30-I51	70.8	65.1
Other degenerative diseases of the nervous system	G30-G31	56.1	52.4
Other external causes of accidental injury	W00-X59	36.8	52.3
Cerebrovascular diseases	I60-I69	38.4	49.1
Chronic lower respiratory diseases	J40-J47	26.5	43.5
Hypertensive diseases	I10-I15	41.2	38.9
Organic, including symptomatic, mental disorders	F01-F09	10.8	33.9

Note: (a) ICD-10 = International Classification of Diseases 10th Revision; (1) Includes COVID-19, adverse effects to COVID-19 vaccines, SARS, and vaping-related disorders; (2) Crude mortality rates are a three-year average covering 2021-2023; (3) Figures cover Clarke County.
Source: Centers for Disease Control and Prevention, National Center for Health Statistics. National Vital Statistics System, Mortality 2018-2023 on CDC WONDER Online Database

Mortality Rates for Selected Causes of Death

Cause of Death	ICD-10[a] Code	Crude Mortality Rate[1] per 100,000 population	
		County[2]	U.S.
Accidental poisoning and exposure to noxious substances	X40-X49	24.7	30.5
Alzheimer disease	G30	27.5	35.4
Assault	X85-Y09	5.7	7.3
COVID-19	U07.1	34.7	65.3
Diabetes mellitus	E10-E14	12.6	30.0
Diseases of the liver	K70-K76	21.1	20.8
Human immunodeficiency virus (HIV) disease	B20-B24	Suppressed	1.5
Influenza and pneumonia	J09-J18	6.4	13.4
Intentional self-harm	X60-X84	12.6	14.7
Malnutrition	E40-E46	9.0	6.0
Obesity and other hyperalimentation	E65-E68	Unreliable	3.1
Renal failure	N17-N19	17.5	16.4
Transport accidents	V01-V99	13.1	14.4

Note: (a) ICD-10 = International Classification of Diseases 10th Revision; (1) Crude mortality rates are a three-year average covering 2021-2023; (2) Figures cover Clarke County; Data are suppressed when the data meet the criteria for confidentiality constraints; Crude mortality rates are flagged as unreliable when the rate would be calculated with a numerator of 20 or less.
Source: Centers for Disease Control and Prevention, National Center for Health Statistics. National Vital Statistics System, Mortality 2018-2023 on CDC WONDER Online Database

Health Insurance Coverage

Area	With Health Insurance	With Private Health Insurance	With Public Health Insurance	Without Health Insurance	Population Under Age 19 Without Health Insurance
City	88.8	72.8	25.0	11.2	8.1
MSA[1]	89.0	71.4	27.8	11.0	7.2
U.S.	91.4	67.3	36.3	8.6	5.4

Note: Figures are percentages that cover the civilian noninstitutionalized population; (1) Figures cover the Athens-Clarke County, GA Metropolitan Statistical Area
Source: U.S. Census Bureau, 2019-2023 American Community Survey 5-Year Estimates

Number of Medical Professionals

Area	MDs[3]	DOs[3,4]	Dentists	Podiatrists	Chiropractors	Optometrists
County[1] (number)	510	23	65	5	28	21
County[1] (rate[2])	392.7	17.7	50.0	3.8	21.5	16.2
U.S. (rate[2])	302.5	29.2	74.6	6.4	29.5	18.0

Note: Data as of 2023 unless noted; (1) Data covers Clarke County; (2) Number of medical professionals per 100,000 population; (3) Data as of 2022 and includes all active, non-federal physicians; (4) Doctor of Osteopathic Medicine
Source: U.S. Department of Health and Human Services, Health Resources and Services Administration, Bureau of Health Professions, Area Resource File (ARF) 2023-2024

EDUCATION

Public School District Statistics

District Name	Schls	Pupils	Pupil/Teacher Ratio	Minority Pupils[1] (%)	Total Rev. per Pupil ($)	Total Exp. per Pupil ($)
Clarke County	21	12,331	10.2	79.1	21,878	19,385
Foothills Charter High School	1	2,157	73.6	56.7	14,504	11,148

Note: Table includes school districts with 2,000 or more students; (1) Percentage of students that are not non-Hispanic white.
Source: U.S. Department of Education, National Center for Education Statistics, Common Core of Data, Local Education Agency (School District) Universe Survey: School Year 2023-2024; U.S. Department of Education, National Center for Education Statistics, Common Core of Data, School District Finance Survey (F-33): School Year 2021–22

Highest Level of Education

Area	Less than H.S.	H.S. Diploma	Some College, No Deg.	Associate Degree	Bachelor's Degree	Master's Degree	Prof. School Degree	Doctorate Degree
City	10.1	17.7	16.5	7.0	24.3	15.3	2.9	6.2
MSA[1]	10.2	21.4	17.5	7.5	21.9	13.4	3.3	4.9
U.S.	10.6	26.2	19.4	8.8	21.3	9.8	2.3	1.6

Note: Figures cover persons age 25 and over; (1) Figures cover the Athens-Clarke County, GA Metropolitan Statistical Area
Source: U.S. Census Bureau, 2019-2023 American Community Survey 5-Year Estimates

Educational Attainment by Race

Area	High School Graduate or Higher (%)					Bachelor's Degree or Higher (%)				
	Total	White	Black	Asian	Hisp.[2]	Total	White	Black	Asian	Hisp.[2]
City	89.9	96.9	82.5	88.5	66.8	48.7	62.8	22.6	67.8	31.7
MSA[1]	89.8	94.2	82.4	85.0	66.0	43.5	49.5	21.4	64.9	30.8
U.S.	89.4	92.9	88.1	88.0	72.5	35.0	37.7	24.7	57.0	19.9

Note: Figures shown cover persons 25 years old and over; (1) Figures cover the Athens-Clarke County, GA Metropolitan Statistical Area; (2) People of Hispanic origin can be of any race
Source: U.S. Census Bureau, 2019-2023 American Community Survey 5-Year Estimates

School Enrollment by Grade and Control

Area	Preschool (%)		Kindergarten (%)		Grades 1 - 4 (%)		Grades 5 - 8 (%)		Grades 9 - 12 (%)	
	Public	Private	Public	Private	Public	Private	Public	Private	Public	Private
City	65.1	34.9	95.8	4.2	88.4	11.6	86.4	13.6	89.2	10.8
MSA[1]	63.8	36.2	93.2	6.8	88.2	11.8	87.2	12.8	88.5	11.5
U.S.	58.7	41.3	85.2	14.8	87.2	12.8	87.9	12.1	89.0	11.0

Note: Figures shown cover persons 3 years old and over; (1) Figures cover the Athens-Clarke County, GA Metropolitan Statistical Area
Source: U.S. Census Bureau, 2019-2023 American Community Survey 5-Year Estimates

Higher Education

Four-Year Colleges			Two-Year Colleges			Medical Schools[1]	Law Schools[2]	Voc/ Tech[3]
Public	Private Non-profit	Private For-profit	Public	Private Non-profit	Private For-profit			
1	1	0	1	0	0	0	1	1

Note: Figures cover institutions located within the Athens-Clarke County, GA Metropolitan Statistical Area and include main campuses only; (1) includes schools accredited by the Liaison Committee on Medical Education and the American Osteopathic Association's Commission on Osteopathic College Accreditation; (2) includes ABA-accredited schools, schools with provisional ABA accreditation, and state accredited schools; (3) includes all schools with programs that are less than 2 years.
Source: National Center for Education Statistics, Integrated Postsecondary Education System (IPEDS), 2023-24; Wikipedia, List of Medical Schools in the United States, accessed May 2, 2025; Wikipedia, List of Law Schools in the United States, accessed May 2, 2025

According to *U.S. News & World Report,* the Athens-Clarke County, GA metro area is home to one of the top 200 national universities in the U.S.: **University of Georgia** (#46 tie). The indicators used to capture academic quality fall into a number of categories: assessment by administrators at peer institutions; retention of students; faculty resources; student selectivity; financial resources; alumni giving; high school counselor ratings of colleges; and graduation rate. *U.S. News & World Report,* "America's Best Colleges 2025"

According to *U.S. News & World Report,* the Athens-Clarke County, GA metro area is home to one of the top 100 law schools in the U.S.: **University of Georgia** (#22 tie). The rankings are based on a weighted average of 12 measures of quality: peer assessment score; assessment score by lawyers/judges; median LSAT scores; median undergrad GPA; acceptance rate; employment rates for graduates; placement success; bar passage rate; faculty resources; expenditures per student; student/faculty ratio; and library resources. *U.S. News & World Report,* "America's Best Graduate Schools, Law, 2025"

According to *U.S. News & World Report,* the Athens-Clarke County, GA metro area is home to one of the top 75 business schools in the U.S.: **University of Georgia (Terry)** (#29 tie). The rankings are based on a weighted average of the following nine measures: quality assessment; peer assessment; recruiter assessment; placement success; mean starting salary and bonus; student selectivity; mean GMAT and GRE scores; mean undergraduate GPA; and acceptance rate. *U.S. News & World Report,* "America's Best Graduate Schools, Business, 2025"

EMPLOYERS

Major Employers

Company Name	Industry
Athens Regional Health Care	Healthcare
Athens-Clarke County	Government
Baldor	Industrial motors
Burton+Burton	Balloons & gifts
Carrier Transicold	Truck refrigeration units
Caterpillar	Excavators
Certainteed	Fiberglass insulation
Clarke County School District	Education
DialAmerica	Telemarketing
Innovative Solution Advisors	Recruitment
Kroger Company	Grocery
McCann	Aerospace products
Merial	Animal health products
Noramco	Medical grade products
Pilgrim's	Food processing
Power Partners	Transformers, chillers, solar panels
Publix Super Markets Inc.	Grocery
Skaps	Non-woven plastics
St. Mary's Healthcare	Healthcare
University of Georgia	Higher education
Wal-Mart Stores	Retail

Note: Companies shown are located within the Athens-Clarke County, GA Metropolitan Statistical Area.
Source: Chambers of Commerce; State Departments of Labor; Wikipedia

PUBLIC SAFETY

Crime Rate

Area	Total Crime Rate	Violent Crime Rate				Property Crime Rate		
		Murder	Rape	Robbery	Aggrav. Assault	Burglary	Larceny-Theft	Motor Vehicle Theft
City	2,950.7	3.9	60.2	61.7	305.6	238.4	2,063.4	217.6
U.S.	2,290.9	5.7	38.0	66.5	264.1	250.7	1,347.2	318.7

Note: Figures are crimes per 100,000 population.
Source: FBI, Table 8, Offenses Known to Law Enforcement, by State by City, 2023

Hate Crimes

Area	Number of Quarters Reported	Number of Incidents per Bias Motivation					
		Race/Ethnicity/Ancestry	Religion	Sexual Orientation	Disability	Gender	Gender Identity
City	4	0	0	0	0	0	0
U.S.	4	5,900	2,699	2,077	187	92	492

Source: Federal Bureau of Investigation, Hate Crime Statistics 2023

Identity Theft Consumer Reports

Area	Reports	Reports per 100,000 Population	Rank[2]
MSA[1]	386	177	206
U.S.	1,135,291	339	-

Note: (1) Figures cover the Athens-Clarke County, GA Metropolitan Statistical Area; (2) Rank ranges from 1 to 401 where 1 indicates greatest number of identity theft reports per 100,000 population
Source: Federal Trade Commission, Consumer Sentinel Network Data Book 2024

Fraud and Other Consumer Reports

Area	Reports	Reports per 100,000 Population	Rank[2]
MSA[1]	1,948	893	276
U.S.	5,360,641	1,601	-

Note: (1) Figures cover the Athens-Clarke County, GA Metropolitan Statistical Area; (2) Rank ranges from 1 to 401 where 1 indicates greatest number of fraud and other consumer reports per 100,000 population
Source: Federal Trade Commission, Consumer Sentinel Network Data Book 2024

POLITICS

2024 Presidential Election Results

Area	Trump (Rep.)	Harris (Dem.)	Stein (Green)	Kennedy (Ind.)	Oliver (Lib.)	Other
Clarke County	30.2	68.3	0.5	0.0	0.6	0.4
U.S.	49.7	48.2	0.6	0.5	0.4	0.6

Note: Results are percentages and may not add to 100% due to rounding
Source: Dave Leip's Atlas of U.S. Presidential Elections

SPORTS

Professional Sports Teams

Team Name	League	Year Established

No teams are located in the metro area
Source: Wikipedia, Major Professional Sports Teams of the United States and Canada, May 1, 2025

CLIMATE

Average and Extreme Temperatures

Temperature	Jan	Feb	Mar	Apr	May	Jun	Jul	Aug	Sep	Oct	Nov	Dec	Yr.
Extreme High (°F)	79	80	85	93	95	101	105	102	98	95	84	77	105
Average High (°F)	52	56	64	73	80	86	88	88	82	73	63	54	72
Average Temp. (°F)	43	46	53	62	70	77	79	79	73	63	53	45	62
Average Low (°F)	33	36	42	51	59	66	70	69	64	52	42	35	52
Extreme Low (°F)	-8	5	10	26	37	46	53	55	36	28	3	0	-8

Note: Figures cover the years 1945-1990
Source: National Climatic Data Center, International Station Meteorological Climate Summary, 9/96

Average Precipitation/Snowfall/Humidity

Precip./Humidity	Jan	Feb	Mar	Apr	May	Jun	Jul	Aug	Sep	Oct	Nov	Dec	Yr.
Avg. Precip. (in.)	4.7	4.6	5.7	4.3	4.0	3.5	5.1	3.6	3.4	2.8	3.8	4.2	49.8
Avg. Snowfall (in.)	1	1	Tr	Tr	0	0	0	0	0	0	Tr	Tr	2
Avg. Rel. Hum. 7am (%)	79	77	78	78	82	83	88	89	88	84	81	79	82
Avg. Rel. Hum. 4pm (%)	56	50	48	45	49	52	57	56	56	51	52	55	52

Note: Figures cover the years 1945-1990; Tr = Trace amounts (<0.05 in. of rain; <0.5 in. of snow)
Source: National Climatic Data Center, International Station Meteorological Climate Summary, 9/96

Weather Conditions

Temperature			Daytime Sky			Precipitation		
10°F & below	32°F & below	90°F & above	Clear	Partly cloudy	Cloudy	0.01 inch or more precip.	0.1 inch or more snow/ice	Thunderstorms
1	49	38	98	147	120	116	3	48

Note: Figures are average number of days per year and cover the years 1945-1990
Source: National Climatic Data Center, International Station Meteorological Climate Summary, 9/96

HAZARDOUS WASTE

Superfund Sites

The Athens-Clarke County, GA metro area has no sites on the EPA's Superfund Final National Priorities List (NPL) or Superfund Alternative Approach (SAA) list. The Superfund alternative approach uses the same investigation and cleanup process and standards that are used for sites listed on the National Priorities List. The SAA is an alternative to listing a site on the NPL; it is not an alternative to Superfund or the Superfund process. There are a total of 1,445 Superfund sites with a status of proposed or final on both lists in the United States. *U.S. Environmental Protection Agency, National Priorities List, May 1, 2025; U.S. Environmental Protection Agency, Superfund Alternative Approach Sites, May 1, 2025*

AIR QUALITY

Air Quality Trends: Ozone

	1990	1995	2000	2005	2010	2015	2020	2021	2022	2023
MSA[1]	n/a	n/a	n/a	n/a	n/a	n/a	n/a	n/a	n/a	n/a
U.S.	0.087	0.089	0.081	0.080	0.072	0.068	0.066	0.067	0.067	0.070

Note: (1) Data covers the Athens-Clarke County, GA Metropolitan Statistical Area; n/a not available. The values shown are the composite ozone concentration averages among trend sites based on the highest fourth daily maximum 8-hour concentration in parts per million. These trends are based on sites having an adequate record of monitoring data during the trend period. Data from exceptional events are included.
Source: U.S. Environmental Protection Agency, Air Quality Monitoring Information, "Air Quality Trends by City, 1990-2023"

Air Quality Index

Area	Percent of Days when Air Quality was...[2]					AQI Statistics[2]	
	Good	Moderate	Unhealthy for Sensitive Groups	Unhealthy	Very Unhealthy	Maximum	Median
MSA[1]	47.4	51.8	0.8	0.0	0.0	147	52

Note: (1) Data covers the Athens-Clarke County, GA Metropolitan Statistical Area; (2) Based on 365 days with AQI data in 2023. Air Quality Index (AQI) is an index for reporting daily air quality. EPA calculates the AQI for five major air pollutants regulated by the Clean Air Act: ground-level ozone, particle pollution (aka particulate matter), carbon monoxide, sulfur dioxide, and nitrogen dioxide. The AQI runs from 0 to 500. The higher the AQI value, the greater the level of air pollution and the greater the health concern. There are six AQI categories: "Good" AQI is between 0 and 50. Air quality is considered satisfactory; "Moderate" AQI is between 51 and 100. Air quality is acceptable; "Unhealthy for Sensitive Groups" When AQI values are between 101 and 150, members of sensitive groups may experience health effects; "Unhealthy" When AQI values are between 151 and 200 everyone may begin to experience health effects; "Very Unhealthy" AQI values between 201 and 300 trigger a health alert; "Hazardous" AQI values over 300 trigger warnings of emergency conditions (not shown).
Source: U.S. Environmental Protection Agency, Air Quality Index Report, 2023

Air Quality Index Pollutants

Area	Percent of Days when AQI Pollutant was...[2]					
	Carbon Monoxide	Nitrogen Dioxide	Ozone	Sulfur Dioxide	Particulate Matter 2.5	Particulate Matter 10
MSA[1]	0.0	0.0	26.8	(3)	73.2	0.0

Note: (1) Data covers the Athens-Clarke County, GA Metropolitan Statistical Area; (2) Based on 365 days with AQI data in 2023. The Air Quality Index (AQI) is an index for reporting daily air quality. EPA calculates the AQI for five major air pollutants regulated by the Clean Air Act: ground-level ozone, particle pollution (also known as particulate matter), carbon monoxide, sulfur dioxide, and nitrogen dioxide. The AQI runs from 0 to 500. The higher the AQI value, the greater the level of air pollution and the greater the health concern; (3) Sulfur dioxide is no longer included in this table because SO_2 concentrations tend to be very localized and not necessarily representative of broad geographical areas like counties and CBSAs.
Source: U.S. Environmental Protection Agency, Air Quality Index Report, 2023

Maximum Air Pollutant Concentrations: Particulate Matter, Ozone, CO and Lead

	Particulate Matter 10 (ug/m^3)	Particulate Matter 2.5 Wtd AM (ug/m^3)	Particulate Matter 2.5 24-Hr (ug/m^3)	Ozone (ppm)	Carbon Monoxide (ppm)	Lead (ug/m^3)
MSA[1] Level	n/a	9.3	26	0.068	n/a	n/a
NAAQS[2]	150	15	35	0.075	9	0.15
Met NAAQS[2]	n/a	Yes	Yes	Yes	n/a	n/a

Note: (1) Data covers the Athens-Clarke County, GA Metropolitan Statistical Area; Data from exceptional events are included; (2) National Ambient Air Quality Standards; ppm = parts per million; ug/m^3 = micrograms per cubic meter; n/a not available.
Concentrations: Particulate Matter 10 (coarse particulate)—highest second maximum 24-hour concentration; Particulate Matter 2.5 Wtd AM (fine particulate)—highest weighted annual mean concentration; Particulate Matter 2.5 24-Hour (fine particulate)—highest 98th percentile 24-hour concentration; Ozone—highest fourth daily maximum 8-hour concentration; Carbon Monoxide—highest second maximum non-overlapping 8-hour concentration; Lead—maximum running 3-month average
Source: U.S. Environmental Protection Agency, Air Quality Monitoring Information, "Air Quality Statistics by City, 2023"

Maximum Air Pollutant Concentrations: Nitrogen Dioxide and Sulfur Dioxide

	Nitrogen Dioxide AM (ppb)	Nitrogen Dioxide 1-Hr (ppb)	Sulfur Dioxide AM (ppb)	Sulfur Dioxide 1-Hr (ppb)	Sulfur Dioxide 24-Hr (ppb)
MSA[1] Level	n/a	n/a	n/a	n/a	n/a
NAAQS[2]	53	100	30	75	140
Met NAAQS[2]	n/a	n/a	n/a	n/a	n/a

Note: (1) Data covers the Athens-Clarke County, GA Metropolitan Statistical Area; Data from exceptional events are included; (2) National Ambient Air Quality Standards; ppm = parts per million; ug/m^3 = micrograms per cubic meter; n/a not available.
Concentrations: Nitrogen Dioxide AM—highest arithmetic mean concentration; Nitrogen Dioxide 1-Hr—highest 98th percentile 1-hour daily maximum concentration; Sulfur Dioxide AM—highest annual mean concentration; Sulfur Dioxide 1-Hr—highest 99th percentile 1-hour daily maximum concentration; Sulfur Dioxide 24-Hr—highest second maximum 24-hour concentration
Source: U.S. Environmental Protection Agency, Air Quality Monitoring Information, "Air Quality Statistics by City, 2023"

Atlanta, Georgia

Background

Atlanta was born of a rough-and-tumble past, as both a natural outgrowth of a thriving railroad in the 1840s, and a resilient go-getter that proudly rose above the rubble of the Civil War.

Blanketed over the rolling hills of the Piedmont Plateau, at the foot of the Blue Ridge Mountains, the state capital stands 1,000 feet above sea level. Atlanta sits in the northwest corner of Georgia where the terrain is rolling to hilly, and slopes downward to the east, west, and south.

Atlanta proper begins at the terminus of the now defunct Western and Atlantic Railroad Line, but its metropolitan area comprises 28 counties. Atlanta is the largest city in the southeast United States with steady population growth for the last decade. It's diversified economy, the 8th largest in the country, comprises manufacturing, retail, and government.

The city has the third-largest concentration of Fortune 500 companies, including CNN and the Centers for Disease Control and Prevention (CDC). Atlanta boasts an involved government that works closely with its business community, which includes HQs of Coca-Cola, The Home Depot, Delta Air Lines, and Arby's.

While schools in Atlanta are predominantly black and suburban schools predominantly white, Atlanta boasts a racially progressive climate. The Martin Luther King, Jr. Historic Site and Preservation District in the Sweet Auburn neighborhood, includes King's birth home and the Ebenezer Baptist Church, where both he and his father preached. The city's consortium of black colleges, including Morehouse College and the Interdenominational Theological Center, testifies to the city's appreciation for those who have always been one-third of Atlanta's population. Atlanta continues to be a major regional center for film and television production, with Tyler Perry Studios, Turner Studios and EVE/ScreenGems Studio located there.

King is one of Atlanta's two Nobel Peace Prize winners. The other is former President Jimmy Carter of Plains, Georgia. The Carter Center sits adjacent to the Jimmy Carter Library and Museum on a hill overlooking the city. Devoted to human rights, the center is operated in partnership with neighboring Emory University. Habitat for Humanity, also founded by Carter, is headquartered in Atlanta.

The city's largest city park, Westside Park at Bellwood Quarry is a 280-acre green space and reservoir that opened in 2021 after major renovation and expansion. It's one of 343 parks, nature preserves, and gardens that cover 3,622 acres.

Atlanta's cultural offerings include the High Museum, the Alliance Theatre, and a number of Westside art galleries. The College Football Hall of Fame and the National Center for Civil and Human Rights are in the city, which will host the 2026 FIFA World Cup, 30 years after hosting the 1996 Summer Olympics. MLB's Atlanta Braves won the World Series in 2021, their first since 1995 and one of four World Series wins.

A film project titled "Bowl Game Armageddon" about the 1956 Sugar Bowl controversy and the Atlanta riots that followed is in development in Atlanta.

Since 1998, Hartsfield-Jackson Atlanta International Airport has been the world's busiest airport. Early in 2025, MARTA (Metropolitan Atlanta Rapid Transit Authority) unveiled its first state-of-the-art CQ400 railcar with more on the way. Construction is underway on the MARTA RapidSummerhill bus line and an upgrade is scheduled for all 38 rail stations, including a major transformation of Five Points Station.

The Appalachian chain of mountains, the Gulf of Mexico, and the Atlantic Ocean influence Atlanta's climate. Temperatures are moderate to hot throughout the year, but extended periods of heat are unusual, and the city rarely reaches 100-degrees. Atlanta winters are mild with a few, short-lived cold spells. Summers can be humid.

Rankings

General Rankings

- To help military veterans find the best places in which to settle down, *WalletHub* compared the 100 largest U.S. cities across 19 key indicators of livability, affordability and veteran-friendliness. They range from the share of military skill-related jobs to veteran income growth to the availability of VA health facilities. Atlanta ranked #51. *Wallethub.com, "Best & Worst Places for Veterans to Live (2025)," November 7, 2024*

- Atlanta was selected as one of the best places to live in the United States by *Money* magazine. The city placed among the top 50. This year's list focused on cities built around community spirit, thoughtful policy and civic engagement. Instead of relying on a predetermined dataset, the cities and towns were grouped according to their strengths and chosen due their affordability, good schools and strong job markets. *Money, "The 50 Best Places to Live in the U.S., 2024" April 8, 2024*

- The human resources consulting firm Mercer ranked 241 major cities worldwide in terms of overall quality of life. Atlanta ranked #53. Criteria: political and personal safety, social, and economic factors; medical and health considerations; schools and education; public services and transportation; recreation; connectivity; housing and infrastructure; and climate. *Mercer, "Mercer 2024 Quality of Living Survey," December 2024*

Business/Finance Rankings

- Payscale.com ranked the 32 largest metro areas in terms of wage growth. The Atlanta metro area ranked #14. Criteria: quarterly changes in private industry employee and education professional wage growth from the previous year. *PayScale, "Wage Trends by Metro Area-4th Quarter," February 4, 2025*

- The Atlanta metro area appeared on the Milken Institute "2025 Best Performing Cities" list. Rank: #61 out of 200 large metro areas (based on performance category). Criteria: job growth; wage growth; high-tech growth and impact; community resilience; housing affordability; household broadband access. *Milken Institute, "Best-Performing Cities 2025," January 14, 2025*

- Mercer Human Resources Consulting ranked 226 cities worldwide in terms of cost-of-living. Atlanta ranked #27 (the lower the ranking, the higher the cost-of-living). The survey measured the comparative cost of over 200 items (such as housing, food, clothing, domestic supplies, transportation, and recreation/entertainment) in each location. *Mercer, "2024 Cost of Living City Ranking," June 17, 2024*

Culture/Performing Arts Rankings

- Atlanta was selected as one of the 25 best cities for moviemakers in North America. Great film cities are places where filmmaking dreams can come true, that offer more creative space, lower costs, and great outdoor locations. NYC & LA were intentionally excluded. Criteria: film industry presence and culture; tax incentives; affordability; and proximity of festivals and schools. The city was ranked #3. *MovieMaker Magazine, "Best Places to Live and Work as a Moviemaker, 2025," January 29, 2025*

Education Rankings

- Personal finance website *WalletHub* analyzed the 150 largest U.S. metropolitan statistical areas to determine where the most educated Americans are putting their degrees to work. Criteria: education levels; percentage of workers with degrees; education quality and attainment gap; public school quality rankings; quality and enrollment of each metro area's universities. Atlanta was ranked #25 (#1 = most educated city). *WalletHub.com, "Most & Least Educated Cities in America, 2025" July 2, 2024*

Environmental Rankings

- The U.S. Environmental Protection Agency (EPA) released its list of U.S. metropolitan areas with the most ENERGY STAR certified buildings in 2023. The Atlanta metro area was ranked #4 out of 25. *U.S. Environmental Protection Agency, "2024 Energy Star Top Cities," May 22, 2024*

Food/Drink Rankings

- WalletHub compared the 100 largest U.S. cities across 17 key indicators of vegan- and vegetarian-friendliness. Atlanta was ranked #16. Cities were selected based on metrics such as the cost of groceries for vegetarians, the share of restaurants serving meatless options and the number of salad shops per capita. *WalletHub.com, "Best Cities for Vegans & Vegetarians (2025)," September 24, 2024*

Health/Fitness Rankings

- For each of the 100 largest cities in the United States, the American Fitness Index®, compiled in partnership between the American College of Sports Medicine and the Elevance Health Foundation, evaluated community infrastructure and more than 30 health behaviors including preventive health, levels of chronic disease conditions, food insecurity, pedestrian safety, air quality, and community/environment resources that support physical activity. Atlanta ranked #8 for "community fitness." *americanfitnessindex.org, "2024 ACSM American Fitness Index Summary Report," July 23, 2024*

- The Atlanta metro area was identified as one of the worst cities for bed bugs in America by pest control company Orkin. The area ranked #13 out of 50 based on the number of bed bug treatments Orkin performed from December 2022 to November 2023. *Orkin, "Chicago Joins Paris In Global Bed Bug Spotlight Ranking As The Worst City On Orkin's U.S. Bed Bug Cities List," January 22, 2024*

- Atlanta was identified as a "2025 Allergy Capital." The area ranked #40 out of the nation's 100 largest metropolitan areas. Three groups of factors were used to identify the most challenging cities for people with allergies: annual tree, grass, and weed pollen scores; over the counter allergy medicine use; number of board-certified allergy specialists. *Asthma and Allergy Foundation of America, "2025 Allergy Capitals: The Most Challenging Places to Live with Allergies," March 18, 2025*

- Atlanta was identified as a "2024 Asthma Capital." The area ranked #43 out of the nation's 100 largest metropolitan areas. Criteria: estimated asthma prevalence; asthma-related mortality; and ER visits due to asthma. Risk factors analyzed but not factored in the rankings: annual air quality including pollution and ozone levels; public smoking laws; indoor air quality; access to asthma specialists; rescue and controller medication use; uninsured rate; pollen allergy; poverty rate. *Asthma and Allergy Foundation of America, "Asthma Capitals 2024: The Most Challenging Places to Live With Asthma," September 10, 2024*

Pet Rankings

- Atlanta appeared on *The Dogington Post* site as one of the top cities for dog lovers, ranking #6 out of 15. The real estate marketplace, Zillow®, and Rover, the largest pet sitter and dog walker network, introduced a new list of "Top Emerging Dog-Friendly Cities" for 2021. Criteria: number of new dog accounts on the Rover platform; and rentals and listings that mention features that attract dog owners (fenced-in yards, dog houses, dog door or proximity to a dog park). *Dogingtonpost.com, "15 Cities Emerging as Dog-Friendliest in 2021," May 11, 2021*

Real Estate Rankings

- *WalletHub* compared the most populated U.S. cities to determine which had the best markets for real estate agents. Atlanta ranked #18 where demand was high and pay was the best. Criteria: sales per agent; annual median wage for real-estate agents; monthly average starting salary for real estate agents; real estate job density and competition; unemployment rate; home turnover rate; housing-market health index; and other relevant metrics. *WalletHub.com, "2021 Best Places to Be a Real Estate Agent," May 12, 2021*

- According to Penske Truck Rental, the Atlanta metro area was named the #4 moving destination in 2023, based on one-way consumer truck rental reservations made through Penske's website, rental locations, and reservations call center. *gopenske.com, "Penske Truck Rental's 2023 Top Moving Destinations," May 7, 2024*

- The Atlanta metro area appeared on Realtor.com's list of hot housing markets to watch in 2025. The area ranked #9. Criteria: forecasted home price and sales growth; overall economy; population trends. *Realtor.com®, "Top 10 Housing Markets Positioned for Growth in 2025," December 10, 2024*

- Atlanta was ranked #82 out of 176 metro areas in terms of cost of housing in 2024 by the National Association of Home Builders (#1 = most affordable). Criteria: the portion of an average family's income necessary to pay the mortgage on a median-priced home. *National Association of Home Builders®, NAHB-Wells Fargo Cost of Housing Index, 4th Quarter 2024*

Safety Rankings

- Allstate ranked the 100 most populous cities in America in terms of driver safety. Atlanta ranked #59. Criteria based on anonymized driving behavior data from Allstate's mobile app powered by Arity: high speed driving (over 80 mph), phone handling, and hard braking. The report helps increase the importance of safety and awareness behind the wheel. *Allstate, "16th Allstate America's Best Drivers Report®" July 11, 2024*

- Atlanta was identified as one of the most dangerous cities in America by NeighborhoodScout. The city ranked #94 out of 100 (#1 = most dangerous). Criteria: number of violent crimes per 1,000 residents. The editors evaluated cities with 25,000 or more residents. *NeighborhoodScout.com, "2023 Top 100 Most Dangerous Cities in the U.S.," January 12, 2023*

Transportation Rankings

- Atlanta was identified as one of the most congested metro areas in the U.S. The area ranked #5 out of 10. Criteria: yearly delay per auto commuter in hours. *Texas A&M Transportation Institute, "2023 Urban Mobility Report," June 2024*

- According to the INRIX "2024 Global Traffic Scorecard," Atlanta was identified as one of the most congested metro areas in the U.S. The area ranked #8 out of 10 in the country and among the top 25 most congested in the world. Criteria: average annual time spent in traffic and average cost of congestion per motorist. *Inrix.com, "Employees & Consumers Returned to Downtowns, Traffic Delays & Costs Grew," January 6, 2025*

Women/Minorities Rankings

- *Travel + Leisure* listed the best cities in and around the U.S. for a memorable and fun girls' trip, even on a budget. Whether it is for a special occasion, to make new memories or just to get away, Atlanta is sure to have something for all the ladies in your tribe. *Travel + Leisure, "25 Affordable Girls Weekend Getaways That Won't Break the Bank," January 30, 2025*

- Personal finance website *WalletHub* compared more than 180 U.S. cities across two key dimensions, "Hispanic Business-Friendliness" and "Hispanic Purchasing Power," to arrive at the most favorable conditions for Hispanic entrepreneurs. Atlanta was ranked #37 out of 182. Criteria includes: share of Hispanic-Owned Businesses; average growth of Hispanic Business revenues; Small Business-Friendliness score; affordability; and number of Hispanics with at least a bachelor's degree. *WalletHub.com, "Best Cities for Hispanic Entrepreneurs," September 4, 2024*

Miscellaneous Rankings

- *MoveHub* ranked 446 hipster cities across 20 countries, using its new and improved alternative Hipster Index and Atlanta came out as #14 among the top 50. Criteria: population over 150,000; number of vintage boutiques; density of tattoo parlors; vegan places to eat; coffee shops; and density of vinyl record stores. *MoveHub.com, "The Hipster Index: Brighton Pips Portland to Global Top Spot," July 28, 2021*

- Atlanta was selected as a 2024 Digital Cities Survey winner. The city ranked #4 in the large city (500,000 or more population) category. The survey examined and assessed how city governments are utilizing new technology and modernized applications to provide residents an array of contactless services and conveniences. Survey questions focused on ten initiatives: cybersecurity; citizen experience; disaster recovery; business intelligence; IT personnel retention; data governance; business automation; AI/machine learning; application modernization; and IT collaboration. *Center for Digital Government, "2024 Digital Cities Survey," November 5, 2024*

- In its roundup of St. Patrick's Day parades, *Gayot* listed the best festivals and parades of all things Irish. The festivities in Atlanta as among the best in North America. *Gayot.com, "Best St. Patrick's Day Parades," March 2025*

- *WalletHub* compared 148 of the most populated U.S. cities to determine their operating efficiency. A "Quality of Services" score was constructed for each city and then measured against the total budget per capita to reveal which were managed the best. Atlanta ranked #102. Criteria: financial stability; economy; education; safety; health; infrastructure and pollution. *WalletHub.com, "2025's Best- & Worst-Run Cities in America," June 18, 2024*

Business Environment

DEMOGRAPHICS

Population Growth

Area	1990 Census	2000 Census	2010 Census	2020 Census	2023 Estimate[2]	Population Growth 1990-2023 (%)
City	394,092	416,474	420,003	498,715	499,287	26.7
MSA[1]	3,069,411	4,247,981	5,268,860	6,089,815	6,176,937	101.2
U.S.	248,709,873	281,421,906	308,745,538	331,449,281	332,387,540	33.6

Note: (1) Figures cover the Atlanta-Sandy Springs-Roswell, GA Metropolitan Statistical Area; (2) 2019-2023 5-year ACS population estimate
Source: U.S. Census Bureau, 1990 Census, 2000 Census, 2010 Census, 2020 Census, 2019-2023 American Community Survey 5-Year Estimates

Race

Area	White Alone[2] (%)	Black Alone[2] (%)	Asian Alone[2] (%)	AIAN[3] Alone[2] (%)	NHOPI[4] Alone[2] (%)	Other Race Alone[2] (%)	Two or More Races (%)
City	39.9	46.9	5.0	0.3	0.1	2.1	5.8
MSA[1]	46.3	34.0	6.4	0.4	0.1	4.9	7.9
U.S.	63.4	12.4	5.8	0.9	0.2	6.6	10.7

Note: (1) Figures cover the Atlanta-Sandy Springs-Roswell, GA Metropolitan Statistical Area; (2) Alone is defined as not being in combination with one or more other races; (3) American Indian and Alaska Native; (4) Native Hawaiian and Other Pacific Islander
Source: U.S. Census Bureau, 2019-2023 American Community Survey 5-Year Estimates

Hispanic or Latino Origin

Area	Total (%)	Mexican (%)	Puerto Rican (%)	Cuban (%)	Other (%)
City	6.3	2.0	0.9	0.3	3.0
MSA[1]	12.1	5.7	1.2	0.4	4.7
U.S.	19.0	11.3	1.8	0.7	5.2

Note: Persons of Hispanic or Latino origin can be of any race; (1) Figures cover the Atlanta-Sandy Springs-Roswell, GA Metropolitan Statistical Area
Source: U.S. Census Bureau, 2019-2023 American Community Survey 5-Year Estimates

Age

Area	Percent of Population									Median Age
	Under Age 5	Age 5–19	Age 20–34	Age 35–44	Age 45–54	Age 55–64	Age 65–74	Age 75–84	Age 85+	
City	5.1	15.7	31.0	14.7	11.4	9.8	7.5	3.5	1.3	34.0
MSA[1]	5.9	20.6	20.5	13.9	13.7	12.2	8.2	3.7	1.2	37.0
U.S.	5.7	19.1	20.2	13.1	12.3	12.8	10.0	4.9	1.9	38.7

Note: (1) Figures cover the Atlanta-Sandy Springs-Roswell, GA Metropolitan Statistical Area
Source: U.S. Census Bureau, 2019-2023 American Community Survey 5-Year Estimates

Disability by Age

Area	All Ages	Under 18 Years Old	18 to 64 Years Old	65 Years and Over
City	11.6	5.4	9.6	32.3
MSA[1]	10.8	4.5	9.0	31.3
U.S.	13.0	4.7	10.7	32.9

Note: Figures show percent of the civilian noninstitutionalized population that reported having a disability. Disability status is determined from six types of difficulty: vision, hearing, cognitive, ambulatory, self-care, and independent living. For children under 5 years old, hearing and vision difficulty are used to determine disability status. For children between the ages of 5 and 14, disability status is determined from hearing, vision, cognitive, ambulatory, and self-care difficulties. For people aged 15 years and older, they are considered to have a disability if they have difficulty with any one of the six difficulty types; Note: (1) Figures cover the Atlanta-Sandy Springs-Roswell, GA Metropolitan Statistical Area
Source: U.S. Census Bureau, 2019-2023 American Community Survey 5-Year Estimates

Ancestry

Area	German	Irish	English	American	Italian	Polish	French[2]	European	Scottish
City	7.1	6.4	9.3	3.8	2.9	1.4	1.7	1.7	1.4
MSA[1]	6.3	6.3	9.1	6.8	2.5	1.2	1.2	1.5	1.6
U.S.	12.6	9.4	9.1	5.5	4.9	2.6	2.0	1.6	1.6

Note: Figures are the percentage of the total population reporting a particular ancestry. The nine most commonly reported ancestries in the U.S. are shown. Figures include multiple ancestries (e.g. if a person reported being Irish and Italian, they were included in both columns); (1) Figures cover the Atlanta-Sandy Springs-Roswell, GA Metropolitan Statistical Area; (2) Excludes Basque
Source: U.S. Census Bureau, 2019-2023 American Community Survey 5-Year Estimates

Foreign-born Population

Area	Percent of Population Born in								
	Any Foreign Country	Asia	Mexico	Europe	Caribbean	Central America[2]	South America	Africa	Canada
City	8.6	3.1	0.7	1.3	0.9	0.3	0.9	1.1	0.3
MSA[1]	14.8	4.8	2.3	1.1	1.7	1.4	1.4	1.8	0.2
U.S.	13.9	4.3	3.3	1.4	1.4	1.2	1.2	0.8	0.2

Note: (1) Figures cover the Atlanta-Sandy Springs-Roswell, GA Metropolitan Statistical Area; (2) Excludes Mexico.
Source: U.S. Census Bureau, 2019-2023 American Community Survey 5-Year Estimates

Household Size

Area	Persons in Household (%)							Average Household Size
	One	Two	Three	Four	Five	Six	Seven or More	
City	47.0	32.0	10.6	6.5	2.3	1.0	0.6	2.01
MSA[1]	27.1	32.0	17.0	13.7	6.2	2.4	1.5	2.67
U.S.	28.5	33.8	15.4	12.7	5.9	2.3	1.4	2.54

Note: (1) Figures cover the Atlanta-Sandy Springs-Roswell, GA Metropolitan Statistical Area
Source: U.S. Census Bureau, 2019-2023 American Community Survey 5-Year Estimates

Household Relationships

Area	Householder	Opposite-sex Spouse	Same-sex Spouse	Opposite-sex Unmarried Partner	Same-sex Unmarried Partner	Child[2]	Grandchild	Other Relatives	Non-relatives
City	45.7	10.4	0.5	3.1	0.6	20.7	2.1	3.9	5.9
MSA[1]	37.1	16.7	0.2	2.1	0.2	30.4	2.7	5.7	3.5
U.S.	38.3	17.5	0.2	2.5	0.2	28.3	2.4	4.8	3.4

Note: Figures are percent of the total population; (1) Figures cover the Atlanta-Sandy Springs-Roswell, GA Metropolitan Statistical Area; (2) Includes biological, adopted, and stepchildren of the householder
Source: U.S. Census Bureau, 2020 Census

Gender

Area	Males	Females	Males per 100 Females
City	242,994	256,293	94.8
MSA[1]	2,998,312	3,178,625	94.3
U.S.	164,545,087	167,842,453	98.0

Note: (1) Figures cover the Atlanta-Sandy Springs-Roswell, GA Metropolitan Statistical Area
Source: U.S. Census Bureau, 2019-2023 American Community Survey 5-Year Estimates

Marital Status

Area	Never Married	Now Married[2]	Separated	Widowed	Divorced
City	55.0	28.9	1.5	4.1	10.5
MSA[1]	36.2	47.1	1.7	4.4	10.6
U.S.	34.1	47.9	1.7	5.6	10.7

Note: Figures are percentages and cover the population 15 years of age and older; (1) Figures cover the Atlanta-Sandy Springs-Roswell, GA Metropolitan Statistical Area; (2) Excludes separated
Source: U.S. Census Bureau, 2019-2023 American Community Survey 5-Year Estimates

Religious Groups by Family

Area	Catholic	Baptist	Methodist	LDS[2]	Pentecostal	Lutheran	Islam	Adventist	Other
MSA[1]	10.7	14.7	6.7	0.8	2.0	0.4	1.9	1.9	12.4
U.S.	18.7	7.3	3.0	2.0	1.8	1.7	1.3	1.3	11.6

Note: Figures are the number of adherents as a percentage of the total population and cover the eight largest religious groups in the U.S; (1) Figures cover the Atlanta-Sandy Springs-Roswell, GA Metropolitan Statistical Area; (2) Church of Jesus Christ of Latter-day Saints
Sources: 2020 U.S. Religion Census, Association of Statisticians of American Religious Bodies; The Association of Religion Data Archives (ARDA)

Religious Groups by Tradition

Area	Catholic	Evangelical Protestant	Mainline Protestant	Black Protestant	Islam	Judaism	Hinduism	Orthodox	Buddhism
MSA[1]	10.7	22.3	7.4	5.3	1.9	0.5	0.7	0.3	0.2
U.S.	18.7	16.5	5.2	2.3	1.3	0.6	0.4	0.4	0.3

Note: Figures are the number of adherents as a percentage of the total population; (1) Figures cover the Atlanta-Sandy Springs-Roswell, GA Metropolitan Statistical Area
Sources: 2020 U.S. Religion Census, Association of Statisticians of American Religious Bodies; The Association of Religion Data Archives (ARDA)

ECONOMY

Real Gross Domestic Product (GDP)

Area	2017	2018	2019	2020	2021	2022	2023	Rank[3]
MSA[1]	398.2	413.0	429.7	416.6	444.7	462.0	471.7	10
U.S.[2]	17,619.1	18,160.7	18,642.5	18,238.9	19,387.6	19,896.6	20,436.3	—

Note: Figures are in billions of chained 2017 dollars; (1) Figures cover the Atlanta-Sandy Springs-Roswell, GA Metropolitan Statistical Area; (2) Figures cover real GDP within metropolitan areas; (3) Rank is based on 2023 data and ranges from 1 to 384
Source: U.S. Bureau of Economic Analysis

Economic Growth

Area	2014	2015	2016	2017	2018	2019	2020	2021	2022	2023
MSA[1]	4.6	5.3	5.3	4.8	3.7	4.0	-3.0	6.7	3.9	2.1
U.S.[2]	2.6	3.2	2.0	2.7	3.1	2.7	-2.2	6.3	2.6	2.7

Note: Figures are real gross domestic product growth rates and represent percent change from preceding period; (1) Figures cover the Atlanta-Sandy Springs-Roswell, GA Metropolitan Statistical Area; (2) Figures are the average growth rates within metropolitan areas
Source: U.S. Bureau of Economic Analysis

Metropolitan Area Exports

Area	2018	2019	2020	2021	2022	2023	Rank[2]
MSA[1]	24,091.6	25,800.8	25,791.0	28,116.4	30,833.1	32,336.4	13
U.S.	1,664,056.1	1,645,173.7	1,431,406.6	1,753,941.4	2,062,937.4	2,019,160.5	—

Note: Figures are in millions of dollars; (1) Figures cover the Atlanta-Sandy Springs-Roswell, GA Metropolitan Statistical Area; (2) Rank is based on 2023 data and ranges from 1 to 386
Source: U.S. Department of Commerce, International Trade Administration, Office of Trade and Economic Analysis, Industry and Analysis, Exports by Metropolitan Area, data extracted April 2, 2025

Building Permits

Area	Single-Family			Multi-Family			Total		
	2023	2024	Pct. Chg.	2023	2024	Pct. Chg.	2023	2024	Pct. Chg.
City	1,139	791	-30.6	6,482	7,318	12.9	7,621	8,109	6.4
MSA[1]	24,022	25,773	7.3	14,617	14,914	2.0	38,639	40,687	5.3
U.S.	920,000	981,900	6.7	591,100	496,100	-16.1	1,511,100	1,478,000	-2.2

Note: (1) Figures cover the Atlanta-Sandy Springs-Roswell, GA Metropolitan Statistical Area; Figures represent new, privately-owned housing units authorized (unadjusted data)
Source: U.S. Census Bureau, Building Permits Survey (BPS), 2023, 2024

Bankruptcy Filings

Area	Business Filings			Nonbusiness Filings		
	2023	2024	% Chg.	2023	2024	% Chg.
Fulton County	318	251	-21.1	2,723	2,846	4.5
U.S.	18,926	23,107	22.1	434,064	494,201	13.9

Note: Business filings include Chapter 7, Chapter 9, Chapter 11, Chapter 12, Chapter 13, Chapter 15, and Section 304; Nonbusiness filings include Chapter 7, Chapter 11, and Chapter 13
Source: Administrative Office of the U.S. Courts, Business and Nonbusiness Bankruptcy, County Cases Commenced by Chapter of the Bankruptcy Code, During the 12-Month Period Ending December 31, 2023 and Business and Nonbusiness Bankruptcy, County Cases Commenced by Chapter of the Bankruptcy Code, During the 12-Month Period Ending December 31, 2024

Housing Vacancy Rates

Area	Gross Vacancy Rate[3] (%)			Year-Round Vacancy Rate[4] (%)			Rental Vacancy Rate[5] (%)			Homeowner Vacancy Rate[6] (%)		
	2022	2023	2024	2022	2023	2024	2022	2023	2024	2022	2023	2024
MSA[1]	5.9	6.6	6.8	5.7	6.4	6.6	6.7	8.7	9.3	0.8	1.2	0.9
U.S.[2]	9.1	9.0	9.1	7.5	7.5	7.6	5.7	6.5	6.8	0.8	0.8	1.0

Note: (1) Figures cover the Atlanta-Sandy Springs-Roswell, GA Metropolitan Statistical Area; (2) Figures cover the 75 largest Metropolitan Statistical Areas; (3) The percentage of the total housing inventory that is vacant; (4) The percentage of the housing inventory (excluding seasonal units) that is year-round vacant; (5) The percentage of rental inventory that is vacant for rent; (6) The percentage of homeowner inventory that is vacant for sale
Source: U.S. Census Bureau, Housing Vacancies and Homeownership Annual Statistics: 2022, 2023, 2024

INCOME

Income

Area	Per Capita ($)	Median Household ($)	Average Household ($)
City	64,063	81,938	135,218
MSA[1]	44,798	86,338	118,625
U.S.	43,289	78,538	110,491

Note: (1) Figures cover the Atlanta-Sandy Springs-Roswell, GA Metropolitan Statistical Area
Source: U.S. Census Bureau, 2019-2023 American Community Survey 5-Year Estimates

Household Income Distribution

Area	Percent of Households Earning							
	Under $15,000	$15,000 -$24,999	$25,000 -$34,999	$35,000 -$49,999	$50,000 -$74,999	$75,000 -$99,999	$100,000 -$149,999	$150,000 and up
City	13.2	6.7	6.1	8.2	12.8	11.5	15.0	26.5
MSA[1]	6.9	5.4	6.0	9.8	15.4	13.4	18.3	24.8
U.S.	8.5	6.6	6.8	10.4	15.7	12.7	17.4	21.9

Note: (1) Figures cover the Atlanta-Sandy Springs-Roswell, GA Metropolitan Statistical Area
Source: U.S. Census Bureau, 2019-2023 American Community Survey 5-Year Estimates

Poverty Rate

Area	All Ages	Under 18 Years Old	18 to 64 Years Old	65 Years and Over
City	17.9	25.9	15.6	18.7
MSA[1]	11.0	15.0	9.7	9.3
U.S.	12.4	16.3	11.6	10.4

Note: Figures are percentage of people whose income during the past 12 months was below the poverty level;
(1) Figures cover the Atlanta-Sandy Springs-Roswell, GA Metropolitan Statistical Area
Source: U.S. Census Bureau, 2019-2023 American Community Survey 5-Year Estimates

EMPLOYMENT

Labor Force and Employment

Area	Civilian Labor Force			Workers Employed		
	Dec. 2023	Dec. 2024	% Chg.	Dec. 2023	Dec. 2024	% Chg.
City	278,364	279,245	0.3	268,161	267,879	-0.1
MD[1]	2,520,105	2,525,607	0.2	2,441,223	2,439,016	-0.1
U.S.	166,661,000	167,746,000	0.7	160,754,000	161,294,000	0.3

Note: Data is not seasonally adjusted and covers workers 16 years of age and older; (1) Figures cover the Atlanta-Sandy Springs-Roswell, GA Metropolitan Division
Source: Bureau of Labor Statistics, Local Area Unemployment Statistics

Unemployment Rate

Area	2024											
	Jan.	Feb.	Mar.	Apr.	May	Jun.	Jul.	Aug.	Sep.	Oct.	Nov.	Dec.
City	3.9	3.9	3.8	3.6	4.0	4.5	4.5	4.6	4.1	4.2	4.2	4.1
MD[1]	3.4	3.4	3.4	3.1	3.5	4.0	3.9	4.0	3.5	3.6	3.6	3.4
U.S.	4.1	4.2	3.9	3.5	3.7	4.3	4.5	4.4	3.9	3.9	4.0	3.8

Note: Data is not seasonally adjusted and covers workers 16 years of age and older; (1) Figures cover the Atlanta-Sandy Springs-Roswell, GA Metropolitan Division
Source: Bureau of Labor Statistics, Local Area Unemployment Statistics

Average Wages

Occupation	$/Hr.	Occupation	$/Hr.
Accountants and Auditors	46.20	Maintenance and Repair Workers	25.02
Automotive Mechanics	28.17	Marketing Managers	82.69
Bookkeepers	24.88	Network and Computer Systems Admin.	48.68
Carpenters	24.84	Nurses, Licensed Practical	29.80
Cashiers	13.99	Nurses, Registered	46.46
Computer Programmers	49.60	Nursing Assistants	18.72
Computer Systems Analysts	53.95	Office Clerks, General	20.88
Computer User Support Specialists	31.11	Physical Therapists	50.04
Construction Laborers	20.30	Physicians	128.59
Cooks, Restaurant	16.66	Plumbers, Pipefitters and Steamfitters	29.64
Customer Service Representatives	21.35	Police and Sheriff's Patrol Officers	30.37
Dentists	102.19	Postal Service Mail Carriers	28.20
Electricians	30.62	Real Estate Sales Agents	34.66
Engineers, Electrical	56.08	Retail Salespersons	16.55
Fast Food and Counter Workers	13.55	Sales Representatives, Technical/Scientific	55.13
Financial Managers	92.61	Secretaries, Exc. Legal/Medical/Executive	20.91
First-Line Supervisors of Office Workers	34.57	Security Guards	19.64
General and Operations Managers	65.51	Surgeons	216.10
Hairdressers/Cosmetologists	22.26	Teacher Assistants, Exc. Postsecondary[1]	14.65
Home Health and Personal Care Aides	14.69	Teachers, Secondary School, Exc. Sp. Ed.[1]	35.49
Janitors and Cleaners	16.89	Telemarketers	16.14
Landscaping/Groundskeeping Workers	18.84	Truck Drivers, Heavy/Tractor-Trailer	28.06
Lawyers	98.50	Truck Drivers, Light/Delivery Services	23.97
Maids and Housekeeping Cleaners	15.44	Waiters and Waitresses	13.74

Note: Wage data covers the Atlanta-Sandy Springs-Roswell, GA Metropolitan Statistical Area; (1) Hourly wages were calculated from annual wage data based on a 40 hour work week
Source: Bureau of Labor Statistics, Metro Area Occupational Employment & Wage Estimates, May 2024

Employment by Industry

Sector	MD[1] Number of Employees	MD[1] Percent of Total	U.S. Percent of Total
Construction	105,600	4.1	5.1
Financial Activities	179,600	7.0	5.8
Government	304,400	11.9	14.9
Information	96,500	3.8	1.9
Leisure and Hospitality	248,100	9.7	10.4
Manufacturing	137,100	5.3	8.0
Mining and Logging	1,800	0.1	0.4
Other Services	93,400	3.6	3.7
Private Education and Health Services	373,900	14.6	16.9
Professional and Business Services	468,300	18.3	14.2
Retail Trade	240,300	9.4	10.0
Transportation, Warehousing, and Utilities	183,300	7.1	4.8
Wholesale Trade	132,000	5.1	3.9

Note: Figures are non-farm employment as of December 2024. Figures are not seasonally adjusted and include workers 16 years of age and older; (1) Figures cover the Atlanta-Sandy Springs-Roswell, GA Metropolitan Division
Source: Bureau of Labor Statistics, Current Employment Statistics, Employment, Hours, and Earnings

Employment by Occupation

Occupation Classification	City (%)	MSA[1] (%)	U.S. (%)
Management, Business, Science, and Arts	59.8	45.0	42.0
Natural Resources, Construction, and Maintenance	2.3	7.4	8.6
Production, Transportation, and Material Moving	7.5	12.6	13.0
Sales and Office	18.2	20.9	19.9
Service	12.2	14.0	16.5

Note: Figures cover employed civilians 16 years of age and older; (1) Figures cover the Atlanta-Sandy Springs-Roswell, GA Metropolitan Statistical Area
Source: U.S. Census Bureau, 2019-2023 American Community Survey 5-Year Estimates

Occupations with Greatest Projected Employment Growth: 2022 – 2032

Occupation[1]	2022 Employment	2032 Projected Employment	Numeric Employment Change	Percent Employment Change
Fast Food and Counter Workers	116,400	132,810	16,410	14.1
Laborers and Freight, Stock, and Material Movers, Hand	122,550	138,390	15,840	12.9
Stockers and Order Fillers	87,050	101,950	14,900	17.1
Cooks, Restaurant	41,200	56,070	14,870	36.1
Software Developers	46,900	60,700	13,800	29.4
General and Operations Managers	101,650	115,240	13,590	13.4
Retail Salespersons	137,730	150,700	12,970	9.4
Registered Nurses	81,800	94,310	12,510	15.3
Heavy and Tractor-Trailer Truck Drivers	78,240	90,230	11,990	15.3
Home Health and Personal Care Aides	36,890	46,020	9,130	24.7

Note: Projections cover Georgia; (1) Sorted by numeric employment change
Source: www.projectionscentral.org, State Occupational Projections, 2022–2032 Long-Term Projections

Fastest-Growing Occupations: 2022 – 2032

Occupation[1]	2022 Employment	2032 Projected Employment	Numeric Employment Change	Percent Employment Change
Nurse Practitioners	7,900	12,500	4,600	58.2
Data Scientists	5,340	7,680	2,340	43.8
Statisticians	520	720	200	38.5
Cooks, Restaurant	41,200	56,070	14,870	36.1
Recreational Vehicle Service Technicians	310	420	110	35.5
Medical and Health Services Managers	8,760	11,860	3,100	35.4
Entertainment Attendants and Related Workers, All Other	600	810	210	35.0
Rail Yard Engineers, Dinkey Operators, and Hostlers	230	310	80	34.8
Information Security Analysts (SOC 2018)	4,990	6,710	1,720	34.5
Actuaries	350	470	120	34.3

Note: Projections cover Georgia; (1) Sorted by percent employment change and excludes occupations with numeric employment change less than 50
Source: www.projectionscentral.org, State Occupational Projections, 2022–2032 Long-Term Projections

CITY FINANCES

City Government Finances

Component	2022 ($000)	2022 ($ per capita)
Total Revenues	2,313,618	4,514
Total Expenditures	1,763,918	3,441
Debt Outstanding	8,260,528	16,117

Source: U.S. Census Bureau, State & Local Government Finances 2022

City Government Revenue by Source

Source	2022 ($000)	2022 ($ per capita)	2022 (%)
General Revenue			
From Federal Government	94,119	184	4.1
From State Government	72,974	142	3.2
From Local Governments	225,726	440	9.8
Taxes			
Property	529,823	1,034	22.9
Sales and Gross Receipts	192,104	375	8.3
Personal Income	0	0	0.0
Corporate Income	0	0	0.0
Motor Vehicle License	0	0	0.0
Other Taxes	154,899	302	6.7
Current Charges	722,567	1,410	31.2
Liquor Store	0	0	0.0
Utility	274,924	536	11.9

Source: U.S. Census Bureau, State & Local Government Finances 2022

City Government Expenditures by Function

Function	2022 ($000)	2022 ($ per capita)	2022 (%)
General Direct Expenditures			
Air Transportation	300,446	586	17.0
Corrections	13,952	27	0.8
Education	0	0	0.0
Employment Security Administration	0	0	0.0
Financial Administration	49,134	95	2.8
Fire Protection	98,242	191	5.6
General Public Buildings	21,186	41	1.2
Governmental Administration, Other	46,805	91	2.7
Health	1,446	2	0.1
Highways	80,831	157	4.6
Hospitals	0	0	0.0
Housing and Community Development	3,525	6	0.2
Interest on General Debt	140,945	275	8.0
Judicial and Legal	37,191	72	2.1
Libraries	0	0	0.0
Parking	0	0	0.0
Parks and Recreation	57,249	111	3.2
Police Protection	213,291	416	12.1
Public Welfare	21,435	41	1.2
Sewerage	15,674	30	0.9
Solid Waste Management	68,491	133	3.9
Veterans' Services	0	0	0.0
Liquor Store	0	0	0.0
Utility	419,168	817	23.8

Source: U.S. Census Bureau, State & Local Government Finances 2022

TAXES

State Corporate Income Tax Rates

State	Tax Rate (%)	Income Brackets ($)	Num. of Brackets	Financial Institution Tax Rate (%)[a]	Federal Income Tax Ded.
Georgia	5.75 - 6.0	Flat rate	1	5.75	No

Note: Tax rates for tax year 2024; (a) Rates listed are the corporate income tax rate applied to financial institutions or excise taxes based on income. Some states have other taxes based upon the value of deposits or shares.

Source: Federation of Tax Administrators, State Corporate Income Tax Rates, January 1, 2025

State Individual Income Tax Rates

State	Tax Rate (%)	Income Brackets ($)	Personal Exemptions ($)			Standard Ded. ($)	
			Single	Married	Depend.	Single	Married
Georgia	5.5	Flat rate	–	–	–	12,000	18,500 (i)

Note: Tax rates for tax year 2024; Local- and county-level taxes are not included; Federal income tax is not deductible on state income tax returns; (i) GA moves to a flat tax rate regime, eliminates the personal exemption and increases the standard deduction amounts for single, HOH and married jointly filers.
Source: Federation of Tax Administrators, State Individual Income Tax Rates, January 1, 2025

Various State Sales and Excise Tax Rates

State	State Sales Tax (%)	Gasoline[1] ($/gal.)	Cigarette[2] ($/pack)	Spirits[3] ($/gal.)	Wine[4] ($/gal.)	Beer[5] ($/gal.)	Recreational Marijuana (%)
Georgia	4	0.34	0.37	3.79	1.51	0.48	Not legal

Note: All tax rates as of January 1, 2025; (1) The American Petroleum Institute has developed a methodology for determining the average tax rate on a gallon of fuel. Rates may include any of the following: excise taxes, environmental fees, storage tank fees, other fees or taxes, general sales tax, and local taxes; (2) The federal excise tax of $1.0066 per pack and local taxes are not included; (3) Rates are those applicable to off-premise sales of 40% alcohol by volume (a.b.v.) distilled spirits in 750ml containers. Local excise taxes are excluded; (4) Rates are those applicable to off-premise sales of 11% a.b.v. non-carbonated wine in 750ml containers; (5) Rates are those applicable to off-premise sales of 4.7% a.b.v. beer in 12 ounce containers.
Source: Tax Foundation, 2025 Facts & Figures: How Does Your State Compare?

State Tax Competitiveness Index

State	Overall Rank	Corporate Tax Rank	Individual Income Tax Rank	Sales Tax Rank	Property Tax Rank	Unemployment Insurance Tax Rank
Georgia	26	12	31	23	34	24

Note: The Tax Foundation's State Tax Competitiveness Index enables policymakers, taxpayers, and business leaders to gauge how their states' tax systems compare. A rank of 1 is best, 50 is worst. Rankings do not average to the total. States without a tax rank equally as 1. DC's scores and rankings do not affect other states. The report shows tax systems as of July 1, 2024 (the beginning of Fiscal Year 2025).
Source: Tax Foundation, State Tax Competitiveness Index 2025

TRANSPORTATION

Means of Transportation to Work

Area	Car/Truck/Van		Public Transportation			Bicycle	Walked	Other Means	Worked at Home
	Drove Alone	Car-pooled	Bus	Subway	Railroad				
City	55.2	4.6	3.6	2.5	0.1	0.7	4.2	2.4	26.6
MSA[1]	68.0	8.7	1.2	0.5	0.1	0.1	1.2	1.8	18.5
U.S.	70.2	8.5	1.7	1.3	0.4	0.4	2.4	1.6	13.5

Note: Figures are percentages and cover workers 16 years of age and older; (1) Figures cover the Atlanta-Sandy Springs-Roswell, GA Metropolitan Statistical Area
Source: U.S. Census Bureau, 2019-2023 American Community Survey 5-Year Estimates

Travel Time to Work

Area	Less Than 10 Minutes	10 to 19 Minutes	20 to 29 Minutes	30 to 44 Minutes	45 to 59 Minutes	60 to 89 Minutes	90 Minutes or More
City	7.8	29.8	25.5	22.5	6.3	5.1	3.0
MSA[1]	7.3	22.7	20.1	25.5	12.0	9.0	3.3
U.S.	12.6	28.6	21.2	20.8	8.1	6.0	2.8

Note: Note: Figures are percentages and include workers 16 years old and over; (1) Figures cover the Atlanta-Sandy Springs-Roswell, GA Metropolitan Statistical Area
Source: U.S. Census Bureau, 2019-2023 American Community Survey 5-Year Estimates

Key Congestion Measures

Measure	2000	2010	2015	2020	2022
Annual Hours of Delay, Total (000)	146,271	184,962	212,509	109,475	232,272
Annual Hours of Delay, Per Auto Commuter	53	60	71	37	82
Annual Congestion Cost, Per Auto Commuter ($)	1,787	1,799	1,908	972	1,953

Note: Figures cover the Atlanta GA urban area
Source: Texas A&M Transportation Institute, 2023 Urban Mobility Report

Freeway Travel Time Index

Measure	1985	1990	1995	2000	2005	2010	2015	2020	2022
Urban Area Index[1]	1.11	1.15	1.22	1.24	1.26	1.23	1.27	1.10	1.25
Urban Area Rank[1,2]	25	22	13	18	22	28	20	29	19

Note: Freeway Travel Time Index—the ratio of travel time in the peak period to the travel time at free-flow conditions. For example, a value of 1.30 indicates a 20-minute free-flow trip takes 26 minutes in the peak (20 minutes x 1.30 = 26 minutes); (1) Covers the Atlanta GA urban area; (2) Rank is based on 101 larger urban areas (#1 = highest travel time index)
Source: Texas A&M Transportation Institute, 2023 Urban Mobility Report

Public Transportation

Agency Name / Mode of Transportation	Vehicles Operated in Maximum Service[1]	Annual Unlinked Passenger Trips[2] (in thous.)	Annual Passenger Miles[3] (in thous.)
Metropolitan Atlanta Rapid Transit Authority (MARTA)			
Bus (directly operated)	384	30,878.8	129,904.4
Demand Response (purchased transportation)	207	683.9	8,612.3
Heavy Rail (directly operated)	160	30,395.5	213,500.3
Streetcar Rail (directly operated)	2	134.8	99.0

Note: (1) Number of revenue vehicles operated by the given mode and type of service to meet the annual maximum service requirement. This is the revenue vehicle count during the peak season of the year; on the week and day that maximum service is provided. Vehicles operated in maximum service (VOMS) exclude atypical days and one-time special events; (2) Number of passengers who boarded public transportation vehicles. Passengers are counted each time they board a vehicle no matter how many vehicles they use to travel from their origin to their destination. (3) Sum of the distances ridden by all passengers during the entire fiscal year.
Source: Federal Transit Administration, National Transit Database, 2023

Air Transportation

Airport Name and Code / Type of Service	Passenger Airlines[1]	Passenger Enplanements	Freight Carriers[2]	Freight (lbs)
Hartsfield-Jackson Atlanta International Airport (ATL)				
Domestic service (U.S. carriers only)	28	45,406,031	16	313,783,404
International service (U.S. carriers only)	6	5,602,240	5	85,295,172

Note: (1) Includes all U.S.-based major, minor and commuter airlines that carried at least one passenger during the year; (2) Includes all U.S.-based airlines and freight carriers that transported at least one pound of freight during the year.
Source: Bureau of Transportation Statistics, The Intermodal Transportation Database, Air Carriers: T-100 Domestic Market (U.S. carriers only), 2024; Bureau of Transportation Statistics, The Intermodal Transportation Database, Air Carriers; T-100 International Market (U.S. carriers only), 2024

BUSINESSES

Major Business Headquarters

Company Name	Industry	Fortune[1]	Forbes[2]
Assurant	Insurance: property and casualty (stock)	365	-
Chick-fil-A	Restaurants	-	73
Coca-Cola	Beverages	95	-
Cox Enterprises	Media	-	13
Delta Air Lines	Airlines	70	-
Genuine Parts	Wholesalers: diversified	175	-
Global Payments	Financial data services	410	-
Graphic Packaging Holding	Packaging, containers	416	-
Holder Construction	Construction	-	133
Home Depot	Specialty retailers: other	23	-
Intercontinental Exchange	Securities	397	-
JM Huber	Chemicals	-	189
King & Spalding	Services	-	261
Newell Brands	Home equipment, furnishings	460	-
Norfolk Southern	Railroads	338	-
PulteGroup	Homebuilders	255	-
RaceTrac	Convenience stores & gas stations	-	24
Southern	Utilities: gas and electric	163	-
US LBM Holdings	Construction	-	62
United Parcel Service	Mail, package and freight delivery	45	-
WestRock	Packaging, containers	202	-

Note: (1) Companies that produce a 10-K are ranked 1 to 500 based on 2023 revenue; (2) All private companies with at least $2 billion in annual revenue through the end of their most current fiscal year are ranked 1 to 275; companies listed are headquartered in the city; dashes indicate no ranking
Source: Fortune, "Fortune 500," 2024; Forbes, "America's Largest Private Companies," 2024

Fastest-Growing Businesses

According to *Inc.*, Atlanta is home to eight of America's 500 fastest-growing private companies: **MintLeads.io** (#81); **VIVA Finance** (#86); **Intown Golf Club** (#204); **adtechnacity** (#218); **Jetset World Travel** (#255); **Spire** (#304); **Mile Auto** (#404); **The ResourceHub** (#462). Criteria: must be an independent, privately-held, for-profit, U.S. corporation, proprietorship or partnership as of December 31, 2023; revenues must be at least $100,000 in 2020 and $2 million in 2023; must have four-year operating/sales history. *Inc., "America's 500 Fastest-Growing Private Companies," 2024*

According to *Initiative for a Competitive Inner City (ICIC)*, Atlanta is home to one of America's 100 fastest-growing "inner city" companies: **WEBMyers Construction** (#25). To be eligible for the IC100, companies have to be independently operated, privately held, for-profit businesses with revenues of at least $50,000 in 2019 and $500,000 in 2023, and headquartered in an under-resourced community. Recognizing that concentrated poverty exists within metropolitan areas outside of big cities (and that poverty overall is suburbanizing), ICIC defines under-resourced communities as large low-income, high-poverty areas located in the urban and suburban parts of all but the smallest metropolitan areas. Companies were ranked overall by revenue growth over the five-year period between 2019 and 2023. *Initiative for a Competitive Inner City (ICIC), "Inner City 100 Companies," 2024*

According to Deloitte, Atlanta is home to 14 of North America's 500 fastest-growing high-technology companies: **PrizePicks** (#8); **VIVA Finance** (#37); **adtechnacity** (#74); **Flock Safety** (#89); **Katalon** (#111); **Relay Payments** (#196); **Popmenu** (#203); **Stord** (#227); **Groundfloor** (#253); **PadSplit** (#263); **PlayOn** (#274); **Cognosos** (#342); **IronScales** (#412); **RoadSync** (#481). Companies are ranked by percentage growth in revenue over a four-year period. Criteria for inclusion: company must be headquartered within North America; must own proprietary intellectual property or technology that is sold to customers in products that contributes to a significant portion of the company's operating revenue; must have been in business for a minumum of four years with 2020 operating revenues of at least $50,000 USD/CD and 2023 operating revenues of at least $5 million USD/CD. *Deloitte, 2024 Technology Fast 500^{TM}*

Living Environment

COST OF LIVING

Cost of Living Index

Composite Index	Groceries	Housing	Utilities	Transportation	Health Care	Misc. Goods/Services
96.0	100.9	86.9	99.7	100.2	107.9	97.6

Note: The Cost of Living Index measures regional differences in the cost of consumer goods and services, excluding taxes and non-consumer expenditures, for professional and managerial households in the top income quintile. It is based on more than 50,000 prices covering almost 60 different items for which prices are collected three times a year by chambers of commerce, economic development organizations or university applied economic centers in each participating urban area. The numbers shown should be read as a percentage above or below the national average of 100. For example, a value of 115.4 in the groceries column indicates that grocery prices are 15.4% higher than the national average. Small differences in the index numbers should not be interpreted as significant; Figures cover the Atlanta GA urban area.
Source: The Council for Community and Economic Research, Cost of Living Index, 2024

Grocery Prices

Area[1]	T-Bone Steak ($/pound)	Frying Chicken ($/pound)	Whole Milk ($/half gal.)	Eggs ($/dozen)	Orange Juice ($/64 oz.)	Coffee ($/11.5 oz.)
City[2]	15.52	1.44	4.67	3.38	4.47	5.59
Avg.	15.42	1.55	4.69	3.25	4.41	5.46
Min.	14.50	1.16	4.43	2.75	4.00	4.85
Max.	17.56	2.89	5.49	4.78	5.54	7.89

Note: (1) Values for the local area are compared with the average, minimum and maximum values for all 276 areas in the Cost of Living Index; (2) Figures cover the Atlanta GA urban area; **T-Bone Steak** (price per pound); **Frying Chicken** (price per pound, whole fryer); **Whole Milk** (half gallon carton); **Eggs** (price per dozen, Grade A, large); **Orange Juice** (64 oz. Tropicana or Florida Natural); **Coffee** (11.5 oz. can, vacuum-packed, Maxwell House, Hills Bros, or Folgers).
Source: The Council for Community and Economic Research, Cost of Living Index, 2024

Housing and Utility Costs

Area[1]	New Home Price ($)	Apartment Rent ($/month)	All Electric ($/month)	Part Electric ($/month)	Other Energy ($/month)	Telephone ($/month)
City[2]	428,946	1,464	-	113.87	91.54	194.22
Avg.	515,975	1,550	210.99	123.07	82.07	194.99
Min.	265,375	692	104.33	53.68	36.26	179.42
Max.	2,775,821	5,719	529.02	397.28	361.63	223.33

Note: (1) Values for the local area are compared with the average, minimum and maximum values for all 276 areas in the Cost of Living Index; (2) Figures cover the Atlanta GA urban area; **New Home Price** (2,400 sf living area, 8,000 sf lot, in urban area with full utilities); **Apartment Rent** (950 sf 2 bedroom/1.5 or 2 bath, unfurnished, excluding all utilities except water); **All Electric** (average monthly cost for an all-electric home); **Part Electric** (average monthly cost for a part-electric home); **Other Energy** (average monthly cost for natural gas, fuel oil, coal, wood, and any other forms of energy except electricity); **Telephone** (price includes the base monthly rate plus taxes and fees for three lines of mobile phone service).
Source: The Council for Community and Economic Research, Cost of Living Index, 2024

Health Care, Transportation, and Other Costs

Area[1]	Doctor ($/visit)	Dentist ($/visit)	Optometrist ($/visit)	Gasoline ($/gallon)	Beauty Salon ($/visit)	Men's Shirt ($)
City[2]	132.58	142.21	130.44	3.22	56.70	30.32
Avg.	143.77	117.51	129.23	3.32	48.57	38.14
Min.	36.74	58.67	67.33	2.80	24.00	13.41
Max.	270.44	216.82	307.33	5.28	94.00	63.89

Note: (1) Values for the local area are compared with the average, minimum and maximum values for all 276 areas in the Cost of Living Index; (2) Figures cover the Atlanta GA urban area; **Doctor** (general practitioners routine exam of an established patient); **Dentist** (adult teeth cleaning and periodic oral examination); **Optometrist** (full vision eye exam for established adult patient); **Gasoline** (one gallon regular unleaded, national brand, including all taxes, cash price at self-service pump if available); **Beauty Salon** (woman's shampoo, trim, and blow-dry); **Men's Shirt** (cotton/polyester dress shirt, pinpoint weave, long sleeves).
Source: The Council for Community and Economic Research, Cost of Living Index, 2024

HOUSING

Homeownership Rate

Area	2017 (%)	2018 (%)	2019 (%)	2020 (%)	2021 (%)	2022 (%)	2023 (%)	2024 (%)
MSA[1]	62.4	64.0	64.2	66.4	64.2	64.4	67.5	67.5
U.S.	63.9	64.4	64.6	66.6	65.5	65.8	65.9	65.6

Note: (1) Figures cover the Atlanta-Sandy Springs-Roswell, GA Metropolitan Statistical Area
Source: U.S. Census Bureau, Housing Vacancies and Homeownership Annual Statistics: 2017-2024

House Price Index (HPI)

Area	National Ranking[2]	Quarterly Change (%)	One-Year Change (%)	Five-Year Change (%)	Since 1991Q1 (%)
MSA[1]	169	-0.09	4.19	66.19	310.49
U.S.[3]	–	1.43	4.51	57.13	327.82

Note: The HPI is a weighted repeat sales index. It measures average price changes in repeat sales or refinancings on the same properties. This information is obtained by reviewing repeat mortgage transactions on single-family properties whose mortgages have been purchased or securitized by Fannie Mae or Freddie Mac since January 1975; (1) Figures cover the Atlanta-Sandy Springs-Roswell, GA Metropolitan Statistical Area; (2) Rankings are based on annual percentage change for all metro areas containing at least 15,000 transactions over the last 10 years and ranges from 1 to 241; (3) figures based on a weighted average of Census Division estimates using a seasonally adjusted, purchase-only index; all figures are for the period ending December 31, 2024
Source: Federal Housing Finance Agency, Change in FHFA Metropolitan Area House Price Indexes, All Transactions Index, 2024Q4

Home Value

Area	Under $100,000	$100,000 -$199,999	$200,000 -$299,999	$300,000 -$399,999	$400,000 -$499,999	$500,000 -$999,999	$1,000,000 or more	Median ($)
City	4.8	10.7	17.8	14.5	11.2	27.8	13.3	420,600
MSA[1]	5.5	13.6	23.9	19.8	13.6	19.9	3.6	335,100
U.S.	12.1	17.8	19.5	14.4	10.5	19.1	6.5	303,400

Note: Figures are percentages except for median and cover owner-occupied housing units; (1) Figures cover the Atlanta-Sandy Springs-Roswell, GA Metropolitan Statistical Area
Source: U.S. Census Bureau, 2019-2023 American Community Survey 5-Year Estimates

Year Housing Structure Built

Area	2020 or Later	2010 -2019	2000 -2009	1990 -1999	1980 -1989	1970 -1979	1960 -1969	1950 -1959	1940 -1949	Before 1940	Median Year
City	2.3	15.8	21.0	8.9	7.8	7.8	10.2	8.8	5.3	12.1	1987
MSA[1]	1.7	11.8	23.5	19.3	16.7	11.5	6.8	4.2	1.7	2.8	1993
U.S.	1.2	8.9	13.6	12.8	13.0	14.4	10.0	9.7	4.5	11.9	1980

Note: Figures are percentages except for Median Year; Note: (1) Figures cover the Atlanta-Sandy Springs-Roswell, GA Metropolitan Statistical Area
Source: U.S. Census Bureau, 2019-2023 American Community Survey 5-Year Estimates

Gross Monthly Rent

Area	Under $500	$500 -$999	$1,000 -$1,499	$1,500 -$1,999	$2,000 -$2,499	$2,500 -$2,999	$3,000 and up	Median ($)
City	9.7	10.8	22.9	28.6	16.1	6.4	5.6	1,617
MSA[1]	3.5	10.4	31.9	33.0	14.4	4.1	2.7	1,563
U.S.	6.5	22.3	29.5	20.2	10.8	4.8	5.9	1,348

Note: Figures are percentages except for median; Gross rent is the contract rent plus the estimated average monthly cost of utilities (electricity, gas, and water and sewer) and fuels (oil, coal, kerosene, wood, etc.) if these are paid by the renter (or paid for the renter by someone else); (1) Figures cover the Atlanta-Sandy Springs-Roswell, GA Metropolitan Statistical Area
Source: U.S. Census Bureau, 2019-2023 American Community Survey 5-Year Estimates

HEALTH

Health Risk Factors

Category	MSA[1] (%)	U.S. (%)
Adults aged 18–64 who have any kind of health care coverage	84.0	90.8
Adults who reported being in good or better health	83.6	81.8
Adults who have been told they have high blood cholesterol	35.1	36.9
Adults who have been told they have high blood pressure	32.7	34.0
Adults who are current smokers	9.8	12.1
Adults who currently use e-cigarettes	6.2	7.7
Adults who currently use chewing tobacco, snuff, or snus	1.9	3.2
Adults who are heavy drinkers[2]	5.7	6.1
Adults who are binge drinkers[3]	14.0	15.2
Adults who are overweight (BMI 25.0 - 29.9)	34.3	34.4
Adults who are obese (BMI 30.0 - 99.8)	33.1	34.3
Adults who participated in any physical activities in the past month	77.6	75.8

Note: All figures are crude prevalence; (1) Figures cover the Atlanta-Sandy Springs-Roswell, GA Metropolitan Statistical Area; (2) Heavy drinkers are classified as adult men having more than 14 drinks per week and adult women having more than 7 drinks per week; (3) Binge drinkers are classified as males having five or more drinks on one occasion or females having four or more drinks on one occasion
Source: Centers for Disease Control and Prevention, Behavioral Risk Factor Surveillance System, SMART: Selected Metropolitan Area Risk Trends, 2023

Acute and Chronic Health Conditions

Category	MSA[1] (%)	U.S. (%)
Adults who have ever been told they had a heart attack	3.2	4.2
Adults who have ever been told they have angina or coronary heart disease	3.4	4.0
Adults who have ever been told they had a stroke	2.5	3.3
Adults who have ever been told they have asthma	15.0	15.7
Adults who have ever been told they have arthritis	19.9	26.3
Adults who have ever been told they have diabetes[2]	10.7	11.5
Adults who have ever been told they had skin cancer	4.5	5.6
Adults who have ever been told they had any other types of cancer	6.7	8.4
Adults who have ever been told they have COPD	4.7	6.4
Adults who have ever been told they have kidney disease	3.3	3.7
Adults who have ever been told they have a form of depression	15.7	22.0

Note: All figures are crude prevalence; (1) Figures cover the Atlanta-Sandy Springs-Roswell, GA Metropolitan Statistical Area; (2) Figures do not include pregnancy-related, borderline, or pre-diabetes
Source: Centers for Disease Control and Prevention, Behavioral Risk Factor Surveillance System, SMART: Selected Metropolitan Area Risk Trends, 2023

Health Screening and Vaccination Rates

Category	MSA[1] (%)	U.S. (%)
Adults who have ever been tested for HIV	46.8	37.5
Adults who have had their blood cholesterol checked within the last five years	88.9	87.0
Adults aged 65+ who have had flu shot within the past year	64.4	63.4
Adults aged 65+ who have ever had a pneumonia vaccination	73.4	71.9

Note: All figures are crude prevalence; (1) Figures cover the Atlanta-Sandy Springs-Roswell, GA Metropolitan Statistical Area.
Source: Centers for Disease Control and Prevention, Behavioral Risk Factor Surveillance System, SMART: Selected Metropolitan Area Risk Trends, 2023

Disability Status

Category	MSA[1] (%)	U.S. (%)
Adults who reported being deaf	4.8	7.4
Are you blind or have serious difficulty seeing, even when wearing glasses?	4.4	4.9
Do you have difficulty doing errands alone?	6.5	7.8
Do you have difficulty dressing or bathing?	2.9	3.6
Do you have serious difficulty concentrating/remembering/making decisions?	12.0	13.7
Do you have serious difficulty walking or climbing stairs?	11.0	13.2

Note: All figures are crude prevalence; (1) Figures cover the Atlanta-Sandy Springs-Roswell, GA Metropolitan Statistical Area.
Source: Centers for Disease Control and Prevention, Behavioral Risk Factor Surveillance System, SMART: Selected Metropolitan Area Risk Trends, 2023

Mortality Rates for the Top 10 Causes of Death in the U.S.

ICD-10[a] Sub-Chapter	ICD-10[a] Code	Crude Mortality Rate[2] per 100,000 population	
		County[3]	U.S.
Malignant neoplasms	C00-C97	138.5	182.7
Ischaemic heart diseases	I20-I25	48.6	109.6
Provisional assignment of new diseases of uncertain etiology[1]	U00-U49	41.0	65.3
Other forms of heart disease	I30-I51	48.7	65.1
Other degenerative diseases of the nervous system	G30-G31	54.3	52.4
Other external causes of accidental injury	W00-X59	40.8	52.3
Cerebrovascular diseases	I60-I69	40.8	49.1
Chronic lower respiratory diseases	J40-J47	20.2	43.5
Hypertensive diseases	I10-I15	50.4	38.9
Organic, including symptomatic, mental disorders	F01-F09	15.4	33.9

Note: (a) ICD-10 = International Classification of Diseases 10th Revision; (1) Includes COVID-19, adverse effects to COVID-19 vaccines, SARS, and vaping-related disorders; (2) Crude mortality rates are a three-year average covering 2021-2023; (3) Figures cover Fulton County.
Source: Centers for Disease Control and Prevention, National Center for Health Statistics. National Vital Statistics System, Mortality 2018-2023 on CDC WONDER Online Database

Mortality Rates for Selected Causes of Death

Cause of Death	ICD-10[a] Code	Crude Mortality Rate[1] per 100,000 population	
		County[2]	U.S.
Accidental poisoning and exposure to noxious substances	X40-X49	26.5	30.5
Alzheimer disease	G30	26.5	35.4
Assault	X85-Y09	17.8	7.3
COVID-19	U07.1	41.0	65.3
Diabetes mellitus	E10-E14	21.3	30.0
Diseases of the liver	K70-K76	12.3	20.8
Human immunodeficiency virus (HIV) disease	B20-B24	4.9	1.5
Influenza and pneumonia	J09-J18	7.9	13.4
Intentional self-harm	X60-X84	13.8	14.7
Malnutrition	E40-E46	6.1	6.0
Obesity and other hyperalimentation	E65-E68	2.6	3.1
Renal failure	N17-N19	16.5	16.4
Transport accidents	V01-V99	13.6	14.4

Note: (a) ICD-10 = International Classification of Diseases 10th Revision; (1) Crude mortality rates are a three-year average covering 2021-2023; (2) Figures cover Fulton County; Data are suppressed when the data meet the criteria for confidentiality constraints; Crude mortality rates are flagged as unreliable when the rate would be calculated with a numerator of 20 or less.
Source: Centers for Disease Control and Prevention, National Center for Health Statistics. National Vital Statistics System, Mortality 2018-2023 on CDC WONDER Online Database

Health Insurance Coverage

Area	With Health Insurance	With Private Health Insurance	With Public Health Insurance	Without Health Insurance	Population Under Age 19 Without Health Insurance
City	89.5	70.4	27.2	10.5	6.2
MSA[1]	87.8	69.1	28.2	12.2	7.2
U.S.	91.4	67.3	36.3	8.6	5.4

Note: Figures are percentages that cover the civilian noninstitutionalized population; (1) Figures cover the Atlanta-Sandy Springs-Roswell, GA Metropolitan Statistical Area
Source: U.S. Census Bureau, 2019-2023 American Community Survey 5-Year Estimates

Number of Medical Professionals

Area	MDs[3]	DOs[3,4]	Dentists	Podiatrists	Chiropractors	Optometrists
County[1] (number)	5,895	197	830	55	653	230
County[1] (rate[2])	548.6	18.3	76.9	5.1	60.5	21.3
U.S. (rate[2])	302.5	29.2	74.6	6.4	29.5	18.0

Note: Data as of 2023 unless noted; (1) Data covers Fulton County; (2) Number of medical professionals per 100,000 population; (3) Data as of 2022 and includes all active, non-federal physicians; (4) Doctor of Osteopathic Medicine
Source: U.S. Department of Health and Human Services, Health Resources and Services Administration, Bureau of Health Professions, Area Resource File (ARF) 2023-2024

Best Hospitals

According to *U.S. News*, the Atlanta-Sandy Springs-Roswell, GA metro area is home to three of the best hospitals in the U.S.: **Emory University Hospital at Wesley Woods** (3 adult specialties); **Emory University Hospital** (3 adult specialties); **Shepherd Center** (1 adult specialty). The hospitals listed were nationally ranked in at least one of 15 adult or 11 pediatric specialties. The number of specialties shown cover the parent hospital. Only 160 U.S. hospitals performed well enough to be nationally ranked in one or more specialties. Twenty hospitals in the U.S. made the Honor Roll. The Best Hospitals Honor Roll takes both the national rankings and the procedure and condition ratings into account. Hospitals received points if they were nationally ranked in one of the 15 adult specialties—the higher they ranked, the more points they got—and how many ratings of "high performing" they earned in the 20 procedures and conditions. *U.S. News Online, "America's Best Hospitals 2024-25"*

According to *U.S. News*, the Atlanta-Sandy Springs-Roswell, GA metro area is home to one of the best children's hospitals in the U.S.: **Children's Healthcare of Atlanta** (10 pediatric specialties). The hospital listed was highly ranked in at least one of 11 pediatric specialties. One hundred five children's hospitals in the U.S. were nationally ranked in at least one specialty. Hospitals received points for being ranked in a specialty, and the 10 hospitals with the most points across the 11 specialties make up the Honor Roll. *U.S. News Online, "America's Best Children's Hospitals 2024-25"*

EDUCATION

Public School District Statistics

District Name	Schls	Pupils	Pupil/Teacher Ratio	Minority Pupils[1] (%)	Total Rev. per Pupil ($)	Total Exp. per Pupil ($)
Atlanta Public Schools	87	49,660	12.0	83.9	27,007	24,033
Fulton County	106	88,043	14.4	75.3	18,138	15,569
State Charter Schls-GA Cyber Acad.	1	9,762	18.5	69.9	10,331	9,416

Note: Table includes school districts with 2,000 or more students; (1) Percentage of students that are not non-Hispanic white.
Source: U.S. Department of Education, National Center for Education Statistics, Common Core of Data, Local Education Agency (School District) Universe Survey: School Year 2023-2024; U.S. Department of Education, National Center for Education Statistics, Common Core of Data, School District Finance Survey (F-33): School Year 2021–22

Highest Level of Education

Area	Less than H.S.	H.S. Diploma	Some College, No Deg.	Associate Degree	Bachelor's Degree	Master's Degree	Prof. School Degree	Doctorate Degree
City	7.0	16.0	13.6	5.0	32.8	16.8	5.7	3.0
MSA[1]	9.2	23.0	18.4	7.9	25.4	11.7	2.6	1.8
U.S.	10.6	26.2	19.4	8.8	21.3	9.8	2.3	1.6

Note: Figures cover persons age 25 and over; (1) Figures cover the Atlanta-Sandy Springs-Roswell, GA Metropolitan Statistical Area
Source: U.S. Census Bureau, 2019-2023 American Community Survey 5-Year Estimates

Educational Attainment by Race

Area	High School Graduate or Higher (%)					Bachelor's Degree or Higher (%)				
	Total	White	Black	Asian	Hisp.[2]	Total	White	Black	Asian	Hisp.[2]
City	93.0	98.5	87.9	97.7	86.1	58.4	81.2	34.6	86.7	50.5
MSA[1]	90.8	93.8	91.9	87.8	69.6	41.5	46.4	34.0	61.2	24.7
U.S.	89.4	92.9	88.1	88.0	72.5	35.0	37.7	24.7	57.0	19.9

Note: Figures shown cover persons 25 years old and over; (1) Figures cover the Atlanta-Sandy Springs-Roswell, GA Metropolitan Statistical Area; (2) People of Hispanic origin can be of any race
Source: U.S. Census Bureau, 2019-2023 American Community Survey 5-Year Estimates

School Enrollment by Grade and Control

Area	Preschool (%)		Kindergarten (%)		Grades 1 - 4 (%)		Grades 5 - 8 (%)		Grades 9 - 12 (%)	
	Public	Private	Public	Private	Public	Private	Public	Private	Public	Private
City	44.5	55.5	67.2	32.8	82.9	17.1	77.0	23.0	78.1	21.9
MSA[1]	56.1	43.9	84.1	15.9	88.3	11.7	87.2	12.8	88.5	11.5
U.S.	58.7	41.3	85.2	14.8	87.2	12.8	87.9	12.1	89.0	11.0

Note: Figures shown cover persons 3 years old and over; (1) Figures cover the Atlanta-Sandy Springs-Roswell, GA Metropolitan Statistical Area
Source: U.S. Census Bureau, 2019-2023 American Community Survey 5-Year Estimates

Higher Education

Four-Year Colleges			Two-Year Colleges			Medical Schools[1]	Law Schools[2]	Voc/Tech[3]
Public	Private Non-profit	Private For-profit	Public	Private Non-profit	Private For-profit			
8	17	5	8	2	10	3	3	20

Note: Figures cover institutions located within the Atlanta-Sandy Springs-Roswell, GA Metropolitan Statistical Area and include main campuses only; (1) includes schools accredited by the Liaison Committee on Medical Education and the American Osteopathic Association's Commission on Osteopathic College Accreditation; (2) includes ABA-accredited schools, schools with provisional ABA accreditation, and state accredited schools; (3) includes all schools with programs that are less than 2 years.
Source: National Center for Education Statistics, Integrated Postsecondary Education System (IPEDS), 2023-24; Wikipedia, List of Medical Schools in the United States, accessed May 2, 2025; Wikipedia, List of Law Schools in the United States, accessed May 2, 2025

According to *U.S. News & World Report*, the Atlanta-Sandy Springs-Roswell, GA metro area is home to three of the top 200 national universities in the U.S.: **Emory University** (#24 tie); **Georgia Institute of Technology** (#33 tie); **Georgia State University** (#196 tie). The indicators used to capture academic quality fall into a number of categories: assessment by administrators at peer institutions; retention of students; faculty resources; student selectivity; financial resources; alumni giving; high school counselor ratings of colleges; and graduation rate. *U.S. News & World Report, "America's Best Colleges 2025"*

According to *U.S. News & World Report*, the Atlanta-Sandy Springs-Roswell, GA metro area is home to three of the top 100 liberal arts colleges in the U.S.: **Spelman College** (#40 tie); **Agnes Scott College** (#63 tie); **Morehouse College** (#95 tie). The indicators used to capture academic quality fall into a number of categories: assessment by administrators at peer institutions; retention of students;

faculty resources; student selectivity; financial resources; alumni giving; high school counselor ratings of colleges; and graduation rate. *U.S. News & World Report, "America's Best Colleges 2025"*

According to *U.S. News & World Report*, the Atlanta-Sandy Springs-Roswell, GA metro area is home to two of the top 100 law schools in the U.S.: **Emory University** (#38 tie); **Georgia State University** (#79 tie). The rankings are based on a weighted average of 12 measures of quality: peer assessment score; assessment score by lawyers/judges; median LSAT scores; median undergrad GPA; acceptance rate; employment rates for graduates; placement success; bar passage rate; faculty resources; expenditures per student; student/faculty ratio; and library resources. *U.S. News & World Report, "America's Best Graduate Schools, Law, 2025"*

According to *U.S. News & World Report*, the Atlanta-Sandy Springs-Roswell, GA metro area is home to one of the top medical schools for research in the U.S.: **Emory University** (Tier 1). *U.S. News* placed medical and osteopathic schools into tiers based on their research productivity, faculty and admissions data. Each school's tier was derived from its overall score, calculated by summing the weighted normalized values generated across several factors of academic quality, outlined below. There are four tiers, with tier 1 medical schools as the highest-performing and tier 4 as the lowest-performing. Only tier 1 and 2 schools are shown. Because of the tier presentation, *U.S. News* calculated overall scores based on their percentile performance among all rated schools instead of dividing against the rescaled score of the No. 1-performing schools. Tier 1 included schools with overall scores of 85 to 99. The cutoffs for tiers 2 through 4 were schools scoring 50 to 84, 15 to 49 and 1 to 14, respectively. The rankings are based on a weighted average of the following measures of quality: total research activity; average research activity per faculty member; total NIH research grants at the medical school and its affiliated hospitals; average NIH research grants per faculty; median MCAT total score; median undergraduate GPA; acceptance rate; and faculty resources. *U.S. News & World Report, "America's Best Graduate Schools, Medical, 2025"*

According to *U.S. News & World Report*, the Atlanta-Sandy Springs-Roswell, GA metro area is home to two of the top 75 business schools in the U.S.: **Emory University (Goizueta)** (#17); **Georgia Institute of Technology (Scheller)** (#21). The rankings are based on a weighted average of the following nine measures: quality assessment; peer assessment; recruiter assessment; placement success; mean starting salary and bonus; student selectivity; mean GMAT and GRE scores; mean undergraduate GPA; and acceptance rate. *U.S. News & World Report, "America's Best Graduate Schools, Business, 2025"*

EMPLOYERS

Major Employers

Company Name	Industry
Apartments.com	Apartment locating service
Aquilex Holdings	Facilities support services
AT&T	Engineering services
Children's Healthcare of Atlanta	Healthcare
Clayton County Board of Education	Public elementary & secondary schools
County of Gwinnett	County government
Delta Air Lines	Air transportation, scheduled
Georgia Department of Behavioral Health	Administration of public health programs
Georgia Department of Human Resources	Administration of public health programs
Georgia Department of Transportation	Regulation, administration of transportation
IBM	Engineering services
Internal Revenue Service	Taxation department, government
Lockheed Martin Aeronautical Company	Aircraft
NCR Corporation	Calculating and accounting equipment
Northide Hospital	Healthcare
Progressive Logistics Services	Labor organizations
Robert Half International	Employment agencies
Saint Joseph's Hospital	Healthcare
The Coca-Cola Company	Bottled and canned soft drinks
The Fulton-Dekalb Hospital Authority	General medical & surgical hospitals

Note: Companies shown are located within the Atlanta-Sandy Springs-Roswell, GA Metropolitan Statistical Area.
Source: Chambers of Commerce; State Departments of Labor; Wikipedia

Best Companies to Work For

Alston & Bird; Delta Air Lines; IHG Hotels & Resorts; OneDigital; PulteGroup, headquartered in Atlanta, are among "The 100 Best Companies to Work For." To pick the best companies, *Fortune* partnered with the Great Place to Work Institute. Using their proprietary Trust Index™ survey, the core of what creates great a workplace is measured—key behaviors that drive trust in management, connection with colleagues, and loyalty to the company. To be eligible for the *Fortune* 100 Best Companies to Work For list, employers must have 1,000 or more employees in the U.S. and cannot be a government agency. *Fortune, "The 100 Best Companies to Work For," 2025*

Alston & Bird; IHG Hotels & Resorts; Invisors, headquartered in Atlanta, are among "Fortune's Best Workplaces for Parents." To pick the best companies, *Fortune* partnered with the Great Place to Work Institute. To be considered for the list, companies must be Great Place To Work-Certified and have at least 50 responses from parents in the US. The survey enables employees to share confidential quantitative and qualitative feedback about their organization's culture by responding to 60 statements on a 5-point scale and answering two open-ended questions. Collectively, these statements describe a great employee experience, defined by high levels of trust, respect, credibility, fairness, pride, and camaraderie. In addition, companies provide organizational data like size, location, industry, demographics, roles, and levels; and provide information about parental leave, adoption, flexible schedule, childcare and dependent health care benefits. *Fortune, "Best Workplaces for Parents," 2024*

Cox Enterprises; IHG Hotels & Resorts; OneDigital; PulteGroup, headquartered in Atlanta, are among "Fortune's Best Workplaces for Women." To pick the best companies, *Fortune* partnered with the Great Place to Work Institute. To be considered for the list, companies must be Great Place To Work-Certified. Companies must also employ at least 50 women, at least 20% of their non-executive managers must be female, and at least one executive must be female. To determine the Best Workplaces for Women, Great Place To Work measured the differences in women's survey responses to those of their peers and assesses the impact of demographics and roles on the quality and consistency of women's experiences. Great Place To Work also analyzed the gender balance of each workplace, how it compared to each company's industry, and patterns in representation as women rise from front-line positions to the board of directors. *Fortune, "Best Workplaces for Women," 2024*

MountainSeed; Walton Communities, headquartered in Atlanta, are among "Best Workplaces in Real Estate." To determine the Best Workplaces in Real Estate list, Great Place To Work analyzed the survey responses of over 29,000 employees from Great Place To Work-Certified companies in the real estate industry. Survey data analysis and company-provided datapoints are then factored into a combined score to compare and rank the companies that create the most consistently positive experience for all employees in this industry. *Fortune, "Best Workplaces in Real Estate," 2024*

Children's Healthcare of Atlanta; Graphic Packaging International, headquartered in Atlanta, are among the "Best Places to Work in IT." To qualify, companies had to have a minimum of 100 total employees and five IT employees. The best places to work were selected based on DEI (diversity, equity, and inclusion) practices; IT turnover, promotions, and growth; IT retention and engagement programs; remote/hybrid working; benefits and perks (such as elder care and child care, flextime, and reimbursement for college tuition); and training and career development opportunities. *Computerworld, "Best Places to Work in IT," 2025*

PUBLIC SAFETY

Crime Rate

Area	Total Crime Rate	Violent Crime Rate				Property Crime Rate		
		Murder	Rape	Robbery	Aggrav. Assault	Burglary	Larceny-Theft	Motor Vehicle Theft
City	4,599.8	26.4	23.2	120.3	537.4	346.9	2,500.1	1,045.6
U.S.	2,290.9	5.7	38.0	66.5	264.1	250.7	1,347.2	318.7

Note: Figures are crimes per 100,000 population.
Source: FBI, Table 8, Offenses Known to Law Enforcement, by State by City, 2023

Hate Crimes

Area	Number of Quarters Reported	Number of Incidents per Bias Motivation					
		Race/Ethnicity/Ancestry	Religion	Sexual Orientation	Disability	Gender	Gender Identity
City[1]	4	3	2	6	0	0	2
U.S.	4	5,900	2,699	2,077	187	92	492

Note: (1) Figures include at least one incident reported with more than one bias motivation.
Source: Federal Bureau of Investigation, Hate Crime Statistics 2023

Identity Theft Consumer Reports

Area	Reports	Reports per 100,000 Population	Rank[2]
MSA[1]	42,616	690	2
U.S.	1,135,291	339	-

Note: (1) Figures cover the Atlanta-Sandy Springs-Roswell, GA Metropolitan Statistical Area; (2) Rank ranges from 1 to 401 where 1 indicates greatest number of identity theft reports per 100,000 population
Source: Federal Trade Commission, Consumer Sentinel Network Data Book 2024

Fraud and Other Consumer Reports

Area	Reports	Reports per 100,000 Population	Rank[2]
MSA[1]	167,515	2,712	2
U.S.	5,360,641	1,601	-

Note: (1) Figures cover the Atlanta-Sandy Springs-Roswell, GA Metropolitan Statistical Area; (2) Rank ranges from 1 to 401 where 1 indicates greatest number of fraud and other consumer reports per 100,000 population
Source: Federal Trade Commission, Consumer Sentinel Network Data Book 2024

POLITICS

2024 Presidential Election Results

Area	Trump (Rep.)	Harris (Dem.)	Stein (Green)	Kennedy (Ind.)	Oliver (Lib.)	Other
Fulton County	26.8	71.3	0.6	0.0	0.5	0.8
U.S.	49.7	48.2	0.6	0.5	0.4	0.6

Note: Results are percentages and may not add to 100% due to rounding
Source: Dave Leip's Atlas of U.S. Presidential Elections

SPORTS

Professional Sports Teams

Team Name	League	Year Established
Atlanta Braves	Major League Baseball (MLB)	1966
Atlanta Falcons	National Football League (NFL)	1966
Atlanta Hawks	National Basketball Association (NBA)	1968
Atlanta United FC	Major League Soccer (MLS)	2017

Note: Includes teams located in the Atlanta-Sandy Springs-Roswell, GA Metropolitan Statistical Area.
Source: Wikipedia, Major Professional Sports Teams of the United States and Canada, May 1, 2025

CLIMATE

Average and Extreme Temperatures

Temperature	Jan	Feb	Mar	Apr	May	Jun	Jul	Aug	Sep	Oct	Nov	Dec	Yr.
Extreme High (°F)	79	80	85	93	95	101	105	102	98	95	84	77	105
Average High (°F)	52	56	64	73	80	86	88	88	82	73	63	54	72
Average Temp. (°F)	43	46	53	62	70	77	79	79	73	63	53	45	62
Average Low (°F)	33	36	42	51	59	66	70	69	64	52	42	35	52
Extreme Low (°F)	-8	5	10	26	37	46	53	55	36	28	3	0	-8

Note: Figures cover the years 1945-1990
Source: National Climatic Data Center, International Station Meteorological Climate Summary, 9/96

Average Precipitation/Snowfall/Humidity

Precip./Humidity	Jan	Feb	Mar	Apr	May	Jun	Jul	Aug	Sep	Oct	Nov	Dec	Yr.
Avg. Precip. (in.)	4.7	4.6	5.7	4.3	4.0	3.5	5.1	3.6	3.4	2.8	3.8	4.2	49.8
Avg. Snowfall (in.)	1	1	Tr	Tr	0	0	0	0	0	0	Tr	Tr	2
Avg. Rel. Hum. 7am (%)	79	77	78	78	82	83	88	89	88	84	81	79	82
Avg. Rel. Hum. 4pm (%)	56	50	48	45	49	52	57	56	56	51	52	55	52

Note: Figures cover the years 1945-1990; Tr = Trace amounts (<0.05 in. of rain; <0.5 in. of snow)
Source: National Climatic Data Center, International Station Meteorological Climate Summary, 9/96

Weather Conditions

Temperature			Daytime Sky			Precipitation		
10°F & below	32°F & below	90°F & above	Clear	Partly cloudy	Cloudy	0.01 inch or more precip.	0.1 inch or more snow/ice	Thunderstorms
1	49	38	98	147	120	116	3	48

Note: Figures are average number of days per year and cover the years 1945-1990
Source: National Climatic Data Center, International Station Meteorological Climate Summary, 9/96

HAZARDOUS WASTE

Superfund Sites

The Atlanta-Sandy Springs-Roswell, GA metro division is home to one site on the EPA's Superfund National Priorities List (NPL) or Superfund Alternative Approach (SAA) list: **Westside Lead** (Final NPL). The Superfund alternative approach uses the same investigation and cleanup process and standards that are used for sites listed on the National Priorities List. The SAA is an alternative to listing a site on the NPL; it is not an alternative to Superfund or the Superfund process. There are a total of 1,445 Superfund sites with a status of proposed or final on both lists in the United States. *U.S. Environmental Protection Agency, National Priorities List, May 1, 2025; U.S. Environmental Protection Agency, Superfund Alternative Approach Sites, May 1, 2025*

AIR QUALITY

Air Quality Trends: Ozone

	1990	1995	2000	2005	2010	2015	2020	2021	2022	2023
MSA[1]	0.088	0.089	0.089	0.077	0.067	0.069	0.059	0.064	0.063	0.072
U.S.	0.087	0.089	0.081	0.080	0.072	0.068	0.066	0.067	0.067	0.070

Note: (1) Data covers the Atlanta-Sandy Springs-Roswell, GA Metropolitan Statistical Area. The values shown are the composite ozone concentration averages among trend sites based on the highest fourth daily maximum 8-hour concentration in parts per million. These trends are based on sites having an adequate record of monitoring data during the trend period. Data from exceptional events are included.
Source: U.S. Environmental Protection Agency, Air Quality Monitoring Information, "Air Quality Trends by City, 1990-2023"

Air Quality Index

Area	Percent of Days when Air Quality was...[2]					AQI Statistics[2]	
	Good	Moderate	Unhealthy for Sensitive Groups	Unhealthy	Very Unhealthy	Maximum	Median
MSA[1]	26.6	67.7	4.9	0.8	0.0	172	57

Note: (1) Data covers the Atlanta-Sandy Springs-Roswell, GA Metropolitan Statistical Area; (2) Based on 365 days with AQI data in 2023. Air Quality Index (AQI) is an index for reporting daily air quality. EPA calculates the AQI for five major air pollutants regulated by the Clean Air Act: ground-level ozone, particle pollution (aka particulate matter), carbon monoxide, sulfur dioxide, and nitrogen dioxide. The AQI runs from 0 to 500. The higher the AQI value, the greater the level of air pollution and the greater the health concern. There are six AQI categories: "Good" AQI is between 0 and 50. Air quality is considered satisfactory; "Moderate" AQI is between 51 and 100. Air quality is acceptable; "Unhealthy for Sensitive Groups" When AQI values are between 101 and 150, members of sensitive groups may experience health effects; "Unhealthy" When AQI values are between 151 and 200 everyone may begin to experience health effects; "Very Unhealthy" AQI values between 201 and 300 trigger a health alert; "Hazardous" AQI values over 300 trigger warnings of emergency conditions (not shown).
Source: U.S. Environmental Protection Agency, Air Quality Index Report, 2023

Air Quality Index Pollutants

Area	Percent of Days when AQI Pollutant was...[2]					
	Carbon Monoxide	Nitrogen Dioxide	Ozone	Sulfur Dioxide	Particulate Matter 2.5	Particulate Matter 10
MSA[1]	0.0	0.8	31.5	(3)	67.7	0.0

Note: (1) Data covers the Atlanta-Sandy Springs-Roswell, GA Metropolitan Statistical Area; (2) Based on 365 days with AQI data in 2023. The Air Quality Index (AQI) is an index for reporting daily air quality. EPA calculates the AQI for five major air pollutants regulated by the Clean Air Act: ground-level ozone, particle pollution (also known as particulate matter), carbon monoxide, sulfur dioxide, and nitrogen dioxide. The AQI runs from 0 to 500. The higher the AQI value, the greater the level of air pollution and the greater the health concern; (3) Sulfur dioxide is no longer included in this table because SO_2 concentrations tend to be very localized and not necessarily representative of broad geographical areas like counties and CBSAs.
Source: U.S. Environmental Protection Agency, Air Quality Index Report, 2023

Maximum Air Pollutant Concentrations: Particulate Matter, Ozone, CO and Lead

	Particulate Matter 10 (ug/m^3)	Particulate Matter 2.5 Wtd AM (ug/m^3)	Particulate Matter 2.5 24-Hr (ug/m^3)	Ozone (ppm)	Carbon Monoxide (ppm)	Lead (ug/m^3)
MSA[1] Level	60	10.6	28	0.077	2	n/a
NAAQS[2]	150	15	35	0.075	9	0.15
Met NAAQS[2]	Yes	Yes	Yes	No	Yes	n/a

Note: (1) Data covers the Atlanta-Sandy Springs-Roswell, GA Metropolitan Statistical Area; Data from exceptional events are included; (2) National Ambient Air Quality Standards; ppm = parts per million; ug/m^3 = micrograms per cubic meter; n/a not available.
Concentrations: Particulate Matter 10 (coarse particulate)—highest second maximum 24-hour concentration; Particulate Matter 2.5 Wtd AM (fine particulate)—highest weighted annual mean concentration; Particulate Matter 2.5 24-Hour (fine particulate)—highest 98th percentile 24-hour concentration; Ozone—highest fourth daily maximum 8-hour concentration; Carbon Monoxide—highest second maximum non-overlapping 8-hour concentration; Lead—maximum running 3-month average
Source: U.S. Environmental Protection Agency, Air Quality Monitoring Information, "Air Quality Statistics by City, 2023"

Maximum Air Pollutant Concentrations: Nitrogen Dioxide and Sulfur Dioxide

	Nitrogen Dioxide AM (ppb)	Nitrogen Dioxide 1-Hr (ppb)	Sulfur Dioxide AM (ppb)	Sulfur Dioxide 1-Hr (ppb)	Sulfur Dioxide 24-Hr (ppb)
MSA[1] Level	15	48	n/a	5	n/a
NAAQS[2]	53	100	30	75	140
Met NAAQS[2]	Yes	Yes	n/a	Yes	n/a

Note: (1) Data covers the Atlanta-Sandy Springs-Roswell, GA Metropolitan Statistical Area; Data from exceptional events are included; (2) National Ambient Air Quality Standards; ppm = parts per million; ug/m³ = micrograms per cubic meter; n/a not available.
Concentrations: Nitrogen Dioxide AM—highest arithmetic mean concentration; Nitrogen Dioxide 1-Hr—highest 98th percentile 1-hour daily maximum concentration; Sulfur Dioxide AM—highest annual mean concentration; Sulfur Dioxide 1-Hr—highest 99th percentile 1-hour daily maximum concentration; Sulfur Dioxide 24-Hr—highest second maximum 24-hour concentration
Source: U.S. Environmental Protection Agency, Air Quality Monitoring Information, "Air Quality Statistics by City, 2023"

Austin, Texas

Background

Starting out in 1730 as a peaceful Spanish mission on the north bank of the Colorado River in south-central Texas, Austin engaged in an imbroglio of territorial wars, beginning when the "Father of Texas," Stephen F. Austin, annexed the territory from Mexico in 1833. The capital was moved from Houston to Austin in 1839.

Austin has been called the "City of the Violet Crown" by short story writer, William Sydney Porter, aka O. Henry, for the purple mist that circles the surrounding hills of the Colorado River Valley.

This city of technological innovation is home to strong computer and electronics industries. Austin offers hundreds of free wireless spots, including city parks, and its technology focus has traditionally drawn numerous high-tech companies. A major Samsung Electronics computer chip plant was built in Austin in the late 1990s with several expansions since. Along with this technology growth came increased traffic, especially on Interstate 35, the main highway linking the U.S. and Mexico. After an 89-mile bypass was built to relieve some of the traffic congestion, Facebook (now Meta) opened a sales and operations facility in the city.

In addition to its traditional business community, Austin is home to the main campus of the University of Texas. The university provides the city with diverse lifestyles, a solid mix of white-collar workers, students, professors, blue-collar workers, musicians and artists, and members of the booming tech industry who all call themselves Austinites.

The influx of young people centered on university life contributes to the city's growth as a thriving live music scene. The Austin Music Commission promotes the local music industry, and South by Southwest Conference (SXSW) returned in-person to Austin in 2022, after a two-year COVID-19 hiatus. SXSW showcases about 2,000 film, interactive media, and music performers at venues throughout the city. It is the highest revenue-producing event, other than athletic events, for the Austin economy.

The civic-minded city operates from a city hall which also houses a public plaza facing Town Lake, and the Long Center for the Performing Arts is one of the town's cultural hubs. The city's first major-league professional sports team, Austin FC, part of the Major League Soccer League, started playing in 2021.

Austinites' pride in their creative and independent culture has spawned a movement to keep the city from excessive corporate development. The slogan "Keep Austin Weird" was adopted by the Austin Independent Business Alliance to promote local and alternative business.

Austin's skyline, dominated for years by the Texas State Capitol and the University of Texas, now includes a significant number of large buildings, including The Austonian (2010), Northshore (2016), The Independent (2019), SXSW Center (2019), and 70 Rainy (aka Rainy Historic District) (2019).

A transit expansion program, Project Connect, was approved in 2024. It's expected to break ground in 2027 and include two new bus routes.

Austin consistently gets high marks in best-of city surveys. It sits at a desirable location along the Colorado River, and many recreational activities center on the water. Austin boasts three spring-fed swimming pools, and the city has more than 100 miles of bike paths, including the Lance Armstrong Crosstown Bikeway.

The climate of Austin is subtropical with hot summers. Winters are mild, with below-freezing temperatures occurring on an average of 25 days a year. Cold spells are short, seldom lasting more than two days; an exception occurred in February 2021, when Austin received 6.4 inches of snow with snow cover lasting five days. Again in 2023, Austin experienced an atypical winter freeze. Daytime temperatures in summer are hot, while summer nights are usually pleasant.

Rankings

General Rankings

- To help military veterans find the best places in which to settle down, *WalletHub* compared the 100 largest U.S. cities across 19 key indicators of livability, affordability and veteran-friendliness. They range from the share of military skill-related jobs to veteran income growth to the availability of VA health facilities. Austin ranked #1. *Wallethub.com, "Best & Worst Places for Veterans to Live (2025)," November 7, 2024*

- *US News & World Report* conducted a survey of more than 3,500 people and analyzed the 150 largest metropolitan areas to determine what matters most when selecting the next place to live. Austin ranked #9 out of the top 25 as having the best combination of desirable factors. Criteria: cost of living; quality of life and education; climate; job market; desirability; and other factors. *realestate.usnews.com, "Best Places to Live in the U.S. in 2024-2025," May 21, 2024*

Business/Finance Rankings

- According to *Business Insider*, the Austin metro area is a prime place to run a startup or move an existing business to. The area ranked #7. More than 300 metro areas were analyzed for factors that were of top concern to new business owners. Data was based on the 2019 U.S. Census Bureau American Community Survey, statistics from the CDC, and University of Chicago analysis. Criteria: business formations; percentage of vaccinated population; percentage of households with internet subscriptions; median household income; and share of work that can be done from home. *BusinessInsider.com, "The 20 Best Cities for Starting a Business in 2022 Include Denver, Raleigh, and Olympia," June 7, 2022*

- Payscale.com ranked the 32 largest metro areas in terms of wage growth. The Austin metro area ranked #14. Criteria: quarterly changes in private industry employee and education professional wage growth from the previous year. *PayScale, "Wage Trends by Metro Area-4th Quarter," February 4, 2025*

- Austin was cited as one of America's top metros for total corporate facility investment projects in 2024. The area ranked #1 in the Tier 1 (large) metro area category (population over 1 million). *Site Selection, "Top Metros of 2024," March 2025*

- The Austin metro area appeared on the Milken Institute "2025 Best Performing Cities" list. Rank: #6 out of 200 large metro areas (based on performance category). Criteria: job growth; wage growth; high-tech growth and impact; community resilience; housing affordability; household broadband access. *Milken Institute, "Best-Performing Cities 2025," January 14, 2025*

Culture/Performing Arts Rankings

- Austin was selected as one of the 25 best cities for moviemakers in North America. Great film cities are places where filmmaking dreams can come true, that offer more creative space, lower costs, and great outdoor locations. NYC & LA were intentionally excluded. Criteria: film industry presence and culture; tax incentives; affordability; and proximity of festivals and schools. The city was ranked #8. *MovieMaker Magazine, "Best Places to Live and Work as a Moviemaker, 2025," January 29, 2025*

Dating/Romance Rankings

- *Apartment List* conducted its Annual Renter Satisfaction Survey and asked renters "how satisfied are you with opportunities for dating in your current city." The cities were ranked from highest to lowest based on their satisfaction scores. Austin ranked #5 out of 10 cities. *Apartment List, "Best Cities for Dating 2022 with Local Dating Insights from Bumble," February 7, 2022*

Education Rankings

- Personal finance website *WalletHub* analyzed the 150 largest U.S. metropolitan statistical areas to determine where the most educated Americans are putting their degrees to work. Criteria: education levels; percentage of workers with degrees; education quality and attainment gap; public school quality rankings; quality and enrollment of each metro area's universities. Austin was ranked #8 (#1 = most educated city). *WalletHub.com, "Most & Least Educated Cities in America, 2025" July 2, 2024*

Environmental Rankings

- Sperling's *BestPlaces* assessed the 50 largest metropolitan areas of the United States for the likelihood of dangerously extreme weather events or earthquakes. In general the Southeast and South-Central regions have the highest risk of weather extremes and earthquakes, while the Pacific Northwest enjoys the lowest risk. Of the most risky metropolitan areas, the Austin metro area was ranked #2. *Bestplaces.net, "Avoid Natural Disasters: BestPlaces Reveals The Top 10 Safest Places to Live," October 25, 2017*

- The U.S. Environmental Protection Agency (EPA) released its list of U.S. metropolitan areas with the most ENERGY STAR certified buildings in 2023. The Austin metro area was ranked #10 out of 25. *U.S. Environmental Protection Agency, "2024 Energy Star Top Cities," May 22, 2024*

Food/Drink Rankings

- WalletHub compared the 100 largest U.S. cities across 17 key indicators of vegan- and vegetarian-friendliness. Austin was ranked #6. Cities were selected based on metrics such as the cost of groceries for vegetarians, the share of restaurants serving meatless options and the number of salad shops per capita. *WalletHub.com, "Best Cities for Vegans & Vegetarians (2025)," September 24, 2024*

Health/Fitness Rankings

- For each of the 100 largest cities in the United States, the American Fitness Index®, compiled in partnership between the American College of Sports Medicine and the Elevance Health Foundation, evaluated community infrastructure and more than 30 health behaviors including preventive health, levels of chronic disease conditions, food insecurity, pedestrian safety, air quality, and community/environment resources that support physical activity. Austin ranked #33 for "community fitness." *americanfitnessindex.org, "2024 ACSM American Fitness Index Summary Report," July 23, 2024*

- Austin was identified as a "2025 Allergy Capital." The area ranked #45 out of the nation's 100 largest metropolitan areas. Three groups of factors were used to identify the most challenging cities for people with allergies: annual tree, grass, and weed pollen scores; over the counter allergy medicine use; number of board-certified allergy specialists. *Asthma and Allergy Foundation of America, "2025 Allergy Capitals: The Most Challenging Places to Live with Allergies," March 18, 2025*

- Austin was identified as a "2024 Asthma Capital." The area ranked #89 out of the nation's 100 largest metropolitan areas. Criteria: estimated asthma prevalence; asthma-related mortality; and ER visits due to asthma. Risk factors analyzed but not factored in the rankings: annual air quality including pollution and ozone levels; public smoking laws; indoor air quality; access to asthma specialists; rescue and controller medication use; uninsured rate; pollen allergy; poverty rate. *Asthma and Allergy Foundation of America, "Asthma Capitals 2024: The Most Challenging Places to Live With Asthma," September 10, 2024*

Pet Rankings

- Austin was selected by *Sniffspot.com* as one of the most dog-friendly cities in the U.S., ranking #2 out of 50. Criteria: dog parks; hiking; sniffspots; public parks; dog-friendly businesses; housing; dog waste cleanliness; leash laws; dog services; and overall cost. *Sniffspot.com, "The Top 50 Most Dog-Friendly Cities in the U.S.," September 30, 2024*

Real Estate Rankings

- *WalletHub* compared the most populated U.S. cities to determine which had the best markets for real estate agents. Austin ranked #9 where demand was high and pay was the best. Criteria: sales per agent; annual median wage for real-estate agents; monthly average starting salary for real estate agents; real estate job density and competition; unemployment rate; home turnover rate; housing-market health index; and other relevant metrics. *WalletHub.com, "2021 Best Places to Be a Real Estate Agent," May 12, 2021*

- According to Penske Truck Rental, the Austin metro area was named the #8 moving destination in 2023, based on one-way consumer truck rental reservations made through Penske's website, rental locations, and reservations call center. *gopenske.com, "Penske Truck Rental's 2023 Top Moving Destinations," May 7, 2024*

- The Austin metro area was identified as one of the top 16 housing markets to invest in for 2025 by *Forbes*. Criteria: stable local economies with good population growth and increase in jobs providing good support for home prices and rents. *Forbes.com, "Best Local Markets For Real Estate Investing In 2025," November 6, 2024*

- The Austin metro area was identified as one of the 20 worst housing markets in the U.S. in 2024. The area ranked #225 out of 226 markets. Criteria: year-over-year change of median sales price of existing single-family homes between the 4th quarter of 2023 and the 4th quarter of 2024. *National Association of Realtors®, Median Sales Price of Existing Single-Family Homes for Metropolitan Areas, 4th Quarter 2024*

- Austin was ranked #102 out of 176 metro areas in terms of cost of housing in 2024 by the National Association of Home Builders (#1 = most affordable). Criteria: the portion of an average family's income necessary to pay the mortgage on a median-priced home. *National Association of Home Builders®, NAHB-Wells Fargo Cost of Housing Index, 4th Quarter 2024*

Safety Rankings

- Allstate ranked the 100 most populous cities in America in terms of driver safety. Austin ranked #64. Criteria based on anonymized driving behavior data from Allstate's mobile app powered by Arity: high speed driving (over 80 mph), phone handling, and hard braking. The report helps increase the importance of safety and awareness behind the wheel. *Allstate, "16th Allstate America's Best Drivers Report®" July 11, 2024*

Women/Minorities Rankings

- *Travel + Leisure* listed the best cities in and around the U.S. for a memorable and fun girls' trip, even on a budget. Whether it is for a special occasion, to make new memories or just to get away, Austin is sure to have something for all the ladies in your tribe. *Travel + Leisure, "25 Affordable Girls Weekend Getaways That Won't Break the Bank," January 30, 2025*

- Personal finance website *WalletHub* compared more than 180 U.S. cities across two key dimensions, "Hispanic Business-Friendliness" and "Hispanic Purchasing Power," to arrive at the most favorable conditions for Hispanic entrepreneurs. Austin was ranked #47 out of 182. Criteria includes: share of Hispanic-Owned Businesses; average growth of Hispanic Business revenues; Small Business-Friendliness score; affordability; and number of Hispanics with at least a bachelor's degree. *WalletHub.com, "Best Cities for Hispanic Entrepreneurs," September 4, 2024*

Miscellaneous Rankings

- *WalletHub* compared 148 of the most populated U.S. cities to determine their operating efficiency. A "Quality of Services" score was constructed for each city and then measured against the total budget per capita to reveal which were managed the best. Austin ranked #89. Criteria: financial stability; economy; education; safety; health; infrastructure and pollution. *WalletHub.com, "2025's Best- & Worst-Run Cities in America," June 18, 2024*

Business Environment

DEMOGRAPHICS

Population Growth

Area	1990 Census	2000 Census	2010 Census	2020 Census	2023 Estimate[2]	Population Growth 1990-2023 (%)
City	499,053	656,562	790,390	961,855	967,862	93.9
MSA[1]	846,217	1,249,763	1,716,289	2,283,371	2,357,497	178.6
U.S.	248,709,873	281,421,906	308,745,538	331,449,281	332,387,540	33.6

Note: (1) Figures cover the Austin-Round Rock-San Marcos, TX Metropolitan Statistical Area; (2) 2019-2023 5-year ACS population estimate
Source: U.S. Census Bureau, 1990 Census, 2000 Census, 2010 Census, 2020 Census, 2019-2023 American Community Survey 5-Year Estimates

Race

Area	White Alone[2] (%)	Black Alone[2] (%)	Asian Alone[2] (%)	AIAN[3] Alone[2] (%)	NHOPI[4] Alone[2] (%)	Other Race Alone[2] (%)	Two or More Races (%)
City	59.9	7.5	8.6	0.7	0.1	7.7	15.5
MSA[1]	61.4	7.2	6.9	0.7	0.1	7.3	16.5
U.S.	63.4	12.4	5.8	0.9	0.2	6.6	10.7

Note: (1) Figures cover the Austin-Round Rock-San Marcos, TX Metropolitan Statistical Area; (2) Alone is defined as not being in combination with one or more other races; (3) American Indian and Alaska Native; (4) Native Hawaiian and Other Pacific Islander
Source: U.S. Census Bureau, 2019-2023 American Community Survey 5-Year Estimates

Hispanic or Latino Origin

Area	Total (%)	Mexican (%)	Puerto Rican (%)	Cuban (%)	Other (%)
City	32.2	23.7	1.0	0.9	6.7
MSA[1]	32.0	24.8	1.0	0.6	5.6
U.S.	19.0	11.3	1.8	0.7	5.2

Note: Persons of Hispanic or Latino origin can be of any race; (1) Figures cover the Austin-Round Rock-San Marcos, TX Metropolitan Statistical Area
Source: U.S. Census Bureau, 2019-2023 American Community Survey 5-Year Estimates

Age

Area	Under Age 5	Age 5–19	Age 20–34	Age 35–44	Age 45–54	Age 55–64	Age 65–74	Age 75–84	Age 85+	Median Age
City	5.4	15.7	29.9	17.3	12.0	9.6	6.4	2.6	1.1	34.5
MSA[1]	5.8	19.0	23.8	16.3	13.0	10.5	7.5	3.1	1.1	35.9
U.S.	5.7	19.1	20.2	13.1	12.3	12.8	10.0	4.9	1.9	38.7

Note: (1) Figures cover the Austin-Round Rock-San Marcos, TX Metropolitan Statistical Area
Source: U.S. Census Bureau, 2019-2023 American Community Survey 5-Year Estimates

Disability by Age

Area	All Ages	Under 18 Years Old	18 to 64 Years Old	65 Years and Over
City	9.5	3.8	8.4	28.3
MSA[1]	10.0	4.3	8.5	29.1
U.S.	13.0	4.7	10.7	32.9

Note: Figures show percent of the civilian noninstitutionalized population that reported having a disability. Disability status is determined from six types of difficulty: vision, hearing, cognitive, ambulatory, self-care, and independent living. For children under 5 years old, hearing and vision difficulty are used to determine disability status. For children between the ages of 5 and 14, disability status is determined from hearing, vision, cognitive, ambulatory, and self-care difficulties. For people aged 15 years and older, they are considered to have a disability if they have difficulty with any one of the six difficulty types; Note: (1) Figures cover the Austin-Round Rock-San Marcos, TX Metropolitan Statistical Area
Source: U.S. Census Bureau, 2019-2023 American Community Survey 5-Year Estimates

Ancestry

Area	German	Irish	English	American	Italian	Polish	French[2]	European	Scottish
City	11.5	8.7	10.2	2.8	3.2	1.9	2.4	2.4	2.2
MSA[1]	12.4	8.3	10.4	3.6	2.9	1.7	2.3	2.4	2.2
U.S.	12.6	9.4	9.1	5.5	4.9	2.6	2.0	1.6	1.6

Note: Figures are the percentage of the total population reporting a particular ancestry. The nine most commonly reported ancestries in the U.S. are shown. Figures include multiple ancestries (e.g. if a person reported being Irish and Italian, they were included in both columns); (1) Figures cover the Austin-Round Rock-San Marcos, TX Metropolitan Statistical Area; (2) Excludes Basque
Source: U.S. Census Bureau, 2019-2023 American Community Survey 5-Year Estimates

Foreign-born Population

Area	Percent of Population Born in								
	Any Foreign Country	Asia	Mexico	Europe	Caribbean	Central America[2]	South America	Africa	Canada
City	18.1	6.2	5.2	1.6	0.8	2.0	0.9	1.0	0.3
MSA[1]	15.5	5.1	5.1	1.3	0.5	1.4	0.8	0.8	0.3
U.S.	13.9	4.3	3.3	1.4	1.4	1.2	1.2	0.8	0.2

Note: (1) Figures cover the Austin-Round Rock-San Marcos, TX Metropolitan Statistical Area; (2) Excludes Mexico.
Source: U.S. Census Bureau, 2019-2023 American Community Survey 5-Year Estimates

Household Size

Area	Persons in Household (%)							Average Household Size
	One	Two	Three	Four	Five	Six	Seven or More	
City	36.9	34.0	13.4	10.0	3.4	1.5	0.7	2.14
MSA[1]	28.7	33.8	15.6	13.2	5.3	2.3	1.1	2.44
U.S.	28.5	33.8	15.4	12.7	5.9	2.3	1.4	2.54

Note: (1) Figures cover the Austin-Round Rock-San Marcos, TX Metropolitan Statistical Area
Source: U.S. Census Bureau, 2019-2023 American Community Survey 5-Year Estimates

Household Relationships

Area	Householder	Opposite-sex Spouse	Same-sex Spouse	Opposite-sex Unmarried Partner	Same-sex Unmarried Partner	Child[2]	Grandchild	Other Relatives	Non-relatives
City	42.7	14.5	0.4	3.6	0.4	23.2	1.5	4.1	6.4
MSA[1]	38.6	17.3	0.3	2.7	0.3	27.8	1.9	4.4	4.6
U.S.	38.3	17.5	0.2	2.5	0.2	28.3	2.4	4.8	3.4

Note: Figures are percent of the total population; (1) Figures cover the Austin-Round Rock-San Marcos, TX Metropolitan Statistical Area; (2) Includes biological, adopted, and stepchildren of the householder
Source: U.S. Census Bureau, 2020 Census

Gender

Area	Males	Females	Males per 100 Females
City	495,563	472,299	104.9
MSA[1]	1,190,277	1,167,220	102.0
U.S.	164,545,087	167,842,453	98.0

Note: (1) Figures cover the Austin-Round Rock-San Marcos, TX Metropolitan Statistical Area
Source: U.S. Census Bureau, 2019-2023 American Community Survey 5-Year Estimates

Marital Status

Area	Never Married	Now Married[2]	Separated	Widowed	Divorced
City	44.0	41.7	1.3	3.0	9.9
MSA[1]	35.9	49.4	1.3	3.5	9.8
U.S.	34.1	47.9	1.7	5.6	10.7

Note: Figures are percentages and cover the population 15 years of age and older; (1) Figures cover the Austin-Round Rock-San Marcos, TX Metropolitan Statistical Area; (2) Excludes separated
Source: U.S. Census Bureau, 2019-2023 American Community Survey 5-Year Estimates

Religious Groups by Family

Area	Catholic	Baptist	Methodist	LDS[2]	Pentecostal	Lutheran	Islam	Adventist	Other
MSA[1]	18.8	6.5	2.2	1.3	0.7	1.1	1.0	1.0	9.9
U.S.	18.7	7.3	3.0	2.0	1.8	1.7	1.3	1.3	11.6

Note: Figures are the number of adherents as a percentage of the total population and cover the eight largest religious groups in the U.S; (1) Figures cover the Austin-Round Rock-San Marcos, TX Metropolitan Statistical Area; (2) Church of Jesus Christ of Latter-day Saints
Sources: 2020 U.S. Religion Census, Association of Statisticians of American Religious Bodies; The Association of Religion Data Archives (ARDA)

Religious Groups by Tradition

Area	Catholic	Evangelical Protestant	Mainline Protestant	Black Protestant	Islam	Judaism	Hinduism	Orthodox	Buddhism
MSA[1]	18.8	13.5	4.0	1.7	1.0	0.2	0.6	0.2	0.3
U.S.	18.7	16.5	5.2	2.3	1.3	0.6	0.4	0.4	0.3

Note: Figures are the number of adherents as a percentage of the total population; (1) Figures cover the Austin-Round Rock-San Marcos, TX Metropolitan Statistical Area
Sources: 2020 U.S. Religion Census, Association of Statisticians of American Religious Bodies; The Association of Religion Data Archives (ARDA)

ECONOMY

Real Gross Domestic Product (GDP)

Area	2017	2018	2019	2020	2021	2022	2023	Rank[3]
MSA[1]	141.1	149.3	159.1	163.6	181.1	198.5	207.5	20
U.S.[2]	17,619.1	18,160.7	18,642.5	18,238.9	19,387.6	19,896.6	20,436.3	—

Note: Figures are in billions of chained 2017 dollars; (1) Figures cover the Austin-Round Rock-San Marcos, TX Metropolitan Statistical Area; (2) Figures cover real GDP within metropolitan areas; (3) Rank is based on 2023 data and ranges from 1 to 384
Source: U.S. Bureau of Economic Analysis

Economic Growth

Area	2014	2015	2016	2017	2018	2019	2020	2021	2022	2023
MSA[1]	5.7	7.7	4.2	4.5	5.8	6.5	2.8	10.7	9.6	4.5
U.S.[2]	2.6	3.2	2.0	2.7	3.1	2.7	-2.2	6.3	2.6	2.7

Note: Figures are real gross domestic product growth rates and represent percent change from preceding period; (1) Figures cover the Austin-Round Rock-San Marcos, TX Metropolitan Statistical Area; (2) Figures are the average growth rates within metropolitan areas
Source: U.S. Bureau of Economic Analysis

Metropolitan Area Exports

Area	2018	2019	2020	2021	2022	2023	Rank[2]
MSA[1]	12,929.9	12,509.0	13,041.5	15,621.9	17,290.7	17,251.5	27
U.S.	1,664,056.1	1,645,173.7	1,431,406.6	1,753,941.4	2,062,937.4	2,019,160.5	—

Note: Figures are in millions of dollars; (1) Figures cover the Austin-Round Rock-San Marcos, TX Metropolitan Statistical Area; (2) Rank is based on 2023 data and ranges from 1 to 386
Source: U.S. Department of Commerce, International Trade Administration, Office of Trade and Economic Analysis, Industry and Analysis, Exports by Metropolitan Area, data extracted April 2, 2025

Building Permits

Area	Single-Family 2023	Single-Family 2024	Pct. Chg.	Multi-Family 2023	Multi-Family 2024	Pct. Chg.	Total 2023	Total 2024	Pct. Chg.
City	1,799	1,946	8.2	11,885	7,498	-36.9	13,684	9,444	-31.0
MSA[1]	16,532	16,435	-0.6	22,241	15,859	-28.7	38,773	32,294	-16.7
U.S.	920,000	981,900	6.7	591,100	496,100	-16.1	1,511,100	1,478,000	-2.2

Note: (1) Figures cover the Austin-Round Rock-San Marcos, TX Metropolitan Statistical Area; Figures represent new, privately-owned housing units authorized (unadjusted data)
Source: U.S. Census Bureau, Building Permits Survey (BPS), 2023, 2024

Bankruptcy Filings

Area	Business Filings 2023	Business Filings 2024	% Chg.	Nonbusiness Filings 2023	Nonbusiness Filings 2024	% Chg.
Travis County	133	121	-9.0	408	619	51.7
U.S.	18,926	23,107	22.1	434,064	494,201	13.9

Note: Business filings include Chapter 7, Chapter 9, Chapter 11, Chapter 12, Chapter 13, Chapter 15, and Section 304; Nonbusiness filings include Chapter 7, Chapter 11, and Chapter 13
Source: Administrative Office of the U.S. Courts, Business and Nonbusiness Bankruptcy, County Cases Commenced by Chapter of the Bankruptcy Code, During the 12-Month Period Ending December 31, 2023 and Business and Nonbusiness Bankruptcy, County Cases Commenced by Chapter of the Bankruptcy Code, During the 12-Month Period Ending December 31, 2024

Housing Vacancy Rates

Area	Gross Vacancy Rate[3] (%) 2022	2023	2024	Year-Round Vacancy Rate[4] (%) 2022	2023	2024	Rental Vacancy Rate[5] (%) 2022	2023	2024	Homeowner Vacancy Rate[6] (%) 2022	2023	2024
MSA[1]	5.5	8.5	8.6	4.9	8.2	8.3	5.6	9.0	8.2	0.6	1.3	1.7
U.S.[2]	9.1	9.0	9.1	7.5	7.5	7.6	5.7	6.5	6.8	0.8	0.8	1.0

Note: (1) Figures cover the Austin-Round Rock-San Marcos, TX Metropolitan Statistical Area; (2) Figures cover the 75 largest Metropolitan Statistical Areas; (3) The percentage of the total housing inventory that is vacant; (4) The percentage of the housing inventory (excluding seasonal units) that is year-round vacant; (5) The percentage of rental inventory that is vacant for rent; (6) The percentage of homeowner inventory that is vacant for sale
Source: U.S. Census Bureau, Housing Vacancies and Homeownership Annual Statistics: 2022, 2023, 2024

INCOME

Income

Area	Per Capita ($)	Median Household ($)	Average Household ($)
City	59,427	91,461	130,163
MSA[1]	53,550	97,638	132,189
U.S.	43,289	78,538	110,491

Note: (1) Figures cover the Austin-Round Rock-San Marcos, TX Metropolitan Statistical Area
Source: U.S. Census Bureau, 2019-2023 American Community Survey 5-Year Estimates

Household Income Distribution

Area	Percent of Households Earning							
	Under $15,000	$15,000 -$24,999	$25,000 -$34,999	$35,000 -$49,999	$50,000 -$74,999	$75,000 -$99,999	$100,000 -$149,999	$150,000 and up
City	7.8	4.6	4.9	9.3	15.1	12.4	17.2	28.7
MSA[1]	6.3	4.1	4.8	8.6	14.8	12.4	19.2	29.9
U.S.	8.5	6.6	6.8	10.4	15.7	12.7	17.4	21.9

Note: (1) Figures cover the Austin-Round Rock-San Marcos, TX Metropolitan Statistical Area
Source: U.S. Census Bureau, 2019-2023 American Community Survey 5-Year Estimates

Poverty Rate

Area	All Ages	Under 18 Years Old	18 to 64 Years Old	65 Years and Over
City	12.3	15.7	11.6	10.9
MSA[1]	9.9	11.5	9.6	8.7
U.S.	12.4	16.3	11.6	10.4

Note: Figures are percentage of people whose income during the past 12 months was below the poverty level; (1) Figures cover the Austin-Round Rock-San Marcos, TX Metropolitan Statistical Area
Source: U.S. Census Bureau, 2019-2023 American Community Survey 5-Year Estimates

EMPLOYMENT

Labor Force and Employment

Area	Civilian Labor Force			Workers Employed		
	Dec. 2023	Dec. 2024	% Chg.	Dec. 2023	Dec. 2024	% Chg.
City	692,732	711,010	2.6	671,863	690,459	2.8
MSA[1]	1,480,563	1,521,172	2.7	1,434,717	1,474,387	2.8
U.S.	166,661,000	167,746,000	0.7	160,754,000	161,294,000	0.3

Note: Data is not seasonally adjusted and covers workers 16 years of age and older; (1) Figures cover the Austin-Round Rock-San Marcos, TX Metropolitan Statistical Area
Source: Bureau of Labor Statistics, Local Area Unemployment Statistics

Unemployment Rate

Area	2024											
	Jan.	Feb.	Mar.	Apr.	May	Jun.	Jul.	Aug.	Sep.	Oct.	Nov.	Dec.
City	3.3	3.5	3.2	2.9	3.1	3.5	3.5	3.5	3.3	3.2	3.2	2.9
MSA[1]	3.5	3.6	3.4	3.0	3.2	3.7	3.7	3.7	3.5	3.4	3.4	3.1
U.S.	4.1	4.2	3.9	3.5	3.7	4.3	4.5	4.4	3.9	3.9	4.0	3.8

Note: Data is not seasonally adjusted and covers workers 16 years of age and older; (1) Figures cover the Austin-Round Rock-San Marcos, TX Metropolitan Statistical Area
Source: Bureau of Labor Statistics, Local Area Unemployment Statistics

Average Wages

Occupation	$/Hr.	Occupation	$/Hr.
Accountants and Auditors	44.19	Maintenance and Repair Workers	24.12
Automotive Mechanics	27.17	Marketing Managers	79.43
Bookkeepers	26.04	Network and Computer Systems Admin.	50.49
Carpenters	24.84	Nurses, Licensed Practical	30.98
Cashiers	15.10	Nurses, Registered	44.74
Computer Programmers	45.82	Nursing Assistants	18.68
Computer Systems Analysts	53.57	Office Clerks, General	21.24
Computer User Support Specialists	29.47	Physical Therapists	50.22
Construction Laborers	20.17	Physicians	140.23
Cooks, Restaurant	17.40	Plumbers, Pipefitters and Steamfitters	30.87
Customer Service Representatives	20.72	Police and Sheriff's Patrol Officers	40.67
Dentists	105.18	Postal Service Mail Carriers	29.21
Electricians	28.24	Real Estate Sales Agents	41.46
Engineers, Electrical	67.90	Retail Salespersons	17.04
Fast Food and Counter Workers	14.09	Sales Representatives, Technical/Scientific	45.57
Financial Managers	89.92	Secretaries, Exc. Legal/Medical/Executive	22.22
First-Line Supervisors of Office Workers	36.88	Security Guards	19.26
General and Operations Managers	68.18	Surgeons	n/a
Hairdressers/Cosmetologists	20.93	Teacher Assistants, Exc. Postsecondary[1]	15.99
Home Health and Personal Care Aides	13.82	Teachers, Secondary School, Exc. Sp. Ed.[1]	29.94
Janitors and Cleaners	16.90	Telemarketers	16.65
Landscaping/Groundskeeping Workers	18.93	Truck Drivers, Heavy/Tractor-Trailer	28.00
Lawyers	83.20	Truck Drivers, Light/Delivery Services	23.95
Maids and Housekeeping Cleaners	15.47	Waiters and Waitresses	17.05

Note: Wage data covers the Austin-Round Rock-San Marcos, TX Metropolitan Statistical Area; (1) Hourly wages were calculated from annual wage data based on a 40 hour work week
Source: Bureau of Labor Statistics, Metro Area Occupational Employment & Wage Estimates, May 2024

Employment by Industry

Sector	MSA[1] Number of Employees	MSA[1] Percent of Total	U.S. Percent of Total
Construction, Mining, and Logging	89,900	6.5	5.5
Financial Activities	89,900	6.5	5.8
Government	211,200	15.3	14.9
Information	49,800	3.6	1.9
Leisure and Hospitality	147,600	10.7	10.4
Manufacturing	73,200	5.3	8.0
Other Services	53,700	3.9	3.7
Private Education and Health Services	165,100	12.0	16.9
Professional and Business Services	282,100	20.5	14.2
Retail Trade	123,600	9.0	10.0
Transportation, Warehousing, and Utilities	37,200	2.7	4.8
Wholesale Trade	56,000	4.1	3.9

Note: Figures are non-farm employment as of December 2024. Figures are not seasonally adjusted and include workers 16 years of age and older; (1) Figures cover the Austin-Round Rock-San Marcos, TX Metropolitan Statistical Area
Source: Bureau of Labor Statistics, Current Employment Statistics, Employment, Hours, and Earnings

Employment by Occupation

Occupation Classification	City (%)	MSA[1] (%)	U.S. (%)
Management, Business, Science, and Arts	57.4	52.4	42.0
Natural Resources, Construction, and Maintenance	5.3	6.9	8.6
Production, Transportation, and Material Moving	6.7	8.3	13.0
Sales and Office	18.0	19.5	19.9
Service	12.6	13.0	16.5

Note: Figures cover employed civilians 16 years of age and older; (1) Figures cover the Austin-Round Rock-San Marcos, TX Metropolitan Statistical Area
Source: U.S. Census Bureau, 2019-2023 American Community Survey 5-Year Estimates

Occupations with Greatest Projected Employment Growth: 2022 – 2032

Occupation[1]	2022 Employment	2032 Projected Employment	Numeric Employment Change	Percent Employment Change
General and Operations Managers	425,560	504,280	78,720	18.5
Fast Food and Counter Workers	333,870	394,290	60,420	18.1
Stockers and Order Fillers	264,810	321,600	56,790	21.4
Home Health and Personal Care Aides	313,670	367,500	53,830	17.2
Software Developers	110,280	161,780	51,500	46.7
Cooks, Restaurant	113,680	158,830	45,150	39.7
Laborers and Freight, Stock, and Material Movers, Hand	225,090	269,120	44,030	19.6
Heavy and Tractor-Trailer Truck Drivers	226,450	270,320	43,870	19.4
Retail Salespersons	319,400	357,630	38,230	12.0
Registered Nurses	233,850	267,980	34,130	14.6

Note: Projections cover Texas; (1) Sorted by numeric employment change
Source: www.projectionscentral.org, State Occupational Projections, 2022–2032 Long-Term Projections

Fastest-Growing Occupations: 2022 – 2032

Occupation[1]	2022 Employment	2032 Projected Employment	Numeric Employment Change	Percent Employment Change
Wind Turbine Service Technicians	4,860	7,950	3,090	63.6
Nurse Practitioners	19,060	30,490	11,430	60.0
Data Scientists	13,220	20,250	7,030	53.2
Computer and Information Research Scientists (SOC 2018)	2,070	3,140	1,070	51.7
Information Security Analysts (SOC 2018)	14,620	21,620	7,000	47.9
Software Developers	110,280	161,780	51,500	46.7
Statisticians	980	1,430	450	45.9
Operations Research Analysts	12,060	17,290	5,230	43.4
Software Quality Assurance Analysts and Testers	17,350	24,440	7,090	40.9
Medical and Health Services Managers	49,430	69,180	19,750	40.0

Note: Projections cover Texas; (1) Sorted by percent employment change and excludes occupations with numeric employment change less than 50
Source: www.projectionscentral.org, State Occupational Projections, 2022–2032 Long-Term Projections

CITY FINANCES

City Government Finances

Component	2022 ($000)	2022 ($ per capita)
Total Revenues	4,324,969	4,345
Total Expenditures	4,312,050	4,332
Debt Outstanding	0	0

Source: U.S. Census Bureau, State & Local Government Finances 2022

City Government Revenue by Source

Source	2022 ($000)	2022 ($ per capita)	2022 (%)
General Revenue			
From Federal Government	120,627	121	2.8
From State Government	17,365	17	0.4
From Local Governments	15,504	16	0.4
Taxes			
Property	645,532	648	14.9
Sales and Gross Receipts	455,612	458	10.5
Personal Income	0	0	0.0
Corporate Income	0	0	0.0
Motor Vehicle License	0	0	0.0
Other Taxes	54,127	54	1.3
Current Charges	936,940	941	21.7
Liquor Store	0	0	0.0
Utility	1,897,933	1,907	43.9

Source: U.S. Census Bureau, State & Local Government Finances 2022

City Government Expenditures by Function

Function	2022 ($000)	2022 ($ per capita)	2022 (%)
General Direct Expenditures			
Air Transportation	177,030	177	4.1
Corrections	0	0	0.0
Education	0	0	0.0
Employment Security Administration	0	0	0.0
Financial Administration	51,161	51	1.2
Fire Protection	215,303	216	5.0
General Public Buildings	0	0	0.0
Governmental Administration, Other	65,448	65	1.5
Health	193,536	194	4.5
Highways	206,689	207	4.8
Hospitals	0	0	0.0
Housing and Community Development	86,075	86	2.0
Interest on General Debt	106,162	106	2.5
Judicial and Legal	48,649	48	1.1
Libraries	89,847	90	2.1
Parking	301	< 1	< 0.1
Parks and Recreation	216,454	217	5.0
Police Protection	445,407	447	10.3
Public Welfare	0	0	0.0
Sewerage	199,731	200	4.6
Solid Waste Management	140,413	141	3.3
Veterans' Services	0	0	0.0
Liquor Store	0	0	0.0
Utility	1,800,310	1,808	41.8

Source: U.S. Census Bureau, State & Local Government Finances 2022

TAXES

State Corporate Income Tax Rates

State	Tax Rate (%)	Income Brackets ($)	Num. of Brackets	Financial Institution Tax Rate (%)[a]	Federal Income Tax Ded.
Texas	(u)	—	—	(u)	No

Note: Tax rates for tax year 2024; (a) Rates listed are the corporate income tax rate applied to financial institutions or excise taxes based on income. Some states have other taxes based upon the value of deposits or shares; (u) Texas imposes a Franchise Tax, otherwise known as margin tax, imposed on entities with more than $2,470,000 total revenues effective in 2024 at rate of 0.75%, or 0.375% for entities primarily engaged in retail or wholesale trade, on lesser of 70% of total revenues or 100% of gross receipts after deductions for either compensation ($450,000 deduction limit) or cost of goods sold. Texas has an EZ rate of 0.331 applicable to a $20 million revenue threshold.

Source: Federation of Tax Administrators, State Corporate Income Tax Rates, January 1, 2025

State Individual Income Tax Rates

State	Tax Rate (%)	Income Brackets ($)	Personal Exemptions ($)			Standard Ded. ($)	
			Single	Married	Depend.	Single	Married
Texas							– No state income tax –

Note: Tax rates for tax year 2024; Local- and county-level taxes are not included
Source: Federation of Tax Administrators, State Individual Income Tax Rates, January 1, 2025

Various State Sales and Excise Tax Rates

State	State Sales Tax (%)	Gasoline[1] ($/gal.)	Cigarette[2] ($/pack)	Spirits[3] ($/gal.)	Wine[4] ($/gal.)	Beer[5] ($/gal.)	Recreational Marijuana (%)
Texas	6.25	0.20	1.41	2.40	0.20	0.19	Not legal

Note: All tax rates as of January 1, 2025; (1) The American Petroleum Institute has developed a methodology for determining the average tax rate on a gallon of fuel. Rates may include any of the following: excise taxes, environmental fees, storage tank fees, other fees or taxes, general sales tax, and local taxes; (2) The federal excise tax of $1.0066 per pack and local taxes are not included; (3) Rates are those applicable to off-premise sales of 40% alcohol by volume (a.b.v.) distilled spirits in 750ml containers. Local excise taxes are excluded; (4) Rates are those applicable to off-premise sales of 11% a.b.v. non-carbonated wine in 750ml containers; (5) Rates are those applicable to off-premise sales of 4.7% a.b.v. beer in 12 ounce containers.
Source: Tax Foundation, 2025 Facts & Figures: How Does Your State Compare?

State Tax Competitiveness Index

State	Overall Rank	Corporate Tax Rank	Individual Income Tax Rank	Sales Tax Rank	Property Tax Rank	Unemployment Insurance Tax Rank
Texas	7	46	1	36	40	30

Note: The Tax Foundation's State Tax Competitiveness Index enables policymakers, taxpayers, and business leaders to gauge how their states' tax systems compare. A rank of 1 is best, 50 is worst. Rankings do not average to the total. States without a tax rank equally as 1. DC's scores and rankings do not affect other states. The report shows tax systems as of July 1, 2024 (the beginning of Fiscal Year 2025).
Source: Tax Foundation, State Tax Competitiveness Index 2025

TRANSPORTATION

Means of Transportation to Work

Area	Car/Truck/Van		Public Transportation			Bicycle	Walked	Other Means	Worked at Home
	Drove Alone	Car-pooled	Bus	Subway	Railroad				
City	58.8	6.9	1.9	0.0	0.0	0.8	2.4	1.6	27.5
MSA[1]	63.4	7.7	1.0	0.0	0.0	0.4	1.8	1.4	24.2
U.S.	70.2	8.5	1.7	1.3	0.4	0.4	2.4	1.6	13.5

Note: Figures are percentages and cover workers 16 years of age and older; (1) Figures cover the Austin-Round Rock-San Marcos, TX Metropolitan Statistical Area
Source: U.S. Census Bureau, 2019-2023 American Community Survey 5-Year Estimates

Travel Time to Work

Area	Less Than 10 Minutes	10 to 19 Minutes	20 to 29 Minutes	30 to 44 Minutes	45 to 59 Minutes	60 to 89 Minutes	90 Minutes or More
City	9.6	33.4	24.5	21.5	6.1	3.5	1.4
MSA[1]	9.5	27.1	21.8	24.0	9.7	6.0	1.9
U.S.	12.6	28.6	21.2	20.8	8.1	6.0	2.8

Note: Note: Figures are percentages and include workers 16 years old and over; (1) Figures cover the Austin-Round Rock-San Marcos, TX Metropolitan Statistical Area
Source: U.S. Census Bureau, 2019-2023 American Community Survey 5-Year Estimates

Key Congestion Measures

Measure	2000	2010	2015	2020	2022
Annual Hours of Delay, Total (000)	25,499	47,034	61,262	48,435	67,840
Annual Hours of Delay, Per Auto Commuter	42	49	61	41	62
Annual Congestion Cost, Per Auto Commuter ($)	836	1,226	1,476	1,057	1,533

Note: Figures cover the Austin TX urban area
Source: Texas A&M Transportation Institute, 2023 Urban Mobility Report

Freeway Travel Time Index

Measure	1985	1990	1995	2000	2005	2010	2015	2020	2022
Urban Area Index[1]	1.12	1.15	1.19	1.26	1.31	1.29	1.33	1.13	1.27
Urban Area Rank[1,2]	21	22	23	13	12	13	11	6	16

Note: Freeway Travel Time Index—the ratio of travel time in the peak period to the travel time at free-flow conditions. For example, a value of 1.30 indicates a 20-minute free-flow trip takes 26 minutes in the peak (20 minutes x 1.30 = 26 minutes); (1) Covers the Austin TX urban area; (2) Rank is based on 101 larger urban areas (#1 = highest travel time index)
Source: Texas A&M Transportation Institute, 2023 Urban Mobility Report

Public Transportation

Agency Name / Mode of Transportation	Vehicles Operated in Maximum Service[1]	Annual Unlinked Passenger Trips[2] (in thous.)	Annual Passenger Miles[3] (in thous.)
Capital Metropolitan Transportation Authority (CMTA)			
Bus (purchased transportation)	290	22,490.9	93,122.3
Commuter Bus (purchased transportation)	12	121.3	2,400.3
Demand Response (purchased transportation)	183	915.0	5,611.3
Hybrid Rail (purchased transportation)	12	477.3	7,330.6
Vanpool (purchased transportation)	160	328.0	13,547.2

Note: (1) Number of revenue vehicles operated by the given mode and type of service to meet the annual maximum service requirement. This is the revenue vehicle count during the peak season of the year; on the week and day that maximum service is provided. Vehicles operated in maximum service (VOMS) exclude atypical days and one-time special events; (2) Number of passengers who boarded public transportation vehicles. Passengers are counted each time they board a vehicle no matter how many vehicles they use to travel from their origin to their destination. (3) Sum of the distances ridden by all passengers during the entire fiscal year.
Source: Federal Transit Administration, National Transit Database, 2023

Air Transportation

Airport Name and Code / Type of Service	Passenger Airlines[1]	Passenger Enplanements	Freight Carriers[2]	Freight (lbs)
Austin-Bergstrom International (AUS)				
Domestic service (U.S. carriers only)	28	10,159,438	16	134,729,553
International service (U.S. carriers only)	9	195,348	4	1,753,048

Note: (1) Includes all U.S.-based major, minor and commuter airlines that carried at least one passenger during the year; (2) Includes all U.S.-based airlines and freight carriers that transported at least one pound of freight during the year.
Source: Bureau of Transportation Statistics, The Intermodal Transportation Database, Air Carriers: T-100 Domestic Market (U.S. carriers only), 2024; Bureau of Transportation Statistics, The Intermodal Transportation Database, Air Carriers: T-100 International Market (U.S. carriers only), 2024

BUSINESSES

Major Business Headquarters

Company Name	Industry	Rankings	
		Fortune[1]	Forbes[2]
Oracle	Computer software	89	-
Tesla	Motor vehicles & parts	40	-

Note: (1) Companies that produce a 10-K are ranked 1 to 500 based on 2023 revenue; (2) All private companies with at least $2 billion in annual revenue through the end of their most current fiscal year are ranked 1 to 275; companies listed are headquartered in the city; dashes indicate no ranking
Source: Fortune, "Fortune 500," 2024; Forbes, "America's Largest Private Companies," 2024

Fastest-Growing Businesses

According to *Inc.*, Austin is home to 16 of America's 500 fastest-growing private companies: **Maev** (#38); **Crave Retail** (#66); **Publishing.com** (#75); **Skydeo** (#79); **Closinglock** (#139); **CloudServus** (#164); **Nok Recommerce** (#165); **Kickfin** (#189); **Pinwheel** (#212); **Incline Insurance Group** (#241); **SyncMatters** (#253); **Divelement Web Services** (#315); **BK Beauty** (#419); **LP First Capital** (#431); **Mainstream Medical Devices** (#485); **Advanced Voice Research Labs** (#496). Criteria: must be an independent, privately-held, for-profit, U.S. corporation, proprietorship or partnership as of December 31, 2023; revenues must be at least $100,000 in 2020 and $2 million in 2023; must have four-year operating/sales history. *Inc.*, "America's 500 Fastest-Growing Private Companies," 2024

According to *Initiative for a Competitive Inner City (ICIC)*, Austin is home to one of America's 100 fastest-growing "inner city" companies: **Mainstream Medical Devices** (#1). To be eligible for the IC100, companies have to be independently operated, privately held, for-profit businesses with revenues of at least $50,000 in 2019 and $500,000 in 2023, and headquartered in an under-resourced community. Recognizing that concentrated poverty exists within metropolitan areas outside of big cities (and that poverty overall is suburbanizing), ICIC defines under-resourced communities as large low-income, high-poverty areas located in the urban and suburban parts of all but the smallest metropolitan areas. Companies were ranked overall by revenue growth over the five-year period between 2019 and 2023. *Initiative for a Competitive Inner City (ICIC), "Inner City 100 Companies," 2024*

According to Deloitte, Austin is home to 13 of North America's 500 fastest-growing high-technology companies: **Kickfin** (#65); **inKind** (#115); **Skimmer** (#225); **VORAGO Technologies** (#285); **NinjaOne** (#302); **Digital Turbine** (#305); **CrowdStrike Holdings** (#320); **Measured** (#327); **Striveworks** (#401); **SpyCloud** (#435); **L7 Informatics** (#466); **ActivTrak** (#468); **Molecular Templates** (#494). Companies are ranked by percentage growth in revenue over a four-year period. Criteria for inclusion: company must be headquartered within North America; must own proprietary intellectual property or technology that is sold to customers in products that contributes to a significant portion of the company's operating revenue; must have been in business for a minumum of four years with 2020 operating revenues of at least $50,000 USD/CD and 2023 operating revenues of at least $5 million USD/CD. *Deloitte, 2024 Technology Fast 500*[TM]

Living Environment

COST OF LIVING

Cost of Living Index

Composite Index	Groceries	Housing	Utilities	Transportation	Health Care	Misc. Goods/Services
97.3	96.6	104.1	98.6	94.9	98.6	92.2

Note: The Cost of Living Index measures regional differences in the cost of consumer goods and services, excluding taxes and non-consumer expenditures, for professional and managerial households in the top income quintile. It is based on more than 50,000 prices covering almost 60 different items for which prices are collected three times a year by chambers of commerce, economic development organizations or university applied economic centers in each participating urban area. The numbers shown should be read as a percentage above or below the national average of 100. For example, a value of 115.4 in the groceries column indicates that grocery prices are 15.4% higher than the national average. Small differences in the index numbers should not be interpreted as significant; Figures cover the Austin TX urban area.
Source: The Council for Community and Economic Research, Cost of Living Index, 2024

Grocery Prices

Area[1]	T-Bone Steak ($/pound)	Frying Chicken ($/pound)	Whole Milk ($/half gal.)	Eggs ($/dozen)	Orange Juice ($/64 oz.)	Coffee ($/11.5 oz.)
City[2]	14.52	1.37	4.62	3.05	4.27	5.19
Avg.	15.42	1.55	4.69	3.25	4.41	5.46
Min.	14.50	1.16	4.43	2.75	4.00	4.85
Max.	17.56	2.89	5.49	4.78	5.54	7.89

Note: (1) Values for the local area are compared with the average, minimum and maximum values for all 276 areas in the Cost of Living Index; (2) Figures cover the Austin TX urban area; **T-Bone Steak** (price per pound); **Frying Chicken** (price per pound, whole fryer); **Whole Milk** (half gallon carton); **Eggs** (price per dozen, Grade A, large); **Orange Juice** (64 oz. Tropicana or Florida Natural); **Coffee** (11.5 oz. can, vacuum-packed, Maxwell House, Hills Bros, or Folgers).
Source: The Council for Community and Economic Research, Cost of Living Index, 2024

Housing and Utility Costs

Area[1]	New Home Price ($)	Apartment Rent ($/month)	All Electric ($/month)	Part Electric ($/month)	Other Energy ($/month)	Telephone ($/month)
City[2]	500,842	1,849	-	137.02	59.06	203.47
Avg.	515,975	1,550	210.99	123.07	82.07	194.99
Min.	265,375	692	104.33	53.68	36.26	179.42
Max.	2,775,821	5,719	529.02	397.28	361.63	223.33

Note: (1) Values for the local area are compared with the average, minimum and maximum values for all 276 areas in the Cost of Living Index; (2) Figures cover the Austin TX urban area; **New Home Price** (2,400 sf living area, 8,000 sf lot, in urban area with full utilities); **Apartment Rent** (950 sf 2 bedroom/1.5 or 2 bath, unfurnished, excluding all utilities except water); **All Electric** (average monthly cost for an all-electric home); **Part Electric** (average monthly cost for a part-electric home); **Other Energy** (average monthly cost for natural gas, fuel oil, coal, wood, and any other forms of energy except electricity); **Telephone** (price includes the base monthly rate plus taxes and fees for three lines of mobile phone service).
Source: The Council for Community and Economic Research, Cost of Living Index, 2024

Health Care, Transportation, and Other Costs

Area[1]	Doctor ($/visit)	Dentist ($/visit)	Optometrist ($/visit)	Gasoline ($/gallon)	Beauty Salon ($/visit)	Men's Shirt ($)
City[2]	109.05	135.58	126.98	2.98	67.39	27.11
Avg.	143.77	117.51	129.23	3.32	48.57	38.14
Min.	36.74	58.67	67.33	2.80	24.00	13.41
Max.	270.44	216.82	307.33	5.28	94.00	63.89

Note: (1) Values for the local area are compared with the average, minimum and maximum values for all 276 areas in the Cost of Living Index; (2) Figures cover the Austin TX urban area; **Doctor** (general practitioners routine exam of an established patient); **Dentist** (adult teeth cleaning and periodic oral examination); **Optometrist** (full vision eye exam for established adult patient); **Gasoline** (one gallon regular unleaded, national brand, including all taxes, cash price at self-service pump if available); **Beauty Salon** (woman's shampoo, trim, and blow-dry); **Men's Shirt** (cotton/polyester dress shirt, pinpoint weave, long sleeves).
Source: The Council for Community and Economic Research, Cost of Living Index, 2024

HOUSING

Homeownership Rate

Area	2017 (%)	2018 (%)	2019 (%)	2020 (%)	2021 (%)	2022 (%)	2023 (%)	2024 (%)
MSA[1]	55.6	56.1	59.0	65.4	62.2	62.4	60.3	56.2
U.S.	63.9	64.4	64.6	66.6	65.5	65.8	65.9	65.6

Note: (1) Figures cover the Austin-Round Rock-San Marcos, TX Metropolitan Statistical Area
Source: U.S. Census Bureau, Housing Vacancies and Homeownership Annual Statistics: 2017-2024

House Price Index (HPI)

Area	National Ranking[2]	Quarterly Change (%)	One-Year Change (%)	Five-Year Change (%)	Since 1991Q1 (%)
MSA[1]	237	-1.06	-0.80	47.35	579.98
U.S.[3]	–	1.43	4.51	57.13	327.82

Note: The HPI is a weighted repeat sales index. It measures average price changes in repeat sales or refinancings on the same properties. This information is obtained by reviewing repeat mortgage transactions on single-family properties whose mortgages have been purchased or securitized by Fannie Mae or Freddie Mac since January 1975; (1) Figures cover the Austin-Round Rock, TX Metropolitan Statistical Area; (2) Rankings are based on annual percentage change for all metro areas containing at least 15,000 transactions over the last 10 years and ranges from 1 to 241; (3) figures based on a weighted average of Census Division estimates using a seasonally adjusted, purchase-only index; all figures are for the period ending December 31, 2024
Source: Federal Housing Finance Agency, Change in FHFA Metropolitan Area House Price Indexes, All Transactions Index, 2024Q4

Home Value

Area	Under $100,000	$100,000 -$199,999	$200,000 -$299,999	$300,000 -$399,999	$400,000 -$499,999	$500,000 -$999,999	$1,000,000 or more	Median ($)
City	2.9	2.8	11.0	14.7	17.1	39.2	12.2	512,700
MSA[1]	5.1	5.2	15.7	18.2	16.6	30.5	8.6	434,800
U.S.	12.1	17.8	19.5	14.4	10.5	19.1	6.5	303,400

Note: Figures are percentages except for median and cover owner-occupied housing units; (1) Figures cover the Austin-Round Rock-San Marcos, TX Metropolitan Statistical Area
Source: U.S. Census Bureau, 2019-2023 American Community Survey 5-Year Estimates

Year Housing Structure Built

Area	2020 or Later	2010 -2019	2000 -2009	1990 -1999	1980 -1989	1970 -1979	1960 -1969	1950 -1959	1940 -1949	Before 1940	Median Year
City	2.5	20.7	17.2	13.0	17.3	13.7	7.2	4.1	2.0	2.3	1993
MSA[1]	4.0	25.5	21.4	14.6	14.3	9.7	4.5	2.8	1.3	2.0	2000
U.S.	1.2	8.9	13.6	12.8	13.0	14.4	10.0	9.7	4.5	11.9	1980

Note: Figures are percentages except for Median Year; Note: (1) Figures cover the Austin-Round Rock-San Marcos, TX Metropolitan Statistical Area
Source: U.S. Census Bureau, 2019-2023 American Community Survey 5-Year Estimates

Gross Monthly Rent

Area	Under $500	$500 -$999	$1,000 -$1,499	$1,500 -$1,999	$2,000 -$2,499	$2,500 -$2,999	$3,000 and up	Median ($)
City	2.5	4.7	32.4	33.5	15.4	6.4	5.0	1,655
MSA[1]	2.2	6.5	32.0	32.0	16.4	6.3	4.6	1,646
U.S.	6.5	22.3	29.5	20.2	10.8	4.8	5.9	1,348

Note: Figures are percentages except for median; Gross rent is the contract rent plus the estimated average monthly cost of utilities (electricity, gas, and water and sewer) and fuels (oil, coal, kerosene, wood, etc.) if these are paid by the renter (or paid for the renter by someone else); (1) Figures cover the Austin-Round Rock-San Marcos, TX Metropolitan Statistical Area
Source: U.S. Census Bureau, 2019-2023 American Community Survey 5-Year Estimates

HEALTH

Health Risk Factors

Category	MSA[1] (%)	U.S. (%)
Adults aged 18–64 who have any kind of health care coverage	81.8	90.8
Adults who reported being in good or better health	82.2	81.8
Adults who have been told they have high blood cholesterol	34.5	36.9
Adults who have been told they have high blood pressure	27.4	34.0
Adults who are current smokers	7.6	12.1
Adults who currently use e-cigarettes	7.1	7.7
Adults who currently use chewing tobacco, snuff, or snus	2.5	3.2
Adults who are heavy drinkers[2]	7.2	6.1
Adults who are binge drinkers[3]	16.5	15.2
Adults who are overweight (BMI 25.0 - 29.9)	32.9	34.4
Adults who are obese (BMI 30.0 - 99.8)	31.2	34.3
Adults who participated in any physical activities in the past month	77.9	75.8

Note: All figures are crude prevalence; (1) Figures cover the Austin-Round Rock, TX Metropolitan Statistical Area; (2) Heavy drinkers are classified as adult men having more than 14 drinks per week and adult women having more than 7 drinks per week; (3) Binge drinkers are classified as males having five or more drinks on one occasion or females having four or more drinks on one occasion
Source: Centers for Disease Control and Prevention, Behaviorial Risk Factor Surveillance System, SMART: Selected Metropolitan Area Risk Trends, 2023

Acute and Chronic Health Conditions

Category	MSA[1] (%)	U.S. (%)
Adults who have ever been told they had a heart attack	2.5	4.2
Adults who have ever been told they have angina or coronary heart disease	3.1	4.0
Adults who have ever been told they had a stroke	1.4	3.3
Adults who have ever been told they have asthma	14.0	15.7
Adults who have ever been told they have arthritis	19.3	26.3
Adults who have ever been told they have diabetes[2]	9.4	11.5
Adults who have ever been told they had skin cancer	4.7	5.6
Adults who have ever been told they had any other types of cancer	5.9	8.4
Adults who have ever been told they have COPD	3.3	6.4
Adults who have ever been told they have kidney disease	3.7	3.7
Adults who have ever been told they have a form of depression	20.1	22.0

Note: All figures are crude prevalence; (1) Figures cover the Austin-Round Rock, TX Metropolitan Statistical Area; (2) Figures do not include pregnancy-related, borderline, or pre-diabetes
Source: Centers for Disease Control and Prevention, Behaviorial Risk Factor Surveillance System, SMART: Selected Metropolitan Area Risk Trends, 2023

Health Screening and Vaccination Rates

Category	MSA[1] (%)	U.S. (%)
Adults who have ever been tested for HIV	42.0	37.5
Adults who have had their blood cholesterol checked within the last five years	89.3	87.0
Adults aged 65+ who have had flu shot within the past year	70.4	63.4
Adults aged 65+ who have ever had a pneumonia vaccination	75.3	71.9

Note: All figures are crude prevalence; (1) Figures cover the Austin-Round Rock, TX Metropolitan Statistical Area.
Source: Centers for Disease Control and Prevention, Behaviorial Risk Factor Surveillance System, SMART: Selected Metropolitan Area Risk Trends, 2023

Disability Status

Category	MSA[1] (%)	U.S. (%)
Adults who reported being deaf	4.3	7.4
Are you blind or have serious difficulty seeing, even when wearing glasses?	2.7	4.9
Do you have difficulty doing errands alone?	6.4	7.8
Do you have difficulty dressing or bathing?	2.7	3.6
Do you have serious difficulty concentrating/remembering/making decisions?	10.6	13.7
Do you have serious difficulty walking or climbing stairs?	10.1	13.2

Note: All figures are crude prevalence; (1) Figures cover the Austin-Round Rock, TX Metropolitan Statistical Area.
Source: Centers for Disease Control and Prevention, Behaviorial Risk Factor Surveillance System, SMART: Selected Metropolitan Area Risk Trends, 2023

Mortality Rates for the Top 10 Causes of Death in the U.S.

ICD-10[a] Sub-Chapter	ICD-10[a] Code	Crude Mortality Rate[2] per 100,000 population	
		County[3]	U.S.
Malignant neoplasms	C00-C97	97.3	182.7
Ischaemic heart diseases	I20-I25	55.5	109.6
Provisional assignment of new diseases of uncertain etiology[1]	U00-U49	30.9	65.3
Other forms of heart disease	I30-I51	24.2	65.1
Other degenerative diseases of the nervous system	G30-G31	42.6	52.4
Other external causes of accidental injury	W00-X59	39.4	52.3
Cerebrovascular diseases	I60-I69	26.3	49.1
Chronic lower respiratory diseases	J40-J47	14.0	43.5
Hypertensive diseases	I10-I15	21.2	38.9
Organic, including symptomatic, mental disorders	F01-F09	16.5	33.9

Note: (a) ICD-10 = International Classification of Diseases 10th Revision; (1) Includes COVID-19, adverse effects to COVID-19 vaccines, SARS, and vaping-related disorders; (2) Crude mortality rates are a three-year average covering 2021-2023; (3) Figures cover Travis County.
Source: Centers for Disease Control and Prevention, National Center for Health Statistics. National Vital Statistics System, Mortality 2018-2023 on CDC WONDER Online Database

Mortality Rates for Selected Causes of Death

Cause of Death	ICD-10[a] Code	Crude Mortality Rate[1] per 100,000 population	
		County[2]	U.S.
Accidental poisoning and exposure to noxious substances	X40-X49	23.2	30.5
Alzheimer disease	G30	22.1	35.4
Assault	X85-Y09	6.0	7.3
COVID-19	U07.1	30.9	65.3
Diabetes mellitus	E10-E14	11.9	30.0
Diseases of the liver	K70-K76	12.6	20.8
Human immunodeficiency virus (HIV) disease	B20-B24	1.3	1.5
Influenza and pneumonia	J09-J18	5.9	13.4
Intentional self-harm	X60-X84	14.2	14.7
Malnutrition	E40-E46	3.2	6.0
Obesity and other hyperalimentation	E65-E68	1.7	3.1
Renal failure	N17-N19	6.6	16.4
Transport accidents	V01-V99	11.4	14.4

Note: (a) ICD-10 = International Classification of Diseases 10th Revision; (1) Crude mortality rates are a three-year average covering 2021-2023; (2) Figures cover Travis County; Data are suppressed when the data meet the criteria for confidentiality constraints; Crude mortality rates are flagged as unreliable when the rate would be calculated with a numerator of 20 or less.
Source: Centers for Disease Control and Prevention, National Center for Health Statistics. National Vital Statistics System, Mortality 2018-2023 on CDC WONDER Online Database

Health Insurance Coverage

Area	With Health Insurance	With Private Health Insurance	With Public Health Insurance	Without Health Insurance	Population Under Age 19 Without Health Insurance
City	87.6	74.8	20.6	12.4	9.2
MSA[1]	87.9	75.2	21.9	12.1	9.0
U.S.	91.4	67.3	36.3	8.6	5.4

Note: Figures are percentages that cover the civilian noninstitutionalized population; (1) Figures cover the Austin-Round Rock-San Marcos, TX Metropolitan Statistical Area
Source: U.S. Census Bureau, 2019-2023 American Community Survey 5-Year Estimates

Number of Medical Professionals

Area	MDs[3]	DOs[3,4]	Dentists	Podiatrists	Chiropractors	Optometrists
County[1] (number)	4,404	291	1,026	59	489	251
County[1] (rate[2])	332.0	21.9	76.9	4.4	36.6	18.8
U.S. (rate[2])	302.5	29.2	74.6	6.4	29.5	18.0

Note: Data as of 2023 unless noted; (1) Data covers Travis County; (2) Number of medical professionals per 100,000 population; (3) Data as of 2022 and includes all active, non-federal physicians; (4) Doctor of Osteopathic Medicine
Source: U.S. Department of Health and Human Services, Health Resources and Services Administration, Bureau of Health Professions, Area Resource File (ARF) 2023-2024

Best Hospitals

According to *U.S. News*, the Austin-Round Rock-San Marcos, TX metro area is home to one of the best hospitals in the U.S.: **St. David's Medical Center** (1 adult specialty). The hospital listed was nationally ranked in at least one of 15 adult or 11 pediatric specialties. The number of specialties shown cover the parent hospital. Only 160 U.S. hospitals performed well enough to be nationally ranked in one or more specialties. Twenty hospitals in the U.S. made the Honor Roll. The Best Hospitals Honor Roll takes both the national rankings and the procedure and condition ratings into account. Hospitals received points if they were nationally ranked in one of the 15 adult specialties—the higher they ranked, the more points they got—and how many ratings of "high performing" they earned in the 20 procedures and conditions. *U.S. News Online, "America's Best Hospitals 2024-25"*

According to *U.S. News*, the Austin-Round Rock-San Marcos, TX metro area is home to one of the best children's hospitals in the U.S.: **Dell Children's Medical Center** (6 pediatric specialties). The hospital listed was highly ranked in at least one of 11 pediatric specialties. One hundred five children's hospitals in the U.S. were nationally ranked in at least one specialty. Hospitals received points for being ranked in a specialty, and the 10 hospitals with the most points across the 11 specialties make up the Honor Roll. *U.S. News Online, "America's Best Children's Hospitals 2024-25"*

EDUCATION

Public School District Statistics

District Name	Schls	Pupils	Pupil/ Teacher Ratio	Minority Pupils[1] (%)	Total Rev. per Pupil ($)	Total Exp. per Pupil ($)
Austin Achieve Public Schools	5	2,647	14.7	97.8	17,017	13,609
Austin ISD	126	72,830	14.3	69.2	15,720	26,950
Eanes ISD	12	7,738	12.8	37.1	14,472	27,865
Harmony Science Academy (Austin)	7	4,509	16.0	84.5	14,050	11,980
Lake Travis ISD	12	11,272	16.6	35.8	14,281	16,997
Valor Public Schools	5	3,159	16.5	49.4	15,972	9,745

Note: Table includes school districts with 2,000 or more students; (1) Percentage of students that are not non-Hispanic white.
Source: U.S. Department of Education, National Center for Education Statistics, Common Core of Data, Local Education Agency (School District) Universe Survey: School Year 2023-2024; U.S. Department of Education, National Center for Education Statistics, Common Core of Data, School District Finance Survey (F-33): School Year 2021–22

Best High Schools

According to *U.S. News,* Austin is home to five of the top 500 high schools in the U.S.: **Liberal Arts and Science Academy (LASA)** (#38); **Richards School for Young Women Leaders** (#121); **Idea Rundberg College Preparatory** (#146); **Chaparral Star Academy** (#347); **Westlake High School** (#409). Nearly 25,000 public, magnet and charter schools were ranked based on their performance on state assessments and how well they prepare students for college. *U.S. News & World Report, "Best High Schools 2024"*

Highest Level of Education

Area	Less than H.S.	H.S. Diploma	Some College, No Deg.	Associate Degree	Bachelor's Degree	Master's Degree	Prof. School Degree	Doctorate Degree
City	8.4	13.2	14.8	5.4	36.2	15.9	3.6	2.5
MSA[1]	8.4	17.1	18.0	6.6	31.6	13.6	2.7	2.1
U.S.	10.6	26.2	19.4	8.8	21.3	9.8	2.3	1.6

Note: Figures cover persons age 25 and over; (1) Figures cover the Austin-Round Rock-San Marcos, TX Metropolitan Statistical Area
Source: U.S. Census Bureau, 2019-2023 American Community Survey 5-Year Estimates

Educational Attainment by Race

Area	High School Graduate or Higher (%)					Bachelor's Degree or Higher (%)				
	Total	White	Black	Asian	Hisp.[2]	Total	White	Black	Asian	Hisp.[2]
City	91.6	95.1	90.6	93.6	78.3	58.2	63.9	36.7	78.4	35.6
MSA[1]	91.6	94.9	93.3	93.8	78.2	49.9	54.2	36.5	76.1	29.0
U.S.	89.4	92.9	88.1	88.0	72.5	35.0	37.7	24.7	57.0	19.9

Note: Figures shown cover persons 25 years old and over; (1) Figures cover the Austin-Round Rock-San Marcos, TX Metropolitan Statistical Area; (2) People of Hispanic origin can be of any race
Source: U.S. Census Bureau, 2019-2023 American Community Survey 5-Year Estimates

School Enrollment by Grade and Control

Area	Preschool (%)		Kindergarten (%)		Grades 1 - 4 (%)		Grades 5 - 8 (%)		Grades 9 - 12 (%)	
	Public	Private	Public	Private	Public	Private	Public	Private	Public	Private
City	51.1	48.9	85.1	14.9	87.7	12.3	86.7	13.3	90.3	9.7
MSA[1]	49.6	50.4	87.0	13.0	90.0	10.0	89.2	10.8	91.1	8.9
U.S.	58.7	41.3	85.2	14.8	87.2	12.8	87.9	12.1	89.0	11.0

Note: Figures shown cover persons 3 years old and over; (1) Figures cover the Austin-Round Rock-San Marcos, TX Metropolitan Statistical Area
Source: U.S. Census Bureau, 2019-2023 American Community Survey 5-Year Estimates

Higher Education

Four-Year Colleges			Two-Year Colleges			Medical Schools[1]	Law Schools[2]	Voc/ Tech[3]
Public	Private Non-profit	Private For-profit	Public	Private Non-profit	Private For-profit			
3	6	4	0	0	5	1	1	11

Note: Figures cover institutions located within the Austin-Round Rock-San Marcos, TX Metropolitan Statistical Area and include main campuses only; (1) includes schools accredited by the Liaison Committee on Medical Education and the American Osteopathic Association's Commission on Osteopathic College Accreditation; (2) includes ABA-accredited schools, schools with provisional ABA accreditation, and state accredited schools; (3) includes all schools with programs that are less than 2 years.
Source: National Center for Education Statistics, Integrated Postsecondary Education System (IPEDS), 2023-24; Wikipedia, List of Medical Schools in the United States, accessed May 2, 2025; Wikipedia, List of Law Schools in the United States, accessed May 2, 2025

According to *U.S. News & World Report*, the Austin-Round Rock-San Marcos, TX metro area is home to one of the top 200 national universities in the U.S.: **The University of Texas—Austin** (#30 tie). The indicators used to capture academic quality fall into a number of categories: assessment by administrators at peer institutions; retention of students; faculty resources; student selectivity; financial resources; alumni giving; high school counselor ratings of colleges; and graduation rate. *U.S. News & World Report, "America's Best Colleges 2025"*

According to *U.S. News & World Report*, the Austin-Round Rock-San Marcos, TX metro area is home to one of the top 100 liberal arts colleges in the U.S.: **Southwestern University** (#83 tie). The indicators used to capture academic quality fall into a number of categories: assessment by administrators at peer institutions; retention of students; faculty resources; student selectivity; financial resources; alumni giving; high school counselor ratings of colleges; and graduation rate. *U.S. News & World Report, "America's Best Colleges 2025"*

According to *U.S. News & World Report*, the Austin-Round Rock-San Marcos, TX metro area is home to one of the top 100 law schools in the U.S.: **University of Texas—Austin** (#14 tie). The rankings are based on a weighted average of 12 measures of quality: peer assessment score; assessment score by lawyers/judges; median LSAT scores; median undergrad GPA; acceptance rate; employment rates for graduates; placement success; bar passage rate; faculty resources; expenditures per student; student/faculty ratio; and library resources. *U.S. News & World Report, "America's Best Graduate Schools, Law, 2025"*

According to *U.S. News & World Report*, the Austin-Round Rock-San Marcos, TX metro area is home to one of the top 75 business schools in the U.S.: **University of Texas—Austin (McCombs)** (#16). The rankings are based on a weighted average of the following nine measures: quality assessment; peer assessment; recruiter assessment; placement success; mean starting salary and bonus; student selectivity; mean GMAT and GRE scores; mean undergraduate GPA; and acceptance rate. *U.S. News & World Report, "America's Best Graduate Schools, Business, 2025"*

EMPLOYERS

Major Employers

Company Name	Industry
Apple	Computer maker's tech & admin support center
Ascension Seton	Healthcare
Austin Independent School District	Education
City of Austin	Government
Dell Technologies	Computer hardware/software
Federal Government	Government
Google	Technology/computing
H-E-B Grocery	Grocery stores
IBM	Computer systems, hardware, software, & chip R&D
Oracle Corp.	Software/IT
St. David's Healthcare Partnership	Healthcare
Tesla	Automotive
The State of Texas	Government
The University of Texas at Austin	Higher education
Under Armour	Apparel

Note: Companies shown are located within the Austin-Round Rock-San Marcos, TX Metropolitan Statistical Area.
Source: Chambers of Commerce; State Departments of Labor; Wikipedia

Best Companies to Work For

CrowdStrike, headquartered in Austin, is among "The 100 Best Companies to Work For." To pick the best companies, *Fortune* partnered with the Great Place to Work Institute. Using their proprietary Trust Index™ survey, the core of what creates great a workplace is measured—key behaviors that drive trust in management, connection with colleagues, and loyalty to the company. To be eligible for the *Fortune* 100 Best Companies to Work For list, employers must have 1,000 or more employees in the U.S. and cannot be a government agency. *Fortune, "The 100 Best Companies to Work For," 2025*

CrowdStrike; SailPoint, headquartered in Austin, are among "Fortune's Best Workplaces for Parents." To pick the best companies, *Fortune* partnered with the Great Place to Work Institute. To be considered for the list, companies must be Great Place To Work-Certified and have at least 50 responses from parents in the US. The survey enables employees to share confidential quantitative and qualitative feedback about their organization's culture by responding to 60 statements on a 5-point scale and answering two open-ended questions. Collectively, these statements describe a great employee experience, defined by high levels of trust, respect, credibility, fairness, pride, and camaraderie. In addition, companies provide organizational data like size, location, industry, demographics, roles, and levels; and provide information about parental leave, adoption, flexible schedule, childcare and dependent health care benefits. *Fortune, "Best Workplaces for Parents," 2024*

Continued; SailPoint, headquartered in Austin, are among "Fortune's Best Workplaces for Women." To pick the best companies, *Fortune* partnered with the Great Place to Work Institute. To be considered for the list, companies must be Great Place To Work-Certified. Companies must also employ at least 50 women, at least 20% of their non-executive managers must be female, and at least one executive must be female. To determine the Best Workplaces for Women, Great Place To Work measured the differences in women's survey responses to those of their peers and assesses the impact of demographics and roles on the quality and consistency of women's experiences. Great Place To Work also analyzed the gender balance of each workplace, how it compared to each company's industry, and patterns in representation as women rise from front-line positions to the board of directors. *Fortune, "Best Workplaces for Women," 2024*

Ownwell, headquartered in Austin, is among "Best Workplaces in Real Estate." To determine the Best Workplaces in Real Estate list, Great Place To Work analyzed the survey responses of over 29,000 employees from Great Place To Work-Certified companies in the real estate industry. Survey data analysis and company-provided datapoints are then factored into a combined score to compare and rank the companies that create the most consistently positive experience for all employees in this industry. *Fortune, "Best Workplaces in Real Estate," 2024*

Tokyo Electron U.S. Holdings, headquartered in Austin, is among the "Best Places to Work in IT." To qualify, companies had to have a minimum of 100 total employees and five IT employees. The best places to work were selected based on DEI (diversity, equity, and inclusion) practices; IT turnover, promotions, and growth; IT retention and engagement programs; remote/hybrid working; benefits and perks (such as elder care and child care, flextime, and reimbursement for college tuition); and training and career development opportunities. *Computerworld, "Best Places to Work in IT," 2025*

PUBLIC SAFETY

Crime Rate

Area	Total Crime Rate	Violent Crime Rate				Property Crime Rate		
		Murder	Rape	Robbery	Aggrav. Assault	Burglary	Larceny-Theft	Motor Vehicle Theft
City	3,804.7	6.7	50.3	93.3	348.8	468.0	2,125.2	712.4
U.S.	2,290.9	5.7	38.0	66.5	264.1	250.7	1,347.2	318.7

Note: Figures are crimes per 100,000 population.
Source: FBI, Table 8, Offenses Known to Law Enforcement, by State by City, 2023

Hate Crimes

Area	Number of Quarters Reported	Number of Incidents per Bias Motivation					
		Race/Ethnicity/Ancestry	Religion	Sexual Orientation	Disability	Gender	Gender Identity
City[1]	4	22	7	20	1	2	0
U.S.	4	5,900	2,699	2,077	187	92	492

Note: (1) Figures include at least one incident reported with more than one bias motivation.
Source: Federal Bureau of Investigation, Hate Crime Statistics 2023

Identity Theft Consumer Reports

Area	Reports	Reports per 100,000 Population	Rank[2]
MSA[1]	7,473	317	55
U.S.	1,135,291	339	-

Note: (1) Figures cover the Austin-Round Rock-San Marcos, TX Metropolitan Statistical Area; (2) Rank ranges from 1 to 401 where 1 indicates greatest number of identity theft reports per 100,000 population
Source: Federal Trade Commission, Consumer Sentinel Network Data Book 2024

Fraud and Other Consumer Reports

Area	Reports	Reports per 100,000 Population	Rank[2]
MSA[1]	35,466	1,504	57
U.S.	5,360,641	1,601	-

Note: (1) Figures cover the Austin-Round Rock-San Marcos, TX Metropolitan Statistical Area; (2) Rank ranges from 1 to 401 where 1 indicates greatest number of fraud and other consumer reports per 100,000 population
Source: Federal Trade Commission, Consumer Sentinel Network Data Book 2024

POLITICS

2024 Presidential Election Results

Area	Trump (Rep.)	Harris (Dem.)	Stein (Green)	Kennedy (Ind.)	Oliver (Lib.)	Other
Travis County	29.2	68.3	1.0	0.0	0.8	0.6
U.S.	49.7	48.2	0.6	0.5	0.4	0.6

Note: Results are percentages and may not add to 100% due to rounding
Source: Dave Leip's Atlas of U.S. Presidential Elections

SPORTS

Professional Sports Teams

Team Name	League	Year Established
Austin FC	Major League Soccer (MLS)	2021

Note: Includes teams located in the Austin-Round Rock-San Marcos, TX Metropolitan Statistical Area.
Source: Wikipedia, Major Professional Sports Teams of the United States and Canada, May 1, 2025

CLIMATE

Average and Extreme Temperatures

Temperature	Jan	Feb	Mar	Apr	May	Jun	Jul	Aug	Sep	Oct	Nov	Dec	Yr.
Extreme High (°F)	90	97	98	98	100	105	109	106	104	98	91	90	109
Average High (°F)	60	64	72	79	85	91	95	96	90	81	70	63	79
Average Temp. (°F)	50	53	61	69	75	82	85	85	80	70	60	52	69
Average Low (°F)	39	43	50	58	65	72	74	74	69	59	49	41	58
Extreme Low (°F)	-2	7	18	35	43	53	64	61	47	32	20	4	-2

Note: Figures cover the years 1948-1990
Source: National Climatic Data Center, International Station Meteorological Climate Summary, 9/96

Average Precipitation/Snowfall/Humidity

Precip./Humidity	Jan	Feb	Mar	Apr	May	Jun	Jul	Aug	Sep	Oct	Nov	Dec	Yr.
Avg. Precip. (in.)	1.6	2.3	1.8	2.9	4.3	3.5	1.9	1.9	3.3	3.5	2.1	1.9	31.1
Avg. Snowfall (in.)	1	Tr	Tr	0	0	0	0	0	0	0	Tr	Tr	1
Avg. Rel. Hum. 6am (%)	79	80	79	83	88	89	88	87	86	84	81	79	84
Avg. Rel. Hum. 3pm (%)	53	51	47	50	53	49	43	42	47	47	49	51	48

Note: Figures cover the years 1948-1990; Tr = Trace amounts (<0.05 in. of rain; <0.5 in. of snow)
Source: National Climatic Data Center, International Station Meteorological Climate Summary, 9/96

Weather Conditions

Temperature			Daytime Sky			Precipitation		
10°F & below	32°F & below	90°F & above	Clear	Partly cloudy	Cloudy	0.01 inch or more precip.	0.1 inch or more snow/ice	Thunderstorms
< 1	20	111	105	148	112	83	1	41

Note: Figures are average number of days per year and cover the years 1948-1990
Source: National Climatic Data Center, International Station Meteorological Climate Summary, 9/96

HAZARDOUS WASTE

Superfund Sites

The Austin-Round Rock-San Marcos, TX metro area has no sites on the EPA's Superfund Final National Priorities List (NPL) or Superfund Alternative Approach (SAA) list. The Superfund alternative approach uses the same investigation and cleanup process and standards that are used for sites listed on the National Priorities List. The SAA is an alternative to listing a site on the NPL; it is not an alternative to Superfund or the Superfund process. There are a total of 1,445 Superfund sites with a status of proposed or final on both lists in the United States. *U.S. Environmental Protection Agency, National Priorities List, May 1, 2025; U.S. Environmental Protection Agency, Superfund Alternative Approach Sites, May 1, 2025*

AIR QUALITY

Air Quality Trends: Ozone

	1990	1995	2000	2005	2010	2015	2020	2021	2022	2023
MSA[1]	0.088	0.089	0.088	0.082	0.074	0.073	0.066	0.066	0.073	0.074
U.S.	0.087	0.089	0.081	0.080	0.072	0.068	0.066	0.067	0.067	0.070

Note: (1) Data covers the Austin-Round Rock-San Marcos, TX Metropolitan Statistical Area. The values shown are the composite ozone concentration averages among trend sites based on the highest fourth daily maximum 8-hour concentration in parts per million. These trends are based on sites having an adequate record of monitoring data during the trend period. Data from exceptional events are included.
Source: U.S. Environmental Protection Agency, Air Quality Monitoring Information, "Air Quality Trends by City, 1990-2023"

Air Quality Index

Area	Percent of Days when Air Quality was...[2]					AQI Statistics[2]	
	Good	Moderate	Unhealthy for Sensitive Groups	Unhealthy	Very Unhealthy	Maximum	Median
MSA[1]	40.3	56.7	3.0	0.0	0.0	122	54

Note: (1) Data covers the Austin-Round Rock-San Marcos, TX Metropolitan Statistical Area; (2) Based on 365 days with AQI data in 2023. Air Quality Index (AQI) is an index for reporting daily air quality. EPA calculates the AQI for five major air pollutants regulated by the Clean Air Act: ground-level ozone, particle pollution (aka particulate matter), carbon monoxide, sulfur dioxide, and nitrogen dioxide. The AQI runs from 0 to 500. The higher the AQI value, the greater the level of air pollution and the greater the health concern. There are six AQI categories: "Good" AQI is between 0 and 50. Air quality is considered satisfactory; "Moderate" AQI is between 51 and 100. Air quality is acceptable; "Unhealthy for Sensitive Groups" When AQI values are between 101 and 150, members of sensitive groups may experience health effects; "Unhealthy" When AQI values are between 151 and 200 everyone may begin to experience health effects; "Very Unhealthy" AQI values between 201 and 300 trigger a health alert; "Hazardous" AQI values over 300 trigger warnings of emergency conditions (not shown).
Source: U.S. Environmental Protection Agency, Air Quality Index Report, 2023

Air Quality Index Pollutants

Area	Percent of Days when AQI Pollutant was...[2]					
	Carbon Monoxide	Nitrogen Dioxide	Ozone	Sulfur Dioxide	Particulate Matter 2.5	Particulate Matter 10
MSA[1]	0.0	1.1	29.3	(3)	69.6	0.0

Note: (1) Data covers the Austin-Round Rock-San Marcos, TX Metropolitan Statistical Area; (2) Based on 365 days with AQI data in 2023. The Air Quality Index (AQI) is an index for reporting daily air quality. EPA calculates the AQI for five major air pollutants regulated by the Clean Air Act: ground-level ozone, particle pollution (also known as particulate matter), carbon monoxide, sulfur dioxide, and nitrogen dioxide. The AQI runs from 0 to 500. The higher the AQI value, the greater the level of air pollution and the greater the health concern; (3) Sulfur dioxide is no longer included in this table because SO_2 concentrations tend to be very localized and not necessarily representative of broad geographical areas like counties and CBSAs.
Source: U.S. Environmental Protection Agency, Air Quality Index Report, 2023

Maximum Air Pollutant Concentrations: Particulate Matter, Ozone, CO and Lead

	Particulate Matter 10 (ug/m^3)	Particulate Matter 2.5 Wtd AM (ug/m^3)	Particulate Matter 2.5 24-Hr (ug/m^3)	Ozone (ppm)	Carbon Monoxide (ppm)	Lead (ug/m^3)
MSA[1] Level	53	10.4	25	0.074	2	n/a
NAAQS[2]	150	15	35	0.075	9	0.15
Met NAAQS[2]	Yes	Yes	Yes	Yes	Yes	n/a

Note: (1) Data covers the Austin-Round Rock-San Marcos, TX Metropolitan Statistical Area; Data from exceptional events are included; (2) National Ambient Air Quality Standards; ppm = parts per million; ug/m^3 = micrograms per cubic meter; n/a not available.
Concentrations: Particulate Matter 10 (coarse particulate)—highest second maximum 24-hour concentration; Particulate Matter 2.5 Wtd AM (fine particulate)—highest weighted annual mean concentration; Particulate Matter 2.5 24-Hour (fine particulate)—highest 98th percentile 24-hour concentration; Ozone—highest fourth daily maximum 8-hour concentration; Carbon Monoxide—highest second maximum non-overlapping 8-hour concentration; Lead—maximum running 3-month average
Source: U.S. Environmental Protection Agency, Air Quality Monitoring Information, "Air Quality Statistics by City, 2023"

Maximum Air Pollutant Concentrations: Nitrogen Dioxide and Sulfur Dioxide

	Nitrogen Dioxide AM (ppb)	Nitrogen Dioxide 1-Hr (ppb)	Sulfur Dioxide AM (ppb)	Sulfur Dioxide 1-Hr (ppb)	Sulfur Dioxide 24-Hr (ppb)
MSA[1] Level	13	n/a	n/a	n/a	n/a
NAAQS[2]	53	100	30	75	140
Met NAAQS[2]	Yes	n/a	n/a	n/a	n/a

Note: (1) Data covers the Austin-Round Rock-San Marcos, TX Metropolitan Statistical Area; Data from exceptional events are included; (2) National Ambient Air Quality Standards; ppm = parts per million; ug/m^3 = micrograms per cubic meter; n/a not available.
Concentrations: Nitrogen Dioxide AM—highest arithmetic mean concentration; Nitrogen Dioxide 1-Hr—highest 98th percentile 1-hour daily maximum concentration; Sulfur Dioxide AM—highest annual mean concentration; Sulfur Dioxide 1-Hr—highest 99th percentile 1-hour daily maximum concentration; Sulfur Dioxide 24-Hr—highest second maximum 24-hour concentration
Source: U.S. Environmental Protection Agency, Air Quality Monitoring Information, "Air Quality Statistics by City, 2023"

Cape Coral, Florida

Background

Cape Coral sits on Florida's Gulf Coast 71 miles south of Sarasota. Developed in 1957 it is now Florida's third-largest city by land mass at 120 square miles, and the largest city between Tampa and Miami. To the east across the Caloosahatchee River lies Fort Myers, and to the west across Pine Island and Pine Island sound lie the fabled barrier islands of Captiva and Sanibel.

Baltimore brothers Leonard and Jack Rosen purchased the former Redfish Point for $678,000 in 1957 and renamed the property Cape Coral. By June of the following year "the Cape," as it is known, was receiving its first residents. The city incorporated in 1970 when its population reached 11,470.

Despite the city's relative youth, this self-named "Waterfront Wonderland" has developed an interest in its roots. It fosters a Cape Coral Historical Museum that is housed in the original snack bar from the local country club; one of its oldest historical documents is the Cape's 1961 phone book.

Four hundred precious miles of salt and fresh water canals slice through the city, providing water access to abundant recreational boaters and numerous opportunities for waterfront living.

Industry-wise, Cape Coral has Foreign Trade Zones in two of its three industrial parks, the 92.5-acre North Cape Industrial Park—home to light manufacturers, service industry and warehouses—and the Mid Cape Commerce Park which, at 143.37 acres, is comprised of service industries and warehouses. The economy of Cape Coral is based on healthcare, retail and real estate.

A VA Clinic was recently built by the U.S. Dept. of Veteran's Affairs at the Hancock Creek Commerce Park and Indian Oaks Trade Centre. It provides a full range of services ranging from mental health and diagnostic radiology to urology and a full complement of imaging services such as CT scans and nuclear medicine. It is the centerpiece of a Veterans Investment Zone initiative designed to draw office, medical parks, and assisted living facilities.

Today the U.S. Bureau of Labor Statistics tracks the success of this retirement and tourism destination in conjunction with that of nearby Fort Myers, and the region boasts trade, transportation, and utilities as its largest economic sector.

Significant recreational opportunities in the area include the Four Mile Cove Ecological Preserve with its nature trail, picnic area, and warm weather kayak rentals, and The Cape Coral Yacht Club with a fishing pier, beach, and community pool. The 18-hole public Coral Oaks Golf Course (replete with pro shop and pub), and Soccer Complex show the city's diverse recreational opportunities.

To the east of Cape Coral—on the other side of Fort Myers—is both the Florida Gulf Coast University and Southwest Florida International Airport.

Cape Coral features a borderline tropical savanna climate. The wet season (May to October) is hot and humid with erratic tropical downpours, while the dry season (November to April) tends to be pleasantly warm and sees only sporadic precipitation. The city receives about 53 inches of rain each year. During the summer months, afternoon thunderstorms are heavy yet brief. The city is affected by the annual hurricane season, which begins officially on June 1 and continues through November. In 2022, Hurricane Ian ripped through the city causing massive damage and several fatalities.

Rankings

General Rankings

- Cape Coral was identified as one of America's fastest-growing areas in terms of population and economy by *Forbes*. Cape Coral ranked #45 out of 50. Over 500 cities with more than 75,000 residents were measured for percentage of population growth over the following three periods: from 2011 to 2016; 2016 to 2021; and then 2011 to 2021. *Forbes.com, "The Fastest Growing Cities in America and Their Change in Income," September 12, 2023*

Business/Finance Rankings

- The Cape Coral metro area appeared on the Milken Institute "2025 Best Performing Cities" list. Rank: #38 out of 200 large metro areas (based on performance category). Criteria: job growth; wage growth; high-tech growth and impact; community resilience; housing affordability; household broadband access. *Milken Institute, "Best-Performing Cities 2025," January 14, 2025*

Education Rankings

- Personal finance website *WalletHub* analyzed the 150 largest U.S. metropolitan statistical areas to determine where the most educated Americans are putting their degrees to work. Criteria: education levels; percentage of workers with degrees; education quality and attainment gap; public school quality rankings; quality and enrollment of each metro area's universities. Cape Coral was ranked #107 (#1 = most educated city). *WalletHub.com, "Most & Least Educated Cities in America, 2025" July 2, 2024*

Health/Fitness Rankings

- Cape Coral was identified as a "2025 Allergy Capital." The area ranked #43 out of the nation's 100 largest metropolitan areas. Three groups of factors were used to identify the most challenging cities for people with allergies: annual tree, grass, and weed pollen scores; over the counter allergy medicine use; number of board-certified allergy specialists. *Asthma and Allergy Foundation of America, "2025 Allergy Capitals: The Most Challenging Places to Live with Allergies," March 18, 2025*

- Cape Coral was identified as a "2024 Asthma Capital." The area ranked #80 out of the nation's 100 largest metropolitan areas. Criteria: estimated asthma prevalence; asthma-related mortality; and ER visits due to asthma. Risk factors analyzed but not factored in the rankings: annual air quality including pollution and ozone levels; public smoking laws; indoor air quality; access to asthma specialists; rescue and controller medication use; uninsured rate; pollen allergy; poverty rate. *Asthma and Allergy Foundation of America, "Asthma Capitals 2024: The Most Challenging Places to Live With Asthma," September 10, 2024*

Real Estate Rankings

- *WalletHub* compared the most populated U.S. cities to determine which had the best markets for real estate agents. Cape Coral ranked #88 where demand was high and pay was the best. Criteria: sales per agent; annual median wage for real-estate agents; monthly average starting salary for real estate agents; real estate job density and competition; unemployment rate; home turnover rate; housing-market health index; and other relevant metrics. *WalletHub.com, "2021 Best Places to Be a Real Estate Agent," May 12, 2021*

- The Cape Coral metro area was identified as one of the 20 worst housing markets in the U.S. in 2024. The area ranked #226 out of 226 markets. Criteria: year-over-year change of median sales price of existing single-family homes between the 4th quarter of 2023 and the 4th quarter of 2024. *National Association of Realtors®, Median Sales Price of Existing Single-Family Homes for Metropolitan Areas, 4th Quarter 2024*

- Cape Coral was ranked #139 out of 176 metro areas in terms of cost of housing in 2024 by the National Association of Home Builders (#1 = most affordable). Criteria: the portion of an average family's income necessary to pay the mortgage on a median-priced home. *National Association of Home Builders®, NAHB-Wells Fargo Cost of Housing Index, 4th Quarter 2024*

Safety Rankings

- Allstate ranked the 100 most populous cities in America in terms of driver safety. Cape Coral ranked #72. Criteria based on anonymized driving behavior data from Allstate's mobile app powered by Arity: high speed driving (over 80 mph), phone handling, and hard braking. The report helps increase the importance of safety and awareness behind the wheel. *Allstate, "16th Allstate America's Best Drivers Report®" July 11, 2024*

Women/Minorities Rankings

- Personal finance website *WalletHub* compared more than 180 U.S. cities across two key dimensions, "Hispanic Business-Friendliness" and "Hispanic Purchasing Power," to arrive at the most favorable conditions for Hispanic entrepreneurs. Cape Coral was ranked #6 out of 182. Criteria includes: share of Hispanic-Owned Businesses; average growth of Hispanic Business revenues; Small Business-Friendliness score; affordability; and number of Hispanics with at least a bachelor's degree. *WalletHub.com, "Best Cities for Hispanic Entrepreneurs," September 4, 2024*

Business Environment

DEMOGRAPHICS

Population Growth

Area	1990 Census	2000 Census	2010 Census	2020 Census	2023 Estimate[2]	Population Growth 1990-2023 (%)
City	75,507	102,286	154,305	194,016	206,387	173.3
MSA[1]	335,113	440,888	618,754	760,822	792,692	136.5
U.S.	248,709,873	281,421,906	308,745,538	331,449,281	332,387,540	33.6

Note: (1) Figures cover the Cape Coral-Fort Myers, FL Metropolitan Statistical Area; (2) 2019-2023 5-year ACS population estimate
Source: U.S. Census Bureau, 1990 Census, 2000 Census, 2010 Census, 2020 Census, 2019-2023 American Community Survey 5-Year Estimates

Race

Area	White Alone[2] (%)	Black Alone[2] (%)	Asian Alone[2] (%)	AIAN[3] Alone[2] (%)	NHOPI[4] Alone[2] (%)	Other Race Alone[2] (%)	Two or More Races (%)
City	72.9	4.5	1.5	0.1	0.0	4.1	16.9
MSA[1]	70.5	8.0	1.7	0.6	0.0	4.3	15.0
U.S.	63.4	12.4	5.8	0.9	0.2	6.6	10.7

Note: (1) Figures cover the Cape Coral-Fort Myers, FL Metropolitan Statistical Area; (2) Alone is defined as not being in combination with one or more other races; (3) American Indian and Alaska Native; (4) Native Hawaiian and Other Pacific Islander
Source: U.S. Census Bureau, 2019-2023 American Community Survey 5-Year Estimates

Hispanic or Latino Origin

Area	Total (%)	Mexican (%)	Puerto Rican (%)	Cuban (%)	Other (%)
City	25.0	1.9	4.9	10.7	7.5
MSA[1]	23.6	4.7	4.5	6.7	7.8
U.S.	19.0	11.3	1.8	0.7	5.2

Note: Persons of Hispanic or Latino origin can be of any race; (1) Figures cover the Cape Coral-Fort Myers, FL Metropolitan Statistical Area
Source: U.S. Census Bureau, 2019-2023 American Community Survey 5-Year Estimates

Age

Area	Percent of Population									Median Age
	Under Age 5	Age 5–19	Age 20–34	Age 35–44	Age 45–54	Age 55–64	Age 65–74	Age 75–84	Age 85+	
City	4.5	14.5	15.7	10.8	13.4	15.9	14.6	7.9	2.5	48.7
MSA[1]	4.5	14.9	15.7	10.6	11.3	14.2	15.4	10.2	3.3	49.3
U.S.	5.7	19.1	20.2	13.1	12.3	12.8	10.0	4.9	1.9	38.7

Note: (1) Figures cover the Cape Coral-Fort Myers, FL Metropolitan Statistical Area
Source: U.S. Census Bureau, 2019-2023 American Community Survey 5-Year Estimates

Disability by Age

Area	All Ages	Under 18 Years Old	18 to 64 Years Old	65 Years and Over
City	14.0	3.8	10.0	30.5
MSA[1]	13.7	4.0	9.6	27.1
U.S.	13.0	4.7	10.7	32.9

Note: Figures show percent of the civilian noninstitutionalized population that reported having a disability. Disability status is determined from six types of difficulty: vision, hearing, cognitive, ambulatory, self-care, and independent living. For children under 5 years old, hearing and vision difficulty are used to determine disability status. For children between the ages of 5 and 14, disability status is determined from hearing, vision, cognitive, ambulatory, and self-care difficulties. For people aged 15 years and older, they are considered to have a disability if they have difficulty with any one of the six difficulty types; Note: (1) Figures cover the Cape Coral-Fort Myers, FL Metropolitan Statistical Area
Source: U.S. Census Bureau, 2019-2023 American Community Survey 5-Year Estimates

Ancestry

Area	German	Irish	English	American	Italian	Polish	French[2]	European	Scottish
City	13.4	11.5	8.5	10.4	9.2	3.3	2.2	1.5	1.3
MSA[1]	13.1	10.6	9.0	10.2	7.9	3.1	2.0	1.4	1.6
U.S.	12.6	9.4	9.1	5.5	4.9	2.6	2.0	1.6	1.6

Note: Figures are the percentage of the total population reporting a particular ancestry. The nine most commonly reported ancestries in the U.S. are shown. Figures include multiple ancestries (e.g. if a person reported being Irish and Italian, they were included in both columns); (1) Figures cover the Cape Coral-Fort Myers, FL Metropolitan Statistical Area; (2) Excludes Basque
Source: U.S. Census Bureau, 2019-2023 American Community Survey 5-Year Estimates

Foreign-born Population

Area	Percent of Population Born in								
	Any Foreign Country	Asia	Mexico	Europe	Caribbean	Central America[2]	South America	Africa	Canada
City	17.9	1.3	0.4	2.2	9.2	1.2	2.8	0.1	0.7
MSA[1]	17.9	1.4	1.7	1.9	7.0	2.4	2.2	0.2	1.0
U.S.	13.9	4.3	3.3	1.4	1.4	1.2	1.2	0.8	0.2

Note: (1) Figures cover the Cape Coral-Fort Myers, FL Metropolitan Statistical Area; (2) Excludes Mexico.
Source: U.S. Census Bureau, 2019-2023 American Community Survey 5-Year Estimates

Household Size

Area	Persons in Household (%)							Average Household Size
	One	Two	Three	Four	Five	Six	Seven or More	
City	24.2	44.1	13.7	10.3	5.5	1.3	0.8	2.59
MSA[1]	28.3	44.7	11.6	8.8	4.4	1.5	0.7	2.44
U.S.	28.5	33.8	15.4	12.7	5.9	2.3	1.4	2.54

Note: (1) Figures cover the Cape Coral-Fort Myers, FL Metropolitan Statistical Area
Source: U.S. Census Bureau, 2019-2023 American Community Survey 5-Year Estimates

Household Relationships

Area	Householder	Opposite-sex Spouse	Same-sex Spouse	Opposite-sex Unmarried Partner	Same-sex Unmarried Partner	Child[2]	Grandchild	Other Relatives	Non-relatives
City	39.5	21.2	0.3	3.2	0.1	25.5	2.1	4.8	2.8
MSA[1]	41.8	20.9	0.3	3.0	0.2	22.4	1.8	4.4	3.3
U.S.	38.3	17.5	0.2	2.5	0.2	28.3	2.4	4.8	3.4

Note: Figures are percent of the total population; (1) Figures cover the Cape Coral-Fort Myers, FL Metropolitan Statistical Area; (2) Includes biological, adopted, and stepchildren of the householder
Source: U.S. Census Bureau, 2020 Census

Gender

Area	Males	Females	Males per 100 Females
City	103,313	103,074	100.2
MSA[1]	389,853	402,839	96.8
U.S.	164,545,087	167,842,453	98.0

Note: (1) Figures cover the Cape Coral-Fort Myers, FL Metropolitan Statistical Area
Source: U.S. Census Bureau, 2019-2023 American Community Survey 5-Year Estimates

Marital Status

Area	Never Married	Now Married[2]	Separated	Widowed	Divorced
City	24.7	52.6	1.5	7.8	13.4
MSA[1]	26.5	51.8	1.5	7.8	12.3
U.S.	34.1	47.9	1.7	5.6	10.7

Note: Figures are percentages and cover the population 15 years of age and older; (1) Figures cover the Cape Coral-Fort Myers, FL Metropolitan Statistical Area; (2) Excludes separated
Source: U.S. Census Bureau, 2019-2023 American Community Survey 5-Year Estimates

Religious Groups by Family

Area	Catholic	Baptist	Methodist	LDS[2]	Pentecostal	Lutheran	Islam	Adventist	Other
MSA[1]	18.8	2.5	1.7	0.6	3.0	0.7	0.2	2.0	12.2
U.S.	18.7	7.3	3.0	2.0	1.8	1.7	1.3	1.3	11.6

Note: Figures are the number of adherents as a percentage of the total population and cover the eight largest religious groups in the U.S; (1) Figures cover the Cape Coral-Fort Myers, FL Metropolitan Statistical Area; (2) Church of Jesus Christ of Latter-day Saints
Sources: 2020 U.S. Religion Census, Association of Statisticians of American Religious Bodies; The Association of Religion Data Archives (ARDA)

Religious Groups by Tradition

Area	Catholic	Evangelical Protestant	Mainline Protestant	Black Protestant	Islam	Judaism	Hinduism	Orthodox	Buddhism
MSA[1]	18.8	16.4	3.0	0.6	0.2	0.2	0.2	0.1	0.1
U.S.	18.7	16.5	5.2	2.3	1.3	0.6	0.4	0.4	0.3

Note: Figures are the number of adherents as a percentage of the total population; (1) Figures cover the Cape Coral-Fort Myers, FL Metropolitan Statistical Area
Sources: 2020 U.S. Religion Census, Association of Statisticians of American Religious Bodies; The Association of Religion Data Archives (ARDA)

ECONOMY

Real Gross Domestic Product (GDP)

Area	2017	2018	2019	2020	2021	2022	2023	Rank[3]
MSA[1]	31.3	32.6	33.3	33.2	36.0	38.8	40.4	84
U.S.[2]	17,619.1	18,160.7	18,642.5	18,238.9	19,387.6	19,896.6	20,436.3	—

Note: Figures are in billions of chained 2017 dollars; (1) Figures cover the Cape Coral-Fort Myers, FL Metropolitan Statistical Area; (2) Figures cover real GDP within metropolitan areas; (3) Rank is based on 2023 data and ranges from 1 to 384
Source: U.S. Bureau of Economic Analysis

Economic Growth

Area	2014	2015	2016	2017	2018	2019	2020	2021	2022	2023
MSA[1]	5.0	6.1	7.5	0.6	4.1	2.4	-0.5	8.5	7.8	4.2
U.S.[2]	2.6	3.2	2.0	2.7	3.1	2.7	-2.2	6.3	2.6	2.7

Note: Figures are real gross domestic product growth rates and represent percent change from preceding period; (1) Figures cover the Cape Coral-Fort Myers, FL Metropolitan Statistical Area; (2) Figures are the average growth rates within metropolitan areas
Source: U.S. Bureau of Economic Analysis

Metropolitan Area Exports

Area	2018	2019	2020	2021	2022	2023	Rank[2]
MSA[1]	668.0	694.9	654.8	797.5	886.9	935.4	177
U.S.	1,664,056.1	1,645,941.7	1,431,406.6	1,753,941.4	2,062,937.4	2,019,160.5	—

Note: Figures are in millions of dollars; (1) Figures cover the Cape Coral-Fort Myers, FL Metropolitan Statistical Area; (2) Rank is based on 2023 data and ranges from 1 to 386
Source: U.S. Department of Commerce, International Trade Administration, Office of Trade and Economic Analysis, Industry and Analysis, Exports by Metropolitan Area, data extracted April 2, 2025

Building Permits

Area	Single-Family			Multi-Family			Total		
	2023	2024	Pct. Chg.	2023	2024	Pct. Chg.	2023	2024	Pct. Chg.
City	2,023	2,671	32.0	1,972	726	-63.2	3,995	3,397	-15.0
MSA[1]	8,654	10,554	22.0	4,902	4,857	-0.9	13,556	15,411	13.7
U.S.	920,000	981,900	6.7	591,100	496,100	-16.1	1,511,100	1,478,000	-2.2

Note: (1) Figures cover the Cape Coral-Fort Myers, FL Metropolitan Statistical Area; Figures represent new, privately-owned housing units authorized (unadjusted data)
Source: U.S. Census Bureau, Building Permits Survey (BPS), 2023, 2024

Bankruptcy Filings

Area	Business Filings			Nonbusiness Filings		
	2023	2024	% Chg.	2023	2024	% Chg.
Lee County	97	64	-34.0	860	1,216	41.4
U.S.	18,926	23,107	22.1	434,064	494,201	13.9

Note: Business filings include Chapter 7, Chapter 9, Chapter 11, Chapter 12, Chapter 13, Chapter 15, and Section 304; Nonbusiness filings include Chapter 7, Chapter 11, and Chapter 13
Source: Administrative Office of the U.S. Courts, Business and Nonbusiness Bankruptcy, County Cases Commenced by Chapter of the Bankruptcy Code, During the 12-Month Period Ending December 31, 2023 and Business and Nonbusiness Bankruptcy, County Cases Commenced by Chapter of the Bankruptcy Code, During the 12-Month Period Ending December 31, 2024

Housing Vacancy Rates

Area	Gross Vacancy Rate[3] (%)			Year-Round Vacancy Rate[4] (%)			Rental Vacancy Rate[5] (%)			Homeowner Vacancy Rate[6] (%)		
	2022	2023	2024	2022	2023	2024	2022	2023	2024	2022	2023	2024
MSA[1]	38.2	38.7	34.1	16.9	16.1	14.7	11.6	15.3	10.1	3.9	2.3	3.0
U.S.[2]	9.1	9.0	9.1	7.5	7.5	7.6	5.7	6.5	6.8	0.8	0.8	1.0

Note: (1) Figures cover the Cape Coral-Fort Myers, FL Metropolitan Statistical Area; (2) Figures cover the 75 largest Metropolitan Statistical Areas; (3) The percentage of the total housing inventory that is vacant; (4) The percentage of the housing inventory (excluding seasonal units) that is year-round vacant; (5) The percentage of rental inventory that is vacant for rent; (6) The percentage of homeowner inventory that is vacant for sale
Source: U.S. Census Bureau, Housing Vacancies and Homeownership Annual Statistics: 2022, 2023, 2024

INCOME

Income

Area	Per Capita ($)	Median Household ($)	Average Household ($)
City	39,603	76,062	97,070
MSA[1]	43,365	73,099	102,290
U.S.	43,289	78,538	110,491

Note: (1) Figures cover the Cape Coral-Fort Myers, FL Metropolitan Statistical Area
Source: U.S. Census Bureau, 2019-2023 American Community Survey 5-Year Estimates

Household Income Distribution

Area	Percent of Households Earning							
	Under $15,000	$15,000 -$24,999	$25,000 -$34,999	$35,000 -$49,999	$50,000 -$74,999	$75,000 -$99,999	$100,000 -$149,999	$150,000 and up
City	6.2	5.0	7.7	10.6	19.9	15.6	19.3	15.7
MSA[1]	7.9	6.2	7.5	11.7	18.0	14.2	17.3	17.2
U.S.	8.5	6.6	6.8	10.4	15.7	12.7	17.4	21.9

Note: (1) Figures cover the Cape Coral-Fort Myers, FL Metropolitan Statistical Area
Source: U.S. Census Bureau, 2019-2023 American Community Survey 5-Year Estimates

Poverty Rate

Area	All Ages	Under 18 Years Old	18 to 64 Years Old	65 Years and Over
City	9.8	13.1	9.1	9.2
MSA[1]	11.7	17.1	11.2	9.5
U.S.	12.4	16.3	11.6	10.4

Note: Figures are percentage of people whose income during the past 12 months was below the poverty level;
(1) Figures cover the Cape Coral-Fort Myers, FL Metropolitan Statistical Area
Source: U.S. Census Bureau, 2019-2023 American Community Survey 5-Year Estimates

EMPLOYMENT

Labor Force and Employment

Area	Civilian Labor Force			Workers Employed		
	Dec. 2023	Dec. 2024	% Chg.	Dec. 2023	Dec. 2024	% Chg.
City	100,486	101,752	1.3	97,397	98,477	1.1
MSA[1]	376,769	381,593	1.3	365,271	369,323	1.1
U.S.	166,661,000	167,746,000	0.7	160,754,000	161,294,000	0.3

Note: Data is not seasonally adjusted and covers workers 16 years of age and older; (1) Figures cover the Cape Coral-Fort Myers, FL Metropolitan Statistical Area
Source: Bureau of Labor Statistics, Local Area Unemployment Statistics

Unemployment Rate

Area	2024											
	Jan.	Feb.	Mar.	Apr.	May	Jun.	Jul.	Aug.	Sep.	Oct.	Nov.	Dec.
City	3.4	3.2	3.2	3.0	3.2	3.8	3.9	3.9	3.6	3.5	3.6	3.2
MSA[1]	3.4	3.3	3.2	3.0	3.2	3.7	4.0	3.9	3.7	3.6	3.6	3.2
U.S.	4.1	4.2	3.9	3.5	3.7	4.3	4.5	4.4	3.9	3.9	4.0	3.8

Note: Data is not seasonally adjusted and covers workers 16 years of age and older; (1) Figures cover the Cape Coral-Fort Myers, FL Metropolitan Statistical Area
Source: Bureau of Labor Statistics, Local Area Unemployment Statistics

Average Wages

Occupation	$/Hr.	Occupation	$/Hr.
Accountants and Auditors	39.76	Maintenance and Repair Workers	23.30
Automotive Mechanics	25.28	Marketing Managers	65.95
Bookkeepers	24.21	Network and Computer Systems Admin.	46.21
Carpenters	23.36	Nurses, Licensed Practical	29.34
Cashiers	14.53	Nurses, Registered	41.84
Computer Programmers	43.02	Nursing Assistants	18.75
Computer Systems Analysts	46.99	Office Clerks, General	22.60
Computer User Support Specialists	28.07	Physical Therapists	46.75
Construction Laborers	21.08	Physicians	178.53
Cooks, Restaurant	17.88	Plumbers, Pipefitters and Steamfitters	25.11
Customer Service Representatives	19.48	Police and Sheriff's Patrol Officers	36.26
Dentists	132.27	Postal Service Mail Carriers	29.05
Electricians	25.82	Real Estate Sales Agents	37.59
Engineers, Electrical	49.73	Retail Salespersons	16.92
Fast Food and Counter Workers	14.23	Sales Representatives, Technical/Scientific	57.39
Financial Managers	82.00	Secretaries, Exc. Legal/Medical/Executive	20.71
First-Line Supervisors of Office Workers	32.80	Security Guards	17.45
General and Operations Managers	57.19	Surgeons	n/a
Hairdressers/Cosmetologists	17.77	Teacher Assistants, Exc. Postsecondary[1]	17.30
Home Health and Personal Care Aides	16.30	Teachers, Secondary School, Exc. Sp. Ed.[1]	27.48
Janitors and Cleaners	16.54	Telemarketers	17.59
Landscaping/Groundskeeping Workers	17.78	Truck Drivers, Heavy/Tractor-Trailer	24.75
Lawyers	72.21	Truck Drivers, Light/Delivery Services	21.61
Maids and Housekeeping Cleaners	16.09	Waiters and Waitresses	18.95

Note: Wage data covers the Cape Coral-Fort Myers, FL Metropolitan Statistical Area; (1) Hourly wages were calculated from annual wage data based on a 40 hour work week
Source: Bureau of Labor Statistics, Metro Area Occupational Employment & Wage Estimates, May 2024

Employment by Industry

Sector	MSA[1] Number of Employees	MSA[1] Percent of Total	U.S. Percent of Total
Construction, Mining, and Logging	43,100	13.6	5.5
Financial Activities	15,600	4.9	5.8
Government	48,600	15.3	14.9
Information	3,600	1.1	1.9
Leisure and Hospitality	41,200	13.0	10.4
Manufacturing	8,400	2.6	8.0
Other Services	12,700	4.0	3.7
Private Education and Health Services	36,400	11.5	16.9
Professional and Business Services	45,200	14.2	14.2
Retail Trade	45,400	14.3	10.0
Transportation, Warehousing, and Utilities	8,100	2.5	4.8
Wholesale Trade	9,400	3.0	3.9

Note: Figures are non-farm employment as of December 2024. Figures are not seasonally adjusted and include workers 16 years of age and older; (1) Figures cover the Cape Coral-Fort Myers, FL Metropolitan Statistical Area
Source: Bureau of Labor Statistics, Current Employment Statistics, Employment, Hours, and Earnings

Employment by Occupation

Occupation Classification	City (%)	MSA[1] (%)	U.S. (%)
Management, Business, Science, and Arts	34.1	35.1	42.0
Natural Resources, Construction, and Maintenance	10.7	11.6	8.6
Production, Transportation, and Material Moving	11.3	9.9	13.0
Sales and Office	24.9	24.0	19.9
Service	19.0	19.3	16.5

Note: Figures cover employed civilians 16 years of age and older; (1) Figures cover the Cape Coral-Fort Myers, FL Metropolitan Statistical Area
Source: U.S. Census Bureau, 2019-2023 American Community Survey 5-Year Estimates

Occupations with Greatest Projected Employment Growth: 2022 – 2032

Occupation[1]	2022 Employment	2032 Projected Employment	Numeric Employment Change	Percent Employment Change
Stockers and Order Fillers	236,990	274,060	37,070	15.6
Retail Salespersons	308,940	340,000	31,060	10.1
Waiters and Waitresses	195,320	223,820	28,500	14.6
Software Developers	75,620	101,940	26,320	34.8
General and Operations Managers	184,790	210,510	25,720	13.9
Registered Nurses	202,780	228,070	25,290	12.5
Fast Food and Counter Workers	185,000	209,460	24,460	13.2
Cooks, Restaurant	120,850	141,640	20,790	17.2
Landscaping and Groundskeeping Workers	112,240	129,030	16,790	15.0
Janitors and Cleaners, Except Maids and Housekeeping Cleaners	136,890	153,490	16,600	12.1

Note: Projections cover Florida; (1) Sorted by numeric employment change
Source: www.projectionscentral.org, State Occupational Projections, 2022–2032 Long-Term Projections

Fastest-Growing Occupations: 2022 – 2032

Occupation[1]	2022 Employment	2032 Projected Employment	Numeric Employment Change	Percent Employment Change
Nurse Practitioners	18,910	29,980	11,070	58.5
Data Scientists	8,470	12,450	3,980	47.0
Information Security Analysts (SOC 2018)	11,060	15,650	4,590	41.5
Statisticians	590	820	230	39.0
Solar Photovoltaic Installers	1,210	1,680	470	38.8
Computer and Information Research Scientists (SOC 2018)	3,160	4,380	1,220	38.6
Physician Assistants	8,830	12,180	3,350	37.9
Actuaries	1,640	2,260	620	37.8
Physical Therapist Assistants	7,430	10,230	2,800	37.7
Medical and Health Services Managers	34,490	47,200	12,710	36.9

Note: Projections cover Florida; (1) Sorted by percent employment change and excludes occupations with numeric employment change less than 50
Source: www.projectionscentral.org, State Occupational Projections, 2022–2032 Long-Term Projections

CITY FINANCES

City Government Finances

Component	2022 ($000)	2022 ($ per capita)
Total Revenues	496,323	2,470
Total Expenditures	406,393	2,022
Debt Outstanding	862,220	4,290

Source: U.S. Census Bureau, State & Local Government Finances 2022

City Government Revenue by Source

Source	2022 ($000)	2022 ($ per capita)	2022 (%)
General Revenue			
From Federal Government	9,273	46	1.9
From State Government	49,646	247	10.0
From Local Governments	22,552	112	4.5
Taxes			
Property	109,971	547	22.2
Sales and Gross Receipts	25,379	126	5.1
Personal Income	0	0	0.0
Corporate Income	0	0	0.0
Motor Vehicle License	0	0	0.0
Other Taxes	18,428	92	3.7
Current Charges	100,514	500	20.3
Liquor Store	0	0	0.0
Utility	34,205	170	6.9

Source: U.S. Census Bureau, State & Local Government Finances 2022

City Government Expenditures by Function

Function	2022 ($000)	2022 ($ per capita)	2022 (%)
General Direct Expenditures			
Air Transportation	0	0	0.0
Corrections	0	0	0.0
Education	29,940	149	7.4
Employment Security Administration	0	0	0.0
Financial Administration	20,259	100	5.0
Fire Protection	39,751	197	9.8
General Public Buildings	0	0	0.0
Governmental Administration, Other	5,689	28	1.4
Health	0	0	0.0
Highways	24,971	124	6.1
Hospitals	0	0	0.0
Housing and Community Development	468	2	0.1
Interest on General Debt	6,045	30	1.5
Judicial and Legal	1,585	7	0.4
Libraries	0	0	0.0
Parking	17	<1	<0.1
Parks and Recreation	24,352	121	6.0
Police Protection	47,676	237	11.7
Public Welfare	0	0	0.0
Sewerage	81,729	406	20.1
Solid Waste Management	0	0	0.0
Veterans' Services	0	0	0.0
Liquor Store	0	0	0.0
Utility	66,058	328	16.3

Source: U.S. Census Bureau, State & Local Government Finances 2022

TAXES

State Corporate Income Tax Rates

State	Tax Rate (%)	Income Brackets ($)	Num. of Brackets	Financial Institution Tax Rate (%)[a]	Federal Income Tax Ded.
Florida	5.5	Flat rate	1	5.5	No

Note: Tax rates for tax year 2024; (a) Rates listed are the corporate income tax rate applied to financial institutions or excise taxes based on income. Some states have other taxes based upon the value of deposits or shares.
Source: Federation of Tax Administrators, State Corporate Income Tax Rates, January 1, 2025

State Individual Income Tax Rates

State	Tax Rate (%)	Income Brackets ($)	Personal Exemptions ($)			Standard Ded. ($)	
			Single	Married	Depend.	Single	Married
Florida						– No state income tax –	

Note: Tax rates for tax year 2024; Local- and county-level taxes are not included
Source: Federation of Tax Administrators, State Individual Income Tax Rates, January 1, 2025

Various State Sales and Excise Tax Rates

State	State Sales Tax (%)	Gasoline[1] ($/gal.)	Cigarette[2] ($/pack)	Spirits[3] ($/gal.)	Wine[4] ($/gal.)	Beer[5] ($/gal.)	Recreational Marijuana (%)
Florida	6	0.39	1.34	6.50	2.25	0.48	Not legal

Note: All tax rates as of January 1, 2025; (1) The American Petroleum Institute has developed a methodology for determining the average tax rate on a gallon of fuel. Rates may include any of the following: excise taxes, environmental fees, storage tank fees, other fees or taxes, general sales tax, and local taxes; (2) The federal excise tax of $1.0066 per pack and local taxes are not included; (3) Rates are those applicable to off-premise sales of 40% alcohol by volume (a.b.v.) distilled spirits in 750ml containers. Local excise taxes are excluded; (4) Rates are those applicable to off-premise sales of 11% a.b.v. non-carbonated wine in 750ml containers; (5) Rates are those applicable to off-premise sales of 4.7% a.b.v. beer in 12 ounce containers.
Source: Tax Foundation, 2025 Facts & Figures: How Does Your State Compare?

State Tax Competitiveness Index

State	Overall Rank	Corporate Tax Rank	Individual Income Tax Rank	Sales Tax Rank	Property Tax Rank	Unemployment Insurance Tax Rank
Florida	4	16	1	14	21	10

Note: The Tax Foundation's State Tax Competitiveness Index enables policymakers, taxpayers, and business leaders to gauge how their states' tax systems compare. A rank of 1 is best, 50 is worst. Rankings do not average to the total. States without a tax rank equally as 1. DC's scores and rankings do not affect other states. The report shows tax systems as of July 1, 2024 (the beginning of Fiscal Year 2025).
Source: Tax Foundation, State Tax Competitiveness Index 2025

TRANSPORTATION

Means of Transportation to Work

Area	Car/Truck/Van		Public Transportation			Bicycle	Walked	Other Means	Worked at Home
	Drove Alone	Car-pooled	Bus	Subway	Railroad				
City	76.0	8.1	0.2	0.0	0.0	0.1	1.0	1.4	13.1
MSA[1]	72.7	9.4	0.4	0.0	0.0	0.6	1.1	1.8	13.8
U.S.	70.2	8.5	1.7	1.3	0.4	0.4	2.4	1.6	13.5

Note: Figures are percentages and cover workers 16 years of age and older; (1) Figures cover the Cape Coral-Fort Myers, FL Metropolitan Statistical Area
Source: U.S. Census Bureau, 2019-2023 American Community Survey 5-Year Estimates

Travel Time to Work

Area	Less Than 10 Minutes	10 to 19 Minutes	20 to 29 Minutes	30 to 44 Minutes	45 to 59 Minutes	60 to 89 Minutes	90 Minutes or More
City	7.8	24.9	22.7	24.9	10.5	6.5	2.7
MSA[1]	8.8	24.5	22.6	25.2	10.2	6.3	2.4
U.S.	12.6	28.6	21.2	20.8	8.1	6.0	2.8

Note: Note: Figures are percentages and include workers 16 years old and over; (1) Figures cover the Cape Coral-Fort Myers, FL Metropolitan Statistical Area
Source: U.S. Census Bureau, 2019-2023 American Community Survey 5-Year Estimates

Key Congestion Measures

Measure	2000	2010	2015	2020	2022
Annual Hours of Delay, Total (000)	6,045	12,851	14,679	7,399	15,674
Annual Hours of Delay, Per Auto Commuter	29	36	36	15	33
Annual Congestion Cost, Per Auto Commuter ($)	457	769	811	377	742

Note: Figures cover the Cape Coral FL urban area
Source: Texas A&M Transportation Institute, 2023 Urban Mobility Report

Freeway Travel Time Index

Measure	1985	1990	1995	2000	2005	2010	2015	2020	2022
Urban Area Index[1]	1.07	1.10	1.13	1.16	1.19	1.10	1.17	1.06	1.15
Urban Area Rank[1,2]	48	47	47	43	38	98	46	75	54

Note: Freeway Travel Time Index—the ratio of travel time in the peak period to the travel time at free-flow conditions. For example, a value of 1.30 indicates a 20-minute free-flow trip takes 26 minutes in the peak (20 minutes x 1.30 = 26 minutes); (1) Covers the Cape Coral FL urban area; (2) Rank is based on 101 larger urban areas (#1 = highest travel time index)
Source: Texas A&M Transportation Institute, 2023 Urban Mobility Report

Public Transportation

Agency Name / Mode of Transportation	Vehicles Operated in Maximum Service[1]	Annual Unlinked Passenger Trips[2] (in thous.)	Annual Passenger Miles[3] (in thous.)
Lee County Transit (LeeTran)			
Bus (directly operated)	41	1,525.8	8,088.6
Demand Response (directly operated)	47	217.1	2,646.5

Note: (1) Number of revenue vehicles operated by the given mode and type of service to meet the annual maximum service requirement. This is the revenue vehicle count during the peak season of the year; on the week and day that maximum service is provided. Vehicles operated in maximum service (VOMS) exclude atypical days and one-time special events; (2) Number of passengers who boarded public transportation vehicles. Passengers are counted each time they board a vehicle no matter how many vehicles they use to travel from their origin to their destination. (3) Sum of the distances ridden by all passengers during the entire fiscal year.
Source: Federal Transit Administration, National Transit Database, 2023

Air Transportation

Airport Name and Code / Type of Service	Passenger Airlines[1]	Passenger Enplanements	Freight Carriers[2]	Freight (lbs)
Southwest Florida International Airport (RSW)				
Domestic service (U.S. carriers only)	22	5,252,997	13	15,430,596
International service (U.S. carriers only)	6	799	0	0

Note: (1) Includes all U.S.-based major, minor and commuter airlines that carried at least one passenger during the year; (2) Includes all U.S.-based airlines and freight carriers that transported at least one pound of freight during the year.
Source: Bureau of Transportation Statistics, The Intermodal Transportation Database, Air Carriers: T-100 Domestic Market (U.S. carriers only), 2024; Bureau of Transportation Statistics, The Intermodal Transportation Database, Air Carriers: T-100 International Market (U.S. carriers only), 2024

BUSINESSES

Major Business Headquarters

Company Name	Industry	Rankings	
		Fortune[1]	Forbes[2]
No companies listed	-	-	-

Note: (1) Companies that produce a 10-K are ranked 1 to 500 based on 2023 revenue; (2) All private companies with at least $2 billion in annual revenue through the end of their most current fiscal year are ranked 1 to 275; companies listed are headquartered in the city; dashes indicate no ranking
Source: Fortune, "Fortune 500," 2024; Forbes, "America's Largest Private Companies," 2024

Living Environment

COST OF LIVING

Cost of Living Index

Composite Index	Groceries	Housing	Utilities	Transportation	Health Care	Misc. Goods/Services
104.9	104.0	105.1	106.5	105.9	111.8	103.5

Note: The Cost of Living Index measures regional differences in the cost of consumer goods and services, excluding taxes and non-consumer expenditures, for professional and managerial households in the top income quintile. It is based on more than 50,000 prices covering almost 60 different items for which prices are collected three times a year by chambers of commerce, economic development organizations or university applied economic centers in each participating urban area. The numbers shown should be read as a percentage above or below the national average of 100. For example, a value of 115.4 in the groceries column indicates that grocery prices are 15.4% higher than the national average. Small differences in the index numbers should not be interpreted as significant; Figures cover the Cape Coral-Fort Myers FL urban area.
Source: The Council for Community and Economic Research, Cost of Living Index, 2024

Grocery Prices

Area[1]	T-Bone Steak ($/pound)	Frying Chicken ($/pound)	Whole Milk ($/half gal.)	Eggs ($/dozen)	Orange Juice ($/64 oz.)	Coffee ($/11.5 oz.)
City[2]	15.51	1.46	4.69	3.46	4.51	5.45
Avg.	15.42	1.55	4.69	3.25	4.41	5.46
Min.	14.50	1.16	4.43	2.75	4.00	4.85
Max.	17.56	2.89	5.49	4.78	5.54	7.89

Note: (1) Values for the local area are compared with the average, minimum and maximum values for all 276 areas in the Cost of Living Index; (2) Figures cover the Cape Coral-Fort Myers FL urban area; **T-Bone Steak** (price per pound); **Frying Chicken** (price per pound, whole fryer); **Whole Milk** (half gallon carton); **Eggs** (price per dozen, Grade A, large); **Orange Juice** (64 oz. Tropicana or Florida Natural); **Coffee** (11.5 oz. can, vacuum-packed, Maxwell House, Hills Bros, or Folgers).
Source: The Council for Community and Economic Research, Cost of Living Index, 2024

Housing and Utility Costs

Area[1]	New Home Price ($)	Apartment Rent ($/month)	All Electric ($/month)	Part Electric ($/month)	Other Energy ($/month)	Telephone ($/month)
City[2]	509,774	1,897	225.95	-	-	197.01
Avg.	515,975	1,550	210.99	123.07	82.07	194.99
Min.	265,375	692	104.33	53.68	36.26	179.42
Max.	2,775,821	5,719	529.02	397.28	361.63	223.33

Note: (1) Values for the local area are compared with the average, minimum and maximum values for all 276 areas in the Cost of Living Index; (2) Figures cover the Cape Coral-Fort Myers FL urban area; **New Home Price** (2,400 sf living area, 8,000 sf lot, in urban area with full utilities); **Apartment Rent** (950 sf 2 bedroom/1.5 or 2 bath, unfurnished, excluding all utilities except water); **All Electric** (average monthly cost for an all-electric home); **Part Electric** (average monthly cost for a part-electric home); **Other Energy** (average monthly cost for natural gas, fuel oil, coal, wood, and any other forms of energy except electricity); **Telephone** (price includes the base monthly rate plus taxes and fees for three lines of mobile phone service).
Source: The Council for Community and Economic Research, Cost of Living Index, 2024

Health Care, Transportation, and Other Costs

Area[1]	Doctor ($/visit)	Dentist ($/visit)	Optometrist ($/visit)	Gasoline ($/gallon)	Beauty Salon ($/visit)	Men's Shirt ($)
City[2]	178.39	133.21	101.13	3.36	54.67	30.93
Avg.	143.77	117.51	129.23	3.32	48.57	38.14
Min.	36.74	58.67	67.33	2.80	24.00	13.41
Max.	270.44	216.82	307.33	5.28	94.00	63.89

Note: (1) Values for the local area are compared with the average, minimum and maximum values for all 276 areas in the Cost of Living Index; (2) Figures cover the Cape Coral-Fort Myers FL urban area; **Doctor** (general practitioners routine exam of an established patient); **Dentist** (adult teeth cleaning and periodic oral examination); **Optometrist** (full vision eye exam for established adult patient); **Gasoline** (one gallon regular unleaded, national brand, including all taxes, cash price at self-service pump if available); **Beauty Salon** (woman's shampoo, trim, and blow-dry); **Men's Shirt** (cotton/polyester dress shirt, pinpoint weave, long sleeves).
Source: The Council for Community and Economic Research, Cost of Living Index, 2024

HOUSING

Homeownership Rate

Area	2017 (%)	2018 (%)	2019 (%)	2020 (%)	2021 (%)	2022 (%)	2023 (%)	2024 (%)
MSA[1]	65.5	75.1	72.0	77.4	76.1	70.8	78.5	77.1
U.S.	63.9	64.4	64.6	66.6	65.5	65.8	65.9	65.6

Note: (1) Figures cover the Cape Coral-Fort Myers, FL Metropolitan Statistical Area
Source: U.S. Census Bureau, Housing Vacancies and Homeownership Annual Statistics: 2017-2024

Cape Coral, Florida

House Price Index (HPI)

Area	National Ranking[2]	Quarterly Change (%)	One-Year Change (%)	Five-Year Change (%)	Since 1991Q1 (%)
MSA[1]	240	-0.39	-2.44	67.84	353.01
U.S.[3]	–	1.43	4.51	57.13	327.82

Note: The HPI is a weighted repeat sales index. It measures average price changes in repeat sales or refinancings on the same properties. This information is obtained by reviewing repeat mortgage transactions on single-family properties whose mortgages have been purchased or securitized by Fannie Mae or Freddie Mac since January 1975; (1) Figures cover the Cape Coral-Fort Myers, FL Metropolitan Statistical Area; (2) Rankings are based on annual percentage change for all metro areas containing at least 15,000 transactions over the last 10 years and ranges from 1 to 241; (3) figures based on a weighted average of Census Division estimates using a seasonally adjusted, purchase-only index; all figures are for the period ending December 31, 2024
Source: Federal Housing Finance Agency, Change in FHFA Metropolitan Area House Price Indexes, All Transactions Index, 2024Q4

Home Value

Area	Under $100,000	$100,000 -$199,999	$200,000 -$299,999	$300,000 -$399,999	$400,000 -$499,999	$500,000 -$999,999	$1,000,000 or more	Median ($)
City	3.1	8.9	28.1	25.5	15.2	16.3	3.0	339,200
MSA[1]	8.7	12.9	23.1	19.9	12.6	17.6	5.1	326,300
U.S.	12.1	17.8	19.5	14.4	10.5	19.1	6.5	303,400

Note: Figures are percentages except for median and cover owner-occupied housing units; (1) Figures cover the Cape Coral-Fort Myers, FL Metropolitan Statistical Area
Source: U.S. Census Bureau, 2019-2023 American Community Survey 5-Year Estimates

Year Housing Structure Built

Area	2020 or Later	2010 -2019	2000 -2009	1990 -1999	1980 -1989	1970 -1979	1960 -1969	1950 -1959	1940 -1949	Before 1940	Median Year
City	2.0	11.6	34.3	15.2	21.1	10.3	4.5	0.8	0.3	0.0	1999
MSA[1]	1.9	11.4	29.2	16.2	20.5	12.9	5.0	1.8	0.4	0.6	1995
U.S.	1.2	8.9	13.6	12.8	13.0	14.4	10.0	9.7	4.5	11.9	1980

Note: Figures are percentages except for Median Year; Note: (1) Figures cover the Cape Coral-Fort Myers, FL Metropolitan Statistical Area
Source: U.S. Census Bureau, 2019-2023 American Community Survey 5-Year Estimates

Gross Monthly Rent

Area	Under $500	$500 -$999	$1,000 -$1,499	$1,500 -$1,999	$2,000 -$2,499	$2,500 -$2,999	$3,000 and up	Median ($)
City	0.8	4.6	24.6	39.7	20.2	6.3	3.7	1,751
MSA[1]	2.9	8.6	31.7	34.5	14.0	4.2	4.1	1,597
U.S.	6.5	22.3	29.5	20.2	10.8	4.8	5.9	1,348

Note: Figures are percentages except for median; Gross rent is the contract rent plus the estimated average monthly cost of utilities (electricity, gas, and water and sewer) and fuels (oil, coal, kerosene, wood, etc.) if these are paid by the renter (or paid for the renter by someone else); (1) Figures cover the Cape Coral-Fort Myers, FL Metropolitan Statistical Area
Source: U.S. Census Bureau, 2019-2023 American Community Survey 5-Year Estimates

HEALTH

Health Risk Factors

Category	MSA[1] (%)	U.S. (%)
Adults aged 18–64 who have any kind of health care coverage	n/a	90.8
Adults who reported being in good or better health	n/a	81.8
Adults who have been told they have high blood cholesterol	n/a	36.9
Adults who have been told they have high blood pressure	n/a	34.0
Adults who are current smokers	n/a	12.1
Adults who currently use e-cigarettes	n/a	7.7
Adults who currently use chewing tobacco, snuff, or snus	n/a	3.2
Adults who are heavy drinkers[2]	n/a	6.1
Adults who are binge drinkers[3]	n/a	15.2
Adults who are overweight (BMI 25.0 - 29.9)	n/a	34.4
Adults who are obese (BMI 30.0 - 99.8)	n/a	34.3
Adults who participated in any physical activities in the past month	n/a	75.8

Note: All figures are crude prevalence; (1) Figures for the Cape Coral-Fort Myers, FL Metropolitan Statistical Area were not available.
(2) Heavy drinkers are classified as adult men having more than 14 drinks per week and adult women having more than 7 drinks per week; (3) Binge drinkers are classified as males having five or more drinks on one occasion or females having four or more drinks on one occasion
Source: Centers for Disease Control and Prevention, Behaviorial Risk Factor Surveillance System, SMART: Selected Metropolitan Area Risk Trends, 2023

Acute and Chronic Health Conditions

Category	MSA[1] (%)	U.S. (%)
Adults who have ever been told they had a heart attack	n/a	4.2
Adults who have ever been told they have angina or coronary heart disease	n/a	4.0
Adults who have ever been told they had a stroke	n/a	3.3
Adults who have ever been told they have asthma	n/a	15.7
Adults who have ever been told they have arthritis	n/a	26.3
Adults who have ever been told they have diabetes[2]	n/a	11.5
Adults who have ever been told they had skin cancer	n/a	5.6
Adults who have ever been told they had any other types of cancer	n/a	8.4
Adults who have ever been told they have COPD	n/a	6.4
Adults who have ever been told they have kidney disease	n/a	3.7
Adults who have ever been told they have a form of depression	n/a	22.0

Note: All figures are crude prevalence; (1) Figures for the Cape Coral-Fort Myers, FL Metropolitan Statistical Area were not available.
(2) Figures do not include pregnancy-related, borderline, or pre-diabetes
Source: Centers for Disease Control and Prevention, Behavioral Risk Factor Surveillance System, SMART: Selected Metropolitan Area Risk Trends, 2023

Health Screening and Vaccination Rates

Category	MSA[1] (%)	U.S. (%)
Adults who have ever been tested for HIV	n/a	37.5
Adults who have had their blood cholesterol checked within the last five years	n/a	87.0
Adults aged 65+ who have had flu shot within the past year	n/a	63.4
Adults aged 65+ who have ever had a pneumonia vaccination	n/a	71.9

Note: All figures are crude prevalence; (1) Figures for the Cape Coral-Fort Myers, FL Metropolitan Statistical Area were not available.
Source: Centers for Disease Control and Prevention, Behavioral Risk Factor Surveillance System, SMART: Selected Metropolitan Area Risk Trends, 2023

Disability Status

Category	MSA[1] (%)	U.S. (%)
Adults who reported being deaf	n/a	7.4
Are you blind or have serious difficulty seeing, even when wearing glasses?	n/a	4.9
Do you have difficulty doing errands alone?	n/a	7.8
Do you have difficulty dressing or bathing?	n/a	3.6
Do you have serious difficulty concentrating/remembering/making decisions?	n/a	13.7
Do you have serious difficulty walking or climbing stairs?	n/a	13.2

Note: All figures are crude prevalence; (1) Figures for the Cape Coral-Fort Myers, FL Metropolitan Statistical Area were not available.
Source: Centers for Disease Control and Prevention, Behavioral Risk Factor Surveillance System, SMART: Selected Metropolitan Area Risk Trends, 2023

Mortality Rates for the Top 10 Causes of Death in the U.S.

ICD-10[a] Sub-Chapter	ICD-10[a] Code	Crude Mortality Rate[2] per 100,000 population	
		County[3]	U.S.
Malignant neoplasms	C00-C97	239.3	182.7
Ischaemic heart diseases	I20-I25	168.5	109.6
Provisional assignment of new diseases of uncertain etiology[1]	U00-U49	63.2	65.3
Other forms of heart disease	I30-I51	42.4	65.1
Other degenerative diseases of the nervous system	G30-G31	100.7	52.4
Other external causes of accidental injury	W00-X59	68.8	52.3
Cerebrovascular diseases	I60-I69	56.2	49.1
Chronic lower respiratory diseases	J40-J47	49.7	43.5
Hypertensive diseases	I10-I15	36.8	38.9
Organic, including symptomatic, mental disorders	F01-F09	16.2	33.9

Note: (a) ICD-10 = International Classification of Diseases 10th Revision; (1) Includes COVID-19, adverse effects to COVID-19 vaccines, SARS, and vaping-related disorders; (2) Crude mortality rates are a three-year average covering 2021-2023; (3) Figures cover Lee County.
Source: Centers for Disease Control and Prevention, National Center for Health Statistics. National Vital Statistics System, Mortality 2018-2023 on CDC WONDER Online Database

Mortality Rates for Selected Causes of Death

Cause of Death	ICD-10[a] Code	Crude Mortality Rate[1] per 100,000 population	
		County[2]	U.S.
Accidental poisoning and exposure to noxious substances	X40-X49	33.4	30.5
Alzheimer disease	G30	32.8	35.4
Assault	X85-Y09	4.3	7.3
COVID-19	U07.1	63.2	65.3
Diabetes mellitus	E10-E14	30.5	30.0
Diseases of the liver	K70-K76	23.1	20.8
Human immunodeficiency virus (HIV) disease	B20-B24	1.8	1.5
Influenza and pneumonia	J09-J18	8.6	13.4
Intentional self-harm	X60-X84	17.4	14.7
Malnutrition	E40-E46	2.9	6.0
Obesity and other hyperalimentation	E65-E68	3.1	3.1
Renal failure	N17-N19	10.4	16.4
Transport accidents	V01-V99	17.0	14.4

Note: (a) ICD-10 = International Classification of Diseases 10th Revision; (1) Crude mortality rates are a three-year average covering 2021-2023; (2) Figures cover Lee County; Data are suppressed when the data meet the criteria for confidentiality constraints; Crude mortality rates are flagged as unreliable when the rate would be calculated with a numerator of 20 or less.
Source: Centers for Disease Control and Prevention, National Center for Health Statistics. National Vital Statistics System, Mortality 2018-2023 on CDC WONDER Online Database

Health Insurance Coverage

Area	With Health Insurance	With Private Health Insurance	With Public Health Insurance	Without Health Insurance	Population Under Age 19 Without Health Insurance
City	88.4	65.5	38.4	11.6	10.1
MSA[1]	87.5	62.0	43.6	12.5	9.7
U.S.	91.4	67.3	36.3	8.6	5.4

Note: Figures are percentages that cover the civilian noninstitutionalized population; (1) Figures cover the Cape Coral-Fort Myers, FL Metropolitan Statistical Area
Source: U.S. Census Bureau, 2019-2023 American Community Survey 5-Year Estimates

Number of Medical Professionals

Area	MDs[3]	DOs[3,4]	Dentists	Podiatrists	Chiropractors	Optometrists
County[1] (number)	1,635	246	468	66	240	111
County[1] (rate[2])	198.8	29.9	56.1	7.9	28.8	13.3
U.S. (rate[2])	302.5	29.2	74.6	6.4	29.5	18.0

Note: Data as of 2023 unless noted; (1) Data covers Lee County; (2) Number of medical professionals per 100,000 population; (3) Data as of 2022 and includes all active, non-federal physicians; (4) Doctor of Osteopathic Medicine
Source: U.S. Department of Health and Human Services, Health Resources and Services Administration, Bureau of Health Professions, Area Resource File (ARF) 2023-2024

EDUCATION

Public School District Statistics

District Name	Schls	Pupils	Pupil/Teacher Ratio	Minority Pupils[1] (%)	Total Rev. per Pupil ($)	Total Exp. per Pupil ($)
Lee	122	100,064	22.7	67.4	13,926	12,577

Note: Table includes school districts with 2,000 or more students; (1) Percentage of students that are not non-Hispanic white.
Source: U.S. Department of Education, National Center for Education Statistics, Common Core of Data, Local Education Agency (School District) Universe Survey: School Year 2023-2024; U.S. Department of Education, National Center for Education Statistics, Common Core of Data, School District Finance Survey (F-33): School Year 2021–22

Highest Level of Education

Area	Less than H.S.	H.S. Diploma	Some College, No Deg.	Associate Degree	Bachelor's Degree	Master's Degree	Prof. School Degree	Doctorate Degree
City	6.8	35.3	22.6	9.5	16.7	6.0	1.7	1.3
MSA[1]	9.6	30.0	19.8	9.8	18.8	8.2	2.3	1.4
U.S.	10.6	26.2	19.4	8.8	21.3	9.8	2.3	1.6

Note: Figures cover persons age 25 and over; (1) Figures cover the Cape Coral-Fort Myers, FL Metropolitan Statistical Area
Source: U.S. Census Bureau, 2019-2023 American Community Survey 5-Year Estimates

Cape Coral, Florida

Educational Attainment by Race

Area	High School Graduate or Higher (%)					Bachelor's Degree or Higher (%)				
	Total	White	Black	Asian	Hisp.[2]	Total	White	Black	Asian	Hisp.[2]
City	93.2	94.9	87.7	90.2	87.3	25.7	26.8	21.3	50.2	18.9
MSA[1]	90.4	94.0	82.6	89.5	75.7	30.8	34.0	16.7	50.3	17.1
U.S.	89.4	92.9	88.1	88.0	72.5	35.0	37.7	24.7	57.0	19.9

Note: Figures shown cover persons 25 years old and over; (1) Figures cover the Cape Coral-Fort Myers, FL Metropolitan Statistical Area; (2) People of Hispanic origin can be of any race
Source: U.S. Census Bureau, 2019-2023 American Community Survey 5-Year Estimates

School Enrollment by Grade and Control

Area	Preschool (%)		Kindergarten (%)		Grades 1 - 4 (%)		Grades 5 - 8 (%)		Grades 9 - 12 (%)	
	Public	Private	Public	Private	Public	Private	Public	Private	Public	Private
City	65.1	34.9	94.7	5.3	84.1	15.9	91.1	8.9	88.5	11.5
MSA[1]	61.4	38.6	86.9	13.1	88.2	11.8	88.7	11.3	90.3	9.7
U.S.	58.7	41.3	85.2	14.8	87.2	12.8	87.9	12.1	89.0	11.0

Note: Figures shown cover persons 3 years old and over; (1) Figures cover the Cape Coral-Fort Myers, FL Metropolitan Statistical Area
Source: U.S. Census Bureau, 2019-2023 American Community Survey 5-Year Estimates

Higher Education

Four-Year Colleges			Two-Year Colleges			Medical Schools[1]	Law Schools[2]	Voc/ Tech[3]
Public	Private Non-profit	Private For-profit	Public	Private Non-profit	Private For-profit			
2	1	0	1	0	2	0	0	7

Note: Figures cover institutions located within the Cape Coral-Fort Myers, FL Metropolitan Statistical Area and include main campuses only; (1) includes schools accredited by the Liaison Committee on Medical Education and the American Osteopathic Association's Commission on Osteopathic College Accreditation; (2) includes ABA-accredited schools, schools with provisional ABA accreditation, and state accredited schools; (3) includes all schools with programs that are less than 2 years.
Source: National Center for Education Statistics, Integrated Postsecondary Education System (IPEDS), 2023-24; Wikipedia, List of Medical Schools in the United States, accessed May 2, 2025; Wikipedia, List of Law Schools in the United States, accessed May 2, 2025

EMPLOYERS

Major Employers

Company Name	Industry
Arthrex	Medical device manufacturer
Charlotte County School District	Education
Charlotte Regional Medical Center	Healthcare
Chico's Fas	Retail
City of Cape Coral	Municipal government
Collier County Administration	Government
Collier County Public Schools	Education
Florida Gulf Coast University	Education
Home Depot	Retail
Lee County School District	Education
Lee County Sherriff's Office	Government
Lee Memorial Health System	Healthcare
NCH Naples Hospitals	Healthcare
Palm Automotive	Auto sales
Publix Supermarkets	Retail grocery
St. Joseph Preferred Healthcare Inc	Healthcare
U.S. Sugar	Manufacturing
United States Postal Service	U.S. postal service
Wal-Mart Stores	Retail
Winn-Dixie	Grocery stores

Note: Companies shown are located within the Cape Coral-Fort Myers, FL Metropolitan Statistical Area.
Source: Chambers of Commerce; State Departments of Labor; Wikipedia

PUBLIC SAFETY

Crime Rate

Area	Total Crime Rate	Violent Crime Rate				Property Crime Rate		
		Murder	Rape	Robbery	Aggrav. Assault	Burglary	Larceny -Theft	Motor Vehicle Theft
City	n/a	n/a	n/a	n/a	n/a	n/a	n/a	n/a
U.S.	2,290.9	5.7	38.0	66.5	264.1	250.7	1,347.2	318.7

Note: Figures are crimes per 100,000 population; n/a not available.
Source: FBI, Table 8, Offenses Known to Law Enforcement, by State by City, 2023

Hate Crimes

Area	Number of Quarters Reported	Number of Incidents per Bias Motivation					
		Race/Ethnicity/Ancestry	Religion	Sexual Orientation	Disability	Gender	Gender Identity
City	1	0	0	0	0	0	0
U.S.	4	5,900	2,699	2,077	187	92	492

Source: Federal Bureau of Investigation, Hate Crime Statistics 2023

Identity Theft Consumer Reports

Area	Reports	Reports per 100,000 Population	Rank[2]
MSA[1]	2,727	344	37
U.S.	1,135,291	339	-

Note: (1) Figures cover the Cape Coral-Fort Myers, FL Metropolitan Statistical Area; (2) Rank ranges from 1 to 401 where 1 indicates greatest number of identity theft reports per 100,000 population
Source: Federal Trade Commission, Consumer Sentinel Network Data Book 2024

Fraud and Other Consumer Reports

Area	Reports	Reports per 100,000 Population	Rank[2]
MSA[1]	12,512	1,578	47
U.S.	5,360,641	1,601	-

Note: (1) Figures cover the Cape Coral-Fort Myers, FL Metropolitan Statistical Area; (2) Rank ranges from 1 to 401 where 1 indicates greatest number of fraud and other consumer reports per 100,000 population
Source: Federal Trade Commission, Consumer Sentinel Network Data Book 2024

POLITICS

2024 Presidential Election Results

Area	Trump (Rep.)	Harris (Dem.)	Stein (Green)	Kennedy (Ind.)	Oliver (Lib.)	Other
Lee County	63.6	35.3	0.2	0.0	0.2	0.6
U.S.	49.7	48.2	0.6	0.5	0.4	0.6

Note: Results are percentages and may not add to 100% due to rounding
Source: Dave Leip's Atlas of U.S. Presidential Elections

SPORTS

Professional Sports Teams

Team Name	League	Year Established

No teams are located in the metro area
Source: Wikipedia, Major Professional Sports Teams of the United States and Canada, May 1, 2025

CLIMATE

Average and Extreme Temperatures

Temperature	Jan	Feb	Mar	Apr	May	Jun	Jul	Aug	Sep	Oct	Nov	Dec	Yr.
Extreme High (°F)	88	91	93	96	99	103	98	98	96	95	95	90	103
Average High (°F)	75	76	80	85	89	91	91	92	90	86	80	76	84
Average Temp. (°F)	65	65	70	74	79	82	83	83	82	77	71	66	75
Average Low (°F)	54	54	59	62	68	73	74	75	74	68	61	55	65
Extreme Low (°F)	28	32	33	39	52	60	66	67	64	48	34	26	26

Note: Figures cover the years 1948-1995
Source: National Climatic Data Center, International Station Meteorological Climate Summary, 9/96

Average Precipitation/Snowfall/Humidity

Precip./Humidity	Jan	Feb	Mar	Apr	May	Jun	Jul	Aug	Sep	Oct	Nov	Dec	Yr.
Avg. Precip. (in.)	2.0	2.2	2.6	1.7	3.6	9.3	8.9	8.9	8.2	3.5	1.4	1.5	53.9
Avg. Snowfall (in.)	0	0	0	0	0	0	0	0	0	0	0	0	0
Avg. Rel. Hum. 7am (%)	90	89	89	88	87	89	90	91	92	90	90	90	90
Avg. Rel. Hum. 4pm (%)	56	54	52	50	53	64	68	67	66	59	58	57	59

Note: Figures cover the years 1948-1995; Tr = Trace amounts (<0.05 in. of rain; <0.5 in. of snow)
Source: National Climatic Data Center, International Station Meteorological Climate Summary, 9/96

Weather Conditions

Temperature			Daytime Sky			Precipitation		
32°F & below	45°F & below	90°F & above	Clear	Partly cloudy	Cloudy	0.01 inch or more precip.	0.1 inch or more snow/ice	Thunderstorms
1	18	115	93	220	52	110	0	92

Note: Figures are average number of days per year and cover the years 1948-1995
Source: National Climatic Data Center, International Station Meteorological Climate Summary, 9/96

HAZARDOUS WASTE

Superfund Sites

The Cape Coral-Fort Myers, FL metro area has no sites on the EPA's Superfund Final National Priorities List (NPL) or Superfund Alternative Approach (SAA) list. The Superfund alternative approach uses the same investigation and cleanup process and standards that are used for sites listed on the National Priorities List. The SAA is an alternative to listing a site on the NPL; it is not an alternative to Superfund or the Superfund process. There are a total of 1,445 Superfund sites with a status of proposed or final on both lists in the United States. *U.S. Environmental Protection Agency, National Priorities List, May 1, 2025; U.S. Environmental Protection Agency, Superfund Alternative Approach Sites, May 1, 2025*

AIR QUALITY

Air Quality Trends: Ozone

	1990	1995	2000	2005	2010	2015	2020	2021	2022	2023
MSA[1]	0.069	0.066	0.073	0.071	0.065	0.058	0.061	0.055	0.058	0.064
U.S.	0.087	0.089	0.081	0.080	0.072	0.068	0.066	0.067	0.067	0.070

Note: (1) Data covers the Cape Coral-Fort Myers, FL Metropolitan Statistical Area. The values shown are the composite ozone concentration averages among trend sites based on the highest fourth daily maximum 8-hour concentration in parts per million. These trends are based on sites having an adequate record of monitoring data during the trend period. Data from exceptional events are included.
Source: U.S. Environmental Protection Agency, Air Quality Monitoring Information, "Air Quality Trends by City, 1990-2023"

Air Quality Index

Area	Percent of Days when Air Quality was...[2]					AQI Statistics[2]	
	Good	Moderate	Unhealthy for Sensitive Groups	Unhealthy	Very Unhealthy	Maximum	Median
MSA[1]	94.5	5.2	0.3	0.0	0.0	101	35

Note: (1) Data covers the Cape Coral-Fort Myers, FL Metropolitan Statistical Area; (2) Based on 363 days with AQI data in 2023. Air Quality Index (AQI) is an index for reporting daily air quality. EPA calculates the AQI for five major air pollutants regulated by the Clean Air Act: ground-level ozone, particle pollution (aka particulate matter), carbon monoxide, sulfur dioxide, and nitrogen dioxide. The AQI runs from 0 to 500. The higher the AQI value, the greater the level of air pollution and the greater the health concern. There are six AQI categories: "Good" AQI is between 0 and 50. Air quality is considered satisfactory; "Moderate" AQI is between 51 and 100. Air quality is acceptable; "Unhealthy for Sensitive Groups" When AQI values are between 101 and 150, members of sensitive groups may experience health effects; "Unhealthy" When AQI values are between 151 and 200 everyone may begin to experience health effects; "Very Unhealthy" AQI values between 201 and 300 trigger a health alert; "Hazardous" AQI values over 300 trigger warnings of emergency conditions (not shown).
Source: U.S. Environmental Protection Agency, Air Quality Index Report, 2023

Air Quality Index Pollutants

Area	Percent of Days when AQI Pollutant was...[2]					
	Carbon Monoxide	Nitrogen Dioxide	Ozone	Sulfur Dioxide	Particulate Matter 2.5	Particulate Matter 10
MSA[1]	0.0	0.0	100.0	(3)	0.0	0.0

Note: (1) Data covers the Cape Coral-Fort Myers, FL Metropolitan Statistical Area; (2) Based on 363 days with AQI data in 2023. The Air Quality Index (AQI) is an index for reporting daily air quality. EPA calculates the AQI for five major air pollutants regulated by the Clean Air Act: ground-level ozone, particle pollution (also known as particulate matter), carbon monoxide, sulfur dioxide, and nitrogen dioxide. The AQI runs from 0 to 500. The higher the AQI value, the greater the level of air pollution and the greater the health concern; (3) Sulfur dioxide is no longer included in this table because SO_2 concentrations tend to be very localized and not necessarily representative of broad geographical areas like counties and CBSAs.
Source: U.S. Environmental Protection Agency, Air Quality Index Report, 2023

Maximum Air Pollutant Concentrations: Particulate Matter, Ozone, CO and Lead

	Particulate Matter 10 (ug/m³)	Particulate Matter 2.5 Wtd AM (ug/m³)	Particulate Matter 2.5 24-Hr (ug/m³)	Ozone (ppm)	Carbon Monoxide (ppm)	Lead (ug/m³)
MSA[1] Level	n/a	n/a	n/a	0.064	n/a	n/a
NAAQS[2]	150	15	35	0.075	9	0.15
Met NAAQS[2]	n/a	n/a	n/a	Yes	n/a	n/a

Note: (1) Data covers the Cape Coral-Fort Myers, FL Metropolitan Statistical Area; Data from exceptional events are included; (2) National Ambient Air Quality Standards; ppm = parts per million; ug/m³ = micrograms per cubic meter; n/a not available.
Concentrations: Particulate Matter 10 (coarse particulate)—highest second maximum 24-hour concentration; Particulate Matter 2.5 Wtd AM (fine particulate)—highest weighted annual mean concentration; Particulate Matter 2.5 24-Hour (fine particulate)—highest 98th percentile 24-hour concentration; Ozone—highest fourth daily maximum 8-hour concentration; Carbon Monoxide—highest second maximum non-overlapping 8-hour concentration; Lead—maximum running 3-month average
Source: U.S. Environmental Protection Agency, Air Quality Monitoring Information, "Air Quality Statistics by City, 2023"

Maximum Air Pollutant Concentrations: Nitrogen Dioxide and Sulfur Dioxide

	Nitrogen Dioxide AM (ppb)	Nitrogen Dioxide 1-Hr (ppb)	Sulfur Dioxide AM (ppb)	Sulfur Dioxide 1-Hr (ppb)	Sulfur Dioxide 24-Hr (ppb)
MSA[1] Level	n/a	n/a	n/a	n/a	n/a
NAAQS[2]	53	100	30	75	140
Met NAAQS[2]	n/a	n/a	n/a	n/a	n/a

Note: (1) Data covers the Cape Coral-Fort Myers, FL Metropolitan Statistical Area; Data from exceptional events are included; (2) National Ambient Air Quality Standards; ppm = parts per million; ug/m³ = micrograms per cubic meter; n/a not available.
Concentrations: Nitrogen Dioxide AM—highest arithmetic mean concentration; Nitrogen Dioxide 1-Hr—highest 98th percentile 1-hour daily maximum concentration; Sulfur Dioxide AM—highest annual mean concentration; Sulfur Dioxide 1-Hr—highest 99th percentile 1-hour daily maximum concentration; Sulfur Dioxide 24-Hr—highest second maximum 24-hour concentration
Source: U.S. Environmental Protection Agency, Air Quality Monitoring Information, "Air Quality Statistics by City, 2023"

Charleston, South Carolina

Background

Charleston is on a bay on the Atlantic coastline, at the end of a peninsula between the Ashley and Cooper rivers. It sits 110 miles southeast of Columbia and 100 miles north of Savannah, Georgia, with low-lying terrain that comprises nearby islands and inlets. Charleston was named for King Charles II of England and is the county seat of Charleston County.

In 1670, English colonists established a nearby settlement, and subsequently moved to Charleston's present site. Charleston became an early trading center for rice, indigo, cotton, and other goods. As the plantation economy grew, Charleston became a slave-trading center. In 1861, the Confederacy fired the cannon shot that launched the Civil War from the city's Battery, aimed at the Union's Fort Sumter in Charleston Harbor. Charleston was under siege during the Civil War and experienced many difficulties during Reconstruction. Manufacturing industries including textiles and ironwork became important in the nineteenth century.

Charleston is part of a commercial and cultural center and southern transportation hub whose port is among the nation's busiest shipping facilities. Charleston's other economic sectors include manufacturing, health care, business and professional services, defense activity, retail and wholesale trade, tourism, education, and construction.

Charleston is a popular tourist area, based on its scenery, history, and recreation. The city center is well known for its historic neighborhoods with distinctive early southern architecture and ambiance. As one of the first American cities in the early twentieth century to actively encourage historic restoration and preservation, Charleston has undertaken numerous revitalization initiatives, including the Charleston Place Hotel and retail complex, and Waterfront Park.

In 2000, the Confederate submarine the *HL Hunley*, which sank in 1864, was raised, and brought to a conservation laboratory at the old Charleston Naval Base. As preservation efforts continue, tours are offered on Saturdays and Sundays. Best-selling crime author Patricia Cornwell has donated $500,000 to help researchers solve the mystery of the sinking of the sub, which was the first submarine in history to sink an enemy warship.

Charleston is a center for health care and medical research. SPAWAR (US Navy Space and Naval Warfare Systems Command) is the area's largest single employer followed by the Medical University of South Carolina. Other area educational institutions include The College of Charleston, The Citadel Military College, Trident Technical College, Charleston Southern University, and a campus of Johnson and Wales University.

The Charleston area has numerous parks, including a skateboard center and public waterfront areas. Coastal recreation activities such as boating, swimming, fishing and beaches are popular, as are golf and other land sports.

The Charleston Museum is the nation's oldest, founded in 1773. In addition to the area's former plantations, attractions include the South Carolina Aquarium, American Military Museum, Drayton Hall Plantation Museum, Gibbes Museum of Art, Karpeles Manuscript Museum, and North Charleston Convention Center and Performing Arts Center. Cultural organizations include the Spoleto Festival and the annual Charleston International Film Festival, CIFF.

In 2015, 21-year-old Dylann Roof entered Charleston's historic Emanuel African Methodist Episcopal Church and opened fire, killing nine people. The attack sparked a debate on racism, Confederate symbolism in Southern states, and gun violence. A month after the attack, the Confederate battle flag was removed from the South Carolina State House and the city has since formally apologized for its role in the American slave trade.

Charleston has a humid subtropical climate, with mild winters, hot humid summers, and significant rainfall all year long. Summer is the wettest season; almost half of the annual rainfall occurs from June to September in the form of thundershowers. Fall remains relatively warm through the middle of November. Winter is short and mild, and is characterized by occasional rain.

Rankings

General Rankings

- *US News & World Report* conducted a survey of more than 3,500 people and analyzed the 150 largest metropolitan areas to determine what matters most when selecting the next place to live. Charleston ranked #13 out of the top 25 as having the best combination of desirable factors. Criteria: cost of living; quality of life and education; climate; job market; desirability; and other factors. *realestate.usnews.com, "Best Places to Live in the U.S. in 2024-2025," May 21, 2024*

- *Insider* listed 23 places in the U.S. that travel industry trends reveal would be popular destinations in 2023. This year the list trends towards cultural and historical happenings, sports events, wellness experiences and invigorating outdoor escapes. According to the website insider.com Charleston is a place to visit in 2023. *Insider, "23 of the Best Places You Should Travel to in the U.S. in 2023," December 17, 2022*

- Charleston appeared on *Travel + Leisure's* list of "The 15 Best Cities in the United States." The city was ranked #1. Criteria: walkability; sights/landmarks; culture; food; friendliness; shopping; and overall value. *Travel + Leisure, "The World's Best Awards 2024" July 9, 2024*

- For its 37th annual "Readers' Choice Awards" survey, *Condé Nast Traveler* ranked its readers' favorite cities in the U.S. Whether it be a longed-for visit or the next big new thing, these are the places travelers loved best. The list was broken into large cities and cities under 250,000. Charleston ranked #1 in the small city category. *Condé Nast Traveler, Readers' Choice Awards 2024, "Best Small Cities in the U.S." October 1, 2024*

- In their annual survey, Livability.com looked at data for more than 2,000 mid-sized U.S. cities to assign a "Livability Score"for each. The top 100 scoring cities make up Livability's "Top 100 Best Places to Live in the U.S." in 2025. Charleston was placed among the top 100 of the customizable list. Criteria: housing and economy; cost of living; environment; education; health care options; transportation; safety; and community amenities. *Livability.com, "Top 100 Best Places to Live in the U.S. in 2025" April 15, 2025*

Business/Finance Rankings

- The Charleston metro area appeared on the Milken Institute "2025 Best Performing Cities" list. Rank: #11 out of 200 large metro areas (based on performance category). Criteria: job growth; wage growth; high-tech growth and impact; community resilience; housing affordability; household broadband access. *Milken Institute, "Best-Performing Cities 2025," January 14, 2025*

Education Rankings

- Personal finance website *WalletHub* analyzed the 150 largest U.S. metropolitan statistical areas to determine where the most educated Americans are putting their degrees to work. Criteria: education levels; percentage of workers with degrees; education quality and attainment gap; public school quality rankings; quality and enrollment of each metro area's universities. Charleston was ranked #36 (#1 = most educated city). *WalletHub.com, "Most & Least Educated Cities in America, 2025" July 2, 2024*

Environmental Rankings

- Charleston was highlighted as one of the top 22 cleanest metro areas for short-term particle pollution (24-hour PM 2.5) in the U.S. during 2021 through 2023. Monitors in these cities reported no days with unhealthful PM 2.5 levels. *American Lung Association, "State of the Air 2025," April 23, 2025*

Health/Fitness Rankings

- Charleston was identified as a "2025 Allergy Capital." The area ranked #58 out of the nation's 100 largest metropolitan areas. Three groups of factors were used to identify the most challenging cities for people with allergies: annual tree, grass, and weed pollen scores; over the counter allergy medicine use; number of board-certified allergy specialists. *Asthma and Allergy Foundation of America, "2025 Allergy Capitals: The Most Challenging Places to Live with Allergies," March 18, 2025*

- Charleston was identified as a "2024 Asthma Capital." The area ranked #9 out of the nation's 100 largest metropolitan areas. Criteria: estimated asthma prevalence; asthma-related mortality; and ER visits due to asthma. Risk factors analyzed but not factored in the rankings: annual air quality including pollution and ozone levels; public smoking laws; indoor air quality; access to asthma specialists; rescue and controller medication use; uninsured rate; pollen allergy; poverty rate. *Asthma and Allergy Foundation of America, "Asthma Capitals 2024: The Most Challenging Places to Live With Asthma," September 10, 2024*

Real Estate Rankings

- *WalletHub* compared the most populated U.S. cities to determine which had the best markets for real estate agents. Charleston ranked #70 where demand was high and pay was the best. Criteria: sales per agent; annual median wage for real-estate agents; monthly average starting salary for real estate agents; real estate job density and competition; unemployment rate; home turnover rate; housing-market health index; and other relevant metrics. *WalletHub.com, "2021 Best Places to Be a Real Estate Agent," May 12, 2021*

- The Charleston metro area was identified as one of the top 16 housing markets to invest in for 2025 by *Forbes*. Criteria: stable local economies with good population growth and increase in jobs providing good support for home prices and rents. *Forbes.com, "Best Local Markets For Real Estate Investing In 2025," November 6, 2024*

- Charleston was ranked #119 out of 176 metro areas in terms of cost of housing in 2024 by the National Association of Home Builders (#1 = most affordable). Criteria: the portion of an average family's income necessary to pay the mortgage on a median-priced home. *National Association of Home Builders®, NAHB-Wells Fargo Cost of Housing Index, 4th Quarter 2024*

Safety Rankings

- Allstate ranked the 100 most populous cities in America in terms of driver safety. Charleston ranked #30. Criteria based on anonymized driving behavior data from Allstate's mobile app powered by Arity: high speed driving (over 80 mph), phone handling, and hard braking. The report helps increase the importance of safety and awareness behind the wheel. *Allstate, "16th Allstate America's Best Drivers Report®" July 11, 2024*

Women/Minorities Rankings

- *Travel + Leisure* listed the best cities in and around the U.S. for a memorable and fun girls' trip, even on a budget. Whether it is for a special occasion, to make new memories or just to get away, Charleston is sure to have something for all the ladies in your tribe. *Travel + Leisure, "25 Affordable Girls Weekend Getaways That Won't Break the Bank," January 30, 2025*

- Personal finance website *WalletHub* compared more than 180 U.S. cities across two key dimensions, "Hispanic Business-Friendliness" and "Hispanic Purchasing Power," to arrive at the most favorable conditions for Hispanic entrepreneurs. Charleston was ranked #106 out of 182. Criteria includes: share of Hispanic-Owned Businesses; average growth of Hispanic Business revenues; Small Business-Friendliness score; affordability; and number of Hispanics with at least a bachelor's degree. *WalletHub.com, "Best Cities for Hispanic Entrepreneurs," September 4, 2024*

Miscellaneous Rankings

- In *Condé Nast Traveler* magazine's 2024 Readers' Choice Survey, Charleston made the top ten list of friendliest American cities. Charleston ranked #8. *Condé Nast Traveler, "The Friendliest Cities in the U.S., According to Our Readers" October 28, 2024*

- *WalletHub* compared 148 of the most populated U.S. cities to determine their operating efficiency. A "Quality of Services" score was constructed for each city and then measured against the total budget per capita to reveal which were managed the best. Charleston ranked #53. Criteria: financial stability; economy; education; safety; health; infrastructure and pollution. *WalletHub.com, "2025's Best- & Worst-Run Cities in America," June 18, 2024*

Business Environment

DEMOGRAPHICS

Population Growth

Area	1990 Census	2000 Census	2010 Census	2020 Census	2023 Estimate[2]	Population Growth 1990-2023 (%)
City	96,102	96,650	120,083	150,227	152,014	58.2
MSA[1]	506,875	549,033	664,607	799,636	817,756	61.3
U.S.	248,709,873	281,421,906	308,745,538	331,449,281	332,387,540	33.6

Note: (1) Figures cover the Charleston-North Charleston, SC Metropolitan Statistical Area; (2) 2019-2023 5-year ACS population estimate
Source: U.S. Census Bureau, 1990 Census, 2000 Census, 2010 Census, 2020 Census, 2019-2023 American Community Survey 5-Year Estimates

Race

Area	White Alone[2] (%)	Black Alone[2] (%)	Asian Alone[2] (%)	AIAN[3] Alone[2] (%)	NHOPI[4] Alone[2] (%)	Other Race Alone[2] (%)	Two or More Races (%)
City	72.9	17.4	2.2	0.6	0.2	1.9	5.0
MSA[1]	64.6	23.9	2.0	0.4	0.2	3.3	5.7
U.S.	63.4	12.4	5.8	0.9	0.2	6.6	10.7

Note: (1) Figures cover the Charleston-North Charleston, SC Metropolitan Statistical Area; (2) Alone is defined as not being in combination with one or more other races; (3) American Indian and Alaska Native; (4) Native Hawaiian and Other Pacific Islander
Source: U.S. Census Bureau, 2019-2023 American Community Survey 5-Year Estimates

Hispanic or Latino Origin

Area	Total (%)	Mexican (%)	Puerto Rican (%)	Cuban (%)	Other (%)
City	5.9	2.6	0.7	0.2	2.4
MSA[1]	7.5	3.5	1.1	0.3	2.7
U.S.	19.0	11.3	1.8	0.7	5.2

Note: Persons of Hispanic or Latino origin can be of any race; (1) Figures cover the Charleston-North Charleston, SC Metropolitan Statistical Area
Source: U.S. Census Bureau, 2019-2023 American Community Survey 5-Year Estimates

Age

Area	Percent of Population									Median Age
	Under Age 5	Age 5–19	Age 20–34	Age 35–44	Age 45–54	Age 55–64	Age 65–74	Age 75–84	Age 85+	
City	5.1	15.6	27.7	14.1	10.2	11.3	9.5	4.5	2.1	36.1
MSA[1]	5.9	18.2	21.0	14.1	12.0	12.6	10.0	4.5	1.6	38.1
U.S.	5.7	19.1	20.2	13.1	12.3	12.8	10.0	4.9	1.9	38.7

Note: (1) Figures cover the Charleston-North Charleston, SC Metropolitan Statistical Area
Source: U.S. Census Bureau, 2019-2023 American Community Survey 5-Year Estimates

Disability by Age

Area	All Ages	Under 18 Years Old	18 to 64 Years Old	65 Years and Over
City	9.7	3.2	6.7	29.6
MSA[1]	12.1	4.5	9.8	31.5
U.S.	13.0	4.7	10.7	32.9

Note: Figures show percent of the civilian noninstitutionalized population that reported having a disability. Disability status is determined from six types of difficulty: vision, hearing, cognitive, ambulatory, self-care, and independent living. For children under 5 years old, hearing and vision difficulty are used to determine disability status. For children between the ages of 5 and 14, disability status is determined from hearing, vision, cognitive, ambulatory, and self-care difficulties. For people aged 15 years and older, they are considered to have a disability if they have difficulty with any one of the six difficulty types; Note: (1) Figures cover the Charleston-North Charleston, SC Metropolitan Statistical Area
Source: U.S. Census Bureau, 2019-2023 American Community Survey 5-Year Estimates

Ancestry

Area	German	Irish	English	American	Italian	Polish	French[2]	European	Scottish
City	11.7	11.0	13.6	13.0	4.8	2.4	2.8	1.9	2.4
MSA[1]	10.5	9.6	12.6	8.7	4.1	1.8	2.1	1.8	2.2
U.S.	12.6	9.4	9.1	5.5	4.9	2.6	2.0	1.6	1.6

Note: Figures are the percentage of the total population reporting a particular ancestry. The nine most commonly reported ancestries in the U.S. are shown. Figures include multiple ancestries (e.g. if a person reported being Irish and Italian, they were included in both columns); (1) Figures cover the Charleston-North Charleston, SC Metropolitan Statistical Area; (2) Excludes Basque
Source: U.S. Census Bureau, 2019-2023 American Community Survey 5-Year Estimates

Foreign-born Population

Area	Percent of Population Born in								
	Any Foreign Country	Asia	Mexico	Europe	Caribbean	Central America[2]	South America	Africa	Canada
City	5.4	1.6	0.6	1.2	0.3	0.3	0.8	0.3	0.2
MSA[1]	6.3	1.5	1.1	1.1	0.4	0.7	1.0	0.3	0.2
U.S.	13.9	4.3	3.3	1.4	1.4	1.2	1.2	0.8	0.2

Note: (1) Figures cover the Charleston-North Charleston, SC Metropolitan Statistical Area; (2) Excludes Mexico.
Source: U.S. Census Bureau, 2019-2023 American Community Survey 5-Year Estimates

Household Size

Area	Persons in Household (%)							Average Household Size
	One	Two	Three	Four	Five	Six	Seven or More	
City	34.5	40.1	12.4	8.7	3.2	0.8	0.3	2.20
MSA[1]	29.3	36.3	15.3	11.8	5.0	1.6	0.7	2.45
U.S.	28.5	33.8	15.4	12.7	5.9	2.3	1.4	2.54

Note: (1) Figures cover the Charleston-North Charleston, SC Metropolitan Statistical Area
Source: U.S. Census Bureau, 2019-2023 American Community Survey 5-Year Estimates

Household Relationships

Area	Householder	Opposite-sex Spouse	Same-sex Spouse	Opposite-sex Unmarried Partner	Same-sex Unmarried Partner	Child[2]	Grandchild	Other Relatives	Non-relatives
City	45.0	17.0	0.3	3.1	0.2	21.8	1.4	2.7	5.3
MSA[1]	39.9	18.1	0.2	2.4	0.1	27.3	2.6	3.8	3.5
U.S.	38.3	17.5	0.2	2.5	0.2	28.3	2.4	4.8	3.4

Note: Figures are percent of the total population; (1) Figures cover the Charleston-North Charleston, SC Metropolitan Statistical Area; (2) Includes biological, adopted, and stepchildren of the householder
Source: U.S. Census Bureau, 2020 Census

Gender

Area	Males	Females	Males per 100 Females
City	72,280	79,734	90.7
MSA[1]	400,382	417,374	95.9
U.S.	164,545,087	167,842,453	98.0

Note: (1) Figures cover the Charleston-North Charleston, SC Metropolitan Statistical Area
Source: U.S. Census Bureau, 2019-2023 American Community Survey 5-Year Estimates

Marital Status

Area	Never Married	Now Married[2]	Separated	Widowed	Divorced
City	39.4	44.3	1.6	4.8	10.0
MSA[1]	33.2	48.9	2.0	5.4	10.5
U.S.	34.1	47.9	1.7	5.6	10.7

Note: Figures are percentages and cover the population 15 years of age and older; (1) Figures cover the Charleston-North Charleston, SC Metropolitan Statistical Area; (2) Excludes separated
Source: U.S. Census Bureau, 2019-2023 American Community Survey 5-Year Estimates

Religious Groups by Family

Area	Catholic	Baptist	Methodist	LDS[2]	Pentecostal	Lutheran	Islam	Adventist	Other
MSA[1]	11.5	7.7	8.0	0.8	1.9	0.7	0.2	1.0	12.8
U.S.	18.7	7.3	3.0	2.0	1.8	1.7	1.3	1.3	11.6

Note: Figures are the number of adherents as a percentage of the total population and cover the eight largest religious groups in the U.S; (1) Figures cover the Charleston-North Charleston, SC Metropolitan Statistical Area; (2) Church of Jesus Christ of Latter-day Saints
Sources: 2020 U.S. Religion Census, Association of Statisticians of American Religious Bodies; The Association of Religion Data Archives (ARDA)

Religious Groups by Tradition

Area	Catholic	Evangelical Protestant	Mainline Protestant	Black Protestant	Islam	Judaism	Hinduism	Orthodox	Buddhism
MSA[1]	11.5	17.1	6.8	6.6	0.2	0.4	<0.1	0.2	n/a
U.S.	18.7	16.5	5.2	2.3	1.3	0.6	0.4	0.4	0.3

Note: Figures are the number of adherents as a percentage of the total population; (1) Figures cover the Charleston-North Charleston, SC Metropolitan Statistical Area
Sources: 2020 U.S. Religion Census, Association of Statisticians of American Religious Bodies; The Association of Religion Data Archives (ARDA)

ECONOMY

Real Gross Domestic Product (GDP)

Area	2017	2018	2019	2020	2021	2022	2023	Rank[3]
MSA[1]	41.7	43.4	45.5	44.2	46.6	49.6	52.1	65
U.S.[2]	17,619.1	18,160.7	18,642.5	18,238.9	19,387.6	19,896.6	20,436.3	—

Note: Figures are in billions of chained 2017 dollars; (1) Figures cover the Charleston-North Charleston, SC Metropolitan Statistical Area; (2) Figures cover real GDP within metropolitan areas; (3) Rank is based on 2023 data and ranges from 1 to 384
Source: U.S. Bureau of Economic Analysis

Economic Growth

Area	2014	2015	2016	2017	2018	2019	2020	2021	2022	2023
MSA[1]	2.8	4.7	5.6	2.0	4.0	4.8	-2.7	5.4	6.4	5.2
U.S.[2]	2.6	3.2	2.0	2.7	3.1	2.7	-2.2	6.3	2.6	2.7

Note: Figures are real gross domestic product growth rates and represent percent change from preceding period; (1) Figures cover the Charleston-North Charleston, SC Metropolitan Statistical Area; (2) Figures are the average growth rates within metropolitan areas
Source: U.S. Bureau of Economic Analysis

Metropolitan Area Exports

Area	2018	2019	2020	2021	2022	2023	Rank[2]
MSA[1]	10,943.2	16,337.9	6,110.5	3,381.6	4,256.0	9,497.6	44
U.S.	1,664,056.1	1,645,173.7	1,431,406.6	1,753,941.4	2,062,937.4	2,019,160.5	—

Note: Figures are in millions of dollars; (1) Figures cover the Charleston-North Charleston, SC Metropolitan Statistical Area; (2) Rank is based on 2023 data and ranges from 1 to 386
Source: U.S. Department of Commerce, International Trade Administration, Office of Trade and Economic Analysis, Industry and Analysis, Exports by Metropolitan Area, data extracted April 2, 2025

Building Permits

Area	Single-Family			Multi-Family			Total		
	2023	2024	Pct. Chg.	2023	2024	Pct. Chg.	2023	2024	Pct. Chg.
City	891	878	-1.5	363	266	-26.7	1,254	1,144	-8.8
MSA[1]	6,184	6,817	10.2	2,389	1,697	-29.0	8,573	8,514	-0.7
U.S.	920,000	981,900	6.7	591,100	496,100	-16.1	1,511,100	1,478,000	-2.2

Note: (1) Figures cover the Charleston-North Charleston, SC Metropolitan Statistical Area; Figures represent new, privately-owned housing units authorized (unadjusted data)
Source: U.S. Census Bureau, Building Permits Survey (BPS), 2023, 2024

Bankruptcy Filings

Area	Business Filings			Nonbusiness Filings		
	2023	2024	% Chg.	2023	2024	% Chg.
Charleston County	7	13	85.7	195	215	10.3
U.S.	18,926	23,107	22.1	434,064	494,201	13.9

Note: Business filings include Chapter 7, Chapter 9, Chapter 11, Chapter 12, Chapter 13, Chapter 15, and Section 304; Nonbusiness filings include Chapter 7, Chapter 11, and Chapter 13
Source: Administrative Office of the U.S. Courts, Business and Nonbusiness Bankruptcy, County Cases Commenced by Chapter of the Bankruptcy Code, During the 12-Month Period Ending December 31, 2023 and Business and Nonbusiness Bankruptcy, County Cases Commenced by Chapter of the Bankruptcy Code, During the 12-Month Period Ending December 31, 2024

Housing Vacancy Rates

Area	Gross Vacancy Rate[3] (%)			Year-Round Vacancy Rate[4] (%)			Rental Vacancy Rate[5] (%)			Homeowner Vacancy Rate[6] (%)		
	2022	2023	2024	2022	2023	2024	2022	2023	2024	2022	2023	2024
MSA[1]	10.6	12.6	11.9	7.5	10.2	9.8	8.8	12.0	12.8	0.4	0.5	0.9
U.S.[2]	9.1	9.0	9.1	7.5	7.5	7.6	5.7	6.5	6.8	0.8	0.8	1.0

Note: (1) Figures cover the Charleston-North Charleston, SC Metropolitan Statistical Area; (2) Figures cover the 75 largest Metropolitan Statistical Areas; (3) The percentage of the total housing inventory that is vacant; (4) The percentage of the housing inventory (excluding seasonal units) that is year-round vacant; (5) The percentage of rental inventory that is vacant for rent; (6) The percentage of homeowner inventory that is vacant for sale
Source: U.S. Census Bureau, Housing Vacancies and Homeownership Annual Statistics: 2022, 2023, 2024

INCOME

Income

Area	Per Capita ($)	Median Household ($)	Average Household ($)
City	58,583	90,038	129,666
MSA[1]	46,863	82,272	114,464
U.S.	43,289	78,538	110,491

Note: (1) Figures cover the Charleston-North Charleston, SC Metropolitan Statistical Area
Source: U.S. Census Bureau, 2019-2023 American Community Survey 5-Year Estimates

Household Income Distribution

Area	Percent of Households Earning							
	Under $15,000	$15,000 -$24,999	$25,000 -$34,999	$35,000 -$49,999	$50,000 -$74,999	$75,000 -$99,999	$100,000 -$149,999	$150,000 and up
City	7.7	6.1	4.3	9.6	14.7	12.7	18.6	26.4
MSA[1]	7.2	6.1	6.1	10.0	16.8	13.0	19.2	21.6
U.S.	8.5	6.6	6.8	10.4	15.7	12.7	17.4	21.9

Note: (1) Figures cover the Charleston-North Charleston, SC Metropolitan Statistical Area
Source: U.S. Census Bureau, 2019-2023 American Community Survey 5-Year Estimates

Poverty Rate

Area	All Ages	Under 18 Years Old	18 to 64 Years Old	65 Years and Over
City	12.0	15.4	12.2	7.3
MSA[1]	11.2	15.6	10.3	9.0
U.S.	12.4	16.3	11.6	10.4

Note: Figures are percentage of people whose income during the past 12 months was below the poverty level; (1) Figures cover the Charleston-North Charleston, SC Metropolitan Statistical Area
Source: U.S. Census Bureau, 2019-2023 American Community Survey 5-Year Estimates

EMPLOYMENT

Labor Force and Employment

Area	Civilian Labor Force			Workers Employed		
	Dec. 2023	Dec. 2024	% Chg.	Dec. 2023	Dec. 2024	% Chg.
City	81,443	83,687	2.8	79,209	80,914	2.2
MSA[1]	433,190	445,523	2.8	421,406	430,483	2.2
U.S.	166,661,000	167,746,000	0.7	160,754,000	161,294,000	0.3

Note: Data is not seasonally adjusted and covers workers 16 years of age and older; (1) Figures cover the Charleston-North Charleston, SC Metropolitan Statistical Area
Source: Bureau of Labor Statistics, Local Area Unemployment Statistics

Unemployment Rate

Area	2024											
	Jan.	Feb.	Mar.	Apr.	May	Jun.	Jul.	Aug.	Sep.	Oct.	Nov.	Dec.
City	3.0	3.3	3.0	2.7	3.2	3.9	4.0	4.1	3.5	3.7	3.6	3.3
MSA[1]	3.1	3.4	3.1	2.7	3.3	4.0	4.2	4.3	3.6	3.8	3.6	3.4
U.S.	4.1	4.2	3.9	3.5	3.7	4.3	4.5	4.4	3.9	3.9	4.0	3.8

Note: Data is not seasonally adjusted and covers workers 16 years of age and older; (1) Figures cover the Charleston-North Charleston, SC Metropolitan Statistical Area
Source: Bureau of Labor Statistics, Local Area Unemployment Statistics

Average Wages

Occupation	$/Hr.	Occupation	$/Hr.
Accountants and Auditors	44.26	Maintenance and Repair Workers	23.84
Automotive Mechanics	24.26	Marketing Managers	66.50
Bookkeepers	23.80	Network and Computer Systems Admin.	46.44
Carpenters	25.54	Nurses, Licensed Practical	29.19
Cashiers	13.77	Nurses, Registered	42.57
Computer Programmers	53.17	Nursing Assistants	18.63
Computer Systems Analysts	52.43	Office Clerks, General	20.56
Computer User Support Specialists	28.38	Physical Therapists	47.07
Construction Laborers	21.91	Physicians	142.06
Cooks, Restaurant	17.47	Plumbers, Pipefitters and Steamfitters	26.91
Customer Service Representatives	20.80	Police and Sheriff's Patrol Officers	30.52
Dentists	78.30	Postal Service Mail Carriers	29.37
Electricians	28.18	Real Estate Sales Agents	n/a
Engineers, Electrical	56.11	Retail Salespersons	16.45
Fast Food and Counter Workers	13.83	Sales Representatives, Technical/Scientific	50.27
Financial Managers	72.75	Secretaries, Exc. Legal/Medical/Executive	21.83
First-Line Supervisors of Office Workers	33.77	Security Guards	18.35
General and Operations Managers	59.32	Surgeons	n/a
Hairdressers/Cosmetologists	18.76	Teacher Assistants, Exc. Postsecondary[1]	13.41
Home Health and Personal Care Aides	15.46	Teachers, Secondary School, Exc. Sp. Ed.[1]	31.47
Janitors and Cleaners	15.59	Telemarketers	n/a
Landscaping/Groundskeeping Workers	18.21	Truck Drivers, Heavy/Tractor-Trailer	27.48
Lawyers	62.85	Truck Drivers, Light/Delivery Services	22.40
Maids and Housekeeping Cleaners	15.15	Waiters and Waitresses	12.20

Note: Wage data covers the Charleston-North Charleston, SC Metropolitan Statistical Area; (1) Hourly wages were calculated from annual wage data based on a 40 hour work week
Source: Bureau of Labor Statistics, Metro Area Occupational Employment & Wage Estimates, May 2024

Employment by Industry

Sector	MSA[1] Number of Employees	MSA[1] Percent of Total	U.S. Percent of Total
Construction, Mining, and Logging	24,400	5.7	5.5
Financial Activities	21,800	5.1	5.8
Government	72,000	16.7	14.9
Information	7,900	1.8	1.9
Leisure and Hospitality	53,400	12.4	10.4
Manufacturing	35,000	8.1	8.0
Other Services	16,600	3.9	3.7
Private Education and Health Services	51,400	11.9	16.9
Professional and Business Services	68,100	15.8	14.2
Retail Trade	46,700	10.9	10.0
Transportation, Warehousing, and Utilities	20,100	4.7	4.8
Wholesale Trade	13,000	3.0	3.9

Note: Figures are non-farm employment as of December 2024. Figures are not seasonally adjusted and include workers 16 years of age and older; (1) Figures cover the Charleston-North Charleston, SC Metropolitan Statistical Area
Source: Bureau of Labor Statistics, Current Employment Statistics, Employment, Hours, and Earnings

Employment by Occupation

Occupation Classification	City (%)	MSA[1] (%)	U.S. (%)
Management, Business, Science, and Arts	53.1	43.8	42.0
Natural Resources, Construction, and Maintenance	5.0	8.9	8.6
Production, Transportation, and Material Moving	7.3	12.1	13.0
Sales and Office	19.6	19.9	19.9
Service	15.1	15.3	16.5

Note: Figures cover employed civilians 16 years of age and older; (1) Figures cover the Charleston-North Charleston, SC Metropolitan Statistical Area
Source: U.S. Census Bureau, 2019-2023 American Community Survey 5-Year Estimates

Occupations with Greatest Projected Employment Growth: 2022 – 2032

Occupation[1]	2022 Employment	2032 Projected Employment	Numeric Employment Change	Percent Employment Change
Laborers and Freight, Stock, and Material Movers, Hand	63,510	75,580	12,070	19.0
Home Health and Personal Care Aides	32,340	43,300	10,960	33.9
Stockers and Order Fillers	38,370	46,800	8,430	22.0
Retail Salespersons	66,680	74,980	8,300	12.4
Cooks, Restaurant	25,700	33,820	8,120	31.6
Fast Food and Counter Workers	55,240	61,930	6,690	12.1
General and Operations Managers	49,750	56,440	6,690	13.4
Miscellaneous Assemblers and Fabricators	46,940	51,780	4,840	10.3
Software Developers	11,550	16,070	4,520	39.1
Registered Nurses	45,140	49,610	4,470	9.9

Note: Projections cover South Carolina; (1) Sorted by numeric employment change
Source: www.projectionscentral.org, State Occupational Projections, 2022–2032 Long-Term Projections

Fastest-Growing Occupations: 2022 – 2032

Occupation[1]	2022 Employment	2032 Projected Employment	Numeric Employment Change	Percent Employment Change
Nurse Practitioners	4,120	6,620	2,500	60.7
Personal Care and Service Workers, All Other	820	1,250	430	52.4
Data Scientists	1,270	1,880	610	48.0
Information Security Analysts (SOC 2018)	1,390	1,990	600	43.2
Statisticians	280	400	120	42.9
Actuaries	120	170	50	41.7
Physician Assistants	1,800	2,510	710	39.4
Software Developers	11,550	16,070	4,520	39.1
Personal Financial Advisors	3,100	4,310	1,210	39.0
Physical Therapist Assistants	2,110	2,910	800	37.9

Note: Projections cover South Carolina; (1) Sorted by percent employment change and excludes occupations with numeric employment change less than 50
Source: www.projectionscentral.org, State Occupational Projections, 2022–2032 Long-Term Projections

CITY FINANCES

City Government Finances

Component	2022 ($000)	2022 ($ per capita)
Total Revenues	509,581	3,647
Total Expenditures	620,644	4,442
Debt Outstanding	1,415,744	10,133

Source: U.S. Census Bureau, State & Local Government Finances 2022

City Government Revenue by Source

Source	2022 ($000)	2022 ($ per capita)	2022 (%)
General Revenue			
From Federal Government	7,619	55	1.5
From State Government	6,660	48	1.3
From Local Governments	0	0	0.0
Taxes			
Property	119,408	855	23.4
Sales and Gross Receipts	63,673	456	12.5
Personal Income	0	0	0.0
Corporate Income	0	0	0.0
Motor Vehicle License	0	0	0.0
Other Taxes	71,706	513	14.1
Current Charges	38,881	278	7.6
Liquor Store	0	0	0.0
Utility	158,902	1,137	31.2

Source: U.S. Census Bureau, State & Local Government Finances 2022

City Government Expenditures by Function

Function	2022 ($000)	2022 ($ per capita)	2022 (%)
General Direct Expenditures			
Air Transportation	0	0	0.0
Corrections	0	0	0.0
Education	0	0	0.0
Employment Security Administration	0	0	0.0
Financial Administration	23,301	166	3.8
Fire Protection	38,632	276	6.2
General Public Buildings	416	3	0.1
Governmental Administration, Other	11,650	83	1.9
Health	0	0	0.0
Highways	6,543	46	1.1
Hospitals	0	0	0.0
Housing and Community Development	3,308	23	0.5
Interest on General Debt	5,949	42	1.0
Judicial and Legal	6,398	45	1.0
Libraries	0	0	0.0
Parking	36,344	260	5.9
Parks and Recreation	38,084	272	6.1
Police Protection	60,972	436	9.8
Public Welfare	1,469	10	0.2
Sewerage	33,443	239	5.4
Solid Waste Management	8,730	62	1.4
Veterans' Services	0	0	0.0
Liquor Store	0	0	0.0
Utility	287,672	2,059	46.4

Source: U.S. Census Bureau, State & Local Government Finances 2022

TAXES

State Corporate Income Tax Rates

State	Tax Rate (%)	Income Brackets ($)	Num. of Brackets	Financial Institution Tax Rate (%)[a]	Federal Income Tax Ded.
South Carolina	5.0	Flat rate	1	4.5 (t)	No

Note: Tax rates for tax year 2024; (a) Rates listed are the corporate income tax rate applied to financial institutions or excise taxes based on income. Some states have other taxes based upon the value of deposits or shares; (t) South Carolina taxes savings and loans at a 6% rate.
Source: Federation of Tax Administrators, State Corporate Income Tax Rates, January 1, 2025

State Individual Income Tax Rates

State	Tax Rate (%)	Income Brackets ($)	Personal Exemptions ($)			Standard Ded. ($)	
			Single	Married	Depend.	Single	Married
South Carolina (a)	0.0 - 6.4 (bb)	3,460 - 17,330	4,610	9,220	4,610 (d)	14,600	29,200 (d)

Note: Tax rates for tax year 2024; Local- and county-level taxes are not included; (a) 16 states have statutory provision for automatically adjusting to the rate of inflation the dollar values of the income tax brackets, standard deductions, and/or personal exemptions. Oregon does not index the income brackets for $125,000 and over See: INFL and SPEC above; (d) These states use the personal exemption/standard deduction amounts provided in the federal Internal Revenue Code. Montana personal exemption subject to repeal under Section 15-30-2114; (bb) Louisiana lawmakers repealed the state's throwout rule, ending the taxation of so-called "nowhere income." Iowa is phasing-in a flat rate by 2027, while Nebraska (LB 754 signed into law) and South Carolina is phasing-in a reduced top rate by 2027.
Source: Federation of Tax Administrators, State Individual Income Tax Rates, January 1, 2025

Various State Sales and Excise Tax Rates

State	State Sales Tax (%)	Gasoline[1] ($/gal.)	Cigarette[2] ($/pack)	Spirits[3] ($/gal.)	Wine[4] ($/gal.)	Beer[5] ($/gal.)	Recreational Marijuana (%)
South Carolina	6	0.29	0.57	5.42	1.08	0.77	Not legal

Note: All tax rates as of January 1, 2025; (1) The American Petroleum Institute has developed a methodology for determining the average tax rate on a gallon of fuel. Rates may include any of the following: excise taxes, environmental fees, storage tank fees, other fees or taxes, general sales tax, and local taxes; (2) The federal excise tax of $1.0066 per pack and local taxes are not included; (3) Rates are those applicable to off-premise sales of 40% alcohol by volume (a.b.v.) distilled spirits in 750ml containers. Local excise taxes are excluded; (4) Rates are those applicable to off-premise sales of 11% a.b.v. non-carbonated wine in 750ml containers; (5) Rates are those applicable to off-premise sales of 4.7% a.b.v. beer in 12 ounce containers.
Source: Tax Foundation, 2025 Facts & Figures: How Does Your State Compare?

State Tax Competitiveness Index

State	Overall Rank	Corporate Tax Rank	Individual Income Tax Rank	Sales Tax Rank	Property Tax Rank	Unemployment Insurance Tax Rank
South Carolina	33	11	24	33	42	28

Note: The Tax Foundation's State Tax Competitiveness Index enables policymakers, taxpayers, and business leaders to gauge how their states' tax systems compare. A rank of 1 is best, 50 is worst. Rankings do not average to the total. States without a tax rank equally as 1. DC's scores and rankings do not affect other states. The report shows tax systems as of July 1, 2024 (the beginning of Fiscal Year 2025).
Source: Tax Foundation, State Tax Competitiveness Index 2025

TRANSPORTATION

Means of Transportation to Work

Area	Car/Truck/Van		Public Transportation			Bicycle	Walked	Other Means	Worked at Home
	Drove Alone	Car-pooled	Bus	Subway	Railroad				
City	68.1	6.5	0.9	0.0	0.0	1.5	4.1	1.2	17.6
MSA[1]	75.3	7.8	0.6	0.0	0.0	0.5	1.7	1.2	12.9
U.S.	70.2	8.5	1.7	1.3	0.4	0.4	2.4	1.6	13.5

Note: Figures are percentages and cover workers 16 years of age and older; (1) Figures cover the Charleston-North Charleston, SC Metropolitan Statistical Area
Source: U.S. Census Bureau, 2019-2023 American Community Survey 5-Year Estimates

Travel Time to Work

Area	Less Than 10 Minutes	10 to 19 Minutes	20 to 29 Minutes	30 to 44 Minutes	45 to 59 Minutes	60 to 89 Minutes	90 Minutes or More
City	11.8	32.8	24.8	19.0	7.2	2.5	1.8
MSA[1]	9.1	26.3	23.3	24.0	9.9	5.4	2.1
U.S.	12.6	28.6	21.2	20.8	8.1	6.0	2.8

Note: Note: Figures are percentages and include workers 16 years old and over; (1) Figures cover the Charleston-North Charleston, SC Metropolitan Statistical Area
Source: U.S. Census Bureau, 2019-2023 American Community Survey 5-Year Estimates

Key Congestion Measures

Measure	2000	2010	2015	2020	2022
Annual Hours of Delay, Total (000)	11,402	17,149	20,047	10,973	25,978
Annual Hours of Delay, Per Auto Commuter	37	45	48	26	63
Annual Congestion Cost, Per Auto Commuter ($)	824	985	1,063	582	1,324

Note: Figures cover the Charleston-North Charleston SC urban area
Source: Texas A&M Transportation Institute, 2023 Urban Mobility Report

Freeway Travel Time Index

Measure	1985	1990	1995	2000	2005	2010	2015	2020	2022
Urban Area Index[1]	1.10	1.14	1.18	1.20	1.22	1.23	1.23	1.07	1.26
Urban Area Rank[1,2]	27	26	26	29	32	28	29	57	18

Note: Freeway Travel Time Index—the ratio of travel time in the peak period to the travel time at free-flow conditions. For example, a value of 1.30 indicates a 20-minute free-flow trip takes 26 minutes in the peak (20 minutes x 1.30 = 26 minutes); (1) Covers the Charleston-North Charleston SC urban area; (2) Rank is based on 101 larger urban areas (#1 = highest travel time index)
Source: Texas A&M Transportation Institute, 2023 Urban Mobility Report

Public Transportation

Agency Name / Mode of Transportation	Vehicles Operated in Maximum Service[1]	Annual Unlinked Passenger Trips[2] (in thous.)	Annual Passenger Miles[3] (in thous.)
Charleston Area Regional Transportation (CARTA)			
Bus (purchased transportation)	66	2,094.0	11,345.6
Commuter Bus (purchased transportation)	6	66.8	773.5
Demand Response (purchased transportation)	20	61.3	549.9
Demand Response - Transportation Network Company	2	8.9	52.4

Note: (1) Number of revenue vehicles operated by the given mode and type of service to meet the annual maximum service requirement. This is the revenue vehicle count during the peak season of the year; on the week and day that maximum service is provided. Vehicles operated in maximum service (VOMS) exclude atypical days and one-time special events; (2) Number of passengers who boarded public transportation vehicles. Passengers are counted each time they board a vehicle no matter how many vehicles they use to travel from their origin to their destination. (3) Sum of the distances ridden by all passengers during the entire fiscal year.
Source: Federal Transit Administration, National Transit Database, 2023

Air Transportation

Airport Name and Code / Type of Service	Passenger Airlines[1]	Passenger Enplanements	Freight Carriers[2]	Freight (lbs)
Charleston International Airport (CHS)				
Domestic service (U.S. carriers only)	25	3,104,355	11	7,758,967
International service (U.S. carriers only)	3	323	5	4,177,151

Note: (1) Includes all U.S.-based major, minor and commuter airlines that carried at least one passenger during the year; (2) Includes all U.S.-based airlines and freight carriers that transported at least one pound of freight during the year.
Source: Bureau of Transportation Statistics, The Intermodal Transportation Database, Air Carriers: T-100 Domestic Market (U.S. carriers only), 2024; Bureau of Transportation Statistics, The Intermodal Transportation Database, Air Carriers: T-100 International Market (U.S. carriers only), 2024

BUSINESSES

Major Business Headquarters

Company Name	Industry	Rankings Fortune[1]	Forbes[2]
No companies listed	-	-	-

Note: (1) Companies that produce a 10-K are ranked 1 to 500 based on 2023 revenue; (2) All private companies with at least $2 billion in annual revenue through the end of their most current fiscal year are ranked 1 to 275; companies listed are headquartered in the city; dashes indicate no ranking
Source: Fortune, "Fortune 500," 2024; Forbes, "America's Largest Private Companies," 2024

Fastest-Growing Businesses

According to *Inc.*, Charleston is home to one of America's 500 fastest-growing private companies: **Compare Credit** (#362). Criteria: must be an independent, privately-held, for-profit, U.S. corporation, proprietorship or partnership as of December 31, 2023; revenues must be at least $100,000 in 2020 and $2 million in 2023; must have four-year operating/sales history. *Inc.*, "America's 500 Fastest-Growing Private Companies," 2024

Living Environment

COST OF LIVING

Cost of Living Index

Composite Index	Groceries	Housing	Utilities	Transportation	Health Care	Misc. Goods/Services
101.9	102.1	103.8	113.9	94.9	85.7	101.2

Note: The Cost of Living Index measures regional differences in the cost of consumer goods and services, excluding taxes and non-consumer expenditures, for professional and managerial households in the top income quintile. It is based on more than 50,000 prices covering almost 60 different items for which prices are collected three times a year by chambers of commerce, economic development organizations or university applied economic centers in each participating urban area. The numbers shown should be read as a percentage above or below the national average of 100. For example, a value of 115.4 in the groceries column indicates that grocery prices are 15.4% higher than the national average. Small differences in the index numbers should not be interpreted as significant; Figures cover the Charleston-N Charleston SC urban area.
Source: The Council for Community and Economic Research, Cost of Living Index, 2024

Grocery Prices

Area[1]	T-Bone Steak ($/pound)	Frying Chicken ($/pound)	Whole Milk ($/half gal.)	Eggs ($/dozen)	Orange Juice ($/64 oz.)	Coffee ($/11.5 oz.)
City[2]	15.51	1.64	4.54	3.41	4.43	5.46
Avg.	15.42	1.55	4.69	3.25	4.41	5.46
Min.	14.50	1.16	4.43	2.75	4.00	4.85
Max.	17.56	2.89	5.49	4.78	5.54	7.89

Note: (1) Values for the local area are compared with the average, minimum and maximum values for all 276 areas in the Cost of Living Index; (2) Figures cover the Charleston-N Charleston SC urban area; **T-Bone Steak** (price per pound); **Frying Chicken** (price per pound, whole fryer); **Whole Milk** (half gallon carton); **Eggs** (price per dozen, Grade A, large); **Orange Juice** (64 oz. Tropicana or Florida Natural); **Coffee** (11.5 oz. can, vacuum-packed, Maxwell House, Hills Bros, or Folgers).
Source: The Council for Community and Economic Research, Cost of Living Index, 2024

Housing and Utility Costs

Area[1]	New Home Price ($)	Apartment Rent ($/month)	All Electric ($/month)	Part Electric ($/month)	Other Energy ($/month)	Telephone ($/month)
City[2]	526,080	1,748	249.82	-	-	197.48
Avg.	515,975	1,550	210.99	123.07	82.07	194.99
Min.	265,375	692	104.33	53.68	36.26	179.42
Max.	2,775,821	5,719	529.02	397.28	361.63	223.33

Note: (1) Values for the local area are compared with the average, minimum and maximum values for all 276 areas in the Cost of Living Index; (2) Figures cover the Charleston-N Charleston SC urban area; **New Home Price** (2,400 sf living area, 8,000 sf lot, in urban area with full utilities); **Apartment Rent** (950 sf 2 bedroom/1.5 or 2 bath, unfurnished, excluding all utilities except water); **All Electric** (average monthly cost for an all-electric home); **Part Electric** (average monthly cost for a part-electric home); **Other Energy** (average monthly cost for natural gas, fuel oil, coal, wood, and any other forms of energy except electricity); **Telephone** (price includes the base monthly rate plus taxes and fees for three lines of mobile phone service).
Source: The Council for Community and Economic Research, Cost of Living Index, 2024

Health Care, Transportation, and Other Costs

Area[1]	Doctor ($/visit)	Dentist ($/visit)	Optometrist ($/visit)	Gasoline ($/gallon)	Beauty Salon ($/visit)	Men's Shirt ($)
City[2]	123.53	99.17	82.86	3.03	56.00	24.77
Avg.	143.77	117.51	129.23	3.32	48.57	38.14
Min.	36.74	58.67	67.33	2.80	24.00	13.41
Max.	270.44	216.82	307.33	5.28	94.00	63.89

Note: (1) Values for the local area are compared with the average, minimum and maximum values for all 276 areas in the Cost of Living Index; (2) Figures cover the Charleston-N Charleston SC urban area; **Doctor** (general practitioners routine exam of an established patient); **Dentist** (adult teeth cleaning and periodic oral examination); **Optometrist** (full vision eye exam for established adult patient); **Gasoline** (one gallon regular unleaded, national brand, including all taxes, cash price at self-service pump if available); **Beauty Salon** (woman's shampoo, trim, and blow-dry); **Men's Shirt** (cotton/polyester dress shirt, pinpoint weave, long sleeves).
Source: The Council for Community and Economic Research, Cost of Living Index, 2024

HOUSING

Homeownership Rate

Area	2017 (%)	2018 (%)	2019 (%)	2020 (%)	2021 (%)	2022 (%)	2023 (%)	2024 (%)
MSA[1]	67.7	68.8	70.7	75.5	73.2	71.9	69.6	68.1
U.S.	63.9	64.4	64.6	66.6	65.5	65.8	65.9	65.6

Note: (1) Figures cover the Charleston-North Charleston, SC Metropolitan Statistical Area
Source: U.S. Census Bureau, Housing Vacancies and Homeownership Annual Statistics: 2017-2024

House Price Index (HPI)

Area	National Ranking[2]	Quarterly Change (%)	One-Year Change (%)	Five-Year Change (%)	Since 1991Q1 (%)
MSA[1]	84	2.18	6.43	77.86	536.36
U.S.[3]	–	1.43	4.51	57.13	327.82

Note: The HPI is a weighted repeat sales index. It measures average price changes in repeat sales or refinancings on the same properties. This information is obtained by reviewing repeat mortgage transactions on single-family properties whose mortgages have been purchased or securitized by Fannie Mae or Freddie Mac since January 1975; (1) Figures cover the Charleston-North Charleston, SC Metropolitan Statistical Area; (2) Rankings are based on annual percentage change for all metro areas containing at least 15,000 transactions over the last 10 years and ranges from 1 to 241; (3) figures based on a weighted average of Census Division estimates using a seasonally adjusted, purchase-only index; all figures are for the period ending December 31, 2024
Source: Federal Housing Finance Agency, Change in FHFA Metropolitan Area House Price Indexes, All Transactions Index, 2024Q4

Home Value

Area	Under $100,000	$100,000 -$199,999	$200,000 -$299,999	$300,000 -$399,999	$400,000 -$499,999	$500,000 -$999,999	$1,000,000 or more	Median ($)
City	2.0	3.6	12.8	18.9	18.2	31.3	13.1	469,100
MSA[1]	8.4	11.0	22.2	18.2	12.1	19.8	8.1	345,400
U.S.	12.1	17.8	19.5	14.4	10.5	19.1	6.5	303,400

Note: Figures are percentages except for median and cover owner-occupied housing units; (1) Figures cover the Charleston-North Charleston, SC Metropolitan Statistical Area
Source: U.S. Census Bureau, 2019-2023 American Community Survey 5-Year Estimates

Year Housing Structure Built

Area	2020 or Later	2010 -2019	2000 -2009	1990 -1999	1980 -1989	1970 -1979	1960 -1969	1950 -1959	1940 -1949	Before 1940	Median Year
City	2.6	22.7	19.1	10.1	10.5	7.5	8.2	5.6	3.0	10.8	1994
MSA[1]	2.9	19.5	20.3	14.1	14.6	11.3	7.2	4.5	2.2	3.4	1995
U.S.	1.2	8.9	13.6	12.8	13.0	14.4	10.0	9.7	4.5	11.9	1980

Note: Figures are percentages except for Median Year; Note: (1) Figures cover the Charleston-North Charleston, SC Metropolitan Statistical Area
Source: U.S. Census Bureau, 2019-2023 American Community Survey 5-Year Estimates

Gross Monthly Rent

Area	Under $500	$500 -$999	$1,000 -$1,499	$1,500 -$1,999	$2,000 -$2,499	$2,500 -$2,999	$3,000 and up	Median ($)
City	4.4	7.5	29.8	31.4	16.4	4.4	6.1	1,632
MSA[1]	3.1	11.1	36.7	27.9	13.4	4.0	3.8	1,488
U.S.	6.5	22.3	29.5	20.2	10.8	4.8	5.9	1,348

Note: Figures are percentages except for median; Gross rent is the contract rent plus the estimated average monthly cost of utilities (electricity, gas, and water and sewer) and fuels (oil, coal, kerosene, wood, etc.) if these are paid by the renter (or paid for the renter by someone else); (1) Figures cover the Charleston-North Charleston, SC Metropolitan Statistical Area
Source: U.S. Census Bureau, 2019-2023 American Community Survey 5-Year Estimates

HEALTH

Health Risk Factors

Category	MSA[1] (%)	U.S. (%)
Adults aged 18–64 who have any kind of health care coverage	87.4	90.8
Adults who reported being in good or better health	83.4	81.8
Adults who have been told they have high blood cholesterol	35.6	36.9
Adults who have been told they have high blood pressure	32.8	34.0
Adults who are current smokers	12.0	12.1
Adults who currently use e-cigarettes	6.0	7.7
Adults who currently use chewing tobacco, snuff, or snus	3.4	3.2
Adults who are heavy drinkers[2]	8.6	6.1
Adults who are binge drinkers[3]	19.1	15.2
Adults who are overweight (BMI 25.0 - 29.9)	32.4	34.4
Adults who are obese (BMI 30.0 - 99.8)	33.1	34.3
Adults who participated in any physical activities in the past month	76.7	75.8

Note: All figures are crude prevalence; (1) Figures cover the Charleston-North Charleston, SC Metropolitan Statistical Area; (2) Heavy drinkers are classified as adult men having more than 14 drinks per week and adult women having more than 7 drinks per week; (3) Binge drinkers are classified as males having five or more drinks on one occasion or females having four or more drinks on one occasion
Source: Centers for Disease Control and Prevention, Behavioral Risk Factor Surveillance System, SMART: Selected Metropolitan Area Risk Trends, 2023

Acute and Chronic Health Conditions

Category	MSA[1] (%)	U.S. (%)
Adults who have ever been told they had a heart attack	3.8	4.2
Adults who have ever been told they have angina or coronary heart disease	3.6	4.0
Adults who have ever been told they had a stroke	3.8	3.3
Adults who have ever been told they have asthma	11.8	15.7
Adults who have ever been told they have arthritis	24.4	26.3
Adults who have ever been told they have diabetes[2]	13.7	11.5
Adults who have ever been told they had skin cancer	7.6	5.6
Adults who have ever been told they had any other types of cancer	8.5	8.4
Adults who have ever been told they have COPD	5.9	6.4
Adults who have ever been told they have kidney disease	4.2	3.7
Adults who have ever been told they have a form of depression	19.4	22.0

Note: All figures are crude prevalence; (1) Figures cover the Charleston-North Charleston, SC Metropolitan Statistical Area; (2) Figures do not include pregnancy-related, borderline, or pre-diabetes
Source: Centers for Disease Control and Prevention, Behavioral Risk Factor Surveillance System, SMART: Selected Metropolitan Area Risk Trends, 2023

Health Screening and Vaccination Rates

Category	MSA[1] (%)	U.S. (%)
Adults who have ever been tested for HIV	40.5	37.5
Adults who have had their blood cholesterol checked within the last five years	88.7	87.0
Adults aged 65+ who have had flu shot within the past year	63.5	63.4
Adults aged 65+ who have ever had a pneumonia vaccination	72.1	71.9

Note: All figures are crude prevalence; (1) Figures cover the Charleston-North Charleston, SC Metropolitan Statistical Area.
Source: Centers for Disease Control and Prevention, Behavioral Risk Factor Surveillance System, SMART: Selected Metropolitan Area Risk Trends, 2023

Disability Status

Category	MSA[1] (%)	U.S. (%)
Adults who reported being deaf	5.8	7.4
Are you blind or have serious difficulty seeing, even when wearing glasses?	4.8	4.9
Do you have difficulty doing errands alone?	7.6	7.8
Do you have difficulty dressing or bathing?	4.5	3.6
Do you have serious difficulty concentrating/remembering/making decisions?	11.9	13.7
Do you have serious difficulty walking or climbing stairs?	14.5	13.2

Note: All figures are crude prevalence; (1) Figures cover the Charleston-North Charleston, SC Metropolitan Statistical Area.
Source: Centers for Disease Control and Prevention, Behavioral Risk Factor Surveillance System, SMART: Selected Metropolitan Area Risk Trends, 2023

Mortality Rates for the Top 10 Causes of Death in the U.S.

ICD-10[a] Sub-Chapter	ICD-10[a] Code	Crude Mortality Rate[2] per 100,000 population	
		County[3]	U.S.
Malignant neoplasms	C00-C97	170.8	182.7
Ischaemic heart diseases	I20-I25	74.3	109.6
Provisional assignment of new diseases of uncertain etiology[1]	U00-U49	46.7	65.3
Other forms of heart disease	I30-I51	70.7	65.1
Other degenerative diseases of the nervous system	G30-G31	66.5	52.4
Other external causes of accidental injury	W00-X59	60.8	52.3
Cerebrovascular diseases	I60-I69	45.0	49.1
Chronic lower respiratory diseases	J40-J47	31.8	43.5
Hypertensive diseases	I10-I15	29.9	38.9
Organic, including symptomatic, mental disorders	F01-F09	23.6	33.9

Note: (a) ICD-10 = International Classification of Diseases 10th Revision; (1) Includes COVID-19, adverse effects to COVID-19 vaccines, SARS, and vaping-related disorders; (2) Crude mortality rates are a three-year average covering 2021-2023; (3) Figures cover Charleston County.
Source: Centers for Disease Control and Prevention, National Center for Health Statistics. National Vital Statistics System, Mortality 2018-2023 on CDC WONDER Online Database

Mortality Rates for Selected Causes of Death

Cause of Death	ICD-10[a] Code	Crude Mortality Rate[1] per 100,000 population	
		County[2]	U.S.
Accidental poisoning and exposure to noxious substances	X40-X49	38.0	30.5
Alzheimer disease	G30	40.7	35.4
Assault	X85-Y09	12.3	7.3
COVID-19	U07.1	46.7	65.3
Diabetes mellitus	E10-E14	24.2	30.0
Diseases of the liver	K70-K76	20.8	20.8
Human immunodeficiency virus (HIV) disease	B20-B24	2.2	1.5
Influenza and pneumonia	J09-J18	5.9	13.4
Intentional self-harm	X60-X84	16.4	14.7
Malnutrition	E40-E46	8.8	6.0
Obesity and other hyperalimentation	E65-E68	1.9	3.1
Renal failure	N17-N19	11.8	16.4
Transport accidents	V01-V99	17.2	14.4

Note: (a) ICD-10 = International Classification of Diseases 10th Revision; (1) Crude mortality rates are a three-year average covering 2021-2023; (2) Figures cover Charleston County; Data are suppressed when the data meet the criteria for confidentiality constraints; Crude mortality rates are flagged as unreliable when the rate would be calculated with a numerator of 20 or less.
Source: Centers for Disease Control and Prevention, National Center for Health Statistics. National Vital Statistics System, Mortality 2018-2023 on CDC WONDER Online Database

Health Insurance Coverage

Area	With Health Insurance	With Private Health Insurance	With Public Health Insurance	Without Health Insurance	Population Under Age 19 Without Health Insurance
City	93.6	79.0	27.0	6.4	2.0
MSA[1]	90.3	71.9	32.2	9.7	6.8
U.S.	91.4	67.3	36.3	8.6	5.4

Note: Figures are percentages that cover the civilian noninstitutionalized population; (1) Figures cover the Charleston-North Charleston, SC Metropolitan Statistical Area
Source: U.S. Census Bureau, 2019-2023 American Community Survey 5-Year Estimates

Number of Medical Professionals

Area	MDs[3]	DOs[3,4]	Dentists	Podiatrists	Chiropractors	Optometrists
County[1] (number)	3,696	191	500	24	232	110
County[1] (rate[2])	881.5	45.6	117.8	5.7	54.7	25.9
U.S. (rate[2])	302.5	29.2	74.6	6.4	29.5	18.0

Note: Data as of 2023 unless noted; (1) Data covers Charleston County; (2) Number of medical professionals per 100,000 population; (3) Data as of 2022 and includes all active, non-federal physicians; (4) Doctor of Osteopathic Medicine
Source: U.S. Department of Health and Human Services, Health Resources and Services Administration, Bureau of Health Professions, Area Resource File (ARF) 2023-2024

Best Hospitals

According to *U.S. News*, the Charleston-North Charleston, SC metro area is home to two of the best hospitals in the U.S.: **MUSC Health-University Medical Center** (2 adult specialties and 4 pediatric specialties); **Roper Hospital** (1 adult specialty). The hospitals listed were nationally ranked in at least one of 15 adult or 11 pediatric specialties. The number of specialties shown cover the parent hospital. Only 160 U.S. hospitals performed well enough to be nationally ranked in one or more specialties. Twenty hospitals in the U.S. made the Honor Roll. The Best Hospitals Honor Roll takes both the national rankings and the procedure and condition ratings into account. Hospitals received points if they were nationally ranked in one of the 15 adult specialties—the higher they ranked, the more points they got—and how many ratings of "high performing" they earned in the 20 procedures and conditions. *U.S. News Online, "America's Best Hospitals 2024-25"*

According to *U.S. News*, the Charleston-North Charleston, SC metro area is home to two of the best children's hospitals in the U.S.: **MUSC Children's Heart Network of South Carolina** (4 pediatric specialties); **MUSC Shawn Jenkins Children's Hospital** (4 pediatric specialties). The hospitals listed were highly ranked in at least one of 11 pediatric specialties. One hundred five children's hospitals in the U.S. were nationally ranked in at least one specialty. Hospitals received points for being ranked in a specialty, and the 10 hospitals with the most points across the 11 specialties make up the Honor Roll. *U.S. News Online, "America's Best Children's Hospitals 2024-25"*

EDUCATION

Public School District Statistics

District Name	Schls	Pupils	Pupil/ Teacher Ratio	Minority Pupils[1] (%)	Total Rev. per Pupil ($)	Total Exp. per Pupil ($)
Charleston 01	82	50,400	13.3	49.9	23,881	20,688

Note: Table includes school districts with 2,000 or more students; (1) Percentage of students that are not non-Hispanic white.
Source: U.S. Department of Education, National Center for Education Statistics, Common Core of Data, Local Education Agency (School District) Universe Survey: School Year 2023-2024; U.S. Department of Education, National Center for Education Statistics, Common Core of Data, School District Finance Survey (F-33): School Year 2021–22

Highest Level of Education

Area	Less than H.S.	H.S. Diploma	Some College, No Deg.	Associate Degree	Bachelor's Degree	Master's Degree	Prof. School Degree	Doctorate Degree
City	4.1	15.4	16.0	6.8	35.5	13.8	5.2	3.2
MSA[1]	8.1	22.9	19.8	9.3	24.9	10.7	2.8	1.6
U.S.	10.6	26.2	19.4	8.8	21.3	9.8	2.3	1.6

Note: Figures cover persons age 25 and over; (1) Figures cover the Charleston-North Charleston, SC Metropolitan Statistical Area
Source: U.S. Census Bureau, 2019-2023 American Community Survey 5-Year Estimates

Educational Attainment by Race

Area	High School Graduate or Higher (%)					Bachelor's Degree or Higher (%)				
	Total	White	Black	Asian	Hisp.[2]	Total	White	Black	Asian	Hisp.[2]
City	95.9	98.3	86.7	92.1	87.9	57.7	65.3	22.9	67.6	39.8
MSA[1]	91.9	95.4	86.5	90.2	72.3	40.0	47.6	20.1	51.7	25.5
U.S.	89.4	92.9	88.1	88.0	72.5	35.0	37.7	24.7	57.0	19.9

Note: Figures shown cover persons 25 years old and over; (1) Figures cover the Charleston-North Charleston, SC Metropolitan Statistical Area; (2) People of Hispanic origin can be of any race
Source: U.S. Census Bureau, 2019-2023 American Community Survey 5-Year Estimates

School Enrollment by Grade and Control

Area	Preschool (%)		Kindergarten (%)		Grades 1 - 4 (%)		Grades 5 - 8 (%)		Grades 9 - 12 (%)	
	Public	Private	Public	Private	Public	Private	Public	Private	Public	Private
City	55.1	44.9	79.8	20.2	86.0	14.0	85.5	14.5	80.9	19.1
MSA[1]	47.5	52.5	82.7	17.3	86.5	13.5	87.9	12.1	87.7	12.3
U.S.	58.7	41.3	85.2	14.8	87.2	12.8	87.9	12.1	89.0	11.0

Note: Figures shown cover persons 3 years old and over; (1) Figures cover the Charleston-North Charleston, SC Metropolitan Statistical Area
Source: U.S. Census Bureau, 2019-2023 American Community Survey 5-Year Estimates

Higher Education

Four-Year Colleges			Two-Year Colleges			Medical Schools[1]	Law Schools[2]	Voc/ Tech[3]
Public	Private Non-profit	Private For-profit	Public	Private Non-profit	Private For-profit			
3	2	1	1	0	2	1	1	5

Note: Figures cover institutions located within the Charleston-North Charleston, SC Metropolitan Statistical Area and include main campuses only; (1) includes schools accredited by the Liaison Committee on Medical Education and the American Osteopathic Association's Commission on Osteopathic College Accreditation; (2) includes ABA-accredited schools, schools with provisional ABA accreditation, and state accredited schools; (3) includes all schools with programs that are less than 2 years.
Source: National Center for Education Statistics, Integrated Postsecondary Education System (IPEDS), 2023-24; Wikipedia, List of Medical Schools in the United States, accessed May 2, 2025; Wikipedia, List of Law Schools in the United States, accessed May 2, 2025

According to *U.S. News & World Report*, the Charleston-North Charleston, SC metro area is home to one of the top medical schools for research in the U.S.: **Medical University of South Carolina** (Tier 2). *U.S. News* placed medical and osteopathic schools into tiers based on their research productivity, faculty and admissions data. Each school's tier was derived from its overall score, calculated by summing the weighted normalized values generated across several factors of academic quality, outlined below. There are four tiers, with tier 1 medical schools as the highest-performing and tier 4 as the lowest-performing. Only tier 1 and 2 schools are shown. Because of the tier presentation, *U.S. News* calculated overall scores based on their percentile performance among all rated schools instead of dividing against the rescaled score of the No. 1-performing schools. Tier 1 included schools with overall scores of 85 to 99. The cutoffs for tiers 2 through 4 were schools scoring 50 to 84, 15 to 49 and 1 to 14, respectively. The rankings are based on a weighted average of the following measures of quality: total research activity; average research activity per faculty member; total NIH research grants at the medical school and its affiliated hospitals; average NIH research grants per faculty; median

MCAT total score; median undergraduate GPA; acceptance rate; and faculty resources. *U.S. News & World Report, "America's Best Graduate Schools, Medical, 2025"*

According to *U.S. News & World Report,* the Charleston-North Charleston, SC metro area is home to one of the top medical schools for primary care in the U.S.: **Medical University of South Carolina** (Tier 2). *U.S. News* placed medical and osteopathic schools into tiers based on their research productivity, faculty and admissions data. Each school's tier was derived from its overall score, calculated by summing the weighted normalized values generated across several factors of academic quality, outlined below. There are four tiers, with tier 1 medical schools as the highest-performing and tier 4 as the lowest-performing. Only tier 1 and 2 schools are shown. Because of the tier presentation, *U.S. News* calculated overall scores based on their percentile performance among all rated schools instead of dividing against the rescaled score of the No. 1-performing schools. Tier 1 included schools with overall scores of 85 to 99. The cutoffs for tiers 2 through 4 were schools scoring 50 to 84, 15 to 49 and 1 to 14, respectively. The rankings are based on a weighted average of the following measures of quality: graduates practicing in primary care specialties; graduates entering primary care residencies; median MCAT total score; median undergraduate GPA; acceptance rate; and faculty resources. *U.S. News & World Report, "America's Best Graduate Schools, Medical, 2025"*

EMPLOYERS

Major Employers

Company Name	Industry
Boeing	Aerospace
Charleston County	Government
Charleston County School District	Education
College of Charleston	Education
Dept. of Defense	Military
Dept. of Veterans Affairs	Military
Harris Teeter LLC	Supermarkets
Joint Base Charleston	Military
Medical University of SC	Healthcare
Publix Supermarkets	Grocery stores
Roper St. Francis Healthcare	Healthcare
South Carolina CVS Pharmacy LLC	Pharmaceutical preparations
Trident Medical Center LLC	Healthcare
University Medical Associates	Healthcare
Wal-Mart Stores	Retail

Note: Companies shown are located within the Charleston-North Charleston, SC Metropolitan Statistical Area.
Source: Chambers of Commerce; State Departments of Labor; Wikipedia

Best Companies to Work For

Roper St. Francis Healthcare, headquartered in Charleston, is among "Best Workplaces in Health Care." To determine the Best Workplaces in Health Care list, Great Place To Work analyzed the survey responses of over 185,000 employees from Great Place To Work-Certified companies in the health care industry. Survey data analysis and company-provided datapoints are then factored into a combined score to compare and rank the companies that create the most consistently positive experience for all employees in this industry. *Fortune, "Best Workplaces in Health Care," 2024*

PUBLIC SAFETY

Crime Rate

Area	Total Crime Rate	Violent Crime Rate				Property Crime Rate		
		Murder	Rape	Robbery	Aggrav. Assault	Burglary	Larceny-Theft	Motor Vehicle Theft
City	2,379.5	6.4	28.4	52.8	314.5	164.3	1,501.0	311.9
U.S.	2,290.9	5.7	38.0	66.5	264.1	250.7	1,347.2	318.7

Note: Figures are crimes per 100,000 population.
Source: FBI, Table 8, Offenses Known to Law Enforcement, by State by City, 2023

Hate Crimes

Area	Number of Quarters Reported	Number of Incidents per Bias Motivation					
		Race/Ethnicity/Ancestry	Religion	Sexual Orientation	Disability	Gender	Gender Identity
City	4	3	0	2	0	0	0
U.S.	4	5,900	2,699	2,077	187	92	492

Source: Federal Bureau of Investigation, Hate Crime Statistics 2023

Identity Theft Consumer Reports

Area	Reports	Reports per 100,000 Population	Rank[2]
MSA[1]	2,790	341	44
U.S.	1,135,291	339	-

Note: (1) Figures cover the Charleston-North Charleston, SC Metropolitan Statistical Area; (2) Rank ranges from 1 to 401 where 1 indicates greatest number of identity theft reports per 100,000 population
Source: Federal Trade Commission, Consumer Sentinel Network Data Book 2024

Fraud and Other Consumer Reports

Area	Reports	Reports per 100,000 Population	Rank[2]
MSA[1]	17,509	2,141	6
U.S.	5,360,641	1,601	-

Note: (1) Figures cover the Charleston-North Charleston, SC Metropolitan Statistical Area; (2) Rank ranges from 1 to 401 where 1 indicates greatest number of fraud and other consumer reports per 100,000 population
Source: Federal Trade Commission, Consumer Sentinel Network Data Book 2024

POLITICS

2024 Presidential Election Results

Area	Trump (Rep.)	Harris (Dem.)	Stein (Green)	Kennedy (Ind.)	Oliver (Lib.)	Other
Charleston County	46.3	51.9	0.5	0.0	0.8	0.6
U.S.	49.7	48.2	0.6	0.5	0.4	0.6

Note: Results are percentages and may not add to 100% due to rounding
Source: Dave Leip's Atlas of U.S. Presidential Elections

SPORTS

Professional Sports Teams

Team Name	League	Year Established

No teams are located in the metro area
Source: Wikipedia, Major Professional Sports Teams of the United States and Canada, May 1, 2025

CLIMATE

Average and Extreme Temperatures

Temperature	Jan	Feb	Mar	Apr	May	Jun	Jul	Aug	Sep	Oct	Nov	Dec	Yr.
Extreme High (°F)	83	87	90	94	98	101	104	102	97	94	88	83	104
Average High (°F)	59	62	68	76	83	88	90	89	85	77	69	61	76
Average Temp. (°F)	49	51	57	65	73	78	81	81	76	67	58	51	66
Average Low (°F)	38	40	46	53	62	69	72	72	67	56	46	39	55
Extreme Low (°F)	6	12	15	30	36	50	58	56	42	27	15	8	6

Note: Figures cover the years 1945-1995
Source: National Climatic Data Center, International Station Meteorological Climate Summary, 9/96

Average Precipitation/Snowfall/Humidity

Precip./Humidity	Jan	Feb	Mar	Apr	May	Jun	Jul	Aug	Sep	Oct	Nov	Dec	Yr.
Avg. Precip. (in.)	3.5	3.1	4.4	2.8	4.1	6.0	7.2	6.9	5.6	3.1	2.5	3.1	52.1
Avg. Snowfall (in.)	Tr	Tr	Tr	0	0	0	0	0	0	0	Tr	Tr	1
Avg. Rel. Hum. 7am (%)	83	81	83	84	85	86	88	90	91	89	86	83	86
Avg. Rel. Hum. 4pm (%)	55	52	51	51	56	62	66	66	65	58	56	55	58

Note: Figures cover the years 1945-1995; Tr = Trace amounts (<0.05 in. of rain; <0.5 in. of snow)
Source: National Climatic Data Center, International Station Meteorological Climate Summary, 9/96

Weather Conditions

Temperature			Daytime Sky			Precipitation		
10°F & below	32°F & below	90°F & above	Clear	Partly cloudy	Cloudy	0.01 inch or more precip.	0.1 inch or more snow/ice	Thunder-storms
<1	33	53	89	162	114	114	1	59

Note: Figures are average number of days per year and cover the years 1945-1995
Source: National Climatic Data Center, International Station Meteorological Climate Summary, 9/96

HAZARDOUS WASTE

Superfund Sites

The Charleston-North Charleston, SC metro area is home to two sites on the EPA's Superfund National Priorities List (NPL) or Superfund Alternative Approach (SAA) list: **Koppers Co., Inc. (Charleston Plant)** (Final NPL); **Macalloy Corporation** (Final NPL). The Superfund alternative approach uses the same investigation and cleanup process and standards that are used for sites listed on the National Priorities List. The SAA is an alternative to listing a site on the NPL; it is not an alternative to Superfund or the Superfund process. There are a total of 1,445 Superfund sites with a status of

AIR QUALITY

Air Quality Trends: Ozone

	1990	1995	2000	2005	2010	2015	2020	2021	2022	2023
MSA[1]	0.059	0.075	0.076	0.077	0.068	0.054	0.053	0.059	0.059	0.056
U.S.	0.087	0.089	0.081	0.080	0.072	0.068	0.066	0.067	0.067	0.070

Note: (1) Data covers the Charleston-North Charleston, SC Metropolitan Statistical Area. The values shown are the composite ozone concentration averages among trend sites based on the highest fourth daily maximum 8-hour concentration in parts per million. These trends are based on sites having an adequate record of monitoring data during the trend period. Data from exceptional events are included.
Source: U.S. Environmental Protection Agency, Air Quality Monitoring Information, "Air Quality Trends by City, 1990-2023"

Air Quality Index

Area	Percent of Days when Air Quality was...[2]					AQI Statistics[2]	
	Good	Moderate	Unhealthy for Sensitive Groups	Unhealthy	Very Unhealthy	Maximum	Median
MSA[1]	57.8	41.6	0.5	0.0	0.0	105	47

Note: (1) Data covers the Charleston-North Charleston, SC Metropolitan Statistical Area; (2) Based on 365 days with AQI data in 2023. Air Quality Index (AQI) is an index for reporting daily air quality. EPA calculates the AQI for five major air pollutants regulated by the Clean Air Act: ground-level ozone, particle pollution (aka particulate matter), carbon monoxide, sulfur dioxide, and nitrogen dioxide. The AQI runs from 0 to 500. The higher the AQI value, the greater the level of air pollution and the greater the health concern. There are six AQI categories: "Good" AQI is between 0 and 50. Air quality is considered satisfactory; "Moderate" AQI is between 51 and 100. Air quality is acceptable; "Unhealthy for Sensitive Groups" When AQI values are between 101 and 150, members of sensitive groups may experience health effects; "Unhealthy" When AQI values are between 151 and 200 everyone may begin to experience health effects; "Very Unhealthy" AQI values between 201 and 300 trigger a health alert; "Hazardous" AQI values over 300 trigger warnings of emergency conditions (not shown).
Source: U.S. Environmental Protection Agency, Air Quality Index Report, 2023

Air Quality Index Pollutants

Area	Percent of Days when AQI Pollutant was...[2]					
	Carbon Monoxide	Nitrogen Dioxide	Ozone	Sulfur Dioxide	Particulate Matter 2.5	Particulate Matter 10
MSA[1]	0.0	0.0	24.4	(3)	75.1	0.5

Note: (1) Data covers the Charleston-North Charleston, SC Metropolitan Statistical Area; (2) Based on 365 days with AQI data in 2023. The Air Quality Index (AQI) is an index for reporting daily air quality. EPA calculates the AQI for five major air pollutants regulated by the Clean Air Act: ground-level ozone, particle pollution (also known as particulate matter), carbon monoxide, sulfur dioxide, and nitrogen dioxide. The AQI runs from 0 to 500. The higher the AQI value, the greater the level of air pollution and the greater the health concern; (3) Sulfur dioxide is no longer included in this table because SO_2 concentrations tend to be very localized and not necessarily representative of broad geographical areas like counties and CBSAs.
Source: U.S. Environmental Protection Agency, Air Quality Index Report, 2023

Maximum Air Pollutant Concentrations: Particulate Matter, Ozone, CO and Lead

	Particulate Matter 10 (ug/m^3)	Particulate Matter 2.5 Wtd AM (ug/m^3)	Particulate Matter 2.5 24-Hr (ug/m^3)	Ozone (ppm)	Carbon Monoxide (ppm)	Lead (ug/m^3)
MSA[1] Level	70	8.1	20	0.062	n/a	n/a
NAAQS[2]	150	15	35	0.075	9	0.15
Met NAAQS[2]	Yes	Yes	Yes	Yes	n/a	n/a

Note: (1) Data covers the Charleston-North Charleston, SC Metropolitan Statistical Area; Data from exceptional events are included; (2) National Ambient Air Quality Standards; ppm = parts per million; ug/m^3 = micrograms per cubic meter; n/a not available.
Concentrations: Particulate Matter 10 (coarse particulate)—highest second maximum 24-hour concentration; Particulate Matter 2.5 Wtd AM (fine particulate)—highest weighted annual mean concentration; Particulate Matter 2.5 24-Hour (fine particulate)—highest 98th percentile 24-hour concentration; Ozone—highest fourth daily maximum 8-hour concentration; Carbon Monoxide—highest second maximum non-overlapping 8-hour concentration; Lead—maximum running 3-month average
Source: U.S. Environmental Protection Agency, Air Quality Monitoring Information, "Air Quality Statistics by City, 2023"

Maximum Air Pollutant Concentrations: Nitrogen Dioxide and Sulfur Dioxide

	Nitrogen Dioxide AM (ppb)	Nitrogen Dioxide 1-Hr (ppb)	Sulfur Dioxide AM (ppb)	Sulfur Dioxide 1-Hr (ppb)	Sulfur Dioxide 24-Hr (ppb)
MSA[1] Level	7	n/a	n/a	6	n/a
NAAQS[2]	53	100	30	75	140
Met NAAQS[2]	Yes	n/a	n/a	Yes	n/a

Note: (1) Data covers the Charleston-North Charleston, SC Metropolitan Statistical Area; Data from exceptional events are included; (2) National Ambient Air Quality Standards; ppm = parts per million; ug/m³ = micrograms per cubic meter; n/a not available.
Concentrations: Nitrogen Dioxide AM—highest arithmetic mean concentration; Nitrogen Dioxide 1-Hr—highest 98th percentile 1-hour daily maximum concentration; Sulfur Dioxide AM—highest annual mean concentration; Sulfur Dioxide 1-Hr—highest 99th percentile 1-hour daily maximum concentration; Sulfur Dioxide 24-Hr—highest second maximum 24-hour concentration
Source: U.S. Environmental Protection Agency, Air Quality Monitoring Information, "Air Quality Statistics by City, 2023"

Clarksville, Tennessee

Background

Just south of the Kentucky border and 47 miles north of Nashville, sits Clarksville, Tennessee's fifth-largest city. Named for Gen. George Rogers Clark, a decorated veteran of the Indian and Revolutionary Wars, the city was founded in 1784, and became incorporated by in 1796.

Located near the confluence of Red and Cumberland rivers, Clarksville was the site of three Confederate forts that the Union defeated in 1862. Fort Defiance, in the 1980s, passed from private hands to the city and became Fort Defiance Civil War Park and Interpretative Center in 2011. In 1942, Fort Campbell (two-thirds in Tennessee and one-third and its post office in Kentucky), became home to the air assault division, known as the Screaming Eagles, with two special ops command units, and a combat support hospital. It houses the U.S. Army's most-deployed contingency forces and the fifth-largest military population. With more than 4,000 civilian jobs, it's the area's largest employer.

Austin Peay State University's main campus is in Clarksville, another of the city's major employers, and named for a local son who became governor. The four-year public master's-level university has seen its enrollment climb steadily throughout the last twenty years. Austin Peay also operates a center at Fort Campbell with fifteen associate, bachelor, and master's level programs.

In 2012, Hemlock Semiconductor Corp, a subsidiary of Dow Corning, opened a $1.2 billion plant in the city, and the state funded a new educational center at APSU to train workers.

F&M Bank Arena is the arena for the Austin Peay Governors men's and women's basketball teams of the ASUN Conference. The arena seats around 6,000 people. The Clarksville Downtown Market—with produce and arts and crafts—is a popular summer event.

Clarksville is also home to the state's second largest general museum, Customs House Museum and Cultural Center, which has seen a recent facelift. Model trains, a gallery devoted to sports champions, and a bubble cave are all part of the experience.

The climate is humid subtropical with hot summers and cold winters. Clarksville is affected by warmer climates of the Gulf of Mexico and the colder temperatures of the Midwest. Snow in winter is common, but large accumulation is sporadic. Precipitation is abundant year-round, with May having the most rain. Generally, the wet season is February through July, the dry season is August through January. Clarksville experienced damaging tornadoes in December 2023 and May 2024.

Rankings

General Rankings

- Clarksville was identified as one of America's fastest-growing areas in terms of population and economy by *Forbes*. Clarksville ranked #47 out of 50. Over 500 cities with more than 75,000 residents were measured for percentage of population growth over the following three periods: from 2011 to 2016; 2016 to 2021; and then 2011 to 2021. *Forbes.com, "The Fastest Growing Cities in America and Their Change in Income," September 12, 2023*

- Clarksville was selected as one of the best places to live in the United States by *Money* magazine. The city placed among the top 50. This year's list focused on cities built around community spirit, thoughtful policy and civic engagement. Instead of relying on a predetermined dataset, the cities and towns were grouped according to their strengths and chosen due their affordability, good schools and strong job markets. *Money, "The 50 Best Places to Live in the U.S., 2024" April 8, 2024*

Business/Finance Rankings

- The Clarksville metro area appeared on the Milken Institute "2025 Best Performing Cities" list. Rank: #70 out of 200 large metro areas (based on performance category). Criteria: job growth; wage growth; high-tech growth and impact; community resilience; housing affordability; household broadband access. *Milken Institute, "Best-Performing Cities 2025," January 14, 2025*

Business Environment

DEMOGRAPHICS

Population Growth

Area	1990 Census	2000 Census	2010 Census	2020 Census	2023 Estimate[2]	Population Growth 1990-2023 (%)
City	78,569	103,455	132,929	166,722	171,897	118.8
MSA[1]	189,277	232,000	273,949	320,535	328,626	73.6
U.S.	248,709,873	281,421,906	308,745,538	331,449,281	332,387,540	33.6

Note: (1) Figures cover the Clarksville, TN-KY Metropolitan Statistical Area; (2) 2019-2023 5-year ACS population estimate
Source: U.S. Census Bureau, 1990 Census, 2000 Census, 2010 Census, 2020 Census, 2019-2023 American Community Survey 5-Year Estimates

Race

Area	White Alone[2] (%)	Black Alone[2] (%)	Asian Alone[2] (%)	AIAN[3] Alone[2] (%)	NHOPI[4] Alone[2] (%)	Other Race Alone[2] (%)	Two or More Races (%)
City	59.4	23.0	2.5	0.4	0.3	2.8	11.7
MSA[1]	67.3	18.5	2.1	0.3	0.3	2.2	9.5
U.S.	63.4	12.4	5.8	0.9	0.2	6.6	10.7

Note: (1) Figures cover the Clarksville, TN-KY Metropolitan Statistical Area; (2) Alone is defined as not being in combination with one or more other races; (3) American Indian and Alaska Native; (4) Native Hawaiian and Other Pacific Islander
Source: U.S. Census Bureau, 2019-2023 American Community Survey 5-Year Estimates

Hispanic or Latino Origin

Area	Total (%)	Mexican (%)	Puerto Rican (%)	Cuban (%)	Other (%)
City	12.5	6.0	3.0	0.3	3.2
MSA[1]	9.7	5.0	2.3	0.2	2.2
U.S.	19.0	11.3	1.8	0.7	5.2

Note: Persons of Hispanic or Latino origin can be of any race; (1) Figures cover the Clarksville, TN-KY Metropolitan Statistical Area
Source: U.S. Census Bureau, 2019-2023 American Community Survey 5-Year Estimates

Age

Area	Percent of Population									Median Age
	Under Age 5	Age 5–19	Age 20–34	Age 35–44	Age 45–54	Age 55–64	Age 65–74	Age 75–84	Age 85+	
City	8.5	21.0	29.2	14.0	9.6	9.0	5.8	2.3	0.7	30.4
MSA[1]	8.1	21.2	25.9	13.1	10.3	10.0	7.1	3.3	1.1	31.9
U.S.	5.7	19.1	20.2	13.1	12.3	12.8	10.0	4.9	1.9	38.7

Note: (1) Figures cover the Clarksville, TN-KY Metropolitan Statistical Area
Source: U.S. Census Bureau, 2019-2023 American Community Survey 5-Year Estimates

Disability by Age

Area	All Ages	Under 18 Years Old	18 to 64 Years Old	65 Years and Over
City	14.8	5.7	15.1	41.8
MSA[1]	16.4	6.5	16.1	41.9
U.S.	13.0	4.7	10.7	32.9

Note: Figures show percent of the civilian noninstitutionalized population that reported having a disability. Disability status is determined from six types of difficulty: vision, hearing, cognitive, ambulatory, self-care, and independent living. For children under 5 years old, hearing and vision difficulty are used to determine disability status. For children between the ages of 5 and 14, disability status is determined from hearing, vision, cognitive, ambulatory, and self-care difficulties. For people aged 15 years and older, they are considered to have a disability if they have difficulty with any one of the six difficulty types; Note: (1) Figures cover the Clarksville, TN-KY Metropolitan Statistical Area
Source: U.S. Census Bureau, 2019-2023 American Community Survey 5-Year Estimates

Ancestry

Area	German	Irish	English	American	Italian	Polish	French[2]	European	Scottish
City	12.5	8.8	8.3	6.0	3.6	1.0	1.6	3.7	1.5
MSA[1]	11.5	8.6	9.9	7.4	2.8	1.0	1.5	3.5	1.7
U.S.	12.6	9.4	9.1	5.5	4.9	2.6	2.0	1.6	1.6

Note: Figures are the percentage of the total population reporting a particular ancestry. The nine most commonly reported ancestries in the U.S. are shown. Figures include multiple ancestries (e.g. if a person reported being Irish and Italian, they were included in both columns); (1) Figures cover the Clarksville, TN-KY Metropolitan Statistical Area; (2) Excludes Basque
Source: U.S. Census Bureau, 2019-2023 American Community Survey 5-Year Estimates

Foreign-born Population

Area	Percent of Population Born in								
	Any Foreign Country	Asia	Mexico	Europe	Caribbean	Central America[2]	South America	Africa	Canada
City	6.8	1.9	1.2	1.0	0.6	0.6	0.6	0.6	0.2
MSA[1]	5.4	1.6	0.9	0.8	0.4	0.4	0.4	0.6	0.2
U.S.	13.9	4.3	3.3	1.4	1.4	1.2	1.2	0.8	0.2

Note: (1) Figures cover the Clarksville, TN-KY Metropolitan Statistical Area; (2) Excludes Mexico.
Source: U.S. Census Bureau, 2019-2023 American Community Survey 5-Year Estimates

Household Size

Area	Persons in Household (%)							Average Household Size
	One	Two	Three	Four	Five	Six	Seven or More	
City	25.7	33.0	18.0	13.6	5.5	2.5	1.6	2.59
MSA[1]	26.0	33.6	17.5	12.8	5.8	2.4	1.9	2.63
U.S.	28.5	33.8	15.4	12.7	5.9	2.3	1.4	2.54

Note: (1) Figures cover the Clarksville, TN-KY Metropolitan Statistical Area
Source: U.S. Census Bureau, 2019-2023 American Community Survey 5-Year Estimates

Household Relationships

Area	Householder	Opposite-sex Spouse	Same-sex Spouse	Opposite-sex Unmarried Partner	Same-sex Unmarried Partner	Child[2]	Grandchild	Other Relatives	Non-relatives
City	36.6	16.9	0.2	2.5	0.1	31.2	2.4	3.9	3.5
MSA[1]	36.7	18.2	0.2	2.2	0.1	30.5	2.5	3.6	3.0
U.S.	38.3	17.5	0.2	2.5	0.2	28.3	2.4	4.8	3.4

Note: Figures are percent of the total population; (1) Figures cover the Clarksville, TN-KY Metropolitan Statistical Area; (2) Includes biological, adopted, and stepchildren of the householder
Source: U.S. Census Bureau, 2020 Census

Gender

Area	Males	Females	Males per 100 Females
City	86,129	85,768	100.4
MSA[1]	165,784	162,842	101.8
U.S.	164,545,087	167,842,453	98.0

Note: (1) Figures cover the Clarksville, TN-KY Metropolitan Statistical Area
Source: U.S. Census Bureau, 2019-2023 American Community Survey 5-Year Estimates

Marital Status

Area	Never Married	Now Married[2]	Separated	Widowed	Divorced
City	30.0	50.9	2.2	4.2	12.7
MSA[1]	29.2	51.6	1.9	5.2	12.0
U.S.	34.1	47.9	1.7	5.6	10.7

Note: Figures are percentages and cover the population 15 years of age and older; (1) Figures cover the Clarksville, TN-KY Metropolitan Statistical Area; (2) Excludes separated
Source: U.S. Census Bureau, 2019-2023 American Community Survey 5-Year Estimates

Religious Groups by Family

Area	Catholic	Baptist	Methodist	LDS[2]	Pentecostal	Lutheran	Islam	Adventist	Other
MSA[1]	4.6	23.2	4.4	1.4	3.2	0.5	0.1	0.8	12.4
U.S.	18.7	7.3	3.0	2.0	1.8	1.7	1.3	1.3	11.6

Note: Figures are the number of adherents as a percentage of the total population and cover the eight largest religious groups in the U.S; (1) Figures cover the Clarksville, TN-KY Metropolitan Statistical Area; (2) Church of Jesus Christ of Latter-day Saints
Sources: 2020 U.S. Religion Census, Association of Statisticians of American Religious Bodies; The Association of Religion Data Archives (ARDA)

Religious Groups by Tradition

Area	Catholic	Evangelical Protestant	Mainline Protestant	Black Protestant	Islam	Judaism	Hinduism	Orthodox	Buddhism
MSA[1]	4.6	35.7	4.8	3.4	0.1	n/a	n/a	0.1	n/a
U.S.	18.7	16.5	5.2	2.3	1.3	0.6	0.4	0.4	0.3

Note: Figures are the number of adherents as a percentage of the total population; (1) Figures cover the Clarksville, TN-KY Metropolitan Statistical Area
Sources: 2020 U.S. Religion Census, Association of Statisticians of American Religious Bodies; The Association of Religion Data Archives (ARDA)

ECONOMY

Real Gross Domestic Product (GDP)

Area	2017	2018	2019	2020	2021	2022	2023	Rank[3]
MSA[1]	12.3	12.4	12.7	12.9	13.6	13.9	14.2	189
U.S.[2]	17,619.1	18,160.7	18,642.5	18,238.9	19,387.6	19,896.6	20,436.3	—

Note: Figures are in billions of chained 2017 dollars; (1) Figures cover the Clarksville, TN-KY Metropolitan Statistical Area; (2) Figures cover real GDP within metropolitan areas; (3) Rank is based on 2023 data and ranges from 1 to 384
Source: U.S. Bureau of Economic Analysis

Economic Growth

Area	2014	2015	2016	2017	2018	2019	2020	2021	2022	2023
MSA[1]	-1.2	0.5	-1.0	0.0	1.1	2.0	1.4	5.9	2.1	1.9
U.S.[2]	2.6	3.2	2.0	2.7	3.1	2.7	-2.2	6.3	2.6	2.7

Note: Figures are real gross domestic product growth rates and represent percent change from preceding period; (1) Figures cover the Clarksville, TN-KY Metropolitan Statistical Area; (2) Figures are the average growth rates within metropolitan areas
Source: U.S. Bureau of Economic Analysis

Metropolitan Area Exports

Area	2018	2019	2020	2021	2022	2023	Rank[2]
MSA[1]	435.5	341.8	246.8	288.7	376.7	445.6	236
U.S.	1,664,056.1	1,645,173.7	1,431,406.6	1,753,941.4	2,062,937.4	2,019,160.5	—

Note: Figures are in millions of dollars; (1) Figures cover the Clarksville, TN-KY Metropolitan Statistical Area; (2) Rank is based on 2023 data and ranges from 1 to 386
Source: U.S. Department of Commerce, International Trade Administration, Office of Trade and Economic Analysis, Industry and Analysis, Exports by Metropolitan Area, data extracted April 2, 2025

Building Permits

Area	Single-Family			Multi-Family			Total		
	2023	2024	Pct. Chg.	2023	2024	Pct. Chg.	2023	2024	Pct. Chg.
City	805	1,366	69.7	1,455	703	-51.7	2,260	2,069	-8.5
MSA[1]	1,385	1,975	42.6	1,554	823	-47.0	2,939	2,798	-4.8
U.S.	920,000	981,900	6.7	591,100	496,100	-16.1	1,511,100	1,478,000	-2.2

Note: (1) Figures cover the Clarksville, TN-KY Metropolitan Statistical Area; Figures represent new, privately-owned housing units authorized (unadjusted data)
Source: U.S. Census Bureau, Building Permits Survey (BPS), 2023, 2024

Bankruptcy Filings

Area	Business Filings			Nonbusiness Filings		
	2023	2024	% Chg.	2023	2024	% Chg.
Montgomery County	4	11	175.0	475	513	8.0
U.S.	18,926	23,107	22.1	434,064	494,201	13.9

Note: Business filings include Chapter 7, Chapter 9, Chapter 11, Chapter 12, Chapter 13, Chapter 15, and Section 304; Nonbusiness filings include Chapter 7, Chapter 11, and Chapter 13
Source: Administrative Office of the U.S. Courts, Business and Nonbusiness Bankruptcy, County Cases Commenced by Chapter of the Bankruptcy Code, During the 12-Month Period Ending December 31, 2023 and Business and Nonbusiness Bankruptcy, County Cases Commenced by Chapter of the Bankruptcy Code, During the 12-Month Period Ending December 31, 2024

Housing Vacancy Rates

Area	Gross Vacancy Rate[3] (%)			Year-Round Vacancy Rate[4] (%)			Rental Vacancy Rate[5] (%)			Homeowner Vacancy Rate[6] (%)		
	2022	2023	2024	2022	2023	2024	2022	2023	2024	2022	2023	2024
MSA[1]	n/a	n/a	n/a	n/a	n/a	n/a	n/a	n/a	n/a	n/a	n/a	n/a
U.S.[2]	9.1	9.0	9.1	7.5	7.5	7.6	5.7	6.5	6.8	0.8	0.8	1.0

Note: (1) Figures cover the Clarksville, TN-KY Metropolitan Statistical Area; (2) Figures cover the 75 largest Metropolitan Statistical Areas; (3) The percentage of the total housing inventory that is vacant; (4) The percentage of the housing inventory (excluding seasonal units) that is year-round vacant; (5) The percentage of rental inventory that is vacant for rent; (6) The percentage of homeowner inventory that is vacant for sale; n/a not available
Source: U.S. Census Bureau, Housing Vacancies and Homeownership Annual Statistics: 2022, 2023, 2024

INCOME

Income

Area	Per Capita ($)	Median Household ($)	Average Household ($)
City	31,266	66,786	79,769
MSA[1]	31,813	66,210	82,303
U.S.	43,289	78,538	110,491

Note: (1) Figures cover the Clarksville, TN-KY Metropolitan Statistical Area
Source: U.S. Census Bureau, 2019-2023 American Community Survey 5-Year Estimates

Household Income Distribution

Area	Percent of Households Earning							
	Under $15,000	$15,000 -$24,999	$25,000 -$34,999	$35,000 -$49,999	$50,000 -$74,999	$75,000 -$99,999	$100,000 -$149,999	$150,000 and up
City	7.7	5.7	7.7	13.4	21.0	16.7	17.8	10.0
MSA[1]	9.1	6.6	8.1	12.3	20.0	15.2	17.1	11.5
U.S.	8.5	6.6	6.8	10.4	15.7	12.7	17.4	21.9

Note: (1) Figures cover the Clarksville, TN-KY Metropolitan Statistical Area
Source: U.S. Census Bureau, 2019-2023 American Community Survey 5-Year Estimates

Poverty Rate

Area	All Ages	Under 18 Years Old	18 to 64 Years Old	65 Years and Over
City	12.8	16.8	11.8	7.7
MSA[1]	13.2	16.4	12.3	10.5
U.S.	12.4	16.3	11.6	10.4

Note: Figures are percentage of people whose income during the past 12 months was below the poverty level; (1) Figures cover the Clarksville, TN-KY Metropolitan Statistical Area
Source: U.S. Census Bureau, 2019-2023 American Community Survey 5-Year Estimates

EMPLOYMENT

Labor Force and Employment

Area	Civilian Labor Force			Workers Employed		
	Dec. 2023	Dec. 2024	% Chg.	Dec. 2023	Dec. 2024	% Chg.
City	65,211	66,900	2.6	62,910	64,067	1.8
MSA[1]	126,537	129,924	2.7	121,844	124,244	2.0
U.S.	166,661,000	167,746,000	0.7	160,754,000	161,294,000	0.3

Note: Data is not seasonally adjusted and covers workers 16 years of age and older; (1) Figures cover the Clarksville, TN-KY Metropolitan Statistical Area
Source: Bureau of Labor Statistics, Local Area Unemployment Statistics

Unemployment Rate

Area	2024											
	Jan.	Feb.	Mar.	Apr.	May	Jun.	Jul.	Aug.	Sep.	Oct.	Nov.	Dec.
City	4.0	3.7	3.8	3.3	3.5	4.6	4.6	4.4	4.2	4.2	4.3	4.2
MSA[1]	4.2	4.1	4.1	3.6	3.8	4.8	4.9	4.6	4.4	4.4	4.5	4.4
U.S.	4.1	4.2	3.9	3.5	3.7	4.3	4.5	4.4	3.9	3.9	4.0	3.8

Note: Data is not seasonally adjusted and covers workers 16 years of age and older; (1) Figures cover the Clarksville, TN-KY Metropolitan Statistical Area
Source: Bureau of Labor Statistics, Local Area Unemployment Statistics

Average Wages

Occupation	$/Hr.	Occupation	$/Hr.
Accountants and Auditors	35.41	Maintenance and Repair Workers	22.72
Automotive Mechanics	23.62	Marketing Managers	56.80
Bookkeepers	22.04	Network and Computer Systems Admin.	57.61
Carpenters	24.61	Nurses, Licensed Practical	26.97
Cashiers	13.04	Nurses, Registered	37.88
Computer Programmers	n/a	Nursing Assistants	17.59
Computer Systems Analysts	39.08	Office Clerks, General	18.67
Computer User Support Specialists	25.48	Physical Therapists	45.46
Construction Laborers	20.62	Physicians	154.95
Cooks, Restaurant	15.08	Plumbers, Pipefitters and Steamfitters	31.80
Customer Service Representatives	18.84	Police and Sheriff's Patrol Officers	26.37
Dentists	87.66	Postal Service Mail Carriers	27.83
Electricians	28.77	Real Estate Sales Agents	25.11
Engineers, Electrical	45.74	Retail Salespersons	16.33
Fast Food and Counter Workers	12.79	Sales Representatives, Technical/Scientific	34.76
Financial Managers	65.73	Secretaries, Exc. Legal/Medical/Executive	19.85
First-Line Supervisors of Office Workers	29.27	Security Guards	19.00
General and Operations Managers	48.25	Surgeons	n/a
Hairdressers/Cosmetologists	16.23	Teacher Assistants, Exc. Postsecondary[1]	15.35
Home Health and Personal Care Aides	15.17	Teachers, Secondary School, Exc. Sp. Ed.[1]	26.88
Janitors and Cleaners	15.39	Telemarketers	n/a
Landscaping/Groundskeeping Workers	17.20	Truck Drivers, Heavy/Tractor-Trailer	26.20
Lawyers	67.51	Truck Drivers, Light/Delivery Services	18.98
Maids and Housekeeping Cleaners	13.62	Waiters and Waitresses	13.57

Note: Wage data covers the Clarksville, TN-KY Metropolitan Statistical Area; (1) Hourly wages were calculated from annual wage data based on a 40 hour work week
Source: Bureau of Labor Statistics, Metro Area Occupational Employment & Wage Estimates, May 2024

Employment by Industry

Sector	MSA[1] Number of Employees	MSA[1] Percent of Total	U.S. Percent of Total
Construction, Mining, and Logging	4,900	4.5	5.5
Financial Activities	4,100	3.8	5.8
Government	22,500	20.6	14.9
Information	1,400	1.3	1.9
Leisure and Hospitality	13,200	12.1	10.4
Manufacturing	14,100	12.9	8.0
Other Services	3,600	3.3	3.7
Private Education and Health Services	14,300	13.1	16.9
Professional and Business Services	9,200	8.4	14.2
Retail Trade	14,400	13.2	10.0
Transportation, Warehousing, and Utilities	4,900	4.5	4.8
Wholesale Trade	2,500	2.3	3.9

Note: Figures are non-farm employment as of December 2024. Figures are not seasonally adjusted and include workers 16 years of age and older; (1) Figures cover the Clarksville, TN-KY Metropolitan Statistical Area
Source: Bureau of Labor Statistics, Current Employment Statistics, Employment, Hours, and Earnings

Employment by Occupation

Occupation Classification	City (%)	MSA[1] (%)	U.S. (%)
Management, Business, Science, and Arts	34.8	35.0	42.0
Natural Resources, Construction, and Maintenance	8.8	10.1	8.6
Production, Transportation, and Material Moving	15.7	16.1	13.0
Sales and Office	21.1	20.5	19.9
Service	19.7	18.3	16.5

Note: Figures cover employed civilians 16 years of age and older; (1) Figures cover the Clarksville, TN-KY Metropolitan Statistical Area
Source: U.S. Census Bureau, 2019-2023 American Community Survey 5-Year Estimates

Occupations with Greatest Projected Employment Growth: 2022 – 2032

Occupation[1]	2022 Employment	2032 Projected Employment	Numeric Employment Change	Percent Employment Change
Laborers and Freight, Stock, and Material Movers, Hand	112,810	131,040	18,230	16.2
Home Health and Personal Care Aides	32,820	46,870	14,050	42.8
General and Operations Managers	66,510	78,660	12,150	18.3
Fast Food and Counter Workers	73,880	86,020	12,140	16.4
Cooks, Restaurant	28,080	38,240	10,160	36.2
Miscellaneous Assemblers and Fabricators	54,300	64,000	9,700	17.9
Construction Laborers	32,750	41,080	8,330	25.4
Nurse Practitioners	13,620	21,500	7,880	57.9
Registered Nurses	60,020	67,720	7,700	12.8
Software Developers	16,540	23,650	7,110	43.0

Note: Projections cover Tennessee; (1) Sorted by numeric employment change
Source: www.projectionscentral.org, State Occupational Projections, 2022–2032 Long-Term Projections

Fastest-Growing Occupations: 2022 – 2032

Occupation[1]	2022 Employment	2032 Projected Employment	Numeric Employment Change	Percent Employment Change
Recreational Vehicle Service Technicians	410	660	250	61.0
Data Scientists	1,840	2,930	1,090	59.2
Nurse Practitioners	13,620	21,500	7,880	57.9
Home Appliance Repairers	650	980	330	50.8
Information Security Analysts (SOC 2018)	2,580	3,850	1,270	49.2
Dancers	170	250	80	47.1
Motor Vehicle Operators, All Other	2,560	3,750	1,190	46.5
Statisticians	940	1,360	420	44.7
Epidemiologists	230	330	100	43.5
Actuaries	370	530	160	43.2

Note: Projections cover Tennessee; (1) Sorted by percent employment change and excludes occupations with numeric employment change less than 50
Source: www.projectionscentral.org, State Occupational Projections, 2022–2032 Long-Term Projections

CITY FINANCES

City Government Finances

Component	2022 ($000)	2022 ($ per capita)
Total Revenues	476,915	2,958
Total Expenditures	470,318	2,917
Debt Outstanding	608,224	3,772

Source: U.S. Census Bureau, State & Local Government Finances 2022

City Government Revenue by Source

Source	2022 ($000)	2022 ($ per capita)	2022 (%)
General Revenue			
From Federal Government	0	0	0.0
From State Government	45,773	284	9.6
From Local Governments	0	0	0.0
Taxes			
Property	42,679	265	8.9
Sales and Gross Receipts	26,785	166	5.6
Personal Income	0	0	0.0
Corporate Income	0	0	0.0
Motor Vehicle License	0	0	0.0
Other Taxes	4,136	26	0.9
Current Charges	51,301	318	10.8
Liquor Store	0	0	0.0
Utility	266,873	1,655	56.0

Source: U.S. Census Bureau, State & Local Government Finances 2022

City Government Expenditures by Function

Function	2022 ($000)	2022 ($ per capita)	2022 (%)
General Direct Expenditures			
Air Transportation	0	0	0.0
Corrections	0	0	0.0
Education	0	0	0.0
Employment Security Administration	0	0	0.0
Financial Administration	2,408	14	0.5
Fire Protection	22,459	139	4.8
General Public Buildings	1,990	12	0.4
Governmental Administration, Other	2,259	14	0.5
Health	129	< 1	< 0.1
Highways	15,433	95	3.3
Hospitals	0	0	0.0
Housing and Community Development	2,698	16	0.6
Interest on General Debt	9,469	58	2.0
Judicial and Legal	847	5	0.2
Libraries	0	0	0.0
Parking	296	1	0.1
Parks and Recreation	9,325	57	2.0
Police Protection	33,828	209	7.2
Public Welfare	0	0	0.0
Sewerage	30,991	192	6.6
Solid Waste Management	0	0	0.0
Veterans' Services	0	0	0.0
Liquor Store	0	0	0.0
Utility	308,973	1,916	65.7

Source: U.S. Census Bureau, State & Local Government Finances 2022

TAXES

State Corporate Income Tax Rates

State	Tax Rate (%)	Income Brackets ($)	Num. of Brackets	Financial Institution Tax Rate (%)[a]	Federal Income Tax Ded.
Tennessee	6.5	Flat rate	1	6.5	No

Note: Tax rates for tax year 2024; (a) Rates listed are the corporate income tax rate applied to financial institutions or excise taxes based on income. Some states have other taxes based upon the value of deposits or shares.

Source: Federation of Tax Administrators, State Corporate Income Tax Rates, January 1, 2025

State Individual Income Tax Rates

State	Tax Rate (%)	Income Brackets ($)	Personal Exemptions ($)			Standard Ded. ($)	
			Single	Married	Depend.	Single	Married
Tennessee							– No state income tax –

Note: Tax rates for tax year 2024; Local- and county-level taxes are not included
Source: Federation of Tax Administrators, State Individual Income Tax Rates, January 1, 2025

Various State Sales and Excise Tax Rates

State	State Sales Tax (%)	Gasoline[1] ($/gal.)	Cigarette[2] ($/pack)	Spirits[3] ($/gal.)	Wine[4] ($/gal.)	Beer[5] ($/gal.)	Recreational Marijuana (%)
Tennessee	7	0.27	0.62	4.46	1.27	1.29	Not legal

Note: All tax rates as of January 1, 2025; (1) The American Petroleum Institute has developed a methodology for determining the average tax rate on a gallon of fuel. Rates may include any of the following: excise taxes, environmental fees, storage tank fees, other fees or taxes, general sales tax, and local taxes; (2) The federal excise tax of $1.0066 per pack and local taxes are not included; (3) Rates are those applicable to off-premise sales of 40% alcohol by volume (a.b.v.) distilled spirits in 750ml containers. Local excise taxes are excluded; (4) Rates are those applicable to off-premise sales of 11% a.b.v. non-carbonated wine in 750ml containers; (5) Rates are those applicable to off-premise sales of 4.7% a.b.v. beer in 12 ounce containers.
Source: Tax Foundation, 2025 Facts & Figures: How Does Your State Compare?

State Tax Competitiveness Index

State	Overall Rank	Corporate Tax Rank	Individual Income Tax Rank	Sales Tax Rank	Property Tax Rank	Unemployment Insurance Tax Rank
Tennessee	8	48	1	47	33	17

Note: The Tax Foundation's State Tax Competitiveness Index enables policymakers, taxpayers, and business leaders to gauge how their states' tax systems compare. A rank of 1 is best, 50 is worst. Rankings do not average to the total. States without a tax rank equally as 1. DC's scores and rankings do not affect other states. The report shows tax systems as of July 1, 2024 (the beginning of Fiscal Year 2025).
Source: Tax Foundation, State Tax Competitiveness Index 2025

TRANSPORTATION

Means of Transportation to Work

Area	Car/Truck/Van		Public Transportation			Bicycle	Walked	Other Means	Worked at Home
	Drove Alone	Car-pooled	Bus	Subway	Railroad				
City	81.0	8.7	0.5	0.0	0.0	0.0	1.2	1.5	7.1
MSA[1]	79.6	9.5	0.4	0.0	0.0	0.2	2.4	1.5	6.5
U.S.	70.2	8.5	1.7	1.3	0.4	0.4	2.4	1.6	13.5

Note: Figures are percentages and cover workers 16 years of age and older; (1) Figures cover the Clarksville, TN-KY Metropolitan Statistical Area
Source: U.S. Census Bureau, 2019-2023 American Community Survey 5-Year Estimates

Travel Time to Work

Area	Less Than 10 Minutes	10 to 19 Minutes	20 to 29 Minutes	30 to 44 Minutes	45 to 59 Minutes	60 to 89 Minutes	90 Minutes or More
City	10.5	32.6	25.9	13.1	7.3	8.3	2.3
MSA[1]	14.1	30.9	22.8	15.1	7.2	6.9	3.0
U.S.	12.6	28.6	21.2	20.8	8.1	6.0	2.8

Note: Note: Figures are percentages and include workers 16 years old and over; (1) Figures cover the Clarksville, TN-KY Metropolitan Statistical Area
Source: U.S. Census Bureau, 2019-2023 American Community Survey 5-Year Estimates

Key Congestion Measures

Measure	2000	2010	2015	2020	2022
Annual Hours of Delay, Total (000)	n/a	n/a	3,611	1,474	3,927
Annual Hours of Delay, Per Auto Commuter	n/a	n/a	21	8	22
Annual Congestion Cost, Per Auto Commuter ($)	n/a	n/a	506	214	519

Note: n/a not available
Source: Texas A&M Transportation Institute, 2023 Urban Mobility Report

Freeway Travel Time Index

Measure	1985	1990	1995	2000	2005	2010	2015	2020	2022
Urban Area Index[1]	n/a	n/a	n/a	n/a	n/a	n/a	1.11	1.04	1.13
Urban Area Rank[1,2]	n/a	n/a	n/a	n/a	n/a	n/a	n/a	n/a	n/a

Note: Freeway Travel Time Index—the ratio of travel time in the peak period to the travel time at free-flow conditions. For example, a value of 1.30 indicates a 20-minute free-flow trip takes 26 minutes in the peak (20 minutes x 1.30 = 26 minutes); (1) Covers the Clarksville TN-KY urban area; (2) Rank is based on 101 larger urban areas (#1 = highest travel time index); n/a not available
Source: Texas A&M Transportation Institute, 2023 Urban Mobility Report

Public Transportation

Agency Name / Mode of Transportation	Vehicles Operated in Maximum Service[1]	Annual Unlinked Passenger Trips[2] (in thous.)	Annual Passenger Miles[3] (in thous.)
Clarksville Transit System (CTS)			
Bus (directly operated)	17	483.7	n/a
Demand Response (directly operated)	12	40.8	n/a

Note: (1) Number of revenue vehicles operated by the given mode and type of service to meet the annual maximum service requirement. This is the revenue vehicle count during the peak season of the year; on the week and day that maximum service is provided. Vehicles operated in maximum service (VOMS) exclude atypical days and one-time special events; (2) Number of passengers who boarded public transportation vehicles. Passengers are counted each time they board a vehicle no matter how many vehicles they use to travel from their origin to their destination. (3) Sum of the distances ridden by all passengers during the entire fiscal year.
Source: Federal Transit Administration, National Transit Database, 2023

Air Transportation

Airport Name and Code / Type of Service	Passenger Airlines[1]	Passenger Enplanements	Freight Carriers[2]	Freight (lbs)
Nashville International (53 miles) (BNA)				
Domestic service (U.S. carriers only)	37	11,798,157	16	65,297,621
International service (U.S. carriers only)	7	27,638	0	0

Note: (1) Includes all U.S.-based major, minor and commuter airlines that carried at least one passenger during the year; (2) Includes all U.S.-based airlines and freight carriers that transported at least one pound of freight during the year.
Source: Bureau of Transportation Statistics, The Intermodal Transportation Database, Air Carriers: T-100 Domestic Market (U.S. carriers only), 2024; Bureau of Transportation Statistics, The Intermodal Transportation Database, Air Carriers: T-100 International Market (U.S. carriers only), 2024

BUSINESSES

Major Business Headquarters

Company Name	Industry	Rankings Fortune[1]	Forbes[2]
No companies listed	-	-	-

Note: (1) Companies that produce a 10-K are ranked 1 to 500 based on 2023 revenue; (2) All private companies with at least $2 billion in annual revenue through the end of their most current fiscal year are ranked 1 to 275; companies listed are headquartered in the city; dashes indicate no ranking
Source: Fortune, "Fortune 500," 2024; Forbes, "America's Largest Private Companies," 2024

Living Environment

COST OF LIVING

Cost of Living Index

Composite Index	Groceries	Housing	Utilities	Transportation	Health Care	Misc. Goods/Services
n/a	n/a	n/a	n/a	n/a	n/a	n/a

Note: The Cost of Living Index measures regional differences in the cost of consumer goods and services, excluding taxes and non-consumer expenditures, for professional and managerial households in the top income quintile. It is based on more than 50,000 prices covering almost 60 different items for which prices are collected three times a year by chambers of commerce, economic development organizations or university applied economic centers in each participating urban area. The numbers shown should be read as a percentage above or below the national average of 100. For example, a value of 115.4 in the groceries column indicates that grocery prices are 15.4% higher than the national average. Small differences in the index numbers should not be interpreted as significant; n/a not available.
Source: The Council for Community and Economic Research, Cost of Living Index, 2024

Grocery Prices

Area[1]	T-Bone Steak ($/pound)	Frying Chicken ($/pound)	Whole Milk ($/half gal.)	Eggs ($/dozen)	Orange Juice ($/64 oz.)	Coffee ($/11.5 oz.)
City[2]	n/a	n/a	n/a	n/a	n/a	n/a
Avg.	15.42	1.55	4.69	3.25	4.41	5.46
Min.	14.50	1.16	4.43	2.75	4.00	4.85
Max.	17.56	2.89	5.49	4.78	5.54	7.89

Note: (1) Values for the local area are compared with the average, minimum and maximum values for all 276 areas in the Cost of Living Index; (2) Figures cover the Clarksville TN urban area; n/a not available; **T-Bone Steak** (price per pound); **Frying Chicken** (price per pound, whole fryer); **Whole Milk** (half gallon carton); **Eggs** (price per dozen, Grade A, large); **Orange Juice** (64 oz. Tropicana or Florida Natural); **Coffee** (11.5 oz. can, vacuum-packed, Maxwell House, Hills Bros, or Folgers).
Source: The Council for Community and Economic Research, Cost of Living Index, 2024

Housing and Utility Costs

Area[1]	New Home Price ($)	Apartment Rent ($/month)	All Electric ($/month)	Part Electric ($/month)	Other Energy ($/month)	Telephone ($/month)
City[2]	n/a	n/a	n/a	n/a	n/a	n/a
Avg.	515,975	1,550	210.99	123.07	82.07	194.99
Min.	265,375	692	104.33	53.68	36.26	179.42
Max.	2,775,821	5,719	529.02	397.28	361.63	223.33

Note: (1) Values for the local area are compared with the average, minimum and maximum values for all 276 areas in the Cost of Living Index; (2) Figures cover the Clarksville TN urban area; n/a not available; **New Home Price** (2,400 sf living area, 8,000 sf lot, in urban area with full utilities); **Apartment Rent** (950 sf 2 bedroom/1.5 or 2 bath, unfurnished, excluding all utilities except water); **All Electric** (average monthly cost for an all-electric home); **Part Electric** (average monthly cost for a part-electric home); **Other Energy** (average monthly cost for natural gas, fuel oil, coal, wood, and any other forms of energy except electricity); **Telephone** (price includes the base monthly rate plus taxes and fees for three lines of mobile phone service).
Source: The Council for Community and Economic Research, Cost of Living Index, 2024

Health Care, Transportation, and Other Costs

Area[1]	Doctor ($/visit)	Dentist ($/visit)	Optometrist ($/visit)	Gasoline ($/gallon)	Beauty Salon ($/visit)	Men's Shirt ($)
City[2]	n/a	n/a	n/a	n/a	n/a	n/a
Avg.	143.77	117.51	129.23	3.32	48.57	38.14
Min.	36.74	58.67	67.33	2.80	24.00	13.41
Max.	270.44	216.82	307.33	5.28	94.00	63.89

Note: (1) Values for the local area are compared with the average, minimum and maximum values for all 276 areas in the Cost of Living Index; (2) Figures cover the Clarksville TN urban area; n/a not available; **Doctor** (general practitioners routine exam of an established patient); **Dentist** (adult teeth cleaning and periodic oral examination); **Optometrist** (full vision eye exam for established adult patient); **Gasoline** (one gallon regular unleaded, national brand, including all taxes, cash price at self-service pump if available); **Beauty Salon** (woman's shampoo, trim, and blow-dry); **Men's Shirt** (cotton/polyester dress shirt, pinpoint weave, long sleeves).
Source: The Council for Community and Economic Research, Cost of Living Index, 2024

HOUSING

Homeownership Rate

Area	2017 (%)	2018 (%)	2019 (%)	2020 (%)	2021 (%)	2022 (%)	2023 (%)	2024 (%)
MSA[1]	n/a	n/a	n/a	n/a	n/a	n/a	n/a	n/a
U.S.	63.9	64.4	64.6	66.6	65.5	65.8	65.9	65.6

Note: (1) Figures cover the Clarksville, TN-KY Metropolitan Statistical Area; n/a not available
Source: U.S. Census Bureau, Housing Vacancies and Homeownership Annual Statistics: 2017-2024

House Price Index (HPI)

Area	National Ranking[2]	Quarterly Change (%)	One-Year Change (%)	Five-Year Change (%)	Since 1991Q1 (%)
MSA[1]	(a)	-0.84	3.55	67.67	n/a
U.S.[3]	—	1.43	4.51	57.13	327.82

Note: The HPI is a weighted repeat sales index. It measures average price changes in repeat sales or refinancings on the same properties. This information is obtained by reviewing repeat mortgage transactions on single-family properties whose mortgages have been purchased or securitized by Fannie Mae or Freddie Mac since January 1975; (1) Figures cover the Clarksville, TN-KY Metropolitan Statistical Area; (2) Rankings are based on annual percentage change for all metro areas containing at least 15,000 transactions over the last 10 years and ranges from 1 to 241; (3) figures based on a weighted average of Census Division estimates using a seasonally adjusted, purchase-only index; all figures are for the period ending December 31, 2024; n/a not available; (a) Not ranked because of increased index variability due to smaller sample size
Source: Federal Housing Finance Agency, Change in FHFA Metropolitan Area House Price Indexes, All Transactions Index, 2024Q4

Home Value

Area	Under $100,000	$100,000 -$199,999	$200,000 -$299,999	$300,000 -$399,999	$400,000 -$499,999	$500,000 -$999,999	$1,000,000 or more	Median ($)
City	7.4	25.5	40.9	15.0	6.3	4.1	0.7	236,100
MSA[1]	13.8	25.6	31.2	14.6	7.2	6.3	1.2	229,400
U.S.	12.1	17.8	19.5	14.4	10.5	19.1	6.5	303,400

Note: Figures are percentages except for median and cover owner-occupied housing units; (1) Figures cover the Clarksville, TN-KY Metropolitan Statistical Area
Source: U.S. Census Bureau, 2019-2023 American Community Survey 5-Year Estimates

Year Housing Structure Built

Area	2020 or Later	2010 -2019	2000 -2009	1990 -1999	1980 -1989	1970 -1979	1960 -1969	1950 -1959	1940 -1949	Before 1940	Median Year
City	3.3	18.0	21.2	18.8	12.9	11.3	6.2	4.2	2.3	1.7	1996
MSA[1]	2.6	16.3	19.0	18.9	12.1	12.6	7.3	5.5	2.6	3.0	1994
U.S.	1.2	8.9	13.6	12.8	13.0	14.4	10.0	9.7	4.5	11.9	1980

Note: Figures are percentages except for Median Year; Note: (1) Figures cover the Clarksville, TN-KY Metropolitan Statistical Area
Source: U.S. Census Bureau, 2019-2023 American Community Survey 5-Year Estimates

Gross Monthly Rent

Area	Under $500	$500 -$999	$1,000 -$1,499	$1,500 -$1,999	$2,000 -$2,499	$2,500 -$2,999	$3,000 and up	Median ($)
City	2.4	26.4	43.4	20.7	6.1	0.8	0.3	1,215
MSA[1]	4.4	33.0	39.4	17.7	4.4	0.6	0.5	1,141
U.S.	6.5	22.3	29.5	20.2	10.8	4.8	5.9	1,348

Note: Figures are percentages except for median; Gross rent is the contract rent plus the estimated average monthly cost of utilities (electricity, gas, and water and sewer) and fuels (oil, coal, kerosene, wood, etc.) if these are paid by the renter (or paid for the renter by someone else); (1) Figures cover the Clarksville, TN-KY Metropolitan Statistical Area
Source: U.S. Census Bureau, 2019-2023 American Community Survey 5-Year Estimates

HEALTH

Health Risk Factors

Category	MSA[1] (%)	U.S. (%)
Adults aged 18–64 who have any kind of health care coverage	n/a	90.8
Adults who reported being in good or better health	n/a	81.8
Adults who have been told they have high blood cholesterol	n/a	36.9
Adults who have been told they have high blood pressure	n/a	34.0
Adults who are current smokers	n/a	12.1
Adults who currently use e-cigarettes	n/a	7.7
Adults who currently use chewing tobacco, snuff, or snus	n/a	3.2
Adults who are heavy drinkers[2]	n/a	6.1
Adults who are binge drinkers[3]	n/a	15.2
Adults who are overweight (BMI 25.0 - 29.9)	n/a	34.4
Adults who are obese (BMI 30.0 - 99.8)	n/a	34.3
Adults who participated in any physical activities in the past month	n/a	75.8

Note: All figures are crude prevalence; (1) Figures for the Clarksville, TN-KY Metropolitan Statistical Area were not available.
(2) Heavy drinkers are classified as adult men having more than 14 drinks per week and adult women having more than 7 drinks per week; (3) Binge drinkers are classified as males having five or more drinks on one occasion or females having four or more drinks on one occasion
Source: Centers for Disease Control and Prevention, Behavioral Risk Factor Surveillance System, SMART: Selected Metropolitan Area Risk Trends, 2023

Acute and Chronic Health Conditions

Category	MSA[1] (%)	U.S. (%)
Adults who have ever been told they had a heart attack	n/a	4.2
Adults who have ever been told they have angina or coronary heart disease	n/a	4.0
Adults who have ever been told they had a stroke	n/a	3.3
Adults who have ever been told they have asthma	n/a	15.7
Adults who have ever been told they have arthritis	n/a	26.3
Adults who have ever been told they have diabetes[2]	n/a	11.5
Adults who have ever been told they had skin cancer	n/a	5.6
Adults who have ever been told they had any other types of cancer	n/a	8.4
Adults who have ever been told they have COPD	n/a	6.4
Adults who have ever been told they have kidney disease	n/a	3.7
Adults who have ever been told they have a form of depression	n/a	22.0

Note: All figures are crude prevalence; (1) Figures for the Clarksville, TN-KY Metropolitan Statistical Area were not available.
(2) Figures do not include pregnancy-related, borderline, or pre-diabetes
Source: Centers for Disease Control and Prevention, Behavioral Risk Factor Surveillance System, SMART: Selected Metropolitan Area Risk Trends, 2023

Health Screening and Vaccination Rates

Category	MSA[1] (%)	U.S. (%)
Adults who have ever been tested for HIV	n/a	37.5
Adults who have had their blood cholesterol checked within the last five years	n/a	87.0
Adults aged 65+ who have had flu shot within the past year	n/a	63.4
Adults aged 65+ who have ever had a pneumonia vaccination	n/a	71.9

Note: All figures are crude prevalence; (1) Figures for the Clarksville, TN-KY Metropolitan Statistical Area were not available.
Source: Centers for Disease Control and Prevention, Behavioral Risk Factor Surveillance System, SMART: Selected Metropolitan Area Risk Trends, 2023

Disability Status

Category	MSA[1] (%)	U.S. (%)
Adults who reported being deaf	n/a	7.4
Are you blind or have serious difficulty seeing, even when wearing glasses?	n/a	4.9
Do you have difficulty doing errands alone?	n/a	7.8
Do you have difficulty dressing or bathing?	n/a	3.6
Do you have serious difficulty concentrating/remembering/making decisions?	n/a	13.7
Do you have serious difficulty walking or climbing stairs?	n/a	13.2

Note: All figures are crude prevalence; (1) Figures for the Clarksville, TN-KY Metropolitan Statistical Area were not available.
Source: Centers for Disease Control and Prevention, Behavioral Risk Factor Surveillance System, SMART: Selected Metropolitan Area Risk Trends, 2023

Mortality Rates for the Top 10 Causes of Death in the U.S.

ICD-10[a] Sub-Chapter	ICD-10[a] Code	Crude Mortality Rate[2] per 100,000 population	
		County[3]	U.S.
Malignant neoplasms	C00-C97	130.4	182.7
Ischaemic heart diseases	I20-I25	84.1	109.6
Provisional assignment of new diseases of uncertain etiology[1]	U00-U49	61.2	65.3
Other forms of heart disease	I30-I51	27.6	65.1
Other degenerative diseases of the nervous system	G30-G31	39.5	52.4
Other external causes of accidental injury	W00-X59	50.9	52.3
Cerebrovascular diseases	I60-I69	37.6	49.1
Chronic lower respiratory diseases	J40-J47	44.5	43.5
Hypertensive diseases	I10-I15	28.7	38.9
Organic, including symptomatic, mental disorders	F01-F09	21.8	33.9

Note: (a) ICD-10 = International Classification of Diseases 10th Revision; (1) Includes COVID-19, adverse effects to COVID-19 vaccines, SARS, and vaping-related disorders; (2) Crude mortality rates are a three-year average covering 2021-2023; (3) Figures cover Montgomery County.
Source: Centers for Disease Control and Prevention, National Center for Health Statistics. National Vital Statistics System, Mortality 2018-2023 on CDC WONDER Online Database

Mortality Rates for Selected Causes of Death

Cause of Death	ICD-10[a] Code	Crude Mortality Rate[1] per 100,000 population	
		County[2]	U.S.
Accidental poisoning and exposure to noxious substances	X40-X49	37.4	30.5
Alzheimer disease	G30	35.7	35.4
Assault	X85-Y09	7.4	7.3
COVID-19	U07.1	61.2	65.3
Diabetes mellitus	E10-E14	29.7	30.0
Diseases of the liver	K70-K76	16.6	20.8
Human immunodeficiency virus (HIV) disease	B20-B24	Suppressed	1.5
Influenza and pneumonia	J09-J18	13.9	13.4
Intentional self-harm	X60-X84	20.6	14.7
Malnutrition	E40-E46	Unreliable	6.0
Obesity and other hyperalimentation	E65-E68	5.3	3.1
Renal failure	N17-N19	8.0	16.4
Transport accidents	V01-V99	17.4	14.4

Note: (a) ICD-10 = International Classification of Diseases 10th Revision; (1) Crude mortality rates are a three-year average covering 2021-2023; (2) Figures cover Montgomery County; Data are suppressed when the data meet the criteria for confidentiality constraints; Crude mortality rates are flagged as unreliable when the rate would be calculated with a numerator of 20 or less.
Source: Centers for Disease Control and Prevention, National Center for Health Statistics. National Vital Statistics System, Mortality 2018-2023 on CDC WONDER Online Database

Health Insurance Coverage

Area	With Health Insurance	With Private Health Insurance	With Public Health Insurance	Without Health Insurance	Population Under Age 19 Without Health Insurance
City	90.7	72.1	34.3	9.3	4.3
MSA[1]	90.7	69.7	36.3	9.3	6.7
U.S.	91.4	67.3	36.3	8.6	5.4

Note: Figures are percentages that cover the civilian noninstitutionalized population; (1) Figures cover the Clarksville, TN-KY Metropolitan Statistical Area
Source: U.S. Census Bureau, 2019-2023 American Community Survey 5-Year Estimates

Number of Medical Professionals

Area	MDs[3]	DOs[3,4]	Dentists	Podiatrists	Chiropractors	Optometrists
County[1] (number)	215	39	108	7	31	25
County[1] (rate[2])	91.4	16.6	45.0	2.9	12.9	10.4
U.S. (rate[2])	302.5	29.2	74.6	6.4	29.5	18.0

Note: Data as of 2023 unless noted; (1) Data covers Montgomery County; (2) Number of medical professionals per 100,000 population; (3) Data as of 2022 and includes all active, non-federal physicians; (4) Doctor of Osteopathic Medicine
Source: U.S. Department of Health and Human Services, Health Resources and Services Administration, Bureau of Health Professions, Area Resource File (ARF) 2023-2024

EDUCATION

Public School District Statistics

District Name	Schls	Pupils	Pupil/ Teacher Ratio	Minority Pupils[1] (%)	Total Rev. per Pupil ($)	Total Exp. per Pupil ($)
Montgomery County	44	39,345	17.9	54.8	11,896	12,015

Note: Table includes school districts with 2,000 or more students; (1) Percentage of students that are not non-Hispanic white.
Source: U.S. Department of Education, National Center for Education Statistics, Common Core of Data, Local Education Agency (School District) Universe Survey: School Year 2023-2024; U.S. Department of Education, National Center for Education Statistics, Common Core of Data, School District Finance Survey (F-33): School Year 2021–22

Highest Level of Education

Area	Less than H.S.	H.S. Diploma	Some College, No Deg.	Associate Degree	Bachelor's Degree	Master's Degree	Prof. School Degree	Doctorate Degree
City	5.8	27.4	24.2	12.0	18.9	9.4	1.2	1.1
MSA[1]	7.7	29.5	23.6	11.2	17.4	8.2	1.3	1.1
U.S.	10.6	26.2	19.4	8.8	21.3	9.8	2.3	1.6

Note: Figures cover persons age 25 and over; (1) Figures cover the Clarksville, TN-KY Metropolitan Statistical Area
Source: U.S. Census Bureau, 2019-2023 American Community Survey 5-Year Estimates

Educational Attainment by Race

Area	High School Graduate or Higher (%)					Bachelor's Degree or Higher (%)				
	Total	White	Black	Asian	Hisp.[2]	Total	White	Black	Asian	Hisp.[2]
City	94.2	95.8	95.2	84.5	84.8	30.6	33.8	27.3	27.8	19.9
MSA[1]	92.3	92.8	93.3	87.6	84.0	28.0	29.3	25.3	35.5	20.5
U.S.	89.4	92.9	88.1	88.0	72.5	35.0	37.7	24.7	57.0	19.9

Note: Figures shown cover persons 25 years old and over; (1) Figures cover the Clarksville, TN-KY Metropolitan Statistical Area; (2) People of Hispanic origin can be of any race
Source: U.S. Census Bureau, 2019-2023 American Community Survey 5-Year Estimates

School Enrollment by Grade and Control

Area	Preschool (%)		Kindergarten (%)		Grades 1 - 4 (%)		Grades 5 - 8 (%)		Grades 9 - 12 (%)	
	Public	Private	Public	Private	Public	Private	Public	Private	Public	Private
City	65.2	34.8	88.2	11.8	93.2	6.8	91.6	8.4	88.3	11.7
MSA[1]	62.8	37.2	85.3	14.7	86.8	13.2	86.0	14.0	87.6	12.4
U.S.	58.7	41.3	85.2	14.8	87.2	12.8	87.9	12.1	89.0	11.0

Note: Figures shown cover persons 3 years old and over; (1) Figures cover the Clarksville, TN-KY Metropolitan Statistical Area
Source: U.S. Census Bureau, 2019-2023 American Community Survey 5-Year Estimates

Higher Education

Four-Year Colleges			Two-Year Colleges			Medical Schools[1]	Law Schools[2]	Voc/ Tech[3]
Public	Private Non-profit	Private For-profit	Public	Private Non-profit	Private For-profit			
1	0	0	1	0	2	0	0	2

Note: Figures cover institutions located within the Clarksville, TN-KY Metropolitan Statistical Area and include main campuses only; (1) includes schools accredited by the Liaison Committee on Medical Education and the American Osteopathic Association's Commission on Osteopathic College Accreditation; (2) includes ABA-accredited schools, schools with provisional ABA accreditation, and state accredited schools; (3) includes all schools with programs that are less than 2 years.
Source: National Center for Education Statistics, Integrated Postsecondary Education System (IPEDS), 2023-24; Wikipedia, List of Medical Schools in the United States, accessed May 2, 2025; Wikipedia, List of Law Schools in the United States, accessed May 2, 2025

EMPLOYERS

Major Employers

Company Name	Industry
Agero	Call center
Akebono	Hubs, rotors
AT&T	Engineering services
Austin Peay State University	University
Bridgestone Metalpha U.S.A.	Steel tire cords & tire cord fabrics
City of Clarksville	Municipal government
Clarksville-Montgomery School System	Education
Gateway Medical Center	General medical & surgical hospitals
Jennie Stuart Medical Center	General medical & surgical hospitals
Jostens	Yearbooks & commercial printing
Montgomery County Government	Government
Trane Company	Heating & air conditioners
Trigg County Board of Education	Elementary & secondary schools
U.S. Army	U.S. military
Wal-Mart Stores	Department stores, discount

Note: Companies shown are located within the Clarksville, TN-KY Metropolitan Statistical Area.
Source: Chambers of Commerce; State Departments of Labor; Wikipedia

PUBLIC SAFETY

Crime Rate

Area	Total Crime Rate	Violent Crime Rate				Property Crime Rate		
		Murder	Rape	Robbery	Aggrav. Assault	Burglary	Larceny -Theft	Motor Vehicle Theft
City	2,193.3	6.0	57.7	29.7	373.8	214.9	1,285.8	225.4
U.S.	2,290.9	5.7	38.0	66.5	264.1	250.7	1,347.2	318.7

Note: Figures are crimes per 100,000 population.
Source: FBI, Table 8, Offenses Known to Law Enforcement, by State by City, 2023

Hate Crimes

Area	Number of Quarters Reported	Number of Incidents per Bias Motivation					
		Race/Ethnicity/Ancestry	Religion	Sexual Orientation	Disability	Gender	Gender Identity
City	4	0	0	0	0	0	0
U.S.	4	5,900	2,699	2,077	187	92	492

Source: Federal Bureau of Investigation, Hate Crime Statistics 2023

Identity Theft Consumer Reports

Area	Reports	Reports per 100,000 Population	Rank[2]
MSA[1]	730	222	130
U.S.	1,135,291	339	-

Note: (1) Figures cover the Clarksville, TN-KY Metropolitan Statistical Area; (2) Rank ranges from 1 to 401 where 1 indicates greatest number of identity theft reports per 100,000 population
Source: Federal Trade Commission, Consumer Sentinel Network Data Book 2024

Fraud and Other Consumer Reports

Area	Reports	Reports per 100,000 Population	Rank[2]
MSA[1]	4,186	1,274	103
U.S.	5,360,641	1,601	-

Note: (1) Figures cover the Clarksville, TN-KY Metropolitan Statistical Area; (2) Rank ranges from 1 to 401 where 1 indicates greatest number of fraud and other consumer reports per 100,000 population
Source: Federal Trade Commission, Consumer Sentinel Network Data Book 2024

POLITICS

2024 Presidential Election Results

Area	Trump (Rep.)	Harris (Dem.)	Stein (Green)	Kennedy (Ind.)	Oliver (Lib.)	Other
Montgomery County	58.3	39.9	0.3	0.8	0.0	0.7
U.S.	49.7	48.2	0.6	0.5	0.4	0.6

Note: Results are percentages and may not add to 100% due to rounding
Source: Dave Leip's Atlas of U.S. Presidential Elections

SPORTS

Professional Sports Teams

Team Name	League	Year Established

No teams are located in the metro area
Source: Wikipedia, Major Professional Sports Teams of the United States and Canada, May 1, 2025

CLIMATE

Average and Extreme Temperatures

Temperature	Jan	Feb	Mar	Apr	May	Jun	Jul	Aug	Sep	Oct	Nov	Dec	Yr.
Extreme High (°F)	78	84	86	91	95	106	107	104	105	94	84	79	107
Average High (°F)	47	51	60	71	79	87	90	89	83	72	60	50	70
Average Temp. (°F)	38	41	50	60	68	76	80	79	72	61	49	41	60
Average Low (°F)	28	31	39	48	57	65	69	68	61	48	39	31	49
Extreme Low (°F)	-17	-13	2	23	34	42	54	49	36	26	-1	-10	-17

Note: Figures cover the years 1948-1990
Source: National Climatic Data Center, International Station Meteorological Climate Summary, 9/96

Average Precipitation/Snowfall/Humidity

Precip./Humidity	Jan	Feb	Mar	Apr	May	Jun	Jul	Aug	Sep	Oct	Nov	Dec	Yr.
Avg. Precip. (in.)	4.4	4.2	5.0	4.1	4.6	3.7	3.8	3.3	3.2	2.6	3.9	4.6	47.4
Avg. Snowfall (in.)	4	3	1	Tr	0	0	0	0	0	Tr	1	1	11
Avg. Rel. Hum. 6am (%)	81	81	80	81	86	86	88	90	90	87	83	82	85
Avg. Rel. Hum. 3pm (%)	61	57	51	48	52	52	54	53	52	49	55	59	54

Note: Figures cover the years 1948-1990; Tr = Trace amounts (<0.05 in. of rain; <0.5 in. of snow)
Source: National Climatic Data Center, International Station Meteorological Climate Summary, 9/96

Weather Conditions

Temperature			Daytime Sky			Precipitation		
10°F & below	32°F & below	90°F & above	Clear	Partly cloudy	Cloudy	0.01 inch or more precip.	0.1 inch or more snow/ice	Thunder-storms
5	76	51	98	135	132	119	8	54

Note: Figures are average number of days per year and cover the years 1948-1990
Source: National Climatic Data Center, International Station Meteorological Climate Summary, 9/96

HAZARDOUS WASTE

Superfund Sites

The Clarksville, TN-KY metro area has no sites on the EPA's Superfund Final National Priorities List (NPL) or Superfund Alternative Approach (SAA) list. The Superfund alternative approach uses the same investigation and cleanup process and standards that are used for sites listed on the National Priorities List. The SAA is an alternative to listing a site on the NPL; it is not an alternative to Superfund or the Superfund process. There are a total of 1,445 Superfund sites with a status of proposed or final on both lists in the United States. *U.S. Environmental Protection Agency, National Priorities List, May 1, 2025; U.S. Environmental Protection Agency, Superfund Alternative Approach Sites, May 1, 2025*

AIR QUALITY

Air Quality Trends: Ozone

	1990	1995	2000	2005	2010	2015	2020	2021	2022	2023
MSA[1]	n/a	n/a	n/a	n/a	n/a	n/a	n/a	n/a	n/a	n/a
U.S.	0.087	0.089	0.081	0.080	0.072	0.068	0.066	0.067	0.067	0.070

Note: (1) Data covers the Clarksville, TN-KY Metropolitan Statistical Area; n/a not available. The values shown are the composite ozone concentration averages among trend sites based on the highest fourth daily maximum 8-hour concentration in parts per million. These trends are based on sites having an adequate record of monitoring data during the trend period. Data from exceptional events are included.
Source: U.S. Environmental Protection Agency, Air Quality Monitoring Information, "Air Quality Trends by City, 1990-2023"

Air Quality Index

Area	Percent of Days when Air Quality was...[2]					AQI Statistics[2]	
	Good	Moderate	Unhealthy for Sensitive Groups	Unhealthy	Very Unhealthy	Maximum	Median
MSA[1]	56.2	42.5	1.4	0.0	0.0	117	47

Note: (1) Data covers the Clarksville, TN-KY Metropolitan Statistical Area; (2) Based on 365 days with AQI data in 2023. Air Quality Index (AQI) is an index for reporting daily air quality. EPA calculates the AQI for five major air pollutants regulated by the Clean Air Act: ground-level ozone, particle pollution (aka particulate matter), carbon monoxide, sulfur dioxide, and nitrogen dioxide. The AQI runs from 0 to 500. The higher the AQI value, the greater the level of air pollution and the greater the health concern. There are six AQI categories: "Good" AQI is between 0 and 50. Air quality is considered satisfactory; "Moderate" AQI is between 51 and 100. Air quality is acceptable; "Unhealthy for Sensitive Groups" When AQI values are between 101 and 150, members of sensitive groups may experience health effects; "Unhealthy" When AQI values are between 151 and 200 everyone may begin to experience health effects; "Very Unhealthy" AQI values between 201 and 300 trigger a health alert; "Hazardous" AQI values over 300 trigger warnings of emergency conditions (not shown).
Source: U.S. Environmental Protection Agency, Air Quality Index Report, 2023

Air Quality Index Pollutants

Area	Percent of Days when AQI Pollutant was...[2]					
	Carbon Monoxide	Nitrogen Dioxide	Ozone	Sulfur Dioxide	Particulate Matter 2.5	Particulate Matter 10
MSA[1]	0.0	0.0	23.3	(3)	76.7	0.0

Note: (1) Data covers the Clarksville, TN-KY Metropolitan Statistical Area; (2) Based on 365 days with AQI data in 2023. The Air Quality Index (AQI) is an index for reporting daily air quality. EPA calculates the AQI for five major air pollutants regulated by the Clean Air Act: ground-level ozone, particle pollution (also known as particulate matter), carbon monoxide, sulfur dioxide, and nitrogen dioxide. The AQI runs from 0 to 500. The higher the AQI value, the greater the level of air pollution and the greater the health concern; (3) Sulfur dioxide is no longer included in this table because SO_2 concentrations tend to be very localized and not necessarily representative of broad geographical areas like counties and CBSAs.
Source: U.S. Environmental Protection Agency, Air Quality Index Report, 2023

Maximum Air Pollutant Concentrations: Particulate Matter, Ozone, CO and Lead

	Particulate Matter 10 (ug/m^3)	Particulate Matter 2.5 Wtd AM (ug/m^3)	Particulate Matter 2.5 24-Hr (ug/m^3)	Ozone (ppm)	Carbon Monoxide (ppm)	Lead (ug/m^3)
MSA[1] Level	n/a	8.6	22	0.07	n/a	n/a
NAAQS[2]	150	15	35	0.075	9	0.15
Met NAAQS[2]	n/a	Yes	Yes	Yes	n/a	n/a

Note: (1) Data covers the Clarksville, TN-KY Metropolitan Statistical Area; Data from exceptional events are included; (2) National Ambient Air Quality Standards; ppm = parts per million; ug/m^3 = micrograms per cubic meter; n/a not available.
Concentrations: Particulate Matter 10 (coarse particulate)—highest second maximum 24-hour concentration; Particulate Matter 2.5 Wtd AM (fine particulate)—highest weighted annual mean concentration; Particulate Matter 2.5 24-Hour (fine particulate)—highest 98th percentile 24-hour concentration; Ozone—highest fourth daily maximum 8-hour concentration; Carbon Monoxide—highest second maximum non-overlapping 8-hour concentration; Lead—maximum running 3-month average
Source: U.S. Environmental Protection Agency, Air Quality Monitoring Information, "Air Quality Statistics by City, 2023"

Maximum Air Pollutant Concentrations: Nitrogen Dioxide and Sulfur Dioxide

	Nitrogen Dioxide AM (ppb)	Nitrogen Dioxide 1-Hr (ppb)	Sulfur Dioxide AM (ppb)	Sulfur Dioxide 1-Hr (ppb)	Sulfur Dioxide 24-Hr (ppb)
MSA[1] Level	n/a	n/a	n/a	n/a	n/a
NAAQS[2]	53	100	30	75	140
Met NAAQS[2]	n/a	n/a	n/a	n/a	n/a

Note: (1) Data covers the Clarksville, TN-KY Metropolitan Statistical Area; Data from exceptional events are included; (2) National Ambient Air Quality Standards; ppm = parts per million; ug/m³ = micrograms per cubic meter; n/a not available.
Concentrations: Nitrogen Dioxide AM—highest arithmetic mean concentration; Nitrogen Dioxide 1-Hr—highest 98th percentile 1-hour daily maximum concentration; Sulfur Dioxide AM—highest annual mean concentration; Sulfur Dioxide 1-Hr—highest 99th percentile 1-hour daily maximum concentration; Sulfur Dioxide 24-Hr—highest second maximum 24-hour concentration
Source: U.S. Environmental Protection Agency, Air Quality Monitoring Information, "Air Quality Statistics by City, 2023"

College Station, Texas

Background

College Station in east-central Texas, sits at the center of the Texas Triangle within Brazos County, and shares a border with the city of Bryan to the northwest. College Station was built alongside the prestigious Texas A&M University (TAMU) during the nation's centennial in 1876. The city's origins date back to 1860, when Houston and Texas Central Railway began to build through the region during the height of railroad expansion in the mid-1800s. Though this railway no longer exists, College Station's location and the university make it important to the state.

The city was not incorporated until 1938. In 1942, the so-called "Father of College Station," became mayor and remained so for 26 years. During Langford's first term, the city adopted a council-manager system of government.

College Station is comprised of three major districts. Northgate, Wolf Pen Creek, and Wellborn combine to create a bustling city populated by students, professors, and their families. The city's population is young, mostly comprised of college-age individuals.

The economy of the city largely relies on the university, which is College Station's largest employer. Many who live in the city both attend TAMU and work in the city's shops and restaurants. Unemployment was among the lowest in Texas in recent years, but underemployment continues to be an issue among the overqualified college students. Post Oak Mall provides much of the business within College Station, being the first to open in the area and the largest mall in Brazos Valley. Over 75 percent of retail sales in the Brazos Valley are comprised here.

TAMU, formerly known as the Agricultural and Mechanical College of Texas, is now known for its triple designation as a Land-, Sea-, and Space-Grant institution, housing ongoing research projects funded by NASA, the National Institutes of Health, the National Science Foundation, and others.

The city's nightlife and entertainment attract a young crowd to events such as the four-day Northgate Music Festival and the live music at Church Street BBQ and Hurricane Harry's. The Texas country music scene thrives here, with many notable musicians getting their start at the city's smaller stages, among them Robert Earl Keen, Grammy-award winner Lyle Lovett, and Roger Creager.

In addition to the college and its music scene, College Station boast several important landmarks, including Church Street, made famous by the Lyle Lovett/Robert Earl Keen duet "The Front Porch Song," and the George Bush Presidential Library, which was dedicated in 1997 in honor of President George H.W. Bush. In 2022, the city became one of the first areas served by Amazon's Prime Air drone service.

The population and popularity of this relatively small city continues to grow every year, with predictions of the population doubling by the year 2030.

With the climate sitting comfortably in the subtropical and temperate zone, College Station enjoys mild winters with low-temperatures lasting less than two months. While snow and ice are rare, February 2021 saw unprecedented frigid temperatures and snowfall that led to days-long power outages. Summers are hot with occasional rain showers.

Rankings

General Rankings

- College Station was identified as one of America's fastest-growing areas in terms of population and economy by *Forbes*. College Station ranked #41 out of 50. Over 500 cities with more than 75,000 residents were measured for percentage of population growth over the following three periods: from 2011 to 2016; 2016 to 2021; and then 2011 to 2021. *Forbes.com, "The Fastest Growing Cities in America and Their Change in Income," September 12, 2023*

- In their annual survey, Livability.com looked at data for more than 2,000 mid-sized U.S. cities to assign a "Livability Score"for each. The top 100 scoring cities make up Livability's "Top 100 Best Places to Live in the U.S." in 2025. College Station was placed among the top 100 of the customizable list. Criteria: housing and economy; cost of living; environment; education; health care options; transportation; safety; and community amenities. *Livability.com, "Top 100 Best Places to Live in the U.S. in 2025" April 15, 2025*

Business/Finance Rankings

- The College Station metro area appeared on the Milken Institute "2025 Best Performing Cities" list. Rank: #37 out of 200 large metro areas (based on performance category). Criteria: job growth; wage growth; high-tech growth and impact; community resilience; housing affordability; household broadband access. *Milken Institute, "Best-Performing Cities 2025," January 14, 2025*

Environmental Rankings

- College Station was highlighted as one of the top 22 cleanest metro areas for short-term particle pollution (24-hour PM 2.5) in the U.S. during 2021 through 2023. Monitors in these cities reported no days with unhealthful PM 2.5 levels. *American Lung Association, "State of the Air 2025," April 23, 2025*

Sports/Recreation Rankings

- College Station was chosen as a bicycle friendly community by the League of American Bicyclists. A "Bicycle Friendly Community" welcomes cyclists by providing safe and supportive accommodation for cycling and encouraging people to bike for transportation and recreation. There are four award levels: Platinum; Gold; Silver; and Bronze. The community achieved an award level of Bronze. *League of American Bicyclists, "2024 Awards-New & Renewing Bicycle Friendly Communities List," January 28, 2025*

Business Environment

DEMOGRAPHICS

Population Growth

Area	1990 Census	2000 Census	2010 Census	2020 Census	2023 Estimate[2]	Population Growth 1990-2023 (%)
City	53,318	67,890	93,857	120,511	122,280	129.3
MSA[1]	150,998	184,885	228,660	268,248	273,280	81.0
U.S.	248,709,873	281,421,906	308,745,538	331,449,281	332,387,540	33.6

Note: (1) Figures cover the College Station-Bryan, TX Metropolitan Statistical Area; (2) 2019-2023 5-year ACS population estimate
Source: U.S. Census Bureau, 1990 Census, 2000 Census, 2010 Census, 2020 Census, 2019-2023 American Community Survey 5-Year Estimates

Race

Area	White Alone[2] (%)	Black Alone[2] (%)	Asian Alone[2] (%)	AIAN[3] Alone[2] (%)	NHOPI[4] Alone[2] (%)	Other Race Alone[2] (%)	Two or More Races (%)
City	67.0	8.8	9.6	0.3	0.1	3.3	10.9
MSA[1]	66.6	11.4	5.1	0.6	0.1	4.4	11.8
U.S.	63.4	12.4	5.8	0.9	0.2	6.6	10.7

Note: (1) Figures cover the College Station-Bryan, TX Metropolitan Statistical Area; (2) Alone is defined as not being in combination with one or more other races; (3) American Indian and Alaska Native; (4) Native Hawaiian and Other Pacific Islander
Source: U.S. Census Bureau, 2019-2023 American Community Survey 5-Year Estimates

Hispanic or Latino Origin

Area	Total (%)	Mexican (%)	Puerto Rican (%)	Cuban (%)	Other (%)
City	18.4	12.9	0.7	0.5	4.3
MSA[1]	26.4	21.9	0.5	0.5	3.6
U.S.	19.0	11.3	1.8	0.7	5.2

Note: Persons of Hispanic or Latino origin can be of any race; (1) Figures cover the College Station-Bryan, TX Metropolitan Statistical Area
Source: U.S. Census Bureau, 2019-2023 American Community Survey 5-Year Estimates

Age

Area	Under Age 5	Age 5-19	Age 20-34	Age 35-44	Age 45-54	Age 55-64	Age 65-74	Age 75-84	Age 85+	Median Age
City	4.8	25.3	40.0	10.3	6.8	6.2	4.2	1.9	0.6	22.9
MSA[1]	5.6	22.3	30.9	11.6	9.2	9.0	6.9	3.0	1.4	28.4
U.S.	5.7	19.1	20.2	13.1	12.3	12.8	10.0	4.9	1.9	38.7

Note: (1) Figures cover the College Station-Bryan, TX Metropolitan Statistical Area
Source: U.S. Census Bureau, 2019-2023 American Community Survey 5-Year Estimates

Disability by Age

Area	All Ages	Under 18 Years Old	18 to 64 Years Old	65 Years and Over
City	8.2	6.2	6.8	29.3
MSA[1]	10.9	5.5	8.8	33.8
U.S.	13.0	4.7	10.7	32.9

Note: Figures show percent of the civilian noninstitutionalized population that reported having a disability. Disability status is determined from six types of difficulty: vision, hearing, cognitive, ambulatory, self-care, and independent living. For children under 5 years old, hearing and vision difficulty are used to determine disability status. For children between the ages of 5 and 14, disability status is determined from hearing, vision, cognitive, ambulatory, and self-care difficulties. For people aged 15 years and older, they are considered to have a disability if they have difficulty with any one of the six difficulty types; Note: (1) Figures cover the College Station-Bryan, TX Metropolitan Statistical Area
Source: U.S. Census Bureau, 2019-2023 American Community Survey 5-Year Estimates

Ancestry

Area	German	Irish	English	American	Italian	Polish	French[2]	European	Scottish
City	14.8	8.0	9.8	3.2	3.3	2.3	1.9	1.8	1.6
MSA[1]	13.5	7.5	9.3	3.8	2.6	2.0	2.1	1.5	1.6
U.S.	12.6	9.4	9.1	5.5	4.9	2.6	2.0	1.6	1.6

Note: Figures are the percentage of the total population reporting a particular ancestry. The nine most commonly reported ancestries in the U.S. are shown. Figures include multiple ancestries (e.g. if a person reported being Irish and Italian, they were included in both columns); (1) Figures cover the College Station-Bryan, TX Metropolitan Statistical Area; (2) Excludes Basque
Source: U.S. Census Bureau, 2019-2023 American Community Survey 5-Year Estimates

Foreign-born Population

Area	Percent of Population Born in								
	Any Foreign Country	Asia	Mexico	Europe	Caribbean	Central America[2]	South America	Africa	Canada
City	12.3	7.1	1.5	0.9	0.1	1.0	1.0	0.5	0.1
MSA[1]	11.7	3.8	4.9	0.7	0.2	0.9	0.7	0.4	0.1
U.S.	13.9	4.3	3.3	1.4	1.4	1.2	1.2	0.8	0.2

Note: (1) Figures cover the College Station-Bryan, TX Metropolitan Statistical Area; (2) Excludes Mexico.
Source: U.S. Census Bureau, 2019-2023 American Community Survey 5-Year Estimates

Household Size

Area	Persons in Household (%)							Average Household Size
	One	Two	Three	Four	Five	Six	Seven or More	
City	31.1	32.3	15.1	15.1	3.5	2.4	0.6	2.42
MSA[1]	30.3	32.8	14.7	13.5	5.3	2.3	1.1	2.48
U.S.	28.5	33.8	15.4	12.7	5.9	2.3	1.4	2.54

Note: (1) Figures cover the College Station-Bryan, TX Metropolitan Statistical Area
Source: U.S. Census Bureau, 2019-2023 American Community Survey 5-Year Estimates

Household Relationships

Area	Householder	Opposite-sex Spouse	Same-sex Spouse	Opposite-sex Unmarried Partner	Same-sex Unmarried Partner	Child[2]	Grandchild	Other Relatives	Non-relatives
City	35.2	11.2	0.2	1.8	0.1	19.7	0.7	2.7	13.7
MSA[1]	36.9	14.6	0.1	2.0	0.1	24.7	1.9	3.5	8.3
U.S.	38.3	17.5	0.2	2.5	0.2	28.3	2.4	4.8	3.4

Note: Figures are percent of the total population; (1) Figures cover the College Station-Bryan, TX Metropolitan Statistical Area; (2) Includes biological, adopted, and stepchildren of the householder
Source: U.S. Census Bureau, 2020 Census

Gender

Area	Males	Females	Males per 100 Females
City	62,870	59,410	105.8
MSA[1]	137,218	136,062	100.8
U.S.	164,545,087	167,842,453	98.0

Note: (1) Figures cover the College Station-Bryan, TX Metropolitan Statistical Area
Source: U.S. Census Bureau, 2019-2023 American Community Survey 5-Year Estimates

Marital Status

Area	Never Married	Now Married[2]	Separated	Widowed	Divorced
City	60.3	31.2	1.2	2.4	5.0
MSA[1]	46.7	39.5	1.6	4.3	7.9
U.S.	34.1	47.9	1.7	5.6	10.7

Note: Figures are percentages and cover the population 15 years of age and older; (1) Figures cover the College Station-Bryan, TX Metropolitan Statistical Area; (2) Excludes separated
Source: U.S. Census Bureau, 2019-2023 American Community Survey 5-Year Estimates

Religious Groups by Family

Area	Catholic	Baptist	Methodist	LDS[2]	Pentecostal	Lutheran	Islam	Adventist	Other
MSA[1]	17.2	10.6	4.3	1.7	0.5	1.1	0.6	0.5	6.8
U.S.	18.7	7.3	3.0	2.0	1.8	1.7	1.3	1.3	11.6

Note: Figures are the number of adherents as a percentage of the total population and cover the eight largest religious groups in the U.S; (1) Figures cover the College Station-Bryan, TX Metropolitan Statistical Area; (2) Church of Jesus Christ of Latter-day Saints
Sources: 2020 U.S. Religion Census, Association of Statisticians of American Religious Bodies; The Association of Religion Data Archives (ARDA)

Religious Groups by Tradition

Area	Catholic	Evangelical Protestant	Mainline Protestant	Black Protestant	Islam	Judaism	Hinduism	Orthodox	Buddhism
MSA[1]	17.2	16.1	5.3	1.8	0.6	n/a	0.1	0.1	n/a
U.S.	18.7	16.5	5.2	2.3	1.3	0.6	0.4	0.4	0.3

Note: Figures are the number of adherents as a percentage of the total population; (1) Figures cover the College Station-Bryan, TX Metropolitan Statistical Area
Sources: 2020 U.S. Religion Census, Association of Statisticians of American Religious Bodies; The Association of Religion Data Archives (ARDA)

ECONOMY

Real Gross Domestic Product (GDP)

Area	2017	2018	2019	2020	2021	2022	2023	Rank[3]
MSA[1]	12.5	13.0	13.6	13.5	14.2	14.7	15.8	171
U.S.[2]	17,619.1	18,160.7	18,642.5	18,238.9	19,387.6	19,896.6	20,436.3	—

Note: Figures are in billions of chained 2017 dollars; (1) Figures cover the College Station-Bryan, TX Metropolitan Statistical Area; (2) Figures cover real GDP within metropolitan areas; (3) Rank is based on 2023 data and ranges from 1 to 384
Source: U.S. Bureau of Economic Analysis

Economic Growth

Area	2014	2015	2016	2017	2018	2019	2020	2021	2022	2023
MSA[1]	6.3	6.2	-0.3	1.7	4.3	4.5	-0.2	4.6	4.0	7.4
U.S.[2]	2.6	3.2	2.0	2.7	3.1	2.7	-2.2	6.3	2.6	2.7

Note: Figures are real gross domestic product growth rates and represent percent change from preceding period; (1) Figures cover the College Station-Bryan, TX Metropolitan Statistical Area; (2) Figures are the average growth rates within metropolitan areas
Source: U.S. Bureau of Economic Analysis

Metropolitan Area Exports

Area	2018	2019	2020	2021	2022	2023	Rank[2]
MSA[1]	153.0	160.5	114.9	110.3	136.2	180.0	323
U.S.	1,664,056.1	1,645,173.7	1,431,406.6	1,753,941.4	2,062,937.4	2,019,160.5	—

Note: Figures are in millions of dollars; (1) Figures cover the College Station-Bryan, TX Metropolitan Statistical Area; (2) Rank is based on 2023 data and ranges from 1 to 386
Source: U.S. Department of Commerce, International Trade Administration, Office of Trade and Economic Analysis, Industry and Analysis, Exports by Metropolitan Area, data extracted April 2, 2025

Building Permits

Area	Single-Family			Multi-Family			Total		
	2023	2024	Pct. Chg.	2023	2024	Pct. Chg.	2023	2024	Pct. Chg.
City	448	650	45.1	293	462	57.7	741	1,112	50.1
MSA[1]	1,155	1,482	28.3	307	839	173.3	1,462	2,321	58.8
U.S.	920,000	981,900	6.7	591,100	496,100	-16.1	1,511,100	1,478,000	-2.2

Note: (1) Figures cover the College Station-Bryan, TX Metropolitan Statistical Area; Figures represent new, privately-owned housing units authorized (unadjusted data)
Source: U.S. Census Bureau, Building Permits Survey (BPS), 2023, 2024

Bankruptcy Filings

Area	Business Filings			Nonbusiness Filings		
	2023	2024	% Chg.	2023	2024	% Chg.
Brazos County	5	7	40.0	65	80	23.1
U.S.	18,926	23,107	22.1	434,064	494,201	13.9

Note: Business filings include Chapter 7, Chapter 9, Chapter 11, Chapter 12, Chapter 13, Chapter 15, and Section 304; Nonbusiness filings include Chapter 7, Chapter 11, and Chapter 13
Source: Administrative Office of the U.S. Courts, Business and Nonbusiness Bankruptcy, County Cases Commenced by Chapter of the Bankruptcy Code, During the 12-Month Period Ending December 31, 2023 and Business and Nonbusiness Bankruptcy, County Cases Commenced by Chapter of the Bankruptcy Code, During the 12-Month Period Ending December 31, 2024

Housing Vacancy Rates

Area	Gross Vacancy Rate[3] (%)			Year-Round Vacancy Rate[4] (%)			Rental Vacancy Rate[5] (%)			Homeowner Vacancy Rate[6] (%)		
	2022	2023	2024	2022	2023	2024	2022	2023	2024	2022	2023	2024
MSA[1]	n/a	n/a	n/a	n/a	n/a	n/a	n/a	n/a	n/a	n/a	n/a	n/a
U.S.[2]	9.1	9.0	9.1	7.5	7.5	7.6	5.7	6.5	6.8	0.8	0.8	1.0

Note: (1) Figures cover the College Station-Bryan, TX Metropolitan Statistical Area; (2) Figures cover the 75 largest Metropolitan Statistical Areas; (3) The percentage of the total housing inventory that is vacant; (4) The percentage of the housing inventory (excluding seasonal units) that is year-round vacant; (5) The percentage of rental inventory that is vacant for rent; (6) The percentage of homeowner inventory that is vacant for sale; n/a not available
Source: U.S. Census Bureau, Housing Vacancies and Homeownership Annual Statistics: 2022, 2023, 2024

INCOME

Income

Area	Per Capita ($)	Median Household ($)	Average Household ($)
City	32,123	51,776	84,849
MSA[1]	34,136	59,691	88,300
U.S.	43,289	78,538	110,491

Note: (1) Figures cover the College Station-Bryan, TX Metropolitan Statistical Area
Source: U.S. Census Bureau, 2019-2023 American Community Survey 5-Year Estimates

Household Income Distribution

Area	Percent of Households Earning							
	Under $15,000	$15,000 -$24,999	$25,000 -$34,999	$35,000 -$49,999	$50,000 -$74,999	$75,000 -$99,999	$100,000 -$149,999	$150,000 and up
City	18.3	8.3	9.5	12.9	12.2	11.0	12.2	15.6
MSA[1]	14.7	7.7	8.7	12.5	14.6	12.2	14.2	15.4
U.S.	8.5	6.6	6.8	10.4	15.7	12.7	17.4	21.9

Note: (1) Figures cover the College Station-Bryan, TX Metropolitan Statistical Area
Source: U.S. Census Bureau, 2019-2023 American Community Survey 5-Year Estimates

Poverty Rate

Area	All Ages	Under 18 Years Old	18 to 64 Years Old	65 Years and Over
City	28.6	14.8	34.5	5.8
MSA[1]	22.6	19.9	26.0	8.5
U.S.	12.4	16.3	11.6	10.4

Note: Figures are percentage of people whose income during the past 12 months was below the poverty level;
(1) Figures cover the College Station-Bryan, TX Metropolitan Statistical Area
Source: U.S. Census Bureau, 2019-2023 American Community Survey 5-Year Estimates

EMPLOYMENT

Labor Force and Employment

Area	Civilian Labor Force			Workers Employed		
	Dec. 2023	Dec. 2024	% Chg.	Dec. 2023	Dec. 2024	% Chg.
City	70,826	73,610	3.9	68,915	71,605	3.9
MSA[1]	154,708	160,796	3.9	150,546	156,418	3.9
U.S.	166,661,000	167,746,000	0.7	160,754,000	161,294,000	0.3

Note: Data is not seasonally adjusted and covers workers 16 years of age and older; (1) Figures cover the College Station-Bryan, TX Metropolitan Statistical Area
Source: Bureau of Labor Statistics, Local Area Unemployment Statistics

Unemployment Rate

Area	2024											
	Jan.	Feb.	Mar.	Apr.	May	Jun.	Jul.	Aug.	Sep.	Oct.	Nov.	Dec.
City	3.4	3.6	3.0	2.5	3.0	3.7	3.8	3.7	3.3	3.2	3.1	2.7
MSA[1]	3.3	3.4	3.0	2.6	3.0	3.6	3.7	3.6	3.2	3.1	3.1	2.7
U.S.	4.1	4.2	3.9	3.5	3.7	4.3	4.5	4.4	3.9	3.9	4.0	3.8

Note: Data is not seasonally adjusted and covers workers 16 years of age and older; (1) Figures cover the College Station-Bryan, TX Metropolitan Statistical Area
Source: Bureau of Labor Statistics, Local Area Unemployment Statistics

Average Wages

Occupation	$/Hr.	Occupation	$/Hr.
Accountants and Auditors	36.32	Maintenance and Repair Workers	20.21
Automotive Mechanics	24.82	Marketing Managers	61.86
Bookkeepers	21.78	Network and Computer Systems Admin.	38.10
Carpenters	22.38	Nurses, Licensed Practical	26.76
Cashiers	13.30	Nurses, Registered	40.15
Computer Programmers	39.46	Nursing Assistants	16.34
Computer Systems Analysts	42.81	Office Clerks, General	n/a
Computer User Support Specialists	24.10	Physical Therapists	49.86
Construction Laborers	17.72	Physicians	118.72
Cooks, Restaurant	14.89	Plumbers, Pipefitters and Steamfitters	26.89
Customer Service Representatives	17.74	Police and Sheriff's Patrol Officers	36.08
Dentists	103.68	Postal Service Mail Carriers	27.95
Electricians	25.02	Real Estate Sales Agents	29.01
Engineers, Electrical	50.62	Retail Salespersons	15.01
Fast Food and Counter Workers	12.43	Sales Representatives, Technical/Scientific	41.37
Financial Managers	70.24	Secretaries, Exc. Legal/Medical/Executive	19.66
First-Line Supervisors of Office Workers	29.93	Security Guards	16.89
General and Operations Managers	51.36	Surgeons	n/a
Hairdressers/Cosmetologists	16.38	Teacher Assistants, Exc. Postsecondary[1]	14.65
Home Health and Personal Care Aides	12.18	Teachers, Secondary School, Exc. Sp. Ed.[1]	28.00
Janitors and Cleaners	15.33	Telemarketers	n/a
Landscaping/Groundskeeping Workers	16.48	Truck Drivers, Heavy/Tractor-Trailer	24.31
Lawyers	67.99	Truck Drivers, Light/Delivery Services	25.81
Maids and Housekeeping Cleaners	13.30	Waiters and Waitresses	15.16

Note: Wage data covers the College Station-Bryan, TX Metropolitan Statistical Area; (1) Hourly wages were calculated from annual wage data based on a 40 hour work week
Source: Bureau of Labor Statistics, Metro Area Occupational Employment & Wage Estimates, May 2024

Employment by Industry

Sector	MSA[1] Number of Employees	MSA[1] Percent of Total	U.S. Percent of Total
Construction, Mining, and Logging	7,800	5.3	5.5
Financial Activities	4,900	3.3	5.8
Government	52,100	35.1	14.9
Information	1,600	1.1	1.9
Leisure and Hospitality	21,400	14.4	10.4
Manufacturing	6,200	4.2	8.0
Other Services	4,100	2.8	3.7
Private Education and Health Services	16,100	10.9	16.9
Professional and Business Services	14,500	9.8	14.2
Retail Trade	13,500	9.1	10.0
Transportation, Warehousing, and Utilities	2,800	1.9	4.8
Wholesale Trade	3,300	2.2	3.9

Note: Figures are non-farm employment as of December 2024. Figures are not seasonally adjusted and include workers 16 years of age and older; (1) Figures cover the College Station-Bryan, TX Metropolitan Statistical Area
Source: Bureau of Labor Statistics, Current Employment Statistics, Employment, Hours, and Earnings

Employment by Occupation

Occupation Classification	City (%)	MSA[1] (%)	U.S. (%)
Management, Business, Science, and Arts	48.3	42.6	42.0
Natural Resources, Construction, and Maintenance	4.3	8.3	8.6
Production, Transportation, and Material Moving	8.5	10.8	13.0
Sales and Office	21.2	20.6	19.9
Service	17.7	17.7	16.5

Note: Figures cover employed civilians 16 years of age and older; (1) Figures cover the College Station-Bryan, TX Metropolitan Statistical Area
Source: U.S. Census Bureau, 2019-2023 American Community Survey 5-Year Estimates

Occupations with Greatest Projected Employment Growth: 2022 – 2032

Occupation[1]	2022 Employment	2032 Projected Employment	Numeric Employment Change	Percent Employment Change
General and Operations Managers	425,560	504,280	78,720	18.5
Fast Food and Counter Workers	333,870	394,290	60,420	18.1
Stockers and Order Fillers	264,810	321,600	56,790	21.4
Home Health and Personal Care Aides	313,670	367,500	53,830	17.2
Software Developers	110,280	161,780	51,500	46.7
Cooks, Restaurant	113,680	158,830	45,150	39.7
Laborers and Freight, Stock, and Material Movers, Hand	225,090	269,120	44,030	19.6
Heavy and Tractor-Trailer Truck Drivers	226,450	270,320	43,870	19.4
Retail Salespersons	319,400	357,630	38,230	12.0
Registered Nurses	233,850	267,980	34,130	14.6

Note: Projections cover Texas; (1) Sorted by numeric employment change
Source: www.projectionscentral.org, State Occupational Projections, 2022–2032 Long-Term Projections

Fastest-Growing Occupations: 2022 – 2032

Occupation[1]	2022 Employment	2032 Projected Employment	Numeric Employment Change	Percent Employment Change
Wind Turbine Service Technicians	4,860	7,950	3,090	63.6
Nurse Practitioners	19,060	30,490	11,430	60.0
Data Scientists	13,220	20,250	7,030	53.2
Computer and Information Research Scientists (SOC 2018)	2,070	3,140	1,070	51.7
Information Security Analysts (SOC 2018)	14,620	21,620	7,000	47.9
Software Developers	110,280	161,780	51,500	46.7
Statisticians	980	1,430	450	45.9
Operations Research Analysts	12,060	17,290	5,230	43.4
Software Quality Assurance Analysts and Testers	17,350	24,440	7,090	40.9
Medical and Health Services Managers	49,430	69,180	19,750	40.0

Note: Projections cover Texas; (1) Sorted by percent employment change and excludes occupations with numeric employment change less than 50
Source: www.projectionscentral.org, State Occupational Projections, 2022–2032 Long-Term Projections

CITY FINANCES

City Government Finances

Component	2022 ($000)	2022 ($ per capita)
Total Revenues	276,902	2,322
Total Expenditures	244,038	2,046
Debt Outstanding	406,981	3,413

Source: U.S. Census Bureau, State & Local Government Finances 2022

City Government Revenue by Source

Source	2022 ($000)	2022 ($ per capita)	2022 (%)
General Revenue			
From Federal Government	1,600	13	0.6
From State Government	992	8	0.4
From Local Governments	560	5	0.2
Taxes			
Property	52,693	442	19.0
Sales and Gross Receipts	40,944	343	14.8
Personal Income	0	0	0.0
Corporate Income	0	0	0.0
Motor Vehicle License	0	0	0.0
Other Taxes	2,599	22	0.9
Current Charges	40,759	342	14.7
Liquor Store	0	0	0.0
Utility	126,667	1,062	45.7

Source: U.S. Census Bureau, State & Local Government Finances 2022

City Government Expenditures by Function

Function	2022 ($000)	2022 ($ per capita)	2022 (%)
General Direct Expenditures			
Air Transportation	0	0	0.0
Corrections	0	0	0.0
Education	0	0	0.0
Employment Security Administration	0	0	0.0
Financial Administration	3,398	28	1.4
Fire Protection	15,203	127	6.2
General Public Buildings	6,745	56	2.8
Governmental Administration, Other	11,386	95	4.7
Health	0	0	0.0
Highways	16,122	135	6.6
Hospitals	0	0	0.0
Housing and Community Development	4,625	38	1.9
Interest on General Debt	2,890	24	1.2
Judicial and Legal	2,479	20	1.0
Libraries	1,266	10	0.5
Parking	544	4	0.2
Parks and Recreation	9,921	83	4.1
Police Protection	17,806	149	7.3
Public Welfare	0	0	0.0
Sewerage	6,353	53	2.6
Solid Waste Management	7,069	59	2.9
Veterans' Services	0	0	0.0
Liquor Store	0	0	0.0
Utility	115,288	966	47.2

Source: U.S. Census Bureau, State & Local Government Finances 2022

TAXES

State Corporate Income Tax Rates

State	Tax Rate (%)	Income Brackets ($)	Num. of Brackets	Financial Institution Tax Rate (%)[a]	Federal Income Tax Ded.
Texas	(u)	–	–	(u)	No

Note: Tax rates for tax year 2024; (a) Rates listed are the corporate income tax rate applied to financial institutions or excise taxes based on income. Some states have other taxes based upon the value of deposits or shares; (u) Texas imposes a Franchise Tax, otherwise known as margin tax, imposed on entities with more than $2,470,000 total revenues effective in 2024 at rate of 0.75%, or 0.375% for entities primarily engaged in retail or wholesale trade, on lesser of 70% of total revenues or 100% of gross receipts after deductions for either compensation ($450,000 deduction limit) or cost of goods sold. Texas has an EZ rate of 0.331 applicable to a $20 million revenue threshold.

Source: Federation of Tax Administrators, State Corporate Income Tax Rates, January 1, 2025

State Individual Income Tax Rates

State	Tax Rate (%)	Income Brackets ($)	Personal Exemptions ($) Single	Married	Depend.	Standard Ded. ($) Single	Married
Texas			– No state income tax –				

Note: Tax rates for tax year 2024; Local- and county-level taxes are not included
Source: Federation of Tax Administrators, State Individual Income Tax Rates, January 1, 2025

Various State Sales and Excise Tax Rates

State	State Sales Tax (%)	Gasoline[1] ($/gal.)	Cigarette[2] ($/pack)	Spirits[3] ($/gal.)	Wine[4] ($/gal.)	Beer[5] ($/gal.)	Recreational Marijuana (%)
Texas	6.25	0.20	1.41	2.40	0.20	0.19	Not legal

Note: All tax rates as of January 1, 2025; (1) The American Petroleum Institute has developed a methodology for determining the average tax rate on a gallon of fuel. Rates may include any of the following: excise taxes, environmental fees, storage tank fees, other fees or taxes, general sales tax, and local taxes; (2) The federal excise tax of $1.0066 per pack and local taxes are not included; (3) Rates are those applicable to off-premise sales of 40% alcohol by volume (a.b.v.) distilled spirits in 750ml containers. Local excise taxes are excluded; (4) Rates are those applicable to off-premise sales of 11% a.b.v. non-carbonated wine in 750ml containers; (5) Rates are those applicable to off-premise sales of 4.7% a.b.v. beer in 12 ounce containers.
Source: Tax Foundation, 2025 Facts & Figures: How Does Your State Compare?

State Tax Competitiveness Index

State	Overall Rank	Corporate Tax Rank	Individual Income Tax Rank	Sales Tax Rank	Property Tax Rank	Unemployment Insurance Tax Rank
Texas	7	46	1	36	40	30

Note: The Tax Foundation's State Tax Competitiveness Index enables policymakers, taxpayers, and business leaders to gauge how their states' tax systems compare. A rank of 1 is best, 50 is worst. Rankings do not average to the total. States without a tax rank equally as 1. DC's scores and rankings do not affect other states. The report shows tax systems as of July 1, 2024 (the beginning of Fiscal Year 2025).
Source: Tax Foundation, State Tax Competitiveness Index 2025

TRANSPORTATION

Means of Transportation to Work

Area	Car/Truck/Van Drove Alone	Car-pooled	Public Transportation Bus	Subway	Railroad	Bicycle	Walked	Other Means	Worked at Home
City	70.8	8.0	2.3	0.0	0.0	1.9	3.9	1.1	12.1
MSA[1]	75.1	9.5	1.3	0.0	0.0	1.0	2.1	1.3	9.7
U.S.	70.2	8.5	1.7	1.3	0.4	0.4	2.4	1.6	13.5

Note: Figures are percentages and cover workers 16 years of age and older; (1) Figures cover the College Station-Bryan, TX Metropolitan Statistical Area
Source: U.S. Census Bureau, 2019-2023 American Community Survey 5-Year Estimates

Travel Time to Work

Area	Less Than 10 Minutes	10 to 19 Minutes	20 to 29 Minutes	30 to 44 Minutes	45 to 59 Minutes	60 to 89 Minutes	90 Minutes or More
City	17.5	54.7	15.3	7.9	1.4	1.8	1.5
MSA[1]	16.2	48.4	17.1	11.0	3.2	2.3	1.9
U.S.	12.6	28.6	21.2	20.8	8.1	6.0	2.8

Note: Note: Figures are percentages and include workers 16 years old and over; (1) Figures cover the College Station-Bryan, TX Metropolitan Statistical Area
Source: U.S. Census Bureau, 2019-2023 American Community Survey 5-Year Estimates

Key Congestion Measures

Measure	2000	2010	2015	2020	2022
Annual Hours of Delay, Total (000)	n/a	n/a	5,235	2,659	6,318
Annual Hours of Delay, Per Auto Commuter	n/a	n/a	31	15	36
Annual Congestion Cost, Per Auto Commuter ($)	n/a	n/a	739	373	855

Note: n/a not available
Source: Texas A&M Transportation Institute, 2023 Urban Mobility Report

Freeway Travel Time Index

Measure	1985	1990	1995	2000	2005	2010	2015	2020	2022
Urban Area Index[1]	n/a	n/a	n/a	n/a	n/a	n/a	1.15	1.05	1.18
Urban Area Rank[1,2]	n/a	n/a	n/a	n/a	n/a	n/a	n/a	n/a	n/a

Note: Freeway Travel Time Index—the ratio of travel time in the peak period to the travel time at free-flow conditions. For example, a value of 1.30 indicates a 20-minute free-flow trip takes 26 minutes in the peak (20 minutes x 1.30 = 26 minutes); (1) Covers the College Station-Bryan TX urban area; (2) Rank is based on 101 larger urban areas (#1 = highest travel time index); n/a not available
Source: Texas A&M Transportation Institute, 2023 Urban Mobility Report

Public Transportation

Agency Name / Mode of Transportation	Vehicles Operated in Maximum Service[1]	Annual Unlinked Passenger Trips[2] (in thous.)	Annual Passenger Miles[3] (in thous.)
Brazos Transit District			
Bus (directly operated)	17	406.7	1,685.4
Demand Response (directly operated)	50	84.3	1,060.7

Note: (1) Number of revenue vehicles operated by the given mode and type of service to meet the annual maximum service requirement. This is the revenue vehicle count during the peak season of the year; on the week and day that maximum service is provided. Vehicles operated in maximum service (VOMS) exclude atypical days and one-time special events; (2) Number of passengers who boarded public transportation vehicles. Passengers are counted each time they board a vehicle no matter how many vehicles they use to travel from their origin to their destination. (3) Sum of the distances ridden by all passengers during the entire fiscal year.
Source: Federal Transit Administration, National Transit Database, 2023

Air Transportation

Airport Name and Code / Type of Service	Passenger Airlines[1]	Passenger Enplanements	Freight Carriers[2]	Freight (lbs)
Easterwood Airport (CLL)				
Domestic service (U.S. carriers only)	16	68,267	2	22,905
International service (U.S. carriers only)	0	0	0	0

Note: (1) Includes all U.S.-based major, minor and commuter airlines that carried at least one passenger during the year; (2) Includes all U.S.-based airlines and freight carriers that transported at least one pound of freight during the year.
Source: Bureau of Transportation Statistics, The Intermodal Transportation Database, Air Carriers: T-100 Domestic Market (U.S. carriers only), 2024; Bureau of Transportation Statistics, The Intermodal Transportation Database, Air Carriers: T-100 International Market (U.S. carriers only), 2024

BUSINESSES

Major Business Headquarters

Company Name	Industry	Rankings	
		Fortune[1]	Forbes[2]
No companies listed	-	-	-

Note: (1) Companies that produce a 10-K are ranked 1 to 500 based on 2023 revenue; (2) All private companies with at least $2 billion in annual revenue through the end of their most current fiscal year are ranked 1 to 275; companies listed are headquartered in the city; dashes indicate no ranking
Source: Fortune, "Fortune 500," 2024; Forbes, "America's Largest Private Companies," 2024

Living Environment

COST OF LIVING

Cost of Living Index

Composite Index	Groceries	Housing	Utilities	Trans-portation	Health Care	Misc. Goods/ Services
n/a	n/a	n/a	n/a	n/a	n/a	n/a

Note: The Cost of Living Index measures regional differences in the cost of consumer goods and services, excluding taxes and non-consumer expenditures, for professional and managerial households in the top income quintile. It is based on more than 50,000 prices covering almost 60 different items for which prices are collected three times a year by chambers of commerce, economic development organizations or university applied economic centers in each participating urban area. The numbers shown should be read as a percentage above or below the national average of 100. For example, a value of 115.4 in the groceries column indicates that grocery prices are 15.4% higher than the national average. Small differences in the index numbers should not be interpreted as significant; n/a not available.
Source: The Council for Community and Economic Research, Cost of Living Index, 2024

Grocery Prices

Area[1]	T-Bone Steak ($/pound)	Frying Chicken ($/pound)	Whole Milk ($/half gal.)	Eggs ($/dozen)	Orange Juice ($/64 oz.)	Coffee ($/11.5 oz.)
City[2]	n/a	n/a	n/a	n/a	n/a	n/a
Avg.	15.42	1.55	4.69	3.25	4.41	5.46
Min.	14.50	1.16	4.43	2.75	4.00	4.85
Max.	17.56	2.89	5.49	4.78	5.54	7.89

Note: (1) Values for the local area are compared with the average, minimum and maximum values for all 276 areas in the Cost of Living Index; (2) Figures cover the College Station TX urban area; n/a not available; **T-Bone Steak** (price per pound); **Frying Chicken** (price per pound, whole fryer); **Whole Milk** (half gallon carton); **Eggs** (price per dozen, Grade A, large); **Orange Juice** (64 oz. Tropicana or Florida Natural); **Coffee** (11.5 oz. can, vacuum-packed, Maxwell House, Hills Bros, or Folgers).
Source: The Council for Community and Economic Research, Cost of Living Index, 2024

Housing and Utility Costs

Area[1]	New Home Price ($)	Apartment Rent ($/month)	All Electric ($/month)	Part Electric ($/month)	Other Energy ($/month)	Telephone ($/month)
City[2]	n/a	n/a	n/a	n/a	n/a	n/a
Avg.	515,975	1,550	210.99	123.07	82.07	194.99
Min.	265,375	692	104.33	53.68	36.26	179.42
Max.	2,775,821	5,719	529.02	397.28	361.63	223.33

Note: (1) Values for the local area are compared with the average, minimum and maximum values for all 276 areas in the Cost of Living Index; (2) Figures cover the College Station TX urban area; n/a not available; **New Home Price** (2,400 sf living area, 8,000 sf lot, in urban area with full utilities); **Apartment Rent** (950 sf 2 bedroom/1.5 or 2 bath, unfurnished, excluding all utilities except water); **All Electric** (average monthly cost for an all-electric home); **Part Electric** (average monthly cost for a part-electric home); **Other Energy** (average monthly cost for natural gas, fuel oil, coal, wood, and any other forms of energy except electricity); **Telephone** (price includes the base monthly rate plus taxes and fees for three lines of mobile phone service).
Source: The Council for Community and Economic Research, Cost of Living Index, 2024

Health Care, Transportation, and Other Costs

Area[1]	Doctor ($/visit)	Dentist ($/visit)	Optometrist ($/visit)	Gasoline ($/gallon)	Beauty Salon ($/visit)	Men's Shirt ($)
City[2]	n/a	n/a	n/a	n/a	n/a	n/a
Avg.	143.77	117.51	129.23	3.32	48.57	38.14
Min.	36.74	58.67	67.33	2.80	24.00	13.41
Max.	270.44	216.82	307.33	5.28	94.00	63.89

Note: (1) Values for the local area are compared with the average, minimum and maximum values for all 276 areas in the Cost of Living Index; (2) Figures cover the College Station TX urban area; n/a not available; **Doctor** (general practitioners routine exam of an established patient); **Dentist** (adult teeth cleaning and periodic oral examination); **Optometrist** (full vision eye exam for established adult patient); **Gasoline** (one gallon regular unleaded, national brand, including all taxes, cash price at self-service pump if available); **Beauty Salon** (woman's shampoo, trim, and blow-dry); **Men's Shirt** (cotton/polyester dress shirt, pinpoint weave, long sleeves).
Source: The Council for Community and Economic Research, Cost of Living Index, 2024

HOUSING

Homeownership Rate

Area	2017 (%)	2018 (%)	2019 (%)	2020 (%)	2021 (%)	2022 (%)	2023 (%)	2024 (%)
MSA[1]	n/a	n/a	n/a	n/a	n/a	n/a	n/a	n/a
U.S.	63.9	64.4	64.6	66.6	65.5	65.8	65.9	65.6

Note: (1) Figures cover the College Station-Bryan, TX Metropolitan Statistical Area; n/a not available
Source: U.S. Census Bureau, Housing Vacancies and Homeownership Annual Statistics: 2017-2024

House Price Index (HPI)

Area	National Ranking[2]	Quarterly Change (%)	One-Year Change (%)	Five-Year Change (%)	Since 1991Q1 (%)
MSA[1]	(a)	-0.47	1.96	50.70	347.63
U.S.[3]	—	1.43	4.51	57.13	327.82

Note: The HPI is a weighted repeat sales index. It measures average price changes in repeat sales or refinancings on the same properties. This information is obtained by reviewing repeat mortgage transactions on single-family properties whose mortgages have been purchased or securitized by Fannie Mae or Freddie Mac since January 1975; (1) Figures cover the College Station-Bryan, TX Metropolitan Statistical Area; (2) Rankings are based on annual percentage change for all metro areas containing at least 15,000 transactions over the last 10 years and ranges from 1 to 241; (3) figures based on a weighted average of Census Division estimates using a seasonally adjusted, purchase-only index; all figures are for the period ending December 31, 2024; n/a not available; (a) Not ranked because of increased index variability due to smaller sample size
Source: Federal Housing Finance Agency, Change in FHFA Metropolitan Area House Price Indexes, All Transactions Index, 2024Q4

Home Value

Area	Under $100,000	$100,000 -$199,999	$200,000 -$299,999	$300,000 -$399,999	$400,000 -$499,999	$500,000 -$999,999	$1,000,000 or more	Median ($)
City	2.4	7.5	32.9	27.0	15.6	12.5	2.1	326,500
MSA[1]	15.0	18.5	26.1	17.3	9.5	11.2	2.3	261,900
U.S.	12.1	17.8	19.5	14.4	10.5	19.1	6.5	303,400

Note: Figures are percentages except for median and cover owner-occupied housing units; (1) Figures cover the College Station-Bryan, TX Metropolitan Statistical Area
Source: U.S. Census Bureau, 2019-2023 American Community Survey 5-Year Estimates

Year Housing Structure Built

Area	2020 or Later	2010 -2019	2000 -2009	1990 -1999	1980 -1989	1970 -1979	1960 -1969	1950 -1959	1940 -1949	Before 1940	Median Year
City	2.4	23.2	20.3	16.5	18.5	12.2	3.9	1.7	0.5	0.7	1998
MSA[1]	2.6	20.0	19.0	15.1	17.1	12.3	5.7	3.9	2.1	2.2	1994
U.S.	1.2	8.9	13.6	12.8	13.0	14.4	10.0	9.7	4.5	11.9	1980

Note: Figures are percentages except for Median Year; Note: (1) Figures cover the College Station-Bryan, TX Metropolitan Statistical Area
Source: U.S. Census Bureau, 2019-2023 American Community Survey 5-Year Estimates

Gross Monthly Rent

Area	Under $500	$500 -$999	$1,000 -$1,499	$1,500 -$1,999	$2,000 -$2,499	$2,500 -$2,999	$3,000 and up	Median ($)
City	2.3	31.8	36.6	18.4	6.6	3.1	1.1	1,168
MSA[1]	4.0	32.0	38.0	16.6	5.7	2.2	1.4	1,146
U.S.	6.5	22.3	29.5	20.2	10.8	4.8	5.9	1,348

Note: Figures are percentages except for median; Gross rent is the contract rent plus the estimated average monthly cost of utilities (electricity, gas, and water and sewer) and fuels (oil, coal, kerosene, wood, etc.) if these are paid by the renter (or paid for the renter by someone else); (1) Figures cover the College Station-Bryan, TX Metropolitan Statistical Area
Source: U.S. Census Bureau, 2019-2023 American Community Survey 5-Year Estimates

HEALTH

Health Risk Factors

Category	MSA[1] (%)	U.S. (%)
Adults aged 18–64 who have any kind of health care coverage	n/a	90.8
Adults who reported being in good or better health	n/a	81.8
Adults who have been told they have high blood cholesterol	n/a	36.9
Adults who have been told they have high blood pressure	n/a	34.0
Adults who are current smokers	n/a	12.1
Adults who currently use e-cigarettes	n/a	7.7
Adults who currently use chewing tobacco, snuff, or snus	n/a	3.2
Adults who are heavy drinkers[2]	n/a	6.1
Adults who are binge drinkers[3]	n/a	15.2
Adults who are overweight (BMI 25.0 - 29.9)	n/a	34.4
Adults who are obese (BMI 30.0 - 99.8)	n/a	34.3
Adults who participated in any physical activities in the past month	n/a	75.8

Note: All figures are crude prevalence; (1) Figures for the College Station-Bryan, TX Metropolitan Statistical Area were not available.
(2) Heavy drinkers are classified as adult men having more than 14 drinks per week and adult women having more than 7 drinks per week; (3) Binge drinkers are classified as males having five or more drinks on one occasion or females having four or more drinks on one occasion
Source: Centers for Disease Control and Prevention, Behavioral Risk Factor Surveillance System, SMART: Selected Metropolitan Area Risk Trends, 2023

Acute and Chronic Health Conditions

Category	MSA[1] (%)	U.S. (%)
Adults who have ever been told they had a heart attack	n/a	4.2
Adults who have ever been told they have angina or coronary heart disease	n/a	4.0
Adults who have ever been told they had a stroke	n/a	3.3
Adults who have ever been told they have asthma	n/a	15.7
Adults who have ever been told they have arthritis	n/a	26.3
Adults who have ever been told they have diabetes[2]	n/a	11.5
Adults who have ever been told they had skin cancer	n/a	5.6
Adults who have ever been told they had any other types of cancer	n/a	8.4
Adults who have ever been told they have COPD	n/a	6.4
Adults who have ever been told they have kidney disease	n/a	3.7
Adults who have ever been told they have a form of depression	n/a	22.0

Note: All figures are crude prevalence; (1) Figures for the College Station-Bryan, TX Metropolitan Statistical Area were not available.
(2) Figures do not include pregnancy-related, borderline, or pre-diabetes
Source: Centers for Disease Control and Prevention, Behavioral Risk Factor Surveillance System, SMART: Selected Metropolitan Area Risk Trends, 2023

Health Screening and Vaccination Rates

Category	MSA[1] (%)	U.S. (%)
Adults who have ever been tested for HIV	n/a	37.5
Adults who have had their blood cholesterol checked within the last five years	n/a	87.0
Adults aged 65+ who have had flu shot within the past year	n/a	63.4
Adults aged 65+ who have ever had a pneumonia vaccination	n/a	71.9

Note: All figures are crude prevalence; (1) Figures for the College Station-Bryan, TX Metropolitan Statistical Area were not available.
Source: Centers for Disease Control and Prevention, Behavioral Risk Factor Surveillance System, SMART: Selected Metropolitan Area Risk Trends, 2023

Disability Status

Category	MSA[1] (%)	U.S. (%)
Adults who reported being deaf	n/a	7.4
Are you blind or have serious difficulty seeing, even when wearing glasses?	n/a	4.9
Do you have difficulty doing errands alone?	n/a	7.8
Do you have difficulty dressing or bathing?	n/a	3.6
Do you have serious difficulty concentrating/remembering/making decisions?	n/a	13.7
Do you have serious difficulty walking or climbing stairs?	n/a	13.2

Note: All figures are crude prevalence; (1) Figures for the College Station-Bryan, TX Metropolitan Statistical Area were not available.
Source: Centers for Disease Control and Prevention, Behavioral Risk Factor Surveillance System, SMART: Selected Metropolitan Area Risk Trends, 2023

Mortality Rates for the Top 10 Causes of Death in the U.S.

ICD-10[a] Sub-Chapter	ICD-10[a] Code	Crude Mortality Rate[2] per 100,000 population	
		County[3]	U.S.
Malignant neoplasms	C00-C97	96.9	182.7
Ischaemic heart diseases	I20-I25	65.2	109.6
Provisional assignment of new diseases of uncertain etiology[1]	U00-U49	41.5	65.3
Other forms of heart disease	I30-I51	58.7	65.1
Other degenerative diseases of the nervous system	G30-G31	37.2	52.4
Other external causes of accidental injury	W00-X59	20.2	52.3
Cerebrovascular diseases	I60-I69	21.3	49.1
Chronic lower respiratory diseases	J40-J47	20.2	43.5
Hypertensive diseases	I10-I15	21.8	38.9
Organic, including symptomatic, mental disorders	F01-F09	23.6	33.9

Note: (a) ICD-10 = International Classification of Diseases 10th Revision; (1) Includes COVID-19, adverse effects to COVID-19 vaccines, SARS, and vaping-related disorders; (2) Crude mortality rates are a three-year average covering 2021-2023; (3) Figures cover Brazos County.
Source: Centers for Disease Control and Prevention, National Center for Health Statistics. National Vital Statistics System, Mortality 2018-2023 on CDC WONDER Online Database

Mortality Rates for Selected Causes of Death

Cause of Death	ICD-10[a] Code	Crude Mortality Rate[1] per 100,000 population	
		County[2]	U.S.
Accidental poisoning and exposure to noxious substances	X40-X49	8.4	30.5
Alzheimer disease	G30	18.7	35.4
Assault	X85-Y09	4.1	7.3
COVID-19	U07.1	41.5	65.3
Diabetes mellitus	E10-E14	13.4	30.0
Diseases of the liver	K70-K76	12.8	20.8
Human immunodeficiency virus (HIV) disease	B20-B24	Suppressed	1.5
Influenza and pneumonia	J09-J18	4.6	13.4
Intentional self-harm	X60-X84	11.1	14.7
Malnutrition	E40-E46	3.7	6.0
Obesity and other hyperalimentation	E65-E68	Unreliable	3.1
Renal failure	N17-N19	6.2	16.4
Transport accidents	V01-V99	9.3	14.4

Note: (a) ICD-10 = International Classification of Diseases 10th Revision; (1) Crude mortality rates are a three-year average covering 2021-2023; (2) Figures cover Brazos County; Data are suppressed when the data meet the criteria for confidentiality constraints; Crude mortality rates are flagged as unreliable when the rate would be calculated with a numerator of 20 or less.
Source: Centers for Disease Control and Prevention, National Center for Health Statistics. National Vital Statistics System, Mortality 2018-2023 on CDC WONDER Online Database

Health Insurance Coverage

Area	With Health Insurance	With Private Health Insurance	With Public Health Insurance	Without Health Insurance	Population Under Age 19 Without Health Insurance
City	91.9	83.0	16.5	8.1	4.7
MSA[1]	88.1	73.2	24.7	11.9	7.6
U.S.	91.4	67.3	36.3	8.6	5.4

Note: Figures are percentages that cover the civilian noninstitutionalized population; (1) Figures cover the College Station-Bryan, TX Metropolitan Statistical Area
Source: U.S. Census Bureau, 2019-2023 American Community Survey 5-Year Estimates

Number of Medical Professionals

Area	MDs[3]	DOs[3,4]	Dentists	Podiatrists	Chiropractors	Optometrists
County[1] (number)	616	49	142	8	48	44
County[1] (rate[2])	254.5	20.2	58.0	3.3	19.6	18.0
U.S. (rate[2])	302.5	29.2	74.6	6.4	29.5	18.0

Note: Data as of 2023 unless noted; (1) Data covers Brazos County; (2) Number of medical professionals per 100,000 population; (3) Data as of 2022 and includes all active, non-federal physicians; (4) Doctor of Osteopathic Medicine
Source: U.S. Department of Health and Human Services, Health Resources and Services Administration, Bureau of Health Professions, Area Resource File (ARF) 2023-2024

EDUCATION

Public School District Statistics

District Name	Schls	Pupils	Pupil/ Teacher Ratio	Minority Pupils[1] (%)	Total Rev. per Pupil ($)	Total Exp. per Pupil ($)
College Station ISD	21	14,366	14.2	49.6	12,884	12,136

Note: Table includes school districts with 2,000 or more students; (1) Percentage of students that are not non-Hispanic white.
Source: U.S. Department of Education, National Center for Education Statistics, Common Core of Data, Local Education Agency (School District) Universe Survey: School Year 2023-2024; U.S. Department of Education, National Center for Education Statistics, Common Core of Data, School District Finance Survey (F-33): School Year 2021–22

Highest Level of Education

Area	Less than H.S.	H.S. Diploma	Some College, No Deg.	Associate Degree	Bachelor's Degree	Master's Degree	Prof. School Degree	Doctorate Degree
City	5.4	14.4	16.9	6.2	29.5	16.1	2.0	9.5
MSA[1]	11.7	23.8	18.7	6.8	22.2	10.2	1.7	5.0
U.S.	10.6	26.2	19.4	8.8	21.3	9.8	2.3	1.6

Note: Figures cover persons age 25 and over; (1) Figures cover the College Station-Bryan, TX Metropolitan Statistical Area
Source: U.S. Census Bureau, 2019-2023 American Community Survey 5-Year Estimates

Educational Attainment by Race

Area	High School Graduate or Higher (%)					Bachelor's Degree or Higher (%)				
	Total	White	Black	Asian	Hisp.[2]	Total	White	Black	Asian	Hisp.[2]
City	94.6	97.4	88.7	95.6	83.0	57.1	60.8	24.5	79.1	40.4
MSA[1]	88.3	91.8	87.1	96.0	69.9	39.1	43.4	15.1	77.8	18.7
U.S.	89.4	92.9	88.1	88.0	72.5	35.0	37.7	24.7	57.0	19.9

Note: Figures shown cover persons 25 years old and over; (1) Figures cover the College Station-Bryan, TX Metropolitan Statistical Area; (2) People of Hispanic origin can be of any race
Source: U.S. Census Bureau, 2019-2023 American Community Survey 5-Year Estimates

School Enrollment by Grade and Control

Area	Preschool (%)		Kindergarten (%)		Grades 1 - 4 (%)		Grades 5 - 8 (%)		Grades 9 - 12 (%)	
	Public	Private	Public	Private	Public	Private	Public	Private	Public	Private
City	57.7	42.3	82.6	17.4	90.0	10.0	87.4	12.6	86.2	13.8
MSA[1]	61.4	38.6	87.5	12.5	90.5	9.5	87.7	12.3	90.5	9.5
U.S.	58.7	41.3	85.2	14.8	87.2	12.8	87.9	12.1	89.0	11.0

Note: Figures shown cover persons 3 years old and over; (1) Figures cover the College Station-Bryan, TX Metropolitan Statistical Area
Source: U.S. Census Bureau, 2019-2023 American Community Survey 5-Year Estimates

Higher Education

Four-Year Colleges			Two-Year Colleges			Medical Schools[1]	Law Schools[2]	Voc/Tech[3]
Public	Private Non-profit	Private For-profit	Public	Private Non-profit	Private For-profit			
1	0	0	0	0	0	1	0	2

Note: Figures cover institutions located within the College Station-Bryan, TX Metropolitan Statistical Area and include main campuses only; (1) includes schools accredited by the Liaison Committee on Medical Education and the American Osteopathic Association's Commission on Osteopathic College Accreditation; (2) includes ABA-accredited schools, schools with provisional ABA accreditation, and state accredited schools; (3) includes all schools with programs that are less than 2 years.
Source: National Center for Education Statistics, Integrated Postsecondary Education System (IPEDS), 2023-24; Wikipedia, List of Medical Schools in the United States, accessed May 2, 2025; Wikipedia, List of Law Schools in the United States, accessed May 2, 2025

According to *U.S. News & World Report,* the College Station-Bryan, TX metro area is home to one of the top 200 national universities in the U.S.: **Texas A&M University** (#51 tie). The indicators used to capture academic quality fall into a number of categories: assessment by administrators at peer institutions; retention of students; faculty resources; student selectivity; financial resources; alumni giving; high school counselor ratings of colleges; and graduation rate. *U.S. News & World Report, "America's Best Colleges 2025"*

According to *U.S. News & World Report,* the College Station-Bryan, TX metro area is home to one of the top medical schools for research in the U.S.: **Texas A&M University** (Tier 2). *U.S. News* placed medical and osteopathic schools into tiers based on their research productivity, faculty and admissions data. Each school's tier was derived from its overall score, calculated by summing the weighted normalized values generated across several factors of academic quality, outlined below. There are four tiers, with tier 1 medical schools as the highest-performing and tier 4 as the lowest-performing. Only tier 1 and 2 schools are shown. Because of the tier presentation, *U.S. News* calculated overall scores based on their percentile performance among all rated schools instead of dividing against the rescaled score of the No. 1-performing schools. Tier 1 included schools with overall scores of 85 to 99. The cutoffs for tiers 2 through 4 were schools scoring 50 to 84, 15 to 49 and 1 to 14, respectively. The rankings are based on a weighted average of the following measures of quality: total research activity; average research activity per faculty member; total NIH research grants at the medical school and its affiliated hospitals; average NIH research grants per faculty; median MCAT total score; median undergraduate GPA; acceptance rate; and faculty resources. *U.S. News & World Report, "America's Best Graduate Schools, Medical, 2025"*

According to *U.S. News & World Report,* the College Station-Bryan, TX metro area is home to one of the top medical schools for primary care in the U.S.: **Texas A&M University** (Tier 1). *U.S. News* placed medical and osteopathic schools into tiers based on their research productivity, faculty and admissions data. Each school's tier was derived from its overall score, calculated by summing the weighted normalized values generated across several factors of academic quality, outlined below. There are four tiers, with tier 1 medical schools as the highest-performing and tier 4 as the lowest-performing. Only tier 1 and 2 schools are shown. Because of the tier presentation, *U.S. News* calculated overall scores based on their percentile performance among all rated schools instead of dividing against the rescaled score of the No. 1-performing schools. Tier 1 included schools with overall scores of 85 to 99. The cutoffs for tiers 2 through 4 were schools scoring 50 to 84, 15 to 49 and 1 to 14, respectively. The rankings are based on a weighted average of the following measures of quality: graduates practicing in primary care specialties; graduates entering primary care residencies; median

MCAT total score; median undergraduate GPA; acceptance rate; and faculty resources. *U.S. News & World Report, "America's Best Graduate Schools, Medical, 2025"*

According to *U.S. News & World Report*, the College Station-Bryan, TX metro area is home to one of the top 75 business schools in the U.S.: **Texas A&M University—College Station (Mays)** (#43 tie). The rankings are based on a weighted average of the following nine measures: quality assessment; peer assessment; recruiter assessment; placement success; mean starting salary and bonus; student selectivity; mean GMAT and GRE scores; mean undergraduate GPA; and acceptance rate. *U.S. News & World Report, "America's Best Graduate Schools, Business, 2025"*

EMPLOYERS

Major Employers

Company Name	Industry
Bryan Independent School District	Education
City of Bryan	Municipal government
City of College Station	Municipal government
College Station ISD	Education
H-E-B Grocery	Grocery stores
New Alenco Windows	Fabricated metal products
Reynolds and Reynolds/Rentsys	Computer hardware/software
Sanderson Farms	Poultry processing
St. Joseph Regional Health Center	Healthcare
Texas A&M University System	Education
Wal-Mart Stores	Retail

Note: Companies shown are located within the College Station-Bryan, TX Metropolitan Statistical Area.
Source: Chambers of Commerce; State Departments of Labor; Wikipedia

PUBLIC SAFETY

Crime Rate

Area	Total Crime Rate	Violent Crime Rate				Property Crime Rate		
		Murder	Rape	Robbery	Aggrav. Assault	Burglary	Larceny-Theft	Motor Vehicle Theft
City	1,493.6	3.2	49.2	17.4	88.8	141.9	1,086.9	106.2
U.S.	2,290.9	5.7	38.0	66.5	264.1	250.7	1,347.2	318.7

Note: Figures are crimes per 100,000 population.
Source: FBI, Table 8, Offenses Known to Law Enforcement, by State by City, 2023

Hate Crimes

Area	Number of Quarters Reported	Number of Incidents per Bias Motivation					
		Race/Ethnicity/Ancestry	Religion	Sexual Orientation	Disability	Gender	Gender Identity
City	4	0	0	0	0	0	0
U.S.	4	5,900	2,699	2,077	187	92	492

Source: Federal Bureau of Investigation, Hate Crime Statistics 2023

Identity Theft Consumer Reports

Area	Reports	Reports per 100,000 Population	Rank[2]
MSA[1]	490	179	198
U.S.	1,135,291	339	-

Note: (1) Figures cover the College Station-Bryan, TX Metropolitan Statistical Area; (2) Rank ranges from 1 to 401 where 1 indicates greatest number of identity theft reports per 100,000 population
Source: Federal Trade Commission, Consumer Sentinel Network Data Book 2024

Fraud and Other Consumer Reports

Area	Reports	Reports per 100,000 Population	Rank[2]
MSA[1]	2,472	905	261
U.S.	5,360,641	1,601	-

Note: (1) Figures cover the College Station-Bryan, TX Metropolitan Statistical Area; (2) Rank ranges from 1 to 401 where 1 indicates greatest number of fraud and other consumer reports per 100,000 population
Source: Federal Trade Commission, Consumer Sentinel Network Data Book 2024

POLITICS

2024 Presidential Election Results

Area	Trump (Rep.)	Harris (Dem.)	Stein (Green)	Kennedy (Ind.)	Oliver (Lib.)	Other
Brazos County	61.6	36.8	0.6	0.0	0.9	0.1
U.S.	49.7	48.2	0.6	0.5	0.4	0.6

Note: Results are percentages and may not add to 100% due to rounding
Source: Dave Leip's Atlas of U.S. Presidential Elections

SPORTS

Professional Sports Teams

Team Name	League	Year Established
No teams are located in the metro area		

Source: Wikipedia, Major Professional Sports Teams of the United States and Canada, May 1, 2025

CLIMATE

Average and Extreme Temperatures

Temperature	Jan	Feb	Mar	Apr	May	Jun	Jul	Aug	Sep	Oct	Nov	Dec	Yr.
Extreme High (°F)	90	97	98	98	100	105	109	106	104	98	91	90	109
Average High (°F)	60	64	72	79	85	91	95	96	90	81	70	63	79
Average Temp. (°F)	50	53	61	69	75	82	85	85	80	70	60	52	69
Average Low (°F)	39	43	50	58	65	72	74	74	69	59	49	41	58
Extreme Low (°F)	-2	7	18	35	43	53	64	61	47	32	20	4	-2

Note: Figures cover the years 1948-1990
Source: National Climatic Data Center, International Station Meteorological Climate Summary, 9/96

Average Precipitation/Snowfall/Humidity

Precip./Humidity	Jan	Feb	Mar	Apr	May	Jun	Jul	Aug	Sep	Oct	Nov	Dec	Yr.
Avg. Precip. (in.)	1.6	2.3	1.8	2.9	4.3	3.5	1.9	1.9	3.3	3.5	2.1	1.9	31.1
Avg. Snowfall (in.)	1	Tr	Tr	0	0	0	0	0	0	0	Tr	Tr	1
Avg. Rel. Hum. 6am (%)	79	80	79	83	88	89	88	87	86	84	81	79	84
Avg. Rel. Hum. 3pm (%)	53	51	47	50	53	49	43	42	47	47	49	51	48

Note: Figures cover the years 1948-1990; Tr = Trace amounts (<0.05 in. of rain; <0.5 in. of snow)
Source: National Climatic Data Center, International Station Meteorological Climate Summary, 9/96

Weather Conditions

Temperature			Daytime Sky			Precipitation		
10°F & below	32°F & below	90°F & above	Clear	Partly cloudy	Cloudy	0.01 inch or more precip.	0.1 inch or more snow/ice	Thunder-storms
< 1	20	111	105	148	112	83	1	41

Note: Figures are average number of days per year and cover the years 1948-1990
Source: National Climatic Data Center, International Station Meteorological Climate Summary, 9/96

HAZARDOUS WASTE

Superfund Sites

The College Station-Bryan, TX metro area has no sites on the EPA's Superfund Final National Priorities List (NPL) or Superfund Alternative Approach (SAA) list. The Superfund alternative approach uses the same investigation and cleanup process and standards that are used for sites listed on the National Priorities List. The SAA is an alternative to listing a site on the NPL; it is not an alternative to Superfund or the Superfund process. There are a total of 1,445 Superfund sites with a status of proposed or final on both lists in the United States. *U.S. Environmental Protection Agency, National Priorities List, May 1, 2025; U.S. Environmental Protection Agency, Superfund Alternative Approach Sites, May 1, 2025*

AIR QUALITY

Air Quality Trends: Ozone

	1990	1995	2000	2005	2010	2015	2020	2021	2022	2023
MSA[1]	n/a	n/a	n/a	n/a	n/a	n/a	n/a	n/a	n/a	n/a
U.S.	0.087	0.089	0.081	0.080	0.072	0.068	0.066	0.067	0.067	0.070

Note: (1) Data covers the College Station-Bryan, TX Metropolitan Statistical Area; n/a not available. The values shown are the composite ozone concentration averages among trend sites based on the highest fourth daily maximum 8-hour concentration in parts per million. These trends are based on sites having an adequate record of monitoring data during the trend period. Data from exceptional events are included.
Source: U.S. Environmental Protection Agency, Air Quality Monitoring Information, "Air Quality Trends by City, 1990-2023"

Air Quality Index

Area	Percent of Days when Air Quality was...[2]					AQI Statistics[2]	
	Good	Moderate	Unhealthy for Sensitive Groups	Unhealthy	Very Unhealthy	Maximum	Median
MSA[1]	67.0	33.0	0.0	0.0	0.0	79	39

Note: (1) Data covers the College Station-Bryan, TX Metropolitan Statistical Area; (2) Based on 348 days with AQI data in 2023. Air Quality Index (AQI) is an index for reporting daily air quality. EPA calculates the AQI for five major air pollutants regulated by the Clean Air Act: ground-level ozone, particle pollution (aka particulate matter), carbon monoxide, sulfur dioxide, and nitrogen dioxide. The AQI runs from 0 to 500. The higher the AQI value, the greater the level of air pollution and the greater the health concern. There are six AQI categories: "Good" AQI is between 0 and 50. Air quality is considered satisfactory; "Moderate" AQI is between 51 and 100. Air quality is acceptable; "Unhealthy for Sensitive Groups" When AQI values are between 101 and 150, members of sensitive groups may experience health effects; "Unhealthy" When AQI values are between 151 and 200 everyone may begin to experience health effects; "Very Unhealthy" AQI values between 201 and 300 trigger a health alert; "Hazardous" AQI values over 300 trigger warnings of emergency conditions (not shown).
Source: U.S. Environmental Protection Agency, Air Quality Index Report, 2023

Air Quality Index Pollutants

Area	Percent of Days when AQI Pollutant was...[2]					
	Carbon Monoxide	Nitrogen Dioxide	Ozone	Sulfur Dioxide	Particulate Matter 2.5	Particulate Matter 10
MSA[1]	0.0	0.0	0.0	(3)	100.0	0.0

Note: (1) Data covers the College Station-Bryan, TX Metropolitan Statistical Area; (2) Based on 348 days with AQI data in 2023. The Air Quality Index (AQI) is an index for reporting daily air quality. EPA calculates the AQI for five major air pollutants regulated by the Clean Air Act: ground-level ozone, particle pollution (also known as particulate matter), carbon monoxide, sulfur dioxide, and nitrogen dioxide. The AQI runs from 0 to 500. The higher the AQI value, the greater the level of air pollution and the greater the health concern; (3) Sulfur dioxide is no longer included in this table because SO_2 concentrations tend to be very localized and not necessarily representative of broad geographical areas like counties and CBSAs.
Source: U.S. Environmental Protection Agency, Air Quality Index Report, 2023

Maximum Air Pollutant Concentrations: Particulate Matter, Ozone, CO and Lead

	Particulate Matter 10 (ug/m³)	Particulate Matter 2.5 Wtd AM (ug/m³)	Particulate Matter 2.5 24-Hr (ug/m³)	Ozone (ppm)	Carbon Monoxide (ppm)	Lead (ug/m³)
MSA[1] Level	n/a	8	20	n/a	n/a	n/a
NAAQS[2]	150	15	35	0.075	9	0.15
Met NAAQS[2]	n/a	Yes	Yes	n/a	n/a	n/a

Note: (1) Data covers the College Station-Bryan, TX Metropolitan Statistical Area; Data from exceptional events are included; (2) National Ambient Air Quality Standards; ppm = parts per million; ug/m³ = micrograms per cubic meter; n/a not available.
Concentrations: Particulate Matter 10 (coarse particulate)—highest second maximum 24-hour concentration; Particulate Matter 2.5 Wtd AM (fine particulate)—highest weighted annual mean concentration; Particulate Matter 2.5 24-Hour (fine particulate)—highest 98th percentile 24-hour concentration; Ozone—highest fourth daily maximum 8-hour concentration; Carbon Monoxide—highest second maximum non-overlapping 8-hour concentration; Lead—maximum running 3-month average
Source: U.S. Environmental Protection Agency, Air Quality Monitoring Information, "Air Quality Statistics by City, 2023"

Maximum Air Pollutant Concentrations: Nitrogen Dioxide and Sulfur Dioxide

	Nitrogen Dioxide AM (ppb)	Nitrogen Dioxide 1-Hr (ppb)	Sulfur Dioxide AM (ppb)	Sulfur Dioxide 1-Hr (ppb)	Sulfur Dioxide 24-Hr (ppb)
MSA[1] Level	n/a	n/a	n/a	29	n/a
NAAQS[2]	53	100	30	75	140
Met NAAQS[2]	n/a	n/a	n/a	Yes	n/a

Note: (1) Data covers the College Station-Bryan, TX Metropolitan Statistical Area; Data from exceptional events are included; (2) National Ambient Air Quality Standards; ppm = parts per million; ug/m³ = micrograms per cubic meter; n/a not available.
Concentrations: Nitrogen Dioxide AM—highest arithmetic mean concentration; Nitrogen Dioxide 1-Hr—highest 98th percentile 1-hour daily maximum concentration; Sulfur Dioxide AM—highest annual mean concentration; Sulfur Dioxide 1-Hr—highest 99th percentile 1-hour daily maximum concentration; Sulfur Dioxide 24-Hr—highest second maximum 24-hour concentration
Source: U.S. Environmental Protection Agency, Air Quality Monitoring Information, "Air Quality Statistics by City, 2023"

Columbia, South Carolina

Background

Located on the Congaree River, Columbia is South Carolina's capital and largest city, and the seat of Richland County. It is a center for local and state government, and important to financial, insurance, and medical industries.

The region has depended on trade since a trading post opened south of the present-day city in 1718. In 1786, Columbia was chosen as the new state capital due to its location in the center of South Carolina, a compromise between residents on the coast and those living further inland.

The nation's second planned city, Columbia was originally 400 acres along the river. The main thoroughfares were designed 150 feet wide and other streets were also wider than most. Much of this spacious layout survives, lending an expansive feel to the city. Columbia was chartered as a town in 1805. Its first mayor—or "intendent"—John Taylor, later served in the state general assembly, the U.S. Congress, and as governor of the state. Columbia was staunchly Confederate during the Civil War, attacked in 1865 by General Sherman's troops and set ablaze by both Union attackers and Confederate evacuees. After the war and Reconstruction, Columbia was revitalized as the state's industrial and farm products hub.

Columbia is home to the University of South Carolina, a major employer alongside BlueCross BlueShield of SC. The USC/Columbia Technology Incubator's more than 40 companies have generated more than $45 million in total revenue by member companies, which employ more than 650. The university has also created the 500-acre Innovista Research District to provide office and lab space to tech and innovation businesses and startups. The health care industry is also significant. The Medical University of South Carolina and the area's largest employer, Palmetto Health, merged their medical practices in 2016 under the banner of Palmetto Health-USC Medical Group. The city's two venerable Providence Hospitals—operated by the Sisters of Charity since 1938—were recently acquired by LifePoint Health, a Tennessee-based for-profit company that operates health care facilities in 22 states.

Other large employers include Fort Jackson, the U.S. Army's largest initial entry training installation and the United Parcel Service, which operates a freight service center in West Columbia.

Columbia is the cultural center for the area, known as South Carolina's Midlands. The Columbia Museum of Art, with its collection of Renaissance and Baroque art, is a major regional museum. The performing arts are onstage year-round at the Koger Center for the Arts at USC. The city's Town Theatre hosted 105th season in 2025, and is the country's oldest community theatre in continuous use. The South Carolina State Museum "Windows to New Worlds" includes a planetarium, observatory, and 4-D theater. Major historic architecture in Columbia includes City Hall, designed by President Ulysses S. Grant's federal architect, Alfred B. Mullet, and the Lutheran Survey Print Building.

In addition to USC, Columbia's other institutions of higher learning are Lutheran Theological Seminary, Columbia College, Benedict College, Allen University, and Columbia International University.

The city broke ground in 2023 on a multi-million dollar redesign of Finlay Park, which will include a rebuilt central fountain, new stage, public art, enhanced lawn areas, strolling gardens and more. Attaining 100 percent clean and renewable energy by 2036 is one of the city's climate goals.

In March 2015, the Confederate battle flag was removed from the state house flagpole by a protester motivated by the Charleston Massacre. Although the flag was raised again minutes after this action, it was permanently removed in July of that year.

Located about 150 miles southeast of the Appalachian Mountains, Columbia has a relatively temperate climate. Summers are long and often hot and humid with frequent thunderstorms. Winters are mild with little snow, while spring is changeable with infrequent tornadoes or hail. Fall is considered the most pleasant season.

Rankings

General Rankings

- In their annual survey, Livability.com looked at data for more than 2,000 mid-sized U.S. cities to assign a "Livability Score"for each. The top 100 scoring cities make up Livability's "Top 100 Best Places to Live in the U.S." in 2025. Columbia was placed among the top 100 of the customizable list. Criteria: housing and economy; cost of living; environment; education; health care options; transportation; safety; and community amenities. *Livability.com, "Top 100 Best Places to Live in the U.S. in 2025" April 15, 2025*

Business/Finance Rankings

- For its annual survey of the "Cheapest U.S. Cities to Live In," Kiplinger applied Cost of Living Index statistics developed by the Council for Community and Economic Research to U.S. Census Bureau population and median household income data for 265 urban areas. Only areas with at least 50,000 residents were considered. In the resulting ranking, Columbia ranked #19. *Kiplinger.com, "The 25 Cheapest Places to Live: U.S. Cities Edition," January 19, 2025*

- The Columbia metro area appeared on the Milken Institute "2025 Best Performing Cities" list. Rank: #54 out of 200 large metro areas (based on performance category). Criteria: job growth; wage growth; high-tech growth and impact; community resilience; housing affordability; household broadband access. *Milken Institute, "Best-Performing Cities 2025," January 14, 2025*

Education Rankings

- Personal finance website *WalletHub* analyzed the 150 largest U.S. metropolitan statistical areas to determine where the most educated Americans are putting their degrees to work. Criteria: education levels; percentage of workers with degrees; education quality and attainment gap; public school quality rankings; quality and enrollment of each metro area's universities. Columbia was ranked #61 (#1 = most educated city). *WalletHub.com, "Most & Least Educated Cities in America, 2025" July 2, 2024*

Health/Fitness Rankings

- Columbia was identified as a "2025 Allergy Capital." The area ranked #44 out of the nation's 100 largest metropolitan areas. Three groups of factors were used to identify the most challenging cities for people with allergies: annual tree, grass, and weed pollen scores; over the counter allergy medicine use; number of board-certified allergy specialists. *Asthma and Allergy Foundation of America, "2025 Allergy Capitals: The Most Challenging Places to Live with Allergies," March 18, 2025*

- Columbia was identified as a "2024 Asthma Capital." The area ranked #30 out of the nation's 100 largest metropolitan areas. Criteria: estimated asthma prevalence; asthma-related mortality; and ER visits due to asthma. Risk factors analyzed but not factored in the rankings: annual air quality including pollution and ozone levels; public smoking laws; indoor air quality; access to asthma specialists; rescue and controller medication use; uninsured rate; pollen allergy; poverty rate. *Asthma and Allergy Foundation of America, "Asthma Capitals 2024: The Most Challenging Places to Live With Asthma," September 10, 2024*

Real Estate Rankings

- *WalletHub* compared the most populated U.S. cities to determine which had the best markets for real estate agents. Columbia ranked #80 where demand was high and pay was the best. Criteria: sales per agent; annual median wage for real-estate agents; monthly average starting salary for real estate agents; real estate job density and competition; unemployment rate; home turnover rate; housing-market health index; and other relevant metrics. *WalletHub.com, "2021 Best Places to Be a Real Estate Agent," May 12, 2021*

- The Columbia metro area was identified as one of the top 16 housing markets to invest in for 2025 by *Forbes*. Criteria: stable local economies with good population growth and increase in jobs providing good support for home prices and rents. *Forbes.com, "Best Local Markets For Real Estate Investing In 2025," November 6, 2024*

- Columbia was ranked #52 out of 176 metro areas in terms of cost of housing in 2024 by the National Association of Home Builders (#1 = most affordable). Criteria: the portion of an average family's income necessary to pay the mortgage on a median-priced home. *National Association of Home Builders®, NAHB-Wells Fargo Cost of Housing Index, 4th Quarter 2024*

Safety Rankings

- Allstate ranked the 100 most populous cities in America in terms of driver safety. Columbia ranked #83. Criteria based on anonymized driving behavior data from Allstate's mobile app powered by Arity: high speed driving (over 80 mph), phone handling, and hard braking. The report helps increase the importance of safety and awareness behind the wheel. *Allstate, "16th Allstate America's Best Drivers Report®" July 11, 2024*

Women/Minorities Rankings

- Personal finance website *WalletHub* compared more than 180 U.S. cities across two key dimensions, "Hispanic Business-Friendliness" and "Hispanic Purchasing Power," to arrive at the most favorable conditions for Hispanic entrepreneurs. Columbia was ranked #64 out of 182. Criteria includes: share of Hispanic-Owned Businesses; average growth of Hispanic Business revenues; Small Business-Friendliness score; affordability; and number of Hispanics with at least a bachelor's degree. *WalletHub.com, "Best Cities for Hispanic Entrepreneurs," September 4, 2024*

Miscellaneous Rankings

- *WalletHub* compared 148 of the most populated U.S. cities to determine their operating efficiency. A "Quality of Services" score was constructed for each city and then measured against the total budget per capita to reveal which were managed the best. Columbia ranked #51. Criteria: financial stability; economy; education; safety; health; infrastructure and pollution. *WalletHub.com, "2025's Best- & Worst-Run Cities in America," June 18, 2024*

Business Environment

DEMOGRAPHICS

Population Growth

Area	1990 Census	2000 Census	2010 Census	2020 Census	2023 Estimate[2]	Population Growth 1990-2023 (%)
City	115,475	116,278	129,272	136,632	138,019	19.5
MSA[1]	548,325	647,158	767,598	829,470	839,868	53.2
U.S.	248,709,873	281,421,906	308,745,538	331,449,281	332,387,540	33.6

Note: (1) Figures cover the Columbia, SC Metropolitan Statistical Area; (2) 2019-2023 5-year ACS population estimate
Source: U.S. Census Bureau, 1990 Census, 2000 Census, 2010 Census, 2020 Census, 2019-2023 American Community Survey 5-Year Estimates

Race

Area	White Alone[2] (%)	Black Alone[2] (%)	Asian Alone[2] (%)	AIAN[3] Alone[2] (%)	NHOPI[4] Alone[2] (%)	Other Race Alone[2] (%)	Two or More Races (%)
City	49.9	39.5	2.7	0.2	0.2	1.7	5.9
MSA[1]	55.4	33.3	2.3	0.2	0.1	2.7	5.9
U.S.	63.4	12.4	5.8	0.9	0.2	6.6	10.7

Note: (1) Figures cover the Columbia, SC Metropolitan Statistical Area; (2) Alone is defined as not being in combination with one or more other races; (3) American Indian and Alaska Native; (4) Native Hawaiian and Other Pacific Islander
Source: U.S. Census Bureau, 2019-2023 American Community Survey 5-Year Estimates

Hispanic or Latino Origin

Area	Total (%)	Mexican (%)	Puerto Rican (%)	Cuban (%)	Other (%)
City	5.7	2.0	1.3	0.2	2.2
MSA[1]	6.8	3.2	1.1	0.3	2.3
U.S.	19.0	11.3	1.8	0.7	5.2

Note: Persons of Hispanic or Latino origin can be of any race; (1) Figures cover the Columbia, SC Metropolitan Statistical Area
Source: U.S. Census Bureau, 2019-2023 American Community Survey 5-Year Estimates

Age

Area	Percent of Population									Median Age
	Under Age 5	Age 5–19	Age 20–34	Age 35–44	Age 45–54	Age 55–64	Age 65–74	Age 75–84	Age 85+	
City	5.4	21.9	32.9	10.9	9.5	8.4	6.8	3.2	1.0	28.7
MSA[1]	5.6	20.1	21.2	12.8	12.1	12.5	9.8	4.5	1.5	37.5
U.S.	5.7	19.1	20.2	13.1	12.3	12.8	10.0	4.9	1.9	38.7

Note: (1) Figures cover the Columbia, SC Metropolitan Statistical Area
Source: U.S. Census Bureau, 2019-2023 American Community Survey 5-Year Estimates

Disability by Age

Area	All Ages	Under 18 Years Old	18 to 64 Years Old	65 Years and Over
City	12.7	3.9	10.7	38.0
MSA[1]	14.3	5.1	12.3	35.3
U.S.	13.0	4.7	10.7	32.9

Note: Figures show percent of the civilian noninstitutionalized population that reported having a disability. Disability status is determined from six types of difficulty: vision, hearing, cognitive, ambulatory, self-care, and independent living. For children under 5 years old, hearing and vision difficulty are used to determine disability status. For children between the ages of 5 and 14, disability status is determined from hearing, vision, cognitive, ambulatory, and self-care difficulties. For people aged 15 years and older, they are considered to have a disability if they have difficulty with any one of the six difficulty types; Note: (1) Figures cover the Columbia, SC Metropolitan Statistical Area
Source: U.S. Census Bureau, 2019-2023 American Community Survey 5-Year Estimates

Ancestry

Area	German	Irish	English	American	Italian	Polish	French[2]	European	Scottish
City	9.0	7.2	8.8	5.3	3.0	1.1	1.7	1.9	2.0
MSA[1]	9.5	7.3	9.5	6.5	2.5	1.3	1.5	1.6	1.9
U.S.	12.6	9.4	9.1	5.5	4.9	2.6	2.0	1.6	1.6

Note: Figures are the percentage of the total population reporting a particular ancestry. The nine most commonly reported ancestries in the U.S. are shown. Figures include multiple ancestries (e.g. if a person reported being Irish and Italian, they were included in both columns); (1) Figures cover the Columbia, SC Metropolitan Statistical Area; (2) Excludes Basque
Source: U.S. Census Bureau, 2019-2023 American Community Survey 5-Year Estimates

Foreign-born Population

Area	Any Foreign Country	Asia	Mexico	Europe	Caribbean	Central America[2]	South America	Africa	Canada
City	5.1	2.0	0.2	0.7	0.8	0.3	0.5	0.4	0.1
MSA[1]	5.6	1.8	1.0	0.7	0.5	0.7	0.5	0.3	0.1
U.S.	13.9	4.3	3.3	1.4	1.4	1.2	1.2	0.8	0.2

Note: (1) Figures cover the Columbia, SC Metropolitan Statistical Area; (2) Excludes Mexico.
Source: U.S. Census Bureau, 2019-2023 American Community Survey 5-Year Estimates

Household Size

Area	One	Two	Three	Four	Five	Six	Seven or More	Average Household Size
City	39.3	33.0	14.2	8.3	3.7	1.2	0.3	2.16
MSA[1]	30.6	34.0	15.5	11.9	5.2	1.9	0.9	2.42
U.S.	28.5	33.8	15.4	12.7	5.9	2.3	1.4	2.54

Note: (1) Figures cover the Columbia, SC Metropolitan Statistical Area
Source: U.S. Census Bureau, 2019-2023 American Community Survey 5-Year Estimates

Household Relationships

Area	Householder	Opposite-sex Spouse	Same-sex Spouse	Opposite-sex Unmarried Partner	Same-sex Unmarried Partner	Child[2]	Grandchild	Other Relatives	Non-relatives
City	39.2	10.5	0.2	2.1	0.2	19.5	1.6	2.8	5.8
MSA[1]	39.9	17.0	0.2	2.1	0.2	27.5	2.7	3.8	3.0
U.S.	38.3	17.5	0.2	2.5	0.2	28.3	2.4	4.8	3.4

Note: Figures are percent of the total population; (1) Figures cover the Columbia, SC Metropolitan Statistical Area; (2) Includes biological, adopted, and stepchildren of the householder
Source: U.S. Census Bureau, 2020 Census

Gender

Area	Males	Females	Males per 100 Females
City	68,245	69,774	97.8
MSA[1]	407,291	432,577	94.2
U.S.	164,545,087	167,842,453	98.0

Note: (1) Figures cover the Columbia, SC Metropolitan Statistical Area
Source: U.S. Census Bureau, 2019-2023 American Community Survey 5-Year Estimates

Marital Status

Area	Never Married	Now Married[2]	Separated	Widowed	Divorced
City	55.8	29.7	2.0	3.9	8.6
MSA[1]	36.0	45.7	2.3	5.7	10.2
U.S.	34.1	47.9	1.7	5.6	10.7

Note: Figures are percentages and cover the population 15 years of age and older; (1) Figures cover the Columbia, SC Metropolitan Statistical Area; (2) Excludes separated
Source: U.S. Census Bureau, 2019-2023 American Community Survey 5-Year Estimates

Religious Groups by Family

Area	Catholic	Baptist	Methodist	LDS[2]	Pentecostal	Lutheran	Islam	Adventist	Other
MSA[1]	6.6	15.1	8.5	1.2	3.8	2.3	0.3	1.3	15.4
U.S.	18.7	7.3	3.0	2.0	1.8	1.7	1.3	1.3	11.6

Note: Figures are the number of adherents as a percentage of the total population and cover the eight largest religious groups in the U.S; (1) Figures cover the Columbia, SC Metropolitan Statistical Area; (2) Church of Jesus Christ of Latter-day Saints
Sources: 2020 U.S. Religion Census, Association of Statisticians of American Religious Bodies; The Association of Religion Data Archives (ARDA)

Religious Groups by Tradition

Area	Catholic	Evangelical Protestant	Mainline Protestant	Black Protestant	Islam	Judaism	Hinduism	Orthodox	Buddhism
MSA[1]	6.6	27.9	10.7	5.6	0.3	0.2	0.4	0.1	0.3
U.S.	18.7	16.5	5.2	2.3	1.3	0.6	0.4	0.4	0.3

Note: Figures are the number of adherents as a percentage of the total population; (1) Figures cover the Columbia, SC Metropolitan Statistical Area
Sources: 2020 U.S. Religion Census, Association of Statisticians of American Religious Bodies; The Association of Religion Data Archives (ARDA)

ECONOMY

Real Gross Domestic Product (GDP)

Area	2017	2018	2019	2020	2021	2022	2023	Rank[3]
MSA[1]	41.0	41.7	42.7	42.2	44.6	45.5	47.0	73
U.S.[2]	17,619.1	18,160.7	18,642.5	18,238.9	19,387.6	19,896.6	20,436.3	—

Note: Figures are in billions of chained 2017 dollars; (1) Figures cover the Columbia, SC Metropolitan Statistical Area; (2) Figures cover real GDP within metropolitan areas; (3) Rank is based on 2023 data and ranges from 1 to 384
Source: U.S. Bureau of Economic Analysis

Economic Growth

Area	2014	2015	2016	2017	2018	2019	2020	2021	2022	2023
MSA[1]	3.6	2.9	2.9	0.3	1.6	2.4	-1.0	5.6	2.0	3.4
U.S.[2]	2.6	3.2	2.0	2.7	3.1	2.7	-2.2	6.3	2.6	2.7

Note: Figures are real gross domestic product growth rates and represent percent change from preceding period; (1) Figures cover the Columbia, SC Metropolitan Statistical Area; (2) Figures are the average growth rates within metropolitan areas
Source: U.S. Bureau of Economic Analysis

Metropolitan Area Exports

Area	2018	2019	2020	2021	2022	2023	Rank[2]
MSA[1]	2,083.8	2,184.6	2,058.8	2,100.2	2,351.3	2,160.3	112
U.S.	1,664,056.1	1,645,173.7	1,431,406.6	1,753,941.4	2,062,937.4	2,019,160.5	—

Note: Figures are in millions of dollars; (1) Figures cover the Columbia, SC Metropolitan Statistical Area; (2) Rank is based on 2023 data and ranges from 1 to 386
Source: U.S. Department of Commerce, International Trade Administration, Office of Trade and Economic Analysis, Industry and Analysis, Exports by Metropolitan Area, data extracted April 2, 2025

Building Permits

Area	Single-Family			Multi-Family			Total		
	2023	2024	Pct. Chg.	2023	2024	Pct. Chg.	2023	2024	Pct. Chg.
City	883	833	-5.7	718	1,315	83.1	1,601	2,148	34.2
MSA[1]	4,634	4,469	-3.6	831	1,423	71.2	5,465	5,892	7.8
U.S.	920,000	981,900	6.7	591,100	496,100	-16.1	1,511,100	1,478,000	-2.2

Note: (1) Figures cover the Columbia, SC Metropolitan Statistical Area; Figures represent new, privately-owned housing units authorized (unadjusted data)
Source: U.S. Census Bureau, Building Permits Survey (BPS), 2023, 2024

Bankruptcy Filings

Area	Business Filings			Nonbusiness Filings		
	2023	2024	% Chg.	2023	2024	% Chg.
Richland County	7	10	42.9	453	584	28.9
U.S.	18,926	23,107	22.1	434,064	494,201	13.9

Note: Business filings include Chapter 7, Chapter 9, Chapter 11, Chapter 12, Chapter 13, Chapter 15, and Section 304; Nonbusiness filings include Chapter 7, Chapter 11, and Chapter 13
Source: Administrative Office of the U.S. Courts, Business and Nonbusiness Bankruptcy, County Cases Commenced by Chapter of the Bankruptcy Code, During the 12-Month Period Ending December 31, 2023 and Business and Nonbusiness Bankruptcy, County Cases Commenced by Chapter of the Bankruptcy Code, During the 12-Month Period Ending December 31, 2024

Housing Vacancy Rates

Area	Gross Vacancy Rate[3] (%)			Year-Round Vacancy Rate[4] (%)			Rental Vacancy Rate[5] (%)			Homeowner Vacancy Rate[6] (%)		
	2022	2023	2024	2022	2023	2024	2022	2023	2024	2022	2023	2024
MSA[1]	12.0	12.7	8.8	12.0	12.6	8.8	6.1	8.5	6.8	0.6	1.0	0.5
U.S.[2]	9.1	9.0	9.1	7.5	7.5	7.6	5.7	6.5	6.8	0.8	0.8	1.0

Note: (1) Figures cover the Columbia, SC Metropolitan Statistical Area; (2) Figures cover the 75 largest Metropolitan Statistical Areas; (3) The percentage of the total housing inventory that is vacant; (4) The percentage of the housing inventory (excluding seasonal units) that is year-round vacant; (5) The percentage of rental inventory that is vacant for rent; (6) The percentage of homeowner inventory that is vacant for sale
Source: U.S. Census Bureau, Housing Vacancies and Homeownership Annual Statistics: 2022, 2023, 2024

INCOME

Income

Area	Per Capita ($)	Median Household ($)	Average Household ($)
City	38,087	55,653	90,935
MSA[1]	37,159	66,146	90,520
U.S.	43,289	78,538	110,491

Note: (1) Figures cover the Columbia, SC Metropolitan Statistical Area
Source: U.S. Census Bureau, 2019-2023 American Community Survey 5-Year Estimates

Household Income Distribution

Area	Percent of Households Earning							
	Under $15,000	$15,000 -$24,999	$25,000 -$34,999	$35,000 -$49,999	$50,000 -$74,999	$75,000 -$99,999	$100,000 -$149,999	$150,000 and up
City	16.5	8.6	8.2	11.7	16.7	10.7	11.7	15.8
MSA[1]	10.1	7.3	8.1	12.5	17.5	13.0	15.8	15.7
U.S.	8.5	6.6	6.8	10.4	15.7	12.7	17.4	21.9

Note: (1) Figures cover the Columbia, SC Metropolitan Statistical Area
Source: U.S. Census Bureau, 2019-2023 American Community Survey 5-Year Estimates

Poverty Rate

Area	All Ages	Under 18 Years Old	18 to 64 Years Old	65 Years and Over
City	23.3	29.4	22.6	17.2
MSA[1]	14.7	19.8	13.9	10.6
U.S.	12.4	16.3	11.6	10.4

Note: Figures are percentage of people whose income during the past 12 months was below the poverty level; (1) Figures cover the Columbia, SC Metropolitan Statistical Area
Source: U.S. Census Bureau, 2019-2023 American Community Survey 5-Year Estimates

EMPLOYMENT

Labor Force and Employment

Area	Civilian Labor Force			Workers Employed		
	Dec. 2023	Dec. 2024	% Chg.	Dec. 2023	Dec. 2024	% Chg.
City	59,838	60,914	1.8	57,599	58,055	0.8
MSA[1]	419,770	426,736	1.7	406,945	410,354	0.8
U.S.	166,661,000	167,746,000	0.7	160,754,000	161,294,000	0.3

Note: Data is not seasonally adjusted and covers workers 16 years of age and older; (1) Figures cover the Columbia, SC Metropolitan Statistical Area
Source: Bureau of Labor Statistics, Local Area Unemployment Statistics

Unemployment Rate

Area	2024											
	Jan.	Feb.	Mar.	Apr.	May	Jun.	Jul.	Aug.	Sep.	Oct.	Nov.	Dec.
City	4.1	4.4	4.1	3.8	5.0	5.8	6.1	5.8	4.9	5.7	5.3	4.7
MSA[1]	3.5	3.7	3.5	3.1	3.8	4.5	4.7	4.8	4.1	4.3	4.1	3.8
U.S.	4.1	4.2	3.9	3.5	3.7	4.3	4.5	4.4	3.9	3.9	4.0	3.8

Note: Data is not seasonally adjusted and covers workers 16 years of age and older; (1) Figures cover the Columbia, SC Metropolitan Statistical Area
Source: Bureau of Labor Statistics, Local Area Unemployment Statistics

Average Wages

Occupation	$/Hr.	Occupation	$/Hr.
Accountants and Auditors	34.91	Maintenance and Repair Workers	23.42
Automotive Mechanics	23.93	Marketing Managers	63.36
Bookkeepers	22.33	Network and Computer Systems Admin.	43.01
Carpenters	24.28	Nurses, Licensed Practical	28.97
Cashiers	12.66	Nurses, Registered	40.80
Computer Programmers	54.49	Nursing Assistants	17.13
Computer Systems Analysts	41.80	Office Clerks, General	19.07
Computer User Support Specialists	27.54	Physical Therapists	45.02
Construction Laborers	21.14	Physicians	172.10
Cooks, Restaurant	16.57	Plumbers, Pipefitters and Steamfitters	25.12
Customer Service Representatives	19.31	Police and Sheriff's Patrol Officers	32.54
Dentists	120.35	Postal Service Mail Carriers	27.58
Electricians	29.62	Real Estate Sales Agents	25.47
Engineers, Electrical	51.67	Retail Salespersons	15.69
Fast Food and Counter Workers	12.71	Sales Representatives, Technical/Scientific	55.80
Financial Managers	64.62	Secretaries, Exc. Legal/Medical/Executive	20.60
First-Line Supervisors of Office Workers	33.15	Security Guards	16.75
General and Operations Managers	54.00	Surgeons	n/a
Hairdressers/Cosmetologists	16.41	Teacher Assistants, Exc. Postsecondary[1]	14.58
Home Health and Personal Care Aides	14.20	Teachers, Secondary School, Exc. Sp. Ed.[1]	28.10
Janitors and Cleaners	15.80	Telemarketers	13.70
Landscaping/Groundskeeping Workers	17.37	Truck Drivers, Heavy/Tractor-Trailer	26.77
Lawyers	65.86	Truck Drivers, Light/Delivery Services	22.11
Maids and Housekeeping Cleaners	13.97	Waiters and Waitresses	11.85

Note: Wage data covers the Columbia, SC Metropolitan Statistical Area; (1) Hourly wages were calculated from annual wage data based on a 40 hour work week
Source: Bureau of Labor Statistics, Metro Area Occupational Employment & Wage Estimates, May 2024

Employment by Industry

Sector	MSA[1] Number of Employees	MSA[1] Percent of Total	U.S. Percent of Total
Construction, Mining, and Logging	18,900	4.3	5.5
Financial Activities	36,400	8.3	5.8
Government	85,300	19.4	14.9
Information	5,000	1.1	1.9
Leisure and Hospitality	41,100	9.4	10.4
Manufacturing	32,400	7.4	8.0
Other Services	18,500	4.2	3.7
Private Education and Health Services	61,200	13.9	16.9
Professional and Business Services	59,600	13.6	14.2
Retail Trade	46,100	10.5	10.0
Transportation, Warehousing, and Utilities	18,400	4.2	4.8
Wholesale Trade	16,200	3.7	3.9

Note: Figures are non-farm employment as of December 2024. Figures are not seasonally adjusted and include workers 16 years of age and older; (1) Figures cover the Columbia, SC Metropolitan Statistical Area
Source: Bureau of Labor Statistics, Current Employment Statistics, Employment, Hours, and Earnings

Employment by Occupation

Occupation Classification	City (%)	MSA[1] (%)	U.S. (%)
Management, Business, Science, and Arts	45.9	41.6	42.0
Natural Resources, Construction, and Maintenance	4.4	7.7	8.6
Production, Transportation, and Material Moving	9.5	13.3	13.0
Sales and Office	21.1	21.7	19.9
Service	19.1	15.7	16.5

Note: Figures cover employed civilians 16 years of age and older; (1) Figures cover the Columbia, SC Metropolitan Statistical Area
Source: U.S. Census Bureau, 2019-2023 American Community Survey 5-Year Estimates

Occupations with Greatest Projected Employment Growth: 2022 – 2032

Occupation[1]	2022 Employment	2032 Projected Employment	Numeric Employment Change	Percent Employment Change
Laborers and Freight, Stock, and Material Movers, Hand	63,510	75,580	12,070	19.0
Home Health and Personal Care Aides	32,340	43,300	10,960	33.9
Stockers and Order Fillers	38,370	46,800	8,430	22.0
Retail Salespersons	66,680	74,980	8,300	12.4
Cooks, Restaurant	25,700	33,820	8,120	31.6
Fast Food and Counter Workers	55,240	61,930	6,690	12.1
General and Operations Managers	49,750	56,440	6,690	13.4
Miscellaneous Assemblers and Fabricators	46,940	51,780	4,840	10.3
Software Developers	11,550	16,070	4,520	39.1
Registered Nurses	45,140	49,610	4,470	9.9

Note: Projections cover South Carolina; (1) Sorted by numeric employment change
Source: www.projectionscentral.org, State Occupational Projections, 2022–2032 Long-Term Projections

Fastest-Growing Occupations: 2022 – 2032

Occupation[1]	2022 Employment	2032 Projected Employment	Numeric Employment Change	Percent Employment Change
Nurse Practitioners	4,120	6,620	2,500	60.7
Personal Care and Service Workers, All Other	820	1,250	430	52.4
Data Scientists	1,270	1,880	610	48.0
Information Security Analysts (SOC 2018)	1,390	1,990	600	43.2
Statisticians	280	400	120	42.9
Actuaries	120	170	50	41.7
Physician Assistants	1,800	2,510	710	39.4
Software Developers	11,550	16,070	4,520	39.1
Personal Financial Advisors	3,100	4,310	1,210	39.0
Physical Therapist Assistants	2,110	2,910	800	37.9

Note: Projections cover South Carolina; (1) Sorted by percent employment change and excludes occupations with numeric employment change less than 50
Source: www.projectionscentral.org, State Occupational Projections, 2022–2032 Long-Term Projections

CITY FINANCES

City Government Finances

Component	2022 ($000)	2022 ($ per capita)
Total Revenues	424,103	3,210
Total Expenditures	478,623	3,622
Debt Outstanding	880,049	6,660

Source: U.S. Census Bureau, State & Local Government Finances 2022

City Government Revenue by Source

Source	2022 ($000)	2022 ($ per capita)	2022 (%)
General Revenue			
From Federal Government	12,952	98	3.1
From State Government	32,233	244	7.6
From Local Governments	28,505	216	6.7
Taxes			
Property	47,594	360	11.2
Sales and Gross Receipts	22,063	167	5.2
Personal Income	0	0	0.0
Corporate Income	0	0	0.0
Motor Vehicle License	0	0	0.0
Other Taxes	41,092	311	9.7
Current Charges	96,190	728	22.7
Liquor Store	0	0	0.0
Utility	114,175	864	26.9

Source: U.S. Census Bureau, State & Local Government Finances 2022

City Government Expenditures by Function

Function	2022 ($000)	2022 ($ per capita)	2022 (%)
General Direct Expenditures			
Air Transportation	0	0	0.0
Corrections	0	0	0.0
Education	0	0	0.0
Employment Security Administration	0	0	0.0
Financial Administration	6,214	47	1.3
Fire Protection	54,127	409	11.3
General Public Buildings	7,059	53	1.5
Governmental Administration, Other	7,984	60	1.7
Health	2,072	15	0.4
Highways	8,186	62	1.7
Hospitals	0	0	0.0
Housing and Community Development	8,694	65	1.8
Interest on General Debt	7,420	56	1.6
Judicial and Legal	4,331	32	0.9
Libraries	0	0	0.0
Parking	5,192	39	1.1
Parks and Recreation	12,810	97	2.7
Police Protection	54,037	409	11.3
Public Welfare	1,611	12	0.3
Sewerage	102,371	774	21.4
Solid Waste Management	12,224	92	2.6
Veterans' Services	0	0	0.0
Liquor Store	0	0	0.0
Utility	152,824	1,156	31.9

Source: U.S. Census Bureau, State & Local Government Finances 2022

TAXES

State Corporate Income Tax Rates

State	Tax Rate (%)	Income Brackets ($)	Num. of Brackets	Financial Institution Tax Rate (%)[a]	Federal Income Tax Ded.
South Carolina	5.0	Flat rate	1	4.5 (t)	No

Note: Tax rates for tax year 2024; (a) Rates listed are the corporate income tax rate applied to financial institutions or excise taxes based on income. Some states have other taxes based upon the value of deposits or shares; (t) South Carolina taxes savings and loans at a 6% rate.
Source: Federation of Tax Administrators, State Corporate Income Tax Rates, January 1, 2025

State Individual Income Tax Rates

State	Tax Rate (%)	Income Brackets ($)	Personal Exemptions ($)			Standard Ded. ($)	
			Single	Married	Depend.	Single	Married
South Carolina (a)	0.0 - 6.4 (bb)	3,460 - 17,330	4,610	9,220	4,610 (d)	14,600	29,200 (d)

Note: Tax rates for tax year 2024; Local- and county-level taxes are not included; (a) 16 states have statutory provision for automatically adjusting to the rate of inflation the dollar values of the income tax brackets, standard deductions, and/or personal exemptions. Oregon does not index the income brackets for $125,000 and over See: INFL and SPEC above; (d) These states use the personal exemption/standard deduction amounts provided in the federal Internal Revenue Code. Montana personal exemption subject to repeal under Section 15-30-2114; (bb) Louisiana lawmakers repealed the state's throwout rule, ending the taxation of so-called "nowhere income." Iowa is phasing-in a flat rate by 2027, while Nebraska (LB 754 signed into law) and South Carolina is phasing-in a reduced top rate by 2027.
Source: Federation of Tax Administrators, State Individual Income Tax Rates, January 1, 2025

Various State Sales and Excise Tax Rates

State	State Sales Tax (%)	Gasoline[1] ($/gal.)	Cigarette[2] ($/pack)	Spirits[3] ($/gal.)	Wine[4] ($/gal.)	Beer[5] ($/gal.)	Recreational Marijuana (%)
South Carolina	6	0.29	0.57	5.42	1.08	0.77	Not legal

Note: All tax rates as of January 1, 2025; (1) The American Petroleum Institute has developed a methodology for determining the average tax rate on a gallon of fuel. Rates may include any of the following: excise taxes, environmental fees, storage tank fees, other fees or taxes, general sales tax, and local taxes; (2) The federal excise tax of $1.0066 per pack and local taxes are not included; (3) Rates are those applicable to off-premise sales of 40% alcohol by volume (a.b.v.) distilled spirits in 750ml containers. Local excise taxes are excluded; (4) Rates are those applicable to off-premise sales of 11% a.b.v. non-carbonated wine in 750ml containers; (5) Rates are those applicable to off-premise sales of 4.7% a.b.v. beer in 12 ounce containers.
Source: Tax Foundation, 2025 Facts & Figures: How Does Your State Compare?

State Tax Competitiveness Index

State	Overall Rank	Corporate Tax Rank	Individual Income Tax Rank	Sales Tax Rank	Property Tax Rank	Unemployment Insurance Tax Rank
South Carolina	33	11	24	33	42	28

Note: The Tax Foundation's State Tax Competitiveness Index enables policymakers, taxpayers, and business leaders to gauge how their states' tax systems compare. A rank of 1 is best, 50 is worst. Rankings do not average to the total. States without a tax rank equally as 1. DC's scores and rankings do not affect other states. The report shows tax systems as of July 1, 2024 (the beginning of Fiscal Year 2025).
Source: Tax Foundation, State Tax Competitiveness Index 2025

TRANSPORTATION

Means of Transportation to Work

Area	Car/Truck/Van		Public Transportation			Bicycle	Walked	Other Means	Worked at Home
	Drove Alone	Car-pooled	Bus	Subway	Railroad				
City	62.9	6.9	1.4	0.0	0.0	0.3	16.4	2.2	9.8
MSA[1]	76.2	8.1	0.5	0.0	0.0	0.1	3.5	1.7	9.9
U.S.	70.2	8.5	1.7	1.3	0.4	0.4	2.4	1.6	13.5

Note: Figures are percentages and cover workers 16 years of age and older; (1) Figures cover the Columbia, SC Metropolitan Statistical Area
Source: U.S. Census Bureau, 2019-2023 American Community Survey 5-Year Estimates

Travel Time to Work

Area	Less Than 10 Minutes	10 to 19 Minutes	20 to 29 Minutes	30 to 44 Minutes	45 to 59 Minutes	60 to 89 Minutes	90 Minutes or More
City	27.7	37.4	19.1	10.0	2.7	1.2	1.8
MSA[1]	12.7	28.9	23.6	22.0	7.3	3.2	2.3
U.S.	12.6	28.6	21.2	20.8	8.1	6.0	2.8

Note: Note: Figures are percentages and include workers 16 years old and over; (1) Figures cover the Columbia, SC Metropolitan Statistical Area
Source: U.S. Census Bureau, 2019-2023 American Community Survey 5-Year Estimates

Key Congestion Measures

Measure	2000	2010	2015	2020	2022
Annual Hours of Delay, Total (000)	7,111	13,675	15,687	7,362	14,890
Annual Hours of Delay, Per Auto Commuter	29	41	44	19	40
Annual Congestion Cost, Per Auto Commuter ($)	539	818	868	414	799

Note: Figures cover the Columbia SC urban area
Source: Texas A&M Transportation Institute, 2023 Urban Mobility Report

Freeway Travel Time Index

Measure	1985	1990	1995	2000	2005	2010	2015	2020	2022
Urban Area Index[1]	1.05	1.07	1.08	1.12	1.14	1.15	1.15	1.05	1.10
Urban Area Rank[1,2]	64	74	84	77	73	65	67	85	89

Note: Freeway Travel Time Index—the ratio of travel time in the peak period to the travel time at free-flow conditions. For example, a value of 1.30 indicates a 20-minute free-flow trip takes 26 minutes in the peak (20 minutes x 1.30 = 26 minutes); (1) Covers the Columbia SC urban area; (2) Rank is based on 101 larger urban areas (#1 = highest travel time index)
Source: Texas A&M Transportation Institute, 2023 Urban Mobility Report

Public Transportation

Agency Name / Mode of Transportation	Vehicles Operated in Maximum Service[1]	Annual Unlinked Passenger Trips[2] (in thous.)	Annual Passenger Miles[3] (in thous.)
Central Midlands Regional Transit Authority			
Bus (purchased transportation)	52	1,783.8	9,558.5
Commuter Bus (purchased transportation)	2	6.4	59.7
Demand Response (purchased transportation)	23	58.7	697.5
Demand Response - Transportation Network Company	134	81.6	198.0
Vanpool (purchased transportation)	19	38.0	1,833.9

Note: (1) Number of revenue vehicles operated by the given mode and type of service to meet the annual maximum service requirement. This is the revenue vehicle count during the peak season of the year; on the week and day that maximum service is provided. Vehicles operated in maximum service (VOMS) exclude atypical days and one-time special events; (2) Number of passengers who boarded public transportation vehicles. Passengers are counted each time they board a vehicle no matter how many vehicles they use to travel from their origin to their destination. (3) Sum of the distances ridden by all passengers during the entire fiscal year.
Source: Federal Transit Administration, National Transit Database, 2023

Air Transportation

Airport Name and Code / Type of Service	Passenger Airlines[1]	Passenger Enplanements	Freight Carriers[2]	Freight (lbs)
Columbia Metropolitan (CAE)				
Domestic service (U.S. carriers only)	19	651,388	11	37,818,801
International service (U.S. carriers only)	1	141	2	59,309

Note: (1) Includes all U.S.-based major, minor and commuter airlines that carried at least one passenger during the year; (2) Includes all U.S.-based airlines and freight carriers that transported at least one pound of freight during the year.
Source: Bureau of Transportation Statistics, The Intermodal Transportation Database, Air Carriers: T-100 Domestic Market (U.S. carriers only), 2024; Bureau of Transportation Statistics, The Intermodal Transportation Database, Air Carriers: T-100 International Market (U.S. carriers only), 2024

BUSINESSES

Major Business Headquarters

Company Name	Industry	Rankings Fortune[1]	Forbes[2]
No companies listed	-	-	-

Note: (1) Companies that produce a 10-K are ranked 1 to 500 based on 2023 revenue; (2) All private companies with at least $2 billion in annual revenue through the end of their most current fiscal year are ranked 1 to 275; companies listed are headquartered in the city; dashes indicate no ranking
Source: Fortune, "Fortune 500," 2024; Forbes, "America's Largest Private Companies," 2024

Living Environment

COST OF LIVING

Cost of Living Index

Composite Index	Groceries	Housing	Utilities	Transportation	Health Care	Misc. Goods/Services
89.2	99.1	69.2	117.6	80.6	75.6	98.3

Note: The Cost of Living Index measures regional differences in the cost of consumer goods and services, excluding taxes and non-consumer expenditures, for professional and managerial households in the top income quintile. It is based on more than 50,000 prices covering almost 60 different items for which prices are collected three times a year by chambers of commerce, economic development organizations or university applied economic centers in each participating urban area. The numbers shown should be read as a percentage above or below the national average of 100. For example, a value of 115.4 in the groceries column indicates that grocery prices are 15.4% higher than the national average. Small differences in the index numbers should not be interpreted as significant; Figures cover the Columbia SC urban area.
Source: The Council for Community and Economic Research, Cost of Living Index, 2024

Grocery Prices

Area[1]	T-Bone Steak ($/pound)	Frying Chicken ($/pound)	Whole Milk ($/half gal.)	Eggs ($/dozen)	Orange Juice ($/64 oz.)	Coffee ($/11.5 oz.)
City[2]	15.51	1.66	4.62	3.28	4.38	5.27
Avg.	15.42	1.55	4.69	3.25	4.41	5.46
Min.	14.50	1.16	4.43	2.75	4.00	4.85
Max.	17.56	2.89	5.49	4.78	5.54	7.89

Note: (1) Values for the local area are compared with the average, minimum and maximum values for all 276 areas in the Cost of Living Index; (2) Figures cover the Columbia SC urban area; **T-Bone Steak** (price per pound); **Frying Chicken** (price per pound, whole fryer); **Whole Milk** (half gallon carton); **Eggs** (price per dozen, Grade A, large); **Orange Juice** (64 oz. Tropicana or Florida Natural); **Coffee** (11.5 oz. can, vacuum-packed, Maxwell House, Hills Bros, or Folgers).
Source: The Council for Community and Economic Research, Cost of Living Index, 2024

Housing and Utility Costs

Area[1]	New Home Price ($)	Apartment Rent ($/month)	All Electric ($/month)	Part Electric ($/month)	Other Energy ($/month)	Telephone ($/month)
City[2]	328,383	1,205	-	119.24	143.41	195.98
Avg.	515,975	1,550	210.99	123.07	82.07	194.99
Min.	265,375	692	104.33	53.68	36.26	179.42
Max.	2,775,821	5,719	529.02	397.28	361.63	223.33

Note: (1) Values for the local area are compared with the average, minimum and maximum values for all 276 areas in the Cost of Living Index; (2) Figures cover the Columbia SC urban area; **New Home Price** (2,400 sf living area, 8,000 sf lot, in urban area with full utilities); **Apartment Rent** (950 sf 2 bedroom/1.5 or 2 bath, unfurnished, excluding all utilities except water); **All Electric** (average monthly cost for an all-electric home); **Part Electric** (average monthly cost for a part-electric home); **Other Energy** (average monthly cost for natural gas, fuel oil, coal, wood, and any other forms of energy except electricity); **Telephone** (price includes the base monthly rate plus taxes and fees for three lines of mobile phone service).
Source: The Council for Community and Economic Research, Cost of Living Index, 2024

Health Care, Transportation, and Other Costs

Area[1]	Doctor ($/visit)	Dentist ($/visit)	Optometrist ($/visit)	Gasoline ($/gallon)	Beauty Salon ($/visit)	Men's Shirt ($)
City[2]	150.00	58.67	67.33	3.12	38.83	34.56
Avg.	143.77	117.51	129.23	3.32	48.57	38.14
Min.	36.74	58.67	67.33	2.80	24.00	13.41
Max.	270.44	216.82	307.33	5.28	94.00	63.89

Note: (1) Values for the local area are compared with the average, minimum and maximum values for all 276 areas in the Cost of Living Index; (2) Figures cover the Columbia SC urban area; **Doctor** (general practitioners routine exam of an established patient); **Dentist** (adult teeth cleaning and periodic oral examination); **Optometrist** (full vision eye exam for established adult patient); **Gasoline** (one gallon regular unleaded, national brand, including all taxes, cash price at self-service pump if available); **Beauty Salon** (woman's shampoo, trim, and blow-dry); **Men's Shirt** (cotton/polyester dress shirt, pinpoint weave, long sleeves).
Source: The Council for Community and Economic Research, Cost of Living Index, 2024

HOUSING

Homeownership Rate

Area	2017 (%)	2018 (%)	2019 (%)	2020 (%)	2021 (%)	2022 (%)	2023 (%)	2024 (%)
MSA[1]	70.7	69.3	65.9	69.7	69.4	70.9	69.2	73.4
U.S.	63.9	64.4	64.6	66.6	65.5	65.8	65.9	65.6

Note: (1) Figures cover the Columbia, SC Metropolitan Statistical Area
Source: U.S. Census Bureau, Housing Vacancies and Homeownership Annual Statistics: 2017-2024

House Price Index (HPI)

Area	National Ranking[2]	Quarterly Change (%)	One-Year Change (%)	Five-Year Change (%)	Since 1991Q1 (%)
MSA[1]	61	0.87	6.97	64.02	248.40
U.S.[3]	–	1.43	4.51	57.13	327.82

Note: The HPI is a weighted repeat sales index. It measures average price changes in repeat sales or refinancings on the same properties. This information is obtained by reviewing repeat mortgage transactions on single-family properties whose mortgages have been purchased or securitized by Fannie Mae or Freddie Mac since January 1975; (1) Figures cover the Columbia, SC Metropolitan Statistical Area; (2) Rankings are based on annual percentage change for all metro areas containing at least 15,000 transactions over the last 10 years and ranges from 1 to 241; (3) figures based on a weighted average of Census Division estimates using a seasonally adjusted, purchase-only index; all figures are for the period ending December 31, 2024
Source: Federal Housing Finance Agency, Change in FHFA Metropolitan Area House Price Indexes, All Transactions Index, 2024Q4

Home Value

Area	Under $100,000	$100,000 -$199,999	$200,000 -$299,999	$300,000 -$399,999	$400,000 -$499,999	$500,000 -$999,999	$1,000,000 or more	Median ($)
City	12.4	26.0	23.5	11.7	8.3	14.7	3.5	243,500
MSA[1]	15.7	30.4	25.4	12.9	6.5	7.4	1.7	213,400
U.S.	12.1	17.8	19.5	14.4	10.5	19.1	6.5	303,400

Note: Figures are percentages except for median and cover owner-occupied housing units; (1) Figures cover the Columbia, SC Metropolitan Statistical Area
Source: U.S. Census Bureau, 2019-2023 American Community Survey 5-Year Estimates

Year Housing Structure Built

Area	2020 or Later	2010 -2019	2000 -2009	1990 -1999	1980 -1989	1970 -1979	1960 -1969	1950 -1959	1940 -1949	Before 1940	Median Year
City	1.0	12.9	14.8	9.8	9.6	9.6	10.1	13.3	8.9	10.1	1978
MSA[1]	1.6	13.8	18.3	16.7	13.5	14.1	8.8	6.7	2.8	3.7	1990
U.S.	1.2	8.9	13.6	12.8	13.0	14.4	10.0	9.7	4.5	11.9	1980

Note: Figures are percentages except for Median Year; Note: (1) Figures cover the Columbia, SC Metropolitan Statistical Area
Source: U.S. Census Bureau, 2019-2023 American Community Survey 5-Year Estimates

Gross Monthly Rent

Area	Under $500	$500 -$999	$1,000 -$1,499	$1,500 -$1,999	$2,000 -$2,499	$2,500 -$2,999	$3,000 and up	Median ($)
City	8.4	26.7	42.3	16.5	5.4	0.5	0.2	1,158
MSA[1]	5.2	31.0	41.5	15.6	5.0	0.9	0.9	1,145
U.S.	6.5	22.3	29.5	20.2	10.8	4.8	5.9	1,348

Note: Figures are percentages except for median; Gross rent is the contract rent plus the estimated average monthly cost of utilities (electricity, gas, and water and sewer) and fuels (oil, coal, kerosene, wood, etc.) if these are paid by the renter (or paid for the renter by someone else); (1) Figures cover the Columbia, SC Metropolitan Statistical Area
Source: U.S. Census Bureau, 2019-2023 American Community Survey 5-Year Estimates

HEALTH

Health Risk Factors

Category	MSA[1] (%)	U.S. (%)
Adults aged 18–64 who have any kind of health care coverage	89.7	90.8
Adults who reported being in good or better health	82.2	81.8
Adults who have been told they have high blood cholesterol	38.9	36.9
Adults who have been told they have high blood pressure	37.0	34.0
Adults who are current smokers	10.8	12.1
Adults who currently use e-cigarettes	8.0	7.7
Adults who currently use chewing tobacco, snuff, or snus	2.9	3.2
Adults who are heavy drinkers[2]	6.5	6.1
Adults who are binge drinkers[3]	15.3	15.2
Adults who are overweight (BMI 25.0 - 29.9)	33.7	34.4
Adults who are obese (BMI 30.0 - 99.8)	35.3	34.3
Adults who participated in any physical activities in the past month	75.5	75.8

Note: All figures are crude prevalence; (1) Figures cover the Columbia, SC Metropolitan Statistical Area; (2) Heavy drinkers are classified as adult men having more than 14 drinks per week and adult women having more than 7 drinks per week; (3) Binge drinkers are classified as males having five or more drinks on one occasion or females having four or more drinks on one occasion
Source: Centers for Disease Control and Prevention, Behaviorial Risk Factor Surveillance System, SMART: Selected Metropolitan Area Risk Trends, 2023

Acute and Chronic Health Conditions

Category	MSA[1] (%)	U.S. (%)
Adults who have ever been told they had a heart attack	3.9	4.2
Adults who have ever been told they have angina or coronary heart disease	3.8	4.0
Adults who have ever been told they had a stroke	3.6	3.3
Adults who have ever been told they have asthma	13.2	15.7
Adults who have ever been told they have arthritis	29.2	26.3
Adults who have ever been told they have diabetes[2]	13.6	11.5
Adults who have ever been told they had skin cancer	5.6	5.6
Adults who have ever been told they had any other types of cancer	8.6	8.4
Adults who have ever been told they have COPD	5.8	6.4
Adults who have ever been told they have kidney disease	3.9	3.7
Adults who have ever been told they have a form of depression	23.5	22.0

Note: All figures are crude prevalence; (1) Figures cover the Columbia, SC Metropolitan Statistical Area; (2) Figures do not include pregnancy-related, borderline, or pre-diabetes
Source: Centers for Disease Control and Prevention, Behaviorial Risk Factor Surveillance System, SMART: Selected Metropolitan Area Risk Trends, 2023

Health Screening and Vaccination Rates

Category	MSA[1] (%)	U.S. (%)
Adults who have ever been tested for HIV	42.0	37.5
Adults who have had their blood cholesterol checked within the last five years	88.0	87.0
Adults aged 65+ who have had flu shot within the past year	61.6	63.4
Adults aged 65+ who have ever had a pneumonia vaccination	76.8	71.9

Note: All figures are crude prevalence; (1) Figures cover the Columbia, SC Metropolitan Statistical Area.
Source: Centers for Disease Control and Prevention, Behaviorial Risk Factor Surveillance System, SMART: Selected Metropolitan Area Risk Trends, 2023

Disability Status

Category	MSA[1] (%)	U.S. (%)
Adults who reported being deaf	6.9	7.4
Are you blind or have serious difficulty seeing, even when wearing glasses?	5.5	4.9
Do you have difficulty doing errands alone?	7.9	7.8
Do you have difficulty dressing or bathing?	4.2	3.6
Do you have serious difficulty concentrating/remembering/making decisions?	13.1	13.7
Do you have serious difficulty walking or climbing stairs?	15.0	13.2

Note: All figures are crude prevalence; (1) Figures cover the Columbia, SC Metropolitan Statistical Area.
Source: Centers for Disease Control and Prevention, Behaviorial Risk Factor Surveillance System, SMART: Selected Metropolitan Area Risk Trends, 2023

Mortality Rates for the Top 10 Causes of Death in the U.S.

ICD-10[a] Sub-Chapter	ICD-10[a] Code	Crude Mortality Rate[2] per 100,000 population	
		County[3]	U.S.
Malignant neoplasms	C00-C97	165.6	182.7
Ischaemic heart diseases	I20-I25	91.2	109.6
Provisional assignment of new diseases of uncertain etiology[1]	U00-U49	51.0	65.3
Other forms of heart disease	I30-I51	45.4	65.1
Other degenerative diseases of the nervous system	G30-G31	56.1	52.4
Other external causes of accidental injury	W00-X59	45.2	52.3
Cerebrovascular diseases	I60-I69	38.7	49.1
Chronic lower respiratory diseases	J40-J47	27.2	43.5
Hypertensive diseases	I10-I15	51.9	38.9
Organic, including symptomatic, mental disorders	F01-F09	25.3	33.9

Note: (a) ICD-10 = International Classification of Diseases 10th Revision; (1) Includes COVID-19, adverse effects to COVID-19 vaccines, SARS, and vaping-related disorders; (2) Crude mortality rates are a three-year average covering 2021-2023; (3) Figures cover Richland County.
Source: Centers for Disease Control and Prevention, National Center for Health Statistics. National Vital Statistics System, Mortality 2018-2023 on CDC WONDER Online Database

Mortality Rates for Selected Causes of Death

Cause of Death	ICD-10[a] Code	Crude Mortality Rate[1] per 100,000 population	
		County[2]	U.S.
Accidental poisoning and exposure to noxious substances	X40-X49	27.0	30.5
Alzheimer disease	G30	36.4	35.4
Assault	X85-Y09	15.7	7.3
COVID-19	U07.1	51.0	65.3
Diabetes mellitus	E10-E14	22.4	30.0
Diseases of the liver	K70-K76	18.3	20.8
Human immunodeficiency virus (HIV) disease	B20-B24	2.8	1.5
Influenza and pneumonia	J09-J18	7.4	13.4
Intentional self-harm	X60-X84	11.5	14.7
Malnutrition	E40-E46	10.9	6.0
Obesity and other hyperalimentation	E65-E68	2.7	3.1
Renal failure	N17-N19	10.8	16.4
Transport accidents	V01-V99	19.8	14.4

Note: (a) ICD-10 = International Classification of Diseases 10th Revision; (1) Crude mortality rates are a three-year average covering 2021-2023; (2) Figures cover Richland County; Data are suppressed when the data meet the criteria for confidentiality constraints; Crude mortality rates are flagged as unreliable when the rate would be calculated with a numerator of 20 or less.
Source: Centers for Disease Control and Prevention, National Center for Health Statistics. National Vital Statistics System, Mortality 2018-2023 on CDC WONDER Online Database

Health Insurance Coverage

Area	With Health Insurance	With Private Health Insurance	With Public Health Insurance	Without Health Insurance	Population Under Age 19 Without Health Insurance
City	91.9	71.0	31.4	8.1	3.2
MSA[1]	91.0	69.6	36.0	9.0	5.2
U.S.	91.4	67.3	36.3	8.6	5.4

Note: Figures are percentages that cover the civilian noninstitutionalized population; (1) Figures cover the Columbia, SC Metropolitan Statistical Area
Source: U.S. Census Bureau, 2019-2023 American Community Survey 5-Year Estimates

Number of Medical Professionals

Area	MDs[3]	DOs[3,4]	Dentists	Podiatrists	Chiropractors	Optometrists
County[1] (number)	1,512	91	396	29	97	80
County[1] (rate[2])	358.7	21.6	93.1	6.8	22.8	18.8
U.S. (rate[2])	302.5	29.2	74.6	6.4	29.5	18.0

Note: Data as of 2023 unless noted; (1) Data covers Richland County; (2) Number of medical professionals per 100,000 population; (3) Data as of 2022 and includes all active, non-federal physicians; (4) Doctor of Osteopathic Medicine
Source: U.S. Department of Health and Human Services, Health Resources and Services Administration, Bureau of Health Professions, Area Resource File (ARF) 2023-2024

EDUCATION

Public School District Statistics

District Name	Schls	Pupils	Pupil/Teacher Ratio	Minority Pupils[1] (%)	Total Rev. per Pupil ($)	Total Exp. per Pupil ($)
Charter Institute at Erskine	27	25,146	17.2	40.9	16,842	18,946
Richland 01	48	22,123	12.3	81.7	24,234	22,848
Richland 02	32	28,917	13.7	84.3	16,580	18,376
SC Public Charter School District	40	18,404	14.1	50.4	24,523	25,770

Note: Table includes school districts with 2,000 or more students; (1) Percentage of students that are not non-Hispanic white.
Source: U.S. Department of Education, National Center for Education Statistics, Common Core of Data, Local Education Agency (School District) Universe Survey: School Year 2023-2024; U.S. Department of Education, National Center for Education Statistics, Common Core of Data, School District Finance Survey (F-33): School Year 2021–22

Highest Level of Education

Area	Less than H.S.	H.S. Diploma	Some College, No Deg.	Associate Degree	Bachelor's Degree	Master's Degree	Prof. School Degree	Doctorate Degree
City	9.1	19.2	18.2	7.4	25.2	12.7	5.0	3.1
MSA[1]	8.9	25.3	21.2	9.6	20.8	10.2	2.2	1.8
U.S.	10.6	26.2	19.4	8.8	21.3	9.8	2.3	1.6

Note: Figures cover persons age 25 and over; (1) Figures cover the Columbia, SC Metropolitan Statistical Area
Source: U.S. Census Bureau, 2019-2023 American Community Survey 5-Year Estimates

Educational Attainment by Race

Area	High School Graduate or Higher (%)					Bachelor's Degree or Higher (%)				
	Total	White	Black	Asian	Hisp.[2]	Total	White	Black	Asian	Hisp.[2]
City	90.9	96.0	85.2	89.9	85.6	46.1	62.6	25.4	73.0	39.5
MSA[1]	91.1	93.5	88.9	91.0	75.3	35.0	39.2	27.3	64.1	22.7
U.S.	89.4	92.9	88.1	88.0	72.5	35.0	37.7	24.7	57.0	19.9

Note: Figures shown cover persons 25 years old and over; (1) Figures cover the Columbia, SC Metropolitan Statistical Area; (2) People of Hispanic origin can be of any race
Source: U.S. Census Bureau, 2019-2023 American Community Survey 5-Year Estimates

School Enrollment by Grade and Control

Area	Preschool (%)		Kindergarten (%)		Grades 1 - 4 (%)		Grades 5 - 8 (%)		Grades 9 - 12 (%)	
	Public	Private	Public	Private	Public	Private	Public	Private	Public	Private
City	33.0	67.0	81.8	18.2	76.7	23.3	85.6	14.4	84.0	16.0
MSA[1]	51.6	48.4	88.3	11.7	87.8	12.2	90.4	9.6	91.7	8.3
U.S.	58.7	41.3	85.2	14.8	87.2	12.8	87.9	12.1	89.0	11.0

Note: Figures shown cover persons 3 years old and over; (1) Figures cover the Columbia, SC Metropolitan Statistical Area
Source: U.S. Census Bureau, 2019-2023 American Community Survey 5-Year Estimates

Higher Education

Four-Year Colleges			Two-Year Colleges			Medical Schools[1]	Law Schools[2]	Voc/Tech[3]
Public	Private Non-profit	Private For-profit	Public	Private Non-profit	Private For-profit			
1	4	1	1	0	2	1	1	6

Note: Figures cover institutions located within the Columbia, SC Metropolitan Statistical Area and include main campuses only; (1) includes schools accredited by the Liaison Committee on Medical Education and the American Osteopathic Association's Commission on Osteopathic College Accreditation; (2) includes ABA-accredited schools, schools with provisional ABA accreditation, and state accredited schools; (3) includes all schools with programs that are less than 2 years.
Source: National Center for Education Statistics, Integrated Postsecondary Education System (IPEDS), 2023-24; Wikipedia, List of Medical Schools in the United States, accessed May 2, 2025; Wikipedia, List of Law Schools in the United States, accessed May 2, 2025

According to *U.S. News & World Report*, the Columbia, SC metro area is home to one of the top 200 national universities in the U.S.: **University of South Carolina** (#121 tie). The indicators used to capture academic quality fall into a number of categories: assessment by administrators at peer institutions; retention of students; faculty resources; student selectivity; financial resources; alumni giving; high school counselor ratings of colleges; and graduation rate. *U.S. News & World Report*, "America's Best Colleges 2025"

According to *U.S. News & World Report*, the Columbia, SC metro area is home to one of the top 100 law schools in the U.S.: **University of South Carolina** (#63 tie). The rankings are based on a weighted average of 12 measures of quality: peer assessment score; assessment score by lawyers/judges; median LSAT scores; median undergrad GPA; acceptance rate; employment rates for graduates; placement success; bar passage rate; faculty resources; expenditures per student; student/faculty ratio; and library resources. *U.S. News & World Report*, "America's Best Graduate Schools, Law, 2025"

According to *U.S. News & World Report*, the Columbia, SC metro area is home to one of the top medical schools for primary care in the U.S.: **University of South Carolina** (Tier 2). *U.S. News* placed medical and osteopathic schools into tiers based on their research productivity, faculty and admissions data. Each school's tier was derived from its overall score, calculated by summing the weighted normalized values generated across several factors of academic quality, outlined below. There are four tiers, with tier 1 medical schools as the highest-performing and tier 4 as the lowest-performing. Only tier 1 and 2 schools are shown. Because of the tier presentation, *U.S. News* calculated overall scores based on their percentile performance among all rated schools instead of dividing against the rescaled score of the No. 1-performing schools. Tier 1 included schools with overall scores of 85 to 99. The cutoffs for tiers 2 through 4 were schools scoring 50 to 84, 15 to 49 and 1 to 14, respectively. The rankings are based on a weighted average of the following measures of quality: graduates practicing in primary care specialties; graduates entering primary care residencies; median MCAT total score; median undergraduate GPA; acceptance rate; and faculty resources. *U.S. News & World Report*, "America's Best Graduate Schools, Medical, 2025"

According to *U.S. News & World Report*, the Columbia, SC metro area is home to one of the top 75 business schools in the U.S.: **University of South Carolina (Moore)** (#71). The rankings are based on a weighted average of the following nine measures: quality assessment; peer assessment; recruiter assessment; placement success; mean starting salary and bonus; student selectivity; mean GMAT and GRE scores; mean undergraduate GPA; and acceptance rate. *U.S. News & World Report*, "America's Best Graduate Schools, Business, 2025"

Columbia, South Carolina

EMPLOYERS

Major Employers

Company Name	Industry
AnMed Health	Healthcare
Baldor Electric Co	Utilities
Ben Arnold Beverage Co	Beverages
Berkeley County School Dist	Education
BlueCross BlueShield of SC	Finance, insurance and real estate
BMW Manufacturing Co	Manufacturing
Bon Secours St Francis Hosp	Healthcare
Charleston AIR Force Base	U.S. military
City of Columbia	Municipal government
Clemson University Research	Healthcare
Continental Tire North America	Wholesaling/manufacturing
Corrections Dept.	Government
Crescent Moon Diving	Professional, scientific, technical
Fluor Enterprises Inc	Engineering services
Greenville Memorial Hospital	Healthcare
Lexington Medical Ctr	Healthcare
McLeod Health	Healthcare
Medical University of SC	Healthcare/university
Palmetto Health	Healthcare & social assistance
Piggly Wiggly	Grocery stores

Note: Companies shown are located within the Columbia, SC Metropolitan Statistical Area.
Source: Chambers of Commerce; State Departments of Labor; Wikipedia

PUBLIC SAFETY

Crime Rate

Area	Total Crime Rate	Violent Crime Rate				Property Crime Rate		
		Murder	Rape	Robbery	Aggrav. Assault	Burglary	Larceny-Theft	Motor Vehicle Theft
City	4,223.4	7.8	45.2	107.4	596.5	455.8	2,537.2	473.5
U.S.	2,290.9	5.7	38.0	66.5	264.1	250.7	1,347.2	318.7

Note: Figures are crimes per 100,000 population.
Source: FBI, Table 8, Offenses Known to Law Enforcement, by State by City, 2023

Hate Crimes

Area	Number of Quarters Reported	Number of Incidents per Bias Motivation					
		Race/Ethnicity/Ancestry	Religion	Sexual Orientation	Disability	Gender	Gender Identity
City	4	1	0	0	0	0	0
U.S.	4	5,900	2,699	2,077	187	92	492

Source: Federal Bureau of Investigation, Hate Crime Statistics 2023

Identity Theft Consumer Reports

Area	Reports	Reports per 100,000 Population	Rank[2]
MSA[1]	2,758	328	47
U.S.	1,135,291	339	-

Note: (1) Figures cover the Columbia, SC Metropolitan Statistical Area; (2) Rank ranges from 1 to 401 where 1 indicates greatest number of identity theft reports per 100,000 population
Source: Federal Trade Commission, Consumer Sentinel Network Data Book 2024

Fraud and Other Consumer Reports

Area	Reports	Reports per 100,000 Population	Rank[2]
MSA[1]	13,548	1,613	42
U.S.	5,360,641	1,601	-

Note: (1) Figures cover the Columbia, SC Metropolitan Statistical Area; (2) Rank ranges from 1 to 401 where 1 indicates greatest number of fraud and other consumer reports per 100,000 population
Source: Federal Trade Commission, Consumer Sentinel Network Data Book 2024

POLITICS

2024 Presidential Election Results

Area	Trump (Rep.)	Harris (Dem.)	Stein (Green)	Kennedy (Ind.)	Oliver (Lib.)	Other
Richland County	31.8	66.4	0.4	0.0	0.5	0.9
U.S.	49.7	48.2	0.6	0.5	0.4	0.6

Note: Results are percentages and may not add to 100% due to rounding
Source: Dave Leip's Atlas of U.S. Presidential Elections

SPORTS

Professional Sports Teams

Team Name	League	Year Established
No teams are located in the metro area		

Source: Wikipedia, Major Professional Sports Teams of the United States and Canada, May 1, 2025

CLIMATE

Average and Extreme Temperatures

Temperature	Jan	Feb	Mar	Apr	May	Jun	Jul	Aug	Sep	Oct	Nov	Dec	Yr.
Extreme High (°F)	84	84	91	94	101	107	107	107	101	101	90	83	107
Average High (°F)	56	60	67	77	84	90	92	91	85	77	67	59	75
Average Temp. (°F)	45	48	55	64	72	78	82	80	75	64	54	47	64
Average Low (°F)	33	35	42	50	59	66	70	69	64	51	41	35	51
Extreme Low (°F)	-1	5	4	26	34	44	54	53	40	23	12	4	-1

Note: Figures cover the years 1948-1990
Source: National Climatic Data Center, International Station Meteorological Climate Summary, 9/96

Average Precipitation/Snowfall/Humidity

Precip./Humidity	Jan	Feb	Mar	Apr	May	Jun	Jul	Aug	Sep	Oct	Nov	Dec	Yr.
Avg. Precip. (in.)	4.0	4.0	4.7	3.4	3.6	4.2	5.5	5.9	4.0	2.9	2.7	3.4	48.3
Avg. Snowfall (in.)	1	1	Tr	0	0	0	0	0	0	0	Tr	Tr	2
Avg. Rel. Hum. 7am (%)	83	83	84	82	84	85	88	91	91	90	88	84	86
Avg. Rel. Hum. 4pm (%)	51	47	44	41	46	50	54	56	54	49	48	51	49

Note: Figures cover the years 1948-1990; Tr = Trace amounts (<0.05 in. of rain; <0.5 in. of snow)
Source: National Climatic Data Center, International Station Meteorological Climate Summary, 9/96

Weather Conditions

Temperature			Daytime Sky			Precipitation		
10°F & below	32°F & below	90°F & above	Clear	Partly cloudy	Cloudy	0.01 inch or more precip.	0.1 inch or more snow/ice	Thunder-storms
< 1	58	77	97	149	119	110	1	53

Note: Figures are average number of days per year and cover the years 1948-1990
Source: National Climatic Data Center, International Station Meteorological Climate Summary, 9/96

HAZARDOUS WASTE

Superfund Sites

The Columbia, SC metro area is home to five sites on the EPA's Superfund National Priorities List (NPL) or Superfund Alternative Approach (SAA) list: **Lexington County Landfill Area** (Final NPL); **Palmetto Wood Preserving** (Final NPL); **SCRDI Bluff Road** (Final NPL); **SCRDI Dixiana** (Final NPL); **Townsend Saw Chain Co.** (Final NPL). The Superfund alternative approach uses the same investigation and cleanup process and standards that are used for sites listed on the National Priorities List. The SAA is an alternative to listing a site on the NPL; it is not an alternative to Superfund or the Superfund process. There are a total of 1,445 Superfund sites with a status of proposed or final on both lists in the United States. *U.S. Environmental Protection Agency, National Priorities List, May 1, 2025; U.S. Environmental Protection Agency, Superfund Alternative Approach Sites, May 1, 2025*

AIR QUALITY

Air Quality Trends: Ozone

	1990	1995	2000	2005	2010	2015	2020	2021	2022	2023
MSA[1]	0.091	0.079	0.089	0.082	0.069	0.058	0.053	0.061	0.061	0.064
U.S.	0.087	0.089	0.081	0.080	0.072	0.068	0.066	0.067	0.067	0.070

Note: (1) Data covers the Columbia, SC Metropolitan Statistical Area. The values shown are the composite ozone concentration averages among trend sites based on the highest fourth daily maximum 8-hour concentration in parts per million. These trends are based on sites having an adequate record of monitoring data during the trend period. Data from exceptional events are included.
Source: U.S. Environmental Protection Agency, Air Quality Monitoring Information, "Air Quality Trends by City, 1990-2023"

Air Quality Index

Area	Percent of Days when Air Quality was...[2]					AQI Statistics[2]	
	Good	Moderate	Unhealthy for Sensitive Groups	Unhealthy	Very Unhealthy	Maximum	Median
MSA[1]	54.5	44.4	1.1	0.0	0.0	123	48

Note: (1) Data covers the Columbia, SC Metropolitan Statistical Area; (2) Based on 365 days with AQI data in 2023. Air Quality Index (AQI) is an index for reporting daily air quality. EPA calculates the AQI for five major air pollutants regulated by the Clean Air Act: ground-level ozone, particle pollution (aka particulate matter), carbon monoxide, sulfur dioxide, and nitrogen dioxide. The AQI runs from 0 to 500. The higher the AQI value, the greater the level of air pollution and the greater the health concern. There are six AQI categories: "Good" AQI is between 0 and 50. Air quality is considered satisfactory; "Moderate" AQI is between 51 and 100. Air quality is acceptable; "Unhealthy for Sensitive Groups" When AQI values are between 101 and 150, members of sensitive groups may experience health effects; "Unhealthy" When AQI values are between 151 and 200 everyone may begin to experience health effects; "Very Unhealthy" AQI values between 201 and 300 trigger a health alert; "Hazardous" AQI values over 300 trigger warnings of emergency conditions (not shown).
Source: U.S. Environmental Protection Agency, Air Quality Index Report, 2023

Air Quality Index Pollutants

Area	Percent of Days when AQI Pollutant was...[2]					
	Carbon Monoxide	Nitrogen Dioxide	Ozone	Sulfur Dioxide	Particulate Matter 2.5	Particulate Matter 10
MSA[1]	0.0	0.3	32.9	(3)	66.8	0.0

Note: (1) Data covers the Columbia, SC Metropolitan Statistical Area; (2) Based on 365 days with AQI data in 2023. The Air Quality Index (AQI) is an index for reporting daily air quality. EPA calculates the AQI for five major air pollutants regulated by the Clean Air Act: ground-level ozone, particle pollution (also known as particulate matter), carbon monoxide, sulfur dioxide, and nitrogen dioxide. The AQI runs from 0 to 500. The higher the AQI value, the greater the level of air pollution and the greater the health concern; (3) Sulfur dioxide is no longer included in this table because SO_2 concentrations tend to be very localized and not necessarily representative of broad geographical areas like counties and CBSAs.
Source: U.S. Environmental Protection Agency, Air Quality Index Report, 2023

Maximum Air Pollutant Concentrations: Particulate Matter, Ozone, CO and Lead

	Particulate Matter 10 (ug/m³)	Particulate Matter 2.5 Wtd AM (ug/m³)	Particulate Matter 2.5 24-Hr (ug/m³)	Ozone (ppm)	Carbon Monoxide (ppm)	Lead (ug/m³)
MSA[1] Level	44	8.2	22	0.069	1	n/a
NAAQS[2]	150	15	35	0.075	9	0.15
Met NAAQS[2]	Yes	Yes	Yes	Yes	Yes	n/a

Note: (1) Data covers the Columbia, SC Metropolitan Statistical Area; Data from exceptional events are included; (2) National Ambient Air Quality Standards; ppm = parts per million; ug/m³ = micrograms per cubic meter; n/a not available.
Concentrations: Particulate Matter 10 (coarse particulate)—highest second maximum 24-hour concentration; Particulate Matter 2.5 Wtd AM (fine particulate)—highest weighted annual mean concentration; Particulate Matter 2.5 24-Hour (fine particulate)—highest 98th percentile 24-hour concentration; Ozone—highest fourth daily maximum 8-hour concentration; Carbon Monoxide—highest second maximum non-overlapping 8-hour concentration; Lead—maximum running 3-month average
Source: U.S. Environmental Protection Agency, Air Quality Monitoring Information, "Air Quality Statistics by City, 2023"

Maximum Air Pollutant Concentrations: Nitrogen Dioxide and Sulfur Dioxide

	Nitrogen Dioxide AM (ppb)	Nitrogen Dioxide 1-Hr (ppb)	Sulfur Dioxide AM (ppb)	Sulfur Dioxide 1-Hr (ppb)	Sulfur Dioxide 24-Hr (ppb)
MSA[1] Level	3	28	n/a	2	n/a
NAAQS[2]	53	100	30	75	140
Met NAAQS[2]	Yes	Yes	n/a	Yes	n/a

Note: (1) Data covers the Columbia, SC Metropolitan Statistical Area; Data from exceptional events are included; (2) National Ambient Air Quality Standards; ppm = parts per million; ug/m³ = micrograms per cubic meter; n/a not available.
Concentrations: Nitrogen Dioxide AM—highest arithmetic mean concentration; Nitrogen Dioxide 1-Hr—highest 98th percentile 1-hour daily maximum concentration; Sulfur Dioxide AM—highest annual mean concentration; Sulfur Dioxide 1-Hr—highest 99th percentile 1-hour daily maximum concentration; Sulfur Dioxide 24-Hr—highest second maximum 24-hour concentration
Source: U.S. Environmental Protection Agency, Air Quality Monitoring Information, "Air Quality Statistics by City, 2023"

Dallas, Texas

Background

Dallas, in northeast Texas, is the largest inland metropolitan area in the U.S. that lacks any navigable link to the sea. Founded in 1841 by Tennessee lawyer and trader, John Neely Bryan, Dallas symbolizes all that is big, exciting, and affluent. The city, combined with its neighbor Fort Worth, has one of the greatest concentrations of billionaires in the world.

Originally one of the largest markets for cotton in the U.S., Dallas is now one of the largest markets for oil in the country. In the 1930s, oil was struck on the eastern fields of Texas. As a result, oil companies were founded and billions were made, creating the face we now associate with Dallas and the state of Texas.

Today, oil still plays a dominant role in the Dallas economy. Outside of Alaska, Texas holds most of the U.S. oil reserves. For that reason, many oil companies choose to headquarter in the silver skyscrapers of Dallas, which is also home to 11 Fortune 500 companies.

In addition to employment opportunities in the oil industry, the Dallas branch of the Federal Reserve Bank, and a host of other banks and investment firms clustering around the Federal Reserve hub, employ thousands. Other important industries important to the city's economy are aircraft, advertising, film, and publishing. The city is sometimes referred to as Texas's "Silicon Prairie" because of a high concentration of telecommunications companies.

The Kay Bailey Hutchison Convention Center Dallas, with more than two million square feet (over one million in exhibit space), is the largest convention center in Texas, and one of the largest in the country, welcoming over a million visitors each year. Plans are moving ahead to expand the KBHCCD by 2029. Dallas also has a significant cultural presence with independent theater groups sponsored by Southern Methodist University; Museum of Art with its collection of modern, especially American, art; and Winspear Opera House as part of the AT&T Performing Arts Center.

Dallas Opera has showcased Maria Callas, Joan Sutherland, and Monserrat Caballe. Dallas is the only city in the world with four buildings within one contiguous block designed by Pritzker Architecture Prize winners. The city also boasts historical districts such as the Swiss Avenue District, and elegant buildings such as the City Hall Building designed by I.M. Pei. A notable city event is the State Fair of Texas, which has been held annually at Fair Park since 1886 with exceptions during WWI and II and COVID-19. Recent numbers report the total annual attendance at 2.4 million with an estimated $680 million impact to the city's economy.

The area's high concentration of wealth contributes to Dallas's wide array of shopping centers and high-end boutiques. Downtown Dallas is home to cafes, restaurants, clubs, and its centrally located "Arts District," named for its many independent theaters and art galleries. Northern districts of the city and the central downtown have seen much urban revival in the last 30 years.

Colleges and universities in the Dallas area include Southern Methodist University, University of Dallas, and University of Texas at Dallas. In 2006, University of North Texas opened a branch in the southern part of the city, in part, to help accelerate development south of downtown Dallas. The city maintains 21,000 acres of park land, with over 400 parks.

Dallas has a humid subtropical climate characteristic of the Southern Plains of the United States. It also has both continental and tropical characteristics, characterized by a relatively wide annual temperature range. Located at the lower end of Tornado Alley, it is prone to extreme weather, tornadoes, and hailstorms. Summers in Dallas are very hot with high humidity, although extended periods of dry weather often occur. Winters in Dallas are usually mild, with occasional cold spells.

Rankings

General Rankings

- To help military veterans find the best places in which to settle down, *WalletHub* compared the 100 largest U.S. cities across 19 key indicators of livability, affordability and veteran-friendliness. They range from the share of military skill-related jobs to veteran income growth to the availability of VA health facilities. Dallas ranked #25. *Wallethub.com, "Best & Worst Places for Veterans to Live (2025)," November 7, 2024*

- The human resources consulting firm Mercer ranked 241 major cities worldwide in terms of overall quality of life. Dallas ranked #59. Criteria: political and personal safety, social, and economic factors; medical and health considerations; schools and education; public services and transportation; recreation; connectivity; housing and infrastructure; and climate. *Mercer, "Mercer 2024 Quality of Living Survey," December 2024*

Business/Finance Rankings

- Payscale.com ranked the 32 largest metro areas in terms of wage growth. The Dallas metro area ranked #6. Criteria: quarterly changes in private industry employee and education professional wage growth from the previous year. *PayScale, "Wage Trends by Metro Area-4th Quarter," February 4, 2025*

- Dallas was cited as one of America's top metros for total corporate facility investment projects in 2024. The area ranked #3 in the Tier 1 (large) metro area category (population over 1 million). *Site Selection, "Top Metros of 2024," March 2025*

- The Dallas metro area appeared on the Milken Institute "2025 Best Performing Cities" list. Rank: #19 out of 200 large metro areas (based on performance category). Criteria: job growth; wage growth; high-tech growth and impact; community resilience; housing affordability; household broadband access. *Milken Institute, "Best-Performing Cities 2025," January 14, 2025*

- Mercer Human Resources Consulting ranked 226 cities worldwide in terms of cost-of-living. Dallas ranked #55 (the lower the ranking, the higher the cost-of-living). The survey measured the comparative cost of over 200 items (such as housing, food, clothing, domestic supplies, transportation, and recreation/entertainment) in each location. *Mercer, "2024 Cost of Living City Ranking," June 17, 2024*

Dating/Romance Rankings

- *Apartment List* conducted its Annual Renter Satisfaction Survey and asked renters "how satisfied are you with opportunities for dating in your current city." The cities were ranked from highest to lowest based on their satisfaction scores. Dallas ranked #10 out of 10 cities. *Apartment List, "Best Cities for Dating 2022 with Local Dating Insights from Bumble," February 7, 2022*

Education Rankings

- Personal finance website *WalletHub* analyzed the 150 largest U.S. metropolitan statistical areas to determine where the most educated Americans are putting their degrees to work. Criteria: education levels; percentage of workers with degrees; education quality and attainment gap; public school quality rankings; quality and enrollment of each metro area's universities. Dallas was ranked #72 (#1 = most educated city). *WalletHub.com, "Most & Least Educated Cities in America, 2025" July 2, 2024*

Environmental Rankings

- Sperling's *BestPlaces* assessed the 50 largest metropolitan areas of the United States for the likelihood of dangerously extreme weather events or earthquakes. In general the Southeast and South-Central regions have the highest risk of weather extremes and earthquakes, while the Pacific Northwest enjoys the lowest risk. Of the most risky metropolitan areas, the Dallas metro area was ranked #4. *Bestplaces.net, "Avoid Natural Disasters: BestPlaces Reveals The Top 10 Safest Places to Live," October 25, 2017*

- The U.S. Environmental Protection Agency (EPA) released its list of U.S. metropolitan areas with the most ENERGY STAR certified buildings in 2023. The Dallas metro area was ranked #6 out of 25. *U.S. Environmental Protection Agency, "2024 Energy Star Top Cities," May 22, 2024*

- Dallas was highlighted as one of the 25 most ozone-polluted metro areas in the U.S. during 2021 through 2023. The area ranked #10. *American Lung Association, "State of the Air 2025," April 23, 2025*

Health/Fitness Rankings

- For each of the 100 largest cities in the United States, the American Fitness Index®, compiled in partnership between the American College of Sports Medicine and the Elevance Health Foundation, evaluated community infrastructure and more than 30 health behaviors including preventive health, levels of chronic disease conditions, food insecurity, pedestrian safety, air quality, and community/environment resources that support physical activity. Dallas ranked #53 for "community fitness." *americanfitnessindex.org, "2024 ACSM American Fitness Index Summary Report," July 23, 2024*

- Dallas was identified as a "2025 Allergy Capital." The area ranked #13 out of the nation's 100 largest metropolitan areas. Three groups of factors were used to identify the most challenging cities for people with allergies: annual tree, grass, and weed pollen scores; over the counter allergy medicine use; number of board-certified allergy specialists. *Asthma and Allergy Foundation of America, "2025 Allergy Capitals: The Most Challenging Places to Live with Allergies," March 18, 2025*

- Dallas was identified as a "2024 Asthma Capital." The area ranked #28 out of the nation's 100 largest metropolitan areas. Criteria: estimated asthma prevalence; asthma-related mortality; and ER visits due to asthma. Risk factors analyzed but not factored in the rankings: annual air quality including pollution and ozone levels; public smoking laws; indoor air quality; access to asthma specialists; rescue and controller medication use; uninsured rate; pollen allergy; poverty rate. *Asthma and Allergy Foundation of America, "Asthma Capitals 2024: The Most Challenging Places to Live With Asthma," September 10, 2024*

Pet Rankings

- Dallas was selected by *Sniffspot.com* as one of the most dog-friendly cities in the U.S., ranking #24 out of 50. Criteria: dog parks; hiking; sniffspots; public parks; dog-friendly businesses; housing; dog waste cleanliness; leash laws; dog services; and overall cost. *Sniffspot.com, "The Top 50 Most Dog-Friendly Cities in the U.S.," September 30, 2024*

Real Estate Rankings

- *WalletHub* compared the most populated U.S. cities to determine which had the best markets for real estate agents. Dallas ranked #62 where demand was high and pay was the best. Criteria: sales per agent; annual median wage for real-estate agents; monthly average starting salary for real estate agents; real estate job density and competition; unemployment rate; home turnover rate; housing-market health index; and other relevant metrics. *WalletHub.com, "2021 Best Places to Be a Real Estate Agent," May 12, 2021*

- Dallas was ranked #111 out of 176 metro areas in terms of cost of housing in 2024 by the National Association of Home Builders (#1 = most affordable). Criteria: the portion of an average family's income necessary to pay the mortgage on a median-priced home. *National Association of Home Builders®, NAHB-Wells Fargo Cost of Housing Index, 4th Quarter 2024*

Safety Rankings

- Allstate ranked the 100 most populous cities in America in terms of driver safety. Dallas ranked #40. Criteria based on anonymized driving behavior data from Allstate's mobile app powered by Arity: high speed driving (over 80 mph), phone handling, and hard braking. The report helps increase the importance of safety and awareness behind the wheel. *Allstate, "16th Allstate America's Best Drivers Report®" July 11, 2024*

- The National Insurance Crime Bureau ranked the largest metro areas in the U.S. in terms of per capita rates of vehicle theft. The Dallas metro area ranked #5 out of the top 10 (#1 = highest rate). Criteria: number of vehicle theft offenses per 100,000 inhabitants in 2023. *National Insurance Crime Bureau, "Vehicle Thefts Surge Nationwide in 2023," April 9, 2024*

Sports/Recreation Rankings

- Dallas was chosen as a bicycle friendly community by the League of American Bicyclists. A "Bicycle Friendly Community" welcomes cyclists by providing safe and supportive accommodation for cycling and encouraging people to bike for transportation and recreation. There are four award levels: Platinum; Gold; Silver; and Bronze. The community achieved an award level of Bronze. *League of American Bicyclists, "2024 Awards-New & Renewing Bicycle Friendly Communities List," January 28, 2025*

Women/Minorities Rankings

- Personal finance website *WalletHub* compared more than 180 U.S. cities across two key dimensions, "Hispanic Business-Friendliness" and "Hispanic Purchasing Power," to arrive at the most favorable conditions for Hispanic entrepreneurs. Dallas was ranked #55 out of 182. Criteria includes: share of Hispanic-Owned Businesses; average growth of Hispanic Business revenues; Small Business-Friendliness score; affordability; and number of Hispanics with at least a bachelor's degree. *WalletHub.com, "Best Cities for Hispanic Entrepreneurs," September 4, 2024*

Miscellaneous Rankings

- *WalletHub* compared 148 of the most populated U.S. cities to determine their operating efficiency. A "Quality of Services" score was constructed for each city and then measured against the total budget per capita to reveal which were managed the best. Dallas ranked #97. Criteria: financial stability; economy; education; safety; health; infrastructure and pollution. *WalletHub.com, "2025's Best- & Worst-Run Cities in America," June 18, 2024*

Business Environment

DEMOGRAPHICS

Population Growth

Area	1990 Census	2000 Census	2010 Census	2020 Census	2023 Estimate[2]	Population Growth 1990-2023 (%)
City	1,006,971	1,188,580	1,197,816	1,304,379	1,299,553	29.1
MSA[1]	3,989,294	5,161,544	6,371,773	7,637,387	7,807,555	95.7
U.S.	248,709,873	281,421,906	308,745,538	331,449,281	332,387,540	33.6

Note: (1) Figures cover the Dallas-Fort Worth-Arlington, TX Metropolitan Statistical Area; (2) 2019-2023 5-year ACS population estimate
Source: U.S. Census Bureau, 1990 Census, 2000 Census, 2010 Census, 2020 Census, 2019-2023 American Community Survey 5-Year Estimates

Race

Area	White Alone[2] (%)	Black Alone[2] (%)	Asian Alone[2] (%)	AIAN[3] Alone[2] (%)	NHOPI[4] Alone[2] (%)	Other Race Alone[2] (%)	Two or More Races (%)
City	41.9	23.7	3.7	0.8	0.1	12.5	17.3
MSA[1]	52.7	16.2	7.8	0.6	0.1	8.0	14.5
U.S.	63.4	12.4	5.8	0.9	0.2	6.6	10.7

Note: (1) Figures cover the Dallas-Fort Worth-Arlington, TX Metropolitan Statistical Area; (2) Alone is defined as not being in combination with one or more other races; (3) American Indian and Alaska Native; (4) Native Hawaiian and Other Pacific Islander
Source: U.S. Census Bureau, 2019-2023 American Community Survey 5-Year Estimates

Hispanic or Latino Origin

Area	Total (%)	Mexican (%)	Puerto Rican (%)	Cuban (%)	Other (%)
City	41.9	33.6	0.6	0.4	7.4
MSA[1]	29.4	23.1	0.9	0.4	5.1
U.S.	19.0	11.3	1.8	0.7	5.2

Note: Persons of Hispanic or Latino origin can be of any race; (1) Figures cover the Dallas-Fort Worth-Arlington, TX Metropolitan Statistical Area
Source: U.S. Census Bureau, 2019-2023 American Community Survey 5-Year Estimates

Age

Area	Percent of Population									Median Age
	Under Age 5	Age 5–19	Age 20–34	Age 35–44	Age 45–54	Age 55–64	Age 65–74	Age 75–84	Age 85+	
City	7.0	19.5	26.0	13.8	11.6	10.7	7.0	3.1	1.3	33.4
MSA[1]	6.4	21.6	21.3	14.4	13.0	11.4	7.4	3.3	1.1	35.5
U.S.	5.7	19.1	20.2	13.1	12.3	12.8	10.0	4.9	1.9	38.7

Note: (1) Figures cover the Dallas-Fort Worth-Arlington, TX Metropolitan Statistical Area
Source: U.S. Census Bureau, 2019-2023 American Community Survey 5-Year Estimates

Disability by Age

Area	All Ages	Under 18 Years Old	18 to 64 Years Old	65 Years and Over
City	11.4	4.7	9.8	34.9
MSA[1]	10.1	4.0	8.5	32.0
U.S.	13.0	4.7	10.7	32.9

Note: Figures show percent of the civilian noninstitutionalized population that reported having a disability. Disability status is determined from six types of difficulty: vision, hearing, cognitive, ambulatory, self-care, and independent living. For children under 5 years old, hearing and vision difficulty are used to determine disability status. For children between the ages of 5 and 14, disability status is determined from hearing, vision, cognitive, ambulatory, and self-care difficulties. For people aged 15 years and older, they are considered to have a disability if they have difficulty with any one of the six difficulty types; Note: (1) Figures cover the Dallas-Fort Worth-Arlington, TX Metropolitan Statistical Area
Source: U.S. Census Bureau, 2019-2023 American Community Survey 5-Year Estimates

Ancestry

Area	German	Irish	English	American	Italian	Polish	French[2]	European	Scottish
City	5.4	4.4	6.0	3.8	1.7	0.8	1.2	1.2	1.1
MSA[1]	8.1	6.4	8.7	5.3	2.2	1.0	1.4	1.4	1.5
U.S.	12.6	9.4	9.1	5.5	4.9	2.6	2.0	1.4	1.6

Note: Figures are the percentage of the total population reporting a particular ancestry. The nine most commonly reported ancestries in the U.S. are shown. Figures include multiple ancestries (e.g. if a person reported being Irish and Italian, they were included in both columns); (1) Figures cover the Dallas-Fort Worth-Arlington, TX Metropolitan Statistical Area; (2) Excludes Basque
Source: U.S. Census Bureau, 2019-2023 American Community Survey 5-Year Estimates

Foreign-born Population

Area	Percent of Population Born in								
	Any Foreign Country	Asia	Mexico	Europe	Caribbean	Central America[2]	South America	Africa	Canada
City	23.4	2.9	12.8	0.8	0.4	3.3	1.0	2.0	0.1
MSA[1]	19.0	6.0	7.4	0.8	0.3	1.7	0.8	1.7	0.2
U.S.	13.9	4.3	3.3	1.4	1.4	1.2	1.2	0.8	0.2

Note: (1) Figures cover the Dallas-Fort Worth-Arlington, TX Metropolitan Statistical Area; (2) Excludes Mexico.
Source: U.S. Census Bureau, 2019-2023 American Community Survey 5-Year Estimates

Household Size

Area	Persons in Household (%)							Average Household Size
	One	Two	Three	Four	Five	Six	Seven or More	
City	37.1	29.7	12.7	10.1	6.1	2.6	1.6	2.43
MSA[1]	25.9	30.9	16.4	14.7	7.5	2.9	1.7	2.73
U.S.	28.5	33.8	15.4	12.7	5.9	2.3	1.4	2.54

Note: (1) Figures cover the Dallas-Fort Worth-Arlington, TX Metropolitan Statistical Area
Source: U.S. Census Bureau, 2019-2023 American Community Survey 5-Year Estimates

Household Relationships

Area	Householder	Opposite-sex Spouse	Same-sex Spouse	Opposite-sex Unmarried Partner	Same-sex Unmarried Partner	Child[2]	Grandchild	Other Relatives	Non-relatives
City	40.1	13.4	0.4	2.6	0.3	28.6	3.2	6.2	4.0
MSA[1]	36.2	17.6	0.2	2.0	0.2	31.7	2.7	5.5	2.9
U.S.	38.3	17.5	0.2	2.5	0.2	28.3	2.4	4.8	3.4

Note: Figures are percent of the total population; (1) Figures cover the Dallas-Fort Worth-Arlington, TX Metropolitan Statistical Area; (2) Includes biological, adopted, and stepchildren of the householder
Source: U.S. Census Bureau, 2020 Census

Gender

Area	Males	Females	Males per 100 Females
City	647,372	652,181	99.3
MSA[1]	3,864,152	3,943,403	98.0
U.S.	164,545,087	167,842,453	98.0

Note: (1) Figures cover the Dallas-Fort Worth-Arlington, TX Metropolitan Statistical Area
Source: U.S. Census Bureau, 2019-2023 American Community Survey 5-Year Estimates

Marital Status

Area	Never Married	Now Married[2]	Separated	Widowed	Divorced
City	43.0	40.2	2.5	4.0	10.2
MSA[1]	33.4	50.6	1.7	4.2	10.0
U.S.	34.1	47.9	1.7	5.6	10.7

Note: Figures are percentages and cover the population 15 years of age and older; (1) Figures cover the Dallas-Fort Worth-Arlington, TX Metropolitan Statistical Area; (2) Excludes separated
Source: U.S. Census Bureau, 2019-2023 American Community Survey 5-Year Estimates

Religious Groups by Family

Area	Catholic	Baptist	Methodist	LDS[2]	Pentecostal	Lutheran	Islam	Adventist	Other
MSA[1]	14.2	14.3	4.7	1.4	2.2	0.5	1.8	1.3	13.8
U.S.	18.7	7.3	3.0	2.0	1.8	1.7	1.3	1.3	11.6

Note: Figures are the number of adherents as a percentage of the total population and cover the eight largest religious groups in the U.S; (1) Figures cover the Dallas-Fort Worth-Arlington, TX Metropolitan Statistical Area; (2) Church of Jesus Christ of Latter-day Saints
Sources: 2020 U.S. Religion Census, Association of Statisticians of American Religious Bodies; The Association of Religion Data Archives (ARDA)

Religious Groups by Tradition

Area	Catholic	Evangelical Protestant	Mainline Protestant	Black Protestant	Islam	Judaism	Hinduism	Orthodox	Buddhism
MSA[1]	14.2	25.4	5.9	3.3	1.8	0.3	0.5	0.3	0.2
U.S.	18.7	16.5	5.2	2.3	1.3	0.6	0.4	0.4	0.3

Note: Figures are the number of adherents as a percentage of the total population; (1) Figures cover the Dallas-Fort Worth-Arlington, TX Metropolitan Statistical Area
Sources: 2020 U.S. Religion Census, Association of Statisticians of American Religious Bodies; The Association of Religion Data Archives (ARDA)

ECONOMY

Real Gross Domestic Product (GDP)

Area	2017	2018	2019	2020	2021	2022	2023	Rank[3]
MSA[1]	483.7	506.2	526.2	520.2	562.1	594.5	613.4	5
U.S.[2]	17,619.1	18,160.7	18,642.5	18,238.9	19,387.6	19,896.6	20,436.3	—

Note: Figures are in billions of chained 2017 dollars; (1) Figures cover the Dallas-Fort Worth-Arlington, TX Metropolitan Statistical Area; (2) Figures cover real GDP within metropolitan areas; (3) Rank is based on 2023 data and ranges from 1 to 384
Source: U.S. Bureau of Economic Analysis

Economic Growth

Area	2014	2015	2016	2017	2018	2019	2020	2021	2022	2023
MSA[1]	3.8	4.8	2.3	3.6	4.6	3.9	-1.1	8.1	5.8	3.2
U.S.[2]	2.6	3.2	2.0	2.7	3.1	2.7	-2.2	6.3	2.6	2.7

Note: Figures are real gross domestic product growth rates and represent percent change from preceding period; (1) Figures cover the Dallas-Fort Worth-Arlington, TX Metropolitan Statistical Area; (2) Figures are the average growth rates within metropolitan areas
Source: U.S. Bureau of Economic Analysis

Metropolitan Area Exports

Area	2018	2019	2020	2021	2022	2023	Rank[2]
MSA[1]	36,260.9	39,474.0	35,642.0	43,189.0	50,632.9	51,863.7	6
U.S.	1,664,056.1	1,645,173.7	1,431,406.6	1,753,941.4	2,062,937.4	2,019,160.5	—

Note: Figures are in millions of dollars; (1) Figures cover the Dallas-Fort Worth-Arlington, TX Metropolitan Statistical Area; (2) Rank is based on 2023 data and ranges from 1 to 386
Source: U.S. Department of Commerce, International Trade Administration, Office of Trade and Economic Analysis, Industry and Analysis, Exports by Metropolitan Area, data extracted April 2, 2025

Building Permits

Area	Single-Family 2023	Single-Family 2024	Pct. Chg.	Multi-Family 2023	Multi-Family 2024	Pct. Chg.	Total 2023	Total 2024	Pct. Chg.
City	1,995	1,957	-1.9	4,429	4,081	-7.9	6,424	6,038	-6.0
MSA[1]	44,366	46,440	4.7	23,663	25,348	7.1	68,029	71,788	5.5
U.S.	920,000	981,900	6.7	591,100	496,100	-16.1	1,511,100	1,478,000	-2.2

Note: (1) Figures cover the Dallas-Fort Worth-Arlington, TX Metropolitan Statistical Area; Figures represent new, privately-owned housing units authorized (unadjusted data)
Source: U.S. Census Bureau, Building Permits Survey (BPS), 2023, 2024

Bankruptcy Filings

Area	Business Filings 2023	Business Filings 2024	% Chg.	Nonbusiness Filings 2023	Nonbusiness Filings 2024	% Chg.
Dallas County	296	496	67.6	2,363	3,025	28.0
U.S.	18,926	23,107	22.1	434,064	494,201	13.9

Note: Business filings include Chapter 7, Chapter 9, Chapter 11, Chapter 12, Chapter 13, Chapter 15, and Section 304; Nonbusiness filings include Chapter 7, Chapter 11, and Chapter 13
Source: Administrative Office of the U.S. Courts, Business and Nonbusiness Bankruptcy, County Cases Commenced by Chapter of the Bankruptcy Code, During the 12-Month Period Ending December 31, 2023 and Business and Nonbusiness Bankruptcy, County Cases Commenced by Chapter of the Bankruptcy Code, During the 12-Month Period Ending December 31, 2024

Housing Vacancy Rates

Area	Gross Vacancy Rate[3] (%) 2022	2023	2024	Year-Round Vacancy Rate[4] (%) 2022	2023	2024	Rental Vacancy Rate[5] (%) 2022	2023	2024	Homeowner Vacancy Rate[6] (%) 2022	2023	2024
MSA[1]	6.6	7.6	7.9	6.3	7.2	7.6	6.8	8.4	8.9	0.7	0.8	1.3
U.S.[2]	9.1	9.0	9.1	7.5	7.5	7.6	5.7	6.5	6.8	0.8	0.8	1.0

Note: (1) Figures cover the Dallas-Fort Worth-Arlington, TX Metropolitan Statistical Area; (2) Figures cover the 75 largest Metropolitan Statistical Areas; (3) The percentage of the total housing inventory that is vacant; (4) The percentage of the housing inventory (excluding seasonal units) that is year-round vacant; (5) The percentage of rental inventory that is vacant for rent; (6) The percentage of homeowner inventory that is vacant for sale
Source: U.S. Census Bureau, Housing Vacancies and Homeownership Annual Statistics: 2022, 2023, 2024

INCOME

Income

Area	Per Capita ($)	Median Household ($)	Average Household ($)
City	44,138	67,760	106,979
MSA[1]	44,447	87,155	120,397
U.S.	43,289	78,538	110,491

Note: (1) Figures cover the Dallas-Fort Worth-Arlington, TX Metropolitan Statistical Area
Source: U.S. Census Bureau, 2019-2023 American Community Survey 5-Year Estimates

Household Income Distribution

Area	Percent of Households Earning							
	Under $15,000	$15,000 -$24,999	$25,000 -$34,999	$35,000 -$49,999	$50,000 -$74,999	$75,000 -$99,999	$100,000 -$149,999	$150,000 and up
City	10.2	6.8	7.7	12.3	17.9	12.5	13.7	18.8
MSA[1]	6.3	4.9	5.8	10.0	16.1	13.1	18.5	25.2
U.S.	8.5	6.6	6.8	10.4	15.7	12.7	17.4	21.9

Note: (1) Figures cover the Dallas-Fort Worth-Arlington, TX Metropolitan Statistical Area
Source: U.S. Census Bureau, 2019-2023 American Community Survey 5-Year Estimates

Poverty Rate

Area	All Ages	Under 18 Years Old	18 to 64 Years Old	65 Years and Over
City	17.2	25.7	14.3	15.0
MSA[1]	10.5	14.5	9.2	9.3
U.S.	12.4	16.3	11.6	10.4

Note: Figures are percentage of people whose income during the past 12 months was below the poverty level; (1) Figures cover the Dallas-Fort Worth-Arlington, TX Metropolitan Statistical Area
Source: U.S. Census Bureau, 2019-2023 American Community Survey 5-Year Estimates

EMPLOYMENT

Labor Force and Employment

Area	Civilian Labor Force			Workers Employed		
	Dec. 2023	Dec. 2024	% Chg.	Dec. 2023	Dec. 2024	% Chg.
City	753,950	773,828	2.6	727,021	746,370	2.7
MD[1]	3,019,102	3,099,037	2.6	2,914,521	2,992,023	2.7
U.S.	166,661,000	167,746,000	0.7	160,754,000	161,294,000	0.3

Note: Data is not seasonally adjusted and covers workers 16 years of age and older; (1) Figures cover the Dallas-Plano-Irving, TX Metropolitan Division
Source: Bureau of Labor Statistics, Local Area Unemployment Statistics

Unemployment Rate

Area	2024											
	Jan.	Feb.	Mar.	Apr.	May	Jun.	Jul.	Aug.	Sep.	Oct.	Nov.	Dec.
City	4.0	4.1	3.9	3.5	3.7	4.3	4.3	4.3	4.0	4.0	4.0	3.5
MD[1]	3.9	4.0	3.8	3.4	3.6	4.2	4.2	4.2	3.9	3.8	3.8	3.5
U.S.	4.1	4.2	3.9	3.5	3.7	4.3	4.5	4.4	3.9	3.9	4.0	3.8

Note: Data is not seasonally adjusted and covers workers 16 years of age and older; (1) Figures cover the Dallas-Plano-Irving, TX Metropolitan Division
Source: Bureau of Labor Statistics, Local Area Unemployment Statistics

Average Wages

Occupation	$/Hr.	Occupation	$/Hr.
Accountants and Auditors	45.03	Maintenance and Repair Workers	24.02
Automotive Mechanics	27.86	Marketing Managers	74.76
Bookkeepers	25.94	Network and Computer Systems Admin.	50.61
Carpenters	24.01	Nurses, Licensed Practical	30.36
Cashiers	14.32	Nurses, Registered	46.50
Computer Programmers	47.68	Nursing Assistants	18.80
Computer Systems Analysts	57.86	Office Clerks, General	21.12
Computer User Support Specialists	29.72	Physical Therapists	52.68
Construction Laborers	19.90	Physicians	105.52
Cooks, Restaurant	17.09	Plumbers, Pipefitters and Steamfitters	30.24
Customer Service Representatives	21.47	Police and Sheriff's Patrol Officers	41.90
Dentists	96.90	Postal Service Mail Carriers	29.14
Electricians	28.56	Real Estate Sales Agents	35.39
Engineers, Electrical	56.38	Retail Salespersons	16.85
Fast Food and Counter Workers	13.48	Sales Representatives, Technical/Scientific	49.39
Financial Managers	83.96	Secretaries, Exc. Legal/Medical/Executive	22.33
First-Line Supervisors of Office Workers	36.12	Security Guards	19.16
General and Operations Managers	67.98	Surgeons	172.43
Hairdressers/Cosmetologists	17.46	Teacher Assistants, Exc. Postsecondary[1]	14.37
Home Health and Personal Care Aides	13.45	Teachers, Secondary School, Exc. Sp. Ed.[1]	31.75
Janitors and Cleaners	16.43	Telemarketers	17.73
Landscaping/Groundskeeping Workers	18.42	Truck Drivers, Heavy/Tractor-Trailer	28.88
Lawyers	85.71	Truck Drivers, Light/Delivery Services	23.68
Maids and Housekeeping Cleaners	15.45	Waiters and Waitresses	15.52

Note: Wage data covers the Dallas-Fort Worth-Arlington, TX Metropolitan Statistical Area; (1) Hourly wages were calculated from annual wage data based on a 40 hour work week
Source: Bureau of Labor Statistics, Metro Area Occupational Employment & Wage Estimates, May 2024

Employment by Industry

Sector	MD[1] Number of Employees	MD[1] Percent of Total	U.S. Percent of Total
Construction, Mining, and Logging	169,300	5.4	5.5
Financial Activities	310,000	10.0	5.8
Government	350,200	11.3	14.9
Information	77,700	2.5	1.9
Leisure and Hospitality	293,400	9.4	10.4
Manufacturing	204,100	6.6	8.0
Other Services	97,200	3.1	3.7
Private Education and Health Services	358,000	11.5	16.9
Professional and Business Services	628,100	20.2	14.2
Retail Trade	278,400	9.0	10.0
Transportation, Warehousing, and Utilities	168,100	5.4	4.8
Wholesale Trade	175,500	5.6	3.9

Note: Figures are non-farm employment as of December 2024. Figures are not seasonally adjusted and include workers 16 years of age and older; (1) Figures cover the Dallas-Plano-Irving, TX Metropolitan Division
Source: Bureau of Labor Statistics, Current Employment Statistics, Employment, Hours, and Earnings

Employment by Occupation

Occupation Classification	City (%)	MSA[1] (%)	U.S. (%)
Management, Business, Science, and Arts	40.4	43.3	42.0
Natural Resources, Construction, and Maintenance	10.7	8.7	8.6
Production, Transportation, and Material Moving	13.1	12.8	13.0
Sales and Office	20.5	21.0	19.9
Service	15.4	14.2	16.5

Note: Figures cover employed civilians 16 years of age and older; (1) Figures cover the Dallas-Fort Worth-Arlington, TX Metropolitan Statistical Area
Source: U.S. Census Bureau, 2019-2023 American Community Survey 5-Year Estimates

Occupations with Greatest Projected Employment Growth: 2022 – 2032

Occupation[1]	2022 Employment	2032 Projected Employment	Numeric Employment Change	Percent Employment Change
General and Operations Managers	425,560	504,280	78,720	18.5
Fast Food and Counter Workers	333,870	394,290	60,420	18.1
Stockers and Order Fillers	264,810	321,600	56,790	21.4
Home Health and Personal Care Aides	313,670	367,500	53,830	17.2
Software Developers	110,280	161,780	51,500	46.7
Cooks, Restaurant	113,680	158,830	45,150	39.7
Laborers and Freight, Stock, and Material Movers, Hand	225,090	269,120	44,030	19.6
Heavy and Tractor-Trailer Truck Drivers	226,450	270,320	43,870	19.4
Retail Salespersons	319,400	357,630	38,230	12.0
Registered Nurses	233,850	267,980	34,130	14.6

Note: Projections cover Texas; (1) Sorted by numeric employment change
Source: www.projectionscentral.org, State Occupational Projections, 2022–2032 Long-Term Projections

Fastest-Growing Occupations: 2022 – 2032

Occupation[1]	2022 Employment	2032 Projected Employment	Numeric Employment Change	Percent Employment Change
Wind Turbine Service Technicians	4,860	7,950	3,090	63.6
Nurse Practitioners	19,060	30,490	11,430	60.0
Data Scientists	13,220	20,250	7,030	53.2
Computer and Information Research Scientists (SOC 2018)	2,070	3,140	1,070	51.7
Information Security Analysts (SOC 2018)	14,620	21,620	7,000	47.9
Software Developers	110,280	161,780	51,500	46.7
Statisticians	980	1,430	450	45.9
Operations Research Analysts	12,060	17,290	5,230	43.4
Software Quality Assurance Analysts and Testers	17,350	24,440	7,090	40.9
Medical and Health Services Managers	49,430	69,180	19,750	40.0

Note: Projections cover Texas; (1) Sorted by percent employment change and excludes occupations with numeric employment change less than 50
Source: www.projectionscentral.org, State Occupational Projections, 2022–2032 Long-Term Projections

CITY FINANCES

City Government Finances

Component	2022 ($000)	2022 ($ per capita)
Total Revenues	4,563,574	3,397
Total Expenditures	4,384,018	3,264
Debt Outstanding	11,664,184	8,683

Source: U.S. Census Bureau, State & Local Government Finances 2022

City Government Revenue by Source

Source	2022 ($000)	2022 ($ per capita)	2022 (%)
General Revenue			
From Federal Government	458,432	341	10.0
From State Government	62,026	46	1.4
From Local Governments	19,144	14	0.4
Taxes			
Property	1,251,922	932	27.4
Sales and Gross Receipts	483,945	360	10.6
Personal Income	0	0	0.0
Corporate Income	0	0	0.0
Motor Vehicle License	0	0	0.0
Other Taxes	47,431	35	1.0
Current Charges	1,687,221	1,256	37.0
Liquor Store	0	0	0.0
Utility	412,158	307	9.0

Source: U.S. Census Bureau, State & Local Government Finances 2022

City Government Expenditures by Function

Function	2022 ($000)	2022 ($ per capita)	2022 (%)
General Direct Expenditures			
Air Transportation	1,225,112	912	27.9
Corrections	3,390	2	0.1
Education	0	0	0.0
Employment Security Administration	0	0	0.0
Financial Administration	43,790	32	1.0
Fire Protection	327,075	243	7.5
General Public Buildings	48,826	36	1.1
Governmental Administration, Other	40,435	30	0.9
Health	38,943	29	0.9
Highways	223,834	166	5.1
Hospitals	0	0	0.0
Housing and Community Development	81,112	60	1.9
Interest on General Debt	308,084	229	7.0
Judicial and Legal	37,442	27	0.9
Libraries	37,652	28	0.9
Parking	504	< 1	< 0.1
Parks and Recreation	241,451	179	5.5
Police Protection	497,575	370	11.3
Public Welfare	18,779	14	0.4
Sewerage	297,917	221	6.8
Solid Waste Management	99,780	74	2.3
Veterans' Services	0	0	0.0
Liquor Store	0	0	0.0
Utility	397,086	295	9.1

Source: U.S. Census Bureau, State & Local Government Finances 2022

TAXES

State Corporate Income Tax Rates

State	Tax Rate (%)	Income Brackets ($)	Num. of Brackets	Financial Institution Tax Rate (%)[a]	Federal Income Tax Ded.
Texas	(u)	—	—	(u)	No

Note: Tax rates for tax year 2024; (a) Rates listed are the corporate income tax rate applied to financial institutions or excise taxes based on income. Some states have other taxes based upon the value of deposits or shares; (u) Texas imposes a Franchise Tax, otherwise known as margin tax, imposed on entities with more than $2,470,000 total revenues effective in 2024 at rate of 0.75%, or 0.375% for entities primarily engaged in retail or wholesale trade, on lesser of 70% of total revenues or 100% of gross receipts after deductions for either compensation ($450,000 deduction limit) or cost of goods sold. Texas has an EZ rate of 0.331 applicable to a $20 million revenue threshold.
Source: Federation of Tax Administrators, State Corporate Income Tax Rates, January 1, 2025

State Individual Income Tax Rates

State	Tax Rate (%)	Income Brackets ($)	Personal Exemptions ($)			Standard Ded. ($)	
			Single	Married	Depend.	Single	Married
Texas	– No state income tax –						

Note: Tax rates for tax year 2024; Local- and county-level taxes are not included
Source: Federation of Tax Administrators, State Individual Income Tax Rates, January 1, 2025

Various State Sales and Excise Tax Rates

State	State Sales Tax (%)	Gasoline[1] ($/gal.)	Cigarette[2] ($/pack)	Spirits[3] ($/gal.)	Wine[4] ($/gal.)	Beer[5] ($/gal.)	Recreational Marijuana (%)
Texas	6.25	0.20	1.41	2.40	0.20	0.19	Not legal

Note: All tax rates as of January 1, 2025; (1) The American Petroleum Institute has developed a methodology for determining the average tax rate on a gallon of fuel. Rates may include any of the following: excise taxes, environmental fees, storage tank fees, other fees or taxes, general sales tax, and local taxes; (2) The federal excise tax of $1.0066 per pack and local taxes are not included; (3) Rates are those applicable to off-premise sales of 40% alcohol by volume (a.b.v.) distilled spirits in 750ml containers. Local excise taxes are excluded; (4) Rates are those applicable to off-premise sales of 11% a.b.v. non-carbonated wine in 750ml containers; (5) Rates are those applicable to off-premise sales of 4.7% a.b.v. beer in 12 ounce containers.
Source: Tax Foundation, 2025 Facts & Figures: How Does Your State Compare?

State Tax Competitiveness Index

State	Overall Rank	Corporate Tax Rank	Individual Income Tax Rank	Sales Tax Rank	Property Tax Rank	Unemployment Insurance Tax Rank
Texas	7	46	1	36	40	30

Note: The Tax Foundation's State Tax Competitiveness Index enables policymakers, taxpayers, and business leaders to gauge how their states' tax systems compare. A rank of 1 is best, 50 is worst. Rankings do not average to the total. States without a tax rank equally as 1. DC's scores and rankings do not affect other states. The report shows tax systems as of July 1, 2024 (the beginning of Fiscal Year 2025).
Source: Tax Foundation, State Tax Competitiveness Index 2025

TRANSPORTATION

Means of Transportation to Work

Area	Car/Truck/Van		Public Transportation			Bicycle	Walked	Other Means	Worked at Home
	Drove Alone	Car-pooled	Bus	Subway	Railroad				
City	68.5	11.4	1.7	0.2	0.1	0.2	2.2	1.7	14.0
MSA[1]	71.2	9.4	0.5	0.1	0.1	0.1	1.2	1.5	15.9
U.S.	70.2	8.5	1.7	1.3	0.4	0.4	2.4	1.6	13.5

Note: Figures are percentages and cover workers 16 years of age and older; (1) Figures cover the Dallas-Fort Worth-Arlington, TX Metropolitan Statistical Area
Source: U.S. Census Bureau, 2019-2023 American Community Survey 5-Year Estimates

Travel Time to Work

Area	Less Than 10 Minutes	10 to 19 Minutes	20 to 29 Minutes	30 to 44 Minutes	45 to 59 Minutes	60 to 89 Minutes	90 Minutes or More
City	8.8	28.5	23.6	24.7	7.4	5.6	1.5
MSA[1]	8.8	25.5	21.7	25.3	10.2	6.5	2.0
U.S.	12.6	28.6	21.2	20.8	8.1	6.0	2.8

Note: Note: Figures are percentages and include workers 16 years old and over; (1) Figures cover the Dallas-Fort Worth-Arlington, TX Metropolitan Statistical Area
Source: U.S. Census Bureau, 2019-2023 American Community Survey 5-Year Estimates

Key Congestion Measures

Measure	2000	2010	2015	2020	2022
Annual Hours of Delay, Total (000)	129,786	175,068	214,718	136,953	217,105
Annual Hours of Delay, Per Auto Commuter	47	50	63	40	68
Annual Congestion Cost, Per Auto Commuter ($)	1,181	1,266	1,434	948	1,523

Note: Figures cover the Dallas-Fort Worth-Arlington TX urban area
Source: Texas A&M Transportation Institute, 2023 Urban Mobility Report

Freeway Travel Time Index

Measure	1985	1990	1995	2000	2005	2010	2015	2020	2022
Urban Area Index[1]	1.19	1.20	1.23	1.24	1.26	1.25	1.26	1.12	1.23
Urban Area Rank[1,2]	6	9	8	18	22	21	23	10	24

Note: Freeway Travel Time Index—the ratio of travel time in the peak period to the travel time at free-flow conditions. For example, a value of 1.30 indicates a 20-minute free-flow trip takes 26 minutes in the peak (20 minutes x 1.30 = 26 minutes); (1) Covers the Dallas-Fort Worth-Arlington TX urban area; (2) Rank is based on 101 larger urban areas (#1 = highest travel time index)
Source: Texas A&M Transportation Institute, 2023 Urban Mobility Report

Public Transportation

Agency Name / Mode of Transportation	Vehicles Operated in Maximum Service[1]	Annual Unlinked Passenger Trips[2] (in thous.)	Annual Passenger Miles[3] (in thous.)
Dallas Area Rapid Transit Authority (DART)			
Bus (directly operated)	465	25,874.9	102,522.5
Commuter Rail (purchased transportation)	23	1,136.1	18,537.5
Demand Response (purchased transportation)	193	1,065.8	9,975.5
Demand Response - Taxi	25	0.3	12.8
Light Rail (directly operated)	75	20,495.4	152,050.9
Streetcar Rail (directly operated)	2	163.9	277.1

Note: (1) Number of revenue vehicles operated by the given mode and type of service to meet the annual maximum service requirement. This is the revenue vehicle count during the peak season of the year; on the week and day that maximum service is provided. Vehicles operated in maximum service (VOMS) exclude atypical days and one-time special events; (2) Number of passengers who boarded public transportation vehicles. Passengers are counted each time they board a vehicle no matter how many vehicles they use to travel from their origin to their destination. (3) Sum of the distances ridden by all passengers during the entire fiscal year.
Source: Federal Transit Administration, National Transit Database, 2023

Air Transportation

Airport Name and Code / Type of Service	Passenger Airlines[1]	Passenger Enplanements	Freight Carriers[2]	Freight (lbs)
Dallas-Fort Worth International (DFW)				
Domestic service (U.S. carriers only)	27	36,327,693	14	400,491,276
International service (U.S. carriers only)	10	4,672,307	7	68,452,785
Dallas Love Field (DAL)				
Domestic service (U.S. carriers only)	24	8,644,402	7	14,460,516
International service (U.S. carriers only)	5	5,554	1	6,750

Note: (1) Includes all U.S.-based major, minor and commuter airlines that carried at least one passenger during the year; (2) Includes all U.S.-based airlines and freight carriers that transported at least one pound of freight during the year.
Source: Bureau of Transportation Statistics, The Intermodal Transportation Database, Air Carriers: T-100 Domestic Market (U.S. carriers only), 2024; Bureau of Transportation Statistics, The Intermodal Transportation Database, Air Carriers: T-100 International Market (U.S. carriers only), 2024

BUSINESSES

Major Business Headquarters

Company Name	Industry	Fortune[1]	Forbes[2]
AECOM	Engineering & construction	291	-
AT&T	Telecommunications	32	-
Austin Industries	Construction	-	147
CBRE Group	Real estate	138	-
Energy Transfer	Pipelines	51	-
HF Sinclair	Petroleum refining	137	-
Highland Homes Holdings	Construction	-	260
Hunt Consolidated/Hunt Oil	Oil & gas operations	-	169
Jacobs Solutions	Diversified outsourcing services	249	-
Mode Global	Transportation	-	249
Sammons Enterprises	Banking and financial services	-	80
Southwest Airlines	Airlines	159	-
Tenet Healthcare	Health care: medical facilities	195	-
Texas Instruments	Semiconductors and other electronic components	234	-

Note: (1) Companies that produce a 10-K are ranked 1 to 500 based on 2023 revenue; (2) All private companies with at least $2 billion in annual revenue through the end of their most current fiscal year are ranked 1 to 275; companies listed are headquartered in the city; dashes indicate no ranking
Source: Fortune, "Fortune 500," 2024; Forbes, "America's Largest Private Companies," 2024

Fastest-Growing Businesses

According to *Inc.*, Dallas is home to six of America's 500 fastest-growing private companies: **Archer Review** (#46); **Built By Grid** (#98); **evolv Consulting** (#295); **Inclusion Cloud** (#323); **Curis Functional Health** (#325); **HighLevel** (#426). Criteria: must be an independent, privately-held, for-profit, U.S. corporation, proprietorship or partnership as of December 31, 2023; revenues must be at least $100,000 in 2020 and $2 million in 2023; must have four-year operating/sales history. *Inc., "America's 500 Fastest-Growing Private Companies," 2024*

According to Deloitte, Dallas is home to four of North America's 500 fastest-growing high-technology companies: **Archer Review** (#33); **HighLevel** (#103); **o9** (#430); **DataBank** (#489). Companies are ranked by percentage growth in revenue over a four-year period. Criteria for inclusion: company must be headquartered within North America; must own proprietary intellectual property or technol-

ogy that is sold to customers in products that contributes to a significant portion of the company's operating revenue; must have been in business for a minumum of four years with 2020 operating revenues of at least $50,000 USD/CD and 2023 operating revenues of at least $5 million USD/CD.
Deloitte, 2024 Technology Fast 500™

Living Environment

COST OF LIVING

Cost of Living Index

Composite Index	Groceries	Housing	Utilities	Transportation	Health Care	Misc. Goods/Services
101.7	98.9	95.1	115.6	91.2	104.5	107.4

Note: The Cost of Living Index measures regional differences in the cost of consumer goods and services, excluding taxes and non-consumer expenditures, for professional and managerial households in the top income quintile. It is based on more than 50,000 prices covering almost 60 different items for which prices are collected three times a year by chambers of commerce, economic development organizations or university applied economic centers in each participating urban area. The numbers shown should be read as a percentage above or below the national average of 100. For example, a value of 115.4 in the groceries column indicates that grocery prices are 15.4% higher than the national average. Small differences in the index numbers should not be interpreted as significant; Figures cover the Dallas TX urban area.
Source: The Council for Community and Economic Research, Cost of Living Index, 2024

Grocery Prices

Area[1]	T-Bone Steak ($/pound)	Frying Chicken ($/pound)	Whole Milk ($/half gal.)	Eggs ($/dozen)	Orange Juice ($/64 oz.)	Coffee ($/11.5 oz.)
City[2]	14.56	1.54	4.61	3.13	4.31	5.41
Avg.	15.42	1.55	4.69	3.25	4.41	5.46
Min.	14.50	1.16	4.43	2.75	4.00	4.85
Max.	17.56	2.89	5.49	4.78	5.54	7.89

Note: (1) Values for the local area are compared with the average, minimum and maximum values for all 276 areas in the Cost of Living Index; (2) Figures cover the Dallas TX urban area; **T-Bone Steak** (price per pound); **Frying Chicken** (price per pound, whole fryer); **Whole Milk** (half gallon carton); **Eggs** (price per dozen, Grade A, large); **Orange Juice** (64 oz. Tropicana or Florida Natural); **Coffee** (11.5 oz. can, vacuum-packed, Maxwell House, Hills Bros, or Folgers).
Source: The Council for Community and Economic Research, Cost of Living Index, 2024

Housing and Utility Costs

Area[1]	New Home Price ($)	Apartment Rent ($/month)	All Electric ($/month)	Part Electric ($/month)	Other Energy ($/month)	Telephone ($/month)
City[2]	477,656	1,572	-	171.06	80.72	203.47
Avg.	515,975	1,550	210.99	123.07	82.07	194.99
Min.	265,375	692	104.33	53.68	36.26	179.42
Max.	2,775,821	5,719	529.02	397.28	361.63	223.33

Note: (1) Values for the local area are compared with the average, minimum and maximum values for all 276 areas in the Cost of Living Index; (2) Figures cover the Dallas TX urban area; **New Home Price** (2,400 sf living area, 8,000 sf lot, in urban area with full utilities); **Apartment Rent** (950 sf 2 bedroom/1.5 or 2 bath, unfurnished, excluding all utilities except water); **All Electric** (average monthly cost for an all-electric home); **Part Electric** (average monthly cost for a part-electric home); **Other Energy** (average monthly cost for natural gas, fuel oil, coal, wood, and any other forms of energy except electricity); **Telephone** (price includes the base monthly rate plus taxes and fees for three lines of mobile phone service).
Source: The Council for Community and Economic Research, Cost of Living Index, 2024

Health Care, Transportation, and Other Costs

Area[1]	Doctor ($/visit)	Dentist ($/visit)	Optometrist ($/visit)	Gasoline ($/gallon)	Beauty Salon ($/visit)	Men's Shirt ($)
City[2]	138.26	133.49	135.65	3.07	72.78	43.45
Avg.	143.77	117.51	129.23	3.32	48.57	38.14
Min.	36.74	58.67	67.33	2.80	24.00	13.41
Max.	270.44	216.82	307.33	5.28	94.00	63.89

Note: (1) Values for the local area are compared with the average, minimum and maximum values for all 276 areas in the Cost of Living Index; (2) Figures cover the Dallas TX urban area; **Doctor** (general practitioners routine exam of an established patient); **Dentist** (adult teeth cleaning and periodic oral examination); **Optometrist** (full vision eye exam for established adult patient); **Gasoline** (one gallon regular unleaded, national brand, including all taxes, cash price at self-service pump if available); **Beauty Salon** (woman's shampoo, trim, and blow-dry); **Men's Shirt** (cotton/polyester dress shirt, pinpoint weave, long sleeves).
Source: The Council for Community and Economic Research, Cost of Living Index, 2024

HOUSING

Homeownership Rate

Area	2017 (%)	2018 (%)	2019 (%)	2020 (%)	2021 (%)	2022 (%)	2023 (%)	2024 (%)
MSA[1]	61.8	62.0	60.6	64.7	61.8	60.4	61.7	61.1
U.S.	63.9	64.4	64.6	66.6	65.5	65.8	65.9	65.6

Note: (1) Figures cover the Dallas-Fort Worth-Arlington, TX Metropolitan Statistical Area
Source: U.S. Census Bureau, Housing Vacancies and Homeownership Annual Statistics: 2017-2024

House Price Index (HPI)

Area	National Ranking[2]	Quarterly Change (%)	One-Year Change (%)	Five-Year Change (%)	Since 1991Q1 (%)
MD[1]	181	0.68	3.91	56.27	350.14
U.S.[3]	—	1.43	4.51	57.13	327.82

Note: The HPI is a weighted repeat sales index. It measures average price changes in repeat sales or refinancings on the same properties. This information is obtained by reviewing repeat mortgage transactions on single-family properties whose mortgages have been purchased or securitized by Fannie Mae or Freddie Mac since January 1975; (1) Figures cover the Dallas-Plano-Irving, TX Metropolitan Division; (2) Rankings are based on annual percentage change for all metro areas containing at least 15,000 transactions over the last 10 years and ranges from 1 to 241; (3) figures based on a weighted average of Census Division estimates using a seasonally adjusted, purchase-only index; all figures are for the period ending December 31, 2024
Source: Federal Housing Finance Agency, Change in FHFA Metropolitan Area House Price Indexes, All Transactions Index, 2024Q4

Home Value

Area	Under $100,000	$100,000 -$199,999	$200,000 -$299,999	$300,000 -$399,999	$400,000 -$499,999	$500,000 -$999,999	$1,000,000 or more	Median ($)
City	9.9	20.3	20.7	12.2	8.8	19.9	8.2	295,300
MSA[1]	6.8	13.3	23.8	20.1	13.1	18.8	4.1	330,300
U.S.	12.1	17.8	19.5	14.4	10.5	19.1	6.5	303,400

Note: Figures are percentages except for median and cover owner-occupied housing units; (1) Figures cover the Dallas-Fort Worth-Arlington, TX Metropolitan Statistical Area
Source: U.S. Census Bureau, 2019-2023 American Community Survey 5-Year Estimates

Year Housing Structure Built

Area	2020 or Later	2010 -2019	2000 -2009	1990 -1999	1980 -1989	1970 -1979	1960 -1969	1950 -1959	1940 -1949	Before 1940	Median Year
City	1.0	12.0	11.0	10.0	16.3	15.0	12.0	12.7	4.6	5.2	1980
MSA[1]	2.6	16.9	18.6	14.3	16.5	12.2	7.6	6.6	2.2	2.5	1992
U.S.	1.2	8.9	13.6	12.8	13.0	14.4	10.0	9.7	4.5	11.9	1980

Note: Figures are percentages except for Median Year; Note: (1) Figures cover the Dallas-Fort Worth-Arlington, TX Metropolitan Statistical Area
Source: U.S. Census Bureau, 2019-2023 American Community Survey 5-Year Estimates

Gross Monthly Rent

Area	Under $500	$500 -$999	$1,000 -$1,499	$1,500 -$1,999	$2,000 -$2,499	$2,500 -$2,999	$3,000 and up	Median ($)
City	3.1	12.2	42.5	25.9	9.5	3.4	3.4	1,403
MSA[1]	2.1	9.7	37.7	28.7	13.8	4.7	3.3	1,509
U.S.	6.5	22.3	29.5	20.2	10.8	4.8	5.9	1,348

Note: Figures are percentages except for median; Gross rent is the contract rent plus the estimated average monthly cost of utilities (electricity, gas, and water and sewer) and fuels (oil, coal, kerosene, wood, etc.) if these are paid by the renter (or paid for the renter by someone else); (1) Figures cover the Dallas-Fort Worth-Arlington, TX Metropolitan Statistical Area
Source: U.S. Census Bureau, 2019-2023 American Community Survey 5-Year Estimates

HEALTH

Health Risk Factors

Category	MD[1] (%)	U.S. (%)
Adults aged 18–64 who have any kind of health care coverage	79.6	90.8
Adults who reported being in good or better health	80.0	81.8
Adults who have been told they have high blood cholesterol	41.1	36.9
Adults who have been told they have high blood pressure	30.2	34.0
Adults who are current smokers	8.7	12.1
Adults who currently use e-cigarettes	5.3	7.7
Adults who currently use chewing tobacco, snuff, or snus	2.1	3.2
Adults who are heavy drinkers[2]	4.8	6.1
Adults who are binge drinkers[3]	15.4	15.2
Adults who are overweight (BMI 25.0 - 29.9)	33.7	34.4
Adults who are obese (BMI 30.0 - 99.8)	36.0	34.3
Adults who participated in any physical activities in the past month	75.0	75.8

Note: All figures are crude prevalence; (1) Figures cover the Dallas-Plano-Irving, TX Metropolitan Division; (2) Heavy drinkers are classified as adult men having more than 14 drinks per week and adult women having more than 7 drinks per week; (3) Binge drinkers are classified as males having five or more drinks on one occasion or females having four or more drinks on one occasion
Source: Centers for Disease Control and Prevention, Behavioral Risk Factor Surveillance System, SMART: Selected Metropolitan Area Risk Trends, 2023

Acute and Chronic Health Conditions

Category	MD[1] (%)	U.S. (%)
Adults who have ever been told they had a heart attack	2.8	4.2
Adults who have ever been told they have angina or coronary heart disease	3.3	4.0
Adults who have ever been told they had a stroke	3.3	3.3
Adults who have ever been told they have asthma	14.5	15.7
Adults who have ever been told they have arthritis	18.9	26.3
Adults who have ever been told they have diabetes[2]	9.3	11.5
Adults who have ever been told they had skin cancer	4.6	5.6
Adults who have ever been told they had any other types of cancer	6.0	8.4
Adults who have ever been told they have COPD	4.4	6.4
Adults who have ever been told they have kidney disease	3.6	3.7
Adults who have ever been told they have a form of depression	17.3	22.0

Note: All figures are crude prevalence; (1) Figures cover the Dallas-Plano-Irving, TX Metropolitan Division; (2) Figures do not include pregnancy-related, borderline, or pre-diabetes
Source: Centers for Disease Control and Prevention, Behavioral Risk Factor Surveillance System, SMART: Selected Metropolitan Area Risk Trends, 2023

Health Screening and Vaccination Rates

Category	MD[1] (%)	U.S. (%)
Adults who have ever been tested for HIV	36.7	37.5
Adults who have had their blood cholesterol checked within the last five years	84.2	87.0
Adults aged 65+ who have had flu shot within the past year	59.3	63.4
Adults aged 65+ who have ever had a pneumonia vaccination	77.8	71.9

Note: All figures are crude prevalence; (1) Figures cover the Dallas-Plano-Irving, TX Metropolitan Division.
Source: Centers for Disease Control and Prevention, Behavioral Risk Factor Surveillance System, SMART: Selected Metropolitan Area Risk Trends, 2023

Disability Status

Category	MD[1] (%)	U.S. (%)
Adults who reported being deaf	6.2	7.4
Are you blind or have serious difficulty seeing, even when wearing glasses?	6.0	4.9
Do you have difficulty doing errands alone?	7.0	7.8
Do you have difficulty dressing or bathing?	3.1	3.6
Do you have serious difficulty concentrating/remembering/making decisions?	13.0	13.7
Do you have serious difficulty walking or climbing stairs?	12.5	13.2

Note: All figures are crude prevalence; (1) Figures cover the Dallas-Plano-Irving, TX Metropolitan Division.
Source: Centers for Disease Control and Prevention, Behavioral Risk Factor Surveillance System, SMART: Selected Metropolitan Area Risk Trends, 2023

Mortality Rates for the Top 10 Causes of Death in the U.S.

ICD-10[a] Sub-Chapter	ICD-10[a] Code	Crude Mortality Rate[2] per 100,000 population	
		County[3]	U.S.
Malignant neoplasms	C00-C97	129.8	182.7
Ischaemic heart diseases	I20-I25	77.2	109.6
Provisional assignment of new diseases of uncertain etiology[1]	U00-U49	60.5	65.3
Other forms of heart disease	I30-I51	38.0	65.1
Other degenerative diseases of the nervous system	G30-G31	50.2	52.4
Other external causes of accidental injury	W00-X59	38.0	52.3
Cerebrovascular diseases	I60-I69	37.4	49.1
Chronic lower respiratory diseases	J40-J47	23.9	43.5
Hypertensive diseases	I10-I15	31.9	38.9
Organic, including symptomatic, mental disorders	F01-F09	16.1	33.9

Note: (a) ICD-10 = International Classification of Diseases 10th Revision; (1) Includes COVID-19, adverse effects to COVID-19 vaccines, SARS, and vaping-related disorders; (2) Crude mortality rates are a three-year average covering 2021-2023; (3) Figures cover Dallas County.
Source: Centers for Disease Control and Prevention, National Center for Health Statistics. National Vital Statistics System, Mortality 2018-2023 on CDC WONDER Online Database

Mortality Rates for Selected Causes of Death

Cause of Death	ICD-10[a] Code	Crude Mortality Rate[1] per 100,000 population	
		County[2]	U.S.
Accidental poisoning and exposure to noxious substances	X40-X49	22.5	30.5
Alzheimer disease	G30	27.5	35.4
Assault	X85-Y09	11.4	7.3
COVID-19	U07.1	60.5	65.3
Diabetes mellitus	E10-E14	24.7	30.0
Diseases of the liver	K70-K76	17.5	20.8
Human immunodeficiency virus (HIV) disease	B20-B24	3.1	1.5
Influenza and pneumonia	J09-J18	7.8	13.4
Intentional self-harm	X60-X84	11.8	14.7
Malnutrition	E40-E46	4.5	6.0
Obesity and other hyperalimentation	E65-E68	2.7	3.1
Renal failure	N17-N19	13.9	16.4
Transport accidents	V01-V99	14.2	14.4

Note: (a) ICD-10 = International Classification of Diseases 10th Revision; (1) Crude mortality rates are a three-year average covering 2021-2023; (2) Figures cover Dallas County; Data are suppressed when the data meet the criteria for confidentiality constraints; Crude mortality rates are flagged as unreliable when the rate would be calculated with a numerator of 20 or less.
Source: Centers for Disease Control and Prevention, National Center for Health Statistics. National Vital Statistics System, Mortality 2018-2023 on CDC WONDER Online Database

Health Insurance Coverage

Area	With Health Insurance	With Private Health Insurance	With Public Health Insurance	Without Health Insurance	Population Under Age 19 Without Health Insurance
City	77.0	54.1	29.3	23.0	15.7
MSA[1]	83.7	66.7	24.5	16.3	11.8
U.S.	91.4	67.3	36.3	8.6	5.4

Note: Figures are percentages that cover the civilian noninstitutionalized population; (1) Figures cover the Dallas-Fort Worth-Arlington, TX Metropolitan Statistical Area
Source: U.S. Census Bureau, 2019-2023 American Community Survey 5-Year Estimates

Number of Medical Professionals

Area	MDs[3]	DOs[3,4]	Dentists	Podiatrists	Chiropractors	Optometrists
County[1] (number)	9,907	641	2,517	116	1,050	406
County[1] (rate[2])	380.9	24.6	96.6	4.5	40.3	15.6
U.S. (rate[2])	302.5	29.2	74.6	6.4	29.5	18.0

Note: Data as of 2023 unless noted; (1) Data covers Dallas County; (2) Number of medical professionals per 100,000 population; (3) Data as of 2022 and includes all active, non-federal physicians; (4) Doctor of Osteopathic Medicine
Source: U.S. Department of Health and Human Services, Health Resources and Services Administration, Bureau of Health Professions, Area Resource File (ARF) 2023-2024

Best Hospitals

According to *U.S. News,* the Dallas-Fort Worth-Arlington, TX metro area is home to five of the best hospitals in the U.S.: **Baylor Scott and White All Saints Medical Center-Fort Worth** (1 adult specialty); **Baylor Scott and White Institute for Rehabilitation-Dallas** (1 adult specialty); **Baylor Scott and White The Heart Hospital Plano** (1 adult specialty); **Baylor University Medical Center** (6 adult specialties); **UT Southwestern Medical Center** (11 adult specialties). The hospitals listed were nationally ranked in at least one of 15 adult or 11 pediatric specialties. The number of specialties shown cover the parent hospital. Only 160 U.S. hospitals performed well enough to be nationally ranked in one or more specialties. Twenty hospitals in the U.S. made the Honor Roll. The Best Hospitals Honor Roll takes both the national rankings and the procedure and condition ratings into account. Hospitals received points if they were nationally ranked in one of the 15 adult specialties—the higher they ranked, the more points they got—and how many ratings of "high performing" they earned in the 20 procedures and conditions. *U.S. News Online, "America's Best Hospitals 2024-25"*

According to *U.S. News,* the Dallas-Fort Worth-Arlington, TX metro area is home to three of the best children's hospitals in the U.S.: **Children's Medical Center Dallas** (11 pediatric specialties); **Children's Medical Center Dallas-Scottish Rite for Children** (1 pediatric specialty); **Cook Children's Medical Center** (7 pediatric specialties). The hospitals listed were highly ranked in at least one of 11 pediatric specialties. One hundred five children's hospitals in the U.S. were nationally ranked in at least one specialty. Hospitals received points for being ranked in a specialty, and the 10 hospitals with the most points across the 11 specialties make up the Honor Roll. *U.S. News Online, "America's Best Children's Hospitals 2024-25"*

EDUCATION

Public School District Statistics

District Name	Schls	Pupils	Pupil/ Teacher Ratio	Minority Pupils[1] (%)	Total Rev. per Pupil ($)	Total Exp. per Pupil ($)
Dallas ISD	249	139,246	13.6	94.0	16,130	18,024
Harmony Science Academy (Waco)	16	10,272	15.5	85.5	13,305	11,223
Highland Park ISD	10	6,437	13.9	18.2	16,387	30,472
Pioneer Technology and Arts Academy	6	2,603	14.7	66.2	12,080	10,876
Texans Can Academies	13	3,608	20.2	98.1	13,203	12,439
Trinity Basin Preparatory	8	6,631	14.7	88.0	13,957	10,617
Uplift Education	45	22,815	17.0	97.2	13,225	11,316

Note: Table includes school districts with 2,000 or more students; (1) Percentage of students that are not non-Hispanic white.
Source: U.S. Department of Education, National Center for Education Statistics, Common Core of Data, Local Education Agency (School District) Universe Survey: School Year 2023-2024; U.S. Department of Education, National Center for Education Statistics, Common Core of Data, School District Finance Survey (F-33): School Year 2021–22

Best High Schools

According to *U.S. News,* Dallas is home to 11 of the top 500 high schools in the U.S.: **The School for the Talented and Gifted (TAG)** (#6); **Irma Lerma Rangel Young Women's Leadership School** (#23); **Science and Engineering Magnet School (SEM)** (#29); **Judge Barefoot Sanders Law Magnet** (#85); **Trinidad Garza Early College at Mt View** (#138); **School of Health Professions** (#166); **School of Business and Management** (#248); **Booker T. Washington SPVA** (#296); **Highland Park High School** (#357); **Rosie Sorrells Education and Social Services High School** (#378); **Barack Obama Male Leadership Academy** (#435). Nearly 25,000 public, magnet and charter schools were ranked based on their performance on state assessments and how well they prepare students for college. *U.S. News & World Report, "Best High Schools 2024"*

Highest Level of Education

Area	Less than H.S.	H.S. Diploma	Some College, No Deg.	Associate Degree	Bachelor's Degree	Master's Degree	Prof. School Degree	Doctorate Degree
City	19.2	21.5	16.7	5.1	22.9	9.7	3.4	1.4
MSA[1]	12.7	21.7	19.7	7.4	24.5	10.7	2.0	1.3
U.S.	10.6	26.2	19.4	8.8	21.3	9.8	2.3	1.6

Note: Figures cover persons age 25 and over; (1) Figures cover the Dallas-Fort Worth-Arlington, TX Metropolitan Statistical Area
Source: U.S. Census Bureau, 2019-2023 American Community Survey 5-Year Estimates

Educational Attainment by Race

Area	High School Graduate or Higher (%)					Bachelor's Degree or Higher (%)				
	Total	White	Black	Asian	Hisp.[2]	Total	White	Black	Asian	Hisp.[2]
City	80.8	87.6	89.0	89.3	58.2	37.4	53.6	23.6	68.5	15.3
MSA[1]	87.3	92.0	92.2	90.0	66.3	38.5	42.8	31.6	65.4	17.8
U.S.	89.4	92.9	88.1	88.0	72.5	35.0	37.7	24.7	57.0	19.9

Note: Figures shown cover persons 25 years old and over; (1) Figures cover the Dallas-Fort Worth-Arlington, TX Metropolitan Statistical Area; (2) People of Hispanic origin can be of any race
Source: U.S. Census Bureau, 2019-2023 American Community Survey 5-Year Estimates

School Enrollment by Grade and Control

Area	Preschool (%)		Kindergarten (%)		Grades 1 - 4 (%)		Grades 5 - 8 (%)		Grades 9 - 12 (%)	
	Public	Private	Public	Private	Public	Private	Public	Private	Public	Private
City	69.0	31.0	88.5	11.5	89.5	10.5	91.1	8.9	89.8	10.2
MSA[1]	57.4	42.6	88.0	12.0	90.4	9.6	91.4	8.6	91.5	8.5
U.S.	58.7	41.3	85.2	14.8	87.2	12.8	87.9	12.1	89.0	11.0

Note: Figures shown cover persons 3 years old and over; (1) Figures cover the Dallas-Fort Worth-Arlington, TX Metropolitan Statistical Area
Source: U.S. Census Bureau, 2019-2023 American Community Survey 5-Year Estimates

Higher Education

Four-Year Colleges			Two-Year Colleges			Medical Schools[1]	Law Schools[2]	Voc/ Tech[3]
Public	Private Non-profit	Private For-profit	Public	Private Non-profit	Private For-profit			
11	25	7	1	3	11	3	3	36

Note: Figures cover institutions located within the Dallas-Fort Worth-Arlington, TX Metropolitan Statistical Area and include main campuses only; (1) includes schools accredited by the Liaison Committee on Medical Education and the American Osteopathic Association's Commission on Osteopathic College Accreditation; (2) includes ABA-accredited schools, schools with provisional ABA accreditation, and state accredited schools; (3) includes all schools with programs that are less than 2 years.
Source: National Center for Education Statistics, Integrated Postsecondary Education System (IPEDS), 2023-24; Wikipedia, List of Medical Schools in the United States, accessed May 2, 2025; Wikipedia, List of Law Schools in the United States, accessed May 2, 2025

According to *U.S. News & World Report,* the Dallas-Fort Worth-Arlington, TX metro area is home to three of the top 200 national universities in the U.S.: **Southern Methodist University** (#91 tie); **Texas Christian University** (#105 tie); **The University of Texas—Dallas** (#109 tie). The indicators used to capture academic quality fall into a number of categories: assessment by administrators at peer institutions; retention of students; faculty resources; student selectivity; financial resources; alumni giving; high school counselor ratings of colleges; and graduation rate. *U.S. News & World Report,* "America's Best Colleges 2025"

According to *U.S. News & World Report,* the Dallas-Fort Worth-Arlington, TX metro area is home to two of the top 100 law schools in the U.S.: **Texas A&M University** (#22 tie); **Southern Methodist University (Dedman)** (#43 tie). The rankings are based on a weighted average of 12 measures of quality: peer assessment score; assessment score by lawyers/judges; median LSAT scores; median undergrad GPA; acceptance rate; employment rates for graduates; placement success; bar passage rate; faculty resources; expenditures per student; student/faculty ratio; and library resources. *U.S. News & World Report,* "America's Best Graduate Schools, Law, 2025"

According to *U.S. News & World Report,* the Dallas-Fort Worth-Arlington, TX metro area is home to one of the top medical schools for research in the U.S.: **University of Texas Southwestern Medical Center** (Tier 1). *U.S. News* placed medical and osteopathic schools into tiers based on their research productivity, faculty and admissions data. Each school's tier was derived from its overall score, calculated by summing the weighted normalized values generated across several factors of academic quality, outlined below. There are four tiers, with tier 1 medical schools as the highest-performing and tier 4 as the lowest-performing. Only tier 1 and 2 schools are shown. Because of the tier presentation, *U.S. News* calculated overall scores based on their percentile performance among all rated schools instead of dividing against the rescaled score of the No. 1-performing schools. Tier 1 included schools with overall scores of 85 to 99. The cutoffs for tiers 2 through 4 were schools scoring 50 to 84, 15 to 49 and 1 to 14, respectively. The rankings are based on a weighted average of the following measures of quality: total research activity; average research activity per faculty member; total NIH research grants at the medical school and its affiliated hospitals; average NIH research grants per faculty; median MCAT total score; median undergraduate GPA; acceptance rate; and faculty resources. *U.S. News & World Report,* "America's Best Graduate Schools, Medical, 2025"

According to *U.S. News & World Report,* the Dallas-Fort Worth-Arlington, TX metro area is home to two of the top medical schools for primary care in the U.S.: **The University of North Texas Health Science Center at Fort Worth** (Tier 2); **University of Texas Southwestern Medical Center** (Tier 2). *U.S. News* placed medical and osteopathic schools into tiers based on their research productivity, faculty and admissions data. Each school's tier was derived from its overall score, calculated by summing the weighted normalized values generated across several factors of academic quality, outlined below. There are four tiers, with tier 1 medical schools as the highest-performing and tier 4 as the lowest-performing. Only tier 1 and 2 schools are shown. Because of the tier presentation, *U.S. News* calculated overall scores based on their percentile performance among all rated schools instead of dividing against the rescaled score of the No. 1-performing schools. Tier 1 included schools with overall scores of 85 to 99. The cutoffs for tiers 2 through 4 were schools scoring 50 to 84, 15 to 49 and 1 to 14, respectively. The rankings are based on a weighted average of the following measures of quality: graduates practicing in primary care specialties; graduates entering primary care residencies; median MCAT total score; median undergraduate GPA; acceptance rate; and faculty resources. *U.S. News & World Report,* "America's Best Graduate Schools, Medical, 2025"

According to *U.S. News & World Report,* the Dallas-Fort Worth-Arlington, TX metro area is home to three of the top 75 business schools in the U.S.: **The University of Texas at Dallas (Jindal)** (#31); **Southern Methodist University (Cox)** (#34); **Texas Christian University (Neeley)** (#43 tie). The rankings are based on a weighted average of the following nine measures: quality assessment; peer assessment; recruiter assessment; placement success; mean starting salary and bonus; student selectivity; mean GMAT and GRE scores; mean undergraduate GPA; and acceptance rate. *U.S. News & World Report,* "America's Best Graduate Schools, Business, 2025"

EMPLOYERS

Major Employers

Company Name	Industry
AMR Corporation	Air transportation, scheduled
Associates First Capital Corporation	Mortgage bankers
Baylor University Medical Center	General medical & surgical hospitals
Children's Medical Center Dallas	Specialty hospitals, except psychiatric
Combat Support Associates	Engineering services
County of Dallas	County government
Dallas County Hospital District	General medical & surgical hospitals
Fort Worth Independent School District	Public elementary & secondary schools
Housewares Holding Company	Toasters, electric: household
HP Enterprise Services	Computer integrated systems design
J.C. Penney Company	Department stores
JCP Publications Corp.	Department stores
L-3 Communications Corporation	Business economic service
Odyssey HealthCare	Home health care services
Romano's Macaroni Grill	Italian restaurant
SFG Management	Milk processing (pasteurizing, homogenizing, bottling)
Texas Instruments Incorporated	Semiconductors & related devices
University of North Texas	Colleges & universities
University of Texas SW Medical Center	Accident & health insurance
Verizon Business Global	Telephone communication, except radio

Note: Companies shown are located within the Dallas-Fort Worth-Arlington, TX Metropolitan Statistical Area.
Source: Chambers of Commerce; State Departments of Labor; Wikipedia

Best Companies to Work For

Ryan, headquartered in Dallas, is among "The 100 Best Companies to Work For." To pick the best companies, *Fortune* partnered with the Great Place to Work Institute. Using their proprietary Trust Index™ survey, the core of what creates great a workplace is measured—key behaviors that drive trust in management, connection with colleagues, and loyalty to the company. To be eligible for the *Fortune* 100 Best Companies to Work For list, employers must have 1,000 or more employees in the U.S. and cannot be a government agency. *Fortune, "The 100 Best Companies to Work For," 2025*

PrimeLending; Ryan, headquartered in Dallas, are among "Fortune's Best Workplaces for Parents." To pick the best companies, *Fortune* partnered with the Great Place to Work Institute. To be considered for the list, companies must be Great Place To Work-Certified and have at least 50 responses from parents in the US. The survey enables employees to share confidential quantitative and qualitative feedback about their organization's culture by responding to 60 statements on a 5-point scale and answering two open-ended questions. Collectively, these statements describe a great employee experience, defined by high levels of trust, respect, credibility, fairness, pride, and camaraderie. In addition, companies provide organizational data like size, location, industry, demographics, roles, and levels; and provide information about parental leave, adoption, flexible schedule, childcare and dependent health care benefits. *Fortune, "Best Workplaces for Parents," 2024*

PMG; PrimeLending; Ryan, headquartered in Dallas, are among "Fortune's Best Workplaces for Women." To pick the best companies, *Fortune* partnered with the Great Place to Work Institute. To be considered for the list, companies must be Great Place To Work-Certified. Companies must also employ at least 50 women, at least 20% of their non-executive managers must be female, and at least one executive must be female. To determine the Best Workplaces for Women, Great Place To Work measured the differences in women's survey responses to those of their peers and assesses the impact of demographics and roles on the quality and consistency of women's experiences. Great Place To Work also analyzed the gender balance of each workplace, how it compared to each company's industry, and patterns in representation as women rise from front-line positions to the board of directors. *Fortune, "Best Workplaces for Women," 2024*

Astanza Laser, headquartered in Dallas, is among "Best Workplaces in Health Care." To determine the Best Workplaces in Health Care list, Great Place To Work analyzed the survey responses of over 185,000 employees from Great Place To Work-Certified companies in the health care industry. Survey data analysis and company-provided datapoints are then factored into a combined score to compare and rank the companies that create the most consistently positive experience for all employees in this industry. *Fortune, "Best Workplaces in Health Care," 2024*

PUBLIC SAFETY

Crime Rate

Area	Total Crime Rate	Violent Crime Rate				Property Crime Rate		
		Murder	Rape	Robbery	Aggrav. Assault	Burglary	Larceny-Theft	Motor Vehicle Theft
City	4,701.5	18.5	36.8	157.8	458.4	470.3	2,126.6	1,433.1
U.S.	2,290.9	5.7	38.0	66.5	264.1	250.7	1,347.2	318.7

Note: Figures are crimes per 100,000 population.
Source: FBI, Table 8, Offenses Known to Law Enforcement, by State by City, 2023

Hate Crimes

Area	Number of Quarters Reported	Number of Incidents per Bias Motivation					
		Race/Ethnicity/Ancestry	Religion	Sexual Orientation	Disability	Gender	Gender Identity
City[1]	4	13	8	9	0	0	3
U.S.	4	5,900	2,699	2,077	187	92	492

Note: (1) Figures include at least one incident reported with more than one bias motivation.
Source: Federal Bureau of Investigation, Hate Crime Statistics 2023

Identity Theft Consumer Reports

Area	Reports	Reports per 100,000 Population	Rank[2]
MSA[1]	37,114	475	10
U.S.	1,135,291	339	-

Note: (1) Figures cover the Dallas-Fort Worth-Arlington, TX Metropolitan Statistical Area; (2) Rank ranges from 1 to 401 where 1 indicates greatest number of identity theft reports per 100,000 population
Source: Federal Trade Commission, Consumer Sentinel Network Data Book 2024

Fraud and Other Consumer Reports

Area	Reports	Reports per 100,000 Population	Rank[2]
MSA[1]	159,709	2,046	10
U.S.	5,360,641	1,601	-

Note: (1) Figures cover the Dallas-Fort Worth-Arlington, TX Metropolitan Statistical Area; (2) Rank ranges from 1 to 401 where 1 indicates greatest number of fraud and other consumer reports per 100,000 population
Source: Federal Trade Commission, Consumer Sentinel Network Data Book 2024

POLITICS

2024 Presidential Election Results

Area	Trump (Rep.)	Harris (Dem.)	Stein (Green)	Kennedy (Ind.)	Oliver (Lib.)	Other
Dallas County	37.8	59.9	1.1	0.0	0.7	0.5
U.S.	49.7	48.2	0.6	0.5	0.4	0.6

Note: Results are percentages and may not add to 100% due to rounding
Source: Dave Leip's Atlas of U.S. Presidential Elections

SPORTS

Professional Sports Teams

Team Name	League	Year Established
Dallas Cowboys	National Football League (NFL)	1960
Dallas Mavericks	National Basketball Association (NBA)	1980
Dallas Stars	National Hockey League (NHL)	1993
FC Dallas	Major League Soccer (MLS)	1996
Texas Rangers	Major League Baseball (MLB)	1972

Note: Includes teams located in the Dallas-Fort Worth-Arlington, TX Metropolitan Statistical Area.
Source: Wikipedia, Major Professional Sports Teams of the United States and Canada, May 1, 2025

CLIMATE

Average and Extreme Temperatures

Temperature	Jan	Feb	Mar	Apr	May	Jun	Jul	Aug	Sep	Oct	Nov	Dec	Yr.
Extreme High (°F)	85	90	100	100	101	112	111	109	107	101	91	87	112
Average High (°F)	55	60	68	76	84	92	96	96	89	79	67	58	77
Average Temp. (°F)	45	50	57	66	74	82	86	86	79	68	56	48	67
Average Low (°F)	35	39	47	56	64	72	76	75	68	57	46	38	56
Extreme Low (°F)	-2	9	12	30	39	53	58	58	42	24	16	0	-2

Note: Figures cover the years 1945-1993
Source: National Climatic Data Center, International Station Meteorological Climate Summary, 9/96

Average Precipitation/Snowfall/Humidity

Precip./Humidity	Jan	Feb	Mar	Apr	May	Jun	Jul	Aug	Sep	Oct	Nov	Dec	Yr.
Avg. Precip. (in.)	1.9	2.3	2.6	3.8	4.9	3.4	2.1	2.3	2.9	3.3	2.3	2.1	33.9
Avg. Snowfall (in.)	1	1	Tr	Tr	0	0	0	0	0	Tr	Tr	Tr	3
Avg. Rel. Hum. 6am (%)	78	77	75	77	82	81	77	76	80	79	78	77	78
Avg. Rel. Hum. 3pm (%)	53	51	47	49	51	48	43	41	46	46	48	51	48

Note: Figures cover the years 1945-1993; Tr = Trace amounts (<0.05 in. of rain; <0.5 in. of snow)
Source: National Climatic Data Center, International Station Meteorological Climate Summary, 9/96

Weather Conditions

Temperature			Daytime Sky			Precipitation		
10°F & below	32°F & below	90°F & above	Clear	Partly cloudy	Cloudy	0.01 inch or more precip.	0.1 inch or more snow/ice	Thunderstorms
1	34	102	108	160	97	78	2	49

Note: Figures are average number of days per year and cover the years 1945-1993
Source: National Climatic Data Center, International Station Meteorological Climate Summary, 9/96

HAZARDOUS WASTE

Superfund Sites

The Dallas-Plano-Irving, TX metro division is home to four sites on the EPA's Superfund National Priorities List (NPL) or Superfund Alternative Approach (SAA) list: **Delfasco Forge** (Final NPL); **Lane Plating Works, Inc** (Final NPL); **RSR Corporation** (Final NPL); **Van Der Horst Usa Corporation** (Final NPL). The Superfund alternative approach uses the same investigation and cleanup process and standards that are used for sites listed on the National Priorities List. The SAA is an alternative to listing a site on the NPL; it is not an alternative to Superfund or the Superfund process. There are a total of 1,445 Superfund sites with a status of proposed or final on both lists in the United States. *U.S. Environmental Protection Agency, National Priorities List, May 1, 2025; U.S. Environmental Protection Agency, Superfund Alternative Approach Sites, May 1, 2025*

AIR QUALITY

Air Quality Trends: Ozone

	1990	1995	2000	2005	2010	2015	2020	2021	2022	2023
MSA[1]	0.094	0.103	0.096	0.096	0.079	0.078	0.070	0.076	0.072	0.081
U.S.	0.087	0.089	0.081	0.080	0.072	0.068	0.066	0.067	0.067	0.070

Note: (1) Data covers the Dallas-Fort Worth-Arlington, TX Metropolitan Statistical Area. The values shown are the composite ozone concentration averages among trend sites based on the highest fourth daily maximum 8-hour concentration in parts per million. These trends are based on sites having an adequate record of monitoring data during the trend period. Data from exceptional events are included.
Source: U.S. Environmental Protection Agency, Air Quality Monitoring Information, "Air Quality Trends by City, 1990-2023"

Air Quality Index

Area	Percent of Days when Air Quality was...[2]					AQI Statistics[2]	
	Good	Moderate	Unhealthy for Sensitive Groups	Unhealthy	Very Unhealthy	Maximum	Median
MSA[1]	20.5	64.9	12.1	2.5	0.0	177	60

Note: (1) Data covers the Dallas-Fort Worth-Arlington, TX Metropolitan Statistical Area; (2) Based on 365 days with AQI data in 2023. Air Quality Index (AQI) is an index for reporting daily air quality. EPA calculates the AQI for five major air pollutants regulated by the Clean Air Act: ground-level ozone, particle pollution (aka particulate matter), carbon monoxide, sulfur dioxide, and nitrogen dioxide. The AQI runs from 0 to 500. The higher the AQI value, the greater the level of air pollution and the greater the health concern. There are six AQI categories: "Good" AQI is between 0 and 50. Air quality is considered satisfactory; "Moderate" AQI is between 51 and 100. Air quality is acceptable; "Unhealthy for Sensitive Groups" When AQI values are between 101 and 150, members of sensitive groups may experience health effects; "Unhealthy" When AQI values are between 151 and 200 everyone may begin to experience health effects; "Very Unhealthy" AQI values between 201 and 300 trigger a health alert; "Hazardous" AQI values over 300 trigger warnings of emergency conditions (not shown).
Source: U.S. Environmental Protection Agency, Air Quality Index Report, 2023

Air Quality Index Pollutants

Area	Percent of Days when AQI Pollutant was...[2]					
	Carbon Monoxide	Nitrogen Dioxide	Ozone	Sulfur Dioxide	Particulate Matter 2.5	Particulate Matter 10
MSA[1]	0.0	0.5	40.5	(3)	58.4	0.5

Note: (1) Data covers the Dallas-Fort Worth-Arlington, TX Metropolitan Statistical Area; (2) Based on 365 days with AQI data in 2023. The Air Quality Index (AQI) is an index for reporting daily air quality. EPA calculates the AQI for five major air pollutants regulated by the Clean Air Act: ground-level ozone, particle pollution (also known as particulate matter), carbon monoxide, sulfur dioxide, and nitrogen dioxide. The AQI runs from 0 to 500. The higher the AQI value, the greater the level of air pollution and the greater the health concern; (3) Sulfur dioxide is no longer included in this table because SO_2 concentrations tend to be very localized and not necessarily representative of broad geographical areas like counties and CBSAs.
Source: U.S. Environmental Protection Agency, Air Quality Index Report, 2023

Maximum Air Pollutant Concentrations: Particulate Matter, Ozone, CO and Lead

	Particulate Matter 10 (ug/m³)	Particulate Matter 2.5 Wtd AM (ug/m³)	Particulate Matter 2.5 24-Hr (ug/m³)	Ozone (ppm)	Carbon Monoxide (ppm)	Lead (ug/m³)
MSA[1] Level	70	10.7	23	0.084	2	0.07
NAAQS[2]	150	15	35	0.075	9	0.15
Met NAAQS[2]	Yes	Yes	Yes	No	Yes	Yes

Note: (1) Data covers the Dallas-Fort Worth-Arlington, TX Metropolitan Statistical Area; Data from exceptional events are included; (2) National Ambient Air Quality Standards; ppm = parts per million; ug/m³ = micrograms per cubic meter; n/a not available.
Concentrations: Particulate Matter 10 (coarse particulate)—highest second maximum 24-hour concentration; Particulate Matter 2.5 Wtd AM (fine particulate)—highest weighted annual mean concentration; Particulate Matter 2.5 24-Hour (fine particulate)—highest 98th percentile 24-hour concentration; Ozone—highest fourth daily maximum 8-hour concentration; Carbon Monoxide—highest second maximum non-overlapping 8-hour concentration; Lead—maximum running 3-month average
Source: U.S. Environmental Protection Agency, Air Quality Monitoring Information, "Air Quality Statistics by City, 2023"

Maximum Air Pollutant Concentrations: Nitrogen Dioxide and Sulfur Dioxide

	Nitrogen Dioxide AM (ppb)	Nitrogen Dioxide 1-Hr (ppb)	Sulfur Dioxide AM (ppb)	Sulfur Dioxide 1-Hr (ppb)	Sulfur Dioxide 24-Hr (ppb)
MSA[1] Level	14	46	n/a	17	n/a
NAAQS[2]	53	100	30	75	140
Met NAAQS[2]	Yes	Yes	n/a	Yes	n/a

Note: (1) Data covers the Dallas-Fort Worth-Arlington, TX Metropolitan Statistical Area; Data from exceptional events are included; (2) National Ambient Air Quality Standards; ppm = parts per million; ug/m³ = micrograms per cubic meter; n/a not available.
Concentrations: Nitrogen Dioxide AM—highest arithmetic mean concentration; Nitrogen Dioxide 1-Hr—highest 98th percentile 1-hour daily maximum concentration; Sulfur Dioxide AM—highest annual mean concentration; Sulfur Dioxide 1-Hr—highest 99th percentile 1-hour daily maximum concentration; Sulfur Dioxide 24-Hr—highest second maximum 24-hour concentration
Source: U.S. Environmental Protection Agency, Air Quality Monitoring Information, "Air Quality Statistics by City, 2023"

El Paso, Texas

Background

El Paso sits in an impressive pass through the Franklin Mountains at an elevation of 3,700 feet and with views of 7,200-foot peaks. It is the fourth-largest city in Texas. It lies just south of New Mexico on the Rio Grande and just north of Juarez, Mexico.

Although there is evidence that early Spanish explorer Alvar Nunez Cabeza de Vaca (circa 1530) passed through this area, the city was named in 1598 by Juan de Onante, El Paso del Rio del Norte—The Pass at the River of the North. It was also Onante who declared the area Spanish, on the authority of King Philip II, but a mission was not established until 1649. El Paso del Norte was the seat of government for northern Mexico, but settlement in and around the present-day city was sparse for many years.

In 1807, Zebulon A. Pike, a United States Army officer, was interned in El Paso after being convicted of trespassing on Spanish territory. He found the area pleasant and well-tended, with many irrigated fields and vineyards and a thriving trade in brandy and wine. Despite Pike's attraction and interest in the area, El Paso remained a Mexican region, escaping most of the military action connected to the Texas Revolution.

In the wake of the Mexican War (1846-1848) and in response to the California gold rush in 1849, El Paso emerged as a significant way station on the road west. Federal garrison Fort Bliss was established there in 1849 and was briefly occupied by Confederate sympathizers in 1862. Federal forces quickly reoccupied the fort, however, and the area became controlled by Union armies. El Paso was incorporated in 1873, and several years later, growth accelerated considerably with the building of rail links through the city, giving rise to ironworks, mills, and breweries.

After the Mexican Revolution (1911), El Paso was an important and disputed city, with Pancho Villa a frequent visitor, and many of his followers' becoming residents of the town. Mexico's national history continued to affect El Paso. In 1967, to settle a historic border dispute, 437 acres of the city was ceded to Mexico. Much of the disputed area on both sides of the border was made into parkland. The U.S. National Parks Service maintains the Chamizal Park on the U.S. side and hosts a variety of community events during the year including the Chamizal Film Festival and the summer concert series, Music Under the Stars.

El Paso is one of the major points of entry to the United States from Mexico, often with hundreds reaching the El Paso's Processing Center daily. El Paso is a vitally important international city and a burgeoning center of rail, road, and air transportation. During the 1990s, the city's economy shifted more toward a service-oriented economy and away from a manufacturing base. In 2021, Amazon opened a 625,000 square-foot fulfillment center in the city and employs about 2,000.

The city is home to Fortune 500 company Western Refining. Transportation services and tourism are growing segments of the economy. Government and military are also sources of employment, with Fort Bliss being the largest Air Defense Artillery Training Center in the world and the city's largest employer. The city hosts the University of Texas at El Paso, and a community college. Cultural amenities include the Tigua Indian Cultural Center, Wilderness Park Museum, El Paso Zoo, a symphony orchestra, a ballet company, and many theaters. The city's "Wild West" qualities have long made it a popular destination for musicians, many of whom have recorded albums at El Paso's Sonic Ranch recording studio.

In 2019, El Paso was awarded its own United Soccer League team.

El Paso's revitalized downtown has increased the city's aesthetic appeal. It includes an open-air mall and "lifestyle center" in the city's central area, Doubletree by Hilton Hotel, and renovations of several historic downtown buildings.

El Paso is home to the world's largest inland desalination plant, designed to produce 27.5 million gallons of fresh water daily making it a critical component of the region's water portfolio.

The weather in El Paso is of the mountain-desert type, with very little precipitation. Summers are hot, humidity is low, and winters are mild. However, temperatures in the flat Rio Grande Valley nearby are notably cooler at night year-round. There is plenty of sunshine and clear skies generally more than 200 days of the year.

Rankings

General Rankings

- To help military veterans find the best places in which to settle down, *WalletHub* compared the 100 largest U.S. cities across 19 key indicators of livability, affordability and veteran-friendliness. They range from the share of military skill-related jobs to veteran income growth to the availability of VA health facilities. El Paso ranked #65. *Wallethub.com, "Best & Worst Places for Veterans to Live (2025)," November 7, 2024*

Business/Finance Rankings

- The El Paso metro area appeared on the Milken Institute "2025 Best Performing Cities" list. Rank: #80 out of 200 large metro areas (based on performance category). Criteria: job growth; wage growth; high-tech growth and impact; community resilience; housing affordability; household broadband access. *Milken Institute, "Best-Performing Cities 2025," January 14, 2025*

Culture/Performing Arts Rankings

- El Paso was selected as one of the 25 best cities for moviemakers in North America. Great film cities are places where filmmaking dreams can come true, that offer more creative space, lower costs, and great outdoor locations. NYC & LA were intentionally excluded. Criteria: film industry presence and culture; tax incentives; affordability; and proximity of festivals and schools. The city was ranked #21. *MovieMaker Magazine, "Best Places to Live and Work as a Moviemaker, 2025," January 29, 2025*

Education Rankings

- Personal finance website *WalletHub* analyzed the 150 largest U.S. metropolitan statistical areas to determine where the most educated Americans are putting their degrees to work. Criteria: education levels; percentage of workers with degrees; education quality and attainment gap; public school quality rankings; quality and enrollment of each metro area's universities. El Paso was ranked #136 (#1 = most educated city). *WalletHub.com, "Most & Least Educated Cities in America, 2025" July 2, 2024*

Environmental Rankings

- El Paso was highlighted as one of the 25 most ozone-polluted metro areas in the U.S. during 2021 through 2023. The area ranked #18. *American Lung Association, "State of the Air 2025," April 23, 2025*

Health/Fitness Rankings

- For each of the 100 largest cities in the United States, the American Fitness Index®, compiled in partnership between the American College of Sports Medicine and the Elevance Health Foundation, evaluated community infrastructure and more than 30 health behaviors including preventive health, levels of chronic disease conditions, food insecurity, pedestrian safety, air quality, and community/environment resources that support physical activity. El Paso ranked #73 for "community fitness." *americanfitnessindex.org, "2024 ACSM American Fitness Index Summary Report," July 23, 2024*

- El Paso was identified as a "2025 Allergy Capital." The area ranked #50 out of the nation's 100 largest metropolitan areas. Three groups of factors were used to identify the most challenging cities for people with allergies: annual tree, grass, and weed pollen scores; over the counter allergy medicine use; number of board-certified allergy specialists. *Asthma and Allergy Foundation of America, "2025 Allergy Capitals: The Most Challenging Places to Live with Allergies," March 18, 2025*

- El Paso was identified as a "2024 Asthma Capital." The area ranked #68 out of the nation's 100 largest metropolitan areas. Criteria: estimated asthma prevalence; asthma-related mortality; and ER visits due to asthma. Risk factors analyzed but not factored in the rankings: annual air quality including pollution and ozone levels; public smoking laws; indoor air quality; access to asthma specialists; rescue and controller medication use; uninsured rate; pollen allergy; poverty rate. *Asthma and Allergy Foundation of America, "Asthma Capitals 2024: The Most Challenging Places to Live With Asthma," September 10, 2024*

Real Estate Rankings

- *WalletHub* compared the most populated U.S. cities to determine which had the best markets for real estate agents. El Paso ranked #156 where demand was high and pay was the best. Criteria: sales per agent; annual median wage for real-estate agents; monthly average starting salary for real estate agents; real estate job density and competition; unemployment rate; home turnover rate; housing-market health index; and other relevant metrics. *WalletHub.com, "2021 Best Places to Be a Real Estate Agent," May 12, 2021*

- The El Paso metro area appeared on Realtor.com's list of hot housing markets to watch in 2025. The area ranked #4. Criteria: forecasted home price and sales growth; overall economy; population trends. *Realtor.com®, "Top 10 Housing Markets Positioned for Growth in 2025," December 10, 2024*

- El Paso was ranked #150 out of 176 metro areas in terms of cost of housing in 2024 by the National Association of Home Builders (#1 = most affordable). Criteria: the portion of an average family's income necessary to pay the mortgage on a median-priced home. *National Association of Home Builders®, NAHB-Wells Fargo Cost of Housing Index, 4th Quarter 2024*

Safety Rankings

- Allstate ranked the 100 most populous cities in America in terms of driver safety. El Paso ranked #25. Criteria based on anonymized driving behavior data from Allstate's mobile app powered by Arity: high speed driving (over 80 mph), phone handling, and hard braking. The report helps increase the importance of safety and awareness behind the wheel. *Allstate, "16th Allstate America's Best Drivers Report®" July 11, 2024*

Women/Minorities Rankings

- Personal finance website *WalletHub* compared more than 180 U.S. cities across two key dimensions, "Hispanic Business-Friendliness" and "Hispanic Purchasing Power," to arrive at the most favorable conditions for Hispanic entrepreneurs. El Paso was ranked #43 out of 182. Criteria includes: share of Hispanic-Owned Businesses; average growth of Hispanic Business revenues; Small Business-Friendliness score; affordability; and number of Hispanics with at least a bachelor's degree. *WalletHub.com, "Best Cities for Hispanic Entrepreneurs," September 4, 2024*

Miscellaneous Rankings

- *WalletHub* compared 148 of the most populated U.S. cities to determine their operating efficiency. A "Quality of Services" score was constructed for each city and then measured against the total budget per capita to reveal which were managed the best. El Paso ranked #48. Criteria: financial stability; economy; education; safety; health; infrastructure and pollution. *WalletHub.com, "2025's Best- & Worst-Run Cities in America," June 18, 2024*

Business Environment

DEMOGRAPHICS

Population Growth

Area	1990 Census	2000 Census	2010 Census	2020 Census	2023 Estimate[2]	Population Growth 1990-2023 (%)
City	515,541	563,662	649,121	678,815	678,147	31.5
MSA[1]	591,610	679,622	800,647	868,859	869,606	47.0
U.S.	248,709,873	281,421,906	308,745,538	331,449,281	332,387,540	33.6

Note: (1) Figures cover the El Paso, TX Metropolitan Statistical Area; (2) 2019-2023 5-year ACS population estimate
Source: U.S. Census Bureau, 1990 Census, 2000 Census, 2010 Census, 2020 Census, 2019-2023 American Community Survey 5-Year Estimates

Race

Area	White Alone[2] (%)	Black Alone[2] (%)	Asian Alone[2] (%)	AIAN[3] Alone[2] (%)	NHOPI[4] Alone[2] (%)	Other Race Alone[2] (%)	Two or More Races (%)
City	39.3	3.6	1.5	0.9	0.2	16.0	38.6
MSA[1]	39.2	3.3	1.3	0.9	0.2	16.3	38.9
U.S.	63.4	12.4	5.8	0.9	0.2	6.6	10.7

Note: (1) Figures cover the El Paso, TX Metropolitan Statistical Area; (2) Alone is defined as not being in combination with one or more other races; (3) American Indian and Alaska Native; (4) Native Hawaiian and Other Pacific Islander
Source: U.S. Census Bureau, 2019-2023 American Community Survey 5-Year Estimates

Hispanic or Latino Origin

Area	Total (%)	Mexican (%)	Puerto Rican (%)	Cuban (%)	Other (%)
City	81.3	76.1	1.1	0.2	3.9
MSA[1]	82.6	77.5	1.0	0.2	4.0
U.S.	19.0	11.3	1.8	0.7	5.2

Note: Persons of Hispanic or Latino origin can be of any race; (1) Figures cover the El Paso, TX Metropolitan Statistical Area
Source: U.S. Census Bureau, 2019-2023 American Community Survey 5-Year Estimates

Age

Area	Percent of Population									Median Age
	Under Age 5	Age 5–19	Age 20–34	Age 35–44	Age 45–54	Age 55–64	Age 65–74	Age 75–84	Age 85+	
City	6.5	21.6	23.2	12.5	11.5	10.8	8.1	4.1	1.8	34.1
MSA[1]	6.8	22.6	23.1	12.8	11.4	10.4	7.6	3.7	1.6	33.3
U.S.	5.7	19.1	20.2	13.1	12.3	12.8	10.0	4.9	1.9	38.7

Note: (1) Figures cover the El Paso, TX Metropolitan Statistical Area
Source: U.S. Census Bureau, 2019-2023 American Community Survey 5-Year Estimates

Disability by Age

Area	All Ages	Under 18 Years Old	18 to 64 Years Old	65 Years and Over
City	14.3	5.5	12.0	40.2
MSA[1]	13.9	5.5	11.7	41.5
U.S.	13.0	4.7	10.7	32.9

Note: Figures show percent of the civilian noninstitutionalized population that reported having a disability. Disability status is determined from six types of difficulty: vision, hearing, cognitive, ambulatory, self-care, and independent living. For children under 5 years old, hearing and vision difficulty are used to determine disability status. For children between the ages of 5 and 14, disability status is determined from hearing, vision, cognitive, ambulatory, and self-care difficulties. For people aged 15 years and older, they are considered to have a disability if they have difficulty with any one of the six difficulty types; Note: (1) Figures cover the El Paso, TX Metropolitan Statistical Area
Source: U.S. Census Bureau, 2019-2023 American Community Survey 5-Year Estimates

Ancestry

Area	German	Irish	English	American	Italian	Polish	French[2]	European	Scottish
City	3.8	2.4	2.2	2.2	1.3	0.5	0.6	0.5	0.4
MSA[1]	3.5	2.2	2.0	2.3	1.2	0.4	0.5	0.5	0.3
U.S.	12.6	9.4	9.1	5.5	4.9	2.6	2.0	1.6	1.6

Note: Figures are the percentage of the total population reporting a particular ancestry. The nine most commonly reported ancestries in the U.S. are shown. Figures include multiple ancestries (e.g. if a person reported being Irish and Italian, they were included in both columns); (1) Figures cover the El Paso, TX Metropolitan Statistical Area; (2) Excludes Basque
Source: U.S. Census Bureau, 2019-2023 American Community Survey 5-Year Estimates

Foreign-born Population

Area	Percent of Population Born in								
	Any Foreign Country	Asia	Mexico	Europe	Caribbean	Central America[2]	South America	Africa	Canada
City	22.3	1.0	19.5	0.6	0.2	0.3	0.2	0.3	0.1
MSA[1]	23.1	0.9	20.6	0.5	0.2	0.4	0.2	0.3	0.1
U.S.	13.9	4.3	3.3	1.4	1.4	1.2	1.2	0.8	0.2

Note: (1) Figures cover the El Paso, TX Metropolitan Statistical Area; (2) Excludes Mexico.
Source: U.S. Census Bureau, 2019-2023 American Community Survey 5-Year Estimates

Household Size

Area	Persons in Household (%)							Average Household Size
	One	Two	Three	Four	Five	Six	Seven or More	
City	25.8	28.2	18.0	15.5	8.0	2.8	1.7	2.77
MSA[1]	23.9	27.3	18.2	16.3	9.0	3.5	1.8	2.88
U.S.	28.5	33.8	15.4	12.7	5.9	2.3	1.4	2.54

Note: (1) Figures cover the El Paso, TX Metropolitan Statistical Area
Source: U.S. Census Bureau, 2019-2023 American Community Survey 5-Year Estimates

Household Relationships

Area	House-holder	Opposite-sex Spouse	Same-sex Spouse	Opposite-sex Unmarried Partner	Same-sex Unmarried Partner	Child[2]	Grand-child	Other Relatives	Non-relatives
City	35.9	15.8	0.2	1.8	0.1	32.7	3.9	6.4	2.0
MSA[1]	34.2	15.8	0.2	1.7	0.1	33.5	4.2	6.5	1.8
U.S.	38.3	17.5	0.2	2.5	0.2	28.3	2.4	4.8	3.4

Note: Figures are percent of the total population; (1) Figures cover the El Paso, TX Metropolitan Statistical Area; (2) Includes biological, adopted, and stepchildren of the householder
Source: U.S. Census Bureau, 2020 Census

Gender

Area	Males	Females	Males per 100 Females
City	333,802	344,345	96.9
MSA[1]	432,470	437,136	98.9
U.S.	164,545,087	167,842,453	98.0

Note: (1) Figures cover the El Paso, TX Metropolitan Statistical Area
Source: U.S. Census Bureau, 2019-2023 American Community Survey 5-Year Estimates

Marital Status

Area	Never Married	Now Married[2]	Separated	Widowed	Divorced
City	35.5	44.8	3.3	5.6	10.9
MSA[1]	35.5	45.7	3.2	5.4	10.2
U.S.	34.1	47.9	1.7	5.6	10.7

Note: Figures are percentages and cover the population 15 years of age and older; (1) Figures cover the El Paso, TX Metropolitan Statistical Area; (2) Excludes separated
Source: U.S. Census Bureau, 2019-2023 American Community Survey 5-Year Estimates

Religious Groups by Family

Area	Catholic	Baptist	Methodist	LDS[2]	Pentecostal	Lutheran	Islam	Adventist	Other
MSA[1]	47.9	2.5	0.4	1.2	1.1	0.2	0.1	2.1	6.9
U.S.	18.7	7.3	3.0	2.0	1.8	1.7	1.3	1.3	11.6

Note: Figures are the number of adherents as a percentage of the total population and cover the eight largest religious groups in the U.S; (1) Figures cover the El Paso, TX Metropolitan Statistical Area; (2) Church of Jesus Christ of Latter-day Saints
Sources: 2020 U.S. Religion Census, Association of Statisticians of American Religious Bodies; The Association of Religion Data Archives (ARDA)

Religious Groups by Tradition

Area	Catholic	Evangelical Protestant	Mainline Protestant	Black Protestant	Islam	Judaism	Hinduism	Orthodox	Buddhism
MSA[1]	47.9	9.9	0.6	0.4	0.1	0.2	<0.1	<0.1	0.2
U.S.	18.7	16.5	5.2	2.3	1.3	0.6	0.4	0.4	0.3

Note: Figures are the number of adherents as a percentage of the total population; (1) Figures cover the El Paso, TX Metropolitan Statistical Area
Sources: 2020 U.S. Religion Census, Association of Statisticians of American Religious Bodies; The Association of Religion Data Archives (ARDA)

ECONOMY

Real Gross Domestic Product (GDP)

Area	2017	2018	2019	2020	2021	2022	2023	Rank[3]
MSA[1]	30.4	31.4	33.1	32.9	35.3	35.9	38.1	87
U.S.[2]	17,619.1	18,160.7	18,642.5	18,238.9	19,387.6	19,896.6	20,436.3	—

Note: Figures are in billions of chained 2017 dollars; (1) Figures cover the El Paso, TX Metropolitan Statistical Area; (2) Figures cover real GDP within metropolitan areas; (3) Rank is based on 2023 data and ranges from 1 to 384
Source: U.S. Bureau of Economic Analysis

Economic Growth

Area	2014	2015	2016	2017	2018	2019	2020	2021	2022	2023
MSA[1]	-1.5	1.5	0.9	2.1	3.1	5.4	-0.5	7.2	1.9	6.1
U.S.[2]	2.6	3.2	2.0	2.7	3.1	2.7	-2.2	6.3	2.6	2.7

Note: Figures are real gross domestic product growth rates and represent percent change from preceding period; (1) Figures cover the El Paso, TX Metropolitan Statistical Area; (2) Figures are the average growth rates within metropolitan areas
Source: U.S. Bureau of Economic Analysis

Metropolitan Area Exports

Area	2018	2019	2020	2021	2022	2023	Rank[2]
MSA[1]	30,052.0	32,749.6	27,154.4	32,397.9	36,488.3	35,223.0	11
U.S.	1,664,056.1	1,645,173.7	1,431,406.6	1,753,941.4	2,062,937.4	2,019,160.5	—

Note: Figures are in millions of dollars; (1) Figures cover the El Paso, TX Metropolitan Statistical Area; (2) Rank is based on 2023 data and ranges from 1 to 386
Source: U.S. Department of Commerce, International Trade Administration, Office of Trade and Economic Analysis, Industry and Analysis, Exports by Metropolitan Area, data extracted April 2, 2025

Building Permits

Area	Single-Family			Multi-Family			Total		
	2023	2024	Pct. Chg.	2023	2024	Pct. Chg.	2023	2024	Pct. Chg.
City	1,572	1,644	4.6	280	243	-13.2	1,852	1,887	1.9
MSA[1]	1,967	2,077	5.6	280	243	-13.2	2,247	2,320	3.2
U.S.	920,000	981,900	6.7	591,100	496,100	-16.1	1,511,100	1,478,000	-2.2

Note: (1) Figures cover the El Paso, TX Metropolitan Statistical Area; Figures represent new, privately-owned housing units authorized (unadjusted data)
Source: U.S. Census Bureau, Building Permits Survey (BPS), 2023, 2024

Bankruptcy Filings

Area	Business Filings			Nonbusiness Filings		
	2023	2024	% Chg.	2023	2024	% Chg.
El Paso County	65	72	10.8	1,351	1,512	11.9
U.S.	18,926	23,107	22.1	434,064	494,201	13.9

Note: Business filings include Chapter 7, Chapter 9, Chapter 11, Chapter 12, Chapter 13, Chapter 15, and Section 304; Nonbusiness filings include Chapter 7, Chapter 11, and Chapter 13
Source: Administrative Office of the U.S. Courts, Business and Nonbusiness Bankruptcy, County Cases Commenced by Chapter of the Bankruptcy Code, During the 12-Month Period Ending December 31, 2023 and Business and Nonbusiness Bankruptcy, County Cases Commenced by Chapter of the Bankruptcy Code, During the 12-Month Period Ending December 31, 2024

Housing Vacancy Rates

Area	Gross Vacancy Rate[3] (%)			Year-Round Vacancy Rate[4] (%)			Rental Vacancy Rate[5] (%)			Homeowner Vacancy Rate[6] (%)		
	2022	2023	2024	2022	2023	2024	2022	2023	2024	2022	2023	2024
MSA[1]	n/a	n/a	n/a	n/a	n/a	n/a	n/a	n/a	n/a	n/a	n/a	n/a
U.S.[2]	9.1	9.0	9.1	7.5	7.5	7.6	5.7	6.5	6.8	0.8	0.8	1.0

Note: (1) Figures cover the El Paso, TX Metropolitan Statistical Area; (2) Figures cover the 75 largest Metropolitan Statistical Areas; (3) The percentage of the total housing inventory that is vacant; (4) The percentage of the housing inventory (excluding seasonal units) that is year-round vacant; (5) The percentage of rental inventory that is vacant for rent; (6) The percentage of homeowner inventory that is vacant for sale; n/a not available
Source: U.S. Census Bureau, Housing Vacancies and Homeownership Annual Statistics: 2022, 2023, 2024

INCOME

Income

Area	Per Capita ($)	Median Household ($)	Average Household ($)
City	28,942	58,734	78,842
MSA[1]	27,509	58,800	77,734
U.S.	43,289	78,538	110,491

Note: (1) Figures cover the El Paso, TX Metropolitan Statistical Area
Source: U.S. Census Bureau, 2019-2023 American Community Survey 5-Year Estimates

Household Income Distribution

Area	Percent of Households Earning							
	Under $15,000	$15,000 -$24,999	$25,000 -$34,999	$35,000 -$49,999	$50,000 -$74,999	$75,000 -$99,999	$100,000 -$149,999	$150,000 and up
City	12.9	9.1	8.9	12.8	18.2	12.6	14.2	11.5
MSA[1]	12.8	8.9	8.9	12.8	18.6	12.6	14.4	11.1
U.S.	8.5	6.6	6.8	10.4	15.7	12.7	17.4	21.9

Note: (1) Figures cover the El Paso, TX Metropolitan Statistical Area
Source: U.S. Census Bureau, 2019-2023 American Community Survey 5-Year Estimates

Poverty Rate

Area	All Ages	Under 18 Years Old	18 to 64 Years Old	65 Years and Over
City	18.4	24.8	15.4	20.0
MSA[1]	18.9	25.1	15.8	20.6
U.S.	12.4	16.3	11.6	10.4

Note: Figures are percentage of people whose income during the past 12 months was below the poverty level; (1) Figures cover the El Paso, TX Metropolitan Statistical Area
Source: U.S. Census Bureau, 2019-2023 American Community Survey 5-Year Estimates

EMPLOYMENT

Labor Force and Employment

Area	Civilian Labor Force			Workers Employed		
	Dec. 2023	Dec. 2024	% Chg.	Dec. 2023	Dec. 2024	% Chg.
City	321,869	330,289	2.6	309,686	317,905	2.7
MSA[1]	388,422	398,643	2.6	372,959	382,859	2.7
U.S.	166,661,000	167,746,000	0.7	160,754,000	161,294,000	0.3

Note: Data is not seasonally adjusted and covers workers 16 years of age and older; (1) Figures cover the El Paso, TX Metropolitan Statistical Area
Source: Bureau of Labor Statistics, Local Area Unemployment Statistics

Unemployment Rate

Area	2024											
	Jan.	Feb.	Mar.	Apr.	May	Jun.	Jul.	Aug.	Sep.	Oct.	Nov.	Dec.
City	4.3	4.5	4.1	3.7	3.9	4.5	4.5	4.5	4.2	4.2	4.2	3.7
MSA[1]	4.5	4.7	4.3	3.9	4.1	4.8	4.8	4.7	4.4	4.4	4.4	4.0
U.S.	4.1	4.2	3.9	3.5	3.7	4.3	4.5	4.4	3.9	3.9	4.0	3.8

Note: Data is not seasonally adjusted and covers workers 16 years of age and older; (1) Figures cover the El Paso, TX Metropolitan Statistical Area
Source: Bureau of Labor Statistics, Local Area Unemployment Statistics

Average Wages

Occupation	$/Hr.	Occupation	$/Hr.
Accountants and Auditors	35.86	Maintenance and Repair Workers	19.68
Automotive Mechanics	22.04	Marketing Managers	55.59
Bookkeepers	20.35	Network and Computer Systems Admin.	39.84
Carpenters	20.00	Nurses, Licensed Practical	27.06
Cashiers	12.41	Nurses, Registered	42.08
Computer Programmers	34.05	Nursing Assistants	16.41
Computer Systems Analysts	44.84	Office Clerks, General	16.95
Computer User Support Specialists	22.07	Physical Therapists	46.74
Construction Laborers	17.25	Physicians	120.70
Cooks, Restaurant	14.12	Plumbers, Pipefitters and Steamfitters	25.72
Customer Service Representatives	17.31	Police and Sheriff's Patrol Officers	36.19
Dentists	101.96	Postal Service Mail Carriers	28.75
Electricians	23.92	Real Estate Sales Agents	31.06
Engineers, Electrical	44.54	Retail Salespersons	14.45
Fast Food and Counter Workers	11.61	Sales Representatives, Technical/Scientific	41.79
Financial Managers	67.83	Secretaries, Exc. Legal/Medical/Executive	18.76
First-Line Supervisors of Office Workers	27.70	Security Guards	14.38
General and Operations Managers	46.07	Surgeons	n/a
Hairdressers/Cosmetologists	15.79	Teacher Assistants, Exc. Postsecondary[1]	13.36
Home Health and Personal Care Aides	11.14	Teachers, Secondary School, Exc. Sp. Ed.[1]	29.30
Janitors and Cleaners	13.49	Telemarketers	n/a
Landscaping/Groundskeeping Workers	15.24	Truck Drivers, Heavy/Tractor-Trailer	25.51
Lawyers	61.03	Truck Drivers, Light/Delivery Services	19.26
Maids and Housekeeping Cleaners	12.61	Waiters and Waitresses	13.84

Note: Wage data covers the El Paso, TX Metropolitan Statistical Area; (1) Hourly wages were calculated from annual wage data based on a 40 hour work week
Source: Bureau of Labor Statistics, Metro Area Occupational Employment & Wage Estimates, May 2024

Employment by Industry

Sector	MSA[1] Number of Employees	MSA[1] Percent of Total	U.S. Percent of Total
Construction, Mining, and Logging	16,100	4.5	5.5
Financial Activities	14,900	4.1	5.8
Government	74,700	20.8	14.9
Information	6,500	1.8	1.9
Leisure and Hospitality	41,500	11.6	10.4
Manufacturing	17,400	4.8	8.0
Other Services	10,100	2.8	3.7
Private Education and Health Services	55,700	15.5	16.9
Professional and Business Services	45,100	12.6	14.2
Retail Trade	41,100	11.4	10.0
Transportation, Warehousing, and Utilities	21,700	6.0	4.8
Wholesale Trade	14,400	4.0	3.9

Note: Figures are non-farm employment as of December 2024. Figures are not seasonally adjusted and include workers 16 years of age and older; (1) Figures cover the El Paso, TX Metropolitan Statistical Area
Source: Bureau of Labor Statistics, Current Employment Statistics, Employment, Hours, and Earnings

Employment by Occupation

Occupation Classification	City (%)	MSA[1] (%)	U.S. (%)
Management, Business, Science, and Arts	34.9	33.2	42.0
Natural Resources, Construction, and Maintenance	8.6	9.9	8.6
Production, Transportation, and Material Moving	13.0	13.9	13.0
Sales and Office	22.6	22.5	19.9
Service	21.0	20.4	16.5

Note: Figures cover employed civilians 16 years of age and older; (1) Figures cover the El Paso, TX Metropolitan Statistical Area
Source: U.S. Census Bureau, 2019-2023 American Community Survey 5-Year Estimates

Occupations with Greatest Projected Employment Growth: 2022 – 2032

Occupation[1]	2022 Employment	2032 Projected Employment	Numeric Employment Change	Percent Employment Change
General and Operations Managers	425,560	504,280	78,720	18.5
Fast Food and Counter Workers	333,870	394,290	60,420	18.1
Stockers and Order Fillers	264,810	321,600	56,790	21.4
Home Health and Personal Care Aides	313,670	367,500	53,830	17.2
Software Developers	110,280	161,780	51,500	46.7
Cooks, Restaurant	113,680	158,830	45,150	39.7
Laborers and Freight, Stock, and Material Movers, Hand	225,090	269,120	44,030	19.6
Heavy and Tractor-Trailer Truck Drivers	226,450	270,320	43,870	19.4
Retail Salespersons	319,400	357,630	38,230	12.0
Registered Nurses	233,850	267,980	34,130	14.6

Note: Projections cover Texas; (1) Sorted by numeric employment change
Source: www.projectionscentral.org, State Occupational Projections, 2022–2032 Long-Term Projections

Fastest-Growing Occupations: 2022 – 2032

Occupation[1]	2022 Employment	2032 Projected Employment	Numeric Employment Change	Percent Employment Change
Wind Turbine Service Technicians	4,860	7,950	3,090	63.6
Nurse Practitioners	19,060	30,490	11,430	60.0
Data Scientists	13,220	20,250	7,030	53.2
Computer and Information Research Scientists (SOC 2018)	2,070	3,140	1,070	51.7
Information Security Analysts (SOC 2018)	14,620	21,620	7,000	47.9
Software Developers	110,280	161,780	51,500	46.7
Statisticians	980	1,430	450	45.9
Operations Research Analysts	12,060	17,290	5,230	43.4
Software Quality Assurance Analysts and Testers	17,350	24,440	7,090	40.9
Medical and Health Services Managers	49,430	69,180	19,750	40.0

Note: Projections cover Texas; (1) Sorted by percent employment change and excludes occupations with numeric employment change less than 50
Source: www.projectionscentral.org, State Occupational Projections, 2022–2032 Long-Term Projections

CITY FINANCES

City Government Finances

Component	2022 ($000)	2022 ($ per capita)
Total Revenues	1,413,090	2,073
Total Expenditures	1,258,805	1,847
Debt Outstanding	2,468,379	3,622

Source: U.S. Census Bureau, State & Local Government Finances 2022

City Government Revenue by Source

Source	2022 ($000)	2022 ($ per capita)	2022 (%)
General Revenue			
From Federal Government	207,645	305	14.7
From State Government	42,765	63	3.0
From Local Governments	4,001	6	0.3
Taxes			
Property	344,586	506	24.4
Sales and Gross Receipts	267,586	393	18.9
Personal Income	0	0	0.0
Corporate Income	0	0	0.0
Motor Vehicle License	0	0	0.0
Other Taxes	15,357	23	1.1
Current Charges	295,507	434	20.9
Liquor Store	0	0	0.0
Utility	178,863	262	12.7

Source: U.S. Census Bureau, State & Local Government Finances 2022

City Government Expenditures by Function

Function	2022 ($000)	2022 ($ per capita)	2022 (%)
General Direct Expenditures			
Air Transportation	38,902	57	3.1
Corrections	0	0	0.0
Education	0	0	0.0
Employment Security Administration	0	0	0.0
Financial Administration	7,906	11	0.6
Fire Protection	156,068	229	12.4
General Public Buildings	0	0	0.0
Governmental Administration, Other	9,768	14	0.8
Health	39,546	58	3.1
Highways	66,303	97	5.3
Hospitals	0	0	0.0
Housing and Community Development	9,138	13	0.7
Interest on General Debt	89,199	130	7.1
Judicial and Legal	9,287	13	0.7
Libraries	5,442	8	0.4
Parking	0	0	0.0
Parks and Recreation	58,236	85	4.6
Police Protection	146,780	215	11.7
Public Welfare	1,517	2	0.1
Sewerage	94,525	138	7.5
Solid Waste Management	33,560	49	2.7
Veterans' Services	0	0	0.0
Liquor Store	0	0	0.0
Utility	274,251	402	21.8

Source: U.S. Census Bureau, State & Local Government Finances 2022

TAXES

State Corporate Income Tax Rates

State	Tax Rate (%)	Income Brackets ($)	Num. of Brackets	Financial Institution Tax Rate (%)[a]	Federal Income Tax Ded.
Texas	(u)	–	–	(u)	No

Note: Tax rates for tax year 2024; (a) Rates listed are the corporate income tax rate applied to financial institutions or excise taxes based on income. Some states have other taxes based upon the value of deposits or shares; (u) Texas imposes a Franchise Tax, otherwise known as margin tax, imposed on entities with more than $2,470,000 total revenues effective in 2024 at rate of 0.75%, or 0.375% for entities primarily engaged in retail or wholesale trade, on lesser of 70% of total revenues or 100% of gross receipts after deductions for either compensation ($450,000 deduction limit) or cost of goods sold. Texas has an EZ rate of 0.331 applicable to a $20 million revenue threshold.
Source: Federation of Tax Administrators, State Corporate Income Tax Rates, January 1, 2025

State Individual Income Tax Rates

State	Tax Rate (%)	Income Brackets ($)	Personal Exemptions ($)			Standard Ded. ($)	
			Single	Married	Depend.	Single	Married
Texas			– No state income tax –				

Note: Tax rates for tax year 2024; Local- and county-level taxes are not included
Source: Federation of Tax Administrators, State Individual Income Tax Rates, January 1, 2025

Various State Sales and Excise Tax Rates

State	State Sales Tax (%)	Gasoline[1] ($/gal.)	Cigarette[2] ($/pack)	Spirits[3] ($/gal.)	Wine[4] ($/gal.)	Beer[5] ($/gal.)	Recreational Marijuana (%)
Texas	6.25	0.20	1.41	2.40	0.20	0.19	Not legal

Note: All tax rates as of January 1, 2025; (1) The American Petroleum Institute has developed a methodology for determining the average tax rate on a gallon of fuel. Rates may include any of the following: excise taxes, environmental fees, storage tank fees, other fees or taxes, general sales tax, and local taxes; (2) The federal excise tax of $1.0066 per pack and local taxes are not included; (3) Rates are those applicable to off-premise sales of 40% alcohol by volume (a.b.v.) distilled spirits in 750ml containers. Local excise taxes are excluded; (4) Rates are those applicable to off-premise sales of 11% a.b.v. non-carbonated wine in 750ml containers; (5) Rates are those applicable to off-premise sales of 4.7% a.b.v. beer in 12 ounce containers.
Source: Tax Foundation, 2025 Facts & Figures: How Does Your State Compare?

State Tax Competitiveness Index

State	Overall Rank	Corporate Tax Rank	Individual Income Tax Rank	Sales Tax Rank	Property Tax Rank	Unemployment Insurance Tax Rank
Texas	7	46	1	36	40	30

Note: The Tax Foundation's State Tax Competitiveness Index enables policymakers, taxpayers, and business leaders to gauge how their states' tax systems compare. A rank of 1 is best, 50 is worst. Rankings do not average to the total. States without a tax rank equally as 1. DC's scores and rankings do not affect other states. The report shows tax systems as of July 1, 2024 (the beginning of Fiscal Year 2025).
Source: Tax Foundation, State Tax Competitiveness Index 2025

TRANSPORTATION

Means of Transportation to Work

Area	Car/Truck/Van Drove Alone	Car/Truck/Van Carpooled	Public Transportation Bus	Public Transportation Subway	Public Transportation Railroad	Bicycle	Walked	Other Means	Worked at Home
City	76.5	11.1	1.0	0.0	0.0	0.1	1.1	2.3	7.8
MSA[1]	76.3	11.4	0.9	0.0	0.0	0.1	1.5	2.0	7.8
U.S.	70.2	8.5	1.7	1.3	0.4	0.4	2.4	1.6	13.5

Note: Figures are percentages and cover workers 16 years of age and older; (1) Figures cover the El Paso, TX Metropolitan Statistical Area
Source: U.S. Census Bureau, 2019-2023 American Community Survey 5-Year Estimates

Travel Time to Work

Area	Less Than 10 Minutes	10 to 19 Minutes	20 to 29 Minutes	30 to 44 Minutes	45 to 59 Minutes	60 to 89 Minutes	90 Minutes or More
City	9.3	33.5	28.5	20.1	4.3	2.4	1.9
MSA[1]	9.7	32.0	27.4	21.6	4.9	2.4	2.0
U.S.	12.6	28.6	21.2	20.8	8.1	6.0	2.8

Note: Note: Figures are percentages and include workers 16 years old and over; (1) Figures cover the El Paso, TX Metropolitan Statistical Area
Source: U.S. Census Bureau, 2019-2023 American Community Survey 5-Year Estimates

Key Congestion Measures

Measure	2000	2010	2015	2020	2022
Annual Hours of Delay, Total (000)	13,636	18,665	21,604	17,490	20,767
Annual Hours of Delay, Per Auto Commuter	32	36	39	32	38
Annual Congestion Cost, Per Auto Commuter ($)	765	834	890	769	903

Note: Figures cover the El Paso TX-NM urban area
Source: Texas A&M Transportation Institute, 2023 Urban Mobility Report

Freeway Travel Time Index

Measure	1985	1990	1995	2000	2005	2010	2015	2020	2022
Urban Area Index[1]	1.05	1.09	1.13	1.16	1.18	1.17	1.16	1.13	1.13
Urban Area Rank[1,2]	64	56	47	43	41	41	57	6	71

Note: Freeway Travel Time Index—the ratio of travel time in the peak period to the travel time at free-flow conditions. For example, a value of 1.30 indicates a 20-minute free-flow trip takes 26 minutes in the peak (20 minutes x 1.30 = 26 minutes); (1) Covers the El Paso TX-NM urban area; (2) Rank is based on 101 larger urban areas (#1 = highest travel time index)
Source: Texas A&M Transportation Institute, 2023 Urban Mobility Report

Public Transportation

Agency Name / Mode of Transportation	Vehicles Operated in Maximum Service[1]	Annual Unlinked Passenger Trips[2] (in thous.)	Annual Passenger Miles[3] (in thous.)
Mass Transit Department-City of El Paso (Sun Metro)			
Bus (directly operated)	97	5,731.6	36,487.3
Demand Response (purchased transportation)	55	252.4	2,417.0
Streetcar Rail (directly operated)	4	89.5	149.4

Note: (1) Number of revenue vehicles operated by the given mode and type of service to meet the annual maximum service requirement. This is the revenue vehicle count during the peak season of the year; on the week and day that maximum service is provided. Vehicles operated in maximum service (VOMS) exclude atypical days and one-time special events; (2) Number of passengers who boarded public transportation vehicles. Passengers are counted each time they board a vehicle no matter how many vehicles they use to travel from their origin to their destination. (3) Sum of the distances ridden by all passengers during the entire fiscal year.
Source: Federal Transit Administration, National Transit Database, 2023

Air Transportation

Airport Name and Code / Type of Service	Passenger Airlines[1]	Passenger Enplanements	Freight Carriers[2]	Freight (lbs)
El Paso International (ELP)				
Domestic service (U.S. carriers only)	23	2,050,734	16	84,763,034
International service (U.S. carriers only)	3	17,452	3	512,294

Note: (1) Includes all U.S.-based major, minor and commuter airlines that carried at least one passenger during the year; (2) Includes all U.S.-based airlines and freight carriers that transported at least one pound of freight during the year.
Source: Bureau of Transportation Statistics, The Intermodal Transportation Database, Air Carriers: T-100 Domestic Market (U.S. carriers only), 2024; Bureau of Transportation Statistics, The Intermodal Transportation Database, Air Carriers: T-100 International Market (U.S. carriers only), 2024

BUSINESSES

Major Business Headquarters

Company Name	Industry	Rankings	
		Fortune[1]	Forbes[2]
No companies listed	-	-	-

Note: (1) Companies that produce a 10-K are ranked 1 to 500 based on 2023 revenue; (2) All private companies with at least $2 billion in annual revenue through the end of their most current fiscal year are ranked 1 to 275; companies listed are headquartered in the city; dashes indicate no ranking
Source: Fortune, "Fortune 500," 2024; Forbes, "America's Largest Private Companies," 2024

Fastest-Growing Businesses

According to *Inc.*, El Paso is home to one of America's 500 fastest-growing private companies: **C. R. Wannamaker Law** (#112). Criteria: must be an independent, privately-held, for-profit, U.S. corporation, proprietorship or partnership as of December 31, 2023; revenues must be at least $100,000 in 2020 and $2 million in 2023; must have four-year operating/sales history. *Inc., "America's 500 Fastest-Growing Private Companies," 2024*

Living Environment

COST OF LIVING

Cost of Living Index

Composite Index	Groceries	Housing	Utilities	Transportation	Health Care	Misc. Goods/Services
88.1	96.7	70.7	91.5	101.2	88.7	94.3

Note: The Cost of Living Index measures regional differences in the cost of consumer goods and services, excluding taxes and non-consumer expenditures, for professional and managerial households in the top income quintile. It is based on more than 50,000 prices covering almost 60 different items for which prices are collected three times a year by chambers of commerce, economic development organizations or university applied economic centers in each participating urban area. The numbers shown should be read as a percentage above or below the national average of 100. For example, a value of 115.4 in the groceries column indicates that grocery prices are 15.4% higher than the national average. Small differences in the index numbers should not be interpreted as significant; Figures cover the El Paso TX urban area.
Source: The Council for Community and Economic Research, Cost of Living Index, 2024

Grocery Prices

Area[1]	T-Bone Steak ($/pound)	Frying Chicken ($/pound)	Whole Milk ($/half gal.)	Eggs ($/dozen)	Orange Juice ($/64 oz.)	Coffee ($/11.5 oz.)
City[2]	14.86	1.41	4.63	2.97	4.27	5.42
Avg.	15.42	1.55	4.69	3.25	4.41	5.46
Min.	14.50	1.16	4.43	2.75	4.00	4.85
Max.	17.56	2.89	5.49	4.78	5.54	7.89

Note: (1) Values for the local area are compared with the average, minimum and maximum values for all 276 areas in the Cost of Living Index; (2) Figures cover the El Paso TX urban area; **T-Bone Steak** (price per pound); **Frying Chicken** (price per pound, whole fryer); **Whole Milk** (half gallon carton); **Eggs** (price per dozen, Grade A, large); **Orange Juice** (64 oz. Tropicana or Florida Natural); **Coffee** (11.5 oz. can, vacuum-packed, Maxwell House, Hills Bros, or Folgers).
Source: The Council for Community and Economic Research, Cost of Living Index, 2024

Housing and Utility Costs

Area[1]	New Home Price ($)	Apartment Rent ($/month)	All Electric ($/month)	Part Electric ($/month)	Other Energy ($/month)	Telephone ($/month)
City[2]	354,072	1,146	-	111.01	62.07	203.47
Avg.	515,975	1,550	210.99	123.07	82.07	194.99
Min.	265,375	692	104.33	53.68	36.26	179.42
Max.	2,775,821	5,719	529.02	397.28	361.63	223.33

Note: (1) Values for the local area are compared with the average, minimum and maximum values for all 276 areas in the Cost of Living Index; (2) Figures cover the El Paso TX urban area; **New Home Price** (2,400 sf living area, 8,000 sf lot, in urban area with full utilities); **Apartment Rent** (950 sf 2 bedroom/1.5 or 2 bath, unfurnished, excluding all utilities except water); **All Electric** (average monthly cost for an all-electric home); **Part Electric** (average monthly cost for a part-electric home); **Other Energy** (average monthly cost for natural gas, fuel oil, coal, wood, and any other forms of energy except electricity); **Telephone** (price includes the base monthly rate plus taxes and fees for three lines of mobile phone service).
Source: The Council for Community and Economic Research, Cost of Living Index, 2024

Health Care, Transportation, and Other Costs

Area[1]	Doctor ($/visit)	Dentist ($/visit)	Optometrist ($/visit)	Gasoline ($/gallon)	Beauty Salon ($/visit)	Men's Shirt ($)
City[2]	129.11	95.03	101.95	3.23	33.64	34.89
Avg.	143.77	117.51	129.23	3.32	48.57	38.14
Min.	36.74	58.67	67.33	2.80	24.00	13.41
Max.	270.44	216.82	307.33	5.28	94.00	63.89

Note: (1) Values for the local area are compared with the average, minimum and maximum values for all 276 areas in the Cost of Living Index; (2) Figures cover the El Paso TX urban area; **Doctor** (general practitioners routine exam of an established patient); **Dentist** (adult teeth cleaning and periodic oral examination); **Optometrist** (full vision eye exam for established adult patient); **Gasoline** (one gallon regular unleaded, national brand, including all taxes, cash price at self-service pump if available); **Beauty Salon** (woman's shampoo, trim, and blow-dry); **Men's Shirt** (cotton/polyester dress shirt, pinpoint weave, long sleeves).
Source: The Council for Community and Economic Research, Cost of Living Index, 2024

HOUSING

Homeownership Rate

Area	2017 (%)	2018 (%)	2019 (%)	2020 (%)	2021 (%)	2022 (%)	2023 (%)	2024 (%)
MSA[1]	n/a	n/a	n/a	n/a	n/a	n/a	n/a	n/a
U.S.	63.9	64.4	64.6	66.6	65.5	65.8	65.9	65.6

Note: (1) Figures cover the El Paso, TX Metropolitan Statistical Area; n/a not available
Source: U.S. Census Bureau, Housing Vacancies and Homeownership Annual Statistics: 2017-2024

House Price Index (HPI)

Area	National Ranking[2]	Quarterly Change (%)	One-Year Change (%)	Five-Year Change (%)	Since 1991Q1 (%)
MSA[1]	67	1.00	6.86	63.01	237.09
U.S.[3]	–	1.43	4.51	57.13	327.82

Note: The HPI is a weighted repeat sales index. It measures average price changes in repeat sales or refinancings on the same properties. This information is obtained by reviewing repeat mortgage transactions on single-family properties whose mortgages have been purchased or securitized by Fannie Mae or Freddie Mac since January 1975; (1) Figures cover the El Paso, TX Metropolitan Statistical Area; (2) Rankings are based on annual percentage change for all metro areas containing at least 15,000 transactions over the last 10 years and ranges from 1 to 241; (3) figures based on a weighted average of Census Division estimates using a seasonally adjusted, purchase-only index; all figures are for the period ending December 31, 2024
Source: Federal Housing Finance Agency, Change in FHFA Metropolitan Area House Price Indexes, All Transactions Index, 2024Q4

Home Value

Area	Under $100,000	$100,000 -$199,999	$200,000 -$299,999	$300,000 -$399,999	$400,000 -$499,999	$500,000 -$999,999	$1,000,000 or more	Median ($)
City	14.2	47.6	24.4	7.7	2.7	2.8	0.7	171,700
MSA[1]	17.9	45.6	23.7	7.1	2.7	2.4	0.6	167,000
U.S.	12.1	17.8	19.5	14.4	10.5	19.1	6.5	303,400

Note: Figures are percentages except for median and cover owner-occupied housing units; (1) Figures cover the El Paso, TX Metropolitan Statistical Area
Source: U.S. Census Bureau, 2019-2023 American Community Survey 5-Year Estimates

Year Housing Structure Built

Area	2020 or Later	2010 -2019	2000 -2009	1990 -1999	1980 -1989	1970 -1979	1960 -1969	1950 -1959	1940 -1949	Before 1940	Median Year
City	0.9	14.1	13.5	11.7	14.9	15.9	10.2	10.9	3.2	4.7	1983
MSA[1]	1.4	16.4	15.2	12.8	14.7	14.6	8.7	9.3	2.8	4.1	1987
U.S.	1.2	8.9	13.6	12.8	13.0	14.4	10.0	9.7	4.5	11.9	1980

Note: Figures are percentages except for Median Year; Note: (1) Figures cover the El Paso, TX Metropolitan Statistical Area
Source: U.S. Census Bureau, 2019-2023 American Community Survey 5-Year Estimates

Gross Monthly Rent

Area	Under $500	$500 -$999	$1,000 -$1,499	$1,500 -$1,999	$2,000 -$2,499	$2,500 -$2,999	$3,000 and up	Median ($)
City	8.8	37.4	37.3	12.4	3.1	0.6	0.5	1,041
MSA[1]	8.7	37.2	37.0	13.0	3.1	0.5	0.4	1,045
U.S.	6.5	22.3	29.5	20.2	10.8	4.8	5.9	1,348

Note: Figures are percentages except for median; Gross rent is the contract rent plus the estimated average monthly cost of utilities (electricity, gas, and water and sewer) and fuels (oil, coal, kerosene, wood, etc.) if these are paid by the renter (or paid for the renter by someone else); (1) Figures cover the El Paso, TX Metropolitan Statistical Area
Source: U.S. Census Bureau, 2019-2023 American Community Survey 5-Year Estimates

HEALTH

Health Risk Factors

Category	MSA[1] (%)	U.S. (%)
Adults aged 18–64 who have any kind of health care coverage	n/a	90.8
Adults who reported being in good or better health	n/a	81.8
Adults who have been told they have high blood cholesterol	n/a	36.9
Adults who have been told they have high blood pressure	n/a	34.0
Adults who are current smokers	n/a	12.1
Adults who currently use e-cigarettes	n/a	7.7
Adults who currently use chewing tobacco, snuff, or snus	n/a	3.2
Adults who are heavy drinkers[2]	n/a	6.1
Adults who are binge drinkers[3]	n/a	15.2
Adults who are overweight (BMI 25.0 - 29.9)	n/a	34.4
Adults who are obese (BMI 30.0 - 99.8)	n/a	34.3
Adults who participated in any physical activities in the past month	n/a	75.8

Note: All figures are crude prevalence; (1) Figures for the El Paso, TX Metropolitan Statistical Area were not available.
(2) Heavy drinkers are classified as adult men having more than 14 drinks per week and adult women having more than 7 drinks per week; (3) Binge drinkers are classified as males having five or more drinks on one occasion or females having four or more drinks on one occasion
Source: Centers for Disease Control and Prevention, Behavioral Risk Factor Surveillance System, SMART: Selected Metropolitan Area Risk Trends, 2023

Acute and Chronic Health Conditions

Category	MSA[1] (%)	U.S. (%)
Adults who have ever been told they had a heart attack	n/a	4.2
Adults who have ever been told they have angina or coronary heart disease	n/a	4.0
Adults who have ever been told they had a stroke	n/a	3.3
Adults who have ever been told they have asthma	n/a	15.7
Adults who have ever been told they have arthritis	n/a	26.3
Adults who have ever been told they have diabetes[2]	n/a	11.5
Adults who have ever been told they had skin cancer	n/a	5.6
Adults who have ever been told they had any other types of cancer	n/a	8.4
Adults who have ever been told they have COPD	n/a	6.4
Adults who have ever been told they have kidney disease	n/a	3.7
Adults who have ever been told they have a form of depression	n/a	22.0

Note: All figures are crude prevalence; (1) Figures for the El Paso, TX Metropolitan Statistical Area were not available.
(2) Figures do not include pregnancy-related, borderline, or pre-diabetes
Source: Centers for Disease Control and Prevention, Behavioral Risk Factor Surveillance System, SMART: Selected Metropolitan Area Risk Trends, 2023

Health Screening and Vaccination Rates

Category	MSA[1] (%)	U.S. (%)
Adults who have ever been tested for HIV	n/a	37.5
Adults who have had their blood cholesterol checked within the last five years	n/a	87.0
Adults aged 65+ who have had flu shot within the past year	n/a	63.4
Adults aged 65+ who have ever had a pneumonia vaccination	n/a	71.9

Note: All figures are crude prevalence; (1) Figures for the El Paso, TX Metropolitan Statistical Area were not available.
Source: Centers for Disease Control and Prevention, Behavioral Risk Factor Surveillance System, SMART: Selected Metropolitan Area Risk Trends, 2023

Disability Status

Category	MSA[1] (%)	U.S. (%)
Adults who reported being deaf	n/a	7.4
Are you blind or have serious difficulty seeing, even when wearing glasses?	n/a	4.9
Do you have difficulty doing errands alone?	n/a	7.8
Do you have difficulty dressing or bathing?	n/a	3.6
Do you have serious difficulty concentrating/remembering/making decisions?	n/a	13.7
Do you have serious difficulty walking or climbing stairs?	n/a	13.2

Note: All figures are crude prevalence; (1) Figures for the El Paso, TX Metropolitan Statistical Area were not available.
Source: Centers for Disease Control and Prevention, Behavioral Risk Factor Surveillance System, SMART: Selected Metropolitan Area Risk Trends, 2023

Mortality Rates for the Top 10 Causes of Death in the U.S.

ICD-10[a] Sub-Chapter	ICD-10[a] Code	Crude Mortality Rate[2] per 100,000 population	
		County[3]	U.S.
Malignant neoplasms	C00-C97	131.4	182.7
Ischaemic heart diseases	I20-I25	88.5	109.6
Provisional assignment of new diseases of uncertain etiology[1]	U00-U49	71.8	65.3
Other forms of heart disease	I30-I51	28.2	65.1
Other degenerative diseases of the nervous system	G30-G31	59.5	52.4
Other external causes of accidental injury	W00-X59	32.6	52.3
Cerebrovascular diseases	I60-I69	28.0	49.1
Chronic lower respiratory diseases	J40-J47	19.8	43.5
Hypertensive diseases	I10-I15	35.8	38.9
Organic, including symptomatic, mental disorders	F01-F09	11.9	33.9

Note: (a) ICD-10 = International Classification of Diseases 10th Revision; (1) Includes COVID-19, adverse effects to COVID-19 vaccines, SARS, and vaping-related disorders; (2) Crude mortality rates are a three-year average covering 2021-2023; (3) Figures cover El Paso County.
Source: Centers for Disease Control and Prevention, National Center for Health Statistics. National Vital Statistics System, Mortality 2018-2023 on CDC WONDER Online Database

Mortality Rates for Selected Causes of Death

Cause of Death	ICD-10[a] Code	Crude Mortality Rate[1] per 100,000 population	
		County[2]	U.S.
Accidental poisoning and exposure to noxious substances	X40-X49	17.8	30.5
Alzheimer disease	G30	40.2	35.4
Assault	X85-Y09	4.7	7.3
COVID-19	U07.1	71.8	65.3
Diabetes mellitus	E10-E14	37.1	30.0
Diseases of the liver	K70-K76	32.6	20.8
Human immunodeficiency virus (HIV) disease	B20-B24	1.5	1.5
Influenza and pneumonia	J09-J18	9.3	13.4
Intentional self-harm	X60-X84	12.2	14.7
Malnutrition	E40-E46	4.3	6.0
Obesity and other hyperalimentation	E65-E68	2.5	3.1
Renal failure	N17-N19	23.7	16.4
Transport accidents	V01-V99	13.0	14.4

Note: (a) ICD-10 = International Classification of Diseases 10th Revision; (1) Crude mortality rates are a three-year average covering 2021-2023; (2) Figures cover El Paso County; Data are suppressed when the data meet the criteria for confidentiality constraints; Crude mortality rates are flagged as unreliable when the rate would be calculated with a numerator of 20 or less.
Source: Centers for Disease Control and Prevention, National Center for Health Statistics. National Vital Statistics System, Mortality 2018-2023 on CDC WONDER Online Database

Health Insurance Coverage

Area	With Health Insurance	With Private Health Insurance	With Public Health Insurance	Without Health Insurance	Population Under Age 19 Without Health Insurance
City	79.0	53.1	34.9	21.0	11.9
MSA[1]	78.1	52.1	34.3	21.9	12.9
U.S.	91.4	67.3	36.3	8.6	5.4

Note: Figures are percentages that cover the civilian noninstitutionalized population; (1) Figures cover the El Paso, TX Metropolitan Statistical Area
Source: U.S. Census Bureau, 2019-2023 American Community Survey 5-Year Estimates

Number of Medical Professionals

Area	MDs[3]	DOs[3,4]	Dentists	Podiatrists	Chiropractors	Optometrists
County[1] (number)	2,009	192	431	41	80	94
County[1] (rate[2])	231.2	22.1	49.5	4.7	9.2	10.8
U.S. (rate[2])	302.5	29.2	74.6	6.4	29.5	18.0

Note: Data as of 2023 unless noted; (1) Data covers El Paso County; (2) Number of medical professionals per 100,000 population; (3) Data as of 2022 and includes all active, non-federal physicians; (4) Doctor of Osteopathic Medicine
Source: U.S. Department of Health and Human Services, Health Resources and Services Administration, Bureau of Health Professions, Area Resource File (ARF) 2023-2024

EDUCATION

Public School District Statistics

District Name	Schls	Pupils	Pupil/ Teacher Ratio	Minority Pupils[1] (%)	Total Rev. per Pupil ($)	Total Exp. per Pupil ($)
Canutillo ISD	11	5,904	14.2	95.3	14,986	13,587
Clint ISD	15	10,260	14.5	96.6	15,866	14,647
El Paso ISD	76	49,139	14.6	91.5	14,172	15,379
Harmony Science Academy (El Paso)	6	5,297	17.0	91.1	13,000	11,628
Socorro ISD	52	47,304	21.6	95.5	12,775	14,281
Ysleta ISD	50	34,918	14.6	97.3	15,450	18,740

Note: Table includes school districts with 2,000 or more students; (1) Percentage of students that are not non-Hispanic white.
Source: U.S. Department of Education, National Center for Education Statistics, Common Core of Data, Local Education Agency (School District) Universe Survey: School Year 2023-2024; U.S. Department of Education, National Center for Education Statistics, Common Core of Data, School District Finance Survey (F-33): School Year 2021–22

Best High Schools

According to *U.S. News,* El Paso is home to two of the top 500 high schools in the U.S.: **Valle Verde Early College High School** (#241); **Mission Early College High School** (#363). Nearly 25,000 public, magnet and charter schools were ranked based on their performance on state assessments and how well they prepare students for college. *U.S. News & World Report, "Best High Schools 2024"*

Highest Level of Education

Area	Less than H.S.	H.S. Diploma	Some College, No Deg.	Associate Degree	Bachelor's Degree	Master's Degree	Prof. School Degree	Doctorate Degree
City	18.1	24.4	21.3	8.8	18.3	6.7	1.4	1.0
MSA[1]	19.4	24.9	21.1	9.2	17.1	6.1	1.2	0.9
U.S.	10.6	26.2	19.4	8.8	21.3	9.8	2.3	1.6

Note: Figures cover persons age 25 and over; (1) Figures cover the El Paso, TX Metropolitan Statistical Area
Source: U.S. Census Bureau, 2019-2023 American Community Survey 5-Year Estimates

Educational Attainment by Race

Area	High School Graduate or Higher (%)					Bachelor's Degree or Higher (%)				
	Total	White	Black	Asian	Hisp.[2]	Total	White	Black	Asian	Hisp.[2]
City	81.9	87.0	94.8	88.4	78.7	27.5	31.5	30.8	52.7	23.9
MSA[1]	80.6	85.8	95.3	88.8	77.4	25.3	29.4	32.0	50.5	21.9
U.S.	89.4	92.9	88.1	88.0	72.5	35.0	37.7	24.7	57.0	19.9

Note: Figures shown cover persons 25 years old and over; (1) Figures cover the El Paso, TX Metropolitan Statistical Area; (2) People of Hispanic origin can be of any race
Source: U.S. Census Bureau, 2019-2023 American Community Survey 5-Year Estimates

School Enrollment by Grade and Control

Area	Preschool (%)		Kindergarten (%)		Grades 1 - 4 (%)		Grades 5 - 8 (%)		Grades 9 - 12 (%)	
	Public	Private	Public	Private	Public	Private	Public	Private	Public	Private
City	87.0	13.0	91.9	8.1	92.8	7.2	94.1	5.9	95.7	4.3
MSA[1]	87.0	13.0	94.1	5.9	93.1	6.9	94.4	5.6	96.2	3.8
U.S.	58.7	41.3	85.2	14.8	87.2	12.8	87.9	12.1	89.0	11.0

Note: Figures shown cover persons 3 years old and over; (1) Figures cover the El Paso, TX Metropolitan Statistical Area
Source: U.S. Census Bureau, 2019-2023 American Community Survey 5-Year Estimates

Higher Education

Four-Year Colleges			Two-Year Colleges			Medical Schools[1]	Law Schools[2]	Voc/Tech[3]
Public	Private Non-profit	Private For-profit	Public	Private Non-profit	Private For-profit			
2	0	3	1	0	1	1	0	5

Note: Figures cover institutions located within the El Paso, TX Metropolitan Statistical Area and include main campuses only; (1) includes schools accredited by the Liaison Committee on Medical Education and the American Osteopathic Association's Commission on Osteopathic College Accreditation; (2) includes ABA-accredited schools, schools with provisional ABA accreditation, and state accredited schools; (3) includes all schools with programs that are less than 2 years.
Source: National Center for Education Statistics, Integrated Postsecondary Education System (IPEDS), 2023-24; Wikipedia, List of Medical Schools in the United States, accessed May 2, 2025; Wikipedia, List of Law Schools in the United States, accessed May 2, 2025

EMPLOYERS

Major Employers

Company Name	Industry
Alorica	Inbound customer service
Automatic Data Processing	Contact center, private
Coca-Cola Enterprises	Bottling & distributing
Datamark	Data processing & related service
Del Sol Medical Center	Healthcare, private
Dish Network	Technical support center
El Paso Electric Corporation	Electric utilities
GC Services	Inbound customer service
Las Palmas Medical Center	Healthcare, private
Redcats USA	Inbound customer service
RM Personnel	Employment services
T&T Staff Management	Employment services
Texas Tech University Health Sci Ctr	Higher education & health care
Union Pacific Railroad Co.	Transportation
University Medical Center	Healthcare, public
Visiting Nurse Association of El Paso	Healthcare & social assistance
West Customer Management Group	Inbound customer service
Western Refining	Corporate headquarters petro chemical refinery

Note: Companies shown are located within the El Paso, TX Metropolitan Statistical Area.
Source: Chambers of Commerce; State Departments of Labor; Wikipedia

PUBLIC SAFETY

Crime Rate

Area	Total Crime Rate	Violent Crime Rate				Property Crime Rate		
		Murder	Rape	Robbery	Aggrav. Assault	Burglary	Larceny-Theft	Motor Vehicle Theft
City	1,955.2	5.0	40.9	48.0	242.2	157.2	1,116.4	345.4
U.S.	2,290.9	5.7	38.0	66.5	264.1	250.7	1,347.2	318.7

Note: Figures are crimes per 100,000 population.
Source: FBI, Table 8, Offenses Known to Law Enforcement, by State by City, 2023

Hate Crimes

Area	Number of Quarters Reported	Number of Incidents per Bias Motivation					
		Race/Ethnicity/Ancestry	Religion	Sexual Orientation	Disability	Gender	Gender Identity
City	4	0	0	0	0	0	0
U.S.	4	5,900	2,699	2,077	187	92	492

Source: Federal Bureau of Investigation, Hate Crime Statistics 2023

Identity Theft Consumer Reports

Area	Reports	Reports per 100,000 Population	Rank[2]
MSA[1]	1,950	224	128
U.S.	1,135,291	339	-

Note: (1) Figures cover the El Paso, TX Metropolitan Statistical Area; (2) Rank ranges from 1 to 401 where 1 indicates greatest number of identity theft reports per 100,000 population
Source: Federal Trade Commission, Consumer Sentinel Network Data Book 2024

Fraud and Other Consumer Reports

Area	Reports	Reports per 100,000 Population	Rank[2]
MSA[1]	10,479	1,205	125
U.S.	5,360,641	1,601	-

Note: (1) Figures cover the El Paso, TX Metropolitan Statistical Area; (2) Rank ranges from 1 to 401 where 1 indicates greatest number of fraud and other consumer reports per 100,000 population
Source: Federal Trade Commission, Consumer Sentinel Network Data Book 2024

POLITICS

2024 Presidential Election Results

Area	Trump (Rep.)	Harris (Dem.)	Stein (Green)	Kennedy (Ind.)	Oliver (Lib.)	Other
El Paso County	41.7	56.8	0.6	0.0	0.6	0.3
U.S.	49.7	48.2	0.6	0.5	0.4	0.6

Note: Results are percentages and may not add to 100% due to rounding
Source: Dave Leip's Atlas of U.S. Presidential Elections

SPORTS

Professional Sports Teams

Team Name	League	Year Established

No teams are located in the metro area
Source: Wikipedia, Major Professional Sports Teams of the United States and Canada, May 1, 2025

CLIMATE

Average and Extreme Temperatures

Temperature	Jan	Feb	Mar	Apr	May	Jun	Jul	Aug	Sep	Oct	Nov	Dec	Yr.
Extreme High (°F)	80	83	89	98	104	114	112	108	104	96	87	80	114
Average High (°F)	57	63	70	79	87	96	95	93	88	79	66	58	78
Average Temp. (°F)	44	49	56	64	73	81	83	81	75	65	52	45	64
Average Low (°F)	31	35	41	49	58	66	70	68	62	50	38	32	50
Extreme Low (°F)	-8	8	14	23	31	46	57	56	42	25	1	5	-8

Note: Figures cover the years 1948-1995
Source: National Climatic Data Center, International Station Meteorological Climate Summary, 9/96

Average Precipitation/Snowfall/Humidity

Precip./Humidity	Jan	Feb	Mar	Apr	May	Jun	Jul	Aug	Sep	Oct	Nov	Dec	Yr.
Avg. Precip. (in.)	0.4	0.4	0.3	0.2	0.3	0.7	1.6	1.5	1.4	0.7	0.3	0.6	8.6
Avg. Snowfall (in.)	1	1	Tr	Tr	0	0	0	0	0	Tr	1	2	6
Avg. Rel. Hum. 6am (%)	68	60	50	43	44	46	63	69	72	66	63	68	59
Avg. Rel. Hum. 3pm (%)	34	27	21	17	17	17	28	30	32	29	30	36	26

Note: Figures cover the years 1948-1995; Tr = Trace amounts (<0.05 in. of rain; <0.5 in. of snow)
Source: National Climatic Data Center, International Station Meteorological Climate Summary, 9/96

Weather Conditions

Temperature			Daytime Sky			Precipitation		
10°F & below	32°F & below	90°F & above	Clear	Partly cloudy	Cloudy	0.01 inch or more precip.	0.1 inch or more snow/ice	Thunder-storms
1	59	106	147	164	54	49	3	35

Note: Figures are average number of days per year and cover the years 1948-1995
Source: National Climatic Data Center, International Station Meteorological Climate Summary, 9/96

HAZARDOUS WASTE

Superfund Sites

The El Paso, TX metro area has no sites on the EPA's Superfund Final National Priorities List (NPL) or Superfund Alternative Approach (SAA) list. The Superfund alternative approach uses the same investigation and cleanup process and standards that are used for sites listed on the National Priorities List. The SAA is an alternative to listing a site on the NPL; it is not an alternative to Superfund or the Superfund process. There are a total of 1,445 Superfund sites with a status of proposed or final on both lists in the United States. *U.S. Environmental Protection Agency, National Priorities List, May 1, 2025; U.S. Environmental Protection Agency, Superfund Alternative Approach Sites, May 1, 2025*

AIR QUALITY

Air Quality Trends: Ozone

	1990	1995	2000	2005	2010	2015	2020	2021	2022	2023
MSA[1]	0.080	0.078	0.082	0.074	0.072	0.071	0.076	0.071	0.071	0.071
U.S.	0.087	0.089	0.081	0.080	0.072	0.068	0.066	0.067	0.067	0.070

Note: (1) Data covers the El Paso, TX Metropolitan Statistical Area. The values shown are the composite ozone concentration averages among trend sites based on the highest fourth daily maximum 8-hour concentration in parts per million. These trends are based on sites having an adequate record of monitoring data during the trend period. Data from exceptional events are included.
Source: U.S. Environmental Protection Agency, Air Quality Monitoring Information, "Air Quality Trends by City, 1990-2023".

Air Quality Index

Area	Percent of Days when Air Quality was...[2]					AQI Statistics[2]	
	Good	Moderate	Unhealthy for Sensitive Groups	Unhealthy	Very Unhealthy	Maximum	Median
MSA[1]	18.9	75.9	4.9	0.3	0.0	155	64

Note: (1) Data covers the El Paso, TX Metropolitan Statistical Area; (2) Based on 365 days with AQI data in 2023. Air Quality Index (AQI) is an index for reporting daily air quality. EPA calculates the AQI for five major air pollutants regulated by the Clean Air Act: ground-level ozone, particle pollution (aka particulate matter), carbon monoxide, sulfur dioxide, and nitrogen dioxide. The AQI runs from 0 to 500. The higher the AQI value, the greater the level of air pollution and the greater the health concern. There are six AQI categories: "Good" AQI is between 0 and 50. Air quality is considered satisfactory; "Moderate" AQI is between 51 and 100. Air quality is acceptable; "Unhealthy for Sensitive Groups" When AQI values are between 101 and 150, members of sensitive groups may experience health effects; "Unhealthy" When AQI values are between 151 and 200 everyone may begin to experience health effects; "Very Unhealthy" AQI values between 201 and 300 trigger a health alert; "Hazardous" AQI values over 300 trigger warnings of emergency conditions (not shown).
Source: U.S. Environmental Protection Agency, Air Quality Index Report, 2023

Air Quality Index Pollutants

Area	Percent of Days when AQI Pollutant was...[2]					
	Carbon Monoxide	Nitrogen Dioxide	Ozone	Sulfur Dioxide	Particulate Matter 2.5	Particulate Matter 10
MSA[1]	0.0	1.4	29.9	(3)	56.4	12.3

Note: (1) Data covers the El Paso, TX Metropolitan Statistical Area; (2) Based on 365 days with AQI data in 2023. The Air Quality Index (AQI) is an index for reporting daily air quality. EPA calculates the AQI for five major air pollutants regulated by the Clean Air Act: ground-level ozone, particle pollution (also known as particulate matter), carbon monoxide, sulfur dioxide, and nitrogen dioxide. The AQI runs from 0 to 500. The higher the AQI value, the greater the level of air pollution and the greater the health concern; (3) Sulfur dioxide is no longer included in this table because SO_2 concentrations tend to be very localized and not necessarily representative of broad geographical areas like counties and CBSAs.
Source: U.S. Environmental Protection Agency, Air Quality Index Report, 2023

Maximum Air Pollutant Concentrations: Particulate Matter, Ozone, CO and Lead

	Particulate Matter 10 (ug/m³)	Particulate Matter 2.5 Wtd AM (ug/m³)	Particulate Matter 2.5 24-Hr (ug/m³)	Ozone (ppm)	Carbon Monoxide (ppm)	Lead (ug/m³)
MSA[1] Level	180	8.6	23	0.074	2	n/a
NAAQS[2]	150	15	35	0.075	9	0.15
Met NAAQS[2]	No	Yes	Yes	Yes	Yes	n/a

Note: (1) Data covers the El Paso, TX Metropolitan Statistical Area; Data from exceptional events are included; (2) National Ambient Air Quality Standards; ppm = parts per million; ug/m³ = micrograms per cubic meter; n/a not available.
Concentrations: Particulate Matter 10 (coarse particulate)—highest second maximum 24-hour concentration; Particulate Matter 2.5 Wtd AM (fine particulate)—highest weighted annual mean concentration; Particulate Matter 2.5 24-Hour (fine particulate)—highest 98th percentile 24-hour concentration; Ozone—highest fourth daily maximum 8-hour concentration; Carbon Monoxide—highest second maximum non-overlapping 8-hour concentration; Lead—maximum running 3-month average
Source: U.S. Environmental Protection Agency, Air Quality Monitoring Information, "Air Quality Statistics by City, 2023"

Maximum Air Pollutant Concentrations: Nitrogen Dioxide and Sulfur Dioxide

	Nitrogen Dioxide AM (ppb)	Nitrogen Dioxide 1-Hr (ppb)	Sulfur Dioxide AM (ppb)	Sulfur Dioxide 1-Hr (ppb)	Sulfur Dioxide 24-Hr (ppb)
MSA[1] Level	15	57	n/a	6	n/a
NAAQS[2]	53	100	30	75	140
Met NAAQS[2]	Yes	Yes	n/a	Yes	n/a

Note: (1) Data covers the El Paso, TX Metropolitan Statistical Area; Data from exceptional events are included; (2) National Ambient Air Quality Standards; ppm = parts per million; ug/m³ = micrograms per cubic meter; n/a not available.
Concentrations: Nitrogen Dioxide AM—highest arithmetic mean concentration; Nitrogen Dioxide 1-Hr—highest 98th percentile 1-hour daily maximum concentration; Sulfur Dioxide AM—highest annual mean concentration; Sulfur Dioxide 1-Hr—highest 99th percentile 1-hour daily maximum concentration; Sulfur Dioxide 24-Hr—highest second maximum 24-hour concentration
Source: U.S. Environmental Protection Agency, Air Quality Monitoring Information, "Air Quality Statistics by City, 2023"

Fort Worth, Texas

Background

Fort Worth lies in north central Texas near the headwaters of the Trinity River. Despite its modern skyscrapers, multiple freeways, shopping malls, and extensive industry, the city is known for its easy-going atmosphere.

The area has seen many travelers. Nomadic Native Americans of the plains rode through on horses bred from those brought by Spanish explorers. The 1840s saw American-Anglos settle in the region. On June 6, 1849, Major Ripley A. Arnold and his U.S. Cavalry troop established an outpost on the Trinity River to protect settlers moving westward. The fort was named for General William J. Worth, Commander of the U.S. Army's Texas department. When the fort was abandoned in 1853, settlers moved in and converted the vacant barracks into trading establishments and homes, stealing the county seat from Birdville (an act made legal in the 1860 election).

In the 1860s, Fort Worth, which was close to the Chisholm Trail, became an oasis for cowboys traveling to and from Kansas. Although the town's growth virtually stopped during the Civil War, Fort Worth was incorporated as a city in 1873. Helped by the completion of the Texas & Pacific Line, Fort Worth survived to be a part of the West Texas oil boom in 1917.

Real prosperity followed at the end of World War II when the city became a center for several military installations. Aviation is the city's principal source of economic growth. Its leading industries include the manufacture of aircraft, automobiles, machinery, and containers, as well as food processing and brewing. Emerging economic sectors in the 21st century include semiconductor manufacturing, and communications equipment manufacturing and distribution. Multinational corporations Bell Textron, American Airlines, and BNSF Railway are headquartered in the city.

Fort Worth contains over 1,000 natural-gas wells tapping the Barnett Shale. Each well site is a bare patch of gravel 2-5 acres in size. As city ordinances permit them in all zoning categories, including residential, well sites can be found in a variety of locations.

Since it first began testing DNA samples in 2003, the DNA Identity Laboratory at the University of North Texas Health Science Center has made hundreds of matches, helping to solve missing-persons cases and close criminal cases. The university is also home to the national Osteopathic Research Center, the only academic DNA Lab qualified to work with the FBI, the Texas Center for Health Disparities, and the Health Institutes of Texas. Other colleges in Fort Worth include Texas Christian University, Southwestern Baptist Seminary, and Texas Wesleyan University.

The Fort Worth Stockyards are a National Historic District. The Stockyards was once among the largest livestock markets in the United States and played a vital role in the city's early growth. Today the neighborhood is characterized by its many bars, restaurants, and notable country music venues such as Billy Bob's. Fort Worth celebrity chef Tim Love of Iron Chef America and Top Chef Masters has operated multiple restaurants in the neighborhood. At the Fort Worth Stockyards, Fort Worth is the only major city that hosts a daily cattle drive.

Fort Worth Zoo houses over 5,000 animals and the city is home to Fort Worth Garden and the Botanical Research Institute of Texas. Fort Worth has 263 parks, including the 4.3 acre Fort Worth Water Gardens.,

Winter temperatures and rainfall are modified by the northeast-northwest mountain barrier, which prevents shallow cold air masses from crossing over from the west. Summer temperatures vary with cloud and shower activity but are generally mild. Summer precipitation is largely from local thunderstorms and varies from year to year. Damaging rains are infrequent. Hurricanes have produced heavy rainfall but are usually not accompanied by destructive winds.

Rankings

General Rankings

- To help military veterans find the best places in which to settle down, *WalletHub* compared the 100 largest U.S. cities across 19 key indicators of livability, affordability and veteran-friendliness. They range from the share of military skill-related jobs to veteran income growth to the availability of VA health facilities. Fort Worth ranked #20. *Wallethub.com, "Best & Worst Places for Veterans to Live (2025)," November 7, 2024*

- Fort Worth was identified as one of America's fastest-growing areas in terms of population and economy by *Forbes*. Fort Worth ranked #50 out of 50. Over 500 cities with more than 75,000 residents were measured for percentage of population growth over the following three periods: from 2011 to 2016; 2016 to 2021; and then 2011 to 2021. *Forbes.com, "The Fastest Growing Cities in America and Their Change in Income," September 12, 2023*

- Fort Worth appeared on *Travel + Leisure's* list of "The 15 Best Cities in the United States." The city was ranked #7. Criteria: walkability; sights/landmarks; culture; food; friendliness; shopping; and overall value. *Travel + Leisure, "The World's Best Awards 2024" July 9, 2024*

Business/Finance Rankings

- Payscale.com ranked the 32 largest metro areas in terms of wage growth. The Dallas metro area ranked #6. Criteria: quarterly changes in private industry employee and education professional wage growth from the previous year. *PayScale, "Wage Trends by Metro Area-4th Quarter," February 4, 2025*

- Fort Worth was cited as one of America's top metros for total corporate facility investment projects in 2024. The area ranked #3 in the Tier 1 (large) metro area category (population over 1 million). *Site Selection, "Top Metros of 2024," March 2025*

- The Fort Worth metro area appeared on the Milken Institute "2025 Best Performing Cities" list. Rank: #30 out of 200 large metro areas (based on performance category). Criteria: job growth; wage growth; high-tech growth and impact; community resilience; housing affordability; household broadband access. *Milken Institute, "Best-Performing Cities 2025," January 14, 2025*

Culture/Performing Arts Rankings

- Fort Worth was selected as one of the 25 best cities for moviemakers in North America. Great film cities are places where filmmaking dreams can come true, that offer more creative space, lower costs, and great outdoor locations. NYC & LA were intentionally excluded. Criteria: film industry presence and culture; tax incentives; affordability; and proximity of festivals and schools. The city was ranked #19. *MovieMaker Magazine, "Best Places to Live and Work as a Moviemaker, 2025," January 29, 2025*

Education Rankings

- Personal finance website *WalletHub* analyzed the 150 largest U.S. metropolitan statistical areas to determine where the most educated Americans are putting their degrees to work. Criteria: education levels; percentage of workers with degrees; education quality and attainment gap; public school quality rankings; quality and enrollment of each metro area's universities. Fort Worth was ranked #72 (#1 = most educated city). *WalletHub.com, "Most & Least Educated Cities in America, 2025" July 2, 2024*

Environmental Rankings

- Sperling's *BestPlaces* assessed the 50 largest metropolitan areas of the United States for the likelihood of dangerously extreme weather events or earthquakes. In general the Southeast and South-Central regions have the highest risk of weather extremes and earthquakes, while the Pacific Northwest enjoys the lowest risk. Of the most risky metropolitan areas, the Fort Worth metro area was ranked #4. *Bestplaces.net, "Avoid Natural Disasters: BestPlaces Reveals The Top 10 Safest Places to Live," October 25, 2017*

- The U.S. Environmental Protection Agency (EPA) released its list of U.S. metropolitan areas with the most ENERGY STAR certified buildings in 2023. The Dallas metro area was ranked #6 out of 25. *U.S. Environmental Protection Agency, "2024 Energy Star Top Cities," May 22, 2024*

- Fort Worth was highlighted as one of the 25 most ozone-polluted metro areas in the U.S. during 2021 through 2023. The area ranked #10. *American Lung Association, "State of the Air 2025," April 23, 2025*

Health/Fitness Rankings

- For each of the 100 largest cities in the United States, the American Fitness Index®, compiled in partnership between the American College of Sports Medicine and the Elevance Health Foundation, evaluated community infrastructure and more than 30 health behaviors including preventive health, levels of chronic disease conditions, food insecurity, pedestrian safety, air quality, and community/environment resources that support physical activity. Fort Worth ranked #75 for "community fitness." *americanfitnessindex.org, "2024 ACSM American Fitness Index Summary Report," July 23, 2024*

- The Fort Worth metro area was identified as one of the worst cities for bed bugs in America by pest control company Orkin. The area ranked #22 out of 50 based on the number of bed bug treatments Orkin performed from December 2022 to November 2023. *Orkin, "Chicago Joins Paris In Global Bed Bug Spotlight Ranking As The Worst City On Orkin's U.S. Bed Bug Cities List," January 22, 2024*

- Dallas was identified as a "2025 Allergy Capital." The area ranked #13 out of the nation's 100 largest metropolitan areas. Three groups of factors were used to identify the most challenging cities for people with allergies: annual tree, grass, and weed pollen scores; over the counter allergy medicine use; number of board-certified allergy specialists. *Asthma and Allergy Foundation of America, "2025 Allergy Capitals: The Most Challenging Places to Live with Allergies," March 18, 2025*

- Dallas was identified as a "2024 Asthma Capital." The area ranked #28 out of the nation's 100 largest metropolitan areas. Criteria: estimated asthma prevalence; asthma-related mortality; and ER visits due to asthma. Risk factors analyzed but not factored in the rankings: annual air quality including pollution and ozone levels; public smoking laws; indoor air quality; access to asthma specialists; rescue and controller medication use; uninsured rate; pollen allergy; poverty rate. *Asthma and Allergy Foundation of America, "Asthma Capitals 2024: The Most Challenging Places to Live With Asthma," September 10, 2024*

Pet Rankings

- Fort Worth appeared on *The Dogington Post* site as one of the top cities for dog lovers, ranking #12 out of 15. The real estate marketplace, Zillow®, and Rover, the largest pet sitter and dog walker network, introduced a new list of "Top Emerging Dog-Friendly Cities" for 2021. Criteria: number of new dog accounts on the Rover platform; and rentals and listings that mention features that attract dog owners (fenced-in yards, dog houses, dog door or proximity to a dog park). *Dogingtonpost.com, "15 Cities Emerging as Dog-Friendliest in 2021," May 11, 2021*

Real Estate Rankings

- *WalletHub* compared the most populated U.S. cities to determine which had the best markets for real estate agents. Fort Worth ranked #76 where demand was high and pay was the best. Criteria: sales per agent; annual median wage for real-estate agents; monthly average starting salary for real estate agents; real estate job density and competition; unemployment rate; home turnover rate; housing-market health index; and other relevant metrics. *WalletHub.com, "2021 Best Places to Be a Real Estate Agent," May 12, 2021*

- The Fort Worth metro area was identified as one of the top 16 housing markets to invest in for 2025 by *Forbes*. Criteria: stable local economies with good population growth and increase in jobs providing good support for home prices and rents. *Forbes.com, "Best Local Markets For Real Estate Investing In 2025," November 6, 2024*

- Fort Worth was ranked #111 out of 176 metro areas in terms of cost of housing in 2024 by the National Association of Home Builders (#1 = most affordable). Criteria: the portion of an average family's income necessary to pay the mortgage on a median-priced home. *National Association of Home Builders®, NAHB-Wells Fargo Cost of Housing Index, 4th Quarter 2024*

Safety Rankings

- The National Insurance Crime Bureau ranked the largest metro areas in the U.S. in terms of per capita rates of vehicle theft. The Fort Worth metro area ranked #5 out of the top 10 (#1 = highest rate). Criteria: number of vehicle theft offenses per 100,000 inhabitants in 2023. *National Insurance Crime Bureau, "Vehicle Thefts Surge Nationwide in 2023," April 9, 2024*

Seniors/Retirement Rankings

- Fort Worth made *Southern Living's* list of southern places—by the beach, in the mountains, or scenic city—to retire. From the incredible views and close knit communities, to the opportunities to put down new roots, and great places to eat and hike, these superb places are perfect for settling down. *Southern Living, "The Best Places to Retire in the South," March 9, 2024*

- *AARP the Magazine* selected Fort Worth as one of the great places in the United States for seniors, as well as younger generations, that represent "a place to call home." For the list, the magazine recognized the change in criteria due to the pandemic, and looked for cities with easy access to exercise/outdoors, quality healthcare, sense of community, relatively affordable housing costs, job markets that accommodate working from home, and reliable internet access. *AARP The Magazine, "Best Places to Live and Retire Now," November 29, 2021*

Women/Minorities Rankings

- Personal finance website *WalletHub* compared more than 180 U.S. cities across two key dimensions, "Hispanic Business-Friendliness" and "Hispanic Purchasing Power," to arrive at the most favorable conditions for Hispanic entrepreneurs. Fort Worth was ranked #25 out of 182. Criteria includes: share of Hispanic-Owned Businesses; average growth of Hispanic Business revenues; Small Business-Friendliness score; affordability; and number of Hispanics with at least a bachelor's degree. *WalletHub.com, "Best Cities for Hispanic Entrepreneurs," September 4, 2024*

Miscellaneous Rankings

- *WalletHub* compared 148 of the most populated U.S. cities to determine their operating efficiency. A "Quality of Services" score was constructed for each city and then measured against the total budget per capita to reveal which were managed the best. Fort Worth ranked #49. Criteria: financial stability; economy; education; safety; health; infrastructure and pollution. *WalletHub.com, "2025's Best- & Worst-Run Cities in America," June 18, 2024*

Business Environment

DEMOGRAPHICS

Population Growth

Area	1990 Census	2000 Census	2010 Census	2020 Census	2023 Estimate[2]	Population Growth 1990-2023 (%)
City	448,311	534,694	741,206	918,915	941,311	110.0
MSA[1]	3,989,294	5,161,544	6,371,773	7,637,387	7,807,555	95.7
U.S.	248,709,873	281,421,906	308,745,538	331,449,281	332,387,540	33.6

Note: (1) Figures cover the Dallas-Fort Worth-Arlington, TX Metropolitan Statistical Area; (2) 2019-2023 5-year ACS population estimate
Source: U.S. Census Bureau, 1990 Census, 2000 Census, 2010 Census, 2020 Census, 2019-2023 American Community Survey 5-Year Estimates

Race

Area	White Alone[2] (%)	Black Alone[2] (%)	Asian Alone[2] (%)	AIAN[3] Alone[2] (%)	NHOPI[4] Alone[2] (%)	Other Race Alone[2] (%)	Two or More Races (%)
City	47.7	19.5	5.2	0.6	0.1	10.4	16.4
MSA[1]	52.7	16.2	7.8	0.6	0.1	8.0	14.5
U.S.	63.4	12.4	5.8	0.9	0.2	6.6	10.7

Note: (1) Figures cover the Dallas-Fort Worth-Arlington, TX Metropolitan Statistical Area; (2) Alone is defined as not being in combination with one or more other races; (3) American Indian and Alaska Native; (4) Native Hawaiian and Other Pacific Islander
Source: U.S. Census Bureau, 2019-2023 American Community Survey 5-Year Estimates

Hispanic or Latino Origin

Area	Total (%)	Mexican (%)	Puerto Rican (%)	Cuban (%)	Other (%)
City	34.6	28.7	1.3	0.4	4.2
MSA[1]	29.4	23.1	0.9	0.4	5.1
U.S.	19.0	11.3	1.8	0.7	5.2

Note: Persons of Hispanic or Latino origin can be of any race; (1) Figures cover the Dallas-Fort Worth-Arlington, TX Metropolitan Statistical Area
Source: U.S. Census Bureau, 2019-2023 American Community Survey 5-Year Estimates

Age

Area	Under Age 5	Age 5–19	Age 20–34	Age 35–44	Age 45–54	Age 55–64	Age 65–74	Age 75–84	Age 85+	Median Age
City	7.3	22.1	23.3	14.4	12.0	10.3	6.5	2.9	1.0	33.4
MSA[1]	6.4	21.6	21.3	14.4	13.0	11.4	7.4	3.3	1.1	35.5
U.S.	5.7	19.1	20.2	13.1	12.3	12.8	10.0	4.9	1.9	38.7

Note: (1) Figures cover the Dallas-Fort Worth-Arlington, TX Metropolitan Statistical Area
Source: U.S. Census Bureau, 2019-2023 American Community Survey 5-Year Estimates

Disability by Age

Area	All Ages	Under 18 Years Old	18 to 64 Years Old	65 Years and Over
City	10.2	3.7	9.0	34.4
MSA[1]	10.1	4.0	8.5	32.0
U.S.	13.0	4.7	10.7	32.9

Note: Figures show percent of the civilian noninstitutionalized population that reported having a disability. Disability status is determined from six types of difficulty: vision, hearing, cognitive, ambulatory, self-care, and independent living. For children under 5 years old, hearing and vision difficulty are used to determine disability status. For children between the ages of 5 and 14, disability status is determined from hearing, vision, cognitive, ambulatory, and self-care difficulties. For people aged 15 years and older, they are considered to have a disability if they have difficulty with any one of the six difficulty types; Note: (1) Figures cover the Dallas-Fort Worth-Arlington, TX Metropolitan Statistical Area
Source: U.S. Census Bureau, 2019-2023 American Community Survey 5-Year Estimates

Ancestry

Area	German	Irish	English	American	Italian	Polish	French[2]	European	Scottish
City	7.1	6.0	7.4	3.7	1.8	0.8	1.3	1.4	1.5
MSA[1]	8.1	6.4	8.7	5.3	2.2	1.0	1.4	1.4	1.5
U.S.	12.6	9.4	9.1	5.5	4.9	2.6	2.0	1.6	1.6

Note: Figures are the percentage of the total population reporting a particular ancestry. The nine most commonly reported ancestries in the U.S. are shown. Figures include multiple ancestries (e.g. if a person reported being Irish and Italian, they were included in both columns); (1) Figures cover the Dallas-Fort Worth-Arlington, TX Metropolitan Statistical Area; (2) Excludes Basque
Source: U.S. Census Bureau, 2019-2023 American Community Survey 5-Year Estimates

Foreign-born Population

Area	Percent of Population Born in								
	Any Foreign Country	Asia	Mexico	Europe	Caribbean	Central America[2]	South America	Africa	Canada
City	17.0	4.1	8.9	0.5	0.3	0.8	0.6	1.6	0.1
MSA[1]	19.0	6.0	7.4	0.8	0.3	1.7	0.8	1.7	0.2
U.S.	13.9	4.3	3.3	1.4	1.4	1.2	1.2	0.8	0.2

Note: (1) Figures cover the Dallas-Fort Worth-Arlington, TX Metropolitan Statistical Area; (2) Excludes Mexico.
Source: U.S. Census Bureau, 2019-2023 American Community Survey 5-Year Estimates

Household Size

Area	Persons in Household (%)							Average Household Size
	One	Two	Three	Four	Five	Six	Seven or More	
City	27.7	29.8	15.6	14.1	7.6	3.1	2.0	2.76
MSA[1]	25.9	30.9	16.4	14.7	7.5	2.9	1.7	2.73
U.S.	28.5	33.8	15.4	12.7	5.9	2.3	1.4	2.54

Note: (1) Figures cover the Dallas-Fort Worth-Arlington, TX Metropolitan Statistical Area
Source: U.S. Census Bureau, 2019-2023 American Community Survey 5-Year Estimates

Household Relationships

Area	Householder	Opposite-sex Spouse	Same-sex Spouse	Opposite-sex Unmarried Partner	Same-sex Unmarried Partner	Child[2]	Grandchild	Other Relatives	Non-relatives
City	35.2	15.8	0.2	2.1	0.1	33.0	3.1	5.6	3.0
MSA[1]	36.2	17.6	0.2	2.0	0.2	31.7	2.7	5.5	2.9
U.S.	38.3	17.5	0.2	2.5	0.2	28.3	2.4	4.8	3.4

Note: Figures are percent of the total population; (1) Figures cover the Dallas-Fort Worth-Arlington, TX Metropolitan Statistical Area; (2) Includes biological, adopted, and stepchildren of the householder
Source: U.S. Census Bureau, 2020 Census

Gender

Area	Males	Females	Males per 100 Females
City	461,317	479,994	96.1
MSA[1]	3,864,152	3,943,403	98.0
U.S.	164,545,087	167,842,453	98.0

Note: (1) Figures cover the Dallas-Fort Worth-Arlington, TX Metropolitan Statistical Area
Source: U.S. Census Bureau, 2019-2023 American Community Survey 5-Year Estimates

Marital Status

Area	Never Married	Now Married[2]	Separated	Widowed	Divorced
City	35.8	46.5	2.2	4.6	10.7
MSA[1]	33.4	50.6	1.7	4.2	10.0
U.S.	34.1	47.9	1.7	5.6	10.7

Note: Figures are percentages and cover the population 15 years of age and older; (1) Figures cover the Dallas-Fort Worth-Arlington, TX Metropolitan Statistical Area; (2) Excludes separated
Source: U.S. Census Bureau, 2019-2023 American Community Survey 5-Year Estimates

Religious Groups by Family

Area	Catholic	Baptist	Methodist	LDS[2]	Pentecostal	Lutheran	Islam	Adventist	Other
MSA[1]	14.2	14.3	4.7	1.4	2.2	0.5	1.8	1.3	13.8
U.S.	18.7	7.3	3.0	2.0	1.8	1.7	1.3	1.3	11.6

Note: Figures are the number of adherents as a percentage of the total population and cover the eight largest religious groups in the U.S; (1) Figures cover the Dallas-Fort Worth-Arlington, TX Metropolitan Statistical Area; (2) Church of Jesus Christ of Latter-day Saints
Sources: 2020 U.S. Religion Census, Association of Statisticians of American Religious Bodies; The Association of Religion Data Archives (ARDA)

Religious Groups by Tradition

Area	Catholic	Evangelical Protestant	Mainline Protestant	Black Protestant	Islam	Judaism	Hinduism	Orthodox	Buddhism
MSA[1]	14.2	25.4	5.9	3.3	1.8	0.3	0.5	0.3	0.2
U.S.	18.7	16.5	5.2	2.3	1.3	0.6	0.4	0.4	0.3

Note: Figures are the number of adherents as a percentage of the total population; (1) Figures cover the Dallas-Fort Worth-Arlington, TX Metropolitan Statistical Area
Sources: 2020 U.S. Religion Census, Association of Statisticians of American Religious Bodies; The Association of Religion Data Archives (ARDA)

ECONOMY

Real Gross Domestic Product (GDP)

Area	2017	2018	2019	2020	2021	2022	2023	Rank[3]
MSA[1]	483.7	506.2	526.2	520.2	562.1	594.5	613.4	5
U.S.[2]	17,619.1	18,160.7	18,642.5	18,238.9	19,387.6	19,896.6	20,436.3	—

Note: Figures are in billions of chained 2017 dollars; (1) Figures cover the Dallas-Fort Worth-Arlington, TX Metropolitan Statistical Area; (2) Figures cover real GDP within metropolitan areas; (3) Rank is based on 2023 data and ranges from 1 to 384
Source: U.S. Bureau of Economic Analysis

Economic Growth

Area	2014	2015	2016	2017	2018	2019	2020	2021	2022	2023
MSA[1]	3.8	4.8	2.3	3.6	4.6	3.9	-1.1	8.1	5.8	3.2
U.S.[2]	2.6	3.2	2.0	2.7	3.1	2.7	-2.2	6.3	2.6	2.7

Note: Figures are real gross domestic product growth rates and represent percent change from preceding period; (1) Figures cover the Dallas-Fort Worth-Arlington, TX Metropolitan Statistical Area; (2) Figures are the average growth rates within metropolitan areas
Source: U.S. Bureau of Economic Analysis

Metropolitan Area Exports

Area	2018	2019	2020	2021	2022	2023	Rank[2]
MSA[1]	36,260.9	39,474.0	35,642.0	43,189.0	50,632.9	51,863.7	6
U.S.	1,664,056.1	1,645,173.7	1,431,406.6	1,753,941.4	2,062,937.4	2,019,160.5	—

Note: Figures are in millions of dollars; (1) Figures cover the Dallas-Fort Worth-Arlington, TX Metropolitan Statistical Area; (2) Rank is based on 2023 data and ranges from 1 to 386
Source: U.S. Department of Commerce, International Trade Administration, Office of Trade and Economic Analysis, Industry and Analysis, Exports by Metropolitan Area, data extracted April 2, 2025

Building Permits

Area	Single-Family			Multi-Family			Total		
	2023	2024	Pct. Chg.	2023	2024	Pct. Chg.	2023	2024	Pct. Chg.
City	6,631	6,257	-5.6	3,429	6,891	101.0	10,060	13,148	30.7
MSA[1]	44,366	46,440	4.7	23,663	25,348	7.1	68,029	71,788	5.5
U.S.	920,000	981,900	6.7	591,100	496,100	-16.1	1,511,100	1,478,000	-2.2

Note: (1) Figures cover the Dallas-Fort Worth-Arlington, TX Metropolitan Statistical Area; Figures represent new, privately-owned housing units authorized (unadjusted data)
Source: U.S. Census Bureau, Building Permits Survey (BPS), 2023, 2024

Bankruptcy Filings

Area	Business Filings			Nonbusiness Filings		
	2023	2024	% Chg.	2023	2024	% Chg.
Tarrant County	200	198	-1.0	2,934	3,513	19.7
U.S.	18,926	23,107	22.1	434,064	494,201	13.9

Note: Business filings include Chapter 7, Chapter 9, Chapter 11, Chapter 12, Chapter 13, Chapter 15, and Section 304; Nonbusiness filings include Chapter 7, Chapter 11, and Chapter 13
Source: Administrative Office of the U.S. Courts, Business and Nonbusiness Bankruptcy, County Cases Commenced by Chapter of the Bankruptcy Code, During the 12-Month Period Ending December 31, 2023 and Business and Nonbusiness Bankruptcy, County Cases Commenced by Chapter of the Bankruptcy Code, During the 12-Month Period Ending December 31, 2024

Housing Vacancy Rates

Area	Gross Vacancy Rate[3] (%)			Year-Round Vacancy Rate[4] (%)			Rental Vacancy Rate[5] (%)			Homeowner Vacancy Rate[6] (%)		
	2022	2023	2024	2022	2023	2024	2022	2023	2024	2022	2023	2024
MSA[1]	6.6	7.6	7.9	6.3	7.2	7.6	6.8	8.4	8.9	0.7	0.8	1.3
U.S.[2]	9.1	9.0	9.1	7.5	7.5	7.6	5.7	6.5	6.8	0.8	0.8	1.0

Note: (1) Figures cover the Dallas-Fort Worth-Arlington, TX Metropolitan Statistical Area; (2) Figures cover the 75 largest Metropolitan Statistical Areas; (3) The percentage of the total housing inventory that is vacant; (4) The percentage of the housing inventory (excluding seasonal units) that is year-round vacant; (5) The percentage of rental inventory that is vacant for rent; (6) The percentage of homeowner inventory that is vacant for sale
Source: U.S. Census Bureau, Housing Vacancies and Homeownership Annual Statistics: 2022, 2023, 2024

INCOME

Income

Area	Per Capita ($)	Median Household ($)	Average Household ($)
City	37,157	76,602	101,838
MSA[1]	44,447	87,155	120,397
U.S.	43,289	78,538	110,491

Note: (1) Figures cover the Dallas-Fort Worth-Arlington, TX Metropolitan Statistical Area
Source: U.S. Census Bureau, 2019-2023 American Community Survey 5-Year Estimates

Household Income Distribution

Area	Percent of Households Earning							
	Under $15,000	$15,000 -$24,999	$25,000 -$34,999	$35,000 -$49,999	$50,000 -$74,999	$75,000 -$99,999	$100,000 -$149,999	$150,000 and up
City	7.4	5.9	6.9	11.1	17.3	13.7	18.1	19.4
MSA[1]	6.3	4.9	5.8	10.0	16.1	13.1	18.5	25.2
U.S.	8.5	6.6	6.8	10.4	15.7	12.7	17.4	21.9

Note: (1) Figures cover the Dallas-Fort Worth-Arlington, TX Metropolitan Statistical Area
Source: U.S. Census Bureau, 2019-2023 American Community Survey 5-Year Estimates

Poverty Rate

Area	All Ages	Under 18 Years Old	18 to 64 Years Old	65 Years and Over
City	12.9	18.0	11.1	10.2
MSA[1]	10.5	14.5	9.2	9.3
U.S.	12.4	16.3	11.6	10.4

Note: Figures are percentage of people whose income during the past 12 months was below the poverty level; (1) Figures cover the Dallas-Fort Worth-Arlington, TX Metropolitan Statistical Area
Source: U.S. Census Bureau, 2019-2023 American Community Survey 5-Year Estimates

EMPLOYMENT

Labor Force and Employment

Area	Civilian Labor Force			Workers Employed		
	Dec. 2023	Dec. 2024	% Chg.	Dec. 2023	Dec. 2024	% Chg.
City	492,810	506,338	2.7	474,900	487,778	2.7
MD[1]	1,397,596	1,435,889	2.7	1,349,809	1,386,446	2.7
U.S.	166,661,000	167,746,000	0.7	160,754,000	161,294,000	0.3

Note: Data is not seasonally adjusted and covers workers 16 years of age and older; (1) Figures cover the Fort Worth-Arlington-Grapevine, TX Metropolitan Division
Source: Bureau of Labor Statistics, Local Area Unemployment Statistics

Unemployment Rate

Area	2024											
	Jan.	Feb.	Mar.	Apr.	May	Jun.	Jul.	Aug.	Sep.	Oct.	Nov.	Dec.
City	4.1	4.3	4.1	3.6	3.9	4.6	4.6	4.4	4.1	4.1	4.1	3.7
MD[1]	3.9	4.1	3.8	3.4	3.6	4.2	4.3	4.2	3.9	3.9	3.9	3.4
U.S.	4.1	4.2	3.9	3.5	3.7	4.3	4.5	4.4	3.9	3.9	4.0	3.8

Note: Data is not seasonally adjusted and covers workers 16 years of age and older; (1) Figures cover the Fort Worth-Arlington-Grapevine, TX Metropolitan Division
Source: Bureau of Labor Statistics, Local Area Unemployment Statistics

Average Wages

Occupation	$/Hr.	Occupation	$/Hr.
Accountants and Auditors	45.03	Maintenance and Repair Workers	24.02
Automotive Mechanics	27.86	Marketing Managers	74.76
Bookkeepers	25.94	Network and Computer Systems Admin.	50.61
Carpenters	24.01	Nurses, Licensed Practical	30.36
Cashiers	14.32	Nurses, Registered	46.50
Computer Programmers	47.68	Nursing Assistants	18.80
Computer Systems Analysts	57.86	Office Clerks, General	21.12
Computer User Support Specialists	29.72	Physical Therapists	52.68
Construction Laborers	19.90	Physicians	105.52
Cooks, Restaurant	17.09	Plumbers, Pipefitters and Steamfitters	30.24
Customer Service Representatives	21.47	Police and Sheriff's Patrol Officers	41.90
Dentists	96.90	Postal Service Mail Carriers	29.14
Electricians	28.56	Real Estate Sales Agents	35.39
Engineers, Electrical	56.38	Retail Salespersons	16.85
Fast Food and Counter Workers	13.48	Sales Representatives, Technical/Scientific	49.39
Financial Managers	83.96	Secretaries, Exc. Legal/Medical/Executive	22.33
First-Line Supervisors of Office Workers	36.12	Security Guards	19.16
General and Operations Managers	67.98	Surgeons	172.43
Hairdressers/Cosmetologists	17.46	Teacher Assistants, Exc. Postsecondary[1]	14.37
Home Health and Personal Care Aides	13.45	Teachers, Secondary School, Exc. Sp. Ed.[1]	31.75
Janitors and Cleaners	16.43	Telemarketers	17.73
Landscaping/Groundskeeping Workers	18.42	Truck Drivers, Heavy/Tractor-Trailer	28.88
Lawyers	85.71	Truck Drivers, Light/Delivery Services	23.68
Maids and Housekeeping Cleaners	15.45	Waiters and Waitresses	15.52

Note: Wage data covers the Dallas-Fort Worth-Arlington, TX Metropolitan Statistical Area; (1) Hourly wages were calculated from annual wage data based on a 40 hour work week
Source: Bureau of Labor Statistics, Metro Area Occupational Employment & Wage Estimates, May 2024

Employment by Industry

Sector	MD[1] Number of Employees	MD[1] Percent of Total	U.S. Percent of Total
Construction, Mining, and Logging	85,700	7.1	5.5
Financial Activities	77,600	6.4	5.8
Government	142,000	11.7	14.9
Information	12,100	1.0	1.9
Leisure and Hospitality	134,800	11.1	10.4
Manufacturing	107,800	8.9	8.0
Other Services	42,000	3.5	3.7
Private Education and Health Services	156,400	12.9	16.9
Professional and Business Services	155,700	12.8	14.2
Retail Trade	132,900	10.9	10.0
Transportation, Warehousing, and Utilities	106,100	8.7	4.8
Wholesale Trade	61,200	5.0	3.9

Note: Figures are non-farm employment as of December 2024. Figures are not seasonally adjusted and include workers 16 years of age and older; (1) Figures cover the Fort Worth-Arlington-Grapevine, TX Metropolitan Division
Source: Bureau of Labor Statistics, Current Employment Statistics, Employment, Hours, and Earnings

Employment by Occupation

Occupation Classification	City (%)	MSA[1] (%)	U.S. (%)
Management, Business, Science, and Arts	38.1	43.3	42.0
Natural Resources, Construction, and Maintenance	9.6	8.7	8.6
Production, Transportation, and Material Moving	16.0	12.8	13.0
Sales and Office	20.6	21.0	19.9
Service	15.8	14.2	16.5

Note: Figures cover employed civilians 16 years of age and older; (1) Figures cover the Dallas-Fort Worth-Arlington, TX Metropolitan Statistical Area
Source: U.S. Census Bureau, 2019-2023 American Community Survey 5-Year Estimates

Occupations with Greatest Projected Employment Growth: 2022 – 2032

Occupation[1]	2022 Employment	2032 Projected Employment	Numeric Employment Change	Percent Employment Change
General and Operations Managers	425,560	504,280	78,720	18.5
Fast Food and Counter Workers	333,870	394,290	60,420	18.1
Stockers and Order Fillers	264,810	321,600	56,790	21.4
Home Health and Personal Care Aides	313,670	367,500	53,830	17.2
Software Developers	110,280	161,780	51,500	46.7
Cooks, Restaurant	113,680	158,830	45,150	39.7
Laborers and Freight, Stock, and Material Movers, Hand	225,090	269,120	44,030	19.6
Heavy and Tractor-Trailer Truck Drivers	226,450	270,320	43,870	19.4
Retail Salespersons	319,400	357,630	38,230	12.0
Registered Nurses	233,850	267,980	34,130	14.6

Note: Projections cover Texas; (1) Sorted by numeric employment change
Source: www.projectionscentral.org, State Occupational Projections, 2022–2032 Long-Term Projections

Fastest-Growing Occupations: 2022 – 2032

Occupation[1]	2022 Employment	2032 Projected Employment	Numeric Employment Change	Percent Employment Change
Wind Turbine Service Technicians	4,860	7,950	3,090	63.6
Nurse Practitioners	19,060	30,490	11,430	60.0
Data Scientists	13,220	20,250	7,030	53.2
Computer and Information Research Scientists (SOC 2018)	2,070	3,140	1,070	51.7
Information Security Analysts (SOC 2018)	14,620	21,620	7,000	47.9
Software Developers	110,280	161,780	51,500	46.7
Statisticians	980	1,430	450	45.9
Operations Research Analysts	12,060	17,290	5,230	43.4
Software Quality Assurance Analysts and Testers	17,350	24,440	7,090	40.9
Medical and Health Services Managers	49,430	69,180	19,750	40.0

Note: Projections cover Texas; (1) Sorted by percent employment change and excludes occupations with numeric employment change less than 50
Source: www.projectionscentral.org, State Occupational Projections, 2022–2032 Long-Term Projections

CITY FINANCES

City Government Finances

Component	2022 ($000)	2022 ($ per capita)
Total Revenues	1,940,882	2,092
Total Expenditures	2,013,853	2,171
Debt Outstanding	2,561,392	2,761

Source: U.S. Census Bureau, State & Local Government Finances 2022

City Government Revenue by Source

Source	2022 ($000)	2022 ($ per capita)	2022 (%)
General Revenue			
From Federal Government	156,871	169	8.1
From State Government	44,745	48	2.3
From Local Governments	0	0	0.0
Taxes			
Property	574,677	619	29.6
Sales and Gross Receipts	353,344	381	18.2
Personal Income	0	0	0.0
Corporate Income	0	0	0.0
Motor Vehicle License	0	0	0.0
Other Taxes	54,634	59	2.8
Current Charges	379,494	409	19.6
Liquor Store	0	0	0.0
Utility	289,914	313	14.9

Source: U.S. Census Bureau, State & Local Government Finances 2022

City Government Expenditures by Function

Function	2022 ($000)	2022 ($ per capita)	2022 (%)
General Direct Expenditures			
Air Transportation	23,540	25	1.2
Corrections	0	0	0.0
Education	0	0	0.0
Employment Security Administration	0	0	0.0
Financial Administration	15,412	16	0.8
Fire Protection	186,944	201	9.3
General Public Buildings	22,125	23	1.1
Governmental Administration, Other	41,965	45	2.1
Health	64,956	70	3.2
Highways	220,790	238	11.0
Hospitals	0	0	0.0
Housing and Community Development	91,550	98	4.5
Interest on General Debt	44,576	48	2.2
Judicial and Legal	20,681	22	1.0
Libraries	20,478	22	1.0
Parking	3,926	4	0.2
Parks and Recreation	93,830	101	4.7
Police Protection	361,883	390	18.0
Public Welfare	0	0	0.0
Sewerage	263,587	284	13.1
Solid Waste Management	62,368	67	3.1
Veterans' Services	0	0	0.0
Liquor Store	0	0	0.0
Utility	304,537	328	15.1

Source: U.S. Census Bureau, State & Local Government Finances 2022

TAXES

State Corporate Income Tax Rates

State	Tax Rate (%)	Income Brackets ($)	Num. of Brackets	Financial Institution Tax Rate (%)[a]	Federal Income Tax Ded.
Texas	(u)	—	—	(u)	No

Note: Tax rates for tax year 2024; (a) Rates listed are the corporate income tax rate applied to financial institutions or excise taxes based on income. Some states have other taxes based upon the value of deposits or shares; (u) Texas imposes a Franchise Tax, otherwise known as margin tax, imposed on entities with more than $2,470,000 total revenues effective in 2024 at rate of 0.75%, or 0.375% for entities primarily engaged in retail or wholesale trade, on lesser of 70% of total revenues or 100% of gross receipts after deductions for either compensation ($450,000 deduction limit) or cost of goods sold. Texas has an EZ rate of 0.331 applicable to a $20 million revenue threshold.
Source: Federation of Tax Administrators, State Corporate Income Tax Rates, January 1, 2025

State Individual Income Tax Rates

State	Tax Rate (%)	Income Brackets ($)	Personal Exemptions ($)			Standard Ded. ($)	
			Single	Married	Depend.	Single	Married
Texas			– No state income tax –				

Note: Tax rates for tax year 2024; Local- and county-level taxes are not included
Source: Federation of Tax Administrators, State Individual Income Tax Rates, January 1, 2025

Various State Sales and Excise Tax Rates

State	State Sales Tax (%)	Gasoline[1] ($/gal.)	Cigarette[2] ($/pack)	Spirits[3] ($/gal.)	Wine[4] ($/gal.)	Beer[5] ($/gal.)	Recreational Marijuana (%)
Texas	6.25	0.20	1.41	2.40	0.20	0.19	Not legal

Note: All tax rates as of January 1, 2025; (1) The American Petroleum Institute has developed a methodology for determining the average tax rate on a gallon of fuel. Rates may include any of the following: excise taxes, environmental fees, storage tank fees, other fees or taxes, general sales tax, and local taxes; (2) The federal excise tax of $1.0066 per pack and local taxes are not included; (3) Rates are those applicable to off-premise sales of 40% alcohol by volume (a.b.v.) distilled spirits in 750ml containers. Local excise taxes are excluded; (4) Rates are those applicable to off-premise sales of 11% a.b.v. non-carbonated wine in 750ml containers; (5) Rates are those applicable to off-premise sales of 4.7% a.b.v. beer in 12 ounce containers.
Source: Tax Foundation, 2025 Facts & Figures: How Does Your State Compare?

State Tax Competitiveness Index

State	Overall Rank	Corporate Tax Rank	Individual Income Tax Rank	Sales Tax Rank	Property Tax Rank	Unemployment Insurance Tax Rank
Texas	7	46	1	36	40	30

Note: The Tax Foundation's State Tax Competitiveness Index enables policymakers, taxpayers, and business leaders to gauge how their states' tax systems compare. A rank of 1 is best, 50 is worst. Rankings do not average to the total. States without a tax rank equally as 1. DC's scores and rankings do not affect other states. The report shows tax systems as of July 1, 2024 (the beginning of Fiscal Year 2025).
Source: Tax Foundation, State Tax Competitiveness Index 2025

TRANSPORTATION

Means of Transportation to Work

Area	Car/Truck/Van		Public Transportation			Bicycle	Walked	Other Means	Worked at Home
	Drove Alone	Car-pooled	Bus	Subway	Railroad				
City	72.9	10.9	0.4	0.0	0.1	0.2	1.2	1.5	12.9
MSA[1]	71.2	9.4	0.5	0.1	0.1	0.1	1.2	1.5	15.9
U.S.	70.2	8.5	1.7	1.3	0.4	0.4	2.4	1.6	13.5

Note: Figures are percentages and cover workers 16 years of age and older; (1) Figures cover the Dallas-Fort Worth-Arlington, TX Metropolitan Statistical Area
Source: U.S. Census Bureau, 2019-2023 American Community Survey 5-Year Estimates

Travel Time to Work

Area	Less Than 10 Minutes	10 to 19 Minutes	20 to 29 Minutes	30 to 44 Minutes	45 to 59 Minutes	60 to 89 Minutes	90 Minutes or More
City	7.4	29.2	23.5	23.5	8.9	5.7	1.8
MSA[1]	8.8	25.5	21.7	25.3	10.2	6.5	2.0
U.S.	12.6	28.6	21.2	20.8	8.1	6.0	2.8

Note: Note: Figures are percentages and include workers 16 years old and over; (1) Figures cover the Dallas-Fort Worth-Arlington, TX Metropolitan Statistical Area
Source: U.S. Census Bureau, 2019-2023 American Community Survey 5-Year Estimates

Key Congestion Measures

Measure	2000	2010	2015	2020	2022
Annual Hours of Delay, Total (000)	129,786	175,068	214,718	136,953	217,105
Annual Hours of Delay, Per Auto Commuter	47	50	63	40	68
Annual Congestion Cost, Per Auto Commuter ($)	1,181	1,266	1,434	948	1,523

Note: Figures cover the Dallas-Fort Worth-Arlington TX urban area
Source: Texas A&M Transportation Institute, 2023 Urban Mobility Report

Freeway Travel Time Index

Measure	1985	1990	1995	2000	2005	2010	2015	2020	2022
Urban Area Index[1]	1.19	1.20	1.23	1.24	1.26	1.25	1.26	1.12	1.23
Urban Area Rank[1,2]	6	9	8	18	22	21	23	10	24

Note: Freeway Travel Time Index—the ratio of travel time in the peak period to the travel time at free-flow conditions. For example, a value of 1.30 indicates a 20-minute free-flow trip takes 26 minutes in the peak (20 minutes x 1.30 = 26 minutes); (1) Covers the Dallas-Fort Worth-Arlington TX urban area; (2) Rank is based on 101 larger urban areas (#1 = highest travel time index)
Source: Texas A&M Transportation Institute, 2023 Urban Mobility Report

Public Transportation

Agency Name / Mode of Transportation	Vehicles Operated in Maximum Service[1]	Annual Unlinked Passenger Trips[2] (in thous.)	Annual Passenger Miles[3] (in thous.)
Fort Worth Transportation Authority (The T)			
Bus (directly operated)	135	3,972.6	14,383.9
Bus (purchased transportation)	7	68.4	158.7
Commuter Rail (purchased transportation)	20	652.2	10,396.5
Demand Response (directly operated)	24	102.6	1,031.2
Demand Response (purchased transportation)	52	188.6	1,654.6
Vanpool (purchased transportation)	197	373.8	12,219.4

Note: (1) Number of revenue vehicles operated by the given mode and type of service to meet the annual maximum service requirement. This is the revenue vehicle count during the peak season of the year; on the week and day that maximum service is provided. Vehicles operated in maximum service (VOMS) exclude atypical days and one-time special events; (2) Number of passengers who boarded public transportation vehicles. Passengers are counted each time they board a vehicle no matter how many vehicles they use to travel from their origin to their destination. (3) Sum of the distances ridden by all passengers during the entire fiscal year.
Source: Federal Transit Administration, National Transit Database, 2023

Air Transportation

Airport Name and Code / Type of Service	Passenger Airlines[1]	Passenger Enplanements	Freight Carriers[2]	Freight (lbs)
Dallas-Fort Worth International (DFW)				
Domestic service (U.S. carriers only)	27	36,327,693	14	400,491,276
International service (U.S. carriers only)	10	4,672,307	7	68,452,785
Dallas Love Field (DAL)				
Domestic service (U.S. carriers only)	24	8,644,402	7	14,460,516
International service (U.S. carriers only)	5	5,554	1	6,750

Note: (1) Includes all U.S.-based major, minor and commuter airlines that carried at least one passenger during the year; (2) Includes all U.S.-based airlines and freight carriers that transported at least one pound of freight during the year.
Source: Bureau of Transportation Statistics, The Intermodal Transportation Database, Air Carriers: T-100 Domestic Market (U.S. carriers only), 2024; Bureau of Transportation Statistics, The Intermodal Transportation Database, Air Carriers: T-100 International Market (U.S. carriers only), 2024

BUSINESSES

Major Business Headquarters

Company Name	Industry	Rankings	
		Fortune[1]	Forbes[2]
American Airlines Group	Airlines	86	-
Ben E Keith	Food, drink & tobacco	-	84

Note: (1) Companies that produce a 10-K are ranked 1 to 500 based on 2023 revenue; (2) All private companies with at least $2 billion in annual revenue through the end of their most current fiscal year are ranked 1 to 275; companies listed are headquartered in the city; dashes indicate no ranking
Source: Fortune, "Fortune 500," 2024; Forbes, "America's Largest Private Companies," 2024

Fastest-Growing Businesses

According to *Inc.*, Fort Worth is home to six of America's 500 fastest-growing private companies: **Archer Review** (#46); **Built By Grid** (#98); **evolv Consulting** (#295); **Inclusion Cloud** (#323); **Curis Functional Health** (#325); **HighLevel** (#426). Criteria: must be an independent, privately-held, for-profit, U.S. corporation, proprietorship or partnership as of December 31, 2023; revenues must be at least $100,000 in 2020 and $2 million in 2023; must have four-year operating/sales history. *Inc., "America's 500 Fastest-Growing Private Companies," 2024*

According to Deloitte, Fort Worth is home to one of North America's 500 fastest-growing high-technology companies: **Sanara MedTech** (#357). Companies are ranked by percentage growth in revenue over a four-year period. Criteria for inclusion: company must be headquartered within North America; must own proprietary intellectual property or technology that is sold to customers in products that contributes to a significant portion of the company's operating revenue; must have been in business for a minumum of four years with 2020 operating revenues of at least $50,000 USD/CD and 2023 operating revenues of at least $5 million USD/CD. *Deloitte, 2024 Technology Fast 500™*

Living Environment

COST OF LIVING

Cost of Living Index

Composite Index	Groceries	Housing	Utilities	Transportation	Health Care	Misc. Goods/Services
96.0	99.3	85.8	116.7	94.7	105.7	97.0

Note: The Cost of Living Index measures regional differences in the cost of consumer goods and services, excluding taxes and non-consumer expenditures, for professional and managerial households in the top income quintile. It is based on more than 50,000 prices covering almost 60 different items for which prices are collected three times a year by chambers of commerce, economic development organizations or university applied economic centers in each participating urban area. The numbers shown should be read as a percentage above or below the national average of 100. For example, a value of 115.4 in the groceries column indicates that grocery prices are 15.4% higher than the national average. Small differences in the index numbers should not be interpreted as significant; Figures cover the Fort Worth TX urban area.
Source: The Council for Community and Economic Research, Cost of Living Index, 2024

Grocery Prices

Area[1]	T-Bone Steak ($/pound)	Frying Chicken ($/pound)	Whole Milk ($/half gal.)	Eggs ($/dozen)	Orange Juice ($/64 oz.)	Coffee ($/11.5 oz.)
City[2]	14.52	1.56	4.61	3.13	4.28	5.46
Avg.	15.42	1.55	4.69	3.25	4.41	5.46
Min.	14.50	1.16	4.43	2.75	4.00	4.85
Max.	17.56	2.89	5.49	4.78	5.54	7.89

Note: (1) Values for the local area are compared with the average, minimum and maximum values for all 276 areas in the Cost of Living Index; (2) Figures cover the Fort Worth TX urban area; **T-Bone Steak** (price per pound); **Frying Chicken** (price per pound, whole fryer); **Whole Milk** (half gallon carton); **Eggs** (price per dozen, Grade A, large); **Orange Juice** (64 oz. Tropicana or Florida Natural); **Coffee** (11.5 oz. can, vacuum-packed, Maxwell House, Hills Bros, or Folgers).
Source: The Council for Community and Economic Research, Cost of Living Index, 2024

Housing and Utility Costs

Area[1]	New Home Price ($)	Apartment Rent ($/month)	All Electric ($/month)	Part Electric ($/month)	Other Energy ($/month)	Telephone ($/month)
City[2]	422,585	1,470	-	170.29	80.72	210.13
Avg.	515,975	1,550	210.99	123.07	82.07	194.99
Min.	265,375	692	104.33	53.68	36.26	179.42
Max.	2,775,821	5,719	529.02	397.28	361.63	223.33

Note: (1) Values for the local area are compared with the average, minimum and maximum values for all 276 areas in the Cost of Living Index; (2) Figures cover the Fort Worth TX urban area; **New Home Price** (2,400 sf living area, 8,000 sf lot, in urban area with full utilities); **Apartment Rent** (950 sf 2 bedroom/1.5 or 2 bath, unfurnished, excluding all utilities except water); **All Electric** (average monthly cost for an all-electric home); **Part Electric** (average monthly cost for a part-electric home); **Other Energy** (average monthly cost for natural gas, fuel oil, coal, wood, and any other forms of energy except electricity); **Telephone** (price includes the base monthly rate plus taxes and fees for three lines of mobile phone service).
Source: The Council for Community and Economic Research, Cost of Living Index, 2024

Health Care, Transportation, and Other Costs

Area[1]	Doctor ($/visit)	Dentist ($/visit)	Optometrist ($/visit)	Gasoline ($/gallon)	Beauty Salon ($/visit)	Men's Shirt ($)
City[2]	138.71	136.11	137.89	3.03	52.39	37.44
Avg.	143.77	117.51	129.23	3.32	48.57	38.14
Min.	36.74	58.67	67.33	2.80	24.00	13.41
Max.	270.44	216.82	307.33	5.28	94.00	63.89

Note: (1) Values for the local area are compared with the average, minimum and maximum values for all 276 areas in the Cost of Living Index; (2) Figures cover the Fort Worth TX urban area; **Doctor** (general practitioners routine exam of an established patient); **Dentist** (adult teeth cleaning and periodic oral examination); **Optometrist** (full vision eye exam for established adult patient); **Gasoline** (one gallon regular unleaded, national brand, including all taxes, cash price at self-service pump if available); **Beauty Salon** (woman's shampoo, trim, and blow-dry); **Men's Shirt** (cotton/polyester dress shirt, pinpoint weave, long sleeves).
Source: The Council for Community and Economic Research, Cost of Living Index, 2024

HOUSING

Homeownership Rate

Area	2017 (%)	2018 (%)	2019 (%)	2020 (%)	2021 (%)	2022 (%)	2023 (%)	2024 (%)
MSA[1]	61.8	62.0	60.6	64.7	61.8	60.4	61.7	61.1
U.S.	63.9	64.4	64.6	66.6	65.5	65.8	65.9	65.6

Note: (1) Figures cover the Dallas-Fort Worth-Arlington, TX Metropolitan Statistical Area
Source: U.S. Census Bureau, Housing Vacancies and Homeownership Annual Statistics: 2017-2024

House Price Index (HPI)

Area	National Ranking[2]	Quarterly Change (%)	One-Year Change (%)	Five-Year Change (%)	Since 1991Q1 (%)
MD[1]	194	0.54	3.30	53.69	324.24
U.S.[3]	—	1.43	4.51	57.13	327.82

Note: The HPI is a weighted repeat sales index. It measures average price changes in repeat sales or refinancings on the same properties. This information is obtained by reviewing repeat mortgage transactions on single-family properties whose mortgages have been purchased or securitized by Fannie Mae or Freddie Mac since January 1975; (1) Figures cover the Fort Worth-Arlington, TX Metropolitan Division; (2) Rankings are based on annual percentage change for all metro areas containing at least 15,000 transactions over the last 10 years and ranges from 1 to 241; (3) figures based on a weighted average of Census Division estimates using a seasonally adjusted, purchase-only index; all figures are for the period ending December 31, 2024
Source: Federal Housing Finance Agency, Change in FHFA Metropolitan Area House Price Indexes, All Transactions Index, 2024Q4

Home Value

Area	Under $100,000	$100,000 -$199,999	$200,000 -$299,999	$300,000 -$399,999	$400,000 -$499,999	$500,000 -$999,999	$1,000,000 or more	Median ($)
City	8.5	18.0	31.0	21.0	10.5	8.9	2.0	277,300
MSA[1]	6.8	13.3	23.8	20.1	13.1	18.8	4.1	330,300
U.S.	12.1	17.8	19.5	14.4	10.5	19.1	6.5	303,400

Note: Figures are percentages except for median and cover owner-occupied housing units; (1) Figures cover the Dallas-Fort Worth-Arlington, TX Metropolitan Statistical Area
Source: U.S. Census Bureau, 2019-2023 American Community Survey 5-Year Estimates

Year Housing Structure Built

Area	2020 or Later	2010 -2019	2000 -2009	1990 -1999	1980 -1989	1970 -1969	1960 -1969	1950 -1959	1940 -1949	Before 1940	Median Year
City	2.4	17.7	20.8	11.1	13.2	8.7	6.9	9.3	4.5	5.6	1992
MSA[1]	2.6	16.9	18.6	14.3	16.5	12.2	7.6	6.6	2.2	2.5	1992
U.S.	1.2	8.9	13.6	12.8	13.0	14.4	10.0	9.7	4.5	11.9	1980

Note: Figures are percentages except for Median Year; Note: (1) Figures cover the Dallas-Fort Worth-Arlington, TX Metropolitan Statistical Area
Source: U.S. Census Bureau, 2019-2023 American Community Survey 5-Year Estimates

Gross Monthly Rent

Area	Under $500	$500 -$999	$1,000 -$1,499	$1,500 -$1,999	$2,000 -$2,499	$2,500 -$2,999	$3,000 and up	Median ($)
City	2.6	13.5	40.6	25.3	12.3	3.4	2.2	1,412
MSA[1]	2.1	9.7	37.7	28.7	13.8	4.7	3.3	1,509
U.S.	6.5	22.3	29.5	20.2	10.8	4.8	5.9	1,348

Note: Figures are percentages except for median; Gross rent is the contract rent plus the estimated average monthly cost of utilities (electricity, gas, and water and sewer) and fuels (oil, coal, kerosene, wood, etc.) if these are paid by the renter (or paid for the renter by someone else); (1) Figures cover the Dallas-Fort Worth-Arlington, TX Metropolitan Statistical Area
Source: U.S. Census Bureau, 2019-2023 American Community Survey 5-Year Estimates

HEALTH

Health Risk Factors

Category	MD[1] (%)	U.S. (%)
Adults aged 18–64 who have any kind of health care coverage	78.7	90.8
Adults who reported being in good or better health	77.9	81.8
Adults who have been told they have high blood cholesterol	30.2	36.9
Adults who have been told they have high blood pressure	28.1	34.0
Adults who are current smokers	13.9	12.1
Adults who currently use e-cigarettes	7.5	7.7
Adults who currently use chewing tobacco, snuff, or snus	4.3	3.2
Adults who are heavy drinkers[2]	5.9	6.1
Adults who are binge drinkers[3]	16.6	15.2
Adults who are overweight (BMI 25.0 - 29.9)	35.2	34.4
Adults who are obese (BMI 30.0 - 99.8)	32.6	34.3
Adults who participated in any physical activities in the past month	71.7	75.8

Note: All figures are crude prevalence; (1) Figures cover the Fort Worth-Arlington, TX Metropolitan Division; (2) Heavy drinkers are classified as adult men having more than 14 drinks per week and adult women having more than 7 drinks per week; (3) Binge drinkers are classified as males having five or more drinks on one occasion or females having four or more drinks on one occasion
Source: Centers for Disease Control and Prevention, Behavioral Risk Factor Surveillance System, SMART: Selected Metropolitan Area Risk Trends, 2023

Acute and Chronic Health Conditions

Category	MD[1] (%)	U.S. (%)
Adults who have ever been told they had a heart attack	3.1	4.2
Adults who have ever been told they have angina or coronary heart disease	3.5	4.0
Adults who have ever been told they had a stroke	3.4	3.3
Adults who have ever been told they have asthma	16.0	15.7
Adults who have ever been told they have arthritis	22.5	26.3
Adults who have ever been told they have diabetes[2]	10.4	11.5
Adults who have ever been told they had skin cancer	3.7	5.6
Adults who have ever been told they had any other types of cancer	5.9	8.4
Adults who have ever been told they have COPD	5.2	6.4
Adults who have ever been told they have kidney disease	4.4	3.7
Adults who have ever been told they have a form of depression	23.3	22.0

Note: All figures are crude prevalence; (1) Figures cover the Fort Worth-Arlington, TX Metropolitan Division; (2) Figures do not include pregnancy-related, borderline, or pre-diabetes
Source: Centers for Disease Control and Prevention, Behavioral Risk Factor Surveillance System, SMART: Selected Metropolitan Area Risk Trends, 2023

Health Screening and Vaccination Rates

Category	MD[1] (%)	U.S. (%)
Adults who have ever been tested for HIV	39.0	37.5
Adults who have had their blood cholesterol checked within the last five years	86.9	87.0
Adults aged 65+ who have had flu shot within the past year	58.9	63.4
Adults aged 65+ who have ever had a pneumonia vaccination	67.9	71.9

Note: All figures are crude prevalence; (1) Figures cover the Fort Worth-Arlington, TX Metropolitan Division.
Source: Centers for Disease Control and Prevention, Behavioral Risk Factor Surveillance System, SMART: Selected Metropolitan Area Risk Trends, 2023

Disability Status

Category	MD[1] (%)	U.S. (%)
Adults who reported being deaf	4.1	7.4
Are you blind or have serious difficulty seeing, even when wearing glasses?	5.2	4.9
Do you have difficulty doing errands alone?	8.3	7.8
Do you have difficulty dressing or bathing?	2.8	3.6
Do you have serious difficulty concentrating/remembering/making decisions?	14.4	13.7
Do you have serious difficulty walking or climbing stairs?	13.0	13.2

Note: All figures are crude prevalence; (1) Figures cover the Fort Worth-Arlington, TX Metropolitan Division.
Source: Centers for Disease Control and Prevention, Behavioral Risk Factor Surveillance System, SMART: Selected Metropolitan Area Risk Trends, 2023

Mortality Rates for the Top 10 Causes of Death in the U.S.

ICD-10[a] Sub-Chapter	ICD-10[a] Code	Crude Mortality Rate[2] per 100,000 population	
		County[3]	U.S.
Malignant neoplasms	C00-C97	134.7	182.7
Ischaemic heart diseases	I20-I25	68.4	109.6
Provisional assignment of new diseases of uncertain etiology[1]	U00-U49	63.9	65.3
Other forms of heart disease	I30-I51	38.4	65.1
Other degenerative diseases of the nervous system	G30-G31	59.8	52.4
Other external causes of accidental injury	W00-X59	35.1	52.3
Cerebrovascular diseases	I60-I69	40.8	49.1
Chronic lower respiratory diseases	J40-J47	30.3	43.5
Hypertensive diseases	I10-I15	35.8	38.9
Organic, including symptomatic, mental disorders	F01-F09	16.9	33.9

Note: (a) ICD-10 = International Classification of Diseases 10th Revision; (1) Includes COVID-19, adverse effects to COVID-19 vaccines, SARS, and vaping-related disorders; (2) Crude mortality rates are a three-year average covering 2021-2023; (3) Figures cover Tarrant County.
Source: Centers for Disease Control and Prevention, National Center for Health Statistics. National Vital Statistics System, Mortality 2018-2023 on CDC WONDER Online Database

Mortality Rates for Selected Causes of Death

Cause of Death	ICD-10[a] Code	Crude Mortality Rate[1] per 100,000 population	
		County[2]	U.S.
Accidental poisoning and exposure to noxious substances	X40-X49	19.7	30.5
Alzheimer disease	G30	31.5	35.4
Assault	X85-Y09	7.5	7.3
COVID-19	U07.1	63.9	65.3
Diabetes mellitus	E10-E14	24.6	30.0
Diseases of the liver	K70-K76	17.4	20.8
Human immunodeficiency virus (HIV) disease	B20-B24	1.6	1.5
Influenza and pneumonia	J09-J18	9.6	13.4
Intentional self-harm	X60-X84	14.5	14.7
Malnutrition	E40-E46	5.5	6.0
Obesity and other hyperalimentation	E65-E68	4.0	3.1
Renal failure	N17-N19	14.0	16.4
Transport accidents	V01-V99	13.0	14.4

Note: (a) ICD-10 = International Classification of Diseases 10th Revision; (1) Crude mortality rates are a three-year average covering 2021-2023; (2) Figures cover Tarrant County; Data are suppressed when the data meet the criteria for confidentiality constraints; Crude mortality rates are flagged as unreliable when the rate would be calculated with a numerator of 20 or less.
Source: Centers for Disease Control and Prevention, National Center for Health Statistics. National Vital Statistics System, Mortality 2018-2023 on CDC WONDER Online Database

Health Insurance Coverage

Area	With Health Insurance	With Private Health Insurance	With Public Health Insurance	Without Health Insurance	Population Under Age 19 Without Health Insurance
City	81.4	61.7	26.4	18.6	12.7
MSA[1]	83.7	66.7	24.5	16.3	11.8
U.S.	91.4	67.3	36.3	8.6	5.4

Note: Figures are percentages that cover the civilian noninstitutionalized population; (1) Figures cover the Dallas-Fort Worth-Arlington, TX Metropolitan Statistical Area
Source: U.S. Census Bureau, 2019-2023 American Community Survey 5-Year Estimates

Number of Medical Professionals

Area	MDs[3]	DOs[3,4]	Dentists	Podiatrists	Chiropractors	Optometrists
County[1] (number)	4,260	849	1,416	99	663	378
County[1] (rate[2])	197.7	39.4	64.9	4.5	30.4	17.3
U.S. (rate[2])	302.5	29.2	74.6	6.4	29.5	18.0

Note: Data as of 2023 unless noted; (1) Data covers Tarrant County; (2) Number of medical professionals per 100,000 population; (3) Data as of 2022 and includes all active, non-federal physicians; (4) Doctor of Osteopathic Medicine
Source: U.S. Department of Health and Human Services, Health Resources and Services Administration, Bureau of Health Professions, Area Resource File (ARF) 2023-2024

Best Hospitals

According to *U.S. News,* the Dallas-Fort Worth-Arlington, TX metro area is home to five of the best hospitals in the U.S.: **Baylor Scott and White All Saints Medical Center-Fort Worth** (1 adult specialty); **Baylor Scott and White Institute for Rehabilitation-Dallas** (1 adult specialty); **Baylor Scott and White The Heart Hospital Plano** (1 adult specialty); **Baylor University Medical Center** (6 adult specialties); **UT Southwestern Medical Center** (11 adult specialties). The hospitals listed were nationally ranked in at least one of 15 adult or 11 pediatric specialties. The number of specialties shown cover the parent hospital. Only 160 U.S. hospitals performed well enough to be nationally ranked in one or more specialties. Twenty hospitals in the U.S. made the Honor Roll. The Best Hospitals Honor Roll takes both the national rankings and the procedure and condition ratings into account. Hospitals received points if they were nationally ranked in one of the 15 adult specialties—the higher they ranked, the more points they got—and how many ratings of "high performing" they earned in the 20 procedures and conditions. *U.S. News Online, "America's Best Hospitals 2024-25"*

According to *U.S. News,* the Dallas-Fort Worth-Arlington, TX metro area is home to three of the best children's hospitals in the U.S.: **Children's Medical Center Dallas** (11 pediatric specialties); **Children's Medical Center Dallas-Scottish Rite for Children** (1 pediatric specialty); **Cook Children's Medical Center** (7 pediatric specialties). The hospitals listed were highly ranked in at least one of 11 pediatric specialties. One hundred five children's hospitals in the U.S. were nationally ranked in at least one specialty. Hospitals received points for being ranked in a specialty, and the 10 hospitals with the most points across the 11 specialties make up the Honor Roll. *U.S. News Online, "America's Best Children's Hospitals 2024-25"*

EDUCATION

Public School District Statistics

District Name	Schls	Pupils	Pupil/ Teacher Ratio	Minority Pupils[1] (%)	Total Rev. per Pupil ($)	Total Exp. per Pupil ($)
Castleberry ISD	8	3,740	13.8	89.0	15,506	13,691
Crowley ISD	25	16,956	13.4	90.6	14,345	17,235
Eagle Mt-Saginaw ISD	32	23,462	15.1	69.6	14,019	16,345
Everman ISD	11	5,139	14.0	96.5	15,692	17,307
Fort Worth ISD	141	71,060	14.8	88.9	15,852	15,887

Note: Table includes school districts with 2,000 or more students; (1) Percentage of students that are not non-Hispanic white.
Source: U.S. Department of Education, National Center for Education Statistics, Common Core of Data, Local Education Agency (School District) Universe Survey: School Year 2023-2024; U.S. Department of Education, National Center for Education Statistics, Common Core of Data, School District Finance Survey (F-33): School Year 2021–22

Best High Schools

According to *U.S. News*, Fort Worth is home to two of the top 500 high schools in the U.S.: **World Languages Institute** (#170); **Young Women's Leadership Academy** (#277). Nearly 25,000 public, magnet and charter schools were ranked based on their performance on state assessments and how well they prepare students for college. *U.S. News & World Report, "Best High Schools 2024"*

Highest Level of Education

Area	Less than H.S.	H.S. Diploma	Some College, No Deg.	Associate Degree	Bachelor's Degree	Master's Degree	Prof. School Degree	Doctorate Degree
City	15.7	24.7	20.5	7.4	20.6	8.4	1.6	1.1
MSA[1]	12.7	21.7	19.7	7.4	24.5	10.7	2.0	1.3
U.S.	10.6	26.2	19.4	8.8	21.3	9.8	2.3	1.6

Note: Figures cover persons age 25 and over; (1) Figures cover the Dallas-Fort Worth-Arlington, TX Metropolitan Statistical Area
Source: U.S. Census Bureau, 2019-2023 American Community Survey 5-Year Estimates

Educational Attainment by Race

Area	High School Graduate or Higher (%)					Bachelor's Degree or Higher (%)				
	Total	White	Black	Asian	Hisp.[2]	Total	White	Black	Asian	Hisp.[2]
City	84.3	91.2	90.0	82.7	64.6	31.7	41.0	23.0	46.0	14.7
MSA[1]	87.3	92.0	92.2	90.0	66.3	38.5	42.8	31.6	65.4	17.8
U.S.	89.4	92.9	88.1	88.0	72.5	35.0	37.7	24.7	57.0	19.9

Note: Figures shown cover persons 25 years old and over; (1) Figures cover the Dallas-Fort Worth-Arlington, TX Metropolitan Statistical Area; (2) People of Hispanic origin can be of any race
Source: U.S. Census Bureau, 2019-2023 American Community Survey 5-Year Estimates

School Enrollment by Grade and Control

Area	Preschool (%)		Kindergarten (%)		Grades 1 - 4 (%)		Grades 5 - 8 (%)		Grades 9 - 12 (%)	
	Public	Private	Public	Private	Public	Private	Public	Private	Public	Private
City	61.4	38.6	86.8	13.2	90.9	9.1	91.0	9.0	91.3	8.7
MSA[1]	57.4	42.6	88.0	12.0	90.4	9.6	91.4	8.6	91.5	8.5
U.S.	58.7	41.3	85.2	14.8	87.2	12.8	87.9	12.1	89.0	11.0

Note: Figures shown cover persons 3 years old and over; (1) Figures cover the Dallas-Fort Worth-Arlington, TX Metropolitan Statistical Area
Source: U.S. Census Bureau, 2019-2023 American Community Survey 5-Year Estimates

Higher Education

Four-Year Colleges			Two-Year Colleges			Medical Schools[1]	Law Schools[2]	Voc/ Tech[3]
Public	Private Non-profit	Private For-profit	Public	Private Non-profit	Private For-profit			
11	25	7	1	3	11	3	3	36

Note: Figures cover institutions located within the Dallas-Fort Worth-Arlington, TX Metropolitan Statistical Area and include main campuses only; (1) includes schools accredited by the Liaison Committee on Medical Education and the American Osteopathic Association's Commission on Osteopathic College Accreditation; (2) includes ABA-accredited schools, schools with provisional ABA accreditation, and state accredited schools; (3) includes all schools with programs that are less than 2 years.
Source: National Center for Education Statistics, Integrated Postsecondary Education System (IPEDS), 2023-24; Wikipedia, List of Medical Schools in the United States, accessed May 2, 2025; Wikipedia, List of Law Schools in the United States, accessed May 2, 2025

According to *U.S. News & World Report,* the Dallas-Fort Worth-Arlington, TX metro area is home to three of the top 200 national universities in the U.S.: **Southern Methodist University** (#91 tie); **Texas Christian University** (#105 tie); **The University of Texas—Dallas** (#109 tie). The indicators used to capture academic quality fall into a number of categories: assessment by administrators at peer institutions; retention of students; faculty resources; student selectivity; financial resources; alumni giving; high school counselor ratings of colleges; and graduation rate. *U.S. News & World Report, "America's Best Colleges 2025"*

According to *U.S. News & World Report,* the Dallas-Fort Worth-Arlington, TX metro area is home to two of the top 100 law schools in the U.S.: **Texas A&M University** (#22 tie); **Southern Methodist University (Dedman)** (#43 tie). The rankings are based on a weighted average of 12 measures of quality: peer assessment score; assessment score by lawyers/judges; median LSAT scores; median undergrad GPA; acceptance rate; employment rates for graduates; placement success; bar passage rate; faculty resources; expenditures per student; student/faculty ratio; and library resources. *U.S. News & World Report, "America's Best Graduate Schools, Law, 2025"*

According to *U.S. News & World Report,* the Dallas-Fort Worth-Arlington, TX metro area is home to one of the top medical schools for research in the U.S.: **University of Texas Southwestern Medical Center** (Tier 1). *U.S. News* placed medical and osteopathic schools into tiers based on their research productivity, faculty and admissions data. Each school's tier was derived from its overall score, calculated by summing the weighted normalized values generated across several factors of academic quality, outlined below. There are four tiers, with tier 1 medical schools as the highest-performing and tier 4 as the lowest-performing. Only tier 1 and 2 schools are shown. Because of the tier presentation, *U.S. News* calculated overall scores based on their percentile performance among all rated schools instead of dividing against the rescaled score of the No. 1-performing schools. Tier 1 included schools with overall scores of 85 to 99. The cutoffs for tiers 2 through 4 were schools scoring 50 to 84, 15 to 49 and 1 to 14, respectively. The rankings are based on a weighted average of the following measures of quality: total research activity; average research activity per faculty member; total NIH research grants at the medical school and its affiliated hospitals; average NIH research grants per faculty; median MCAT total score; median undergraduate GPA; acceptance rate; and faculty resources. *U.S. News & World Report, "America's Best Graduate Schools, Medical, 2025"*

According to *U.S. News & World Report,* the Dallas-Fort Worth-Arlington, TX metro area is home to two of the top medical schools for primary care in the U.S.: **The University of North Texas Health Science Center at Fort Worth** (Tier 2); **University of Texas Southwestern Medical Center** (Tier 2). *U.S. News* placed medical and osteopathic schools into tiers based on their research productivity, faculty and admissions data. Each school's tier was derived from its overall score, calculated by summing the weighted normalized values generated across several factors of academic quality, outlined below. There are four tiers, with tier 1 medical schools as the highest-performing and tier 4 as the lowest-performing. Only tier 1 and 2 schools are shown. Because of the tier presentation, *U.S. News* calculated overall scores based on their percentile performance among all rated schools instead of dividing against the rescaled score of the No. 1-performing schools. Tier 1 included schools with overall scores of 85 to 99. The cutoffs for tiers 2 through 4 were schools scoring 50 to 84, 15 to 49 and 1 to 14, respectively. The rankings are based on a weighted average of the following measures of quality: graduates practicing in primary care specialties; graduates entering primary care residencies; median MCAT total score; median undergraduate GPA; acceptance rate; and faculty resources. *U.S. News & World Report, "America's Best Graduate Schools, Medical, 2025"*

According to *U.S. News & World Report,* the Dallas-Fort Worth-Arlington, TX metro area is home to three of the top 75 business schools in the U.S.: **The University of Texas at Dallas (Jindal)** (#31); **Southern Methodist University (Cox)** (#34); **Texas Christian University (Neeley)** (#43 tie). The rankings are based on a weighted average of the following nine measures: quality assessment; peer assessment; recruiter assessment; placement success; mean starting salary and bonus; student selectivity; mean GMAT and GRE scores; mean undergraduate GPA; and acceptance rate. *U.S. News & World Report, "America's Best Graduate Schools, Business, 2025"*

EMPLOYERS

Major Employers

Company Name	Industry
AMR Corporation	Air transportation, scheduled
Associates First Capital Corporation	Mortgage bankers
Baylor University Medical Center	General medical & surgical hospitals
Children's Medical Center Dallas	Specialty hospitals, except psychiatric
Combat Support Associates	Engineering services
County of Dallas	County government
Dallas County Hospital District	General medical & surgical hospitals
Fort Worth Independent School District	Public elementary & secondary schools
Housewares Holding Company	Toasters, electric: household
HP Enterprise Services	Computer integrated systems design
J.C. Penney Company	Department stores
JCP Publications Corp.	Department stores
L-3 Communications Corporation	Business economic service
Odyssey HealthCare	Home health care services
Romano's Macaroni Grill	Italian restaurant
SFG Management	Milk processing (pasteurizing, homogenizing, bottling)
Texas Instruments Incorporated	Semiconductors & related devices
University of North Texas	Colleges & universities
University of Texas SW Medical Center	Accident & health insurance
Verizon Business Global	Telephone communication, except radio

Note: Companies shown are located within the Dallas-Fort Worth-Arlington, TX Metropolitan Statistical Area.
Source: Chambers of Commerce; State Departments of Labor; Wikipedia

Best Companies to Work For

Freese and Nichols, headquartered in Fort Worth, is among "Fortune's Best Workplaces for Women." To pick the best companies, *Fortune* partnered with the Great Place to Work Institute. To be considered for the list, companies must be Great Place To Work-Certified. Companies must also employ at least 50 women, at least 20% of their non-executive managers must be female, and at least one executive must be female. To determine the Best Workplaces for Women, Great Place To Work measured the differences in women's survey responses to those of their peers and assesses the impact of demographics and roles on the quality and consistency of women's experiences. Great Place To Work also analyzed the gender balance of each workplace, how it compared to each company's industry, and patterns in representation as women rise from front-line positions to the board of directors. *Fortune, "Best Workplaces for Women," 2024*

TimelyCare, headquartered in Fort Worth, is among "Best Workplaces in Health Care." To determine the Best Workplaces in Health Care list, Great Place To Work analyzed the survey responses of over 185,000 employees from Great Place To Work-Certified companies in the health care industry. Survey data analysis and company-provided datapoints are then factored into a combined score to compare and rank the companies that create the most consistently positive experience for all employees in this industry. *Fortune, "Best Workplaces in Health Care," 2024*

Fort; M2G Ventures, headquartered in Fort Worth, are among "Best Workplaces in Real Estate." To determine the Best Workplaces in Real Estate list, Great Place To Work analyzed the survey responses of over 29,000 employees from Great Place To Work-Certified companies in the real estate industry. Survey data analysis and company-provided datapoints are then factored into a combined score to compare and rank the companies that create the most consistently positive experience for all employees in this industry. *Fortune, "Best Workplaces in Real Estate," 2024*

PUBLIC SAFETY

Crime Rate

Area	Total Crime Rate	Violent Crime Rate				Property Crime Rate		
		Murder	Rape	Robbery	Aggrav. Assault	Burglary	Larceny-Theft	Motor Vehicle Theft
City	3,135.9	8.7	69.1	71.2	340.8	391.4	1,763.5	491.2
U.S.	2,290.9	5.7	38.0	66.5	264.1	250.7	1,347.2	318.7

Note: Figures are crimes per 100,000 population.
Source: FBI, Table 8, Offenses Known to Law Enforcement, by State by City, 2023

Hate Crimes

Area	Number of Quarters Reported	Number of Incidents per Bias Motivation					
		Race/Ethnicity/Ancestry	Religion	Sexual Orientation	Disability	Gender	Gender Identity
City[1]	4	8	2	5	0	0	0
U.S.	4	5,900	2,699	2,077	187	92	492

Note: (1) Figures include at least one incident reported with more than one bias motivation.
Source: Federal Bureau of Investigation, Hate Crime Statistics 2023

Identity Theft Consumer Reports

Area	Reports	Reports per 100,000 Population	Rank[2]
MSA[1]	37,114	475	10
U.S.	1,135,291	339	-

Note: (1) Figures cover the Dallas-Fort Worth-Arlington, TX Metropolitan Statistical Area; (2) Rank ranges from 1 to 401 where 1 indicates greatest number of identity theft reports per 100,000 population
Source: Federal Trade Commission, Consumer Sentinel Network Data Book 2024

Fraud and Other Consumer Reports

Area	Reports	Reports per 100,000 Population	Rank[2]
MSA[1]	159,709	2,046	10
U.S.	5,360,641	1,601	-

Note: (1) Figures cover the Dallas-Fort Worth-Arlington, TX Metropolitan Statistical Area; (2) Rank ranges from 1 to 401 where 1 indicates greatest number of fraud and other consumer reports per 100,000 population
Source: Federal Trade Commission, Consumer Sentinel Network Data Book 2024

POLITICS

2024 Presidential Election Results

Area	Trump (Rep.)	Harris (Dem.)	Stein (Green)	Kennedy (Ind.)	Oliver (Lib.)	Other
Tarrant County	51.8	46.7	0.7	0.0	0.7	0.1
U.S.	49.7	48.2	0.6	0.5	0.4	0.6

Note: Results are percentages and may not add to 100% due to rounding
Source: Dave Leip's Atlas of U.S. Presidential Elections

SPORTS

Professional Sports Teams

Team Name	League	Year Established
Dallas Cowboys	National Football League (NFL)	1960
Dallas Mavericks	National Basketball Association (NBA)	1980
Dallas Stars	National Hockey League (NHL)	1993
FC Dallas	Major League Soccer (MLS)	1996
Texas Rangers	Major League Baseball (MLB)	1972

Note: Includes teams located in the Dallas-Fort Worth-Arlington, TX Metropolitan Statistical Area.
Source: Wikipedia, Major Professional Sports Teams of the United States and Canada, May 1, 2025

CLIMATE

Average and Extreme Temperatures

Temperature	Jan	Feb	Mar	Apr	May	Jun	Jul	Aug	Sep	Oct	Nov	Dec	Yr.
Extreme High (°F)	88	88	96	98	103	113	110	108	107	106	89	90	113
Average High (°F)	54	59	67	76	83	92	96	96	88	79	67	58	76
Average Temp. (°F)	44	49	57	66	73	81	85	85	78	68	56	47	66
Average Low (°F)	33	38	45	54	63	71	75	74	67	56	45	37	55
Extreme Low (°F)	4	6	11	29	41	51	59	56	43	29	19	-1	-1

Note: Figures cover the years 1953-1990
Source: National Climatic Data Center, International Station Meteorological Climate Summary, 9/96

Average Precipitation/Snowfall/Humidity

Precip./Humidity	Jan	Feb	Mar	Apr	May	Jun	Jul	Aug	Sep	Oct	Nov	Dec	Yr.
Avg. Precip. (in.)	1.8	2.2	2.6	3.7	4.9	2.8	2.1	1.9	3.0	3.3	2.1	1.7	32.3
Avg. Snowfall (in.)	1	1	Tr	0	0	0	0	0	0	0	Tr	Tr	3
Avg. Rel. Hum. 6am (%)	79	79	79	81	86	85	80	79	83	82	80	79	81
Avg. Rel. Hum. 3pm (%)	52	51	48	50	53	47	42	41	46	47	49	51	48

Note: Figures cover the years 1953-1990; Tr = Trace amounts (<0.05 in. of rain; <0.5 in. of snow)
Source: National Climatic Data Center, International Station Meteorological Climate Summary, 9/96

Weather Conditions

Temperature			Daytime Sky			Precipitation		
10°F & below	32°F & below	90°F & above	Clear	Partly cloudy	Cloudy	0.01 inch or more precip.	0.1 inch or more snow/ice	Thunder-storms
1	40	100	123	136	106	79	3	47

Note: Figures are average number of days per year and cover the years 1953-1990
Source: National Climatic Data Center, International Station Meteorological Climate Summary, 9/96

HAZARDOUS WASTE

Superfund Sites

The Fort Worth-Arlington-Grapevine, TX metro division is home to three sites on the EPA's Superfund National Priorities List (NPL) or Superfund Alternative Approach (SAA) list: **Air Force**

Plant #4 (General Dynamics) (Final NPL); **Circle Court Ground Water Plume** (Final NPL); **Sandy Beach Road Ground Water Plume** (Final NPL). The Superfund alternative approach uses the same investigation and cleanup process and standards that are used for sites listed on the National Priorities List. The SAA is an alternative to listing a site on the NPL; it is not an alternative to Superfund or the Superfund process. There are a total of 1,445 Superfund sites with a status of proposed or final on both lists in the United States. *U.S. Environmental Protection Agency, National Priorities List, May 1, 2025; U.S. Environmental Protection Agency, Superfund Alternative Approach Sites, May 1, 2025*

AIR QUALITY

Air Quality Trends: Ozone

	1990	1995	2000	2005	2010	2015	2020	2021	2022	2023
MSA[1]	0.094	0.103	0.096	0.096	0.079	0.078	0.070	0.076	0.072	0.081
U.S.	0.087	0.089	0.081	0.080	0.072	0.068	0.066	0.067	0.067	0.070

Note: (1) Data covers the Dallas-Fort Worth-Arlington, TX Metropolitan Statistical Area. The values shown are the composite ozone concentration averages among trend sites based on the highest fourth daily maximum 8-hour concentration in parts per million. These trends are based on sites having an adequate record of monitoring data during the trend period. Data from exceptional events are included.
Source: U.S. Environmental Protection Agency, Air Quality Monitoring Information, "Air Quality Trends by City, 1990-2023"

Air Quality Index

Area	Percent of Days when Air Quality was...[2]					AQI Statistics[2]	
	Good	Moderate	Unhealthy for Sensitive Groups	Unhealthy	Very Unhealthy	Maximum	Median
MSA[1]	20.5	64.9	12.1	2.5	0.0	177	60

Note: (1) Data covers the Dallas-Fort Worth-Arlington, TX Metropolitan Statistical Area; (2) Based on 365 days with AQI data in 2023. Air Quality Index (AQI) is an index for reporting daily air quality. EPA calculates the AQI for five major air pollutants regulated by the Clean Air Act: ground-level ozone, particle pollution (aka particulate matter), carbon monoxide, sulfur dioxide, and nitrogen dioxide. The AQI runs from 0 to 500. The higher the AQI value, the greater the level of air pollution and the greater the health concern. There are six AQI categories: "Good" AQI is between 0 and 50. Air quality is considered satisfactory; "Moderate" AQI is between 51 and 100. Air quality is acceptable; "Unhealthy for Sensitive Groups" When AQI values are between 101 and 150, members of sensitive groups may experience health effects; "Unhealthy" When AQI values are between 151 and 200 everyone may begin to experience health effects; "Very Unhealthy" AQI values between 201 and 300 trigger a health alert; "Hazardous" AQI values over 300 trigger warnings of emergency conditions (not shown).
Source: U.S. Environmental Protection Agency, Air Quality Index Report, 2023

Air Quality Index Pollutants

Area	Percent of Days when AQI Pollutant was...[2]					
	Carbon Monoxide	Nitrogen Dioxide	Ozone	Sulfur Dioxide	Particulate Matter 2.5	Particulate Matter 10
MSA[1]	0.0	0.5	40.5	(3)	58.4	0.5

Note: (1) Data covers the Dallas-Fort Worth-Arlington, TX Metropolitan Statistical Area; (2) Based on 365 days with AQI data in 2023. The Air Quality Index (AQI) is an index for reporting daily air quality. EPA calculates the AQI for five major air pollutants regulated by the Clean Air Act: ground-level ozone, particle pollution (also known as particulate matter), carbon monoxide, sulfur dioxide, and nitrogen dioxide. The AQI runs from 0 to 500. The higher the AQI value, the greater the level of air pollution and the greater the health concern; (3) Sulfur dioxide is no longer included in this table because SO_2 concentrations tend to be very localized and not necessarily representative of broad geographical areas like counties and CBSAs.
Source: U.S. Environmental Protection Agency, Air Quality Index Report, 2023

Maximum Air Pollutant Concentrations: Particulate Matter, Ozone, CO and Lead

	Particulate Matter 10 (ug/m³)	Particulate Matter 2.5 Wtd AM (ug/m³)	Particulate Matter 2.5 24-Hr (ug/m³)	Ozone (ppm)	Carbon Monoxide (ppm)	Lead (ug/m³)
MSA[1] Level	70	10.7	23	0.084	2	0.07
NAAQS[2]	150	15	35	0.075	9	0.15
Met NAAQS[2]	Yes	Yes	Yes	No	Yes	Yes

Note: (1) Data covers the Dallas-Fort Worth-Arlington, TX Metropolitan Statistical Area; Data from exceptional events are included; (2) National Ambient Air Quality Standards; ppm = parts per million; ug/m³ = micrograms per cubic meter; n/a not available.
Concentrations: Particulate Matter 10 (coarse particulate)—highest second maximum 24-hour concentration; Particulate Matter 2.5 Wtd AM (fine particulate)—highest weighted annual mean concentration; Particulate Matter 2.5 24-Hour (fine particulate)—highest 98th percentile 24-hour concentration; Ozone—highest fourth daily maximum 8-hour concentration; Carbon Monoxide—highest second maximum non-overlapping 8-hour concentration; Lead—maximum running 3-month average
Source: U.S. Environmental Protection Agency, Air Quality Monitoring Information, "Air Quality Statistics by City, 2023"

Maximum Air Pollutant Concentrations: Nitrogen Dioxide and Sulfur Dioxide

	Nitrogen Dioxide AM (ppb)	Nitrogen Dioxide 1-Hr (ppb)	Sulfur Dioxide AM (ppb)	Sulfur Dioxide 1-Hr (ppb)	Sulfur Dioxide 24-Hr (ppb)
MSA[1] Level	14	46	n/a	17	n/a
NAAQS[2]	53	100	30	75	140
Met NAAQS[2]	Yes	Yes	n/a	Yes	n/a

Note: (1) Data covers the Dallas-Fort Worth-Arlington, TX Metropolitan Statistical Area; Data from exceptional events are included; (2) National Ambient Air Quality Standards; ppm = parts per million; ug/m^3 = micrograms per cubic meter; n/a not available.
Concentrations: Nitrogen Dioxide AM—highest arithmetic mean concentration; Nitrogen Dioxide 1-Hr—highest 98th percentile 1-hour daily maximum concentration; Sulfur Dioxide AM—highest annual mean concentration; Sulfur Dioxide 1-Hr—highest 99th percentile 1-hour daily maximum concentration; Sulfur Dioxide 24-Hr—highest second maximum 24-hour concentration
Source: U.S. Environmental Protection Agency, Air Quality Monitoring Information, "Air Quality Statistics by City, 2023"

Gainesville, Florida

Background

Gainesville sits in between the Atlantic Ocean and the Gulf of Mexico. The cultural and educational hub of North Florida, Alachua County's largest city is known for its subtropical locale and its largest employer, the University of Florida (UF). Innovation is the name of the game when it comes to the region's push for businesses emerging from the university's numerous research centers. Gainesville is only a short drive to the Paynes Prairie Preserve with bison, alligators, and hundreds of bird species, and found at Paynes Prairie Preserve and part of North Florida large concentration of freshwater springs.

Originally a Timucuan Native American village, present-day Gainesville was part of a Spanish land grant by 1817. The United States annexed Florida in 1825, and just over a quarter-century later came plans for the Florida Railroad. In 1853, the local citizenry opted to create a new county seat along the railroad line, and Gainesville was founded and named for Seminole Indian War General Edmund P. Gaines. After the Civil War, a Union veteran established a successful cotton shipping station here, and in 1906 UF was founded. Through the years, fire and development has destroyed many of Gainesville's early buildings; those few that remain include the Hippodrome State Theatre which was once the local Federal Building.

Emerging from the University of Florida (the nation's fourth largest university), are projects from dozens of research centers and institutes. An early success was Gatorade, invented in 1965 to hydrate the Gator football team. Alternative energy research draws accolades, and the city proper became the nation's first to implement a solar feed-in tariff, which means consumers who invest in the appropriate technology can sell their electricity back to the utility. The university's Sid Martin Biotechnology Incubator was ranked "World's Best University Biotechnology Incubator," and its annual economic impact is nearly $16 billion, and state-wide its activities are estimated to generate more than 135,000 jobs.

In addition to the biotechnology incubator, UF Innovate | Accelerate at The Hub is a business incubator with a mission to build, drive and support the spirit of innovation. The original 48,000-square-foot facility was built with an $8.2 million grant from the federal Economic Development Administration and a $5 million commitment from the University of Florida. After it opened in October 2011, the incubator demonstrated such success that the EDA awarded a second $8 million grant, to which UF added an additional $9 million in 2015. The expansion opened in January 2018, doubling the facility to a total of 100,000 square feet.

A long list of rankings lauds Gainesville's quality of life for young people and retirees. As with many college towns, there's a robust music scene. Tom Petty and the Heartbreakers emerged from Gainesville. Cultural resources include the Florida Museum of Natural History, founded in 1891, fueled by donations from interested professors. In addition to its central museum and collections, it operates the Randell Research Center (a significant Calusa Indian archaeological and ancient ecological site in Lee County northwest of Fort Myers) and the McGuire Center for Lepidoptera and Biodiversity that boasts one of the world's largest butterfly and moth collections. Public exhibitions include the 6,800 square-foot living Butterfly Rainforest. The museum closed in early 2025 for a large-scale expansion project and will reopen in 2026.

In addition, UF's Harn Museum of Art exhibits traveling shows and collections of photography and Ancient American, Asian, African, modern and contemporary art. Also in the city are the Hippodrome State Theatre, showcasing cinema and traveling theater, and the Curtis M. Phillips Center for Performing Arts. Gainesville is also known for "Gainesville Green," a potent strain of marijuana.

Famously humid, Gainesville's subtropical climate means freezes are not unheard of in winter, with December through February average highs in the 50s. June through August is notably wet, averaging more than six inches of rain the first two months of summer and eight inches in August. Gainesville's inland location tends to mitigate the threat of hurricanes that face Florida's coasts. Temperatures often climb into the 90s from April to October.

Rankings

General Rankings

- In their annual survey, Livability.com looked at data for more than 2,000 mid-sized U.S. cities to assign a "Livability Score"for each. The top 100 scoring cities make up Livability's "Top 100 Best Places to Live in the U.S." in 2025. Gainesville was placed among the top 100 of the customizable list. Criteria: housing and economy; cost of living; environment; education; health care options; transportation; safety; and community amenities. *Livability.com, "Top 100 Best Places to Live in the U.S. in 2025" April 15, 2025*

Business/Finance Rankings

- The Gainesville metro area appeared on the Milken Institute "2025 Best Performing Cities" list. Rank: #127 out of 200 large metro areas (based on performance category). Criteria: job growth; wage growth; high-tech growth and impact; community resilience; housing affordability; household broadband access. *Milken Institute, "Best-Performing Cities 2025," January 14, 2025*

Environmental Rankings

- Gainesville was highlighted as one of the cleanest metro areas for ozone air pollution in the U.S. during 2021 through 2023. The list represents cities with no monitored ozone air pollution in unhealthful ranges. *American Lung Association, "State of the Air 2025," April 23, 2025*

- Gainesville was highlighted as one of the top 25 cleanest metro areas for year-round particle pollution (Annual PM 2.5) in the U.S. during 2021 through 2023. The area ranked #15. *American Lung Association, "State of the Air 2025," April 23, 2025*

Pet Rankings

- Gainesville was selected by *Sniffspot.com* as one of the most dog-friendly cities in the U.S., ranking #49 out of 50. Criteria: dog parks; hiking; sniffspots; public parks; dog-friendly businesses; housing; dog waste cleanliness; leash laws; dog services; and overall cost. *Sniffspot.com, "The Top 50 Most Dog-Friendly Cities in the U.S.," September 30, 2024*

Real Estate Rankings

- Gainesville was ranked #89 out of 176 metro areas in terms of cost of housing in 2024 by the National Association of Home Builders (#1 = most affordable). Criteria: the portion of an average family's income necessary to pay the mortgage on a median-priced home. *National Association of Home Builders®, NAHB-Wells Fargo Cost of Housing Index, 4th Quarter 2024*

Business Environment

DEMOGRAPHICS

Population Growth

Area	1990 Census	2000 Census	2010 Census	2020 Census	2023 Estimate[2]	Population Growth 1990-2023 (%)
City	90,519	95,447	124,354	141,085	143,611	58.7
MSA[1]	191,263	232,392	264,275	339,247	344,521	80.1
U.S.	248,709,873	281,421,906	308,745,538	331,449,281	332,387,540	33.6

Note: (1) Figures cover the Gainesville, FL Metropolitan Statistical Area; (2) 2019-2023 5-year ACS population estimate
Source: U.S. Census Bureau, 1990 Census, 2000 Census, 2010 Census, 2020 Census, 2019-2023 American Community Survey 5-Year Estimates

Race

Area	White Alone[2] (%)	Black Alone[2] (%)	Asian Alone[2] (%)	AIAN[3] Alone[2] (%)	NHOPI[4] Alone[2] (%)	Other Race Alone[2] (%)	Two or More Races (%)
City	59.2	21.6	6.2	0.2	0.1	3.0	9.7
MSA[1]	66.6	17.1	4.9	0.2	0.0	2.5	8.7
U.S.	63.4	12.4	5.8	0.9	0.2	6.6	10.7

Note: (1) Figures cover the Gainesville, FL Metropolitan Statistical Area; (2) Alone is defined as not being in combination with one or more other races; (3) American Indian and Alaska Native; (4) Native Hawaiian and Other Pacific Islander
Source: U.S. Census Bureau, 2019-2023 American Community Survey 5-Year Estimates

Hispanic or Latino Origin

Area	Total (%)	Mexican (%)	Puerto Rican (%)	Cuban (%)	Other (%)
City	13.4	1.3	2.9	2.9	6.3
MSA[1]	11.6	1.8	2.8	2.1	4.9
U.S.	19.0	11.3	1.8	0.7	5.2

Note: Persons of Hispanic or Latino origin can be of any race; (1) Figures cover the Gainesville, FL Metropolitan Statistical Area
Source: U.S. Census Bureau, 2019-2023 American Community Survey 5-Year Estimates

Age

Area	Under Age 5	Age 5–19	Age 20–34	Age 35–44	Age 45–54	Age 55–64	Age 65–74	Age 75–84	Age 85+	Median Age
City	3.7	19.7	40.6	9.6	7.3	7.3	6.7	3.3	1.7	26.5
MSA[1]	4.9	18.6	27.4	11.4	10.1	11.2	9.9	4.7	2.0	34.3
U.S.	5.7	19.1	20.2	13.1	12.3	12.8	10.0	4.9	1.9	38.7

Note: (1) Figures cover the Gainesville, FL Metropolitan Statistical Area
Source: U.S. Census Bureau, 2019-2023 American Community Survey 5-Year Estimates

Disability by Age

Area	All Ages	Under 18 Years Old	18 to 64 Years Old	65 Years and Over
City	10.5	3.9	8.3	33.6
MSA[1]	13.3	5.4	10.2	34.6
U.S.	13.0	4.7	10.7	32.9

Note: Figures show percent of the civilian noninstitutionalized population that reported having a disability. Disability status is determined from six types of difficulty: vision, hearing, cognitive, ambulatory, self-care, and independent living. For children under 5 years old, hearing and vision difficulty are used to determine disability status. For children between the ages of 5 and 14, disability status is determined from hearing, vision, cognitive, ambulatory, and self-care difficulties. For people aged 15 years and older, they are considered to have a disability if they have difficulty with any one of the six difficulty types; Note: (1) Figures cover the Gainesville, FL Metropolitan Statistical Area
Source: U.S. Census Bureau, 2019-2023 American Community Survey 5-Year Estimates

Ancestry

Area	German	Irish	English	American	Italian	Polish	French[2]	European	Scottish
City	10.6	8.9	10.5	3.4	5.1	2.5	1.6	1.3	2.6
MSA[1]	11.6	10.3	12.1	4.6	4.5	2.1	2.0	1.7	2.9
U.S.	12.6	9.4	9.1	5.5	4.9	2.6	2.0	1.6	1.6

Note: Figures are the percentage of the total population reporting a particular ancestry. The nine most commonly reported ancestries in the U.S. are shown. Figures include multiple ancestries (e.g. if a person reported being Irish and Italian, they were included in both columns); (1) Figures cover the Gainesville, FL Metropolitan Statistical Area; (2) Excludes Basque
Source: U.S. Census Bureau, 2019-2023 American Community Survey 5-Year Estimates

Foreign-born Population

Area	Percent of Population Born in								
	Any Foreign Country	Asia	Mexico	Europe	Caribbean	Central America[2]	South America	Africa	Canada
City	12.1	4.6	0.2	1.7	1.7	0.4	2.3	0.8	0.4
MSA[1]	10.2	3.7	0.5	1.5	1.3	0.6	1.7	0.5	0.4
U.S.	13.9	4.3	3.3	1.4	1.4	1.2	1.2	0.8	0.2

Note: (1) Figures cover the Gainesville, FL Metropolitan Statistical Area; (2) Excludes Mexico.
Source: U.S. Census Bureau, 2019-2023 American Community Survey 5-Year Estimates

Household Size

Area	Persons in Household (%)							Average Household Size
	One	Two	Three	Four	Five	Six	Seven or More	
City	39.2	33.2	14.6	8.8	3.1	0.5	0.6	2.17
MSA[1]	32.9	35.5	15.3	10.3	3.9	1.2	0.9	2.36
U.S.	28.5	33.8	15.4	12.7	5.9	2.3	1.4	2.54

Note: (1) Figures cover the Gainesville, FL Metropolitan Statistical Area
Source: U.S. Census Bureau, 2019-2023 American Community Survey 5-Year Estimates

Household Relationships

Area	House-holder	Opposite-sex Spouse	Same-sex Spouse	Opposite-sex Unmarried Partner	Same-sex Unmarried Partner	Child[2]	Grand-child	Other Relatives	Non-relatives
City	41.0	9.4	0.3	3.0	0.3	17.0	1.5	3.4	12.5
MSA[1]	40.4	14.9	0.2	2.8	0.2	22.9	2.2	3.9	6.9
U.S.	38.3	17.5	0.2	2.5	0.2	28.3	2.4	4.8	3.4

Note: Figures are percent of the total population; (1) Figures cover the Gainesville, FL Metropolitan Statistical Area; (2) Includes biological, adopted, and stepchildren of the householder
Source: U.S. Census Bureau, 2020 Census

Gender

Area	Males	Females	Males per 100 Females
City	68,593	75,018	91.4
MSA[1]	166,988	177,533	94.1
U.S.	164,545,087	167,842,453	98.0

Note: (1) Figures cover the Gainesville, FL Metropolitan Statistical Area
Source: U.S. Census Bureau, 2019-2023 American Community Survey 5-Year Estimates

Marital Status

Area	Never Married	Now Married[2]	Separated	Widowed	Divorced
City	62.8	24.3	1.3	2.9	8.8
MSA[1]	43.5	39.6	1.3	5.1	10.4
U.S.	34.1	47.9	1.7	5.6	10.7

Note: Figures are percentages and cover the population 15 years of age and older; (1) Figures cover the Gainesville, FL Metropolitan Statistical Area; (2) Excludes separated
Source: U.S. Census Bureau, 2019-2023 American Community Survey 5-Year Estimates

Religious Groups by Family

Area	Catholic	Baptist	Methodist	LDS[2]	Pentecostal	Lutheran	Islam	Adventist	Other
MSA[1]	8.5	10.6	4.8	1.4	3.2	0.3	0.4	1.3	14.5
U.S.	18.7	7.3	3.0	2.0	1.8	1.7	1.3	1.3	11.6

Note: Figures are the number of adherents as a percentage of the total population and cover the eight largest religious groups in the U.S; (1) Figures cover the Gainesville, FL Metropolitan Statistical Area; (2) Church of Jesus Christ of Latter-day Saints
Sources: 2020 U.S. Religion Census, Association of Statisticians of American Religious Bodies; The Association of Religion Data Archives (ARDA)

Religious Groups by Tradition

Area	Catholic	Evangelical Protestant	Mainline Protestant	Black Protestant	Islam	Judaism	Hinduism	Orthodox	Buddhism
MSA[1]	8.5	25.3	5.4	2.0	0.4	0.3	0.3	<0.1	0.3
U.S.	18.7	16.5	5.2	2.3	1.3	0.6	0.4	0.4	0.3

Note: Figures are the number of adherents as a percentage of the total population; (1) Figures cover the Gainesville, FL Metropolitan Statistical Area
Sources: 2020 U.S. Religion Census, Association of Statisticians of American Religious Bodies; The Association of Religion Data Archives (ARDA)

ECONOMY

Real Gross Domestic Product (GDP)

Area	2017	2018	2019	2020	2021	2022	2023	Rank[3]
MSA[1]	14.5	15.0	15.4	15.4	16.4	17.0	17.7	159
U.S.[2]	17,619.1	18,160.7	18,642.5	18,238.9	19,387.6	19,896.6	20,436.3	—

Note: Figures are in billions of chained 2017 dollars; (1) Figures cover the Gainesville, FL Metropolitan Statistical Area; (2) Figures cover real GDP within metropolitan areas; (3) Rank is based on 2023 data and ranges from 1 to 384
Source: U.S. Bureau of Economic Analysis

Economic Growth

Area	2014	2015	2016	2017	2018	2019	2020	2021	2022	2023
MSA[1]	3.2	1.9	2.1	3.8	3.3	2.9	0.1	6.5	3.4	4.5
U.S.[2]	2.6	3.2	2.0	2.7	3.1	2.7	-2.2	6.3	2.6	2.7

Note: Figures are real gross domestic product growth rates and represent percent change from preceding period; (1) Figures cover the Gainesville, FL Metropolitan Statistical Area; (2) Figures are the average growth rates within metropolitan areas
Source: U.S. Bureau of Economic Analysis

Metropolitan Area Exports

Area	2018	2019	2020	2021	2022	2023	Rank[2]
MSA[1]	370.2	297.2	260.9	320.7	307.2	306.6	274
U.S.	1,664,056.1	1,645,173.7	1,431,406.6	1,753,941.4	2,062,937.4	2,019,160.5	—

Note: Figures are in millions of dollars; (1) Figures cover the Gainesville, FL Metropolitan Statistical Area; (2) Rank is based on 2023 data and ranges from 1 to 386
Source: U.S. Department of Commerce, International Trade Administration, Office of Trade and Economic Analysis, Industry and Analysis, Exports by Metropolitan Area, data extracted April 2, 2025

Building Permits

Area	Single-Family			Multi-Family			Total		
	2023	2024	Pct. Chg.	2023	2024	Pct. Chg.	2023	2024	Pct. Chg.
City	236	296	25.4	544	922	69.5	780	1,218	56.2
MSA[1]	1,247	1,115	-10.6	698	928	33.0	1,945	2,043	5.0
U.S.	920,000	981,900	6.7	591,100	496,100	-16.1	1,511,100	1,478,000	-2.2

Note: (1) Figures cover the Gainesville, FL Metropolitan Statistical Area; Figures represent new, privately-owned housing units authorized (unadjusted data)
Source: U.S. Census Bureau, Building Permits Survey (BPS), 2023, 2024

Bankruptcy Filings

Area	Business Filings			Nonbusiness Filings		
	2023	2024	% Chg.	2023	2024	% Chg.
Alachua County	11	30	172.7	153	177	15.7
U.S.	18,926	23,107	22.1	434,064	494,201	13.9

Note: Business filings include Chapter 7, Chapter 9, Chapter 11, Chapter 12, Chapter 13, Chapter 15, and Section 304; Nonbusiness filings include Chapter 7, Chapter 11, and Chapter 13
Source: Administrative Office of the U.S. Courts, Business and Nonbusiness Bankruptcy, County Cases Commenced by Chapter of the Bankruptcy Code, During the 12-Month Period Ending December 31, 2023 and Business and Nonbusiness Bankruptcy, County Cases Commenced by Chapter of the Bankruptcy Code, During the 12-Month Period Ending December 31, 2024

Housing Vacancy Rates

Area	Gross Vacancy Rate[3] (%)			Year-Round Vacancy Rate[4] (%)			Rental Vacancy Rate[5] (%)			Homeowner Vacancy Rate[6] (%)		
	2022	2023	2024	2022	2023	2024	2022	2023	2024	2022	2023	2024
MSA[1]	n/a	n/a	n/a	n/a	n/a	n/a	n/a	n/a	n/a	n/a	n/a	n/a
U.S.[2]	9.1	9.0	9.1	7.5	7.5	7.6	5.7	6.5	6.8	0.8	0.8	1.0

Note: (1) Figures cover the Gainesville, FL Metropolitan Statistical Area; (2) Figures cover the 75 largest Metropolitan Statistical Areas; (3) The percentage of the total housing inventory that is vacant; (4) The percentage of the housing inventory (excluding seasonal units) that is year-round vacant; (5) The percentage of rental inventory that is vacant for rent; (6) The percentage of homeowner inventory that is vacant for sale; n/a not available
Source: U.S. Census Bureau, Housing Vacancies and Homeownership Annual Statistics: 2022, 2023, 2024

INCOME

Income

Area	Per Capita ($)	Median Household ($)	Average Household ($)
City	30,282	45,611	71,640
MSA[1]	36,810	58,946	89,302
U.S.	43,289	78,538	110,491

Note: (1) Figures cover the Gainesville, FL Metropolitan Statistical Area
Source: U.S. Census Bureau, 2019-2023 American Community Survey 5-Year Estimates

Household Income Distribution

Area	Percent of Households Earning							
	Under $15,000	$15,000 -$24,999	$25,000 -$34,999	$35,000 -$49,999	$50,000 -$74,999	$75,000 -$99,999	$100,000 -$149,999	$150,000 and up
City	18.0	10.4	11.2	14.8	14.8	10.2	10.4	10.2
MSA[1]	13.2	8.5	9.1	12.6	16.2	11.1	14.0	15.2
U.S.	8.5	6.6	6.8	10.4	15.7	12.7	17.4	21.9

Note: (1) Figures cover the Gainesville, FL Metropolitan Statistical Area
Source: U.S. Census Bureau, 2019-2023 American Community Survey 5-Year Estimates

Poverty Rate

Area	All Ages	Under 18 Years Old	18 to 64 Years Old	65 Years and Over
City	28.0	18.0	32.8	11.4
MSA[1]	18.9	16.3	21.8	10.7
U.S.	12.4	16.3	11.6	10.4

Note: Figures are percentage of people whose income during the past 12 months was below the poverty level; (1) Figures cover the Gainesville, FL Metropolitan Statistical Area
Source: U.S. Census Bureau, 2019-2023 American Community Survey 5-Year Estimates

EMPLOYMENT

Labor Force and Employment

Area	Civilian Labor Force			Workers Employed		
	Dec. 2023	Dec. 2024	% Chg.	Dec. 2023	Dec. 2024	% Chg.
City	71,265	72,407	1.6	68,797	69,722	1.3
MSA[1]	168,667	171,235	1.5	163,355	165,582	1.4
U.S.	166,661,000	167,746,000	0.7	160,754,000	161,294,000	0.3

Note: Data is not seasonally adjusted and covers workers 16 years of age and older; (1) Figures cover the Gainesville, FL Metropolitan Statistical Area
Source: Bureau of Labor Statistics, Local Area Unemployment Statistics

Unemployment Rate

Area	2024											
	Jan.	Feb.	Mar.	Apr.	May	Jun.	Jul.	Aug.	Sep.	Oct.	Nov.	Dec.
City	3.8	3.6	4.0	3.4	3.8	4.6	4.4	4.6	3.9	4.2	4.4	3.7
MSA[1]	3.5	3.3	3.5	3.1	3.4	4.0	4.0	4.0	3.5	3.7	3.8	3.3
U.S.	4.1	4.2	3.9	3.5	3.7	4.3	4.5	4.4	3.9	3.9	4.0	3.8

Note: Data is not seasonally adjusted and covers workers 16 years of age and older; (1) Figures cover the Gainesville, FL Metropolitan Statistical Area
Source: Bureau of Labor Statistics, Local Area Unemployment Statistics

Average Wages

Occupation	$/Hr.	Occupation	$/Hr.
Accountants and Auditors	38.54	Maintenance and Repair Workers	23.13
Automotive Mechanics	24.87	Marketing Managers	64.71
Bookkeepers	23.70	Network and Computer Systems Admin.	41.00
Carpenters	23.37	Nurses, Licensed Practical	27.62
Cashiers	14.25	Nurses, Registered	42.66
Computer Programmers	44.12	Nursing Assistants	18.80
Computer Systems Analysts	41.84	Office Clerks, General	21.26
Computer User Support Specialists	25.88	Physical Therapists	46.21
Construction Laborers	19.68	Physicians	130.80
Cooks, Restaurant	16.92	Plumbers, Pipefitters and Steamfitters	24.73
Customer Service Representatives	19.63	Police and Sheriff's Patrol Officers	29.02
Dentists	98.53	Postal Service Mail Carriers	28.67
Electricians	25.55	Real Estate Sales Agents	29.50
Engineers, Electrical	51.00	Retail Salespersons	16.05
Fast Food and Counter Workers	14.25	Sales Representatives, Technical/Scientific	48.82
Financial Managers	67.20	Secretaries, Exc. Legal/Medical/Executive	21.09
First-Line Supervisors of Office Workers	30.71	Security Guards	17.73
General and Operations Managers	55.75	Surgeons	n/a
Hairdressers/Cosmetologists	15.92	Teacher Assistants, Exc. Postsecondary[1]	15.81
Home Health and Personal Care Aides	15.70	Teachers, Secondary School, Exc. Sp. Ed.[1]	33.04
Janitors and Cleaners	16.07	Telemarketers	n/a
Landscaping/Groundskeeping Workers	17.73	Truck Drivers, Heavy/Tractor-Trailer	24.90
Lawyers	53.79	Truck Drivers, Light/Delivery Services	21.27
Maids and Housekeeping Cleaners	15.37	Waiters and Waitresses	18.15

Note: Wage data covers the Gainesville, FL Metropolitan Statistical Area; (1) Hourly wages were calculated from annual wage data based on a 40 hour work week
Source: Bureau of Labor Statistics, Metro Area Occupational Employment & Wage Estimates, May 2024

Employment by Industry

Sector	MSA[1] Number of Employees	MSA[1] Percent of Total	U.S. Percent of Total
Construction, Mining, and Logging	7,300	4.3	5.5
Financial Activities	6,700	4.0	5.8
Government	48,500	28.7	14.9
Information	2,000	1.2	1.9
Leisure and Hospitality	17,700	10.5	10.4
Manufacturing	5,200	3.1	8.0
Other Services	5,000	3.0	3.7
Private Education and Health Services	33,200	19.7	16.9
Professional and Business Services	18,000	10.7	14.2
Retail Trade	16,900	10.0	10.0
Transportation, Warehousing, and Utilities	4,800	2.8	4.8
Wholesale Trade	3,500	2.1	3.9

Note: Figures are non-farm employment as of December 2024. Figures are not seasonally adjusted and include workers 16 years of age and older; (1) Figures cover the Gainesville, FL Metropolitan Statistical Area
Source: Bureau of Labor Statistics, Current Employment Statistics, Employment, Hours, and Earnings

Employment by Occupation

Occupation Classification	City (%)	MSA[1] (%)	U.S. (%)
Management, Business, Science, and Arts	48.1	46.3	42.0
Natural Resources, Construction, and Maintenance	4.0	7.0	8.6
Production, Transportation, and Material Moving	7.0	8.4	13.0
Sales and Office	23.4	21.2	19.9
Service	17.5	17.1	16.5

Note: Figures cover employed civilians 16 years of age and older; (1) Figures cover the Gainesville, FL Metropolitan Statistical Area
Source: U.S. Census Bureau, 2019-2023 American Community Survey 5-Year Estimates

Occupations with Greatest Projected Employment Growth: 2022 – 2032

Occupation[1]	2022 Employment	2032 Projected Employment	Numeric Employment Change	Percent Employment Change
Stockers and Order Fillers	236,990	274,060	37,070	15.6
Retail Salespersons	308,940	340,000	31,060	10.1
Waiters and Waitresses	195,320	223,820	28,500	14.6
Software Developers	75,620	101,940	26,320	34.8
General and Operations Managers	184,790	210,510	25,720	13.9
Registered Nurses	202,780	228,070	25,290	12.5
Fast Food and Counter Workers	185,000	209,460	24,460	13.2
Cooks, Restaurant	120,850	141,640	20,790	17.2
Landscaping and Groundskeeping Workers	112,240	129,030	16,790	15.0
Janitors and Cleaners, Except Maids and Housekeeping Cleaners	136,890	153,490	16,600	12.1

Note: Projections cover Florida; (1) Sorted by numeric employment change
Source: www.projectionscentral.org, State Occupational Projections, 2022–2032 Long-Term Projections

Fastest-Growing Occupations: 2022 – 2032

Occupation[1]	2022 Employment	2032 Projected Employment	Numeric Employment Change	Percent Employment Change
Nurse Practitioners	18,910	29,980	11,070	58.5
Data Scientists	8,470	12,450	3,980	47.0
Information Security Analysts (SOC 2018)	11,060	15,650	4,590	41.5
Statisticians	590	820	230	39.0
Solar Photovoltaic Installers	1,210	1,680	470	38.8
Computer and Information Research Scientists (SOC 2018)	3,160	4,380	1,220	38.6
Physician Assistants	8,830	12,180	3,350	37.9
Actuaries	1,640	2,260	620	37.8
Physical Therapist Assistants	7,430	10,230	2,800	37.7
Medical and Health Services Managers	34,490	47,200	12,710	36.9

Note: Projections cover Florida; (1) Sorted by percent employment change and excludes occupations with numeric employment change less than 50
Source: www.projectionscentral.org, State Occupational Projections, 2022–2032 Long-Term Projections

CITY FINANCES

City Government Finances

Component	2022 ($000)	2022 ($ per capita)
Total Revenues	621,664	4,605
Total Expenditures	719,678	5,331
Debt Outstanding	2,187,750	16,205

Source: U.S. Census Bureau, State & Local Government Finances 2022

City Government Revenue by Source

Source	2022 ($000)	2022 ($ per capita)	2022 (%)
General Revenue			
From Federal Government	22,896	170	3.7
From State Government	22,674	168	3.6
From Local Governments	5,734	42	0.9
Taxes			
Property	38,926	288	6.3
Sales and Gross Receipts	32,295	239	5.2
Personal Income	0	0	0.0
Corporate Income	0	0	0.0
Motor Vehicle License	0	0	0.0
Other Taxes	15,863	118	2.6
Current Charges	96,350	714	15.5
Liquor Store	0	0	0.0
Utility	371,973	2,755	59.8

Source: U.S. Census Bureau, State & Local Government Finances 2022

City Government Expenditures by Function

Function	2022 ($000)	2022 ($ per capita)	2022 (%)
General Direct Expenditures			
Air Transportation	468	3	0.1
Corrections	0	0	0.0
Education	0	0	0.0
Employment Security Administration	0	0	0.0
Financial Administration	6,716	49	0.9
Fire Protection	20,427	151	2.8
General Public Buildings	0	0	0.0
Governmental Administration, Other	7,131	52	1.0
Health	3,225	23	0.4
Highways	17,240	127	2.4
Hospitals	0	0	0.0
Housing and Community Development	24,480	181	3.4
Interest on General Debt	12,150	90	1.7
Judicial and Legal	1,438	10	0.2
Libraries	0	0	0.0
Parking	540	4	0.1
Parks and Recreation	14,730	109	2.0
Police Protection	39,267	290	5.5
Public Welfare	2,187	16	0.3
Sewerage	33,269	246	4.6
Solid Waste Management	7,689	57	1.1
Veterans' Services	0	0	0.0
Liquor Store	0	0	0.0
Utility	449,413	3,328	62.4

Source: U.S. Census Bureau, State & Local Government Finances 2022

TAXES

State Corporate Income Tax Rates

State	Tax Rate (%)	Income Brackets ($)	Num. of Brackets	Financial Institution Tax Rate (%)[a]	Federal Income Tax Ded.
Florida	5.5	Flat rate	1	5.5	No

Note: Tax rates for tax year 2024; (a) Rates listed are the corporate income tax rate applied to financial institutions or excise taxes based on income. Some states have other taxes based upon the value of deposits or shares.
Source: Federation of Tax Administrators, State Corporate Income Tax Rates, January 1, 2025

State Individual Income Tax Rates

State	Tax Rate (%)	Income Brackets ($)	Personal Exemptions ($)			Standard Ded. ($)	
			Single	Married	Depend.	Single	Married
Florida			– No state income tax –				

Note: Tax rates for tax year 2024; Local- and county-level taxes are not included
Source: Federation of Tax Administrators, State Individual Income Tax Rates, January 1, 2025

Various State Sales and Excise Tax Rates

State	State Sales Tax (%)	Gasoline[1] ($/gal.)	Cigarette[2] ($/pack)	Spirits[3] ($/gal.)	Wine[4] ($/gal.)	Beer[5] ($/gal.)	Recreational Marijuana (%)
Florida	6	0.39	1.34	6.50	2.25	0.48	Not legal

Note: All tax rates as of January 1, 2025; (1) The American Petroleum Institute has developed a methodology for determining the average tax rate on a gallon of fuel. Rates may include any of the following: excise taxes, environmental fees, storage tank fees, other fees or taxes, general sales tax, and local taxes; (2) The federal excise tax of $1.0066 per pack and local taxes are not included; (3) Rates are those applicable to off-premise sales of 40% alcohol by volume (a.b.v.) distilled spirits in 750ml containers. Local excise taxes are excluded; (4) Rates are those applicable to off-premise sales of 11% a.b.v. non-carbonated wine in 750ml containers; (5) Rates are those applicable to off-premise sales of 4.7% a.b.v. beer in 12 ounce containers.
Source: Tax Foundation, 2025 Facts & Figures: How Does Your State Compare?

State Tax Competitiveness Index

State	Overall Rank	Corporate Tax Rank	Individual Income Tax Rank	Sales Tax Rank	Property Tax Rank	Unemployment Insurance Tax Rank
Florida	4	16	1	14	21	10

Note: The Tax Foundation's State Tax Competitiveness Index enables policymakers, taxpayers, and business leaders to gauge how their states' tax systems compare. A rank of 1 is best, 50 is worst. Rankings do not average to the total. States without a tax rank equally as 1. DC's scores and rankings do not affect other states. The report shows tax systems as of July 1, 2024 (the beginning of Fiscal Year 2025).
Source: Tax Foundation, State Tax Competitiveness Index 2025

TRANSPORTATION

Means of Transportation to Work

Area	Car/Truck/Van		Public Transportation			Bicycle	Walked	Other Means	Worked at Home
	Drove Alone	Car-pooled	Bus	Subway	Railroad				
City	62.9	9.0	4.9	0.0	0.0	3.5	5.0	2.3	12.4
MSA[1]	71.5	8.8	2.4	0.0	0.0	1.6	2.9	1.5	11.2
U.S.	70.2	8.5	1.7	1.3	0.4	0.4	2.4	1.6	13.5

Note: Figures are percentages and cover workers 16 years of age and older; (1) Figures cover the Gainesville, FL Metropolitan Statistical Area
Source: U.S. Census Bureau, 2019-2023 American Community Survey 5-Year Estimates

Travel Time to Work

Area	Less Than 10 Minutes	10 to 19 Minutes	20 to 29 Minutes	30 to 44 Minutes	45 to 59 Minutes	60 to 89 Minutes	90 Minutes or More
City	16.1	43.8	23.4	11.6	2.6	1.6	0.9
MSA[1]	12.2	32.8	25.2	19.2	5.7	3.2	1.7
U.S.	12.6	28.6	21.2	20.8	8.1	6.0	2.8

Note: Note: Figures are percentages and include workers 16 years old and over; (1) Figures cover the Gainesville, FL Metropolitan Statistical Area
Source: U.S. Census Bureau, 2019-2023 American Community Survey 5-Year Estimates

Key Congestion Measures

Measure	2000	2010	2015	2020	2022
Annual Hours of Delay, Total (000)	n/a	n/a	5,558	2,263	5,231
Annual Hours of Delay, Per Auto Commuter	n/a	n/a	27	11	25
Annual Congestion Cost, Per Auto Commuter ($)	n/a	n/a	636	268	585

Note: n/a not available
Source: Texas A&M Transportation Institute, 2023 Urban Mobility Report

Freeway Travel Time Index

Measure	1985	1990	1995	2000	2005	2010	2015	2020	2022
Urban Area Index[1]	n/a	n/a	n/a	n/a	n/a	n/a	1.17	1.08	1.16
Urban Area Rank[1,2]	n/a	n/a	n/a	n/a	n/a	n/a	n/a	n/a	n/a

Note: Freeway Travel Time Index—the ratio of travel time in the peak period to the travel time at free-flow conditions. For example, a value of 1.30 indicates a 20-minute free-flow trip takes 26 minutes in the peak (20 minutes x 1.30 = 26 minutes); (1) Covers the Gainesville FL urban area; (2) Rank is based on 101 larger urban areas (#1 = highest travel time index); n/a not available
Source: Texas A&M Transportation Institute, 2023 Urban Mobility Report

Public Transportation

Agency Name / Mode of Transportation	Vehicles Operated in Maximum Service[1]	Annual Unlinked Passenger Trips[2] (in thous.)	Annual Passenger Miles[3] (in thous.)
Gainesville Regional Transit System (RTS)			
Bus (directly operated)	90	5,106.6	16,586.3
Demand Response (purchased transportation)	35	44.3	405.3
Vanpool (purchased transportation)	9	19.6	917.3

Note: (1) Number of revenue vehicles operated by the given mode and type of service to meet the annual maximum service requirement. This is the revenue vehicle count during the peak season of the year; on the week and day that maximum service is provided. Vehicles operated in maximum service (VOMS) exclude atypical days and one-time special events; (2) Number of passengers who boarded public transportation vehicles. Passengers are counted each time they board a vehicle no matter how many vehicles they use to travel from their origin to their destination. (3) Sum of the distances ridden by all passengers during the entire fiscal year.
Source: Federal Transit Administration, National Transit Database, 2023

Air Transportation

Airport Name and Code / Type of Service	Passenger Airlines[1]	Passenger Enplanements	Freight Carriers[2]	Freight (lbs)
Gainesville Regional Airport (GNV)				
Domestic service (U.S. carriers only)	17	290,395	5	54,489
International service (U.S. carriers only)	0	0	0	0

Note: (1) Includes all U.S.-based major, minor and commuter airlines that carried at least one passenger during the year; (2) Includes all U.S.-based airlines and freight carriers that transported at least one pound of freight during the year.
Source: Bureau of Transportation Statistics, The Intermodal Transportation Database, Air Carriers: T-100 Domestic Market (U.S. carriers only), 2024; Bureau of Transportation Statistics, The Intermodal Transportation Database, Air Carriers: T-100 International Market (U.S. carriers only), 2024

BUSINESSES

Major Business Headquarters

Company Name	Industry	Rankings	
		Fortune[1]	Forbes[2]
No companies listed	-	-	-

Note: (1) Companies that produce a 10-K are ranked 1 to 500 based on 2023 revenue; (2) All private companies with at least $2 billion in annual revenue through the end of their most current fiscal year are ranked 1 to 275; companies listed are headquartered in the city; dashes indicate no ranking
Source: Fortune, "Fortune 500," 2024; Forbes, "America's Largest Private Companies," 2024

Living Environment

COST OF LIVING

Cost of Living Index

Composite Index	Groceries	Housing	Utilities	Transportation	Health Care	Misc. Goods/Services
n/a	n/a	n/a	n/a	n/a	n/a	n/a

Note: The Cost of Living Index measures regional differences in the cost of consumer goods and services, excluding taxes and non-consumer expenditures, for professional and managerial households in the top income quintile. It is based on more than 50,000 prices covering almost 60 different items for which prices are collected three times a year by chambers of commerce, economic development organizations or university applied economic centers in each participating urban area. The numbers shown should be read as a percentage above or below the national average of 100. For example, a value of 115.4 in the groceries column indicates that grocery prices are 15.4% higher than the national average. Small differences in the index numbers should not be interpreted as significant; n/a not available.
Source: The Council for Community and Economic Research, Cost of Living Index, 2024

Grocery Prices

Area[1]	T-Bone Steak ($/pound)	Frying Chicken ($/pound)	Whole Milk ($/half gal.)	Eggs ($/dozen)	Orange Juice ($/64 oz.)	Coffee ($/11.5 oz.)
City[2]	n/a	n/a	n/a	n/a	n/a	n/a
Avg.	15.42	1.55	4.69	3.25	4.41	5.46
Min.	14.50	1.16	4.43	2.75	4.00	4.85
Max.	17.56	2.89	5.49	4.78	5.54	7.89

Note: (1) Values for the local area are compared with the average, minimum and maximum values for all 276 areas in the Cost of Living Index; (2) Figures cover the Gainesville FL urban area; n/a not available; **T-Bone Steak** (price per pound); **Frying Chicken** (price per pound, whole fryer); **Whole Milk** (half gallon carton); **Eggs** (price per dozen, Grade A, large); **Orange Juice** (64 oz. Tropicana or Florida Natural); **Coffee** (11.5 oz. can, vacuum-packed, Maxwell House, Hills Bros, or Folgers).
Source: The Council for Community and Economic Research, Cost of Living Index, 2024

Housing and Utility Costs

Area[1]	New Home Price ($)	Apartment Rent ($/month)	All Electric ($/month)	Part Electric ($/month)	Other Energy ($/month)	Telephone ($/month)
City[2]	n/a	n/a	n/a	n/a	n/a	n/a
Avg.	515,975	1,550	210.99	123.07	82.07	194.99
Min.	265,375	692	104.33	53.68	36.26	179.42
Max.	2,775,821	5,719	529.02	397.28	361.63	223.33

Note: (1) Values for the local area are compared with the average, minimum and maximum values for all 276 areas in the Cost of Living Index; (2) Figures cover the Gainesville FL urban area; n/a not available; **New Home Price** (2,400 sf living area, 8,000 sf lot, in urban area with full utilities); **Apartment Rent** (950 sf 2 bedroom/1.5 or 2 bath, unfurnished, excluding all utilities except water); **All Electric** (average monthly cost for an all-electric home); **Part Electric** (average monthly cost for a part-electric home); **Other Energy** (average monthly cost for natural gas, fuel oil, coal, wood, and any other forms of energy except electricity); **Telephone** (price includes the base monthly rate plus taxes and fees for three lines of mobile phone service).
Source: The Council for Community and Economic Research, Cost of Living Index, 2024

Health Care, Transportation, and Other Costs

Area[1]	Doctor ($/visit)	Dentist ($/visit)	Optometrist ($/visit)	Gasoline ($/gallon)	Beauty Salon ($/visit)	Men's Shirt ($)
City[2]	n/a	n/a	n/a	n/a	n/a	n/a
Avg.	143.77	117.51	129.23	3.32	48.57	38.14
Min.	36.74	58.67	67.33	2.80	24.00	13.41
Max.	270.44	216.82	307.33	5.28	94.00	63.89

Note: (1) Values for the local area are compared with the average, minimum and maximum values for all 276 areas in the Cost of Living Index; (2) Figures cover the Gainesville FL urban area; n/a not available; **Doctor** (general practitioners routine exam of an established patient); **Dentist** (adult teeth cleaning and periodic oral examination); **Optometrist** (full vision eye exam for established adult patient); **Gasoline** (one gallon regular unleaded, national brand, including all taxes, cash price at self-service pump if available); **Beauty Salon** (woman's shampoo, trim, and blow-dry); **Men's Shirt** (cotton/polyester dress shirt, pinpoint weave, long sleeves).
Source: The Council for Community and Economic Research, Cost of Living Index, 2024

HOUSING

Homeownership Rate

Area	2017 (%)	2018 (%)	2019 (%)	2020 (%)	2021 (%)	2022 (%)	2023 (%)	2024 (%)
MSA[1]	n/a	n/a	n/a	n/a	n/a	n/a	n/a	n/a
U.S.	63.9	64.4	64.6	66.6	65.5	65.8	65.9	65.6

Note: (1) Figures cover the Gainesville, FL Metropolitan Statistical Area; n/a not available
Source: U.S. Census Bureau, Housing Vacancies and Homeownership Annual Statistics: 2017-2024

House Price Index (HPI)

Area	National Ranking[2]	Quarterly Change (%)	One-Year Change (%)	Five-Year Change (%)	Since 1991Q1 (%)
MSA[1]	(a)	-0.72	5.55	65.26	357.21
U.S.[3]	—	1.43	4.51	57.13	327.82

Note: The HPI is a weighted repeat sales index. It measures average price changes in repeat sales or refinancings on the same properties. This information is obtained by reviewing repeat mortgage transactions on single-family properties whose mortgages have been purchased or securitized by Fannie Mae or Freddie Mac since January 1975; (1) Figures cover the Gainesville, FL Metropolitan Statistical Area; (2) Rankings are based on annual percentage change for all metro areas containing at least 15,000 transactions over the last 10 years and ranges from 1 to 241; (3) figures based on a weighted average of Census Division estimates using a seasonally adjusted, purchase-only index; all figures are for the period ending December 31, 2024; n/a not available; (a) Not ranked because of increased index variability due to smaller sample size
Source: Federal Housing Finance Agency, Change in FHFA Metropolitan Area House Price Indexes, All Transactions Index, 2024Q4

Home Value

Area	Under $100,000	$100,000 -$199,999	$200,000 -$299,999	$300,000 -$399,999	$400,000 -$499,999	$500,000 -$999,999	$1,000,000 or more	Median ($)
City	7.9	27.4	35.1	16.9	5.7	6.3	0.7	235,000
MSA[1]	13.9	23.8	25.3	16.2	9.0	10.1	1.6	245,800
U.S.	12.1	17.8	19.5	14.4	10.5	19.1	6.5	303,400

Note: Figures are percentages except for median and cover owner-occupied housing units; (1) Figures cover the Gainesville, FL Metropolitan Statistical Area
Source: U.S. Census Bureau, 2019-2023 American Community Survey 5-Year Estimates

Year Housing Structure Built

Area	2020 or Later	2010 -2019	2000 -2009	1990 -1999	1980 -1989	1970 -1979	1960 -1969	1950 -1959	1940 -1949	Before 1940	Median Year
City	1.3	6.5	14.0	14.2	19.5	20.2	11.8	7.0	2.7	2.9	1983
MSA[1]	1.8	9.8	17.7	17.7	18.9	16.6	8.4	4.7	1.9	2.5	1988
U.S.	1.2	8.9	13.6	12.8	13.0	14.4	10.0	9.7	4.5	11.9	1980

Note: Figures are percentages except for Median Year; Note: (1) Figures cover the Gainesville, FL Metropolitan Statistical Area
Source: U.S. Census Bureau, 2019-2023 American Community Survey 5-Year Estimates

Gross Monthly Rent

Area	Under $500	$500 -$999	$1,000 -$1,499	$1,500 -$1,999	$2,000 -$2,499	$2,500 -$2,999	$3,000 and up	Median ($)
City	3.6	27.6	37.8	20.0	7.3	2.2	1.6	1,214
MSA[1]	3.9	27.5	36.4	20.0	7.2	2.6	2.3	1,219
U.S.	6.5	22.3	29.5	20.2	10.8	4.8	5.9	1,348

Note: Figures are percentages except for median; Gross rent is the contract rent plus the estimated average monthly cost of utilities (electricity, gas, and water and sewer) and fuels (oil, coal, kerosene, wood, etc.) if these are paid by the renter (or paid for the renter by someone else); (1) Figures cover the Gainesville, FL Metropolitan Statistical Area
Source: U.S. Census Bureau, 2019-2023 American Community Survey 5-Year Estimates

HEALTH

Health Risk Factors

Category	MSA[1] (%)	U.S. (%)
Adults aged 18–64 who have any kind of health care coverage	90.8	90.8
Adults who reported being in good or better health	81.9	81.8
Adults who have been told they have high blood cholesterol	35.4	36.9
Adults who have been told they have high blood pressure	30.6	34.0
Adults who are current smokers	5.6	12.1
Adults who currently use e-cigarettes	n/a	7.7
Adults who currently use chewing tobacco, snuff, or snus	2.2	3.2
Adults who are heavy drinkers[2]	6.9	6.1
Adults who are binge drinkers[3]	19.0	15.2
Adults who are overweight (BMI 25.0 - 29.9)	25.5	34.4
Adults who are obese (BMI 30.0 - 99.8)	35.0	34.3
Adults who participated in any physical activities in the past month	77.8	75.8

Note: All figures are crude prevalence; (1) Figures cover the Gainesville, FL Metropolitan Statistical Area; (2) Heavy drinkers are classified as adult men having more than 14 drinks per week and adult women having more than 7 drinks per week; (3) Binge drinkers are classified as males having five or more drinks on one occasion or females having four or more drinks on one occasion
Source: Centers for Disease Control and Prevention, Behavioral Risk Factor Surveillance System, SMART: Selected Metropolitan Area Risk Trends, 2023

Acute and Chronic Health Conditions

Category	MSA[1] (%)	U.S. (%)
Adults who have ever been told they had a heart attack	n/a	4.2
Adults who have ever been told they have angina or coronary heart disease	n/a	4.0
Adults who have ever been told they had a stroke	n/a	3.3
Adults who have ever been told they have asthma	22.7	15.7
Adults who have ever been told they have arthritis	24.9	26.3
Adults who have ever been told they have diabetes[2]	13.3	11.5
Adults who have ever been told they had skin cancer	8.8	5.6
Adults who have ever been told they had any other types of cancer	9.2	8.4
Adults who have ever been told they have COPD	6.6	6.4
Adults who have ever been told they have kidney disease	n/a	3.7
Adults who have ever been told they have a form of depression	18.4	22.0

Note: All figures are crude prevalence; (1) Figures cover the Gainesville, FL Metropolitan Statistical Area; (2) Figures do not include pregnancy-related, borderline, or pre-diabetes
Source: Centers for Disease Control and Prevention, Behaviorial Risk Factor Surveillance System, SMART: Selected Metropolitan Area Risk Trends, 2023

Health Screening and Vaccination Rates

Category	MSA[1] (%)	U.S. (%)
Adults who have ever been tested for HIV	46.4	37.5
Adults who have had their blood cholesterol checked within the last five years	84.7	87.0
Adults aged 65+ who have had flu shot within the past year	69.5	63.4
Adults aged 65+ who have ever had a pneumonia vaccination	77.4	71.9

Note: All figures are crude prevalence; (1) Figures cover the Gainesville, FL Metropolitan Statistical Area.
Source: Centers for Disease Control and Prevention, Behaviorial Risk Factor Surveillance System, SMART: Selected Metropolitan Area Risk Trends, 2023

Disability Status

Category	MSA[1] (%)	U.S. (%)
Adults who reported being deaf	7.1	7.4
Are you blind or have serious difficulty seeing, even when wearing glasses?	n/a	4.9
Do you have difficulty doing errands alone?	6.7	7.8
Do you have difficulty dressing or bathing?	n/a	3.6
Do you have serious difficulty concentrating/remembering/making decisions?	14.6	13.7
Do you have serious difficulty walking or climbing stairs?	13.0	13.2

Note: All figures are crude prevalence; (1) Figures cover the Gainesville, FL Metropolitan Statistical Area.
Source: Centers for Disease Control and Prevention, Behaviorial Risk Factor Surveillance System, SMART: Selected Metropolitan Area Risk Trends, 2023

Mortality Rates for the Top 10 Causes of Death in the U.S.

ICD-10[a] Sub-Chapter	ICD-10[a] Code	Crude Mortality Rate[2] per 100,000 population	
		County[3]	U.S.
Malignant neoplasms	C00-C97	163.3	182.7
Ischaemic heart diseases	I20-I25	74.7	109.6
Provisional assignment of new diseases of uncertain etiology[1]	U00-U49	51.2	65.3
Other forms of heart disease	I30-I51	46.9	65.1
Other degenerative diseases of the nervous system	G30-G31	32.7	52.4
Other external causes of accidental injury	W00-X59	42.4	52.3
Cerebrovascular diseases	I60-I69	55.0	49.1
Chronic lower respiratory diseases	J40-J47	33.2	43.5
Hypertensive diseases	I10-I15	21.7	38.9
Organic, including symptomatic, mental disorders	F01-F09	41.3	33.9

Note: (a) ICD-10 = International Classification of Diseases 10th Revision; (1) Includes COVID-19, adverse effects to COVID-19 vaccines, SARS, and vaping-related disorders; (2) Crude mortality rates are a three-year average covering 2021-2023; (3) Figures cover Alachua County.
Source: Centers for Disease Control and Prevention, National Center for Health Statistics. National Vital Statistics System, Mortality 2018-2023 on CDC WONDER Online Database

Mortality Rates for Selected Causes of Death

Cause of Death	ICD-10[a] Code	Crude Mortality Rate[1] per 100,000 population	
		County[2]	U.S.
Accidental poisoning and exposure to noxious substances	X40-X49	17.3	30.5
Alzheimer disease	G30	20.3	35.4
Assault	X85-Y09	6.6	7.3
COVID-19	U07.1	51.2	65.3
Diabetes mellitus	E10-E14	22.1	30.0
Diseases of the liver	K70-K76	17.8	20.8
Human immunodeficiency virus (HIV) disease	B20-B24	3.1	1.5
Influenza and pneumonia	J09-J18	8.8	13.4
Intentional self-harm	X60-X84	14.2	14.7
Malnutrition	E40-E46	2.5	6.0
Obesity and other hyperalimentation	E65-E68	Unreliable	3.1
Renal failure	N17-N19	11.4	16.4
Transport accidents	V01-V99	16.2	14.4

Note: (a) ICD-10 = International Classification of Diseases 10th Revision; (1) Crude mortality rates are a three-year average covering 2021-2023; (2) Figures cover Alachua County; Data are suppressed when the data meet the criteria for confidentiality constraints; Crude mortality rates are flagged as unreliable when the rate would be calculated with a numerator of 20 or less.
Source: Centers for Disease Control and Prevention, National Center for Health Statistics. National Vital Statistics System, Mortality 2018-2023 on CDC WONDER Online Database

Health Insurance Coverage

Area	With Health Insurance	With Private Health Insurance	With Public Health Insurance	Without Health Insurance	Population Under Age 19 Without Health Insurance
City	91.8	76.6	23.8	8.2	5.0
MSA[1]	90.9	71.2	30.8	9.1	5.2
U.S.	91.4	67.3	36.3	8.6	5.4

Note: Figures are percentages that cover the civilian noninstitutionalized population; (1) Figures cover the Gainesville, FL Metropolitan Statistical Area
Source: U.S. Census Bureau, 2019-2023 American Community Survey 5-Year Estimates

Number of Medical Professionals

Area	MDs[3]	DOs[3,4]	Dentists	Podiatrists	Chiropractors	Optometrists
County[1] (number)	3,009	194	553	16	77	55
County[1] (rate[2])	1,059.4	68.3	193.4	5.6	26.9	19.2
U.S. (rate[2])	302.5	29.2	74.6	6.4	29.5	18.0

Note: Data as of 2023 unless noted; (1) Data covers Alachua County; (2) Number of medical professionals per 100,000 population; (3) Data as of 2022 and includes all active, non-federal physicians; (4) Doctor of Osteopathic Medicine
Source: U.S. Department of Health and Human Services, Health Resources and Services Administration, Bureau of Health Professions, Area Resource File (ARF) 2023-2024

Best Hospitals

According to *U.S. News,* the Gainesville, FL metro area is home to one of the best hospitals in the U.S.: **UF Health Shands Hospital** (7 adult specialties and 5 pediatric specialties). The hospital listed was nationally ranked in at least one of 15 adult or 11 pediatric specialties. The number of specialties shown cover the parent hospital. Only 160 U.S. hospitals performed well enough to be nationally ranked in one or more specialties. Twenty hospitals in the U.S. made the Honor Roll. The Best Hospitals Honor Roll takes both the national rankings and the procedure and condition ratings into account. Hospitals received points if they were nationally ranked in one of the 15 adult specialties—the higher they ranked, the more points they got—and how many ratings of "high performing" they earned in the 20 procedures and conditions. *U.S. News Online, "America's Best Hospitals 2024-25"*

According to *U.S. News,* the Gainesville, FL metro area is home to one of the best children's hospitals in the U.S.: **UF Health Shands Children's Hospital** (5 pediatric specialties). The hospital listed was highly ranked in at least one of 11 pediatric specialties. One hundred five children's hospitals in the U.S. were nationally ranked in at least one specialty. Hospitals received points for being ranked in a specialty, and the 10 hospitals with the most points across the 11 specialties make up the Honor Roll. *U.S. News Online, "America's Best Children's Hospitals 2024-25"*

EDUCATION

Public School District Statistics

District Name	Schls	Pupils	Pupil/Teacher Ratio	Minority Pupils[1] (%)	Total Rev. per Pupil ($)	Total Exp. per Pupil ($)
Alachua	68	28,749	17.3	61.2	12,719	12,950

Note: Table includes school districts with 2,000 or more students; (1) Percentage of students that are not non-Hispanic white.
Source: U.S. Department of Education, National Center for Education Statistics, Common Core of Data, Local Education Agency (School District) Universe Survey: School Year 2023-2024; U.S. Department of Education, National Center for Education Statistics, Common Core of Data, School District Finance Survey (F-33): School Year 2021–22

Highest Level of Education

Area	Less than H.S.	H.S. Diploma	Some College, No Deg.	Associate Degree	Bachelor's Degree	Master's Degree	Prof. School Degree	Doctorate Degree
City	5.7	17.7	14.9	10.0	25.7	15.1	4.2	6.8
MSA[1]	7.3	24.2	16.4	11.1	20.3	11.8	4.0	4.8
U.S.	10.6	26.2	19.4	8.8	21.3	9.8	2.3	1.6

Note: Figures cover persons age 25 and over; (1) Figures cover the Gainesville, FL Metropolitan Statistical Area
Source: U.S. Census Bureau, 2019-2023 American Community Survey 5-Year Estimates

Educational Attainment by Race

Area	High School Graduate or Higher (%)					Bachelor's Degree or Higher (%)				
	Total	White	Black	Asian	Hisp.[2]	Total	White	Black	Asian	Hisp.[2]
City	94.3	96.5	87.4	96.9	94.7	51.7	57.0	28.8	77.5	61.4
MSA[1]	92.7	93.9	87.4	94.6	89.8	40.9	41.6	24.2	73.6	49.6
U.S.	89.4	92.9	88.1	88.0	72.5	35.0	37.7	24.7	57.0	19.9

Note: Figures shown cover persons 25 years old and over; (1) Figures cover the Gainesville, FL Metropolitan Statistical Area; (2) People of Hispanic origin can be of any race
Source: U.S. Census Bureau, 2019-2023 American Community Survey 5-Year Estimates

School Enrollment by Grade and Control

Area	Preschool (%)		Kindergarten (%)		Grades 1 - 4 (%)		Grades 5 - 8 (%)		Grades 9 - 12 (%)	
	Public	Private	Public	Private	Public	Private	Public	Private	Public	Private
City	61.4	38.6	70.4	29.6	82.4	17.6	88.7	11.3	92.3	7.7
MSA[1]	53.9	46.1	72.0	28.0	76.7	23.3	78.1	21.9	86.5	13.5
U.S.	58.7	41.3	85.2	14.8	87.2	12.8	87.9	12.1	89.0	11.0

Note: Figures shown cover persons 3 years old and over; (1) Figures cover the Gainesville, FL Metropolitan Statistical Area
Source: U.S. Census Bureau, 2019-2023 American Community Survey 5-Year Estimates

Higher Education

Four-Year Colleges			Two-Year Colleges			Medical Schools[1]	Law Schools[2]	Voc/Tech[3]
Public	Private Non-profit	Private For-profit	Public	Private Non-profit	Private For-profit			
3	2	1	0	1	1	1	1	2

Note: Figures cover institutions located within the Gainesville, FL Metropolitan Statistical Area and include main campuses only; (1) includes schools accredited by the Liaison Committee on Medical Education and the American Osteopathic Association's Commission on Osteopathic College Accreditation; (2) includes ABA-accredited schools, schools with provisional ABA accreditation, and state accredited schools; (3) includes all schools with programs that are less than 2 years.
Source: National Center for Education Statistics, Integrated Postsecondary Education System (IPEDS), 2023-24; Wikipedia, List of Medical Schools in the United States, accessed May 2, 2025; Wikipedia, List of Law Schools in the United States, accessed May 2, 2025

According to *U.S. News & World Report*, the Gainesville, FL metro area is home to one of the top 200 national universities in the U.S.: **University of Florida** (#30 tie). The indicators used to capture academic quality fall into a number of categories: assessment by administrators at peer institutions; retention of students; faculty resources; student selectivity; financial resources; alumni giving; high school counselor ratings of colleges; and graduation rate. *U.S. News & World Report, "America's Best Colleges 2025"*

According to *U.S. News & World Report*, the Gainesville, FL metro area is home to one of the top 100 law schools in the U.S.: **University of Florida (Levin)** (#38 tie). The rankings are based on a weighted average of 12 measures of quality: peer assessment score; assessment score by lawyers/judges; median LSAT scores; median undergrad GPA; acceptance rate; employment rates for graduates; placement success; bar passage rate; faculty resources; expenditures per student; student/faculty ratio; and library resources. *U.S. News & World Report, "America's Best Graduate Schools, Law, 2025"*

According to *U.S. News & World Report*, the Gainesville, FL metro area is home to one of the top medical schools for research in the U.S.: **University of Florida** (Tier 2). *U.S. News* placed medical and osteopathic schools into tiers based on their research productivity, faculty and admissions data. Each school's tier was derived from its overall score, calculated by summing the weighted normalized values generated across several factors of academic quality, outlined below. There are four tiers, with tier 1 medical schools as the highest-performing and tier 4 as the lowest-performing. Only tier 1 and 2 schools are shown. Because of the tier presentation, *U.S. News* calculated overall scores based on their percentile performance among all rated schools instead of dividing against the rescaled score of the No. 1-performing schools. Tier 1 included schools with overall scores of 85 to 99. The cutoffs for tiers 2 through 4 were schools scoring 50 to 84, 15 to 49 and 1 to 14, respectively. The rankings are based on a weighted average of the following measures of quality: total research activity; average research activity per faculty member; total NIH research grants at the medical school and its affiliated hospitals; average NIH research grants per faculty; median MCAT total score; median undergraduate GPA; acceptance rate; and faculty resources. *U.S. News & World Report*, "America's Best Graduate Schools, Medical, 2025"

According to *U.S. News & World Report*, the Gainesville, FL metro area is home to one of the top 75 business schools in the U.S.: **University of Florida (Warrington)** (#38 tie). The rankings are based on a weighted average of the following nine measures: quality assessment; peer assessment; recruiter assessment; placement success; mean starting salary and bonus; student selectivity; mean GMAT and GRE scores; mean undergraduate GPA; and acceptance rate. *U.S. News & World Report*, "America's Best Graduate Schools, Business, 2025"

EMPLOYERS

Major Employers

Company Name	Industry
Alachua County	Government
Alachua County School Board	Education
City of Gainesville	Municipal government
Dollar General Distribution Center	Retail
Gator Dining Services	Food services
Nationwide Insurance Company	Insurance
North Florida Regional Medical Center	Healthcare
Publix Supermarkets	Retail grocery
RTI Surgical	Medical manufacturing
Santa Fe College	Education
UF Health	Healthcare
University of Florida	Education
Veterans Affairs Medical Center	Healthcare
Wal-Mart Distribution Center	Retail
Wal-Mart Stores	Retail

Note: Companies shown are located within the Gainesville, FL Metropolitan Statistical Area.
Source: Chambers of Commerce; State Departments of Labor; Wikipedia

PUBLIC SAFETY

Crime Rate

Area	Total Crime Rate	Violent Crime Rate				Property Crime Rate		
		Murder	Rape	Robbery	Aggrav. Assault	Burglary	Larceny-Theft	Motor Vehicle Theft
City	3,608.3	10.9	100.9	119.3	507.7	286.2	2,572.5	10.9
U.S.	2,290.9	5.7	38.0	66.5	264.1	250.7	1,347.2	318.7

Note: Figures are crimes per 100,000 population.
Source: FBI, Table 8, Offenses Known to Law Enforcement, by State by City, 2023

Hate Crimes

Area	Number of Quarters Reported	Number of Incidents per Bias Motivation					
		Race/Ethnicity/Ancestry	Religion	Sexual Orientation	Disability	Gender	Gender Identity
City	4	0	3	0	0	0	0
U.S.	4	5,900	2,699	2,077	187	92	492

Source: Federal Bureau of Investigation, Hate Crime Statistics 2023

Identity Theft Consumer Reports

Area	Reports	Reports per 100,000 Population	Rank[2]
MSA[1]	783	227	123
U.S.	1,135,291	339	-

Note: (1) Figures cover the Gainesville, FL Metropolitan Statistical Area; (2) Rank ranges from 1 to 401 where 1 indicates greatest number of identity theft reports per 100,000 population
Source: Federal Trade Commission, Consumer Sentinel Network Data Book 2024

Fraud and Other Consumer Reports

Area	Reports	Reports per 100,000 Population	Rank[2]
MSA[1]	5,211	1,513	54
U.S.	5,360,641	1,601	-

Note: (1) Figures cover the Gainesville, FL Metropolitan Statistical Area; (2) Rank ranges from 1 to 401 where 1 indicates greatest number of fraud and other consumer reports per 100,000 population
Source: Federal Trade Commission, Consumer Sentinel Network Data Book 2024

POLITICS

2024 Presidential Election Results

Area	Trump (Rep.)	Harris (Dem.)	Stein (Green)	Kennedy (Ind.)	Oliver (Lib.)	Other
Alachua County	38.6	59.4	0.6	0.0	0.5	0.9
U.S.	49.7	48.2	0.6	0.5	0.4	0.6

Note: Results are percentages and may not add to 100% due to rounding
Source: Dave Leip's Atlas of U.S. Presidential Elections

SPORTS

Professional Sports Teams

Team Name	League	Year Established

No teams are located in the metro area
Source: Wikipedia, Major Professional Sports Teams of the United States and Canada, May 1, 2025

CLIMATE

Average and Extreme Temperatures

Temperature	Jan	Feb	Mar	Apr	May	Jun	Jul	Aug	Sep	Oct	Nov	Dec	Yr.
Extreme High (°F)	83	85	90	95	98	102	99	99	95	92	88	85	102
Average High (°F)	66	68	74	81	86	89	90	90	87	81	74	68	79
Average Temp. (°F)	55	57	63	69	75	79	81	81	78	71	63	56	69
Average Low (°F)	43	45	50	56	63	69	71	71	69	60	51	44	58
Extreme Low (°F)	10	19	28	35	42	50	62	62	48	33	28	13	10

Note: Figures cover the years 1962-1995
Source: National Climatic Data Center, International Station Meteorological Climate Summary, 9/96

Average Precipitation/Snowfall/Humidity

Precip./Humidity	Jan	Feb	Mar	Apr	May	Jun	Jul	Aug	Sep	Oct	Nov	Dec	Yr.
Avg. Precip. (in.)	3.7	4.0	3.9	2.3	3.3	6.9	6.5	7.7	5.1	2.8	2.2	2.6	50.9
Avg. Snowfall (in.)	0	Tr	0	0	0	0	0	0	0	0	0	Tr	Tr
Avg. Rel. Hum. 7am (%)	90	90	92	92	91	93	94	96	96	94	94	92	93
Avg. Rel. Hum. 4pm (%)	60	55	52	50	51	61	67	67	67	63	63	61	60

Note: Figures cover the years 1962-1995; Tr = Trace amounts (<0.05 in. of rain; <0.5 in. of snow)
Source: National Climatic Data Center, International Station Meteorological Climate Summary, 9/96

Weather Conditions

Temperature			Daytime Sky			Precipitation		
32°F & below	45°F & below	90°F & above	Clear	Partly cloudy	Cloudy	0.01 inch or more precip.	0.1 inch or more snow/ice	Thunderstorms
16	73	77	88	196	81	119	0	78

Note: Figures are average number of days per year and cover the years 1962-1995
Source: National Climatic Data Center, International Station Meteorological Climate Summary, 9/96

HAZARDOUS WASTE

Superfund Sites

The Gainesville, FL metro area is home to one site on the EPA's Superfund National Priorities List (NPL) or Superfund Alternative Approach (SAA) list: **Cabot/Koppers** (Final NPL). The Superfund alternative approach uses the same investigation and cleanup process and standards that are used for sites listed on the National Priorities List. The SAA is an alternative to listing a site on the NPL; it is not an alternative to Superfund or the Superfund process. There are a total of 1,445 Superfund sites with a status of proposed or final on both lists in the United States. *U.S. Environmental Protection Agency, National Priorities List, May 1, 2025; U.S. Environmental Protection Agency, Superfund Alternative Approach Sites, May 1, 2025*

AIR QUALITY

Air Quality Trends: Ozone

	1990	1995	2000	2005	2010	2015	2020	2021	2022	2023
MSA[1]	n/a	n/a	n/a	n/a	n/a	n/a	n/a	n/a	n/a	n/a
U.S.	0.087	0.089	0.081	0.080	0.072	0.068	0.066	0.067	0.067	0.070

Note: (1) Data covers the Gainesville, FL Metropolitan Statistical Area; n/a not available. The values shown are the composite ozone concentration averages among trend sites based on the highest fourth daily maximum 8-hour concentration in parts per million. These trends are based on sites having an adequate record of monitoring data during the trend period. Data from exceptional events are included.
Source: U.S. Environmental Protection Agency, Air Quality Monitoring Information, "Air Quality Trends by City, 1990-2023"

Air Quality Index

Area	Percent of Days when Air Quality was...[2]					AQI Statistics[2]	
	Good	Moderate	Unhealthy for Sensitive Groups	Unhealthy	Very Unhealthy	Maximum	Median
MSA[1]	74.0	25.8	0.3	0.0	0.0	104	40

Note: (1) Data covers the Gainesville, FL Metropolitan Statistical Area; (2) Based on 365 days with AQI data in 2023. Air Quality Index (AQI) is an index for reporting daily air quality. EPA calculates the AQI for five major air pollutants regulated by the Clean Air Act: ground-level ozone, particle pollution (aka particulate matter), carbon monoxide, sulfur dioxide, and nitrogen dioxide. The AQI runs from 0 to 500. The higher the AQI value, the greater the level of air pollution and the greater the health concern. There are six AQI categories: "Good" AQI is between 0 and 50. Air quality is considered satisfactory; "Moderate" AQI is between 51 and 100. Air quality is acceptable; "Unhealthy for Sensitive Groups" When AQI values are between 101 and 150, members of sensitive groups may experience health effects; "Unhealthy" When AQI values are between 151 and 200 everyone may begin to experience health effects; "Very Unhealthy" AQI values between 201 and 300 trigger a health alert; "Hazardous" AQI values over 300 trigger warnings of emergency conditions (not shown).
Source: U.S. Environmental Protection Agency, Air Quality Index Report, 2023

Air Quality Index Pollutants

Area	Percent of Days when AQI Pollutant was...[2]					
	Carbon Monoxide	Nitrogen Dioxide	Ozone	Sulfur Dioxide	Particulate Matter 2.5	Particulate Matter 10
MSA[1]	0.0	0.0	38.1	(3)	61.9	0.0

Note: (1) Data covers the Gainesville, FL Metropolitan Statistical Area; (2) Based on 365 days with AQI data in 2023. The Air Quality Index (AQI) is an index for reporting daily air quality. EPA calculates the AQI for five major air pollutants regulated by the Clean Air Act: ground-level ozone, particle pollution (also known as particulate matter), carbon monoxide, sulfur dioxide, and nitrogen dioxide. The AQI runs from 0 to 500. The higher the AQI value, the greater the level of air pollution and the greater the health concern; (3) Sulfur dioxide is no longer included in this table because SO_2 concentrations tend to be very localized and not necessarily representative of broad geographical areas like counties and CBSAs.
Source: U.S. Environmental Protection Agency, Air Quality Index Report, 2023

Maximum Air Pollutant Concentrations: Particulate Matter, Ozone, CO and Lead

	Particulate Matter 10 (ug/m^3)	Particulate Matter 2.5 Wtd AM (ug/m^3)	Particulate Matter 2.5 24-Hr (ug/m^3)	Ozone (ppm)	Carbon Monoxide (ppm)	Lead (ug/m^3)
MSA[1] Level	n/a	6.3	17	0.058	n/a	n/a
NAAQS[2]	150	15	35	0.075	9	0.15
Met NAAQS[2]	n/a	Yes	Yes	Yes	n/a	n/a

Note: (1) Data covers the Gainesville, FL Metropolitan Statistical Area; Data from exceptional events are included; (2) National Ambient Air Quality Standards; ppm = parts per million; ug/m^3 = micrograms per cubic meter; n/a not available.
Concentrations: Particulate Matter 10 (coarse particulate)—highest second maximum 24-hour concentration; Particulate Matter 2.5 Wtd AM (fine particulate)—highest weighted annual mean concentration; Particulate Matter 2.5 24-Hour (fine particulate)—highest 98th percentile 24-hour concentration; Ozone—highest fourth daily maximum 8-hour concentration; Carbon Monoxide—highest second maximum non-overlapping 8-hour concentration; Lead—maximum running 3-month average
Source: U.S. Environmental Protection Agency, Air Quality Monitoring Information, "Air Quality Statistics by City, 2023"

Maximum Air Pollutant Concentrations: Nitrogen Dioxide and Sulfur Dioxide

	Nitrogen Dioxide AM (ppb)	Nitrogen Dioxide 1-Hr (ppb)	Sulfur Dioxide AM (ppb)	Sulfur Dioxide 1-Hr (ppb)	Sulfur Dioxide 24-Hr (ppb)
MSA[1] Level	n/a	n/a	n/a	n/a	n/a
NAAQS[2]	53	100	30	75	140
Met NAAQS[2]	n/a	n/a	n/a	n/a	n/a

Note: (1) Data covers the Gainesville, FL Metropolitan Statistical Area; Data from exceptional events are included; (2) National Ambient Air Quality Standards; ppm = parts per million; ug/m³ = micrograms per cubic meter; n/a not available.
Concentrations: Nitrogen Dioxide AM—highest arithmetic mean concentration; Nitrogen Dioxide 1-Hr—highest 98th percentile 1-hour daily maximum concentration; Sulfur Dioxide AM—highest annual mean concentration; Sulfur Dioxide 1-Hr—highest 99th percentile 1-hour daily maximum concentration; Sulfur Dioxide 24-Hr—highest second maximum 24-hour concentration
Source: U.S. Environmental Protection Agency, Air Quality Monitoring Information, "Air Quality Statistics by City, 2023"

Houston, Texas

Background

Houston began as a 6,642-acre tract of marshy, mosquito-infested land 56 miles north of the Gulf of Mexico bought by brothers John K. and Augustus C. Allen in 1836. They named it Houston, after the hero of San Jacinto. Since then, Houston has experienced continued growth, with 1,500 residents by the end of its first year in the Republic of Texas. In its first three years, Houston had a theater, churches, and its first steamship, establishing its position as one of the top-ranking ports in the country.

Certainly, Houston owes much to the Houston ship channel, the "golden strip" on which oil refineries, chemical plants, cement factories, and grain elevators conduct their bustling economic activity. The diversity of these industries is a testament to Houston's economy in general. Tonnage through the Port of Houston has grown to number one in the nation for foreign tonnage. The regions is important to the cruise industry as well, and the Norwegian Cruise Line sails out of the major cruise port of Galveston, 50 miles southeast of Houston.

As Texas' biggest city, Houston has also enjoyed manufacturing expansion in its diversified economy. The city is home to 24 Fortune 500 companies, behind Chicago and New York City.

Houston is also one of the major scientific research areas in the world. The presence of the Johnson Space Center has spawned several related industries in medical and technological research. The Texas Medical Center oversees a network of 45 medical institutions, including St. Luke's Episcopal Hospital, the Texas Children's Hospital, and the Methodist Hospital. As a city whose reputation rests upon advanced research, Houston is also devoted to education and the arts. Rice University, for example, whose admission standards rank as one of the highest in the nation, is in Houston, as are Dominican College and the University of St. Thomas.

Today, this relatively young city is home to a diverse range of ethnicities, including Mexican American, Nigerian, American Indian, and Pakistani.

Houston also is patron to the Museum of Fine Arts, the Contemporary Arts Museum, and the Houston Ballet and Grand Opera. A host of smaller cultural institutions, such as the Gilbert and Sullivan Society, the Virtuoso Quartet, and the Houston Harpsichord Society enliven the scene. Two privately funded museums, the Holocaust Museum Houston, and the Houston Museum of Natural Science, are historical and educational attractions.

Houstonians eagerly embrace continued revitalization. Recent years have seen an explosion of dining and entertainment options in the heart of the city. The opening of the Bayou Place, Houston's largest entertainment complex, has especially generated excitement, providing a variety of restaurants and entertainment options in one facility. An active urban park sits on 12 acres in front of the George R. Brown Convention Center. NRG, formerly Reliant, Stadium in downtown Houston is home to the NFL's Houston Texans, and hosted Superbowl XXXVIII in 2004 and LI in 2017, and WrestleMania XXV in 2009. Major league baseball team Houston Astros won the 2017 and 2022 World Series and play in Daikin, formerly Minute Maid Park. The city has sports teams for every major professional league except the National Hockey League.

Located in the flat coastal plains, Houston's climate is predominantly marine. The terrain includes many small streams and bayous which, together with the nearness to Galveston Bay, create foggy conditions. Temperatures are moderated by the influence of winds from the Gulf of Mexico, which is 50 miles away. Mild winters are the norm, as is abundant rainfall. Polar air penetrates the area frequently enough to provide variability in the weather. In August 2017, Hurricane Harvey caused severe flooding in the Houston area, with some regions receiving over 50 inches of rain. Damage from the hurricane was estimated at $125 billion. It is considered one of the worst natural disasters in the history of the United States.

Rankings

General Rankings

- To help military veterans find the best places in which to settle down, *WalletHub* compared the 100 largest U.S. cities across 19 key indicators of livability, affordability and veteran-friendliness. They range from the share of military skill-related jobs to veteran income growth to the availability of VA health facilities. Houston ranked #59. *Wallethub.com, "Best & Worst Places for Veterans to Live (2025)," November 7, 2024*

- The human resources consulting firm Mercer ranked 241 major cities worldwide in terms of overall quality of life. Houston ranked #65. Criteria: political and personal safety, social, and economic factors; medical and health considerations; schools and education; public services and transportation; recreation; connectivity; housing and infrastructure; and climate. *Mercer, "Mercer 2024 Quality of Living Survey," December 2024*

Business/Finance Rankings

- Payscale.com ranked the 32 largest metro areas in terms of wage growth. The Houston metro area ranked #2. Criteria: quarterly changes in private industry employee and education professional wage growth from the previous year. *PayScale, "Wage Trends by Metro Area-4th Quarter," February 4, 2025*

- Houston was cited as one of America's top metros for total corporate facility investment projects in 2024. The area ranked #4 in the Tier 1 (large) metro area category (population over 1 million). *Site Selection, "Top Metros of 2024," March 2025*

- The Houston metro area appeared on the Milken Institute "2025 Best Performing Cities" list. Rank: #27 out of 200 large metro areas (based on performance category). Criteria: job growth; wage growth; high-tech growth and impact; community resilience; housing affordability; household broadband access. *Milken Institute, "Best-Performing Cities 2025," January 14, 2025*

- Mercer Human Resources Consulting ranked 226 cities worldwide in terms of cost-of-living. Houston ranked #50 (the lower the ranking, the higher the cost-of-living). The survey measured the comparative cost of over 200 items (such as housing, food, clothing, domestic supplies, transportation, and recreation/entertainment) in each location. *Mercer, "2024 Cost of Living City Ranking," June 17, 2024*

Culture/Performing Arts Rankings

- Houston was selected as one of the 25 best cities for moviemakers in North America. Great film cities are places where filmmaking dreams can come true, that offer more creative space, lower costs, and great outdoor locations. NYC & LA were intentionally excluded. Criteria: film industry presence and culture; tax incentives; affordability; and proximity of festivals and schools. The city was ranked #12. *MovieMaker Magazine, "Best Places to Live and Work as a Moviemaker, 2025," January 29, 2025*

Dating/Romance Rankings

- *Apartment List* conducted its Annual Renter Satisfaction Survey and asked renters "how satisfied are you with opportunities for dating in your current city." The cities were ranked from highest to lowest based on their satisfaction scores. Houston ranked #3 out of 10 cities. *Apartment List, "Best Cities for Dating 2022 with Local Dating Insights from Bumble," February 7, 2022*

Education Rankings

- Personal finance website *WalletHub* analyzed the 150 largest U.S. metropolitan statistical areas to determine where the most educated Americans are putting their degrees to work. Criteria: education levels; percentage of workers with degrees; education quality and attainment gap; public school quality rankings; quality and enrollment of each metro area's universities. Houston was ranked #84 (#1 = most educated city). *WalletHub.com, "Most & Least Educated Cities in America, 2025" July 2, 2024*

Environmental Rankings

- Sperling's *BestPlaces* assessed the 50 largest metropolitan areas of the United States for the likelihood of dangerously extreme weather events or earthquakes. In general the Southeast and South-Central regions have the highest risk of weather extremes and earthquakes, while the Pacific Northwest enjoys the lowest risk. Of the most risky metropolitan areas, the Houston metro area was ranked #5. *Bestplaces.net, "Avoid Natural Disasters: BestPlaces Reveals The Top 10 Safest Places to Live," October 25, 2017*

- The U.S. Environmental Protection Agency (EPA) released its list of U.S. metropolitan areas with the most ENERGY STAR certified buildings in 2023. The Houston metro area was ranked #8 out of 25. *U.S. Environmental Protection Agency, "2024 Energy Star Top Cities," May 22, 2024*

- Houston was highlighted as one of the 25 most ozone-polluted metro areas in the U.S. during 2021 through 2023. The area ranked #7. *American Lung Association, "State of the Air 2025," April 23, 2025*

- Houston was highlighted as one of the 25 metro areas most polluted by year-round particle pollution (Annual PM 2.5) in the U.S. during 2021 through 2023. The area ranked #8. *American Lung Association, "State of the Air 2025," April 23, 2025*

Food/Drink Rankings

- WalletHub compared the 100 largest U.S. cities across 17 key indicators of vegan- and vegetarian-friendliness. Houston was ranked #18. Cities were selected based on metrics such as the cost of groceries for vegetarians, the share of restaurants serving meatless options and the number of salad shops per capita. *WalletHub.com, "Best Cities for Vegans & Vegetarians (2025)," September 24, 2024*

Health/Fitness Rankings

- For each of the 100 largest cities in the United States, the American Fitness Index®, compiled in partnership between the American College of Sports Medicine and the Elevance Health Foundation, evaluated community infrastructure and more than 30 health behaviors including preventive health, levels of chronic disease conditions, food insecurity, pedestrian safety, air quality, and community/environment resources that support physical activity. Houston ranked #61 for "community fitness." *americanfitnessindex.org, "2024 ACSM American Fitness Index Summary Report," July 23, 2024*

- The Houston metro area was identified as one of the worst cities for bed bugs in America by pest control company Orkin. The area ranked #38 out of 50 based on the number of bed bug treatments Orkin performed from December 2022 to November 2023. *Orkin, "Chicago Joins Paris In Global Bed Bug Spotlight Ranking As The Worst City On Orkin's U.S. Bed Bug Cities List," January 22, 2024*

- Houston was identified as a "2025 Allergy Capital." The area ranked #26 out of the nation's 100 largest metropolitan areas. Three groups of factors were used to identify the most challenging cities for people with allergies: annual tree, grass, and weed pollen scores; over the counter allergy medicine use; number of board-certified allergy specialists. *Asthma and Allergy Foundation of America, "2025 Allergy Capitals: The Most Challenging Places to Live with Allergies," March 18, 2025*

- Houston was identified as a "2024 Asthma Capital." The area ranked #70 out of the nation's 100 largest metropolitan areas. Criteria: estimated asthma prevalence; asthma-related mortality; and ER visits due to asthma. Risk factors analyzed but not factored in the rankings: annual air quality including pollution and ozone levels; public smoking laws; indoor air quality; access to asthma specialists; rescue and controller medication use; uninsured rate; pollen allergy; poverty rate. *Asthma and Allergy Foundation of America, "Asthma Capitals 2024: The Most Challenging Places to Live With Asthma," September 10, 2024*

Real Estate Rankings

- *WalletHub* compared the most populated U.S. cities to determine which had the best markets for real estate agents. Houston ranked #149 where demand was high and pay was the best. Criteria: sales per agent; annual median wage for real-estate agents; monthly average starting salary for real estate agents; real estate job density and competition; unemployment rate; home turnover rate; housing-market health index; and other relevant metrics. *WalletHub.com, "2021 Best Places to Be a Real Estate Agent," May 12, 2021*

- According to Penske Truck Rental, the Houston metro area was named the #1 moving destination in 2023, based on one-way consumer truck rental reservations made through Penske's website, rental locations, and reservations call center. *gopenske.com, "Penske Truck Rental's 2023 Top Moving Destinations," May 7, 2024*

- The Houston metro area was identified as one of the top 16 housing markets to invest in for 2025 by *Forbes*. Criteria: stable local economies with good population growth and increase in jobs providing good support for home prices and rents. *Forbes.com, "Best Local Markets For Real Estate Investing In 2025," November 6, 2024*

- The Houston metro area was identified as one of the 20 worst housing markets in the U.S. in 2024. The area ranked #207 out of 226 markets. Criteria: year-over-year change of median sales price of existing single-family homes between the 4th quarter of 2023 and the 4th quarter of 2024. *National Association of Realtors®, Median Sales Price of Existing Single-Family Homes for Metropolitan Areas, 4th Quarter 2024*

- Houston was ranked #111 out of 176 metro areas in terms of cost of housing in 2024 by the National Association of Home Builders (#1 = most affordable). Criteria: the portion of an average family's income necessary to pay the mortgage on a median-priced home. *National Association of Home Builders®, NAHB-Wells Fargo Cost of Housing Index, 4th Quarter 2024*

- The nation's largest metro areas were analyzed in terms of the percentage of households entering some stage of foreclosure in 2024. The Houston metro area ranked #3 out of 5 (#1 = highest foreclosure rate). *ATTOM Data Solutions, "2024 Year-End U.S. Foreclosure Market Report™," January 15, 2025*

Safety Rankings

- To identify the most dangerous cities in America, *24/7 Wall St.* focused on violent crime categories—murder, non-negligent manslaughter, rape, robbery, and aggravated assault—as reported for every 100,000 residents using data from the FBI's 2020 annual Uniform Crime Report. For cities with populations over 25,000, Houston was ranked #34. *247wallst.com, "America's Most Dangerous Cities" November 12, 2021*

- Statistics drawn from the FBI's Uniform Crime Report were used to rank the cities where violent crime rose the most year over year from 2019 to 2020. Only cities with 25,000 or more residents were included. *24/7 Wall St.* found that Houston placed #38 of those with a notable surge in incidents of violent crime. *247wallst.com, "American Cities Where Crime Is Soaring," March 4, 2022*

- Allstate ranked the 100 most populous cities in America in terms of driver safety. Houston ranked #26. Criteria based on anonymized driving behavior data from Allstate's mobile app powered by Arity: high speed driving (over 80 mph), phone handling, and hard braking. The report helps increase the importance of safety and awareness behind the wheel. *Allstate, "16th Allstate America's Best Drivers Report®" July 11, 2024*

- Houston was identified as one of the most dangerous cities in America by NeighborhoodScout. The city ranked #43 out of 100 (#1 = most dangerous). Criteria: number of violent crimes per 1,000 residents. The editors evaluated cities with 25,000 or more residents. *NeighborhoodScout.com, "2023 Top 100 Most Dangerous Cities in the U.S.," January 12, 2023*

- The National Insurance Crime Bureau ranked the largest metro areas in the U.S. in terms of per capita rates of vehicle theft. The Houston metro area ranked #4 out of the top 10 (#1 = highest rate). Criteria: number of vehicle theft offenses per 100,000 inhabitants in 2023. *National Insurance Crime Bureau, "Vehicle Thefts Surge Nationwide in 2023," April 9, 2024*

Transportation Rankings

- According to the INRIX "2024 Global Traffic Scorecard," Houston was identified as one of the most congested metro areas in the U.S. The area ranked #7 out of 10 in the country and among the top 25 most congested in the world. Criteria: average annual time spent in traffic and average cost of congestion per motorist. *Inrix.com, "Employees & Consumers Returned to Downtowns, Traffic Delays & Costs Grew," January 6, 2025*

Women/Minorities Rankings

- Personal finance website *WalletHub* compared more than 180 U.S. cities across two key dimensions, "Hispanic Business-Friendliness" and "Hispanic Purchasing Power," to arrive at the most favorable conditions for Hispanic entrepreneurs. Houston was ranked #80 out of 182. Criteria includes: share of Hispanic-Owned Businesses; average growth of Hispanic Business revenues; Small Business-Friendliness score; affordability; and number of Hispanics with at least a bachelor's degree. *WalletHub.com, "Best Cities for Hispanic Entrepreneurs," September 4, 2024*

Miscellaneous Rankings

- *WalletHub* compared 148 of the most populated U.S. cities to determine their operating efficiency. A "Quality of Services" score was constructed for each city and then measured against the total budget per capita to reveal which were managed the best. Houston ranked #85. Criteria: financial stability; economy; education; safety; health; infrastructure and pollution. *WalletHub.com, "2025's Best- & Worst-Run Cities in America," June 18, 2024*

Business Environment

DEMOGRAPHICS

Population Growth

Area	1990 Census	2000 Census	2010 Census	2020 Census	2023 Estimate[2]	Population Growth 1990-2023 (%)
City	1,697,610	1,953,631	2,099,451	2,304,580	2,300,419	35.5
MSA[1]	3,767,335	4,715,407	5,946,800	7,122,240	7,274,714	93.1
U.S.	248,709,873	281,421,906	308,745,538	331,449,281	332,387,540	33.6

Note: (1) Figures cover the Houston-Pasadena-The Woodlands, TX Metropolitan Statistical Area; (2) 2019-2023 5-year ACS population estimate
Source: U.S. Census Bureau, 1990 Census, 2000 Census, 2010 Census, 2020 Census, 2019-2023 American Community Survey 5-Year Estimates

Race

Area	White Alone[2] (%)	Black Alone[2] (%)	Asian Alone[2] (%)	AIAN[3] Alone[2] (%)	NHOPI[4] Alone[2] (%)	Other Race Alone[2] (%)	Two or More Races (%)
City	35.5	22.9	6.9	0.9	0.1	14.6	19.2
MSA[1]	45.3	17.3	8.2	0.7	0.1	10.7	17.8
U.S.	63.4	12.4	5.8	0.9	0.2	6.6	10.7

Note: (1) Figures cover the Houston-Pasadena-The Woodlands, TX Metropolitan Statistical Area; (2) Alone is defined as not being in combination with one or more other races; (3) American Indian and Alaska Native; (4) Native Hawaiian and Other Pacific Islander
Source: U.S. Census Bureau, 2019-2023 American Community Survey 5-Year Estimates

Hispanic or Latino Origin

Area	Total (%)	Mexican (%)	Puerto Rican (%)	Cuban (%)	Other (%)
City	44.1	28.5	0.8	0.8	14.0
MSA[1]	37.8	26.1	0.8	0.8	10.1
U.S.	19.0	11.3	1.8	0.7	5.2

Note: Persons of Hispanic or Latino origin can be of any race; (1) Figures cover the Houston-Pasadena-The Woodlands, TX Metropolitan Statistical Area
Source: U.S. Census Bureau, 2019-2023 American Community Survey 5-Year Estimates

Age

Area	Under Age 5	Age 5–19	Age 20–34	Age 35–44	Age 45–54	Age 55–64	Age 65–74	Age 75–84	Age 85+	Median Age
City	6.7	19.4	25.1	14.5	11.7	10.6	7.3	3.4	1.3	34.3
MSA[1]	6.7	22.0	20.8	14.5	12.8	11.1	7.7	3.3	1.1	35.3
U.S.	5.7	19.1	20.2	13.1	12.3	12.8	10.0	4.9	1.9	38.7

Note: (1) Figures cover the Houston-Pasadena-The Woodlands, TX Metropolitan Statistical Area
Source: U.S. Census Bureau, 2019-2023 American Community Survey 5-Year Estimates

Disability by Age

Area	All Ages	Under 18 Years Old	18 to 64 Years Old	65 Years and Over
City	11.0	4.7	8.9	35.1
MSA[1]	10.4	4.3	8.6	32.8
U.S.	13.0	4.7	10.7	32.9

Note: Figures show percent of the civilian noninstitutionalized population that reported having a disability. Disability status is determined from six types of difficulty: vision, hearing, cognitive, ambulatory, self-care, and independent living. For children under 5 years old, hearing and vision difficulty are used to determine disability status. For children between the ages of 5 and 14, disability status is determined from hearing, vision, cognitive, ambulatory, and self-care difficulties. For people aged 15 years and older, they are considered to have a disability if they have difficulty with any one of the six difficulty types; Note: (1) Figures cover the Houston-Pasadena-The Woodlands, TX Metropolitan Statistical Area
Source: U.S. Census Bureau, 2019-2023 American Community Survey 5-Year Estimates

Ancestry

Area	German	Irish	English	American	Italian	Polish	French[2]	European	Scottish
City	5.0	3.6	5.0	3.1	1.6	0.9	1.4	1.0	0.9
MSA[1]	7.1	5.0	6.6	3.6	2.0	1.1	1.8	1.2	1.1
U.S.	12.6	9.4	9.1	5.5	4.9	2.6	2.0	1.6	1.6

Note: Figures are the percentage of the total population reporting a particular ancestry. The nine most commonly reported ancestries in the U.S. are shown. Figures include multiple ancestries (e.g. if a person reported being Irish and Italian, they were included in both columns); (1) Figures cover the Houston-Pasadena-The Woodlands, TX Metropolitan Statistical Area; (2) Excludes Basque
Source: U.S. Census Bureau, 2019-2023 American Community Survey 5-Year Estimates

Foreign-born Population

| Area | Percent of Population Born in | | | | | | | | |
	Any Foreign Country	Asia	Mexico	Europe	Caribbean	Central America[2]	South America	Africa	Canada
City	28.8	5.7	9.9	1.2	1.0	6.8	1.9	2.0	0.2
MSA[1]	23.8	6.2	8.0	1.0	1.0	3.9	1.8	1.6	0.3
U.S.	13.9	4.3	3.3	1.4	1.4	1.2	1.2	0.8	0.2

Note: (1) Figures cover the Houston-Pasadena-The Woodlands, TX Metropolitan Statistical Area; (2) Excludes Mexico.
Source: U.S. Census Bureau, 2019-2023 American Community Survey 5-Year Estimates

Household Size

| Area | Persons in Household (%) | | | | | | | Average Household Size |
	One	Two	Three	Four	Five	Six	Seven or More	
City	34.1	29.2	15.6	11.6	5.7	2.3	1.5	2.47
MSA[1]	24.8	29.9	17.2	15.3	8.0	3.0	1.8	2.76
U.S.	28.5	33.8	15.4	12.7	5.9	2.3	1.4	2.54

Note: (1) Figures cover the Houston-Pasadena-The Woodlands, TX Metropolitan Statistical Area
Source: U.S. Census Bureau, 2019-2023 American Community Survey 5-Year Estimates

Household Relationships

Area	Householder	Opposite-sex Spouse	Same-sex Spouse	Opposite-sex Unmarried Partner	Same-sex Unmarried Partner	Child[2]	Grandchild	Other Relatives	Non-relatives
City	38.9	14.0	0.3	2.4	0.2	29.5	2.9	6.5	3.6
MSA[1]	35.2	17.1	0.2	2.0	0.1	32.7	2.8	6.1	2.6
U.S.	38.3	17.5	0.2	2.5	0.2	28.3	2.4	4.8	3.4

Note: Figures are percent of the total population; (1) Figures cover the Houston-Pasadena-The Woodlands, TX Metropolitan Statistical Area; (2) Includes biological, adopted, and stepchildren of the householder
Source: U.S. Census Bureau, 2020 Census

Gender

Area	Males	Females	Males per 100 Females
City	1,138,504	1,161,915	98.0
MSA[1]	3,616,570	3,658,144	98.9
U.S.	164,545,087	167,842,453	98.0

Note: (1) Figures cover the Houston-Pasadena-The Woodlands, TX Metropolitan Statistical Area
Source: U.S. Census Bureau, 2019-2023 American Community Survey 5-Year Estimates

Marital Status

Area	Never Married	Now Married[2]	Separated	Widowed	Divorced
City	42.2	40.5	2.8	4.4	10.0
MSA[1]	34.3	50.1	2.1	4.3	9.2
U.S.	34.1	47.9	1.7	5.6	10.7

Note: Figures are percentages and cover the population 15 years of age and older; (1) Figures cover the Houston-Pasadena-The Woodlands, TX Metropolitan Statistical Area; (2) Excludes separated
Source: U.S. Census Bureau, 2019-2023 American Community Survey 5-Year Estimates

Religious Groups by Family

Area	Catholic	Baptist	Methodist	LDS[2]	Pentecostal	Lutheran	Islam	Adventist	Other
MSA[1]	18.3	13.1	3.7	1.2	1.6	0.7	1.7	1.5	13.1
U.S.	18.7	7.3	3.0	2.0	1.8	1.7	1.3	1.3	11.6

Note: Figures are the number of adherents as a percentage of the total population and cover the eight largest religious groups in the U.S; (1) Figures cover the Houston-Pasadena-The Woodlands, TX Metropolitan Statistical Area; (2) Church of Jesus Christ of Latter-day Saints
Sources: 2020 U.S. Religion Census, Association of Statisticians of American Religious Bodies; The Association of Religion Data Archives (ARDA)

Religious Groups by Tradition

Area	Catholic	Evangelical Protestant	Mainline Protestant	Black Protestant	Islam	Judaism	Hinduism	Orthodox	Buddhism
MSA[1]	18.3	23.8	4.7	2.3	1.7	0.3	0.7	0.3	0.3
U.S.	18.7	16.5	5.2	2.3	1.3	0.6	0.4	0.4	0.3

Note: Figures are the number of adherents as a percentage of the total population; (1) Figures cover the Houston-Pasadena-The Woodlands, TX Metropolitan Statistical Area
Sources: 2020 U.S. Religion Census, Association of Statisticians of American Religious Bodies; The Association of Religion Data Archives (ARDA)

ECONOMY

Real Gross Domestic Product (GDP)

Area	2017	2018	2019	2020	2021	2022	2023	Rank[3]
MSA[1]	470.7	491.2	486.9	478.0	501.2	522.6	550.8	7
U.S.[2]	17,619.1	18,160.7	18,642.5	18,238.9	19,387.6	19,896.6	20,436.3	—

Note: Figures are in billions of chained 2017 dollars; (1) Figures cover the Houston-Pasadena-The Woodlands, TX Metropolitan Statistical Area; (2) Figures cover real GDP within metropolitan areas; (3) Rank is based on 2023 data and ranges from 1 to 384
Source: U.S. Bureau of Economic Analysis

Economic Growth

Area	2014	2015	2016	2017	2018	2019	2020	2021	2022	2023
MSA[1]	1.7	5.5	-2.1	0.7	4.4	-0.9	-1.8	4.8	4.3	5.4
U.S.[2]	2.6	3.2	2.0	2.7	3.1	2.7	-2.2	6.3	2.6	2.7

Note: Figures are real gross domestic product growth rates and represent percent change from preceding period; (1) Figures cover the Houston-Pasadena-The Woodlands, TX Metropolitan Statistical Area; (2) Figures are the average growth rates within metropolitan areas
Source: U.S. Bureau of Economic Analysis

Metropolitan Area Exports

Area	2018	2019	2020	2021	2022	2023	Rank[2]
MSA[1]	120,714.3	129,656.0	104,538.2	140,750.4	191,846.9	175,470.1	1
U.S.	1,664,056.1	1,645,173.7	1,431,406.6	1,753,941.4	2,062,937.4	2,019,160.5	—

Note: Figures are in millions of dollars; (1) Figures cover the Houston-Pasadena-The Woodlands, TX Metropolitan Statistical Area; (2) Rank is based on 2023 data and ranges from 1 to 386
Source: U.S. Department of Commerce, International Trade Administration, Office of Trade and Economic Analysis, Industry and Analysis, Exports by Metropolitan Area, data extracted April 2, 2025

Building Permits

Area	Single-Family			Multi-Family			Total		
	2023	2024	Pct. Chg.	2023	2024	Pct. Chg.	2023	2024	Pct. Chg.
City	6,609	6,808	3.0	9,821	5,090	-48.2	16,430	11,898	-27.6
MSA[1]	50,444	52,703	4.5	18,311	13,044	-28.8	68,755	65,747	-4.4
U.S.	920,000	981,900	6.7	591,100	496,100	-16.1	1,511,100	1,478,000	-2.2

Note: (1) Figures cover the Houston-Pasadena-The Woodlands, TX Metropolitan Statistical Area; Figures represent new, privately-owned housing units authorized (unadjusted data)
Source: U.S. Census Bureau, Building Permits Survey (BPS), 2023, 2024

Bankruptcy Filings

Area	Business Filings			Nonbusiness Filings		
	2023	2024	% Chg.	2023	2024	% Chg.
Harris County	356	426	19.7	3,285	3,853	17.3
U.S.	18,926	23,107	22.1	434,064	494,201	13.9

Note: Business filings include Chapter 7, Chapter 9, Chapter 11, Chapter 12, Chapter 13, Chapter 15, and Section 304; Nonbusiness filings include Chapter 7, Chapter 11, and Chapter 13
Source: Administrative Office of the U.S. Courts, Business and Nonbusiness Bankruptcy, County Cases Commenced by Chapter of the Bankruptcy Code, During the 12-Month Period Ending December 31, 2023 and Business and Nonbusiness Bankruptcy, County Cases Commenced by Chapter of the Bankruptcy Code, During the 12-Month Period Ending December 31, 2024

Housing Vacancy Rates

Area	Gross Vacancy Rate[3] (%)			Year-Round Vacancy Rate[4] (%)			Rental Vacancy Rate[5] (%)			Homeowner Vacancy Rate[6] (%)		
	2022	2023	2024	2022	2023	2024	2022	2023	2024	2022	2023	2024
MSA[1]	6.9	7.9	7.8	6.3	7.3	7.2	8.9	10.9	9.8	0.6	1.4	1.2
U.S.[2]	9.1	9.0	9.1	7.5	7.5	7.6	5.7	6.5	6.8	0.8	0.8	1.0

Note: (1) Figures cover the Houston-Pasadena-The Woodlands, TX Metropolitan Statistical Area; (2) Figures cover the 75 largest Metropolitan Statistical Areas; (3) The percentage of the total housing inventory that is vacant; (4) The percentage of the housing inventory (excluding seasonal units) that is year-round vacant; (5) The percentage of rental inventory that is vacant for rent; (6) The percentage of homeowner inventory that is vacant for sale
Source: U.S. Census Bureau, Housing Vacancies and Homeownership Annual Statistics: 2022, 2023, 2024

INCOME

Income

Area	Per Capita ($)	Median Household ($)	Average Household ($)
City	41,142	62,894	101,848
MSA[1]	41,559	80,458	115,043
U.S.	43,289	78,538	110,491

Note: (1) Figures cover the Houston-Pasadena-The Woodlands, TX Metropolitan Statistical Area
Source: U.S. Census Bureau, 2019-2023 American Community Survey 5-Year Estimates

Household Income Distribution

Area	Percent of Households Earning							
	Under $15,000	$15,000 -$24,999	$25,000 -$34,999	$35,000 -$49,999	$50,000 -$74,999	$75,000 -$99,999	$100,000 -$149,999	$150,000 and up
City	10.9	8.2	8.5	12.6	17.4	11.6	13.1	17.7
MSA[1]	7.7	6.2	6.7	10.5	15.9	12.5	16.9	23.6
U.S.	8.5	6.6	6.8	10.4	15.7	12.7	17.4	21.9

Note: (1) Figures cover the Houston-Pasadena-The Woodlands, TX Metropolitan Statistical Area
Source: U.S. Census Bureau, 2019-2023 American Community Survey 5-Year Estimates

Poverty Rate

Area	All Ages	Under 18 Years Old	18 to 64 Years Old	65 Years and Over
City	19.7	29.9	16.6	16.0
MSA[1]	13.6	19.1	11.7	11.3
U.S.	12.4	16.3	11.6	10.4

Note: Figures are percentage of people whose income during the past 12 months was below the poverty level; (1) Figures cover the Houston-Pasadena-The Woodlands, TX Metropolitan Statistical Area
Source: U.S. Census Bureau, 2019-2023 American Community Survey 5-Year Estimates

EMPLOYMENT

Labor Force and Employment

Area	Civilian Labor Force			Workers Employed		
	Dec. 2023	Dec. 2024	% Chg.	Dec. 2023	Dec. 2024	% Chg.
City	1,221,575	1,251,524	2.5	1,168,408	1,201,001	2.8
MSA[1]	3,704,314	3,811,882	2.9	3,557,779	3,657,192	2.8
U.S.	166,661,000	167,746,000	0.7	160,754,000	161,294,000	0.3

Note: Data is not seasonally adjusted and covers workers 16 years of age and older; (1) Figures cover the Houston-Pasadena-The Woodlands, TX Metropolitan Statistical Area
Source: Bureau of Labor Statistics, Local Area Unemployment Statistics

Unemployment Rate

Area	2024											
	Jan.	Feb.	Mar.	Apr.	May	Jun.	Jul.	Aug.	Sep.	Oct.	Nov.	Dec.
City	4.4	4.4	4.2	3.8	4.0	4.7	5.1	4.9	4.5	4.4	4.5	4.0
MSA[1]	4.4	4.5	4.1	3.8	4.0	4.7	5.0	4.8	4.5	4.4	4.4	4.1
U.S.	4.1	4.2	3.9	3.5	3.7	4.3	4.5	4.4	3.9	3.9	4.0	3.8

Note: Data is not seasonally adjusted and covers workers 16 years of age and older; (1) Figures cover the Houston-Pasadena-The Woodlands, TX Metropolitan Statistical Area
Source: Bureau of Labor Statistics, Local Area Unemployment Statistics

Average Wages

Occupation	$/Hr.	Occupation	$/Hr.
Accountants and Auditors	45.33	Maintenance and Repair Workers	23.29
Automotive Mechanics	27.12	Marketing Managers	75.23
Bookkeepers	24.69	Network and Computer Systems Admin.	48.11
Carpenters	24.93	Nurses, Licensed Practical	30.16
Cashiers	14.10	Nurses, Registered	46.51
Computer Programmers	n/a	Nursing Assistants	18.77
Computer Systems Analysts	56.46	Office Clerks, General	19.64
Computer User Support Specialists	29.02	Physical Therapists	53.94
Construction Laborers	20.13	Physicians	123.51
Cooks, Restaurant	15.99	Plumbers, Pipefitters and Steamfitters	29.30
Customer Service Representatives	20.40	Police and Sheriff's Patrol Officers	35.97
Dentists	115.55	Postal Service Mail Carriers	28.58
Electricians	28.39	Real Estate Sales Agents	36.58
Engineers, Electrical	57.48	Retail Salespersons	16.26
Fast Food and Counter Workers	12.78	Sales Representatives, Technical/Scientific	50.66
Financial Managers	88.07	Secretaries, Exc. Legal/Medical/Executive	22.14
First-Line Supervisors of Office Workers	35.05	Security Guards	18.23
General and Operations Managers	66.82	Surgeons	n/a
Hairdressers/Cosmetologists	19.05	Teacher Assistants, Exc. Postsecondary[1]	14.01
Home Health and Personal Care Aides	12.11	Teachers, Secondary School, Exc. Sp. Ed.[1]	31.15
Janitors and Cleaners	15.20	Telemarketers	18.64
Landscaping/Groundskeeping Workers	17.42	Truck Drivers, Heavy/Tractor-Trailer	27.49
Lawyers	78.80	Truck Drivers, Light/Delivery Services	23.30
Maids and Housekeeping Cleaners	14.99	Waiters and Waitresses	15.23

Note: Wage data covers the Houston-Pasadena-The Woodlands, TX Metropolitan Statistical Area; (1) Hourly wages were calculated from annual wage data based on a 40 hour work week
Source: Bureau of Labor Statistics, Metro Area Occupational Employment & Wage Estimates, May 2024

Employment by Industry

Sector	MSA[1] Number of Employees	MSA[1] Percent of Total	U.S. Percent of Total
Construction	234,700	6.7	5.1
Financial Activities	182,400	5.2	5.8
Government	467,100	13.4	14.9
Information	30,400	0.9	1.9
Leisure and Hospitality	362,100	10.4	10.4
Manufacturing	240,700	6.9	8.0
Mining and Logging	78,600	2.3	0.4
Other Services	134,500	3.9	3.7
Private Education and Health Services	462,600	13.3	16.9
Professional and Business Services	569,700	16.4	14.2
Retail Trade	333,800	9.6	10.0
Transportation, Warehousing, and Utilities	200,900	5.8	4.8
Wholesale Trade	181,700	5.2	3.9

Note: Figures are non-farm employment as of December 2024. Figures are not seasonally adjusted and include workers 16 years of age and older; (1) Figures cover the Houston-Pasadena-The Woodlands, TX Metropolitan Statistical Area
Source: Bureau of Labor Statistics, Current Employment Statistics, Employment, Hours, and Earnings

Employment by Occupation

Occupation Classification	City (%)	MSA[1] (%)	U.S. (%)
Management, Business, Science, and Arts	39.2	41.2	42.0
Natural Resources, Construction, and Maintenance	11.5	10.4	8.6
Production, Transportation, and Material Moving	12.6	12.8	13.0
Sales and Office	18.8	20.0	19.9
Service	17.8	15.6	16.5

Note: Figures cover employed civilians 16 years of age and older; (1) Figures cover the Houston-Pasadena-The Woodlands, TX Metropolitan Statistical Area
Source: U.S. Census Bureau, 2019-2023 American Community Survey 5-Year Estimates

Occupations with Greatest Projected Employment Growth: 2022 – 2032

Occupation[1]	2022 Employment	2032 Projected Employment	Numeric Employment Change	Percent Employment Change
General and Operations Managers	425,560	504,280	78,720	18.5
Fast Food and Counter Workers	333,870	394,290	60,420	18.1
Stockers and Order Fillers	264,810	321,600	56,790	21.4
Home Health and Personal Care Aides	313,670	367,500	53,830	17.2
Software Developers	110,280	161,780	51,500	46.7
Cooks, Restaurant	113,680	158,830	45,150	39.7
Laborers and Freight, Stock, and Material Movers, Hand	225,090	269,120	44,030	19.6
Heavy and Tractor-Trailer Truck Drivers	226,450	270,320	43,870	19.4
Retail Salespersons	319,400	357,630	38,230	12.0
Registered Nurses	233,850	267,980	34,130	14.6

Note: Projections cover Texas; (1) Sorted by numeric employment change
Source: www.projectionscentral.org, State Occupational Projections, 2022–2032 Long-Term Projections

Fastest-Growing Occupations: 2022 – 2032

Occupation[1]	2022 Employment	2032 Projected Employment	Numeric Employment Change	Percent Employment Change
Wind Turbine Service Technicians	4,860	7,950	3,090	63.6
Nurse Practitioners	19,060	30,490	11,430	60.0
Data Scientists	13,220	20,250	7,030	53.2
Computer and Information Research Scientists (SOC 2018)	2,070	3,140	1,070	51.7
Information Security Analysts (SOC 2018)	14,620	21,620	7,000	47.9
Software Developers	110,280	161,780	51,500	46.7
Statisticians	980	1,430	450	45.9
Operations Research Analysts	12,060	17,290	5,230	43.4
Software Quality Assurance Analysts and Testers	17,350	24,440	7,090	40.9
Medical and Health Services Managers	49,430	69,180	19,750	40.0

Note: Projections cover Texas; (1) Sorted by percent employment change and excludes occupations with numeric employment change less than 50
Source: www.projectionscentral.org, State Occupational Projections, 2022–2032 Long-Term Projections

CITY FINANCES

City Government Finances

Component	2022 ($000)	2022 ($ per capita)
Total Revenues	7,131,732	3,079
Total Expenditures	5,441,392	2,349
Debt Outstanding	13,110,985	5,661

Source: U.S. Census Bureau, State & Local Government Finances 2022

City Government Revenue by Source

Source	2022 ($000)	2022 ($ per capita)	2022 (%)
General Revenue			
From Federal Government	562,901	243	7.9
From State Government	550,916	238	7.7
From Local Governments	489,744	211	6.9
Taxes			
Property	1,593,612	688	22.3
Sales and Gross Receipts	1,071,313	463	15.0
Personal Income	0	0	0.0
Corporate Income	0	0	0.0
Motor Vehicle License	0	0	0.0
Other Taxes	193,581	84	2.7
Current Charges	1,441,988	623	20.2
Liquor Store	0	0	0.0
Utility	730,861	316	10.2

Source: U.S. Census Bureau, State & Local Government Finances 2022

City Government Expenditures by Function

Function	2022 ($000)	2022 ($ per capita)	2022 (%)
General Direct Expenditures			
Air Transportation	568,839	245	10.5
Corrections	0	0	0.0
Education	0	0	0.0
Employment Security Administration	0	0	0.0
Financial Administration	60,228	26	1.1
Fire Protection	433,739	187	8.0
General Public Buildings	40,573	17	0.7
Governmental Administration, Other	399,773	172	7.3
Health	218,193	94	4.0
Highways	221,049	95	4.1
Hospitals	0	0	0.0
Housing and Community Development	207,759	89	3.8
Interest on General Debt	552,256	238	10.1
Judicial and Legal	51,273	22	0.9
Libraries	46,074	19	0.8
Parking	9,337	4	0.2
Parks and Recreation	98,845	42	1.8
Police Protection	813,817	351	15.0
Public Welfare	0	0	0.0
Sewerage	690,413	298	12.7
Solid Waste Management	78,848	34	1.4
Veterans' Services	0	0	0.0
Liquor Store	0	0	0.0
Utility	533,181	230	9.8

Source: U.S. Census Bureau, State & Local Government Finances 2022

TAXES

State Corporate Income Tax Rates

State	Tax Rate (%)	Income Brackets ($)	Num. of Brackets	Financial Institution Tax Rate (%)[a]	Federal Income Tax Ded.
Texas	(u)	–	–	(u)	No

Note: Tax rates for tax year 2024; (a) Rates listed are the corporate income tax rate applied to financial institutions or excise taxes based on income. Some states have other taxes based upon the value of deposits or shares; (u) Texas imposes a Franchise Tax, otherwise known as margin tax, imposed on entities with more than $2,470,000 total revenues effective in 2024 at rate of 0.75%, or 0.375% for entities primarily engaged in retail or wholesale trade, on lesser of 70% of total revenues or 100% of gross receipts after deductions for either compensation ($450,000 deduction limit) or cost of goods sold. Texas has an EZ rate of 0.331 applicable to a $20 million revenue threshold.

Source: Federation of Tax Administrators, State Corporate Income Tax Rates, January 1, 2025

State Individual Income Tax Rates

State	Tax Rate (%)	Income Brackets ($)	Personal Exemptions ($)			Standard Ded. ($)	
			Single	Married	Depend.	Single	Married
Texas	– No state income tax –						

Note: Tax rates for tax year 2024; Local- and county-level taxes are not included
Source: Federation of Tax Administrators, State Individual Income Tax Rates, January 1, 2025

Various State Sales and Excise Tax Rates

State	State Sales Tax (%)	Gasoline[1] ($/gal.)	Cigarette[2] ($/pack)	Spirits[3] ($/gal.)	Wine[4] ($/gal.)	Beer[5] ($/gal.)	Recreational Marijuana (%)
Texas	6.25	0.20	1.41	2.40	0.20	0.19	Not legal

Note: All tax rates as of January 1, 2025; (1) The American Petroleum Institute has developed a methodology for determining the average tax rate on a gallon of fuel. Rates may include any of the following: excise taxes, environmental fees, storage tank fees, other fees or taxes, general sales tax, and local taxes; (2) The federal excise tax of $1.0066 per pack and local taxes are not included; (3) Rates are those applicable to off-premise sales of 40% alcohol by volume (a.b.v.) distilled spirits in 750ml containers. Local excise taxes are excluded; (4) Rates are those applicable to off-premise sales of 11% a.b.v. non-carbonated wine in 750ml containers; (5) Rates are those applicable to off-premise sales of 4.7% a.b.v. beer in 12 ounce containers.
Source: Tax Foundation, 2025 Facts & Figures: How Does Your State Compare?

State Tax Competitiveness Index

State	Overall Rank	Corporate Tax Rank	Individual Income Tax Rank	Sales Tax Rank	Property Tax Rank	Unemployment Insurance Tax Rank
Texas	7	46	1	36	40	30

Note: The Tax Foundation's State Tax Competitiveness Index enables policymakers, taxpayers, and business leaders to gauge how their states' tax systems compare. A rank of 1 is best, 50 is worst. Rankings do not average to the total. States without a tax rank equally as 1. DC's scores and rankings do not affect other states. The report shows tax systems as of July 1, 2024 (the beginning of Fiscal Year 2025).
Source: Tax Foundation, State Tax Competitiveness Index 2025

TRANSPORTATION

Means of Transportation to Work

Area	Car/Truck/Van		Public Transportation			Bicycle	Walked	Other Means	Worked at Home
	Drove Alone	Car-pooled	Bus	Subway	Railroad				
City	69.7	10.1	2.9	0.1	0.0	0.4	1.9	3.1	11.7
MSA[1]	73.5	9.7	1.4	0.0	0.0	0.2	1.2	2.0	11.9
U.S.	70.2	8.5	1.7	1.3	0.4	0.4	2.4	1.6	13.5

Note: Figures are percentages and cover workers 16 years of age and older; (1) Figures cover the Houston-Pasadena-The Woodlands, TX Metropolitan Statistical Area
Source: U.S. Census Bureau, 2019-2023 American Community Survey 5-Year Estimates

Travel Time to Work

Area	Less Than 10 Minutes	10 to 19 Minutes	20 to 29 Minutes	30 to 44 Minutes	45 to 59 Minutes	60 to 89 Minutes	90 Minutes or More
City	7.5	25.3	23.6	27.7	8.6	5.5	1.8
MSA[1]	7.7	22.9	20.7	26.9	11.5	7.9	2.5
U.S.	12.6	28.6	21.2	20.8	8.1	6.0	2.8

Note: Note: Figures are percentages and include workers 16 years old and over; (1) Figures cover the Houston-Pasadena-The Woodlands, TX Metropolitan Statistical Area
Source: U.S. Census Bureau, 2019-2023 American Community Survey 5-Year Estimates

Key Congestion Measures

Measure	2000	2010	2015	2020	2022
Annual Hours of Delay, Total (000)	111,210	176,796	236,989	169,765	233,366
Annual Hours of Delay, Per Auto Commuter	43	55	72	49	69
Annual Congestion Cost, Per Auto Commuter ($)	1,089	1,376	1,705	1,226	1,645

Note: Figures cover the Houston TX urban area
Source: Texas A&M Transportation Institute, 2023 Urban Mobility Report

Freeway Travel Time Index

Measure	1985	1990	1995	2000	2005	2010	2015	2020	2022
Urban Area Index[1]	1.25	1.22	1.22	1.23	1.28	1.28	1.33	1.15	1.27
Urban Area Rank[1,2]	3	5	13	22	14	16	11	4	16

Note: Freeway Travel Time Index—the ratio of travel time in the peak period to the travel time at free-flow conditions. For example, a value of 1.30 indicates a 20-minute free-flow trip takes 26 minutes in the peak (20 minutes x 1.30 = 26 minutes); (1) Covers the Houston TX urban area; (2) Rank is based on 101 larger urban areas (#1 = highest travel time index)
Source: Texas A&M Transportation Institute, 2023 Urban Mobility Report

Public Transportation

Agency Name / Mode of Transportation	Vehicles Operated in Maximum Service[1]	Annual Unlinked Passenger Trips[2] (in thous.)	Annual Passenger Miles[3] (in thous.)
Metropolitan Transit Authority of Harris County (METRO)			
Bus (directly operated)	520	38,937.8	205,905.2
Bus (purchased transportation)	126	10,085.8	54,318.2
Bus Rapid Transit (directly operated)	6	298.8	872.8
Commuter Bus (directly operated)	141	2,001.7	38,956.6
Commuter Bus (purchased transportation)	59	1,267.7	25,578.9
Demand Response (purchased transportation)	402	1,900.3	18,263.1
Light Rail (directly operated)	52	13,670.6	38,200.8
Vanpool (directly operated)	199	413.2	12,621.3

Note: (1) Number of revenue vehicles operated by the given mode and type of service to meet the annual maximum service requirement. This is the revenue vehicle count during the peak season of the year; on the week and day that maximum service is provided. Vehicles operated in maximum service (VOMS) exclude atypical days and one-time special events; (2) Number of passengers who boarded public transportation vehicles. Passengers are counted each time they board a vehicle no matter how many vehicles they use to travel from their origin to their destination. (3) Sum of the distances ridden by all passengers during the entire fiscal year.
Source: Federal Transit Administration, National Transit Database, 2023

Air Transportation

Airport Name and Code / Type of Service	Passenger Airlines[1]	Passenger Enplanements	Freight Carriers[2]	Freight (lbs)
George Bush Intercontinental (IAH)				
Domestic service (U.S. carriers only)	24	17,464,743	16	330,696,032
International service (U.S. carriers only)	12	4,113,542	5	54,374,761
William P. Hobby (HOU)				
Domestic service (U.S. carriers only)	25	6,639,433	5	11,572,579
International service (U.S. carriers only)	4	476,246	3	99,103

Note: (1) Includes all U.S.-based major, minor and commuter airlines that carried at least one passenger during the year; (2) Includes all U.S.-based airlines and freight carriers that transported at least one pound of freight during the year.
Source: Bureau of Transportation Statistics, The Intermodal Transportation Database, Air Carriers: T-100 Domestic Market (U.S. carriers only), 2024; Bureau of Transportation Statistics, The Intermodal Transportation Database, Air Carriers: T-100 International Market (U.S. carriers only), 2024

BUSINESSES

Major Business Headquarters

Company Name	Industry	Fortune[1]	Forbes[2]
APA	Mining, crude-oil production	455	-
BMC Software	IT software & services	-	266
Baker Hughes	Oil and gas equipment, services	161	-
Calpine	Utilities	-	32
CenterPoint Energy	Utilities: gas and electric	441	-
Cheniere Energy	Pipelines	200	-
ConocoPhillips	Mining, crude-oil production	68	-
David Weekley Homes	Construction	-	198
EOG Resources	Mining, crude-oil production	169	-
Enterprise Products Partners	Pipelines	90	-
Fertitta Entertainment	Hotels, restaurants & leisure	-	140
Group 1 Automotive	Automotive retailing, services	229	-
Halliburton	Oil and gas equipment, services	177	-
Kinder Morgan	Pipelines	268	-
NOV	Oil and gas equipment, services	444	-
NRG Energy	Energy	150	-
Occidental Petroleum	Mining, crude-oil production	149	-
Par Pacific Holdings	Petroleum refining	454	-
Perry Homes	Construction	-	242
Phillips 66	Petroleum refining	26	-
Plains GP Holdings	Pipelines	92	-
Quanta Services	Engineering & construction	192	-
Sysco	Wholesalers: food and grocery	54	-
Targa Resources	Pipelines	256	-
Tauber Oil	Oil & gas operations	-	188
The Friedkin Group	Multicompany	-	34
Waste Management	Waste management	199	-
Westlake	Chemicals	326	-

Note: (1) Companies that produce a 10-K are ranked 1 to 500 based on 2023 revenue; (2) All private companies with at least $2 billion in annual revenue through the end of their most current fiscal year are ranked 1 to 275; companies listed are headquartered in the city; dashes indicate no ranking
Source: Fortune, "Fortune 500," 2024; Forbes, "America's Largest Private Companies," 2024

Fastest-Growing Businesses

According to *Inc.*, Houston is home to six of America's 500 fastest-growing private companies: **Realty.com** (#107); **Turtlebox Audio** (#209); **Amundson Group** (#332); **Valiant Business Lending** (#337); **Strategic Office Support** (#367); **10xTravel** (#401). Criteria: must be an independent, privately-held, for-profit, U.S. corporation, proprietorship or partnership as of December 31, 2023; revenues must be at least $100,000 in 2020 and $2 million in 2023; must have four-year operating/sales history. *Inc., "America's 500 Fastest-Growing Private Companies," 2024*

According to *Initiative for a Competitive Inner City (ICIC)*, Houston is home to five of America's 100 fastest-growing "inner city" companies: **Premier Wireless Business Technology Solutions** (#17); **Heaven on Earth** (#24); **Three Brothers Bakery** (#80); **Classy Act** (#82); **Star Building Services** (#92). To be eligible for the IC100, companies have to be independently operated, privately held, for-profit businesses with revenues of at least $50,000 in 2019 and $500,000 in 2023, and headquartered in an under-resourced community. Recognizing that concentrated poverty exists within metropolitan areas outside of big cities (and that poverty overall is suburbanizing), ICIC defines under-resourced communities as large low-income, high-poverty areas located in the urban and suburban parts of all but the smallest metropolitan areas. Companies were ranked overall by revenue growth over the five-year period between 2019 and 2023. *Initiative for a Competitive Inner City (ICIC), "Inner City 100 Companies," 2024*

According to Deloitte, Houston is home to three of North America's 500 fastest-growing high-technology companies: **Direct Digital Holdings** (#101); **NatGasHub.com** (#286); **Liongard** (#437). Companies are ranked by percentage growth in revenue over a four-year period. Criteria for inclusion: company must be headquartered within North America; must own proprietary intellectual property or technology that is sold to customers in products that contributes to a significant portion of the company's operating revenue; must have been in business for a minumum of four years with 2020 operating revenues of at least $50,000 USD/CD and 2023 operating revenues of at least $5 million USD/CD. *Deloitte, 2024 Technology Fast 500™*

Living Environment

COST OF LIVING

Cost of Living Index

Composite Index	Groceries	Housing	Utilities	Transportation	Health Care	Misc. Goods/Services
94.1	99.3	79.2	92.4	94.0	97.5	104.1

Note: The Cost of Living Index measures regional differences in the cost of consumer goods and services, excluding taxes and non-consumer expenditures, for professional and managerial households in the top income quintile. It is based on more than 50,000 prices covering almost 60 different items for which prices are collected three times a year by chambers of commerce, economic development organizations or university applied economic centers in each participating urban area. The numbers shown should be read as a percentage above or below the national average of 100. For example, a value of 115.4 in the groceries column indicates that grocery prices are 15.4% higher than the national average. Small differences in the index numbers should not be interpreted as significant; Figures cover the Houston TX urban area.
Source: The Council for Community and Economic Research, Cost of Living Index, 2024

Grocery Prices

Area[1]	T-Bone Steak ($/pound)	Frying Chicken ($/pound)	Whole Milk ($/half gal.)	Eggs ($/dozen)	Orange Juice ($/64 oz.)	Coffee ($/11.5 oz.)
City[2]	14.53	1.62	4.64	3.18	4.33	5.40
Avg.	15.42	1.55	4.69	3.25	4.41	5.46
Min.	14.50	1.16	4.43	2.75	4.00	4.85
Max.	17.56	2.89	5.49	4.78	5.54	7.89

Note: (1) Values for the local area are compared with the average, minimum and maximum values for all 276 areas in the Cost of Living Index; (2) Figures cover the Houston TX urban area; **T-Bone Steak** (price per pound); **Frying Chicken** (price per pound, whole fryer); **Whole Milk** (half gallon carton); **Eggs** (price per dozen, Grade A, large); **Orange Juice** (64 oz. Tropicana or Florida Natural); **Coffee** (11.5 oz. can, vacuum-packed, Maxwell House, Hills Bros, or Folgers).
Source: The Council for Community and Economic Research, Cost of Living Index, 2024

Housing and Utility Costs

Area[1]	New Home Price ($)	Apartment Rent ($/month)	All Electric ($/month)	Part Electric ($/month)	Other Energy ($/month)	Telephone ($/month)
City[2]	388,197	1,322	-	124.12	48.31	209.27
Avg.	515,975	1,550	210.99	123.07	82.07	194.99
Min.	265,375	692	104.33	53.68	36.26	179.42
Max.	2,775,821	5,719	529.02	397.28	361.63	223.33

Note: (1) Values for the local area are compared with the average, minimum and maximum values for all 276 areas in the Cost of Living Index; (2) Figures cover the Houston TX urban area; **New Home Price** (2,400 sf living area, 8,000 sf lot, in urban area with full utilities); **Apartment Rent** (950 sf 2 bedroom/1.5 or 2 bath, unfurnished, excluding all utilities except water); **All Electric** (average monthly cost for an all-electric home); **Part Electric** (average monthly cost for a part-electric home); **Other Energy** (average monthly cost for natural gas, fuel oil, coal, wood, and any other forms of energy except electricity); **Telephone** (price includes the base monthly rate plus taxes and fees for three lines of mobile phone service).
Source: The Council for Community and Economic Research, Cost of Living Index, 2024

Health Care, Transportation, and Other Costs

Area[1]	Doctor ($/visit)	Dentist ($/visit)	Optometrist ($/visit)	Gasoline ($/gallon)	Beauty Salon ($/visit)	Men's Shirt ($)
City[2]	97.07	129.17	137.54	2.98	73.30	50.68
Avg.	143.77	117.51	129.23	3.32	48.57	38.14
Min.	36.74	58.67	67.33	2.80	24.00	13.41
Max.	270.44	216.82	307.33	5.28	94.00	63.89

Note: (1) Values for the local area are compared with the average, minimum and maximum values for all 276 areas in the Cost of Living Index; (2) Figures cover the Houston TX urban area; **Doctor** (general practitioners routine exam of an established patient); **Dentist** (adult teeth cleaning and periodic oral examination); **Optometrist** (full vision eye exam for established adult patient); **Gasoline** (one gallon regular unleaded, national brand, including all taxes, cash price at self-service pump if available); **Beauty Salon** (woman's shampoo, trim, and blow-dry); **Men's Shirt** (cotton/polyester dress shirt, pinpoint weave, long sleeves).
Source: The Council for Community and Economic Research, Cost of Living Index, 2024

HOUSING

Homeownership Rate

Area	2017 (%)	2018 (%)	2019 (%)	2020 (%)	2021 (%)	2022 (%)	2023 (%)	2024 (%)
MSA[1]	58.9	60.1	61.3	65.3	64.1	63.7	61.8	61.6
U.S.	63.9	64.4	64.6	66.6	65.5	65.8	65.9	65.6

Note: (1) Figures cover the Houston-Pasadena-The Woodlands, TX Metropolitan Statistical Area
Source: U.S. Census Bureau, Housing Vacancies and Homeownership Annual Statistics: 2017-2024

House Price Index (HPI)

Area	National Ranking[2]	Quarterly Change (%)	One-Year Change (%)	Five-Year Change (%)	Since 1991Q1 (%)
MSA[1]	195	0.35	3.29	44.19	326.50
U.S.[3]	–	1.43	4.51	57.13	327.82

Note: The HPI is a weighted repeat sales index. It measures average price changes in repeat sales or refinancings on the same properties. This information is obtained by reviewing repeat mortgage transactions on single-family properties whose mortgages have been purchased or securitized by Fannie Mae or Freddie Mac since January 1975; (1) Figures cover the Houston-The Woodlands-Sugar Land, TX Metropolitan Statistical Area; (2) Rankings are based on annual percentage change for all metro areas containing at least 15,000 transactions over the last 10 years and ranges from 1 to 241; (3) figures based on a weighted average of Census Division estimates using a seasonally adjusted, purchase-only index; all figures are for the period ending December 31, 2024
Source: Federal Housing Finance Agency, Change in FHFA Metropolitan Area House Price Indexes, All Transactions Index, 2024Q4

Home Value

Area	Under $100,000	$100,000 -$199,999	$200,000 -$299,999	$300,000 -$399,999	$400,000 -$499,999	$500,000 -$999,999	$1,000,000 or more	Median ($)
City	11.1	24.9	22.9	12.3	8.6	14.1	6.1	253,400
MSA[1]	9.2	18.8	28.6	17.5	10.0	12.4	3.6	275,200
U.S.	12.1	17.8	19.5	14.4	10.5	19.1	6.5	303,400

Note: Figures are percentages except for median and cover owner-occupied housing units; (1) Figures cover the Houston-Pasadena-The Woodlands, TX Metropolitan Statistical Area
Source: U.S. Census Bureau, 2019-2023 American Community Survey 5-Year Estimates

Year Housing Structure Built

Area	2020 or Later	2010 -2019	2000 -2009	1990 -1999	1980 -1989	1970 -1979	1960 -1969	1950 -1959	1940 -1949	Before 1940	Median Year
City	1.4	14.0	13.0	9.3	14.1	19.0	12.1	9.4	3.7	4.1	1981
MSA[1]	2.3	18.1	19.6	12.8	14.7	15.1	7.6	5.4	2.1	2.3	1992
U.S.	1.2	8.9	13.6	12.8	13.0	14.4	10.0	9.7	4.5	11.9	1980

Note: Figures are percentages except for Median Year; Note: (1) Figures cover the Houston-Pasadena-The Woodlands, TX Metropolitan Statistical Area
Source: U.S. Census Bureau, 2019-2023 American Community Survey 5-Year Estimates

Gross Monthly Rent

Area	Under $500	$500 -$999	$1,000 -$1,499	$1,500 -$1,999	$2,000 -$2,499	$2,500 -$2,999	$3,000 and up	Median ($)
City	2.7	21.1	39.5	23.4	8.1	2.6	2.7	1,313
MSA[1]	2.6	17.5	39.1	24.9	10.1	3.2	2.6	1,378
U.S.	6.5	22.3	29.5	20.2	10.8	4.8	5.9	1,348

Note: Figures are percentages except for median; Gross rent is the contract rent plus the estimated average monthly cost of utilities (electricity, gas, and water and sewer) and fuels (oil, coal, kerosene, wood, etc.) if these are paid by the renter (or paid for the renter by someone else); (1) Figures cover the Houston-Pasadena-The Woodlands, TX Metropolitan Statistical Area
Source: U.S. Census Bureau, 2019-2023 American Community Survey 5-Year Estimates

HEALTH

Health Risk Factors

Category	MSA[1] (%)	U.S. (%)
Adults aged 18–64 who have any kind of health care coverage	74.9	90.8
Adults who reported being in good or better health	81.8	81.8
Adults who have been told they have high blood cholesterol	38.7	36.9
Adults who have been told they have high blood pressure	30.1	34.0
Adults who are current smokers	9.0	12.1
Adults who currently use e-cigarettes	8.7	7.7
Adults who currently use chewing tobacco, snuff, or snus	4.0	3.2
Adults who are heavy drinkers[2]	4.8	6.1
Adults who are binge drinkers[3]	18.3	15.2
Adults who are overweight (BMI 25.0 - 29.9)	36.7	34.4
Adults who are obese (BMI 30.0 - 99.8)	30.7	34.3
Adults who participated in any physical activities in the past month	74.5	75.8

Note: All figures are crude prevalence; (1) Figures cover the Houston-The Woodlands-Sugar Land, TX Metropolitan Statistical Area; (2) Heavy drinkers are classified as adult men having more than 14 drinks per week and adult women having more than 7 drinks per week; (3) Binge drinkers are classified as males having five or more drinks on one occasion or females having four or more drinks on one occasion
Source: Centers for Disease Control and Prevention, Behavioral Risk Factor Surveillance System, SMART: Selected Metropolitan Area Risk Trends, 2023

Acute and Chronic Health Conditions

Category	MSA[1] (%)	U.S. (%)
Adults who have ever been told they had a heart attack	3.0	4.2
Adults who have ever been told they have angina or coronary heart disease	2.4	4.0
Adults who have ever been told they had a stroke	3.1	3.3
Adults who have ever been told they have asthma	12.0	15.7
Adults who have ever been told they have arthritis	19.0	26.3
Adults who have ever been told they have diabetes[2]	11.6	11.5
Adults who have ever been told they had skin cancer	3.7	5.6
Adults who have ever been told they had any other types of cancer	5.1	8.4
Adults who have ever been told they have COPD	3.6	6.4
Adults who have ever been told they have kidney disease	2.6	3.7
Adults who have ever been told they have a form of depression	16.0	22.0

Note: All figures are crude prevalence; (1) Figures cover the Houston-The Woodlands-Sugar Land, TX Metropolitan Statistical Area; (2) Figures do not include pregnancy-related, borderline, or pre-diabetes
Source: Centers for Disease Control and Prevention, Behavioral Risk Factor Surveillance System, SMART: Selected Metropolitan Area Risk Trends, 2023

Health Screening and Vaccination Rates

Category	MSA[1] (%)	U.S. (%)
Adults who have ever been tested for HIV	46.2	37.5
Adults who have had their blood cholesterol checked within the last five years	85.5	87.0
Adults aged 65+ who have had flu shot within the past year	59.0	63.4
Adults aged 65+ who have ever had a pneumonia vaccination	72.8	71.9

Note: All figures are crude prevalence; (1) Figures cover the Houston-The Woodlands-Sugar Land, TX Metropolitan Statistical Area.
Source: Centers for Disease Control and Prevention, Behavioral Risk Factor Surveillance System, SMART: Selected Metropolitan Area Risk Trends, 2023

Disability Status

Category	MSA[1] (%)	U.S. (%)
Adults who reported being deaf	5.7	7.4
Are you blind or have serious difficulty seeing, even when wearing glasses?	8.0	4.9
Do you have difficulty doing errands alone?	4.1	7.8
Do you have difficulty dressing or bathing?	2.1	3.6
Do you have serious difficulty concentrating/remembering/making decisions?	14.9	13.7
Do you have serious difficulty walking or climbing stairs?	8.7	13.2

Note: All figures are crude prevalence; (1) Figures cover the Houston-The Woodlands-Sugar Land, TX Metropolitan Statistical Area.
Source: Centers for Disease Control and Prevention, Behavioral Risk Factor Surveillance System, SMART: Selected Metropolitan Area Risk Trends, 2023

Mortality Rates for the Top 10 Causes of Death in the U.S.

ICD-10[a] Sub-Chapter	ICD-10[a] Code	Crude Mortality Rate[2] per 100,000 population	
		County[3]	U.S.
Malignant neoplasms	C00-C97	120.6	182.7
Ischaemic heart diseases	I20-I25	72.5	109.6
Provisional assignment of new diseases of uncertain etiology[1]	U00-U49	56.1	65.3
Other forms of heart disease	I30-I51	41.1	65.1
Other degenerative diseases of the nervous system	G30-G31	37.4	52.4
Other external causes of accidental injury	W00-X59	38.1	52.3
Cerebrovascular diseases	I60-I69	35.1	49.1
Chronic lower respiratory diseases	J40-J47	19.0	43.5
Hypertensive diseases	I10-I15	24.0	38.9
Organic, including symptomatic, mental disorders	F01-F09	12.4	33.9

Note: (a) ICD-10 = International Classification of Diseases 10th Revision; (1) Includes COVID-19, adverse effects to COVID-19 vaccines, SARS, and vaping-related disorders; (2) Crude mortality rates are a three-year average covering 2021-2023; (3) Figures cover Harris County.
Source: Centers for Disease Control and Prevention, National Center for Health Statistics. National Vital Statistics System, Mortality 2018-2023 on CDC WONDER Online Database

Mortality Rates for Selected Causes of Death

Cause of Death	ICD-10[a] Code	Crude Mortality Rate[1] per 100,000 population	
		County[2]	U.S.
Accidental poisoning and exposure to noxious substances	X40-X49	21.9	30.5
Alzheimer disease	G30	20.6	35.4
Assault	X85-Y09	12.1	7.3
COVID-19	U07.1	56.1	65.3
Diabetes mellitus	E10-E14	20.7	30.0
Diseases of the liver	K70-K76	16.2	20.8
Human immunodeficiency virus (HIV) disease	B20-B24	3.1	1.5
Influenza and pneumonia	J09-J18	8.9	13.4
Intentional self-harm	X60-X84	12.2	14.7
Malnutrition	E40-E46	4.6	6.0
Obesity and other hyperalimentation	E65-E68	3.0	3.1
Renal failure	N17-N19	13.8	16.4
Transport accidents	V01-V99	13.9	14.4

Note: (a) ICD-10 = International Classification of Diseases 10th Revision; (1) Crude mortality rates are a three-year average covering 2021-2023; (2) Figures cover Harris County; Data are suppressed when the data meet the criteria for confidentiality constraints; Crude mortality rates are flagged as unreliable when the rate would be calculated with a numerator of 20 or less.
Source: Centers for Disease Control and Prevention, National Center for Health Statistics. National Vital Statistics System, Mortality 2018-2023 on CDC WONDER Online Database

Health Insurance Coverage

Area	With Health Insurance	With Private Health Insurance	With Public Health Insurance	Without Health Insurance	Population Under Age 19 Without Health Insurance
City	76.0	52.1	30.3	24.0	16.0
MSA[1]	81.3	61.4	27.1	18.7	12.6
U.S.	91.4	67.3	36.3	8.6	5.4

Note: Figures are percentages that cover the civilian noninstitutionalized population; (1) Figures cover the Houston-Pasadena-The Woodlands, TX Metropolitan Statistical Area
Source: U.S. Census Bureau, 2019-2023 American Community Survey 5-Year Estimates

Number of Medical Professionals

Area	MDs[3]	DOs[3,4]	Dentists	Podiatrists	Chiropractors	Optometrists
County[1] (number)	17,384	763	3,643	242	1,162	1,042
County[1] (rate[2])	363.6	16.0	75.3	5.0	24.0	21.6
U.S. (rate[2])	302.5	29.2	74.6	6.4	29.5	18.0

Note: Data as of 2023 unless noted; (1) Data covers Harris County; (2) Number of medical professionals per 100,000 population; (3) Data as of 2022 and includes all active, non-federal physicians; (4) Doctor of Osteopathic Medicine
Source: U.S. Department of Health and Human Services, Health Resources and Services Administration, Bureau of Health Professions, Area Resource File (ARF) 2023-2024

Best Hospitals

According to *U.S. News,* the Houston-Pasadena-The Woodlands, TX metro area is home to eight of the best hospitals in the U.S.: **Baylor St. Luke's Medical Center** (4 adult specialties); **Cullen Eye Institute at Baylor St. Luke's Medical Center** (4 adult specialties); **Houston Methodist Hospital** (Honor Roll/10 adult specialties); **Memorial Hermann Greater Heights Hospital** (1 adult specialty); **Memorial Hermann Hospital** (1 adult specialty and 4 pediatric specialties); **TIRR Memorial Hermann** (1 adult specialty); **Texas Heart Institute at Baylor St. Luke's Medical Center** (4 adult specialties); **University of Texas MD Anderson Cancer Center** (4 adult specialties and 1 pediatric specialty). The hospitals listed were nationally ranked in at least one of 15 adult or 11 pediatric specialties. The number of specialties shown cover the parent hospital. Only 160 U.S. hospitals performed well enough to be nationally ranked in one or more specialties. Twenty hospitals in the U.S. made the Honor Roll. The Best Hospitals Honor Roll takes both the national rankings and the procedure and condition ratings into account. Hospitals received points if they were nationally ranked in one of the 15 adult specialties—the higher they ranked, the more points they got—and how many ratings of "high performing" they earned in the 20 procedures and conditions. *U.S. News Online,* "America's Best Hospitals 2024-25"

According to *U.S. News,* the Houston-Pasadena-The Woodlands, TX metro area is home to three of the best children's hospitals in the U.S.: **Children's Cancer Hospital-University of Texas M.D. Anderson Cancer Center** (1 pediatric specialty); **Children's Memorial Hermann Hospital** (4 pediatric specialties); **Texas Children's Hospital** (Honor Roll/11 pediatric specialties). The hospitals listed were highly ranked in at least one of 11 pediatric specialties. One hundred five children's hospitals in the U.S. were nationally ranked in at least one specialty. Hospitals received points for being ranked in a specialty, and the 10 hospitals with the most points across the 11 specialties make up the Honor Roll. *U.S. News Online,* "America's Best Children's Hospitals 2024-25"

EDUCATION

Public School District Statistics

District Name	Schls	Pupils	Pupil/Teacher Ratio	Minority Pupils[1] (%)	Total Rev. per Pupil ($)	Total Exp. per Pupil ($)
Aldine ISD	80	57,844	14.6	98.1	15,073	12,943
Alief ISD	48	39,474	13.3	96.7	15,379	15,230
Cypress-Fairbanks ISD	94	118,470	14.7	80.4	12,692	14,636
Galena Park ISD	25	21,105	15.1	97.1	15,183	15,150
Harmony School of Excellence	10	7,107	16.1	89.5	13,541	11,557
Houston Gateway Academy	3	2,157	21.8	98.9	14,620	8,072
Houston ISD	274	184,109	15.6	90.1	15,124	14,515
Kipp Texas Public Schools	58	34,111	19.1	98.1	14,372	12,423
Sheldon ISD	14	11,028	16.8	96.0	15,114	14,236
Spring Branch ISD	50	33,407	15.5	72.0	16,332	18,524
Spring ISD	43	33,935	14.9	95.6	14,322	12,850
Yes Prep Public Schools Inc	21	17,622	16.3	97.8	15,049	12,372

Note: Table includes school districts with 2,000 or more students; (1) Percentage of students that are not non-Hispanic white.
Source: U.S. Department of Education, National Center for Education Statistics, Common Core of Data, Local Education Agency (School District) Universe Survey: School Year 2023-2024; U.S. Department of Education, National Center for Education Statistics, Common Core of Data, School District Finance Survey (F-33): School Year 2021–22

Best High Schools

According to *U.S. News*, Houston is home to 11 of the top 500 high schools in the U.S.: **Carnegie Vanguard High School** (#31); **DeBakey High School for Health Professions** (#70); **Kinder High School for Performing and Visual Arts** (#159); **Challenge Early College High School** (#162); **Young Women's College Prep Academy** (#171); **Eastwood Academy** (#195); **Kerr High School** (#289); **Houston Academy for International Studies** (#299); **East Early College High School** (#360); **Clear Horizons Early College High School** (#446); **Early College Academy at Southridge** (#472). Nearly 25,000 public, magnet and charter schools were ranked based on their performance on state assessments and how well they prepare students for college. *U.S. News & World Report, "Best High Schools 2024"*

Highest Level of Education

Area	Less than H.S.	H.S. Diploma	Some College, No Deg.	Associate Degree	Bachelor's Degree	Master's Degree	Prof. School Degree	Doctorate Degree
City	19.7	21.5	16.6	6.2	21.3	9.6	3.2	1.9
MSA[1]	14.9	22.7	19.5	7.5	22.1	9.3	2.3	1.7
U.S.	10.6	26.2	19.4	8.8	21.3	9.8	2.3	1.6

Note: Figures cover persons age 25 and over; (1) Figures cover the Houston-Pasadena-The Woodlands, TX Metropolitan Statistical Area
Source: U.S. Census Bureau, 2019-2023 American Community Survey 5-Year Estimates

Educational Attainment by Race

Area	High School Graduate or Higher (%)					Bachelor's Degree or Higher (%)				
	Total	White	Black	Asian	Hisp.[2]	Total	White	Black	Asian	Hisp.[2]
City	80.3	88.5	89.9	86.6	60.7	36.0	50.8	27.4	61.7	16.7
MSA[1]	85.1	90.6	92.3	87.6	67.9	35.4	40.8	32.1	58.0	17.8
U.S.	89.4	92.9	88.1	88.0	72.5	35.0	37.7	24.7	57.0	19.9

Note: Figures shown cover persons 25 years old and over; (1) Figures cover the Houston-Pasadena-The Woodlands, TX Metropolitan Statistical Area; (2) People of Hispanic origin can be of any race
Source: U.S. Census Bureau, 2019-2023 American Community Survey 5-Year Estimates

School Enrollment by Grade and Control

Area	Preschool (%)		Kindergarten (%)		Grades 1 - 4 (%)		Grades 5 - 8 (%)		Grades 9 - 12 (%)	
	Public	Private	Public	Private	Public	Private	Public	Private	Public	Private
City	65.2	34.8	87.6	12.4	91.1	8.9	91.5	8.5	91.7	8.3
MSA[1]	57.2	42.8	88.1	11.9	90.9	9.1	92.0	8.0	91.7	8.3
U.S.	58.7	41.3	85.2	14.8	87.2	12.8	87.9	12.1	89.0	11.0

Note: Figures shown cover persons 3 years old and over; (1) Figures cover the Houston-Pasadena-The Woodlands, TX Metropolitan Statistical Area
Source: U.S. Census Bureau, 2019-2023 American Community Survey 5-Year Estimates

Higher Education

Four-Year Colleges			Two-Year Colleges			Medical Schools[1]	Law Schools[2]	Voc/ Tech[3]
Public	Private Non-profit	Private For-profit	Public	Private Non-profit	Private For-profit			
14	10	6	2	3	18	5	3	22

Note: Figures cover institutions located within the Houston-Pasadena-The Woodlands, TX Metropolitan Statistical Area and include main campuses only; (1) includes schools accredited by the Liaison Committee on Medical Education and the American Osteopathic Association's Commission on Osteopathic College Accreditation; (2) includes ABA-accredited schools, schools with provisional ABA accreditation, and state accredited schools; (3) includes all schools with programs that are less than 2 years.
Source: National Center for Education Statistics, Integrated Postsecondary Education System (IPEDS), 2023-24; Wikipedia, List of Medical Schools in the United States, accessed May 2, 2025; Wikipedia, List of Law Schools in the United States, accessed May 2, 2025

According to *U.S. News & World Report,* the Houston-Pasadena-The Woodlands, TX metro area is home to two of the top 200 national universities in the U.S.: **Rice University** (#18 tie); **University of Houston** (#144 tie). The indicators used to capture academic quality fall into a number of categories: assessment by administrators at peer institutions; retention of students; faculty resources; student selectivity; financial resources; alumni giving; high school counselor ratings of colleges; and graduation rate. *U.S. News & World Report, "America's Best Colleges 2025"*

According to *U.S. News & World Report,* the Houston-Pasadena-The Woodlands, TX metro area is home to one of the top 100 law schools in the U.S.: **University of Houston Law Center** (#63 tie). The rankings are based on a weighted average of 12 measures of quality: peer assessment score; assessment score by lawyers/judges; median LSAT scores; median undergrad GPA; acceptance rate; employment rates for graduates; placement success; bar passage rate; faculty resources; expenditures per student; student/faculty ratio; and library resources. *U.S. News & World Report, "America's Best Graduate Schools, Law, 2025"*

According to *U.S. News & World Report,* the Houston-Pasadena-The Woodlands, TX metro area is home to two of the top medical schools for research in the U.S.: **Baylor College of Medicine** (Tier 1); **University of Texas Health Science Center—Houston (McGovern)** (Tier 2). *U.S. News* placed medical and osteopathic schools into tiers based on their research productivity, faculty and admissions data. Each school's tier was derived from its overall score, calculated by summing the weighted normalized values generated across several factors of academic quality, outlined below. There are four tiers, with tier 1 medical schools as the highest-performing and tier 4 as the lowest-performing. Only tier 1 and 2 schools are shown. Because of the tier presentation, *U.S. News* calculated overall scores based on their percentile performance among all rated schools instead of dividing against the rescaled score of the No. 1-performing schools. Tier 1 included schools with overall scores of 85 to 99. The cutoffs for tiers 2 through 4 were schools scoring 50 to 84, 15 to 49 and 1 to 14, respectively. The rankings are based on a weighted average of the following measures of quality: total research activity; average research activity per faculty member; total NIH research grants at the medical school and its affiliated hospitals; average NIH research grants per faculty; median MCAT total score; median undergraduate GPA; acceptance rate; and faculty resources. *U.S. News & World Report, "America's Best Graduate Schools, Medical, 2025"*

According to *U.S. News & World Report,* the Houston-Pasadena-The Woodlands, TX metro area is home to one of the top medical schools for primary care in the U.S.: **University of Texas Health Science Center—Houston (McGovern)** (Tier 2). *U.S. News* placed medical and osteopathic schools into tiers based on their research productivity, faculty and admissions data. Each school's tier was derived from its overall score, calculated by summing the weighted normalized values generated across several factors of academic quality, outlined below. There are four tiers, with tier 1 medical schools as the highest-performing and tier 4 as the lowest-performing. Only tier 1 and 2 schools are shown. Because of the tier presentation, *U.S. News* calculated overall scores based on their percentile performance among all rated schools instead of dividing against the rescaled score of the No. 1-performing schools. Tier 1 included schools with overall scores of 85 to 99. The cutoffs for tiers 2 through 4 were schools scoring 50 to 84, 15 to 49 and 1 to 14, respectively. The rankings are based on a weighted average of the following measures of quality: graduates practicing in primary care specialties; graduates entering primary care residencies; median MCAT total score; median undergraduate GPA; acceptance rate; and faculty resources. *U.S. News & World Report, "America's Best Graduate Schools, Medical, 2025"*

According to *U.S. News & World Report,* the Houston-Pasadena-The Woodlands, TX metro area is home to one of the top 75 business schools in the U.S.: **Rice University (Jones)** (#29 tie). The rankings are based on a weighted average of the following nine measures: quality assessment; peer assessment; recruiter assessment; placement success; mean starting salary and bonus; student selectivity; mean GMAT and GRE scores; mean undergraduate GPA; and acceptance rate. *U.S. News & World Report, "America's Best Graduate Schools, Business, 2025"*

EMPLOYERS

Major Employers

Company Name	Industry
Amazon.com	Online retail
City of Houston	Local government
ConocoPhillips	Exploration and production
Enterprise Products Partners	Pipeline transportation, processing, storage
H.E.B.	Grocery stores
HCA Houston Healthcare	Healthcare
Houston Methodist	Healthcare
Kroger	Grocery stores
Memorial Herman Health Systems	Healthcare
Phillips 66	Energy
Plains All American Pipeline	Oil & gas
Sysco	Food distribution, restaurant supplies
Texas Children's Hospital	Healthcare
U.S. Dept of Veteran Affairs	Administration of veterans' affairs
United Airlines	Airline
Univ of Texas Medical Branch at Galveston	Accident & health insurance
University of Houston System	University
University of Texas System	General medical & surgical hospitals
Veterans Health Administration	Administration of veterans' affairs
Wal-Mart Stores	Retail

Note: Companies shown are located within the Houston-Pasadena-The Woodlands, TX Metropolitan Statistical Area.
Source: Chambers of Commerce; State Departments of Labor; Wikipedia

Best Companies to Work For

Camden Property Trust; David Weekley Homes; Hewlett Packard Enterprise Company; Hilcorp Energy Company, headquartered in Houston, are among "The 100 Best Companies to Work For." To pick the best companies, *Fortune* partnered with the Great Place to Work Institute. Using their proprietary Trust Index™ survey, the core of what creates great a workplace is measured—key behaviors that drive trust in management, connection with colleagues, and loyalty to the company. To be eligible for the *Fortune* 100 Best Companies to Work For list, employers must have 1,000 or more employees in the U.S. and cannot be a government agency. *Fortune, "The 100 Best Companies to Work For," 2025*

Hewlett Packard Enterprise Company, headquartered in Houston, is among "Fortune's Best Workplaces for Parents." To pick the best companies, *Fortune* partnered with the Great Place to Work Institute. To be considered for the list, companies must be Great Place To Work-Certified and have at least 50 responses from parents in the US. The survey enables employees to share confidential quantitative and qualitative feedback about their organization's culture by responding to 60 statements on a 5-point scale and answering two open-ended questions. Collectively, these statements describe a great employee experience, defined by high levels of trust, respect, credibility, fairness, pride, and camaraderie. In addition, companies provide organizational data like size, location, industry, demographics, roles, and levels; and provide information about parental leave, adoption, flexible schedule, childcare and dependent health care benefits. *Fortune, "Best Workplaces for Parents," 2024*

Camden Property Trust; David Weekley Homes; Venterra Realty, headquartered in Houston, are among "Fortune's Best Workplaces for Women." To pick the best companies, *Fortune* partnered with the Great Place to Work Institute. To be considered for the list, companies must be Great Place To Work-Certified. Companies must also employ at least 50 women, at least 20% of their non-executive managers must be female, and at least one executive must be female. To determine the Best Workplaces for Women, Great Place To Work measured the differences in women's survey responses to those of their peers and assesses the impact of demographics and roles on the quality and consistency of women's experiences. Great Place To Work also analyzed the gender balance of each workplace, how it compared to each company's industry, and patterns in representation as women rise from front-line positions to the board of directors. *Fortune, "Best Workplaces for Women," 2024*

Service Corporation International, headquartered in Houston, is among "Best Workplaces in Health Care." To determine the Best Workplaces in Health Care list, Great Place To Work analyzed the survey responses of over 185,000 employees from Great Place To Work-Certified companies in the health care industry. Survey data analysis and company-provided datapoints are then factored into a combined score to compare and rank the companies that create the most consistently positive experience for all employees in this industry. *Fortune, "Best Workplaces in Health Care," 2024*

Camden Property Trust; Hilltop Residential; The Morgan Group; Transwestern; Venterra Realty, headquartered in Houston, are among "Best Workplaces in Real Estate." To determine the Best Workplaces in Real Estate list, Great Place To Work analyzed the survey responses of over 29,000 employees from Great Place To Work-Certified companies in the real estate industry. Survey data analysis and company-provided datapoints are then factored into a combined score to compare and rank the companies that create the most consistently positive experience for all employees in this industry. *Fortune, "Best Workplaces in Real Estate," 2024*

PUBLIC SAFETY

Crime Rate

Area	Total Crime Rate	Violent Crime Rate				Property Crime Rate		
		Murder	Rape	Robbery	Aggrav. Assault	Burglary	Larceny-Theft	Motor Vehicle Theft
City	5,599.2	14.9	61.1	295.7	720.0	606.3	3,034.5	866.7
U.S.	2,290.9	5.7	38.0	66.5	264.1	250.7	1,347.2	318.7

Note: Figures are crimes per 100,000 population.
Source: FBI, Table 8, Offenses Known to Law Enforcement, by State by City, 2023

Hate Crimes

Area	Number of Quarters Reported	Number of Incidents per Bias Motivation					
		Race/Ethnicity/Ancestry	Religion	Sexual Orientation	Disability	Gender	Gender Identity
City[1]	4	12	6	15	0	0	1
U.S.	4	5,900	2,699	2,077	187	92	492

Note: (1) Figures include at least one incident reported with more than one bias motivation.
Source: Federal Bureau of Investigation, Hate Crime Statistics 2023

Identity Theft Consumer Reports

Area	Reports	Reports per 100,000 Population	Rank[2]
MSA[1]	41,668	573	3
U.S.	1,135,291	339	-

Note: (1) Figures cover the Houston-Pasadena-The Woodlands, TX Metropolitan Statistical Area; (2) Rank ranges from 1 to 401 where 1 indicates greatest number of identity theft reports per 100,000 population
Source: Federal Trade Commission, Consumer Sentinel Network Data Book 2024

Fraud and Other Consumer Reports

Area	Reports	Reports per 100,000 Population	Rank[2]
MSA[1]	136,239	1,873	18
U.S.	5,360,641	1,601	-

Note: (1) Figures cover the Houston-Pasadena-The Woodlands, TX Metropolitan Statistical Area; (2) Rank ranges from 1 to 401 where 1 indicates greatest number of fraud and other consumer reports per 100,000 population
Source: Federal Trade Commission, Consumer Sentinel Network Data Book 2024

POLITICS

2024 Presidential Election Results

Area	Trump (Rep.)	Harris (Dem.)	Stein (Green)	Kennedy (Ind.)	Oliver (Lib.)	Other
Harris County	46.4	51.9	1.0	0.0	0.6	0.1
U.S.	49.7	48.2	0.6	0.5	0.4	0.6

Note: Results are percentages and may not add to 100% due to rounding
Source: Dave Leip's Atlas of U.S. Presidential Elections

SPORTS

Professional Sports Teams

Team Name	League	Year Established
Houston Astros	Major League Baseball (MLB)	1962
Houston Dynamo	Major League Soccer (MLS)	2006
Houston Rockets	National Basketball Association (NBA)	1971
Houston Texans	National Football League (NFL)	2002

Note: Includes teams located in the Houston-Pasadena-The Woodlands, TX Metropolitan Statistical Area.
Source: Wikipedia, Major Professional Sports Teams of the United States and Canada, May 1, 2025

CLIMATE

Average and Extreme Temperatures

Temperature	Jan	Feb	Mar	Apr	May	Jun	Jul	Aug	Sep	Oct	Nov	Dec	Yr.
Extreme High (°F)	84	91	91	95	97	103	104	107	102	94	89	83	107
Average High (°F)	61	65	73	79	85	91	93	93	89	81	72	65	79
Average Temp. (°F)	51	54	62	69	75	81	83	83	79	70	61	54	69
Average Low (°F)	41	43	51	58	65	71	73	73	68	58	50	43	58
Extreme Low (°F)	12	20	22	31	44	52	62	62	48	32	19	7	7

Note: Figures cover the years 1969-1990
Source: National Climatic Data Center, International Station Meteorological Climate Summary, 9/96

Average Precipitation/Snowfall/Humidity

Precip./Humidity	Jan	Feb	Mar	Apr	May	Jun	Jul	Aug	Sep	Oct	Nov	Dec	Yr.
Avg. Precip. (in.)	3.3	2.7	3.3	3.3	5.6	4.9	3.7	3.7	4.8	4.7	3.7	3.3	46.9
Avg. Snowfall (in.)	Tr	Tr	0	0	0	0	0	0	0	0	Tr	Tr	Tr
Avg. Rel. Hum. 6am (%)	85	86	87	89	91	92	93	93	93	91	89	86	90
Avg. Rel. Hum. 3pm (%)	58	55	54	54	57	56	55	55	57	53	55	57	55

Note: Figures cover the years 1969-1990; Tr = Trace amounts (<0.05 in. of rain; <0.5 in. of snow)
Source: National Climatic Data Center, International Station Meteorological Climate Summary, 9/96

Weather Conditions

Temperature			Daytime Sky			Precipitation		
32°F & below	45°F & below	90°F & above	Clear	Partly cloudy	Cloudy	0.01 inch or more precip.	0.1 inch or more snow/ice	Thunder-storms
21	87	96	83	167	115	101	1	62

Note: Figures are average number of days per year and cover the years 1969-1990
Source: National Climatic Data Center, International Station Meteorological Climate Summary, 9/96

HAZARDOUS WASTE

Superfund Sites

The Houston-Pasadena-The Woodlands, TX metro area is home to 21 sites on the EPA's Superfund National Priorities List (NPL) or Superfund Alternative Approach (SAA) list: **Conroe Creosoting Co.** (Final NPL); **Crystal Chemical Co.** (Final NPL); **French, Ltd.** (Final NPL); **Geneva Industries/Fuhrmann Energy** (Final NPL); **Gulfco Marine Maintenance** (Final NPL); **Highlands Acid Pit** (Final NPL); **Jones Road Ground Water Plume** (Final NPL); **Malone Service Co - Swan Lake Plant** (Final NPL); **Many Diversified Interests, Inc.** (Final NPL); **Motco, Inc.** (Final NPL); **North Cavalcade Street** (Final NPL); **Patrick Bayou** (Final NPL); **Petro-Chemical Systems, Inc. (Turtle Bayou)** (Final NPL); **San Jacinto River Waste Pits** (Final NPL); **Sheridan Disposal Services** (Final NPL); **Sikes Disposal Pits** (Final NPL); **Sol Lynn/Industrial Transformers** (Final NPL); **South Cavalcade Street** (Final NPL); **Tex-tin Corp.** (Final NPL); **United Creosoting Co.** (Final NPL); **US Oil Recovery** (Final NPL). The Superfund alternative approach uses the same investigation and cleanup process and standards that are used for sites listed on the National Priorities List. The SAA is an alternative to listing a site on the NPL; it is not an alternative to Superfund or the Superfund process. There are a total of 1,445 Superfund sites with a status of proposed or final on both lists in the United States. *U.S. Environmental Protection Agency, National Priorities List, May 1, 2025; U.S. Environmental Protection Agency, Superfund Alternative Approach Sites, May 1, 2025*

AIR QUALITY

Air Quality Trends: Ozone

	1990	1995	2000	2005	2010	2015	2020	2021	2022	2023
MSA[1]	0.119	0.114	0.102	0.087	0.079	0.083	0.067	0.072	0.068	0.079
U.S.	0.087	0.089	0.081	0.080	0.072	0.068	0.066	0.067	0.067	0.070

Note: (1) Data covers the Houston-Pasadena-The Woodlands, TX Metropolitan Statistical Area. The values shown are the composite ozone concentration averages among trend sites based on the highest fourth daily maximum 8-hour concentration in parts per million. These trends are based on sites having an adequate record of monitoring data during the trend period. Data from exceptional events are included.
Source: U.S. Environmental Protection Agency, Air Quality Monitoring Information, "Air Quality Trends by City, 1990-2023"

Air Quality Index

Area	Percent of Days when Air Quality was...[2]					AQI Statistics[2]	
	Good	Moderate	Unhealthy for Sensitive Groups	Unhealthy	Very Unhealthy	Maximum	Median
MSA[1]	9.9	74.5	12.3	3.0	0.3	205	65

Note: (1) Data covers the Houston-Pasadena-The Woodlands, TX Metropolitan Statistical Area; (2) Based on 365 days with AQI data in 2023. Air Quality Index (AQI) is an index for reporting daily air quality. EPA calculates the AQI for five major air pollutants regulated by the Clean Air Act: ground-level ozone, particle pollution (aka particulate matter), carbon monoxide, sulfur dioxide, and nitrogen dioxide. The AQI runs from 0 to 500. The higher the AQI value, the greater the level of air pollution and the greater the health concern. There are six AQI categories: "Good" AQI is between 0 and 50. Air quality is considered satisfactory; "Moderate" AQI is between 51 and 100. Air quality is acceptable; "Unhealthy for Sensitive Groups" When AQI values are between 101 and 150, members of sensitive groups may experience health effects; "Unhealthy" When AQI values are between 151 and 200 everyone may begin to experience health effects; "Very Unhealthy" AQI values between 201 and 300 trigger a health alert; "Hazardous" AQI values over 300 trigger warnings of emergency conditions (not shown).
Source: U.S. Environmental Protection Agency, Air Quality Index Report, 2023

Air Quality Index Pollutants

Area	Percent of Days when AQI Pollutant was...[2]					
	Carbon Monoxide	Nitrogen Dioxide	Ozone	Sulfur Dioxide	Particulate Matter 2.5	Particulate Matter 10
MSA[1]	0.0	0.3	31.5	(3)	62.7	5.5

Note: (1) Data covers the Houston-Pasadena-The Woodlands, TX Metropolitan Statistical Area; (2) Based on 365 days with AQI data in 2023. The Air Quality Index (AQI) is an index for reporting daily air quality. EPA calculates the AQI for five major air pollutants regulated by the Clean Air Act: ground-level ozone, particle pollution (also known as particulate matter), carbon monoxide, sulfur dioxide, and nitrogen dioxide. The AQI runs from 0 to 500. The higher the AQI value, the greater the level of air pollution and the greater the health concern; (3) Sulfur dioxide is no longer included in this table because SO_2 concentrations tend to be very localized and not necessarily representative of broad geographical areas like counties and CBSAs.
Source: U.S. Environmental Protection Agency, Air Quality Index Report, 2023

Maximum Air Pollutant Concentrations: Particulate Matter, Ozone, CO and Lead

	Particulate Matter 10 (ug/m^3)	Particulate Matter 2.5 Wtd AM (ug/m^3)	Particulate Matter 2.5 24-Hr (ug/m^3)	Ozone (ppm)	Carbon Monoxide (ppm)	Lead (ug/m^3)
MSA[1] Level	161	13.1	28	0.09	2	n/a
NAAQS[2]	150	15	35	0.075	9	0.15
Met NAAQS[2]	No	Yes	Yes	No	Yes	n/a

Note: (1) Data covers the Houston-Pasadena-The Woodlands, TX Metropolitan Statistical Area; Data from exceptional events are included; (2) National Ambient Air Quality Standards; ppm = parts per million; ug/m^3 = micrograms per cubic meter; n/a not available.
Concentrations: Particulate Matter 10 (coarse particulate)—highest second maximum 24-hour concentration; Particulate Matter 2.5 Wtd AM (fine particulate)—highest weighted annual mean concentration; Particulate Matter 2.5 24-Hour (fine particulate)—highest 98th percentile 24-hour concentration; Ozone—highest fourth daily maximum 8-hour concentration; Carbon Monoxide—highest second maximum non-overlapping 8-hour concentration; Lead—maximum running 3-month average
Source: U.S. Environmental Protection Agency, Air Quality Monitoring Information, "Air Quality Statistics by City, 2023"

Maximum Air Pollutant Concentrations: Nitrogen Dioxide and Sulfur Dioxide

	Nitrogen Dioxide AM (ppb)	Nitrogen Dioxide 1-Hr (ppb)	Sulfur Dioxide AM (ppb)	Sulfur Dioxide 1-Hr (ppb)	Sulfur Dioxide 24-Hr (ppb)
MSA[1] Level	18	60	n/a	13	n/a
NAAQS[2]	53	100	30	75	140
Met NAAQS[2]	Yes	Yes	n/a	Yes	n/a

Note: (1) Data covers the Houston-Pasadena-The Woodlands, TX Metropolitan Statistical Area; Data from exceptional events are included; (2) National Ambient Air Quality Standards; ppm = parts per million; ug/m^3 = micrograms per cubic meter; n/a not available.
Concentrations: Nitrogen Dioxide AM—highest arithmetic mean concentration; Nitrogen Dioxide 1-Hr—highest 98th percentile 1-hour daily maximum concentration; Sulfur Dioxide AM—highest annual mean concentration; Sulfur Dioxide 1-Hr—highest 99th percentile 1-hour daily maximum concentration; Sulfur Dioxide 24-Hr—highest second maximum 24-hour concentration
Source: U.S. Environmental Protection Agency, Air Quality Monitoring Information, "Air Quality Statistics by City, 2023"

Huntsville, Alabama

Background

Huntsville is richly evocative of the antebellum Deep South, uniquely cosmopolitan, and one of the South's fastest growing city. It was named for John Hunt, its first white settler from Virginia and Revolutionary War Veteran, who built a cabin in 1805 on the corner of today's Bank Street and Oak Avenue. The seat of Madison County, Huntsville was originally home to Cherokee and Chickasaw Native Americans, and rich in forests and game animals.

The fertility of the valley attracted both smaller farmers and wealthy plantation investors. Leroy Pope, having donated land to the municipality, wanted to rename it Twickenham, after a London suburb home to his kin, poet Alexander Pope, but resentment against all things British, prevented it.

Huntsville was the largest town in the Alabama Territory by 1819, the year Alabama received statehood. It was the site of the state's first constitutional convention and, briefly, the capital. It quickly became a hub for processing corn, tobacco, and cotton, which became its economic mainstay. In 1852, the Memphis and Charleston Railway was completed, and planters, merchants, and shippers transformed Huntsville into a main commercial southern city.

Because many wealthy residents had remained loyal to the Union at the outset of the Civil War, the town was largely undamaged by occupying forces and, as a result, Huntsville boasts one of the largest collections of antebellum houses in the South. Walking tours of the Twickenham historic district offer the 1819 Weeden House Museum and the 1860 Huntsville Depot Museum. Restored nineteenth-century cabins and farm buildings are displayed at the mountaintop Burritt Museum and Park.

Huntsville's U.S. Space and Rocket Center, the state's largest tourist attraction, showcases space technology and houses Space Camp, opportunities for children and adults that promote science, engineering, aviation, and exploration. The Huntsville Botanical Garden features year-long floral and aquatic gardens, and the Huntsville Museum of Art features both contemporary and classical exhibits.

In 2021, the Singing River Trail project joined forces with the Tennessee RiverLine project, resulting in a 150-mile, 8-county system of hiking, biking, and on-water experience along the Tennessee River. Also in 2021 Huntsville saw the opening of a new Mazda Toyota manufacturing facility, which employs more than 4,000.

The city's modern Von Braun Center hosts national and international trade shows, local sports teams, concerts, and theater, and the city has a well-regarded symphony orchestra.

More than 25 biotechnology firms are in the city due to the Huntsville Biotech Initiative. The HudsonAlpha Institute for Biotechnology is the centerpiece of the Cummings Research Park Biotech Campus, and contributes genomics and genetics work to the Encyclopedia of DNA Elements (ENCODE). The University of Alabama in Huntsville's (UAH) doctoral program in biotechnology supports HudsonAlpha and the emerging biotechnology economy in Huntsville.

Huntsville's institutions of higher learning include a campus of the University of Alabama, Oakwood College, and Alabama A&M University in nearby Normal, Alabama.

Redstone Arsenal, home to U.S. Army Aviation and Missile Command, propelled Huntsville into a high-tech hub, and is a strategic research site for rocketry, aviation, and related programs. In 1950, German rocket scientists, most notably the famous Wernher von Braun developed rockets for the U.S. Army here. The Redstone complex developed the rocket that launched America's first satellite into space, and rockets that put astronauts into space and landed them on the moon.

Huntsville has a humid subtropical climate. It experiences hot, humid summers and generally mild winters. The city has maximum precipitation in the winter and spring, with the annual average is more than 54 inches. Droughts can occur, primarily August through October, but usually there is enough rainfall to keep soils moist and vegetation lush. Thunderstorms are most frequent during the spring. Severe storms during the spring and late fall can deliver large hail, damaging straight-line winds, and tornadoes. Huntsville lies in a region more prone to violent, long-track tornadoes than most other parts of the U.S.

Rankings

General Rankings

- *US News & World Report* conducted a survey of more than 3,500 people and analyzed the 150 largest metropolitan areas to determine what matters most when selecting the next place to live. Huntsville ranked #7 out of the top 25 as having the best combination of desirable factors. Criteria: cost of living; quality of life and education; climate; job market; desirability; and other factors. *realestate.usnews.com, "Best Places to Live in the U.S. in 2024-2025," May 21, 2024*

- In their annual survey, Livability.com looked at data for more than 2,000 mid-sized U.S. cities to assign a "Livability Score" for each. The top 100 scoring cities make up Livability's "Top 100 Best Places to Live in the U.S." in 2025. Huntsville was placed among the top 100 of the customizable list. Criteria: housing and economy; cost of living; environment; education; health care options; transportation; safety; and community amenities. *Livability.com, "Top 100 Best Places to Live in the U.S. in 2025" April 15, 2025*

Business/Finance Rankings

- The Huntsville metro area appeared on the Milken Institute "2025 Best Performing Cities" list. Rank: #4 out of 200 large metro areas (based on performance category). Criteria: job growth; wage growth; high-tech growth and impact; community resilience; housing affordability; household broadband access. *Milken Institute, "Best-Performing Cities 2025," January 14, 2025*

Education Rankings

- Personal finance website *WalletHub* analyzed the 150 largest U.S. metropolitan statistical areas to determine where the most educated Americans are putting their degrees to work. Criteria: education levels; percentage of workers with degrees; education quality and attainment gap; public school quality rankings; quality and enrollment of each metro area's universities. Huntsville was ranked #13 (#1 = most educated city). *WalletHub.com, "Most & Least Educated Cities in America, 2025" July 2, 2024*

Real Estate Rankings

- *WalletHub* compared the most populated U.S. cities to determine which had the best markets for real estate agents. Huntsville ranked #8 where demand was high and pay was the best. Criteria: sales per agent; annual median wage for real-estate agents; monthly average starting salary for real estate agents; real estate job density and competition; unemployment rate; home turnover rate; housing-market health index; and other relevant metrics. *WalletHub.com, "2021 Best Places to Be a Real Estate Agent," May 12, 2021*

- The Huntsville metro area was identified as one of the 20 worst housing markets in the U.S. in 2024. The area ranked #213 out of 226 markets. Criteria: year-over-year change of median sales price of existing single-family homes between the 4th quarter of 2023 and the 4th quarter of 2024. *National Association of Realtors®, Median Sales Price of Existing Single-Family Homes for Metropolitan Areas, 4th Quarter 2024*

- Huntsville was ranked #32 out of 176 metro areas in terms of cost of housing in 2024 by the National Association of Home Builders (#1 = most affordable). Criteria: the portion of an average family's income necessary to pay the mortgage on a median-priced home. *National Association of Home Builders®, NAHB-Wells Fargo Cost of Housing Index, 4th Quarter 2024*

Safety Rankings

- Huntsville was identified as one of the most dangerous cities in America by NeighborhoodScout. The city ranked #84 out of 100 (#1 = most dangerous). Criteria: number of violent crimes per 1,000 residents. The editors evaluated cities with 25,000 or more residents. *NeighborhoodScout.com, "2023 Top 100 Most Dangerous Cities in the U.S.," January 12, 2023*

Seniors/Retirement Rankings

- Huntsville made *Southern Living's* list of southern places—by the beach, in the mountains, or scenic city—to retire. From the incredible views and close knit communities, to the opportunities to put down new roots, and great places to eat and hike, these superb places are perfect for settling down. *Southern Living, "The Best Places to Retire in the South," March 9, 2024*

Women/Minorities Rankings

- Personal finance website *WalletHub* compared more than 180 U.S. cities across two key dimensions, "Hispanic Business-Friendliness" and "Hispanic Purchasing Power," to arrive at the most favorable conditions for Hispanic entrepreneurs. Huntsville was ranked #86 out of 182. Criteria includes: share of Hispanic-Owned Businesses; average growth of Hispanic Business revenues; Small Business-Friendliness score; affordability; and number of Hispanics with at least a bachelor's degree. *WalletHub.com, "Best Cities for Hispanic Entrepreneurs," September 4, 2024*

Business Environment

DEMOGRAPHICS

Population Growth

Area	1990 Census	2000 Census	2010 Census	2020 Census	2023 Estimate[2]	Population Growth 1990-2023 (%)
City	161,842	158,216	180,105	215,006	218,814	35.2
MSA[1]	293,047	342,376	417,593	491,723	504,712	72.2
U.S.	248,709,873	281,421,906	308,745,538	331,449,281	332,387,540	33.6

Note: (1) Figures cover the Huntsville, AL Metropolitan Statistical Area; (2) 2019-2023 5-year ACS population estimate
Source: U.S. Census Bureau, 1990 Census, 2000 Census, 2010 Census, 2020 Census, 2019-2023 American Community Survey 5-Year Estimates

Race

Area	White Alone[2] (%)	Black Alone[2] (%)	Asian Alone[2] (%)	AIAN[3] Alone[2] (%)	NHOPI[4] Alone[2] (%)	Other Race Alone[2] (%)	Two or More Races (%)
City	58.4	29.7	2.0	0.6	0.1	2.9	6.2
MSA[1]	66.6	21.8	2.4	0.7	0.1	2.2	6.2
U.S.	63.4	12.4	5.8	0.9	0.2	6.6	10.7

Note: (1) Figures cover the Huntsville, AL Metropolitan Statistical Area; (2) Alone is defined as not being in combination with one or more other races; (3) American Indian and Alaska Native; (4) Native Hawaiian and Other Pacific Islander
Source: U.S. Census Bureau, 2019-2023 American Community Survey 5-Year Estimates

Hispanic or Latino Origin

Area	Total (%)	Mexican (%)	Puerto Rican (%)	Cuban (%)	Other (%)
City	8.1	4.3	1.0	0.2	2.5
MSA[1]	6.7	3.6	0.9	0.2	1.9
U.S.	19.0	11.3	1.8	0.7	5.2

Note: Persons of Hispanic or Latino origin can be of any race; (1) Figures cover the Huntsville, AL Metropolitan Statistical Area
Source: U.S. Census Bureau, 2019-2023 American Community Survey 5-Year Estimates

Age

Area	Under Age 5	Age 5–19	Age 20–34	Age 35–44	Age 45–54	Age 55–64	Age 65–74	Age 75–84	Age 85+	Median Age
City	5.6	17.5	24.7	12.3	10.9	12.5	9.2	5.2	2.1	36.4
MSA[1]	5.6	18.9	20.4	13.1	12.5	14.0	9.2	4.7	1.5	38.8
U.S.	5.7	19.1	20.2	13.1	12.3	12.8	10.0	4.9	1.9	38.7

Note: (1) Figures cover the Huntsville, AL Metropolitan Statistical Area
Source: U.S. Census Bureau, 2019-2023 American Community Survey 5-Year Estimates

Disability by Age

Area	All Ages	Under 18 Years Old	18 to 64 Years Old	65 Years and Over
City	14.3	5.4	11.8	34.8
MSA[1]	13.5	4.5	11.5	34.9
U.S.	13.0	4.7	10.7	32.9

Note: Figures show percent of the civilian noninstitutionalized population that reported having a disability. Disability status is determined from six types of difficulty: vision, hearing, cognitive, ambulatory, self-care, and independent living. For children under 5 years old, hearing and vision difficulty are used to determine disability status. For children between the ages of 5 and 14, disability status is determined from hearing, vision, cognitive, ambulatory, and self-care difficulties. For people aged 15 years and older, they are considered to have a disability if they have difficulty with any one of the six difficulty types; Note: (1) Figures cover the Huntsville, AL Metropolitan Statistical Area
Source: U.S. Census Bureau, 2019-2023 American Community Survey 5-Year Estimates

Ancestry

Area	German	Irish	English	American	Italian	Polish	French[2]	European	Scottish
City	9.2	8.5	13.0	10.2	2.4	1.3	1.8	2.2	2.1
MSA[1]	9.4	9.3	13.8	11.4	2.3	1.2	1.5	2.2	2.1
U.S.	12.6	9.4	9.1	5.5	4.9	2.6	2.0	1.6	1.6

Note: Figures are the percentage of the total population reporting a particular ancestry. The nine most commonly reported ancestries in the U.S. are shown. Figures include multiple ancestries (e.g. if a person reported being Irish and Italian, they were included in both columns); (1) Figures cover the Huntsville, AL Metropolitan Statistical Area; (2) Excludes Basque
Source: U.S. Census Bureau, 2019-2023 American Community Survey 5-Year Estimates

Foreign-born Population

Area	Any Foreign Country	Asia	Mexico	Europe	Caribbean	Central America[2]	South America	Africa	Canada
City	6.6	1.7	1.6	0.8	0.7	0.5	0.3	0.5	0.2
MSA[1]	5.4	1.8	1.1	0.8	0.4	0.4	0.3	0.3	0.2
U.S.	13.9	4.3	3.3	1.4	1.4	1.2	1.2	0.8	0.2

Percent of Population Born in

Note: (1) Figures cover the Huntsville, AL Metropolitan Statistical Area; (2) Excludes Mexico.
Source: U.S. Census Bureau, 2019-2023 American Community Survey 5-Year Estimates

Household Size

Area	One	Two	Three	Four	Five	Six	Seven or More	Average Household Size
City	36.9	35.6	13.6	8.6	3.8	1.2	0.4	2.21
MSA[1]	29.4	36.4	15.1	12.1	4.8	1.5	0.6	2.42
U.S.	28.5	33.8	15.4	12.7	5.9	2.3	1.4	2.54

Note: (1) Figures cover the Huntsville, AL Metropolitan Statistical Area
Source: U.S. Census Bureau, 2019-2023 American Community Survey 5-Year Estimates

Household Relationships

Area	Householder	Opposite-sex Spouse	Same-sex Spouse	Opposite-sex Unmarried Partner	Same-sex Unmarried Partner	Child[2]	Grandchild	Other Relatives	Non-relatives
City	42.8	16.5	0.2	2.2	0.2	25.1	2.1	3.5	3.1
MSA[1]	40.1	19.3	0.1	1.9	0.1	27.8	2.3	3.4	2.3
U.S.	38.3	17.5	0.2	2.5	0.2	28.3	2.4	4.8	3.4

Note: Figures are percent of the total population; (1) Figures cover the Huntsville, AL Metropolitan Statistical Area; (2) Includes biological, adopted, and stepchildren of the householder
Source: U.S. Census Bureau, 2020 Census

Gender

Area	Males	Females	Males per 100 Females
City	107,036	111,778	95.8
MSA[1]	249,354	255,358	97.6
U.S.	164,545,087	167,842,453	98.0

Note: (1) Figures cover the Huntsville, AL Metropolitan Statistical Area
Source: U.S. Census Bureau, 2019-2023 American Community Survey 5-Year Estimates

Marital Status

Area	Never Married	Now Married[2]	Separated	Widowed	Divorced
City	37.9	42.7	1.9	6.0	11.6
MSA[1]	30.6	51.3	1.4	5.5	11.2
U.S.	34.1	47.9	1.7	5.6	10.7

Note: Figures are percentages and cover the population 15 years of age and older; (1) Figures cover the Huntsville, AL Metropolitan Statistical Area; (2) Excludes separated
Source: U.S. Census Bureau, 2019-2023 American Community Survey 5-Year Estimates

Religious Groups by Family

Area	Catholic	Baptist	Methodist	LDS[2]	Pentecostal	Lutheran	Islam	Adventist	Other
MSA[1]	7.5	23.6	6.6	1.4	1.2	0.4	0.8	2.7	17.5
U.S.	18.7	7.3	3.0	2.0	1.8	1.7	1.3	1.3	11.6

Note: Figures are the number of adherents as a percentage of the total population and cover the eight largest religious groups in the U.S; (1) Figures cover the Huntsville, AL Metropolitan Statistical Area; (2) Church of Jesus Christ of Latter-day Saints
Sources: 2020 U.S. Religion Census, Association of Statisticians of American Religious Bodies; The Association of Religion Data Archives (ARDA)

Religious Groups by Tradition

Area	Catholic	Evangelical Protestant	Mainline Protestant	Black Protestant	Islam	Judaism	Hinduism	Orthodox	Buddhism
MSA[1]	7.5	34.8	8.2	7.2	0.8	0.1	0.9	0.1	0.1
U.S.	18.7	16.5	5.2	2.3	1.3	0.6	0.4	0.4	0.3

Note: Figures are the number of adherents as a percentage of the total population; (1) Figures cover the Huntsville, AL Metropolitan Statistical Area
Sources: 2020 U.S. Religion Census, Association of Statisticians of American Religious Bodies; The Association of Religion Data Archives (ARDA)

ECONOMY

Real Gross Domestic Product (GDP)

Area	2017	2018	2019	2020	2021	2022	2023	Rank[3]
MSA[1]	27.5	28.6	30.2	30.7	32.6	34.1	36.1	92
U.S.[2]	17,619.1	18,160.7	18,642.5	18,238.9	19,387.6	19,896.6	20,436.3	—

Note: Figures are in billions of chained 2017 dollars; (1) Figures cover the Huntsville, AL Metropolitan Statistical Area; (2) Figures cover real GDP within metropolitan areas; (3) Rank is based on 2023 data and ranges from 1 to 384
Source: U.S. Bureau of Economic Analysis

Economic Growth

Area	2014	2015	2016	2017	2018	2019	2020	2021	2022	2023
MSA[1]	0.3	1.8	3.1	3.8	3.9	5.7	1.6	6.0	4.6	6.0
U.S.[2]	2.6	3.2	2.0	2.7	3.1	2.7	-2.2	6.3	2.6	2.7

Note: Figures are real gross domestic product growth rates and represent percent change from preceding period; (1) Figures cover the Huntsville, AL Metropolitan Statistical Area; (2) Figures are the average growth rates within metropolitan areas
Source: U.S. Bureau of Economic Analysis

Metropolitan Area Exports

Area	2018	2019	2020	2021	2022	2023	Rank[2]
MSA[1]	1,608.7	1,534.2	1,263.0	1,579.5	1,558.7	1,762.1	125
U.S.	1,664,056.1	1,645,173.7	1,431,406.6	1,753,941.4	2,062,937.4	2,019,160.5	—

Note: Figures are in millions of dollars; (1) Figures cover the Huntsville, AL Metropolitan Statistical Area; (2) Rank is based on 2023 data and ranges from 1 to 386
Source: U.S. Department of Commerce, International Trade Administration, Office of Trade and Economic Analysis, Industry and Analysis, Exports by Metropolitan Area, data extracted April 2, 2025

Building Permits

Area	Single-Family			Multi-Family			Total		
	2023	2024	Pct. Chg.	2023	2024	Pct. Chg.	2023	2024	Pct. Chg.
City	1,403	1,245	-11.3	1,197	240	-79.9	2,600	1,485	-42.9
MSA[1]	3,908	3,972	1.6	2,032	1,234	-39.3	5,940	5,206	-12.4
U.S.	920,000	981,900	6.7	591,100	496,100	-16.1	1,511,100	1,478,000	-2.2

Note: (1) Figures cover the Huntsville, AL Metropolitan Statistical Area; Figures represent new, privately-owned housing units authorized (unadjusted data)
Source: U.S. Census Bureau, Building Permits Survey (BPS), 2023, 2024

Bankruptcy Filings

Area	Business Filings			Nonbusiness Filings		
	2023	2024	% Chg.	2023	2024	% Chg.
Madison County	20	35	75.0	902	946	4.9
U.S.	18,926	23,107	22.1	434,064	494,201	13.9

Note: Business filings include Chapter 7, Chapter 9, Chapter 11, Chapter 12, Chapter 13, Chapter 15, and Section 304; Nonbusiness filings include Chapter 7, Chapter 11, and Chapter 13
Source: Administrative Office of the U.S. Courts, Business and Nonbusiness Bankruptcy, County Cases Commenced by Chapter of the Bankruptcy Code, During the 12-Month Period Ending December 31, 2023 and Business and Nonbusiness Bankruptcy, County Cases Commenced by Chapter of the Bankruptcy Code, During the 12-Month Period Ending December 31, 2024

Housing Vacancy Rates

Area	Gross Vacancy Rate[3] (%)			Year-Round Vacancy Rate[4] (%)			Rental Vacancy Rate[5] (%)			Homeowner Vacancy Rate[6] (%)		
	2022	2023	2024	2022	2023	2024	2022	2023	2024	2022	2023	2024
MSA[1]	n/a	n/a	n/a	n/a	n/a	n/a	n/a	n/a	n/a	n/a	n/a	n/a
U.S.[2]	9.1	9.0	9.1	7.5	7.5	7.6	5.7	6.5	6.8	0.8	0.8	1.0

Note: (1) Figures cover the Huntsville, AL Metropolitan Statistical Area; (2) Figures cover the 75 largest Metropolitan Statistical Areas; (3) The percentage of the total housing inventory that is vacant; (4) The percentage of the housing inventory (excluding seasonal units) that is year-round vacant; (5) The percentage of rental inventory that is vacant for rent; (6) The percentage of homeowner inventory that is vacant for sale; n/a not available
Source: U.S. Census Bureau, Housing Vacancies and Homeownership Annual Statistics: 2022, 2023, 2024

INCOME

Income

Area	Per Capita ($)	Median Household ($)	Average Household ($)
City	44,733	70,778	101,671
MSA[1]	45,250	83,529	110,607
U.S.	43,289	78,538	110,491

Note: (1) Figures cover the Huntsville, AL Metropolitan Statistical Area
Source: U.S. Census Bureau, 2019-2023 American Community Survey 5-Year Estimates

Household Income Distribution

Area	Percent of Households Earning							
	Under $15,000	$15,000 -$24,999	$25,000 -$34,999	$35,000 -$49,999	$50,000 -$74,999	$75,000 -$99,999	$100,000 -$149,999	$150,000 and up
City	9.2	8.0	8.7	11.3	15.0	12.6	15.6	19.6
MSA[1]	7.3	6.6	6.8	10.1	15.1	12.5	18.2	23.4
U.S.	8.5	6.6	6.8	10.4	15.7	12.7	17.4	21.9

Note: (1) Figures cover the Huntsville, AL Metropolitan Statistical Area
Source: U.S. Census Bureau, 2019-2023 American Community Survey 5-Year Estimates

Poverty Rate

Area	All Ages	Under 18 Years Old	18 to 64 Years Old	65 Years and Over
City	13.8	19.5	13.3	8.9
MSA[1]	10.4	13.1	9.8	9.1
U.S.	12.4	16.3	11.6	10.4

Note: Figures are percentage of people whose income during the past 12 months was below the poverty level; (1) Figures cover the Huntsville, AL Metropolitan Statistical Area
Source: U.S. Census Bureau, 2019-2023 American Community Survey 5-Year Estimates

EMPLOYMENT

Labor Force and Employment

Area	Civilian Labor Force			Workers Employed		
	Dec. 2023	Dec. 2024	% Chg.	Dec. 2023	Dec. 2024	% Chg.
City	110,121	113,202	2.8	107,585	109,886	2.1
MSA[1]	257,532	264,722	2.8	252,062	257,486	2.2
U.S.	166,661,000	167,746,000	0.7	160,754,000	161,294,000	0.3

Note: Data is not seasonally adjusted and covers workers 16 years of age and older; (1) Figures cover the Huntsville, AL Metropolitan Statistical Area
Source: Bureau of Labor Statistics, Local Area Unemployment Statistics

Unemployment Rate

Area	2024											
	Jan.	Feb.	Mar.	Apr.	May	Jun.	Jul.	Aug.	Sep.	Oct.	Nov.	Dec.
City	2.8	2.8	2.6	2.1	2.1	2.9	3.1	3.1	2.7	2.8	2.9	2.9
MSA[1]	2.6	2.7	2.4	2.0	2.0	2.7	2.9	3.0	2.6	2.7	2.8	2.7
U.S.	4.1	4.2	3.9	3.5	3.7	4.3	4.5	4.4	3.9	3.9	4.0	3.8

Note: Data is not seasonally adjusted and covers workers 16 years of age and older; (1) Figures cover the Huntsville, AL Metropolitan Statistical Area
Source: Bureau of Labor Statistics, Local Area Unemployment Statistics

Average Wages

Occupation	$/Hr.	Occupation	$/Hr.
Accountants and Auditors	41.06	Maintenance and Repair Workers	22.69
Automotive Mechanics	25.69	Marketing Managers	67.44
Bookkeepers	22.10	Network and Computer Systems Admin.	48.12
Carpenters	23.65	Nurses, Licensed Practical	25.96
Cashiers	13.43	Nurses, Registered	35.22
Computer Programmers	52.24	Nursing Assistants	16.31
Computer Systems Analysts	59.51	Office Clerks, General	16.03
Computer User Support Specialists	25.12	Physical Therapists	47.20
Construction Laborers	18.37	Physicians	140.44
Cooks, Restaurant	16.05	Plumbers, Pipefitters and Steamfitters	26.63
Customer Service Representatives	19.29	Police and Sheriff's Patrol Officers	30.79
Dentists	n/a	Postal Service Mail Carriers	27.93
Electricians	27.47	Real Estate Sales Agents	22.98
Engineers, Electrical	63.59	Retail Salespersons	16.48
Fast Food and Counter Workers	13.10	Sales Representatives, Technical/Scientific	52.53
Financial Managers	78.84	Secretaries, Exc. Legal/Medical/Executive	21.47
First-Line Supervisors of Office Workers	31.88	Security Guards	19.04
General and Operations Managers	74.54	Surgeons	n/a
Hairdressers/Cosmetologists	15.09	Teacher Assistants, Exc. Postsecondary[1]	11.76
Home Health and Personal Care Aides	13.34	Teachers, Secondary School, Exc. Sp. Ed.[1]	30.28
Janitors and Cleaners	15.09	Telemarketers	n/a
Landscaping/Groundskeeping Workers	17.69	Truck Drivers, Heavy/Tractor-Trailer	27.09
Lawyers	69.83	Truck Drivers, Light/Delivery Services	22.62
Maids and Housekeeping Cleaners	13.23	Waiters and Waitresses	12.42

Note: Wage data covers the Huntsville, AL Metropolitan Statistical Area; (1) Hourly wages were calculated from annual wage data based on a 40 hour work week
Source: Bureau of Labor Statistics, Metro Area Occupational Employment & Wage Estimates, May 2024

Employment by Industry

Sector	MSA[1] Number of Employees	MSA[1] Percent of Total	U.S. Percent of Total
Construction, Mining, and Logging	11,700	4.0	5.5
Financial Activities	9,000	3.1	5.8
Government	60,400	20.8	14.9
Information	2,800	1.0	1.9
Leisure and Hospitality	24,300	8.4	10.4
Manufacturing	36,000	12.4	8.0
Other Services	9,500	3.3	3.7
Private Education and Health Services	26,200	9.0	16.9
Professional and Business Services	68,600	23.6	14.2
Retail Trade	28,800	9.9	10.0
Transportation, Warehousing, and Utilities	6,300	2.2	4.8
Wholesale Trade	7,200	2.5	3.9

Note: Figures are non-farm employment as of December 2024. Figures are not seasonally adjusted and include workers 16 years of age and older; (1) Figures cover the Huntsville, AL Metropolitan Statistical Area
Source: Bureau of Labor Statistics, Current Employment Statistics, Employment, Hours, and Earnings

Employment by Occupation

Occupation Classification	City (%)	MSA[1] (%)	U.S. (%)
Management, Business, Science, and Arts	49.7	48.8	42.0
Natural Resources, Construction, and Maintenance	6.3	7.3	8.6
Production, Transportation, and Material Moving	11.1	12.5	13.0
Sales and Office	17.5	17.7	19.9
Service	15.5	13.6	16.5

Note: Figures cover employed civilians 16 years of age and older; (1) Figures cover the Huntsville, AL Metropolitan Statistical Area
Source: U.S. Census Bureau, 2019-2023 American Community Survey 5-Year Estimates

Occupations with Greatest Projected Employment Growth: 2022 – 2032

Occupation[1]	2022 Employment	2032 Projected Employment	Numeric Employment Change	Percent Employment Change
Cooks, Restaurant	16,350	21,910	5,560	34.0
Fast Food and Counter Workers	39,120	44,250	5,130	13.1
Stockers and Order Fillers	44,310	48,390	4,080	9.2
Industrial Machinery Mechanics	16,070	20,040	3,970	24.7
Retail Salespersons	58,920	62,440	3,520	6.0
First-Line Supervisors of Food Preparation and Serving Workers	20,720	24,200	3,480	16.8
Registered Nurses	52,030	55,370	3,340	6.4
Laborers and Freight, Stock, and Material Movers, Hand	40,700	44,010	3,310	8.1
Software Developers	16,860	20,120	3,260	19.3
Heavy and Tractor-Trailer Truck Drivers	39,300	42,470	3,170	8.1

Note: Projections cover Alabama; (1) Sorted by numeric employment change
Source: www.projectionscentral.org, State Occupational Projections, 2022–2032 Long-Term Projections

Fastest-Growing Occupations: 2022 – 2032

Occupation[1]	2022 Employment	2032 Projected Employment	Numeric Employment Change	Percent Employment Change
Nurse Practitioners	4,540	6,810	2,270	50.0
Cooks, Restaurant	16,350	21,910	5,560	34.0
Occupational Therapy Assistants	460	610	150	32.6
Physician Assistants	770	1,020	250	32.5
Statisticians	230	300	70	30.4
Medical and Health Services Managers	9,130	11,810	2,680	29.4
Physical Therapist Assistants	2,060	2,660	600	29.1
Information Security Analysts (SOC 2018)	2,720	3,460	740	27.2
Speech-Language Pathologists	2,430	3,040	610	25.1
Industrial Machinery Mechanics	16,070	20,040	3,970	24.7

Note: Projections cover Alabama; (1) Sorted by percent employment change and excludes occupations with numeric employment change less than 50
Source: www.projectionscentral.org, State Occupational Projections, 2022–2032 Long-Term Projections

CITY FINANCES

City Government Finances

Component	2022 ($000)	2022 ($ per capita)
Total Revenues	1,276,269	6,288
Total Expenditures	1,175,254	5,790
Debt Outstanding	1,080,608	5,324

Source: U.S. Census Bureau, State & Local Government Finances 2022

City Government Revenue by Source

Source	2022 ($000)	2022 ($ per capita)	2022 (%)
General Revenue			
From Federal Government	0	0	0.0
From State Government	54,812	270	4.3
From Local Governments	0	0	0.0
Taxes			
Property	76,367	376	6.0
Sales and Gross Receipts	326,383	1,608	25.6
Personal Income	0	0	0.0
Corporate Income	0	0	0.0
Motor Vehicle License	0	0	0.0
Other Taxes	36,532	180	2.9
Current Charges	76,771	378	6.0
Liquor Store	0	0	0.0
Utility	638,803	3,147	50.1

Source: U.S. Census Bureau, State & Local Government Finances 2022

City Government Expenditures by Function

Function	2022 ($000)	2022 ($ per capita)	2022 (%)
General Direct Expenditures			
Air Transportation	0	0	0.0
Corrections	0	0	0.0
Education	0	0	0.0
Employment Security Administration	0	0	0.0
Financial Administration	4,628	22	0.4
Fire Protection	39,873	196	3.4
General Public Buildings	8,286	40	0.7
Governmental Administration, Other	18,602	91	1.6
Health	2,388	11	0.2
Highways	31,836	156	2.7
Hospitals	0	0	0.0
Housing and Community Development	11,872	58	1.0
Interest on General Debt	34,137	168	2.9
Judicial and Legal	8,820	43	0.8
Libraries	6,160	30	0.5
Parking	2,728	13	0.2
Parks and Recreation	27,067	133	2.3
Police Protection	53,990	266	4.6
Public Welfare	0	0	0.0
Sewerage	36,500	179	3.1
Solid Waste Management	0	0	0.0
Veterans' Services	0	0	0.0
Liquor Store	0	0	0.0
Utility	606,682	2,989	51.6

Source: U.S. Census Bureau, State & Local Government Finances 2022

TAXES

State Corporate Income Tax Rates

State	Tax Rate (%)	Income Brackets ($)	Num. of Brackets	Financial Institution Tax Rate (%)[a]	Federal Income Tax Ded.
Alabama	6.5	Flat rate	1	6.5	Yes

Note: Tax rates for tax year 2024; (a) Rates listed are the corporate income tax rate applied to financial institutions or excise taxes based on income. Some states have other taxes based upon the value of deposits or shares.
Source: Federation of Tax Administrators, State Corporate Income Tax Rates, January 1, 2025

State Individual Income Tax Rates

State	Tax Rate (%)	Income Brackets ($)	Personal Exemptions ($)			Standard Ded. ($)	
			Single	Married	Depend.	Single	Married
Alabama	2.0 - 5.0	500 - 3,001 (b)	1,500	3,000	300 (e)	4,000	10,500 (z)

Note: Tax rates for tax year 2024; Local- and county-level taxes are not included; Federal income tax is deductible on state income tax returns; (b) For joint returns, taxes are twice the tax on half the couple's income. California brackets violate this formula at the two highest tax brackets in 2024; (e) In Alabama, the per-dependent exemption is $1,000 for taxpayers with state AGI of $50,000 or less, $500 with AGI from $50,001 to $100,000, and $300 with AGI over $100,000 - 2023; (z) Alabama standard deduction is phased out for incomes over $25,500 after 2017 (MFJ, HOH and Single); $12,750 for MFS. Rhode Island exemptions & standard deductions phased out for incomes over $274,650; Wisconsin standard deduciton phases out for income over $124,500.
Source: Federation of Tax Administrators, State Individual Income Tax Rates, January 1, 2025

Various State Sales and Excise Tax Rates

State	State Sales Tax (%)	Gasoline[1] ($/gal.)	Cigarette[2] ($/pack)	Spirits[3] ($/gal.)	Wine[4] ($/gal.)	Beer[5] ($/gal.)	Recreational Marijuana (%)
Alabama	4	0.30	0.68	22.87	1.70	0.53	Not legal

Note: All tax rates as of January 1, 2025; (1) The American Petroleum Institute has developed a methodology for determining the average tax rate on a gallon of fuel. Rates may include any of the following: excise taxes, environmental fees, storage tank fees, other fees or taxes, general sales tax, and local taxes; (2) The federal excise tax of $1.0066 per pack and local taxes are not included; (3) Rates are those applicable to off-premise sales of 40% alcohol by volume (a.b.v.) distilled spirits in 750ml containers. Local excise taxes are excluded; (4) Rates are those applicable to off-premise sales of 11% a.b.v. non-carbonated wine in 750ml containers; (5) Rates are those applicable to off-premise sales of 4.7% a.b.v. beer in 12 ounce containers.
Source: Tax Foundation, 2025 Facts & Figures: How Does Your State Compare?

State Tax Competitiveness Index

State	Overall Rank	Corporate Tax Rank	Individual Income Tax Rank	Sales Tax Rank	Property Tax Rank	Unemployment Insurance Tax Rank
Alabama	38	14	34	49	14	18

Note: The Tax Foundation's State Tax Competitiveness Index enables policymakers, taxpayers, and business leaders to gauge how their states' tax systems compare. A rank of 1 is best, 50 is worst. Rankings do not average to the total. States without a tax rank equally as 1. DC's scores and rankings do not affect other states. The report shows tax systems as of July 1, 2024 (the beginning of Fiscal Year 2025).
Source: Tax Foundation, State Tax Competitiveness Index 2025

TRANSPORTATION

Means of Transportation to Work

Area	Car/Truck/Van		Public Transportation			Bicycle	Walked	Other Means	Worked at Home
	Drove Alone	Car-pooled	Bus	Subway	Railroad				
City	77.5	6.8	0.3	0.0	0.0	0.0	1.3	1.0	13.1
MSA[1]	78.3	6.8	0.2	0.0	0.0	0.0	0.8	1.1	12.7
U.S.	70.2	8.5	1.7	1.3	0.4	0.4	2.4	1.6	13.5

Note: Figures are percentages and cover workers 16 years of age and older; (1) Figures cover the Huntsville, AL Metropolitan Statistical Area
Source: U.S. Census Bureau, 2019-2023 American Community Survey 5-Year Estimates

Travel Time to Work

Area	Less Than 10 Minutes	10 to 19 Minutes	20 to 29 Minutes	30 to 44 Minutes	45 to 59 Minutes	60 to 89 Minutes	90 Minutes or More
City	13.9	39.8	27.2	14.9	2.2	1.2	0.7
MSA[1]	10.8	30.8	28.1	22.2	4.9	1.9	1.2
U.S.	12.6	28.6	21.2	20.8	8.1	6.0	2.8

Note: Note: Figures are percentages and include workers 16 years old and over; (1) Figures cover the Huntsville, AL Metropolitan Statistical Area
Source: U.S. Census Bureau, 2019-2023 American Community Survey 5-Year Estimates

Key Congestion Measures

Measure	2000	2010	2015	2020	2022
Annual Hours of Delay, Total (000)	n/a	n/a	7,460	5,232	9,912
Annual Hours of Delay, Per Auto Commuter	n/a	n/a	23	14	26
Annual Congestion Cost, Per Auto Commuter ($)	n/a	n/a	528	333	588

Note: n/a not available
Source: Texas A&M Transportation Institute, 2023 Urban Mobility Report

Freeway Travel Time Index

Measure	1985	1990	1995	2000	2005	2010	2015	2020	2022
Urban Area Index[1]	n/a	n/a	n/a	n/a	n/a	n/a	1.11	1.06	1.14
Urban Area Rank[1,2]	n/a	n/a	n/a	n/a	n/a	n/a	n/a	n/a	n/a

Note: Freeway Travel Time Index—the ratio of travel time in the peak period to the travel time at free-flow conditions. For example, a value of 1.30 indicates a 20-minute free-flow trip takes 26 minutes in the peak (20 minutes x 1.30 = 26 minutes); (1) Covers the Huntsville AL urban area; (2) Rank is based on 101 larger urban areas (#1 = highest travel time index); n/a not available
Source: Texas A&M Transportation Institute, 2023 Urban Mobility Report

Public Transportation

Agency Name / Mode of Transportation	Vehicles Operated in Maximum Service[1]	Annual Unlinked Passenger Trips[2] (in thous.)	Annual Passenger Miles[3] (in thous.)
City of Huntsville - Public Transportation Division			
Bus (directly operated)	16	603.7	2,651.8
Demand Response (directly operated)	19	97.8	576.7

Note: (1) Number of revenue vehicles operated by the given mode and type of service to meet the annual maximum service requirement. This is the revenue vehicle count during the peak season of the year; on the week and day that maximum service is provided. Vehicles operated in maximum service (VOMS) exclude atypical days and one-time special events; (2) Number of passengers who boarded public transportation vehicles. Passengers are counted each time they board a vehicle no matter how many vehicles they use to travel from their origin to their destination. (3) Sum of the distances ridden by all passengers during the entire fiscal year.
Source: Federal Transit Administration, National Transit Database, 2023

Air Transportation

Airport Name and Code / Type of Service	Passenger Airlines[1]	Passenger Enplanements	Freight Carriers[2]	Freight (lbs)
Huntsville International (HSV)				
Domestic service (U.S. carriers only)	17	804,260	6	25,048,430
International service (U.S. carriers only)	0	0	0	0

Note: (1) Includes all U.S.-based major, minor and commuter airlines that carried at least one passenger during the year; (2) Includes all U.S.-based airlines and freight carriers that transported at least one pound of freight during the year.
Source: Bureau of Transportation Statistics, The Intermodal Transportation Database, Air Carriers: T-100 Domestic Market (U.S. carriers only), 2024; Bureau of Transportation Statistics, The Intermodal Transportation Database, Air Carriers: T-100 International Market (U.S. carriers only), 2024

BUSINESSES

Major Business Headquarters

Company Name	Industry	Rankings Fortune[1]	Rankings Forbes[2]
No companies listed	-	-	-

Note: (1) Companies that produce a 10-K are ranked 1 to 500 based on 2023 revenue; (2) All private companies with at least $2 billion in annual revenue through the end of their most current fiscal year are ranked 1 to 275; companies listed are headquartered in the city; dashes indicate no ranking
Source: Fortune, "Fortune 500," 2024; Forbes, "America's Largest Private Companies," 2024

Fastest-Growing Businesses

According to *Inc.*, Huntsville is home to one of America's 500 fastest-growing private companies: **LaunchTech** (#269). Criteria: must be an independent, privately-held, for-profit, U.S. corporation, proprietorship or partnership as of December 31, 2023; revenues must be at least $100,000 in 2020 and $2 million in 2023; must have four-year operating/sales history. *Inc.*, "America's 500 Fastest-Growing Private Companies," 2024

Living Environment

COST OF LIVING

Cost of Living Index

Composite Index	Groceries	Housing	Utilities	Transportation	Health Care	Misc. Goods/Services
90.8	100.2	72.3	88.7	96.5	92.5	100.7

Note: The Cost of Living Index measures regional differences in the cost of consumer goods and services, excluding taxes and non-consumer expenditures, for professional and managerial households in the top income quintile. It is based on more than 50,000 prices covering almost 60 different items for which prices are collected three times a year by chambers of commerce, economic development organizations or university applied economic centers in each participating urban area. The numbers shown should be read as a percentage above or below the national average of 100. For example, a value of 115.4 in the groceries column indicates that grocery prices are 15.4% higher than the national average. Small differences in the index numbers should not be interpreted as significant; Figures cover the Huntsville AL urban area.
Source: The Council for Community and Economic Research, Cost of Living Index, 2024

Grocery Prices

Area[1]	T-Bone Steak ($/pound)	Frying Chicken ($/pound)	Whole Milk ($/half gal.)	Eggs ($/dozen)	Orange Juice ($/64 oz.)	Coffee ($/11.5 oz.)
City[2]	15.52	1.41	4.54	3.35	4.41	5.49
Avg.	15.42	1.55	4.69	3.25	4.41	5.46
Min.	14.50	1.16	4.43	2.75	4.00	4.85
Max.	17.56	2.89	5.49	4.78	5.54	7.89

Note: (1) Values for the local area are compared with the average, minimum and maximum values for all 276 areas in the Cost of Living Index; (2) Figures cover the Huntsville AL urban area; **T-Bone Steak** (price per pound); **Frying Chicken** (price per pound, whole fryer); **Whole Milk** (half gallon carton); **Eggs** (price per dozen, Grade A, large); **Orange Juice** (64 oz. Tropicana or Florida Natural); **Coffee** (11.5 oz. can, vacuum-packed, Maxwell House, Hills Bros, or Folgers).
Source: The Council for Community and Economic Research, Cost of Living Index, 2024

Housing and Utility Costs

Area[1]	New Home Price ($)	Apartment Rent ($/month)	All Electric ($/month)	Part Electric ($/month)	Other Energy ($/month)	Telephone ($/month)
City[2]	361,221	1,123	172.74	-	-	189.28
Avg.	515,975	1,550	210.99	123.07	82.07	194.99
Min.	265,375	692	104.33	53.68	36.26	179.42
Max.	2,775,821	5,719	529.02	397.28	361.63	223.33

Note: (1) Values for the local area are compared with the average, minimum and maximum values for all 276 areas in the Cost of Living Index; (2) Figures cover the Huntsville AL urban area; **New Home Price** (2,400 sf living area, 8,000 sf lot, in urban area with full utilities); **Apartment Rent** (950 sf 2 bedroom/1.5 or 2 bath, unfurnished, excluding all utilities except water); **All Electric** (average monthly cost for an all-electric home); **Part Electric** (average monthly cost for a part-electric home); **Other Energy** (average monthly cost for natural gas, fuel oil, coal, wood, and any other forms of energy except electricity); **Telephone** (price includes the base monthly rate plus taxes and fees for three lines of mobile phone service).
Source: The Council for Community and Economic Research, Cost of Living Index, 2024

Health Care, Transportation, and Other Costs

Area[1]	Doctor ($/visit)	Dentist ($/visit)	Optometrist ($/visit)	Gasoline ($/gallon)	Beauty Salon ($/visit)	Men's Shirt ($)
City[2]	121.00	115.28	99.56	3.04	58.56	30.30
Avg.	143.77	117.51	129.23	3.32	48.57	38.14
Min.	36.74	58.67	67.33	2.80	24.00	13.41
Max.	270.44	216.82	307.33	5.28	94.00	63.89

Note: (1) Values for the local area are compared with the average, minimum and maximum values for all 276 areas in the Cost of Living Index; (2) Figures cover the Huntsville AL urban area; **Doctor** (general practitioners routine exam of an established patient); **Dentist** (adult teeth cleaning and periodic oral examination); **Optometrist** (full vision eye exam for established adult patient); **Gasoline** (one gallon regular unleaded, national brand, including all taxes, cash price at self-service pump if available); **Beauty Salon** (woman's shampoo, trim, and blow-dry); **Men's Shirt** (cotton/polyester dress shirt, pinpoint weave, long sleeves).
Source: The Council for Community and Economic Research, Cost of Living Index, 2024

HOUSING

Homeownership Rate

Area	2017 (%)	2018 (%)	2019 (%)	2020 (%)	2021 (%)	2022 (%)	2023 (%)	2024 (%)
MSA[1]	n/a	n/a	n/a	n/a	n/a	n/a	n/a	n/a
U.S.	63.9	64.4	64.6	66.6	65.5	65.8	65.9	65.6

Note: (1) Figures cover the Huntsville, AL Metropolitan Statistical Area; n/a not available
Source: U.S. Census Bureau, Housing Vacancies and Homeownership Annual Statistics: 2017-2024

House Price Index (HPI)

Area	National Ranking[2]	Quarterly Change (%)	One-Year Change (%)	Five-Year Change (%)	Since 1991Q1 (%)
MSA[1]	76	-1.12	6.65	66.60	239.11
U.S.[3]	–	1.43	4.51	57.13	327.82

Note: The HPI is a weighted repeat sales index. It measures average price changes in repeat sales or refinancings on the same properties. This information is obtained by reviewing repeat mortgage transactions on single-family properties whose mortgages have been purchased or securitized by Fannie Mae or Freddie Mac since January 1975; (1) Figures cover the Huntsville, AL Metropolitan Statistical Area; (2) Rankings are based on annual percentage change for all metro areas containing at least 15,000 transactions over the last 10 years and ranges from 1 to 241; (3) figures based on a weighted average of Census Division estimates using a seasonally adjusted, purchase-only index; all figures are for the period ending December 31, 2024
Source: Federal Housing Finance Agency, Change in FHFA Metropolitan Area House Price Indexes, All Transactions Index, 2024Q4

Home Value

Area	Under $100,000	$100,000 -$199,999	$200,000 -$299,999	$300,000 -$399,999	$400,000 -$499,999	$500,000 -$999,999	$1,000,000 or more	Median ($)
City	11.8	23.6	22.4	17.3	9.3	12.8	2.7	263,100
MSA[1]	10.6	22.2	26.0	17.6	10.3	11.7	1.6	265,000
U.S.	12.1	17.8	19.5	14.4	10.5	19.1	6.5	303,400

Note: Figures are percentages except for median and cover owner-occupied housing units; (1) Figures cover the Huntsville, AL Metropolitan Statistical Area
Source: U.S. Census Bureau, 2019-2023 American Community Survey 5-Year Estimates

Year Housing Structure Built

Area	2020 or Later	2010 -2019	2000 -2009	1990 -1999	1980 -1989	1970 -1979	1960 -1969	1950 -1959	1940 -1949	Before 1940	Median Year
City	2.3	15.6	12.4	10.8	14.8	11.9	20.1	7.8	1.8	2.6	1984
MSA[1]	2.9	16.7	18.5	15.2	14.9	9.8	12.7	5.5	1.4	2.3	1992
U.S.	1.2	8.9	13.6	12.8	13.0	14.4	10.0	9.7	4.5	11.9	1980

Note: Figures are percentages except for Median Year; Note: (1) Figures cover the Huntsville, AL Metropolitan Statistical Area
Source: U.S. Census Bureau, 2019-2023 American Community Survey 5-Year Estimates

Gross Monthly Rent

Area	Under $500	$500 -$999	$1,000 -$1,499	$1,500 -$1,999	$2,000 -$2,499	$2,500 -$2,999	$3,000 and up	Median ($)
City	4.8	38.7	37.7	14.0	2.9	0.5	1.3	1,078
MSA[1]	4.8	37.6	36.8	14.6	4.3	0.6	1.2	1,091
U.S.	6.5	22.3	29.5	20.2	10.8	4.8	5.9	1,348

Note: Figures are percentages except for median; Gross rent is the contract rent plus the estimated average monthly cost of utilities (electricity, gas, and water and sewer) and fuels (oil, coal, kerosene, wood, etc.) if these are paid by the renter (or paid for the renter by someone else); (1) Figures cover the Huntsville, AL Metropolitan Statistical Area
Source: U.S. Census Bureau, 2019-2023 American Community Survey 5-Year Estimates

HEALTH

Health Risk Factors

Category	MSA[1] (%)	U.S. (%)
Adults aged 18–64 who have any kind of health care coverage	n/a	90.8
Adults who reported being in good or better health	n/a	81.8
Adults who have been told they have high blood cholesterol	n/a	36.9
Adults who have been told they have high blood pressure	n/a	34.0
Adults who are current smokers	n/a	12.1
Adults who currently use e-cigarettes	n/a	7.7
Adults who currently use chewing tobacco, snuff, or snus	n/a	3.2
Adults who are heavy drinkers[2]	n/a	6.1
Adults who are binge drinkers[3]	n/a	15.2
Adults who are overweight (BMI 25.0 - 29.9)	n/a	34.4
Adults who are obese (BMI 30.0 - 99.8)	n/a	34.3
Adults who participated in any physical activities in the past month	n/a	75.8

Note: All figures are crude prevalence; (1) Figures for the Huntsville, AL Metropolitan Statistical Area were not available.
(2) Heavy drinkers are classified as adult men having more than 14 drinks per week and adult women having more than 7 drinks per week; (3) Binge drinkers are classified as males having five or more drinks on one occasion or females having four or more drinks on one occasion
Source: Centers for Disease Control and Prevention, Behaviorial Risk Factor Surveillance System, SMART: Selected Metropolitan Area Risk Trends, 2023

Acute and Chronic Health Conditions

Category	MSA[1] (%)	U.S. (%)
Adults who have ever been told they had a heart attack	n/a	4.2
Adults who have ever been told they have angina or coronary heart disease	n/a	4.0
Adults who have ever been told they had a stroke	n/a	3.3
Adults who have ever been told they have asthma	n/a	15.7
Adults who have ever been told they have arthritis	n/a	26.3
Adults who have ever been told they have diabetes[2]	n/a	11.5
Adults who have ever been told they had skin cancer	n/a	5.6
Adults who have ever been told they had any other types of cancer	n/a	8.4
Adults who have ever been told they have COPD	n/a	6.4
Adults who have ever been told they have kidney disease	n/a	3.7
Adults who have ever been told they have a form of depression	n/a	22.0

Note: All figures are crude prevalence; (1) Figures for the Huntsville, AL Metropolitan Statistical Area were not available.
(2) Figures do not include pregnancy-related, borderline, or pre-diabetes
Source: Centers for Disease Control and Prevention, Behavioral Risk Factor Surveillance System, SMART: Selected Metropolitan Area Risk Trends, 2023

Health Screening and Vaccination Rates

Category	MSA[1] (%)	U.S. (%)
Adults who have ever been tested for HIV	n/a	37.5
Adults who have had their blood cholesterol checked within the last five years	n/a	87.0
Adults aged 65+ who have had flu shot within the past year	n/a	63.4
Adults aged 65+ who have ever had a pneumonia vaccination	n/a	71.9

Note: All figures are crude prevalence; (1) Figures for the Huntsville, AL Metropolitan Statistical Area were not available.
Source: Centers for Disease Control and Prevention, Behavioral Risk Factor Surveillance System, SMART: Selected Metropolitan Area Risk Trends, 2023

Disability Status

Category	MSA[1] (%)	U.S. (%)
Adults who reported being deaf	n/a	7.4
Are you blind or have serious difficulty seeing, even when wearing glasses?	n/a	4.9
Do you have difficulty doing errands alone?	n/a	7.8
Do you have difficulty dressing or bathing?	n/a	3.6
Do you have serious difficulty concentrating/remembering/making decisions?	n/a	13.7
Do you have serious difficulty walking or climbing stairs?	n/a	13.2

Note: All figures are crude prevalence; (1) Figures for the Huntsville, AL Metropolitan Statistical Area were not available.
Source: Centers for Disease Control and Prevention, Behavioral Risk Factor Surveillance System, SMART: Selected Metropolitan Area Risk Trends, 2023

Mortality Rates for the Top 10 Causes of Death in the U.S.

ICD-10[a] Sub-Chapter	ICD-10[a] Code	Crude Mortality Rate[2] per 100,000 population	
		County[3]	U.S.
Malignant neoplasms	C00-C97	166.3	182.7
Ischaemic heart diseases	I20-I25	73.0	109.6
Provisional assignment of new diseases of uncertain etiology[1]	U00-U49	59.4	65.3
Other forms of heart disease	I30-I51	127.5	65.1
Other degenerative diseases of the nervous system	G30-G31	68.6	52.4
Other external causes of accidental injury	W00-X59	41.9	52.3
Cerebrovascular diseases	I60-I69	56.5	49.1
Chronic lower respiratory diseases	J40-J47	36.6	43.5
Hypertensive diseases	I10-I15	43.8	38.9
Organic, including symptomatic, mental disorders	F01-F09	15.4	33.9

Note: (a) ICD-10 = International Classification of Diseases 10th Revision; (1) Includes COVID-19, adverse effects to COVID-19 vaccines, SARS, and vaping-related disorders; (2) Crude mortality rates are a three-year average covering 2021-2023; (3) Figures cover Madison County.
Source: Centers for Disease Control and Prevention, National Center for Health Statistics. National Vital Statistics System, Mortality 2018-2023 on CDC WONDER Online Database

Mortality Rates for Selected Causes of Death

Cause of Death	ICD-10[a] Code	Crude Mortality Rate[1] per 100,000 population	
		County[2]	U.S.
Accidental poisoning and exposure to noxious substances	X40-X49	27.6	30.5
Alzheimer disease	G30	47.3	35.4
Assault	X85-Y09	8.7	7.3
COVID-19	U07.1	59.4	65.3
Diabetes mellitus	E10-E14	19.5	30.0
Diseases of the liver	K70-K76	25.8	20.8
Human immunodeficiency virus (HIV) disease	B20-B24	Unreliable	1.5
Influenza and pneumonia	J09-J18	11.8	13.4
Intentional self-harm	X60-X84	15.8	14.7
Malnutrition	E40-E46	14.4	6.0
Obesity and other hyperalimentation	E65-E68	Unreliable	3.1
Renal failure	N17-N19	21.1	16.4
Transport accidents	V01-V99	14.9	14.4

Note: (a) ICD-10 = International Classification of Diseases 10th Revision; (1) Crude mortality rates are a three-year average covering 2021-2023; (2) Figures cover Madison County; Data are suppressed when the data meet the criteria for confidentiality constraints; Crude mortality rates are flagged as unreliable when the rate would be calculated with a numerator of 20 or less.
Source: Centers for Disease Control and Prevention, National Center for Health Statistics. National Vital Statistics System, Mortality 2018-2023 on CDC WONDER Online Database

Health Insurance Coverage

Area	With Health Insurance	With Private Health Insurance	With Public Health Insurance	Without Health Insurance	Population Under Age 19 Without Health Insurance
City	90.6	73.2	32.5	9.4	3.2
MSA[1]	92.2	77.5	29.4	7.8	2.8
U.S.	91.4	67.3	36.3	8.6	5.4

Note: Figures are percentages that cover the civilian noninstitutionalized population; (1) Figures cover the Huntsville, AL Metropolitan Statistical Area
Source: U.S. Census Bureau, 2019-2023 American Community Survey 5-Year Estimates

Number of Medical Professionals

Area	MDs[3]	DOs[3,4]	Dentists	Podiatrists	Chiropractors	Optometrists
County[1] (number)	1,111	65	220	12	95	83
County[1] (rate[2])	275.3	16.1	53.3	2.9	23.0	20.1
U.S. (rate[2])	302.5	29.2	74.6	6.4	29.5	18.0

Note: Data as of 2023 unless noted; (1) Data covers Madison County; (2) Number of medical professionals per 100,000 population; (3) Data as of 2022 and includes all active, non-federal physicians; (4) Doctor of Osteopathic Medicine
Source: U.S. Department of Health and Human Services, Health Resources and Services Administration, Bureau of Health Professions, Area Resource File (ARF) 2023-2024

EDUCATION

Public School District Statistics

District Name	Schls	Pupils	Pupil/ Teacher Ratio	Minority Pupils[1] (%)	Total Rev. per Pupil ($)	Total Exp. per Pupil ($)
Huntsville City	45	23,649	17.1	64.4	15,959	13,040
Madison County	30	20,639	18.2	44.2	12,904	11,512

Note: Table includes school districts with 2,000 or more students; (1) Percentage of students that are not non-Hispanic white.
Source: U.S. Department of Education, National Center for Education Statistics, Common Core of Data, Local Education Agency (School District) Universe Survey: School Year 2023-2024; U.S. Department of Education, National Center for Education Statistics, Common Core of Data, School District Finance Survey (F-33): School Year 2021–22

Best High Schools

According to *U.S. News,* Huntsville is home to one of the top 500 high schools in the U.S.: **New Century Tech Demo High School** (#282). Nearly 25,000 public, magnet and charter schools were ranked based on their performance on state assessments and how well they prepare students for college. *U.S. News & World Report, "Best High Schools 2024"*

Highest Level of Education

Area	Less than H.S.	H.S. Diploma	Some College, No Deg.	Associate Degree	Bachelor's Degree	Master's Degree	Prof. School Degree	Doctorate Degree
City	8.4	17.3	20.8	7.3	26.7	14.8	2.3	2.3
MSA[1]	8.5	20.7	20.4	8.0	25.3	13.5	1.7	1.9
U.S.	10.6	26.2	19.4	8.8	21.3	9.8	2.3	1.6

Note: Figures cover persons age 25 and over; (1) Figures cover the Huntsville, AL Metropolitan Statistical Area
Source: U.S. Census Bureau, 2019-2023 American Community Survey 5-Year Estimates

Educational Attainment by Race

Area	High School Graduate or Higher (%)					Bachelor's Degree or Higher (%)				
	Total	White	Black	Asian	Hisp.[2]	Total	White	Black	Asian	Hisp.[2]
City	91.6	94.8	86.8	91.0	77.4	46.2	54.1	30.1	57.6	29.7
MSA[1]	91.5	93.3	88.5	91.9	77.4	42.4	45.2	33.2	63.5	30.7
U.S.	89.4	92.9	88.1	88.0	72.5	35.0	37.7	24.7	57.0	19.9

Note: Figures shown cover persons 25 years old and over; (1) Figures cover the Huntsville, AL Metropolitan Statistical Area; (2) People of Hispanic origin can be of any race
Source: U.S. Census Bureau, 2019-2023 American Community Survey 5-Year Estimates

School Enrollment by Grade and Control

Area	Preschool (%)		Kindergarten (%)		Grades 1 - 4 (%)		Grades 5 - 8 (%)		Grades 9 - 12 (%)	
	Public	Private	Public	Private	Public	Private	Public	Private	Public	Private
City	63.7	36.3	80.9	19.1	81.8	18.2	78.2	21.8	84.2	15.8
MSA[1]	56.0	44.0	79.7	20.3	82.9	17.1	82.3	17.7	83.1	16.9
U.S.	58.7	41.3	85.2	14.8	87.2	12.8	87.9	12.1	89.0	11.0

Note: Figures shown cover persons 3 years old and over; (1) Figures cover the Huntsville, AL Metropolitan Statistical Area
Source: U.S. Census Bureau, 2019-2023 American Community Survey 5-Year Estimates

Higher Education

Four-Year Colleges			Two-Year Colleges			Medical Schools[1]	Law Schools[2]	Voc/Tech[3]
Public	Private Non-profit	Private For-profit	Public	Private Non-profit	Private For-profit			
3	2	0	2	0	0	0	0	3

Note: Figures cover institutions located within the Huntsville, AL Metropolitan Statistical Area and include main campuses only; (1) includes schools accredited by the Liaison Committee on Medical Education and the American Osteopathic Association's Commission on Osteopathic College Accreditation; (2) includes ABA-accredited schools, schools with provisional ABA accreditation, and state accredited schools; (3) includes all schools with programs that are less than 2 years.
Source: National Center for Education Statistics, Integrated Postsecondary Education System (IPEDS), 2023-24; Wikipedia, List of Medical Schools in the United States, accessed May 2, 2025; Wikipedia, List of Law Schools in the United States, accessed May 2, 2025

EMPLOYERS

Major Employers

Company Name	Industry
Avocent Corporation	Computer peripheral equip
City of Huntsville	Municipal government
City of Huntsville	Municipal government
COLSA Corporation	Commercial research laboratory
County of Madison	County government
Dynetics	Engineering laboratory/except testing
General Dynamics C4 Systems	Defense systems equipment
Healthcare Auth - City of Huntsville	General government
Intergraph Process & Bldg Solutions	Systems software development
Qualitest Products	Drugs & drug proprietaries
Science Applications Int'l Corporation	Computer processing services/commercial research lab
Teledyne Brown Engineering	Energy research
The Boeing Company	Aircraft/guided missiles/space vehicles
U.S. Army	U.S. military
United States Department of the Army	Army

Note: Companies shown are located within the Huntsville, AL Metropolitan Statistical Area.
Source: Chambers of Commerce; State Departments of Labor; Wikipedia

PUBLIC SAFETY

Crime Rate

Area	Total Crime Rate	Violent Crime Rate				Property Crime Rate		
		Murder	Rape	Robbery	Aggrav. Assault	Burglary	Larceny-Theft	Motor Vehicle Theft
City	834.6	2.7	15.1	17.4	94.8	101.9	521.4	81.4
U.S.	2,290.9	5.7	38.0	66.5	264.1	250.7	1,347.2	318.7

Note: Figures are crimes per 100,000 population.
Source: FBI, Table 8, Offenses Known to Law Enforcement, by State by City, 2023

Hate Crimes

Area	Number of Quarters Reported	Number of Incidents per Bias Motivation					
		Race/Ethnicity/Ancestry	Religion	Sexual Orientation	Disability	Gender	Gender Identity
City[1]	4	8	4	0	0	0	5
U.S.	4	5,900	2,699	2,077	187	92	492

Note: (1) Figures include at least one incident reported with more than one bias motivation.
Source: Federal Bureau of Investigation, Hate Crime Statistics 2023

Identity Theft Consumer Reports

Area	Reports	Reports per 100,000 Population	Rank[2]
MSA[1]	1,459	289	74
U.S.	1,135,291	339	-

Note: (1) Figures cover the Huntsville, AL Metropolitan Statistical Area; (2) Rank ranges from 1 to 401 where 1 indicates greatest number of identity theft reports per 100,000 population
Source: Federal Trade Commission, Consumer Sentinel Network Data Book 2024

Fraud and Other Consumer Reports

Area	Reports	Reports per 100,000 Population	Rank[2]
MSA[1]	7,978	1,581	46
U.S.	5,360,641	1,601	-

Note: (1) Figures cover the Huntsville, AL Metropolitan Statistical Area; (2) Rank ranges from 1 to 401 where 1 indicates greatest number of fraud and other consumer reports per 100,000 population
Source: Federal Trade Commission, Consumer Sentinel Network Data Book 2024

POLITICS

2024 Presidential Election Results

Area	Trump (Rep.)	Harris (Dem.)	Stein (Green)	Kennedy (Ind.)	Oliver (Lib.)	Other
Madison County	53.4	44.4	0.3	0.8	0.5	0.6
U.S.	49.7	48.2	0.6	0.5	0.4	0.6

Note: Results are percentages and may not add to 100% due to rounding
Source: Dave Leip's Atlas of U.S. Presidential Elections

SPORTS

Professional Sports Teams

Team Name	League	Year Established

No teams are located in the metro area
Source: Wikipedia, Major Professional Sports Teams of the United States and Canada, May 1, 2025

CLIMATE

Average and Extreme Temperatures

Temperature	Jan	Feb	Mar	Apr	May	Jun	Jul	Aug	Sep	Oct	Nov	Dec	Yr.
Extreme High (°F)	76	82	88	92	96	101	104	103	101	91	84	77	104
Average High (°F)	49	54	63	73	80	87	90	89	83	73	62	52	71
Average Temp. (°F)	39	44	52	61	69	76	80	79	73	62	51	43	61
Average Low (°F)	30	33	41	49	58	65	69	68	62	50	40	33	50
Extreme Low (°F)	-11	5	6	26	36	45	53	52	37	28	15	-3	-11

Note: Figures cover the years 1958-1995
Source: National Climatic Data Center, International Station Meteorological Climate Summary, 9/96

Average Precipitation/Snowfall/Humidity

Precip./Humidity	Jan	Feb	Mar	Apr	May	Jun	Jul	Aug	Sep	Oct	Nov	Dec	Yr.
Avg. Precip. (in.)	5.0	5.0	6.6	4.8	5.1	4.3	4.6	3.5	4.1	3.3	4.7	5.7	56.8
Avg. Snowfall (in.)	2	1	1	Tr	0	0	0	0	0	Tr	Tr	1	4
Avg. Rel. Hum. 7am (%)	82	81	79	78	79	81	84	86	85	86	84	81	82
Avg. Rel. Hum. 4pm (%)	60	56	51	46	51	53	56	55	54	51	55	60	54

Note: Figures cover the years 1958-1995; Tr = Trace amounts (<0.05 in. of rain; <0.5 in. of snow)
Source: National Climatic Data Center, International Station Meteorological Climate Summary, 9/96

Weather Conditions

Temperature			Daytime Sky			Precipitation		
10°F & below	32°F & below	90°F & above	Clear	Partly cloudy	Cloudy	0.01 inch or more precip.	0.1 inch or more snow/ice	Thunderstorms
2	66	49	70	118	177	116	2	54

Note: Figures are average number of days per year and cover the years 1958-1995
Source: National Climatic Data Center, International Station Meteorological Climate Summary, 9/96

HAZARDOUS WASTE

Superfund Sites

The Huntsville, AL metro area is home to one site on the EPA's Superfund National Priorities List (NPL) or Superfund Alternative Approach (SAA) list: **USARMY/NASA Redstone Arsenal** (Final NPL). The Superfund alternative approach uses the same investigation and cleanup process and standards that are used for sites listed on the National Priorities List. The SAA is an alternative to listing a site on the NPL; it is not an alternative to Superfund or the Superfund process. There are a total of 1,445 Superfund sites with a status of proposed or final on both lists in the United States. *U.S. Environmental Protection Agency, National Priorities List, May 1, 2025; U.S. Environmental Protection Agency, Superfund Alternative Approach Sites, May 1, 2025*

AIR QUALITY

Air Quality Trends: Ozone

	1990	1995	2000	2005	2010	2015	2020	2021	2022	2023
MSA[1]	0.079	0.080	0.088	0.075	0.071	0.063	0.057	0.061	0.065	0.064
U.S.	0.087	0.089	0.081	0.080	0.072	0.068	0.066	0.067	0.067	0.070

Note: (1) Data covers the Huntsville, AL Metropolitan Statistical Area. The values shown are the composite ozone concentration averages among trend sites based on the highest fourth daily maximum 8-hour concentration in parts per million. These trends are based on sites having an adequate record of monitoring data during the trend period. Data from exceptional events are included.
Source: U.S. Environmental Protection Agency, Air Quality Monitoring Information, "Air Quality Trends by City, 1990-2023"

Air Quality Index

Area	Percent of Days when Air Quality was...[2]					AQI Statistics[2]	
	Good	Moderate	Unhealthy for Sensitive Groups	Unhealthy	Very Unhealthy	Maximum	Median
MSA[1]	56.0	43.1	0.8	0.0	0.0	135	49

Note: (1) Data covers the Huntsville, AL Metropolitan Statistical Area; (2) Based on 364 days with AQI data in 2023. Air Quality Index (AQI) is an index for reporting daily air quality. EPA calculates the AQI for five major air pollutants regulated by the Clean Air Act: ground-level ozone, particle pollution (aka particulate matter), carbon monoxide, sulfur dioxide, and nitrogen dioxide. The AQI runs from 0 to 500. The higher the AQI value, the greater the level of air pollution and the greater the health concern. There are six AQI categories: "Good" AQI is between 0 and 50. Air quality is considered satisfactory; "Moderate" AQI is between 51 and 100. Air quality is acceptable; "Unhealthy for Sensitive Groups" When AQI values are between 101 and 150, members of sensitive groups may experience health effects; "Unhealthy" When AQI values are between 151 and 200 everyone may begin to experience health effects; "Very Unhealthy" AQI values between 201 and 300 trigger a health alert; "Hazardous" AQI values over 300 trigger warnings of emergency conditions (not shown).
Source: U.S. Environmental Protection Agency, Air Quality Index Report, 2023

Air Quality Index Pollutants

Area	Percent of Days when AQI Pollutant was...[2]					
	Carbon Monoxide	Nitrogen Dioxide	Ozone	Sulfur Dioxide	Particulate Matter 2.5	Particulate Matter 10
MSA[1]	0.0	0.0	25.3	(3)	74.7	0.0

Note: (1) Data covers the Huntsville, AL Metropolitan Statistical Area; (2) Based on 364 days with AQI data in 2023. The Air Quality Index (AQI) is an index for reporting daily air quality. EPA calculates the AQI for five major air pollutants regulated by the Clean Air Act: ground-level ozone, particle pollution (also known as particulate matter), carbon monoxide, sulfur dioxide, and nitrogen dioxide. The AQI runs from 0 to 500. The higher the AQI value, the greater the level of air pollution and the greater the health concern; (3) Sulfur dioxide is no longer included in this table because SO_2 concentrations tend to be very localized and not necessarily representative of broad geographical areas like counties and CBSAs.
Source: U.S. Environmental Protection Agency, Air Quality Index Report, 2023

Maximum Air Pollutant Concentrations: Particulate Matter, Ozone, CO and Lead

	Particulate Matter 10 (ug/m^3)	Particulate Matter 2.5 Wtd AM (ug/m^3)	Particulate Matter 2.5 24-Hr (ug/m^3)	Ozone (ppm)	Carbon Monoxide (ppm)	Lead (ug/m^3)
MSA[1] Level	61	8.6	21	0.067	n/a	n/a
NAAQS[2]	150	15	35	0.075	9	0.15
Met NAAQS[2]	Yes	Yes	Yes	Yes	n/a	n/a

Note: (1) Data covers the Huntsville, AL Metropolitan Statistical Area; Data from exceptional events are included; (2) National Ambient Air Quality Standards; ppm = parts per million; ug/m^3 = micrograms per cubic meter; n/a not available.
Concentrations: Particulate Matter 10 (coarse particulate)—highest second maximum 24-hour concentration; Particulate Matter 2.5 Wtd AM (fine particulate)—highest weighted annual mean concentration; Particulate Matter 2.5 24-Hour (fine particulate)—highest 98th percentile 24-hour concentration; Ozone—highest fourth daily maximum 8-hour concentration; Carbon Monoxide—highest second maximum non-overlapping 8-hour concentration; Lead—maximum running 3-month average
Source: U.S. Environmental Protection Agency, Air Quality Monitoring Information, "Air Quality Statistics by City, 2023"

Maximum Air Pollutant Concentrations: Nitrogen Dioxide and Sulfur Dioxide

	Nitrogen Dioxide AM (ppb)	Nitrogen Dioxide 1-Hr (ppb)	Sulfur Dioxide AM (ppb)	Sulfur Dioxide 1-Hr (ppb)	Sulfur Dioxide 24-Hr (ppb)
MSA[1] Level	n/a	n/a	n/a	n/a	n/a
NAAQS[2]	53	100	30	75	140
Met NAAQS[2]	n/a	n/a	n/a	n/a	n/a

Note: (1) Data covers the Huntsville, AL Metropolitan Statistical Area; Data from exceptional events are included; (2) National Ambient Air Quality Standards; ppm = parts per million; ug/m^3 = micrograms per cubic meter; n/a not available.
Concentrations: Nitrogen Dioxide AM—highest arithmetic mean concentration; Nitrogen Dioxide 1-Hr—highest 98th percentile 1-hour daily maximum concentration; Sulfur Dioxide AM—highest annual mean concentration; Sulfur Dioxide 1-Hr—highest 99th percentile 1-hour daily maximum concentration; Sulfur Dioxide 24-Hr—highest second maximum 24-hour concentration
Source: U.S. Environmental Protection Agency, Air Quality Monitoring Information, "Air Quality Statistics by City, 2023"

Jacksonville, Florida

Background

Today's Jacksonville is largely a product of the reconstruction that occurred during the 1940s after a fire razed 147 city blocks a few decades earlier. Lying under the modern structures, however, is a history that dates back earlier than the settlement of Plymouth by the Pilgrims.

Located in the northeast part of Florida on the St. John's River, Jacksonville, the largest city in land area in the contiguous United States, was settled by English, Spanish, and French explorers from the sixteenth through the eighteenth centuries. Sites commemorating their presence include Fort Caroline National Monument, marking the French settlement led by Rene Goulaine de Laudonniere in 1564; Spanish Pond one-quarter of a mile east of Fort Caroline, where Spanish forces led by Pedro Menendez captured the Fort; and Fort George Island, from which General James Oglethorpe led English attacks against the Spanish during the eighteenth century.

Jacksonville was attractive to these early settlers because of its easy access to the Atlantic Ocean, a favorable port. Today, Jacksonville remains a military and civilian deep-water port. The city is home to Naval Station Mayport, Naval Air Station Jacksonville, the U.S. Marine Corps Bount Island command, and the Port of Jacksonville, Florida's third largest seaport. Jacksonville's military bases and the nearby Naval Submarine Base Kings Bay form the third largest military presence in the United States.

Jacksonville is the financial hub of Florida, and many business and financial companies are headquartered in the city. As with much of Florida, tourism is important to Jacksonville, particularly tourism related to golf.

Jacksonville voters approved The Better Jacksonville Plan in 2000, which authorized a half-penny sales tax to generate revenue for major improvement city projects, environmental protection and economic development. Improvements to the city's highway system are designed to reduce congestion, and will continue through 2030.

On the cultural front, Jacksonville boasts a range of options, including the Children's Museum, the Jacksonville Symphony Orchestra, the Gator Bowl, and the beach. The Jacksonville Jazz Festival, held every April, is the second-largest jazz festival in the nation. The city is home to several theaters, including Little Theatre, which, operating since 1919, is one of the oldest operating community theaters in the nation.

The city also boasts the largest urban park system in the United States, providing services at more than 337 locations on more than 80,000 acres located throughout the city. The Timucuan Preserve is a U.S. National Preserve comprising over 46,000 acres of wetlands and waterways. It includes natural and historic areas such as the Fort Caroline National Memorial and the Kingsley Plantation, the oldest standing plantation in the state.

Summers are long, warm, and relatively humid. Winters are generally mild, although cold northern air can bring the temperature down. Temperatures along the beaches rarely rise above 90 degrees. Summer coastal thunderstorms usually occur before noon and move inland in the afternoons. The greatest rainfall, as localized thundershowers, occurs during the summer months. Although in the hurricane belt, this section of the coast has escaped hurricane-force winds in recent history until 2016, when Hurricane Matthew caused major flooding and damage to the city, Jacksonville Beach, Atlantic Beach, and Neptune Beach. In September 2017, Hurricane Irma caused record breaking floods in Jacksonville.

Rankings

General Rankings

- To help military veterans find the best places in which to settle down, *WalletHub* compared the 100 largest U.S. cities across 19 key indicators of livability, affordability and veteran-friendliness. They range from the share of military skill-related jobs to veteran income growth to the availability of VA health facilities. Jacksonville ranked #10. *Wallethub.com, "Best & Worst Places for Veterans to Live (2025)," November 7, 2024*

Business/Finance Rankings

- The Jacksonville metro area appeared on the Milken Institute "2025 Best Performing Cities" list. Rank: #22 out of 200 large metro areas (based on performance category). Criteria: job growth; wage growth; high-tech growth and impact; community resilience; housing affordability; household broadband access. *Milken Institute, "Best-Performing Cities 2025," January 14, 2025*

Education Rankings

- Personal finance website *WalletHub* analyzed the 150 largest U.S. metropolitan statistical areas to determine where the most educated Americans are putting their degrees to work. Criteria: education levels; percentage of workers with degrees; education quality and attainment gap; public school quality rankings; quality and enrollment of each metro area's universities. Jacksonville was ranked #76 (#1 = most educated city). *WalletHub.com, "Most & Least Educated Cities in America, 2025" July 2, 2024*

Environmental Rankings

- The U.S. Environmental Protection Agency (EPA) released its list of mid-size U.S. metropolitan areas with the most ENERGY STAR certified buildings in 2023. The Jacksonville metro area was ranked #4 out of 10. *U.S. Environmental Protection Agency, "2024 Energy Star Top Cities," May 22, 2024*

Health/Fitness Rankings

- For each of the 100 largest cities in the United States, the American Fitness Index®, compiled in partnership between the American College of Sports Medicine and the Elevance Health Foundation, evaluated community infrastructure and more than 30 health behaviors including preventive health, levels of chronic disease conditions, food insecurity, pedestrian safety, air quality, and community/environment resources that support physical activity. Jacksonville ranked #68 for "community fitness." *americanfitnessindex.org, "2024 ACSM American Fitness Index Summary Report," July 23, 2024*

- Jacksonville was identified as a "2025 Allergy Capital." The area ranked #20 out of the nation's 100 largest metropolitan areas. Three groups of factors were used to identify the most challenging cities for people with allergies: annual tree, grass, and weed pollen scores; over the counter allergy medicine use; number of board-certified allergy specialists. *Asthma and Allergy Foundation of America, "2025 Allergy Capitals: The Most Challenging Places to Live with Allergies," March 18, 2025*

- Jacksonville was identified as a "2024 Asthma Capital." The area ranked #42 out of the nation's 100 largest metropolitan areas. Criteria: estimated asthma prevalence; asthma-related mortality; and ER visits due to asthma. Risk factors analyzed but not factored in the rankings: annual air quality including pollution and ozone levels; public smoking laws; indoor air quality; access to asthma specialists; rescue and controller medication use; uninsured rate; pollen allergy; poverty rate. *Asthma and Allergy Foundation of America, "Asthma Capitals 2024: The Most Challenging Places to Live With Asthma," September 10, 2024*

Pet Rankings

- Jacksonville was selected by *Sniffspot.com* as one of the most dog-friendly cities in the U.S., ranking #27 out of 50. Criteria: dog parks; hiking; sniffspots; public parks; dog-friendly businesses; housing; dog waste cleanliness; leash laws; dog services; and overall cost. *Sniffspot.com, "The Top 50 Most Dog-Friendly Cities in the U.S.," September 30, 2024*

Real Estate Rankings

- *WalletHub* compared the most populated U.S. cities to determine which had the best markets for real estate agents. Jacksonville ranked #21 where demand was high and pay was the best. Criteria: sales per agent; annual median wage for real-estate agents; monthly average starting salary for real estate agents; real estate job density and competition; unemployment rate; home turnover rate; housing-market health index; and other relevant metrics. *WalletHub.com, "2021 Best Places to Be a Real Estate Agent," May 12, 2021*

- According to Penske Truck Rental, the Jacksonville metro area was named the #10 moving destination in 2023, based on one-way consumer truck rental reservations made through Penske's website, rental locations, and reservations call center. *gopenske.com, "Penske Truck Rental's 2023 Top Moving Destinations," May 7, 2024*
- The Jacksonville metro area was identified as one of the top 16 housing markets to invest in for 2025 by *Forbes*. Criteria: stable local economies with good population growth and increase in jobs providing good support for home prices and rents. *Forbes.com, "Best Local Markets For Real Estate Investing In 2025," November 6, 2024*
- Jacksonville was ranked #119 out of 176 metro areas in terms of cost of housing in 2024 by the National Association of Home Builders (#1 = most affordable). Criteria: the portion of an average family's income necessary to pay the mortgage on a median-priced home. *National Association of Home Builders®, NAHB-Wells Fargo Cost of Housing Index, 4th Quarter 2024*

Safety Rankings

- Allstate ranked the 100 most populous cities in America in terms of driver safety. Jacksonville ranked #20. Criteria based on anonymized driving behavior data from Allstate's mobile app powered by Arity: high speed driving (over 80 mph), phone handling, and hard braking. The report helps increase the importance of safety and awareness behind the wheel. *Allstate, "16th Allstate America's Best Drivers Report®" July 11, 2024*

Women/Minorities Rankings

- Personal finance website *WalletHub* compared more than 180 U.S. cities across two key dimensions, "Hispanic Business-Friendliness" and "Hispanic Purchasing Power," to arrive at the most favorable conditions for Hispanic entrepreneurs. Jacksonville was ranked #19 out of 182. Criteria includes: share of Hispanic-Owned Businesses; average growth of Hispanic Business revenues; Small Business-Friendliness score; affordability; and number of Hispanics with at least a bachelor's degree. *WalletHub.com, "Best Cities for Hispanic Entrepreneurs," September 4, 2024*

Miscellaneous Rankings

- *WalletHub* compared 148 of the most populated U.S. cities to determine their operating efficiency. A "Quality of Services" score was constructed for each city and then measured against the total budget per capita to reveal which were managed the best. Jacksonville ranked #42. Criteria: financial stability; economy; education; safety; health; infrastructure and pollution. *WalletHub.com, "2025's Best- & Worst-Run Cities in America," June 18, 2024*

Business Environment

DEMOGRAPHICS

Population Growth

Area	1990 Census	2000 Census	2010 Census	2020 Census	2023 Estimate[2]	Population Growth 1990-2023 (%)
City	635,221	735,617	821,784	949,611	961,739	51.4
MSA[1]	925,213	1,122,750	1,345,596	1,605,848	1,645,707	77.9
U.S.	248,709,873	281,421,906	308,745,538	331,449,281	332,387,540	33.6

Note: (1) Figures cover the Jacksonville, FL Metropolitan Statistical Area; (2) 2019-2023 5-year ACS population estimate
Source: U.S. Census Bureau, 1990 Census, 2000 Census, 2010 Census, 2020 Census, 2019-2023 American Community Survey 5-Year Estimates

Race

Area	White Alone[2] (%)	Black Alone[2] (%)	Asian Alone[2] (%)	AIAN[3] Alone[2] (%)	NHOPI[4] Alone[2] (%)	Other Race Alone[2] (%)	Two or More Races (%)
City	51.2	30.1	4.9	0.2	0.1	3.9	9.6
MSA[1]	62.8	20.7	4.0	0.2	0.1	3.2	9.0
U.S.	63.4	12.4	5.8	0.9	0.2	6.6	10.7

Note: (1) Figures cover the Jacksonville, FL Metropolitan Statistical Area; (2) Alone is defined as not being in combination with one or more other races; (3) American Indian and Alaska Native; (4) Native Hawaiian and Other Pacific Islander
Source: U.S. Census Bureau, 2019-2023 American Community Survey 5-Year Estimates

Hispanic or Latino Origin

Area	Total (%)	Mexican (%)	Puerto Rican (%)	Cuban (%)	Other (%)
City	12.0	2.0	3.9	1.8	4.3
MSA[1]	10.6	1.8	3.3	1.5	4.0
U.S.	19.0	11.3	1.8	0.7	5.2

Note: Persons of Hispanic or Latino origin can be of any race; (1) Figures cover the Jacksonville, FL Metropolitan Statistical Area
Source: U.S. Census Bureau, 2019-2023 American Community Survey 5-Year Estimates

Age

Area	Percent of Population									Median Age
	Under Age 5	Age 5–19	Age 20–34	Age 35–44	Age 45–54	Age 55–64	Age 65–74	Age 75–84	Age 85+	
City	6.5	18.7	22.6	13.4	11.8	12.5	9.0	4.1	1.6	36.4
MSA[1]	5.8	18.7	19.8	13.3	12.4	13.2	10.2	4.8	1.7	39.1
U.S.	5.7	19.1	20.2	13.1	12.3	12.8	10.0	4.9	1.9	38.7

Note: (1) Figures cover the Jacksonville, FL Metropolitan Statistical Area
Source: U.S. Census Bureau, 2019-2023 American Community Survey 5-Year Estimates

Disability by Age

Area	All Ages	Under 18 Years Old	18 to 64 Years Old	65 Years and Over
City	13.5	5.0	11.8	34.1
MSA[1]	13.1	4.8	11.1	31.8
U.S.	13.0	4.7	10.7	32.9

Note: Figures show percent of the civilian noninstitutionalized population that reported having a disability. Disability status is determined from six types of difficulty: vision, hearing, cognitive, ambulatory, self-care, and independent living. For children under 5 years old, hearing and vision difficulty are used to determine disability status. For children between the ages of 5 and 14, disability status is determined from hearing, vision, cognitive, ambulatory, and self-care difficulties. For people aged 15 years and older, they are considered to have a disability if they have difficulty with any one of the six difficulty types; Note: (1) Figures cover the Jacksonville, FL Metropolitan Statistical Area
Source: U.S. Census Bureau, 2019-2023 American Community Survey 5-Year Estimates

Ancestry

Area	German	Irish	English	American	Italian	Polish	French[2]	European	Scottish
City	7.8	7.7	7.6	6.3	3.6	1.4	1.4	2.2	1.6
MSA[1]	9.6	9.6	10.2	7.5	4.5	1.8	1.8	2.1	2.0
U.S.	12.6	9.4	9.1	5.5	4.9	2.6	2.0	1.6	1.6

Note: Figures are the percentage of the total population reporting a particular ancestry. The nine most commonly reported ancestries in the U.S. are shown. Figures include multiple ancestries (e.g. if a person reported being Irish and Italian, they were included in both columns); (1) Figures cover the Jacksonville, FL Metropolitan Statistical Area; (2) Excludes Basque
Source: U.S. Census Bureau, 2019-2023 American Community Survey 5-Year Estimates

Foreign-born Population

Area	Any Foreign Country	Asia	Mexico	Europe	Caribbean	Central America[2]	South America	Africa	Canada
City	12.2	4.1	0.5	1.7	2.5	0.8	1.7	0.8	0.1
MSA[1]	10.0	3.2	0.5	1.7	1.8	0.6	1.4	0.5	0.2
U.S.	13.9	4.3	3.3	1.4	1.4	1.2	1.2	0.8	0.2

Note: (1) Figures cover the Jacksonville, FL Metropolitan Statistical Area; (2) Excludes Mexico.
Source: U.S. Census Bureau, 2019-2023 American Community Survey 5-Year Estimates

Household Size

Area	One	Two	Three	Four	Five	Six	Seven or More	Average Household Size
City	32.2	33.3	16.2	10.6	5.0	1.8	0.9	2.44
MSA[1]	27.8	35.6	16.4	11.8	5.5	1.9	1.0	2.51
U.S.	28.5	33.8	15.4	12.7	5.9	2.3	1.4	2.54

Note: (1) Figures cover the Jacksonville, FL Metropolitan Statistical Area
Source: U.S. Census Bureau, 2019-2023 American Community Survey 5-Year Estimates

Household Relationships

Area	Householder	Opposite-sex Spouse	Same-sex Spouse	Opposite-sex Unmarried Partner	Same-sex Unmarried Partner	Child[2]	Grandchild	Other Relatives	Non-relatives
City	39.9	15.6	0.2	2.8	0.2	27.7	2.8	4.9	3.6
MSA[1]	39.1	17.9	0.2	2.6	0.2	28.0	2.6	4.3	3.2
U.S.	38.3	17.5	0.2	2.5	0.2	28.3	2.4	4.8	3.4

Note: Figures are percent of the total population; (1) Figures cover the Jacksonville, FL Metropolitan Statistical Area; (2) Includes biological, adopted, and stepchildren of the householder
Source: U.S. Census Bureau, 2020 Census

Gender

Area	Males	Females	Males per 100 Females
City	466,421	495,318	94.2
MSA[1]	804,019	841,688	95.5
U.S.	164,545,087	167,842,453	98.0

Note: (1) Figures cover the Jacksonville, FL Metropolitan Statistical Area
Source: U.S. Census Bureau, 2019-2023 American Community Survey 5-Year Estimates

Marital Status

Area	Never Married	Now Married[2]	Separated	Widowed	Divorced
City	36.2	42.5	2.1	5.5	13.6
MSA[1]	31.4	48.4	1.8	5.6	12.7
U.S.	34.1	47.9	1.7	5.6	10.7

Note: Figures are percentages and cover the population 15 years of age and older; (1) Figures cover the Jacksonville, FL Metropolitan Statistical Area; (2) Excludes separated
Source: U.S. Census Bureau, 2019-2023 American Community Survey 5-Year Estimates

Religious Groups by Family

Area	Catholic	Baptist	Methodist	LDS[2]	Pentecostal	Lutheran	Islam	Adventist	Other
MSA[1]	13.0	14.5	3.0	1.0	1.4	0.4	0.6	1.3	20.5
U.S.	18.7	7.3	3.0	2.0	1.8	1.7	1.3	1.3	11.6

Note: Figures are the number of adherents as a percentage of the total population and cover the eight largest religious groups in the U.S; (1) Figures cover the Jacksonville, FL Metropolitan Statistical Area; (2) Church of Jesus Christ of Latter-day Saints
Sources: 2020 U.S. Religion Census, Association of Statisticians of American Religious Bodies; The Association of Religion Data Archives (ARDA)

Religious Groups by Tradition

Area	Catholic	Evangelical Protestant	Mainline Protestant	Black Protestant	Islam	Judaism	Hinduism	Orthodox	Buddhism
MSA[1]	13.0	29.8	3.5	5.6	0.6	0.3	0.3	0.3	0.2
U.S.	18.7	16.5	5.2	2.3	1.3	0.6	0.4	0.4	0.3

Note: Figures are the number of adherents as a percentage of the total population; (1) Figures cover the Jacksonville, FL Metropolitan Statistical Area
Sources: 2020 U.S. Religion Census, Association of Statisticians of American Religious Bodies; The Association of Religion Data Archives (ARDA)

ECONOMY

Real Gross Domestic Product (GDP)

Area	2017	2018	2019	2020	2021	2022	2023	Rank[3]
MSA[1]	80.3	83.0	86.5	87.7	94.4	100.4	104.7	40
U.S.[2]	17,619.1	18,160.7	18,642.5	18,238.9	19,387.6	19,896.6	20,436.3	—

Note: Figures are in billions of chained 2017 dollars; (1) Figures cover the Jacksonville, FL Metropolitan Statistical Area; (2) Figures cover real GDP within metropolitan areas; (3) Rank is based on 2023 data and ranges from 1 to 384
Source: U.S. Bureau of Economic Analysis

Economic Growth

Area	2014	2015	2016	2017	2018	2019	2020	2021	2022	2023
MSA[1]	2.4	4.2	3.8	4.5	3.3	4.3	1.3	7.7	6.3	4.3
U.S.[2]	2.6	3.2	2.0	2.7	3.1	2.7	-2.2	6.3	2.6	2.7

Note: Figures are real gross domestic product growth rates and represent percent change from preceding period; (1) Figures cover the Jacksonville, FL Metropolitan Statistical Area; (2) Figures are the average growth rates within metropolitan areas
Source: U.S. Bureau of Economic Analysis

Metropolitan Area Exports

Area	2018	2019	2020	2021	2022	2023	Rank[2]
MSA[1]	2,406.7	2,975.5	2,473.3	2,683.7	3,007.8	2,730.8	92
U.S.	1,664,056.1	1,645,173.7	1,431,406.6	1,753,941.4	2,062,937.4	2,019,160.5	—

Note: Figures are in millions of dollars; (1) Figures cover the Jacksonville, FL Metropolitan Statistical Area; (2) Rank is based on 2023 data and ranges from 1 to 386
Source: U.S. Department of Commerce, International Trade Administration, Office of Trade and Economic Analysis, Industry and Analysis, Exports by Metropolitan Area, data extracted April 2, 2025

Building Permits

Area	Single-Family			Multi-Family			Total		
	2023	2024	Pct. Chg.	2023	2024	Pct. Chg.	2023	2024	Pct. Chg.
City	4,223	5,037	19.3	5,485	1,361	-75.2	9,708	6,398	-34.1
MSA[1]	12,479	12,936	3.7	7,847	2,066	-73.7	20,326	15,002	-26.2
U.S.	920,000	981,900	6.7	591,100	496,100	-16.1	1,511,100	1,478,000	-2.2

Note: (1) Figures cover the Jacksonville, FL Metropolitan Statistical Area; Figures represent new, privately-owned housing units authorized (unadjusted data)
Source: U.S. Census Bureau, Building Permits Survey (BPS), 2023, 2024

Bankruptcy Filings

Area	Business Filings			Nonbusiness Filings		
	2023	2024	% Chg.	2023	2024	% Chg.
Duval County	73	83	13.7	1,514	1,784	17.8
U.S.	18,926	23,107	22.1	434,064	494,201	13.9

Note: Business filings include Chapter 7, Chapter 9, Chapter 11, Chapter 12, Chapter 13, Chapter 15, and Section 304; Nonbusiness filings include Chapter 7, Chapter 11, and Chapter 13
Source: Administrative Office of the U.S. Courts, Business and Nonbusiness Bankruptcy, County Cases Commenced by Chapter of the Bankruptcy Code, During the 12-Month Period Ending December 31, 2023 and Business and Nonbusiness Bankruptcy, County Cases Commenced by Chapter of the Bankruptcy Code, During the 12-Month Period Ending December 31, 2024

Housing Vacancy Rates

Area	Gross Vacancy Rate[3] (%)			Year-Round Vacancy Rate[4] (%)			Rental Vacancy Rate[5] (%)			Homeowner Vacancy Rate[6] (%)		
	2022	2023	2024	2022	2023	2024	2022	2023	2024	2022	2023	2024
MSA[1]	8.9	8.6	9.2	7.7	7.8	8.5	6.2	9.4	8.8	1.7	0.7	1.0
U.S.[2]	9.1	9.0	9.1	7.5	7.5	7.6	5.7	6.5	6.8	0.8	0.8	1.0

Note: (1) Figures cover the Jacksonville, FL Metropolitan Statistical Area; (2) Figures cover the 75 largest Metropolitan Statistical Areas; (3) The percentage of the total housing inventory that is vacant; (4) The percentage of the housing inventory (excluding seasonal units) that is year-round vacant; (5) The percentage of rental inventory that is vacant for rent; (6) The percentage of homeowner inventory that is vacant for sale
Source: U.S. Census Bureau, Housing Vacancies and Homeownership Annual Statistics: 2022, 2023, 2024

INCOME

Income

Area	Per Capita ($)	Median Household ($)	Average Household ($)
City	37,269	66,981	90,429
MSA[1]	41,987	77,013	104,828
U.S.	43,289	78,538	110,491

Note: (1) Figures cover the Jacksonville, FL Metropolitan Statistical Area
Source: U.S. Census Bureau, 2019-2023 American Community Survey 5-Year Estimates

Household Income Distribution

Area	Percent of Households Earning							
	Under $15,000	$15,000 -$24,999	$25,000 -$34,999	$35,000 -$49,999	$50,000 -$74,999	$75,000 -$99,999	$100,000 -$149,999	$150,000 and up
City	10.0	7.3	7.5	12.7	17.9	13.3	16.9	14.5
MSA[1]	8.0	6.1	6.7	11.1	16.9	13.3	18.3	19.7
U.S.	8.5	6.6	6.8	10.4	15.7	12.7	17.4	21.9

Note: (1) Figures cover the Jacksonville, FL Metropolitan Statistical Area
Source: U.S. Census Bureau, 2019-2023 American Community Survey 5-Year Estimates

Poverty Rate

Area	All Ages	Under 18 Years Old	18 to 64 Years Old	65 Years and Over
City	15.0	20.9	13.1	14.2
MSA[1]	12.1	16.9	10.9	10.2
U.S.	12.4	16.3	11.6	10.4

Note: Figures are percentage of people whose income during the past 12 months was below the poverty level; (1) Figures cover the Jacksonville, FL Metropolitan Statistical Area
Source: U.S. Census Bureau, 2019-2023 American Community Survey 5-Year Estimates

EMPLOYMENT

Labor Force and Employment

Area	Civilian Labor Force			Workers Employed		
	Dec. 2023	Dec. 2024	% Chg.	Dec. 2023	Dec. 2024	% Chg.
City	491,737	495,209	0.7	476,373	479,227	0.6
MSA[1]	845,904	852,367	0.8	820,842	825,781	0.6
U.S.	166,661,000	167,746,000	0.7	160,754,000	161,294,000	0.3

Note: Data is not seasonally adjusted and covers workers 16 years of age and older; (1) Figures cover the Jacksonville, FL Metropolitan Statistical Area
Source: Bureau of Labor Statistics, Local Area Unemployment Statistics

Unemployment Rate

Area	2024											
	Jan.	Feb.	Mar.	Apr.	May	Jun.	Jul.	Aug.	Sep.	Oct.	Nov.	Dec.
City	3.5	3.4	3.3	3.1	3.3	3.9	4.1	4.0	3.6	3.6	3.5	3.2
MSA[1]	3.3	3.2	3.2	2.9	3.1	3.7	3.9	3.8	3.4	3.4	3.5	3.1
U.S.	4.1	4.2	3.9	3.5	3.7	4.3	4.5	4.4	3.9	3.9	4.0	3.8

Note: Data is not seasonally adjusted and covers workers 16 years of age and older; (1) Figures cover the Jacksonville, FL Metropolitan Statistical Area
Source: Bureau of Labor Statistics, Local Area Unemployment Statistics

Average Wages

Occupation	$/Hr.	Occupation	$/Hr.
Accountants and Auditors	41.72	Maintenance and Repair Workers	23.93
Automotive Mechanics	25.10	Marketing Managers	69.06
Bookkeepers	23.66	Network and Computer Systems Admin.	44.92
Carpenters	24.55	Nurses, Licensed Practical	28.41
Cashiers	14.62	Nurses, Registered	41.31
Computer Programmers	50.71	Nursing Assistants	18.27
Computer Systems Analysts	50.41	Office Clerks, General	21.57
Computer User Support Specialists	28.60	Physical Therapists	46.05
Construction Laborers	20.35	Physicians	130.38
Cooks, Restaurant	16.89	Plumbers, Pipefitters and Steamfitters	26.34
Customer Service Representatives	20.86	Police and Sheriff's Patrol Officers	33.29
Dentists	86.80	Postal Service Mail Carriers	29.28
Electricians	27.03	Real Estate Sales Agents	35.39
Engineers, Electrical	52.71	Retail Salespersons	16.85
Fast Food and Counter Workers	13.94	Sales Representatives, Technical/Scientific	47.51
Financial Managers	80.15	Secretaries, Exc. Legal/Medical/Executive	21.36
First-Line Supervisors of Office Workers	33.12	Security Guards	17.65
General and Operations Managers	59.57	Surgeons	n/a
Hairdressers/Cosmetologists	17.54	Teacher Assistants, Exc. Postsecondary[1]	16.11
Home Health and Personal Care Aides	15.94	Teachers, Secondary School, Exc. Sp. Ed.[1]	33.35
Janitors and Cleaners	16.39	Telemarketers	17.68
Landscaping/Groundskeeping Workers	17.93	Truck Drivers, Heavy/Tractor-Trailer	27.47
Lawyers	62.65	Truck Drivers, Light/Delivery Services	22.53
Maids and Housekeeping Cleaners	15.49	Waiters and Waitresses	18.38

Note: Wage data covers the Jacksonville, FL Metropolitan Statistical Area; (1) Hourly wages were calculated from annual wage data based on a 40 hour work week
Source: Bureau of Labor Statistics, Metro Area Occupational Employment & Wage Estimates, May 2024

Employment by Industry

Sector	MSA[1] Number of Employees	MSA[1] Percent of Total	U.S. Percent of Total
Construction	54,100	6.6	5.1
Financial Activities	73,700	9.0	5.8
Government	82,600	10.1	14.9
Information	14,700	1.8	1.9
Leisure and Hospitality	92,600	11.3	10.4
Manufacturing	36,500	4.5	8.0
Mining and Logging	400	<0.1	0.4
Other Services	29,400	3.6	3.7
Private Education and Health Services	134,000	16.3	16.9
Professional and Business Services	122,400	14.9	14.2
Retail Trade	89,900	11.0	10.0
Transportation, Warehousing, and Utilities	59,500	7.3	4.8
Wholesale Trade	30,400	3.7	3.9

Note: Figures are non-farm employment as of December 2024. Figures are not seasonally adjusted and include workers 16 years of age and older; (1) Figures cover the Jacksonville, FL Metropolitan Statistical Area
Source: Bureau of Labor Statistics, Current Employment Statistics, Employment, Hours, and Earnings

Employment by Occupation

Occupation Classification	City (%)	MSA[1] (%)	U.S. (%)
Management, Business, Science, and Arts	38.8	41.5	42.0
Natural Resources, Construction, and Maintenance	7.8	7.8	8.6
Production, Transportation, and Material Moving	12.7	11.3	13.0
Sales and Office	24.0	23.6	19.9
Service	16.8	15.9	16.5

Note: Figures cover employed civilians 16 years of age and older; (1) Figures cover the Jacksonville, FL Metropolitan Statistical Area
Source: U.S. Census Bureau, 2019-2023 American Community Survey 5-Year Estimates

Occupations with Greatest Projected Employment Growth: 2022 – 2032

Occupation[1]	2022 Employment	2032 Projected Employment	Numeric Employment Change	Percent Employment Change
Stockers and Order Fillers	236,990	274,060	37,070	15.6
Retail Salespersons	308,940	340,000	31,060	10.1
Waiters and Waitresses	195,320	223,820	28,500	14.6
Software Developers	75,620	101,940	26,320	34.8
General and Operations Managers	184,790	210,510	25,720	13.9
Registered Nurses	202,780	228,070	25,290	12.5
Fast Food and Counter Workers	185,000	209,460	24,460	13.2
Cooks, Restaurant	120,850	141,640	20,790	17.2
Landscaping and Groundskeeping Workers	112,240	129,030	16,790	15.0
Janitors and Cleaners, Except Maids and Housekeeping Cleaners	136,890	153,490	16,600	12.1

Note: Projections cover Florida; (1) Sorted by numeric employment change
Source: www.projectionscentral.org, State Occupational Projections, 2022–2032 Long-Term Projections

Fastest-Growing Occupations: 2022 – 2032

Occupation[1]	2022 Employment	2032 Projected Employment	Numeric Employment Change	Percent Employment Change
Nurse Practitioners	18,910	29,980	11,070	58.5
Data Scientists	8,470	12,450	3,980	47.0
Information Security Analysts (SOC 2018)	11,060	15,650	4,590	41.5
Statisticians	590	820	230	39.0
Solar Photovoltaic Installers	1,210	1,680	470	38.8
Computer and Information Research Scientists (SOC 2018)	3,160	4,380	1,220	38.6
Physician Assistants	8,830	12,180	3,350	37.9
Actuaries	1,640	2,260	620	37.8
Physical Therapist Assistants	7,430	10,230	2,800	37.7
Medical and Health Services Managers	34,490	47,200	12,710	36.9

Note: Projections cover Florida; (1) Sorted by percent employment change and excludes occupations with numeric employment change less than 50
Source: www.projectionscentral.org, State Occupational Projections, 2022–2032 Long-Term Projections

CITY FINANCES

City Government Finances

Component	2022 ($000)	2022 ($ per capita)
Total Revenues	4,255,431	4,623
Total Expenditures	4,286,041	4,656
Debt Outstanding	5,087,365	5,526

Source: U.S. Census Bureau, State & Local Government Finances 2022

City Government Revenue by Source

Source	2022 ($000)	2022 ($ per capita)	2022 (%)
General Revenue			
From Federal Government	198,347	215	4.7
From State Government	192,652	209	4.5
From Local Governments	351,237	382	8.3
Taxes			
Property	786,826	855	18.5
Sales and Gross Receipts	391,139	425	9.2
Personal Income	0	0	0.0
Corporate Income	0	0	0.0
Motor Vehicle License	0	0	0.0
Other Taxes	117,868	128	2.8
Current Charges	634,746	690	14.9
Liquor Store	0	0	0.0
Utility	1,487,236	1,616	34.9

Source: U.S. Census Bureau, State & Local Government Finances 2022

City Government Expenditures by Function

Function	2022 ($000)	2022 ($ per capita)	2022 (%)
General Direct Expenditures			
Air Transportation	78,758	85	1.8
Corrections	328	< 1	< 0.1
Education	0	0	0.0
Employment Security Administration	0	0	0.0
Financial Administration	316,812	344	7.4
Fire Protection	213,893	232	5.0
General Public Buildings	0	0	0.0
Governmental Administration, Other	25,741	28	0.6
Health	114,539	124	2.7
Highways	56,675	61	1.3
Hospitals	0	0	0.0
Housing and Community Development	60,806	66	1.4
Interest on General Debt	75,864	82	1.8
Judicial and Legal	44,868	48	1.0
Libraries	36,841	40	0.9
Parking	3,710	4	0.1
Parks and Recreation	130,409	141	3.0
Police Protection	501,617	544	11.7
Public Welfare	6,080	6	0.1
Sewerage	113,638	123	2.7
Solid Waste Management	87,364	94	2.0
Veterans' Services	0	0	0.0
Liquor Store	0	0	0.0
Utility	1,753,769	1,905	40.9

Source: U.S. Census Bureau, State & Local Government Finances 2022

TAXES

State Corporate Income Tax Rates

State	Tax Rate (%)	Income Brackets ($)	Num. of Brackets	Financial Institution Tax Rate (%)[a]	Federal Income Tax Ded.
Florida	5.5	Flat rate	1	5.5	No

Note: Tax rates for tax year 2024; (a) Rates listed are the corporate income tax rate applied to financial institutions or excise taxes based on income. Some states have other taxes based upon the value of deposits or shares.
Source: Federation of Tax Administrators, State Corporate Income Tax Rates, January 1, 2025

State Individual Income Tax Rates

State	Tax Rate (%)	Income Brackets ($)	Personal Exemptions ($)			Standard Ded. ($)	
			Single	Married	Depend.	Single	Married
Florida	— No state income tax —						

Note: Tax rates for tax year 2024; Local- and county-level taxes are not included
Source: Federation of Tax Administrators, State Individual Income Tax Rates, January 1, 2025

Various State Sales and Excise Tax Rates

State	State Sales Tax (%)	Gasoline[1] ($/gal.)	Cigarette[2] ($/pack)	Spirits[3] ($/gal.)	Wine[4] ($/gal.)	Beer[5] ($/gal.)	Recreational Marijuana (%)
Florida	6	0.39	1.34	6.50	2.25	0.48	Not legal

Note: All tax rates as of January 1, 2025; (1) The American Petroleum Institute has developed a methodology for determining the average tax rate on a gallon of fuel. Rates may include any of the following: excise taxes, environmental fees, storage tank fees, other fees or taxes, general sales tax, and local taxes; (2) The federal excise tax of $1.0066 per pack and local taxes are not included; (3) Rates are those applicable to off-premise sales of 40% alcohol by volume (a.b.v.) distilled spirits in 750ml containers. Local excise taxes are excluded; (4) Rates are those applicable to off-premise sales of 11% a.b.v. non-carbonated wine in 750ml containers; (5) Rates are those applicable to off-premise sales of 4.7% a.b.v. beer in 12 ounce containers.
Source: Tax Foundation, 2025 Facts & Figures: How Does Your State Compare?

State Tax Competitiveness Index

State	Overall Rank	Corporate Tax Rank	Individual Income Tax Rank	Sales Tax Rank	Property Tax Rank	Unemployment Insurance Tax Rank
Florida	4	16	1	14	21	10

Note: The Tax Foundation's State Tax Competitiveness Index enables policymakers, taxpayers, and business leaders to gauge how their states' tax systems compare. A rank of 1 is best, 50 is worst. Rankings do not average to the total. States without a tax rank equally as 1. DC's scores and rankings do not affect other states. The report shows tax systems as of July 1, 2024 (the beginning of Fiscal Year 2025).
Source: Tax Foundation, State Tax Competitiveness Index 2025

TRANSPORTATION

Means of Transportation to Work

Area	Car/Truck/Van Drove Alone	Car/Truck/Van Car-pooled	Public Transportation Bus	Public Transportation Subway	Public Transportation Railroad	Bicycle	Walked	Other Means	Worked at Home
City	72.8	9.0	1.2	0.0	0.0	0.4	1.2	2.0	13.5
MSA[1]	72.1	8.2	0.7	0.0	0.0	0.4	1.1	1.8	15.6
U.S.	70.2	8.5	1.7	1.3	0.4	0.4	2.4	1.6	13.5

Note: Figures are percentages and cover workers 16 years of age and older; (1) Figures cover the Jacksonville, FL Metropolitan Statistical Area
Source: U.S. Census Bureau, 2019-2023 American Community Survey 5-Year Estimates

Travel Time to Work

Area	Less Than 10 Minutes	10 to 19 Minutes	20 to 29 Minutes	30 to 44 Minutes	45 to 59 Minutes	60 to 89 Minutes	90 Minutes or More
City	8.7	29.0	28.0	24.9	5.6	2.5	1.3
MSA[1]	9.2	26.2	24.8	26.0	8.2	3.9	1.7
U.S.	12.6	28.6	21.2	20.8	8.1	6.0	2.8

Note: Note: Figures are percentages and include workers 16 years old and over; (1) Figures cover the Jacksonville, FL Metropolitan Statistical Area
Source: U.S. Census Bureau, 2019-2023 American Community Survey 5-Year Estimates

Key Congestion Measures

Measure	2000	2010	2015	2020	2022
Annual Hours of Delay, Total (000)	21,108	29,864	33,457	16,143	41,318
Annual Hours of Delay, Per Auto Commuter	37	41	44	21	54
Annual Congestion Cost, Per Auto Commuter ($)	872	980	1,013	501	1,217

Note: Figures cover the Jacksonville FL urban area
Source: Texas A&M Transportation Institute, 2023 Urban Mobility Report

Freeway Travel Time Index

Measure	1985	1990	1995	2000	2005	2010	2015	2020	2022
Urban Area Index[1]	1.08	1.12	1.14	1.17	1.20	1.18	1.19	1.06	1.19
Urban Area Rank[1,2]	40	35	41	36	38	36	38	75	37

Note: Freeway Travel Time Index—the ratio of travel time in the peak period to the travel time at free-flow conditions. For example, a value of 1.30 indicates a 20-minute free-flow trip takes 26 minutes in the peak (20 minutes x 1.30 = 26 minutes); (1) Covers the Jacksonville FL urban area; (2) Rank is based on 101 larger urban areas (#1 = highest travel time index)
Source: Texas A&M Transportation Institute, 2023 Urban Mobility Report

Public Transportation

Agency Name / Mode of Transportation	Vehicles Operated in Maximum Service[1]	Annual Unlinked Passenger Trips[2] (in thous.)	Annual Passenger Miles[3] (in thous.)
Jacksonville Transportation Authority (JTA)			
Bus (directly operated)	115	5,748.3	33,172.2
Bus (purchased transportation)	7	22.7	250.6
Commuter Bus (purchased transportation)	6	4.8	148.2
Demand Response (purchased transportation)	93	297.9	2,774.7
Ferryboat (purchased transportation)	1	304.9	146.3
Monorail and Automated Guideway (directly operated)	3	299.5	284.6

Note: (1) Number of revenue vehicles operated by the given mode and type of service to meet the annual maximum service requirement. This is the revenue vehicle count during the peak season of the year; on the week and day that maximum service is provided. Vehicles operated in maximum service (VOMS) exclude atypical days and one-time special events; (2) Number of passengers who boarded public transportation vehicles. Passengers are counted each time they board a vehicle no matter how many vehicles they use to travel from their origin to their destination. (3) Sum of the distances ridden by all passengers during the entire fiscal year.
Source: Federal Transit Administration, National Transit Database, 2023

Air Transportation

Airport Name and Code / Type of Service	Passenger Airlines[1]	Passenger Enplanements	Freight Carriers[2]	Freight (lbs)
Jacksonville International (JAX)				
Domestic service (U.S. carriers only)	20	3,749,052	9	62,826,279
International service (U.S. carriers only)	3	351	1	66,663

Note: (1) Includes all U.S.-based major, minor and commuter airlines that carried at least one passenger during the year; (2) Includes all U.S.-based airlines and freight carriers that transported at least one pound of freight during the year.
Source: Bureau of Transportation Statistics, The Intermodal Transportation Database, Air Carriers: T-100 Domestic Market (U.S. carriers only), 2024; Bureau of Transportation Statistics, The Intermodal Transportation Database, Air Carriers: T-100 International Market (U.S. carriers only), 2024

BUSINESSES

Major Business Headquarters

Company Name	Industry	Rankings Fortune[1]	Rankings Forbes[2]
CSX	Railroads	290	-
Crowley	Transportation	-	175
Fanatics	Retailing	-	68
Fidelity National Financial	Insurance: property and casualty (stock)	351	-
Fidelity National Information Services	Financial data services	288	-

Note: (1) Companies that produce a 10-K are ranked 1 to 500 based on 2023 revenue; (2) All private companies with at least $2 billion in annual revenue through the end of their most current fiscal year are ranked 1 to 275; companies listed are headquartered in the city; dashes indicate no ranking
Source: Fortune, "Fortune 500," 2024; Forbes, "America's Largest Private Companies," 2024

Fastest-Growing Businesses

According to *Inc.*, Jacksonville is home to two of America's 500 fastest-growing private companies: **Demons Behind Me** (#207); **Pulse Clinical Alliance** (#341). Criteria: must be an independent, privately-held, for-profit, U.S. corporation, proprietorship or partnership as of December 31, 2023; revenues must be at least $100,000 in 2020 and $2 million in 2023; must have four-year operating/sales history. *Inc.*, "America's 500 Fastest-Growing Private Companies," 2024

Living Environment

COST OF LIVING

Cost of Living Index

Composite Index	Groceries	Housing	Utilities	Transportation	Health Care	Misc. Goods/Services
92.9	104.0	87.1	89.7	87.2	85.2	96.0

Note: The Cost of Living Index measures regional differences in the cost of consumer goods and services, excluding taxes and non-consumer expenditures, for professional and managerial households in the top income quintile. It is based on more than 50,000 prices covering almost 60 different items for which prices are collected three times a year by chambers of commerce, economic development organizations or university applied economic centers in each participating urban area. The numbers shown should be read as a percentage above or below the national average of 100. For example, a value of 115.4 in the groceries column indicates that grocery prices are 15.4% higher than the national average. Small differences in the index numbers should not be interpreted as significant; Figures cover the Jacksonville FL urban area.
Source: The Council for Community and Economic Research, Cost of Living Index, 2024

Grocery Prices

Area[1]	T-Bone Steak ($/pound)	Frying Chicken ($/pound)	Whole Milk ($/half gal.)	Eggs ($/dozen)	Orange Juice ($/64 oz.)	Coffee ($/11.5 oz.)
City[2]	15.52	1.42	4.72	3.41	4.53	5.38
Avg.	15.42	1.55	4.69	3.25	4.41	5.46
Min.	14.50	1.16	4.43	2.75	4.00	4.85
Max.	17.56	2.89	5.49	4.78	5.54	7.89

Note: (1) Values for the local area are compared with the average, minimum and maximum values for all 276 areas in the Cost of Living Index; (2) Figures cover the Jacksonville FL urban area; **T-Bone Steak** (price per pound); **Frying Chicken** (price per pound, whole fryer); **Whole Milk** (half gallon carton); **Eggs** (price per dozen, Grade A, large); **Orange Juice** (64 oz. Tropicana or Florida Natural); **Coffee** (11.5 oz. can, vacuum-packed, Maxwell House, Hills Bros, or Folgers).
Source: The Council for Community and Economic Research, Cost of Living Index, 2024

Housing and Utility Costs

Area[1]	New Home Price ($)	Apartment Rent ($/month)	All Electric ($/month)	Part Electric ($/month)	Other Energy ($/month)	Telephone ($/month)
City[2]	391,862	1,714	170.55	-	-	197.76
Avg.	515,975	1,550	210.99	123.07	82.07	194.99
Min.	265,375	692	104.33	53.68	36.26	179.42
Max.	2,775,821	5,719	529.02	397.28	361.63	223.33

Note: (1) Values for the local area are compared with the average, minimum and maximum values for all 276 areas in the Cost of Living Index; (2) Figures cover the Jacksonville FL urban area; **New Home Price** (2,400 sf living area, 8,000 sf lot, in urban area with full utilities); **Apartment Rent** (950 sf 2 bedroom/1.5 or 2 bath, unfurnished, excluding all utilities except water); **All Electric** (average monthly cost for an all-electric home); **Part Electric** (average monthly cost for a part-electric home); **Other Energy** (average monthly cost for natural gas, fuel oil, coal, wood, and any other forms of energy except electricity); **Telephone** (price includes the base monthly rate plus taxes and fees for three lines of mobile phone service).
Source: The Council for Community and Economic Research, Cost of Living Index, 2024

Health Care, Transportation, and Other Costs

Area[1]	Doctor ($/visit)	Dentist ($/visit)	Optometrist ($/visit)	Gasoline ($/gallon)	Beauty Salon ($/visit)	Men's Shirt ($)
City[2]	106.53	98.40	97.76	3.34	79.67	30.27
Avg.	143.77	117.51	129.23	3.32	48.57	38.14
Min.	36.74	58.67	67.33	2.80	24.00	13.41
Max.	270.44	216.82	307.33	5.28	94.00	63.89

Note: (1) Values for the local area are compared with the average, minimum and maximum values for all 276 areas in the Cost of Living Index; (2) Figures cover the Jacksonville FL urban area; **Doctor** (general practitioners routine exam of an established patient); **Dentist** (adult teeth cleaning and periodic oral examination); **Optometrist** (full vision eye exam for established adult patient); **Gasoline** (one gallon regular unleaded, national brand, including all taxes, cash price at self-service pump if available); **Beauty Salon** (woman's shampoo, trim, and blow-dry); **Men's Shirt** (cotton/polyester dress shirt, pinpoint weave, long sleeves).
Source: The Council for Community and Economic Research, Cost of Living Index, 2024

HOUSING

Homeownership Rate

Area	2017 (%)	2018 (%)	2019 (%)	2020 (%)	2021 (%)	2022 (%)	2023 (%)	2024 (%)
MSA[1]	65.2	61.4	63.1	64.8	68.1	70.6	72.9	67.0
U.S.	63.9	64.4	64.6	66.6	65.5	65.8	65.9	65.6

Note: (1) Figures cover the Jacksonville, FL Metropolitan Statistical Area
Source: U.S. Census Bureau, Housing Vacancies and Homeownership Annual Statistics: 2017-2024

House Price Index (HPI)

Area	National Ranking[2]	Quarterly Change (%)	One-Year Change (%)	Five-Year Change (%)	Since 1991Q1 (%)
MSA[1]	168	-0.18	4.19	65.48	401.54
U.S.[3]	—	1.43	4.51	57.13	327.82

Note: The HPI is a weighted repeat sales index. It measures average price changes in repeat sales or refinancings on the same properties. This information is obtained by reviewing repeat mortgage transactions on single-family properties whose mortgages have been purchased or securitized by Fannie Mae or Freddie Mac since January 1975; (1) Figures cover the Jacksonville, FL Metropolitan Statistical Area; (2) Rankings are based on annual percentage change for all metro areas containing at least 15,000 transactions over the last 10 years and ranges from 1 to 241; (3) figures based on a weighted average of Census Division estimates using a seasonally adjusted, purchase-only index; all figures are for the period ending December 31, 2024
Source: Federal Housing Finance Agency, Change in FHFA Metropolitan Area House Price Indexes, All Transactions Index, 2024Q4

Home Value

Area	Under $100,000	$100,000 -$199,999	$200,000 -$299,999	$300,000 -$399,999	$400,000 -$499,999	$500,000 -$999,999	$1,000,000 or more	Median ($)
City	11.0	20.4	27.6	19.5	10.1	9.1	2.2	266,100
MSA[1]	8.7	15.7	24.0	19.1	12.4	16.2	4.0	308,900
U.S.	12.1	17.8	19.5	14.4	10.5	19.1	6.5	303,400

Note: Figures are percentages except for median and cover owner-occupied housing units; (1) Figures cover the Jacksonville, FL Metropolitan Statistical Area
Source: U.S. Census Bureau, 2019-2023 American Community Survey 5-Year Estimates

Year Housing Structure Built

Area	2020 or Later	2010 -2019	2000 -2009	1990 -1999	1980 -1989	1970 -1979	1960 -1969	1950 -1959	1940 -1949	Before 1940	Median Year
City	2.4	10.6	17.4	13.1	15.9	11.9	9.3	10.3	4.1	5.0	1986
MSA[1]	3.2	13.5	20.2	14.3	16.1	11.4	7.3	7.2	2.9	3.8	1991
U.S.	1.2	8.9	13.6	12.8	13.0	14.4	10.0	9.7	4.5	11.9	1980

Note: Figures are percentages except for Median Year; Note: (1) Figures cover the Jacksonville, FL Metropolitan Statistical Area
Source: U.S. Census Bureau, 2019-2023 American Community Survey 5-Year Estimates

Gross Monthly Rent

Area	Under $500	$500 -$999	$1,000 -$1,499	$1,500 -$1,999	$2,000 -$2,499	$2,500 -$2,999	$3,000 and up	Median ($)
City	4.9	16.1	38.9	26.9	9.7	2.3	1.2	1,375
MSA[1]	4.3	15.8	36.2	27.0	11.0	2.9	2.7	1,416
U.S.	6.5	22.3	29.5	20.2	10.8	4.8	5.9	1,348

Note: Figures are percentages except for median; Gross rent is the contract rent plus the estimated average monthly cost of utilities (electricity, gas, and water and sewer) and fuels (oil, coal, kerosene, wood, etc.) if these are paid by the renter (or paid for the renter by someone else); (1) Figures cover the Jacksonville, FL Metropolitan Statistical Area
Source: U.S. Census Bureau, 2019-2023 American Community Survey 5-Year Estimates

HEALTH

Health Risk Factors

Category	MSA[1] (%)	U.S. (%)
Adults aged 18–64 who have any kind of health care coverage	89.5	90.8
Adults who reported being in good or better health	84.8	81.8
Adults who have been told they have high blood cholesterol	33.5	36.9
Adults who have been told they have high blood pressure	34.8	34.0
Adults who are current smokers	11.2	12.1
Adults who currently use e-cigarettes	11.2	7.7
Adults who currently use chewing tobacco, snuff, or snus	2.6	3.2
Adults who are heavy drinkers[2]	6.5	6.1
Adults who are binge drinkers[3]	15.3	15.2
Adults who are overweight (BMI 25.0 - 29.9)	33.7	34.4
Adults who are obese (BMI 30.0 - 99.8)	33.0	34.3
Adults who participated in any physical activities in the past month	72.5	75.8

Note: All figures are crude prevalence; (1) Figures cover the Jacksonville, FL Metropolitan Statistical Area; (2) Heavy drinkers are classified as adult men having more than 14 drinks per week and adult women having more than 7 drinks per week; (3) Binge drinkers are classified as males having five or more drinks on one occasion or females having four or more drinks on one occasion
Source: Centers for Disease Control and Prevention, Behavioral Risk Factor Surveillance System, SMART: Selected Metropolitan Area Risk Trends, 2023

Acute and Chronic Health Conditions

Category	MSA[1] (%)	U.S. (%)
Adults who have ever been told they had a heart attack	3.9	4.2
Adults who have ever been told they have angina or coronary heart disease	n/a	4.0
Adults who have ever been told they had a stroke	2.0	3.3
Adults who have ever been told they have asthma	20.1	15.7
Adults who have ever been told they have arthritis	25.2	26.3
Adults who have ever been told they have diabetes[2]	12.4	11.5
Adults who have ever been told they had skin cancer	6.7	5.6
Adults who have ever been told they had any other types of cancer	10.1	8.4
Adults who have ever been told they have COPD	11.8	6.4
Adults who have ever been told they have kidney disease	3.6	3.7
Adults who have ever been told they have a form of depression	19.7	22.0

Note: All figures are crude prevalence; (1) Figures cover the Jacksonville, FL Metropolitan Statistical Area; (2) Figures do not include pregnancy-related, borderline, or pre-diabetes
Source: Centers for Disease Control and Prevention, Behavioral Risk Factor Surveillance System, SMART: Selected Metropolitan Area Risk Trends, 2023

Health Screening and Vaccination Rates

Category	MSA[1] (%)	U.S. (%)
Adults who have ever been tested for HIV	42.5	37.5
Adults who have had their blood cholesterol checked within the last five years	89.4	87.0
Adults aged 65+ who have had flu shot within the past year	66.0	63.4
Adults aged 65+ who have ever had a pneumonia vaccination	76.6	71.9

Note: All figures are crude prevalence; (1) Figures cover the Jacksonville, FL Metropolitan Statistical Area.
Source: Centers for Disease Control and Prevention, Behavioral Risk Factor Surveillance System, SMART: Selected Metropolitan Area Risk Trends, 2023

Disability Status

Category	MSA[1] (%)	U.S. (%)
Adults who reported being deaf	5.7	7.4
Are you blind or have serious difficulty seeing, even when wearing glasses?	10.4	4.9
Do you have difficulty doing errands alone?	9.9	7.8
Do you have difficulty dressing or bathing?	4.2	3.6
Do you have serious difficulty concentrating/remembering/making decisions?	17.7	13.7
Do you have serious difficulty walking or climbing stairs?	13.5	13.2

Note: All figures are crude prevalence; (1) Figures cover the Jacksonville, FL Metropolitan Statistical Area.
Source: Centers for Disease Control and Prevention, Behavioral Risk Factor Surveillance System, SMART: Selected Metropolitan Area Risk Trends, 2023

Mortality Rates for the Top 10 Causes of Death in the U.S.

ICD-10[a] Sub-Chapter	ICD-10[a] Code	Crude Mortality Rate[2] per 100,000 population	
		County[3]	U.S.
Malignant neoplasms	C00-C97	187.8	182.7
Ischaemic heart diseases	I20-I25	98.9	109.6
Provisional assignment of new diseases of uncertain etiology[1]	U00-U49	80.7	65.3
Other forms of heart disease	I30-I51	52.1	65.1
Other degenerative diseases of the nervous system	G30-G31	50.2	52.4
Other external causes of accidental injury	W00-X59	66.3	52.3
Cerebrovascular diseases	I60-I69	58.7	49.1
Chronic lower respiratory diseases	J40-J47	44.1	43.5
Hypertensive diseases	I10-I15	40.1	38.9
Organic, including symptomatic, mental disorders	F01-F09	23.5	33.9

Note: (a) ICD-10 = International Classification of Diseases 10th Revision; (1) Includes COVID-19, adverse effects to COVID-19 vaccines, SARS, and vaping-related disorders; (2) Crude mortality rates are a three-year average covering 2021-2023; (3) Figures cover Duval County.
Source: Centers for Disease Control and Prevention, National Center for Health Statistics. National Vital Statistics System, Mortality 2018-2023 on CDC WONDER Online Database

Mortality Rates for Selected Causes of Death

Cause of Death	ICD-10[a] Code	Crude Mortality Rate[1] per 100,000 population	
		County[2]	U.S.
Accidental poisoning and exposure to noxious substances	X40-X49	47.9	30.5
Alzheimer disease	G30	10.5	35.4
Assault	X85-Y09	14.3	7.3
COVID-19	U07.1	80.7	65.3
Diabetes mellitus	E10-E14	32.7	30.0
Diseases of the liver	K70-K76	22.7	20.8
Human immunodeficiency virus (HIV) disease	B20-B24	4.9	1.5
Influenza and pneumonia	J09-J18	10.8	13.4
Intentional self-harm	X60-X84	16.4	14.7
Malnutrition	E40-E46	5.2	6.0
Obesity and other hyperalimentation	E65-E68	3.2	3.1
Renal failure	N17-N19	25.1	16.4
Transport accidents	V01-V99	17.8	14.4

Note: (a) ICD-10 = International Classification of Diseases 10th Revision; (1) Crude mortality rates are a three-year average covering 2021-2023; (2) Figures cover Duval County; Data are suppressed when the data meet the criteria for confidentiality constraints; Crude mortality rates are flagged as unreliable when the rate would be calculated with a numerator of 20 or less.
Source: Centers for Disease Control and Prevention, National Center for Health Statistics. National Vital Statistics System, Mortality 2018-2023 on CDC WONDER Online Database

Health Insurance Coverage

Area	With Health Insurance	With Private Health Insurance	With Public Health Insurance	Without Health Insurance	Population Under Age 19 Without Health Insurance
City	88.3	64.4	34.4	11.7	7.1
MSA[1]	90.1	69.3	33.4	9.9	6.3
U.S.	91.4	67.3	36.3	8.6	5.4

Note: Figures are percentages that cover the civilian noninstitutionalized population; (1) Figures cover the Jacksonville, FL Metropolitan Statistical Area
Source: U.S. Census Bureau, 2019-2023 American Community Survey 5-Year Estimates

Number of Medical Professionals

Area	MDs[3]	DOs[3,4]	Dentists	Podiatrists	Chiropractors	Optometrists
County[1] (number)	3,753	386	798	71	285	169
County[1] (rate[2])	369.2	38.0	77.4	6.9	27.6	16.4
U.S. (rate[2])	302.5	29.2	74.6	6.4	29.5	18.0

Note: Data as of 2023 unless noted; (1) Data covers Duval County; (2) Number of medical professionals per 100,000 population; (3) Data as of 2022 and includes all active, non-federal physicians; (4) Doctor of Osteopathic Medicine
Source: U.S. Department of Health and Human Services, Health Resources and Services Administration, Bureau of Health Professions, Area Resource File (ARF) 2023-2024

Best Hospitals

According to *U.S. News*, the Jacksonville, FL metro area is home to two of the best hospitals in the U.S.: **Brooks Rehabilitation Hospital** (1 adult specialty); **Mayo Clinic-Florida** (10 adult specialties). The hospitals listed were nationally ranked in at least one of 15 adult or 11 pediatric specialties. The number of specialties shown cover the parent hospital. Only 160 U.S. hospitals performed well enough to be nationally ranked in one or more specialties. Twenty hospitals in the U.S. made the Honor Roll. The Best Hospitals Honor Roll takes both the national rankings and the procedure and condition ratings into account. Hospitals received points if they were nationally ranked in one of the 15 adult specialties—the higher they ranked, the more points they got—and how many ratings of "high performing" they earned in the 20 procedures and conditions. *U.S. News Online, "America's Best Hospitals 2024-25"*

According to *U.S. News*, the Jacksonville, FL metro area is home to one of the best children's hospitals in the U.S.: **Wolfson Children's Hospital** (4 pediatric specialties). The hospital listed was highly ranked in at least one of 11 pediatric specialties. One hundred five children's hospitals in the U.S. were nationally ranked in at least one specialty. Hospitals received points for being ranked in a specialty, and the 10 hospitals with the most points across the 11 specialties make up the Honor Roll. *U.S. News Online, "America's Best Children's Hospitals 2024-25"*

EDUCATION

Public School District Statistics

District Name	Schls	Pupils	Pupil/ Teacher Ratio	Minority Pupils[1] (%)	Total Rev. per Pupil ($)	Total Exp. per Pupil ($)
Duval	210	127,971	22.4	68.9	12,451	11,534

Note: Table includes school districts with 2,000 or more students; (1) Percentage of students that are not non-Hispanic white.
Source: U.S. Department of Education, National Center for Education Statistics, Common Core of Data, Local Education Agency (School District) Universe Survey: School Year 2023-2024; U.S. Department of Education, National Center for Education Statistics, Common Core of Data, School District Finance Survey (F-33): School Year 2021–22

Best High Schools

According to *U.S. News,* Jacksonville is home to five of the top 500 high schools in the U.S.: **Stanton College Preparatory School** (#55); **Paxon School/Advanced Studies** (#189); **Darnell Cookman Middle/High School** (#200); **Douglas Anderson School of the Arts** (#345); **Samuel W. Wolfson High School** (#439). Nearly 25,000 public, magnet and charter schools were ranked based on their performance on state assessments and how well they prepare students for college. *U.S. News & World Report, "Best High Schools 2024"*

Highest Level of Education

Area	Less than H.S.	H.S. Diploma	Some College, No Deg.	Associate Degree	Bachelor's Degree	Master's Degree	Prof. School Degree	Doctorate Degree
City	9.2	28.2	20.7	10.0	21.6	7.4	1.7	1.1
MSA[1]	7.9	26.4	20.5	10.0	23.0	8.9	2.0	1.3
U.S.	10.6	26.2	19.4	8.8	21.3	9.8	2.3	1.6

Note: Figures cover persons age 25 and over; (1) Figures cover the Jacksonville, FL Metropolitan Statistical Area
Source: U.S. Census Bureau, 2019-2023 American Community Survey 5-Year Estimates

Educational Attainment by Race

Area	High School Graduate or Higher (%)					Bachelor's Degree or Higher (%)				
	Total	White	Black	Asian	Hisp.[2]	Total	White	Black	Asian	Hisp.[2]
City	90.8	93.0	88.6	88.9	84.8	31.8	35.1	22.6	52.6	28.1
MSA[1]	92.1	93.8	88.5	89.6	87.1	35.1	37.9	23.6	52.4	30.2
U.S.	89.4	92.9	88.1	88.0	72.5	35.0	37.7	24.7	57.0	19.9

Note: Figures shown cover persons 25 years old and over; (1) Figures cover the Jacksonville, FL Metropolitan Statistical Area; (2) People of Hispanic origin can be of any race
Source: U.S. Census Bureau, 2019-2023 American Community Survey 5-Year Estimates

School Enrollment by Grade and Control

Area	Preschool (%)		Kindergarten (%)		Grades 1 - 4 (%)		Grades 5 - 8 (%)		Grades 9 - 12 (%)	
	Public	Private	Public	Private	Public	Private	Public	Private	Public	Private
City	56.5	43.5	83.5	16.5	83.4	16.6	80.0	20.0	83.7	16.3
MSA[1]	56.0	44.0	85.4	14.6	84.0	16.0	82.8	17.2	85.6	14.4
U.S.	58.7	41.3	85.2	14.8	87.2	12.8	87.9	12.1	89.0	11.0

Note: Figures shown cover persons 3 years old and over; (1) Figures cover the Jacksonville, FL Metropolitan Statistical Area
Source: U.S. Census Bureau, 2019-2023 American Community Survey 5-Year Estimates

Higher Education

Four-Year Colleges			Two-Year Colleges			Medical Schools[1]	Law Schools[2]	Voc/ Tech[3]
Public	Private Non-profit	Private For-profit	Public	Private Non-profit	Private For-profit			
2	4	1	0	1	2	0	0	12

Note: Figures cover institutions located within the Jacksonville, FL Metropolitan Statistical Area and include main campuses only; (1) includes schools accredited by the Liaison Committee on Medical Education and the American Osteopathic Association's Commission on Osteopathic College Accreditation; (2) includes ABA-accredited schools, schools with provisional ABA accreditation, and state accredited schools; (3) includes all schools with programs that are less than 2 years.
Source: National Center for Education Statistics, Integrated Postsecondary Education System (IPEDS), 2023-24; Wikipedia, List of Medical Schools in the United States, accessed May 2, 2025; Wikipedia, List of Law Schools in the United States, accessed May 2, 2025

EMPLOYERS

Major Employers

Company Name	Industry
Amazon.com	Online retail
Bank of America, Merrill Lynch	Financial services
Baptist Health	Healthcare
Citi	Financial services
City of Jacksonville	Local government
Duval County Public Schools	Education
Fidelity National	Financial services
FIS	Financial services
Fleet Readiness Center SE	Aviation & aerospace
Florida Blue	Financial services
Mayo Clinic	Healthcare
Southeastern Grocers	Grocery stores
St. Vincent's Medical Center - Riverside	Healthcare
State of Florida	Government
UF Health	Healthcare

Note: Companies shown are located within the Jacksonville, FL Metropolitan Statistical Area.
Source: Chambers of Commerce; State Departments of Labor; Wikipedia

Best Companies to Work For

Florida Blue, headquartered in Jacksonville, is among "Fortune's Best Workplaces for Parents." To pick the best companies, *Fortune* partnered with the Great Place to Work Institute. To be considered for the list, companies must be Great Place To Work-Certified and have at least 50 responses from parents in the US. The survey enables employees to share confidential quantitative and qualitative feedback about their organization's culture by responding to 60 statements on a 5-point scale and answering two open-ended questions. Collectively, these statements describe a great employee experience, defined by high levels of trust, respect, credibility, fairness, pride, and camaraderie. In addition, companies provide organizational data like size, location, industry, demographics, roles, and levels; and provide information about parental leave, adoption, flexible schedule, childcare and dependent health care benefits. *Fortune, "Best Workplaces for Parents," 2024*

Florida Blue, headquartered in Jacksonville, is among "Fortune's Best Workplaces for Women." To pick the best companies, *Fortune* partnered with the Great Place to Work Institute. To be considered for the list, companies must be Great Place To Work-Certified. Companies must also employ at least 50 women, at least 20% of their non-executive managers must be female, and at least one executive must be female. To determine the Best Workplaces for Women, Great Place To Work measured the differences in women's survey responses to those of their peers and assesses the impact of demographics and roles on the quality and consistency of women's experiences. Great Place To Work also analyzed the gender balance of each workplace, how it compared to each company's industry, and patterns in representation as women rise from front-line positions to the board of directors. *Fortune, "Best Workplaces for Women," 2024*

Florida Blue; Forcura, headquartered in Jacksonville, are among "Best Workplaces in Health Care." To determine the Best Workplaces in Health Care list, Great Place To Work analyzed the survey responses of over 185,000 employees from Great Place To Work-Certified companies in the health care industry. Survey data analysis and company-provided datapoints are then factored into a combined score to compare and rank the companies that create the most consistently positive experience for all employees in this industry. *Fortune, "Best Workplaces in Health Care," 2024*

Baptist Health System - Jacksonville; VyStar Credit Union, headquartered in Jacksonville, are among the "Best Places to Work in IT." To qualify, companies had to have a minimum of 100 total employees and five IT employees. The best places to work were selected based on DEI (diversity, equity, and inclusion) practices; IT turnover, promotions, and growth; IT retention and engagement programs; remote/hybrid working; benefits and perks (such as elder care and child care, flextime, and reimbursement for college tuition); and training and career development opportunities.
Computerworld, "Best Places to Work in IT," 2025

PUBLIC SAFETY

Crime Rate

Area	Total Crime Rate	Violent Crime Rate				Property Crime Rate		
		Murder	Rape	Robbery	Aggrav. Assault	Burglary	Larceny-Theft	Motor Vehicle Theft
City	n/a	n/a	n/a	n/a	n/a	n/a	n/a	n/a
U.S.	2,290.9	5.7	38.0	66.5	264.1	250.7	1,347.2	318.7

Note: Figures are crimes per 100,000 population; n/a not available.
Source: FBI, Table 8, Offenses Known to Law Enforcement, by State by City, 2023

Hate Crimes

Area	Number of Quarters Reported	Number of Incidents per Bias Motivation					
		Race/Ethnicity/Ancestry	Religion	Sexual Orientation	Disability	Gender	Gender Identity
City	n/a	n/a	n/a	n/a	n/a	n/a	n/a
U.S.	4	5,900	2,699	2,077	187	92	492

Note: n/a not available.
Source: Federal Bureau of Investigation, Hate Crime Statistics 2023

Identity Theft Consumer Reports

Area	Reports	Reports per 100,000 Population	Rank[2]
MSA[1]	5,986	364	31
U.S.	1,135,291	339	-

Note: (1) Figures cover the Jacksonville, FL Metropolitan Statistical Area; (2) Rank ranges from 1 to 401 where 1 indicates greatest number of identity theft reports per 100,000 population
Source: Federal Trade Commission, Consumer Sentinel Network Data Book 2024

Fraud and Other Consumer Reports

Area	Reports	Reports per 100,000 Population	Rank[2]
MSA[1]	31,560	1,918	15
U.S.	5,360,641	1,601	-

Note: (1) Figures cover the Jacksonville, FL Metropolitan Statistical Area; (2) Rank ranges from 1 to 401 where 1 indicates greatest number of fraud and other consumer reports per 100,000 population
Source: Federal Trade Commission, Consumer Sentinel Network Data Book 2024

POLITICS

2024 Presidential Election Results

Area	Trump (Rep.)	Harris (Dem.)	Stein (Green)	Kennedy (Ind.)	Oliver (Lib.)	Other
Duval County	49.9	48.5	0.5	0.0	0.4	0.7
U.S.	49.7	48.2	0.6	0.5	0.4	0.6

Note: Results are percentages and may not add to 100% due to rounding
Source: Dave Leip's Atlas of U.S. Presidential Elections

SPORTS

Professional Sports Teams

Team Name	League	Year Established
Jacksonville Jaguars	National Football League (NFL)	1995

Note: Includes teams located in the Jacksonville, FL Metropolitan Statistical Area.
Source: Wikipedia, Major Professional Sports Teams of the United States and Canada, May 1, 2025

CLIMATE

Average and Extreme Temperatures

Temperature	Jan	Feb	Mar	Apr	May	Jun	Jul	Aug	Sep	Oct	Nov	Dec	Yr.
Extreme High (°F)	84	88	91	95	100	103	103	102	98	96	88	84	103
Average High (°F)	65	68	74	80	86	90	92	91	87	80	73	67	79
Average Temp. (°F)	54	57	62	69	75	80	83	82	79	71	62	56	69
Average Low (°F)	43	45	51	57	64	70	73	73	70	61	51	44	58
Extreme Low (°F)	7	22	23	34	45	47	61	63	48	36	21	11	7

Note: Figures cover the years 1948-1990
Source: National Climatic Data Center, International Station Meteorological Climate Summary, 9/96

Average Precipitation/Snowfall/Humidity

Precip./Humidity	Jan	Feb	Mar	Apr	May	Jun	Jul	Aug	Sep	Oct	Nov	Dec	Yr.
Avg. Precip. (in.)	3.0	3.7	3.8	3.0	3.6	5.3	6.2	7.4	7.8	3.7	2.0	2.6	52.0
Avg. Snowfall (in.)	Tr	Tr	Tr	0	0	0	0	0	0	0	0	Tr	0
Avg. Rel. Hum. 7am (%)	86	86	87	86	86	88	89	91	92	91	89	88	88
Avg. Rel. Hum. 4pm (%)	56	53	50	49	54	61	64	65	66	62	58	58	58

Note: Figures cover the years 1948-1990; Tr = Trace amounts (<0.05 in. of rain; <0.5 in. of snow)
Source: National Climatic Data Center, International Station Meteorological Climate Summary, 9/96

Weather Conditions

Temperature			Daytime Sky			Precipitation		Thunder-storms
10°F & below	32°F & below	90°F & above	Clear	Partly cloudy	Cloudy	0.01 inch or more precip.	0.1 inch or more snow/ice	
<1	16	83	86	181	98	114	1	65

Note: Figures are average number of days per year and cover the years 1948-1990
Source: National Climatic Data Center, International Station Meteorological Climate Summary, 9/96

HAZARDOUS WASTE

Superfund Sites

The Jacksonville, FL metro area is home to six sites on the EPA's Superfund National Priorities List (NPL) or Superfund Alternative Approach (SAA) list: **Brown's Dump** (SAA); **Jacksonville Ash Site** (SAA); **Jacksonville Naval Air Station** (Final NPL); **Kerr-Mcgee Chemical Corp - Jacksonville** (Final NPL); **Pickettville Road Landfill** (Final NPL); **USN Air Station Cecil Field** (Final NPL). The Superfund alternative approach uses the same investigation and cleanup process and standards that are used for sites listed on the National Priorities List. The SAA is an alternative to listing a site on the NPL; it is not an alternative to Superfund or the Superfund process. There are a total of 1,445 Superfund sites with a status of proposed or final on both lists in the United States. *U.S. Environmental Protection Agency, National Priorities List, May 1, 2025; U.S. Environmental Protection Agency, Superfund Alternative Approach Sites, May 1, 2025*

AIR QUALITY

Air Quality Trends: Ozone

	1990	1995	2000	2005	2010	2015	2020	2021	2022	2023
MSA[1]	0.080	0.068	0.072	0.076	0.068	0.060	0.057	0.061	0.062	0.060
U.S.	0.087	0.089	0.081	0.080	0.072	0.068	0.066	0.067	0.067	0.070

Note: (1) Data covers the Jacksonville, FL Metropolitan Statistical Area. The values shown are the composite ozone concentration averages among trend sites based on the highest fourth daily maximum 8-hour concentration in parts per million. These trends are based on sites having an adequate record of monitoring data during the trend period. Data from exceptional events are included.
Source: U.S. Environmental Protection Agency, Air Quality Monitoring Information, "Air Quality Trends by City, 1990-2023"

Air Quality Index

Area	Percent of Days when Air Quality was...[2]					AQI Statistics[2]	
	Good	Moderate	Unhealthy for Sensitive Groups	Unhealthy	Very Unhealthy	Maximum	Median
MSA[1]	41.6	57.8	0.5	0.0	0.0	124	52

Note: (1) Data covers the Jacksonville, FL Metropolitan Statistical Area; (2) Based on 365 days with AQI data in 2023. Air Quality Index (AQI) is an index for reporting daily air quality. EPA calculates the AQI for five major air pollutants regulated by the Clean Air Act: ground-level ozone, particle pollution (aka particulate matter), carbon monoxide, sulfur dioxide, and nitrogen dioxide. The AQI runs from 0 to 500. The higher the AQI value, the greater the level of air pollution and the greater the health concern. There are six AQI categories: "Good" AQI is between 0 and 50. Air quality is considered satisfactory; "Moderate" AQI is between 51 and 100. Air quality is acceptable; "Unhealthy for Sensitive Groups" When AQI values are between 101 and 150, members of sensitive groups may experience health effects; "Unhealthy" When AQI values are between 151 and 200 everyone may begin to experience health effects; "Very Unhealthy" AQI values between 201 and 300 trigger a health alert; "Hazardous" AQI values over 300 trigger warnings of emergency conditions (not shown).
Source: U.S. Environmental Protection Agency, Air Quality Index Report, 2023

Air Quality Index Pollutants

Area	Percent of Days when AQI Pollutant was...[2]					
	Carbon Monoxide	Nitrogen Dioxide	Ozone	Sulfur Dioxide	Particulate Matter 2.5	Particulate Matter 10
MSA[1]	0.0	0.0	17.0	(3)	83.0	0.0

Note: (1) Data covers the Jacksonville, FL Metropolitan Statistical Area; (2) Based on 365 days with AQI data in 2023. The Air Quality Index (AQI) is an index for reporting daily air quality. EPA calculates the AQI for five major air pollutants regulated by the Clean Air Act: ground-level ozone, particle pollution (also known as particulate matter), carbon monoxide, sulfur dioxide, and nitrogen dioxide. The AQI runs from 0 to 500. The higher the AQI value, the greater the level of air pollution and the greater the health concern; (3) Sulfur dioxide is no longer included in this table because SO_2 concentrations tend to be very localized and not necessarily representative of broad geographical areas like counties and CBSAs.
Source: U.S. Environmental Protection Agency, Air Quality Index Report, 2023

Maximum Air Pollutant Concentrations: Particulate Matter, Ozone, CO and Lead

	Particulate Matter 10 (ug/m^3)	Particulate Matter 2.5 Wtd AM (ug/m^3)	Particulate Matter 2.5 24-Hr (ug/m^3)	Ozone (ppm)	Carbon Monoxide (ppm)	Lead (ug/m^3)
MSA[1] Level	55	7.9	20	0.062	1	n/a
NAAQS[2]	150	15	35	0.075	9	0.15
Met NAAQS[2]	Yes	Yes	Yes	Yes	Yes	n/a

Note: (1) Data covers the Jacksonville, FL Metropolitan Statistical Area; Data from exceptional events are included; (2) National Ambient Air Quality Standards; ppm = parts per million; ug/m^3 = micrograms per cubic meter; n/a not available.
Concentrations: Particulate Matter 10 (coarse particulate)—highest second maximum 24-hour concentration; Particulate Matter 2.5 Wtd AM (fine particulate)—highest weighted annual mean concentration; Particulate Matter 2.5 24-Hour (fine particulate)—highest 98th percentile 24-hour concentration; Ozone—highest fourth daily maximum 8-hour concentration; Carbon Monoxide—highest second maximum non-overlapping 8-hour concentration; Lead—maximum running 3-month average
Source: U.S. Environmental Protection Agency, Air Quality Monitoring Information, "Air Quality Statistics by City, 2023"

Maximum Air Pollutant Concentrations: Nitrogen Dioxide and Sulfur Dioxide

	Nitrogen Dioxide AM (ppb)	Nitrogen Dioxide 1-Hr (ppb)	Sulfur Dioxide AM (ppb)	Sulfur Dioxide 1-Hr (ppb)	Sulfur Dioxide 24-Hr (ppb)
MSA[1] Level	10	40	n/a	40	n/a
NAAQS[2]	53	100	30	75	140
Met NAAQS[2]	Yes	Yes	n/a	Yes	n/a

Note: (1) Data covers the Jacksonville, FL Metropolitan Statistical Area; Data from exceptional events are included; (2) National Ambient Air Quality Standards; ppm = parts per million; ug/m^3 = micrograms per cubic meter; n/a not available.
Concentrations: Nitrogen Dioxide AM—highest arithmetic mean concentration; Nitrogen Dioxide 1-Hr—highest 98th percentile 1-hour daily maximum concentration; Sulfur Dioxide AM—highest annual mean concentration; Sulfur Dioxide 1-Hr—highest 99th percentile 1-hour daily maximum concentration; Sulfur Dioxide 24-Hr—highest second maximum 24-hour concentration
Source: U.S. Environmental Protection Agency, Air Quality Monitoring Information, "Air Quality Statistics by City, 2023"

Lafayette, Louisiana

Background

Lafayette is located 100 miles west of New Orleans and 40 miles north of the Gulf of Mexico. It's cultural origins originated in Nova Scotia, Canada, in 1755, when British governor Charles Lawrence, expelled the entire population of Canadians known as the Acadians, whose roots were French and Catholic, when they refused to pledge loyalty to the British crown. Many lost their lives in their quest for a new home, as they settled all along the eastern seaboard of the United States. A large majority of Acadians settled in southern Louisiana, in the area surrounding New Orleans.

Prior to the Acadian expulsion, southern Louisiana had remained unsettled. The first known inhabitants were the Attakapas Native American tribe. A sparse population of French trappers, traders, and ranchers occupied the region until the Spanish occupation of 1766. The 1789 French Revolution brought teams of French immigrants fleeing the brutal conditions at home. In 1803, the French sold the Louisiana territory to the United States—known as the Louisiana Purchase.

An important early event for Lafayette, originally named Vermillionville, was the donation of land to the Catholic Church by Acadian Jean Mouton. The population began to grow in the parish then known as St. John the Evangelist of Vermillion. The community was renamed in 1884 in honor of the French Marquis de Lafayette, a Frenchman who fought under General George Washington in the American Revolution. Lafayette is credited with bringing some of the ideals of the American Revolution to the French, partly precipitating the French Revolution. By the time of his death, Lafayette had visited all 24 of the United States, and was an American citizen.

The word "cajun," is derived from the early Acadian settlers. In French, "Les Acadians" became "le Cadiens," which later became just "Cadien." The French pronunciation was difficult for non-French Americans to say, so Cadien became Cajun. A primary characteristic of the Acadian/Cajun culture is what's known as "joie de vivre" (joy of living). The Cajun reputation is one of hard work and hard play, full of passion that can turn on a dime. Contributions of the Cajun culture to the fabric of America have been many, but their food and their music have made an indelible mark.

Lafayette is often referred to as the center of Cajun culture not because of its geography, but because of the strong Cajun influence in everyday life. Celebration is a major part of the Cajun culture, and this is reflected in Lafayette's many festivals, one of the most being the annual Mari Gras. Others include The Festival International de Louisiana, which celebrates the French-speaking heritage of much of the population and Festival Acadians, which celebrates everything that is uniquely Cajun.

With over 600 oil-related businesses in Lafayette Parish alone, the city is known for its oil and natural gas industries. Other important industry sectors are healthcare and education. The University of Louisiana at Lafayette which started out as a small agricultural college with about 100 students, today has more than 18,000 students in more than 100 programs housed on 1,300-acres. It is the second largest public university in the state with a focus on hands-on research. UL is considered among the top universities in computer science, engineering, and nursing.

Lafayette's climate is classified as humid subtropical. It has year-round precipitation, especially during summertime. It is typical of areas along the Gulf of Mexico with hot, humid summers and mild winters.

Rankings

Business/Finance Rankings

- The Lafayette metro area appeared on the Milken Institute "2025 Best Performing Cities" list. Rank: #198 out of 200 large metro areas (based on performance category). Criteria: job growth; wage growth; high-tech growth and impact; community resilience; housing affordability; household broadband access. *Milken Institute, "Best-Performing Cities 2025," January 14, 2025*

Education Rankings

- Personal finance website *WalletHub* analyzed the 150 largest U.S. metropolitan statistical areas to determine where the most educated Americans are putting their degrees to work. Criteria: education levels; percentage of workers with degrees; education quality and attainment gap; public school quality rankings; quality and enrollment of each metro area's universities. Lafayette was ranked #135 (#1 = most educated city). *WalletHub.com, "Most & Least Educated Cities in America, 2025" July 2, 2024*

Business Environment

DEMOGRAPHICS

Population Growth

Area	1990 Census	2000 Census	2010 Census	2020 Census	2023 Estimate[2]	Population Growth 1990-2023 (%)
City	104,735	110,257	120,623	121,374	121,537	16.0
MSA[1]	208,740	239,086	273,738	478,384	410,883	96.8
U.S.	248,709,873	281,421,906	308,745,538	331,449,281	332,387,540	33.6

Note: (1) Figures cover the Lafayette, LA Metropolitan Statistical Area; (2) 2019-2023 5-year ACS population estimate
Source: U.S. Census Bureau, 1990 Census, 2000 Census, 2010 Census, 2020 Census, 2019-2023 American Community Survey 5-Year Estimates

Race

Area	White Alone[2] (%)	Black Alone[2] (%)	Asian Alone[2] (%)	AIAN[3] Alone[2] (%)	NHOPI[4] Alone[2] (%)	Other Race Alone[2] (%)	Two or More Races (%)
City	59.1	28.6	2.1	0.1	0.1	1.2	8.8
MSA[1]	68.0	22.7	1.5	0.2	0.1	1.1	6.4
U.S.	63.4	12.4	5.8	0.9	0.2	6.6	10.7

Note: (1) Figures cover the Lafayette, LA Metropolitan Statistical Area; (2) Alone is defined as not being in combination with one or more other races; (3) American Indian and Alaska Native; (4) Native Hawaiian and Other Pacific Islander
Source: U.S. Census Bureau, 2019-2023 American Community Survey 5-Year Estimates

Hispanic or Latino Origin

Area	Total (%)	Mexican (%)	Puerto Rican (%)	Cuban (%)	Other (%)
City	7.6	1.9	0.4	0.5	4.8
MSA[1]	5.3	1.9	0.2	0.2	3.0
U.S.	19.0	11.3	1.8	0.7	5.2

Note: Persons of Hispanic or Latino origin can be of any race; (1) Figures cover the Lafayette, LA Metropolitan Statistical Area
Source: U.S. Census Bureau, 2019-2023 American Community Survey 5-Year Estimates

Age

Area	Percent of Population									Median Age
	Under Age 5	Age 5–19	Age 20–34	Age 35–44	Age 45–54	Age 55–64	Age 65–74	Age 75–84	Age 85+	
City	6.1	18.0	22.9	12.8	10.2	12.9	10.9	4.5	1.8	37.1
MSA[1]	6.6	20.1	20.1	13.6	11.7	12.8	9.5	4.2	1.4	37.2
U.S.	5.7	19.1	20.2	13.1	12.3	12.8	10.0	4.9	1.9	38.7

Note: (1) Figures cover the Lafayette, LA Metropolitan Statistical Area
Source: U.S. Census Bureau, 2019-2023 American Community Survey 5-Year Estimates

Disability by Age

Area	All Ages	Under 18 Years Old	18 to 64 Years Old	65 Years and Over
City	12.9	3.5	10.3	33.9
MSA[1]	14.5	4.7	12.9	37.2
U.S.	13.0	4.7	10.7	32.9

Note: Figures show percent of the civilian noninstitutionalized population that reported having a disability. Disability status is determined from six types of difficulty: vision, hearing, cognitive, ambulatory, self-care, and independent living. For children under 5 years old, hearing and vision difficulty are used to determine disability status. For children between the ages of 5 and 14, disability status is determined from hearing, vision, cognitive, ambulatory, and self-care difficulties. For people aged 15 years and older, they are considered to have a disability if they have difficulty with any one of the six difficulty types; Note: (1) Figures cover the Lafayette, LA Metropolitan Statistical Area
Source: U.S. Census Bureau, 2019-2023 American Community Survey 5-Year Estimates

Ancestry

Area	German	Irish	English	American	Italian	Polish	French[2]	European	Scottish
City	9.2	5.6	6.7	5.2	3.8	0.5	16.7	0.7	1.1
MSA[1]	7.1	4.5	5.3	6.2	3.0	0.6	17.1	0.7	0.7
U.S.	12.6	9.4	9.1	5.5	4.9	2.6	2.0	1.6	1.6

Note: Figures are the percentage of the total population reporting a particular ancestry. The nine most commonly reported ancestries in the U.S. are shown. Figures include multiple ancestries (e.g. if a person reported being Irish and Italian, they were included in both columns); (1) Figures cover the Lafayette, LA Metropolitan Statistical Area; (2) Excludes Basque
Source: U.S. Census Bureau, 2019-2023 American Community Survey 5-Year Estimates

Foreign-born Population

Area	Any Foreign Country	Percent of Population Born in							
		Asia	Mexico	Europe	Caribbean	Central America[2]	South America	Africa	Canada
City	6.6	2.1	0.5	0.4	0.2	1.8	0.8	0.4	0.1
MSA[1]	3.8	1.2	0.5	0.2	0.2	1.0	0.4	0.1	0.0
U.S.	13.9	4.3	3.3	1.4	1.4	1.2	1.2	0.8	0.2

Note: (1) Figures cover the Lafayette, LA Metropolitan Statistical Area; (2) Excludes Mexico.
Source: U.S. Census Bureau, 2019-2023 American Community Survey 5-Year Estimates

Household Size

Area	Persons in Household (%)							Average Household Size
	One	Two	Three	Four	Five	Six	Seven or More	
City	33.8	36.5	13.4	9.1	5.0	1.4	0.9	2.25
MSA[1]	29.1	33.5	16.1	12.4	5.4	2.1	1.2	2.49
U.S.	28.5	33.8	15.4	12.7	5.9	2.3	1.4	2.54

Note: (1) Figures cover the Lafayette, LA Metropolitan Statistical Area
Source: U.S. Census Bureau, 2019-2023 American Community Survey 5-Year Estimates

Household Relationships

Area	Householder	Opposite-sex Spouse	Same-sex Spouse	Opposite-sex Unmarried Partner	Same-sex Unmarried Partner	Child[2]	Grandchild	Other Relatives	Non-relatives
City	43.0	15.3	0.2	2.8	0.2	27.0	2.3	3.5	3.8
MSA[1]	39.5	17.1	0.2	2.7	0.2	30.4	2.9	3.5	2.5
U.S.	38.3	17.5	0.2	2.5	0.2	28.3	2.4	4.8	3.4

Note: Figures are percent of the total population; (1) Figures cover the Lafayette, LA Metropolitan Statistical Area; (2) Includes biological, adopted, and stepchildren of the householder
Source: U.S. Census Bureau, 2020 Census

Gender

Area	Males	Females	Males per 100 Females
City	58,993	62,544	94.3
MSA[1]	200,575	210,308	95.4
U.S.	164,545,087	167,842,453	98.0

Note: (1) Figures cover the Lafayette, LA Metropolitan Statistical Area
Source: U.S. Census Bureau, 2019-2023 American Community Survey 5-Year Estimates

Marital Status

Area	Never Married	Now Married[2]	Separated	Widowed	Divorced
City	40.0	42.8	2.2	5.1	9.9
MSA[1]	33.9	47.8	2.0	5.4	10.9
U.S.	34.1	47.9	1.7	5.6	10.7

Note: Figures are percentages and cover the population 15 years of age and older; (1) Figures cover the Lafayette, LA Metropolitan Statistical Area; (2) Excludes separated
Source: U.S. Census Bureau, 2019-2023 American Community Survey 5-Year Estimates

Religious Groups by Family

Area	Catholic	Baptist	Methodist	LDS[2]	Pentecostal	Lutheran	Islam	Adventist	Other
MSA[1]	44.3	9.3	2.0	0.4	1.8	0.1	0.1	0.8	7.0
U.S.	18.7	7.3	3.0	2.0	1.8	1.7	1.3	1.3	11.6

Note: Figures are the number of adherents as a percentage of the total population and cover the eight largest religious groups in the U.S; (1) Figures cover the Lafayette, LA Metropolitan Statistical Area; (2) Church of Jesus Christ of Latter-day Saints
Sources: 2020 U.S. Religion Census, Association of Statisticians of American Religious Bodies; The Association of Religion Data Archives (ARDA)

Religious Groups by Tradition

Area	Catholic	Evangelical Protestant	Mainline Protestant	Black Protestant	Islam	Judaism	Hinduism	Orthodox	Buddhism
MSA[1]	44.3	12.6	2.4	5.0	0.1	n/a	<0.1	<0.1	0.1
U.S.	18.7	16.5	5.2	2.3	1.3	0.6	0.4	0.4	0.3

Note: Figures are the number of adherents as a percentage of the total population; (1) Figures cover the Lafayette, LA Metropolitan Statistical Area
Sources: 2020 U.S. Religion Census, Association of Statisticians of American Religious Bodies; The Association of Religion Data Archives (ARDA)

ECONOMY

Real Gross Domestic Product (GDP)

Area	2017	2018	2019	2020	2021	2022	2023	Rank[3]
MSA[1]	21.1	22.0	21.8	20.8	21.8	21.8	22.6	132
U.S.[2]	17,619.1	18,160.7	18,642.5	18,238.9	19,387.6	19,896.6	20,436.3	—

Note: Figures are in billions of chained 2017 dollars; (1) Figures cover the Lafayette, LA Metropolitan Statistical Area; (2) Figures cover real GDP within metropolitan areas; (3) Rank is based on 2023 data and ranges from 1 to 384
Source: U.S. Bureau of Economic Analysis

Economic Growth

Area	2014	2015	2016	2017	2018	2019	2020	2021	2022	2023
MSA[1]	1.4	-7.6	-9.3	0.0	4.4	-1.0	-4.5	4.6	0.1	3.8
U.S.[2]	2.6	3.2	2.0	2.7	3.1	2.7	-2.2	6.3	2.6	2.7

Note: Figures are real gross domestic product growth rates and represent percent change from preceding period; (1) Figures cover the Lafayette, LA Metropolitan Statistical Area; (2) Figures are the average growth rates within metropolitan areas
Source: U.S. Bureau of Economic Analysis

Metropolitan Area Exports

Area	2018	2019	2020	2021	2022	2023	Rank[2]
MSA[1]	1,001.7	1,086.2	946.2	895.7	911.8	836.2	189
U.S.	1,664,056.1	1,645,173.7	1,431,406.6	1,753,941.4	2,062,937.4	2,019,160.5	—

Note: Figures are in millions of dollars; (1) Figures cover the Lafayette, LA Metropolitan Statistical Area; (2) Rank is based on 2023 data and ranges from 1 to 386
Source: U.S. Department of Commerce, International Trade Administration, Office of Trade and Economic Analysis, Industry and Analysis, Exports by Metropolitan Area, data extracted April 2, 2025

Building Permits

Area	Single-Family			Multi-Family			Total		
	2023	2024	Pct. Chg.	2023	2024	Pct. Chg.	2023	2024	Pct. Chg.
City	n/a	n/a	n/a	n/a	n/a	n/a	n/a	n/a	n/a
MSA[1]	2,008	2,001	-0.3	378	18	-95.2	2,386	2,019	-15.4
U.S.	920,000	981,900	6.7	591,100	496,100	-16.1	1,511,100	1,478,000	-2.2

Note: (1) Figures cover the Lafayette, LA Metropolitan Statistical Area; Figures represent new, privately-owned housing units authorized (unadjusted data)
Source: U.S. Census Bureau, Building Permits Survey (BPS), 2023, 2024

Bankruptcy Filings

Area	Business Filings			Nonbusiness Filings		
	2023	2024	% Chg.	2023	2024	% Chg.
Lafayette Parish	19	44	131.6	335	410	22.4
U.S.	18,926	23,107	22.1	434,064	494,201	13.9

Note: Business filings include Chapter 7, Chapter 9, Chapter 11, Chapter 12, Chapter 13, Chapter 15, and Section 304; Nonbusiness filings include Chapter 7, Chapter 11, and Chapter 13
Source: Administrative Office of the U.S. Courts, Business and Nonbusiness Bankruptcy, County Cases Commenced by Chapter of the Bankruptcy Code, During the 12-Month Period Ending December 31, 2023 and Business and Nonbusiness Bankruptcy, County Cases Commenced by Chapter of the Bankruptcy Code, During the 12-Month Period Ending December 31, 2024

Housing Vacancy Rates

Area	Gross Vacancy Rate[3] (%)			Year-Round Vacancy Rate[4] (%)			Rental Vacancy Rate[5] (%)			Homeowner Vacancy Rate[6] (%)		
	2022	2023	2024	2022	2023	2024	2022	2023	2024	2022	2023	2024
MSA[1]	n/a	n/a	n/a	n/a	n/a	n/a	n/a	n/a	n/a	n/a	n/a	n/a
U.S.[2]	9.1	9.0	9.1	7.5	7.5	7.6	5.7	6.5	6.8	0.8	0.8	1.0

Note: (1) Figures cover the Lafayette, LA Metropolitan Statistical Area; (2) Figures cover the 75 largest Metropolitan Statistical Areas; (3) The percentage of the total housing inventory that is vacant; (4) The percentage of the housing inventory (excluding seasonal units) that is year-round vacant; (5) The percentage of rental inventory that is vacant for rent; (6) The percentage of homeowner inventory that is vacant for sale; n/a not available
Source: U.S. Census Bureau, Housing Vacancies and Homeownership Annual Statistics: 2022, 2023, 2024

INCOME

Income

Area	Per Capita ($)	Median Household ($)	Average Household ($)
City	39,861	61,454	91,871
MSA[1]	34,845	60,910	86,057
U.S.	43,289	78,538	110,491

Note: (1) Figures cover the Lafayette, LA Metropolitan Statistical Area
Source: U.S. Census Bureau, 2019-2023 American Community Survey 5-Year Estimates

Household Income Distribution

Area	Percent of Households Earning							
	Under $15,000	$15,000 -$24,999	$25,000 -$34,999	$35,000 -$49,999	$50,000 -$74,999	$75,000 -$99,999	$100,000 -$149,999	$150,000 and up
City	13.8	8.8	8.0	11.5	14.6	12.8	14.9	15.6
MSA[1]	13.1	9.6	8.3	12.0	14.7	12.2	15.8	14.3
U.S.	8.5	6.6	6.8	10.4	15.7	12.7	17.4	21.9

Note: (1) Figures cover the Lafayette, LA Metropolitan Statistical Area
Source: U.S. Census Bureau, 2019-2023 American Community Survey 5-Year Estimates

Poverty Rate

Area	All Ages	Under 18 Years Old	18 to 64 Years Old	65 Years and Over
City	19.1	28.3	17.1	14.8
MSA[1]	18.5	25.0	16.8	14.8
U.S.	12.4	16.3	11.6	10.4

Note: Figures are percentage of people whose income during the past 12 months was below the poverty level; (1) Figures cover the Lafayette, LA Metropolitan Statistical Area
Source: U.S. Census Bureau, 2019-2023 American Community Survey 5-Year Estimates

EMPLOYMENT

Labor Force and Employment

Area	Civilian Labor Force			Workers Employed		
	Dec. 2023	Dec. 2024	% Chg.	Dec. 2023	Dec. 2024	% Chg.
City	59,760	59,993	0.4	57,644	57,720	0.1
MSA[1]	185,004	185,747	0.4	178,352	178,532	0.1
U.S.	166,661,000	167,746,000	0.7	160,754,000	161,294,000	0.3

Note: Data is not seasonally adjusted and covers workers 16 years of age and older; (1) Figures cover the Lafayette, LA Metropolitan Statistical Area
Source: Bureau of Labor Statistics, Local Area Unemployment Statistics

Unemployment Rate

Area	2024											
	Jan.	Feb.	Mar.	Apr.	May	Jun.	Jul.	Aug.	Sep.	Oct.	Nov.	Dec.
City	4.0	3.9	3.8	3.4	3.6	4.5	4.4	4.4	4.3	4.3	4.1	3.8
MSA[1]	4.1	4.0	3.8	3.4	3.6	4.5	4.4	4.4	4.3	4.3	4.2	3.9
U.S.	4.1	4.2	3.9	3.5	3.7	4.3	4.5	4.4	3.9	3.9	4.0	3.8

Note: Data is not seasonally adjusted and covers workers 16 years of age and older; (1) Figures cover the Lafayette, LA Metropolitan Statistical Area
Source: Bureau of Labor Statistics, Local Area Unemployment Statistics

Average Wages

Occupation	$/Hr.	Occupation	$/Hr.
Accountants and Auditors	35.63	Maintenance and Repair Workers	19.43
Automotive Mechanics	23.75	Marketing Managers	52.19
Bookkeepers	20.97	Network and Computer Systems Admin.	45.64
Carpenters	22.46	Nurses, Licensed Practical	24.52
Cashiers	11.84	Nurses, Registered	38.87
Computer Programmers	40.56	Nursing Assistants	14.75
Computer Systems Analysts	49.57	Office Clerks, General	15.09
Computer User Support Specialists	30.51	Physical Therapists	45.77
Construction Laborers	20.27	Physicians	127.73
Cooks, Restaurant	13.44	Plumbers, Pipefitters and Steamfitters	26.64
Customer Service Representatives	18.01	Police and Sheriff's Patrol Officers	26.21
Dentists	82.38	Postal Service Mail Carriers	28.33
Electricians	26.35	Real Estate Sales Agents	20.17
Engineers, Electrical	47.69	Retail Salespersons	14.62
Fast Food and Counter Workers	12.06	Sales Representatives, Technical/Scientific	53.76
Financial Managers	57.76	Secretaries, Exc. Legal/Medical/Executive	19.61
First-Line Supervisors of Office Workers	27.80	Security Guards	15.29
General and Operations Managers	57.89	Surgeons	n/a
Hairdressers/Cosmetologists	12.82	Teacher Assistants, Exc. Postsecondary[1]	12.65
Home Health and Personal Care Aides	10.36	Teachers, Secondary School, Exc. Sp. Ed.[1]	24.74
Janitors and Cleaners	13.40	Telemarketers	n/a
Landscaping/Groundskeeping Workers	15.75	Truck Drivers, Heavy/Tractor-Trailer	26.47
Lawyers	66.98	Truck Drivers, Light/Delivery Services	19.63
Maids and Housekeeping Cleaners	12.04	Waiters and Waitresses	11.17

Note: Wage data covers the Lafayette, LA Metropolitan Statistical Area; (1) Hourly wages were calculated from annual wage data based on a 40 hour work week
Source: Bureau of Labor Statistics, Metro Area Occupational Employment & Wage Estimates, May 2024

Employment by Industry

Sector	MSA[1] Number of Employees	MSA[1] Percent of Total	U.S. Percent of Total
Construction	10,200	5.5	5.1
Financial Activities	8,800	4.7	5.8
Government	23,400	12.6	14.9
Information	1,500	0.8	1.9
Leisure and Hospitality	20,700	11.1	10.4
Manufacturing	14,300	7.7	8.0
Mining and Logging	7,600	4.1	0.4
Other Services	6,700	3.6	3.7
Private Education and Health Services	34,000	18.3	16.9
Professional and Business Services	21,000	11.3	14.2
Retail Trade	23,500	12.6	10.0
Transportation, Warehousing, and Utilities	6,200	3.3	4.8
Wholesale Trade	8,100	4.4	3.9

Note: Figures are non-farm employment as of December 2024. Figures are not seasonally adjusted and include workers 16 years of age and older; (1) Figures cover the Lafayette, LA Metropolitan Statistical Area
Source: Bureau of Labor Statistics, Current Employment Statistics, Employment, Hours, and Earnings

Employment by Occupation

Occupation Classification	City (%)	MSA[1] (%)	U.S. (%)
Management, Business, Science, and Arts	45.3	38.7	42.0
Natural Resources, Construction, and Maintenance	7.0	11.2	8.6
Production, Transportation, and Material Moving	7.5	11.3	13.0
Sales and Office	22.3	22.5	19.9
Service	17.9	16.3	16.5

Note: Figures cover employed civilians 16 years of age and older; (1) Figures cover the Lafayette, LA Metropolitan Statistical Area
Source: U.S. Census Bureau, 2019-2023 American Community Survey 5-Year Estimates

Occupations with Greatest Projected Employment Growth: 2022 – 2032

Occupation[1]	2022 Employment	2032 Projected Employment	Numeric Employment Change	Percent Employment Change
Home Health and Personal Care Aides	36,540	44,950	8,410	23.0
Construction Laborers	31,390	35,600	4,210	13.4
Registered Nurses	43,740	47,040	3,300	7.5
Cooks, Restaurant	14,130	17,300	3,170	22.4
Stockers and Order Fillers	27,540	30,190	2,650	9.6
General and Operations Managers	38,680	40,940	2,260	5.8
Nurse Practitioners	4,470	6,420	1,950	43.6
Medical and Health Services Managers	6,570	8,470	1,900	28.9
Managers, All Other	33,510	35,250	1,740	5.2
Laborers and Freight, Stock, and Material Movers, Hand	37,120	38,820	1,700	4.6

Note: Projections cover Louisiana; (1) Sorted by numeric employment change
Source: www.projectionscentral.org, State Occupational Projections, 2022–2032 Long-Term Projections

Fastest-Growing Occupations: 2022 – 2032

Occupation[1]	2022 Employment	2032 Projected Employment	Numeric Employment Change	Percent Employment Change
Nurse Practitioners	4,470	6,420	1,950	43.6
Epidemiologists	150	200	50	33.3
Data Scientists	560	740	180	32.1
Medical and Health Services Managers	6,570	8,470	1,900	28.9
Information Security Analysts (SOC 2018)	480	610	130	27.1
Occupational Therapy Assistants	740	940	200	27.0
Orthotists and Prosthetists	230	290	60	26.1
Physical Therapist Assistants	1,580	1,990	410	25.9
Taxi Drivers	240	300	60	25.0
Software Developers	2,680	3,330	650	24.3

Note: Projections cover Louisiana; (1) Sorted by percent employment change and excludes occupations with numeric employment change less than 50
Source: www.projectionscentral.org, State Occupational Projections, 2022–2032 Long-Term Projections

CITY FINANCES

City Government Finances

Component	2022 ($000)	2022 ($ per capita)
Total Revenues	713,198	5,636
Total Expenditures	664,803	5,254
Debt Outstanding	460,067	3,636

Source: U.S. Census Bureau, State & Local Government Finances 2022

City Government Revenue by Source

Source	2022 ($000)	2022 ($ per capita)	2022 (%)
General Revenue			
From Federal Government	28,974	229	4.1
From State Government	10,466	83	1.5
From Local Governments	2,954	23	0.4
Taxes			
Property	131,962	1,043	18.5
Sales and Gross Receipts	126,938	1,003	17.8
Personal Income	0	0	0.0
Corporate Income	0	0	0.0
Motor Vehicle License	0	0	0.0
Other Taxes	6,044	48	0.8
Current Charges	129,690	1,025	18.2
Liquor Store	0	0	0.0
Utility	258,283	2,041	36.2

Source: U.S. Census Bureau, State & Local Government Finances 2022

City Government Expenditures by Function

Function	2022 ($000)	2022 ($ per capita)	2022 (%)
General Direct Expenditures			
Air Transportation	7,547	59	1.1
Corrections	7,126	56	1.1
Education	0	0	0.0
Employment Security Administration	0	0	0.0
Financial Administration	21,966	173	3.3
Fire Protection	30,006	237	4.5
General Public Buildings	4,883	38	0.7
Governmental Administration, Other	7,552	59	1.1
Health	4,605	36	0.7
Highways	59,246	468	8.9
Hospitals	0	0	0.0
Housing and Community Development	19,930	157	3.0
Interest on General Debt	11,027	87	1.7
Judicial and Legal	19,844	156	3.0
Libraries	10,899	86	1.6
Parking	754	6	0.1
Parks and Recreation	17,603	139	2.6
Police Protection	110,134	870	16.6
Public Welfare	0	0	0.0
Sewerage	33,781	267	5.1
Solid Waste Management	16,015	126	2.4
Veterans' Services	0	0	0.0
Liquor Store	0	0	0.0
Utility	236,190	1,866	35.5

Source: U.S. Census Bureau, State & Local Government Finances 2022

TAXES

State Corporate Income Tax Rates

State	Tax Rate (%)	Income Brackets ($)	Num. of Brackets	Financial Institution Tax Rate (%)[a]	Federal Income Tax Ded.
Louisiana	3.5 - 7.5	50,000 - 150,000	3	3.5 - 7.5	Yes

Note: Tax rates for tax year 2024; (a) Rates listed are the corporate income tax rate applied to financial institutions or excise taxes based on income. Some states have other taxes based upon the value of deposits or shares.
Source: Federation of Tax Administrators, State Corporate Income Tax Rates, January 1, 2025

State Individual Income Tax Rates

State	Tax Rate (%)	Income Brackets ($)	Personal Exemptions ($)			Standard Ded. ($)	
			Single	Married	Depend.	Single	Married
Louisiana (aa)	1.85 - 4.25 (bb)	12,500 - 50,001 (b)	4,500	9,000	1,000 (k)	14,600 (k)	29,000 (k)

Note: Tax rates for tax year 2024; Local- and county-level taxes are not included; Federal income tax is not deductible on state income tax returns; (b) For joint returns, taxes are twice the tax on half the couple's income. California brackets violate this formula at the two highest tax brackets in 2024; (k) The amounts reported for Louisiana are a combined personal exemption-standard deduction. Louisiana provides for a an adjustment of federal itemized medical and dentals expenses above the federal standard deduction; (aa) Standard deduction amounts reported are maximums, Maryland standard deduction is 15% of AGI with an increased deduction above $17,000 - S/$34,333 - MFJ in 2023; Montana, 20% of AGI; (bb) Louisiana lawmakers repealed the state's throwout rule, ending the taxation of so-called "nowhere income." Iowa is phasing-in a flat rate by 2027, while Nebraska (LB 754 signed into law) and South Carolina is phasing-in a reduced top rate by 2027.
Source: Federation of Tax Administrators, State Individual Income Tax Rates, January 1, 2025

Various State Sales and Excise Tax Rates

State	State Sales Tax (%)	Gasoline[1] ($/gal.)	Cigarette[2] ($/pack)	Spirits[3] ($/gal.)	Wine[4] ($/gal.)	Beer[5] ($/gal.)	Recreational Marijuana (%)
Louisiana	5	0.21	1.08	3.03	0.76	0.40	Not legal

Note: All tax rates as of January 1, 2025; (1) The American Petroleum Institute has developed a methodology for determining the average tax rate on a gallon of fuel. Rates may include any of the following: excise taxes, environmental fees, storage tank fees, other fees or taxes, general sales tax, and local taxes; (2) The federal excise tax of $1.0066 per pack and local taxes are not included; (3) Rates are those applicable to off-premise sales of 40% alcohol by volume (a.b.v.) distilled spirits in 750ml containers. Local excise taxes are excluded; (4) Rates are those applicable to off-premise sales of 11% a.b.v. non-carbonated wine in 750ml containers; (5) Rates are those applicable to off-premise sales of 4.7% a.b.v. beer in 12 ounce containers.
Source: Tax Foundation, 2025 Facts & Figures: How Does Your State Compare?

State Tax Competitiveness Index

State	Overall Rank	Corporate Tax Rank	Individual Income Tax Rank	Sales Tax Rank	Property Tax Rank	Unemployment Insurance Tax Rank
Louisiana	40	29	33	48	16	9

Note: The Tax Foundation's State Tax Competitiveness Index enables policymakers, taxpayers, and business leaders to gauge how their states' tax systems compare. A rank of 1 is best, 50 is worst. Rankings do not average to the total. States without a tax rank equally as 1. DC's scores and rankings do not affect other states. The report shows tax systems as of July 1, 2024 (the beginning of Fiscal Year 2025).
Source: Tax Foundation, State Tax Competitiveness Index 2025

TRANSPORTATION

Means of Transportation to Work

Area	Car/Truck/Van		Public Transportation			Bicycle	Walked	Other Means	Worked at Home
	Drove Alone	Car-pooled	Bus	Subway	Railroad				
City	80.4	5.6	0.6	0.0	0.0	0.5	2.2	1.2	9.5
MSA[1]	82.4	6.3	0.3	0.0	0.0	0.3	1.8	1.3	7.7
U.S.	70.2	8.5	1.7	1.3	0.4	0.4	2.4	1.6	13.5

Note: Figures are percentages and cover workers 16 years of age and older; (1) Figures cover the Lafayette, LA Metropolitan Statistical Area
Source: U.S. Census Bureau, 2019-2023 American Community Survey 5-Year Estimates

Travel Time to Work

Area	Less Than 10 Minutes	10 to 19 Minutes	20 to 29 Minutes	30 to 44 Minutes	45 to 59 Minutes	60 to 89 Minutes	90 Minutes or More
City	16.4	44.8	19.9	11.5	2.3	3.6	1.6
MSA[1]	13.7	32.9	21.8	19.4	5.2	3.8	3.2
U.S.	12.6	28.6	21.2	20.8	8.1	6.0	2.8

Note: Note: Figures are percentages and include workers 16 years old and over; (1) Figures cover the Lafayette, LA Metropolitan Statistical Area
Source: U.S. Census Bureau, 2019-2023 American Community Survey 5-Year Estimates

Key Congestion Measures

Measure	2000	2010	2015	2020	2022
Annual Hours of Delay, Total (000)	n/a	n/a	8,208	3,331	8,021
Annual Hours of Delay, Per Auto Commuter	n/a	n/a	30	13	32
Annual Congestion Cost, Per Auto Commuter ($)	n/a	n/a	754	344	820

Note: n/a not available
Source: Texas A&M Transportation Institute, 2023 Urban Mobility Report

Freeway Travel Time Index

Measure	1985	1990	1995	2000	2005	2010	2015	2020	2022
Urban Area Index[1]	n/a	n/a	n/a	n/a	n/a	n/a	1.13	1.06	1.11
Urban Area Rank[1,2]	n/a	n/a	n/a	n/a	n/a	n/a	n/a	n/a	n/a

Note: Freeway Travel Time Index—the ratio of travel time in the peak period to the travel time at free-flow conditions. For example, a value of 1.30 indicates a 20-minute free-flow trip takes 26 minutes in the peak (20 minutes x 1.30 = 26 minutes); (1) Covers the Lafayette LA urban area; (2) Rank is based on 101 larger urban areas (#1 = highest travel time index); n/a not available
Source: Texas A&M Transportation Institute, 2023 Urban Mobility Report

Public Transportation

Agency Name / Mode of Transportation	Vehicles Operated in Maximum Service[1]	Annual Unlinked Passenger Trips[2] (in thous.)	Annual Passenger Miles[3] (in thous.)
Lafayette Transit System			
Bus (directly operated)	11	1,008.6	5,681.4
Demand Response (purchased transportation)	8	30.1	318.7

Note: (1) Number of revenue vehicles operated by the given mode and type of service to meet the annual maximum service requirement. This is the revenue vehicle count during the peak season of the year; on the week and day that maximum service is provided. Vehicles operated in maximum service (VOMS) exclude atypical days and one-time special events; (2) Number of passengers who boarded public transportation vehicles. Passengers are counted each time they board a vehicle no matter how many vehicles they use to travel from their origin to their destination. (3) Sum of the distances ridden by all passengers during the entire fiscal year.
Source: Federal Transit Administration, National Transit Database, 2023

Air Transportation

Airport Name and Code / Type of Service	Passenger Airlines[1]	Passenger Enplanements	Freight Carriers[2]	Freight (lbs)
Lafayette Regional Airport (LFT)				
Domestic service (U.S. carriers only)	10	264,454	4	9,336,691
International service (U.S. carriers only)	0	0	0	0

Note: (1) Includes all U.S.-based major, minor and commuter airlines that carried at least one passenger during the year; (2) Includes all U.S.-based airlines and freight carriers that transported at least one pound of freight during the year.
Source: Bureau of Transportation Statistics, The Intermodal Transportation Database, Air Carriers: T-100 Domestic Market (U.S. carriers only), 2024; Bureau of Transportation Statistics, The Intermodal Transportation Database, Air Carriers: T-100 International Market (U.S. carriers only), 2024

BUSINESSES

Major Business Headquarters

Company Name	Industry	Rankings	
		Fortune[1]	Forbes[2]
No companies listed	-	-	-

Note: (1) Companies that produce a 10-K are ranked 1 to 500 based on 2023 revenue; (2) All private companies with at least $2 billion in annual revenue through the end of their most current fiscal year are ranked 1 to 275; companies listed are headquartered in the city; dashes indicate no ranking
Source: Fortune, "Fortune 500," 2024; Forbes, "America's Largest Private Companies," 2024

Living Environment

COST OF LIVING

Cost of Living Index

Composite Index	Groceries	Housing	Utilities	Transportation	Health Care	Misc. Goods/Services
87.2	97.1	64.5	84.1	97.9	80.7	100.5

Note: The Cost of Living Index measures regional differences in the cost of consumer goods and services, excluding taxes and non-consumer expenditures, for professional and managerial households in the top income quintile. It is based on more than 50,000 prices covering almost 60 different items for which prices are collected three times a year by chambers of commerce, economic development organizations or university applied economic centers in each participating urban area. The numbers shown should be read as a percentage above or below the national average of 100. For example, a value of 115.4 in the groceries column indicates that grocery prices are 15.4% higher than the national average. Small differences in the index numbers should not be interpreted as significant; Figures cover the Lafayette LA urban area.
Source: The Council for Community and Economic Research, Cost of Living Index, 2024

Grocery Prices

Area[1]	T-Bone Steak ($/pound)	Frying Chicken ($/pound)	Whole Milk ($/half gal.)	Eggs ($/dozen)	Orange Juice ($/64 oz.)	Coffee ($/11.5 oz.)
City[2]	15.29	1.41	4.60	3.05	4.38	5.07
Avg.	15.42	1.55	4.69	3.25	4.41	5.46
Min.	14.50	1.16	4.43	2.75	4.00	4.85
Max.	17.56	2.89	5.49	4.78	5.54	7.89

Note: (1) Values for the local area are compared with the average, minimum and maximum values for all 276 areas in the Cost of Living Index; (2) Figures cover the Lafayette LA urban area; **T-Bone Steak** (price per pound); **Frying Chicken** (price per pound, whole fryer); **Whole Milk** (half gallon carton); **Eggs** (price per dozen, Grade A, large); **Orange Juice** (64 oz. Tropicana or Florida Natural); **Coffee** (11.5 oz. can, vacuum-packed, Maxwell House, Hills Bros, or Folgers).
Source: The Council for Community and Economic Research, Cost of Living Index, 2024

Housing and Utility Costs

Area[1]	New Home Price ($)	Apartment Rent ($/month)	All Electric ($/month)	Part Electric ($/month)	Other Energy ($/month)	Telephone ($/month)
City[2]	306,872	1,150	-	96.15	60.82	190.09
Avg.	515,975	1,550	210.99	123.07	82.07	194.99
Min.	265,375	692	104.33	53.68	36.26	179.42
Max.	2,775,821	5,719	529.02	397.28	361.63	223.33

Note: (1) Values for the local area are compared with the average, minimum and maximum values for all 276 areas in the Cost of Living Index; (2) Figures cover the Lafayette LA urban area; **New Home Price** (2,400 sf living area, 8,000 sf lot, in urban area with full utilities); **Apartment Rent** (950 sf 2 bedroom/1.5 or 2 bath, unfurnished, excluding all utilities except water); **All Electric** (average monthly cost for an all-electric home); **Part Electric** (average monthly cost for a part-electric home); **Other Energy** (average monthly cost for natural gas, fuel oil, coal, wood, and any other forms of energy except electricity); **Telephone** (price includes the base monthly rate plus taxes and fees for three lines of mobile phone service).
Source: The Council for Community and Economic Research, Cost of Living Index, 2024

Health Care, Transportation, and Other Costs

Area[1]	Doctor ($/visit)	Dentist ($/visit)	Optometrist ($/visit)	Gasoline ($/gallon)	Beauty Salon ($/visit)	Men's Shirt ($)
City[2]	95.33	95.87	120.20	3.01	40.73	44.86
Avg.	143.77	117.51	129.23	3.32	48.57	38.14
Min.	36.74	58.67	67.33	2.80	24.00	13.41
Max.	270.44	216.82	307.33	5.28	94.00	63.89

Note: (1) Values for the local area are compared with the average, minimum and maximum values for all 276 areas in the Cost of Living Index; (2) Figures cover the Lafayette LA urban area; **Doctor** (general practitioners routine exam of an established patient); **Dentist** (adult teeth cleaning and periodic oral examination); **Optometrist** (full vision eye exam for established adult patient); **Gasoline** (one gallon regular unleaded, national brand, including all taxes, cash price at self-service pump if available); **Beauty Salon** (woman's shampoo, trim, and blow-dry); **Men's Shirt** (cotton/polyester dress shirt, pinpoint weave, long sleeves).
Source: The Council for Community and Economic Research, Cost of Living Index, 2024

HOUSING

Homeownership Rate

Area	2017 (%)	2018 (%)	2019 (%)	2020 (%)	2021 (%)	2022 (%)	2023 (%)	2024 (%)
MSA[1]	n/a	n/a	n/a	n/a	n/a	n/a	n/a	n/a
U.S.	63.9	64.4	64.6	66.6	65.5	65.8	65.9	65.6

Note: (1) Figures cover the Lafayette, LA Metropolitan Statistical Area; n/a not available
Source: U.S. Census Bureau, Housing Vacancies and Homeownership Annual Statistics: 2017-2024

House Price Index (HPI)

Area	National Ranking[2]	Quarterly Change (%)	One-Year Change (%)	Five-Year Change (%)	Since 1991Q1 (%)
MSA[1]	132	3.26	5.15	25.86	238.79
U.S.[3]	–	1.43	4.51	57.13	327.82

Note: The HPI is a weighted repeat sales index. It measures average price changes in repeat sales or refinancings on the same properties. This information is obtained by reviewing repeat mortgage transactions on single-family properties whose mortgages have been purchased or securitized by Fannie Mae or Freddie Mac since January 1975; (1) Figures cover the Lafayette, LA Metropolitan Statistical Area; (2) Rankings are based on annual percentage change for all metro areas containing at least 15,000 transactions over the last 10 years and ranges from 1 to 241; (3) figures based on a weighted average of Census Division estimates using a seasonally adjusted, purchase-only index; all figures are for the period ending December 31, 2024
Source: Federal Housing Finance Agency, Change in FHFA Metropolitan Area House Price Indexes, All Transactions Index, 2024Q4

Home Value

Area	Under $100,000	$100,000 -$199,999	$200,000 -$299,999	$300,000 -$399,999	$400,000 -$499,999	$500,000 -$999,999	$1,000,000 or more	Median ($)
City	11.2	23.8	28.6	14.9	9.3	10.0	2.2	251,300
MSA[1]	22.9	24.9	27.1	12.6	6.3	5.2	1.0	206,900
U.S.	12.1	17.8	19.5	14.4	10.5	19.1	6.5	303,400

Note: Figures are percentages except for median and cover owner-occupied housing units; (1) Figures cover the Lafayette, LA Metropolitan Statistical Area
Source: U.S. Census Bureau, 2019-2023 American Community Survey 5-Year Estimates

Year Housing Structure Built

Area	2020 or Later	2010 -2019	2000 -2009	1990 -1999	1980 -1989	1970 -1979	1960 -1969	1950 -1959	1940 -1949	Before 1940	Median Year
City	0.8	12.4	11.5	9.3	18.6	21.5	12.8	8.7	2.7	1.6	1981
MSA[1]	1.4	15.7	15.9	12.0	15.0	15.9	9.4	8.3	3.2	3.4	1987
U.S.	1.2	8.9	13.6	12.8	13.0	14.4	10.0	9.7	4.5	11.9	1980

Note: Figures are percentages except for Median Year; Note: (1) Figures cover the Lafayette, LA Metropolitan Statistical Area
Source: U.S. Census Bureau, 2019-2023 American Community Survey 5-Year Estimates

Gross Monthly Rent

Area	Under $500	$500 -$999	$1,000 -$1,499	$1,500 -$1,999	$2,000 -$2,499	$2,500 -$2,999	$3,000 and up	Median ($)
City	6.5	37.0	39.7	13.7	2.6	0.2	0.4	1,065
MSA[1]	11.3	44.1	33.2	9.1	1.7	0.3	0.2	954
U.S.	6.5	22.3	29.5	20.2	10.8	4.6	5.9	1,348

Note: Figures are percentages except for median; Gross rent is the contract rent plus the estimated average monthly cost of utilities (electricity, gas, and water and sewer) and fuels (oil, coal, kerosene, wood, etc.) if these are paid by the renter (or paid for the renter by someone else); (1) Figures cover the Lafayette, LA Metropolitan Statistical Area
Source: U.S. Census Bureau, 2019-2023 American Community Survey 5-Year Estimates

HEALTH

Health Risk Factors

Category	MSA[1] (%)	U.S. (%)
Adults aged 18–64 who have any kind of health care coverage	92.8	90.8
Adults who reported being in good or better health	78.1	81.8
Adults who have been told they have high blood cholesterol	38.1	36.9
Adults who have been told they have high blood pressure	39.7	34.0
Adults who are current smokers	16.2	12.1
Adults who currently use e-cigarettes	10.4	7.7
Adults who currently use chewing tobacco, snuff, or snus	3.4	3.2
Adults who are heavy drinkers[2]	7.3	6.1
Adults who are binge drinkers[3]	16.4	15.2
Adults who are overweight (BMI 25.0 - 29.9)	32.9	34.4
Adults who are obese (BMI 30.0 - 99.8)	38.4	34.3
Adults who participated in any physical activities in the past month	73.6	75.8

Note: All figures are crude prevalence; (1) Figures cover the Lafayette, LA Metropolitan Statistical Area; (2) Heavy drinkers are classified as adult men having more than 14 drinks per week and adult women having more than 7 drinks per week; (3) Binge drinkers are classified as males having five or more drinks on one occasion or females having four or more drinks on one occasion
Source: Centers for Disease Control and Prevention, Behavioral Risk Factor Surveillance System, SMART: Selected Metropolitan Area Risk Trends, 2023

Acute and Chronic Health Conditions

Category	MSA[1] (%)	U.S. (%)
Adults who have ever been told they had a heart attack	n/a	4.2
Adults who have ever been told they have angina or coronary heart disease	4.7	4.0
Adults who have ever been told they had a stroke	4.8	3.3
Adults who have ever been told they have asthma	16.6	15.7
Adults who have ever been told they have arthritis	28.4	26.3
Adults who have ever been told they have diabetes[2]	15.8	11.5
Adults who have ever been told they had skin cancer	4.0	5.6
Adults who have ever been told they had any other types of cancer	5.7	8.4
Adults who have ever been told they have COPD	8.1	6.4
Adults who have ever been told they have kidney disease	3.8	3.7
Adults who have ever been told they have a form of depression	27.0	22.0

Note: All figures are crude prevalence; (1) Figures cover the Lafayette, LA Metropolitan Statistical Area; (2) Figures do not include pregnancy-related, borderline, or pre-diabetes
Source: Centers for Disease Control and Prevention, Behavioral Risk Factor Surveillance System, SMART: Selected Metropolitan Area Risk Trends, 2023

Health Screening and Vaccination Rates

Category	MSA[1] (%)	U.S. (%)
Adults who have ever been tested for HIV	39.7	37.5
Adults who have had their blood cholesterol checked within the last five years	89.0	87.0
Adults aged 65+ who have had flu shot within the past year	48.0	63.4
Adults aged 65+ who have ever had a pneumonia vaccination	65.7	71.9

Note: All figures are crude prevalence; (1) Figures cover the Lafayette, LA Metropolitan Statistical Area.
Source: Centers for Disease Control and Prevention, Behavioral Risk Factor Surveillance System, SMART: Selected Metropolitan Area Risk Trends, 2023

Disability Status

Category	MSA[1] (%)	U.S. (%)
Adults who reported being deaf	9.5	7.4
Are you blind or have serious difficulty seeing, even when wearing glasses?	6.6	4.9
Do you have difficulty doing errands alone?	9.5	7.8
Do you have difficulty dressing or bathing?	5.7	3.6
Do you have serious difficulty concentrating/remembering/making decisions?	16.4	13.7
Do you have serious difficulty walking or climbing stairs?	18.9	13.2

Note: All figures are crude prevalence; (1) Figures cover the Lafayette, LA Metropolitan Statistical Area.
Source: Centers for Disease Control and Prevention, Behavioral Risk Factor Surveillance System, SMART: Selected Metropolitan Area Risk Trends, 2023

Mortality Rates for the Top 10 Causes of Death in the U.S.

ICD-10[a] Sub-Chapter	ICD-10[a] Code	Crude Mortality Rate[2] per 100,000 population	
		County[3]	U.S.
Malignant neoplasms	C00-C97	178.6	182.7
Ischaemic heart diseases	I20-I25	53.2	109.6
Provisional assignment of new diseases of uncertain etiology[1]	U00-U49	36.0	65.3
Other forms of heart disease	I30-I51	65.1	65.1
Other degenerative diseases of the nervous system	G30-G31	65.9	52.4
Other external causes of accidental injury	W00-X59	57.4	52.3
Cerebrovascular diseases	I60-I69	45.4	49.1
Chronic lower respiratory diseases	J40-J47	28.8	43.5
Hypertensive diseases	I10-I15	108.5	38.9
Organic, including symptomatic, mental disorders	F01-F09	8.5	33.9

Note: (a) ICD-10 = International Classification of Diseases 10th Revision; (1) Includes COVID-19, adverse effects to COVID-19 vaccines, SARS, and vaping-related disorders; (2) Crude mortality rates are a three-year average covering 2021-2023; (3) Figures cover Lafayette Parish.
Source: Centers for Disease Control and Prevention, National Center for Health Statistics. National Vital Statistics System, Mortality 2018-2023 on CDC WONDER Online Database

Mortality Rates for Selected Causes of Death

Cause of Death	ICD-10[a] Code	Crude Mortality Rate[1] per 100,000 population	
		County[2]	U.S.
Accidental poisoning and exposure to noxious substances	X40-X49	42.6	30.5
Alzheimer disease	G30	59.2	35.4
Assault	X85-Y09	14.8	7.3
COVID-19	U07.1	36.0	65.3
Diabetes mellitus	E10-E14	31.4	30.0
Diseases of the liver	K70-K76	13.9	20.8
Human immunodeficiency virus (HIV) disease	B20-B24	Suppressed	1.5
Influenza and pneumonia	J09-J18	9.8	13.4
Intentional self-harm	X60-X84	14.6	14.7
Malnutrition	E40-E46	5.3	6.0
Obesity and other hyperalimentation	E65-E68	4.2	3.1
Renal failure	N17-N19	15.5	16.4
Transport accidents	V01-V99	16.9	14.4

Note: (a) ICD-10 = International Classification of Diseases 10th Revision; (1) Crude mortality rates are a three-year average covering 2021-2023; (2) Figures cover Lafayette Parish; Data are suppressed when the data meet the criteria for confidentiality constraints; Crude mortality rates are flagged as unreliable when the rate would be calculated with a numerator of 20 or less.
Source: Centers for Disease Control and Prevention, National Center for Health Statistics. National Vital Statistics System, Mortality 2018-2023 on CDC WONDER Online Database

Health Insurance Coverage

Area	With Health Insurance	With Private Health Insurance	With Public Health Insurance	Without Health Insurance	Population Under Age 19 Without Health Insurance
City	90.5	60.7	41.3	9.5	4.4
MSA[1]	92.3	60.4	42.4	7.7	3.2
U.S.	91.4	67.3	36.3	8.6	5.4

Note: Figures are percentages that cover the civilian noninstitutionalized population; (1) Figures cover the Lafayette, LA Metropolitan Statistical Area
Source: U.S. Census Bureau, 2019-2023 American Community Survey 5-Year Estimates

Number of Medical Professionals

Area	MDs[3]	DOs[3,4]	Dentists	Podiatrists	Chiropractors	Optometrists
Parish[1] (number)	951	43	178	10	84	36
Parish[1] (rate[2])	383.7	17.3	71.3	4.0	33.6	14.4
U.S. (rate[2])	302.5	29.2	74.6	6.4	29.5	18.0

Note: Data as of 2023 unless noted; (1) Data covers Lafayette Parish; (2) Number of medical professionals per 100,000 population; (3) Data as of 2022 and includes all active, non-federal physicians; (4) Doctor of Osteopathic Medicine
Source: U.S. Department of Health and Human Services, Health Resources and Services Administration, Bureau of Health Professions, Area Resource File (ARF) 2023-2024

EDUCATION

Public School District Statistics

District Name	Schls	Pupils	Pupil/Teacher Ratio	Minority Pupils[1] (%)	Total Rev. per Pupil ($)	Total Exp. per Pupil ($)
Lafayette Parish	44	30,991	16.0	58.3	15,395	13,877

Note: Table includes school districts with 2,000 or more students; (1) Percentage of students that are not non-Hispanic white.
Source: U.S. Department of Education, National Center for Education Statistics, Common Core of Data, Local Education Agency (School District) Universe Survey: School Year 2023-2024; U.S. Department of Education, National Center for Education Statistics, Common Core of Data, School District Finance Survey (F-33): School Year 2021–22

Highest Level of Education

Area	Less than H.S.	H.S. Diploma	Some College, No Deg.	Associate Degree	Bachelor's Degree	Master's Degree	Prof. School Degree	Doctorate Degree
City	9.1	25.3	18.9	6.0	27.1	7.7	4.0	1.9
MSA[1]	13.0	34.8	17.9	7.3	19.0	5.3	1.8	0.9
U.S.	10.6	26.2	19.4	8.8	21.3	9.8	2.3	1.6

Note: Figures cover persons age 25 and over; (1) Figures cover the Lafayette, LA Metropolitan Statistical Area
Source: U.S. Census Bureau, 2019-2023 American Community Survey 5-Year Estimates

Educational Attainment by Race

Area	High School Graduate or Higher (%)					Bachelor's Degree or Higher (%)				
	Total	White	Black	Asian	Hisp.[2]	Total	White	Black	Asian	Hisp.[2]
City	90.9	95.4	81.2	91.6	83.8	40.6	50.4	17.4	55.0	36.6
MSA[1]	87.0	90.1	79.6	72.7	76.8	27.0	30.1	15.1	36.6	27.1
U.S.	89.4	92.9	88.1	88.0	72.5	35.0	37.7	24.7	57.0	19.9

Note: Figures shown cover persons 25 years old and over; (1) Figures cover the Lafayette, LA Metropolitan Statistical Area; (2) People of Hispanic origin can be of any race
Source: U.S. Census Bureau, 2019-2023 American Community Survey 5-Year Estimates

School Enrollment by Grade and Control

Area	Preschool (%)		Kindergarten (%)		Grades 1 - 4 (%)		Grades 5 - 8 (%)		Grades 9 - 12 (%)	
	Public	Private	Public	Private	Public	Private	Public	Private	Public	Private
City	55.1	44.9	71.4	28.6	76.8	23.2	72.2	27.8	78.4	21.6
MSA[1]	56.7	43.3	78.8	21.2	77.7	22.3	77.9	22.1	79.1	20.9
U.S.	58.7	41.3	85.2	14.8	87.2	12.8	87.9	12.1	89.0	11.0

Note: Figures shown cover persons 3 years old and over; (1) Figures cover the Lafayette, LA Metropolitan Statistical Area
Source: U.S. Census Bureau, 2019-2023 American Community Survey 5-Year Estimates

Higher Education

Four-Year Colleges			Two-Year Colleges			Medical Schools[1]	Law Schools[2]	Voc/ Tech[3]
Public	Private Non-profit	Private For-profit	Public	Private Non-profit	Private For-profit			
1	0	0	2	2	2	0	0	4

Note: Figures cover institutions located within the Lafayette, LA Metropolitan Statistical Area and include main campuses only; (1) includes schools accredited by the Liaison Committee on Medical Education and the American Osteopathic Association's Commission on Osteopathic College Accreditation; (2) includes ABA-accredited schools, schools with provisional ABA accreditation, and state accredited schools; (3) includes all schools with programs that are less than 2 years.
Source: National Center for Education Statistics, Integrated Postsecondary Education System (IPEDS), 2023-24; Wikipedia, List of Medical Schools in the United States, accessed May 2, 2025; Wikipedia, List of Law Schools in the United States, accessed May 2, 2025

EMPLOYERS

Major Employers

Company Name	Industry
Acadian Companies	Healthcare
American Legion Hospital	Healthcare
AT&T Wireless	Telecommunications
Baker Hughes	Oil field service
Cal Dive Intl Inc	Diving instruction
Cameron Valves & Measurement	Valves, manufacturers
Cheveron USA Production Co.	Oil & gas
Fieldwood Energy	Oil & gas
Frank's Casing Crew & Rental	Oil field service
Halliburton Energy SVC	Oil field service
Lafayette General Medical Ctr	Healthcare
LHC Group Inc	Healthcare
McDonald's of Acadiana	Services
Offshore Energy Inc	Oil field service
Opelousas Health Systems	Healthcare
Our Lady of Lourdes Regional Medical Ctr	Healthcare
Petroleum Helicopters	Transportation
Quality Construction & Production	General contractors
Regional Medical Center-Acadiana	Healthcare
Schlumberger	Oil field service

Note: Companies shown are located within the Lafayette, LA Metropolitan Statistical Area.
Source: Chambers of Commerce; State Departments of Labor; Wikipedia

PUBLIC SAFETY

Crime Rate

Area	Total Crime Rate	Violent Crime Rate				Property Crime Rate		
		Murder	Rape	Robbery	Aggrav. Assault	Burglary	Larceny -Theft	Motor Vehicle Theft
City	5,421.0	23.1	24.7	98.1	672.4	1,017.6	3,291.8	293.3
U.S.	2,290.9	5.7	38.0	66.5	264.1	250.7	1,347.2	318.7

Note: Figures are crimes per 100,000 population.
Source: FBI, Table 8, Offenses Known to Law Enforcement, by State by City, 2023

Hate Crimes

Area	Number of Quarters Reported	Number of Incidents per Bias Motivation					
		Race/Ethnicity/Ancestry	Religion	Sexual Orientation	Disability	Gender	Gender Identity
City	n/a	n/a	n/a	n/a	n/a	n/a	n/a
U.S.	4	5,900	2,699	2,077	187	92	492

Note: n/a not available.
Source: Federal Bureau of Investigation, Hate Crime Statistics 2023

Identity Theft Consumer Reports

Area	Reports	Reports per 100,000 Population	Rank[2]
MSA[1]	1,168	284	79
U.S.	1,135,291	339	-

Note: (1) Figures cover the Lafayette, LA Metropolitan Statistical Area; (2) Rank ranges from 1 to 401 where 1 indicates greatest number of identity theft reports per 100,000 population
Source: Federal Trade Commission, Consumer Sentinel Network Data Book 2024

Fraud and Other Consumer Reports

Area	Reports	Reports per 100,000 Population	Rank[2]
MSA[1]	6,545	1,593	43
U.S.	5,360,641	1,601	-

Note: (1) Figures cover the Lafayette, LA Metropolitan Statistical Area; (2) Rank ranges from 1 to 401 where 1 indicates greatest number of fraud and other consumer reports per 100,000 population
Source: Federal Trade Commission, Consumer Sentinel Network Data Book 2024

POLITICS

2024 Presidential Election Results

Area	Trump (Rep.)	Harris (Dem.)	Stein (Green)	Kennedy (Ind.)	Oliver (Lib.)	Other
Lafayette Parish	64.8	33.5	0.4	0.4	0.4	0.5
U.S.	49.7	48.2	0.6	0.5	0.4	0.6

Note: Results are percentages and may not add to 100% due to rounding
Source: Dave Leip's Atlas of U.S. Presidential Elections

SPORTS

Professional Sports Teams

Team Name	League	Year Established

No teams are located in the metro area
Source: Wikipedia, Major Professional Sports Teams of the United States and Canada, May 1, 2025

CLIMATE

Average and Extreme Temperatures

Temperature	Jan	Feb	Mar	Apr	May	Jun	Jul	Aug	Sep	Oct	Nov	Dec	Yr.
Extreme High (°F)	82	85	91	92	98	103	101	102	99	94	87	85	103
Average High (°F)	61	65	71	79	85	90	91	91	87	80	70	64	78
Average Temp. (°F)	51	54	61	68	75	81	82	82	78	69	59	53	68
Average Low (°F)	41	44	50	57	64	70	73	72	68	57	48	43	57
Extreme Low (°F)	9	13	20	32	44	53	58	59	43	30	21	8	8

Note: Figures cover the years 1948-1995
Source: National Climatic Data Center, International Station Meteorological Climate Summary, 9/96

Average Precipitation/Snowfall/Humidity

Precip./Humidity	Jan	Feb	Mar	Apr	May	Jun	Jul	Aug	Sep	Oct	Nov	Dec	Yr.
Avg. Precip. (in.)	4.9	5.1	4.8	5.5	5.0	4.4	6.6	5.4	4.1	3.1	4.2	5.3	58.5
Avg. Snowfall (in.)	Tr	Tr	Tr	0	0	0	0	0	0	0	Tr	Tr	Tr
Avg. Rel. Hum. 6am (%)	85	85	86	89	91	91	92	93	91	89	88	86	89
Avg. Rel. Hum. 3pm (%)	59	55	52	52	54	57	62	61	59	51	53	57	56

Note: Figures cover the years 1948-1995; Tr = Trace amounts (<0.05 in. of rain; <0.5 in. of snow)
Source: National Climatic Data Center, International Station Meteorological Climate Summary, 9/96

Weather Conditions

Temperature			Daytime Sky			Precipitation		
10°F & below	32°F & below	90°F & above	Clear	Partly cloudy	Cloudy	0.01 inch or more precip.	0.1 inch or more snow/ice	Thunderstorms
< 1	21	86	99	150	116	113	< 1	73

Note: Figures are average number of days per year and cover the years 1948-1995
Source: National Climatic Data Center, International Station Meteorological Climate Summary, 9/96

HAZARDOUS WASTE

Superfund Sites

The Lafayette, LA metro area is home to one site on the EPA's Superfund National Priorities List (NPL) or Superfund Alternative Approach (SAA) list: **Evr-Wood Treating/Evangeline Refining Company** (Final NPL). The Superfund alternative approach uses the same investigation and cleanup process and standards that are used for sites listed on the National Priorities List. The SAA is an alternative to listing a site on the NPL; it is not an alternative to Superfund or the Superfund process. There are a total of 1,445 Superfund sites with a status of proposed or final on both lists in the United States. *U.S. Environmental Protection Agency, National Priorities List, May 1, 2025; U.S. Environmental Protection Agency, Superfund Alternative Approach Sites, May 1, 2025*

AIR QUALITY

Air Quality Trends: Ozone

	1990	1995	2000	2005	2010	2015	2020	2021	2022	2023
MSA[1]	n/a	n/a	n/a	n/a	n/a	n/a	n/a	n/a	n/a	n/a
U.S.	0.087	0.089	0.081	0.080	0.072	0.068	0.066	0.067	0.067	0.070

Note: (1) Data covers the Lafayette, LA Metropolitan Statistical Area; n/a not available. The values shown are the composite ozone concentration averages among trend sites based on the highest fourth daily maximum 8-hour concentration in parts per million. These trends are based on sites having an adequate record of monitoring data during the trend period. Data from exceptional events are included.
Source: U.S. Environmental Protection Agency, Air Quality Monitoring Information, "Air Quality Trends by City, 1990-2023"

Air Quality Index

Area	Percent of Days when Air Quality was...[2]					AQI Statistics[2]	
	Good	Moderate	Unhealthy for Sensitive Groups	Unhealthy	Very Unhealthy	Maximum	Median
MSA[1]	56.7	43.0	0.3	0.0	0.0	112	47

Note: (1) Data covers the Lafayette, LA Metropolitan Statistical Area; (2) Based on 365 days with AQI data in 2023. Air Quality Index (AQI) is an index for reporting daily air quality. EPA calculates the AQI for five major air pollutants regulated by the Clean Air Act: ground-level ozone, particle pollution (aka particulate matter), carbon monoxide, sulfur dioxide, and nitrogen dioxide. The AQI runs from 0 to 500. The higher the AQI value, the greater the level of air pollution and the greater the health concern. There are six AQI categories: "Good" AQI is between 0 and 50. Air quality is considered satisfactory; "Moderate" AQI is between 51 and 100. Air quality is acceptable; "Unhealthy for Sensitive Groups" When AQI values are between 101 and 150, members of sensitive groups may experience health effects; "Unhealthy" When AQI values are between 151 and 200 everyone may begin to experience health effects; "Very Unhealthy" AQI values between 201 and 300 trigger a health alert; "Hazardous" AQI values over 300 trigger warnings of emergency conditions (not shown).
Source: U.S. Environmental Protection Agency, Air Quality Index Report, 2023

Air Quality Index Pollutants

Area	Percent of Days when AQI Pollutant was...[2]					
	Carbon Monoxide	Nitrogen Dioxide	Ozone	Sulfur Dioxide	Particulate Matter 2.5	Particulate Matter 10
MSA[1]	0.0	0.0	54.8	(3)	44.7	0.5

Note: (1) Data covers the Lafayette, LA Metropolitan Statistical Area; (2) Based on 365 days with AQI data in 2023. The Air Quality Index (AQI) is an index for reporting daily air quality. EPA calculates the AQI for five major air pollutants regulated by the Clean Air Act: ground-level ozone, particle pollution (also known as particulate matter), carbon monoxide, sulfur dioxide, and nitrogen dioxide. The AQI runs from 0 to 500. The higher the AQI value, the greater the level of air pollution and the greater the health concern; (3) Sulfur dioxide is no longer included in this table because SO_2 concentrations tend to be very localized and not necessarily representative of broad geographical areas like counties and CBSAs.
Source: U.S. Environmental Protection Agency, Air Quality Index Report, 2023

Maximum Air Pollutant Concentrations: Particulate Matter, Ozone, CO and Lead

	Particulate Matter 10 (ug/m³)	Particulate Matter 2.5 Wtd AM (ug/m³)	Particulate Matter 2.5 24-Hr (ug/m³)	Ozone (ppm)	Carbon Monoxide (ppm)	Lead (ug/m³)
MSA[1] Level	48	8.2	15	0.068	n/a	n/a
NAAQS[2]	150	15	35	0.075	9	0.15
Met NAAQS[2]	Yes	Yes	Yes	Yes	n/a	n/a

Note: (1) Data covers the Lafayette, LA Metropolitan Statistical Area; Data from exceptional events are included; (2) National Ambient Air Quality Standards; ppm = parts per million; ug/m³ = micrograms per cubic meter; n/a not available.
Concentrations: Particulate Matter 10 (coarse particulate)—highest second maximum 24-hour concentration; Particulate Matter 2.5 Wtd AM (fine particulate)—highest weighted annual mean concentration; Particulate Matter 2.5 24-Hour (fine particulate)—highest 98th percentile 24-hour concentration; Ozone—highest fourth daily maximum 8-hour concentration; Carbon Monoxide—highest second maximum non-overlapping 8-hour concentration; Lead—maximum running 3-month average
Source: U.S. Environmental Protection Agency, Air Quality Monitoring Information, "Air Quality Statistics by City, 2023"

Maximum Air Pollutant Concentrations: Nitrogen Dioxide and Sulfur Dioxide

	Nitrogen Dioxide AM (ppb)	Nitrogen Dioxide 1-Hr (ppb)	Sulfur Dioxide AM (ppb)	Sulfur Dioxide 1-Hr (ppb)	Sulfur Dioxide 24-Hr (ppb)
MSA[1] Level	n/a	n/a	n/a	n/a	n/a
NAAQS[2]	53	100	30	75	140
Met NAAQS[2]	n/a	n/a	n/a	n/a	n/a

Note: (1) Data covers the Lafayette, LA Metropolitan Statistical Area; Data from exceptional events are included; (2) National Ambient Air Quality Standards; ppm = parts per million; ug/m³ = micrograms per cubic meter; n/a not available.
Concentrations: Nitrogen Dioxide AM—highest arithmetic mean concentration; Nitrogen Dioxide 1-Hr—highest 98th percentile 1-hour daily maximum concentration; Sulfur Dioxide AM—highest annual mean concentration; Sulfur Dioxide 1-Hr—highest 99th percentile 1-hour daily maximum concentration; Sulfur Dioxide 24-Hr—highest second maximum 24-hour concentration
Source: U.S. Environmental Protection Agency, Air Quality Monitoring Information, "Air Quality Statistics by City, 2023"

McAllen, Texas

Background

McAllen is the largest city in Hidalgo County, located near the tip of southern Texas, across the Rio Grande from Reynosa, Mexico, a location key to its commercial transformation. The city grew while agriculture and petroleum were its economic mainstays, but since the North American Free Trade Agreement in 1994, international trade, health care, government administration, and tourism have become its economic engines. Tourism in McAllen has fueled the highest retail spending per capita in Texas.

In 1904 John McAllen, together with his son, James, and other partners, established a town site eight miles north of the county seat, Hidalgo. In 1907, two miles to the east, William Briggs, O. Jones, and John Closner founded a settlement called East McAllen, while the original town was called West McAllen. By 1911 East McAllen had a thousand residents and West McAllen had withered, and the larger town incorporated as the city of McAllen.

John McAllen experimented growing sugarcane, cotton, alfalfa, broom corn, citrus fruits, grapes, and figs. Eventually farming displaced ranching as the primary economic activity. By the 1920s the city had some 6,000 residents.

From 1926 McAllen was linked to Reynosa by bridge. The McAllen-Hidalgo-Reynosa International Bridge proved crucial to McAllen after oil was discovered near Reynosa in the late 1940s. The bridge became the second-most-important port of entry into Mexico. Tourism and retail businesses flourished, bolstered by the cheap labor supply.

McAllen's population grew sporadically over the next several decades. In the 1970s and 1980s the population boomed, owing to the *maquiladora* economy (in which U.S. companies, taking advantage of low Mexican labor costs, ship components of manufactured goods across the border to be assembled and shipped back). The McAllen Foreign-Trade Zone (FTZ), created in 1973, was the first inland U.S. foreign trade zone; there is also an FTZ site at McAllen-Miller International Airport. Anzalduas International Bridge opened in 2009 and, today the city is more than three-quarters Hispanic.

South Texas College was founded in 1993. Three of its five campuses are in McAllen, including the Technical Campus. Edinburg-based University of Texas–Pan American has a branch in McAllen.

McAllen's cultural institutions include Quinta Mazatlan, a Spanish Revival Style hacienda built in 1935 and now a sanctuary known for its environmental stewardship programs. Quinta Mazatlan is one of nine Rio Grande Valley preserves administered by the World Birding Center. The oldest stand of native forest in the area is preserved in the McAllen Botanical Garden. Nearby nature preserves include the Edinburg Scenic Wetlands, Santa Ana National Wildlife Refuge, and Bentsen State Park.

McAllen has several notable museums: the International Museum of Art & Science, the Museum of South Texas History, and the McAllen Heritage Center. The Valley Symphony Orchestra and Chorale and two VSO-affiliated youth orchestras perform in McAllen and at the University of Texas–Pan American. An arts scene is coalescing, thanks to the city's Creative Arts Incubator, which sponsors a public art program, studio space for artists and performers, a monthly Artwalk, and a music series. Notable among the region's yearly festivals are the February Borderfest, at Hidalgo, and the mid-March Rio Grande Valley Livestock Show, in Mercedes. Plus, the city boasts the 18.5-acre McAllen Convention Center complex.

The Rio Grande Valley Vipers are an American professional basketball team of the NBA G League based in nearby Edinburg, Texas, and are affiliated with the Houston Rockets. The Vipers play their home games at the Bert Ogden Arena. The Vipers have won four league titles in 2010, 2013, 2019, and 2022.

The "City of Palms," as McAllen is known, has a hot semi-arid climate, featuring long, very hot and humid summers, and brief, warm winters. The city's two distinct seasons are a wet season from May to October and a dry season from November to April.

Rankings

Business/Finance Rankings

- For its annual survey of the "Cheapest U.S. Cities to Live In," Kiplinger applied Cost of Living Index statistics developed by the Council for Community and Economic Research to U.S. Census Bureau population and median household income data for 265 urban areas. Only areas with at least 50,000 residents were considered. In the resulting ranking, McAllen ranked #13. *Kiplinger.com, "The 25 Cheapest Places to Live: U.S. Cities Edition," January 19, 2025*

- The McAllen metro area appeared on the Milken Institute "2025 Best Performing Cities" list. Rank: #94 out of 200 large metro areas (based on performance category). Criteria: job growth; wage growth; high-tech growth and impact; community resilience; housing affordability; household broadband access. *Milken Institute, "Best-Performing Cities 2025," January 14, 2025*

Education Rankings

- Personal finance website *WalletHub* analyzed the 150 largest U.S. metropolitan statistical areas to determine where the most educated Americans are putting their degrees to work. Criteria: education levels; percentage of workers with degrees; education quality and attainment gap; public school quality rankings; quality and enrollment of each metro area's universities. McAllen was ranked #149 (#1 = most educated city). *WalletHub.com, "Most & Least Educated Cities in America, 2025" July 2, 2024*

Health/Fitness Rankings

- McAllen was identified as a "2025 Allergy Capital." The area ranked #27 out of the nation's 100 largest metropolitan areas. Three groups of factors were used to identify the most challenging cities for people with allergies: annual tree, grass, and weed pollen scores; over the counter allergy medicine use; number of board-certified allergy specialists. *Asthma and Allergy Foundation of America, "2025 Allergy Capitals: The Most Challenging Places to Live with Allergies," March 18, 2025*

- McAllen was identified as a "2024 Asthma Capital." The area ranked #63 out of the nation's 100 largest metropolitan areas. Criteria: estimated asthma prevalence; asthma-related mortality; and ER visits due to asthma. Risk factors analyzed but not factored in the rankings: annual air quality including pollution and ozone levels; public smoking laws; indoor air quality; access to asthma specialists; rescue and controller medication use; uninsured rate; pollen allergy; poverty rate. *Asthma and Allergy Foundation of America, "Asthma Capitals 2024: The Most Challenging Places to Live With Asthma," September 10, 2024*

- The Sharecare Community Well-Being Index evaluates 10 individual and social health factors in order to measure what matters to Americans in the communities in which they live. The McAllen metro area ranked #379 in the bottom 10 across all 10 domains. Criteria: access to healthcare, food, and community resources; housing and transportation; economic security; feeling of purpose; and physical, financial, social, and community well-being. *Sharecare.com, "Community Well-Being Index: 2020 Metro Area & County Rankings Report," August 30, 2021*

Real Estate Rankings

- The McAllen metro area appeared on Realtor.com's list of hot housing markets to watch in 2025. The area ranked #7. Criteria: forecasted home price and sales growth; overall economy; population trends. *Realtor.com®, "Top 10 Housing Markets Positioned for Growth in 2025," December 10, 2024*

Safety Rankings

- Allstate ranked the 100 most populous cities in America in terms of driver safety. McAllen ranked #76. Criteria based on anonymized driving behavior data from Allstate's mobile app powered by Arity: high speed driving (over 80 mph), phone handling, and hard braking. The report helps increase the importance of safety and awareness behind the wheel. *Allstate, "16th Allstate America's Best Drivers Report®" July 11, 2024*

Business Environment

DEMOGRAPHICS

Population Growth

Area	1990 Census	2000 Census	2010 Census	2020 Census	2023 Estimate[2]	Population Growth 1990-2023 (%)
City	86,145	106,414	129,877	142,210	143,789	66.9
MSA[1]	383,545	569,463	774,769	870,781	880,921	129.7
U.S.	248,709,873	281,421,906	308,745,538	331,449,281	332,387,540	33.6

Note: (1) Figures cover the McAllen-Edinburg-Mission, TX Metropolitan Statistical Area; (2) 2019-2023 5-year ACS population estimate
Source: U.S. Census Bureau, 1990 Census, 2000 Census, 2010 Census, 2020 Census, 2019-2023 American Community Survey 5-Year Estimates

Race

Area	White Alone[2] (%)	Black Alone[2] (%)	Asian Alone[2] (%)	AIAN[3] Alone[2] (%)	NHOPI[4] Alone[2] (%)	Other Race Alone[2] (%)	Two or More Races (%)
City	43.1	0.9	2.9	0.6	0.0	17.5	35.1
MSA[1]	39.5	0.7	1.0	0.4	0.0	10.8	47.6
U.S.	63.4	12.4	5.8	0.9	0.2	6.6	10.7

Note: (1) Figures cover the McAllen-Edinburg-Mission, TX Metropolitan Statistical Area; (2) Alone is defined as not being in combination with one or more other races; (3) American Indian and Alaska Native; (4) Native Hawaiian and Other Pacific Islander
Source: U.S. Census Bureau, 2019-2023 American Community Survey 5-Year Estimates

Hispanic or Latino Origin

Area	Total (%)	Mexican (%)	Puerto Rican (%)	Cuban (%)	Other (%)
City	86.5	81.1	0.5	0.1	4.8
MSA[1]	91.9	87.6	0.3	0.1	3.9
U.S.	19.0	11.3	1.8	0.7	5.2

Note: Persons of Hispanic or Latino origin can be of any race; (1) Figures cover the McAllen-Edinburg-Mission, TX Metropolitan Statistical Area
Source: U.S. Census Bureau, 2019-2023 American Community Survey 5-Year Estimates

Age

Area	Under Age 5	Age 5–19	Age 20–34	Age 35–44	Age 45–54	Age 55–64	Age 65–74	Age 75–84	Age 85+	Median Age
City	7.0	23.3	21.2	13.3	12.4	9.4	8.1	3.8	1.5	34.0
MSA[1]	8.0	26.8	21.3	12.3	11.4	8.6	6.5	3.8	1.2	30.3
U.S.	5.7	19.1	20.2	13.1	12.3	12.8	10.0	4.9	1.9	38.7

Note: (1) Figures cover the McAllen-Edinburg-Mission, TX Metropolitan Statistical Area
Source: U.S. Census Bureau, 2019-2023 American Community Survey 5-Year Estimates

Disability by Age

Area	All Ages	Under 18 Years Old	18 to 64 Years Old	65 Years and Over
City	13.0	6.1	9.4	43.8
MSA[1]	12.5	5.5	9.7	45.5
U.S.	13.0	4.7	10.7	32.9

Note: Figures show percent of the civilian noninstitutionalized population that reported having a disability. Disability status is determined from six types of difficulty: vision, hearing, cognitive, ambulatory, self-care, and independent living. For children under 5 years old, hearing and vision difficulty are used to determine disability status. For children between the ages of 5 and 14, disability status is determined from hearing, vision, cognitive, ambulatory, and self-care difficulties. For people aged 15 years and older, they are considered to have a disability if they have difficulty with any one of the six difficulty types; Note: (1) Figures cover the McAllen-Edinburg-Mission, TX Metropolitan Statistical Area
Source: U.S. Census Bureau, 2019-2023 American Community Survey 5-Year Estimates

Ancestry

Area	German	Irish	English	American	Italian	Polish	French[2]	European	Scottish
City	2.6	1.6	1.9	3.1	0.9	0.4	1.0	0.3	0.2
MSA[1]	1.7	1.0	1.1	2.1	0.4	0.2	0.4	0.2	0.2
U.S.	12.6	9.4	9.1	5.5	4.9	2.6	2.0	1.6	1.6

Note: Figures are the percentage of the total population reporting a particular ancestry. The nine most commonly reported ancestries in the U.S. are shown. Figures include multiple ancestries (e.g. if a person reported being Irish and Italian, they were included in both columns); (1) Figures cover the McAllen-Edinburg-Mission, TX Metropolitan Statistical Area; (2) Excludes Basque
Source: U.S. Census Bureau, 2019-2023 American Community Survey 5-Year Estimates

Foreign-born Population

Area	Percent of Population Born in								
	Any Foreign Country	Asia	Mexico	Europe	Caribbean	Central America[2]	South America	Africa	Canada
City	25.7	2.2	22.0	0.2	0.3	0.5	0.4	0.1	0.0
MSA[1]	26.0	0.8	24.1	0.1	0.1	0.5	0.2	0.1	0.1
U.S.	13.9	4.3	3.3	1.4	1.4	1.2	1.2	0.8	0.2

Note: (1) Figures cover the McAllen-Edinburg-Mission, TX Metropolitan Statistical Area; (2) Excludes Mexico.
Source: U.S. Census Bureau, 2019-2023 American Community Survey 5-Year Estimates

Household Size

Area	Persons in Household (%)							Average Household Size
	One	Two	Three	Four	Five	Six	Seven or More	
City	21.4	28.2	18.3	16.3	10.9	2.4	2.5	2.96
MSA[1]	18.5	25.1	16.9	17.1	12.2	5.6	4.5	3.30
U.S.	28.5	33.8	15.4	12.7	5.9	2.3	1.4	2.54

Note: (1) Figures cover the McAllen-Edinburg-Mission, TX Metropolitan Statistical Area
Source: U.S. Census Bureau, 2019-2023 American Community Survey 5-Year Estimates

Household Relationships

Area	Householder	Opposite-sex Spouse	Same-sex Spouse	Opposite-sex Unmarried Partner	Same-sex Unmarried Partner	Child[2]	Grandchild	Other Relatives	Non-relatives
City	34.3	16.0	0.1	1.7	0.1	34.6	3.5	6.8	2.0
MSA[1]	29.7	15.0	0.1	1.6	0.1	38.3	5.2	7.5	1.6
U.S.	38.3	17.5	0.2	2.5	0.2	28.3	2.4	4.8	3.4

Note: Figures are percent of the total population; (1) Figures cover the McAllen-Edinburg-Mission, TX Metropolitan Statistical Area; (2) Includes biological, adopted, and stepchildren of the householder
Source: U.S. Census Bureau, 2020 Census

Gender

Area	Males	Females	Males per 100 Females
City	71,212	72,577	98.1
MSA[1]	434,784	446,137	97.5
U.S.	164,545,087	167,842,453	98.0

Note: (1) Figures cover the McAllen-Edinburg-Mission, TX Metropolitan Statistical Area
Source: U.S. Census Bureau, 2019-2023 American Community Survey 5-Year Estimates

Marital Status

Area	Never Married	Now Married[2]	Separated	Widowed	Divorced
City	35.1	48.8	2.1	5.6	8.4
MSA[1]	36.7	47.8	3.0	4.9	7.6
U.S.	34.1	47.9	1.7	5.6	10.7

Note: Figures are percentages and cover the population 15 years of age and older; (1) Figures cover the McAllen-Edinburg-Mission, TX Metropolitan Statistical Area; (2) Excludes separated
Source: U.S. Census Bureau, 2019-2023 American Community Survey 5-Year Estimates

Religious Groups by Family

Area	Catholic	Baptist	Methodist	LDS[2]	Pentecostal	Lutheran	Islam	Adventist	Other
MSA[1]	46.6	2.2	0.8	1.2	1.0	0.3	0.2	3.2	6.0
U.S.	18.7	7.3	3.0	2.0	1.8	1.7	1.3	1.3	11.6

Note: Figures are the number of adherents as a percentage of the total population and cover the eight largest religious groups in the U.S; (1) Figures cover the McAllen-Edinburg-Mission, TX Metropolitan Statistical Area; (2) Church of Jesus Christ of Latter-day Saints
Sources: 2020 U.S. Religion Census, Association of Statisticians of American Religious Bodies; The Association of Religion Data Archives (ARDA)

Religious Groups by Tradition

Area	Catholic	Evangelical Protestant	Mainline Protestant	Black Protestant	Islam	Judaism	Hinduism	Orthodox	Buddhism
MSA[1]	46.6	10.0	1.1	0.1	0.2	<0.1	<0.1	<0.1	n/a
U.S.	18.7	16.5	5.2	2.3	1.3	0.6	0.4	0.4	0.3

Note: Figures are the number of adherents as a percentage of the total population; (1) Figures cover the McAllen-Edinburg-Mission, TX Metropolitan Statistical Area
Sources: 2020 U.S. Religion Census, Association of Statisticians of American Religious Bodies; The Association of Religion Data Archives (ARDA)

ECONOMY

Real Gross Domestic Product (GDP)

Area	2017	2018	2019	2020	2021	2022	2023	Rank[3]
MSA[1]	20.7	21.2	22.0	21.5	22.7	23.1	24.0	124
U.S.[2]	17,619.1	18,160.7	18,642.5	18,238.9	19,387.6	19,896.6	20,436.3	—

Note: Figures are in billions of chained 2017 dollars; (1) Figures cover the McAllen-Edinburg-Mission, TX Metropolitan Statistical Area; (2) Figures cover real GDP within metropolitan areas; (3) Rank is based on 2023 data and ranges from 1 to 384
Source: U.S. Bureau of Economic Analysis

Economic Growth

Area	2014	2015	2016	2017	2018	2019	2020	2021	2022	2023
MSA[1]	1.7	1.1	-0.4	0.5	2.2	3.8	-2.1	5.4	1.9	3.8
U.S.[2]	2.6	3.2	2.0	2.7	3.1	2.7	-2.2	6.3	2.6	2.7

Note: Figures are real gross domestic product growth rates and represent percent change from preceding period; (1) Figures cover the McAllen-Edinburg-Mission, TX Metropolitan Statistical Area; (2) Figures are the average growth rates within metropolitan areas
Source: U.S. Bureau of Economic Analysis

Metropolitan Area Exports

Area	2018	2019	2020	2021	2022	2023	Rank[2]
MSA[1]	6,627.9	5,234.1	4,087.6	5,164.6	5,677.1	7,072.4	51
U.S.	1,664,056.1	1,645,173.7	1,431,406.6	1,753,941.4	2,062,937.4	2,019,160.5	—

Note: Figures are in millions of dollars; (1) Figures cover the McAllen-Edinburg-Mission, TX Metropolitan Statistical Area; (2) Rank is based on 2023 data and ranges from 1 to 386
Source: U.S. Department of Commerce, International Trade Administration, Office of Trade and Economic Analysis, Industry and Analysis, Exports by Metropolitan Area, data extracted April 2, 2025

Building Permits

Area	Single-Family			Multi-Family			Total		
	2023	2024	Pct. Chg.	2023	2024	Pct. Chg.	2023	2024	Pct. Chg.
City	428	669	56.3	753	1,053	39.8	1,181	1,722	45.8
MSA[1]	4,143	4,336	4.7	2,756	2,956	7.3	6,899	7,292	5.7
U.S.	920,000	981,900	6.7	591,100	496,100	-16.1	1,511,100	1,478,000	-2.2

Note: (1) Figures cover the McAllen-Edinburg-Mission, TX Metropolitan Statistical Area; Figures represent new, privately-owned housing units authorized (unadjusted data)
Source: U.S. Census Bureau, Building Permits Survey (BPS), 2023, 2024

Bankruptcy Filings

Area	Business Filings			Nonbusiness Filings		
	2023	2024	% Chg.	2023	2024	% Chg.
Hidalgo County	13	11	-15.4	263	274	4.2
U.S.	18,926	23,107	22.1	434,064	494,201	13.9

Note: Business filings include Chapter 7, Chapter 9, Chapter 11, Chapter 12, Chapter 13, Chapter 15, and Section 304; Nonbusiness filings include Chapter 7, Chapter 11, and Chapter 13
Source: Administrative Office of the U.S. Courts, Business and Nonbusiness Bankruptcy, County Cases Commenced by Chapter of the Bankruptcy Code, During the 12-Month Period Ending December 31, 2023 and Business and Nonbusiness Bankruptcy, County Cases Commenced by Chapter of the Bankruptcy Code, During the 12-Month Period Ending December 31, 2024

Housing Vacancy Rates

Area	Gross Vacancy Rate[3] (%)			Year-Round Vacancy Rate[4] (%)			Rental Vacancy Rate[5] (%)			Homeowner Vacancy Rate[6] (%)		
	2022	2023	2024	2022	2023	2024	2022	2023	2024	2022	2023	2024
MSA[1]	n/a	n/a	n/a	n/a	n/a	n/a	n/a	n/a	n/a	n/a	n/a	n/a
U.S.[2]	9.1	9.0	9.1	7.5	7.5	7.6	5.7	6.5	6.8	0.8	0.8	1.0

Note: (1) Figures cover the McAllen-Edinburg-Mission, TX Metropolitan Statistical Area; (2) Figures cover the 75 largest Metropolitan Statistical Areas; (3) The percentage of the total housing inventory that is vacant; (4) The percentage of the housing inventory (excluding seasonal units) that is year-round vacant; (5) The percentage of rental inventory that is vacant for rent; (6) The percentage of homeowner inventory that is vacant for sale; n/a not available
Source: U.S. Census Bureau, Housing Vacancies and Homeownership Annual Statistics: 2022, 2023, 2024

INCOME

Income

Area	Per Capita ($)	Median Household ($)	Average Household ($)
City	29,406	60,165	86,175
MSA[1]	22,005	52,281	71,722
U.S.	43,289	78,538	110,491

Note: (1) Figures cover the McAllen-Edinburg-Mission, TX Metropolitan Statistical Area
Source: U.S. Census Bureau, 2019-2023 American Community Survey 5-Year Estimates

Household Income Distribution

Area	Percent of Households Earning							
	Under $15,000	$15,000 -$24,999	$25,000 -$34,999	$35,000 -$49,999	$50,000 -$74,999	$75,000 -$99,999	$100,000 -$149,999	$150,000 and up
City	11.9	10.2	9.3	11.4	16.1	11.7	15.7	13.7
MSA[1]	14.0	11.7	10.0	12.6	16.7	11.7	13.8	9.5
U.S.	8.5	6.6	6.8	10.4	15.7	12.7	17.4	21.9

Note: (1) Figures cover the McAllen-Edinburg-Mission, TX Metropolitan Statistical Area
Source: U.S. Census Bureau, 2019-2023 American Community Survey 5-Year Estimates

Poverty Rate

Area	All Ages	Under 18 Years Old	18 to 64 Years Old	65 Years and Over
City	20.2	27.2	17.6	17.0
MSA[1]	27.2	37.1	22.6	22.9
U.S.	12.4	16.3	11.6	10.4

Note: Figures are percentage of people whose income during the past 12 months was below the poverty level;
(1) Figures cover the McAllen-Edinburg-Mission, TX Metropolitan Statistical Area
Source: U.S. Census Bureau, 2019-2023 American Community Survey 5-Year Estimates

EMPLOYMENT

Labor Force and Employment

Area	Civilian Labor Force			Workers Employed		
	Dec. 2023	Dec. 2024	% Chg.	Dec. 2023	Dec. 2024	% Chg.
City	72,499	74,052	2.1	69,572	71,063	2.1
MSA[1]	385,693	394,540	2.3	362,243	370,007	2.1
U.S.	166,661,000	167,746,000	0.7	160,754,000	161,294,000	0.3

Note: Data is not seasonally adjusted and covers workers 16 years of age and older; (1) Figures cover the McAllen-Edinburg-Mission, TX Metropolitan Statistical Area
Source: Bureau of Labor Statistics, Local Area Unemployment Statistics

Unemployment Rate

Area	2024											
	Jan.	Feb.	Mar.	Apr.	May	Jun.	Jul.	Aug.	Sep.	Oct.	Nov.	Dec.
City	4.5	4.6	4.3	4.0	4.2	4.9	4.9	4.8	4.3	4.2	4.3	4.0
MSA[1]	6.5	6.0	5.8	5.4	5.7	6.9	6.9	6.5	5.9	5.4	6.0	6.2
U.S.	4.1	4.2	3.9	3.5	3.7	4.3	4.5	4.4	3.9	3.9	4.0	3.8

Note: Data is not seasonally adjusted and covers workers 16 years of age and older; (1) Figures cover the McAllen-Edinburg-Mission, TX Metropolitan Statistical Area
Source: Bureau of Labor Statistics, Local Area Unemployment Statistics

Average Wages

Occupation	$/Hr.	Occupation	$/Hr.
Accountants and Auditors	33.75	Maintenance and Repair Workers	17.79
Automotive Mechanics	22.30	Marketing Managers	54.38
Bookkeepers	19.81	Network and Computer Systems Admin.	37.41
Carpenters	18.97	Nurses, Licensed Practical	24.78
Cashiers	12.40	Nurses, Registered	36.77
Computer Programmers	38.07	Nursing Assistants	15.66
Computer Systems Analysts	37.09	Office Clerks, General	16.04
Computer User Support Specialists	21.73	Physical Therapists	50.03
Construction Laborers	15.75	Physicians	144.98
Cooks, Restaurant	13.57	Plumbers, Pipefitters and Steamfitters	22.61
Customer Service Representatives	17.73	Police and Sheriff's Patrol Officers	29.67
Dentists	106.72	Postal Service Mail Carriers	30.28
Electricians	21.99	Real Estate Sales Agents	28.28
Engineers, Electrical	46.39	Retail Salespersons	14.03
Fast Food and Counter Workers	11.81	Sales Representatives, Technical/Scientific	39.87
Financial Managers	63.80	Secretaries, Exc. Legal/Medical/Executive	18.47
First-Line Supervisors of Office Workers	28.02	Security Guards	13.98
General and Operations Managers	44.25	Surgeons	n/a
Hairdressers/Cosmetologists	14.51	Teacher Assistants, Exc. Postsecondary[1]	13.28
Home Health and Personal Care Aides	11.34	Teachers, Secondary School, Exc. Sp. Ed.[1]	30.53
Janitors and Cleaners	14.44	Telemarketers	n/a
Landscaping/Groundskeeping Workers	14.92	Truck Drivers, Heavy/Tractor-Trailer	24.00
Lawyers	57.98	Truck Drivers, Light/Delivery Services	19.17
Maids and Housekeeping Cleaners	12.70	Waiters and Waitresses	13.40

Note: Wage data covers the McAllen-Edinburg-Mission, TX Metropolitan Statistical Area; (1) Hourly wages were calculated from annual wage data based on a 40 hour work week
Source: Bureau of Labor Statistics, Metro Area Occupational Employment & Wage Estimates, May 2024

Employment by Industry

Sector	MSA[1] Number of Employees	MSA[1] Percent of Total	U.S. Percent of Total
Construction, Mining, and Logging	9,300	3.0	5.5
Financial Activities	10,100	3.3	5.8
Government	62,100	20.3	14.9
Information	3,100	1.0	1.9
Leisure and Hospitality	30,000	9.8	10.4
Manufacturing	7,000	2.3	8.0
Other Services	6,600	2.2	3.7
Private Education and Health Services	91,900	30.1	16.9
Professional and Business Services	27,100	8.9	14.2
Retail Trade	38,800	12.7	10.0
Transportation, Warehousing, and Utilities	10,200	3.3	4.8
Wholesale Trade	9,500	3.1	3.9

Note: Figures are non-farm employment as of December 2024. Figures are not seasonally adjusted and include workers 16 years of age and older; (1) Figures cover the McAllen-Edinburg-Mission, TX Metropolitan Statistical Area
Source: Bureau of Labor Statistics, Current Employment Statistics, Employment, Hours, and Earnings

Employment by Occupation

Occupation Classification	City (%)	MSA[1] (%)	U.S. (%)
Management, Business, Science, and Arts	38.5	28.4	42.0
Natural Resources, Construction, and Maintenance	7.6	13.9	8.6
Production, Transportation, and Material Moving	9.8	13.0	13.0
Sales and Office	24.0	22.2	19.9
Service	20.1	22.4	16.5

Note: Figures cover employed civilians 16 years of age and older; (1) Figures cover the McAllen-Edinburg-Mission, TX Metropolitan Statistical Area
Source: U.S. Census Bureau, 2019-2023 American Community Survey 5-Year Estimates

Occupations with Greatest Projected Employment Growth: 2022 – 2032

Occupation[1]	2022 Employment	2032 Projected Employment	Numeric Employment Change	Percent Employment Change
General and Operations Managers	425,560	504,280	78,720	18.5
Fast Food and Counter Workers	333,870	394,290	60,420	18.1
Stockers and Order Fillers	264,810	321,600	56,790	21.4
Home Health and Personal Care Aides	313,670	367,500	53,830	17.2
Software Developers	110,280	161,780	51,500	46.7
Cooks, Restaurant	113,680	158,830	45,150	39.7
Laborers and Freight, Stock, and Material Movers, Hand	225,090	269,120	44,030	19.6
Heavy and Tractor-Trailer Truck Drivers	226,450	270,320	43,870	19.4
Retail Salespersons	319,400	357,630	38,230	12.0
Registered Nurses	233,850	267,980	34,130	14.6

Note: Projections cover Texas; (1) Sorted by numeric employment change
Source: www.projectionscentral.org, State Occupational Projections, 2022–2032 Long-Term Projections

Fastest-Growing Occupations: 2022 – 2032

Occupation[1]	2022 Employment	2032 Projected Employment	Numeric Employment Change	Percent Employment Change
Wind Turbine Service Technicians	4,860	7,950	3,090	63.6
Nurse Practitioners	19,060	30,490	11,430	60.0
Data Scientists	13,220	20,250	7,030	53.2
Computer and Information Research Scientists (SOC 2018)	2,070	3,140	1,070	51.7
Information Security Analysts (SOC 2018)	14,620	21,620	7,000	47.9
Software Developers	110,280	161,780	51,500	46.7
Statisticians	980	1,430	450	45.9
Operations Research Analysts	12,060	17,290	5,230	43.4
Software Quality Assurance Analysts and Testers	17,350	24,440	7,090	40.9
Medical and Health Services Managers	49,430	69,180	19,750	40.0

Note: Projections cover Texas; (1) Sorted by percent employment change and excludes occupations with numeric employment change less than 50
Source: www.projectionscentral.org, State Occupational Projections, 2022–2032 Long-Term Projections

CITY FINANCES

City Government Finances

Component	2022 ($000)	2022 ($ per capita)
Total Revenues	292,722	2,036
Total Expenditures	280,995	1,955
Debt Outstanding	59,553	414

Source: U.S. Census Bureau, State & Local Government Finances 2022

City Government Revenue by Source

Source	2022 ($000)	2022 ($ per capita)	2022 (%)
General Revenue			
From Federal Government	18,630	130	6.4
From State Government	1,168	8	0.4
From Local Governments	351	2	0.1
Taxes			
Property	52,359	364	17.9
Sales and Gross Receipts	93,884	653	32.1
Personal Income	0	0	0.0
Corporate Income	0	0	0.0
Motor Vehicle License	0	0	0.0
Other Taxes	2,411	17	0.8
Current Charges	80,344	559	27.4
Liquor Store	0	0	0.0
Utility	24,643	171	8.4

Source: U.S. Census Bureau, State & Local Government Finances 2022

City Government Expenditures by Function

Function	2022 ($000)	2022 ($ per capita)	2022 (%)
General Direct Expenditures			
Air Transportation	8,887	61	3.2
Corrections	0	0	0.0
Education	0	0	0.0
Employment Security Administration	0	0	0.0
Financial Administration	8,533	59	3.0
Fire Protection	22,830	158	8.1
General Public Buildings	1,731	12	0.6
Governmental Administration, Other	5,942	41	2.1
Health	3,453	24	1.2
Highways	29,533	205	10.5
Hospitals	0	0	0.0
Housing and Community Development	2,544	17	0.9
Interest on General Debt	3,990	27	1.4
Judicial and Legal	3,920	27	1.4
Libraries	5,152	35	1.8
Parking	1,401	9	0.5
Parks and Recreation	23,042	160	8.2
Police Protection	43,441	302	15.5
Public Welfare	2,189	15	0.8
Sewerage	42,524	295	15.1
Solid Waste Management	25,915	180	9.2
Veterans' Services	0	0	0.0
Liquor Store	0	0	0.0
Utility	27,308	190	9.7

Source: U.S. Census Bureau, State & Local Government Finances 2022

TAXES

State Corporate Income Tax Rates

State	Tax Rate (%)	Income Brackets ($)	Num. of Brackets	Financial Institution Tax Rate (%)[a]	Federal Income Tax Ded.
Texas	(u)	—	—	(u)	No

Note: Tax rates for tax year 2024; (a) Rates listed are the corporate income tax rate applied to financial institutions or excise taxes based on income. Some states have other taxes based upon the value of deposits or shares; (u) Texas imposes a Franchise Tax, otherwise known as margin tax, imposed on entities with more than $2,470,000 total revenues effective in 2024 at rate of 0.75%, or 0.375% for entities primarily engaged in retail or wholesale trade, on lesser of 70% of total revenues or 100% of gross receipts after deductions for either compensation ($450,000 deduction limit) or cost of goods sold. Texas has an EZ rate of 0.331 applicable to a $20 million revenue threshold.
Source: Federation of Tax Administrators, State Corporate Income Tax Rates, January 1, 2025

State Individual Income Tax Rates

State	Tax Rate (%)	Income Brackets ($)	Personal Exemptions ($)			Standard Ded. ($)	
			Single	Married	Depend.	Single	Married
Texas							– No state income tax –

Note: Tax rates for tax year 2024; Local- and county-level taxes are not included
Source: Federation of Tax Administrators, State Individual Income Tax Rates, January 1, 2025

Various State Sales and Excise Tax Rates

State	State Sales Tax (%)	Gasoline[1] ($/gal.)	Cigarette[2] ($/pack)	Spirits[3] ($/gal.)	Wine[4] ($/gal.)	Beer[5] ($/gal.)	Recreational Marijuana (%)
Texas	6.25	0.20	1.41	2.40	0.20	0.19	Not legal

Note: All tax rates as of January 1, 2025; (1) The American Petroleum Institute has developed a methodology for determining the average tax rate on a gallon of fuel. Rates may include any of the following: excise taxes, environmental fees, storage tank fees, other fees or taxes, general sales tax, and local taxes; (2) The federal excise tax of $1.0066 per pack and local taxes are not included; (3) Rates are those applicable to off-premise sales of 40% alcohol by volume (a.b.v.) distilled spirits in 750ml containers. Local excise taxes are excluded; (4) Rates are those applicable to off-premise sales of 11% a.b.v. non-carbonated wine in 750ml containers; (5) Rates are those applicable to off-premise sales of 4.7% a.b.v. beer in 12 ounce containers.
Source: Tax Foundation, 2025 Facts & Figures: How Does Your State Compare?

State Tax Competitiveness Index

State	Overall Rank	Corporate Tax Rank	Individual Income Tax Rank	Sales Tax Rank	Property Tax Rank	Unemployment Insurance Tax Rank
Texas	7	46	1	36	40	30

Note: The Tax Foundation's State Tax Competitiveness Index enables policymakers, taxpayers, and business leaders to gauge how their states' tax systems compare. A rank of 1 is best, 50 is worst. Rankings do not average to the total. States without a tax rank equally as 1. DC's scores and rankings do not affect other states. The report shows tax systems as of July 1, 2024 (the beginning of Fiscal Year 2025).
Source: Tax Foundation, State Tax Competitiveness Index 2025

TRANSPORTATION

Means of Transportation to Work

Area	Car/Truck/Van		Public Transportation			Bicycle	Walked	Other Means	Worked at Home
	Drove Alone	Car-pooled	Bus	Subway	Railroad				
City	72.2	10.4	0.4	0.0	0.0	0.3	0.9	4.3	11.5
MSA[1]	75.8	10.3	0.2	0.0	0.0	0.1	1.2	3.7	8.6
U.S.	70.2	8.5	1.7	1.3	0.4	0.4	2.4	1.6	13.5

Note: Figures are percentages and cover workers 16 years of age and older; (1) Figures cover the McAllen-Edinburg-Mission, TX Metropolitan Statistical Area
Source: U.S. Census Bureau, 2019-2023 American Community Survey 5-Year Estimates

Travel Time to Work

Area	Less Than 10 Minutes	10 to 19 Minutes	20 to 29 Minutes	30 to 44 Minutes	45 to 59 Minutes	60 to 89 Minutes	90 Minutes or More
City	14.6	39.5	23.9	15.2	2.9	2.1	1.7
MSA[1]	15.4	33.5	24.2	18.6	3.8	2.4	2.2
U.S.	12.6	28.6	21.2	20.8	8.1	6.0	2.8

Note: Note: Figures are percentages and include workers 16 years old and over; (1) Figures cover the McAllen-Edinburg-Mission, TX Metropolitan Statistical Area
Source: U.S. Census Bureau, 2019-2023 American Community Survey 5-Year Estimates

Key Congestion Measures

Measure	2000	2010	2015	2020	2022
Annual Hours of Delay, Total (000)	6,118	13,842	17,969	13,202	21,501
Annual Hours of Delay, Per Auto Commuter	29	30	36	25	40
Annual Congestion Cost, Per Auto Commuter ($)	362	650	765	566	886

Note: Figures cover the McAllen TX urban area
Source: Texas A&M Transportation Institute, 2023 Urban Mobility Report

Freeway Travel Time Index

Measure	1985	1990	1995	2000	2005	2010	2015	2020	2022
Urban Area Index[1]	1.03	1.05	1.09	1.15	1.16	1.14	1.16	1.12	1.14
Urban Area Rank[1,2]	89	89	77	53	57	71	57	10	64

Note: Freeway Travel Time Index—the ratio of travel time in the peak period to the travel time at free-flow conditions. For example, a value of 1.30 indicates a 20-minute free-flow trip takes 26 minutes in the peak (20 minutes x 1.30 = 26 minutes); (1) Covers the McAllen TX urban area; (2) Rank is based on 101 larger urban areas (#1 = highest travel time index)
Source: Texas A&M Transportation Institute, 2023 Urban Mobility Report

McAllen, Texas

Public Transportation

Agency Name / Mode of Transportation	Vehicles Operated in Maximum Service[1]	Annual Unlinked Passenger Trips[2] (in thous.)	Annual Passenger Miles[3] (in thous.)
City of McAllen - McAllen Express Transit			
Bus (directly operated)	12	590.2	n/a
Demand Response (directly operated)	3	13.3	n/a

Note: (1) Number of revenue vehicles operated by the given mode and type of service to meet the annual maximum service requirement. This is the revenue vehicle count during the peak season of the year; on the week and day that maximum service is provided. Vehicles operated in maximum service (VOMS) exclude atypical days and one-time special events; (2) Number of passengers who boarded public transportation vehicles. Passengers are counted each time they board a vehicle no matter how many vehicles they use to travel from their origin to their destination. (3) Sum of the distances ridden by all passengers during the entire fiscal year.
Source: Federal Transit Administration, National Transit Database, 2023

Air Transportation

Airport Name and Code / Type of Service	Passenger Airlines[1]	Passenger Enplanements	Freight Carriers[2]	Freight (lbs)
McAllen-Miller International Airport (MFE)				
Domestic service (U.S. carriers only)	12	600,610	9	7,551,670
International service (U.S. carriers only)	2	1,948	1	64,566

Note: (1) Includes all U.S.-based major, minor and commuter airlines that carried at least one passenger during the year; (2) Includes all U.S.-based airlines and freight carriers that transported at least one pound of freight during the year.
Source: Bureau of Transportation Statistics, The Intermodal Transportation Database, Air Carriers: T-100 Domestic Market (U.S. carriers only), 2024; Bureau of Transportation Statistics, The Intermodal Transportation Database, Air Carriers: T-100 International Market (U.S. carriers only), 2024

BUSINESSES

Major Business Headquarters

Company Name	Industry	Rankings Fortune[1]	Forbes[2]
No companies listed	-	-	-

Note: (1) Companies that produce a 10-K are ranked 1 to 500 based on 2023 revenue; (2) All private companies with at least $2 billion in annual revenue through the end of their most current fiscal year are ranked 1 to 275; companies listed are headquartered in the city; dashes indicate no ranking
Source: Fortune, "Fortune 500," 2024; Forbes, "America's Largest Private Companies," 2024

Living Environment

COST OF LIVING

Cost of Living Index

Composite Index	Groceries	Housing	Utilities	Transportation	Health Care	Misc. Goods/Services
85.1	93.4	60.2	119.6	94.1	79.2	92.1

Note: The Cost of Living Index measures regional differences in the cost of consumer goods and services, excluding taxes and non-consumer expenditures, for professional and managerial households in the top income quintile. It is based on more than 50,000 prices covering almost 60 different items for which prices are collected three times a year by chambers of commerce, economic development organizations or university applied economic centers in each participating urban area. The numbers shown should be read as a percentage above or below the national average of 100. For example, a value of 115.4 in the groceries column indicates that grocery prices are 15.4% higher than the national average. Small differences in the index numbers should not be interpreted as significant; Figures cover the McAllen TX urban area.
Source: The Council for Community and Economic Research, Cost of Living Index, 2024

Grocery Prices

Area[1]	T-Bone Steak ($/pound)	Frying Chicken ($/pound)	Whole Milk ($/half gal.)	Eggs ($/dozen)	Orange Juice ($/64 oz.)	Coffee ($/11.5 oz.)
City[2]	14.52	1.28	4.54	2.96	4.22	5.08
Avg.	15.42	1.55	4.69	3.25	4.41	5.46
Min.	14.50	1.16	4.43	2.75	4.00	4.85
Max.	17.56	2.89	5.49	4.78	5.54	7.89

Note: (1) Values for the local area are compared with the average, minimum and maximum values for all 276 areas in the Cost of Living Index; (2) Figures cover the McAllen TX urban area; **T-Bone Steak** (price per pound); **Frying Chicken** (price per pound, whole fryer); **Whole Milk** (half gallon carton); **Eggs** (price per dozen, Grade A, large); **Orange Juice** (64 oz. Tropicana or Florida Natural); **Coffee** (11.5 oz. can, vacuum-packed, Maxwell House, Hills Bros, or Folgers).
Source: The Council for Community and Economic Research, Cost of Living Index, 2024

Housing and Utility Costs

Area[1]	New Home Price ($)	Apartment Rent ($/month)	All Electric ($/month)	Part Electric ($/month)	Other Energy ($/month)	Telephone ($/month)
City[2]	291,921	981	-	176.13	88.49	203.47
Avg.	515,975	1,550	210.99	123.07	82.07	194.99
Min.	265,375	692	104.33	53.68	36.26	179.42
Max.	2,775,821	5,719	529.02	397.28	361.63	223.33

Note: (1) Values for the local area are compared with the average, minimum and maximum values for all 276 areas in the Cost of Living Index; (2) Figures cover the McAllen TX urban area; **New Home Price** (2,400 sf living area, 8,000 sf lot, in urban area with full utilities); **Apartment Rent** (950 sf 2 bedroom/1.5 or 2 bath, unfurnished, excluding all utilities except water); **All Electric** (average monthly cost for an all-electric home); **Part Electric** (average monthly cost for a part-electric home); **Other Energy** (average monthly cost for natural gas, fuel oil, coal, wood, and any other forms of energy except electricity); **Telephone** (price includes the base monthly rate plus taxes and fees for three lines of mobile phone service).
Source: The Council for Community and Economic Research, Cost of Living Index, 2024

Health Care, Transportation, and Other Costs

Area[1]	Doctor ($/visit)	Dentist ($/visit)	Optometrist ($/visit)	Gasoline ($/gallon)	Beauty Salon ($/visit)	Men's Shirt ($)
City[2]	91.69	88.11	100.21	2.96	47.50	32.95
Avg.	143.77	117.51	129.23	3.32	48.57	38.14
Min.	36.74	58.67	67.33	2.80	24.00	13.41
Max.	270.44	216.82	307.33	5.28	94.00	63.89

Note: (1) Values for the local area are compared with the average, minimum and maximum values for all 276 areas in the Cost of Living Index; (2) Figures cover the McAllen TX urban area; **Doctor** (general practitioners routine exam of an established patient); **Dentist** (adult teeth cleaning and periodic oral examination); **Optometrist** (full vision eye exam for established adult patient); **Gasoline** (one gallon regular unleaded, national brand, including all taxes, cash price at self-service pump if available); **Beauty Salon** (woman's shampoo, trim, and blow-dry); **Men's Shirt** (cotton/polyester dress shirt, pinpoint weave, long sleeves).
Source: The Council for Community and Economic Research, Cost of Living Index, 2024

HOUSING

Homeownership Rate

Area	2017 (%)	2018 (%)	2019 (%)	2020 (%)	2021 (%)	2022 (%)	2023 (%)	2024 (%)
MSA[1]	n/a	n/a	n/a	n/a	n/a	n/a	n/a	n/a
U.S.	63.9	64.4	64.6	66.6	65.5	65.8	65.9	65.6

Note: (1) Figures cover the McAllen-Edinburg-Mission, TX Metropolitan Statistical Area; n/a not available
Source: U.S. Census Bureau, Housing Vacancies and Homeownership Annual Statistics: 2017-2024

House Price Index (HPI)

Area	National Ranking[2]	Quarterly Change (%)	One-Year Change (%)	Five-Year Change (%)	Since 1991Q1 (%)
MSA[1]	(a)	0.07	8.58	59.26	234.64
U.S.[3]	—	1.43	4.51	57.13	327.82

Note: The HPI is a weighted repeat sales index. It measures average price changes in repeat sales or refinancings on the same properties. This information is obtained by reviewing repeat mortgage transactions on single-family properties whose mortgages have been purchased or securitized by Fannie Mae or Freddie Mac since January 1975; (1) Figures cover the McAllen-Edinburg-Mission, TX Metropolitan Statistical Area; (2) Rankings are based on annual percentage change for all metro areas containing at least 15,000 transactions over the last 10 years and ranges from 1 to 241; (3) figures based on a weighted average of Census Division estimates using a seasonally adjusted, purchase-only index; all figures are for the period ending December 31, 2024; n/a not available; (a) Not ranked because of increased index variability due to smaller sample size
Source: Federal Housing Finance Agency, Change in FHFA Metropolitan Area House Price Indexes, All Transactions Index, 2024Q4

Home Value

Area	Under $100,000	$100,000 -$199,999	$200,000 -$299,999	$300,000 -$399,999	$400,000 -$499,999	$500,000 -$999,999	$1,000,000 or more	Median ($)
City	20.0	40.0	22.5	10.6	3.3	3.0	0.8	173,800
MSA[1]	39.7	34.5	16.0	5.7	2.2	1.6	0.4	124,000
U.S.	12.1	17.8	19.5	14.4	10.5	19.1	6.5	303,400

Note: Figures are percentages except for median and cover owner-occupied housing units; (1) Figures cover the McAllen-Edinburg-Mission, TX Metropolitan Statistical Area
Source: U.S. Census Bureau, 2019-2023 American Community Survey 5-Year Estimates

Year Housing Structure Built

Area	2020 or Later	2010 -2019	2000 -2009	1990 -1999	1980 -1989	1970 -1979	1960 -1969	1950 -1959	1940 -1949	Before 1940	Median Year
City	1.2	13.0	24.8	16.8	18.5	15.3	5.0	2.3	1.2	1.9	1993
MSA[1]	1.6	18.0	27.8	19.0	15.8	9.7	3.9	2.1	1.1	1.1	1999
U.S.	1.2	8.9	13.6	12.8	13.0	14.4	10.0	9.7	4.5	11.9	1980

Note: Figures are percentages except for Median Year; Note: (1) Figures cover the McAllen-Edinburg-Mission, TX Metropolitan Statistical Area
Source: U.S. Census Bureau, 2019-2023 American Community Survey 5-Year Estimates

Gross Monthly Rent

Area	Under $500	$500 -$999	$1,000 -$1,499	$1,500 -$1,999	$2,000 -$2,499	$2,500 -$2,999	$3,000 and up	Median ($)
City	8.3	40.3	37.2	11.2	2.0	0.9	0.0	1,017
MSA[1]	11.1	48.5	30.9	7.4	1.4	0.5	0.2	925
U.S.	6.5	22.3	29.5	20.2	10.8	4.8	5.9	1,348

Note: Figures are percentages except for median; Gross rent is the contract rent plus the estimated average monthly cost of utilities (electricity, gas, and water and sewer) and fuels (oil, coal, kerosene, wood, etc.) if these are paid by the renter (or paid for the renter by someone else); (1) Figures cover the McAllen-Edinburg-Mission, TX Metropolitan Statistical Area
Source: U.S. Census Bureau, 2019-2023 American Community Survey 5-Year Estimates

HEALTH

Health Risk Factors

Category	MSA[1] (%)	U.S. (%)
Adults aged 18–64 who have any kind of health care coverage	n/a	90.8
Adults who reported being in good or better health	n/a	81.8
Adults who have been told they have high blood cholesterol	n/a	36.9
Adults who have been told they have high blood pressure	n/a	34.0
Adults who are current smokers	n/a	12.1
Adults who currently use e-cigarettes	n/a	7.7
Adults who currently use chewing tobacco, snuff, or snus	n/a	3.2
Adults who are heavy drinkers[2]	n/a	6.1
Adults who are binge drinkers[3]	n/a	15.2
Adults who are overweight (BMI 25.0 - 29.9)	n/a	34.4
Adults who are obese (BMI 30.0 - 99.8)	n/a	34.3
Adults who participated in any physical activities in the past month	n/a	75.8

Note: All figures are crude prevalence; (1) Figures for the McAllen-Edinburg-Mission, TX Metropolitan Statistical Area were not available.
(2) Heavy drinkers are classified as adult men having more than 14 drinks per week and adult women having more than 7 drinks per week; (3) Binge drinkers are classified as males having five or more drinks on one occasion or females having four or more drinks on one occasion
Source: Centers for Disease Control and Prevention, Behaviorial Risk Factor Surveillance System, SMART: Selected Metropolitan Area Risk Trends, 2023

Acute and Chronic Health Conditions

Category	MSA[1] (%)	U.S. (%)
Adults who have ever been told they had a heart attack	n/a	4.2
Adults who have ever been told they have angina or coronary heart disease	n/a	4.0
Adults who have ever been told they had a stroke	n/a	3.3
Adults who have ever been told they have asthma	n/a	15.7
Adults who have ever been told they have arthritis	n/a	26.3
Adults who have ever been told they have diabetes[2]	n/a	11.5
Adults who have ever been told they had skin cancer	n/a	5.6
Adults who have ever been told they had any other types of cancer	n/a	8.4
Adults who have ever been told they have COPD	n/a	6.4
Adults who have ever been told they have kidney disease	n/a	3.7
Adults who have ever been told they have a form of depression	n/a	22.0

Note: All figures are crude prevalence; (1) Figures for the McAllen-Edinburg-Mission, TX Metropolitan Statistical Area were not available.
(2) Figures do not include pregnancy-related, borderline, or pre-diabetes
Source: Centers for Disease Control and Prevention, Behavioral Risk Factor Surveillance System, SMART: Selected Metropolitan Area Risk Trends, 2023

Health Screening and Vaccination Rates

Category	MSA[1] (%)	U.S. (%)
Adults who have ever been tested for HIV	n/a	37.5
Adults who have had their blood cholesterol checked within the last five years	n/a	87.0
Adults aged 65+ who have had flu shot within the past year	n/a	63.4
Adults aged 65+ who have ever had a pneumonia vaccination	n/a	71.9

Note: All figures are crude prevalence; (1) Figures for the McAllen-Edinburg-Mission, TX Metropolitan Statistical Area were not available.
Source: Centers for Disease Control and Prevention, Behavioral Risk Factor Surveillance System, SMART: Selected Metropolitan Area Risk Trends, 2023

Disability Status

Category	MSA[1] (%)	U.S. (%)
Adults who reported being deaf	n/a	7.4
Are you blind or have serious difficulty seeing, even when wearing glasses?	n/a	4.9
Do you have difficulty doing errands alone?	n/a	7.8
Do you have difficulty dressing or bathing?	n/a	3.6
Do you have serious difficulty concentrating/remembering/making decisions?	n/a	13.7
Do you have serious difficulty walking or climbing stairs?	n/a	13.2

Note: All figures are crude prevalence; (1) Figures for the McAllen-Edinburg-Mission, TX Metropolitan Statistical Area were not available.
Source: Centers for Disease Control and Prevention, Behavioral Risk Factor Surveillance System, SMART: Selected Metropolitan Area Risk Trends, 2023

Mortality Rates for the Top 10 Causes of Death in the U.S.

ICD-10[a] Sub-Chapter	ICD-10[a] Code	Crude Mortality Rate[2] per 100,000 population	
		County[3]	U.S.
Malignant neoplasms	C00-C97	106.0	182.7
Ischaemic heart diseases	I20-I25	89.7	109.6
Provisional assignment of new diseases of uncertain etiology[1]	U00-U49	64.6	65.3
Other forms of heart disease	I30-I51	43.8	65.1
Other degenerative diseases of the nervous system	G30-G31	46.9	52.4
Other external causes of accidental injury	W00-X59	13.9	52.3
Cerebrovascular diseases	I60-I69	28.5	49.1
Chronic lower respiratory diseases	J40-J47	13.9	43.5
Hypertensive diseases	I10-I15	18.5	38.9
Organic, including symptomatic, mental disorders	F01-F09	10.8	33.9

Note: (a) ICD-10 = International Classification of Diseases 10th Revision; (1) Includes COVID-19, adverse effects to COVID-19 vaccines, SARS, and vaping-related disorders; (2) Crude mortality rates are a three-year average covering 2021-2023; (3) Figures cover Hidalgo County.
Source: Centers for Disease Control and Prevention, National Center for Health Statistics. National Vital Statistics System, Mortality 2018-2023 on CDC WONDER Online Database

Mortality Rates for Selected Causes of Death

Cause of Death	ICD-10[a] Code	Crude Mortality Rate[1] per 100,000 population	
		County[2]	U.S.
Accidental poisoning and exposure to noxious substances	X40-X49	5.3	30.5
Alzheimer disease	G30	37.8	35.4
Assault	X85-Y09	4.1	7.3
COVID-19	U07.1	64.6	65.3
Diabetes mellitus	E10-E14	30.1	30.0
Diseases of the liver	K70-K76	22.2	20.8
Human immunodeficiency virus (HIV) disease	B20-B24	1.2	1.5
Influenza and pneumonia	J09-J18	10.5	13.4
Intentional self-harm	X60-X84	7.0	14.7
Malnutrition	E40-E46	3.0	6.0
Obesity and other hyperalimentation	E65-E68	1.6	3.1
Renal failure	N17-N19	11.8	16.4
Transport accidents	V01-V99	10.6	14.4

Note: (a) ICD-10 = International Classification of Diseases 10th Revision; (1) Crude mortality rates are a three-year average covering 2021-2023; (2) Figures cover Hidalgo County; Data are suppressed when the data meet the criteria for confidentiality constraints; Crude mortality rates are flagged as unreliable when the rate would be calculated with a numerator of 20 or less.
Source: Centers for Disease Control and Prevention, National Center for Health Statistics. National Vital Statistics System, Mortality 2018-2023 on CDC WONDER Online Database

Health Insurance Coverage

Area	With Health Insurance	With Private Health Insurance	With Public Health Insurance	Without Health Insurance	Population Under Age 19 Without Health Insurance
City	74.2	48.4	32.3	25.8	14.9
MSA[1]	70.3	37.7	37.5	29.7	15.7
U.S.	91.4	67.3	36.3	8.6	5.4

Note: Figures are percentages that cover the civilian noninstitutionalized population; (1) Figures cover the McAllen-Edinburg-Mission, TX Metropolitan Statistical Area
Source: U.S. Census Bureau, 2019-2023 American Community Survey 5-Year Estimates

Number of Medical Professionals

Area	MDs[3]	DOs[3,4]	Dentists	Podiatrists	Chiropractors	Optometrists
County[1] (number)	1,295	42	282	14	72	65
County[1] (rate[2])	145.8	4.7	31.4	1.6	8.0	7.2
U.S. (rate[2])	302.5	29.2	74.6	6.4	29.5	18.0

Note: Data as of 2023 unless noted; (1) Data covers Hidalgo County; (2) Number of medical professionals per 100,000 population; (3) Data as of 2022 and includes all active, non-federal physicians; (4) Doctor of Osteopathic Medicine
Source: U.S. Department of Health and Human Services, Health Resources and Services Administration, Bureau of Health Professions, Area Resource File (ARF) 2023-2024

EDUCATION

Public School District Statistics

District Name	Schls	Pupils	Pupil/ Teacher Ratio	Minority Pupils[1] (%)	Total Rev. per Pupil ($)	Total Exp. per Pupil ($)
McAllen ISD	31	20,095	13.1	95.7	17,351	15,178

Note: Table includes school districts with 2,000 or more students; (1) Percentage of students that are not non-Hispanic white.
Source: U.S. Department of Education, National Center for Education Statistics, Common Core of Data, Local Education Agency (School District) Universe Survey: School Year 2023-2024; U.S. Department of Education, National Center for Education Statistics, Common Core of Data, School District Finance Survey (F-33): School Year 2021–22

Best High Schools

According to *U.S. News,* McAllen is home to two of the top 500 high schools in the U.S.: **IDEA McAllen College Preparatory** (#107); **Achieve Early College High School** (#165). Nearly 25,000 public, magnet and charter schools were ranked based on their performance on state assessments and how well they prepare students for college. *U.S. News & World Report, "Best High Schools 2024"*

Highest Level of Education

Area	Less than H.S.	H.S. Diploma	Some College, No Deg.	Associate Degree	Bachelor's Degree	Master's Degree	Prof. School Degree	Doctorate Degree
City	20.1	20.7	20.6	6.5	20.3	7.6	2.9	1.2
MSA[1]	30.7	25.2	18.3	5.6	13.9	4.8	1.0	0.6
U.S.	10.6	26.2	19.4	8.8	21.3	9.8	2.3	1.6

Note: Figures cover persons age 25 and over; (1) Figures cover the McAllen-Edinburg-Mission, TX Metropolitan Statistical Area
Source: U.S. Census Bureau, 2019-2023 American Community Survey 5-Year Estimates

Educational Attainment by Race

Area	High School Graduate or Higher (%)					Bachelor's Degree or Higher (%)				
	Total	White	Black	Asian	Hisp.[2]	Total	White	Black	Asian	Hisp.[2]
City	79.9	85.7	99.5	89.7	77.2	32.0	35.4	31.6	64.7	28.6
MSA[1]	69.3	76.0	84.4	92.3	66.7	20.3	22.9	23.5	67.0	18.2
U.S.	89.4	92.9	88.1	88.0	72.5	35.0	37.7	24.7	57.0	19.9

Note: Figures shown cover persons 25 years old and over; (1) Figures cover the McAllen-Edinburg-Mission, TX Metropolitan Statistical Area; (2) People of Hispanic origin can be of any race
Source: U.S. Census Bureau, 2019-2023 American Community Survey 5-Year Estimates

School Enrollment by Grade and Control

Area	Preschool (%)		Kindergarten (%)		Grades 1 - 4 (%)		Grades 5 - 8 (%)		Grades 9 - 12 (%)	
	Public	Private	Public	Private	Public	Private	Public	Private	Public	Private
City	81.6	18.4	90.0	10.0	94.4	5.6	96.7	3.3	98.3	1.7
MSA[1]	93.3	6.7	96.4	3.6	97.7	2.3	98.1	1.9	98.7	1.3
U.S.	58.7	41.3	85.2	14.8	87.2	12.8	87.9	12.1	89.0	11.0

Note: Figures shown cover persons 3 years old and over; (1) Figures cover the McAllen-Edinburg-Mission, TX Metropolitan Statistical Area
Source: U.S. Census Bureau, 2019-2023 American Community Survey 5-Year Estimates

Higher Education

Four-Year Colleges			Two-Year Colleges			Medical Schools[1]	Law Schools[2]	Voc/Tech[3]
Public	Private Non-profit	Private For-profit	Public	Private Non-profit	Private For-profit			
2	0	0	0	0	3	0	0	12

Note: Figures cover institutions located within the McAllen-Edinburg-Mission, TX Metropolitan Statistical Area and include main campuses only; (1) includes schools accredited by the Liaison Committee on Medical Education and the American Osteopathic Association's Commission on Osteopathic College Accreditation; (2) includes ABA-accredited schools, schools with provisional ABA accreditation, and state accredited schools; (3) includes all schools with programs that are less than 2 years.
Source: National Center for Education Statistics, Integrated Postsecondary Education System (IPEDS), 2023-24; Wikipedia, List of Medical Schools in the United States, accessed May 2, 2025; Wikipedia, List of Law Schools in the United States, accessed May 2, 2025

EMPLOYERS

Major Employers

Company Name	Industry
BBVA Compass Bank	Financial services
City of McAllen	Municipal government
GE Engines	Manufacturing
IBC Bank	Financial services
McAllen Independent School District	Education
McAllen Medical Center	Healthcare
Mercedes Independent School District	Public elementary & secondary schools
Mid Valley Health System	Investment holding companies, except banks
Mission Consolidated Ind. School District	Public elementary & secondary schools
Panasonic Industrial Devices Corporation	Audio electronic systems
Pharr-San Juan-Alamo Ind. School District	Public elementary & secondary schools
Rio Grande Regional Hospital	Healthcare
Sharyland ISB	Public elementary & secondary schools
South Texas College	Education
Tex-Best Travel Centers	Fast-food restaurant, chain
Texas Regional Delaware	State commercial banks
TST NA Trim	Personal service agents, brokers, & bureaus
University of Texas - Pan American	Colleges & universities
Weslaco Independent School District	Public elementary & secondary schools
Woodcrafters Home Products Holding	Vanities, bathroom, wood

Note: Companies shown are located within the McAllen-Edinburg-Mission, TX Metropolitan Statistical Area.
Source: Chambers of Commerce; State Departments of Labor; Wikipedia

PUBLIC SAFETY

Crime Rate

Area	Total Crime Rate	Violent Crime Rate				Property Crime Rate		
		Murder	Rape	Robbery	Aggrav. Assault	Burglary	Larceny-Theft	Motor Vehicle Theft
City	2,092.9	4.8	35.7	24.0	79.6	111.2	1,774.4	63.2
U.S.	2,290.9	5.7	38.0	66.5	264.1	250.7	1,347.2	318.7

Note: Figures are crimes per 100,000 population.
Source: FBI, Table 8, Offenses Known to Law Enforcement, by State by City, 2023

Hate Crimes

Area	Number of Quarters Reported	Number of Incidents per Bias Motivation					
		Race/Ethnicity/Ancestry	Religion	Sexual Orientation	Disability	Gender	Gender Identity
City	4	0	0	0	0	0	0
U.S.	4	5,900	2,699	2,077	187	92	492

Source: Federal Bureau of Investigation, Hate Crime Statistics 2023

Identity Theft Consumer Reports

Area	Reports	Reports per 100,000 Population	Rank[2]
MSA[1]	1,867	212	141
U.S.	1,135,291	339	-

Note: (1) Figures cover the McAllen-Edinburg-Mission, TX Metropolitan Statistical Area; (2) Rank ranges from 1 to 401 where 1 indicates greatest number of identity theft reports per 100,000 population
Source: Federal Trade Commission, Consumer Sentinel Network Data Book 2024

Fraud and Other Consumer Reports

Area	Reports	Reports per 100,000 Population	Rank[2]
MSA[1]	5,061	575	391
U.S.	5,360,641	1,601	-

Note: (1) Figures cover the McAllen-Edinburg-Mission, TX Metropolitan Statistical Area; (2) Rank ranges from 1 to 401 where 1 indicates greatest number of fraud and other consumer reports per 100,000 population
Source: Federal Trade Commission, Consumer Sentinel Network Data Book 2024

POLITICS

2024 Presidential Election Results

Area	Trump (Rep.)	Harris (Dem.)	Stein (Green)	Kennedy (Ind.)	Oliver (Lib.)	Other
Hidalgo County	51.0	48.1	0.5	0.0	0.4	0.0
U.S.	49.7	48.2	0.6	0.5	0.4	0.6

Note: Results are percentages and may not add to 100% due to rounding
Source: Dave Leip's Atlas of U.S. Presidential Elections

SPORTS

Professional Sports Teams

Team Name	League	Year Established

No teams are located in the metro area
Source: Wikipedia, Major Professional Sports Teams of the United States and Canada, May 1, 2025

CLIMATE

Average and Extreme Temperatures

Temperature	Jan	Feb	Mar	Apr	May	Jun	Jul	Aug	Sep	Oct	Nov	Dec	Yr.
Extreme High (°F)	93	94	106	102	102	102	101	102	99	96	97	94	106
Average High (°F)	70	73	78	83	87	91	93	93	90	85	78	72	83
Average Temp. (°F)	60	63	69	75	80	83	84	85	82	76	68	63	74
Average Low (°F)	51	53	59	66	72	75	76	76	73	66	59	53	65
Extreme Low (°F)	19	22	32	38	52	60	67	63	56	40	33	16	16

Note: Figures cover the years 1948-1990
Source: National Climatic Data Center, International Station Meteorological Climate Summary, 9/96

Average Precipitation/Snowfall/Humidity

Precip./Humidity	Jan	Feb	Mar	Apr	May	Jun	Jul	Aug	Sep	Oct	Nov	Dec	Yr.
Avg. Precip. (in.)	1.4	1.4	0.6	1.5	2.5	2.8	1.8	2.6	5.6	3.2	1.5	1.1	25.8
Avg. Snowfall (in.)	Tr	Tr	0	0	0	0	0	0	0	0	Tr	Tr	Tr
Avg. Rel. Hum. 6am (%)	88	89	88	89	90	91	92	92	91	89	87	87	89
Avg. Rel. Hum. 3pm (%)	62	60	57	58	60	59	54	55	60	58	59	61	59

Note: Figures cover the years 1948-1990; Tr = Trace amounts (<0.05 in. of rain; <0.5 in. of snow)
Source: National Climatic Data Center, International Station Meteorological Climate Summary, 9/96

Weather Conditions

Temperature			Daytime Sky			Precipitation		
32°F & below	45°F & below	90°F & above	Clear	Partly cloudy	Cloudy	0.01 inch or more precip.	0.1 inch or more snow/ice	Thunder-storms
2	30	116	86	180	99	72	0	27

Note: Figures are average number of days per year and cover the years 1948-1990
Source: National Climatic Data Center, International Station Meteorological Climate Summary, 9/96

HAZARDOUS WASTE

Superfund Sites

The McAllen-Edinburg-Mission, TX metro area is home to one site on the EPA's Superfund National Priorities List (NPL) or Superfund Alternative Approach (SAA) list: **Donna Reservoir and Canal System** (Final NPL). The Superfund alternative approach uses the same investigation and cleanup process and standards that are used for sites listed on the National Priorities List. The SAA is an alternative to listing a site on the NPL; it is not an alternative to Superfund or the Superfund process. There are a total of 1,445 Superfund sites with a status of proposed or final on both lists in the United States. *U.S. Environmental Protection Agency, National Priorities List, May 1, 2025; U.S. Environmental Protection Agency, Superfund Alternative Approach Sites, May 1, 2025*

AIR QUALITY

Air Quality Trends: Ozone

	1990	1995	2000	2005	2010	2015	2020	2021	2022	2023
MSA[1]	n/a	n/a	n/a	n/a	n/a	n/a	n/a	n/a	n/a	n/a
U.S.	0.087	0.089	0.081	0.080	0.072	0.068	0.066	0.067	0.067	0.070

Note: (1) Data covers the McAllen-Edinburg-Mission, TX Metropolitan Statistical Area; n/a not available. The values shown are the composite ozone concentration averages among trend sites based on the highest fourth daily maximum 8-hour concentration in parts per million. These trends are based on sites having an adequate record of monitoring data during the trend period. Data from exceptional events are included.
Source: U.S. Environmental Protection Agency, Air Quality Monitoring Information, "Air Quality Trends by City, 1990-2023"

Air Quality Index

Area	Percent of Days when Air Quality was...[2]					AQI Statistics[2]	
	Good	Moderate	Unhealthy for Sensitive Groups	Unhealthy	Very Unhealthy	Maximum	Median
MSA[1]	57.7	42.3	0.0	0.0	0.0	95	44

Note: (1) Data covers the McAllen-Edinburg-Mission, TX Metropolitan Statistical Area; (2) Based on 357 days with AQI data in 2023. Air Quality Index (AQI) is an index for reporting daily air quality. EPA calculates the AQI for five major air pollutants regulated by the Clean Air Act: ground-level ozone, particle pollution (aka particulate matter), carbon monoxide, sulfur dioxide, and nitrogen dioxide. The AQI runs from 0 to 500. The higher the AQI value, the greater the level of air pollution and the greater the health concern. There are six AQI categories: "Good" AQI is between 0 and 50. Air quality is considered satisfactory; "Moderate" AQI is between 51 and 100. Air quality is acceptable; "Unhealthy for Sensitive Groups" When AQI values are between 101 and 150, members of sensitive groups may experience health effects; "Unhealthy" When AQI values are between 151 and 200 everyone may begin to experience health effects; "Very Unhealthy" AQI values between 201 and 300 trigger a health alert; "Hazardous" AQI values over 300 trigger warnings of emergency conditions (not shown).
Source: U.S. Environmental Protection Agency, Air Quality Index Report, 2023

Air Quality Index Pollutants

Area	Percent of Days when AQI Pollutant was...[2]					
	Carbon Monoxide	Nitrogen Dioxide	Ozone	Sulfur Dioxide	Particulate Matter 2.5	Particulate Matter 10
MSA[1]	0.0	0.0	5.3	(3)	94.7	0.0

Note: (1) Data covers the McAllen-Edinburg-Mission, TX Metropolitan Statistical Area; (2) Based on 357 days with AQI data in 2023. The Air Quality Index (AQI) is an index for reporting daily air quality. EPA calculates the AQI for five major air pollutants regulated by the Clean Air Act: ground-level ozone, particle pollution (also known as particulate matter), carbon monoxide, sulfur dioxide, and nitrogen dioxide. The AQI runs from 0 to 500. The higher the AQI value, the greater the level of air pollution and the greater the health concern; (3) Sulfur dioxide is no longer included in this table because SO_2 concentrations tend to be very localized and not necessarily representative of broad geographical areas like counties and CBSAs.
Source: U.S. Environmental Protection Agency, Air Quality Index Report, 2023

Maximum Air Pollutant Concentrations: Particulate Matter, Ozone, CO and Lead

	Particulate Matter 10 (ug/m^3)	Particulate Matter 2.5 Wtd AM (ug/m^3)	Particulate Matter 2.5 24-Hr (ug/m^3)	Ozone (ppm)	Carbon Monoxide (ppm)	Lead (ug/m^3)
MSA[1] Level	47	n/a	n/a	0.051	n/a	n/a
NAAQS[2]	150	15	35	0.075	9	0.15
Met NAAQS[2]	Yes	n/a	n/a	Yes	n/a	n/a

Note: (1) Data covers the McAllen-Edinburg-Mission, TX Metropolitan Statistical Area; Data from exceptional events are included; (2) National Ambient Air Quality Standards; ppm = parts per million; ug/m^3 = micrograms per cubic meter; n/a not available.
Concentrations: Particulate Matter 10 (coarse particulate)—highest second maximum 24-hour concentration; Particulate Matter 2.5 Wtd AM (fine particulate)—highest weighted annual mean concentration; Particulate Matter 2.5 24-Hour (fine particulate)—highest 98th percentile 24-hour concentration; Ozone—highest fourth daily maximum 8-hour concentration; Carbon Monoxide—highest second maximum non-overlapping 8-hour concentration; Lead—maximum running 3-month average
Source: U.S. Environmental Protection Agency, Air Quality Monitoring Information, "Air Quality Statistics by City, 2023"

Maximum Air Pollutant Concentrations: Nitrogen Dioxide and Sulfur Dioxide

	Nitrogen Dioxide AM (ppb)	Nitrogen Dioxide 1-Hr (ppb)	Sulfur Dioxide AM (ppb)	Sulfur Dioxide 1-Hr (ppb)	Sulfur Dioxide 24-Hr (ppb)
MSA[1] Level	n/a	n/a	n/a	n/a	n/a
NAAQS[2]	53	100	30	75	140
Met NAAQS[2]	n/a	n/a	n/a	n/a	n/a

Note: (1) Data covers the McAllen-Edinburg-Mission, TX Metropolitan Statistical Area; Data from exceptional events are included; (2) National Ambient Air Quality Standards; ppm = parts per million; ug/m^3 = micrograms per cubic meter; n/a not available.
Concentrations: Nitrogen Dioxide AM—highest arithmetic mean concentration; Nitrogen Dioxide 1-Hr—highest 98th percentile 1-hour daily maximum concentration; Sulfur Dioxide AM—highest annual mean concentration; Sulfur Dioxide 1-Hr—highest 99th percentile 1-hour daily maximum concentration; Sulfur Dioxide 24-Hr—highest second maximum 24-hour concentration
Source: U.S. Environmental Protection Agency, Air Quality Monitoring Information, "Air Quality Statistics by City, 2023"

Memphis, Tennessee

Background

Memphis is named after an ancient city in Egypt. As a natural inland port on the Mississippi River, it was inhabited for centuries by the Chickasaws Native Americans. It came to the attention of early white explorers, among them Hernando de Soto in 1541. French explorers followed. By the 1783 Treaty of Paris, the western lands up to the Mississippi claimed by the British crown passed to the newly independent United States, and the Chickasaws gave up their claim to the area in 1818. The next year a trio of American citizens, James Winchester, John Overton, and General Andrew Jackson, the last fresh from his victory at the Battle of New Orleans in 1815, organized a settlement.

In the years before the Civil War, Memphis flourished because of its advantageous location on the Mississippi. At the opening of the Civil War, it was a prize of both Northern and Southern armies. As the war lengthened and the North drew a cordon around its Southern foes, Memphis fell, but the city survived. By the end of the nineteenth century, it was clearly flourishing. In the next century, Memphis took its place as the virtual economic capital of Tennessee and the state's largest city. The driving forces in the early expansion of Memphis were cotton, and, by the end of the nineteenth century, the burgeoning lumber trade. After World War II, the city's other industries, namely food stuffs, chemicals, and electrical goods grew in importance.

Livestock and meatpacking have proved highly profitable, and the city has attracted such agricultural products from across the Upper South, earning the sobriquet America's Distribution Center. Healthcare employs a majority of residents, with a large hospital complex, the Memphis Medical Center, including the famous St. Jude Children's Research Hospital, located in the city. FedEx, ServiceMaster AutoZone, and International Paper have their corporate headquarters here.

The recording industry, too, has flourished in Memphis, and music has long been a mainstay of its growth. The composer W.C. Handy developed the blues in Memphis, and the late rock-and-roll idol Elvis Presley and his home Graceland have brought renown to the city.

In the 60s and early 70s, the city was declining, with many core buildings being vacated or razed. But in the late 1970s, the city fathers undertook to revive the core area, and launched a project that, by the 1990s, had spent three-quarters of a billion dollars to both renovate and build new. The Orpheum Theater and the Peabody Hotel, both early landmarks, were restored to their previous grandeur. The city built a convention center and Mud Island River Park, which is connected by monorail to the downtown area as part of the Memphis Riverfront Concept.

Fabled Beale Street continues to be a center for blues and music and a major tourist draw as is Memphis-style barbecue, one of four predominant regional styles of barbecue in the United States. Memphis-style barbecue, well known due to the World Championship Barbecue Cooking Contest, an event held annually in Memphis and listed in *Guinness World Records* as the largest pork barbecue contest in the world.

In 2018, the Memphis Cook Convention Center underwent a $200 million expansion and renovation and is now known as the Renasant Convention Center. The nearby Cannon Center for the Performing Arts is a 2,100-seat multi-purpose venue that is home to the Memphis Symphony Orchestra and hosts other entertainment including comedians, stage plays and children's theater, ballet, opera, and a wide variety of concerts.

In early 2022, The Memphis Medical District received nearly $3 million from the Hyde Family Foundation to grow existing programming and foster further economic development in the neighborhood. The district—increasing called the Biomedical District—is home to several large hospital systems and medical education providers. It hosts more than 30,000 employees and students and more than 10,000 residents and is served by Memphis Area Transit Authority (MATA) rail.

The $250 million NBA FedExForum, home of NBA's Memphis Grizzlies and the NCAA Division I men's basketball program of the University of Memphis, has been a catalyst for new growth and development in the sports and entertainment district.

Memphis has a humid subtropical climate, with four distinct seasons. Winter weather comes from the upper Great Plains and the Gulf of Mexico, leading to drastic swings in temperature. Summer weather can be hot and humid. Most precipitation occurs during winter and spring, with a secondary surge in rainfall due to thunderstorm activity. Severe storms are relatively infrequent.

Rankings

General Rankings

- To help military veterans find the best places in which to settle down, *WalletHub* compared the 100 largest U.S. cities across 19 key indicators of livability, affordability and veteran-friendliness. They range from the share of military skill-related jobs to veteran income growth to the availability of VA health facilities. Memphis ranked #98. *Wallethub.com, "Best & Worst Places for Veterans to Live (2025)," November 7, 2024*

Business/Finance Rankings

- WalletHub's latest report ranked 182 cities by the average credit score of its residents. Memphis was ranked #181 among the ten cities with the lowest average credit score, based on WalletHub's 2024 fourth quarter data. *WalletHub.com, "2025's Cities With the Highest & Lowest Credit Scores," March 6, 2025*

- The Memphis metro area appeared on the Milken Institute "2025 Best Performing Cities" list. Rank: #196 out of 200 large metro areas (based on performance category). Criteria: job growth; wage growth; high-tech growth and impact; community resilience; housing affordability; household broadband access. *Milken Institute, "Best-Performing Cities 2025," January 14, 2025*

Education Rankings

- Personal finance website *WalletHub* analyzed the 150 largest U.S. metropolitan statistical areas to determine where the most educated Americans are putting their degrees to work. Criteria: education levels; percentage of workers with degrees; education quality and attainment gap; public school quality rankings; quality and enrollment of each metro area's universities. Memphis was ranked #108 (#1 = most educated city). *WalletHub.com, "Most & Least Educated Cities in America, 2025" July 2, 2024*

Environmental Rankings

- Sperling's *BestPlaces* assessed the 50 largest metropolitan areas of the United States for the likelihood of dangerously extreme weather events or earthquakes. In general the Southeast and South-Central regions have the highest risk of weather extremes and earthquakes, while the Pacific Northwest enjoys the lowest risk. Of the most risky metropolitan areas, the Memphis metro area was ranked #7. *Bestplaces.net, "Avoid Natural Disasters: BestPlaces Reveals The Top 10 Safest Places to Live," October 25, 2017*

Health/Fitness Rankings

- For each of the 100 largest cities in the United States, the American Fitness Index®, compiled in partnership between the American College of Sports Medicine and the Elevance Health Foundation, evaluated community infrastructure and more than 30 health behaviors including preventive health, levels of chronic disease conditions, food insecurity, pedestrian safety, air quality, and community/environment resources that support physical activity. Memphis ranked #98 for "community fitness." *americanfitnessindex.org, "2024 ACSM American Fitness Index Summary Report," July 23, 2024*

- Memphis was identified as a "2025 Allergy Capital." The area ranked #5 out of the nation's 100 largest metropolitan areas. Three groups of factors were used to identify the most challenging cities for people with allergies: annual tree, grass, and weed pollen scores; over the counter allergy medicine use; number of board-certified allergy specialists. *Asthma and Allergy Foundation of America, "2025 Allergy Capitals: The Most Challenging Places to Live with Allergies," March 18, 2025*

- Memphis was identified as a "2024 Asthma Capital." The area ranked #15 out of the nation's 100 largest metropolitan areas. Criteria: estimated asthma prevalence; asthma-related mortality; and ER visits due to asthma. Risk factors analyzed but not factored in the rankings: annual air quality including pollution and ozone levels; public smoking laws; indoor air quality; access to asthma specialists; rescue and controller medication use; uninsured rate; pollen allergy; poverty rate. *Asthma and Allergy Foundation of America, "Asthma Capitals 2024: The Most Challenging Places to Live With Asthma," September 10, 2024*

Real Estate Rankings

- *WalletHub* compared the most populated U.S. cities to determine which had the best markets for real estate agents. Memphis ranked #131 where demand was high and pay was the best. Criteria: sales per agent; annual median wage for real-estate agents; monthly average starting salary for real estate agents; real estate job density and competition; unemployment rate; home turnover rate; housing-market health index; and other relevant metrics. *WalletHub.com, "2021 Best Places to Be a Real Estate Agent," May 12, 2021*

- Memphis was ranked #72 out of 176 metro areas in terms of cost of housing in 2024 by the National Association of Home Builders (#1 = most affordable). Criteria: the portion of an average family's income necessary to pay the mortgage on a median-priced home. *National Association of Home Builders®, NAHB-Wells Fargo Cost of Housing Index, 4th Quarter 2024*

Safety Rankings

- To identify the most dangerous cities in America, *24/7 Wall St.* focused on violent crime categories—murder, non-negligent manslaughter, rape, robbery, and aggravated assault—as reported for every 100,000 residents using data from the FBI's 2020 annual Uniform Crime Report. For cities with populations over 25,000, Memphis was ranked #2. *247wallst.com, "America's Most Dangerous Cities" November 12, 2021*

- Statistics drawn from the FBI's Uniform Crime Report were used to rank the cities where violent crime rose the most year over year from 2019 to 2020. Only cities with 25,000 or more residents were included. *24/7 Wall St.* found that Memphis placed #3 of those with a notable surge in incidents of violent crime. *247wallst.com, "American Cities Where Crime Is Soaring," March 4, 2022*

- Allstate ranked the 100 most populous cities in America in terms of driver safety. Memphis ranked #94. Criteria based on anonymized driving behavior data from Allstate's mobile app powered by Arity: high speed driving (over 80 mph), phone handling, and hard braking. The report helps increase the importance of safety and awareness behind the wheel. *Allstate, "16th Allstate America's Best Drivers Report®" July 11, 2024*

- Memphis was identified as one of the most dangerous cities in America by NeighborhoodScout. The city ranked #5 out of 100 (#1 = most dangerous). Criteria: number of violent crimes per 1,000 residents. The editors evaluated cities with 25,000 or more residents. *NeighborhoodScout.com, "2023 Top 100 Most Dangerous Cities in the U.S.," January 12, 2023*

Sports/Recreation Rankings

- Memphis was chosen as a bicycle friendly community by the League of American Bicyclists. A "Bicycle Friendly Community" welcomes cyclists by providing safe and supportive accommodation for cycling and encouraging people to bike for transportation and recreation. There are four award levels: Platinum; Gold; Silver; and Bronze. The community achieved an award level of Bronze. *League of American Bicyclists, "2024 Awards-New & Renewing Bicycle Friendly Communities List," January 28, 2025*

Women/Minorities Rankings

- Personal finance website *WalletHub* compared more than 180 U.S. cities across two key dimensions, "Hispanic Business-Friendliness" and "Hispanic Purchasing Power," to arrive at the most favorable conditions for Hispanic entrepreneurs. Memphis was ranked #141 out of 182. Criteria includes: share of Hispanic-Owned Businesses; average growth of Hispanic Business revenues; Small Business-Friendliness score; affordability; and number of Hispanics with at least a bachelor's degree. *WalletHub.com, "Best Cities for Hispanic Entrepreneurs," September 4, 2024*

Miscellaneous Rankings

- *WalletHub* compared 148 of the most populated U.S. cities to determine their operating efficiency. A "Quality of Services" score was constructed for each city and then measured against the total budget per capita to reveal which were managed the best. Memphis ranked #134. Criteria: financial stability; economy; education; safety; health; infrastructure and pollution. *WalletHub.com, "2025's Best- & Worst-Run Cities in America," June 18, 2024*

Business Environment

DEMOGRAPHICS

Population Growth

Area	1990 Census	2000 Census	2010 Census	2020 Census	2023 Estimate[2]	Population Growth 1990-2023 (%)
City	660,536	650,100	646,889	633,104	629,063	-4.8
MSA[1]	1,067,263	1,205,204	1,316,100	1,337,779	1,341,606	25.7
U.S.	248,709,873	281,421,906	308,745,538	331,449,281	332,387,540	33.6

Note: (1) Figures cover the Memphis, TN-MS-AR Metropolitan Statistical Area; (2) 2019-2023 5-year ACS population estimate
Source: U.S. Census Bureau, 1990 Census, 2000 Census, 2010 Census, 2020 Census, 2019-2023 American Community Survey 5-Year Estimates

Race

Area	White Alone[2] (%)	Black Alone[2] (%)	Asian Alone[2] (%)	AIAN[3] Alone[2] (%)	NHOPI[4] Alone[2] (%)	Other Race Alone[2] (%)	Two or More Races (%)
City	25.0	62.9	1.7	0.5	0.1	5.1	4.6
MSA[1]	42.5	46.8	2.2	0.3	0.1	3.4	4.7
U.S.	63.4	12.4	5.8	0.9	0.2	6.6	10.7

Note: (1) Figures cover the Memphis, TN-MS-AR Metropolitan Statistical Area; (2) Alone is defined as not being in combination with one or more other races; (3) American Indian and Alaska Native; (4) Native Hawaiian and Other Pacific Islander
Source: U.S. Census Bureau, 2019-2023 American Community Survey 5-Year Estimates

Hispanic or Latino Origin

Area	Total (%)	Mexican (%)	Puerto Rican (%)	Cuban (%)	Other (%)
City	10.2	5.7	0.3	0.2	3.9
MSA[1]	7.2	4.2	0.3	0.2	2.5
U.S.	19.0	11.3	1.8	0.7	5.2

Note: Persons of Hispanic or Latino origin can be of any race; (1) Figures cover the Memphis, TN-MS-AR Metropolitan Statistical Area
Source: U.S. Census Bureau, 2019-2023 American Community Survey 5-Year Estimates

Age

Area	Percent of Population									Median Age
	Under Age 5	Age 5–19	Age 20–34	Age 35–44	Age 45–54	Age 55–64	Age 65–74	Age 75–84	Age 85+	
City	7.2	20.2	23.7	12.1	11.1	11.6	8.9	3.9	1.3	34.3
MSA[1]	6.5	20.8	20.4	12.9	12.2	12.4	9.3	4.1	1.4	36.7
U.S.	5.7	19.1	20.2	13.1	12.3	12.8	10.0	4.9	1.9	38.7

Note: (1) Figures cover the Memphis, TN-MS-AR Metropolitan Statistical Area
Source: U.S. Census Bureau, 2019-2023 American Community Survey 5-Year Estimates

Disability by Age

Area	All Ages	Under 18 Years Old	18 to 64 Years Old	65 Years and Over
City	13.6	4.6	12.5	34.6
MSA[1]	13.5	5.0	12.1	34.6
U.S.	13.0	4.7	10.7	32.9

Note: Figures show percent of the civilian noninstitutionalized population that reported having a disability. Disability status is determined from six types of difficulty: vision, hearing, cognitive, ambulatory, self-care, and independent living. For children under 5 years old, hearing and vision difficulty are used to determine disability status. For children between the ages of 5 and 14, disability status is determined from hearing, vision, cognitive, ambulatory, and self-care difficulties. For people aged 15 years and older, they are considered to have a disability if they have difficulty with any one of the six difficulty types; Note: (1) Figures cover the Memphis, TN-MS-AR Metropolitan Statistical Area
Source: U.S. Census Bureau, 2019-2023 American Community Survey 5-Year Estimates

Ancestry

Area	German	Irish	English	American	Italian	Polish	French[2]	European	Scottish
City	3.3	3.6	4.9	3.3	1.5	0.5	0.7	1.6	0.9
MSA[1]	5.1	5.9	7.7	6.6	2.0	0.7	1.0	1.6	1.2
U.S.	12.6	9.4	9.1	5.5	4.9	2.6	2.0	1.6	1.6

Note: Figures are the percentage of the total population reporting a particular ancestry. The nine most commonly reported ancestries in the U.S. are shown. Figures include multiple ancestries (e.g. if a person reported being Irish and Italian, they were included in both columns); (1) Figures cover the Memphis, TN-MS-AR Metropolitan Statistical Area; (2) Excludes Basque
Source: U.S. Census Bureau, 2019-2023 American Community Survey 5-Year Estimates

Foreign-born Population

Area	Percent of Population Born in								
	Any Foreign Country	Asia	Mexico	Europe	Caribbean	Central America[2]	South America	Africa	Canada
City	7.4	1.3	2.3	0.3	0.3	1.9	0.5	0.7	0.1
MSA[1]	6.1	1.7	1.6	0.4	0.2	1.0	0.4	0.6	0.1
U.S.	13.9	4.3	3.3	1.4	1.4	1.2	1.2	0.8	0.2

Note: (1) Figures cover the Memphis, TN-MS-AR Metropolitan Statistical Area; (2) Excludes Mexico.
Source: U.S. Census Bureau, 2019-2023 American Community Survey 5-Year Estimates

Household Size

Area	Persons in Household (%)							Average Household Size
	One	Two	Three	Four	Five	Six	Seven or More	
City	38.9	29.6	14.5	9.4	4.3	1.8	1.5	2.42
MSA[1]	31.2	31.7	16.4	11.7	5.5	2.0	1.5	2.55
U.S.	28.5	33.8	15.4	12.7	5.9	2.3	1.4	2.54

Note: (1) Figures cover the Memphis, TN-MS-AR Metropolitan Statistical Area
Source: U.S. Census Bureau, 2019-2023 American Community Survey 5-Year Estimates

Household Relationships

Area	House-holder	Opposite-sex Spouse	Same-sex Spouse	Opposite-sex Unmarried Partner	Same-sex Unmarried Partner	Child[2]	Grand-child	Other Relatives	Non-relatives
City	40.4	10.9	0.2	2.7	0.2	29.7	4.3	6.1	3.7
MSA[1]	38.6	15.1	0.1	2.2	0.1	30.4	3.9	5.2	2.7
U.S.	38.3	17.5	0.2	2.5	0.2	28.3	2.4	4.8	3.4

Note: Figures are percent of the total population; (1) Figures cover the Memphis, TN-MS-AR Metropolitan Statistical Area; (2) Includes biological, adopted, and stepchildren of the householder
Source: U.S. Census Bureau, 2020 Census

Gender

Area	Males	Females	Males per 100 Females
City	298,855	330,208	90.5
MSA[1]	642,599	699,007	91.9
U.S.	164,545,087	167,842,453	98.0

Note: (1) Figures cover the Memphis, TN-MS-AR Metropolitan Statistical Area
Source: U.S. Census Bureau, 2019-2023 American Community Survey 5-Year Estimates

Marital Status

Area	Never Married	Now Married[2]	Separated	Widowed	Divorced
City	48.1	30.9	3.3	5.9	11.7
MSA[1]	38.5	42.0	2.5	5.9	11.1
U.S.	34.1	47.9	1.7	5.6	10.7

Note: Figures are percentages and cover the population 15 years of age and older; (1) Figures cover the Memphis, TN-MS-AR Metropolitan Statistical Area; (2) Excludes separated
Source: U.S. Census Bureau, 2019-2023 American Community Survey 5-Year Estimates

Religious Groups by Family

Area	Catholic	Baptist	Methodist	LDS[2]	Pentecostal	Lutheran	Islam	Adventist	Other
MSA[1]	4.8	26.6	6.0	0.7	5.1	0.3	1.3	1.3	18.4
U.S.	18.7	7.3	3.0	2.0	1.8	1.7	1.3	1.3	11.6

Note: Figures are the number of adherents as a percentage of the total population and cover the eight largest religious groups in the U.S; (1) Figures cover the Memphis, TN-MS-AR Metropolitan Statistical Area; (2) Church of Jesus Christ of Latter-day Saints
Sources: 2020 U.S. Religion Census, Association of Statisticians of American Religious Bodies; The Association of Religion Data Archives (ARDA)

Religious Groups by Tradition

Area	Catholic	Evangelical Protestant	Mainline Protestant	Black Protestant	Islam	Judaism	Hinduism	Orthodox	Buddhism
MSA[1]	4.8	32.4	5.8	17.2	1.3	0.6	0.4	0.1	0.1
U.S.	18.7	16.5	5.2	2.3	1.3	0.6	0.4	0.4	0.3

Note: Figures are the number of adherents as a percentage of the total population; (1) Figures cover the Memphis, TN-MS-AR Metropolitan Statistical Area
Sources: 2020 U.S. Religion Census, Association of Statisticians of American Religious Bodies; The Association of Religion Data Archives (ARDA)

ECONOMY

Real Gross Domestic Product (GDP)

Area	2017	2018	2019	2020	2021	2022	2023	Rank[3]
MSA[1]	75.3	76.0	76.6	75.7	79.9	79.7	81.2	47
U.S.[2]	17,619.1	18,160.7	18,642.5	18,238.9	19,387.6	19,896.6	20,436.3	—

Note: Figures are in billions of chained 2017 dollars; (1) Figures cover the Memphis, TN-MS-AR Metropolitan Statistical Area; (2) Figures cover real GDP within metropolitan areas; (3) Rank is based on 2023 data and ranges from 1 to 384
Source: U.S. Bureau of Economic Analysis

Economic Growth

Area	2014	2015	2016	2017	2018	2019	2020	2021	2022	2023
MSA[1]	-0.2	2.0	1.3	1.8	0.8	0.9	-1.2	5.5	-0.2	1.9
U.S.[2]	2.6	3.2	2.0	2.7	3.1	2.7	-2.2	6.3	2.6	2.7

Note: Figures are real gross domestic product growth rates and represent percent change from preceding period; (1) Figures cover the Memphis, TN-MS-AR Metropolitan Statistical Area; (2) Figures are the average growth rates within metropolitan areas
Source: U.S. Bureau of Economic Analysis

Metropolitan Area Exports

Area	2018	2019	2020	2021	2022	2023	Rank[2]
MSA[1]	12,695.4	13,751.7	13,350.3	16,761.5	17,835.3	17,853.5	25
U.S.	1,664,056.1	1,645,173.7	1,431,406.6	1,753,941.4	2,062,937.4	2,019,160.5	—

Note: Figures are in millions of dollars; (1) Figures cover the Memphis, TN-MS-AR Metropolitan Statistical Area; (2) Rank is based on 2023 data and ranges from 1 to 386
Source: U.S. Department of Commerce, International Trade Administration, Office of Trade and Economic Analysis, Industry and Analysis, Exports by Metropolitan Area, data extracted April 2, 2025

Building Permits

Area	Single-Family			Multi-Family			Total		
	2023	2024	Pct. Chg.	2023	2024	Pct. Chg.	2023	2024	Pct. Chg.
City	n/a	n/a	n/a	n/a	n/a	n/a	n/a	n/a	n/a
MSA[1]	3,062	2,773	-9.4	996	1,467	47.3	4,058	4,240	4.5
U.S.	920,000	981,900	6.7	591,100	496,100	-16.1	1,511,100	1,478,000	-2.2

Note: (1) Figures cover the Memphis, TN-MS-AR Metropolitan Statistical Area; Figures represent new, privately-owned housing units authorized (unadjusted data)
Source: U.S. Census Bureau, Building Permits Survey (BPS), 2023, 2024

Bankruptcy Filings

Area	Business Filings			Nonbusiness Filings		
	2023	2024	% Chg.	2023	2024	% Chg.
Shelby County	48	45	-6.3	5,959	6,030	1.2
U.S.	18,926	23,107	22.1	434,064	494,201	13.9

Note: Business filings include Chapter 7, Chapter 9, Chapter 11, Chapter 12, Chapter 13, Chapter 15, and Section 304; Nonbusiness filings include Chapter 7, Chapter 11, and Chapter 13
Source: Administrative Office of the U.S. Courts, Business and Nonbusiness Bankruptcy, County Cases Commenced by Chapter of the Bankruptcy Code, During the 12-Month Period Ending December 31, 2023 and Business and Nonbusiness Bankruptcy, County Cases Commenced by Chapter of the Bankruptcy Code, During the 12-Month Period Ending December 31, 2024

Housing Vacancy Rates

Area	Gross Vacancy Rate[3] (%)			Year-Round Vacancy Rate[4] (%)			Rental Vacancy Rate[5] (%)			Homeowner Vacancy Rate[6] (%)		
	2022	2023	2024	2022	2023	2024	2022	2023	2024	2022	2023	2024
MSA[1]	6.2	7.0	7.4	6.1	6.9	7.2	6.4	11.4	12.0	0.4	0.4	0.9
U.S.[2]	9.1	9.0	9.1	7.5	7.5	7.6	5.7	6.5	6.8	0.8	0.8	1.0

Note: (1) Figures cover the Memphis, TN-MS-AR Metropolitan Statistical Area; (2) Figures cover the 75 largest Metropolitan Statistical Areas; (3) The percentage of the total housing inventory that is vacant; (4) The percentage of the housing inventory (excluding seasonal units) that is year-round vacant; (5) The percentage of rental inventory that is vacant for rent; (6) The percentage of homeowner inventory that is vacant for sale
Source: U.S. Census Bureau, Housing Vacancies and Homeownership Annual Statistics: 2022, 2023, 2024

INCOME

Income

Area	Per Capita ($)	Median Household ($)	Average Household ($)
City	32,314	51,211	77,102
MSA[1]	36,519	64,743	92,389
U.S.	43,289	78,538	110,491

Note: (1) Figures cover the Memphis, TN-MS-AR Metropolitan Statistical Area
Source: U.S. Census Bureau, 2019-2023 American Community Survey 5-Year Estimates

Household Income Distribution

Area	Percent of Households Earning							
	Under $15,000	$15,000 -$24,999	$25,000 -$34,999	$35,000 -$49,999	$50,000 -$74,999	$75,000 -$99,999	$100,000 -$149,999	$150,000 and up
City	14.7	9.9	10.1	14.4	17.9	10.9	11.6	10.5
MSA[1]	10.9	8.0	8.2	12.2	16.7	12.1	16.0	15.9
U.S.	8.5	6.6	6.8	10.4	15.7	12.7	17.4	21.9

Note: (1) Figures cover the Memphis, TN-MS-AR Metropolitan Statistical Area
Source: U.S. Census Bureau, 2019-2023 American Community Survey 5-Year Estimates

Poverty Rate

Area	All Ages	Under 18 Years Old	18 to 64 Years Old	65 Years and Over
City	22.5	34.7	18.9	16.4
MSA[1]	16.3	24.2	14.0	12.2
U.S.	12.4	16.3	11.6	10.4

Note: Figures are percentage of people whose income during the past 12 months was below the poverty level; (1) Figures cover the Memphis, TN-MS-AR Metropolitan Statistical Area
Source: U.S. Census Bureau, 2019-2023 American Community Survey 5-Year Estimates

EMPLOYMENT

Labor Force and Employment

Area	Civilian Labor Force			Workers Employed		
	Dec. 2023	Dec. 2024	% Chg.	Dec. 2023	Dec. 2024	% Chg.
City	283,933	286,196	0.8	271,779	271,426	-0.1
MSA[1]	620,716	627,549	1.1	598,585	600,246	0.3
U.S.	166,661,000	167,746,000	0.7	160,754,000	161,294,000	0.3

Note: Data is not seasonally adjusted and covers workers 16 years of age and older; (1) Figures cover the Memphis, TN-MS-AR Metropolitan Statistical Area
Source: Bureau of Labor Statistics, Local Area Unemployment Statistics

Unemployment Rate

Area	2024											
	Jan.	Feb.	Mar.	Apr.	May	Jun.	Jul.	Aug.	Sep.	Oct.	Nov.	Dec.
City	4.9	4.5	4.7	4.2	4.4	5.8	6.2	5.8	5.3	5.4	5.3	5.2
MSA[1]	4.0	3.7	3.8	3.4	3.7	4.9	5.0	4.8	4.4	4.5	4.5	4.4
U.S.	4.1	4.2	3.9	3.5	3.7	4.3	4.5	4.4	3.9	3.9	4.0	3.8

Note: Data is not seasonally adjusted and covers workers 16 years of age and older; (1) Figures cover the Memphis, TN-MS-AR Metropolitan Statistical Area
Source: Bureau of Labor Statistics, Local Area Unemployment Statistics

Average Wages

Occupation	$/Hr.	Occupation	$/Hr.
Accountants and Auditors	39.28	Maintenance and Repair Workers	23.77
Automotive Mechanics	25.26	Marketing Managers	70.27
Bookkeepers	23.48	Network and Computer Systems Admin.	43.88
Carpenters	25.20	Nurses, Licensed Practical	25.70
Cashiers	13.30	Nurses, Registered	40.79
Computer Programmers	43.86	Nursing Assistants	17.76
Computer Systems Analysts	48.38	Office Clerks, General	19.17
Computer User Support Specialists	28.25	Physical Therapists	48.19
Construction Laborers	22.21	Physicians	143.52
Cooks, Restaurant	16.20	Plumbers, Pipefitters and Steamfitters	28.45
Customer Service Representatives	21.10	Police and Sheriff's Patrol Officers	32.26
Dentists	91.70	Postal Service Mail Carriers	28.14
Electricians	27.81	Real Estate Sales Agents	27.09
Engineers, Electrical	53.37	Retail Salespersons	16.86
Fast Food and Counter Workers	13.12	Sales Representatives, Technical/Scientific	48.33
Financial Managers	76.07	Secretaries, Exc. Legal/Medical/Executive	21.52
First-Line Supervisors of Office Workers	34.04	Security Guards	18.00
General and Operations Managers	61.94	Surgeons	n/a
Hairdressers/Cosmetologists	17.10	Teacher Assistants, Exc. Postsecondary[1]	14.32
Home Health and Personal Care Aides	15.01	Teachers, Secondary School, Exc. Sp. Ed.[1]	28.90
Janitors and Cleaners	15.76	Telemarketers	13.76
Landscaping/Groundskeeping Workers	18.30	Truck Drivers, Heavy/Tractor-Trailer	29.58
Lawyers	71.60	Truck Drivers, Light/Delivery Services	29.29
Maids and Housekeeping Cleaners	15.17	Waiters and Waitresses	13.80

Note: Wage data covers the Memphis, TN-MS-AR Metropolitan Statistical Area; (1) Hourly wages were calculated from annual wage data based on a 40 hour work week
Source: Bureau of Labor Statistics, Metro Area Occupational Employment & Wage Estimates, May 2024

Employment by Industry

Sector	MSA[1] Number of Employees	MSA[1] Percent of Total	U.S. Percent of Total
Construction, Mining, and Logging	25,100	3.8	5.5
Financial Activities	30,300	4.5	5.8
Government	87,800	13.2	14.9
Information	5,400	0.8	1.9
Leisure and Hospitality	61,900	9.3	10.4
Manufacturing	40,900	6.1	8.0
Other Services	28,000	4.2	3.7
Private Education and Health Services	101,400	15.2	16.9
Professional and Business Services	90,200	13.5	14.2
Retail Trade	62,400	9.4	10.0
Transportation, Warehousing, and Utilities	94,000	14.1	4.8
Wholesale Trade	38,700	5.8	3.9

Note: Figures are non-farm employment as of December 2024. Figures are not seasonally adjusted and include workers 16 years of age and older; (1) Figures cover the Memphis, TN-MS-AR Metropolitan Statistical Area
Source: Bureau of Labor Statistics, Current Employment Statistics, Employment, Hours, and Earnings

Employment by Occupation

Occupation Classification	City (%)	MSA[1] (%)	U.S. (%)
Management, Business, Science, and Arts	32.6	37.0	42.0
Natural Resources, Construction, and Maintenance	7.1	7.6	8.6
Production, Transportation, and Material Moving	21.1	18.8	13.0
Sales and Office	21.4	21.0	19.9
Service	17.8	15.7	16.5

Note: Figures cover employed civilians 16 years of age and older; (1) Figures cover the Memphis, TN-MS-AR Metropolitan Statistical Area
Source: U.S. Census Bureau, 2019-2023 American Community Survey 5-Year Estimates

Occupations with Greatest Projected Employment Growth: 2022 – 2032

Occupation[1]	2022 Employment	2032 Projected Employment	Numeric Employment Change	Percent Employment Change
Laborers and Freight, Stock, and Material Movers, Hand	112,810	131,040	18,230	16.2
Home Health and Personal Care Aides	32,820	46,870	14,050	42.8
General and Operations Managers	66,510	78,660	12,150	18.3
Fast Food and Counter Workers	73,880	86,020	12,140	16.4
Cooks, Restaurant	28,080	38,240	10,160	36.2
Miscellaneous Assemblers and Fabricators	54,300	64,000	9,700	17.9
Construction Laborers	32,750	41,080	8,330	25.4
Nurse Practitioners	13,620	21,500	7,880	57.9
Registered Nurses	60,020	67,720	7,700	12.8
Software Developers	16,540	23,650	7,110	43.0

Note: Projections cover Tennessee; (1) Sorted by numeric employment change
Source: www.projectionscentral.org, State Occupational Projections, 2022–2032 Long-Term Projections

Fastest-Growing Occupations: 2022 – 2032

Occupation[1]	2022 Employment	2032 Projected Employment	Numeric Employment Change	Percent Employment Change
Recreational Vehicle Service Technicians	410	660	250	61.0
Data Scientists	1,840	2,930	1,090	59.2
Nurse Practitioners	13,620	21,500	7,880	57.9
Home Appliance Repairers	650	980	330	50.8
Information Security Analysts (SOC 2018)	2,580	3,850	1,270	49.2
Dancers	170	250	80	47.1
Motor Vehicle Operators, All Other	2,560	3,750	1,190	46.5
Statisticians	940	1,360	420	44.7
Epidemiologists	230	330	100	43.5
Actuaries	370	530	160	43.2

Note: Projections cover Tennessee; (1) Sorted by percent employment change and excludes occupations with numeric employment change less than 50
Source: www.projectionscentral.org, State Occupational Projections, 2022–2032 Long-Term Projections

CITY FINANCES

City Government Finances

Component	2022 ($000)	2022 ($ per capita)
Total Revenues	3,315,648	5,103
Total Expenditures	3,040,102	4,679
Debt Outstanding	2,161,600	3,327

Source: U.S. Census Bureau, State & Local Government Finances 2022

City Government Revenue by Source

Source	2022 ($000)	2022 ($ per capita)	2022 (%)
General Revenue			
From Federal Government	130,910	201	3.9
From State Government	131,839	203	4.0
From Local Governments	101,430	156	3.1
Taxes			
Property	419,174	645	12.6
Sales and Gross Receipts	282,128	434	8.5
Personal Income	0	0	0.0
Corporate Income	0	0	0.0
Motor Vehicle License	12,004	18	0.4
Other Taxes	4,523	7	0.1
Current Charges	336,867	518	10.2
Liquor Store	0	0	0.0
Utility	1,647,395	2,536	49.7

Source: U.S. Census Bureau, State & Local Government Finances 2022

City Government Expenditures by Function

Function	2022 ($000)	2022 ($ per capita)	2022 (%)
General Direct Expenditures			
Air Transportation	0	0	0.0
Corrections	432	< 1	< 0.1
Education	0	0	0.0
Employment Security Administration	0	0	0.0
Financial Administration	39,243	60	1.3
Fire Protection	215,210	331	7.1
General Public Buildings	11,428	17	0.4
Governmental Administration, Other	58,871	90	1.9
Health	414	< 1	< 0.1
Highways	72,682	111	2.4
Hospitals	0	0	0.0
Housing and Community Development	88,322	135	2.9
Interest on General Debt	21,796	33	0.7
Judicial and Legal	22,271	34	0.7
Libraries	23,630	36	0.8
Parking	3,511	5	0.1
Parks and Recreation	80,755	124	2.7
Police Protection	290,805	447	9.6
Public Welfare	596	< 1	< 0.1
Sewerage	138,708	213	4.6
Solid Waste Management	76,736	118	2.5
Veterans' Services	0	0	0.0
Liquor Store	0	0	0.0
Utility	1,611,486	2,480	53.0

Source: U.S. Census Bureau, State & Local Government Finances 2022

TAXES

State Corporate Income Tax Rates

State	Tax Rate (%)	Income Brackets ($)	Num. of Brackets	Financial Institution Tax Rate (%)[a]	Federal Income Tax Ded.
Tennessee	6.5	Flat rate	1	6.5	No

Note: Tax rates for tax year 2024; (a) Rates listed are the corporate income tax rate applied to financial institutions or excise taxes based on income. Some states have other taxes based upon the value of deposits or shares.
Source: Federation of Tax Administrators, State Corporate Income Tax Rates, January 1, 2025

State Individual Income Tax Rates

State	Tax Rate (%)	Income Brackets ($)	Personal Exemptions ($)			Standard Ded. ($)	
			Single	Married	Depend.	Single	Married
Tennessee					– No state income tax –		

Note: Tax rates for tax year 2024; Local- and county-level taxes are not included
Source: Federation of Tax Administrators, State Individual Income Tax Rates, January 1, 2025

Various State Sales and Excise Tax Rates

State	State Sales Tax (%)	Gasoline[1] ($/gal.)	Cigarette[2] ($/pack)	Spirits[3] ($/gal.)	Wine[4] ($/gal.)	Beer[5] ($/gal.)	Recreational Marijuana (%)
Tennessee	7	0.27	0.62	4.46	1.27	1.29	Not legal

Note: All tax rates as of January 1, 2025; (1) The American Petroleum Institute has developed a methodology for determining the average tax rate on a gallon of fuel. Rates may include any of the following: excise taxes, environmental fees, storage tank fees, other fees or taxes, general sales tax, and local taxes; (2) The federal excise tax of $1.0066 per pack and local taxes are not included; (3) Rates are those applicable to off-premise sales of 40% alcohol by volume (a.b.v.) distilled spirits in 750ml containers. Local excise taxes are excluded; (4) Rates are those applicable to off-premise sales of 11% a.b.v. non-carbonated wine in 750ml containers; (5) Rates are those applicable to off-premise sales of 4.7% a.b.v. beer in 12 ounce containers.
Source: Tax Foundation, 2025 Facts & Figures: How Does Your State Compare?

State Tax Competitiveness Index

State	Overall Rank	Corporate Tax Rank	Individual Income Tax Rank	Sales Tax Rank	Property Tax Rank	Unemployment Insurance Tax Rank
Tennessee	8	48	1	47	33	17

Note: The Tax Foundation's State Tax Competitiveness Index enables policymakers, taxpayers, and business leaders to gauge how their states' tax systems compare. A rank of 1 is best, 50 is worst. Rankings do not average to the total. States without a tax rank equally as 1. DC's scores and rankings do not affect other states. The report shows tax systems as of July 1, 2024 (the beginning of Fiscal Year 2025).
Source: Tax Foundation, State Tax Competitiveness Index 2025

TRANSPORTATION

Means of Transportation to Work

Area	Car/Truck/Van Drove Alone	Car/Truck/Van Car-pooled	Public Transportation Bus	Public Transportation Subway	Public Transportation Railroad	Bicycle	Walked	Other Means	Worked at Home
City	77.8	10.0	0.8	0.0	0.0	0.2	1.7	1.5	8.0
MSA[1]	79.5	9.2	0.4	0.0	0.0	0.1	1.0	1.1	8.6
U.S.	70.2	8.5	1.7	1.3	0.4	0.4	2.4	1.6	13.5

Note: Figures are percentages and cover workers 16 years of age and older; (1) Figures cover the Memphis, TN-MS-AR Metropolitan Statistical Area
Source: U.S. Census Bureau, 2019-2023 American Community Survey 5-Year Estimates

Travel Time to Work

Area	Less Than 10 Minutes	10 to 19 Minutes	20 to 29 Minutes	30 to 44 Minutes	45 to 59 Minutes	60 to 89 Minutes	90 Minutes or More
City	11.2	31.8	33.7	18.2	2.7	1.5	1.0
MSA[1]	11.0	26.8	27.9	23.6	6.6	2.6	1.4
U.S.	12.6	28.6	21.2	20.8	8.1	6.0	2.8

Note: Note: Figures are percentages and include workers 16 years old and over; (1) Figures cover the Memphis, TN-MS-AR Metropolitan Statistical Area
Source: U.S. Census Bureau, 2019-2023 American Community Survey 5-Year Estimates

Key Congestion Measures

Measure	2000	2010	2015	2020	2022
Annual Hours of Delay, Total (000)	18,184	23,506	26,996	16,285	33,115
Annual Hours of Delay, Per Auto Commuter	35	40	45	28	58
Annual Congestion Cost, Per Auto Commuter ($)	679	697	739	477	926

Note: Figures cover the Memphis TN-MS-AR urban area
Source: Texas A&M Transportation Institute, 2023 Urban Mobility Report

Freeway Travel Time Index

Measure	1985	1990	1995	2000	2005	2010	2015	2020	2022
Urban Area Index[1]	1.05	1.11	1.14	1.16	1.17	1.17	1.18	1.08	1.13
Urban Area Rank[1,2]	64	42	41	43	49	41	41	44	71

Note: Freeway Travel Time Index—the ratio of travel time in the peak period to the travel time at free-flow conditions. For example, a value of 1.30 indicates a 20-minute free-flow trip takes 26 minutes in the peak (20 minutes x 1.30 = 26 minutes); (1) Covers the Memphis TN-MS-AR urban area; (2) Rank is based on 101 larger urban areas (#1 = highest travel time index)
Source: Texas A&M Transportation Institute, 2023 Urban Mobility Report

Public Transportation

Agency Name / Mode of Transportation	Vehicles Operated in Maximum Service[1]	Annual Unlinked Passenger Trips[2] (in thous.)	Annual Passenger Miles[3] (in thous.)
Memphis Area Transit Authority (MATA)			
Bus (directly operated)	73	2,208.2	12,290.5
Demand Response (directly operated)	54	252.8	1,749.8
Streetcar Rail (directly operated)	4	358.7	434.8

Note: (1) Number of revenue vehicles operated by the given mode and type of service to meet the annual maximum service requirement. This is the revenue vehicle count during the peak season of the year; on the week and day that maximum service is provided. Vehicles operated in maximum service (VOMS) exclude atypical days and one-time special events; (2) Number of passengers who boarded public transportation vehicles. Passengers are counted each time they board a vehicle no matter how many vehicles they use to travel from their origin to their destination. (3) Sum of the distances ridden by all passengers during the entire fiscal year.
Source: Federal Transit Administration, National Transit Database, 2023

Air Transportation

Airport Name and Code / Type of Service	Passenger Airlines[1]	Passenger Enplanements	Freight Carriers[2]	Freight (lbs)
Memphis International (MEM)				
Domestic service (U.S. carriers only)	27	2,437,316	16	3,709,000,031
International service (U.S. carriers only)	1	889	3	390,350,366

Note: (1) Includes all U.S.-based major, minor and commuter airlines that carried at least one passenger during the year; (2) Includes all U.S.-based airlines and freight carriers that transported at least one pound of freight during the year.
Source: Bureau of Transportation Statistics, The Intermodal Transportation Database, Air Carriers: T-100 Domestic Market (U.S. carriers only), 2024; Bureau of Transportation Statistics, The Intermodal Transportation Database, Air Carriers: T-100 International Market (U.S. carriers only), 2024

BUSINESSES

Major Business Headquarters

Company Name	Industry	Rankings Fortune[1]	Rankings Forbes[2]
AutoZone	Specialty retailers: other	236	-
FedEx	Mail, package and freight delivery	46	-
International Paper	Packaging, containers	218	-

Note: (1) Companies that produce a 10-K are ranked 1 to 500 based on 2023 revenue; (2) All private companies with at least $2 billion in annual revenue through the end of their most current fiscal year are ranked 1 to 275; companies listed are headquartered in the city; dashes indicate no ranking
Source: Fortune, "Fortune 500," 2024; Forbes, "America's Largest Private Companies," 2024

Fastest-Growing Businesses

According to *Initiative for a Competitive Inner City (ICIC)*, Memphis is home to three of America's 100 fastest-growing "inner city" companies: **Electronic Responsible Recyclers** (#49); **neMarc Professional Services** (#55); **Global Café** (#89). To be eligible for the IC100, companies have to be independently operated, privately held, for-profit businesses with revenues of at least $50,000 in 2019 and $500,000 in 2023, and headquartered in an under-resourced community. Recognizing that concentrated poverty exists within metropolitan areas outside of big cities (and that poverty overall is suburbanizing), ICIC defines under-resourced communities as large low-income, high-poverty areas located in the urban and suburban parts of all but the smallest metropolitan areas. Companies were ranked overall by revenue growth over the five-year period between 2019 and 2023. *Initiative for a Competitive Inner City (ICIC), "Inner City 100 Companies," 2024*

Living Environment

COST OF LIVING

Cost of Living Index

Composite Index	Groceries	Housing	Utilities	Transportation	Health Care	Misc. Goods/Services
89.8	98.8	86.2	80.9	88.8	86.0	91.7

Note: The Cost of Living Index measures regional differences in the cost of consumer goods and services, excluding taxes and non-consumer expenditures, for professional and managerial households in the top income quintile. It is based on more than 50,000 prices covering almost 60 different items for which prices are collected three times a year by chambers of commerce, economic development organizations or university applied economic centers in each participating urban area. The numbers shown should be read as a percentage above or below the national average of 100. For example, a value of 115.4 in the groceries column indicates that grocery prices are 15.4% higher than the national average. Small differences in the index numbers should not be interpreted as significant; Figures cover the Memphis TN urban area.
Source: The Council for Community and Economic Research, Cost of Living Index, 2024

Grocery Prices

Area[1]	T-Bone Steak ($/pound)	Frying Chicken ($/pound)	Whole Milk ($/half gal.)	Eggs ($/dozen)	Orange Juice ($/64 oz.)	Coffee ($/11.5 oz.)
City[2]	15.53	1.31	4.67	3.47	4.35	5.24
Avg.	15.42	1.55	4.69	3.25	4.41	5.46
Min.	14.50	1.16	4.43	2.75	4.00	4.85
Max.	17.56	2.89	5.49	4.78	5.54	7.89

Note: (1) Values for the local area are compared with the average, minimum and maximum values for all 276 areas in the Cost of Living Index; (2) Figures cover the Memphis TN urban area; **T-Bone Steak** (price per pound); **Frying Chicken** (price per pound, whole fryer); **Whole Milk** (half gallon carton); **Eggs** (price per dozen, Grade A, large); **Orange Juice** (64 oz. Tropicana or Florida Natural); **Coffee** (11.5 oz. can, vacuum-packed, Maxwell House, Hills Bros, or Folgers).
Source: The Council for Community and Economic Research, Cost of Living Index, 2024

Housing and Utility Costs

Area[1]	New Home Price ($)	Apartment Rent ($/month)	All Electric ($/month)	Part Electric ($/month)	Other Energy ($/month)	Telephone ($/month)
City[2]	404,407	1,598	-	105.22	38.46	195.12
Avg.	515,975	1,550	210.99	123.07	82.07	194.99
Min.	265,375	692	104.33	53.68	36.26	179.42
Max.	2,775,821	5,719	529.02	397.28	361.63	223.33

Note: (1) Values for the local area are compared with the average, minimum and maximum values for all 276 areas in the Cost of Living Index; (2) Figures cover the Memphis TN urban area; **New Home Price** (2,400 sf living area, 8,000 sf lot, in urban area with full utilities); **Apartment Rent** (950 sf 2 bedroom/1.5 or 2 bath, unfurnished, excluding all utilities except water); **All Electric** (average monthly cost for an all-electric home); **Part Electric** (average monthly cost for a part-electric home); **Other Energy** (average monthly cost for natural gas, fuel oil, coal, wood, and any other forms of energy except electricity); **Telephone** (price includes the base monthly rate plus taxes and fees for three lines of mobile phone service).
Source: The Council for Community and Economic Research, Cost of Living Index, 2024

Health Care, Transportation, and Other Costs

Area[1]	Doctor ($/visit)	Dentist ($/visit)	Optometrist ($/visit)	Gasoline ($/gallon)	Beauty Salon ($/visit)	Men's Shirt ($)
City[2]	112.80	97.80	83.95	3.00	46.92	27.44
Avg.	143.77	117.51	129.23	3.32	48.57	38.14
Min.	36.74	58.67	67.33	2.80	24.00	13.41
Max.	270.44	216.82	307.33	5.28	94.00	63.89

Note: (1) Values for the local area are compared with the average, minimum and maximum values for all 276 areas in the Cost of Living Index; (2) Figures cover the Memphis TN urban area; **Doctor** (general practitioners routine exam of an established patient); **Dentist** (adult teeth cleaning and periodic oral examination); **Optometrist** (full vision eye exam for established adult patient); **Gasoline** (one gallon regular unleaded, national brand, including all taxes, cash price at self-service pump if available); **Beauty Salon** (woman's shampoo, trim, and blow-dry); **Men's Shirt** (cotton/polyester dress shirt, pinpoint weave, long sleeves).
Source: The Council for Community and Economic Research, Cost of Living Index, 2024

HOUSING

Homeownership Rate

Area	2017 (%)	2018 (%)	2019 (%)	2020 (%)	2021 (%)	2022 (%)	2023 (%)	2024 (%)
MSA[1]	62.4	63.5	63.7	62.5	60.7	59.7	63.2	60.1
U.S.	63.9	64.4	64.6	66.6	65.5	65.8	65.9	65.6

Note: (1) Figures cover the Memphis, TN-MS-AR Metropolitan Statistical Area
Source: U.S. Census Bureau, Housing Vacancies and Homeownership Annual Statistics: 2017-2024

House Price Index (HPI)

Area	National Ranking[2]	Quarterly Change (%)	One-Year Change (%)	Five-Year Change (%)	Since 1991Q1 (%)
MSA[1]	206	-0.64	2.99	49.80	207.31
U.S.[3]	–	1.43	4.51	57.13	327.82

Note: The HPI is a weighted repeat sales index. It measures average price changes in repeat sales or refinancings on the same properties. This information is obtained by reviewing repeat mortgage transactions on single-family properties whose mortgages have been purchased or securitized by Fannie Mae or Freddie Mac since January 1975; (1) Figures cover the Memphis, TN-MS-AR Metropolitan Statistical Area; (2) Rankings are based on annual percentage change for all metro areas containing at least 15,000 transactions over the last 10 years and ranges from 1 to 241; (3) figures based on a weighted average of Census Division estimates using a seasonally adjusted, purchase-only index; all figures are for the period ending December 31, 2024
Source: Federal Housing Finance Agency, Change in FHFA Metropolitan Area House Price Indexes, All Transactions Index, 2024Q4

Home Value

Area	Under $100,000	$100,000 -$199,999	$200,000 -$299,999	$300,000 -$399,999	$400,000 -$499,999	$500,000 -$999,999	$1,000,000 or more	Median ($)
City	31.7	28.3	18.4	8.8	4.5	6.3	1.9	157,100
MSA[1]	18.7	24.3	22.8	15.3	8.1	9.3	1.6	228,100
U.S.	12.1	17.8	19.5	14.4	10.5	19.1	6.5	303,400

Note: Figures are percentages except for median and cover owner-occupied housing units; (1) Figures cover the Memphis, TN-MS-AR Metropolitan Statistical Area
Source: U.S. Census Bureau, 2019-2023 American Community Survey 5-Year Estimates

Year Housing Structure Built

Area	2020 or Later	2010 -2019	2000 -2009	1990 -1999	1980 -1989	1970 -1979	1960 -1969	1950 -1959	1940 -1949	Before 1940	Median Year
City	0.5	3.6	6.5	9.7	12.4	17.3	14.6	20.0	7.7	7.7	1970
MSA[1]	0.9	7.4	15.0	16.1	13.3	15.3	10.5	11.7	4.8	4.9	1982
U.S.	1.2	8.9	13.6	12.8	13.0	14.4	10.0	9.7	4.5	11.9	1980

Note: Figures are percentages except for Median Year; Note: (1) Figures cover the Memphis, TN-MS-AR Metropolitan Statistical Area
Source: U.S. Census Bureau, 2019-2023 American Community Survey 5-Year Estimates

Gross Monthly Rent

Area	Under $500	$500 -$999	$1,000 -$1,499	$1,500 -$1,999	$2,000 -$2,499	$2,500 -$2,999	$3,000 and up	Median ($)
City	4.9	32.5	43.3	15.2	2.8	0.7	0.6	1,123
MSA[1]	4.9	30.4	42.2	16.0	4.3	1.2	1.0	1,153
U.S.	6.5	22.3	29.5	20.2	10.8	4.8	5.9	1,348

Note: Figures are percentages except for median; Gross rent is the contract rent plus the estimated average monthly cost of utilities (electricity, gas, and water and sewer) and fuels (oil, coal, kerosene, wood, etc.) if these are paid by the renter (or paid for the renter by someone else); (1) Figures cover the Memphis, TN-MS-AR Metropolitan Statistical Area
Source: U.S. Census Bureau, 2019-2023 American Community Survey 5-Year Estimates

HEALTH

Health Risk Factors

Category	MSA[1] (%)	U.S. (%)
Adults aged 18–64 who have any kind of health care coverage	90.7	90.8
Adults who reported being in good or better health	79.4	81.8
Adults who have been told they have high blood cholesterol	41.9	36.9
Adults who have been told they have high blood pressure	42.5	34.0
Adults who are current smokers	17.8	12.1
Adults who currently use e-cigarettes	7.6	7.7
Adults who currently use chewing tobacco, snuff, or snus	4.7	3.2
Adults who are heavy drinkers[2]	5.0	6.1
Adults who are binge drinkers[3]	14.7	15.2
Adults who are overweight (BMI 25.0 - 29.9)	35.3	34.4
Adults who are obese (BMI 30.0 - 99.8)	36.0	34.3
Adults who participated in any physical activities in the past month	73.6	75.8

Note: All figures are crude prevalence; (1) Figures cover the Memphis, TN-MS-AR Metropolitan Statistical Area; (2) Heavy drinkers are classified as adult men having more than 14 drinks per week and adult women having more than 7 drinks per week; (3) Binge drinkers are classified as males having five or more drinks on one occasion or females having four or more drinks on one occasion
Source: Centers for Disease Control and Prevention, Behavioral Risk Factor Surveillance System, SMART: Selected Metropolitan Area Risk Trends, 2023

Acute and Chronic Health Conditions

Category	MSA[1] (%)	U.S. (%)
Adults who have ever been told they had a heart attack	4.1	4.2
Adults who have ever been told they have angina or coronary heart disease	4.4	4.0
Adults who have ever been told they had a stroke	5.9	3.3
Adults who have ever been told they have asthma	15.3	15.7
Adults who have ever been told they have arthritis	26.2	26.3
Adults who have ever been told they have diabetes[2]	17.2	11.5
Adults who have ever been told they had skin cancer	3.1	5.6
Adults who have ever been told they had any other types of cancer	8.8	8.4
Adults who have ever been told they have COPD	8.6	6.4
Adults who have ever been told they have kidney disease	5.4	3.7
Adults who have ever been told they have a form of depression	23.9	22.0

Note: All figures are crude prevalence; (1) Figures cover the Memphis, TN-MS-AR Metropolitan Statistical Area; (2) Figures do not include pregnancy-related, borderline, or pre-diabetes
Source: Centers for Disease Control and Prevention, Behavioral Risk Factor Surveillance System, SMART: Selected Metropolitan Area Risk Trends, 2023

Health Screening and Vaccination Rates

Category	MSA[1] (%)	U.S. (%)
Adults who have ever been tested for HIV	47.6	37.5
Adults who have had their blood cholesterol checked within the last five years	88.2	87.0
Adults aged 65+ who have had flu shot within the past year	61.2	63.4
Adults aged 65+ who have ever had a pneumonia vaccination	64.1	71.9

Note: All figures are crude prevalence; (1) Figures cover the Memphis, TN-MS-AR Metropolitan Statistical Area.
Source: Centers for Disease Control and Prevention, Behavioral Risk Factor Surveillance System, SMART: Selected Metropolitan Area Risk Trends, 2023

Disability Status

Category	MSA[1] (%)	U.S. (%)
Adults who reported being deaf	8.9	7.4
Are you blind or have serious difficulty seeing, even when wearing glasses?	10.8	4.9
Do you have difficulty doing errands alone?	11.5	7.8
Do you have difficulty dressing or bathing?	5.7	3.6
Do you have serious difficulty concentrating/remembering/making decisions?	19.6	13.7
Do you have serious difficulty walking or climbing stairs?	17.5	13.2

Note: All figures are crude prevalence; (1) Figures cover the Memphis, TN-MS-AR Metropolitan Statistical Area.
Source: Centers for Disease Control and Prevention, Behavioral Risk Factor Surveillance System, SMART: Selected Metropolitan Area Risk Trends, 2023

Mortality Rates for the Top 10 Causes of Death in the U.S.

ICD-10[a] Sub-Chapter	ICD-10[a] Code	Crude Mortality Rate[2] per 100,000 population	
		County[3]	U.S.
Malignant neoplasms	C00-C97	175.8	182.7
Ischaemic heart diseases	I20-I25	114.7	109.6
Provisional assignment of new diseases of uncertain etiology[1]	U00-U49	79.8	65.3
Other forms of heart disease	I30-I51	52.9	65.1
Other degenerative diseases of the nervous system	G30-G31	44.3	52.4
Other external causes of accidental injury	W00-X59	78.4	52.3
Cerebrovascular diseases	I60-I69	53.9	49.1
Chronic lower respiratory diseases	J40-J47	30.3	43.5
Hypertensive diseases	I10-I15	70.6	38.9
Organic, including symptomatic, mental disorders	F01-F09	23.7	33.9

Note: (a) ICD-10 = International Classification of Diseases 10th Revision; (1) Includes COVID-19, adverse effects to COVID-19 vaccines, SARS, and vaping-related disorders; (2) Crude mortality rates are a three-year average covering 2021-2023; (3) Figures cover Shelby County.
Source: Centers for Disease Control and Prevention, National Center for Health Statistics. National Vital Statistics System, Mortality 2018-2023 on CDC WONDER Online Database

Mortality Rates for Selected Causes of Death

Cause of Death	ICD-10[a] Code	Crude Mortality Rate[1] per 100,000 population	
		County[2]	U.S.
Accidental poisoning and exposure to noxious substances	X40-X49	58.2	30.5
Alzheimer disease	G30	24.6	35.4
Assault	X85-Y09	36.6	7.3
COVID-19	U07.1	79.8	65.3
Diabetes mellitus	E10-E14	34.8	30.0
Diseases of the liver	K70-K76	16.8	20.8
Human immunodeficiency virus (HIV) disease	B20-B24	4.7	1.5
Influenza and pneumonia	J09-J18	17.5	13.4
Intentional self-harm	X60-X84	13.0	14.7
Malnutrition	E40-E46	7.5	6.0
Obesity and other hyperalimentation	E65-E68	3.9	3.1
Renal failure	N17-N19	20.1	16.4
Transport accidents	V01-V99	29.5	14.4

Note: (a) ICD-10 = International Classification of Diseases 10th Revision; (1) Crude mortality rates are a three-year average covering 2021-2023; (2) Figures cover Shelby County; Data are suppressed when the data meet the criteria for confidentiality constraints; Crude mortality rates are flagged as unreliable when the rate would be calculated with a numerator of 20 or less.
Source: Centers for Disease Control and Prevention, National Center for Health Statistics. National Vital Statistics System, Mortality 2018-2023 on CDC WONDER Online Database

Health Insurance Coverage

Area	With Health Insurance	With Private Health Insurance	With Public Health Insurance	Without Health Insurance	Population Under Age 19 Without Health Insurance
City	85.2	55.1	41.3	14.8	8.6
MSA[1]	88.9	64.1	36.1	11.1	6.4
U.S.	91.4	67.3	36.3	8.6	5.4

Note: Figures are percentages that cover the civilian noninstitutionalized population; (1) Figures cover the Memphis, TN-MS-AR Metropolitan Statistical Area
Source: U.S. Census Bureau, 2019-2023 American Community Survey 5-Year Estimates

Number of Medical Professionals

Area	MDs[3]	DOs[3,4]	Dentists	Podiatrists	Chiropractors	Optometrists
County[1] (number)	3,934	163	717	36	141	300
County[1] (rate[2])	429.3	17.8	78.8	4.0	15.5	33.0
U.S. (rate[2])	302.5	29.2	74.6	6.4	29.5	18.0

Note: Data as of 2023 unless noted; (1) Data covers Shelby County; (2) Number of medical professionals per 100,000 population; (3) Data as of 2022 and includes all active, non-federal physicians; (4) Doctor of Osteopathic Medicine
Source: U.S. Department of Health and Human Services, Health Resources and Services Administration, Bureau of Health Professions, Area Resource File (ARF) 2023-2024

Best Hospitals

According to *U.S. News,* the Memphis, TN-MS-AR metro area is home to two of the best children's hospitals in the U.S.: **Le Bonheur Children's Hospital** (8 pediatric specialties); **St. Jude Children's Research Hospital** (1 pediatric specialty). The hospitals listed were highly ranked in at least one of 11 pediatric specialties. One hundred five children's hospitals in the U.S. were nationally ranked in at least one specialty. Hospitals received points for being ranked in a specialty, and the 10 hospitals with the most points across the 11 specialties make up the Honor Roll. *U.S. News Online, "America's Best Children's Hospitals 2024-25"*

EDUCATION

Public School District Statistics

District Name	Schls	Pupils	Pupil/ Teacher Ratio	Minority Pupils[1] (%)	Total Rev. per Pupil ($)	Total Exp. per Pupil ($)
Shelby County	222	110,057	16.3	94.8	15,499	15,292

Note: Table includes school districts with 2,000 or more students; (1) Percentage of students that are not non-Hispanic white.
Source: U.S. Department of Education, National Center for Education Statistics, Common Core of Data, Local Education Agency (School District) Universe Survey: School Year 2023-2024; U.S. Department of Education, National Center for Education Statistics, Common Core of Data, School District Finance Survey (F-33): School Year 2021–22

Highest Level of Education

Area	Less than H.S.	H.S. Diploma	Some College, No Deg.	Associate Degree	Bachelor's Degree	Master's Degree	Prof. School Degree	Doctorate Degree
City	12.6	30.6	22.5	6.1	16.9	7.9	2.0	1.4
MSA[1]	10.5	29.1	22.1	7.6	18.5	8.9	2.0	1.4
U.S.	10.6	26.2	19.4	8.8	21.3	9.8	2.3	1.6

Note: Figures cover persons age 25 and over; (1) Figures cover the Memphis, TN-MS-AR Metropolitan Statistical Area
Source: U.S. Census Bureau, 2019-2023 American Community Survey 5-Year Estimates

Educational Attainment by Race

Area	High School Graduate or Higher (%)					Bachelor's Degree or Higher (%)				
	Total	White	Black	Asian	Hisp.[2]	Total	White	Black	Asian	Hisp.[2]
City	87.4	93.9	87.8	86.8	52.0	28.2	49.9	17.9	60.0	17.8
MSA[1]	89.5	93.3	88.5	88.2	57.9	30.7	39.1	21.4	64.8	19.0
U.S.	89.4	92.9	88.1	88.0	72.5	35.0	37.7	24.7	57.0	19.9

Note: Figures shown cover persons 25 years old and over; (1) Figures cover the Memphis, TN-MS-AR Metropolitan Statistical Area; (2) People of Hispanic origin can be of any race
Source: U.S. Census Bureau, 2019-2023 American Community Survey 5-Year Estimates

School Enrollment by Grade and Control

Area	Preschool (%)		Kindergarten (%)		Grades 1 - 4 (%)		Grades 5 - 8 (%)		Grades 9 - 12 (%)	
	Public	Private	Public	Private	Public	Private	Public	Private	Public	Private
City	60.2	39.8	87.7	12.3	88.1	11.9	88.5	11.5	85.6	14.4
MSA[1]	59.8	40.2	87.5	12.5	86.3	13.7	87.0	13.0	84.8	15.2
U.S.	58.7	41.3	85.2	14.8	87.2	12.8	87.9	12.1	89.0	11.0

Note: Figures shown cover persons 3 years old and over; (1) Figures cover the Memphis, TN-MS-AR Metropolitan Statistical Area
Source: U.S. Census Bureau, 2019-2023 American Community Survey 5-Year Estimates

Higher Education

Four-Year Colleges			Two-Year Colleges			Medical Schools[1]	Law Schools[2]	Voc/Tech[3]
Public	Private Non-profit	Private For-profit	Public	Private Non-profit	Private For-profit			
2	9	1	4	2	2	1	1	9

Note: Figures cover institutions located within the Memphis, TN-MS-AR Metropolitan Statistical Area and include main campuses only; (1) includes schools accredited by the Liaison Committee on Medical Education and the American Osteopathic Association's Commission on Osteopathic College Accreditation; (2) includes ABA-accredited schools, schools with provisional ABA accreditation, and state accredited schools; (3) includes all schools with programs that are less than 2 years.
Source: National Center for Education Statistics, Integrated Postsecondary Education System (IPEDS), 2023-24; Wikipedia, List of Medical Schools in the United States, accessed May 2, 2025; Wikipedia, List of Law Schools in the United States, accessed May 2, 2025

According to *U.S. News & World Report*, the Memphis, TN-MS-AR metro area is home to one of the top 100 liberal arts colleges in the U.S.: **Rhodes College** (#59 tie). The indicators used to capture academic quality fall into a number of categories: assessment by administrators at peer institutions; retention of students; faculty resources; student selectivity; financial resources; alumni giving; high school counselor ratings of colleges; and graduation rate. *U.S. News & World Report, "America's Best Colleges 2025"*

According to *U.S. News & World Report*, the Memphis, TN-MS-AR metro area is home to one of the top medical schools for research in the U.S.: **University of Tennessee Health Science Center** (Tier 2). *U.S. News* placed medical and osteopathic schools into tiers based on their research productivity, faculty and admissions data. Each school's tier was derived from its overall score, calculated by summing the weighted normalized values generated across several factors of academic quality, outlined below. There are four tiers, with tier 1 medical schools as the highest-performing and tier 4 as the lowest-performing. Only tier 1 and 2 schools are shown. Because of the tier presentation, *U.S. News* calculated overall scores based on their percentile performance among all rated schools instead of dividing against the rescaled score of the No. 1-performing schools. Tier 1 included schools with overall scores of 85 to 99. The cutoffs for tiers 2 through 4 were schools scoring 50 to 84, 15 to 49 and 1 to 14, respectively. The rankings are based on a weighted average of the following measures of quality: total research activity; average research activity per faculty member; total NIH research grants at the medical school and its affiliated hospitals; average NIH research grants per faculty; median MCAT total score; median undergraduate GPA; acceptance rate; and faculty resources. *U.S. News & World Report, "America's Best Graduate Schools, Medical, 2025"*

EMPLOYERS

Major Employers

Company Name	Industry
Baptist Memorial Healthcare Corp.	Healthcare system
Baptist Memorial Healthcare Corp.	Integrated health care delivery system
City of Memphis	Municipal government
FedEx Corp.	Transportation, e-commerce & business services
First Tennessee Bank	Commercial banking
Horseshoe Casino & Hotel	Casinos & hotel resorts
International Paper	Printing & writing paper
Kroger Delta Marketing	Grocery stores
Memphis City Schools	Primary & secondary education
Memphis Light, Gas & Water	Utilities
Methodist Le Bonheur Healthcare	Integrated health care delivery system
Naval Support Activity Mid-South	Federal government
Park Place Entertainment	Casinos & hotel resorts
Shelby County Government	County government
Shelby County Schools	Primary & secondary education
St. Jude Children's Research Hospital	Specialty hospitals, except psychiatric
Tennessee State Government	State government
United States Government	Federal government
University of Memphis	Colleges & universities
University of Tennessee, Memphis	Colleges & universities

Note: Companies shown are located within the Memphis, TN-MS-AR Metropolitan Statistical Area.
Source: Chambers of Commerce; State Departments of Labor; Wikipedia

Best Companies to Work For

FedEx Corporation; International Paper, headquartered in Memphis, are among the "Best Places to Work in IT." To qualify, companies had to have a minimum of 100 total employees and five IT employees. The best places to work were selected based on DEI (diversity, equity, and inclusion) practices; IT turnover, promotions, and growth; IT retention and engagement programs; remote/hybrid working; benefits and perks (such as elder care and child care, flextime, and reimbursement for college tuition); and training and career development opportunities. *Computerworld, "Best Places to Work in IT," 2025*

PUBLIC SAFETY

Crime Rate

Area	Total Crime Rate	Violent Crime Rate				Property Crime Rate		
		Murder	Rape	Robbery	Aggrav. Assault	Burglary	Larceny-Theft	Motor Vehicle Theft
City	11,214.8	57.0	73.4	451.1	2,030.5	1,110.9	4,942.0	2,549.9
U.S.	2,290.9	5.7	38.0	66.5	264.1	250.7	1,347.2	318.7

Note: Figures are crimes per 100,000 population.
Source: FBI, Table 8, Offenses Known to Law Enforcement, by State by City, 2023

Hate Crimes

Area	Number of Quarters Reported	Number of Incidents per Bias Motivation					
		Race/Ethnicity/Ancestry	Religion	Sexual Orientation	Disability	Gender	Gender Identity
City	4	2	1	1	0	0	1
U.S.	4	5,900	2,699	2,077	187	92	492

Source: Federal Bureau of Investigation, Hate Crime Statistics 2023

Identity Theft Consumer Reports

Area	Reports	Reports per 100,000 Population	Rank[2]
MSA[1]	5,502	410	19
U.S.	1,135,291	339	-

Note: (1) Figures cover the Memphis, TN-MS-AR Metropolitan Statistical Area; (2) Rank ranges from 1 to 401 where 1 indicates greatest number of identity theft reports per 100,000 population
Source: Federal Trade Commission, Consumer Sentinel Network Data Book 2024

Fraud and Other Consumer Reports

Area	Reports	Reports per 100,000 Population	Rank[2]
MSA[1]	25,046	1,867	19
U.S.	5,360,641	1,601	-

Note: (1) Figures cover the Memphis, TN-MS-AR Metropolitan Statistical Area; (2) Rank ranges from 1 to 401 where 1 indicates greatest number of fraud and other consumer reports per 100,000 population
Source: Federal Trade Commission, Consumer Sentinel Network Data Book 2024

Memphis, Tennessee

POLITICS

2024 Presidential Election Results

Area	Trump (Rep.)	Harris (Dem.)	Stein (Green)	Kennedy (Ind.)	Oliver (Lib.)	Other
Shelby County	36.2	61.5	0.6	0.8	0.0	1.0
U.S.	49.7	48.2	0.6	0.5	0.4	0.6

Note: Results are percentages and may not add to 100% due to rounding
Source: Dave Leip's Atlas of U.S. Presidential Elections

SPORTS

Professional Sports Teams

Team Name	League	Year Established
Memphis Grizzlies	National Basketball Association (NBA)	2001

Note: Includes teams located in the Memphis, TN-MS-AR Metropolitan Statistical Area.
Source: Wikipedia, Major Professional Sports Teams of the United States and Canada, May 1, 2025

CLIMATE

Average and Extreme Temperatures

Temperature	Jan	Feb	Mar	Apr	May	Jun	Jul	Aug	Sep	Oct	Nov	Dec	Yr.
Extreme High (°F)	83	85	90	95	99	104	107	104	105	97	86	82	107
Average High (°F)	57	62	69	78	84	90	92	92	87	78	68	60	77
Average Temp. (°F)	46	50	57	65	72	79	81	81	76	65	55	48	65
Average Low (°F)	34	37	44	51	59	67	70	69	64	51	42	36	52
Extreme Low (°F)	0	8	15	28	38	42	55	53	34	24	16	2	0

Note: Figures cover the years 1948-1990
Source: National Climatic Data Center, International Station Meteorological Climate Summary, 9/96

Average Precipitation/Snowfall/Humidity

Precip./Humidity	Jan	Feb	Mar	Apr	May	Jun	Jul	Aug	Sep	Oct	Nov	Dec	Yr.
Avg. Precip. (in.)	4.9	5.1	6.6	5.2	4.3	3.7	5.3	3.5	3.6	2.7	4.2	5.6	54.8
Avg. Snowfall (in.)	1	Tr	Tr	Tr	0	0	0	0	0	0	Tr	Tr	1
Avg. Rel. Hum. 6am (%)	87	86	87	90	91	91	93	93	92	91	88	87	90
Avg. Rel. Hum. 3pm (%)	56	51	47	46	50	52	57	54	54	48	49	54	51

Note: Figures cover the years 1948-1990; Tr = Trace amounts (<0.05 in. of rain; <0.5 in. of snow)
Source: National Climatic Data Center, International Station Meteorological Climate Summary, 9/96

Weather Conditions

Temperature			Daytime Sky			Precipitation		
10°F & below	32°F & below	90°F & above	Clear	Partly cloudy	Cloudy	0.01 inch or more precip.	0.1 inch or more snow/ice	Thunder-storms
1	53	86	101	152	112	104	2	59

Note: Figures are average number of days per year and cover the years 1948-1990
Source: National Climatic Data Center, International Station Meteorological Climate Summary, 9/96

HAZARDOUS WASTE

Superfund Sites

The Memphis, TN-MS-AR metro area is home to 10 sites on the EPA's Superfund National Priorities List (NPL) or Superfund Alternative Approach (SAA) list: **Arlington Blending & Packaging** (Final NPL); **Carrier Air Conditioning Co.** (Final NPL); **Former Custom Cleaners** (Final NPL); **Illinois Central Railroad Company's Johnston Yard Superfund Site** (SAA); **Memphis Defense Depot (DLA)** (Final NPL); **National Fireworks** (Final NPL); **Ross Metals Inc.** (Final NPL); **Sixty One Industrial Park** (SAA); **Smalley-Piper** (Final NPL); **Walker Machine Products, Inc.** (Final NPL). The Superfund alternative approach uses the same investigation and cleanup process and standards that are used for sites listed on the National Priorities List. The SAA is an alternative to listing a site on the NPL; it is not an alternative to Superfund or the Superfund process. There are a total of 1,445 Superfund sites with a status of proposed or final on both lists in the United States. *U.S. Environmental Protection Agency, National Priorities List, May 1, 2025; U.S. Environmental Protection Agency, Superfund Alternative Approach Sites, May 1, 2025*

AIR QUALITY

Air Quality Trends: Ozone

	1990	1995	2000	2005	2010	2015	2020	2021	2022	2023
MSA[1]	0.088	0.095	0.092	0.086	0.076	0.065	0.063	0.067	0.071	0.071
U.S.	0.087	0.089	0.081	0.080	0.072	0.068	0.066	0.067	0.067	0.070

Note: (1) Data covers the Memphis, TN-MS-AR Metropolitan Statistical Area. The values shown are the composite ozone concentration averages among trend sites based on the highest fourth daily maximum 8-hour concentration in parts per million. These trends are based on sites having an adequate record of monitoring data during the trend period. Data from exceptional events are included.
Source: U.S. Environmental Protection Agency, Air Quality Monitoring Information, "Air Quality Trends by City, 1990-2023"

Air Quality Index

Area	Percent of Days when Air Quality was...[2]					AQI Statistics[2]	
	Good	Moderate	Unhealthy for Sensitive Groups	Unhealthy	Very Unhealthy	Maximum	Median
MSA[1]	28.5	67.4	4.1	0.0	0.0	140	55

Note: (1) Data covers the Memphis, TN-MS-AR Metropolitan Statistical Area; (2) Based on 365 days with AQI data in 2023. Air Quality Index (AQI) is an index for reporting daily air quality. EPA calculates the AQI for five major air pollutants regulated by the Clean Air Act: ground-level ozone, particle pollution (aka particulate matter), carbon monoxide, sulfur dioxide, and nitrogen dioxide. The AQI runs from 0 to 500. The higher the AQI value, the greater the level of air pollution and the greater the health concern. There are six AQI categories: "Good" AQI is between 0 and 50. Air quality is considered satisfactory; "Moderate" AQI is between 51 and 100. Air quality is acceptable; "Unhealthy for Sensitive Groups" When AQI values are between 101 and 150, members of sensitive groups may experience health effects; "Unhealthy" When AQI values are between 151 and 200 everyone may begin to experience health effects; "Very Unhealthy" AQI values between 201 and 300 trigger a health alert; "Hazardous" AQI values over 300 trigger warnings of emergency conditions (not shown).
Source: U.S. Environmental Protection Agency, Air Quality Index Report, 2023

Air Quality Index Pollutants

Area	Percent of Days when AQI Pollutant was...[2]					
	Carbon Monoxide	Nitrogen Dioxide	Ozone	Sulfur Dioxide	Particulate Matter 2.5	Particulate Matter 10
MSA[1]	0.0	0.0	34.2	(3)	65.8	0.0

Note: (1) Data covers the Memphis, TN-MS-AR Metropolitan Statistical Area; (2) Based on 365 days with AQI data in 2023. The Air Quality Index (AQI) is an index for reporting daily air quality. EPA calculates the AQI for five major air pollutants regulated by the Clean Air Act: ground-level ozone, particle pollution (also known as particulate matter), carbon monoxide, sulfur dioxide, and nitrogen dioxide. The AQI runs from 0 to 500. The higher the AQI value, the greater the level of air pollution and the greater the health concern; (3) Sulfur dioxide is no longer included in this table because SO_2 concentrations tend to be very localized and not necessarily representative of broad geographical areas like counties and CBSAs.
Source: U.S. Environmental Protection Agency, Air Quality Index Report, 2023

Maximum Air Pollutant Concentrations: Particulate Matter, Ozone, CO and Lead

	Particulate Matter 10 (ug/m^3)	Particulate Matter 2.5 Wtd AM (ug/m^3)	Particulate Matter 2.5 24-Hr (ug/m^3)	Ozone (ppm)	Carbon Monoxide (ppm)	Lead (ug/m^3)
MSA[1] Level	67	10.6	27	0.074	1	n/a
NAAQS[2]	150	15	35	0.075	9	0.15
Met NAAQS[2]	Yes	Yes	Yes	Yes	Yes	n/a

Note: (1) Data covers the Memphis, TN-MS-AR Metropolitan Statistical Area; Data from exceptional events are included; (2) National Ambient Air Quality Standards; ppm = parts per million; ug/m^3 = micrograms per cubic meter; n/a not available.
Concentrations: Particulate Matter 10 (coarse particulate)—highest second maximum 24-hour concentration; Particulate Matter 2.5 Wtd AM (fine particulate)—highest weighted annual mean concentration; Particulate Matter 2.5 24-Hour (fine particulate)—highest 98th percentile 24-hour concentration; Ozone—highest fourth daily maximum 8-hour concentration; Carbon Monoxide—highest second maximum non-overlapping 8-hour concentration; Lead—maximum running 3-month average
Source: U.S. Environmental Protection Agency, Air Quality Monitoring Information, "Air Quality Statistics by City, 2023"

Maximum Air Pollutant Concentrations: Nitrogen Dioxide and Sulfur Dioxide

	Nitrogen Dioxide AM (ppb)	Nitrogen Dioxide 1-Hr (ppb)	Sulfur Dioxide AM (ppb)	Sulfur Dioxide 1-Hr (ppb)	Sulfur Dioxide 24-Hr (ppb)
MSA[1] Level	9	38	n/a	2	n/a
NAAQS[2]	53	100	30	75	140
Met NAAQS[2]	Yes	Yes	n/a	Yes	n/a

Note: (1) Data covers the Memphis, TN-MS-AR Metropolitan Statistical Area; Data from exceptional events are included; (2) National Ambient Air Quality Standards; ppm = parts per million; ug/m^3 = micrograms per cubic meter; n/a not available.
Concentrations: Nitrogen Dioxide AM—highest arithmetic mean concentration; Nitrogen Dioxide 1-Hr—highest 98th percentile 1-hour daily maximum concentration; Sulfur Dioxide AM—highest annual mean concentration; Sulfur Dioxide 1-Hr—highest 99th percentile 1-hour daily maximum concentration; Sulfur Dioxide 24-Hr—highest second maximum 24-hour concentration
Source: U.S. Environmental Protection Agency, Air Quality Monitoring Information, "Air Quality Statistics by City, 2023"

Miami, Florida

Background

Miami is comprised mostly of Latinos. With three official languages—English, Spanish, and Haitian Creole—and large numbers of Cubans, Puerto Ricans, and Haitians, the city is a flavorful Latin American, Caribbean mix.

In 1896 railroad magnate Henry Flagler extended the East Coast Railroad to Miami and within 15 years the city became known as the "Gold Coast." The land boom of the 1920s brought wealthy socialites, as well as African Americans in search of work. Pink- and aquamarine-hued art deco hotels were squeezed onto a tiny tract of land called Miami Beach, and the population of the Miami metro area swelled.

Miami's tourist economy is one of the largest in the country. The city offers many leisurely activities, including swimming, scuba diving, golf, tennis, and boating. For those who enjoy professional sports, the city is host to the Miami Dolphins, football; Florida Marlins, baseball; Miami Heat, basketball; and Florida Panthers, hockey. Cultural activities range from the Miami City Ballet and the Coconut Grove Playhouse to numerous art galleries and museums, including the Bass Museum of Art. The Villa Vizcaya, a gorgeous palazzo built by industrialist James Deering in the Italian Renaissance style, and the Miami MetroZoo are popular destinations.

Miami's prime location on Biscayne Bay in the southeastern United States makes it a perfect nexus for travel and trade. The Port of Miami is a bustling center for many cruise and cargo ships. The Port is also a base for the National Oceanic and Atmospheric Administration. The Miami International Airport is a busy one, serving nearly 56 million passengers in 2024. It is expected to process 77 million passengers annually by 2040, and a $5 billion improvement plan is in the works.

Miami is at the trading crossroads of the Western Hemisphere as the chief shipment point for exports and imports with Latin America and the Caribbean. One out of every three North American cruise passengers sails from Miami.

Miami is the home to the National Hurricane Center and the headquarters of the United States Southern Command, responsible for military operations in Central and South America. Miami is also a center for stone quarrying and warehousing, industries that are centered largely on the western fringes of the city near Doral and Hialeah.

The sultry, subtropical climate against a backdrop of Spanish, art deco, and modern architecture makes Miami a uniquely cosmopolitan city. The Art Deco Historic District, known as South Beach is located on the tip of Miami Beach with an international reputation in the fashion, film, and music industries. Greater Miami is a national center for film, television, and print production.

Miami has a tropical monsoon climate with hot and wet summers and warm and dry winters. The marine influence is evidenced by a narrow temperature range and the rapid warming of cold air. During the summer months, rainfall occurs in early morning near the ocean and in early afternoon further inland. Hurricanes occasionally affect the Miami area, usually in September and October, while destructive tornadoes are quite rare. Funnel clouds are occasionally sighted and a few touch the ground briefly, but significant destruction is unusual. Waterspouts are visible from the beaches during the summer months but seldom cause any damage. June, July, and August see numerous beautiful, but dangerous, lightning events.

Miami is one of the major coastal cities and major cities in the United States that will be most affected by climate change. Globally, it is one of the most at-risk cities according to a 2020 report by Resources for the Future. Global sea level rise, which in Miami is projected to be 21 inches to 40 inches by 2070, will lead to an increase in storm damage, more intense flooding, and threaten the city's water supply. Other potential impacts of climate change include higher hurricane wind speeds and more severe thunderstorms. Some protective efforts are in place, including nourishing beaches and adding protective barriers, raising buildings and roads that are vulnerable, and restoring natural habitats such as wetlands.

Rankings

General Rankings

- To help military veterans find the best places in which to settle down, *WalletHub* compared the 100 largest U.S. cities across 19 key indicators of livability, affordability and veteran-friendliness. They range from the share of military skill-related jobs to veteran income growth to the availability of VA health facilities. Miami ranked #11. *Wallethub.com, "Best & Worst Places for Veterans to Live (2025)," November 7, 2024*

- The human resources consulting firm Mercer ranked 241 major cities worldwide in terms of overall quality of life. Miami ranked #70. Criteria: political and personal safety, social, and economic factors; medical and health considerations; schools and education; public services and transportation; recreation; connectivity; housing and infrastructure; and climate. *Mercer, "Mercer 2024 Quality of Living Survey," December 2024*

- For its 37th annual "Readers' Choice Awards" survey, *Condé Nast Traveler* ranked its readers' favorite cities in the U.S. Whether it be a longed-for visit or the next big new thing, these are the places travelers loved best. The list was broken into large cities and cities under 250,000. Miami ranked #10 in the big city category. *Condé Nast Traveler, Readers' Choice Awards 2024, "Best Big Cities in the U.S." October 1, 2024*

Business/Finance Rankings

- Mercer Human Resources Consulting ranked 226 cities worldwide in terms of cost-of-living. Miami ranked #17 (the lower the ranking, the higher the cost-of-living). The survey measured the comparative cost of over 200 items (such as housing, food, clothing, domestic supplies, transportation, and recreation/entertainment) in each location. *Mercer, "2024 Cost of Living City Ranking," June 17, 2024*

Culture/Performing Arts Rankings

- Miami was selected as one of the 25 best cities for moviemakers in North America. Great film cities are places where filmmaking dreams can come true, that offer more creative space, lower costs, and great outdoor locations. NYC & LA were intentionally excluded. Criteria: film industry presence and culture; tax incentives; affordability; and proximity of festivals and schools. The city was ranked #7. *MovieMaker Magazine, "Best Places to Live and Work as a Moviemaker, 2025," January 29, 2025*

Dating/Romance Rankings

- *Apartment List* conducted its Annual Renter Satisfaction Survey and asked renters "how satisfied are you with opportunities for dating in your current city." The cities were ranked from highest to lowest based on their satisfaction scores. Miami ranked #9 out of 10 cities. *Apartment List, "Best Cities for Dating 2022 with Local Dating Insights from Bumble," February 7, 2022*

Environmental Rankings

- Sperling's *BestPlaces* assessed the 50 largest metropolitan areas of the United States for the likelihood of dangerously extreme weather events or earthquakes. In general the Southeast and South-Central regions have the highest risk of weather extremes and earthquakes, while the Pacific Northwest enjoys the lowest risk. Of the most risky metropolitan areas, the Miami metro area was ranked #1. *Bestplaces.net, "Avoid Natural Disasters: BestPlaces Reveals The Top 10 Safest Places to Live," October 25, 2017*

- The U.S. Environmental Protection Agency (EPA) released its list of U.S. metropolitan areas with the most ENERGY STAR certified buildings in 2023. The Miami metro area was ranked #22 out of 25. *U.S. Environmental Protection Agency, "2024 Energy Star Top Cities," May 22, 2024*

Food/Drink Rankings

- Miami was identified as one of the cities in America ordering the most vegan food options by GrubHub.com. The city ranked #4 out of 5. Criteria: percentage of vegan, vegetarian and plant-based food orders compared to the overall number of orders. *GrubHub.com, "State of the Plate Report 2021: Top Cities for Vegans," June 20, 2021*

- WalletHub compared the 100 largest U.S. cities across 17 key indicators of vegan- and vegetarian-friendliness. Miami was ranked #8. Cities were selected based on metrics such as the cost of groceries for vegetarians, the share of restaurants serving meatless options and the number of salad shops per capita. *WalletHub.com, "Best Cities for Vegans & Vegetarians (2025)," September 24, 2024*

Health/Fitness Rankings

- For each of the 100 largest cities in the United States, the American Fitness Index®, compiled in partnership between the American College of Sports Medicine and the Elevance Health Foundation, evaluated community infrastructure and more than 30 health behaviors including preventive health, levels of chronic disease conditions, food insecurity, pedestrian safety, air quality, and community/environment resources that support physical activity. Miami ranked #13 for "community fitness." *americanfitnessindex.org, "2024 ACSM American Fitness Index Summary Report," July 23, 2024*

- Miami was identified as one of the 10 most walkable cities in the U.S. by Walk Score. The city ranked #5. Walk Score measures walkability by analyzing hundreds of walking routes to nearby amenities, and also measures pedestrian friendliness by analyzing population density and road metrics such as block length and intersection density. *WalkScore.com, April 13, 2021*

- Miami was identified as a "2025 Allergy Capital." The area ranked #65 out of the nation's 100 largest metropolitan areas. Three groups of factors were used to identify the most challenging cities for people with allergies: annual tree, grass, and weed pollen scores; over the counter allergy medicine use; number of board-certified allergy specialists. *Asthma and Allergy Foundation of America, "2025 Allergy Capitals: The Most Challenging Places to Live with Allergies," March 18, 2025*

- Miami was identified as a "2024 Asthma Capital." The area ranked #29 out of the nation's 100 largest metropolitan areas. Criteria: estimated asthma prevalence; asthma-related mortality; and ER visits due to asthma. Risk factors analyzed but not factored in the rankings: annual air quality including pollution and ozone levels; public smoking laws; indoor air quality; access to asthma specialists; rescue and controller medication use; uninsured rate; pollen allergy; poverty rate. *Asthma and Allergy Foundation of America, "Asthma Capitals 2024: The Most Challenging Places to Live With Asthma," September 10, 2024*

Pet Rankings

- Miami appeared on *The Dogington Post* site as one of the top cities for dog lovers, ranking #13 out of 15. The real estate marketplace, Zillow®, and Rover, the largest pet sitter and dog walker network, introduced a new list of "Top Emerging Dog-Friendly Cities" for 2021. Criteria: number of new dog accounts on the Rover platform; and rentals and listings that mention features that attract dog owners (fenced-in yards, dog houses, dog door or proximity to a dog park). *Dogingtonpost.com, "15 Cities Emerging as Dog-Friendliest in 2021," May 11, 2021*

- Miami was selected by *Sniffspot.com* as one of the most dog-friendly cities in the U.S., ranking #30 out of 50. Criteria: dog parks; hiking; sniffspots; public parks; dog-friendly businesses; housing; dog waste cleanliness; leash laws; dog services; and overall cost. *Sniffspot.com, "The Top 50 Most Dog-Friendly Cities in the U.S.," September 30, 2024*

Real Estate Rankings

- *WalletHub* compared the most populated U.S. cities to determine which had the best markets for real estate agents. Miami ranked #155 where demand was high and pay was the best. Criteria: sales per agent; annual median wage for real-estate agents; monthly average starting salary for real estate agents; real estate job density and competition; unemployment rate; home turnover rate; housing-market health index; and other relevant metrics. *WalletHub.com, "2021 Best Places to Be a Real Estate Agent," May 12, 2021*

Safety Rankings

- Allstate ranked the 100 most populous cities in America in terms of driver safety. Miami ranked #90. Criteria based on anonymized driving behavior data from Allstate's mobile app powered by Arity: high speed driving (over 80 mph), phone handling, and hard braking. The report helps increase the importance of safety and awareness behind the wheel. *Allstate, "16th Allstate America's Best Drivers Report®" July 11, 2024*

Transportation Rankings

- According to the INRIX "2024 Global Traffic Scorecard," Miami was identified as one of the most congested metro areas in the U.S. The area ranked #6 out of 10 in the country and among the top 25 most congested in the world. Criteria: average annual time spent in traffic and average cost of congestion per motorist. *Inrix.com, "Employees & Consumers Returned to Downtowns, Traffic Delays & Costs Grew," January 6, 2025*

Women/Minorities Rankings

- Personal finance website *WalletHub* compared more than 180 U.S. cities across two key dimensions, "Hispanic Business-Friendliness" and "Hispanic Purchasing Power," to arrive at the most favorable conditions for Hispanic entrepreneurs. Miami was ranked #5 out of 182. Criteria includes: share of Hispanic-Owned Businesses; average growth of Hispanic Business revenues; Small Business-Friendliness score; affordability; and number of Hispanics with at least a bachelor's degree. *WalletHub.com, "Best Cities for Hispanic Entrepreneurs," September 4, 2024*

Miscellaneous Rankings

- *MoveHub* ranked 446 hipster cities across 20 countries, using its new and improved alternative Hipster Index and Miami came out as #7 among the top 50. Criteria: population over 150,000; number of vintage boutiques; density of tattoo parlors; vegan places to eat; coffee shops; and density of vinyl record stores. *MoveHub.com, "The Hipster Index: Brighton Pips Portland to Global Top Spot," July 28, 2021*

- *WalletHub* compared 148 of the most populated U.S. cities to determine their operating efficiency. A "Quality of Services" score was constructed for each city and then measured against the total budget per capita to reveal which were managed the best. Miami ranked #62. Criteria: financial stability; economy; education; safety; health; infrastructure and pollution. *WalletHub.com, "2025's Best- & Worst-Run Cities in America," June 18, 2024*

Business Environment

DEMOGRAPHICS

Population Growth

Area	1990 Census	2000 Census	2010 Census	2020 Census	2023 Estimate[2]	Population Growth 1990-2023 (%)
City	358,843	362,470	399,457	442,241	446,663	24.5
MSA[1]	4,056,100	5,007,564	5,564,635	6,138,333	6,138,876	51.3
U.S.	248,709,873	281,421,906	308,745,538	331,449,281	332,387,540	33.6

Note: (1) Figures cover the Miami-Fort Lauderdale-West Palm Beach, FL Metropolitan Statistical Area; (2) 2019-2023 5-year ACS population estimate
Source: U.S. Census Bureau, 1990 Census, 2000 Census, 2010 Census, 2020 Census, 2019-2023 American Community Survey 5-Year Estimates

Race

Area	White Alone[2] (%)	Black Alone[2] (%)	Asian Alone[2] (%)	AIAN[3] Alone[2] (%)	NHOPI[4] Alone[2] (%)	Other Race Alone[2] (%)	Two or More Races (%)
City	34.2	13.7	1.6	0.4	0.0	7.5	42.6
MSA[1]	43.7	20.3	2.6	0.2	0.0	6.6	26.6
U.S.	63.4	12.4	5.8	0.9	0.2	6.6	10.7

Note: (1) Figures cover the Miami-Fort Lauderdale-West Palm Beach, FL Metropolitan Statistical Area; (2) Alone is defined as not being in combination with one or more other races; (3) American Indian and Alaska Native; (4) Native Hawaiian and Other Pacific Islander
Source: U.S. Census Bureau, 2019-2023 American Community Survey 5-Year Estimates

Hispanic or Latino Origin

Area	Total (%)	Mexican (%)	Puerto Rican (%)	Cuban (%)	Other (%)
City	71.2	2.2	3.3	31.0	34.8
MSA[1]	46.0	2.5	3.7	18.4	21.5
U.S.	19.0	11.3	1.8	0.7	5.2

Note: Persons of Hispanic or Latino origin can be of any race; (1) Figures cover the Miami-Fort Lauderdale-West Palm Beach, FL Metropolitan Statistical Area
Source: U.S. Census Bureau, 2019-2023 American Community Survey 5-Year Estimates

Age

Area	Under Age 5	Age 5–19	Age 20–34	Age 35–44	Age 45–54	Age 55–64	Age 65–74	Age 75–84	Age 85+	Median Age
City	5.3	12.8	23.8	15.4	13.5	12.8	8.5	5.2	2.6	39.7
MSA[1]	5.4	16.9	18.5	13.2	13.6	13.4	10.2	6.1	2.7	41.9
U.S.	5.7	19.1	20.3	13.1	12.3	12.8	10.0	4.9	1.9	38.7

Note: (1) Figures cover the Miami-Fort Lauderdale-West Palm Beach, FL Metropolitan Statistical Area
Source: U.S. Census Bureau, 2019-2023 American Community Survey 5-Year Estimates

Disability by Age

Area	All Ages	Under 18 Years Old	18 to 64 Years Old	65 Years and Over
City	11.5	3.7	7.0	38.2
MSA[1]	11.0	4.0	7.2	30.9
U.S.	13.0	4.7	10.7	32.9

Note: Figures show percent of the civilian noninstitutionalized population that reported having a disability. Disability status is determined from six types of difficulty: vision, hearing, cognitive, ambulatory, self-care, and independent living. For children under 5 years old, hearing and vision difficulty are used to determine disability status. For children between the ages of 5 and 14, disability status is determined from hearing, vision, cognitive, ambulatory, and self-care difficulties. For people aged 15 years and older, they are considered to have a disability if they have difficulty with any one of the six difficulty types; Note: (1) Figures cover the Miami-Fort Lauderdale-West Palm Beach, FL Metropolitan Statistical Area
Source: U.S. Census Bureau, 2019-2023 American Community Survey 5-Year Estimates

Ancestry

Area	German	Irish	English	American	Italian	Polish	French[2]	European	Scottish
City	1.9	1.3	1.3	2.6	3.0	0.7	0.9	0.6	0.2
MSA[1]	4.2	4.1	3.1	5.6	4.9	1.8	1.1	0.9	0.6
U.S.	12.6	9.4	9.1	5.5	4.9	2.6	2.0	1.6	1.6

Note: Figures are the percentage of the total population reporting a particular ancestry. The nine most commonly reported ancestries in the U.S. are shown. Figures include multiple ancestries (e.g. if a person reported being Irish and Italian, they were included in both columns); (1) Figures cover the Miami-Fort Lauderdale-West Palm Beach, FL Metropolitan Statistical Area; (2) Excludes Basque
Source: U.S. Census Bureau, 2019-2023 American Community Survey 5-Year Estimates

Foreign-born Population

Area	Percent of Population Born in								
	Any Foreign Country	Asia	Mexico	Europe	Caribbean	Central America[2]	South America	Africa	Canada
City	57.7	1.5	1.2	2.2	28.5	11.8	11.9	0.4	0.2
MSA[1]	41.9	2.2	1.1	2.4	20.6	4.3	10.2	0.4	0.5
U.S.	13.9	4.3	3.3	1.4	1.4	1.2	1.2	0.8	0.2

Note: (1) Figures cover the Miami-Fort Lauderdale-West Palm Beach, FL Metropolitan Statistical Area; (2) Excludes Mexico.
Source: U.S. Census Bureau, 2019-2023 American Community Survey 5-Year Estimates

Household Size

Area	Persons in Household (%)							Average Household Size
	One	Two	Three	Four	Five	Six	Seven or More	
City	36.5	32.1	15.8	9.5	3.8	1.1	1.2	2.30
MSA[1]	27.9	32.2	17.3	13.3	6.0	2.1	1.3	2.62
U.S.	28.5	33.8	15.4	12.7	5.9	2.3	1.4	2.54

Note: (1) Figures cover the Miami-Fort Lauderdale-West Palm Beach, FL Metropolitan Statistical Area
Source: U.S. Census Bureau, 2019-2023 American Community Survey 5-Year Estimates

Household Relationships

Area	House-holder	Opposite-sex Spouse	Same-sex Spouse	Opposite-sex Unmarried Partner	Same-sex Unmarried Partner	Child[2]	Grand-child	Other Relatives	Non-relatives
City	42.4	12.6	0.5	3.3	0.3	22.5	2.4	8.7	5.8
MSA[1]	38.0	16.0	0.3	2.6	0.2	27.6	2.5	7.8	3.7
U.S.	38.3	17.5	0.2	2.5	0.2	28.3	2.4	4.8	3.4

Note: Figures are percent of the total population; (1) Figures cover the Miami-Fort Lauderdale-West Palm Beach, FL Metropolitan Statistical Area; (2) Includes biological, adopted, and stepchildren of the householder
Source: U.S. Census Bureau, 2020 Census

Gender

Area	Males	Females	Males per 100 Females
City	226,349	220,314	102.7
MSA[1]	3,005,200	3,133,676	95.9
U.S.	164,545,087	167,842,453	98.0

Note: (1) Figures cover the Miami-Fort Lauderdale-West Palm Beach, FL Metropolitan Statistical Area
Source: U.S. Census Bureau, 2019-2023 American Community Survey 5-Year Estimates

Marital Status

Area	Never Married	Now Married[2]	Separated	Widowed	Divorced
City	40.4	37.0	3.3	5.7	13.5
MSA[1]	34.0	44.7	2.4	6.1	12.8
U.S.	34.1	47.9	1.7	5.6	10.7

Note: Figures are percentages and cover the population 15 years of age and older; (1) Figures cover the Miami-Fort Lauderdale-West Palm Beach, FL Metropolitan Statistical Area; (2) Excludes separated
Source: U.S. Census Bureau, 2019-2023 American Community Survey 5-Year Estimates

Religious Groups by Family

Area	Catholic	Baptist	Methodist	LDS[2]	Pentecostal	Lutheran	Islam	Adventist	Other
MSA[1]	23.8	5.1	0.9	0.5	1.3	0.3	0.8	2.4	11.1
U.S.	18.7	7.3	3.0	2.0	1.8	1.7	1.3	1.3	11.6

Note: Figures are the number of adherents as a percentage of the total population and cover the eight largest religious groups in the U.S; (1) Figures cover the Miami-Fort Lauderdale-West Palm Beach, FL Metropolitan Statistical Area; (2) Church of Jesus Christ of Latter-day Saints
Sources: 2020 U.S. Religion Census, Association of Statisticians of American Religious Bodies; The Association of Religion Data Archives (ARDA)

Religious Groups by Tradition

Area	Catholic	Evangelical Protestant	Mainline Protestant	Black Protestant	Islam	Judaism	Hinduism	Orthodox	Buddhism
MSA[1]	23.8	13.7	1.6	2.2	0.8	1.2	0.3	0.2	0.3
U.S.	18.7	16.5	5.2	2.3	0.6	0.4	0.4	0.4	0.3

Note: Figures are the number of adherents as a percentage of the total population; (1) Figures cover the Miami-Fort Lauderdale-West Palm Beach, FL Metropolitan Statistical Area
Sources: 2020 U.S. Religion Census, Association of Statisticians of American Religious Bodies; The Association of Religion Data Archives (ARDA)

ECONOMY

Real Gross Domestic Product (GDP)

Area	2017	2018	2019	2020	2021	2022	2023	Rank[3]
MSA[1]	347.0	359.9	367.6	353.8	391.4	415.2	431.9	12
U.S.[2]	17,619.1	18,160.7	18,642.5	18,238.9	19,387.6	19,896.6	20,436.3	—

Note: Figures are in billions of chained 2017 dollars; (1) Figures cover the Miami-Fort Lauderdale-West Palm Beach, FL Metropolitan Statistical Area; (2) Figures cover real GDP within metropolitan areas; (3) Rank is based on 2023 data and ranges from 1 to 384
Source: U.S. Bureau of Economic Analysis

Economic Growth

Area	2014	2015	2016	2017	2018	2019	2020	2021	2022	2023
MSA[1]	3.4	4.4	3.1	4.5	3.7	2.1	-3.7	10.6	6.1	4.0
U.S.[2]	2.6	3.2	2.0	2.7	3.1	2.7	-2.2	6.3	2.6	2.7

Note: Figures are real gross domestic product growth rates and represent percent change from preceding period; (1) Figures cover the Miami-Fort Lauderdale-West Palm Beach, FL Metropolitan Statistical Area; (2) Figures are the average growth rates within metropolitan areas
Source: U.S. Bureau of Economic Analysis

Metropolitan Area Exports

Area	2018	2019	2020	2021	2022	2023	Rank[2]
MSA[1]	35,650.2	35,498.9	29,112.1	36,011.3	41,517.8	44,256.4	8
U.S.	1,664,056.1	1,645,173.7	1,431,406.6	1,753,941.4	2,062,937.4	2,019,160.5	—

Note: Figures are in millions of dollars; (1) Figures cover the Miami-Fort Lauderdale-West Palm Beach, FL Metropolitan Statistical Area; (2) Rank is based on 2023 data and ranges from 1 to 386
Source: U.S. Department of Commerce, International Trade Administration, Office of Trade and Economic Analysis, Industry and Analysis, Exports by Metropolitan Area, data extracted April 2, 2025

Building Permits

Area	Single-Family 2023	Single-Family 2024	Pct. Chg.	Multi-Family 2023	Multi-Family 2024	Pct. Chg.	Total 2023	Total 2024	Pct. Chg.
City	113	145	28.3	5,307	5,878	10.8	5,420	6,023	11.1
MSA[1]	5,512	5,825	5.7	15,808	10,527	-33.4	21,320	16,352	-23.3
U.S.	920,000	981,900	6.7	591,100	496,100	-16.1	1,511,100	1,478,000	-2.2

Note: (1) Figures cover the Miami-Fort Lauderdale-West Palm Beach, FL Metropolitan Statistical Area; Figures represent new, privately-owned housing units authorized (unadjusted data)
Source: U.S. Census Bureau, Building Permits Survey (BPS), 2023, 2024

Bankruptcy Filings

Area	Business Filings 2023	Business Filings 2024	% Chg.	Nonbusiness Filings 2023	Nonbusiness Filings 2024	% Chg.
Miami-Dade County	242	413	70.7	5,320	6,779	27.4
U.S.	18,926	23,107	22.1	434,064	494,201	13.9

Note: Business filings include Chapter 7, Chapter 9, Chapter 11, Chapter 12, Chapter 13, Chapter 15, and Section 304; Nonbusiness filings include Chapter 7, Chapter 11, and Chapter 13
Source: Administrative Office of the U.S. Courts, Business and Nonbusiness Bankruptcy, County Cases Commenced by Chapter of the Bankruptcy Code, During the 12-Month Period Ending December 31, 2023 and Business and Nonbusiness Bankruptcy, County Cases Commenced by Chapter of the Bankruptcy Code, During the 12-Month Period Ending December 31, 2024

Housing Vacancy Rates

Area	Gross Vacancy Rate[3] (%) 2022	2023	2024	Year-Round Vacancy Rate[4] (%) 2022	2023	2024	Rental Vacancy Rate[5] (%) 2022	2023	2024	Homeowner Vacancy Rate[6] (%) 2022	2023	2024
MSA[1]	12.6	14.7	14.8	7.5	8.9	9.3	6.3	8.4	9.5	1.1	0.9	1.4
U.S.[2]	9.1	9.0	9.1	7.5	7.5	7.6	5.7	6.5	6.8	0.8	0.8	1.0

Note: (1) Figures cover the Miami-Fort Lauderdale-West Palm Beach, FL Metropolitan Statistical Area; (2) Figures cover the 75 largest Metropolitan Statistical Areas; (3) The percentage of the total housing inventory that is vacant; (4) The percentage of the housing inventory (excluding seasonal units) that is year-round vacant; (5) The percentage of rental inventory that is vacant for rent; (6) The percentage of homeowner inventory that is vacant for sale
Source: U.S. Census Bureau, Housing Vacancies and Homeownership Annual Statistics: 2022, 2023, 2024

INCOME

Income

Area	Per Capita ($)	Median Household ($)	Average Household ($)
City	42,528	59,390	97,643
MSA[1]	42,369	73,481	109,356
U.S.	43,289	78,538	110,491

Note: (1) Figures cover the Miami-Fort Lauderdale-West Palm Beach, FL Metropolitan Statistical Area
Source: U.S. Census Bureau, 2019-2023 American Community Survey 5-Year Estimates

Household Income Distribution

Area	Percent of Households Earning							
	Under $15,000	$15,000 -$24,999	$25,000 -$34,999	$35,000 -$49,999	$50,000 -$74,999	$75,000 -$99,999	$100,000 -$149,999	$150,000 and up
City	14.4	9.3	8.1	11.9	15.7	10.2	13.1	17.4
MSA[1]	9.3	7.1	7.4	10.9	16.1	12.6	16.3	20.1
U.S.	8.5	6.6	6.8	10.4	15.7	12.7	17.4	21.9

Note: (1) Figures cover the Miami-Fort Lauderdale-West Palm Beach, FL Metropolitan Statistical Area
Source: U.S. Census Bureau, 2019-2023 American Community Survey 5-Year Estimates

Poverty Rate

Area	All Ages	Under 18 Years Old	18 to 64 Years Old	65 Years and Over
City	19.2	23.4	15.3	31.4
MSA[1]	13.1	16.9	11.0	15.9
U.S.	12.4	16.3	11.6	10.4

Note: Figures are percentage of people whose income during the past 12 months was below the poverty level; (1) Figures cover the Miami-Fort Lauderdale-West Palm Beach, FL Metropolitan Statistical Area
Source: U.S. Census Bureau, 2019-2023 American Community Survey 5-Year Estimates

EMPLOYMENT

Labor Force and Employment

Area	Civilian Labor Force			Workers Employed		
	Dec. 2023	Dec. 2024	% Chg.	Dec. 2023	Dec. 2024	% Chg.
City	247,114	249,197	0.8	242,276	243,343	0.4
MD[1]	1,433,283	1,445,779	0.9	1,404,765	1,410,954	0.4
U.S.	166,661,000	167,746,000	0.7	160,754,000	161,294,000	0.3

Note: Data is not seasonally adjusted and covers workers 16 years of age and older; (1) Figures cover the Miami-Miami Beach-Kendall, FL Metropolitan Division
Source: Bureau of Labor Statistics, Local Area Unemployment Statistics

Unemployment Rate

Area	2024											
	Jan.	Feb.	Mar.	Apr.	May	Jun.	Jul.	Aug.	Sep.	Oct.	Nov.	Dec.
City	1.8	2.0	2.2	2.2	2.2	2.4	2.8	2.8	2.4	2.4	2.3	2.3
MD[1]	1.9	2.0	2.3	2.3	2.3	2.6	2.8	2.9	2.4	2.4	2.4	2.4
U.S.	4.1	4.2	3.9	3.5	3.7	4.3	4.5	4.4	3.9	3.9	4.0	3.8

Note: Data is not seasonally adjusted and covers workers 16 years of age and older; (1) Figures cover the Miami-Miami Beach-Kendall, FL Metropolitan Division
Source: Bureau of Labor Statistics, Local Area Unemployment Statistics

Average Wages

Occupation	$/Hr.	Occupation	$/Hr.
Accountants and Auditors	43.02	Maintenance and Repair Workers	23.66
Automotive Mechanics	26.45	Marketing Managers	69.64
Bookkeepers	24.75	Network and Computer Systems Admin.	47.57
Carpenters	24.57	Nurses, Licensed Practical	30.32
Cashiers	14.99	Nurses, Registered	44.26
Computer Programmers	57.85	Nursing Assistants	19.01
Computer Systems Analysts	54.87	Office Clerks, General	22.54
Computer User Support Specialists	32.66	Physical Therapists	42.79
Construction Laborers	21.69	Physicians	117.21
Cooks, Restaurant	17.30	Plumbers, Pipefitters and Steamfitters	27.27
Customer Service Representatives	20.41	Police and Sheriff's Patrol Officers	50.84
Dentists	89.88	Postal Service Mail Carriers	28.58
Electricians	27.58	Real Estate Sales Agents	35.78
Engineers, Electrical	53.23	Retail Salespersons	17.72
Fast Food and Counter Workers	14.62	Sales Representatives, Technical/Scientific	72.39
Financial Managers	85.42	Secretaries, Exc. Legal/Medical/Executive	22.74
First-Line Supervisors of Office Workers	34.06	Security Guards	19.47
General and Operations Managers	64.93	Surgeons	n/a
Hairdressers/Cosmetologists	18.78	Teacher Assistants, Exc. Postsecondary[1]	15.86
Home Health and Personal Care Aides	16.09	Teachers, Secondary School, Exc. Sp. Ed.[1]	28.86
Janitors and Cleaners	15.94	Telemarketers	18.31
Landscaping/Groundskeeping Workers	18.25	Truck Drivers, Heavy/Tractor-Trailer	26.65
Lawyers	78.54	Truck Drivers, Light/Delivery Services	23.18
Maids and Housekeeping Cleaners	16.01	Waiters and Waitresses	18.71

Note: Wage data covers the Miami-Fort Lauderdale-West Palm Beach, FL Metropolitan Statistical Area; (1) Hourly wages were calculated from annual wage data based on a 40 hour work week
Source: Bureau of Labor Statistics, Metro Area Occupational Employment & Wage Estimates, May 2024

Employment by Industry

Sector	MD[1] Number of Employees	MD[1] Percent of Total	U.S. Percent of Total
Construction	61,100	4.5	5.1
Financial Activities	97,500	7.1	5.8
Government	144,600	10.6	14.9
Information	23,100	1.7	1.9
Leisure and Hospitality	155,500	11.4	10.4
Manufacturing	48,200	3.5	8.0
Mining and Logging	600	<0.1	0.4
Other Services	49,900	3.7	3.7
Private Education and Health Services	226,600	16.6	16.9
Professional and Business Services	213,900	15.7	14.2
Retail Trade	152,700	11.2	10.0
Transportation, Warehousing, and Utilities	105,900	7.8	4.8
Wholesale Trade	84,700	6.2	3.9

Note: Figures are non-farm employment as of December 2024. Figures are not seasonally adjusted and include workers 16 years of age and older; (1) Figures cover the Miami-Miami Beach-Kendall, FL Metropolitan Division
Source: Bureau of Labor Statistics, Current Employment Statistics, Employment, Hours, and Earnings

Employment by Occupation

Occupation Classification	City (%)	MSA[1] (%)	U.S. (%)
Management, Business, Science, and Arts	37.5	38.6	42.0
Natural Resources, Construction, and Maintenance	11.4	9.1	8.6
Production, Transportation, and Material Moving	9.8	10.5	13.0
Sales and Office	19.7	22.5	19.9
Service	21.5	19.2	16.5

Note: Figures cover employed civilians 16 years of age and older; (1) Figures cover the Miami-Fort Lauderdale-West Palm Beach, FL Metropolitan Statistical Area
Source: U.S. Census Bureau, 2019-2023 American Community Survey 5-Year Estimates

Occupations with Greatest Projected Employment Growth: 2022 – 2032

Occupation[1]	2022 Employment	2032 Projected Employment	Numeric Employment Change	Percent Employment Change
Stockers and Order Fillers	236,990	274,060	37,070	15.6
Retail Salespersons	308,940	340,000	31,060	10.1
Waiters and Waitresses	195,320	223,820	28,500	14.6
Software Developers	75,620	101,940	26,320	34.8
General and Operations Managers	184,790	210,510	25,720	13.9
Registered Nurses	202,780	228,070	25,290	12.5
Fast Food and Counter Workers	185,000	209,460	24,460	13.2
Cooks, Restaurant	120,850	141,640	20,790	17.2
Landscaping and Groundskeeping Workers	112,240	129,030	16,790	15.0
Janitors and Cleaners, Except Maids and Housekeeping Cleaners	136,890	153,490	16,600	12.1

Note: Projections cover Florida; (1) Sorted by numeric employment change
Source: www.projectionscentral.org, State Occupational Projections, 2022–2032 Long-Term Projections

Fastest-Growing Occupations: 2022 – 2032

Occupation[1]	2022 Employment	2032 Projected Employment	Numeric Employment Change	Percent Employment Change
Nurse Practitioners	18,910	29,980	11,070	58.5
Data Scientists	8,470	12,450	3,980	47.0
Information Security Analysts (SOC 2018)	11,060	15,650	4,590	41.5
Statisticians	590	820	230	39.0
Solar Photovoltaic Installers	1,210	1,680	470	38.8
Computer and Information Research Scientists (SOC 2018)	3,160	4,380	1,220	38.6
Physician Assistants	8,830	12,180	3,350	37.9
Actuaries	1,640	2,260	620	37.8
Physical Therapist Assistants	7,430	10,230	2,800	37.7
Medical and Health Services Managers	34,490	47,200	12,710	36.9

Note: Projections cover Florida; (1) Sorted by percent employment change and excludes occupations with numeric employment change less than 50
Source: www.projectionscentral.org, State Occupational Projections, 2022–2032 Long-Term Projections

CITY FINANCES

City Government Finances

Component	2022 ($000)	2022 ($ per capita)
Total Revenues	1,151,404	2,442
Total Expenditures	1,050,669	2,228
Debt Outstanding	667,122	1,415

Source: U.S. Census Bureau, State & Local Government Finances 2022

City Government Revenue by Source

Source	2022 ($000)	2022 ($ per capita)	2022 (%)
General Revenue			
From Federal Government	104,243	221	9.1
From State Government	59,055	125	5.1
From Local Governments	73,473	156	6.4
Taxes			
Property	524,897	1,113	45.6
Sales and Gross Receipts	86,880	184	7.5
Personal Income	0	0	0.0
Corporate Income	0	0	0.0
Motor Vehicle License	0	0	0.0
Other Taxes	107,761	229	9.4
Current Charges	132,062	280	11.5
Liquor Store	0	0	0.0
Utility	9	0	0.0

Source: U.S. Census Bureau, State & Local Government Finances 2022

City Government Expenditures by Function

Function	2022 ($000)	2022 ($ per capita)	2022 (%)
General Direct Expenditures			
Air Transportation	0	0	0.0
Corrections	0	0	0.0
Education	0	0	0.0
Employment Security Administration	0	0	0.0
Financial Administration	66,124	140	6.3
Fire Protection	189,567	402	18.0
General Public Buildings	0	0	0.0
Governmental Administration, Other	61,434	130	5.8
Health	0	0	0.0
Highways	22,393	47	2.1
Hospitals	0	0	0.0
Housing and Community Development	48,696	103	4.6
Interest on General Debt	18,036	38	1.7
Judicial and Legal	10,473	22	1.0
Libraries	0	0	0.0
Parking	36,681	77	3.5
Parks and Recreation	117,953	250	11.2
Police Protection	281,039	596	26.7
Public Welfare	13,870	29	1.3
Sewerage	0	0	0.0
Solid Waste Management	44,451	94	4.2
Veterans' Services	0	0	0.0
Liquor Store	0	0	0.0
Utility	0	0	0.0

Source: U.S. Census Bureau, State & Local Government Finances 2022

TAXES

State Corporate Income Tax Rates

State	Tax Rate (%)	Income Brackets ($)	Num. of Brackets	Financial Institution Tax Rate (%)[a]	Federal Income Tax Ded.
Florida	5.5	Flat rate	1	5.5	No

Note: Tax rates for tax year 2024; (a) Rates listed are the corporate income tax rate applied to financial institutions or excise taxes based on income. Some states have other taxes based upon the value of deposits or shares.
Source: Federation of Tax Administrators, State Corporate Income Tax Rates, January 1, 2025

State Individual Income Tax Rates

State	Tax Rate (%)	Income Brackets ($)	Personal Exemptions ($)			Standard Ded. ($)	
			Single	Married	Depend.	Single	Married
Florida			– No state income tax –				

Note: Tax rates for tax year 2024; Local- and county-level taxes are not included
Source: Federation of Tax Administrators, State Individual Income Tax Rates, January 1, 2025

Various State Sales and Excise Tax Rates

State	State Sales Tax (%)	Gasoline[1] ($/gal.)	Cigarette[2] ($/pack)	Spirits[3] ($/gal.)	Wine[4] ($/gal.)	Beer[5] ($/gal.)	Recreational Marijuana (%)
Florida	6	0.39	1.34	6.50	2.25	0.48	Not legal

Note: All tax rates as of January 1, 2025; (1) The American Petroleum Institute has developed a methodology for determining the average tax rate on a gallon of fuel. Rates may include any of the following: excise taxes, environmental fees, storage tank fees, other fees or taxes, general sales tax, and local taxes; (2) The federal excise tax of $1.0066 per pack and local taxes are not included; (3) Rates are those applicable to off-premise sales of 40% alcohol by volume (a.b.v.) distilled spirits in 750ml containers. Local excise taxes are excluded; (4) Rates are those applicable to off-premise sales of 11% a.b.v. non-carbonated wine in 750ml containers; (5) Rates are those applicable to off-premise sales of 4.7% a.b.v. beer in 12 ounce containers.
Source: Tax Foundation, 2025 Facts & Figures: How Does Your State Compare?

State Tax Competitiveness Index

State	Overall Rank	Corporate Tax Rank	Individual Income Tax Rank	Sales Tax Rank	Property Tax Rank	Unemployment Insurance Tax Rank
Florida	4	16	1	14	21	10

Note: The Tax Foundation's State Tax Competitiveness Index enables policymakers, taxpayers, and business leaders to gauge how their states' tax systems compare. A rank of 1 is best, 50 is worst. Rankings do not average to the total. States without a tax rank equally as 1. DC's scores and rankings do not affect other states. The report shows tax systems as of July 1, 2024 (the beginning of Fiscal Year 2025).
Source: Tax Foundation, State Tax Competitiveness Index 2025

TRANSPORTATION

Means of Transportation to Work

Area	Car/Truck/Van		Public Transportation			Bicycle	Walked	Other Means	Worked at Home
	Drove Alone	Car-pooled	Bus	Subway	Railroad				
City	61.7	7.9	5.4	1.1	0.1	0.8	5.4	3.5	14.2
MSA[1]	71.3	9.2	2.0	0.2	0.1	0.4	1.6	2.3	12.9
U.S.	70.2	8.5	1.7	1.3	0.4	0.4	2.4	1.6	13.5

Note: Figures are percentages and cover workers 16 years of age and older; (1) Figures cover the Miami-Fort Lauderdale-West Palm Beach, FL Metropolitan Statistical Area
Source: U.S. Census Bureau, 2019-2023 American Community Survey 5-Year Estimates

Travel Time to Work

Area	Less Than 10 Minutes	10 to 19 Minutes	20 to 29 Minutes	30 to 44 Minutes	45 to 59 Minutes	60 to 89 Minutes	90 Minutes or More
City	6.4	24.1	25.7	27.6	8.7	6.0	1.5
MSA[1]	6.8	23.2	23.1	27.1	9.9	7.2	2.6
U.S.	12.6	28.6	21.2	20.8	8.1	6.0	2.8

Note: Note: Figures are percentages and include workers 16 years old and over; (1) Figures cover the Miami-Fort Lauderdale-West Palm Beach, FL Metropolitan Statistical Area
Source: U.S. Census Bureau, 2019-2023 American Community Survey 5-Year Estimates

Key Congestion Measures

Measure	2000	2010	2015	2020	2022
Annual Hours of Delay, Total (000)	184,437	226,862	270,637	112,879	315,984
Annual Hours of Delay, Per Auto Commuter	49	55	65	27	79
Annual Congestion Cost, Per Auto Commuter ($)	1,461	1,428	1,574	680	1,852

Note: Figures cover the Miami FL urban area
Source: Texas A&M Transportation Institute, 2023 Urban Mobility Report

Freeway Travel Time Index

Measure	1985	1990	1995	2000	2005	2010	2015	2020	2022
Urban Area Index[1]	1.16	1.18	1.21	1.27	1.29	1.28	1.31	1.11	1.34
Urban Area Rank[1,2]	10	15	13	16	10	13	16	15	20	6

Note: Freeway Travel Time Index—the ratio of travel time in the peak period to the travel time at free-flow conditions. For example, a value of 1.30 indicates a 20-minute free-flow trip takes 26 minutes in the peak (20 minutes x 1.30 = 26 minutes); (1) Covers the Miami FL urban area; (2) Rank is based on 101 larger urban areas (#1 = highest travel time index)
Source: Texas A&M Transportation Institute, 2023 Urban Mobility Report

Public Transportation

Agency Name / Mode of Transportation	Vehicles Operated in Maximum Service[1]	Annual Unlinked Passenger Trips[2] (in thous.)	Annual Passenger Miles[3] (in thous.)
Miami-Dade Transit (MDT)			
Bus (directly operated)	571	54,697.0	248,850.9
Bus (purchased transportation)	53	1,225.0	4,820.1
Commuter Bus (purchased transportation)	9	362.7	14,001.7
Demand Response (purchased transportation)	339	1,424.1	18,527.0
Heavy Rail (directly operated)	84	13,261.3	106,633.0
Monorail and Automated Guideway (directly operated)	21	6,546.1	7,163.4
Vanpool (purchased transportation)	220	445.8	14,132.9
South Florida Regional Transportation Authority (TRI-Rail)			
Bus (purchased transportation)	3	386.2	1,196.1
Commuter Rail (purchased transportation)	43	3,735.9	105,501.7

Note: (1) Number of revenue vehicles operated by the given mode and type of service to meet the annual maximum service requirement. This is the revenue vehicle count during the peak season of the year; on the week and day that maximum service is provided. Vehicles operated in maximum service (VOMS) exclude atypical days and one-time special events; (2) Number of passengers who boarded public transportation vehicles. Passengers are counted each time they board a vehicle no matter how many vehicles they use to travel from their origin to their destination. (3) Sum of the distances ridden by all passengers during the entire fiscal year.
Source: Federal Transit Administration, National Transit Database, 2023

Air Transportation

Airport Name and Code / Type of Service	Passenger Airlines[1]	Passenger Enplanements	Freight Carriers[2]	Freight (lbs)
Miami International (MIA)				
Domestic service (U.S. carriers only)	28	14,921,318	22	500,786,329
International service (U.S. carriers only)	19	6,900,883	17	853,849,928

Note: (1) Includes all U.S.-based major, minor and commuter airlines that carried at least one passenger during the year; (2) Includes all U.S.-based airlines and freight carriers that transported at least one pound of freight during the year.
Source: Bureau of Transportation Statistics, The Intermodal Transportation Database, Air Carriers: T-100 Domestic Market (U.S. carriers only), 2024; Bureau of Transportation Statistics, The Intermodal Transportation Database, Air Carriers: T-100 International Market (U.S. carriers only), 2024

BUSINESSES

Major Business Headquarters

Company Name	Industry	Rankings Fortune[1]	Rankings Forbes[2]
Greenberg Traurig	Business services & supplies	-	246
Lennar	Homebuilders	126	-
Southern Glazer's Wine & Spirits	Food, drink & tobacco	-	10
Watsco	Wholesalers: diversified	489	-
World Kinect	Energy	93	-

Note: (1) Companies that produce a 10-K are ranked 1 to 500 based on 2023 revenue; (2) All private companies with at least $2 billion in annual revenue through the end of their most current fiscal year are ranked 1 to 275; companies listed are headquartered in the city; dashes indicate no ranking
Source: Fortune, "Fortune 500," 2024; Forbes, "America's Largest Private Companies," 2024

Fastest-Growing Businesses

According to *Inc.*, Miami is home to 12 of America's 500 fastest-growing private companies: **StatusPro** (#15); **GoTu Technology** (#42); **Spot Pet Insurance** (#62); **Novo** (#77); **Body20** (#205); **Payabli** (#223); **Blankfactor** (#280); **HCM Unlocked** (#334); **Guardian Dentistry** (#384); **Get Staffed Up** (#433); **Condor Agency** (#445); **Superhuman** (#465). Criteria: must be an independent, privately-held, for-profit, U.S. corporation, proprietorship or partnership as of December 31, 2023; revenues must be at least $100,000 in 2020 and $2 million in 2023; must have four-year operating/sales history. *Inc., "America's 500 Fastest-Growing Private Companies," 2024*

According to *Initiative for a Competitive Inner City (ICIC)*, Miami is home to one of America's 100 fastest-growing "inner city" companies: **M. Gill & Associates** (#29). To be eligible for the IC100, companies have to be independently operated, privately held, for-profit businesses with revenues of at least $50,000 in 2019 and $500,000 in 2023, and headquartered in an under-resourced community. Recognizing that concentrated poverty exists within metropolitan areas outside of big cities (and that poverty overall is suburbanizing), ICIC defines under-resourced communities as large low-income, high-poverty areas located in the urban and suburban parts of all but the smallest metropolitan areas. Companies were ranked overall by revenue growth over the five-year period between 2019 and 2023. *Initiative for a Competitive Inner City (ICIC), "Inner City 100 Companies," 2024*

According to Deloitte, Miami is home to three of North America's 500 fastest-growing high-technology companies: **GoTu** (#31); **The Real Brokerage** (#38); **the COOL company** (#314). Companies are ranked by percentage growth in revenue over a four-year period. Criteria for inclusion: company must be headquartered within North America; must own proprietary intellectual property or technology that is sold to customers in products that contributes to a significant portion of the company's operating revenue; must have been in business for a minumum of four years with 2020 operating revenues of at least $50,000 USD/CD and 2023 operating revenues of at least $5 million USD/CD. *Deloitte, 2024 Technology Fast 500*[TM]

Living Environment

COST OF LIVING

Cost of Living Index

Composite Index	Groceries	Housing	Utilities	Trans-portation	Health Care	Misc. Goods/Services
120.9	110.8	157.4	104.9	100.6	98.1	107.4

Note: The Cost of Living Index measures regional differences in the cost of consumer goods and services, excluding taxes and non-consumer expenditures, for professional and managerial households in the top income quintile. It is based on more than 50,000 prices covering almost 60 different items for which prices are collected three times a year by chambers of commerce, economic development organizations or university applied economic centers in each participating urban area. The numbers shown should be read as a percentage above or below the national average of 100. For example, a value of 115.4 in the groceries column indicates that grocery prices are 15.4% higher than the national average. Small differences in the index numbers should not be interpreted as significant; Figures cover the Miami-Dade County FL urban area.
Source: The Council for Community and Economic Research, Cost of Living Index, 2024

Grocery Prices

Area[1]	T-Bone Steak ($/pound)	Frying Chicken ($/pound)	Whole Milk ($/half gal.)	Eggs ($/dozen)	Orange Juice ($/64 oz.)	Coffee ($/11.5 oz.)
City[2]	15.52	1.45	4.80	3.77	4.78	5.91
Avg.	15.42	1.55	4.69	3.25	4.41	5.46
Min.	14.50	1.16	4.43	2.75	4.00	4.85
Max.	17.56	2.89	5.49	4.78	5.54	7.89

Note: (1) Values for the local area are compared with the average, minimum and maximum values for all 276 areas in the Cost of Living Index; (2) Figures cover the Miami-Dade County FL urban area; **T-Bone Steak** (price per pound); **Frying Chicken** (price per pound, whole fryer); **Whole Milk** (half gallon carton); **Eggs** (price per dozen, Grade A, large); **Orange Juice** (64 oz. Tropicana or Florida Natural); **Coffee** (11.5 oz. can, vacuum-packed, Maxwell House, Hills Bros, or Folgers).
Source: The Council for Community and Economic Research, Cost of Living Index, 2024

Housing and Utility Costs

Area[1]	New Home Price ($)	Apartment Rent ($/month)	All Electric ($/month)	Part Electric ($/month)	Other Energy ($/month)	Telephone ($/month)
City[2]	711,025	3,211	220.47	-	-	197.31
Avg.	515,975	1,550	210.99	123.07	82.07	194.99
Min.	265,375	692	104.33	53.68	36.26	179.42
Max.	2,775,821	5,719	529.02	397.28	361.63	223.33

Note: (1) Values for the local area are compared with the average, minimum and maximum values for all 276 areas in the Cost of Living Index; (2) Figures cover the Miami-Dade County FL urban area; **New Home Price** (2,400 sf living area, 8,000 sf lot, in urban area with full utilities); **Apartment Rent** (950 sf 2 bedroom/1.5 or 2 bath, unfurnished, excluding all utilities except water); **All Electric** (average monthly cost for an all-electric home); **Part Electric** (average monthly cost for a part-electric home); **Other Energy** (average monthly cost for natural gas, fuel oil, coal, wood, and any other forms of energy except electricity); **Telephone** (price includes the base monthly rate plus taxes and fees for three lines of mobile phone service).
Source: The Council for Community and Economic Research, Cost of Living Index, 2024

Health Care, Transportation, and Other Costs

Area[1]	Doctor ($/visit)	Dentist ($/visit)	Optometrist ($/visit)	Gasoline ($/gallon)	Beauty Salon ($/visit)	Men's Shirt ($)
City[2]	134.75	118.47	110.39	3.43	87.63	28.46
Avg.	143.77	117.51	129.23	3.32	48.57	38.14
Min.	36.74	58.67	67.33	2.80	24.00	13.41
Max.	270.44	216.82	307.33	5.28	94.00	63.89

Note: (1) Values for the local area are compared with the average, minimum and maximum values for all 276 areas in the Cost of Living Index; (2) Figures cover the Miami-Dade County FL urban area; **Doctor** (general practitioners routine exam of an established patient); **Dentist** (adult teeth cleaning and periodic oral examination); **Optometrist** (full vision eye exam for established adult patient); **Gasoline** (one gallon regular unleaded, national brand, including all taxes, cash price at self-service pump if available); **Beauty Salon** (woman's shampoo, trim, and blow-dry); **Men's Shirt** (cotton/polyester dress shirt, pinpoint weave, long sleeves).
Source: The Council for Community and Economic Research, Cost of Living Index, 2024

HOUSING

Homeownership Rate

Area	2017 (%)	2018 (%)	2019 (%)	2020 (%)	2021 (%)	2022 (%)	2023 (%)	2024 (%)
MSA[1]	57.9	59.9	60.4	60.6	59.4	58.3	58.6	60.8
U.S.	63.9	64.4	64.6	66.6	65.5	65.8	65.9	65.6

Note: (1) Figures cover the Miami-Fort Lauderdale-West Palm Beach, FL Metropolitan Statistical Area
Source: U.S. Census Bureau, Housing Vacancies and Homeownership Annual Statistics: 2017-2024

House Price Index (HPI)

Area	National Ranking[2]	Quarterly Change (%)	One-Year Change (%)	Five-Year Change (%)	Since 1991Q1 (%)
MD[1]	19	2.12	8.69	89.36	668.91
U.S.[3]	–	1.43	4.51	57.13	327.82

Note: The HPI is a weighted repeat sales index. It measures average price changes in repeat sales or refinancings on the same properties. This information is obtained by reviewing repeat mortgage transactions on single-family properties whose mortgages have been purchased or securitized by Fannie Mae or Freddie Mac since January 1975; (1) Figures cover the Miami-Miami Beach-Kendall, FL Metropolitan Division; (2) Rankings are based on annual percentage change for all metro areas containing at least 15,000 transactions over the last 10 years and ranges from 1 to 241; (3) figures based on a weighted average of Census Division estimates using a seasonally adjusted, purchase-only index; all figures are for the period ending December 31, 2024
Source: Federal Housing Finance Agency, Change in FHFA Metropolitan Area House Price Indexes, All Transactions Index, 2024Q4

Home Value

Area	Under $100,000	$100,000 -$199,999	$200,000 -$299,999	$300,000 -$399,999	$400,000 -$499,999	$500,000 -$999,999	$1,000,000 or more	Median ($)
City	2.9	5.9	12.9	14.6	18.1	31.4	14.1	475,200
MSA[1]	6.3	9.6	15.7	17.5	16.5	26.1	8.3	405,600
U.S.	12.1	17.8	19.5	14.4	10.5	19.1	6.5	303,400

Note: Figures are percentages except for median and cover owner-occupied housing units; (1) Figures cover the Miami-Fort Lauderdale-West Palm Beach, FL Metropolitan Statistical Area
Source: U.S. Census Bureau, 2019-2023 American Community Survey 5-Year Estimates

Year Housing Structure Built

Area	2020 or Later	2010 -2019	2000 -2009	1990 -1999	1980 -1989	1970 -1979	1960 -1969	1950 -1959	1940 -1949	Before 1940	Median Year
City	1.8	15.4	17.0	6.0	7.4	11.9	10.0	13.5	9.1	7.9	1978
MSA[1]	1.0	7.4	12.8	13.8	19.0	20.4	11.5	9.6	2.6	2.0	1982
U.S.	1.2	8.9	13.6	12.8	13.0	14.4	10.0	9.7	4.5	11.9	1980

Note: Figures are percentages except for Median Year; Note: (1) Figures cover the Miami-Fort Lauderdale-West Palm Beach, FL Metropolitan Statistical Area
Source: U.S. Census Bureau, 2019-2023 American Community Survey 5-Year Estimates

Gross Monthly Rent

Area	Under $500	$500 -$999	$1,000 -$1,499	$1,500 -$1,999	$2,000 -$2,499	$2,500 -$2,999	$3,000 and up	Median ($)
City	8.4	9.2	25.4	22.3	16.1	8.1	10.5	1,657
MSA[1]	3.9	6.5	23.2	30.3	19.3	8.6	8.2	1,770
U.S.	6.5	22.3	29.5	20.2	10.8	4.8	5.9	1,348

Note: Figures are percentages except for median; Gross rent is the contract rent plus the estimated average monthly cost of utilities (electricity, gas, and water and sewer) and fuels (oil, coal, kerosene, wood, etc.) if these are paid by the renter (or paid for the renter by someone else); (1) Figures cover the Miami-Fort Lauderdale-West Palm Beach, FL Metropolitan Statistical Area
Source: U.S. Census Bureau, 2019-2023 American Community Survey 5-Year Estimates

HEALTH

Health Risk Factors

Category	MSA[1] (%)	U.S. (%)
Adults aged 18–64 who have any kind of health care coverage	80.9	90.8
Adults who reported being in good or better health	82.3	81.8
Adults who have been told they have high blood cholesterol	36.0	36.9
Adults who have been told they have high blood pressure	31.0	34.0
Adults who are current smokers	10.1	12.1
Adults who currently use e-cigarettes	5.9	7.7
Adults who currently use chewing tobacco, snuff, or snus	0.5	3.2
Adults who are heavy drinkers[2]	3.7	6.1
Adults who are binge drinkers[3]	14.5	15.2
Adults who are overweight (BMI 25.0 - 29.9)	37.3	34.4
Adults who are obese (BMI 30.0 - 99.8)	24.5	34.3
Adults who participated in any physical activities in the past month	71.3	75.8

Note: All figures are crude prevalence; (1) Figures cover the Miami-Fort Lauderdale-West Palm Beach, FL Metropolitan Statistical Area; (2) Heavy drinkers are classified as adult men having more than 14 drinks per week and adult women having more than 7 drinks per week; (3) Binge drinkers are classified as males having five or more drinks on one occasion or females having four or more drinks on one occasion
Source: Centers for Disease Control and Prevention, Behavioral Risk Factor Surveillance System, SMART: Selected Metropolitan Area Risk Trends, 2023

Acute and Chronic Health Conditions

Category	MSA[1] (%)	U.S. (%)
Adults who have ever been told they had a heart attack	6.7	4.2
Adults who have ever been told they have angina or coronary heart disease	4.6	4.0
Adults who have ever been told they had a stroke	3.1	3.3
Adults who have ever been told they have asthma	9.6	15.7
Adults who have ever been told they have arthritis	19.7	26.3
Adults who have ever been told they have diabetes[2]	10.7	11.5
Adults who have ever been told they had skin cancer	5.9	5.6
Adults who have ever been told they had any other types of cancer	7.6	8.4
Adults who have ever been told they have COPD	4.1	6.4
Adults who have ever been told they have kidney disease	4.7	3.7
Adults who have ever been told they have a form of depression	10.9	22.0

Note: All figures are crude prevalence; (1) Figures cover the Miami-Fort Lauderdale-West Palm Beach, FL Metropolitan Statistical Area; (2) Figures do not include pregnancy-related, borderline, or pre-diabetes
Source: Centers for Disease Control and Prevention, Behavioral Risk Factor Surveillance System, SMART: Selected Metropolitan Area Risk Trends, 2023

Health Screening and Vaccination Rates

Category	MSA[1] (%)	U.S. (%)
Adults who have ever been tested for HIV	49.4	37.5
Adults who have had their blood cholesterol checked within the last five years	86.9	87.0
Adults aged 65+ who have had flu shot within the past year	61.2	63.4
Adults aged 65+ who have ever had a pneumonia vaccination	55.3	71.9

Note: All figures are crude prevalence; (1) Figures cover the Miami-Fort Lauderdale-West Palm Beach, FL Metropolitan Statistical Area.
Source: Centers for Disease Control and Prevention, Behavioral Risk Factor Surveillance System, SMART: Selected Metropolitan Area Risk Trends, 2023

Disability Status

Category	MSA[1] (%)	U.S. (%)
Adults who reported being deaf	6.3	7.4
Are you blind or have serious difficulty seeing, even when wearing glasses?	7.4	4.9
Do you have difficulty doing errands alone?	5.9	7.8
Do you have difficulty dressing or bathing?	3.1	3.6
Do you have serious difficulty concentrating/remembering/making decisions?	9.6	13.7
Do you have serious difficulty walking or climbing stairs?	12.1	13.2

Note: All figures are crude prevalence; (1) Figures cover the Miami-Fort Lauderdale-West Palm Beach, FL Metropolitan Statistical Area.
Source: Centers for Disease Control and Prevention, Behavioral Risk Factor Surveillance System, SMART: Selected Metropolitan Area Risk Trends, 2023

Mortality Rates for the Top 10 Causes of Death in the U.S.

ICD-10[a] Sub-Chapter	ICD-10[a] Code	Crude Mortality Rate[2] per 100,000 population	
		County[3]	U.S.
Malignant neoplasms	C00-C97	162.1	182.7
Ischaemic heart diseases	I20-I25	120.9	109.6
Provisional assignment of new diseases of uncertain etiology[1]	U00-U49	73.7	65.3
Other forms of heart disease	I30-I51	38.7	65.1
Other degenerative diseases of the nervous system	G30-G31	49.1	52.4
Other external causes of accidental injury	W00-X59	25.5	52.3
Cerebrovascular diseases	I60-I69	73.0	49.1
Chronic lower respiratory diseases	J40-J47	31.3	43.5
Hypertensive diseases	I10-I15	43.8	38.9
Organic, including symptomatic, mental disorders	F01-F09	30.9	33.9

Note: (a) ICD-10 = International Classification of Diseases 10th Revision; (1) Includes COVID-19, adverse effects to COVID-19 vaccines, SARS, and vaping-related disorders; (2) Crude mortality rates are a three-year average covering 2021-2023; (3) Figures cover Miami-Dade County.
Source: Centers for Disease Control and Prevention, National Center for Health Statistics. National Vital Statistics System, Mortality 2018-2023 on CDC WONDER Online Database

Mortality Rates for Selected Causes of Death

Cause of Death	ICD-10[a] Code	Crude Mortality Rate[1] per 100,000 population	
		County[2]	U.S.
Accidental poisoning and exposure to noxious substances	X40-X49	13.5	30.5
Alzheimer disease	G30	39.5	35.4
Assault	X85-Y09	7.8	7.3
COVID-19	U07.1	73.7	65.3
Diabetes mellitus	E10-E14	36.8	30.0
Diseases of the liver	K70-K76	12.9	20.8
Human immunodeficiency virus (HIV) disease	B20-B24	4.2	1.5
Influenza and pneumonia	J09-J18	9.5	13.4
Intentional self-harm	X60-X84	9.1	14.7
Malnutrition	E40-E46	0.7	6.0
Obesity and other hyperalimentation	E65-E68	2.9	3.1
Renal failure	N17-N19	11.4	16.4
Transport accidents	V01-V99	14.7	14.4

Note: (a) ICD-10 = International Classification of Diseases 10th Revision; (1) Crude mortality rates are a three-year average covering 2021-2023; (2) Figures cover Miami-Dade County; Data are suppressed when the data meet the criteria for confidentiality constraints; Crude mortality rates are flagged as unreliable when the rate would be calculated with a numerator of 20 or less.
Source: Centers for Disease Control and Prevention, National Center for Health Statistics. National Vital Statistics System, Mortality 2018-2023 on CDC WONDER Online Database

Health Insurance Coverage

Area	With Health Insurance	With Private Health Insurance	With Public Health Insurance	Without Health Insurance	Population Under Age 19 Without Health Insurance
City	82.4	52.6	33.5	17.6	8.8
MSA[1]	86.3	60.5	33.6	13.7	8.2
U.S.	91.4	67.3	36.3	8.6	5.4

Note: Figures are percentages that cover the civilian noninstitutionalized population; (1) Figures cover the Miami-Fort Lauderdale-West Palm Beach, FL Metropolitan Statistical Area
Source: U.S. Census Bureau, 2019-2023 American Community Survey 5-Year Estimates

Number of Medical Professionals

Area	MDs[3]	DOs[3,4]	Dentists	Podiatrists	Chiropractors	Optometrists
County[1] (number)	11,103	727	2,190	268	540	438
County[1] (rate[2])	415.2	27.2	81.5	10.0	20.1	16.3
U.S. (rate[2])	302.5	29.2	74.6	6.4	29.5	18.0

Note: Data as of 2023 unless noted; (1) Data covers Miami-Dade County; (2) Number of medical professionals per 100,000 population; (3) Data as of 2022 and includes all active, non-federal physicians; (4) Doctor of Osteopathic Medicine
Source: U.S. Department of Health and Human Services, Health Resources and Services Administration, Bureau of Health Professions, Area Resource File (ARF) 2023-2024

Best Hospitals

According to *U.S. News,* the Miami-Fort Lauderdale-West Palm Beach, FL metro area is home to five of the best hospitals in the U.S.: **Bascom Palmer Eye Institute-University of Miami Hospital and Clinics** (2 adult specialties); **Cleveland Clinic Weston** (1 adult specialty); **Lynn Rehabilitation Center at UHealth/Jackson Memorial Hospital** (1 adult specialty); **Memorial Regional Hospital** (1 adult specialty and 3 pediatric specialties); **University of Miami Hospital and Clinics-UHealth Tower** (2 adult specialties). The hospitals listed were nationally ranked in at least one of 15 adult or 11 pediatric specialties. The number of specialties shown cover the parent hospital. Only 160 U.S. hospitals performed well enough to be nationally ranked in one or more specialties. Twenty hospitals in the U.S. made the Honor Roll. The Best Hospitals Honor Roll takes both the national rankings and the procedure and condition ratings into account. Hospitals received points if they were nationally ranked in one of the 15 adult specialties—the higher they ranked, the more points they got—and how many ratings of "high performing" they earned in the 20 procedures and conditions. *U.S. News Online, "America's Best Hospitals 2024-25"*

According to *U.S. News,* the Miami-Fort Lauderdale-West Palm Beach, FL metro area is home to two of the best children's hospitals in the U.S.: **Joe DiMaggio Children's Hospital at Memorial** (3 pediatric specialties); **Nicklaus Children's Hospital** (5 pediatric specialties). The hospitals listed were highly ranked in at least one of 11 pediatric specialties. One hundred five children's hospitals in the U.S. were nationally ranked in at least one specialty. Hospitals received points for being ranked in a specialty, and the 10 hospitals with the most points across the 11 specialties make up the Honor Roll. *U.S. News Online, "America's Best Children's Hospitals 2024-25"*

EDUCATION

Public School District Statistics

District Name	Schls	Pupils	Pupil/ Teacher Ratio	Minority Pupils[1] (%)	Total Rev. per Pupil ($)	Total Exp. per Pupil ($)
Miami-Dade	537	335,500	20.0	94.0	13,452	13,577

Note: Table includes school districts with 2,000 or more students; (1) Percentage of students that are not non-Hispanic white.
Source: U.S. Department of Education, National Center for Education Statistics, Common Core of Data, Local Education Agency (School District) Universe Survey: School Year 2023-2024; U.S. Department of Education, National Center for Education Statistics, Common Core of Data, School District Finance Survey (F-33): School Year 2021–22

Best High Schools

According to *U.S. News,* Miami is home to 10 of the top 500 high schools in the U.S.: **Archimedean Upper Conservatory Charter School** (#51); **Design and Architecture Senior High School** (#73); **Young Women's Preparatory Academy** (#102); **Terra Environmental Research Institute** (#119); **International Studies Charter High School** (#126); **iPrep Academy** (#152); **New World School of the Arts** (#303); **Coral Reef Senior High School** (#371); **Miami Arts Studio** (#449); **Pinecrest Glades Preparatory Academy Middle High School** (#470). Nearly 25,000 public, magnet and charter schools were ranked based on their performance on state assessments and how well they prepare students for college. *U.S. News & World Report, "Best High Schools 2024"*

Highest Level of Education

Area	Less than H.S.	H.S. Diploma	Some College, No Deg.	Associate Degree	Bachelor's Degree	Master's Degree	Prof. School Degree	Doctorate Degree
City	20.0	25.2	11.6	7.5	21.5	8.8	4.1	1.3
MSA[1]	13.1	25.7	16.0	9.5	21.8	9.0	3.4	1.4
U.S.	10.6	26.2	19.4	8.8	21.3	9.8	2.3	1.6

Note: Figures cover persons age 25 and over; (1) Figures cover the Miami-Fort Lauderdale-West Palm Beach, FL Metropolitan Statistical Area
Source: U.S. Census Bureau, 2019-2023 American Community Survey 5-Year Estimates

Educational Attainment by Race

Area	High School Graduate or Higher (%)					Bachelor's Degree or Higher (%)				
	Total	White	Black	Asian	Hisp.[2]	Total	White	Black	Asian	Hisp.[2]
City	80.0	82.6	78.1	95.4	76.7	35.6	44.7	17.5	69.4	31.3
MSA[1]	86.9	90.6	84.2	88.6	81.7	35.6	42.4	22.4	56.3	31.2
U.S.	89.4	92.9	88.1	88.0	72.5	35.0	37.7	24.7	57.0	19.9

Note: Figures shown cover persons 25 years old and over; (1) Figures cover the Miami-Fort Lauderdale-West Palm Beach, FL Metropolitan Statistical Area; (2) People of Hispanic origin can be of any race
Source: U.S. Census Bureau, 2019-2023 American Community Survey 5-Year Estimates

School Enrollment by Grade and Control

Area	Preschool (%)		Kindergarten (%)		Grades 1 - 4 (%)		Grades 5 - 8 (%)		Grades 9 - 12 (%)	
	Public	Private	Public	Private	Public	Private	Public	Private	Public	Private
City	61.1	38.9	80.7	19.3	85.9	14.1	86.9	13.1	91.6	8.4
MSA[1]	50.2	49.8	80.4	19.6	84.2	15.8	85.0	15.0	85.7	14.3
U.S.	58.7	41.3	85.2	14.8	87.2	12.8	87.9	12.1	89.0	11.0

Note: Figures shown cover persons 3 years old and over; (1) Figures cover the Miami-Fort Lauderdale-West Palm Beach, FL Metropolitan Statistical Area
Source: U.S. Census Bureau, 2019-2023 American Community Survey 5-Year Estimates

Higher Education

Four-Year Colleges			Two-Year Colleges			Medical Schools[1]	Law Schools[2]	Voc/ Tech[3]
Public	Private Non-profit	Private For-profit	Public	Private Non-profit	Private For-profit			
5	20	21	6	2	25	5	5	49

Note: Figures cover institutions located within the Miami-Fort Lauderdale-West Palm Beach, FL Metropolitan Statistical Area and include main campuses only; (1) includes schools accredited by the Liaison Committee on Medical Education and the American Osteopathic Association's Commission on Osteopathic College Accreditation; (2) includes ABA-accredited schools, schools with provisional ABA accreditation, and state accredited schools; (3) includes all schools with programs that are less than 2 years.
Source: National Center for Education Statistics, Integrated Postsecondary Education System (IPEDS), 2023-24; Wikipedia, List of Medical Schools in the United States, accessed May 2, 2025; Wikipedia, List of Law Schools in the United States, accessed May 2, 2025

According to *U.S. News & World Report,* the Miami-Fort Lauderdale-West Palm Beach, FL metro area is home to three of the top 200 national universities in the U.S.: **University of Miami** (#63 tie); **Florida International University** (#98 tie); **Florida Atlantic University** (#189 tie). The indicators used to capture academic quality fall into a number of categories: assessment by administrators at peer institutions; retention of students; faculty resources; student selectivity; financial resources; alumni giving; high school counselor ratings of colleges; and graduation rate. *U.S. News & World Report, "America's Best Colleges 2025"*

According to *U.S. News & World Report*, the Miami-Fort Lauderdale-West Palm Beach, FL metro area is home to two of the top 100 law schools in the U.S.: **Florida International University** (#84 tie); **University of Miami** (#92 tie). The rankings are based on a weighted average of 12 measures of quality: peer assessment score; assessment score by lawyers/judges; median LSAT scores; median undergrad GPA; acceptance rate; employment rates for graduates; placement success; bar passage rate; faculty resources; expenditures per student; student/faculty ratio; and library resources. *U.S. News & World Report, "America's Best Graduate Schools, Law, 2025"*

According to *U.S. News & World Report*, the Miami-Fort Lauderdale-West Palm Beach, FL metro area is home to one of the top medical schools for research in the U.S.: **University of Miami (Miller)** (Tier 2). *U.S. News* placed medical and osteopathic schools into tiers based on their research productivity, faculty and admissions data. Each school's tier was derived from its overall score, calculated by summing the weighted normalized values generated across several factors of academic quality, outlined below. There are four tiers, with tier 1 medical schools as the highest-performing and tier 4 as the lowest-performing. Only tier 1 and 2 schools are shown. Because of the tier presentation, *U.S. News* calculated overall scores based on their percentile performance among all rated schools instead of dividing against the rescaled score of the No. 1-performing schools. Tier 1 included schools with overall scores of 85 to 99. The cutoffs for tiers 2 through 4 were schools scoring 50 to 84, 15 to 49 and 1 to 14, respectively. The rankings are based on a weighted average of the following measures of quality: total research activity; average research activity per faculty member; total NIH research grants at the medical school and its affiliated hospitals; average NIH research grants per faculty; median MCAT total score; median undergraduate GPA; acceptance rate; and faculty resources. *U.S. News & World Report, "America's Best Graduate Schools, Medical, 2025"*

According to *U.S. News & World Report*, the Miami-Fort Lauderdale-West Palm Beach, FL metro area is home to one of the top 75 business schools in the U.S.: **University of Miami (Herbert)** (#50 tie). The rankings are based on a weighted average of the following nine measures: quality assessment; peer assessment; recruiter assessment; placement success; mean starting salary and bonus; student selectivity; mean GMAT and GRE scores; mean undergraduate GPA; and acceptance rate. *U.S. News & World Report, "America's Best Graduate Schools, Business, 2025"*

EMPLOYERS

Major Employers

Company Name	Industry
Baptist Health South Florida	General medical & surgical hospitals
Baptist Hospital of Miami	General medical & surgical hospitals
County of Miami-Dade	County government
Florida International University	Colleges & universities
Intercoastal Health Systems	Management services
Miami Dade College	Community college
Mount Sinai Medical Center of Florida	General medical & surgical hospitals
North Broward Hospital District	General medical & surgical hospitals
Palm Beach County	County government
Royal Caribbean Cruises Ltd	Deep sea passenger transportation, except ferry
School Board of Palm Beach County	Public elementary & secondary schools
Style View Products	Storm doors of windows, metal
The Answer Group	Custom computer programming services
University of Miami	Colleges & universities
Veterans Health Administration	General medical & surgical hospitals

Note: Companies shown are located within the Miami-Fort Lauderdale-West Palm Beach, FL Metropolitan Statistical Area.
Source: Chambers of Commerce; State Departments of Labor; Wikipedia

Best Companies to Work For

Community Medical Group; Lennar Corporation, headquartered in Miami, are among "Fortune's Best Workplaces for Women." To pick the best companies, *Fortune* partnered with the Great Place to Work Institute. To be considered for the list, companies must be Great Place To Work-Certified. Companies must also employ at least 50 women, at least 20% of their non-executive managers must be female, and at least one executive must be female. To determine the Best Workplaces for Women, Great Place To Work measured the differences in women's survey responses to those of their peers and assesses the impact of demographics and roles on the quality and consistency of women's experiences. Great Place To Work also analyzed the gender balance of each workplace, how it compared to each company's industry, and patterns in representation as women rise from front-line positions to the board of directors. *Fortune, "Best Workplaces for Women," 2024*

Community Medical Group, headquartered in Miami, is among "Best Workplaces in Health Care." To determine the Best Workplaces in Health Care list, Great Place To Work analyzed the survey responses of over 185,000 employees from Great Place To Work-Certified companies in the health care industry. Survey data analysis and company-provided datapoints are then factored into a combined score to compare and rank the companies that create the most consistently positive experience for all employees in this industry. *Fortune, "Best Workplaces in Health Care," 2024*

ChenMed, headquartered in Miami, is among the "Best Places to Work in IT." To qualify, companies had to have a minimum of 100 total employees and five IT employees. The best places to work were selected based on DEI (diversity, equity, and inclusion) practices; IT turnover, promotions, and growth; IT retention and engagement programs; remote/hybrid working; benefits and perks (such as elder care and child care, flextime, and reimbursement for college tuition); and training and career development opportunities. *Computerworld, "Best Places to Work in IT," 2025*

PUBLIC SAFETY

Crime Rate

Area	Total Crime Rate	Violent Crime Rate				Property Crime Rate		
		Murder	Rape	Robbery	Aggrav. Assault	Burglary	Larceny-Theft	Motor Vehicle Theft
City	3,436.7	7.1	28.3	109.7	346.9	254.1	2,223.1	467.6
U.S.	2,290.9	5.7	38.0	66.5	264.1	250.7	1,347.2	318.7

Note: Figures are crimes per 100,000 population.
Source: FBI, Table 8, Offenses Known to Law Enforcement, by State by City, 2023

Hate Crimes

Area	Number of Quarters Reported	Number of Incidents per Bias Motivation					
		Race/Ethnicity/Ancestry	Religion	Sexual Orientation	Disability	Gender	Gender Identity
City[1]	4	6	6	5	0	0	1
U.S.	4	5,900	2,699	2,077	187	92	492

Note: (1) Figures include at least one incident reported with more than one bias motivation.
Source: Federal Bureau of Investigation, Hate Crime Statistics 2023

Identity Theft Consumer Reports

Area	Reports	Reports per 100,000 Population	Rank[2]
MSA[1]	55,457	903	1
U.S.	1,135,291	339	-

Note: (1) Figures cover the Miami-Fort Lauderdale-West Palm Beach, FL Metropolitan Statistical Area; (2) Rank ranges from 1 to 401 where 1 indicates greatest number of identity theft reports per 100,000 population
Source: Federal Trade Commission, Consumer Sentinel Network Data Book 2024

Fraud and Other Consumer Reports

Area	Reports	Reports per 100,000 Population	Rank[2]
MSA[1]	171,462	2,793	1
U.S.	5,360,641	1,601	-

Note: (1) Figures cover the Miami-Fort Lauderdale-West Palm Beach, FL Metropolitan Statistical Area; (2) Rank ranges from 1 to 401 where 1 indicates greatest number of fraud and other consumer reports per 100,000 population
Source: Federal Trade Commission, Consumer Sentinel Network Data Book 2024

POLITICS

2024 Presidential Election Results

Area	Trump (Rep.)	Harris (Dem.)	Stein (Green)	Kennedy (Ind.)	Oliver (Lib.)	Other
Miami-Dade County	55.2	43.8	0.3	0.0	0.2	0.5
U.S.	49.7	48.2	0.6	0.5	0.4	0.6

Note: Results are percentages and may not add to 100% due to rounding
Source: Dave Leip's Atlas of U.S. Presidential Elections

SPORTS

Professional Sports Teams

Team Name	League	Year Established
Florida Panthers	National Hockey League (NHL)	1993
Inter Miami CF	Major League Soccer (MLS)	2020
Miami Dolphins	National Football League (NFL)	1966
Miami Heat	National Basketball Association (NBA)	1988
Miami Marlins	Major League Baseball (MLB)	1993

Note: Includes teams located in the Miami-Fort Lauderdale-West Palm Beach, FL Metropolitan Statistical Area.
Source: Wikipedia, Major Professional Sports Teams of the United States and Canada, May 1, 2025

CLIMATE

Average and Extreme Temperatures

Temperature	Jan	Feb	Mar	Apr	May	Jun	Jul	Aug	Sep	Oct	Nov	Dec	Yr.
Extreme High (°F)	88	89	92	96	95	98	98	98	97	95	89	87	98
Average High (°F)	75	77	79	82	85	88	89	90	88	85	80	77	83
Average Temp. (°F)	68	69	72	75	79	82	83	83	82	78	73	69	76
Average Low (°F)	59	60	64	68	72	75	76	76	76	72	66	61	69
Extreme Low (°F)	30	35	32	42	55	60	69	68	68	53	39	30	30

Note: Figures cover the years 1948-1990
Source: National Climatic Data Center, International Station Meteorological Climate Summary, 9/96

Average Precipitation/Snowfall/Humidity

Precip./Humidity	Jan	Feb	Mar	Apr	May	Jun	Jul	Aug	Sep	Oct	Nov	Dec	Yr.
Avg. Precip. (in.)	1.9	2.0	2.3	3.0	6.2	8.7	6.1	7.5	8.2	6.6	2.7	1.8	57.1
Avg. Snowfall (in.)	0	0	0	0	0	0	0	0	0	0	0	0	0
Avg. Rel. Hum. 7am (%)	84	84	82	80	81	84	84	86	88	87	85	84	84
Avg. Rel. Hum. 4pm (%)	59	57	57	57	62	68	66	67	69	65	63	60	63

Note: Figures cover the years 1948-1990; Tr = Trace amounts (<0.05 in. of rain; <0.5 in. of snow)
Source: National Climatic Data Center, International Station Meteorological Climate Summary, 9/96

Weather Conditions

Temperature			Daytime Sky			Precipitation		
32°F & below	45°F & below	90°F & above	Clear	Partly cloudy	Cloudy	0.01 inch or more precip.	0.1 inch or more snow/ice	Thunder-storms
< 1	7	55	48	263	54	128	0	74

Note: Figures are average number of days per year and cover the years 1948-1990
Source: National Climatic Data Center, International Station Meteorological Climate Summary, 9/96

HAZARDOUS WASTE

Superfund Sites

The Miami-Miami Beach-Kendall, FL metro division is home to six sites on the EPA's Superfund National Priorities List (NPL) or Superfund Alternative Approach (SAA) list: **Airco Plating Co.** (Final NPL); **Anodyne, Inc.** (Final NPL); **Continental Cleaners** (Final NPL); **Homestead Air Force Base** (Final NPL); **Miami Drum Services** (Final NPL); **Pepper Steel & Alloys, Inc.** (Final NPL). The Superfund alternative approach uses the same investigation and cleanup process and standards that are used for sites listed on the National Priorities List. The SAA is an alternative to listing a site on the NPL; it is not an alternative to Superfund or the Superfund process. There are a total of 1,445 Superfund sites with a status of proposed or final on both lists in the United States. *U.S. Environmental Protection Agency, National Priorities List, May 1, 2025; U.S. Environmental Protection Agency, Superfund Alternative Approach Sites, May 1, 2025*

AIR QUALITY

Air Quality Trends: Ozone

	1990	1995	2000	2005	2010	2015	2020	2021	2022	2023
MSA[1]	0.068	0.072	0.075	0.065	0.064	0.061	0.058	0.057	0.063	0.061
U.S.	0.087	0.089	0.081	0.080	0.072	0.068	0.066	0.067	0.067	0.070

Note: (1) Data covers the Miami-Fort Lauderdale-West Palm Beach, FL Metropolitan Statistical Area. The values shown are the composite ozone concentration averages among trend sites based on the highest fourth daily maximum 8-hour concentration in parts per million. These trends are based on sites having an adequate record of monitoring data during the trend period. Data from exceptional events are included.
Source: U.S. Environmental Protection Agency, Air Quality Monitoring Information, "Air Quality Trends by City, 1990-2023"

Air Quality Index

Area	Percent of Days when Air Quality was...[2]					AQI Statistics[2]	
	Good	Moderate	Unhealthy for Sensitive Groups	Unhealthy	Very Unhealthy	Maximum	Median
MSA[1]	37.3	61.6	0.3	0.8	0.0	170	53

Note: (1) Data covers the Miami-Fort Lauderdale-West Palm Beach, FL Metropolitan Statistical Area; (2) Based on 365 days with AQI data in 2023. Air Quality Index (AQI) is an index for reporting daily air quality. EPA calculates the AQI for five major air pollutants regulated by the Clean Air Act: ground-level ozone, particle pollution (aka particulate matter), carbon monoxide, sulfur dioxide, and nitrogen dioxide. The AQI runs from 0 to 500. The higher the AQI value, the greater the level of air pollution and the greater the health concern. There are six AQI categories: "Good" AQI is between 0 and 50. Air quality is considered satisfactory; "Moderate" AQI is between 51 and 100. Air quality is acceptable; "Unhealthy for Sensitive Groups" When AQI values are between 101 and 150, members of sensitive groups may experience health effects; "Unhealthy" When AQI values are between 151 and 200 everyone may begin to experience health effects; "Very Unhealthy" AQI values between 201 and 300 trigger a health alert; "Hazardous" AQI values over 300 trigger warnings of emergency conditions (not shown).
Source: U.S. Environmental Protection Agency, Air Quality Index Report, 2023

Air Quality Index Pollutants

Area	Percent of Days when AQI Pollutant was...[2]					
	Carbon Monoxide	Nitrogen Dioxide	Ozone	Sulfur Dioxide	Particulate Matter 2.5	Particulate Matter 10
MSA[1]	0.0	3.6	13.7	(3)	82.7	0.0

Note: (1) Data covers the Miami-Fort Lauderdale-West Palm Beach, FL Metropolitan Statistical Area; (2) Based on 365 days with AQI data in 2023. The Air Quality Index (AQI) is an index for reporting daily air quality. EPA calculates the AQI for five major air pollutants regulated by the Clean Air Act: ground-level ozone, particle pollution (also known as particulate matter), carbon monoxide, sulfur dioxide, and nitrogen dioxide. The AQI runs from 0 to 500. The higher the AQI value, the greater the level of air pollution and the greater the health concern; (3) Sulfur dioxide is no longer included in this table because SO_2 concentrations tend to be very localized and not necessarily representative of broad geographical areas like counties and CBSAs.
Source: U.S. Environmental Protection Agency, Air Quality Index Report, 2023

Maximum Air Pollutant Concentrations: Particulate Matter, Ozone, CO and Lead

	Particulate Matter 10 (ug/m^3)	Particulate Matter 2.5 Wtd AM (ug/m^3)	Particulate Matter 2.5 24-Hr (ug/m^3)	Ozone (ppm)	Carbon Monoxide (ppm)	Lead (ug/m^3)
MSA[1] Level	65	9.4	24	0.066	2	n/a
NAAQS[2]	150	15	35	0.075	9	0.15
Met NAAQS[2]	Yes	Yes	Yes	Yes	Yes	n/a

Note: (1) Data covers the Miami-Fort Lauderdale-West Palm Beach, FL Metropolitan Statistical Area; Data from exceptional events are included; (2) National Ambient Air Quality Standards; ppm = parts per million; ug/m^3 = micrograms per cubic meter; n/a not available.
Concentrations: Particulate Matter 10 (coarse particulate)—highest second maximum 24-hour concentration; Particulate Matter 2.5 Wtd AM (fine particulate)—highest weighted annual mean concentration; Particulate Matter 2.5 24-Hour (fine particulate)—highest 98th percentile 24-hour concentration; Ozone—highest fourth daily maximum 8-hour concentration; Carbon Monoxide—highest second maximum non-overlapping 8-hour concentration; Lead—maximum running 3-month average
Source: U.S. Environmental Protection Agency, Air Quality Monitoring Information, "Air Quality Statistics by City, 2023"

Maximum Air Pollutant Concentrations: Nitrogen Dioxide and Sulfur Dioxide

	Nitrogen Dioxide AM (ppb)	Nitrogen Dioxide 1-Hr (ppb)	Sulfur Dioxide AM (ppb)	Sulfur Dioxide 1-Hr (ppb)	Sulfur Dioxide 24-Hr (ppb)
MSA[1] Level	15	53	n/a	2	n/a
NAAQS[2]	53	100	30	75	140
Met NAAQS[2]	Yes	Yes	n/a	Yes	n/a

Note: (1) Data covers the Miami-Fort Lauderdale-West Palm Beach, FL Metropolitan Statistical Area; Data from exceptional events are included; (2) National Ambient Air Quality Standards; ppm = parts per million; ug/m^3 = micrograms per cubic meter; n/a not available.
Concentrations: Nitrogen Dioxide AM—highest arithmetic mean concentration; Nitrogen Dioxide 1-Hr—highest 98th percentile 1-hour daily maximum concentration; Sulfur Dioxide AM—highest annual mean concentration; Sulfur Dioxide 1-Hr—highest 99th percentile 1-hour daily maximum concentration; Sulfur Dioxide 24-Hr—highest second maximum 24-hour concentration
Source: U.S. Environmental Protection Agency, Air Quality Monitoring Information, "Air Quality Statistics by City, 2023"

Midland, Texas

Background

In 1881, Midland, Texas might have been called the middle of nowhere, almost exactly at the midpoint between Fort Worth and El Paso. Then barely a whistle-stop, Midland provided a small shelter where Texas and Pacific Railroad crews could rest and store maintenance equipment. Ten years later, it was a vital shipping center for the cattle trade. Today the locals say Midland is in the middle of somewhere.

Little is known about the first inhabitants in the region, though they left plenty of evidence of their existence. The Pecos Trail Region, 22 counties in West Texas rich in Western heritage including Native American petroglyphs and pictographs. Anthropologists surmise these early scribes are the ancestors of the Comanche, Apache, Kiowa, and Kickapoo nations.

In 1882, Herman Garrett, a sheep rancher from California, was the first westerner to make Midland his permanent home. Within three years, 100 families lived there, and by 1900, the population was 1,000. Midland became known as the "Windmill Town," as individual homes used windmills to pump water. After devastating fires in 1905 and 1909, the town put in a municipal water system and created a fire department.

Midland remained a center of ranching and shipping until 1923, when the Santa Rita oil rig "blew" just southeast of the city and the oil industry overtook the town, marking the start of Midland's roller coaster ride of the highs and lows of oil prices. By 1929, there were 36 oil companies in Midland. Roads were paved, streetlights were raised, and Midland's downtown skyline took shape, nicknaming the city The Tall City; the Hogal Building was twelve stories high, a major change from the previously flat landscape. When the Great Depression hit, the demand for petroleum decreased and prices plummeted. By 1932, one third of Midland's workers were unemployed.

The surge in energy prices in the mid-1980s sparked another building boom downtown. The 22-story Wilco Building in downtown, the tallest building between Fort Worth and Phoenix for many years, lost that honor to the 24-story Bank of America Building, still Midland's tallest building. World War II brought an increase in oil prices, along with the Midland Army Air Force Base to the city, giving Midland's economy a much-needed boost. By 1950, 250 oil companies had set up shop in the city.

Today, Midland's economy is still driven by its prominence in the oil industry, with significant technological advancements in fracking fueling a boom in both employment and population. Midland's top employers include Midland Independent School District, Midland Memorial Hospital and Medical Center, Dawson Geophysical, and Walmart.

Higher education in the city includes Midland College, which hosts the Davidson Distinguished Lecture Series twice a year, bringing to Midland Ken Burns, Richard Leakey, Bill Moyers, Mark Russell, Sandra Day O'Connor, Richard Rodriguez, Shelby Foote, Anna Deavere, Bill Nye, John Updike and Neil deGrasse Tyson. Midland College is also home to the McCormick Gallery. In 2020, the city voted to change the name of the former Robert E. Lee High School to Legacy High School in the wake of the George Floyd protests.

Recreation in the city includes 50 parks and the Rockhounds minor league baseball team. Also a popular attraction in Midland is The Bush Family Home State Historic Site at 1412 W. Ohio Ave., home to former U.S. Presidents George W. Bush and George H. W. Bush from 1951 to 1955. Laura Bush was born and raised in Midland and Barbara and Jeb Bush also lived in the city.

Cultural opportunities in Midland include Museum of the Southwest and Permian Basin Petroleum, community theater, the Midland-Odessa Symphony & Chorale, and the Marian Blakemore planetarium.

Midland features a semi-arid climate with long, hot summers and short, moderate winters. The city is occasionally subject to cold waves during the winter, but it rarely sees extended periods of below-freezing cold. Midland receives approximately 14.6 inches of precipitation per year, much of which falls in the summer. Highs exceed 90 degrees on 101 days per year, and 100 degrees on 16 days.

Rankings

General Rankings

- In their annual survey, Livability.com looked at data for more than 2,000 mid-sized U.S. cities to assign a "Livability Score" for each. The top 100 scoring cities make up Livability's "Top 100 Best Places to Live in the U.S." in 2025. Midland was placed among the top 100 of the customizable list. Criteria: housing and economy; cost of living; environment; education; health care options; transportation; safety; and community amenities. *Livability.com, "Top 100 Best Places to Live in the U.S. in 2025" April 15, 2025*

Business/Finance Rankings

- The Midland metro area appeared on the Milken Institute "2025 Best Performing Cities" list. Rank: #5 out of 203 small metro areas (based on performance category). Criteria: job growth; wage growth; high-tech growth and impact; community resilience; housing affordability; household broadband access. *Milken Institute, "Best-Performing Cities 2025," January 14, 2025*

Environmental Rankings

- Midland was highlighted as one of the top 22 cleanest metro areas for short-term particle pollution (24-hour PM 2.5) in the U.S. during 2021 through 2023. Monitors in these cities reported no days with unhealthful PM 2.5 levels. *American Lung Association, "State of the Air 2025," April 23, 2025*

Business Environment

DEMOGRAPHICS

Population Growth

Area	1990 Census	2000 Census	2010 Census	2020 Census	2023 Estimate[2]	Population Growth 1990-2023 (%)
City	89,358	94,996	111,147	132,524	133,998	50.0
MSA[1]	106,611	116,009	136,872	175,220	176,726	65.8
U.S.	248,709,873	281,421,906	308,745,538	331,449,281	332,387,540	33.6

Note: (1) Figures cover the Midland, TX Metropolitan Statistical Area; (2) 2019-2023 5-year ACS population estimate
Source: U.S. Census Bureau, 1990 Census, 2000 Census, 2010 Census, 2020 Census, 2019-2023 American Community Survey 5-Year Estimates

Race

Area	White Alone[2] (%)	Black Alone[2] (%)	Asian Alone[2] (%)	AIAN[3] Alone[2] (%)	NHOPI[4] Alone[2] (%)	Other Race Alone[2] (%)	Two or More Races (%)
City	58.8	8.6	2.1	0.7	0.0	12.0	17.9
MSA[1]	60.4	7.1	2.1	0.6	0.0	12.8	17.1
U.S.	63.4	12.4	5.8	0.9	0.2	6.6	10.7

Note: (1) Figures cover the Midland, TX Metropolitan Statistical Area; (2) Alone is defined as not being in combination with one or more other races; (3) American Indian and Alaska Native; (4) Native Hawaiian and Other Pacific Islander
Source: U.S. Census Bureau, 2019-2023 American Community Survey 5-Year Estimates

Hispanic or Latino Origin

Area	Total (%)	Mexican (%)	Puerto Rican (%)	Cuban (%)	Other (%)
City	44.3	38.1	0.6	1.3	4.3
MSA[1]	44.8	39.3	0.6	1.2	3.8
U.S.	19.0	11.3	1.8	0.7	5.2

Note: Persons of Hispanic or Latino origin can be of any race; (1) Figures cover the Midland, TX Metropolitan Statistical Area
Source: U.S. Census Bureau, 2019-2023 American Community Survey 5-Year Estimates

Age

Area	Under Age 5	Age 5-19	Age 20-34	Age 35-44	Age 45-54	Age 55-64	Age 65-74	Age 75-84	Age 85+	Median Age
City	8.8	22.6	24.9	14.7	9.6	8.9	6.0	2.9	1.6	31.6
MSA[1]	8.3	23.1	22.7	15.3	10.2	9.9	6.5	2.7	1.4	32.7
U.S.	5.7	19.1	20.2	13.1	12.3	12.8	10.0	4.9	1.9	38.7

Note: (1) Figures cover the Midland, TX Metropolitan Statistical Area
Source: U.S. Census Bureau, 2019-2023 American Community Survey 5-Year Estimates

Disability by Age

Area	All Ages	Under 18 Years Old	18 to 64 Years Old	65 Years and Over
City	10.4	3.4	8.7	40.3
MSA[1]	10.9	3.5	9.3	40.7
U.S.	13.0	4.7	10.7	32.9

Note: Figures show percent of the civilian noninstitutionalized population that reported having a disability. Disability status is determined from six types of difficulty: vision, hearing, cognitive, ambulatory, self-care, and independent living. For children under 5 years old, hearing and vision difficulty are used to determine disability status. For children between the ages of 5 and 14, disability status is determined from hearing, vision, cognitive, ambulatory, and self-care difficulties. For people aged 15 years and older, they are considered to have a disability if they have difficulty with any one of the six difficulty types; Note: (1) Figures cover the Midland, TX Metropolitan Statistical Area
Source: U.S. Census Bureau, 2019-2023 American Community Survey 5-Year Estimates

Ancestry

Area	German	Irish	English	American	Italian	Polish	French[2]	European	Scottish
City	6.6	6.1	7.8	4.6	0.9	0.4	1.3	1.1	1.5
MSA[1]	7.0	5.8	7.6	5.2	0.9	0.3	1.3	1.0	1.4
U.S.	12.6	9.4	9.1	5.5	4.9	2.6	2.0	1.6	1.6

Note: Figures are the percentage of the total population reporting a particular ancestry. The nine most commonly reported ancestries in the U.S. are shown. Figures include multiple ancestries (e.g. if a person reported being Irish and Italian, they were included in both columns); (1) Figures cover the Midland, TX Metropolitan Statistical Area; (2) Excludes Basque
Source: U.S. Census Bureau, 2019-2023 American Community Survey 5-Year Estimates

Foreign-born Population

Area	Percent of Population Born in								
	Any Foreign Country	Asia	Mexico	Europe	Caribbean	Central America[2]	South America	Africa	Canada
City	13.7	2.0	7.1	0.4	1.0	0.5	1.1	1.0	0.6
MSA[1]	13.0	1.9	7.2	0.3	0.9	0.4	0.9	0.8	0.5
U.S.	13.9	4.3	3.3	1.4	1.4	1.2	1.2	0.8	0.2

Note: (1) Figures cover the Midland, TX Metropolitan Statistical Area; (2) Excludes Mexico.
Source: U.S. Census Bureau, 2019-2023 American Community Survey 5-Year Estimates

Household Size

Area	Persons in Household (%)							Average Household Size
	One	Two	Three	Four	Five	Six	Seven or More	
City	29.9	27.2	15.3	16.3	7.6	2.6	1.1	2.51
MSA[1]	28.9	27.1	15.8	16.0	8.2	2.7	1.4	2.53
U.S.	28.5	33.8	15.4	12.7	5.9	2.3	1.4	2.54

Note: (1) Figures cover the Midland, TX Metropolitan Statistical Area
Source: U.S. Census Bureau, 2019-2023 American Community Survey 5-Year Estimates

Household Relationships

Area	Householder	Opposite-sex Spouse	Same-sex Spouse	Opposite-sex Unmarried Partner	Same-sex Unmarried Partner	Child[2]	Grandchild	Other Relatives	Non-relatives
City	36.4	18.5	0.1	2.1	0.1	31.9	3.0	4.2	2.5
MSA[1]	35.8	18.6	0.1	2.0	0.1	32.3	3.2	4.4	2.6
U.S.	38.3	17.5	0.2	2.5	0.2	28.3	2.4	4.8	3.4

Note: Figures are percent of the total population; (1) Figures cover the Midland, TX Metropolitan Statistical Area; (2) Includes biological, adopted, and stepchildren of the householder
Source: U.S. Census Bureau, 2020 Census

Gender

Area	Males	Females	Males per 100 Females
City	68,527	65,471	104.7
MSA[1]	90,328	86,398	104.5
U.S.	164,545,087	167,842,453	98.0

Note: (1) Figures cover the Midland, TX Metropolitan Statistical Area
Source: U.S. Census Bureau, 2019-2023 American Community Survey 5-Year Estimates

Marital Status

Area	Never Married	Now Married[2]	Separated	Widowed	Divorced
City	29.3	54.5	1.9	4.8	9.6
MSA[1]	28.6	55.2	1.6	4.9	9.8
U.S.	34.1	47.9	1.7	5.6	10.7

Note: Figures are percentages and cover the population 15 years of age and older; (1) Figures cover the Midland, TX Metropolitan Statistical Area; (2) Excludes separated
Source: U.S. Census Bureau, 2019-2023 American Community Survey 5-Year Estimates

Religious Groups by Family

Area	Catholic	Baptist	Methodist	LDS[2]	Pentecostal	Lutheran	Islam	Adventist	Other
MSA[1]	15.4	25.5	2.5	2.0	1.2	0.3	0.4	1.3	16.5
U.S.	18.7	7.3	3.0	2.0	1.8	1.7	1.3	1.3	11.6

Note: Figures are the number of adherents as a percentage of the total population and cover the eight largest religious groups in the U.S; (1) Figures cover the Midland, TX Metropolitan Statistical Area; (2) Church of Jesus Christ of Latter-day Saints
Sources: 2020 U.S. Religion Census, Association of Statisticians of American Religious Bodies; The Association of Religion Data Archives (ARDA)

Religious Groups by Tradition

Area	Catholic	Evangelical Protestant	Mainline Protestant	Black Protestant	Islam	Judaism	Hinduism	Orthodox	Buddhism
MSA[1]	15.4	35.5	3.0	7.6	0.4	n/a	0.2	n/a	n/a
U.S.	18.7	16.5	5.2	2.3	1.3	0.6	0.4	0.4	0.3

Note: Figures are the number of adherents as a percentage of the total population; (1) Figures cover the Midland, TX Metropolitan Statistical Area
Sources: 2020 U.S. Religion Census, Association of Statisticians of American Religious Bodies; The Association of Religion Data Archives (ARDA)

ECONOMY

Real Gross Domestic Product (GDP)

Area	2017	2018	2019	2020	2021	2022	2023	Rank[3]
MSA[1]	21.9	27.6	33.1	31.1	31.7	31.0	44.2	78
U.S.[2]	17,619.1	18,160.7	18,642.5	18,238.9	19,387.6	19,896.6	20,436.3	—

Note: Figures are in billions of chained 2017 dollars; (1) Figures cover the Midland, TX Metropolitan Statistical Area; (2) Figures cover real GDP within metropolitan areas; (3) Rank is based on 2023 data and ranges from 1 to 384
Source: U.S. Bureau of Economic Analysis

Economic Growth

Area	2014	2015	2016	2017	2018	2019	2020	2021	2022	2023
MSA[1]	9.0	9.5	-1.7	14.0	25.9	20.3	-6.1	1.8	-2.3	42.9
U.S.[2]	2.6	3.2	2.0	2.7	3.1	2.7	-2.2	6.3	2.6	2.7

Note: Figures are real gross domestic product growth rates and represent percent change from preceding period; (1) Figures cover the Midland, TX Metropolitan Statistical Area; (2) Figures are the average growth rates within metropolitan areas
Source: U.S. Bureau of Economic Analysis

Metropolitan Area Exports

Area	2018	2019	2020	2021	2022	2023	Rank[2]
MSA[1]	63.6	63.7	57.7	49.9	76.2	72.4	365
U.S.	1,664,056.1	1,645,173.7	1,431,406.6	1,753,941.4	2,062,937.4	2,019,160.5	—

Note: Figures are in millions of dollars; (1) Figures cover the Midland, TX Metropolitan Statistical Area; (2) Rank is based on 2023 data and ranges from 1 to 386
Source: U.S. Department of Commerce, International Trade Administration, Office of Trade and Economic Analysis, Industry and Analysis, Exports by Metropolitan Area, data extracted April 2, 2025

Building Permits

Area	Single-Family			Multi-Family			Total		
	2023	2024	Pct. Chg.	2023	2024	Pct. Chg.	2023	2024	Pct. Chg.
City	805	1,504	86.8	0	0	0.0	805	1,504	86.8
MSA[1]	810	1,505	85.8	8	4	-50.0	818	1,509	84.5
U.S.	920,000	981,900	6.7	591,100	496,100	-16.1	1,511,100	1,478,000	-2.2

Note: (1) Figures cover the Midland, TX Metropolitan Statistical Area; Figures represent new, privately-owned housing units authorized (unadjusted data)
Source: U.S. Census Bureau, Building Permits Survey (BPS), 2023, 2024

Bankruptcy Filings

Area	Business Filings			Nonbusiness Filings		
	2023	2024	% Chg.	2023	2024	% Chg.
Midland County	14	17	21.4	66	93	40.9
U.S.	18,926	23,107	22.1	434,064	494,201	13.9

Note: Business filings include Chapter 7, Chapter 9, Chapter 11, Chapter 12, Chapter 13, Chapter 15, and Section 304; Nonbusiness filings include Chapter 7, Chapter 11, and Chapter 13
Source: Administrative Office of the U.S. Courts, Business and Nonbusiness Bankruptcy, County Cases Commenced by Chapter of the Bankruptcy Code, During the 12-Month Period Ending December 31, 2023 and Business and Nonbusiness Bankruptcy, County Cases Commenced by Chapter of the Bankruptcy Code, During the 12-Month Period Ending December 31, 2024

Housing Vacancy Rates

Area	Gross Vacancy Rate[3] (%)			Year-Round Vacancy Rate[4] (%)			Rental Vacancy Rate[5] (%)			Homeowner Vacancy Rate[6] (%)		
	2022	2023	2024	2022	2023	2024	2022	2023	2024	2022	2023	2024
MSA[1]	n/a	n/a	n/a	n/a	n/a	n/a	n/a	n/a	n/a	n/a	n/a	n/a
U.S.[2]	9.1	9.0	9.1	7.5	7.5	7.6	5.7	6.5	6.8	0.8	0.8	1.0

Note: (1) Figures cover the Midland, TX Metropolitan Statistical Area; (2) Figures cover the 75 largest Metropolitan Statistical Areas; (3) The percentage of the total housing inventory that is vacant; (4) The percentage of the housing inventory (excluding seasonal units) that is year-round vacant; (5) The percentage of rental inventory that is vacant for rent; (6) The percentage of homeowner inventory that is vacant for sale; n/a not available
Source: U.S. Census Bureau, Housing Vacancies and Homeownership Annual Statistics: 2022, 2023, 2024

INCOME

Income

Area	Per Capita ($)	Median Household ($)	Average Household ($)
City	49,327	91,169	126,317
MSA[1]	48,843	93,442	126,152
U.S.	43,289	78,538	110,491

Note: (1) Figures cover the Midland, TX Metropolitan Statistical Area
Source: U.S. Census Bureau, 2019-2023 American Community Survey 5-Year Estimates

Household Income Distribution

Area	Percent of Households Earning							
	Under $15,000	$15,000 -$24,999	$25,000 -$34,999	$35,000 -$49,999	$50,000 -$74,999	$75,000 -$99,999	$100,000 -$149,999	$150,000 and up
City	9.1	4.8	5.8	9.2	14.3	10.1	18.0	28.6
MSA[1]	8.0	4.3	5.9	9.4	13.7	11.6	18.6	28.4
U.S.	8.5	6.6	6.8	10.4	15.7	12.7	17.4	21.9

Note: (1) Figures cover the Midland, TX Metropolitan Statistical Area
Source: U.S. Census Bureau, 2019-2023 American Community Survey 5-Year Estimates

Poverty Rate

Area	All Ages	Under 18 Years Old	18 to 64 Years Old	65 Years and Over
City	11.7	14.0	10.6	11.5
MSA[1]	10.6	12.7	9.3	11.6
U.S.	12.4	16.3	11.6	10.4

Note: Figures are percentage of people whose income during the past 12 months was below the poverty level; (1) Figures cover the Midland, TX Metropolitan Statistical Area
Source: U.S. Census Bureau, 2019-2023 American Community Survey 5-Year Estimates

EMPLOYMENT

Labor Force and Employment

Area	Civilian Labor Force			Workers Employed		
	Dec. 2023	Dec. 2024	% Chg.	Dec. 2023	Dec. 2024	% Chg.
City	93,937	96,111	2.3	91,915	93,872	2.1
MSA[1]	116,721	119,415	2.3	114,162	116,595	2.1
U.S.	166,661,000	167,746,000	0.7	160,754,000	161,294,000	0.3

Note: Data is not seasonally adjusted and covers workers 16 years of age and older; (1) Figures cover the Midland, TX Metropolitan Statistical Area
Source: Bureau of Labor Statistics, Local Area Unemployment Statistics

Unemployment Rate

Area	2024											
	Jan.	Feb.	Mar.	Apr.	May	Jun.	Jul.	Aug.	Sep.	Oct.	Nov.	Dec.
City	2.6	2.8	2.4	2.2	2.4	2.8	2.8	2.9	2.6	2.7	2.7	2.3
MSA[1]	2.6	2.8	2.5	2.2	2.5	2.8	2.9	2.9	2.7	2.7	2.7	2.4
U.S.	4.1	4.2	3.9	3.5	3.7	4.3	4.5	4.4	3.9	3.9	4.0	3.8

Note: Data is not seasonally adjusted and covers workers 16 years of age and older; (1) Figures cover the Midland, TX Metropolitan Statistical Area
Source: Bureau of Labor Statistics, Local Area Unemployment Statistics

Average Wages

Occupation	$/Hr.	Occupation	$/Hr.
Accountants and Auditors	47.51	Maintenance and Repair Workers	23.89
Automotive Mechanics	26.20	Marketing Managers	73.71
Bookkeepers	25.44	Network and Computer Systems Admin.	47.24
Carpenters	24.81	Nurses, Licensed Practical	30.11
Cashiers	14.69	Nurses, Registered	42.82
Computer Programmers	42.10	Nursing Assistants	18.39
Computer Systems Analysts	57.62	Office Clerks, General	23.20
Computer User Support Specialists	27.70	Physical Therapists	54.19
Construction Laborers	20.63	Physicians	n/a
Cooks, Restaurant	16.62	Plumbers, Pipefitters and Steamfitters	27.83
Customer Service Representatives	20.78	Police and Sheriff's Patrol Officers	40.49
Dentists	n/a	Postal Service Mail Carriers	27.68
Electricians	28.92	Real Estate Sales Agents	57.72
Engineers, Electrical	61.86	Retail Salespersons	17.23
Fast Food and Counter Workers	13.82	Sales Representatives, Technical/Scientific	n/a
Financial Managers	87.54	Secretaries, Exc. Legal/Medical/Executive	22.14
First-Line Supervisors of Office Workers	36.53	Security Guards	23.02
General and Operations Managers	69.94	Surgeons	n/a
Hairdressers/Cosmetologists	n/a	Teacher Assistants, Exc. Postsecondary[1]	15.30
Home Health and Personal Care Aides	12.83	Teachers, Secondary School, Exc. Sp. Ed.[1]	31.99
Janitors and Cleaners	16.27	Telemarketers	n/a
Landscaping/Groundskeeping Workers	18.44	Truck Drivers, Heavy/Tractor-Trailer	28.32
Lawyers	95.87	Truck Drivers, Light/Delivery Services	23.98
Maids and Housekeeping Cleaners	14.15	Waiters and Waitresses	15.93

Note: Wage data covers the Midland, TX Metropolitan Statistical Area; (1) Hourly wages were calculated from annual wage data based on a 40 hour work week
Source: Bureau of Labor Statistics, Metro Area Occupational Employment & Wage Estimates, May 2024

Employment by Industry

Sector	MSA[1] Number of Employees	MSA[1] Percent of Total	U.S. Percent of Total
Construction, Mining, and Logging	41,700	33.1	5.5
Financial Activities	6,300	5.0	5.8
Government	11,000	8.7	14.9
Information	1,000	0.8	1.9
Leisure and Hospitality	11,600	9.2	10.4
Manufacturing	4,700	3.7	8.0
Other Services	4,300	3.4	3.7
Private Education and Health Services	9,700	7.7	16.9
Professional and Business Services	12,000	9.5	14.2
Retail Trade	10,000	7.9	10.0
Transportation, Warehousing, and Utilities	6,500	5.2	4.8
Wholesale Trade	7,300	5.8	3.9

Note: Figures are non-farm employment as of December 2024. Figures are not seasonally adjusted and include workers 16 years of age and older; (1) Figures cover the Midland, TX Metropolitan Statistical Area
Source: Bureau of Labor Statistics, Current Employment Statistics, Employment, Hours, and Earnings

Employment by Occupation

Occupation Classification	City (%)	MSA[1] (%)	U.S. (%)
Management, Business, Science, and Arts	41.0	39.9	42.0
Natural Resources, Construction, and Maintenance	12.8	13.2	8.6
Production, Transportation, and Material Moving	11.6	13.1	13.0
Sales and Office	21.9	21.1	19.9
Service	12.7	12.7	16.5

Note: Figures cover employed civilians 16 years of age and older; (1) Figures cover the Midland, TX Metropolitan Statistical Area
Source: U.S. Census Bureau, 2019-2023 American Community Survey 5-Year Estimates

Occupations with Greatest Projected Employment Growth: 2022 – 2032

Occupation[1]	2022 Employment	2032 Projected Employment	Numeric Employment Change	Percent Employment Change
General and Operations Managers	425,560	504,280	78,720	18.5
Fast Food and Counter Workers	333,870	394,290	60,420	18.1
Stockers and Order Fillers	264,810	321,600	56,790	21.4
Home Health and Personal Care Aides	313,670	367,500	53,830	17.2
Software Developers	110,280	161,780	51,500	46.7
Cooks, Restaurant	113,680	158,830	45,150	39.7
Laborers and Freight, Stock, and Material Movers, Hand	225,090	269,120	44,030	19.6
Heavy and Tractor-Trailer Truck Drivers	226,450	270,320	43,870	19.4
Retail Salespersons	319,400	357,630	38,230	12.0
Registered Nurses	233,850	267,980	34,130	14.6

Note: Projections cover Texas; (1) Sorted by numeric employment change
Source: www.projectionscentral.org, State Occupational Projections, 2022–2032 Long-Term Projections

Fastest-Growing Occupations: 2022 – 2032

Occupation[1]	2022 Employment	2032 Projected Employment	Numeric Employment Change	Percent Employment Change
Wind Turbine Service Technicians	4,860	7,950	3,090	63.6
Nurse Practitioners	19,060	30,490	11,430	60.0
Data Scientists	13,220	20,250	7,030	53.2
Computer and Information Research Scientists (SOC 2018)	2,070	3,140	1,070	51.7
Information Security Analysts (SOC 2018)	14,620	21,620	7,000	47.9
Software Developers	110,280	161,780	51,500	46.7
Statisticians	980	1,430	450	45.9
Operations Research Analysts	12,060	17,290	5,230	43.4
Software Quality Assurance Analysts and Testers	17,350	24,440	7,090	40.9
Medical and Health Services Managers	49,430	69,180	19,750	40.0

Note: Projections cover Texas; (1) Sorted by percent employment change and excludes occupations with numeric employment change less than 50
Source: www.projectionscentral.org, State Occupational Projections, 2022–2032 Long-Term Projections

CITY FINANCES

City Government Finances

Component	2022 ($000)	2022 ($ per capita)
Total Revenues	307,291	2,089
Total Expenditures	387,833	2,637
Debt Outstanding	143,646	977

Source: U.S. Census Bureau, State & Local Government Finances 2022

City Government Revenue by Source

Source	2022 ($000)	2022 ($ per capita)	2022 (%)
General Revenue			
From Federal Government	16,472	112	5.4
From State Government	1,005	7	0.3
From Local Governments	0	0	0.0
Taxes			
Property	61,553	419	20.0
Sales and Gross Receipts	76,744	522	25.0
Personal Income	0	0	0.0
Corporate Income	0	0	0.0
Motor Vehicle License	0	0	0.0
Other Taxes	2,522	17	0.8
Current Charges	66,406	452	21.6
Liquor Store	0	0	0.0
Utility	66,499	452	21.6

Source: U.S. Census Bureau, State & Local Government Finances 2022

City Government Expenditures by Function

Function	2022 ($000)	2022 ($ per capita)	2022 (%)
General Direct Expenditures			
Air Transportation	14,828	100	3.8
Corrections	0	0	0.0
Education	0	0	0.0
Employment Security Administration	0	0	0.0
Financial Administration	8,029	54	2.1
Fire Protection	28,750	195	7.4
General Public Buildings	1,831	12	0.5
Governmental Administration, Other	144,430	982	37.2
Health	2,216	15	0.6
Highways	34,574	235	8.9
Hospitals	0	0	0.0
Housing and Community Development	5,258	35	1.4
Interest on General Debt	5,376	36	1.4
Judicial and Legal	0	0	0.0
Libraries	0	0	0.0
Parking	0	0	0.0
Parks and Recreation	8,428	57	2.2
Police Protection	0	0	0.0
Public Welfare	0	0	0.0
Sewerage	17,540	119	4.5
Solid Waste Management	81,762	555	21.1
Veterans' Services	0	0	0.0
Liquor Store	0	0	0.0
Utility	304	2	0.1

Source: U.S. Census Bureau, State & Local Government Finances 2022

TAXES

State Corporate Income Tax Rates

State	Tax Rate (%)	Income Brackets ($)	Num. of Brackets	Financial Institution Tax Rate (%)[a]	Federal Income Tax Ded.
Texas	(u)	–	–	(u)	No

Note: Tax rates for tax year 2024; (a) Rates listed are the corporate income tax rate applied to financial institutions or excise taxes based on income. Some states have other taxes based upon the value of deposits or shares; (u) Texas imposes a Franchise Tax, otherwise known as margin tax, imposed on entities with more than $2,470,000 total revenues effective in 2024 at rate of 0.75%, or 0.375% for entities primarily engaged in retail or wholesale trade, on lesser of 70% of total revenues or 100% of gross receipts after deductions for either compensation ($450,000 deduction limit) or cost of goods sold. Texas has an EZ rate of 0.331 applicable to a $20 million revenue threshold.

Source: Federation of Tax Administrators, State Corporate Income Tax Rates, January 1, 2025

State Individual Income Tax Rates

State	Tax Rate (%)	Income Brackets ($)	Personal Exemptions ($)			Standard Ded. ($)	
			Single	Married	Depend.	Single	Married
Texas							– No state income tax –

Note: Tax rates for tax year 2024; Local- and county-level taxes are not included
Source: Federation of Tax Administrators, State Individual Income Tax Rates, January 1, 2025

Various State Sales and Excise Tax Rates

State	State Sales Tax (%)	Gasoline[1] ($/gal.)	Cigarette[2] ($/pack)	Spirits[3] ($/gal.)	Wine[4] ($/gal.)	Beer[5] ($/gal.)	Recreational Marijuana (%)
Texas	6.25	0.20	1.41	2.40	0.20	0.19	Not legal

Note: All tax rates as of January 1, 2025; (1) The American Petroleum Institute has developed a methodology for determining the average tax rate on a gallon of fuel. Rates may include any of the following: excise taxes, environmental fees, storage tank fees, other fees or taxes, general sales tax, and local taxes; (2) The federal excise tax of $1.0066 per pack and local taxes are not included; (3) Rates are those applicable to off-premise sales of 40% alcohol by volume (a.b.v.) distilled spirits in 750ml containers. Local excise taxes are excluded; (4) Rates are those applicable to off-premise sales of 11% a.b.v. non-carbonated wine in 750ml containers; (5) Rates are those applicable to off-premise sales of 4.7% a.b.v. beer in 12 ounce containers.
Source: Tax Foundation, 2025 Facts & Figures: How Does Your State Compare?

State Tax Competitiveness Index

State	Overall Rank	Corporate Tax Rank	Individual Income Tax Rank	Sales Tax Rank	Property Tax Rank	Unemployment Insurance Tax Rank
Texas	7	46	1	36	40	30

Note: The Tax Foundation's State Tax Competitiveness Index enables policymakers, taxpayers, and business leaders to gauge how their states' tax systems compare. A rank of 1 is best, 50 is worst. Rankings do not average to the total. States without a tax rank equally as 1. DC's scores and rankings do not affect other states. The report shows tax systems as of July 1, 2024 (the beginning of Fiscal Year 2025).
Source: Tax Foundation, State Tax Competitiveness Index 2025

TRANSPORTATION

Means of Transportation to Work

Area	Car/Truck/Van		Public Transportation			Bicycle	Walked	Other Means	Worked at Home
	Drove Alone	Car-pooled	Bus	Subway	Railroad				
City	79.9	12.2	0.4	0.0	0.0	0.2	0.7	1.0	5.6
MSA[1]	79.8	12.0	0.3	0.0	0.0	0.2	1.1	1.3	5.2
U.S.	70.2	8.5	1.7	1.3	0.4	0.4	2.4	1.6	13.5

Note: Figures are percentages and cover workers 16 years of age and older; (1) Figures cover the Midland, TX Metropolitan Statistical Area
Source: U.S. Census Bureau, 2019-2023 American Community Survey 5-Year Estimates

Travel Time to Work

Area	Less Than 10 Minutes	10 to 19 Minutes	20 to 29 Minutes	30 to 44 Minutes	45 to 59 Minutes	60 to 89 Minutes	90 Minutes or More
City	16.2	45.2	18.6	11.9	4.0	2.3	1.9
MSA[1]	15.7	40.3	20.4	14.4	4.2	2.3	2.7
U.S.	12.6	28.6	21.2	20.8	8.1	6.0	2.8

Note: Note: Figures are percentages and include workers 16 years old and over; (1) Figures cover the Midland, TX Metropolitan Statistical Area
Source: U.S. Census Bureau, 2019-2023 American Community Survey 5-Year Estimates

Key Congestion Measures

Measure	2000	2010	2015	2020	2022
Annual Hours of Delay, Total (000)	n/a	n/a	2,945	3,167	4,144
Annual Hours of Delay, Per Auto Commuter	n/a	n/a	21	18	24
Annual Congestion Cost, Per Auto Commuter ($)	n/a	n/a	506	465	578

Note: n/a not available
Source: Texas A&M Transportation Institute, 2023 Urban Mobility Report

Freeway Travel Time Index

Measure	1985	1990	1995	2000	2005	2010	2015	2020	2022
Urban Area Index[1]	n/a	n/a	n/a	n/a	n/a	n/a	1.08	1.09	1.11
Urban Area Rank[1,2]	n/a	n/a	n/a	n/a	n/a	n/a	n/a	n/a	n/a

Note: Freeway Travel Time Index—the ratio of travel time in the peak period to the travel time at free-flow conditions. For example, a value of 1.30 indicates a 20-minute free-flow trip takes 26 minutes in the peak (20 minutes x 1.30 = 26 minutes); (1) Covers the Midland TX urban area; (2) Rank is based on 101 larger urban areas (#1 = highest travel time index); n/a not available
Source: Texas A&M Transportation Institute, 2023 Urban Mobility Report

Public Transportation

Agency Name / Mode of Transportation	Vehicles Operated in Maximum Service[1]	Annual Unlinked Passenger Trips[2] (in thous.)	Annual Passenger Miles[3] (in thous.)
Midland-Odessa Urban Transit District			
Bus (directly operated)	12	199.8	n/a
Commuter Bus (directly operated)	2	4.4	n/a
Demand Response (directly operated)	9	29.3	n/a

Note: (1) Number of revenue vehicles operated by the given mode and type of service to meet the annual maximum service requirement. This is the revenue vehicle count during the peak season of the year; on the week and day that maximum service is provided. Vehicles operated in maximum service (VOMS) exclude atypical days and one-time special events; (2) Number of passengers who boarded public transportation vehicles. Passengers are counted each time they board a vehicle no matter how many vehicles they use to travel from their origin to their destination. (3) Sum of the distances ridden by all passengers during the entire fiscal year.
Source: Federal Transit Administration, National Transit Database, 2023

Air Transportation

Airport Name and Code / Type of Service	Passenger Airlines[1]	Passenger Enplanements	Freight Carriers[2]	Freight (lbs)
Midland International Airport (MAF)				
Domestic service (U.S. carriers only)	10	761,708	4	2,336,648
International service (U.S. carriers only)	1	8	0	0

Note: (1) Includes all U.S.-based major, minor and commuter airlines that carried at least one passenger during the year; (2) Includes all U.S.-based airlines and freight carriers that transported at least one pound of freight during the year.
Source: Bureau of Transportation Statistics, The Intermodal Transportation Database, Air Carriers: T-100 Domestic Market (U.S. carriers only), 2024; Bureau of Transportation Statistics, The Intermodal Transportation Database, Air Carriers: T-100 International Market (U.S. carriers only), 2024

BUSINESSES

Major Business Headquarters

Company Name	Industry	Rankings	
		Fortune[1]	Forbes[2]
Diamondback Energy	Mining, crude-oil production	449	-

Note: (1) Companies that produce a 10-K are ranked 1 to 500 based on 2023 revenue; (2) All private companies with at least $2 billion in annual revenue through the end of their most current fiscal year are ranked 1 to 275; companies listed are headquartered in the city; dashes indicate no ranking
Source: Fortune, "Fortune 500," 2024; Forbes, "America's Largest Private Companies," 2024

Living Environment

COST OF LIVING

Cost of Living Index

Composite Index	Groceries	Housing	Utilities	Transportation	Health Care	Misc. Goods/ Services
96.4	96.2	83.8	100.9	94.3	87.6	107.5

Note: The Cost of Living Index measures regional differences in the cost of consumer goods and services, excluding taxes and non-consumer expenditures, for professional and managerial households in the top income quintile. It is based on more than 50,000 prices covering almost 60 different items for which prices are collected three times a year by chambers of commerce, economic development organizations or university applied economic centers in each participating urban area. The numbers shown should be read as a percentage above or below the national average of 100. For example, a value of 115.4 in the groceries column indicates that grocery prices are 15.4% higher than the national average. Small differences in the index numbers should not be interpreted as significant; Figures cover the Midland TX urban area.
Source: The Council for Community and Economic Research, Cost of Living Index, 2024

Grocery Prices

Area[1]	T-Bone Steak ($/pound)	Frying Chicken ($/pound)	Whole Milk ($/half gal.)	Eggs ($/dozen)	Orange Juice ($/64 oz.)	Coffee ($/11.5 oz.)
City[2]	14.53	1.41	4.61	3.04	4.30	4.99
Avg.	15.42	1.55	4.69	3.25	4.41	5.46
Min.	14.50	1.16	4.43	2.75	4.00	4.85
Max.	17.56	2.89	5.49	4.78	5.54	7.89

Note: (1) Values for the local area are compared with the average, minimum and maximum values for all 276 areas in the Cost of Living Index; (2) Figures cover the Midland TX urban area; **T-Bone Steak** (price per pound); **Frying Chicken** (price per pound, whole fryer); **Whole Milk** (half gallon carton); **Eggs** (price per dozen, Grade A, large); **Orange Juice** (64 oz. Tropicana or Florida Natural); **Coffee** (11.5 oz. can, vacuum-packed, Maxwell House, Hills Bros, or Folgers).
Source: The Council for Community and Economic Research, Cost of Living Index, 2024

Housing and Utility Costs

Area[1]	New Home Price ($)	Apartment Rent ($/month)	All Electric ($/month)	Part Electric ($/month)	Other Energy ($/month)	Telephone ($/month)
City[2]	400,707	1,483	-	150.59	53.85	202.34
Avg.	515,975	1,550	210.99	123.07	82.07	194.99
Min.	265,375	692	104.33	53.68	36.26	179.42
Max.	2,775,821	5,719	529.02	397.28	361.63	223.33

Note: (1) Values for the local area are compared with the average, minimum and maximum values for all 276 areas in the Cost of Living Index; (2) Figures cover the Midland TX urban area; **New Home Price** (2,400 sf living area, 8,000 sf lot, in urban area with full utilities); **Apartment Rent** (950 sf 2 bedroom/1.5 or 2 bath, unfurnished, excluding all utilities except water); **All Electric** (average monthly cost for an all-electric home); **Part Electric** (average monthly cost for a part-electric home); **Other Energy** (average monthly cost for natural gas, fuel oil, coal, wood, and any other forms of energy except electricity); **Telephone** (price includes the base monthly rate plus taxes and fees for three lines of mobile phone service).
Source: The Council for Community and Economic Research, Cost of Living Index, 2024

Health Care, Transportation, and Other Costs

Area[1]	Doctor ($/visit)	Dentist ($/visit)	Optometrist ($/visit)	Gasoline ($/gallon)	Beauty Salon ($/visit)	Men's Shirt ($)
City[2]	97.50	108.17	132.67	3.13	69.08	43.45
Avg.	143.77	117.51	129.23	3.32	48.57	38.14
Min.	36.74	58.67	67.33	2.80	24.00	13.41
Max.	270.44	216.82	307.33	5.28	94.00	63.89

Note: (1) Values for the local area are compared with the average, minimum and maximum values for all 276 areas in the Cost of Living Index; (2) Figures cover the Midland TX urban area; **Doctor** (general practitioners routine exam of an established patient); **Dentist** (adult teeth cleaning and periodic oral examination); **Optometrist** (full vision eye exam for established adult patient); **Gasoline** (one gallon regular unleaded, national brand, including all taxes, cash price at self-service pump if available); **Beauty Salon** (woman's shampoo, trim, and blow-dry); **Men's Shirt** (cotton/polyester dress shirt, pinpoint weave, long sleeves).
Source: The Council for Community and Economic Research, Cost of Living Index, 2024

HOUSING

Homeownership Rate

Area	2017 (%)	2018 (%)	2019 (%)	2020 (%)	2021 (%)	2022 (%)	2023 (%)	2024 (%)
MSA[1]	n/a	n/a	n/a	n/a	n/a	n/a	n/a	n/a
U.S.	63.9	64.4	64.6	66.6	65.5	65.8	65.9	65.6

Note: (1) Figures cover the Midland, TX Metropolitan Statistical Area; n/a not available
Source: U.S. Census Bureau, Housing Vacancies and Homeownership Annual Statistics: 2017-2024

House Price Index (HPI)

Area	National Ranking[2]	Quarterly Change (%)	One-Year Change (%)	Five-Year Change (%)	Since 1991Q1 (%)
MSA[1]	(a)	1.03	1.09	21.00	383.65
U.S.[3]	—	1.43	4.51	57.13	327.82

Note: The HPI is a weighted repeat sales index. It measures average price changes in repeat sales or refinancings on the same properties. This information is obtained by reviewing repeat mortgage transactions on single-family properties whose mortgages have been purchased or securitized by Fannie Mae or Freddie Mac since January 1975; (1) Figures cover the Midland, TX Metropolitan Statistical Area; (2) Rankings are based on annual percentage change for all metro areas containing at least 15,000 transactions over the last 10 years and ranges from 1 to 241; (3) figures based on a weighted average of Census Division estimates using a seasonally adjusted, purchase-only index; all figures are for the period ending December 31, 2024; n/a not available; (a) Not ranked because of increased index variability due to smaller sample size
Source: Federal Housing Finance Agency, Change in FHFA Metropolitan Area House Price Indexes, All Transactions Index, 2024Q4

Home Value

Area	Under $100,000	$100,000 -$199,999	$200,000 -$299,999	$300,000 -$399,999	$400,000 -$499,999	$500,000 -$999,999	$1,000,000 or more	Median ($)
City	7.8	12.9	29.7	24.9	10.4	11.8	2.5	298,600
MSA[1]	12.7	13.2	26.8	21.6	10.8	12.6	2.4	290,300
U.S.	12.1	17.8	19.5	14.4	10.5	19.1	6.5	303,400

Note: Figures are percentages except for median and cover owner-occupied housing units; (1) Figures cover the Midland, TX Metropolitan Statistical Area
Source: U.S. Census Bureau, 2019-2023 American Community Survey 5-Year Estimates

Year Housing Structure Built

Area	2020 or Later	2010 -2019	2000 -2009	1990 -1999	1980 -1989	1970 -1979	1960 -1969	1950 -1959	1940 -1949	Before 1940	Median Year
City	2.2	21.9	10.1	9.7	17.3	10.9	7.7	16.6	2.5	1.1	1986
MSA[1]	2.4	24.0	11.8	9.7	17.4	10.3	6.8	13.7	2.4	1.3	1989
U.S.	1.2	8.9	13.6	12.8	13.0	14.4	10.0	9.7	4.5	11.9	1980

Note: Figures are percentages except for Median Year; Note: (1) Figures cover the Midland, TX Metropolitan Statistical Area
Source: U.S. Census Bureau, 2019-2023 American Community Survey 5-Year Estimates

Gross Monthly Rent

Area	Under $500	$500 -$999	$1,000 -$1,499	$1,500 -$1,999	$2,000 -$2,499	$2,500 -$2,999	$3,000 and up	Median ($)
City	3.2	15.5	38.6	24.4	11.7	4.2	2.3	1,407
MSA[1]	3.7	17.8	38.4	23.7	10.7	3.8	2.0	1,377
U.S.	6.5	22.3	29.5	20.2	10.8	4.8	5.9	1,348

Note: Figures are percentages except for median; Gross rent is the contract rent plus the estimated average monthly cost of utilities (electricity, gas, and water and sewer) and fuels (oil, coal, kerosene, wood, etc.) if these are paid by the renter (or paid for the renter by someone else); (1) Figures cover the Midland, TX Metropolitan Statistical Area
Source: U.S. Census Bureau, 2019-2023 American Community Survey 5-Year Estimates

HEALTH

Health Risk Factors

Category	MSA[1] (%)	U.S. (%)
Adults aged 18–64 who have any kind of health care coverage	n/a	90.8
Adults who reported being in good or better health	n/a	81.8
Adults who have been told they have high blood cholesterol	n/a	36.9
Adults who have been told they have high blood pressure	n/a	34.0
Adults who are current smokers	n/a	12.1
Adults who currently use e-cigarettes	n/a	7.7
Adults who currently use chewing tobacco, snuff, or snus	n/a	3.2
Adults who are heavy drinkers[2]	n/a	6.1
Adults who are binge drinkers[3]	n/a	15.2
Adults who are overweight (BMI 25.0 - 29.9)	n/a	34.4
Adults who are obese (BMI 30.0 - 99.8)	n/a	34.3
Adults who participated in any physical activities in the past month	n/a	75.8

Note: All figures are crude prevalence; (1) Figures for the Midland, TX Metropolitan Statistical Area were not available.
(2) Heavy drinkers are classified as adult men having more than 14 drinks per week and adult women having more than 7 drinks per week; (3) Binge drinkers are classified as males having five or more drinks on one occasion or females having four or more drinks on one occasion
Source: Centers for Disease Control and Prevention, Behaviorial Risk Factor Surveillance System, SMART: Selected Metropolitan Area Risk Trends, 2023

Acute and Chronic Health Conditions

Category	MSA[1] (%)	U.S. (%)
Adults who have ever been told they had a heart attack	n/a	4.2
Adults who have ever been told they have angina or coronary heart disease	n/a	4.0
Adults who have ever been told they had a stroke	n/a	3.3
Adults who have ever been told they have asthma	n/a	15.7
Adults who have ever been told they have arthritis	n/a	26.3
Adults who have ever been told they have diabetes[2]	n/a	11.5
Adults who have ever been told they had skin cancer	n/a	5.6
Adults who have ever been told they had any other types of cancer	n/a	8.4
Adults who have ever been told they have COPD	n/a	6.4
Adults who have ever been told they have kidney disease	n/a	3.7
Adults who have ever been told they have a form of depression	n/a	22.0

Note: All figures are crude prevalence; (1) Figures for the Midland, TX Metropolitan Statistical Area were not available.
(2) Figures do not include pregnancy-related, borderline, or pre-diabetes
Source: Centers for Disease Control and Prevention, Behavioral Risk Factor Surveillance System, SMART: Selected Metropolitan Area Risk Trends, 2023

Health Screening and Vaccination Rates

Category	MSA[1] (%)	U.S. (%)
Adults who have ever been tested for HIV	n/a	37.5
Adults who have had their blood cholesterol checked within the last five years	n/a	87.0
Adults aged 65+ who have had flu shot within the past year	n/a	63.4
Adults aged 65+ who have ever had a pneumonia vaccination	n/a	71.9

Note: All figures are crude prevalence; (1) Figures for the Midland, TX Metropolitan Statistical Area were not available.
Source: Centers for Disease Control and Prevention, Behavioral Risk Factor Surveillance System, SMART: Selected Metropolitan Area Risk Trends, 2023

Disability Status

Category	MSA[1] (%)	U.S. (%)
Adults who reported being deaf	n/a	7.4
Are you blind or have serious difficulty seeing, even when wearing glasses?	n/a	4.9
Do you have difficulty doing errands alone?	n/a	7.8
Do you have difficulty dressing or bathing?	n/a	3.6
Do you have serious difficulty concentrating/remembering/making decisions?	n/a	13.7
Do you have serious difficulty walking or climbing stairs?	n/a	13.2

Note: All figures are crude prevalence; (1) Figures for the Midland, TX Metropolitan Statistical Area were not available.
Source: Centers for Disease Control and Prevention, Behavioral Risk Factor Surveillance System, SMART: Selected Metropolitan Area Risk Trends, 2023

Mortality Rates for the Top 10 Causes of Death in the U.S.

ICD-10[a] Sub-Chapter	ICD-10[a] Code	Crude Mortality Rate[2] per 100,000 population	
		County[3]	U.S.
Malignant neoplasms	C00-C97	116.8	182.7
Ischaemic heart diseases	I20-I25	74.5	109.6
Provisional assignment of new diseases of uncertain etiology[1]	U00-U49	65.4	65.3
Other forms of heart disease	I30-I51	48.0	65.1
Other degenerative diseases of the nervous system	G30-G31	74.7	52.4
Other external causes of accidental injury	W00-X59	26.1	52.3
Cerebrovascular diseases	I60-I69	35.8	49.1
Chronic lower respiratory diseases	J40-J47	33.8	43.5
Hypertensive diseases	I10-I15	33.1	38.9
Organic, including symptomatic, mental disorders	F01-F09	7.2	33.9

Note: (a) ICD-10 = International Classification of Diseases 10th Revision; (1) Includes COVID-19, adverse effects to COVID-19 vaccines, SARS, and vaping-related disorders; (2) Crude mortality rates are a three-year average covering 2021-2023; (3) Figures cover Midland County.
Source: Centers for Disease Control and Prevention, National Center for Health Statistics. National Vital Statistics System, Mortality 2018-2023 on CDC WONDER Online Database

Mortality Rates for Selected Causes of Death

Cause of Death	ICD-10[a] Code	Crude Mortality Rate[1] per 100,000 population	
		County[2]	U.S.
Accidental poisoning and exposure to noxious substances	X40-X49	15.1	30.5
Alzheimer disease	G30	66.3	35.4
Assault	X85-Y09	7.7	7.3
COVID-19	U07.1	65.4	65.3
Diabetes mellitus	E10-E14	30.0	30.0
Diseases of the liver	K70-K76	22.6	20.8
Human immunodeficiency virus (HIV) disease	B20-B24	Unreliable	1.5
Influenza and pneumonia	J09-J18	7.9	13.4
Intentional self-harm	X60-X84	16.8	14.7
Malnutrition	E40-E46	7.9	6.0
Obesity and other hyperalimentation	E65-E68	4.4	3.1
Renal failure	N17-N19	12.0	16.4
Transport accidents	V01-V99	26.5	14.4

Note: (a) ICD-10 = International Classification of Diseases 10th Revision; (1) Crude mortality rates are a three-year average covering 2021-2023; (2) Figures cover Midland County; Data are suppressed when the data meet the criteria for confidentiality constraints; Crude mortality rates are flagged as unreliable when the rate would be calculated with a numerator of 20 or less.
Source: Centers for Disease Control and Prevention, National Center for Health Statistics. National Vital Statistics System, Mortality 2018-2023 on CDC WONDER Online Database

Health Insurance Coverage

Area	With Health Insurance	With Private Health Insurance	With Public Health Insurance	Without Health Insurance	Population Under Age 19 Without Health Insurance
City	85.2	72.0	21.3	14.8	11.7
MSA[1]	84.7	70.7	21.7	15.3	12.1
U.S.	91.4	67.3	36.3	8.6	5.4

Note: Figures are percentages that cover the civilian noninstitutionalized population; (1) Figures cover the Midland, TX Metropolitan Statistical Area
Source: U.S. Census Bureau, 2019-2023 American Community Survey 5-Year Estimates

Number of Medical Professionals

Area	MDs[3]	DOs[3,4]	Dentists	Podiatrists	Chiropractors	Optometrists
County[1] (number)	265	11	107	4	25	21
County[1] (rate[2])	154.1	6.4	60.4	2.3	14.1	11.9
U.S. (rate[2])	302.5	29.2	74.6	6.4	29.5	18.0

Note: Data as of 2023 unless noted; (1) Data covers Midland County; (2) Number of medical professionals per 100,000 population; (3) Data as of 2022 and includes all active, non-federal physicians; (4) Doctor of Osteopathic Medicine
Source: U.S. Department of Health and Human Services, Health Resources and Services Administration, Bureau of Health Professions, Area Resource File (ARF) 2023-2024

EDUCATION

Public School District Statistics

District Name	Schls	Pupils	Pupil/Teacher Ratio	Minority Pupils[1] (%)	Total Rev. per Pupil ($)	Total Exp. per Pupil ($)
Greenwood ISD	4	3,257	14.9	55.6	14,557	15,055
Midland ISD	40	28,752	18.7	78.5	13,694	16,821

Note: Table includes school districts with 2,000 or more students; (1) Percentage of students that are not non-Hispanic white.
Source: U.S. Department of Education, National Center for Education Statistics, Common Core of Data, Local Education Agency (School District) Universe Survey: School Year 2023-2024; U.S. Department of Education, National Center for Education Statistics, Common Core of Data, School District Finance Survey (F-33): School Year 2021–22

Highest Level of Education

Area	Less than H.S.	H.S. Diploma	Some College, No Deg.	Associate Degree	Bachelor's Degree	Master's Degree	Prof. School Degree	Doctorate Degree
City	13.5	22.5	22.4	8.0	23.9	7.4	1.4	1.0
MSA[1]	13.8	24.0	23.3	8.2	20.9	7.4	1.4	0.8
U.S.	10.6	26.2	19.4	8.8	21.3	9.8	2.3	1.6

Note: Figures cover persons age 25 and over; (1) Figures cover the Midland, TX Metropolitan Statistical Area
Source: U.S. Census Bureau, 2019-2023 American Community Survey 5-Year Estimates

Educational Attainment by Race

Area	High School Graduate or Higher (%)					Bachelor's Degree or Higher (%)				
	Total	White	Black	Asian	Hisp.[2]	Total	White	Black	Asian	Hisp.[2]
City	86.5	91.9	90.5	70.2	74.6	33.7	40.3	20.1	39.1	22.1
MSA[1]	86.2	91.5	91.3	74.8	74.3	30.6	35.7	20.6	48.7	19.3
U.S.	89.4	92.9	88.1	88.0	72.5	35.0	37.7	24.7	57.0	19.9

Note: Figures shown cover persons 25 years old and over; (1) Figures cover the Midland, TX Metropolitan Statistical Area; (2) People of Hispanic origin can be of any race
Source: U.S. Census Bureau, 2019-2023 American Community Survey 5-Year Estimates

School Enrollment by Grade and Control

Area	Preschool (%)		Kindergarten (%)		Grades 1 - 4 (%)		Grades 5 - 8 (%)		Grades 9 - 12 (%)	
	Public	Private	Public	Private	Public	Private	Public	Private	Public	Private
City	57.2	42.8	67.9	32.1	78.9	21.1	76.4	23.6	84.3	15.7
MSA[1]	65.0	35.0	65.8	34.2	80.9	19.1	78.8	21.2	83.9	16.1
U.S.	58.7	41.3	85.2	14.8	87.2	12.8	87.9	12.1	89.0	11.0

Note: Figures shown cover persons 3 years old and over; (1) Figures cover the Midland, TX Metropolitan Statistical Area
Source: U.S. Census Bureau, 2019-2023 American Community Survey 5-Year Estimates

Higher Education

Four-Year Colleges			Two-Year Colleges			Medical Schools[1]	Law Schools[2]	Voc/Tech[3]
Public	Private Non-profit	Private For-profit	Public	Private Non-profit	Private For-profit			
1	0	0	0	0	0	0	0	0

Note: Figures cover institutions located within the Midland, TX Metropolitan Statistical Area and include main campuses only; (1) includes schools accredited by the Liaison Committee on Medical Education and the American Osteopathic Association's Commission on Osteopathic College Accreditation; (2) includes ABA-accredited schools, schools with provisional ABA accreditation, and state accredited schools; (3) includes all schools with programs that are less than 2 years.
Source: National Center for Education Statistics, Integrated Postsecondary Education System (IPEDS), 2023-24; Wikipedia, List of Medical Schools in the United States, accessed May 2, 2025; Wikipedia, List of Law Schools in the United States, accessed May 2, 2025

EMPLOYERS

Major Employers

Company Name	Industry
Albertsons Companies	Grocery stores
Bobby Cox Companies	Retail, restaurants
City of Odessa	Municipal government
Cudd Energy	Oil & gas
Dixie Electric	Electric
Ector County	Government
Ector County ISD	Public education
Family Dollar	Distribution
Halliburton Services	Oil & gas
HEB	Grocery stores
Holloman Construction	Oil field construction
Investment Corp. of America	Financial services
Lithia Motors	Automotive
Medical Center Hospital	County hospital
Nurses Unlimited	Medical
Odessa College	Education
Odessa Regional Medical Center	Medical
REXtac	Manufacturer
Saulsbury Companies	Electric & construction
Sewell Family of Dealerships	Automotive
Southwest Convenience Stores	Retail, service
Texas Tech University Health Sci Ctr	Education/medical
The University of Texas Permian Basin	Education
Wal-Mart Stores	Retail
Weatherford	Oil & gas

Note: Companies shown are located within the Midland, TX Metropolitan Statistical Area.
Source: Chambers of Commerce; State Departments of Labor; Wikipedia

PUBLIC SAFETY

Crime Rate

Area	Total Crime Rate	Violent Crime Rate				Property Crime Rate		
		Murder	Rape	Robbery	Aggrav. Assault	Burglary	Larceny-Theft	Motor Vehicle Theft
City	2,321.6	5.2	63.6	33.3	328.3	274.3	1,354.5	262.5
U.S.	2,290.9	5.7	38.0	66.5	264.1	250.7	1,347.2	318.7

Note: Figures are crimes per 100,000 population.
Source: FBI, Table 8, Offenses Known to Law Enforcement, by State by City, 2023

Hate Crimes

Area	Number of Quarters Reported	Number of Incidents per Bias Motivation					
		Race/Ethnicity/Ancestry	Religion	Sexual Orientation	Disability	Gender	Gender Identity
City	4	2	0	1	0	0	0
U.S.	4	5,900	2,699	2,077	187	92	492

Source: Federal Bureau of Investigation, Hate Crime Statistics 2023

Identity Theft Consumer Reports

Area	Reports	Reports per 100,000 Population	Rank[2]
MSA[1]	707	400	23
U.S.	1,135,291	339	-

Note: (1) Figures cover the Midland, TX Metropolitan Statistical Area; (2) Rank ranges from 1 to 401 where 1 indicates greatest number of identity theft reports per 100,000 population
Source: Federal Trade Commission, Consumer Sentinel Network Data Book 2024

Fraud and Other Consumer Reports

Area	Reports	Reports per 100,000 Population	Rank[2]
MSA[1]	2,247	1,271	104
U.S.	5,360,641	1,601	-

Note: (1) Figures cover the Midland, TX Metropolitan Statistical Area; (2) Rank ranges from 1 to 401 where 1 indicates greatest number of fraud and other consumer reports per 100,000 population
Source: Federal Trade Commission, Consumer Sentinel Network Data Book 2024

POLITICS

2024 Presidential Election Results

Area	Trump (Rep.)	Harris (Dem.)	Stein (Green)	Kennedy (Ind.)	Oliver (Lib.)	Other
Midland County	79.6	19.2	0.2	0.0	0.6	0.3
U.S.	49.7	48.2	0.6	0.5	0.4	0.6

Note: Results are percentages and may not add to 100% due to rounding
Source: Dave Leip's Atlas of U.S. Presidential Elections

SPORTS

Professional Sports Teams

Team Name	League	Year Established

No teams are located in the metro area
Source: Wikipedia, Major Professional Sports Teams of the United States and Canada, May 1, 2025

CLIMATE

Average and Extreme Temperatures

Temperature	Jan	Feb	Mar	Apr	May	Jun	Jul	Aug	Sep	Oct	Nov	Dec	Yr.
Extreme High (°F)	84	90	95	101	108	116	112	107	107	100	89	85	116
Average High (°F)	57	62	70	79	86	93	94	93	86	78	66	59	77
Average Temp. (°F)	43	48	55	64	73	80	82	81	74	65	53	46	64
Average Low (°F)	30	34	40	49	59	67	69	68	62	51	39	32	50
Extreme Low (°F)	-8	-11	9	20	34	47	53	54	36	24	13	-1	-11

Note: Figures cover the years 1948-1995
Source: National Climatic Data Center, International Station Meteorological Climate Summary, 9/96

Average Precipitation/Snowfall/Humidity

Precip./Humidity	Jan	Feb	Mar	Apr	May	Jun	Jul	Aug	Sep	Oct	Nov	Dec	Yr.
Avg. Precip. (in.)	0.6	0.6	0.5	0.8	2.1	1.6	1.9	1.7	2.1	1.6	0.6	0.5	14.6
Avg. Snowfall (in.)	2	1	Tr	Tr	0	0	0	0	0	Tr	Tr	1	4
Avg. Rel. Hum. 6am (%)	72	72	65	67	75	76	73	74	79	78	74	71	73
Avg. Rel. Hum. 3pm (%)	38	35	27	27	31	32	34	34	40	37	35	37	34

Note: Figures cover the years 1948-1995; Tr = Trace amounts (<0.05 in. of rain; <0.5 in. of snow)
Source: National Climatic Data Center, International Station Meteorological Climate Summary, 9/96

Weather Conditions

Temperature			Daytime Sky			Precipitation		
10°F & below	32°F & below	90°F & above	Clear	Partly cloudy	Cloudy	0.01 inch or more precip.	0.1 inch or more snow/ice	Thunder-storms
1	62	102	144	138	83	52	3	38

Note: Figures are average number of days per year and cover the years 1948-1995
Source: National Climatic Data Center, International Station Meteorological Climate Summary, 9/96

HAZARDOUS WASTE

Superfund Sites

The Midland, TX metro area is home to two sites on the EPA's Superfund National Priorities List (NPL) or Superfund Alternative Approach (SAA) list: **Midessa Ground Water Plume** (Final NPL); **West County Road 112 Ground Water** (Final NPL). The Superfund alternative approach uses the same investigation and cleanup process and standards that are used for sites listed on the National Priorities List. The SAA is an alternative to listing a site on the NPL; it is not an alternative to Superfund or the Superfund process. There are a total of 1,445 Superfund sites with a status of proposed or final on both lists in the United States. *U.S. Environmental Protection Agency, National Priorities List, May 1, 2025; U.S. Environmental Protection Agency, Superfund Alternative Approach Sites, May 1, 2025*

AIR QUALITY

Air Quality Trends: Ozone

	1990	1995	2000	2005	2010	2015	2020	2021	2022	2023
MSA[1]	n/a	n/a	n/a	n/a	n/a	n/a	n/a	n/a	n/a	n/a
U.S.	0.087	0.089	0.081	0.080	0.072	0.068	0.066	0.067	0.067	0.070

Note: (1) Data covers the Midland, TX Metropolitan Statistical Area; n/a not available. The values shown are the composite ozone concentration averages among trend sites based on the highest fourth daily maximum 8-hour concentration in parts per million. These trends are based on sites having an adequate record of monitoring data during the trend period. Data from exceptional events are included.
Source: U.S. Environmental Protection Agency, Air Quality Monitoring Information, "Air Quality Trends by City, 1990-2023"

Air Quality Index

Area	Percent of Days when Air Quality was...[2]					AQI Statistics[2]	
	Good	Moderate	Unhealthy for Sensitive Groups	Unhealthy	Very Unhealthy	Maximum	Median
MSA[1]	n/a	n/a	n/a	n/a	n/a	n/a	n/a

Note: (1) Data covers the Midland, TX Metropolitan Statistical Area; (2) Based on days with AQI data in 2023. Air Quality Index (AQI) is an index for reporting daily air quality. EPA calculates the AQI for five major air pollutants regulated by the Clean Air Act: ground-level ozone, particle pollution (aka particulate matter), carbon monoxide, sulfur dioxide, and nitrogen dioxide. The AQI runs from 0 to 500. The higher the AQI value, the greater the level of air pollution and the greater the health concern. There are six AQI categories: "Good" AQI is between 0 and 50. Air quality is considered satisfactory; "Moderate" AQI is between 51 and 100. Air quality is acceptable; "Unhealthy for Sensitive Groups" When AQI values are between 101 and 150, members of sensitive groups may experience health effects; "Unhealthy" When AQI values are between 151 and 200 everyone may begin to experience health effects; "Very Unhealthy" AQI values between 201 and 300 trigger a health alert; "Hazardous" AQI values over 300 trigger warnings of emergency conditions (not shown).
Source: U.S. Environmental Protection Agency, Air Quality Index Report, 2023

Air Quality Index Pollutants

Area	Percent of Days when AQI Pollutant was...[2]					
	Carbon Monoxide	Nitrogen Dioxide	Ozone	Sulfur Dioxide	Particulate Matter 2.5	Particulate Matter 10
MSA[1]	n/a	n/a	n/a	(3)	n/a	n/a

Note: (1) Data covers the Midland, TX Metropolitan Statistical Area; (2) Based on days with AQI data in 2023. The Air Quality Index (AQI) is an index for reporting daily air quality. EPA calculates the AQI for five major air pollutants regulated by the Clean Air Act: ground-level ozone, particle pollution (also known as particulate matter), carbon monoxide, sulfur dioxide, and nitrogen dioxide. The AQI runs from 0 to 500. The higher the AQI value, the greater the level of air pollution and the greater the health concern; (3) Sulfur dioxide is no longer included in this table because SO_2 concentrations tend to be very localized and not necessarily representative of broad geographical areas like counties and CBSAs.
Source: U.S. Environmental Protection Agency, Air Quality Index Report, 2023

Maximum Air Pollutant Concentrations: Particulate Matter, Ozone, CO and Lead

	Particulate Matter 10 (ug/m^3)	Particulate Matter 2.5 Wtd AM (ug/m^3)	Particulate Matter 2.5 24-Hr (ug/m^3)	Ozone (ppm)	Carbon Monoxide (ppm)	Lead (ug/m^3)
MSA[1] Level	n/a	n/a	n/a	n/a	n/a	n/a
NAAQS[2]	150	15	35	0.075	9	0.15
Met NAAQS[2]	Yes	Yes	Yes	Yes	Yes	Yes

Note: (1) Data covers the Midland, TX Metropolitan Statistical Area; Data from exceptional events are included; (2) National Ambient Air Quality Standards; ppm = parts per million; ug/m³ = micrograms per cubic meter; n/a not available.
Concentrations: Particulate Matter 10 (coarse particulate)—highest second maximum 24-hour concentration; Particulate Matter 2.5 Wtd AM (fine particulate)—highest weighted annual mean concentration; Particulate Matter 2.5 24-Hour (fine particulate)—highest 98th percentile 24-hour concentration; Ozone—highest fourth daily maximum 8-hour concentration; Carbon Monoxide—highest second maximum non-overlapping 8-hour concentration; Lead—maximum running 3-month average
Source: U.S. Environmental Protection Agency, Air Quality Monitoring Information, "Air Quality Statistics by City, 2023"

Maximum Air Pollutant Concentrations: Nitrogen Dioxide and Sulfur Dioxide

	Nitrogen Dioxide AM (ppb)	Nitrogen Dioxide 1-Hr (ppb)	Sulfur Dioxide AM (ppb)	Sulfur Dioxide 1-Hr (ppb)	Sulfur Dioxide 24-Hr (ppb)
MSA[1] Level	n/a	n/a	n/a	n/a	n/a
NAAQS[2]	53	100	30	75	140
Met NAAQS[2]	Yes	Yes	Yes	Yes	Yes

Note: (1) Data covers the Midland, TX Metropolitan Statistical Area; Data from exceptional events are included; (2) National Ambient Air Quality Standards; ppm = parts per million; ug/m³ = micrograms per cubic meter; n/a not available.
Concentrations: Nitrogen Dioxide AM—highest arithmetic mean concentration; Nitrogen Dioxide 1-Hr—highest 98th percentile 1-hour daily maximum concentration; Sulfur Dioxide AM—highest annual mean concentration; Sulfur Dioxide 1-Hr—highest 99th percentile 1-hour daily maximum concentration; Sulfur Dioxide 24-Hr—highest second maximum 24-hour concentration
Source: U.S. Environmental Protection Agency, Air Quality Monitoring Information, "Air Quality Statistics by City, 2023"

Nashville, Tennessee

Background

Nashville, the capital of Tennessee, was in 1779 by James Robertson and John Donelson and is considered the country music capital of the world. It is home to the Grand Ole Opry—the longest-running radio show in the country, with millions of devoted listeners, and to Music Row just southwest of downtown, with hundreds of businesses related to the country music, gospel music, and contemporary Christian music industries. The USA Network's *Nashville Star*, a country music singing competition, is held in the Acuff Theatre.

Industries other than the recording industry that are important to its economy include health care management, automobile production, and printing and publishing. Nashville is consistently ranked a high job-growth region and has been called "Nowville" and "It City." Nashville's first female mayor, Megan Barry, performed the city's first same-sex wedding in Nashville. The city recently received accolades for its economy and robust housing market.

Nashville is a devoted patron of education. The Davidson Academy, forerunner of the George Peabody College for Teachers, was founded in Nashville, as were Vanderbilt and Fisk universities, the latter being the first private black university in the United States. Vanderbilt University and Medical Center is the region's largest non-governmental employer.

Nashville citizens take pride in their museums, including the Adventure Science Center, with its Sudekum Planetarium; the Aaron Douglas Gallery at Fisk University, which features a remarkable collection of African American art; and the Carl Van Vechten Gallery, also at Fisk University, home to works by Alfred Stieglitz, Picasso, Cezanne, and Georgia O'Keefe. The Cheekwood Botanical Garden and Museum of Art includes 55 acres of gardens and contemporary art galleries.

The city's majestic mansions and plantations testify to the nineteenth-century splendor for which the South is famous. The Belle Meade Plantation is an 1853 Greek Revival mansion crowning a 5,400-acre thoroughbred stud farm and nursery. The Belmont Mansion, built in 1850 by Adelicia Acklen, one of the wealthiest women in America, is constructed in the style of an Italian villa and was originally intended to be the summer home of the Acklens. Travelers' Rest Plantation, built in 1799, is Nashville's oldest plantation home open to the public. Carnton Plantation was the site of the Civil War's Battle of Franklin, and The Hermitage was the home of Andrew Jackson, the seventh president of the United States. Tennessee's historic State Capitol Building, completed in 1859, has had much of its interior restored to its original grandeur.

The Nashville area comprises many urban, suburban, rural, and historic districts, which differ immensely from each other. Restaurants, clubs, and shops are on the west side of the Cumberland River, while the east side encompasses residential neighborhoods with a variety of house styles and upscale shopping.

Located in nearby Lebanon, the Nashville Superspeedway is a 1.33-mile, tri-oval intermediate speedway. The track has held a variety of racing series since its opening in 2001, including NASCAR and the IndyCar Series. The area is also home to three major professional sports teams, the Predators (hockey), Titans (football), and Nashville SC (soccer).

The city as nearly 200 parks and 100 miles of greenways. Outdoor activities include camping, fishing, hiking, and biking at the many scenic and accessible lakes in the region.

Located on the Cumberland River in central Tennessee, Nashville has a humid subtropical climate, with hot, humid summers and generally cool winters typical of the Upper South. Snowfall, usually light, occurs during the winter months. Rainfall is typically greater in spring and summer, while the autumn months are the driest on average. Spring and fall are prone to severe thunderstorms, which may bring tornadoes, large hail, flash floods and damaging wind.

Rankings

General Rankings

- To help military veterans find the best places in which to settle down, *WalletHub* compared the 100 largest U.S. cities across 19 key indicators of livability, affordability and veteran-friendliness. They range from the share of military skill-related jobs to veteran income growth to the availability of VA health facilities. Nashville ranked #81. *Wallethub.com, "Best & Worst Places for Veterans to Live (2025)," November 7, 2024*

- *Insider* listed 23 places in the U.S. that travel industry trends reveal would be popular destinations in 2023. This year the list trends towards cultural and historical happenings, sports events, wellness experiences and invigorating outdoor escapes. According to the website insider.com Nashville is a place to visit in 2023. *Insider, "23 of the Best Places You Should Travel to in the U.S. in 2023," December 17, 2022*

- Nashville appeared on *Travel + Leisure's* list of "The 15 Best Cities in the United States." The city was ranked #13. Criteria: walkability; sights/landmarks; culture; food; friendliness; shopping; and overall value. *Travel + Leisure, "The World's Best Awards 2024" July 9, 2024*

Business/Finance Rankings

- Payscale.com ranked the 32 largest metro areas in terms of wage growth. The Nashville metro area ranked #31. Criteria: quarterly changes in private industry employee and education professional wage growth from the previous year. *PayScale, "Wage Trends by Metro Area-4th Quarter," February 4, 2025*

- The Nashville metro area appeared on the Milken Institute "2025 Best Performing Cities" list. Rank: #20 out of 200 large metro areas (based on performance category). Criteria: job growth; wage growth; high-tech growth and impact; community resilience; housing affordability; household broadband access. *Milken Institute, "Best-Performing Cities 2025," January 14, 2025*

Education Rankings

- Personal finance website *WalletHub* analyzed the 150 largest U.S. metropolitan statistical areas to determine where the most educated Americans are putting their degrees to work. Criteria: education levels; percentage of workers with degrees; education quality and attainment gap; public school quality rankings; quality and enrollment of each metro area's universities. Nashville was ranked #43 (#1 = most educated city). *WalletHub.com, "Most & Least Educated Cities in America, 2025" July 2, 2024*

Health/Fitness Rankings

- For each of the 100 largest cities in the United States, the American Fitness Index®, compiled in partnership between the American College of Sports Medicine and the Elevance Health Foundation, evaluated community infrastructure and more than 30 health behaviors including preventive health, levels of chronic disease conditions, food insecurity, pedestrian safety, air quality, and community/environment resources that support physical activity. Nashville ranked #67 for "community fitness." *americanfitnessindex.org, "2024 ACSM American Fitness Index Summary Report," July 23, 2024*

- The Nashville metro area was identified as one of the worst cities for bed bugs in America by pest control company Orkin. The area ranked #30 out of 50 based on the number of bed bug treatments Orkin performed from December 2022 to November 2023. *Orkin, "Chicago Joins Paris In Global Bed Bug Spotlight Ranking As The Worst City On Orkin's U.S. Bed Bug Cities List," January 22, 2024*

- Nashville was identified as a "2025 Allergy Capital." The area ranked #29 out of the nation's 100 largest metropolitan areas. Three groups of factors were used to identify the most challenging cities for people with allergies: annual tree, grass, and weed pollen scores; over the counter allergy medicine use; number of board-certified allergy specialists. *Asthma and Allergy Foundation of America, "2025 Allergy Capitals: The Most Challenging Places to Live with Allergies," March 18, 2025*

- Nashville was identified as a "2024 Asthma Capital." The area ranked #32 out of the nation's 100 largest metropolitan areas. Criteria: estimated asthma prevalence; asthma-related mortality; and ER visits due to asthma. Risk factors analyzed but not factored in the rankings: annual air quality including pollution and ozone levels; public smoking laws; indoor air quality; access to asthma specialists; rescue and controller medication use; uninsured rate; pollen allergy; poverty rate. *Asthma and Allergy Foundation of America, "Asthma Capitals 2024: The Most Challenging Places to Live With Asthma," September 10, 2024*

Pet Rankings

- Nashville appeared on *The Dogington Post* site as one of the top cities for dog lovers, ranking #14 out of 15. The real estate marketplace, Zillow®, and Rover, the largest pet sitter and dog walker network, introduced a new list of "Top Emerging Dog-Friendly Cities" for 2021. Criteria: number of new dog accounts on the Rover platform; and rentals and listings that mention features that attract dog owners (fenced-in yards, dog houses, dog door or proximity to a dog park). *Dogingtonpost.com, "15 Cities Emerging as Dog-Friendliest in 2021," May 11, 2021*

- Nashville was selected by *Sniffspot.com* as one of the most dog-friendly cities in the U.S., ranking #41 out of 50. Criteria: dog parks; hiking; sniffspots; public parks; dog-friendly businesses; housing; dog waste cleanliness; leash laws; dog services; and overall cost. *Sniffspot.com, "The Top 50 Most Dog-Friendly Cities in the U.S.," September 30, 2024*

Real Estate Rankings

- *WalletHub* compared the most populated U.S. cities to determine which had the best markets for real estate agents. Nashville ranked #6 where demand was high and pay was the best. Criteria: sales per agent; annual median wage for real-estate agents; monthly average starting salary for real estate agents; real estate job density and competition; unemployment rate; home turnover rate; housing-market health index; and other relevant metrics. *WalletHub.com, "2021 Best Places to Be a Real Estate Agent," May 12, 2021*

- Nashville was ranked #96 out of 176 metro areas in terms of cost of housing in 2024 by the National Association of Home Builders (#1 = most affordable). Criteria: the portion of an average family's income necessary to pay the mortgage on a median-priced home. *National Association of Home Builders®, NAHB-Wells Fargo Cost of Housing Index, 4th Quarter 2024*

Safety Rankings

- To identify the most dangerous cities in America, *24/7 Wall St.* focused on violent crime categories—murder, non-negligent manslaughter, rape, robbery, and aggravated assault—as reported for every 100,000 residents using data from the FBI's 2020 annual Uniform Crime Report. For cities with populations over 25,000, Nashville was ranked #47. *247wallst.com, "America's Most Dangerous Cities" November 12, 2021*

- Allstate ranked the 100 most populous cities in America in terms of driver safety. Nashville ranked #49. Criteria based on anonymized driving behavior data from Allstate's mobile app powered by Arity: high speed driving (over 80 mph), phone handling, and hard braking. The report helps increase the importance of safety and awareness behind the wheel. *Allstate, "16th Allstate America's Best Drivers Report®" July 11, 2024*

- Nashville was identified as one of the most dangerous cities in America by NeighborhoodScout. The city ranked #52 out of 100 (#1 = most dangerous). Criteria: number of violent crimes per 1,000 residents. The editors evaluated cities with 25,000 or more residents. *NeighborhoodScout.com, "2023 Top 100 Most Dangerous Cities in the U.S.," January 12, 2023*

Sports/Recreation Rankings

- Nashville was chosen as a bicycle friendly community by the League of American Bicyclists. A "Bicycle Friendly Community" welcomes cyclists by providing safe and supportive accommodation for cycling and encouraging people to bike for transportation and recreation. There are four award levels: Platinum; Gold; Silver; and Bronze. The community achieved an award level of Bronze. *League of American Bicyclists, "2024 Awards-New & Renewing Bicycle Friendly Communities List," January 28, 2025*

Women/Minorities Rankings

- *Travel + Leisure* listed the best cities in and around the U.S. for a memorable and fun girls' trip, even on a budget. Whether it is for a special occasion, to make new memories or just to get away, Nashville is sure to have something for all the ladies in your tribe. *Travel + Leisure, "25 Affordable Girls Weekend Getaways That Won't Break the Bank," January 30, 2025*

- Personal finance website *WalletHub* compared more than 180 U.S. cities across two key dimensions, "Hispanic Business-Friendliness" and "Hispanic Purchasing Power," to arrive at the most favorable conditions for Hispanic entrepreneurs. Nashville was ranked #123 out of 182. Criteria includes: share of Hispanic-Owned Businesses; average growth of Hispanic Business revenues; Small Business-Friendliness score; affordability; and number of Hispanics with at least a bachelor's degree. *WalletHub.com, "Best Cities for Hispanic Entrepreneurs," September 4, 2024*

Miscellaneous Rankings

- *WalletHub* compared 148 of the most populated U.S. cities to determine their operating efficiency. A "Quality of Services" score was constructed for each city and then measured against the total budget per capita to reveal which were managed the best. Nashville ranked #124. Criteria: financial stability; economy; education; safety; health; infrastructure and pollution. *WalletHub.com, "2025's Best- & Worst-Run Cities in America," June 18, 2024*

Business Environment

DEMOGRAPHICS

Population Growth

Area	1990 Census	2000 Census	2010 Census	2020 Census	2023 Estimate[2]	Population Growth 1990-2023 (%)
City	488,364	545,524	601,222	689,447	684,298	40.1
MSA[1]	1,048,218	1,311,789	1,589,934	1,989,519	2,043,713	95.0
U.S.	248,709,873	281,421,906	308,745,538	331,449,281	332,387,540	33.6

Note: (1) Figures cover the Nashville-Davidson—Murfreesboro—Franklin, TN Metropolitan Statistical Area; (2) 2019-2023 5-year ACS population estimate
Source: U.S. Census Bureau, 1990 Census, 2000 Census, 2010 Census, 2020 Census, 2019-2023 American Community Survey 5-Year Estimates

Race

Area	White Alone[2] (%)	Black Alone[2] (%)	Asian Alone[2] (%)	AIAN[3] Alone[2] (%)	NHOPI[4] Alone[2] (%)	Other Race Alone[2] (%)	Two or More Races (%)
City	56.5	25.5	3.5	0.3	0.1	4.9	9.2
MSA[1]	71.6	14.3	2.9	0.2	0.1	3.4	7.6
U.S.	63.4	12.4	5.8	0.9	0.2	6.6	10.7

Note: (1) Figures cover the Nashville-Davidson—Murfreesboro—Franklin, TN Metropolitan Statistical Area; (2) Alone is defined as not being in combination with one or more other races; (3) American Indian and Alaska Native; (4) Native Hawaiian and Other Pacific Islander
Source: U.S. Census Bureau, 2019-2023 American Community Survey 5-Year Estimates

Hispanic or Latino Origin

Area	Total (%)	Mexican (%)	Puerto Rican (%)	Cuban (%)	Other (%)
City	13.8	6.8	0.7	0.6	5.7
MSA[1]	9.7	5.1	0.7	0.4	3.5
U.S.	19.0	11.3	1.8	0.7	5.2

Note: Persons of Hispanic or Latino origin can be of any race; (1) Figures cover the Nashville-Davidson—Murfreesboro—Franklin, TN Metropolitan Statistical Area
Source: U.S. Census Bureau, 2019-2023 American Community Survey 5-Year Estimates

Age

Area	Percent of Population									Median Age
	Under Age 5	Age 5–19	Age 20–34	Age 35–44	Age 45–54	Age 55–64	Age 65–74	Age 75–84	Age 85+	
City	6.6	16.9	27.6	14.5	11.2	10.8	7.9	3.4	1.2	34.4
MSA[1]	6.1	19.3	21.9	14.2	12.6	12.1	8.6	4.0	1.2	36.8
U.S.	5.7	19.1	20.2	13.1	12.3	12.8	10.0	4.9	1.9	38.7

Note: (1) Figures cover the Nashville-Davidson—Murfreesboro—Franklin, TN Metropolitan Statistical Area
Source: U.S. Census Bureau, 2019-2023 American Community Survey 5-Year Estimates

Disability by Age

Area	All Ages	Under 18 Years Old	18 to 64 Years Old	65 Years and Over
City	11.0	4.5	8.8	33.8
MSA[1]	11.4	4.2	9.4	32.9
U.S.	13.0	4.7	10.7	32.9

Note: Figures show percent of the civilian noninstitutionalized population that reported having a disability. Disability status is determined from six types of difficulty: vision, hearing, cognitive, ambulatory, self-care, and independent living. For children under 5 years old, hearing and vision difficulty are used to determine disability status. For children between the ages of 5 and 14, disability status is determined from hearing, vision, cognitive, ambulatory, and self-care difficulties. For people aged 15 years and older, they are considered to have a disability if they have difficulty with any one of the six difficulty types; Note: (1) Figures cover the Nashville-Davidson—Murfreesboro—Franklin, TN Metropolitan Statistical Area
Source: U.S. Census Bureau, 2019-2023 American Community Survey 5-Year Estimates

Ancestry

Area	German	Irish	English	American	Italian	Polish	French[2]	European	Scottish
City	8.7	7.9	10.2	5.9	2.7	1.4	1.5	1.7	1.9
MSA[1]	9.6	8.9	12.9	10.5	2.6	1.2	1.6	2.3	2.2
U.S.	12.6	9.4	9.1	5.5	4.9	2.6	2.0	1.6	1.6

Note: Figures are the percentage of the total population reporting a particular ancestry. The nine most commonly reported ancestries in the U.S. are shown. Figures include multiple ancestries (e.g. if a person reported being Irish and Italian, they were included in both columns); (1) Figures cover the Nashville-Davidson—Murfreesboro—Franklin, TN Metropolitan Statistical Area; (2) Excludes Basque
Source: U.S. Census Bureau, 2019-2023 American Community Survey 5-Year Estimates

Foreign-born Population

Area	Percent of Population Born in								
	Any Foreign Country	Asia	Mexico	Europe	Caribbean	Central America[2]	South America	Africa	Canada
City	15.1	3.6	3.1	0.8	0.6	3.1	0.6	2.9	0.3
MSA[1]	9.4	2.4	2.1	0.7	0.4	1.6	0.5	1.4	0.3
U.S.	13.9	4.3	3.3	1.4	1.4	1.2	1.2	0.8	0.2

Note: (1) Figures cover the Nashville-Davidson—Murfreesboro—Franklin, TN Metropolitan Statistical Area; (2) Excludes Mexico.
Source: U.S. Census Bureau, 2019-2023 American Community Survey 5-Year Estimates

Household Size

Area	Persons in Household (%)							Average Household Size
	One	Two	Three	Four	Five	Six	Seven or More	
City	36.9	33.0	13.6	9.2	4.6	1.5	1.2	2.19
MSA[1]	28.0	34.5	16.1	12.7	5.7	1.9	1.1	2.49
U.S.	28.5	33.8	15.4	12.7	5.9	2.3	1.4	2.54

Note: (1) Figures cover the Nashville-Davidson—Murfreesboro—Franklin, TN Metropolitan Statistical Area
Source: U.S. Census Bureau, 2019-2023 American Community Survey 5-Year Estimates

Household Relationships

Area	House- holder	Opposite- sex Spouse	Same-sex Spouse	Opposite-sex Unmarried Partner	Same-sex Unmarried Partner	Child[2]	Grand- child	Other Relatives	Non- relatives
City	42.1	14.3	0.3	3.0	0.3	24.0	1.9	4.7	5.7
MSA[1]	38.8	18.2	0.2	2.4	0.2	28.1	2.2	4.1	3.8
U.S.	38.3	17.5	0.2	2.5	0.2	28.3	2.4	4.8	3.4

Note: Figures are percent of the total population; (1) Figures cover the Nashville-Davidson—Murfreesboro—Franklin, TN Metropolitan Statistical Area; (2) Includes biological, adopted, and stepchildren of the householder
Source: U.S. Census Bureau, 2020 Census

Gender

Area	Males	Females	Males per 100 Females
City	331,646	352,652	94.0
MSA[1]	1,004,473	1,039,240	96.7
U.S.	164,545,087	167,842,453	98.0

Note: (1) Figures cover the Nashville-Davidson—Murfreesboro—Franklin, TN Metropolitan Statistical Area
Source: U.S. Census Bureau, 2019-2023 American Community Survey 5-Year Estimates

Marital Status

Area	Never Married	Now Married[2]	Separated	Widowed	Divorced
City	41.6	41.4	1.7	4.3	11.0
MSA[1]	32.8	50.3	1.4	4.9	10.6
U.S.	34.1	47.9	1.7	5.6	10.7

Note: Figures are percentages and cover the population 15 years of age and older; (1) Figures cover the Nashville-Davidson—Murfreesboro—Franklin, TN Metropolitan Statistical Area; (2) Excludes separated
Source: U.S. Census Bureau, 2019-2023 American Community Survey 5-Year Estimates

Religious Groups by Family

Area	Catholic	Baptist	Methodist	LDS[2]	Pentecostal	Lutheran	Islam	Adventist	Other
MSA[1]	6.2	16.4	4.8	0.9	1.6	0.4	0.8	1.3	19.4
U.S.	18.7	7.3	3.0	2.0	1.8	1.7	1.3	1.3	11.6

Note: Figures are the number of adherents as a percentage of the total population and cover the eight largest religious groups in the U.S; (1) Figures cover the Nashville-Davidson—Murfreesboro—Franklin, TN Metropolitan Statistical Area; (2) Church of Jesus Christ of Latter-day Saints
Sources: 2020 U.S. Religion Census, Association of Statisticians of American Religious Bodies; The Association of Religion Data Archives (ARDA)

Religious Groups by Tradition

Area	Catholic	Evangelical Protestant	Mainline Protestant	Black Protestant	Islam	Judaism	Hinduism	Orthodox	Buddhism
MSA[1]	6.2	30.1	6.0	5.2	0.8	0.2	0.4	1.1	0.2
U.S.	18.7	16.5	5.2	2.3	1.3	0.6	0.4	0.4	0.3

Note: Figures are the number of adherents as a percentage of the total population; (1) Figures cover the Nashville-Davidson—Murfreesboro—Franklin, TN Metropolitan Statistical Area
Sources: 2020 U.S. Religion Census, Association of Statisticians of American Religious Bodies; The Association of Religion Data Archives (ARDA)

ECONOMY

Real Gross Domestic Product (GDP)

Area	2017	2018	2019	2020	2021	2022	2023	Rank[3]
MSA[1]	130.5	134.6	139.3	138.4	154.0	163.2	168.2	27
U.S.[2]	17,619.1	18,160.7	18,642.5	18,238.9	19,387.6	19,896.6	20,436.3	—

Note: Figures are in billions of chained 2017 dollars; (1) Figures cover the Nashville-Davidson—Murfreesboro—Franklin, TN Metropolitan Statistical Area; (2) Figures cover real GDP within metropolitan areas; (3) Rank is based on 2023 data and ranges from 1 to 384
Source: U.S. Bureau of Economic Analysis

Economic Growth

Area	2014	2015	2016	2017	2018	2019	2020	2021	2022	2023
MSA[1]	4.6	6.7	3.7	4.6	3.1	3.6	-0.7	11.3	6.0	3.1
U.S.[2]	2.6	3.2	2.0	2.7	3.1	2.7	-2.2	6.3	2.6	2.7

Note: Figures are real gross domestic product growth rates and represent percent change from preceding period; (1) Figures cover the Nashville-Davidson—Murfreesboro—Franklin, TN Metropolitan Statistical Area; (2) Figures are the average growth rates within metropolitan areas
Source: U.S. Bureau of Economic Analysis

Metropolitan Area Exports

Area	2018	2019	2020	2021	2022	2023	Rank[2]
MSA[1]	8,723.7	7,940.7	6,569.9	8,256.1	9,347.5	10,385.4	41
U.S.	1,664,056.1	1,645,173.7	1,431,406.6	1,753,941.4	2,062,937.4	2,019,160.5	—

Note: Figures are in millions of dollars; (1) Figures cover the Nashville-Davidson—Murfreesboro—Franklin, TN Metropolitan Statistical Area; (2) Rank is based on 2023 data and ranges from 1 to 386
Source: U.S. Department of Commerce, International Trade Administration, Office of Trade and Economic Analysis, Industry and Analysis, Exports by Metropolitan Area, data extracted April 2, 2025

Building Permits

Area	Single-Family			Multi-Family			Total		
	2023	2024	Pct. Chg.	2023	2024	Pct. Chg.	2023	2024	Pct. Chg.
City	3,106	2,662	-14.3	8,052	4,137	-48.6	11,158	6,799	-39.1
MSA[1]	13,842	14,465	4.5	9,716	5,573	-42.6	23,558	20,038	-14.9
U.S.	920,000	981,900	6.7	591,100	496,100	-16.1	1,511,100	1,478,000	-2.2

Note: (1) Figures cover the Nashville-Davidson—Murfreesboro—Franklin, TN Metropolitan Statistical Area; Figures represent new, privately-owned housing units authorized (unadjusted data)
Source: U.S. Census Bureau, Building Permits Survey (BPS), 2023, 2024

Bankruptcy Filings

Area	Business Filings			Nonbusiness Filings		
	2023	2024	% Chg.	2023	2024	% Chg.
Davidson County	303	123	-59.4	1,109	1,195	7.8
U.S.	18,926	23,107	22.1	434,064	494,201	13.9

Note: Business filings include Chapter 7, Chapter 9, Chapter 11, Chapter 12, Chapter 13, Chapter 15, and Section 304; Nonbusiness filings include Chapter 7, Chapter 11, and Chapter 13
Source: Administrative Office of the U.S. Courts, Business and Nonbusiness Bankruptcy, County Cases Commenced by Chapter of the Bankruptcy Code, During the 12-Month Period Ending December 31, 2023 and Business and Nonbusiness Bankruptcy, County Cases Commenced by Chapter of the Bankruptcy Code, During the 12-Month Period Ending December 31, 2024

Housing Vacancy Rates

Area	Gross Vacancy Rate[3] (%)			Year-Round Vacancy Rate[4] (%)			Rental Vacancy Rate[5] (%)			Homeowner Vacancy Rate[6] (%)		
	2022	2023	2024	2022	2023	2024	2022	2023	2024	2022	2023	2024
MSA[1]	7.6	7.5	7.0	7.1	7.0	6.4	6.4	9.3	8.6	0.9	0.9	1.5
U.S.[2]	9.1	9.0	9.1	7.5	7.5	7.6	5.7	6.5	6.8	0.8	0.8	1.0

Note: (1) Figures cover the Nashville-Davidson—Murfreesboro—Franklin, TN Metropolitan Statistical Area; (2) Figures cover the 75 largest Metropolitan Statistical Areas; (3) The percentage of the total housing inventory that is vacant; (4) The percentage of the housing inventory (excluding seasonal units) that is year-round vacant; (5) The percentage of rental inventory that is vacant for rent; (6) The percentage of homeowner inventory that is vacant for sale
Source: U.S. Census Bureau, Housing Vacancies and Homeownership Annual Statistics: 2022, 2023, 2024

INCOME

Income

Area	Per Capita ($)	Median Household ($)	Average Household ($)
City	46,820	75,197	106,483
MSA[1]	45,266	82,499	113,441
U.S.	43,289	78,538	110,491

Note: (1) Figures cover the Nashville-Davidson—Murfreesboro—Franklin, TN Metropolitan Statistical Area
Source: U.S. Census Bureau, 2019-2023 American Community Survey 5-Year Estimates

Household Income Distribution

Area	Percent of Households Earning							
	Under $15,000	$15,000 -$24,999	$25,000 -$34,999	$35,000 -$49,999	$50,000 -$74,999	$75,000 -$99,999	$100,000 -$149,999	$150,000 and up
City	8.5	5.6	6.6	11.8	17.4	13.6	17.2	19.3
MSA[1]	6.6	5.5	5.8	10.7	16.8	13.9	19.0	21.7
U.S.	8.5	6.6	6.8	10.4	15.7	12.7	17.4	21.9

Note: (1) Figures cover the Nashville-Davidson—Murfreesboro—Franklin, TN Metropolitan Statistical Area
Source: U.S. Census Bureau, 2019-2023 American Community Survey 5-Year Estimates

Poverty Rate

Area	All Ages	Under 18 Years Old	18 to 64 Years Old	65 Years and Over
City	14.1	21.2	12.5	11.2
MSA[1]	10.4	13.6	9.5	8.9
U.S.	12.4	16.3	11.6	10.4

Note: Figures are percentage of people whose income during the past 12 months was below the poverty level;
(1) Figures cover the Nashville-Davidson—Murfreesboro—Franklin, TN Metropolitan Statistical Area
Source: U.S. Census Bureau, 2019-2023 American Community Survey 5-Year Estimates

EMPLOYMENT

Labor Force and Employment

Area	Civilian Labor Force			Workers Employed		
	Dec. 2023	Dec. 2024	% Chg.	Dec. 2023	Dec. 2024	% Chg.
City	421,198	426,189	1.2	411,304	413,569	0.6
MSA[1]	1,150,386	1,163,681	1.2	1,123,659	1,129,538	0.5
U.S.	166,661,000	167,746,000	0.7	160,754,000	161,294,000	0.3

Note: Data is not seasonally adjusted and covers workers 16 years of age and older; (1) Figures cover the Nashville-Davidson—Murfreesboro—Franklin, TN Metropolitan Statistical Area
Source: Bureau of Labor Statistics, Local Area Unemployment Statistics

Unemployment Rate

Area	2024											
	Jan.	Feb.	Mar.	Apr.	May	Jun.	Jul.	Aug.	Sep.	Oct.	Nov.	Dec.
City	2.6	2.5	2.6	2.4	2.5	3.1	3.2	3.1	2.9	3.0	3.1	3.0
MSA[1]	2.6	2.5	2.5	2.3	2.4	3.1	3.2	3.1	2.9	3.0	3.0	2.9
U.S.	4.1	4.2	3.9	3.5	3.7	4.3	4.5	4.4	3.9	3.9	4.0	3.8

Note: Data is not seasonally adjusted and covers workers 16 years of age and older; (1) Figures cover the Nashville-Davidson—Murfreesboro—Franklin, TN Metropolitan Statistical Area
Source: Bureau of Labor Statistics, Local Area Unemployment Statistics

Average Wages

Occupation	$/Hr.	Occupation	$/Hr.
Accountants and Auditors	41.77	Maintenance and Repair Workers	24.27
Automotive Mechanics	26.05	Marketing Managers	70.23
Bookkeepers	24.43	Network and Computer Systems Admin.	54.49
Carpenters	25.67	Nurses, Licensed Practical	28.30
Cashiers	14.57	Nurses, Registered	42.71
Computer Programmers	n/a	Nursing Assistants	19.32
Computer Systems Analysts	42.96	Office Clerks, General	20.60
Computer User Support Specialists	29.95	Physical Therapists	47.86
Construction Laborers	22.45	Physicians	134.22
Cooks, Restaurant	18.35	Plumbers, Pipefitters and Steamfitters	29.46
Customer Service Representatives	21.72	Police and Sheriff's Patrol Officers	30.96
Dentists	97.05	Postal Service Mail Carriers	29.67
Electricians	29.83	Real Estate Sales Agents	24.17
Engineers, Electrical	55.61	Retail Salespersons	17.69
Fast Food and Counter Workers	14.12	Sales Representatives, Technical/Scientific	49.18
Financial Managers	79.15	Secretaries, Exc. Legal/Medical/Executive	22.79
First-Line Supervisors of Office Workers	35.70	Security Guards	20.23
General and Operations Managers	66.64	Surgeons	n/a
Hairdressers/Cosmetologists	20.68	Teacher Assistants, Exc. Postsecondary[1]	14.83
Home Health and Personal Care Aides	16.69	Teachers, Secondary School, Exc. Sp. Ed.[1]	29.56
Janitors and Cleaners	17.04	Telemarketers	15.16
Landscaping/Groundskeeping Workers	19.47	Truck Drivers, Heavy/Tractor-Trailer	28.95
Lawyers	80.00	Truck Drivers, Light/Delivery Services	23.69
Maids and Housekeeping Cleaners	15.97	Waiters and Waitresses	15.99

Note: Wage data covers the Nashville-Davidson—Murfreesboro—Franklin, TN Metropolitan Statistical Area;
(1) Hourly wages were calculated from annual wage data based on a 40 hour work week
Source: Bureau of Labor Statistics, Metro Area Occupational Employment & Wage Estimates, May 2024

Employment by Industry

Sector	MSA[1] Number of Employees	MSA[1] Percent of Total	U.S. Percent of Total
Construction, Mining, and Logging	66,200	5.5	5.5
Financial Activities	81,400	6.8	5.8
Government	135,000	11.2	14.9
Information	32,200	2.7	1.9
Leisure and Hospitality	134,700	11.2	10.4
Manufacturing	88,900	7.4	8.0
Other Services	50,300	4.2	3.7
Private Education and Health Services	181,600	15.1	16.9
Professional and Business Services	193,400	16.1	14.2
Retail Trade	109,900	9.2	10.0
Transportation, Warehousing, and Utilities	76,600	6.4	4.8
Wholesale Trade	50,600	4.2	3.9

Note: Figures are non-farm employment as of December 2024. Figures are not seasonally adjusted and include workers 16 years of age and older; (1) Figures cover the Nashville-Davidson—Murfreesboro—Franklin, TN Metropolitan Statistical Area
Source: Bureau of Labor Statistics, Current Employment Statistics, Employment, Hours, and Earnings

Employment by Occupation

Occupation Classification	City (%)	MSA[1] (%)	U.S. (%)
Management, Business, Science, and Arts	48.6	44.6	42.0
Natural Resources, Construction, and Maintenance	6.7	7.7	8.6
Production, Transportation, and Material Moving	11.3	13.2	13.0
Sales and Office	19.1	20.7	19.9
Service	14.1	13.8	16.5

Note: Figures cover employed civilians 16 years of age and older; (1) Figures cover the Nashville-Davidson—Murfreesboro—Franklin, TN Metropolitan Statistical Area
Source: U.S. Census Bureau, 2019-2023 American Community Survey 5-Year Estimates

Occupations with Greatest Projected Employment Growth: 2022 – 2032

Occupation[1]	2022 Employment	2032 Projected Employment	Numeric Employment Change	Percent Employment Change
Laborers and Freight, Stock, and Material Movers, Hand	112,810	131,040	18,230	16.2
Home Health and Personal Care Aides	32,820	46,870	14,050	42.8
General and Operations Managers	66,510	78,660	12,150	18.3
Fast Food and Counter Workers	73,880	86,020	12,140	16.4
Cooks, Restaurant	28,080	38,240	10,160	36.2
Miscellaneous Assemblers and Fabricators	54,300	64,000	9,700	17.9
Construction Laborers	32,750	41,080	8,330	25.4
Nurse Practitioners	13,620	21,500	7,880	57.9
Registered Nurses	60,020	67,720	7,700	12.8
Software Developers	16,540	23,650	7,110	43.0

Note: Projections cover Tennessee; (1) Sorted by numeric employment change
Source: www.projectionscentral.org, State Occupational Projections, 2022–2032 Long-Term Projections

Fastest-Growing Occupations: 2022 – 2032

Occupation[1]	2022 Employment	2032 Projected Employment	Numeric Employment Change	Percent Employment Change
Recreational Vehicle Service Technicians	410	660	250	61.0
Data Scientists	1,840	2,930	1,090	59.2
Nurse Practitioners	13,620	21,500	7,880	57.9
Home Appliance Repairers	650	980	330	50.8
Information Security Analysts (SOC 2018)	2,580	3,850	1,270	49.2
Dancers	170	250	80	47.1
Motor Vehicle Operators, All Other	2,560	3,750	1,190	46.5
Statisticians	940	1,360	420	44.7
Epidemiologists	230	330	100	43.5
Actuaries	370	530	160	43.2

Note: Projections cover Tennessee; (1) Sorted by percent employment change and excludes occupations with numeric employment change less than 50
Source: www.projectionscentral.org, State Occupational Projections, 2022–2032 Long-Term Projections

CITY FINANCES

City Government Finances

Component	2022 ($000)	2022 ($ per capita)
Total Revenues	5,942,736	8,561
Total Expenditures	5,471,526	7,882
Debt Outstanding	10,075,751	14,515

Source: U.S. Census Bureau, State & Local Government Finances 2022

City Government Revenue by Source

Source	2022 ($000)	2022 ($ per capita)	2022 (%)
General Revenue			
From Federal Government	149,908	216	2.5
From State Government	685,689	988	11.5
From Local Governments	2,431	4	0.0
Taxes			
Property	1,566,384	2,256	26.4
Sales and Gross Receipts	888,067	1,279	14.9
Personal Income	0	0	0.0
Corporate Income	0	0	0.0
Motor Vehicle License	35,662	51	0.6
Other Taxes	47,919	69	0.8
Current Charges	432,283	623	7.3
Liquor Store	0	0	0.0
Utility	1,538,304	2,216	25.9

Source: U.S. Census Bureau, State & Local Government Finances 2022

City Government Expenditures by Function

Function	2022 ($000)	2022 ($ per capita)	2022 (%)
General Direct Expenditures			
Air Transportation	0	0	0.0
Corrections	91,606	132	1.7
Education	1,345,981	1,939	24.6
Employment Security Administration	0	0	0.0
Financial Administration	34,643	49	0.6
Fire Protection	162,314	233	3.0
General Public Buildings	883	1	0.0
Governmental Administration, Other	114,374	164	2.1
Health	97,956	141	1.8
Highways	124,418	179	2.3
Hospitals	126,868	182	2.3
Housing and Community Development	137,302	197	2.5
Interest on General Debt	175,793	253	3.2
Judicial and Legal	101,472	146	1.9
Libraries	39,385	56	0.7
Parking	3,316	4	0.1
Parks and Recreation	260,553	375	4.8
Police Protection	273,023	393	5.0
Public Welfare	108,969	157	2.0
Sewerage	220,581	317	4.0
Solid Waste Management	13,244	19	0.2
Veterans' Services	0	0	0.0
Liquor Store	0	0	0.0
Utility	1,646,907	2,372	30.1

Source: U.S. Census Bureau, State & Local Government Finances 2022

TAXES

State Corporate Income Tax Rates

State	Tax Rate (%)	Income Brackets ($)	Num. of Brackets	Financial Institution Tax Rate (%)[a]	Federal Income Tax Ded.
Tennessee	6.5	Flat rate	1	6.5	No

Note: Tax rates for tax year 2024; (a) Rates listed are the corporate income tax rate applied to financial institutions or excise taxes based on income. Some states have other taxes based upon the value of deposits or shares.
Source: Federation of Tax Administrators, State Corporate Income Tax Rates, January 1, 2025

State Individual Income Tax Rates

State	Tax Rate (%)	Income Brackets ($)	Personal Exemptions ($)			Standard Ded. ($)	
			Single	Married	Depend.	Single	Married
Tennessee			– No state income tax –				

Note: Tax rates for tax year 2024; Local- and county-level taxes are not included
Source: Federation of Tax Administrators, State Individual Income Tax Rates, January 1, 2025

Various State Sales and Excise Tax Rates

State	State Sales Tax (%)	Gasoline[1] ($/gal.)	Cigarette[2] ($/pack)	Spirits[3] ($/gal.)	Wine[4] ($/gal.)	Beer[5] ($/gal.)	Recreational Marijuana (%)
Tennessee	7	0.27	0.62	4.46	1.27	1.29	Not legal

Note: All tax rates as of January 1, 2025; (1) The American Petroleum Institute has developed a methodology for determining the average tax rate on a gallon of fuel. Rates may include any of the following: excise taxes, environmental fees, storage tank fees, other fees or taxes, general sales tax, and local taxes; (2) The federal excise tax of $1.0066 per pack and local taxes are not included; (3) Rates are those applicable to off-premise sales of 40% alcohol by volume (a.b.v.) distilled spirits in 750ml containers. Local excise taxes are excluded; (4) Rates are those applicable to off-premise sales of 11% a.b.v. non-carbonated wine in 750ml containers; (5) Rates are those applicable to off-premise sales of 4.7% a.b.v. beer in 12 ounce containers.
Source: Tax Foundation, 2025 Facts & Figures: How Does Your State Compare?

State Tax Competitiveness Index

State	Overall Rank	Corporate Tax Rank	Individual Income Tax Rank	Sales Tax Rank	Property Tax Rank	Unemployment Insurance Tax Rank
Tennessee	8	48	1	47	33	17

Note: The Tax Foundation's State Tax Competitiveness Index enables policymakers, taxpayers, and business leaders to gauge how their states' tax systems compare. A rank of 1 is best, 50 is worst. Rankings do not average to the total. States without a tax rank equally as 1. DC's scores and rankings do not affect other states. The report shows tax systems as of July 1, 2024 (the beginning of Fiscal Year 2025).
Source: Tax Foundation, State Tax Competitiveness Index 2025

TRANSPORTATION

Means of Transportation to Work

Area	Car/Truck/Van		Public Transportation			Bicycle	Walked	Other Means	Worked at Home
	Drove Alone	Car-pooled	Bus	Subway	Railroad				
City	68.1	8.3	1.6	0.0	0.0	0.3	1.9	1.5	18.3
MSA[1]	72.4	8.2	0.7	0.0	0.0	0.1	1.1	1.2	16.3
U.S.	70.2	8.5	1.7	1.3	0.4	0.4	2.4	1.6	13.5

Note: Figures are percentages and cover workers 16 years of age and older; (1) Figures cover the Nashville-Davidson—Murfreesboro—Franklin, TN Metropolitan Statistical Area
Source: U.S. Census Bureau, 2019-2023 American Community Survey 5-Year Estimates

Travel Time to Work

Area	Less Than 10 Minutes	10 to 19 Minutes	20 to 29 Minutes	30 to 44 Minutes	45 to 59 Minutes	60 to 89 Minutes	90 Minutes or More
City	9.2	28.7	26.8	23.2	7.0	3.8	1.3
MSA[1]	9.6	26.0	21.1	24.2	10.7	6.6	1.8
U.S.	12.6	28.6	21.2	20.8	8.1	6.0	2.8

Note: Note: Figures are percentages and include workers 16 years old and over; (1) Figures cover the Nashville-Davidson—Murfreesboro—Franklin, TN Metropolitan Statistical Area
Source: U.S. Census Bureau, 2019-2023 American Community Survey 5-Year Estimates

Key Congestion Measures

Measure	2000	2010	2015	2020	2022
Annual Hours of Delay, Total (000)	25,497	39,786	49,865	25,770	61,536
Annual Hours of Delay, Per Auto Commuter	43	46	57	28	72
Annual Congestion Cost, Per Auto Commuter ($)	954	1,183	1,371	737	1,685

Note: Figures cover the Nashville-Davidson TN urban area
Source: Texas A&M Transportation Institute, 2023 Urban Mobility Report

Freeway Travel Time Index

Measure	1985	1990	1995	2000	2005	2010	2015	2020	2022
Urban Area Index[1]	1.10	1.12	1.15	1.19	1.22	1.20	1.22	1.06	1.23
Urban Area Rank[1,2]	27	35	36	34	32	36	34	75	24

Note: Freeway Travel Time Index—the ratio of travel time in the peak period to the travel time at free-flow conditions. For example, a value of 1.30 indicates a 20-minute free-flow trip takes 26 minutes in the peak (20 minutes x 1.30 = 26 minutes); (1) Covers the Nashville-Davidson TN urban area; (2) Rank is based on 101 larger urban areas (#1 = highest travel time index)
Source: Texas A&M Transportation Institute, 2023 Urban Mobility Report

Public Transportation

Agency Name / Mode of Transportation	Vehicles Operated in Maximum Service[1]	Annual Unlinked Passenger Trips[2] (in thous.)	Annual Passenger Miles[3] (in thous.)
Metropolitan Transit Authority (MTA)			
Bus (directly operated)	136	7,806.9	31,254.5
Demand Response (directly operated)	48	233.6	2,172.7
Demand Response - Taxi	69	122.3	1,474.3

Note: (1) Number of revenue vehicles operated by the given mode and type of service to meet the annual maximum service requirement. This is the revenue vehicle count during the peak season of the year; on the week and day that maximum service is provided. Vehicles operated in maximum service (VOMS) exclude atypical days and one-time special events; (2) Number of passengers who boarded public transportation vehicles. Passengers are counted each time they board a vehicle no matter how many vehicles they use to travel from their origin to their destination. (3) Sum of the distances ridden by all passengers during the entire fiscal year.
Source: Federal Transit Administration, National Transit Database, 2023

Air Transportation

Airport Name and Code / Type of Service	Passenger Airlines[1]	Passenger Enplanements	Freight Carriers[2]	Freight (lbs)
Nashville International (BNA)				
Domestic service (U.S. carriers only)	37	11,798,157	16	65,297,621
International service (U.S. carriers only)	7	27,638	0	0

Note: (1) Includes all U.S.-based major, minor and commuter airlines that carried at least one passenger during the year; (2) Includes all U.S.-based airlines and freight carriers that transported at least one pound of freight during the year.
Source: Bureau of Transportation Statistics, The Intermodal Transportation Database, Air Carriers: T-100 Domestic Market (U.S. carriers only), 2024; Bureau of Transportation Statistics, The Intermodal Transportation Database, Air Carriers: T-100 International Market (U.S. carriers only), 2024

BUSINESSES

Major Business Headquarters

Company Name	Industry	Rankings Fortune[1]	Rankings Forbes[2]
HCA Healthcare	Health care: medical facilities	61	-
Ingram Industries	Multicompany	-	223

Note: (1) Companies that produce a 10-K are ranked 1 to 500 based on 2023 revenue; (2) All private companies with at least $2 billion in annual revenue through the end of their most current fiscal year are ranked 1 to 275; companies listed are headquartered in the city; dashes indicate no ranking
Source: Fortune, "Fortune 500," 2024; Forbes, "America's Largest Private Companies," 2024

Fastest-Growing Businesses

According to *Inc.*, Nashville is home to one of America's 500 fastest-growing private companies: **Daily Crunch** (#270). Criteria: must be an independent, privately-held, for-profit, U.S. corporation, proprietorship or partnership as of December 31, 2023; revenues must be at least $100,000 in 2020 and $2 million in 2023; must have four-year operating/sales history. *Inc., "America's 500 Fastest-Growing Private Companies," 2024*

According to Deloitte, Nashville is home to one of North America's 500 fastest-growing high-technology companies: **XOi** (#464). Companies are ranked by percentage growth in revenue over a four-year period. Criteria for inclusion: company must be headquartered within North America; must own proprietary intellectual property or technology that is sold to customers in products that contributes to a significant portion of the company's operating revenue; must have been in business for a minumum of four years with 2020 operating revenues of at least $50,000 USD/CD and 2023 operating revenues of at least $5 million USD/CD. *Deloitte, 2024 Technology Fast 500™*

Living Environment

COST OF LIVING

Cost of Living Index

Composite Index	Groceries	Housing	Utilities	Transportation	Health Care	Misc. Goods/Services
98.7	99.5	101.4	98.2	90.8	95.5	98.7

Note: The Cost of Living Index measures regional differences in the cost of consumer goods and services, excluding taxes and non-consumer expenditures, for professional and managerial households in the top income quintile. It is based on more than 50,000 prices covering almost 60 different items for which prices are collected three times a year by chambers of commerce, economic development organizations or university applied economic centers in each participating urban area. The numbers shown should be read as a percentage above or below the national average of 100. For example, a value of 115.4 in the groceries column indicates that grocery prices are 15.4% higher than the national average. Small differences in the index numbers should not be interpreted as significant; Figures cover the Nashville-Murfreesboro TN urban area.
Source: The Council for Community and Economic Research, Cost of Living Index, 2024

Grocery Prices

Area[1]	T-Bone Steak ($/pound)	Frying Chicken ($/pound)	Whole Milk ($/half gal.)	Eggs ($/dozen)	Orange Juice ($/64 oz.)	Coffee ($/11.5 oz.)
City[2]	15.51	1.43	4.63	3.32	4.40	5.35
Avg.	15.42	1.55	4.69	3.25	4.41	5.46
Min.	14.50	1.16	4.43	2.75	4.00	4.85
Max.	17.56	2.89	5.49	4.78	5.54	7.89

Note: (1) Values for the local area are compared with the average, minimum and maximum values for all 276 areas in the Cost of Living Index; (2) Figures cover the Nashville-Murfreesboro TN urban area; **T-Bone Steak** (price per pound); **Frying Chicken** (price per pound, whole fryer); **Whole Milk** (half gallon carton); **Eggs** (price per dozen, Grade A, large); **Orange Juice** (64 oz. Tropicana or Florida Natural); **Coffee** (11.5 oz. can, vacuum-packed, Maxwell House, Hills Bros, or Folgers).
Source: The Council for Community and Economic Research, Cost of Living Index, 2024

Housing and Utility Costs

Area[1]	New Home Price ($)	Apartment Rent ($/month)	All Electric ($/month)	Part Electric ($/month)	Other Energy ($/month)	Telephone ($/month)
City[2]	519,432	1,670	-	105.42	77.00	223.33
Avg.	515,975	1,550	210.99	123.07	82.07	194.99
Min.	265,375	692	104.33	53.68	36.26	179.42
Max.	2,775,821	5,719	529.02	397.28	361.63	223.33

Note: (1) Values for the local area are compared with the average, minimum and maximum values for all 276 areas in the Cost of Living Index; (2) Figures cover the Nashville-Murfreesboro TN urban area; **New Home Price** (2,400 sf living area, 8,000 sf lot, in urban area with full utilities); **Apartment Rent** (950 sf 2 bedroom/1.5 or 2 bath, unfurnished, excluding all utilities except water); **All Electric** (average monthly cost for an all-electric home); **Part Electric** (average monthly cost for a part-electric home); **Other Energy** (average monthly cost for natural gas, fuel oil, coal, wood, and any other forms of energy except electricity); **Telephone** (price includes the base monthly rate plus taxes and fees for three lines of mobile phone service).
Source: The Council for Community and Economic Research, Cost of Living Index, 2024

Health Care, Transportation, and Other Costs

Area[1]	Doctor ($/visit)	Dentist ($/visit)	Optometrist ($/visit)	Gasoline ($/gallon)	Beauty Salon ($/visit)	Men's Shirt ($)
City[2]	122.71	110.37	114.45	3.08	48.65	32.66
Avg.	143.77	117.51	129.23	3.32	48.57	38.14
Min.	36.74	58.67	67.33	2.80	24.00	13.41
Max.	270.44	216.82	307.33	5.28	94.00	63.89

Note: (1) Values for the local area are compared with the average, minimum and maximum values for all 276 areas in the Cost of Living Index; (2) Figures cover the Nashville-Murfreesboro TN urban area; **Doctor** (general practitioners routine exam of an established patient); **Dentist** (adult teeth cleaning and periodic oral examination); **Optometrist** (full vision eye exam for established adult patient); **Gasoline** (one gallon regular unleaded, national brand, including all taxes, cash price at self-service pump if available); **Beauty Salon** (woman's shampoo, trim, and blow-dry); **Men's Shirt** (cotton/polyester dress shirt, pinpoint weave, long sleeves).
Source: The Council for Community and Economic Research, Cost of Living Index, 2024

HOUSING

Homeownership Rate

Area	2017 (%)	2018 (%)	2019 (%)	2020 (%)	2021 (%)	2022 (%)	2023 (%)	2024 (%)
MSA[1]	69.4	68.3	69.8	69.8	65.7	70.4	70.7	71.6
U.S.	63.9	64.4	64.6	66.6	65.5	65.8	65.9	65.6

Note: (1) Figures cover the Nashville-Davidson—Murfreesboro—Franklin, TN Metropolitan Statistical Area
Source: U.S. Census Bureau, Housing Vacancies and Homeownership Annual Statistics: 2017-2024

House Price Index (HPI)

Area	National Ranking[2]	Quarterly Change (%)	One-Year Change (%)	Five-Year Change (%)	Since 1991Q1 (%)
MSA[1]	164	-0.12	4.28	65.94	467.10
U.S.[3]	—	1.43	4.51	57.13	327.82

Note: The HPI is a weighted repeat sales index. It measures average price changes in repeat sales or refinancings on the same properties. This information is obtained by reviewing repeat mortgage transactions on single-family properties whose mortgages have been purchased or securitized by Fannie Mae or Freddie Mac since January 1975; (1) Figures cover the Nashville-Davidson—Murfreesboro—Franklin, TN Metropolitan Statistical Area; (2) Rankings are based on annual percentage change for all metro areas containing at least 15,000 transactions over the last 10 years and ranges from 1 to 241; (3) figures based on a weighted average of Census Division estimates using a seasonally adjusted, purchase-only index; all figures are for the period ending December 31, 2024
Source: Federal Housing Finance Agency, Change in FHFA Metropolitan Area House Price Indexes, All Transactions Index, 2024Q4

Home Value

Area	Under $100,000	$100,000 -$199,999	$200,000 -$299,999	$300,000 -$399,999	$400,000 -$499,999	$500,000 -$999,999	$1,000,000 or more	Median ($)
City	3.4	6.6	21.4	22.5	16.9	22.1	7.1	383,100
MSA[1]	4.8	8.7	20.9	20.4	15.0	23.6	6.7	376,800
U.S.	12.1	17.8	19.5	14.4	10.5	19.1	6.5	303,400

Note: Figures are percentages except for median and cover owner-occupied housing units; (1) Figures cover the Nashville-Davidson—Murfreesboro—Franklin, TN Metropolitan Statistical Area
Source: U.S. Census Bureau, 2019-2023 American Community Survey 5-Year Estimates

Year Housing Structure Built

Area	2020 or Later	2010 -2019	2000 -2009	1990 -1999	1980 -1989	1970 -1979	1960 -1969	1950 -1959	1940 -1949	Before 1940	Median Year
City	3.2	15.4	13.9	11.0	14.2	12.8	10.9	9.0	3.4	6.2	1985
MSA[1]	3.1	17.7	18.1	15.3	13.0	11.9	8.2	6.0	2.5	4.3	1993
U.S.	1.2	8.9	13.6	12.8	13.0	14.4	10.0	9.7	4.5	11.9	1980

Note: Figures are percentages except for Median Year; Note: (1) Figures cover the Nashville-Davidson—Murfreesboro—Franklin, TN Metropolitan Statistical Area
Source: U.S. Census Bureau, 2019-2023 American Community Survey 5-Year Estimates

Gross Monthly Rent

Area	Under $500	$500 -$999	$1,000 -$1,499	$1,500 -$1,999	$2,000 -$2,499	$2,500 -$2,999	$3,000 and up	Median ($)
City	6.2	10.7	34.1	28.4	12.8	4.5	3.3	1,486
MSA[1]	5.4	15.0	34.3	27.1	11.6	3.7	2.8	1,434
U.S.	6.5	22.3	29.5	20.2	10.8	4.8	5.9	1,348

Note: Figures are percentages except for median; Gross rent is the contract rent plus the estimated average monthly cost of utilities (electricity, gas, and water and sewer) and fuels (oil, coal, kerosene, wood, etc.) if these are paid by the renter (or paid for the renter by someone else); (1) Figures cover the Nashville-Davidson—Murfreesboro—Franklin, TN Metropolitan Statistical Area
Source: U.S. Census Bureau, 2019-2023 American Community Survey 5-Year Estimates

HEALTH

Health Risk Factors

Category	MSA[1] (%)	U.S. (%)
Adults aged 18–64 who have any kind of health care coverage	89.3	90.8
Adults who reported being in good or better health	81.0	81.8
Adults who have been told they have high blood cholesterol	37.3	36.9
Adults who have been told they have high blood pressure	34.1	34.0
Adults who are current smokers	11.9	12.1
Adults who currently use e-cigarettes	8.6	7.7
Adults who currently use chewing tobacco, snuff, or snus	5.4	3.2
Adults who are heavy drinkers[2]	6.4	6.1
Adults who are binge drinkers[3]	15.7	15.2
Adults who are overweight (BMI 25.0 - 29.9)	33.4	34.4
Adults who are obese (BMI 30.0 - 99.8)	33.3	34.3
Adults who participated in any physical activities in the past month	76.3	75.8

Note: All figures are crude prevalence; (1) Figures cover the Nashville-Davidson—Murfreesboro—Franklin, TN Metropolitan Statistical Area; (2) Heavy drinkers are classified as adult men having more than 14 drinks per week and adult women having more than 7 drinks per week; (3) Binge drinkers are classified as males having five or more drinks on one occasion or females having four or more drinks on one occasion
Source: Centers for Disease Control and Prevention, Behavioral Risk Factor Surveillance System, SMART: Selected Metropolitan Area Risk Trends, 2023

Acute and Chronic Health Conditions

Category	MSA[1] (%)	U.S. (%)
Adults who have ever been told they had a heart attack	4.1	4.2
Adults who have ever been told they have angina or coronary heart disease	3.1	4.0
Adults who have ever been told they had a stroke	4.5	3.3
Adults who have ever been told they have asthma	17.9	15.7
Adults who have ever been told they have arthritis	30.4	26.3
Adults who have ever been told they have diabetes[2]	10.6	11.5
Adults who have ever been told they had skin cancer	4.8	5.6
Adults who have ever been told they had any other types of cancer	7.3	8.4
Adults who have ever been told they have COPD	7.5	6.4
Adults who have ever been told they have kidney disease	4.0	3.7
Adults who have ever been told they have a form of depression	24.5	22.0

Note: All figures are crude prevalence; (1) Figures cover the Nashville-Davidson—Murfreesboro—Franklin, TN Metropolitan Statistical Area; (2) Figures do not include pregnancy-related, borderline, or pre-diabetes
Source: Centers for Disease Control and Prevention, Behavioral Risk Factor Surveillance System, SMART: Selected Metropolitan Area Risk Trends, 2023

Health Screening and Vaccination Rates

Category	MSA[1] (%)	U.S. (%)
Adults who have ever been tested for HIV	37.0	37.5
Adults who have had their blood cholesterol checked within the last five years	90.0	87.0
Adults aged 65+ who have had flu shot within the past year	64.1	63.4
Adults aged 65+ who have ever had a pneumonia vaccination	69.9	71.9

Note: All figures are crude prevalence; (1) Figures cover the Nashville-Davidson—Murfreesboro—Franklin, TN Metropolitan Statistical Area.
Source: Centers for Disease Control and Prevention, Behavioral Risk Factor Surveillance System, SMART: Selected Metropolitan Area Risk Trends, 2023

Disability Status

Category	MSA[1] (%)	U.S. (%)
Adults who reported being deaf	8.7	7.4
Are you blind or have serious difficulty seeing, even when wearing glasses?	8.0	4.9
Do you have difficulty doing errands alone?	9.0	7.8
Do you have difficulty dressing or bathing?	n/a	3.6
Do you have serious difficulty concentrating/remembering/making decisions?	16.8	13.7
Do you have serious difficulty walking or climbing stairs?	13.9	13.2

Note: All figures are crude prevalence; (1) Figures cover the Nashville-Davidson—Murfreesboro—Franklin, TN Metropolitan Statistical Area.
Source: Centers for Disease Control and Prevention, Behavioral Risk Factor Surveillance System, SMART: Selected Metropolitan Area Risk Trends, 2023

Mortality Rates for the Top 10 Causes of Death in the U.S.

ICD-10[a] Sub-Chapter	ICD-10[a] Code	Crude Mortality Rate[2] per 100,000 population	
		County[3]	U.S.
Malignant neoplasms	C00-C97	145.9	182.7
Ischaemic heart diseases	I20-I25	86.1	109.6
Provisional assignment of new diseases of uncertain etiology[1]	U00-U49	51.5	65.3
Other forms of heart disease	I30-I51	45.7	65.1
Other degenerative diseases of the nervous system	G30-G31	44.3	52.4
Other external causes of accidental injury	W00-X59	99.5	52.3
Cerebrovascular diseases	I60-I69	44.5	49.1
Chronic lower respiratory diseases	J40-J47	35.3	43.5
Hypertensive diseases	I10-I15	46.6	38.9
Organic, including symptomatic, mental disorders	F01-F09	26.8	33.9

Note: (a) ICD-10 = International Classification of Diseases 10th Revision; (1) Includes COVID-19, adverse effects to COVID-19 vaccines, SARS, and vaping-related disorders; (2) Crude mortality rates are a three-year average covering 2021-2023; (3) Figures cover Davidson County.
Source: Centers for Disease Control and Prevention, National Center for Health Statistics. National Vital Statistics System, Mortality 2018-2023 on CDC WONDER Online Database

Mortality Rates for Selected Causes of Death

Cause of Death	ICD-10[a] Code	Crude Mortality Rate[1] per 100,000 population	
		County[2]	U.S.
Accidental poisoning and exposure to noxious substances	X40-X49	74.0	30.5
Alzheimer disease	G30	28.3	35.4
Assault	X85-Y09	14.5	7.3
COVID-19	U07.1	51.5	65.3
Diabetes mellitus	E10-E14	28.8	30.0
Diseases of the liver	K70-K76	15.3	20.8
Human immunodeficiency virus (HIV) disease	B20-B24	1.9	1.5
Influenza and pneumonia	J09-J18	9.5	13.4
Intentional self-harm	X60-X84	14.3	14.7
Malnutrition	E40-E46	2.0	6.0
Obesity and other hyperalimentation	E65-E68	3.6	3.1
Renal failure	N17-N19	11.3	16.4
Transport accidents	V01-V99	16.6	14.4

Note: (a) ICD-10 = International Classification of Diseases 10th Revision; (1) Crude mortality rates are a three-year average covering 2021-2023; (2) Figures cover Davidson County; Data are suppressed when the data meet the criteria for confidentiality constraints; Crude mortality rates are flagged as unreliable when the rate would be calculated with a numerator of 20 or less.
Source: Centers for Disease Control and Prevention, National Center for Health Statistics. National Vital Statistics System, Mortality 2018-2023 on CDC WONDER Online Database

Health Insurance Coverage

Area	With Health Insurance	With Private Health Insurance	With Public Health Insurance	Without Health Insurance	Population Under Age 19 Without Health Insurance
City	87.4	69.0	29.0	12.6	9.0
MSA[1]	90.6	72.8	28.6	9.4	5.8
U.S.	91.4	67.3	36.3	8.6	5.4

Note: Figures are percentages that cover the civilian noninstitutionalized population; (1) Figures cover the Nashville-Davidson—Murfreesboro—Franklin, TN Metropolitan Statistical Area
Source: U.S. Census Bureau, 2019-2023 American Community Survey 5-Year Estimates

Number of Medical Professionals

Area	MDs[3]	DOs[3,4]	Dentists	Podiatrists	Chiropractors	Optometrists
County[1] (number)	4,949	136	605	38	212	127
County[1] (rate[2])	698.9	19.2	84.9	5.3	29.8	17.8
U.S. (rate[2])	302.5	29.2	74.6	6.4	29.5	18.0

Note: Data as of 2023 unless noted; (1) Data covers Davidson County; (2) Number of medical professionals per 100,000 population; (3) Data as of 2022 and includes all active, non-federal physicians; (4) Doctor of Osteopathic Medicine
Source: U.S. Department of Health and Human Services, Health Resources and Services Administration, Bureau of Health Professions, Area Resource File (ARF) 2023-2024

Best Hospitals

According to *U.S. News*, the Nashville-Davidson—Murfreesboro—Franklin, TN metro area is home to one of the best hospitals in the U.S.: **Vanderbilt University Medical Center** (7 adult specialties and 10 pediatric specialties). The hospital listed was nationally ranked in at least one of 15 adult or 11 pediatric specialties. The number of specialties shown cover the parent hospital. Only 160 U.S. hospitals performed well enough to be nationally ranked in one or more specialties. Twenty hospitals in the U.S. made the Honor Roll. The Best Hospitals Honor Roll takes both the national rankings and the procedure and condition ratings into account. Hospitals received points if they were nationally ranked in one of the 15 adult specialties—the higher they ranked, the more points they got—and how many ratings of "high performing" they earned in the 20 procedures and conditions. *U.S. News Online,* "America's Best Hospitals 2024-25"

According to *U.S. News*, the Nashville-Davidson—Murfreesboro—Franklin, TN metro area is home to one of the best children's hospitals in the U.S.: **Monroe Carell Jr. Children's Hospital at Vanderbilt** (10 pediatric specialties). The hospital listed was highly ranked in at least one of 11 pediatric specialties. One hundred five children's hospitals in the U.S. were nationally ranked in at least one specialty. Hospitals received points for being ranked in a specialty, and the 10 hospitals with the most points across the 11 specialties make up the Honor Roll. *U.S. News Online, "America's Best Children's Hospitals 2024-25"*

EDUCATION

Public School District Statistics

District Name	Schls	Pupils	Pupil/ Teacher Ratio	Minority Pupils[1] (%)	Total Rev. per Pupil ($)	Total Exp. per Pupil ($)
Achievement School District	13	4,501	21.3	98.8	n/a	n/a
Davidson County	162	80,468	16.4	76.0	21,610	17,219
Tennessee Public Charter School Comm.	13	4,975	18.1	85.7	25,654	13,599

Note: Table includes school districts with 2,000 or more students; (1) Percentage of students that are not non-Hispanic white.
Source: U.S. Department of Education, National Center for Education Statistics, Common Core of Data, Local Education Agency (School District) Universe Survey: School Year 2023-2024; U.S. Department of Education, National Center for Education Statistics, Common Core of Data, School District Finance Survey (F-33): School Year 2021–22

Best High Schools

According to *U.S. News*, Nashville is home to three of the top 500 high schools in the U.S.: **Hume Fogg Magnet High School** (#48); **Martin Luther King Jr. Magnet School** (#154); **Valor Flagship Academy** (#385). Nearly 25,000 public, magnet and charter schools were ranked based on their performance on state assessments and how well they prepare students for college. *U.S. News & World Report, "Best High Schools 2024"*

Highest Level of Education

Area	Less than H.S.	H.S. Diploma	Some College, No Deg.	Associate Degree	Bachelor's Degree	Master's Degree	Prof. School Degree	Doctorate Degree
City	9.8	20.2	17.0	6.0	29.1	11.7	3.4	2.7
MSA[1]	8.5	25.7	18.7	7.3	25.6	10.0	2.4	1.9
U.S.	10.6	26.2	19.4	8.8	21.3	9.8	2.3	1.6

Note: Figures cover persons age 25 and over; (1) Figures cover the Nashville-Davidson—Murfreesboro—Franklin, TN Metropolitan Statistical Area
Source: U.S. Census Bureau, 2019-2023 American Community Survey 5-Year Estimates

Educational Attainment by Race

Area	High School Graduate or Higher (%)					Bachelor's Degree or Higher (%)				
	Total	White	Black	Asian	Hisp.[2]	Total	White	Black	Asian	Hisp.[2]
City	90.2	93.9	89.5	83.4	61.8	46.9	56.0	29.8	55.1	20.5
MSA[1]	91.5	93.4	90.4	85.7	68.4	39.9	42.0	30.5	56.8	22.2
U.S.	89.4	92.9	88.1	88.0	72.5	35.0	37.7	24.7	57.0	19.9

Note: Figures shown cover persons 25 years old and over; (1) Figures cover the Nashville-Davidson—Murfreesboro—Franklin, TN Metropolitan Statistical Area; (2) People of Hispanic origin can be of any race
Source: U.S. Census Bureau, 2019-2023 American Community Survey 5-Year Estimates

School Enrollment by Grade and Control

Area	Preschool (%)		Kindergarten (%)		Grades 1 - 4 (%)		Grades 5 - 8 (%)		Grades 9 - 12 (%)	
	Public	Private	Public	Private	Public	Private	Public	Private	Public	Private
City	51.0	49.0	82.7	17.3	82.9	17.1	78.2	21.8	81.2	18.8
MSA[1]	50.1	49.9	82.5	17.5	84.8	15.2	83.3	16.7	83.0	17.0
U.S.	58.7	41.3	85.2	14.8	87.2	12.8	87.9	12.1	89.0	11.0

Note: Figures shown cover persons 3 years old and over; (1) Figures cover the Nashville-Davidson—Murfreesboro—Franklin, TN Metropolitan Statistical Area
Source: U.S. Census Bureau, 2019-2023 American Community Survey 5-Year Estimates

Higher Education

Four-Year Colleges			Two-Year Colleges			Medical Schools[1]	Law Schools[2]	Voc/ Tech[3]
Public	Private Non-profit	Private For-profit	Public	Private Non-profit	Private For-profit			
2	12	3	7	2	4	3	3	11

Note: Figures cover institutions located within the Nashville-Davidson—Murfreesboro—Franklin, TN Metropolitan Statistical Area and include main campuses only; (1) includes schools accredited by the Liaison Committee on Medical Education and the American Osteopathic Association's Commission on Osteopathic College Accreditation; (2) includes ABA-accredited schools, schools with provisional ABA accreditation, and state accredited schools; (3) includes all schools with programs that are less than 2 years.
Source: National Center for Education Statistics, Integrated Postsecondary Education System (IPEDS), 2023-24; Wikipedia, List of Medical Schools in the United States, accessed May 2, 2025; Wikipedia, List of Law Schools in the United States, accessed May 2, 2025

According to *U.S. News & World Report*, the Nashville-Davidson—Murfreesboro—Franklin, TN metro area is home to one of the top 200 national universities in the U.S.: **Vanderbilt University** (#18 tie). The indicators used to capture academic quality fall into a number of categories: assessment by administrators at peer institutions; retention of students; faculty resources; student selectivity; financial resources; alumni giving; high school counselor ratings of colleges; and graduation rate. *U.S. News & World Report, "America's Best Colleges 2025"*

According to *U.S. News & World Report*, the Nashville-Davidson—Murfreesboro—Franklin, TN metro area is home to two of the top 100 law schools in the U.S.: **Vanderbilt University** (#14 tie); **Belmont University** (#84 tie). The rankings are based on a weighted average of 12 measures of quality: peer assessment score; assessment score by lawyers/judges; median LSAT scores; median undergrad GPA; acceptance rate; employment rates for graduates; placement success; bar passage rate; faculty resources; expenditures per student; student/faculty ratio; and library resources. *U.S. News & World Report, "America's Best Graduate Schools, Law, 2025"*

According to *U.S. News & World Report*, the Nashville-Davidson—Murfreesboro—Franklin, TN metro area is home to one of the top medical schools for research in the U.S.: **Vanderbilt University** (Tier 1). *U.S. News* placed medical and osteopathic schools into tiers based on their research productivity, faculty and admissions data. Each school's tier was derived from its overall score, calculated by summing the weighted normalized values generated across several factors of academic quality, outlined below. There are four tiers, with tier 1 medical schools as the highest-performing and tier 4 as the lowest-performing. Only tier 1 and 2 schools are shown. Because of the tier presentation, *U.S. News* calculated overall scores based on their percentile performance among all rated schools instead of dividing against the rescaled score of the No. 1-performing schools. Tier 1 included schools with overall scores of 85 to 99. The cutoffs for tiers 2 through 4 were schools scoring 50 to 84, 15 to 49 and 1 to 14, respectively. The rankings are based on a weighted average of the following measures of quality: total research activity; average research activity per faculty member; total NIH research grants at the medical school and its affiliated hospitals; average NIH research grants per faculty; median MCAT total score; median undergraduate GPA; acceptance rate; and faculty resources. *U.S. News & World Report, "America's Best Graduate Schools, Medical, 2025"*

According to *U.S. News & World Report*, the Nashville-Davidson—Murfreesboro—Franklin, TN metro area is home to one of the top 75 business schools in the U.S.: **Vanderbilt University (Owen)** (#18 tie). The rankings are based on a weighted average of the following nine measures: quality assessment; peer assessment; recruiter assessment; placement success; mean starting salary and bonus; student selectivity; mean GMAT and GRE scores; mean undergraduate GPA; and acceptance rate. *U.S. News & World Report, "America's Best Graduate Schools, Business, 2025"*

EMPLOYERS

Major Employers

Company Name	Industry
AHOM Holdings	Home health care services
Asurion Corporation	Business services nec
Baptist Hospital	General medical & surgical hospitals
Cannon County Knitting Mills	Apparel & outerwear broadwoven fabrics
County of Rutherford	County government
County of Sumner	County government
Gaylord Entertainment Company	Hotels & motels
Gaylord Opryland USA	Hotels & motels
Ingram Book Company	Books, periodicals, & newspapers
International Automotive	Automotive storage garage
LifeWay Christian Resources of the SBC	Religious organizations
Middle Tennessee State University	Colleges & universities
Newspaper Printing Corporation	Newspapers, publishing & printing
Nissan North America	Motor vehicles & car bodies
Primus Automotive Financial Services	Automobile loans including insurance
Psychiatric Solutions	Psychiatric clinic
State Industries	Hot water heaters, household
State of Tennessee	State government
Tennessee Department of Transportation	Regulation, administration of transportation
Vanderbilt Childrens Hospital	General medical & surgical hospitals

Note: Companies shown are located within the Nashville-Davidson—Murfreesboro—Franklin, TN Metropolitan Statistical Area.
Source: Chambers of Commerce; State Departments of Labor; Wikipedia

Best Companies to Work For

Pinnacle Financial Partners, headquartered in Nashville, is among "The 100 Best Companies to Work For." To pick the best companies, *Fortune* partnered with the Great Place to Work Institute. Using their proprietary Trust Index™ survey, the core of what creates great a workplace is measured—key behaviors that drive trust in management, connection with colleagues, and loyalty to the company. To be eligible for the *Fortune* 100 Best Companies to Work For list, employers must have 1,000 or more employees in the U.S. and cannot be a government agency. *Fortune, "The 100 Best Companies to Work For," 2025*

Pinnacle Financial Partners, headquartered in Nashville, is among "Fortune's Best Workplaces for Parents." To pick the best companies, *Fortune* partnered with the Great Place to Work Institute. To be considered for the list, companies must be Great Place To Work-Certified and have at least 50 responses from parents in the US. The survey enables employees to share confidential quantitative and qualitative feedback about their organization's culture by responding to 60 statements on a 5-point scale and answering two open-ended questions. Collectively, these statements describe a great employee experience, defined by high levels of trust, respect, credibility, fairness, pride, and camaraderie. In addition, companies provide organizational data like size, location, industry, demographics, roles, and levels; and provide information about parental leave, adoption, flexible schedule, childcare and dependent health care benefits. *Fortune, "Best Workplaces for Parents," 2024*

Pinnacle Financial Partners, headquartered in Nashville, is among "Fortune's Best Workplaces for Women." To pick the best companies, *Fortune* partnered with the Great Place to Work Institute. To be considered for the list, companies must be Great Place To Work-Certified. Companies must also employ at least 50 women, at least 20% of their non-executive managers must be female, and at least one executive must be female. To determine the Best Workplaces for Women, Great Place To Work measured the differences in women's survey responses to those of their peers and assesses the impact of demographics and roles on the quality and consistency of women's experiences. Great Place To Work also analyzed the gender balance of each workplace, how it compared to each company's industry, and patterns in representation as women rise from front-line positions to the board of directors. *Fortune, "Best Workplaces for Women," 2024*

PUBLIC SAFETY

Crime Rate

Area	Total Crime Rate	Violent Crime Rate				Property Crime Rate		
		Murder	Rape	Robbery	Aggrav. Assault	Burglary	Larceny-Theft	Motor Vehicle Theft
City	5,533.6	14.5	59.1	163.4	892.0	401.7	3,232.8	770.2
U.S.	2,290.9	5.7	38.0	66.5	264.1	250.7	1,347.2	318.7

Note: Figures are crimes per 100,000 population.
Source: FBI, Table 8, Offenses Known to Law Enforcement, by State by City, 2023

Hate Crimes

Area	Number of Quarters Reported	Number of Incidents per Bias Motivation					
		Race/Ethnicity/Ancestry	Religion	Sexual Orientation	Disability	Gender	Gender Identity
City	n/a	n/a	n/a	n/a	n/a	n/a	n/a
U.S.	4	5,900	2,699	2,077	187	92	492

Note: n/a not available.
Source: Federal Bureau of Investigation, Hate Crime Statistics 2023

Identity Theft Consumer Reports

Area	Reports	Reports per 100,000 Population	Rank[2]
MSA[1]	4,470	219	134
U.S.	1,135,291	339	-

Note: (1) Figures cover the Nashville-Davidson—Murfreesboro—Franklin, TN Metropolitan Statistical Area; (2) Rank ranges from 1 to 401 where 1 indicates greatest number of identity theft reports per 100,000 population
Source: Federal Trade Commission, Consumer Sentinel Network Data Book 2024

Fraud and Other Consumer Reports

Area	Reports	Reports per 100,000 Population	Rank[2]
MSA[1]	25,458	1,246	113
U.S.	5,360,641	1,601	-

Note: (1) Figures cover the Nashville-Davidson—Murfreesboro—Franklin, TN Metropolitan Statistical Area; (2) Rank ranges from 1 to 401 where 1 indicates greatest number of fraud and other consumer reports per 100,000 population
Source: Federal Trade Commission, Consumer Sentinel Network Data Book 2024

POLITICS

2024 Presidential Election Results

Area	Trump (Rep.)	Harris (Dem.)	Stein (Green)	Kennedy (Ind.)	Oliver (Lib.)	Other
Davidson County	35.0	62.2	0.6	0.9	0.0	1.2
U.S.	49.7	48.2	0.6	0.5	0.4	0.6

Note: Results are percentages and may not add to 100% due to rounding
Source: Dave Leip's Atlas of U.S. Presidential Elections

SPORTS

Professional Sports Teams

Team Name	League	Year Established
Nashville Predators	National Hockey League (NHL)	1998
Nashville SC	Major League Soccer (MLS)	1997
Tennessee Titans	National Football League (NFL)	1997

Note: Includes teams located in the Nashville-Davidson—Murfreesboro—Franklin, TN Metropolitan Statistical Area.
Source: Wikipedia, Major Professional Sports Teams of the United States and Canada, May 1, 2025

CLIMATE

Average and Extreme Temperatures

Temperature	Jan	Feb	Mar	Apr	May	Jun	Jul	Aug	Sep	Oct	Nov	Dec	Yr.
Extreme High (°F)	78	84	86	91	95	106	107	104	105	94	84	79	107
Average High (°F)	47	51	60	71	79	87	90	89	83	72	60	50	70
Average Temp. (°F)	38	41	50	60	68	76	80	79	72	61	49	41	60
Average Low (°F)	28	31	39	48	57	65	69	68	61	48	39	31	49
Extreme Low (°F)	-17	-13	2	23	34	42	54	49	36	26	-1	-10	-17

Note: Figures cover the years 1948-1990
Source: National Climatic Data Center, International Station Meteorological Climate Summary, 9/96

Average Precipitation/Snowfall/Humidity

Precip./Humidity	Jan	Feb	Mar	Apr	May	Jun	Jul	Aug	Sep	Oct	Nov	Dec	Yr.
Avg. Precip. (in.)	4.4	4.2	5.0	4.1	4.6	3.7	3.8	3.3	3.2	2.6	3.9	4.6	47.4
Avg. Snowfall (in.)	4	3	1	Tr	0	0	0	0	0	Tr	1	1	11
Avg. Rel. Hum. 6am (%)	81	81	80	81	86	86	88	90	90	87	83	82	85
Avg. Rel. Hum. 3pm (%)	61	57	51	48	52	52	54	53	52	49	55	59	54

Note: Figures cover the years 1948-1990; Tr = Trace amounts (<0.05 in. of rain; <0.5 in. of snow)
Source: National Climatic Data Center, International Station Meteorological Climate Summary, 9/96

Weather Conditions

Temperature			Daytime Sky			Precipitation		
10°F & below	32°F & below	90°F & above	Clear	Partly cloudy	Cloudy	0.01 inch or more precip.	0.1 inch or more snow/ice	Thunder-storms
5	76	51	98	135	132	119	8	54

Note: Figures are average number of days per year and cover the years 1948-1990
Source: National Climatic Data Center, International Station Meteorological Climate Summary, 9/96

HAZARDOUS WASTE

Superfund Sites

The Nashville-Davidson—Murfreesboro—Franklin, TN metro area is home to one site on the EPA's Superfund National Priorities List (NPL) or Superfund Alternative Approach (SAA) list: **Wrigley Charcoal Plant** (Final NPL). The Superfund alternative approach uses the same investigation and cleanup process and standards that are used for sites listed on the National Priorities List. The SAA is an alternative to listing a site on the NPL; it is not an alternative to Superfund or the Superfund process. There are a total of 1,445 Superfund sites with a status of proposed or final on both lists in the United States. *U.S. Environmental Protection Agency, National Priorities List, May 1, 2025; U.S. Environmental Protection Agency, Superfund Alternative Approach Sites, May 1, 2025*

AIR QUALITY

Air Quality Trends: Ozone

	1990	1995	2000	2005	2010	2015	2020	2021	2022	2023
MSA[1]	0.089	0.092	0.084	0.078	0.073	0.065	0.061	0.064	0.065	0.071
U.S.	0.087	0.089	0.081	0.080	0.072	0.068	0.066	0.067	0.067	0.070

Note: (1) Data covers the Nashville-Davidson—Murfreesboro—Franklin, TN Metropolitan Statistical Area. The values shown are the composite ozone concentration averages among trend sites based on the highest fourth daily maximum 8-hour concentration in parts per million. These trends are based on sites having an adequate record of monitoring data during the trend period. Data from exceptional events are included.
Source: U.S. Environmental Protection Agency, Air Quality Monitoring Information, "Air Quality Trends by City, 1990-2023"

Air Quality Index

Area	Percent of Days when Air Quality was...[2]					AQI Statistics[2]	
	Good	Moderate	Unhealthy for Sensitive Groups	Unhealthy	Very Unhealthy	Maximum	Median
MSA[1]	34.8	62.5	2.7	0.0	0.0	133	54

Note: (1) Data covers the Nashville-Davidson—Murfreesboro—Franklin, TN Metropolitan Statistical Area; (2) Based on 365 days with AQI data in 2023. Air Quality Index (AQI) is an index for reporting daily air quality. EPA calculates the AQI for five major air pollutants regulated by the Clean Air Act: ground-level ozone, particle pollution (aka particulate matter), carbon monoxide, sulfur dioxide, and nitrogen dioxide. The AQI runs from 0 to 500. The higher the AQI value, the greater the level of air pollution and the greater the health concern. There are six AQI categories: "Good" AQI is between 0 and 50. Air quality is considered satisfactory; "Moderate" AQI is between 51 and 100. Air quality is acceptable; "Unhealthy for Sensitive Groups" When AQI values are between 101 and 150, members of sensitive groups may experience health effects; "Unhealthy" When AQI values are between 151 and 200 everyone may begin to experience health effects; "Very Unhealthy" AQI values between 201 and 300 trigger a health alert; "Hazardous" AQI values over 300 trigger warnings of emergency conditions (not shown).
Source: U.S. Environmental Protection Agency, Air Quality Index Report, 2023

Air Quality Index Pollutants

Area	Percent of Days when AQI Pollutant was...[2]					
	Carbon Monoxide	Nitrogen Dioxide	Ozone	Sulfur Dioxide	Particulate Matter 2.5	Particulate Matter 10
MSA[1]	0.0	0.5	26.0	(3)	73.4	0.0

Note: (1) Data covers the Nashville-Davidson—Murfreesboro—Franklin, TN Metropolitan Statistical Area; (2) Based on 365 days with AQI data in 2023. The Air Quality Index (AQI) is an index for reporting daily air quality. EPA calculates the AQI for five major air pollutants regulated by the Clean Air Act: ground-level ozone, particle pollution (also known as particulate matter), carbon monoxide, sulfur dioxide, and nitrogen dioxide. The AQI runs from 0 to 500. The higher the AQI value, the greater the level of air pollution and the greater the health concern; (3) Sulfur dioxide is no longer included in this table because SO_2 concentrations tend to be very localized and not necessarily representative of broad geographical areas like counties and CBSAs.
Source: U.S. Environmental Protection Agency, Air Quality Index Report, 2023

Maximum Air Pollutant Concentrations: Particulate Matter, Ozone, CO and Lead

	Particulate Matter 10 (ug/m^3)	Particulate Matter 2.5 Wtd AM (ug/m^3)	Particulate Matter 2.5 24-Hr (ug/m^3)	Ozone (ppm)	Carbon Monoxide (ppm)	Lead (ug/m^3)
MSA[1] Level	57	10.2	25	0.076	2	n/a
NAAQS[2]	150	15	35	0.075	9	0.15
Met NAAQS[2]	Yes	Yes	Yes	No	Yes	n/a

Note: (1) Data covers the Nashville-Davidson—Murfreesboro—Franklin, TN Metropolitan Statistical Area; Data from exceptional events are included; (2) National Ambient Air Quality Standards; ppm = parts per million; ug/m^3 = micrograms per cubic meter; n/a not available.
Concentrations: Particulate Matter 10 (coarse particulate)—highest second maximum 24-hour concentration; Particulate Matter 2.5 Wtd AM (fine particulate)—highest weighted annual mean concentration; Particulate Matter 2.5 24-Hour (fine particulate)—highest 98th percentile 24-hour concentration; Ozone—highest fourth daily maximum 8-hour concentration; Carbon Monoxide—highest second maximum non-overlapping 8-hour concentration; Lead—maximum running 3-month average
Source: U.S. Environmental Protection Agency, Air Quality Monitoring Information, "Air Quality Statistics by City, 2023"

Maximum Air Pollutant Concentrations: Nitrogen Dioxide and Sulfur Dioxide

	Nitrogen Dioxide AM (ppb)	Nitrogen Dioxide 1-Hr (ppb)	Sulfur Dioxide AM (ppb)	Sulfur Dioxide 1-Hr (ppb)	Sulfur Dioxide 24-Hr (ppb)
MSA[1] Level	13	52	n/a	6	n/a
NAAQS[2]	53	100	30	75	140
Met NAAQS[2]	Yes	Yes	n/a	Yes	n/a

Note: (1) Data covers the Nashville-Davidson—Murfreesboro—Franklin, TN Metropolitan Statistical Area; Data from exceptional events are included; (2) National Ambient Air Quality Standards; ppm = parts per million; ug/m^3 = micrograms per cubic meter; n/a not available.
Concentrations: Nitrogen Dioxide AM—highest arithmetic mean concentration; Nitrogen Dioxide 1-Hr—highest 98th percentile 1-hour daily maximum concentration; Sulfur Dioxide AM—highest annual mean concentration; Sulfur Dioxide 1-Hr—highest 99th percentile 1-hour daily maximum concentration; Sulfur Dioxide 24-Hr—highest second maximum 24-hour concentration
Source: U.S. Environmental Protection Agency, Air Quality Monitoring Information, "Air Quality Statistics by City, 2023"

New Orleans, Louisiana

Background

New Orleans, a port city upriver from the mouth of the Mississippi River, is one of the country's most interesting cities. This birthplace of jazz is rich in unique local history, distinctive neighborhoods, and an unmistakably individual character.

New Orleans was founded on behalf of France by the brothers Le Moyne, Sieurs d'Iberville, and de Bienville, in 1718. Despite disease, starvation, and an unwilling working class, New Orleans emerged as a genteel antebellum slave society, fashioning itself after the rigid social hierarchy of Versailles. After New Orleans was ceded to Spain after the French & Indian War, this unequal lifestyle persisted.

The became a crown jewel in the 1803 Louisiana Purchase to the U.S. The transfer of control changed New Orleans's Old-World isolation. American settlers introduced aggressive business acumen to the area, as well as the idea of respect for the self-made man. As trade opened with countries around the world, this made for a happy union. New Orleans became "Queen City of the South," growing prosperous from adventurous riverboat traders and speculators, as well as the cotton trade. Today, New Orleans' diverse economy focuses on energy, advanced manufacturing, international trade, healthcare, and tourism.

Much of the city's Old-World charm remains, resulting from Southern, Creole, African American, and European cultures. New Orleans' cuisine, indigenous music, unique festivals, and sultry, pleasing atmosphere, drew nearly 18 million domestic visitors in 2023. The Ernest N. Morial Convention Center's numerous convention goers continuously fill more than 35,000 rooms. Another economic pillar is the Port of New Orleans, one of the nation's leading general cargo ports. In recent years, it has seen $400 million invested in new facilities.

In 2005, failure of federal levees following Hurricane Katrina put 80 percent of the city under floodwaters for weeks. The Crescent City's revival since then is a testament to her unique spirit, an influx of federal dollars, and an outpouring from volunteers ranging from church groups to spring breakers who returned year after year to help rebuild, giving rise to a new start-up spirit. State tax breaks have helped to turn New Orleans into "Hollywood South," where more the number of films and TV shows produced there increases every year. New Orleans has given birth to a mother lode of cultural phenomena: Dixieland jazz, musicians Louis Armstrong, Mahalia Jackson, Dr. John, and chefs Emeril Lagasse and John Besh. The city is aware of its "cultural economy," which employs nearly 14 percent of the local workforce. Popular tourist draws include the annual Mardi Gras celebration—which spans two long spring weekends leading up to Fat Tuesday—and the annual New Orleans Jazz & Heritage Festival.

The Louisiana Superdome—a home for the homeless after Katrina—was renovated and renamed in 2011 the Mercedes Benz Superdome. It is home to the 2010 Super Bowl champion New Orleans Saints and hosted the 2013 Super Bowl. In 2021 it was renamed Caesars Superdome.

Louis Armstrong New Orleans International Airport was made more efficient for travelers by the expansion of the Consolidated Rental Car Facility project that has also brought scattered facilities under one roof. Billions of dollars have been spent in recent years for bridge, airport, road, hospital, and school updates. Post Katrina, most New Orleans public schools became charter schools under the Recovery School District (RSD). In 2018, the RSD returned all its schools to the Orleans Parish School Board. Higher education campuses include Tulane University (including a medical school and law school), Loyola University, and the University of New Orleans. Louisiana State University Medical Center New Orleans opened in 2015.

Cultural amenities include the New Orleans Museum of Art located in the live oak filled City Park, the Ogden Museum of Southern Art, and Audubon Park, designed by John Charles Olmsted with its golf course and the Audubon Zoo.

The New Orleans metro area is virtually surrounded by water, which influences its climate. Between mid-June and September, temperatures are kept down by near-daily sporadic thunderstorms. Cold spells sometimes reach the area in winter but seldom last. Frequent and sometimes heavy rains are typical. Hurricane season officially runs from June 1 to November 30 but typically reaches its height in late summer.

Rankings

General Rankings

- To help military veterans find the best places in which to settle down, *WalletHub* compared the 100 largest U.S. cities across 19 key indicators of livability, affordability and veteran-friendliness. They range from the share of military skill-related jobs to veteran income growth to the availability of VA health facilities. New Orleans ranked #94. *Wallethub.com, "Best & Worst Places for Veterans to Live (2025)," November 7, 2024*

- *Insider* listed 23 places in the U.S. that travel industry trends reveal would be popular destinations in 2023. This year the list trends towards cultural and historical happenings, sports events, wellness experiences and invigorating outdoor escapes. According to the website insider.com New Orleans is a place to visit in 2023. *Insider, "23 of the Best Places You Should Travel to in the U.S. in 2023," December 17, 2022*

- New Orleans was selected as one of the happiest places to live in America by *Outside Magazine*. Criteria centered on overall well being; effect of climate change; inclusivity; affordability; outdoor access; and other demographic and population figures. Local experts shared highlights from hands-on experience in each location. *Outside Magazine, "The 15 Happiest Places to Live in the U.S.," September 18, 2023*

- New Orleans appeared on *Travel + Leisure's* list of "The 15 Best Cities in the United States." The city was ranked #5. Criteria: walkability; sights/landmarks; culture; food; friendliness; shopping; and overall value. *Travel + Leisure, "The World's Best Awards 2024" July 9, 2024*

- For its 37th annual "Readers' Choice Awards" survey, *Condé Nast Traveler* ranked its readers' favorite cities in the U.S. Whether it be a longed-for visit or the next big new thing, these are the places travelers loved best. The list was broken into large cities and cities under 250,000. New Orleans ranked #4 in the big city category. *Condé Nast Traveler, Readers' Choice Awards 2024, "Best Big Cities in the U.S." October 1, 2024*

Business/Finance Rankings

- New Orleans was cited as one of America's top metros for total major capital investment facility projects in 2024. The area ranked #10 in the Tier 2 (mid-sized) metro area category (population 200,000 to 1 million). *Site Selection, "Top Metros of 2024," March 2025*

- The New Orleans metro area appeared on the Milken Institute "2025 Best Performing Cities" list. Rank: #200 out of 200 large metro areas (based on performance category). Criteria: job growth; wage growth; high-tech growth and impact; community resilience; housing affordability; household broadband access. *Milken Institute, "Best-Performing Cities 2025," January 14, 2025*

Culture/Performing Arts Rankings

- New Orleans was selected as one of the 25 best cities for moviemakers in North America. Great film cities are places where filmmaking dreams can come true, that offer more creative space, lower costs, and great outdoor locations. NYC & LA were intentionally excluded. Criteria: film industry presence and culture; tax incentives; affordability; and proximity of festivals and schools. The city was ranked #6. *MovieMaker Magazine, "Best Places to Live and Work as a Moviemaker, 2025," January 29, 2025*

Education Rankings

- Personal finance website *WalletHub* analyzed the 150 largest U.S. metropolitan statistical areas to determine where the most educated Americans are putting their degrees to work. Criteria: education levels; percentage of workers with degrees; education quality and attainment gap; public school quality rankings; quality and enrollment of each metro area's universities. New Orleans was ranked #95 (#1 = most educated city). *WalletHub.com, "Most & Least Educated Cities in America, 2025" July 2, 2024*

Environmental Rankings

- Sperling's *BestPlaces* assessed the 50 largest metropolitan areas of the United States for the likelihood of dangerously extreme weather events or earthquakes. In general the Southeast and South-Central regions have the highest risk of weather extremes and earthquakes, while the Pacific Northwest enjoys the lowest risk. Of the most risky metropolitan areas, the New Orleans metro area was ranked #10. *Bestplaces.net, "Avoid Natural Disasters: BestPlaces Reveals The Top 10 Safest Places to Live," October 25, 2017*

Health/Fitness Rankings

- For each of the 100 largest cities in the United States, the American Fitness Index®, compiled in partnership between the American College of Sports Medicine and the Elevance Health Foundation, evaluated community infrastructure and more than 30 health behaviors including preventive health, levels of chronic disease conditions, food insecurity, pedestrian safety, air quality, and community/environment resources that support physical activity. New Orleans ranked #52 for "community fitness." *americanfitnessindex.org, "2024 ACSM American Fitness Index Summary Report," July 23, 2024*

- New Orleans was identified as a "2025 Allergy Capital." The area ranked #2 out of the nation's 100 largest metropolitan areas. Three groups of factors were used to identify the most challenging cities for people with allergies: annual tree, grass, and weed pollen scores; over the counter allergy medicine use; number of board-certified allergy specialists. *Asthma and Allergy Foundation of America, "2025 Allergy Capitals: The Most Challenging Places to Live with Allergies," March 18, 2025*

- New Orleans was identified as a "2024 Asthma Capital." The area ranked #55 out of the nation's 100 largest metropolitan areas. Criteria: estimated asthma prevalence; asthma-related mortality; and ER visits due to asthma. Risk factors analyzed but not factored in the rankings: annual air quality including pollution and ozone levels; public smoking laws; indoor air quality; access to asthma specialists; rescue and controller medication use; uninsured rate; pollen allergy; poverty rate. *Asthma and Allergy Foundation of America, "Asthma Capitals 2024: The Most Challenging Places to Live With Asthma," September 10, 2024*

Pet Rankings

- New Orleans appeared on *The Dogington Post* site as one of the top cities for dog lovers, ranking #9 out of 15. The real estate marketplace, Zillow®, and Rover, the largest pet sitter and dog walker network, introduced a new list of "Top Emerging Dog-Friendly Cities" for 2021. Criteria: number of new dog accounts on the Rover platform; and rentals and listings that mention features that attract dog owners (fenced-in yards, dog houses, dog door or proximity to a dog park). *Dogingtonpost.com, "15 Cities Emerging as Dog-Friendliest in 2021," May 11, 2021*

- New Orleans was selected by *Sniffspot.com* as one of the most dog-friendly cities in the U.S., ranking #19 out of 50. Criteria: dog parks; hiking; sniffspots; public parks; dog-friendly businesses; housing; dog waste cleanliness; leash laws; dog services; and overall cost. *Sniffspot.com, "The Top 50 Most Dog-Friendly Cities in the U.S.," September 30, 2024*

Real Estate Rankings

- *WalletHub* compared the most populated U.S. cities to determine which had the best markets for real estate agents. New Orleans ranked #148 where demand was high and pay was the best. Criteria: sales per agent; annual median wage for real-estate agents; monthly average starting salary for real estate agents; real estate job density and competition; unemployment rate; home turnover rate; housing-market health index; and other relevant metrics. *WalletHub.com, "2021 Best Places to Be a Real Estate Agent," May 12, 2021*

- The New Orleans metro area was identified as one of the 10 worst condo markets in the U.S. in 2024. The area ranked #54 out of 63 markets. Criteria: year-over-year change of median sales price of existing apartment condo-coop homes between the 4th quarter of 2023 and the 4th quarter of 2024. *National Association of Realtors®, Median Sales Price of Existing Apartment Condo-Coops Homes for Metropolitan Areas, 4th Quarter 2024*

- New Orleans was ranked #76 out of 176 metro areas in terms of cost of housing in 2024 by the National Association of Home Builders (#1 = most affordable). Criteria: the portion of an average family's income necessary to pay the mortgage on a median-priced home. *National Association of Home Builders®, NAHB-Wells Fargo Cost of Housing Index, 4th Quarter 2024*

Safety Rankings

- To identify the most dangerous cities in America, *24/7 Wall St.* focused on violent crime categories—murder, non-negligent manslaughter, rape, robbery, and aggravated assault—as reported for every 100,000 residents using data from the FBI's 2020 annual Uniform Crime Report. For cities with populations over 25,000, New Orleans was ranked #29. *247wallst.com, "America's Most Dangerous Cities" November 12, 2021*

- Statistics drawn from the FBI's Uniform Crime Report were used to rank the cities where violent crime rose the most year over year from 2019 to 2020. Only cities with 25,000 or more residents were included. *24/7 Wall St.* found that New Orleans placed #41 of those with a notable surge in incidents of violent crime. *247wallst.com, "American Cities Where Crime Is Soaring," March 4, 2022*

- Allstate ranked the 100 most populous cities in America in terms of driver safety. New Orleans ranked #36. Criteria based on anonymized driving behavior data from Allstate's mobile app powered by Arity: high speed driving (over 80 mph), phone handling, and hard braking. The report helps increase the importance of safety and awareness behind the wheel. *Allstate, "16th Allstate America's Best Drivers Report®" July 11, 2024*

- New Orleans was identified as one of the most dangerous cities in America by NeighborhoodScout. The city ranked #33 out of 100 (#1 = most dangerous). Criteria: number of violent crimes per 1,000 residents. The editors evaluated cities with 25,000 or more residents. *NeighborhoodScout.com, "2023 Top 100 Most Dangerous Cities in the U.S.," January 12, 2023*

Women/Minorities Rankings

- *Travel + Leisure* listed the best cities in and around the U.S. for a memorable and fun girls' trip, even on a budget. Whether it is for a special occasion, to make new memories or just to get away, New Orleans is sure to have something for all the ladies in your tribe. *Travel + Leisure, "25 Affordable Girls Weekend Getaways That Won't Break the Bank," January 30, 2025*

- New Orleans was listed as one of the most LGBTQ-friendly cities in America by *The Advocate*, as compiled by the real estate data site *Clever*. The city ranked #10 out of 15. Criteria, among many: Pride events; gay bars; LGBTQ-affirming healthcare options; state and local laws; number of PFLAG chapters; LGBTQ+ population. *The Advocate, "These Are the 15 Most LGBTQ-Friendly Cities in the U.S." November 1, 2023*

- Personal finance website *WalletHub* compared more than 180 U.S. cities across two key dimensions, "Hispanic Business-Friendliness" and "Hispanic Purchasing Power," to arrive at the most favorable conditions for Hispanic entrepreneurs. New Orleans was ranked #96 out of 182. Criteria includes: share of Hispanic-Owned Businesses; average growth of Hispanic Business revenues; Small Business-Friendliness score; affordability; and number of Hispanics with at least a bachelor's degree. *WalletHub.com, "Best Cities for Hispanic Entrepreneurs," September 4, 2024*

Miscellaneous Rankings

- *MoveHub* ranked 446 hipster cities across 20 countries, using its new and improved alternative Hipster Index and New Orleans came out as #22 among the top 50. Criteria: population over 150,000; number of vintage boutiques; density of tattoo parlors; vegan places to eat; coffee shops; and density of vinyl record stores. *MoveHub.com, "The Hipster Index: Brighton Pips Portland to Global Top Spot," July 28, 2021*

- In its roundup of St. Patrick's Day parades, *Gayot* listed the best festivals and parades of all things Irish. The festivities in New Orleans as among the best in North America. *Gayot.com, "Best St. Patrick's Day Parades," March 2025*

- *WalletHub* compared 148 of the most populated U.S. cities to determine their operating efficiency. A "Quality of Services" score was constructed for each city and then measured against the total budget per capita to reveal which were managed the best. New Orleans ranked #120. Criteria: financial stability; economy; education; safety; health; infrastructure and pollution. *WalletHub.com, "2025's Best- & Worst-Run Cities in America," June 18, 2024*

Business Environment

DEMOGRAPHICS

Population Growth

Area	1990 Census	2000 Census	2010 Census	2020 Census	2023 Estimate[2]	Population Growth 1990-2023 (%)
City	496,938	484,674	343,829	383,997	376,035	-24.3
MSA[1]	1,264,391	1,316,510	1,167,764	1,271,845	988,763	-21.8
U.S.	248,709,873	281,421,906	308,745,538	331,449,281	332,387,540	33.6

Note: (1) Figures cover the New Orleans-Metairie, LA Metropolitan Statistical Area; (2) 2019-2023 5-year ACS population estimate
Source: U.S. Census Bureau, 1990 Census, 2000 Census, 2010 Census, 2020 Census, 2019-2023 American Community Survey 5-Year Estimates

Race

Area	White Alone[2] (%)	Black Alone[2] (%)	Asian Alone[2] (%)	AIAN[3] Alone[2] (%)	NHOPI[4] Alone[2] (%)	Other Race Alone[2] (%)	Two or More Races (%)
City	31.6	55.2	2.8	0.3	0.0	2.8	7.3
MSA[1]	45.0	38.5	3.2	0.6	0.0	4.4	8.4
U.S.	63.4	12.4	5.8	0.9	0.2	6.6	10.7

Note: (1) Figures cover the New Orleans-Metairie, LA Metropolitan Statistical Area; (2) Alone is defined as not being in combination with one or more other races; (3) American Indian and Alaska Native; (4) Native Hawaiian and Other Pacific Islander
Source: U.S. Census Bureau, 2019-2023 American Community Survey 5-Year Estimates

Hispanic or Latino Origin

Area	Total (%)	Mexican (%)	Puerto Rican (%)	Cuban (%)	Other (%)
City	7.9	1.5	0.4	0.8	5.3
MSA[1]	12.6	2.0	0.7	0.9	9.1
U.S.	19.0	11.3	1.8	0.7	5.2

Note: Persons of Hispanic or Latino origin can be of any race; (1) Figures cover the New Orleans-Metairie, LA Metropolitan Statistical Area
Source: U.S. Census Bureau, 2019-2023 American Community Survey 5-Year Estimates

Age

Area	Under Age 5	Age 5–19	Age 20–34	Age 35–44	Age 45–54	Age 55–64	Age 65–74	Age 75–84	Age 85+	Median Age
City	5.5	16.9	22.0	14.9	11.5	12.7	10.4	4.3	1.7	38.4
MSA[1]	5.9	18.1	20.2	13.9	11.8	13.3	10.5	4.5	1.9	38.9
U.S.	5.7	19.1	20.2	13.1	12.3	12.8	10.0	4.9	1.9	38.7

Note: (1) Figures cover the New Orleans-Metairie, LA Metropolitan Statistical Area
Source: U.S. Census Bureau, 2019-2023 American Community Survey 5-Year Estimates

Disability by Age

Area	All Ages	Under 18 Years Old	18 to 64 Years Old	65 Years and Over
City	14.1	5.7	11.6	34.2
MSA[1]	15.3	6.1	12.9	36.3
U.S.	13.0	4.7	10.7	32.9

Note: Figures show percent of the civilian noninstitutionalized population that reported having a disability. Disability status is determined from six types of difficulty: vision, hearing, cognitive, ambulatory, self-care, and independent living. For children under 5 years old, hearing and vision difficulty are used to determine disability status. For children between the ages of 5 and 14, disability status is determined from hearing, vision, cognitive, ambulatory, and self-care difficulties. For people aged 15 years and older, they are considered to have a disability if they have difficulty with any one of the six difficulty types; Note: (1) Figures cover the New Orleans-Metairie, LA Metropolitan Statistical Area
Source: U.S. Census Bureau, 2019-2023 American Community Survey 5-Year Estimates

Ancestry

Area	German	Irish	English	American	Italian	Polish	French[2]	European	Scottish
City	6.4	6.0	5.3	2.3	4.0	0.9	5.4	1.2	1.1
MSA[1]	8.2	6.6	5.2	3.8	6.7	0.6	9.1	0.9	0.8
U.S.	12.6	9.4	9.1	5.5	4.9	2.6	2.0	1.6	1.6

Note: Figures are the percentage of the total population reporting a particular ancestry. The nine most commonly reported ancestries in the U.S. are shown. Figures include multiple ancestries (e.g. if a person reported being Irish and Italian, they were included in both columns); (1) Figures cover the New Orleans-Metairie, LA Metropolitan Statistical Area; (2) Excludes Basque
Source: U.S. Census Bureau, 2019-2023 American Community Survey 5-Year Estimates

Foreign-born Population

Area	Percent of Population Born in								
	Any Foreign Country	Asia	Mexico	Europe	Caribbean	Central America[2]	South America	Africa	Canada
City	6.6	2.0	0.4	0.6	0.6	1.9	0.5	0.3	0.2
MSA[1]	9.5	2.4	0.6	0.5	1.1	3.9	0.5	0.4	0.1
U.S.	13.9	4.3	3.3	1.4	1.4	1.2	1.2	0.8	0.2

Note: (1) Figures cover the New Orleans-Metairie, LA Metropolitan Statistical Area; (2) Excludes Mexico.
Source: U.S. Census Bureau, 2019-2023 American Community Survey 5-Year Estimates

Household Size

Area	Persons in Household (%)							Average Household Size
	One	Two	Three	Four	Five	Six	Seven or More	
City	44.7	29.3	13.2	8.0	3.3	1.0	0.5	2.34
MSA[1]	36.4	30.5	15.4	10.8	4.4	1.6	0.9	2.44
U.S.	28.5	33.8	15.4	12.7	5.9	2.3	1.4	2.54

Note: (1) Figures cover the New Orleans-Metairie, LA Metropolitan Statistical Area
Source: U.S. Census Bureau, 2019-2023 American Community Survey 5-Year Estimates

Household Relationships

Area	House-holder	Opposite-sex Spouse	Same-sex Spouse	Opposite-sex Unmarried Partner	Same-sex Unmarried Partner	Child[2]	Grand-child	Other Relatives	Non-relatives
City	43.0	11.0	0.3	3.1	0.4	26.1	3.2	4.6	4.3
MSA[1]	40.3	15.3	0.2	2.7	0.2	28.8	3.1	4.6	2.9
U.S.	38.3	17.5	0.2	2.5	0.2	28.3	2.4	4.8	3.4

Note: Figures are percent of the total population; (1) Figures cover the New Orleans-Metairie, LA Metropolitan Statistical Area; (2) Includes biological, adopted, and stepchildren of the householder
Source: U.S. Census Bureau, 2020 Census

Gender

Area	Males	Females	Males per 100 Females
City	177,299	198,736	89.2
MSA[1]	476,985	511,778	93.2
U.S.	164,545,087	167,842,453	98.0

Note: (1) Figures cover the New Orleans-Metairie, LA Metropolitan Statistical Area
Source: U.S. Census Bureau, 2019-2023 American Community Survey 5-Year Estimates

Marital Status

Area	Never Married	Now Married[2]	Separated	Widowed	Divorced
City	49.2	30.8	2.3	5.2	12.5
MSA[1]	40.3	38.9	2.3	6.0	12.4
U.S.	34.1	47.9	1.7	5.6	10.7

Note: Figures are percentages and cover the population 15 years of age and older; (1) Figures cover the New Orleans-Metairie, LA Metropolitan Statistical Area; (2) Excludes separated
Source: U.S. Census Bureau, 2019-2023 American Community Survey 5-Year Estimates

Religious Groups by Family

Area	Catholic	Baptist	Methodist	LDS[2]	Pentecostal	Lutheran	Islam	Adventist	Other
MSA[1]	42.1	9.3	2.5	0.5	2.1	0.5	1.4	1.0	8.0
U.S.	18.7	7.3	3.0	2.0	1.8	1.7	1.3	1.3	11.6

Note: Figures are the number of adherents as a percentage of the total population and cover the eight largest religious groups in the U.S; (1) Figures cover the New Orleans-Metairie, LA Metropolitan Statistical Area; (2) Church of Jesus Christ of Latter-day Saints
Sources: 2020 U.S. Religion Census, Association of Statisticians of American Religious Bodies; The Association of Religion Data Archives (ARDA)

Religious Groups by Tradition

Area	Catholic	Evangelical Protestant	Mainline Protestant	Black Protestant	Islam	Judaism	Hinduism	Orthodox	Buddhism
MSA[1]	42.1	13.5	3.0	4.9	1.4	0.4	0.3	0.1	0.3
U.S.	18.7	16.5	5.2	2.3	1.3	0.6	0.4	0.4	0.3

Note: Figures are the number of adherents as a percentage of the total population; (1) Figures cover the New Orleans-Metairie, LA Metropolitan Statistical Area
Sources: 2020 U.S. Religion Census, Association of Statisticians of American Religious Bodies; The Association of Religion Data Archives (ARDA)

ECONOMY

Real Gross Domestic Product (GDP)

Area	2017	2018	2019	2020	2021	2022	2023	Rank[3]
MSA[1]	78.2	78.1	79.8	73.4	76.8	75.7	79.6	48
U.S.[2]	17,619.1	18,160.7	18,642.5	18,238.9	19,387.6	19,896.6	20,436.3	—

Note: Figures are in billions of chained 2017 dollars; (1) Figures cover the New Orleans-Metairie, LA Metropolitan Statistical Area; (2) Figures cover real GDP within metropolitan areas; (3) Rank is based on 2023 data and ranges from 1 to 384
Source: U.S. Bureau of Economic Analysis

Economic Growth

Area	2014	2015	2016	2017	2018	2019	2020	2021	2022	2023
MSA[1]	1.2	0.3	0.8	5.8	-0.1	2.1	-8.0	4.6	-1.3	5.0
U.S.[2]	2.6	3.2	2.0	2.7	3.1	2.7	-2.2	6.3	2.6	2.7

Note: Figures are real gross domestic product growth rates and represent percent change from preceding period; (1) Figures cover the New Orleans-Metairie, LA Metropolitan Statistical Area; (2) Figures are the average growth rates within metropolitan areas
Source: U.S. Bureau of Economic Analysis

Metropolitan Area Exports

Area	2018	2019	2020	2021	2022	2023	Rank[2]
MSA[1]	36,570.4	34,109.6	31,088.4	35,773.5	52,912.9	38,978.6	9
U.S.	1,664,056.1	1,645,173.7	1,431,406.6	1,753,941.4	2,062,937.4	2,019,160.5	—

Note: Figures are in millions of dollars; (1) Figures cover the New Orleans-Metairie, LA Metropolitan Statistical Area; (2) Rank is based on 2023 data and ranges from 1 to 386
Source: U.S. Department of Commerce, International Trade Administration, Office of Trade and Economic Analysis, Industry and Analysis, Exports by Metropolitan Area, data extracted April 2, 2025

Building Permits

Area	Single-Family			Multi-Family			Total		
	2023	2024	Pct. Chg.	2023	2024	Pct. Chg.	2023	2024	Pct. Chg.
City	249	202	-18.9	818	508	-37.9	1,067	710	-33.5
MSA[1]	1,865	1,007	-46.0	1,207	604	-50.0	3,072	1,611	-47.6
U.S.	920,000	981,900	6.7	591,100	496,100	-16.1	1,511,100	1,478,000	-2.2

Note: (1) Figures cover the New Orleans-Metairie, LA Metropolitan Statistical Area; Figures represent new, privately-owned housing units authorized (unadjusted data)
Source: U.S. Census Bureau, Building Permits Survey (BPS), 2023, 2024

Bankruptcy Filings

Area	Business Filings			Nonbusiness Filings		
	2023	2024	% Chg.	2023	2024	% Chg.
Orleans Parish	28	35	25.0	388	446	14.9
U.S.	18,926	23,107	22.1	434,064	494,201	13.9

Note: Business filings include Chapter 7, Chapter 9, Chapter 11, Chapter 12, Chapter 13, Chapter 15, and Section 304; Nonbusiness filings include Chapter 7, Chapter 11, and Chapter 13
Source: Administrative Office of the U.S. Courts, Business and Nonbusiness Bankruptcy, County Cases Commenced by Chapter of the Bankruptcy Code, During the 12-Month Period Ending December 31, 2023 and Business and Nonbusiness Bankruptcy, County Cases Commenced by Chapter of the Bankruptcy Code, During the 12-Month Period Ending December 31, 2024

Housing Vacancy Rates

Area	Gross Vacancy Rate[3] (%)			Year-Round Vacancy Rate[4] (%)			Rental Vacancy Rate[5] (%)			Homeowner Vacancy Rate[6] (%)		
	2022	2023	2024	2022	2023	2024	2022	2023	2024	2022	2023	2024
MSA[1]	13.4	10.9	11.9	11.5	9.8	10.8	6.6	9.2	9.1	1.6	1.6	1.4
U.S.[2]	9.1	9.0	9.1	7.5	7.5	7.6	5.7	6.5	6.8	0.8	0.8	1.0

Note: (1) Figures cover the New Orleans-Metairie, LA Metropolitan Statistical Area; (2) Figures cover the 75 largest Metropolitan Statistical Areas; (3) The percentage of the total housing inventory that is vacant; (4) The percentage of the housing inventory (excluding seasonal units) that is year-round vacant; (5) The percentage of rental inventory that is vacant for rent; (6) The percentage of homeowner inventory that is vacant for sale
Source: U.S. Census Bureau, Housing Vacancies and Homeownership Annual Statistics: 2022, 2023, 2024

INCOME

Income

Area	Per Capita ($)	Median Household ($)	Average Household ($)
City	39,698	55,339	89,943
MSA[1]	37,547	62,271	90,627
U.S.	43,289	78,538	110,491

Note: (1) Figures cover the New Orleans-Metairie, LA Metropolitan Statistical Area
Source: U.S. Census Bureau, 2019-2023 American Community Survey 5-Year Estimates

Household Income Distribution

Area	Percent of Households Earning							
	Under $15,000	$15,000 -$24,999	$25,000 -$34,999	$35,000 -$49,999	$50,000 -$74,999	$75,000 -$99,999	$100,000 -$149,999	$150,000 and up
City	18.7	9.7	7.7	10.8	14.8	9.6	12.8	15.8
MSA[1]	13.6	8.8	8.5	11.2	15.6	11.7	14.6	15.9
U.S.	8.5	6.6	6.8	10.4	15.7	12.7	17.4	21.9

Note: (1) Figures cover the New Orleans-Metairie, LA Metropolitan Statistical Area
Source: U.S. Census Bureau, 2019-2023 American Community Survey 5-Year Estimates

Poverty Rate

Area	All Ages	Under 18 Years Old	18 to 64 Years Old	65 Years and Over
City	22.6	32.2	20.1	20.7
MSA[1]	18.3	25.6	16.5	14.9
U.S.	12.4	16.3	11.6	10.4

Note: Figures are percentage of people whose income during the past 12 months was below the poverty level;
(1) Figures cover the New Orleans-Metairie, LA Metropolitan Statistical Area
Source: U.S. Census Bureau, 2019-2023 American Community Survey 5-Year Estimates

EMPLOYMENT

Labor Force and Employment

Area	Civilian Labor Force			Workers Employed		
	Dec. 2023	Dec. 2024	% Chg.	Dec. 2023	Dec. 2024	% Chg.
City	173,294	173,800	0.3	165,506	165,809	0.2
MSA[1]	461,088	463,007	0.4	442,552	443,450	0.2
U.S.	166,661,000	167,746,000	0.7	160,754,000	161,294,000	0.3

Note: Data is not seasonally adjusted and covers workers 16 years of age and older; (1) Figures cover the New Orleans-Metairie, LA Metropolitan Statistical Area
Source: Bureau of Labor Statistics, Local Area Unemployment Statistics

Unemployment Rate

Area	2024											
	Jan.	Feb.	Mar.	Apr.	May	Jun.	Jul.	Aug.	Sep.	Oct.	Nov.	Dec.
City	5.3	4.8	4.7	4.3	4.4	5.7	5.8	5.5	5.2	5.3	4.9	4.6
MSA[1]	4.6	4.3	4.2	3.8	3.9	5.0	5.0	4.9	4.7	4.7	4.5	4.2
U.S.	4.1	4.2	3.9	3.5	3.7	4.3	4.5	4.4	3.9	3.9	4.0	3.8

Note: Data is not seasonally adjusted and covers workers 16 years of age and older; (1) Figures cover the New Orleans-Metairie, LA Metropolitan Statistical Area
Source: Bureau of Labor Statistics, Local Area Unemployment Statistics

Average Wages

Occupation	$/Hr.	Occupation	$/Hr.
Accountants and Auditors	40.08	Maintenance and Repair Workers	22.29
Automotive Mechanics	24.79	Marketing Managers	60.16
Bookkeepers	22.70	Network and Computer Systems Admin.	47.36
Carpenters	25.98	Nurses, Licensed Practical	28.31
Cashiers	13.04	Nurses, Registered	43.12
Computer Programmers	39.98	Nursing Assistants	16.45
Computer Systems Analysts	48.21	Office Clerks, General	16.23
Computer User Support Specialists	28.92	Physical Therapists	51.00
Construction Laborers	21.90	Physicians	147.27
Cooks, Restaurant	15.42	Plumbers, Pipefitters and Steamfitters	29.90
Customer Service Representatives	19.43	Police and Sheriff's Patrol Officers	27.76
Dentists	97.54	Postal Service Mail Carriers	28.47
Electricians	29.41	Real Estate Sales Agents	24.83
Engineers, Electrical	56.07	Retail Salespersons	15.83
Fast Food and Counter Workers	13.66	Sales Representatives, Technical/Scientific	70.24
Financial Managers	67.51	Secretaries, Exc. Legal/Medical/Executive	20.08
First-Line Supervisors of Office Workers	30.04	Security Guards	17.58
General and Operations Managers	62.93	Surgeons	n/a
Hairdressers/Cosmetologists	14.33	Teacher Assistants, Exc. Postsecondary[1]	14.58
Home Health and Personal Care Aides	11.68	Teachers, Secondary School, Exc. Sp. Ed.[1]	28.89
Janitors and Cleaners	14.73	Telemarketers	n/a
Landscaping/Groundskeeping Workers	16.51	Truck Drivers, Heavy/Tractor-Trailer	25.97
Lawyers	66.68	Truck Drivers, Light/Delivery Services	22.33
Maids and Housekeeping Cleaners	14.95	Waiters and Waitresses	12.40

Note: Wage data covers the New Orleans-Metairie, LA Metropolitan Statistical Area; (1) Hourly wages were calculated from annual wage data based on a 40 hour work week
Source: Bureau of Labor Statistics, Metro Area Occupational Employment & Wage Estimates, May 2024

Employment by Industry

Sector	MSA[1] Number of Employees	MSA[1] Percent of Total	U.S. Percent of Total
Construction	26,800	5.6	5.1
Financial Activities	24,100	5.0	5.8
Government	55,500	11.6	14.9
Information	6,600	1.4	1.9
Leisure and Hospitality	69,100	14.5	10.4
Manufacturing	26,500	5.5	8.0
Mining and Logging	1,800	0.4	0.4
Other Services	20,400	4.3	3.7
Private Education and Health Services	97,100	20.3	16.9
Professional and Business Services	61,600	12.9	14.2
Retail Trade	44,700	9.3	10.0
Transportation, Warehousing, and Utilities	26,800	5.6	4.8
Wholesale Trade	17,200	3.6	3.9

Note: Figures are non-farm employment as of December 2024. Figures are not seasonally adjusted and include workers 16 years of age and older; (1) Figures cover the New Orleans-Metairie, LA Metropolitan Statistical Area
Source: Bureau of Labor Statistics, Current Employment Statistics, Employment, Hours, and Earnings

Employment by Occupation

Occupation Classification	City (%)	MSA[1] (%)	U.S. (%)
Management, Business, Science, and Arts	49.3	41.8	42.0
Natural Resources, Construction, and Maintenance	5.5	9.2	8.6
Production, Transportation, and Material Moving	7.6	10.7	13.0
Sales and Office	18.0	19.4	19.9
Service	19.5	18.8	16.5

Note: Figures cover employed civilians 16 years of age and older; (1) Figures cover the New Orleans-Metairie, LA Metropolitan Statistical Area
Source: U.S. Census Bureau, 2019-2023 American Community Survey 5-Year Estimates

Occupations with Greatest Projected Employment Growth: 2022 – 2032

Occupation[1]	2022 Employment	2032 Projected Employment	Numeric Employment Change	Percent Employment Change
Home Health and Personal Care Aides	36,540	44,950	8,410	23.0
Construction Laborers	31,390	35,600	4,210	13.4
Registered Nurses	43,740	47,040	3,300	7.5
Cooks, Restaurant	14,130	17,300	3,170	22.4
Stockers and Order Fillers	27,540	30,190	2,650	9.6
General and Operations Managers	38,680	40,940	2,260	5.8
Nurse Practitioners	4,470	6,420	1,950	43.6
Medical and Health Services Managers	6,570	8,470	1,900	28.9
Managers, All Other	33,510	35,250	1,740	5.2
Laborers and Freight, Stock, and Material Movers, Hand	37,120	38,820	1,700	4.6

Note: Projections cover Louisiana; (1) Sorted by numeric employment change
Source: www.projectionscentral.org, State Occupational Projections, 2022–2032 Long-Term Projections

Fastest-Growing Occupations: 2022 – 2032

Occupation[1]	2022 Employment	2032 Projected Employment	Numeric Employment Change	Percent Employment Change
Nurse Practitioners	4,470	6,420	1,950	43.6
Epidemiologists	150	200	50	33.3
Data Scientists	560	740	180	32.1
Medical and Health Services Managers	6,570	8,470	1,900	28.9
Information Security Analysts (SOC 2018)	480	610	130	27.1
Occupational Therapy Assistants	740	940	200	27.0
Orthotists and Prosthetists	230	290	60	26.1
Physical Therapist Assistants	1,580	1,990	410	25.9
Taxi Drivers	240	300	60	25.0
Software Developers	2,680	3,330	650	24.3

Note: Projections cover Louisiana; (1) Sorted by percent employment change and excludes occupations with numeric employment change less than 50
Source: www.projectionscentral.org, State Occupational Projections, 2022–2032 Long-Term Projections

CITY FINANCES

City Government Finances

Component	2022 ($000)	2022 ($ per capita)
Total Revenues	2,239,216	5,749
Total Expenditures	2,081,178	5,344
Debt Outstanding	1,197,419	3,074

Source: U.S. Census Bureau, State & Local Government Finances 2022

City Government Revenue by Source

Source	2022 ($000)	2022 ($ per capita)	2022 (%)
General Revenue			
From Federal Government	440,077	1,130	19.7
From State Government	414,938	1,065	18.5
From Local Governments	11,320	29	0.5
Taxes			
Property	342,166	879	15.3
Sales and Gross Receipts	283,263	727	12.7
Personal Income	0	0	0.0
Corporate Income	0	0	0.0
Motor Vehicle License	1,792	5	0.1
Other Taxes	32,219	83	1.4
Current Charges	463,325	1,190	20.7
Liquor Store	0	0	0.0
Utility	124,517	320	5.6

Source: U.S. Census Bureau, State & Local Government Finances 2022

City Government Expenditures by Function

Function	2022 ($000)	2022 ($ per capita)	2022 (%)
General Direct Expenditures			
Air Transportation	112,569	289	5.4
Corrections	0	0	0.0
Education	0	0	0.0
Employment Security Administration	0	0	0.0
Financial Administration	30,546	78	1.5
Fire Protection	117,130	300	5.6
General Public Buildings	9,583	24	0.5
Governmental Administration, Other	135,949	349	6.5
Health	35,999	92	1.7
Highways	34,244	87	1.6
Hospitals	68,620	176	3.3
Housing and Community Development	307,156	788	14.8
Interest on General Debt	91,429	234	4.4
Judicial and Legal	104,918	269	5.0
Libraries	17,232	44	0.8
Parking	0	0	0.0
Parks and Recreation	66,498	170	3.2
Police Protection	175,149	449	8.4
Public Welfare	0	0	0.0
Sewerage	194,268	498	9.3
Solid Waste Management	34,483	88	1.7
Veterans' Services	0	0	0.0
Liquor Store	0	0	0.0
Utility	200,051	513	9.6

Source: U.S. Census Bureau, State & Local Government Finances 2022

TAXES

State Corporate Income Tax Rates

State	Tax Rate (%)	Income Brackets ($)	Num. of Brackets	Financial Institution Tax Rate (%)[a]	Federal Income Tax Ded.
Louisiana	3.5 - 7.5	50,000 - 150,000	3	3.5 - 7.5	Yes

Note: Tax rates for tax year 2024; (a) Rates listed are the corporate income tax rate applied to financial institutions or excise taxes based on income. Some states have other taxes based upon the value of deposits or shares.
Source: Federation of Tax Administrators, State Corporate Income Tax Rates, January 1, 2025

State Individual Income Tax Rates

State	Tax Rate (%)	Income Brackets ($)	Personal Exemptions ($)			Standard Ded. ($)	
			Single	Married	Depend.	Single	Married
Louisiana (aa)	1.85 - 4.25 (bb)	12,500 - 50,001 (b)	4,500	9,000	1,000 (k)	14,600 (k)	29,000 (k)

Note: Tax rates for tax year 2024; Local- and county-level taxes are not included; Federal income tax is not deductible on state income tax returns; (b) For joint returns, taxes are twice the tax on half the couple's income. California brackets violate this formula at the two highest tax brackets in 2024; (k) The amounts reported for Louisiana are a combined personal exemption-standard deduction. Louisiana provides for a an adjustment of federal itemized medical and dentals expenses above the federal standard deduction; (aa) Standard deduction amounts reported are maximums, Maryland standard deduction is 15% of AGI with an increased deduction above $17,000 - S/$34,333 - MFJ in 2023; Montana, 20% of AGI; (bb) Louisiana lawmakers repealed the state's throwout rule, ending the taxation of so-called "nowhere income." Iowa is phasing-in a flat rate by 2027, while Nebraska (LB 754 signed into law) and South Carolina is phasing-in a reduced top rate by 2027.
Source: Federation of Tax Administrators, State Individual Income Tax Rates, January 1, 2025

Various State Sales and Excise Tax Rates

State	State Sales Tax (%)	Gasoline[1] ($/gal.)	Cigarette[2] ($/pack)	Spirits[3] ($/gal.)	Wine[4] ($/gal.)	Beer[5] ($/gal.)	Recreational Marijuana (%)
Louisiana	5	0.21	1.08	3.03	0.76	0.40	Not legal

Note: All tax rates as of January 1, 2025; (1) The American Petroleum Institute has developed a methodology for determining the average tax rate on a gallon of fuel. Rates may include any of the following: excise taxes, environmental fees, storage tank fees, other fees or taxes, general sales tax, and local taxes; (2) The federal excise tax of $1.0066 per pack and local taxes are not included; (3) Rates are those applicable to off-premise sales of 40% alcohol by volume (a.b.v.) distilled spirits in 750ml containers. Local excise taxes are excluded; (4) Rates are those applicable to off-premise sales of 11% a.b.v. non-carbonated wine in 750ml containers; (5) Rates are those applicable to off-premise sales of 4.7% a.b.v. beer in 12 ounce containers.
Source: Tax Foundation, 2025 Facts & Figures: How Does Your State Compare?

State Tax Competitiveness Index

State	Overall Rank	Corporate Tax Rank	Individual Income Tax Rank	Sales Tax Rank	Property Tax Rank	Unemployment Insurance Tax Rank
Louisiana	40	29	33	48	16	9

Note: The Tax Foundation's State Tax Competitiveness Index enables policymakers, taxpayers, and business leaders to gauge how their states' tax systems compare. A rank of 1 is best, 50 is worst. Rankings do not average to the total. States without a tax rank equally as 1. DC's scores and rankings do not affect other states. The report shows tax systems as of July 1, 2024 (the beginning of Fiscal Year 2025).
Source: Tax Foundation, State Tax Competitiveness Index 2025

TRANSPORTATION

Means of Transportation to Work

Area	Car/Truck/Van		Public Transportation			Bicycle	Walked	Other Means	Worked at Home
	Drove Alone	Car-pooled	Bus	Subway	Railroad				
City	63.2	8.7	3.8	0.1	0.0	1.9	5.6	3.0	13.7
MSA[1]	73.0	9.7	1.8	0.0	0.0	0.9	3.1	1.9	9.6
U.S.	70.2	8.5	1.7	1.3	0.4	0.4	2.4	1.6	13.5

Note: Figures are percentages and cover workers 16 years of age and older; (1) Figures cover the New Orleans-Metairie, LA Metropolitan Statistical Area
Source: U.S. Census Bureau, 2019-2023 American Community Survey 5-Year Estimates

Travel Time to Work

Area	Less Than 10 Minutes	10 to 19 Minutes	20 to 29 Minutes	30 to 44 Minutes	45 to 59 Minutes	60 to 89 Minutes	90 Minutes or More
City	11.9	35.1	24.3	18.7	5.2	3.1	1.7
MSA[1]	11.4	31.5	22.9	21.7	6.6	3.9	2.0
U.S.	12.6	28.6	21.2	20.8	8.1	6.0	2.8

Note: Note: Figures are percentages and include workers 16 years old and over; (1) Figures cover the New Orleans-Metairie, LA Metropolitan Statistical Area
Source: U.S. Census Bureau, 2019-2023 American Community Survey 5-Year Estimates

Key Congestion Measures

Measure	2000	2010	2015	2020	2022
Annual Hours of Delay, Total (000)	35,168	47,211	53,514	24,668	49,631
Annual Hours of Delay, Per Auto Commuter	30	45	56	26	53
Annual Congestion Cost, Per Auto Commuter ($)	1,223	1,304	1,367	667	1,422

Note: Figures cover the New Orleans LA urban area
Source: Texas A&M Transportation Institute, 2023 Urban Mobility Report

Freeway Travel Time Index

Measure	1985	1990	1995	2000	2005	2010	2015	2020	2022
Urban Area Index[1]	1.14	1.16	1.20	1.22	1.23	1.32	1.34	1.11	1.29
Urban Area Rank[1,2]	18	19	21	24	28	8	9	20	13

Note: Freeway Travel Time Index—the ratio of travel time in the peak period to the travel time at free-flow conditions. For example, a value of 1.30 indicates a 20-minute free-flow trip takes 26 minutes in the peak (20 minutes x 1.30 = 26 minutes); (1) Covers the New Orleans LA urban area; (2) Rank is based on 101 larger urban areas (#1 = highest travel time index)
Source: Texas A&M Transportation Institute, 2023 Urban Mobility Report

Public Transportation

Agency Name / Mode of Transportation	Vehicles Operated in Maximum Service[1]	Annual Unlinked Passenger Trips[2] (in thous.)	Annual Passenger Miles[3] (in thous.)
New Orleans Regional Transit Authority (NORTA)			
Bus (directly operated)	98	8,726.5	34,866.0
Demand Response (directly operated)	51	226.5	1,856.5
Ferryboat (purchased transportation)	3	967.6	483.8
Streetcar Rail (directly operated)	21	3,859.3	6,830.9

Note: (1) Number of revenue vehicles operated by the given mode and type of service to meet the annual maximum service requirement. This is the revenue vehicle count during the peak season of the year; on the week and day that maximum service is provided. Vehicles operated in maximum service (VOMS) exclude atypical days and one-time special events; (2) Number of passengers who boarded public transportation vehicles. Passengers are counted each time they board a vehicle no matter how many vehicles they use to travel from their origin to their destination. (3) Sum of the distances ridden by all passengers during the entire fiscal year.
Source: Federal Transit Administration, National Transit Database, 2023

Air Transportation

Airport Name and Code / Type of Service	Passenger Airlines[1]	Passenger Enplanements	Freight Carriers[2]	Freight (lbs)
New Orleans International (MSY)				
Domestic service (U.S. carriers only)	28	6,414,251	16	46,172,823
International service (U.S. carriers only)	6	48,435	2	27,053

Note: (1) Includes all U.S.-based major, minor and commuter airlines that carried at least one passenger during the year; (2) Includes all U.S.-based airlines and freight carriers that transported at least one pound of freight during the year.
Source: Bureau of Transportation Statistics, The Intermodal Transportation Database, Air Carriers: T-100 Domestic Market (U.S. carriers only), 2024; Bureau of Transportation Statistics, The Intermodal Transportation Database, Air Carriers: T-100 International Market (U.S. carriers only), 2024

BUSINESSES

Major Business Headquarters

Company Name	Industry	Rankings Fortune[1]	Rankings Forbes[2]
Entergy	Utilities: gas and electric	339	-
Sazerac Company	Food, drink & tobacco	-	213

Note: (1) Companies that produce a 10-K are ranked 1 to 500 based on 2023 revenue; (2) All private companies with at least $2 billion in annual revenue through the end of their most current fiscal year are ranked 1 to 275; companies listed are headquartered in the city; dashes indicate no ranking
Source: Fortune, "Fortune 500," 2024; Forbes, "America's Largest Private Companies," 2024

Fastest-Growing Businesses

According to *Initiative for a Competitive Inner City (ICIC)*, New Orleans is home to three of America's 100 fastest-growing "inner city" companies: **El Guapo** (#15); **Ready Power** (#19); **Online Optimism** (#72). To be eligible for the IC100, companies have to be independently operated, privately held, for-profit businesses with revenues of at least $50,000 in 2019 and $500,000 in 2023, and headquartered in an under-resourced community. Recognizing that concentrated poverty exists within metropolitan areas outside of big cities (and that poverty overall is suburbanizing), ICIC defines under-resourced communities as large low-income, high-poverty areas located in the urban and suburban parts of all but the smallest metropolitan areas. Companies were ranked overall by revenue growth over the five-year period between 2019 and 2023. *Initiative for a Competitive Inner City (ICIC), "Inner City 100 Companies," 2024*

Living Environment

COST OF LIVING

Cost of Living Index

Composite Index	Groceries	Housing	Utilities	Transportation	Health Care	Misc. Goods/Services
112.4	99.2	148.7	71.6	95.6	102.6	104.0

Note: The Cost of Living Index measures regional differences in the cost of consumer goods and services, excluding taxes and non-consumer expenditures, for professional and managerial households in the top income quintile. It is based on more than 50,000 prices covering almost 60 different items for which prices are collected three times a year by chambers of commerce, economic development organizations or university applied economic centers in each participating urban area. The numbers shown should be read as a percentage above or below the national average of 100. For example, a value of 115.4 in the groceries column indicates that grocery prices are 15.4% higher than the national average. Small differences in the index numbers should not be interpreted as significant; Figures cover the New Orleans LA urban area.
Source: The Council for Community and Economic Research, Cost of Living Index, 2024

Grocery Prices

Area[1]	T-Bone Steak ($/pound)	Frying Chicken ($/pound)	Whole Milk ($/half gal.)	Eggs ($/dozen)	Orange Juice ($/64 oz.)	Coffee ($/11.5 oz.)
City[2]	15.51	1.36	4.66	3.19	4.38	4.94
Avg.	15.42	1.55	4.69	3.25	4.41	5.46
Min.	14.50	1.16	4.43	2.75	4.00	4.85
Max.	17.56	2.89	5.49	4.78	5.54	7.89

Note: (1) Values for the local area are compared with the average, minimum and maximum values for all 276 areas in the Cost of Living Index; (2) Figures cover the New Orleans LA urban area; **T-Bone Steak** (price per pound); **Frying Chicken** (price per pound, whole fryer); **Whole Milk** (half gallon carton); **Eggs** (price per dozen, Grade A, large); **Orange Juice** (64 oz. Tropicana or Florida Natural); **Coffee** (11.5 oz. can, vacuum-packed, Maxwell House, Hills Bros, or Folgers).
Source: The Council for Community and Economic Research, Cost of Living Index, 2024

Housing and Utility Costs

Area[1]	New Home Price ($)	Apartment Rent ($/month)	All Electric ($/month)	Part Electric ($/month)	Other Energy ($/month)	Telephone ($/month)
City[2]	812,851	2,128	-	68.38	47.92	190.09
Avg.	515,975	1,550	210.99	123.07	82.07	194.99
Min.	265,375	692	104.33	53.68	36.26	179.42
Max.	2,775,821	5,719	529.02	397.28	361.63	223.33

Note: (1) Values for the local area are compared with the average, minimum and maximum values for all 276 areas in the Cost of Living Index; (2) Figures cover the New Orleans LA urban area; **New Home Price** (2,400 sf living area, 8,000 sf lot, in urban area with full utilities); **Apartment Rent** (950 sf 2 bedroom/1.5 or 2 bath, unfurnished, excluding all utilities except water); **All Electric** (average monthly cost for an all-electric home); **Part Electric** (average monthly cost for a part-electric home); **Other Energy** (average monthly cost for natural gas, fuel oil, coal, wood, and any other forms of energy except electricity); **Telephone** (price includes the base monthly rate plus taxes and fees for three lines of mobile phone service).
Source: The Council for Community and Economic Research, Cost of Living Index, 2024

Health Care, Transportation, and Other Costs

Area[1]	Doctor ($/visit)	Dentist ($/visit)	Optometrist ($/visit)	Gasoline ($/gallon)	Beauty Salon ($/visit)	Men's Shirt ($)
City[2]	161.78	121.36	115.44	3.11	48.33	49.00
Avg.	143.77	117.51	129.23	3.32	48.57	38.14
Min.	36.74	58.67	67.33	2.80	24.00	13.41
Max.	270.44	216.82	307.33	5.28	94.00	63.89

Note: (1) Values for the local area are compared with the average, minimum and maximum values for all 276 areas in the Cost of Living Index; (2) Figures cover the New Orleans LA urban area; **Doctor** (general practitioners routine exam of an established patient); **Dentist** (adult teeth cleaning and periodic oral examination); **Optometrist** (full vision eye exam for established adult patient); **Gasoline** (one gallon regular unleaded, national brand, including all taxes, cash price at self-service pump if available); **Beauty Salon** (woman's shampoo, trim, and blow-dry); **Men's Shirt** (cotton/polyester dress shirt, pinpoint weave, long sleeves).
Source: The Council for Community and Economic Research, Cost of Living Index, 2024

HOUSING

Homeownership Rate

Area	2017 (%)	2018 (%)	2019 (%)	2020 (%)	2021 (%)	2022 (%)	2023 (%)	2024 (%)
MSA[1]	61.7	62.6	61.1	66.3	66.2	66.3	63.2	63.2
U.S.	63.9	64.4	64.6	66.6	65.5	65.8	65.9	65.6

Note: (1) Figures cover the New Orleans-Metairie, LA Metropolitan Statistical Area
Source: U.S. Census Bureau, Housing Vacancies and Homeownership Annual Statistics: 2017-2024

House Price Index (HPI)

Area	National Ranking[2]	Quarterly Change (%)	One-Year Change (%)	Five-Year Change (%)	Since 1991Q1 (%)
MSA[1]	233	0.13	0.85	25.47	285.27
U.S.[3]	–	1.43	4.51	57.13	327.82

Note: The HPI is a weighted repeat sales index. It measures average price changes in repeat sales or refinancings on the same properties. This information is obtained by reviewing repeat mortgage transactions on single-family properties whose mortgages have been purchased or securitized by Fannie Mae or Freddie Mac since January 1975; (1) Figures cover the New Orleans-Metairie, LA Metropolitan Statistical Area; (2) Rankings are based on annual percentage change for all metro areas containing at least 15,000 transactions over the last 10 years and ranges from 1 to 241; (3) figures based on a weighted average of Census Division estimates using a seasonally adjusted, purchase-only index; all figures are for the period ending December 31, 2024
Source: Federal Housing Finance Agency, Change in FHFA Metropolitan Area House Price Indexes, All Transactions Index, 2024Q4

Home Value

Area	Under $100,000	$100,000 -$199,999	$200,000 -$299,999	$300,000 -$399,999	$400,000 -$499,999	$500,000 -$999,999	$1,000,000 or more	Median ($)
City	6.4	21.2	23.1	13.8	9.7	19.4	6.4	296,400
MSA[1]	8.9	25.9	28.3	15.3	7.8	10.8	3.0	248,000
U.S.	12.1	17.8	19.5	14.4	10.5	19.1	6.5	303,400

Note: Figures are percentages except for median and cover owner-occupied housing units; (1) Figures cover the New Orleans-Metairie, LA Metropolitan Statistical Area
Source: U.S. Census Bureau, 2019-2023 American Community Survey 5-Year Estimates

Year Housing Structure Built

Area	2020 or Later	2010 -2019	2000 -2009	1990 -1999	1980 -1989	1970 -1979	1960 -1969	1950 -1959	1940 -1949	Before 1940	Median Year
City	0.4	5.7	7.6	3.0	7.8	13.9	10.2	12.0	7.1	32.1	1959
MSA[1]	0.4	5.1	9.9	6.8	13.1	19.6	13.9	10.8	5.1	15.2	1973
U.S.	1.2	8.9	13.6	12.8	13.0	14.4	10.0	9.7	4.5	11.9	1980

Note: Figures are percentages except for Median Year; Note: (1) Figures cover the New Orleans-Metairie, LA Metropolitan Statistical Area
Source: U.S. Census Bureau, 2019-2023 American Community Survey 5-Year Estimates

Gross Monthly Rent

Area	Under $500	$500 -$999	$1,000 -$1,499	$1,500 -$1,999	$2,000 -$2,499	$2,500 -$2,999	$3,000 and up	Median ($)
City	10.0	21.7	38.2	19.5	6.2	2.7	1.7	1,211
MSA[1]	7.3	24.9	41.7	18.2	5.0	1.7	1.1	1,182
U.S.	6.5	22.3	29.5	20.2	10.8	4.8	5.9	1,348

Note: Figures are percentages except for median; Gross rent is the contract rent plus the estimated average monthly cost of utilities (electricity, gas, and water and sewer) and fuels (oil, coal, kerosene, wood, etc.) if these are paid by the renter (or paid for the renter by someone else); (1) Figures cover the New Orleans-Metairie, LA Metropolitan Statistical Area
Source: U.S. Census Bureau, 2019-2023 American Community Survey 5-Year Estimates

HEALTH

Health Risk Factors

Category	MSA[1] (%)	U.S. (%)
Adults aged 18–64 who have any kind of health care coverage	92.8	90.8
Adults who reported being in good or better health	79.3	81.8
Adults who have been told they have high blood cholesterol	36.1	36.9
Adults who have been told they have high blood pressure	39.8	34.0
Adults who are current smokers	11.5	12.1
Adults who currently use e-cigarettes	9.2	7.7
Adults who currently use chewing tobacco, snuff, or snus	2.0	3.2
Adults who are heavy drinkers[2]	5.7	6.1
Adults who are binge drinkers[3]	17.3	15.2
Adults who are overweight (BMI 25.0 - 29.9)	32.8	34.4
Adults who are obese (BMI 30.0 - 99.8)	36.4	34.3
Adults who participated in any physical activities in the past month	72.5	75.8

Note: All figures are crude prevalence; (1) Figures cover the New Orleans-Metairie, LA Metropolitan Statistical Area; (2) Heavy drinkers are classified as adult men having more than 14 drinks per week and adult women having more than 7 drinks per week; (3) Binge drinkers are classified as males having five or more drinks on one occasion or females having four or more drinks on one occasion
Source: Centers for Disease Control and Prevention, Behavioral Risk Factor Surveillance System, SMART: Selected Metropolitan Area Risk Trends, 2023

Acute and Chronic Health Conditions

Category	MSA[1] (%)	U.S. (%)
Adults who have ever been told they had a heart attack	4.0	4.2
Adults who have ever been told they have angina or coronary heart disease	4.9	4.0
Adults who have ever been told they had a stroke	4.3	3.3
Adults who have ever been told they have asthma	19.0	15.7
Adults who have ever been told they have arthritis	26.1	26.3
Adults who have ever been told they have diabetes[2]	15.8	11.5
Adults who have ever been told they had skin cancer	4.8	5.6
Adults who have ever been told they had any other types of cancer	6.7	8.4
Adults who have ever been told they have COPD	7.4	6.4
Adults who have ever been told they have kidney disease	4.1	3.7
Adults who have ever been told they have a form of depression	25.5	22.0

Note: All figures are crude prevalence; (1) Figures cover the New Orleans-Metairie, LA Metropolitan Statistical Area; (2) Figures do not include pregnancy-related, borderline, or pre-diabetes
Source: Centers for Disease Control and Prevention, Behavioral Risk Factor Surveillance System, SMART: Selected Metropolitan Area Risk Trends, 2023

Health Screening and Vaccination Rates

Category	MSA[1] (%)	U.S. (%)
Adults who have ever been tested for HIV	52.2	37.5
Adults who have had their blood cholesterol checked within the last five years	89.9	87.0
Adults aged 65+ who have had flu shot within the past year	54.9	63.4
Adults aged 65+ who have ever had a pneumonia vaccination	68.8	71.9

Note: All figures are crude prevalence; (1) Figures cover the New Orleans-Metairie, LA Metropolitan Statistical Area.
Source: Centers for Disease Control and Prevention, Behavioral Risk Factor Surveillance System, SMART: Selected Metropolitan Area Risk Trends, 2023

Disability Status

Category	MSA[1] (%)	U.S. (%)
Adults who reported being deaf	8.2	7.4
Are you blind or have serious difficulty seeing, even when wearing glasses?	7.6	4.9
Do you have difficulty doing errands alone?	8.1	7.8
Do you have difficulty dressing or bathing?	5.4	3.6
Do you have serious difficulty concentrating/remembering/making decisions?	16.2	13.7
Do you have serious difficulty walking or climbing stairs?	15.8	13.2

Note: All figures are crude prevalence; (1) Figures cover the New Orleans-Metairie, LA Metropolitan Statistical Area.
Source: Centers for Disease Control and Prevention, Behavioral Risk Factor Surveillance System, SMART: Selected Metropolitan Area Risk Trends, 2023

Mortality Rates for the Top 10 Causes of Death in the U.S.

ICD-10[a] Sub-Chapter	ICD-10[a] Code	Crude Mortality Rate[2] per 100,000 population	
		County[3]	U.S.
Malignant neoplasms	C00-C97	178.6	182.7
Ischaemic heart diseases	I20-I25	87.9	109.6
Provisional assignment of new diseases of uncertain etiology[1]	U00-U49	34.6	65.3
Other forms of heart disease	I30-I51	80.5	65.1
Other degenerative diseases of the nervous system	G30-G31	47.2	52.4
Other external causes of accidental injury	W00-X59	118.7	52.3
Cerebrovascular diseases	I60-I69	45.0	49.1
Chronic lower respiratory diseases	J40-J47	24.3	43.5
Hypertensive diseases	I10-I15	38.1	38.9
Organic, including symptomatic, mental disorders	F01-F09	14.0	33.9

Note: (a) ICD-10 = International Classification of Diseases 10th Revision; (1) Includes COVID-19, adverse effects to COVID-19 vaccines, SARS, and vaping-related disorders; (2) Crude mortality rates are a three-year average covering 2021-2023; (3) Figures cover Orleans Parish.
Source: Centers for Disease Control and Prevention, National Center for Health Statistics. National Vital Statistics System, Mortality 2018-2023 on CDC WONDER Online Database

Mortality Rates for Selected Causes of Death

Cause of Death	ICD-10[a] Code	Crude Mortality Rate[1] per 100,000 population	
		County[2]	U.S.
Accidental poisoning and exposure to noxious substances	X40-X49	99.6	30.5
Alzheimer disease	G30	23.1	35.4
Assault	X85-Y09	51.3	7.3
COVID-19	U07.1	34.6	65.3
Diabetes mellitus	E10-E14	49.2	30.0
Diseases of the liver	K70-K76	17.5	20.8
Human immunodeficiency virus (HIV) disease	B20-B24	5.3	1.5
Influenza and pneumonia	J09-J18	7.8	13.4
Intentional self-harm	X60-X84	11.5	14.7
Malnutrition	E40-E46	9.4	6.0
Obesity and other hyperalimentation	E65-E68	3.5	3.1
Renal failure	N17-N19	24.1	16.4
Transport accidents	V01-V99	18.4	14.4

Note: (a) ICD-10 = International Classification of Diseases 10th Revision; (1) Crude mortality rates are a three-year average covering 2021-2023; (2) Figures cover Orleans Parish; Data are suppressed when the data meet the criteria for confidentiality constraints; Crude mortality rates are flagged as unreliable when the rate would be calculated with a numerator of 20 or less.
Source: Centers for Disease Control and Prevention, National Center for Health Statistics. National Vital Statistics System, Mortality 2018-2023 on CDC WONDER Online Database

Health Insurance Coverage

Area	With Health Insurance	With Private Health Insurance	With Public Health Insurance	Without Health Insurance	Population Under Age 19 Without Health Insurance
City	91.6	55.4	45.3	8.4	5.4
MSA[1]	90.8	55.9	45.1	9.2	5.6
U.S.	91.4	67.3	36.3	8.6	5.4

Note: Figures are percentages that cover the civilian noninstitutionalized population; (1) Figures cover the New Orleans-Metairie, LA Metropolitan Statistical Area
Source: U.S. Census Bureau, 2019-2023 American Community Survey 5-Year Estimates

Number of Medical Professionals

Area	MDs[3]	DOs[3,4]	Dentists	Podiatrists	Chiropractors	Optometrists
Parish[1] (number)	3,716	125	315	18	37	32
Parish[1] (rate[2])	1,005.0	33.8	86.5	4.9	10.2	8.8
U.S. (rate[2])	302.5	29.2	74.6	6.4	29.5	18.0

Note: Data as of 2023 unless noted; (1) Data covers Orleans Parish; (2) Number of medical professionals per 100,000 population; (3) Data as of 2022 and includes all active, non-federal physicians; (4) Doctor of Osteopathic Medicine
Source: U.S. Department of Health and Human Services, Health Resources and Services Administration, Bureau of Health Professions, Area Resource File (ARF) 2023-2024

Best Hospitals

According to *U.S. News*, the New Orleans-Metairie, LA metro area is home to one of the best hospitals in the U.S.: **Ochsner Medical Center** (3 pediatric specialties). The hospital listed was nationally ranked in at least one of 15 adult or 11 pediatric specialties. The number of specialties shown cover the parent hospital. Only 160 U.S. hospitals performed well enough to be nationally ranked in one or more specialties. Twenty hospitals in the U.S. made the Honor Roll. The Best Hospitals Honor Roll takes both the national rankings and the procedure and condition ratings into account. Hospitals received points if they were nationally ranked in one of the 15 adult specialties—the higher they ranked, the more points they got—and how many ratings of "high performing" they earned in the 20 procedures and conditions. *U.S. News Online, "America's Best Hospitals 2024-25"*

According to *U.S. News*, the New Orleans-Metairie, LA metro area is home to one of the best children's hospitals in the U.S.: **Ochsner Children's Hospital** (3 pediatric specialties). The hospital listed was highly ranked in at least one of 11 pediatric specialties. One hundred five children's hospitals in the U.S. were nationally ranked in at least one specialty. Hospitals received points for being ranked in a specialty, and the 10 hospitals with the most points across the 11 specialties make up the Honor Roll. *U.S. News Online, "America's Best Children's Hospitals 2024-25"*

EDUCATION

Public School District Statistics

District Name	Schls	Pupils	Pupil/ Teacher Ratio	Minority Pupils[1] (%)	Total Rev. per Pupil ($)	Total Exp. per Pupil ($)
Orleans Parrish School Board	5	2,128	11.8	98.9	345,835	65,041

Note: Table includes school districts with 2,000 or more students; (1) Percentage of students that are not non-Hispanic white.
Source: U.S. Department of Education, National Center for Education Statistics, Common Core of Data, Local Education Agency (School District) Universe Survey: School Year 2023-2024; U.S. Department of Education, National Center for Education Statistics, Common Core of Data, School District Finance Survey (F-33): School Year 2021–22

Best High Schools

According to *U.S. News,* New Orleans is home to two of the top 500 high schools in the U.S.: **Benjamin Franklin High School** (#103); **Lusher Charter School** (#178). Nearly 25,000 public, magnet and charter schools were ranked based on their performance on state assessments and how well they prepare students for college. *U.S. News & World Report, "Best High Schools 2024"*

Highest Level of Education

Area	Less than H.S.	H.S. Diploma	Some College, No Deg.	Associate Degree	Bachelor's Degree	Master's Degree	Prof. School Degree	Doctorate Degree
City	10.9	21.3	20.7	5.2	22.5	12.0	4.8	2.6
MSA[1]	12.5	26.2	21.5	6.7	19.6	8.7	3.1	1.6
U.S.	10.6	26.2	19.4	8.8	21.3	9.8	2.3	1.6

Note: Figures cover persons age 25 and over; (1) Figures cover the New Orleans-Metairie, LA Metropolitan Statistical Area
Source: U.S. Census Bureau, 2019-2023 American Community Survey 5-Year Estimates

Educational Attainment by Race

Area	High School Graduate or Higher (%)					Bachelor's Degree or Higher (%)				
	Total	White	Black	Asian	Hisp.[2]	Total	White	Black	Asian	Hisp.[2]
City	89.1	96.8	85.9	77.4	79.1	42.0	68.0	24.1	50.4	42.2
MSA[1]	87.5	92.2	85.3	80.0	74.8	33.0	41.2	22.5	47.7	25.0
U.S.	89.4	92.9	88.1	88.0	72.5	35.0	37.7	24.7	57.0	19.9

Note: Figures shown cover persons 25 years old and over; (1) Figures cover the New Orleans-Metairie, LA Metropolitan Statistical Area; (2) People of Hispanic origin can be of any race
Source: U.S. Census Bureau, 2019-2023 American Community Survey 5-Year Estimates

School Enrollment by Grade and Control

Area	Preschool (%)		Kindergarten (%)		Grades 1 - 4 (%)		Grades 5 - 8 (%)		Grades 9 - 12 (%)	
	Public	Private	Public	Private	Public	Private	Public	Private	Public	Private
City	42.8	57.2	76.0	24.0	75.5	24.5	80.0	20.0	78.6	21.4
MSA[1]	50.8	49.2	76.7	23.3	76.5	23.5	78.6	21.4	75.1	24.9
U.S.	58.7	41.3	85.2	14.8	87.2	12.8	87.9	12.1	89.0	11.0

Note: Figures shown cover persons 3 years old and over; (1) Figures cover the New Orleans-Metairie, LA Metropolitan Statistical Area
Source: U.S. Census Bureau, 2019-2023 American Community Survey 5-Year Estimates

Higher Education

Four-Year Colleges			Two-Year Colleges			Medical Schools[1]	Law Schools[2]	Voc/ Tech[3]
Public	Private Non-profit	Private For-profit	Public	Private Non-profit	Private For-profit			
3	10	1	2	0	2	2	2	7

Note: Figures cover institutions located within the New Orleans-Metairie, LA Metropolitan Statistical Area and include main campuses only; (1) includes schools accredited by the Liaison Committee on Medical Education and the American Osteopathic Association's Commission on Osteopathic College Accreditation; (2) includes ABA-accredited schools, schools with provisional ABA accreditation, and state accredited schools; (3) includes all schools with programs that are less than 2 years.
Source: National Center for Education Statistics, Integrated Postsecondary Education System (IPEDS), 2023-24; Wikipedia, List of Medical Schools in the United States, accessed May 2, 2025; Wikipedia, List of Law Schools in the United States, accessed May 2, 2025

According to *U.S. News & World Report,* the New Orleans-Metairie, LA metro area is home to one of the top 200 national universities in the U.S.: **Tulane University of Louisiana** (#63 tie). The indicators used to capture academic quality fall into a number of categories: assessment by administrators at peer institutions; retention of students; faculty resources; student selectivity; financial resources; alumni giving; high school counselor ratings of colleges; and graduation rate. *U.S. News & World Report, "America's Best Colleges 2025"*

According to *U.S. News & World Report*, the New Orleans-Metairie, LA metro area is home to one of the top 100 law schools in the U.S.: **Tulane University 1** (#71 tie). The rankings are based on a weighted average of 12 measures of quality: peer assessment score; assessment score by lawyers/judges; median LSAT scores; median undergrad GPA; acceptance rate; employment rates for graduates; placement success; bar passage rate; faculty resources; expenditures per student; student/faculty ratio; and library resources. *U.S. News & World Report, "America's Best Graduate Schools, Law, 2025"*

According to *U.S. News & World Report*, the New Orleans-Metairie, LA metro area is home to one of the top 75 business schools in the U.S.: **Tulane University (Freeman)** (#54 tie). The rankings are based on a weighted average of the following nine measures: quality assessment; peer assessment; recruiter assessment; placement success; mean starting salary and bonus; student selectivity; mean GMAT and GRE scores; mean undergraduate GPA; and acceptance rate. *U.S. News & World Report, "America's Best Graduate Schools, Business, 2025"*

EMPLOYERS

Major Employers

Company Name	Industry
Capital One	Commercial banking
City of New Orleans	Local government
Dow Chemical Co.	Chemical manufacturing
DXC Technology	Technology
Entergy	Energy
First Horizon	Financial services
Harrah's New Orleans	Casino hotels
Jefferson Parish	Government
Jefferson Parish School Board	Elementary & secondary schools
Jefferson Parish Sheriff's Office	Government
Laitram	Manufacturing
Lakeview Regional Medical Center	Healthcare
NOLA Public Schools	Education
Ochsner Health	Healthcare
Pan-American	Life insurance
Southeastern Louisiana University	Colleges & universities
Tulane Health System	Healthcare
Tulane University	Higher education
United States Postal Service	U.S. postal service
West Jefferson Medical Center	Healthcare

Note: Companies shown are located within the New Orleans-Metairie, LA Metropolitan Statistical Area.
Source: Chambers of Commerce; State Departments of Labor; Wikipedia

Best Companies to Work For

Ochsner Health, headquartered in New Orleans, is among "Best Workplaces in Health Care." To determine the Best Workplaces in Health Care list, Great Place To Work analyzed the survey responses of over 185,000 employees from Great Place To Work-Certified companies in the health care industry. Survey data analysis and company-provided datapoints are then factored into a combined score to compare and rank the companies that create the most consistently positive experience for all employees in this industry. *Fortune, "Best Workplaces in Health Care," 2024*

PUBLIC SAFETY

Crime Rate

Area	Total Crime Rate	Violent Crime Rate				Property Crime Rate		
		Murder	Rape	Robbery	Aggrav. Assault	Burglary	Larceny-Theft	Motor Vehicle Theft
City	6,450.6	53.0	187.0	180.1	941.0	478.3	2,770.8	1,840.5
U.S.	2,290.9	5.7	38.0	66.5	264.1	250.7	1,347.2	318.7

Note: Figures are crimes per 100,000 population.
Source: FBI, Table 8, Offenses Known to Law Enforcement, by State by City, 2023

Hate Crimes

Area	Number of Quarters Reported	Number of Incidents per Bias Motivation					
		Race/Ethnicity/Ancestry	Religion	Sexual Orientation	Disability	Gender	Gender Identity
City	n/a	n/a	n/a	n/a	n/a	n/a	n/a
U.S.	4	5,900	2,699	2,077	187	92	492

Note: n/a not available.
Source: Federal Bureau of Investigation, Hate Crime Statistics 2023

Identity Theft Consumer Reports

Area	Reports	Reports per 100,000 Population	Rank[2]
MSA[1]	4,268	432	16
U.S.	1,135,291	339	-

Note: (1) Figures cover the New Orleans-Metairie, LA Metropolitan Statistical Area; (2) Rank ranges from 1 to 401 where 1 indicates greatest number of identity theft reports per 100,000 population
Source: Federal Trade Commission, Consumer Sentinel Network Data Book 2024

Fraud and Other Consumer Reports

Area	Reports	Reports per 100,000 Population	Rank[2]
MSA[1]	17,332	1,753	28
U.S.	5,360,641	1,601	-

Note: (1) Figures cover the New Orleans-Metairie, LA Metropolitan Statistical Area; (2) Rank ranges from 1 to 401 where 1 indicates greatest number of fraud and other consumer reports per 100,000 population
Source: Federal Trade Commission, Consumer Sentinel Network Data Book 2024

POLITICS

2024 Presidential Election Results

Area	Trump (Rep.)	Harris (Dem.)	Stein (Green)	Kennedy (Ind.)	Oliver (Lib.)	Other
Orleans Parish	15.2	82.2	0.9	0.3	0.5	1.0
U.S.	49.7	48.2	0.6	0.5	0.4	0.6

Note: Results are percentages and may not add to 100% due to rounding
Source: Dave Leip's Atlas of U.S. Presidential Elections

SPORTS

Professional Sports Teams

Team Name	League	Year Established
New Orleans Pelicans	National Basketball Association (NBA)	2002
New Orleans Saints	National Football League (NFL)	1967

Note: Includes teams located in the New Orleans-Metairie, LA Metropolitan Statistical Area.
Source: Wikipedia, Major Professional Sports Teams of the United States and Canada, May 1, 2025

CLIMATE

Average and Extreme Temperatures

Temperature	Jan	Feb	Mar	Apr	May	Jun	Jul	Aug	Sep	Oct	Nov	Dec	Yr.
Extreme High (°F)	83	85	89	92	96	100	101	102	101	92	87	84	102
Average High (°F)	62	65	71	78	85	89	91	90	87	80	71	64	78
Average Temp. (°F)	53	56	62	69	75	81	82	82	79	70	61	55	69
Average Low (°F)	43	46	52	59	66	71	73	73	70	59	51	45	59
Extreme Low (°F)	14	19	25	32	41	50	60	60	42	35	24	11	11

Note: Figures cover the years 1948-1990
Source: National Climatic Data Center, International Station Meteorological Climate Summary, 9/96

Average Precipitation/Snowfall/Humidity

Precip./Humidity	Jan	Feb	Mar	Apr	May	Jun	Jul	Aug	Sep	Oct	Nov	Dec	Yr.
Avg. Precip. (in.)	4.7	5.6	5.2	4.7	4.4	5.4	6.4	5.9	5.5	2.8	4.4	5.5	60.6
Avg. Snowfall (in.)	Tr	Tr	Tr	0	0	0	0	0	0	0	0	Tr	Tr
Avg. Rel. Hum. 6am (%)	85	84	84	88	89	89	91	91	89	87	86	85	88
Avg. Rel. Hum. 3pm (%)	62	59	57	57	58	61	66	65	63	56	59	62	60

Note: Figures cover the years 1948-1990; Tr = Trace amounts (<0.05 in. of rain; <0.5 in. of snow)
Source: National Climatic Data Center, International Station Meteorological Climate Summary, 9/96

Weather Conditions

Temperature			Daytime Sky			Precipitation		
10°F & below	32°F & below	90°F & above	Clear	Partly cloudy	Cloudy	0.01 inch or more precip.	0.1 inch or more snow/ice	Thunderstorms
0	13	70	90	169	106	114	1	69

Note: Figures are average number of days per year and cover the years 1948-1990
Source: National Climatic Data Center, International Station Meteorological Climate Summary, 9/96

HAZARDOUS WASTE

Superfund Sites

The New Orleans-Metairie, LA metro area is home to one site on the EPA's Superfund National Priorities List (NPL) or Superfund Alternative Approach (SAA) list: **Agriculture Street Landfill** (Final NPL). The Superfund alternative approach uses the same investigation and cleanup process and standards that are used for sites listed on the National Priorities List. The SAA is an alternative to listing a site on the NPL; it is not an alternative to Superfund or the Superfund process. There are a total of

AIR QUALITY

Air Quality Trends: Ozone

	1990	1995	2000	2005	2010	2015	2020	2021	2022	2023
MSA[1]	0.082	0.088	0.091	0.079	0.074	0.067	0.061	0.060	0.061	0.068
U.S.	0.087	0.089	0.081	0.080	0.072	0.068	0.066	0.067	0.067	0.070

Note: (1) Data covers the New Orleans-Metairie, LA Metropolitan Statistical Area. The values shown are the composite ozone concentration averages among trend sites based on the highest fourth daily maximum 8-hour concentration in parts per million. These trends are based on sites having an adequate record of monitoring data during the trend period. Data from exceptional events are included.
Source: U.S. Environmental Protection Agency, Air Quality Monitoring Information, "Air Quality Trends by City, 1990-2023"

Air Quality Index

Area	Percent of Days when Air Quality was...[2]					AQI Statistics[2]	
	Good	Moderate	Unhealthy for Sensitive Groups	Unhealthy	Very Unhealthy	Maximum	Median
MSA[1]	38.1	59.2	2.7	0.0	0.0	126	53

Note: (1) Data covers the New Orleans-Metairie, LA Metropolitan Statistical Area; (2) Based on 365 days with AQI data in 2023. Air Quality Index (AQI) is an index for reporting daily air quality. EPA calculates the AQI for five major air pollutants regulated by the Clean Air Act: ground-level ozone, particle pollution (aka particulate matter), carbon monoxide, sulfur dioxide, and nitrogen dioxide. The AQI runs from 0 to 500. The higher the AQI value, the greater the level of air pollution and the greater the health concern. There are six AQI categories: "Good" AQI is between 0 and 50. Air quality is considered satisfactory; "Moderate" AQI is between 51 and 100. Air quality is acceptable; "Unhealthy for Sensitive Groups" When AQI values are between 101 and 150, members of sensitive groups may experience health effects; "Unhealthy" When AQI values are between 151 and 200 everyone may begin to experience health effects; "Very Unhealthy" AQI values between 201 and 300 trigger a health alert; "Hazardous" AQI values over 300 trigger warnings of emergency conditions (not shown).
Source: U.S. Environmental Protection Agency, Air Quality Index Report, 2023

Air Quality Index Pollutants

Area	Percent of Days when AQI Pollutant was...[2]					
	Carbon Monoxide	Nitrogen Dioxide	Ozone	Sulfur Dioxide	Particulate Matter 2.5	Particulate Matter 10
MSA[1]	0.0	0.3	37.5	(3)	62.2	0.0

Note: (1) Data covers the New Orleans-Metairie, LA Metropolitan Statistical Area; (2) Based on 365 days with AQI data in 2023. The Air Quality Index (AQI) is an index for reporting daily air quality. EPA calculates the AQI for five major air pollutants regulated by the Clean Air Act: ground-level ozone, particle pollution (also known as particulate matter), carbon monoxide, sulfur dioxide, and nitrogen dioxide. The AQI runs from 0 to 500. The higher the AQI value, the greater the level of air pollution and the greater the health concern; (3) Sulfur dioxide is no longer included in this table because SO_2 concentrations tend to be very localized and not necessarily representative of broad geographical areas like counties and CBSAs.
Source: U.S. Environmental Protection Agency, Air Quality Index Report, 2023

Maximum Air Pollutant Concentrations: Particulate Matter, Ozone, CO and Lead

	Particulate Matter 10 (ug/m³)	Particulate Matter 2.5 Wtd AM (ug/m³)	Particulate Matter 2.5 24-Hr (ug/m³)	Ozone (ppm)	Carbon Monoxide (ppm)	Lead (ug/m³)
MSA[1] Level	49	9.4	19	0.071	2	0.02
NAAQS[2]	150	15	35	0.075	9	0.15
Met NAAQS[2]	Yes	Yes	Yes	Yes	Yes	Yes

Note: (1) Data covers the New Orleans-Metairie, LA Metropolitan Statistical Area; Data from exceptional events are included; (2) National Ambient Air Quality Standards; ppm = parts per million; ug/m³ = micrograms per cubic meter; n/a not available.
Concentrations: Particulate Matter 10 (coarse particulate)—highest second maximum 24-hour concentration; Particulate Matter 2.5 Wtd AM (fine particulate)—highest weighted annual mean concentration; Particulate Matter 2.5 24-Hour (fine particulate)—highest 98th percentile 24-hour concentration; Ozone—highest fourth daily maximum 8-hour concentration; Carbon Monoxide—highest second maximum non-overlapping 8-hour concentration; Lead—maximum running 3-month average
Source: U.S. Environmental Protection Agency, Air Quality Monitoring Information, "Air Quality Statistics by City, 2023"

Maximum Air Pollutant Concentrations: Nitrogen Dioxide and Sulfur Dioxide

	Nitrogen Dioxide AM (ppb)	Nitrogen Dioxide 1-Hr (ppb)	Sulfur Dioxide AM (ppb)	Sulfur Dioxide 1-Hr (ppb)	Sulfur Dioxide 24-Hr (ppb)
MSA[1] Level	8	39	n/a	52	n/a
NAAQS[2]	53	100	30	75	140
Met NAAQS[2]	Yes	Yes	n/a	Yes	n/a

Note: (1) Data covers the New Orleans-Metairie, LA Metropolitan Statistical Area; Data from exceptional events are included; (2) National Ambient Air Quality Standards; ppm = parts per million; ug/m^3 = micrograms per cubic meter; n/a not available.
Concentrations: Nitrogen Dioxide AM—highest arithmetic mean concentration; Nitrogen Dioxide 1-Hr—highest 98th percentile 1-hour daily maximum concentration; Sulfur Dioxide AM—highest annual mean concentration; Sulfur Dioxide 1-Hr—highest 99th percentile 1-hour daily maximum concentration; Sulfur Dioxide 24-Hr—highest second maximum 24-hour concentration
Source: U.S. Environmental Protection Agency, Air Quality Monitoring Information, "Air Quality Statistics by City, 2023"

Orlando, Florida

Background

The city of Orlando, in central Florida, is a hub for tourists and home to the worldwide attractions of Walt Disney World, Universal Studios Florida, and Sea World, Medieval Times Dinner & Tournament, Ripley's Believe It or Not Museum, and Sleuths Mystery Dinner Shows. It's nickname is "The Theme Park Capital of the World."

Orlando has its own high-tech corridor due to the University of Central Florida's College of Optics and Photonics. Manufacturing, government, business service, health care, high-tech research, and tourism supply significant numbers of jobs. The city is also one of the busiest American cities for conferences and conventions; Orange County Convention Center's annual numbers include approximately $3 billion to Central Florida's economy, 200 events, and more than 1.5 million attendees.

Aside from the glitz that pumps most of the money into its economy "The City Beautiful," with its warm climate and abundant rains, produce a variety of lush flora and fauna—an attractive setting for the many young people who settle in the area. There are numerous jazz clubs, restaurants, and pubs along Orange Avenue and Church Street. Known as the land of orange juice and sunshine, Orlando is also the city for young job seekers and professionals. It is one of Florida's fastest growing cities, and number two behind Miami in most new construction.

This genteel setting is a far cry from Orlando's rough-and-tumble origins. The city started out as a makeshift campsite in the middle of a cotton plantation. The Civil War and devastating rains brought an end to the cotton trade, and its settlers turned to raising livestock, a transition that resulted in daily chaotic brawls and senseless shootings, causing martial law to be imposed by several large ranching families.

The greatest impetus toward modernity came when Cape Canaveral was founded in 1963, 50 miles away. Called Cape Kennedy until 1973, it brought missile assembly and electronic component production to the area. In 1971 the opening of Walt Disney World, created out of 27,000 acres of unexplored swampland, set the tone for Orlando as a tourist-oriented economy.

Orlando's University of Central Florida (UCF) is a public research university with its main campus in unincorporated Orange County. It is part of the State University System of Florida. With over 430,000 students enrolled in its 12 universities at last count. It has the fourth-largest on-campus student body of any public university in the United States.

Also a leading destination for film, television, commercial and web production, the city is home to Universal Studios, and a variety of arts and entertainment facilities. Amway Center opened in 2009 in Orlando, which is also home to the NBA's Orlando Magic, the Orlando Solar Bears of the ECHL (AA Hockey League) and the Orlando Predators of the National Arena League.

Orlando has a large LGBTQ+ population and is recognized as one of the most accepting and tolerant cities in the Southeast. The city is host to Gay Days every June (a Pride Month event at Walt Disney World), holds a Pride festival and parade every October, and is home to Florida's first openly gay City Commissioner, Patty Sheehan.

The city is also remembered for one of the deadliest mass shootings by a lone gunman when, in October 2016, more than 100 people were shot at Pulse, a gay nightclub in Orlando.

Orlando is surrounded by many lakes and its relative humidity remains high year-round, although winters are generally less humid. June through September is the rainy season, when scattered afternoon thunderstorms are an almost daily occurrence. During the winter months rainfall is light and the afternoons are most pleasant.

Orlando has a considerable hurricane risk, although it is not as high as in South Florida's urban corridor or other coastal regions. Since the city is located 42 miles inland from the Atlantic and 77 miles inland from the Gulf of Mexico, hurricanes usually weaken before arriving. Storm surges are not a concern since the region is 100 feet above mean sea level.

Rankings

General Rankings

- To help military veterans find the best places in which to settle down, *WalletHub* compared the 100 largest U.S. cities across 19 key indicators of livability, affordability and veteran-friendliness. They range from the share of military skill-related jobs to veteran income growth to the availability of VA health facilities. Orlando ranked #2. *Wallethub.com, "Best & Worst Places for Veterans to Live (2025)," November 7, 2024*

- *Insider* listed 23 places in the U.S. that travel industry trends reveal would be popular destinations in 2023. This year the list trends towards cultural and historical happenings, sports events, wellness experiences and invigorating outdoor escapes. According to the website insider.com Orlando is a place to visit in 2023. *Insider, "23 of the Best Places You Should Travel to in the U.S. in 2023," December 17, 2022*

- Orlando was identified as one of America's fastest-growing areas in terms of population and economy by *Forbes*. Orlando ranked #38 out of 50. Over 500 cities with more than 75,000 residents were measured for percentage of population growth over the following three periods: from 2011 to 2016; 2016 to 2021; and then 2011 to 2021. *Forbes.com, "The Fastest Growing Cities in America and Their Change in Income," September 12, 2023*

- In their annual survey, Livability.com looked at data for more than 2,000 mid-sized U.S. cities to assign a "Livability Score"for each. The top 100 scoring cities make up Livability's "Top 100 Best Places to Live in the U.S." in 2025. Orlando was placed among the top 100 of the customizable list. Criteria: housing and economy; cost of living; environment; education; health care options; transportation; safety; and community amenities. *Livability.com, "Top 100 Best Places to Live in the U.S. in 2025" April 15, 2025*

Business/Finance Rankings

- Payscale.com ranked the 32 largest metro areas in terms of wage growth. The Orlando metro area ranked #22. Criteria: quarterly changes in private industry employee and education professional wage growth from the previous year. *PayScale, "Wage Trends by Metro Area-4th Quarter," February 4, 2025*

- The Orlando metro area appeared on the Milken Institute "2025 Best Performing Cities" list. Rank: #17 out of 200 large metro areas (based on performance category). Criteria: job growth; wage growth; high-tech growth and impact; community resilience; housing affordability; household broadband access. *Milken Institute, "Best-Performing Cities 2025," January 14, 2025*

Education Rankings

- Personal finance website *WalletHub* analyzed the 150 largest U.S. metropolitan statistical areas to determine where the most educated Americans are putting their degrees to work. Criteria: education levels; percentage of workers with degrees; education quality and attainment gap; public school quality rankings; quality and enrollment of each metro area's universities. Orlando was ranked #56 (#1 = most educated city). *WalletHub.com, "Most & Least Educated Cities in America, 2025" July 2, 2024*

Environmental Rankings

- The U.S. Environmental Protection Agency (EPA) released its list of U.S. metropolitan areas with the most ENERGY STAR certified buildings in 2023. The Orlando metro area was ranked #25 out of 25. *U.S. Environmental Protection Agency, "2024 Energy Star Top Cities," May 22, 2024*

Food/Drink Rankings

- WalletHub compared the 100 largest U.S. cities across 17 key indicators of vegan- and vegetarian-friendliness. Orlando was ranked #2. Cities were selected based on metrics such as the cost of groceries for vegetarians, the share of restaurants serving meatless options and the number of salad shops per capita. *WalletHub.com, "Best Cities for Vegans & Vegetarians (2025)," September 24, 2024*

Health/Fitness Rankings

- For each of the 100 largest cities in the United States, the American Fitness Index®, compiled in partnership between the American College of Sports Medicine and the Elevance Health Foundation, evaluated community infrastructure and more than 30 health behaviors including preventive health, levels of chronic disease conditions, food insecurity, pedestrian safety, air quality, and community/environment resources that support physical activity. Orlando ranked #46 for "community fitness." *americanfitnessindex.org, "2024 ACSM American Fitness Index Summary Report," July 23, 2024*

- The Orlando metro area was identified as one of the worst cities for bed bugs in America by pest control company Orkin. The area ranked #46 out of 50 based on the number of bed bug treatments Orkin performed from December 2022 to November 2023. *Orkin, "Chicago Joins Paris In Global Bed Bug Spotlight Ranking As The Worst City On Orkin's U.S. Bed Bug Cities List," January 22, 2024*

- Orlando was identified as a "2025 Allergy Capital." The area ranked #34 out of the nation's 100 largest metropolitan areas. Three groups of factors were used to identify the most challenging cities for people with allergies: annual tree, grass, and weed pollen scores; over the counter allergy medicine use; number of board-certified allergy specialists. *Asthma and Allergy Foundation of America, "2025 Allergy Capitals: The Most Challenging Places to Live with Allergies," March 18, 2025*

- Orlando was identified as a "2024 Asthma Capital." The area ranked #33 out of the nation's 100 largest metropolitan areas. Criteria: estimated asthma prevalence; asthma-related mortality; and ER visits due to asthma. Risk factors analyzed but not factored in the rankings: annual air quality including pollution and ozone levels; public smoking laws; indoor air quality; access to asthma specialists; rescue and controller medication use; uninsured rate; pollen allergy; poverty rate. *Asthma and Allergy Foundation of America, "Asthma Capitals 2024: The Most Challenging Places to Live With Asthma," September 10, 2024*

Pet Rankings

- Orlando appeared on *The Dogington Post* site as one of the top cities for dog lovers, ranking #2 out of 15. The real estate marketplace, Zillow®, and Rover, the largest pet sitter and dog walker network, introduced a new list of "Top Emerging Dog-Friendly Cities" for 2021. Criteria: number of new dog accounts on the Rover platform; and rentals and listings that mention features that attract dog owners (fenced-in yards, dog houses, dog door or proximity to a dog park). *Dogingtonpost.com, "15 Cities Emerging as Dog-Friendliest in 2021," May 11, 2021*

- Orlando was selected by *Sniffspot.com* as one of the most dog-friendly cities in the U.S., ranking #33 out of 50. Criteria: dog parks; hiking; sniffspots; public parks; dog-friendly businesses; housing; dog waste cleanliness; leash laws; dog services; and overall cost. *Sniffspot.com, "The Top 50 Most Dog-Friendly Cities in the U.S.," September 30, 2024*

Real Estate Rankings

- *WalletHub* compared the most populated U.S. cities to determine which had the best markets for real estate agents. Orlando ranked #115 where demand was high and pay was the best. Criteria: sales per agent; annual median wage for real-estate agents; monthly average starting salary for real estate agents; real estate job density and competition; unemployment rate; home turnover rate; housing-market health index; and other relevant metrics. *WalletHub.com, "2021 Best Places to Be a Real Estate Agent," May 12, 2021*

- According to Penske Truck Rental, the Orlando metro area was named the #7 moving destination in 2023, based on one-way consumer truck rental reservations made through Penske's website, rental locations, and reservations call center. *gopenske.com, "Penske Truck Rental's 2023 Top Moving Destinations," May 7, 2024*

- The Orlando metro area appeared on Realtor.com's list of hot housing markets to watch in 2025. The area ranked #6. Criteria: forecasted home price and sales growth; overall economy; population trends. *Realtor.com®, "Top 10 Housing Markets Positioned for Growth in 2025," December 10, 2024*

- The Orlando metro area was identified as one of the 20 worst housing markets in the U.S. in 2024. The area ranked #219 out of 226 markets. Criteria: year-over-year change of median sales price of existing single-family homes between the 4th quarter of 2023 and the 4th quarter of 2024. *National Association of Realtors®, Median Sales Price of Existing Single-Family Homes for Metropolitan Areas, 4th Quarter 2024*

- Orlando was ranked #159 out of 176 metro areas in terms of cost of housing in 2024 by the National Association of Home Builders (#1 = most affordable). Criteria: the portion of an average family's income necessary to pay the mortgage on a median-priced home. *National Association of Home Builders®, NAHB-Wells Fargo Cost of Housing Index, 4th Quarter 2024*

Safety Rankings

- Allstate ranked the 100 most populous cities in America in terms of driver safety. Orlando ranked #57. Criteria based on anonymized driving behavior data from Allstate's mobile app powered by Arity: high speed driving (over 80 mph), phone handling, and hard braking. The report helps increase the importance of safety and awareness behind the wheel. *Allstate, "16th Allstate America's Best Drivers Report®" July 11, 2024*

Sports/Recreation Rankings

- Orlando was chosen as a bicycle friendly community by the League of American Bicyclists. A "Bicycle Friendly Community" welcomes cyclists by providing safe and supportive accommodation for cycling and encouraging people to bike for transportation and recreation. There are four award levels: Platinum; Gold; Silver; and Bronze. The community achieved an award level of Silver. *League of American Bicyclists, "2024 Awards-New & Renewing Bicycle Friendly Communities List," January 28, 2025*

Women/Minorities Rankings

- Personal finance website *WalletHub* compared more than 180 U.S. cities across two key dimensions, "Hispanic Business-Friendliness" and "Hispanic Purchasing Power," to arrive at the most favorable conditions for Hispanic entrepreneurs. Orlando was ranked #2 out of 182. Criteria includes: share of Hispanic-Owned Businesses; average growth of Hispanic Business revenues; Small Business-Friendliness score; affordability; and number of Hispanics with at least a bachelor's degree. *WalletHub.com, "Best Cities for Hispanic Entrepreneurs," September 4, 2024*

Miscellaneous Rankings

- *MoveHub* ranked 446 hipster cities across 20 countries, using its new and improved alternative Hipster Index and Orlando came out as #8 among the top 50. Criteria: population over 150,000; number of vintage boutiques; density of tattoo parlors; vegan places to eat; coffee shops; and density of vinyl record stores. *MoveHub.com, "The Hipster Index: Brighton Pips Portland to Global Top Spot," July 28, 2021*

- *WalletHub* compared 148 of the most populated U.S. cities to determine their operating efficiency. A "Quality of Services" score was constructed for each city and then measured against the total budget per capita to reveal which were managed the best. Orlando ranked #87. Criteria: financial stability; economy; education; safety; health; infrastructure and pollution. *WalletHub.com, "2025's Best- & Worst-Run Cities in America," June 18, 2024*

Business Environment

DEMOGRAPHICS

Population Growth

Area	1990 Census	2000 Census	2010 Census	2020 Census	2023 Estimate[2]	Population Growth 1990-2023 (%)
City	161,172	185,951	238,300	307,573	311,732	93.4
MSA[1]	1,224,852	1,644,561	2,134,411	2,673,376	2,721,022	122.2
U.S.	248,709,873	281,421,906	308,745,538	331,449,281	332,387,540	33.6

Note: (1) Figures cover the Orlando-Kissimmee-Sanford, FL Metropolitan Statistical Area; (2) 2019-2023 5-year ACS population estimate
Source: U.S. Census Bureau, 1990 Census, 2000 Census, 2010 Census, 2020 Census, 2019-2023 American Community Survey 5-Year Estimates

Race

Area	White Alone[2] (%)	Black Alone[2] (%)	Asian Alone[2] (%)	AIAN[3] Alone[2] (%)	NHOPI[4] Alone[2] (%)	Other Race Alone[2] (%)	Two or More Races (%)
City	43.2	22.9	4.4	0.1	0.1	8.4	21.0
MSA[1]	52.5	16.0	4.5	0.3	0.1	9.5	17.2
U.S.	63.4	12.4	5.8	0.9	0.2	6.6	10.7

Note: (1) Figures cover the Orlando-Kissimmee-Sanford, FL Metropolitan Statistical Area; (2) Alone is defined as not being in combination with one or more other races; (3) American Indian and Alaska Native; (4) Native Hawaiian and Other Pacific Islander
Source: U.S. Census Bureau, 2019-2023 American Community Survey 5-Year Estimates

Hispanic or Latino Origin

Area	Total (%)	Mexican (%)	Puerto Rican (%)	Cuban (%)	Other (%)
City	35.6	2.0	15.2	2.6	15.8
MSA[1]	32.5	2.7	14.3	2.6	12.9
U.S.	19.0	11.3	1.8	0.7	5.2

Note: Persons of Hispanic or Latino origin can be of any race; (1) Figures cover the Orlando-Kissimmee-Sanford, FL Metropolitan Statistical Area
Source: U.S. Census Bureau, 2019-2023 American Community Survey 5-Year Estimates

Age

Area	Under Age 5	Age 5–19	Age 20–34	Age 35–44	Age 45–54	Age 55–64	Age 65–74	Age 75–84	Age 85+	Median Age
City	6.2	16.8	26.7	16.5	12.4	10.2	6.6	3.2	1.3	35.1
MSA[1]	5.5	18.5	21.4	14.2	12.9	12.0	9.1	4.7	1.8	38.3
U.S.	5.7	19.1	20.2	13.1	12.3	12.8	10.0	4.9	1.9	38.7

Note: (1) Figures cover the Orlando-Kissimmee-Sanford, FL Metropolitan Statistical Area
Source: U.S. Census Bureau, 2019-2023 American Community Survey 5-Year Estimates

Disability by Age

Area	All Ages	Under 18 Years Old	18 to 64 Years Old	65 Years and Over
City	10.3	5.2	8.3	33.4
MSA[1]	12.3	5.6	9.5	33.1
U.S.	13.0	4.7	10.7	32.9

Note: Figures show percent of the civilian noninstitutionalized population that reported having a disability. Disability status is determined from six types of difficulty: vision, hearing, cognitive, ambulatory, self-care, and independent living. For children under 5 years old, hearing and vision difficulty are used to determine disability status. For children between the ages of 5 and 14, disability status is determined from hearing, vision, cognitive, ambulatory, and self-care difficulties. For people aged 15 years and older, they are considered to have a disability if they have difficulty with any one of the six difficulty types; Note: (1) Figures cover the Orlando-Kissimmee-Sanford, FL Metropolitan Statistical Area
Source: U.S. Census Bureau, 2019-2023 American Community Survey 5-Year Estimates

Ancestry

Area	German	Irish	English	American	Italian	Polish	French[2]	European	Scottish
City	6.4	5.4	5.9	6.1	4.5	1.6	1.5	0.8	0.9
MSA[1]	8.2	7.2	7.1	9.1	5.0	1.7	1.6	1.1	1.2
U.S.	12.6	9.4	9.1	5.5	4.9	2.6	2.0	1.6	1.6

Note: Figures are the percentage of the total population reporting a particular ancestry. The nine most commonly reported ancestries in the U.S. are shown. Figures include multiple ancestries (e.g. if a person reported being Irish and Italian, they were included in both columns); (1) Figures cover the Orlando-Kissimmee-Sanford, FL Metropolitan Statistical Area; (2) Excludes Basque
Source: U.S. Census Bureau, 2019-2023 American Community Survey 5-Year Estimates

Foreign-born Population

Area	Percent of Population Born in								
	Any Foreign Country	Asia	Mexico	Europe	Caribbean	Central America[2]	South America	Africa	Canada
City	24.1	3.0	0.8	1.8	6.5	1.2	10.1	0.5	0.2
MSA[1]	20.3	3.1	0.9	1.6	5.9	1.2	6.8	0.6	0.3
U.S.	13.9	4.3	3.3	1.4	1.4	1.2	1.2	0.8	0.2

Note: (1) Figures cover the Orlando-Kissimmee-Sanford, FL Metropolitan Statistical Area; (2) Excludes Mexico.
Source: U.S. Census Bureau, 2019-2023 American Community Survey 5-Year Estimates

Household Size

Area	Persons in Household (%)							Average Household Size
	One	Two	Three	Four	Five	Six	Seven or More	
City	32.4	33.5	15.9	11.2	4.5	1.4	1.1	2.44
MSA[1]	24.5	34.1	17.0	14.3	6.5	2.2	1.3	2.71
U.S.	28.5	33.8	15.4	12.7	5.9	2.3	1.4	2.54

Note: (1) Figures cover the Orlando-Kissimmee-Sanford, FL Metropolitan Statistical Area
Source: U.S. Census Bureau, 2019-2023 American Community Survey 5-Year Estimates

Household Relationships

Area	House-holder	Opposite-sex Spouse	Same-sex Spouse	Opposite-sex Unmarried Partner	Same-sex Unmarried Partner	Child[2]	Grand-child	Other Relatives	Non-relatives
City	41.7	13.7	0.5	3.5	0.4	26.1	2.0	5.9	5.0
MSA[1]	37.0	17.0	0.3	2.7	0.2	28.4	2.4	6.0	4.2
U.S.	38.3	17.5	0.2	2.5	0.2	28.3	2.4	4.8	3.4

Note: Figures are percent of the total population; (1) Figures cover the Orlando-Kissimmee-Sanford, FL Metropolitan Statistical Area; (2) Includes biological, adopted, and stepchildren of the householder
Source: U.S. Census Bureau, 2020 Census

Gender

Area	Males	Females	Males per 100 Females
City	153,714	158,018	97.3
MSA[1]	1,336,264	1,384,758	96.5
U.S.	164,545,087	167,842,453	98.0

Note: (1) Figures cover the Orlando-Kissimmee-Sanford, FL Metropolitan Statistical Area
Source: U.S. Census Bureau, 2019-2023 American Community Survey 5-Year Estimates

Marital Status

Area	Never Married	Now Married[2]	Separated	Widowed	Divorced
City	42.9	38.6	2.4	3.7	12.5
MSA[1]	35.1	47.0	1.8	4.9	11.2
U.S.	34.1	47.9	1.7	5.6	10.7

Note: Figures are percentages and cover the population 15 years of age and older; (1) Figures cover the Orlando-Kissimmee-Sanford, FL Metropolitan Statistical Area; (2) Excludes separated
Source: U.S. Census Bureau, 2019-2023 American Community Survey 5-Year Estimates

Religious Groups by Family

Area	Catholic	Baptist	Methodist	LDS[2]	Pentecostal	Lutheran	Islam	Adventist	Other
MSA[1]	17.6	5.7	2.1	0.9	2.7	0.6	1.3	2.8	14.6
U.S.	18.7	7.3	3.0	2.0	1.8	1.7	1.3	1.3	11.6

Note: Figures are the number of adherents as a percentage of the total population and cover the eight largest religious groups in the U.S; (1) Figures cover the Orlando-Kissimmee-Sanford, FL Metropolitan Statistical Area; (2) Church of Jesus Christ of Latter-day Saints
Sources: 2020 U.S. Religion Census, Association of Statisticians of American Religious Bodies; The Association of Religion Data Archives (ARDA)

Religious Groups by Tradition

Area	Catholic	Evangelical Protestant	Mainline Protestant	Black Protestant	Islam	Judaism	Hinduism	Orthodox	Buddhism
MSA[1]	17.6	20.6	2.5	2.7	1.3	0.2	0.5	0.3	0.3
U.S.	18.7	16.5	5.2	2.3	1.3	0.6	0.4	0.4	0.3

Note: Figures are the number of adherents as a percentage of the total population; (1) Figures cover the Orlando-Kissimmee-Sanford, FL Metropolitan Statistical Area
Sources: 2020 U.S. Religion Census, Association of Statisticians of American Religious Bodies; The Association of Religion Data Archives (ARDA)

ECONOMY

Real Gross Domestic Product (GDP)

Area	2017	2018	2019	2020	2021	2022	2023	Rank[3]
MSA[1]	136.2	141.2	146.8	140.3	156.9	167.8	175.3	26
U.S.[2]	17,619.1	18,160.7	18,642.5	18,238.9	19,387.6	19,896.6	20,436.3	—

Note: Figures are in billions of chained 2017 dollars; (1) Figures cover the Orlando-Kissimmee-Sanford, FL Metropolitan Statistical Area; (2) Figures cover real GDP within metropolitan areas; (3) Rank is based on 2023 data and ranges from 1 to 384
Source: U.S. Bureau of Economic Analysis

Economic Growth

Area	2014	2015	2016	2017	2018	2019	2020	2021	2022	2023
MSA[1]	3.8	5.5	3.8	5.5	3.7	4.0	-4.4	11.9	6.9	4.5
U.S.[2]	2.6	3.2	2.0	2.7	3.1	2.7	-2.2	6.3	2.6	2.7

Note: Figures are real gross domestic product growth rates and represent percent change from preceding period; (1) Figures cover the Orlando-Kissimmee-Sanford, FL Metropolitan Statistical Area; (2) Figures are the average growth rates within metropolitan areas
Source: U.S. Bureau of Economic Analysis

Metropolitan Area Exports

Area	2018	2019	2020	2021	2022	2023	Rank[2]
MSA[1]	3,131.7	3,363.9	2,849.8	3,313.6	4,096.9	4,443.5	71
U.S.	1,664,056.1	1,645,173.7	1,431,406.6	1,753,941.4	2,062,937.4	2,019,160.5	—

Note: Figures are in millions of dollars; (1) Figures cover the Orlando-Kissimmee-Sanford, FL Metropolitan Statistical Area; (2) Rank is based on 2023 data and ranges from 1 to 386
Source: U.S. Department of Commerce, International Trade Administration, Office of Trade and Economic Analysis, Industry and Analysis, Exports by Metropolitan Area, data extracted April 2, 2025

Building Permits

Area	Single-Family			Multi-Family			Total		
	2023	2024	Pct. Chg.	2023	2024	Pct. Chg.	2023	2024	Pct. Chg.
City	887	914	3.0	1,514	1,056	-30.3	2,401	1,970	-18.0
MSA[1]	17,049	15,364	-9.9	8,366	8,771	4.8	25,415	24,135	-5.0
U.S.	920,000	981,900	6.7	591,100	496,100	-16.1	1,511,100	1,478,000	-2.2

Note: (1) Figures cover the Orlando-Kissimmee-Sanford, FL Metropolitan Statistical Area; Figures represent new, privately-owned housing units authorized (unadjusted data)
Source: U.S. Census Bureau, Building Permits Survey (BPS), 2023, 2024

Bankruptcy Filings

Area	Business Filings			Nonbusiness Filings		
	2023	2024	% Chg.	2023	2024	% Chg.
Orange County	152	231	52.0	1,832	2,279	24.4
U.S.	18,926	23,107	22.1	434,064	494,201	13.9

Note: Business filings include Chapter 7, Chapter 9, Chapter 11, Chapter 12, Chapter 13, Chapter 15, and Section 304; Nonbusiness filings include Chapter 7, Chapter 11, and Chapter 13
Source: Administrative Office of the U.S. Courts, Business and Nonbusiness Bankruptcy, County Cases Commenced by Chapter of the Bankruptcy Code, During the 12-Month Period Ending December 31, 2023 and Business and Nonbusiness Bankruptcy, County Cases Commenced by Chapter of the Bankruptcy Code, During the 12-Month Period Ending December 31, 2024

Housing Vacancy Rates

Area	Gross Vacancy Rate[3] (%)			Year-Round Vacancy Rate[4] (%)			Rental Vacancy Rate[5] (%)			Homeowner Vacancy Rate[6] (%)		
	2022	2023	2024	2022	2023	2024	2022	2023	2024	2022	2023	2024
MSA[1]	9.6	9.5	9.8	7.4	7.6	8.4	6.5	7.0	9.4	1.4	1.1	1.5
U.S.[2]	9.1	9.0	9.1	7.5	7.5	7.6	5.7	6.5	6.8	0.8	0.8	1.0

Note: (1) Figures cover the Orlando-Kissimmee-Sanford, FL Metropolitan Statistical Area; (2) Figures cover the 75 largest Metropolitan Statistical Areas; (3) The percentage of the total housing inventory that is vacant; (4) The percentage of the housing inventory (excluding seasonal units) that is year-round vacant; (5) The percentage of rental inventory that is vacant for rent; (6) The percentage of homeowner inventory that is vacant for sale
Source: U.S. Census Bureau, Housing Vacancies and Homeownership Annual Statistics: 2022, 2023, 2024

INCOME

Income

Area	Per Capita ($)	Median Household ($)	Average Household ($)
City	41,985	69,268	100,135
MSA[1]	38,776	75,611	103,312
U.S.	43,289	78,538	110,491

Note: (1) Figures cover the Orlando-Kissimmee-Sanford, FL Metropolitan Statistical Area
Source: U.S. Census Bureau, 2019-2023 American Community Survey 5-Year Estimates

Household Income Distribution

Area	Percent of Households Earning							
	Under $15,000	$15,000 -$24,999	$25,000 -$34,999	$35,000 -$49,999	$50,000 -$74,999	$75,000 -$99,999	$100,000 -$149,999	$150,000 and up
City	9.5	7.0	8.7	11.7	17.1	12.5	16.3	17.2
MSA[1]	7.3	6.3	7.3	11.1	17.7	13.5	18.0	18.9
U.S.	8.5	6.6	6.8	10.4	15.7	12.7	17.4	21.9

Note: (1) Figures cover the Orlando-Kissimmee-Sanford, FL Metropolitan Statistical Area
Source: U.S. Census Bureau, 2019-2023 American Community Survey 5-Year Estimates

Poverty Rate

Area	All Ages	Under 18 Years Old	18 to 64 Years Old	65 Years and Over
City	15.5	23.0	12.9	16.8
MSA[1]	11.8	15.0	11.0	10.5
U.S.	12.4	16.3	11.6	10.4

Note: Figures are percentage of people whose income during the past 12 months was below the poverty level; (1) Figures cover the Orlando-Kissimmee-Sanford, FL Metropolitan Statistical Area
Source: U.S. Census Bureau, 2019-2023 American Community Survey 5-Year Estimates

EMPLOYMENT

Labor Force and Employment

Area	Civilian Labor Force			Workers Employed		
	Dec. 2023	Dec. 2024	% Chg.	Dec. 2023	Dec. 2024	% Chg.
City	181,418	181,948	0.3	176,377	176,719	0.2
MSA[1]	1,476,354	1,481,986	0.4	1,432,973	1,435,926	0.2
U.S.	166,661,000	167,746,000	0.7	160,754,000	161,294,000	0.3

Note: Data is not seasonally adjusted and covers workers 16 years of age and older; (1) Figures cover the Orlando-Kissimmee-Sanford, FL Metropolitan Statistical Area
Source: Bureau of Labor Statistics, Local Area Unemployment Statistics

Unemployment Rate

Area	2024											
	Jan.	Feb.	Mar.	Apr.	May	Jun.	Jul.	Aug.	Sep.	Oct.	Nov.	Dec.
City	3.0	2.8	2.7	2.7	2.9	3.3	3.5	3.5	3.2	3.1	3.1	2.9
MSA[1]	3.2	3.1	3.1	2.9	3.1	3.6	3.8	3.8	3.4	3.4	3.5	3.1
U.S.	4.1	4.2	3.9	3.5	3.7	4.3	4.5	4.4	3.9	3.9	4.0	3.8

Note: Data is not seasonally adjusted and covers workers 16 years of age and older; (1) Figures cover the Orlando-Kissimmee-Sanford, FL Metropolitan Statistical Area
Source: Bureau of Labor Statistics, Local Area Unemployment Statistics

Average Wages

Occupation	$/Hr.	Occupation	$/Hr.
Accountants and Auditors	42.38	Maintenance and Repair Workers	23.02
Automotive Mechanics	25.24	Marketing Managers	75.25
Bookkeepers	23.73	Network and Computer Systems Admin.	45.79
Carpenters	24.25	Nurses, Licensed Practical	28.81
Cashiers	15.21	Nurses, Registered	41.57
Computer Programmers	46.42	Nursing Assistants	17.96
Computer Systems Analysts	49.67	Office Clerks, General	21.36
Computer User Support Specialists	28.57	Physical Therapists	47.77
Construction Laborers	21.13	Physicians	152.34
Cooks, Restaurant	18.25	Plumbers, Pipefitters and Steamfitters	26.02
Customer Service Representatives	19.99	Police and Sheriff's Patrol Officers	32.01
Dentists	85.11	Postal Service Mail Carriers	28.68
Electricians	26.17	Real Estate Sales Agents	33.44
Engineers, Electrical	56.13	Retail Salespersons	16.93
Fast Food and Counter Workers	14.19	Sales Representatives, Technical/Scientific	50.60
Financial Managers	78.11	Secretaries, Exc. Legal/Medical/Executive	21.59
First-Line Supervisors of Office Workers	32.58	Security Guards	18.05
General and Operations Managers	58.33	Surgeons	n/a
Hairdressers/Cosmetologists	17.70	Teacher Assistants, Exc. Postsecondary[1]	15.02
Home Health and Personal Care Aides	16.03	Teachers, Secondary School, Exc. Sp. Ed.[1]	27.08
Janitors and Cleaners	16.19	Telemarketers	17.71
Landscaping/Groundskeeping Workers	17.82	Truck Drivers, Heavy/Tractor-Trailer	26.28
Lawyers	68.56	Truck Drivers, Light/Delivery Services	22.34
Maids and Housekeeping Cleaners	16.98	Waiters and Waitresses	18.62

Note: Wage data covers the Orlando-Kissimmee-Sanford, FL Metropolitan Statistical Area; (1) Hourly wages were calculated from annual wage data based on a 40 hour work week
Source: Bureau of Labor Statistics, Metro Area Occupational Employment & Wage Estimates, May 2024

Employment by Industry

Sector	MSA[1] Number of Employees	MSA[1] Percent of Total	U.S. Percent of Total
Construction	96,500	6.3	5.1
Financial Activities	93,300	6.1	5.8
Government	136,100	8.9	14.9
Information	28,200	1.8	1.9
Leisure and Hospitality	293,200	19.2	10.4
Manufacturing	52,800	3.5	8.0
Mining and Logging	300	<0.1	0.4
Other Services	56,400	3.7	3.7
Private Education and Health Services	197,200	12.9	16.9
Professional and Business Services	291,800	19.1	14.2
Retail Trade	161,000	10.5	10.0
Transportation, Warehousing, and Utilities	68,700	4.5	4.8
Wholesale Trade	53,300	3.5	3.9

Note: Figures are non-farm employment as of December 2024. Figures are not seasonally adjusted and include workers 16 years of age and older; (1) Figures cover the Orlando-Kissimmee-Sanford, FL Metropolitan Statistical Area
Source: Bureau of Labor Statistics, Current Employment Statistics, Employment, Hours, and Earnings

Employment by Occupation

Occupation Classification	City (%)	MSA[1] (%)	U.S. (%)
Management, Business, Science, and Arts	43.1	39.9	42.0
Natural Resources, Construction, and Maintenance	5.7	7.9	8.6
Production, Transportation, and Material Moving	11.3	10.7	13.0
Sales and Office	22.4	23.2	19.9
Service	17.5	18.3	16.5

Note: Figures cover employed civilians 16 years of age and older; (1) Figures cover the Orlando-Kissimmee-Sanford, FL Metropolitan Statistical Area
Source: U.S. Census Bureau, 2019-2023 American Community Survey 5-Year Estimates

Occupations with Greatest Projected Employment Growth: 2022 – 2032

Occupation[1]	2022 Employment	2032 Projected Employment	Numeric Employment Change	Percent Employment Change
Stockers and Order Fillers	236,990	274,060	37,070	15.6
Retail Salespersons	308,940	340,000	31,060	10.1
Waiters and Waitresses	195,320	223,820	28,500	14.6
Software Developers	75,620	101,940	26,320	34.8
General and Operations Managers	184,790	210,510	25,720	13.9
Registered Nurses	202,780	228,070	25,290	12.5
Fast Food and Counter Workers	185,000	209,460	24,460	13.2
Cooks, Restaurant	120,850	141,640	20,790	17.2
Landscaping and Groundskeeping Workers	112,240	129,030	16,790	15.0
Janitors and Cleaners, Except Maids and Housekeeping Cleaners	136,890	153,490	16,600	12.1

Note: Projections cover Florida; (1) Sorted by numeric employment change
Source: www.projectionscentral.org, State Occupational Projections, 2022–2032 Long-Term Projections

Fastest-Growing Occupations: 2022 – 2032

Occupation[1]	2022 Employment	2032 Projected Employment	Numeric Employment Change	Percent Employment Change
Nurse Practitioners	18,910	29,980	11,070	58.5
Data Scientists	8,470	12,450	3,980	47.0
Information Security Analysts (SOC 2018)	11,060	15,650	4,590	41.5
Statisticians	590	820	230	39.0
Solar Photovoltaic Installers	1,210	1,680	470	38.8
Computer and Information Research Scientists (SOC 2018)	3,160	4,380	1,220	38.6
Physician Assistants	8,830	12,180	3,350	37.9
Actuaries	1,640	2,260	620	37.8
Physical Therapist Assistants	7,430	10,230	2,800	37.7
Medical and Health Services Managers	34,490	47,200	12,710	36.9

Note: Projections cover Florida; (1) Sorted by percent employment change and excludes occupations with numeric employment change less than 50
Source: www.projectionscentral.org, State Occupational Projections, 2022–2032 Long-Term Projections

CITY FINANCES

City Government Finances

Component	2022 ($000)	2022 ($ per capita)
Total Revenues	1,062,439	3,670
Total Expenditures	1,039,925	3,593
Debt Outstanding	910,494	3,146

Source: U.S. Census Bureau, State & Local Government Finances 2022

City Government Revenue by Source

Source	2022 ($000)	2022 ($ per capita)	2022 (%)
General Revenue			
From Federal Government	31,602	109	3.0
From State Government	48,317	167	4.5
From Local Governments	192,061	664	18.1
Taxes			
Property	241,849	836	22.8
Sales and Gross Receipts	64,397	222	6.1
Personal Income	0	0	0.0
Corporate Income	0	0	0.0
Motor Vehicle License	0	0	0.0
Other Taxes	62,016	214	5.8
Current Charges	283,508	979	26.7
Liquor Store	0	0	0.0
Utility	28	0	0.0

Source: U.S. Census Bureau, State & Local Government Finances 2022

City Government Expenditures by Function

Function	2022 ($000)	2022 ($ per capita)	2022 (%)
General Direct Expenditures			
Air Transportation	0	0	0.0
Corrections	0	0	0.0
Education	0	0	0.0
Employment Security Administration	0	0	0.0
Financial Administration	34,951	120	3.4
Fire Protection	127,891	441	12.3
General Public Buildings	0	0	0.0
Governmental Administration, Other	104,592	361	10.1
Health	0	0	0.0
Highways	41,312	142	4.0
Hospitals	0	0	0.0
Housing and Community Development	20,192	69	1.9
Interest on General Debt	31,671	109	3.0
Judicial and Legal	5,562	19	0.5
Libraries	0	0	0.0
Parking	19,322	66	1.9
Parks and Recreation	113,914	393	11.0
Police Protection	191,683	662	18.4
Public Welfare	0	0	0.0
Sewerage	109,208	377	10.5
Solid Waste Management	37,377	129	3.6
Veterans' Services	0	0	0.0
Liquor Store	0	0	0.0
Utility	0	0	0.0

Source: U.S. Census Bureau, State & Local Government Finances 2022

TAXES

State Corporate Income Tax Rates

State	Tax Rate (%)	Income Brackets ($)	Num. of Brackets	Financial Institution Tax Rate (%)[a]	Federal Income Tax Ded.
Florida	5.5	Flat rate	1	5.5	No

Note: Tax rates for tax year 2024; (a) Rates listed are the corporate income tax rate applied to financial institutions or excise taxes based on income. Some states have other taxes based upon the value of deposits or shares.
Source: Federation of Tax Administrators, State Corporate Income Tax Rates, January 1, 2025

State Individual Income Tax Rates

State	Tax Rate (%)	Income Brackets ($)	Personal Exemptions ($)			Standard Ded. ($)	
			Single	Married	Depend.	Single	Married
Florida	– No state income tax –						

Note: Tax rates for tax year 2024; Local- and county-level taxes are not included
Source: Federation of Tax Administrators, State Individual Income Tax Rates, January 1, 2025

Various State Sales and Excise Tax Rates

State	State Sales Tax (%)	Gasoline[1] ($/gal.)	Cigarette[2] ($/pack)	Spirits[3] ($/gal.)	Wine[4] ($/gal.)	Beer[5] ($/gal.)	Recreational Marijuana (%)
Florida	6	0.39	1.34	6.50	2.25	0.48	Not legal

Note: All tax rates as of January 1, 2025; (1) The American Petroleum Institute has developed a methodology for determining the average tax rate on a gallon of fuel. Rates may include any of the following: excise taxes, environmental fees, storage tank fees, other fees or taxes, general sales tax, and local taxes; (2) The federal excise tax of $1.0066 per pack and local taxes are not included; (3) Rates are those applicable to off-premise sales of 40% alcohol by volume (a.b.v.) distilled spirits in 750ml containers. Local excise taxes are excluded; (4) Rates are those applicable to off-premise sales of 11% a.b.v. non-carbonated wine in 750ml containers; (5) Rates are those applicable to off-premise sales of 4.7% a.b.v. beer in 12 ounce containers.
Source: Tax Foundation, 2025 Facts & Figures: How Does Your State Compare?

State Tax Competitiveness Index

State	Overall Rank	Corporate Tax Rank	Individual Income Tax Rank	Sales Tax Rank	Property Tax Rank	Unemployment Insurance Tax Rank
Florida	4	16	1	14	21	10

Note: The Tax Foundation's State Tax Competitiveness Index enables policymakers, taxpayers, and business leaders to gauge how their states' tax systems compare. A rank of 1 is best, 50 is worst. Rankings do not average to the total. States without a tax rank equally as 1. DC's scores and rankings do not affect other states. The report shows tax systems as of July 1, 2024 (the beginning of Fiscal Year 2025).
Source: Tax Foundation, State Tax Competitiveness Index 2025

TRANSPORTATION

Means of Transportation to Work

Area	Car/Truck/Van		Public Transportation			Bicycle	Walked	Other Means	Worked at Home
	Drove Alone	Car-pooled	Bus	Subway	Railroad				
City	69.5	8.9	1.8	0.0	0.0	0.5	1.6	2.5	15.1
MSA[1]	70.8	9.2	1.0	0.0	0.1	0.3	1.2	1.8	15.6
U.S.	70.2	8.5	1.7	1.3	0.4	0.4	2.4	1.6	13.5

Note: Figures are percentages and cover workers 16 years of age and older; (1) Figures cover the Orlando-Kissimmee-Sanford, FL Metropolitan Statistical Area
Source: U.S. Census Bureau, 2019-2023 American Community Survey 5-Year Estimates

Travel Time to Work

Area	Less Than 10 Minutes	10 to 19 Minutes	20 to 29 Minutes	30 to 44 Minutes	45 to 59 Minutes	60 to 89 Minutes	90 Minutes or More
City	7.5	26.1	27.4	26.5	6.4	3.9	2.2
MSA[1]	7.1	23.4	22.2	27.8	10.6	6.3	2.5
U.S.	12.6	28.6	21.2	20.8	8.1	6.0	2.8

Note: Note: Figures are percentages and include workers 16 years old and over; (1) Figures cover the Orlando-Kissimmee-Sanford, FL Metropolitan Statistical Area
Source: U.S. Census Bureau, 2019-2023 American Community Survey 5-Year Estimates

Key Congestion Measures

Measure	2000	2010	2015	2020	2022
Annual Hours of Delay, Total (000)	34,970	51,679	58,893	25,458	68,736
Annual Hours of Delay, Per Auto Commuter	43	48	53	22	62
Annual Congestion Cost, Per Auto Commuter ($)	980	1,152	1,212	527	1,392

Note: Figures cover the Orlando FL urban area
Source: Texas A&M Transportation Institute, 2023 Urban Mobility Report

Freeway Travel Time Index

Measure	1985	1990	1995	2000	2005	2010	2015	2020	2022
Urban Area Index[1]	1.09	1.14	1.16	1.20	1.23	1.22	1.23	1.07	1.22
Urban Area Rank[1,2]	36	26	32	29	28	32	29	57	28

Note: Freeway Travel Time Index—the ratio of travel time in the peak period to the travel time at free-flow conditions. For example, a value of 1.30 indicates a 20-minute free-flow trip takes 26 minutes in the peak (20 minutes x 1.30 = 26 minutes); (1) Covers the Orlando FL urban area; (2) Rank is based on 101 larger urban areas (#1 = highest travel time index)
Source: Texas A&M Transportation Institute, 2023 Urban Mobility Report

Public Transportation

Agency Name / Mode of Transportation	Vehicles Operated in Maximum Service[1]	Annual Unlinked Passenger Trips[2] (in thous.)	Annual Passenger Miles[3] (in thous.)
Central Florida Regional Transportation Authority (Lynx)			
Bus (directly operated)	248	16,995.2	97,732.3
Bus (purchased transportation)	13	66.1	363.3
Bus Rapid Transit (directly operated)	8	431.1	451.9
Demand Response (purchased transportation)	163	668.9	6,835.5
Vanpool (purchased transportation)	133	256.9	5,635.3

Note: (1) Number of revenue vehicles operated by the given mode and type of service to meet the annual maximum service requirement. This is the revenue vehicle count during the peak season of the year; on the week and day that maximum service is provided. Vehicles operated in maximum service (VOMS) exclude atypical days and one-time special events; (2) Number of passengers who boarded public transportation vehicles. Passengers are counted each time they board a vehicle no matter how many vehicles they use to travel from their origin to their destination. (3) Sum of the distances ridden by all passengers during the entire fiscal year.
Source: Federal Transit Administration, National Transit Database, 2023

Air Transportation

Airport Name and Code / Type of Service	Passenger Airlines[1]	Passenger Enplanements	Freight Carriers[2]	Freight (lbs)
Orlando International (MCO)				
Domestic service (U.S. carriers only)	27	24,109,668	15	150,564,423
International service (U.S. carriers only)	9	1,103,050	3	999,348

Note: (1) Includes all U.S.-based major, minor and commuter airlines that carried at least one passenger during the year; (2) Includes all U.S.-based airlines and freight carriers that transported at least one pound of freight during the year.
Source: Bureau of Transportation Statistics, The Intermodal Transportation Database, Air Carriers: T-100 Domestic Market (U.S. carriers only), 2024; Bureau of Transportation Statistics, The Intermodal Transportation Database, Air Carriers: T-100 International Market (U.S. carriers only), 2024

BUSINESSES

Major Business Headquarters

Company Name	Industry	Rankings Fortune[1]	Rankings Forbes[2]
Darden Restaurants	Food services	383	-
Red Lobster	Restaurants	-	273

Note: (1) Companies that produce a 10-K are ranked 1 to 500 based on 2023 revenue; (2) All private companies with at least $2 billion in annual revenue through the end of their most current fiscal year are ranked 1 to 275; companies listed are headquartered in the city; dashes indicate no ranking
Source: Fortune, "Fortune 500," 2024; Forbes, "America's Largest Private Companies," 2024

Fastest-Growing Businesses

According to *Inc.*, Orlando is home to three of America's 500 fastest-growing private companies: **ThreatLocker(r)** (#120); **Biller Genie** (#259); **Charter Research** (#285). Criteria: must be an independent, privately-held, for-profit, U.S. corporation, proprietorship or partnership as of December 31, 2023; revenues must be at least $100,000 in 2020 and $2 million in 2023; must have four-year operating/sales history. *Inc., "America's 500 Fastest-Growing Private Companies," 2024*

According to Deloitte, Orlando is home to two of North America's 500 fastest-growing high-technology companies: **ThreatLocker** (#49); **OneRail** (#66). Companies are ranked by percentage growth in revenue over a four-year period. Criteria for inclusion: company must be headquartered within North America; must own proprietary intellectual property or technology that is sold to customers in products that contributes to a significant portion of the company's operating revenue; must have been in business for a minumum of four years with 2020 operating revenues of at least $50,000 USD/CD and 2023 operating revenues of at least $5 million USD/CD. *Deloitte, 2024 Technology Fast 500*™

Living Environment

COST OF LIVING

Cost of Living Index

Composite Index	Groceries	Housing	Utilities	Transportation	Health Care	Misc. Goods/Services
96.4	104.7	91.7	103.7	97.4	91.9	95.2

Note: The Cost of Living Index measures regional differences in the cost of consumer goods and services, excluding taxes and non-consumer expenditures, for professional and managerial households in the top income quintile. It is based on more than 50,000 prices covering almost 60 different items for which prices are collected three times a year by chambers of commerce, economic development organizations or university applied economic centers in each participating urban area. The numbers shown should be read as a percentage above or below the national average of 100. For example, a value of 115.4 in the groceries column indicates that grocery prices are 15.4% higher than the national average. Small differences in the index numbers should not be interpreted as significant; Figures cover the Orlando FL urban area.
Source: The Council for Community and Economic Research, Cost of Living Index, 2024

Grocery Prices

Area[1]	T-Bone Steak ($/pound)	Frying Chicken ($/pound)	Whole Milk ($/half gal.)	Eggs ($/dozen)	Orange Juice ($/64 oz.)	Coffee ($/11.5 oz.)
City[2]	15.52	1.45	4.63	3.47	4.53	5.53
Avg.	15.42	1.55	4.69	3.25	4.41	5.46
Min.	14.50	1.16	4.43	2.75	4.00	4.85
Max.	17.56	2.89	5.49	4.78	5.54	7.89

Note: (1) Values for the local area are compared with the average, minimum and maximum values for all 276 areas in the Cost of Living Index; (2) Figures cover the Orlando FL urban area; **T-Bone Steak** (price per pound); **Frying Chicken** (price per pound, whole fryer); **Whole Milk** (half gallon carton); **Eggs** (price per dozen, Grade A, large); **Orange Juice** (64 oz. Tropicana or Florida Natural); **Coffee** (11.5 oz. can, vacuum-packed, Maxwell House, Hills Bros, or Folgers).
Source: The Council for Community and Economic Research, Cost of Living Index, 2024

Housing and Utility Costs

Area[1]	New Home Price ($)	Apartment Rent ($/month)	All Electric ($/month)	Part Electric ($/month)	Other Energy ($/month)	Telephone ($/month)
City[2]	441,765	1,690	216.79	-	-	197.01
Avg.	515,975	1,550	210.99	123.07	82.07	194.99
Min.	265,375	692	104.33	53.68	36.26	179.42
Max.	2,775,821	5,719	529.02	397.28	361.63	223.33

Note: (1) Values for the local area are compared with the average, minimum and maximum values for all 276 areas in the Cost of Living Index; (2) Figures cover the Orlando FL urban area; **New Home Price** (2,400 sf living area, 8,000 sf lot, in urban area with full utilities); **Apartment Rent** (950 sf 2 bedroom/1.5 or 2 bath, unfurnished, excluding all utilities except water); **All Electric** (average monthly cost for an all-electric home); **Part Electric** (average monthly cost for a part-electric home); **Other Energy** (average monthly cost for natural gas, fuel oil, coal, wood, and any other forms of energy except electricity); **Telephone** (price includes the base monthly rate plus taxes and fees for three lines of mobile phone service).
Source: The Council for Community and Economic Research, Cost of Living Index, 2024

Health Care, Transportation, and Other Costs

Area[1]	Doctor ($/visit)	Dentist ($/visit)	Optometrist ($/visit)	Gasoline ($/gallon)	Beauty Salon ($/visit)	Men's Shirt ($)
City[2]	123.06	110.00	97.28	3.34	53.19	32.49
Avg.	143.77	117.51	129.23	3.32	48.57	38.14
Min.	36.74	58.67	67.33	2.80	24.00	13.41
Max.	270.44	216.82	307.33	5.28	94.00	63.89

Note: (1) Values for the local area are compared with the average, minimum and maximum values for all 276 areas in the Cost of Living Index; (2) Figures cover the Orlando FL urban area; **Doctor** (general practitioners routine exam of an established patient); **Dentist** (adult teeth cleaning and periodic oral examination); **Optometrist** (full vision eye exam for established adult patient); **Gasoline** (one gallon regular unleaded, national brand, including all taxes, cash price at self-service pump if available); **Beauty Salon** (woman's shampoo, trim, and blow-dry); **Men's Shirt** (cotton/polyester dress shirt, pinpoint weave, long sleeves).
Source: The Council for Community and Economic Research, Cost of Living Index, 2024

HOUSING

Homeownership Rate

Area	2017 (%)	2018 (%)	2019 (%)	2020 (%)	2021 (%)	2022 (%)	2023 (%)	2024 (%)
MSA[1]	59.5	58.5	56.1	64.2	63.0	62.1	61.9	62.6
U.S.	63.9	64.4	64.6	66.6	65.5	65.8	65.9	65.6

Note: (1) Figures cover the Orlando-Kissimmee-Sanford, FL Metropolitan Statistical Area
Source: U.S. Census Bureau, Housing Vacancies and Homeownership Annual Statistics: 2017-2024

House Price Index (HPI)

Area	National Ranking[2]	Quarterly Change (%)	One-Year Change (%)	Five-Year Change (%)	Since 1991Q1 (%)
MSA[1]	56	2.87	7.06	70.73	377.10
U.S.[3]	–	1.43	4.51	57.13	327.82

Note: The HPI is a weighted repeat sales index. It measures average price changes in repeat sales or refinancings on the same properties. This information is obtained by reviewing repeat mortgage transactions on single-family properties whose mortgages have been purchased or securitized by Fannie Mae or Freddie Mac since January 1975; (1) Figures cover the Orlando-Kissimmee-Sanford, FL Metropolitan Statistical Area; (2) Rankings are based on annual percentage change for all metro areas containing at least 15,000 transactions over the last 10 years and ranges from 1 to 241; (3) figures based on a weighted average of Census Division estimates using a seasonally adjusted, purchase-only index; all figures are for the period ending December 31, 2024
Source: Federal Housing Finance Agency, Change in FHFA Metropolitan Area House Price Indexes, All Transactions Index, 2024Q4

Home Value

Area	Under $100,000	$100,000 -$199,999	$200,000 -$299,999	$300,000 -$399,999	$400,000 -$499,999	$500,000 -$999,999	$1,000,000 or more	Median ($)
City	3.5	15.0	19.9	19.6	14.5	22.0	5.4	359,000
MSA[1]	7.9	10.2	22.8	23.6	15.2	17.1	3.2	338,500
U.S.	12.1	17.8	19.5	14.4	10.5	19.1	6.5	303,400

Note: Figures are percentages except for median and cover owner-occupied housing units; (1) Figures cover the Orlando-Kissimmee-Sanford, FL Metropolitan Statistical Area
Source: U.S. Census Bureau, 2019-2023 American Community Survey 5-Year Estimates

Year Housing Structure Built

Area	2020 or Later	2010 -2019	2000 -2009	1990 -1999	1980 -1989	1970 -1979	1960 -1969	1950 -1959	1940 -1949	Before 1940	Median Year
City	1.3	16.1	21.0	13.1	15.1	12.7	7.2	8.4	2.6	2.6	1991
MSA[1]	2.1	15.3	21.5	17.9	18.5	11.6	5.5	4.9	1.1	1.5	1994
U.S.	1.2	8.9	13.6	12.8	13.0	14.4	10.0	9.7	4.5	11.9	1980

Note: Figures are percentages except for Median Year; Note: (1) Figures cover the Orlando-Kissimmee-Sanford, FL Metropolitan Statistical Area
Source: U.S. Census Bureau, 2019-2023 American Community Survey 5-Year Estimates

Gross Monthly Rent

Area	Under $500	$500 -$999	$1,000 -$1,499	$1,500 -$1,999	$2,000 -$2,499	$2,500 -$2,999	$3,000 and up	Median ($)
City	3.1	6.0	30.0	36.5	17.1	4.7	2.6	1,650
MSA[1]	2.1	8.2	28.7	34.6	18.0	5.3	3.0	1,659
U.S.	6.5	22.3	29.5	20.2	10.8	4.8	5.9	1,348

Note: Figures are percentages except for median; Gross rent is the contract rent plus the estimated average monthly cost of utilities (electricity, gas, and water and sewer) and fuels (oil, coal, kerosene, wood, etc.) if these are paid by the renter (or paid for the renter by someone else); (1) Figures cover the Orlando-Kissimmee-Sanford, FL Metropolitan Statistical Area
Source: U.S. Census Bureau, 2019-2023 American Community Survey 5-Year Estimates

HEALTH

Health Risk Factors

Category	MSA[1] (%)	U.S. (%)
Adults aged 18–64 who have any kind of health care coverage	87.5	90.8
Adults who reported being in good or better health	83.9	81.8
Adults who have been told they have high blood cholesterol	36.4	36.9
Adults who have been told they have high blood pressure	34.1	34.0
Adults who are current smokers	8.7	12.1
Adults who currently use e-cigarettes	6.8	7.7
Adults who currently use chewing tobacco, snuff, or snus	0.8	3.2
Adults who are heavy drinkers[2]	8.5	6.1
Adults who are binge drinkers[3]	13.4	15.2
Adults who are overweight (BMI 25.0 - 29.9)	36.0	34.4
Adults who are obese (BMI 30.0 - 99.8)	32.5	34.3
Adults who participated in any physical activities in the past month	77.0	75.8

Note: All figures are crude prevalence; (1) Figures cover the Orlando-Kissimmee-Sanford, FL Metropolitan Statistical Area; (2) Heavy drinkers are classified as adult men having more than 14 drinks per week and adult women having more than 7 drinks per week; (3) Binge drinkers are classified as males having five or more drinks on one occasion or females having four or more drinks on one occasion
Source: Centers for Disease Control and Prevention, Behavioral Risk Factor Surveillance System, SMART: Selected Metropolitan Area Risk Trends, 2023

Acute and Chronic Health Conditions

Category	MSA[1] (%)	U.S. (%)
Adults who have ever been told they had a heart attack	5.3	4.2
Adults who have ever been told they have angina or coronary heart disease	5.6	4.0
Adults who have ever been told they had a stroke	4.0	3.3
Adults who have ever been told they have asthma	11.8	15.7
Adults who have ever been told they have arthritis	22.9	26.3
Adults who have ever been told they have diabetes[2]	12.8	11.5
Adults who have ever been told they had skin cancer	6.4	5.6
Adults who have ever been told they had any other types of cancer	8.3	8.4
Adults who have ever been told they have COPD	5.1	6.4
Adults who have ever been told they have kidney disease	3.8	3.7
Adults who have ever been told they have a form of depression	14.6	22.0

Note: All figures are crude prevalence; (1) Figures cover the Orlando-Kissimmee-Sanford, FL Metropolitan Statistical Area; (2) Figures do not include pregnancy-related, borderline, or pre-diabetes
Source: Centers for Disease Control and Prevention, Behavioral Risk Factor Surveillance System, SMART: Selected Metropolitan Area Risk Trends, 2023

Health Screening and Vaccination Rates

Category	MSA[1] (%)	U.S. (%)
Adults who have ever been tested for HIV	42.5	37.5
Adults who have had their blood cholesterol checked within the last five years	90.2	87.0
Adults aged 65+ who have had flu shot within the past year	60.9	63.4
Adults aged 65+ who have ever had a pneumonia vaccination	68.4	71.9

Note: All figures are crude prevalence; (1) Figures cover the Orlando-Kissimmee-Sanford, FL Metropolitan Statistical Area.
Source: Centers for Disease Control and Prevention, Behavioral Risk Factor Surveillance System, SMART: Selected Metropolitan Area Risk Trends, 2023

Disability Status

Category	MSA[1] (%)	U.S. (%)
Adults who reported being deaf	4.3	7.4
Are you blind or have serious difficulty seeing, even when wearing glasses?	6.6	4.9
Do you have difficulty doing errands alone?	6.6	7.8
Do you have difficulty dressing or bathing?	2.4	3.6
Do you have serious difficulty concentrating/remembering/making decisions?	12.2	13.7
Do you have serious difficulty walking or climbing stairs?	10.5	13.2

Note: All figures are crude prevalence; (1) Figures cover the Orlando-Kissimmee-Sanford, FL Metropolitan Statistical Area.
Source: Centers for Disease Control and Prevention, Behavioral Risk Factor Surveillance System, SMART: Selected Metropolitan Area Risk Trends, 2023

Mortality Rates for the Top 10 Causes of Death in the U.S.

ICD-10[a] Sub-Chapter	ICD-10[a] Code	Crude Mortality Rate[2] per 100,000 population	
		County[3]	U.S.
Malignant neoplasms	C00-C97	133.9	182.7
Ischaemic heart diseases	I20-I25	78.6	109.6
Provisional assignment of new diseases of uncertain etiology[1]	U00-U49	47.9	65.3
Other forms of heart disease	I30-I51	34.0	65.1
Other degenerative diseases of the nervous system	G30-G31	22.8	52.4
Other external causes of accidental injury	W00-X59	44.5	52.3
Cerebrovascular diseases	I60-I69	49.0	49.1
Chronic lower respiratory diseases	J40-J47	24.0	43.5
Hypertensive diseases	I10-I15	25.2	38.9
Organic, including symptomatic, mental disorders	F01-F09	30.0	33.9

Note: (a) ICD-10 = International Classification of Diseases 10th Revision; (1) Includes COVID-19, adverse effects to COVID-19 vaccines, SARS, and vaping-related disorders; (2) Crude mortality rates are a three-year average covering 2021-2023; (3) Figures cover Orange County.
Source: Centers for Disease Control and Prevention, National Center for Health Statistics. National Vital Statistics System, Mortality 2018-2023 on CDC WONDER Online Database

Mortality Rates for Selected Causes of Death

Cause of Death	ICD-10[a] Code	Crude Mortality Rate[1] per 100,000 population	
		County[2]	U.S.
Accidental poisoning and exposure to noxious substances	X40-X49	26.7	30.5
Alzheimer disease	G30	18.2	35.4
Assault	X85-Y09	7.2	7.3
COVID-19	U07.1	47.9	65.3
Diabetes mellitus	E10-E14	23.6	30.0
Diseases of the liver	K70-K76	13.7	20.8
Human immunodeficiency virus (HIV) disease	B20-B24	2.7	1.5
Influenza and pneumonia	J09-J18	7.6	13.4
Intentional self-harm	X60-X84	10.5	14.7
Malnutrition	E40-E46	3.7	6.0
Obesity and other hyperalimentation	E65-E68	1.6	3.1
Renal failure	N17-N19	11.2	16.4
Transport accidents	V01-V99	14.2	14.4

Note: (a) ICD-10 = International Classification of Diseases 10th Revision; (1) Crude mortality rates are a three-year average covering 2021-2023; (2) Figures cover Orange County; Data are suppressed when the data meet the criteria for confidentiality constraints; Crude mortality rates are flagged as unreliable when the rate would be calculated with a numerator of 20 or less.
Source: Centers for Disease Control and Prevention, National Center for Health Statistics. National Vital Statistics System, Mortality 2018-2023 on CDC WONDER Online Database

Health Insurance Coverage

Area	With Health Insurance	With Private Health Insurance	With Public Health Insurance	Without Health Insurance	Population Under Age 19 Without Health Insurance
City	86.1	64.6	27.6	13.9	8.0
MSA[1]	88.7	66.6	31.4	11.3	6.3
U.S.	91.4	67.3	36.3	8.6	5.4

Note: Figures are percentages that cover the civilian noninstitutionalized population; (1) Figures cover the Orlando-Kissimmee-Sanford, FL Metropolitan Statistical Area
Source: U.S. Census Bureau, 2019-2023 American Community Survey 5-Year Estimates

Number of Medical Professionals

Area	MDs[3]	DOs[3,4]	Dentists	Podiatrists	Chiropractors	Optometrists
County[1] (number)	5,075	420	796	61	438	208
County[1] (rate[2])	349.3	28.9	54.1	4.1	29.8	14.1
U.S. (rate[2])	302.5	29.2	74.6	6.4	29.5	18.0

Note: Data as of 2023 unless noted; (1) Data covers Orange County; (2) Number of medical professionals per 100,000 population; (3) Data as of 2022 and includes all active, non-federal physicians; (4) Doctor of Osteopathic Medicine
Source: U.S. Department of Health and Human Services, Health Resources and Services Administration, Bureau of Health Professions, Area Resource File (ARF) 2023-2024

Best Hospitals

According to *U.S. News,* the Orlando-Kissimmee-Sanford, FL metro area is home to two of the best hospitals in the U.S.: **AdventHealth Orlando** (4 adult specialties and 3 pediatric specialties); **Orlando Health-Orlando Regional Medical Center** (2 adult specialties and 5 pediatric specialties). The hospitals listed were nationally ranked in at least one of 15 adult or 11 pediatric specialties. The number of specialties shown cover the parent hospital. Only 160 U.S. hospitals performed well enough to be nationally ranked in one or more specialties. Twenty hospitals in the U.S. made the Honor Roll. The Best Hospitals Honor Roll takes both the national rankings and the procedure and condition ratings into account. Hospitals received points if they were nationally ranked in one of the 15 adult specialties—the higher they ranked, the more points they got—and how many ratings of "high performing" they earned in the 20 procedures and conditions. *U.S. News Online, "America's Best Hospitals 2024-25"*

According to *U.S. News,* the Orlando-Kissimmee-Sanford, FL metro area is home to three of the best children's hospitals in the U.S.: **AdventHealth for Children** (3 pediatric specialties); **Nemours Children's Hospital-Florida** (2 pediatric specialties); **Orlando Health Arnold Palmer Hospital for Children** (5 pediatric specialties). The hospitals listed were highly ranked in at least one of 11 pediatric specialties. One hundred five children's hospitals in the U.S. were nationally ranked in at least one specialty. Hospitals received points for being ranked in a specialty, and the 10 hospitals with the most points across the 11 specialties make up the Honor Roll. *U.S. News Online, "America's Best Children's Hospitals 2024-25"*

EDUCATION

Public School District Statistics

District Name	Schls	Pupils	Pupil/ Teacher Ratio	Minority Pupils[1] (%)	Total Rev. per Pupil ($)	Total Exp. per Pupil ($)
FL Virtual	3	8,902	26.7	52.4	n/a	n/a
Orange	277	206,815	18.1	76.2	14,962	13,040

Note: Table includes school districts with 2,000 or more students; (1) Percentage of students that are not non-Hispanic white.
Source: U.S. Department of Education, National Center for Education Statistics, Common Core of Data, Local Education Agency (School District) Universe Survey: School Year 2023-2024; U.S. Department of Education, National Center for Education Statistics, Common Core of Data, School District Finance Survey (F-33): School Year 2021–22

Best High Schools

According to *U.S. News,* Orlando is home to one of the top 500 high schools in the U.S.: **Orlando Science Middle High Charter** (#224). Nearly 25,000 public, magnet and charter schools were ranked based on their performance on state assessments and how well they prepare students for college. *U.S. News & World Report, "Best High Schools 2024"*

Highest Level of Education

Area	Less than H.S.	H.S. Diploma	Some College, No Deg.	Associate Degree	Bachelor's Degree	Master's Degree	Prof. School Degree	Doctorate Degree
City	8.1	23.1	15.7	10.9	26.1	11.2	3.2	1.8
MSA[1]	9.3	25.1	18.5	11.2	23.2	9.2	2.1	1.3
U.S.	10.6	26.2	19.4	8.8	21.3	9.8	2.3	1.6

Note: Figures cover persons age 25 and over; (1) Figures cover the Orlando-Kissimmee-Sanford, FL Metropolitan Statistical Area
Source: U.S. Census Bureau, 2019-2023 American Community Survey 5-Year Estimates

Educational Attainment by Race

Area	High School Graduate or Higher (%)					Bachelor's Degree or Higher (%)				
	Total	White	Black	Asian	Hisp.[2]	Total	White	Black	Asian	Hisp.[2]
City	91.9	95.6	84.1	93.4	90.9	42.2	53.5	21.7	59.3	33.9
MSA[1]	90.7	93.5	85.8	90.2	86.5	35.8	39.4	25.0	54.9	28.8
U.S.	89.4	92.9	88.1	88.0	72.5	35.0	37.7	24.7	57.0	19.9

Note: Figures shown cover persons 25 years old and over; (1) Figures cover the Orlando-Kissimmee-Sanford, FL Metropolitan Statistical Area; (2) People of Hispanic origin can be of any race
Source: U.S. Census Bureau, 2019-2023 American Community Survey 5-Year Estimates

School Enrollment by Grade and Control

Area	Preschool (%)		Kindergarten (%)		Grades 1 - 4 (%)		Grades 5 - 8 (%)		Grades 9 - 12 (%)	
	Public	Private	Public	Private	Public	Private	Public	Private	Public	Private
City	60.7	39.3	81.8	18.2	85.9	14.1	90.0	10.0	88.0	12.0
MSA[1]	48.9	51.1	79.8	20.2	82.1	17.9	85.3	14.7	87.0	13.0
U.S.	58.7	41.3	85.2	14.8	87.2	12.8	87.9	12.1	89.0	11.0

Note: Figures shown cover persons 3 years old and over; (1) Figures cover the Orlando-Kissimmee-Sanford, FL Metropolitan Statistical Area
Source: U.S. Census Bureau, 2019-2023 American Community Survey 5-Year Estimates

Higher Education

Four-Year Colleges			Two-Year Colleges			Medical Schools[1]	Law Schools[2]	Voc/ Tech[3]
Public	Private Non-profit	Private For-profit	Public	Private Non-profit	Private For-profit			
4	7	5	3	0	6	1	2	10

Note: Figures cover institutions located within the Orlando-Kissimmee-Sanford, FL Metropolitan Statistical Area and include main campuses only; (1) includes schools accredited by the Liaison Committee on Medical Education and the American Osteopathic Association's Commission on Osteopathic College Accreditation; (2) includes ABA-accredited schools, schools with provisional ABA accreditation, and state accredited schools; (3) includes all schools with programs that are less than 2 years.
Source: National Center for Education Statistics, Integrated Postsecondary Education System (IPEDS), 2023-24; Wikipedia, List of Medical Schools in the United States, accessed May 2, 2025; Wikipedia, List of Law Schools in the United States, accessed May 2, 2025

According to *U.S. News & World Report,* the Orlando-Kissimmee-Sanford, FL metro area is home to one of the top 200 national universities in the U.S.: **University of Central Florida** (#121 tie). The indicators used to capture academic quality fall into a number of categories: assessment by administrators at peer institutions; retention of students; faculty resources; student selectivity; financial resources; alumni giving; high school counselor ratings of colleges; and graduation rate. *U.S. News & World Report, "America's Best Colleges 2025"*

EMPLOYERS

Major Employers

Company Name	Industry
Adventist Health System/Sunbelt	General medical & surgical hospitals
Airtran Airways	Air passenger carrier, scheduled
Central Florida Health Alliance	Hospital management
CNL Lifestyle Properties	Real estate agents & managers
Connextions	Communication services
Florida Department of Children & Families	Individual & family services
Florida Hospital Medical Center	General medical & surgical hospitals
Gaylord Palms Resort & Conv Ctr	Hotel franchised
Leesburg Regional Medical Center	General medical & surgical hospitals
Lockheed Martin Corporation	Aircraft
Marriott International	Hotels & motels
Orlando Health	General medical & surgical hospitals
Rosen 9939	Hotels & motels
Sea World of Florida	Theme park, amusement
Sears Termite & Pest Control	Pest control in structures
Siemens Energy	Power plant construction
Universal City Florida Partners	Amusement & theme parks
University of Central Florida	Colleges & universities
Winter Park Healthcare Group	Hospital affiliated with AMA residency

Note: Companies shown are located within the Orlando-Kissimmee-Sanford, FL Metropolitan Statistical Area.
Source: Chambers of Commerce; State Departments of Labor; Wikipedia

Best Companies to Work For

Orlando Health, headquartered in Orlando, is among "Fortune's Best Workplaces for Women." To pick the best companies, *Fortune* partnered with the Great Place to Work Institute. To be considered for the list, companies must be Great Place To Work-Certified. Companies must also employ at least 50 women, at least 20% of their non-executive managers must be female, and at least one executive must be female. To determine the Best Workplaces for Women, Great Place To Work measured the differences in women's survey responses to those of their peers and assesses the impact of demographics and roles on the quality and consistency of women's experiences. Great Place To Work also analyzed the gender balance of each workplace, how it compared to each company's industry, and patterns in representation as women rise from front-line positions to the board of directors. *Fortune, "Best Workplaces for Women," 2024*

Orlando Health, headquartered in Orlando, is among "Best Workplaces in Health Care." To determine the Best Workplaces in Health Care list, Great Place To Work analyzed the survey responses of over 185,000 employees from Great Place To Work-Certified companies in the health care industry. Survey data analysis and company-provided datapoints are then factored into a combined score to compare and rank the companies that create the most consistently positive experience for all employees in this industry. *Fortune, "Best Workplaces in Health Care," 2024*

PUBLIC SAFETY

Crime Rate

Area	Total Crime Rate	Violent Crime Rate				Property Crime Rate		
		Murder	Rape	Robbery	Aggrav. Assault	Burglary	Larceny-Theft	Motor Vehicle Theft
City	4,864.3	10.3	72.7	137.1	615.7	449.9	3,173.7	404.9
U.S.	2,362.5	6.5	42.1	67.1	273.0	272.7	1,416.6	284.5

Note: Figures are crimes per 100,000 population and cover 2022. Data for 2023 was not available.
Source: FBI, Table 8, Offenses Known to Law Enforcement, by State by City, 2022

Hate Crimes

Area	Number of Quarters Reported	Number of Incidents per Bias Motivation					
		Race/Ethnicity/Ancestry	Religion	Sexual Orientation	Disability	Gender	Gender Identity
City	2	0	0	0	0	0	0
U.S.	4	5,900	2,699	2,077	187	92	492

Source: Federal Bureau of Investigation, Hate Crime Statistics 2023

Identity Theft Consumer Reports

Area	Reports	Reports per 100,000 Population	Rank[2]
MSA[1]	15,099	555	5
U.S.	1,135,291	339	-

Note: (1) Figures cover the Orlando-Kissimmee-Sanford, FL Metropolitan Statistical Area; (2) Rank ranges from 1 to 401 where 1 indicates greatest number of identity theft reports per 100,000 population
Source: Federal Trade Commission, Consumer Sentinel Network Data Book 2024

Fraud and Other Consumer Reports

Area	Reports	Reports per 100,000 Population	Rank[2]
MSA[1]	63,405	2,330	4
U.S.	5,360,641	1,601	-

Note: (1) Figures cover the Orlando-Kissimmee-Sanford, FL Metropolitan Statistical Area; (2) Rank ranges from 1 to 401 where 1 indicates greatest number of fraud and other consumer reports per 100,000 population
Source: Federal Trade Commission, Consumer Sentinel Network Data Book 2024

POLITICS

2024 Presidential Election Results

Area	Trump (Rep.)	Harris (Dem.)	Stein (Green)	Kennedy (Ind.)	Oliver (Lib.)	Other
Orange County	42.4	55.9	0.7	0.0	0.3	0.7
U.S.	49.7	48.2	0.6	0.5	0.4	0.6

Note: Results are percentages and may not add to 100% due to rounding
Source: Dave Leip's Atlas of U.S. Presidential Elections

SPORTS

Professional Sports Teams

Team Name	League	Year Established
Orlando City SC	Major League Soccer (MLS)	2015
Orlando Magic	National Basketball Association (NBA)	1989

Note: Includes teams located in the Orlando-Kissimmee-Sanford, FL Metropolitan Statistical Area.
Source: Wikipedia, Major Professional Sports Teams of the United States and Canada, May 1, 2025

CLIMATE

Average and Extreme Temperatures

Temperature	Jan	Feb	Mar	Apr	May	Jun	Jul	Aug	Sep	Oct	Nov	Dec	Yr.
Extreme High (°F)	86	89	90	95	100	100	99	100	98	95	89	90	100
Average High (°F)	70	72	77	82	87	90	91	91	89	83	78	72	82
Average Temp. (°F)	59	62	67	72	77	81	82	82	81	75	68	62	72
Average Low (°F)	48	51	56	60	66	71	73	74	72	66	58	51	62
Extreme Low (°F)	19	29	25	38	51	53	64	65	57	44	32	20	19

Note: Figures cover the years 1952-1990
Source: National Climatic Data Center, International Station Meteorological Climate Summary, 9/96

Average Precipitation/Snowfall/Humidity

Precip./Humidity	Jan	Feb	Mar	Apr	May	Jun	Jul	Aug	Sep	Oct	Nov	Dec	Yr.
Avg. Precip. (in.)	2.3	2.8	3.4	2.0	3.2	7.0	7.2	5.8	5.8	2.7	3.5	2.0	47.7
Avg. Snowfall (in.)	Tr	0	0	0	0	0	0	0	0	0	0	0	Tr
Avg. Rel. Hum. 7am (%)	87	87	88	87	88	89	90	92	92	89	89	87	89
Avg. Rel. Hum. 4pm (%)	53	51	49	47	51	61	65	66	66	59	56	55	57

Note: Figures cover the years 1952-1990; Tr = Trace amounts (<0.05 in. of rain; <0.5 in. of snow)
Source: National Climatic Data Center, International Station Meteorological Climate Summary, 9/96

Weather Conditions

Temperature			Daytime Sky			Precipitation		
32°F & below	45°F & below	90°F & above	Clear	Partly cloudy	Cloudy	0.01 inch or more precip.	0.1 inch or more snow/ice	Thunderstorms
3	35	90	76	208	81	115	0	80

Note: Figures are average number of days per year and cover the years 1952-1990
Source: National Climatic Data Center, International Station Meteorological Climate Summary, 9/96

HAZARDOUS WASTE

Superfund Sites

The Orlando-Kissimmee-Sanford, FL metro area is home to nine sites on the EPA's Superfund National Priorities List (NPL) or Superfund Alternative Approach (SAA) list: **Chevron Chemical Co. (Ortho Division)** (Final NPL); **City Industries, Inc.** (Final NPL); **General Dynamics Longwood** (Final NPL); **Orlando Gasification Plant** (SAA); **Sanford Dry Cleaners** (Final NPL); **Sanford Gasification Plant** (SAA); **Sprague Electric Company** (SAA); **Tower Chemical Co.** (Final NPL); **Zellwood Ground Water Contamination** (Final NPL). The Superfund alternative approach uses the same investigation and cleanup process and standards that are used for sites listed on the National Priorities List. The SAA is an alternative to listing a site on the NPL; it is not an alternative to Superfund or the Superfund process. There are a total of 1,445 Superfund sites with a status of proposed or final on both lists in the United States. *U.S. Environmental Protection Agency, National Priorities List, May 1, 2025; U.S. Environmental Protection Agency, Superfund Alternative Approach Sites, May 1, 2025*

AIR QUALITY

Air Quality Trends: Ozone

	1990	1995	2000	2005	2010	2015	2020	2021	2022	2023
MSA[1]	0.081	0.075	0.080	0.083	0.069	0.060	0.059	0.061	0.062	0.066
U.S.	0.087	0.089	0.081	0.080	0.072	0.068	0.066	0.067	0.067	0.070

Note: (1) Data covers the Orlando-Kissimmee-Sanford, FL Metropolitan Statistical Area. The values shown are the composite ozone concentration averages among trend sites based on the highest fourth daily maximum 8-hour concentration in parts per million. These trends are based on sites having an adequate record of monitoring data during the trend period. Data from exceptional events are included.
Source: U.S. Environmental Protection Agency, Air Quality Monitoring Information, "Air Quality Trends by City, 1990-2023"

Air Quality Index

Area	Percent of Days when Air Quality was...[2]					AQI Statistics[2]	
	Good	Moderate	Unhealthy for Sensitive Groups	Unhealthy	Very Unhealthy	Maximum	Median
MSA[1]	71.0	28.2	0.8	0.0	0.0	115	44

Note: (1) Data covers the Orlando-Kissimmee-Sanford, FL Metropolitan Statistical Area; (2) Based on 365 days with AQI data in 2023. Air Quality Index (AQI) is an index for reporting daily air quality. EPA calculates the AQI for five major air pollutants regulated by the Clean Air Act: ground-level ozone, particle pollution (aka particulate matter), carbon monoxide, sulfur dioxide, and nitrogen dioxide. The AQI runs from 0 to 500. The higher the AQI value, the greater the level of air pollution and the greater the health concern. There are six AQI categories: "Good" AQI is between 0 and 50. Air quality is considered satisfactory; "Moderate" AQI is between 51 and 100. Air quality is acceptable; "Unhealthy for Sensitive Groups" When AQI values are between 101 and 150, members of sensitive groups may experience health effects; "Unhealthy" When AQI values are between 151 and 200 everyone may begin to experience health effects; "Very Unhealthy" AQI values between 201 and 300 trigger a health alert; "Hazardous" AQI values over 300 trigger warnings of emergency conditions (not shown).
Source: U.S. Environmental Protection Agency, Air Quality Index Report, 2023

Air Quality Index Pollutants

Area	Percent of Days when AQI Pollutant was...[2]					
	Carbon Monoxide	Nitrogen Dioxide	Ozone	Sulfur Dioxide	Particulate Matter 2.5	Particulate Matter 10
MSA[1]	0.0	0.5	55.1	(3)	44.4	0.0

Note: (1) Data covers the Orlando-Kissimmee-Sanford, FL Metropolitan Statistical Area; (2) Based on 365 days with AQI data in 2023. The Air Quality Index (AQI) is an index for reporting daily air quality. EPA calculates the AQI for five major air pollutants regulated by the Clean Air Act: ground-level ozone, particle pollution (also known as particulate matter), carbon monoxide, sulfur dioxide, and nitrogen dioxide. The AQI runs from 0 to 500. The higher the AQI value, the greater the level of air pollution and the greater the health concern; (3) Sulfur dioxide is no longer included in this table because SO_2 concentrations tend to be very localized and not necessarily representative of broad geographical areas like counties and CBSAs.
Source: U.S. Environmental Protection Agency, Air Quality Index Report, 2023

Maximum Air Pollutant Concentrations: Particulate Matter, Ozone, CO and Lead

	Particulate Matter 10 (ug/m³)	Particulate Matter 2.5 Wtd AM (ug/m³)	Particulate Matter 2.5 24-Hr (ug/m³)	Ozone (ppm)	Carbon Monoxide (ppm)	Lead (ug/m³)
MSA[1] Level	54	6.8	16	0.069	1	n/a
NAAQS[2]	150	15	35	0.075	9	0.15
Met NAAQS[2]	Yes	Yes	Yes	Yes	Yes	n/a

Note: (1) Data covers the Orlando-Kissimmee-Sanford, FL Metropolitan Statistical Area; Data from exceptional events are included; (2) National Ambient Air Quality Standards; ppm = parts per million; ug/m³ = micrograms per cubic meter; n/a not available.
Concentrations: Particulate Matter 10 (coarse particulate)—highest second maximum 24-hour concentration; Particulate Matter 2.5 Wtd AM (fine particulate)—highest weighted annual mean concentration; Particulate Matter 2.5 24-Hour (fine particulate)—highest 98th percentile 24-hour concentration; Ozone—highest fourth daily maximum 8-hour concentration; Carbon Monoxide—highest second maximum non-overlapping 8-hour concentration; Lead—maximum running 3-month average
Source: U.S. Environmental Protection Agency, Air Quality Monitoring Information, "Air Quality Statistics by City, 2023"

Maximum Air Pollutant Concentrations: Nitrogen Dioxide and Sulfur Dioxide

	Nitrogen Dioxide AM (ppb)	Nitrogen Dioxide 1-Hr (ppb)	Sulfur Dioxide AM (ppb)	Sulfur Dioxide 1-Hr (ppb)	Sulfur Dioxide 24-Hr (ppb)
MSA[1] Level	n/a	n/a	n/a	4	n/a
NAAQS[2]	53	100	30	75	140
Met NAAQS[2]	n/a	n/a	n/a	Yes	n/a

Note: (1) Data covers the Orlando-Kissimmee-Sanford, FL Metropolitan Statistical Area; Data from exceptional events are included; (2) National Ambient Air Quality Standards; ppm = parts per million; ug/m^3 = micrograms per cubic meter; n/a not available.
Concentrations: Nitrogen Dioxide AM—highest arithmetic mean concentration; Nitrogen Dioxide 1-Hr—highest 98th percentile 1-hour daily maximum concentration; Sulfur Dioxide AM—highest annual mean concentration; Sulfur Dioxide 1-Hr—highest 99th percentile 1-hour daily maximum concentration; Sulfur Dioxide 24-Hr—highest second maximum 24-hour concentration
Source: U.S. Environmental Protection Agency, Air Quality Monitoring Information, "Air Quality Statistics by City, 2023"

San Antonio, Texas

Background

San Antonio is located in south central Texas at the head of the San Antonio River, a testament to its Mexican-Spanish heritage. The city's famous Paseo Del Rio is known for cream-colored stucco structures, seashell ornamented facades, and gently illuminating tiny lights.

San Antonio began in the early eighteenth century as a cohesion of different Spanish missions, whose aim was to convert the Coahuiltecan Native Americans to Christianity and European ways of farming. A debilitating epidemic, however, thwarted those plans. In 1836, San Antonio became of interest again, when a small band of American soldiers were unable to successfully defend themselves against an army of 4,000 Mexican soldiers, led by General Antonio de Lopez Santa Anna. Fighting desperately from within the walls of the Mission San Antonio de Valero, or The Alamo, all 183 men were killed. This inspired the cry "Remember the Alamo" from every American soldier led by General Sam Houston, who fought with determination to wrest Texas territory and independence from Mexico.

Despite San Antonio becoming part of the United States in 1846, Mexican culture and its influence remain strong, evidenced by its architecture, the Franciscan educational system, the variety of Spanish-language media, and a population that is 64 percent Latino.

This blend of old and new makes San Antonio unique among American cities. It is home to the first museum of modern art in Texas, McNay Art Museum. Other art institutions and museums include ArtPace, Blue Star Contemporary Art Center, Briscoe Western Art Museum, Buckhorn Saloon & Museum (heavy on the cowboy culture), San Antonio Museum of Art, formerly Lonestar Brewery, Say Si (mentoring San Antonio artistic youth), Southwest School of Art, Texas Rangers Museum, Texas Transportation Museum, Witte Museum and the DoSeum. An outdoor display at North Star Mall features 40-foot-tall cowboy boots.

The five missions in the city, four in the San Antonio Missions National Historical Park and the Alamo, were named a UNESCO World Heritage Site in 2015. The San Antonio Missions became the 23rd U.S. site on the World Heritage List, which includes the Grand Canyon and the Statue of Liberty. It is the first such site in the state of Texas.

The city continues to draw tourists who come to visit the Alamo, theme parks like Six Flags Fiesta Texas and SeaWorld, and the famed River Walk. Kelly Air Force Base, decommissioned in 2001, is now a nearly 5,000-acre business park, Kelly USA. Port San Antonio, a warehouse on the site was used to house refugees from Hurricane Katrina. Sego Lily Dam was constructed in 2017 to prevent further flooding in the city.

Businesses at the port receive favorable property tax and pay no state, city, or corporate income taxes. With a continuing increase in professional jobs, San Antonio has become a destination for a college-education workforce. The city's economy focuses on military, healthcare, financial services, oil and gas, and tourism. Its major employers include RBFCU, Broadway Bank, Whataburger, and Accenture.

The city airport's current major renovation is ongoing. New gates opened in 2022, and a new terminal and Ground Transportation Center will open in 2028.

Yearly events, such as Fiesta San Antonio (the city's signature event), Luminaria (a contemporary arts festival) and Fiesta Noche del Rio, add a variety of entertainment options to the area. The city also plays host to SAFILM-San Antonio Film Festival every summer in August. Founded in 1994, the film festival is the largest in South Texas.

San Antonio's location on the edge of the Gulf Coastal Plains exposes it to a modified subtropical climate. Summers are hot, although extremely high temperatures are rare. Winters are mild. Located 140 miles from the Gulf of Mexico, tropical storms occasionally occur, bringing strong winds and heavy rains. Relative humidity is high in the morning but tends to drop by late afternoon. San Antonio is one of the most flood-prone regions in North America. In recent years, the region is experiencing increased earthquake activity, which experts say is likely caused by saltwater disposal wells, where wastewater and chemicals from fracking are pumped into the ground.

Rankings

General Rankings

- To help military veterans find the best places in which to settle down, *WalletHub* compared the 100 largest U.S. cities across 19 key indicators of livability, affordability and veteran-friendliness. They range from the share of military skill-related jobs to veteran income growth to the availability of VA health facilities. San Antonio ranked #28. *Wallethub.com, "Best & Worst Places for Veterans to Live (2025)," November 7, 2024*

- *Insider* listed 23 places in the U.S. that travel industry trends reveal would be popular destinations in 2023. This year the list trends towards cultural and historical happenings, sports events, wellness experiences and invigorating outdoor escapes. According to the website insider.com San Antonio is a place to visit in 2023. *Insider, "23 of the Best Places You Should Travel to in the U.S. in 2023," December 17, 2022*

- San Antonio appeared on *Travel + Leisure's* list of "The 15 Best Cities in the United States." The city was ranked #6. Criteria: walkability; sights/landmarks; culture; food; friendliness; shopping; and overall value. *Travel + Leisure, "The World's Best Awards 2024" July 9, 2024*

Business/Finance Rankings

- The San Antonio metro area appeared on the Milken Institute "2025 Best Performing Cities" list. Rank: #26 out of 200 large metro areas (based on performance category). Criteria: job growth; wage growth; high-tech growth and impact; community resilience; housing affordability; household broadband access. *Milken Institute, "Best-Performing Cities 2025," January 14, 2025*

Culture/Performing Arts Rankings

- San Antonio was selected as one of the 25 best cities for moviemakers in North America. Great film cities are places where filmmaking dreams can come true, that offer more creative space, lower costs, and great outdoor locations. NYC & LA were intentionally excluded. Criteria: film industry presence and culture; tax incentives; affordability; and proximity of festivals and schools. The city was ranked #20. *MovieMaker Magazine, "Best Places to Live and Work as a Moviemaker, 2025," January 29, 2025*

Dating/Romance Rankings

- *Apartment List* conducted its Annual Renter Satisfaction Survey and asked renters "how satisfied are you with opportunities for dating in your current city." The cities were ranked from highest to lowest based on their satisfaction scores. San Antonio ranked #8 out of 10 cities. *Apartment List, "Best Cities for Dating 2022 with Local Dating Insights from Bumble," February 7, 2022*

Education Rankings

- Personal finance website *WalletHub* analyzed the 150 largest U.S. metropolitan statistical areas to determine where the most educated Americans are putting their degrees to work. Criteria: education levels; percentage of workers with degrees; education quality and attainment gap; public school quality rankings; quality and enrollment of each metro area's universities. San Antonio was ranked #103 (#1 = most educated city). *WalletHub.com, "Most & Least Educated Cities in America, 2025" July 2, 2024*

Environmental Rankings

- San Antonio was highlighted as one of the 25 most ozone-polluted metro areas in the U.S. during 2021 through 2023. The area ranked #20. *American Lung Association, "State of the Air 2025," April 23, 2025*

Food/Drink Rankings

- WalletHub compared the 100 largest U.S. cities across 17 key indicators of vegan- and vegetarian-friendliness. San Antonio was ranked #20. Cities were selected based on metrics such as the cost of groceries for vegetarians, the share of restaurants serving meatless options and the number of salad shops per capita. *WalletHub.com, "Best Cities for Vegans & Vegetarians (2025)," September 24, 2024*

Health/Fitness Rankings

- For each of the 100 largest cities in the United States, the American Fitness Index®, compiled in partnership between the American College of Sports Medicine and the Elevance Health Foundation, evaluated community infrastructure and more than 30 health behaviors including preventive health, levels of chronic disease conditions, food insecurity, pedestrian safety, air quality, and community/environment resources that support physical activity. San Antonio ranked #89 for "community fitness." *americanfitnessindex.org, "2024 ACSM American Fitness Index Summary Report," July 23, 2024*

- San Antonio was identified as a "2025 Allergy Capital." The area ranked #37 out of the nation's 100 largest metropolitan areas. Three groups of factors were used to identify the most challenging cities for people with allergies: annual tree, grass, and weed pollen scores; over the counter allergy medicine use; number of board-certified allergy specialists. *Asthma and Allergy Foundation of America, "2025 Allergy Capitals: The Most Challenging Places to Live with Allergies," March 18, 2025*

- San Antonio was identified as a "2024 Asthma Capital." The area ranked #57 out of the nation's 100 largest metropolitan areas. Criteria: estimated asthma prevalence; asthma-related mortality; and ER visits due to asthma. Risk factors analyzed but not factored in the rankings: annual air quality including pollution and ozone levels; public smoking laws; indoor air quality; access to asthma specialists; rescue and controller medication use; uninsured rate; pollen allergy; poverty rate. *Asthma and Allergy Foundation of America, "Asthma Capitals 2024: The Most Challenging Places to Live With Asthma," September 10, 2024*

Pet Rankings

- San Antonio was selected by *Sniffspot.com* as one of the most dog-friendly cities in the U.S., ranking #43 out of 50. Criteria: dog parks; hiking; sniffspots; public parks; dog-friendly businesses; housing; dog waste cleanliness; leash laws; dog services; and overall cost. *Sniffspot.com, "The Top 50 Most Dog-Friendly Cities in the U.S.," September 30, 2024*

Real Estate Rankings

- *WalletHub* compared the most populated U.S. cities to determine which had the best markets for real estate agents. San Antonio ranked #133 where demand was high and pay was the best. Criteria: sales per agent; annual median wage for real-estate agents; monthly average starting salary for real estate agents; real estate job density and competition; unemployment rate; home turnover rate; housing-market health index; and other relevant metrics. *WalletHub.com, "2021 Best Places to Be a Real Estate Agent," May 12, 2021*

- According to Penske Truck Rental, the San Antonio metro area was named the #2 moving destination in 2023, based on one-way consumer truck rental reservations made through Penske's website, rental locations, and reservations call center. *gopenske.com, "Penske Truck Rental's 2023 Top Moving Destinations," May 7, 2024*

- The San Antonio metro area was identified as one of the top 16 housing markets to invest in for 2025 by *Forbes*. Criteria: stable local economies with good population growth and increase in jobs providing good support for home prices and rents. *Forbes.com, "Best Local Markets For Real Estate Investing In 2025," November 6, 2024*

- The San Antonio metro area was identified as one of the 20 worst housing markets in the U.S. in 2024. The area ranked #220 out of 226 markets. Criteria: year-over-year change of median sales price of existing single-family homes between the 4th quarter of 2023 and the 4th quarter of 2024. *National Association of Realtors®, Median Sales Price of Existing Single-Family Homes for Metropolitan Areas, 4th Quarter 2024*

- San Antonio was ranked #102 out of 176 metro areas in terms of cost of housing in 2024 by the National Association of Home Builders (#1 = most affordable). Criteria: the portion of an average family's income necessary to pay the mortgage on a median-priced home. *National Association of Home Builders®, NAHB-Wells Fargo Cost of Housing Index, 4th Quarter 2024*

Safety Rankings

- Allstate ranked the 100 most populous cities in America in terms of driver safety. San Antonio ranked #12. Criteria based on anonymized driving behavior data from Allstate's mobile app powered by Arity: high speed driving (over 80 mph), phone handling, and hard braking. The report helps increase the importance of safety and awareness behind the wheel. *Allstate, "16th Allstate America's Best Drivers Report®" July 11, 2024*

Women/Minorities Rankings

- Personal finance website *WalletHub* compared more than 180 U.S. cities across two key dimensions, "Hispanic Business-Friendliness" and "Hispanic Purchasing Power," to arrive at the most favorable conditions for Hispanic entrepreneurs. San Antonio was ranked #24 out of 182. Criteria includes: share of Hispanic-Owned Businesses; average growth of Hispanic Business revenues; Small Business-Friendliness score; affordability; and number of Hispanics with at least a bachelor's degree. *WalletHub.com, "Best Cities for Hispanic Entrepreneurs," September 4, 2024*

Miscellaneous Rankings

- *WalletHub* compared 148 of the most populated U.S. cities to determine their operating efficiency. A "Quality of Services" score was constructed for each city and then measured against the total budget per capita to reveal which were managed the best. San Antonio ranked #94. Criteria: financial stability; economy; education; safety; health; infrastructure and pollution. *WalletHub.com, "2025's Best- & Worst-Run Cities in America," June 18, 2024*

Business Environment

DEMOGRAPHICS

Population Growth

Area	1990 Census	2000 Census	2010 Census	2020 Census	2023 Estimate[2]	Population Growth 1990-2023 (%)
City	997,258	1,144,646	1,327,407	1,434,625	1,458,954	46.3
MSA[1]	1,407,745	1,711,703	2,142,508	2,558,143	2,612,802	85.6
U.S.	248,709,873	281,421,906	308,745,538	331,449,281	332,387,540	33.6

Note: (1) Figures cover the San Antonio-New Braunfels, TX Metropolitan Statistical Area; (2) 2019-2023 5-year ACS population estimate
Source: U.S. Census Bureau, 1990 Census, 2000 Census, 2010 Census, 2020 Census, 2019-2023 American Community Survey 5-Year Estimates

Race

Area	White Alone[2] (%)	Black Alone[2] (%)	Asian Alone[2] (%)	AIAN[3] Alone[2] (%)	NHOPI[4] Alone[2] (%)	Other Race Alone[2] (%)	Two or More Races (%)
City	48.3	6.9	3.1	1.1	0.1	10.9	29.6
MSA[1]	53.5	7.0	2.8	0.9	0.1	9.5	26.2
U.S.	63.4	12.4	5.8	0.9	0.2	6.6	10.7

Note: (1) Figures cover the San Antonio-New Braunfels, TX Metropolitan Statistical Area; (2) Alone is defined as not being in combination with one or more other races; (3) American Indian and Alaska Native; (4) Native Hawaiian and Other Pacific Islander
Source: U.S. Census Bureau, 2019-2023 American Community Survey 5-Year Estimates

Hispanic or Latino Origin

Area	Total (%)	Mexican (%)	Puerto Rican (%)	Cuban (%)	Other (%)
City	64.4	54.1	1.4	0.4	8.6
MSA[1]	54.5	45.5	1.5	0.3	7.2
U.S.	19.0	11.3	1.8	0.7	5.2

Note: Persons of Hispanic or Latino origin can be of any race; (1) Figures cover the San Antonio-New Braunfels, TX Metropolitan Statistical Area
Source: U.S. Census Bureau, 2019-2023 American Community Survey 5-Year Estimates

Age

Area	Under Age 5	Age 5–19	Age 20–34	Age 35–44	Age 45–54	Age 55–64	Age 65–74	Age 75–84	Age 85+	Median Age
City	6.3	20.5	23.7	13.8	11.8	10.7	7.9	3.7	1.6	34.6
MSA[1]	6.3	21.1	21.5	14.1	12.2	11.2	8.3	3.8	1.5	35.7
U.S.	5.7	19.1	20.2	13.1	12.3	12.8	10.0	4.9	1.9	38.7

Note: (1) Figures cover the San Antonio-New Braunfels, TX Metropolitan Statistical Area
Source: U.S. Census Bureau, 2019-2023 American Community Survey 5-Year Estimates

Disability by Age

Area	All Ages	Under 18 Years Old	18 to 64 Years Old	65 Years and Over
City	15.5	6.7	13.5	41.8
MSA[1]	14.6	6.3	12.6	39.1
U.S.	13.0	4.7	10.7	32.9

Note: Figures show percent of the civilian noninstitutionalized population that reported having a disability. Disability status is determined from six types of difficulty: vision, hearing, cognitive, ambulatory, self-care, and independent living. For children under 5 years old, hearing and vision difficulty are used to determine disability status. For children between the ages of 5 and 14, disability status is determined from hearing, vision, cognitive, ambulatory, and self-care difficulties. For people aged 15 years and older, they are considered to have a disability if they have difficulty with any one of the six difficulty types; Note: (1) Figures cover the San Antonio-New Braunfels, TX Metropolitan Statistical Area
Source: U.S. Census Bureau, 2019-2023 American Community Survey 5-Year Estimates

Ancestry

Area	German	Irish	English	American	Italian	Polish	French[2]	European	Scottish
City	7.2	4.6	4.7	3.4	2.0	0.9	1.2	0.8	0.9
MSA[1]	10.0	5.8	6.6	3.8	2.2	1.4	1.5	1.1	1.3
U.S.	12.6	9.4	9.1	5.5	4.9	2.6	2.0	1.6	1.6

Note: Figures are the percentage of the total population reporting a particular ancestry. The nine most commonly reported ancestries in the U.S. are shown. Figures include multiple ancestries (e.g. if a person reported being Irish and Italian, they were included in both columns); (1) Figures cover the San Antonio-New Braunfels, TX Metropolitan Statistical Area; (2) Excludes Basque
Source: U.S. Census Bureau, 2019-2023 American Community Survey 5-Year Estimates

Foreign-born Population

Area	Percent of Population Born in								
	Any Foreign Country	Asia	Mexico	Europe	Caribbean	Central America[2]	South America	Africa	Canada
City	14.3	2.6	8.8	0.6	0.3	1.0	0.6	0.4	0.1
MSA[1]	11.8	2.2	6.8	0.6	0.3	0.8	0.5	0.4	0.1
U.S.	13.9	4.3	3.3	1.4	1.4	1.2	1.2	0.8	0.2

Note: (1) Figures cover the San Antonio-New Braunfels, TX Metropolitan Statistical Area; (2) Excludes Mexico.
Source: U.S. Census Bureau, 2019-2023 American Community Survey 5-Year Estimates

Household Size

Area	Persons in Household (%)							Average Household Size
	One	Two	Three	Four	Five	Six	Seven or More	
City	31.3	29.4	15.5	12.5	6.7	2.8	1.8	2.62
MSA[1]	26.8	31.1	16.3	13.8	7.3	2.8	1.9	2.71
U.S.	28.5	33.8	15.4	12.7	5.9	2.3	1.4	2.54

Note: (1) Figures cover the San Antonio-New Braunfels, TX Metropolitan Statistical Area
Source: U.S. Census Bureau, 2019-2023 American Community Survey 5-Year Estimates

Household Relationships

Area	House-holder	Opposite-sex Spouse	Same-sex Spouse	Opposite-sex Unmarried Partner	Same-sex Unmarried Partner	Child[2]	Grand-child	Other Relatives	Non-relatives
City	37.5	14.7	0.3	2.7	0.2	30.3	3.8	5.5	3.2
MSA[1]	36.2	16.9	0.2	2.3	0.2	31.0	3.5	5.1	2.8
U.S.	38.3	17.5	0.2	2.5	0.2	28.3	2.4	4.8	3.4

Note: Figures are percent of the total population; (1) Figures cover the San Antonio-New Braunfels, TX Metropolitan Statistical Area; (2) Includes biological, adopted, and stepchildren of the householder
Source: U.S. Census Bureau, 2020 Census

Gender

Area	Males	Females	Males per 100 Females
City	722,875	736,079	98.2
MSA[1]	1,298,427	1,314,375	98.8
U.S.	164,545,087	167,842,453	98.0

Note: (1) Figures cover the San Antonio-New Braunfels, TX Metropolitan Statistical Area
Source: U.S. Census Bureau, 2019-2023 American Community Survey 5-Year Estimates

Marital Status

Area	Never Married	Now Married[2]	Separated	Widowed	Divorced
City	39.1	40.8	2.9	5.3	12.0
MSA[1]	34.3	47.2	2.3	5.1	11.1
U.S.	34.1	47.9	1.7	5.6	10.7

Note: Figures are percentages and cover the population 15 years of age and older; (1) Figures cover the San Antonio-New Braunfels, TX Metropolitan Statistical Area; (2) Excludes separated
Source: U.S. Census Bureau, 2019-2023 American Community Survey 5-Year Estimates

Religious Groups by Family

Area	Catholic	Baptist	Methodist	LDS[2]	Pentecostal	Lutheran	Islam	Adventist	Other
MSA[1]	27.3	6.4	2.1	1.4	1.6	1.1	0.5	1.5	11.0
U.S.	18.7	7.3	3.0	2.0	1.8	1.7	1.3	1.3	11.6

Note: Figures are the number of adherents as a percentage of the total population and cover the eight largest religious groups in the U.S; (1) Figures cover the San Antonio-New Braunfels, TX Metropolitan Statistical Area; (2) Church of Jesus Christ of Latter-day Saints
Sources: 2020 U.S. Religion Census, Association of Statisticians of American Religious Bodies; The Association of Religion Data Archives (ARDA)

Religious Groups by Tradition

Area	Catholic	Evangelical Protestant	Mainline Protestant	Black Protestant	Islam	Judaism	Hinduism	Orthodox	Buddhism
MSA[1]	27.3	17.7	3.1	0.8	0.5	0.2	0.1	0.1	0.3
U.S.	18.7	16.5	5.2	2.3	1.3	0.6	0.4	0.4	0.3

Note: Figures are the number of adherents as a percentage of the total population; (1) Figures cover the San Antonio-New Braunfels, TX Metropolitan Statistical Area
Sources: 2020 U.S. Religion Census, Association of Statisticians of American Religious Bodies; The Association of Religion Data Archives (ARDA)

ECONOMY

Real Gross Domestic Product (GDP)

Area	2017	2018	2019	2020	2021	2022	2023	Rank[3]
MSA[1]	118.9	124.5	129.0	127.4	134.2	143.7	150.3	33
U.S.[2]	17,619.1	18,160.7	18,642.5	18,238.9	19,387.6	19,896.6	20,436.3	—

Note: Figures are in billions of chained 2017 dollars; (1) Figures cover the San Antonio-New Braunfels, TX Metropolitan Statistical Area; (2) Figures cover real GDP within metropolitan areas; (3) Rank is based on 2023 data and ranges from 1 to 384
Source: U.S. Bureau of Economic Analysis

Economic Growth

Area	2014	2015	2016	2017	2018	2019	2020	2021	2022	2023
MSA[1]	5.3	5.7	0.9	0.3	4.7	3.6	-1.3	5.4	7.1	4.6
U.S.[2]	2.6	3.2	2.0	2.7	3.1	2.7	-2.2	6.3	2.6	2.7

Note: Figures are real gross domestic product growth rates and represent percent change from preceding period; (1) Figures cover the San Antonio-New Braunfels, TX Metropolitan Statistical Area; (2) Figures are the average growth rates within metropolitan areas
Source: U.S. Bureau of Economic Analysis

Metropolitan Area Exports

Area	2018	2019	2020	2021	2022	2023	Rank[2]
MSA[1]	11,678.1	11,668.0	10,987.9	13,086.4	13,173.6	12,821.8	31
U.S.	1,664,056.1	1,645,173.7	1,431,406.6	1,753,941.4	2,062,937.4	2,019,160.5	—

Note: Figures are in millions of dollars; (1) Figures cover the San Antonio-New Braunfels, TX Metropolitan Statistical Area; (2) Rank is based on 2023 data and ranges from 1 to 386
Source: U.S. Department of Commerce, International Trade Administration, Office of Trade and Economic Analysis, Industry and Analysis, Exports by Metropolitan Area, data extracted April 2, 2025

Building Permits

Area	Single-Family			Multi-Family			Total		
	2023	2024	Pct. Chg.	2023	2024	Pct. Chg.	2023	2024	Pct. Chg.
City	4,299	5,000	16.3	4,860	1,258	-74.1	9,159	6,258	-31.7
MSA[1]	8,718	10,999	26.2	7,767	3,858	-50.3	16,485	14,857	-9.9
U.S.	920,000	981,900	6.7	591,100	496,100	-16.1	1,511,100	1,478,000	-2.2

Note: (1) Figures cover the San Antonio-New Braunfels, TX Metropolitan Statistical Area; Figures represent new, privately-owned housing units authorized (unadjusted data)
Source: U.S. Census Bureau, Building Permits Survey (BPS), 2023, 2024

Bankruptcy Filings

Area	Business Filings			Nonbusiness Filings		
	2023	2024	% Chg.	2023	2024	% Chg.
Bexar County	126	169	34.1	1,270	1,813	42.8
U.S.	18,926	23,107	22.1	434,064	494,201	13.9

Note: Business filings include Chapter 7, Chapter 9, Chapter 11, Chapter 12, Chapter 13, Chapter 15, and Section 304; Nonbusiness filings include Chapter 7, Chapter 11, and Chapter 13
Source: Administrative Office of the U.S. Courts, Business and Nonbusiness Bankruptcy, County Cases Commenced by Chapter of the Bankruptcy Code, During the 12-Month Period Ending December 31, 2023 and Business and Nonbusiness Bankruptcy, County Cases Commenced by Chapter of the Bankruptcy Code, During the 12-Month Period Ending December 31, 2024

Housing Vacancy Rates

Area	Gross Vacancy Rate[3] (%)			Year-Round Vacancy Rate[4] (%)			Rental Vacancy Rate[5] (%)			Homeowner Vacancy Rate[6] (%)		
	2022	2023	2024	2022	2023	2024	2022	2023	2024	2022	2023	2024
MSA[1]	7.5	7.4	9.9	7.1	6.9	7.9	8.1	8.8	10.0	0.9	1.3	1.9
U.S.[2]	9.1	9.0	9.1	7.5	7.5	7.6	5.7	6.5	6.8	0.8	0.8	1.0

Note: (1) Figures cover the San Antonio-New Braunfels, TX Metropolitan Statistical Area; (2) Figures cover the 75 largest Metropolitan Statistical Areas; (3) The percentage of the total housing inventory that is vacant; (4) The percentage of the housing inventory (excluding seasonal units) that is year-round vacant; (5) The percentage of rental inventory that is vacant for rent; (6) The percentage of homeowner inventory that is vacant for sale
Source: U.S. Census Bureau, Housing Vacancies and Homeownership Annual Statistics: 2022, 2023, 2024

INCOME

Income

Area	Per Capita ($)	Median Household ($)	Average Household ($)
City	32,983	62,917	85,107
MSA[1]	37,425	74,297	100,400
U.S.	43,289	78,538	110,491

Note: (1) Figures cover the San Antonio-New Braunfels, TX Metropolitan Statistical Area
Source: U.S. Census Bureau, 2019-2023 American Community Survey 5-Year Estimates

Household Income Distribution

Area	Percent of Households Earning							
	Under $15,000	$15,000 -$24,999	$25,000 -$34,999	$35,000 -$49,999	$50,000 -$74,999	$75,000 -$99,999	$100,000 -$149,999	$150,000 and up
City	10.3	7.9	9.2	12.4	18.6	13.4	15.0	13.4
MSA[1]	8.2	6.5	7.5	10.9	17.2	13.3	17.4	18.9
U.S.	8.5	6.6	6.8	10.4	15.7	12.7	17.4	21.9

Note: (1) Figures cover the San Antonio-New Braunfels, TX Metropolitan Statistical Area
Source: U.S. Census Bureau, 2019-2023 American Community Survey 5-Year Estimates

Poverty Rate

Area	All Ages	Under 18 Years Old	18 to 64 Years Old	65 Years and Over
City	17.1	24.8	14.8	14.2
MSA[1]	13.4	18.5	11.9	11.4
U.S.	12.4	16.3	11.6	10.4

Note: Figures are percentage of people whose income during the past 12 months was below the poverty level; (1) Figures cover the San Antonio-New Braunfels, TX Metropolitan Statistical Area
Source: U.S. Census Bureau, 2019-2023 American Community Survey 5-Year Estimates

EMPLOYMENT

Labor Force and Employment

Area	Civilian Labor Force			Workers Employed		
	Dec. 2023	Dec. 2024	% Chg.	Dec. 2023	Dec. 2024	% Chg.
City	780,314	813,666	4.3	753,069	786,995	4.5
MSA[1]	1,308,187	1,349,973	3.2	1,265,057	1,304,101	3.1
U.S.	166,661,000	167,746,000	0.7	160,754,000	161,294,000	0.3

Note: Data is not seasonally adjusted and covers workers 16 years of age and older; (1) Figures cover the San Antonio-New Braunfels, TX Metropolitan Statistical Area
Source: Bureau of Labor Statistics, Local Area Unemployment Statistics

Unemployment Rate

Area	2024											
	Jan.	Feb.	Mar.	Apr.	May	Jun.	Jul.	Aug.	Sep.	Oct.	Nov.	Dec.
City	3.9	4.1	3.6	3.4	3.4	4.5	4.3	4.2	3.8	3.8	4.0	3.3
MSA[1]	3.8	4.0	3.6	3.3	3.5	4.1	4.2	4.1	3.8	3.8	3.8	3.4
U.S.	4.1	4.2	3.9	3.5	3.7	4.3	4.5	4.4	3.9	3.9	4.0	3.8

Note: Data is not seasonally adjusted and covers workers 16 years of age and older; (1) Figures cover the San Antonio-New Braunfels, TX Metropolitan Statistical Area
Source: Bureau of Labor Statistics, Local Area Unemployment Statistics

Average Wages

Occupation	$/Hr.	Occupation	$/Hr.
Accountants and Auditors	41.41	Maintenance and Repair Workers	22.06
Automotive Mechanics	25.74	Marketing Managers	67.10
Bookkeepers	23.19	Network and Computer Systems Admin.	43.87
Carpenters	23.06	Nurses, Licensed Practical	29.23
Cashiers	14.39	Nurses, Registered	42.93
Computer Programmers	62.03	Nursing Assistants	17.50
Computer Systems Analysts	51.53	Office Clerks, General	19.72
Computer User Support Specialists	27.32	Physical Therapists	48.60
Construction Laborers	19.44	Physicians	148.25
Cooks, Restaurant	15.83	Plumbers, Pipefitters and Steamfitters	28.13
Customer Service Representatives	20.34	Police and Sheriff's Patrol Officers	33.62
Dentists	78.33	Postal Service Mail Carriers	28.61
Electricians	26.69	Real Estate Sales Agents	27.84
Engineers, Electrical	55.23	Retail Salespersons	16.14
Fast Food and Counter Workers	13.32	Sales Representatives, Technical/Scientific	48.30
Financial Managers	77.30	Secretaries, Exc. Legal/Medical/Executive	21.21
First-Line Supervisors of Office Workers	32.68	Security Guards	17.26
General and Operations Managers	57.15	Surgeons	n/a
Hairdressers/Cosmetologists	16.98	Teacher Assistants, Exc. Postsecondary[1]	12.78
Home Health and Personal Care Aides	12.52	Teachers, Secondary School, Exc. Sp. Ed.[1]	29.49
Janitors and Cleaners	15.75	Telemarketers	16.58
Landscaping/Groundskeeping Workers	17.39	Truck Drivers, Heavy/Tractor-Trailer	25.47
Lawyers	73.65	Truck Drivers, Light/Delivery Services	21.43
Maids and Housekeeping Cleaners	14.28	Waiters and Waitresses	15.16

Note: Wage data covers the San Antonio-New Braunfels, TX Metropolitan Statistical Area; (1) Hourly wages were calculated from annual wage data based on a 40 hour work week
Source: Bureau of Labor Statistics, Metro Area Occupational Employment & Wage Estimates, May 2024

Employment by Industry

Sector	MSA[1] Number of Employees	MSA[1] Percent of Total	U.S. Percent of Total
Construction	69,000	5.7	5.1
Financial Activities	102,000	8.5	5.8
Government	193,700	16.1	14.9
Information	19,800	1.6	1.9
Leisure and Hospitality	146,700	12.2	10.4
Manufacturing	63,000	5.2	8.0
Mining and Logging	7,100	0.6	0.4
Other Services	42,000	3.5	3.7
Private Education and Health Services	182,400	15.2	16.9
Professional and Business Services	160,400	13.3	14.2
Retail Trade	128,400	10.7	10.0
Transportation, Warehousing, and Utilities	48,500	4.0	4.8
Wholesale Trade	38,900	3.2	3.9

Note: Figures are non-farm employment as of December 2024. Figures are not seasonally adjusted and include workers 16 years of age and older; (1) Figures cover the San Antonio-New Braunfels, TX Metropolitan Statistical Area
Source: Bureau of Labor Statistics, Current Employment Statistics, Employment, Hours, and Earnings

Employment by Occupation

Occupation Classification	City (%)	MSA[1] (%)	U.S. (%)
Management, Business, Science, and Arts	36.0	39.2	42.0
Natural Resources, Construction, and Maintenance	10.1	9.6	8.6
Production, Transportation, and Material Moving	11.5	11.5	13.0
Sales and Office	22.8	22.1	19.9
Service	19.6	17.6	16.5

Note: Figures cover employed civilians 16 years of age and older; (1) Figures cover the San Antonio-New Braunfels, TX Metropolitan Statistical Area
Source: U.S. Census Bureau, 2019-2023 American Community Survey 5-Year Estimates

Occupations with Greatest Projected Employment Growth: 2022 – 2032

Occupation[1]	2022 Employment	2032 Projected Employment	Numeric Employment Change	Percent Employment Change
General and Operations Managers	425,560	504,280	78,720	18.5
Fast Food and Counter Workers	333,870	394,290	60,420	18.1
Stockers and Order Fillers	264,810	321,600	56,790	21.4
Home Health and Personal Care Aides	313,670	367,500	53,830	17.2
Software Developers	110,280	161,780	51,500	46.7
Cooks, Restaurant	113,680	158,830	45,150	39.7
Laborers and Freight, Stock, and Material Movers, Hand	225,090	269,120	44,030	19.6
Heavy and Tractor-Trailer Truck Drivers	226,450	270,320	43,870	19.4
Retail Salespersons	319,400	357,630	38,230	12.0
Registered Nurses	233,850	267,980	34,130	14.6

Note: Projections cover Texas; (1) Sorted by numeric employment change
Source: www.projectionscentral.org, State Occupational Projections, 2022–2032 Long-Term Projections

Fastest-Growing Occupations: 2022 – 2032

Occupation[1]	2022 Employment	2032 Projected Employment	Numeric Employment Change	Percent Employment Change
Wind Turbine Service Technicians	4,860	7,950	3,090	63.6
Nurse Practitioners	19,060	30,490	11,430	60.0
Data Scientists	13,220	20,250	7,030	53.2
Computer and Information Research Scientists (SOC 2018)	2,070	3,140	1,070	51.7
Information Security Analysts (SOC 2018)	14,620	21,620	7,000	47.9
Software Developers	110,280	161,780	51,500	46.7
Statisticians	980	1,430	450	45.9
Operations Research Analysts	12,060	17,290	5,230	43.4
Software Quality Assurance Analysts and Testers	17,350	24,440	7,090	40.9
Medical and Health Services Managers	49,430	69,180	19,750	40.0

Note: Projections cover Texas; (1) Sorted by percent employment change and excludes occupations with numeric employment change less than 50
Source: www.projectionscentral.org, State Occupational Projections, 2022–2032 Long-Term Projections

CITY FINANCES

City Government Finances

Component	2022 ($000)	2022 ($ per capita)
Total Revenues	6,277,961	4,006
Total Expenditures	6,121,112	3,906
Debt Outstanding	11,964,157	7,634

Source: U.S. Census Bureau, State & Local Government Finances 2022

City Government Revenue by Source

Source	2022 ($000)	2022 ($ per capita)	2022 (%)
General Revenue			
From Federal Government	153,298	98	2.4
From State Government	369,706	236	5.9
From Local Governments	127,330	81	2.0
Taxes			
Property	644,788	411	10.3
Sales and Gross Receipts	523,353	334	8.3
Personal Income	0	0	0.0
Corporate Income	0	0	0.0
Motor Vehicle License	0	0	0.0
Other Taxes	76,117	49	1.2
Current Charges	703,662	449	11.2
Liquor Store	0	0	0.0
Utility	3,261,866	2,081	52.0

Source: U.S. Census Bureau, State & Local Government Finances 2022

City Government Expenditures by Function

Function	2022 ($000)	2022 ($ per capita)	2022 (%)
General Direct Expenditures			
Air Transportation	85,180	54	1.4
Corrections	0	0	0.0
Education	93,053	59	1.5
Employment Security Administration	0	0	0.0
Financial Administration	98,412	62	1.6
Fire Protection	309,981	197	5.1
General Public Buildings	23,721	15	0.4
Governmental Administration, Other	32,906	21	0.5
Health	71,353	45	1.2
Highways	194,306	124	3.2
Hospitals	0	0	0.0
Housing and Community Development	168,392	107	2.8
Interest on General Debt	188,884	120	3.1
Judicial and Legal	29,337	18	0.5
Libraries	40,760	26	0.7
Parking	7,016	4	0.1
Parks and Recreation	168,286	107	2.7
Police Protection	445,353	284	7.3
Public Welfare	139,794	89	2.3
Sewerage	299,383	191	4.9
Solid Waste Management	144,565	92	2.4
Veterans' Services	0	0	0.0
Liquor Store	0	0	0.0
Utility	3,262,615	2,081	53.3

Source: U.S. Census Bureau, State & Local Government Finances 2022

TAXES

State Corporate Income Tax Rates

State	Tax Rate (%)	Income Brackets ($)	Num. of Brackets	Financial Institution Tax Rate (%)[a]	Federal Income Tax Ded.
Texas	(u)	–	–	(u)	No

Note: Tax rates for tax year 2024; (a) Rates listed are the corporate income tax rate applied to financial institutions or excise taxes based on income. Some states have other taxes based upon the value of deposits or shares; (u) Texas imposes a Franchise Tax, otherwise known as margin tax, imposed on entities with more than $2,470,000 total revenues effective in 2024 at rate of 0.75%, or 0.375% for entities primarily engaged in retail or wholesale trade, on lesser of 70% of total revenues or 100% of gross receipts after deductions for either compensation ($450,000 deduction limit) or cost of goods sold. Texas has an EZ rate of 0.331 applicable to a $20 million revenue threshold.
Source: Federation of Tax Administrators, State Corporate Income Tax Rates, January 1, 2025

State Individual Income Tax Rates

State	Tax Rate (%)	Income Brackets ($)	Personal Exemptions ($)			Standard Ded. ($)	
			Single	Married	Depend.	Single	Married
Texas					– No state income tax –		

Note: Tax rates for tax year 2024; Local- and county-level taxes are not included
Source: Federation of Tax Administrators, State Individual Income Tax Rates, January 1, 2025

Various State Sales and Excise Tax Rates

State	State Sales Tax (%)	Gasoline[1] ($/gal.)	Cigarette[2] ($/pack)	Spirits[3] ($/gal.)	Wine[4] ($/gal.)	Beer[5] ($/gal.)	Recreational Marijuana (%)
Texas	6.25	0.20	1.41	2.40	0.20	0.19	Not legal

Note: All tax rates as of January 1, 2025; (1) The American Petroleum Institute has developed a methodology for determining the average tax rate on a gallon of fuel. Rates may include any of the following: excise taxes, environmental fees, storage tank fees, other fees or taxes, general sales tax, and local taxes; (2) The federal excise tax of $1.0066 per pack and local taxes are not included; (3) Rates are those applicable to off-premise sales of 40% alcohol by volume (a.b.v.) distilled spirits in 750ml containers. Local excise taxes are excluded; (4) Rates are those applicable to off-premise sales of 11% a.b.v. non-carbonated wine in 750ml containers; (5) Rates are those applicable to off-premise sales of 4.7% a.b.v. beer in 12 ounce containers.
Source: Tax Foundation, 2025 Facts & Figures: How Does Your State Compare?

State Tax Competitiveness Index

State	Overall Rank	Corporate Tax Rank	Individual Income Tax Rank	Sales Tax Rank	Property Tax Rank	Unemployment Insurance Tax Rank
Texas	7	46	1	36	40	30

Note: The Tax Foundation's State Tax Competitiveness Index enables policymakers, taxpayers, and business leaders to gauge how their states' tax systems compare. A rank of 1 is best, 50 is worst. Rankings do not average to the total. States without a tax rank equally as 1. DC's scores and rankings do not affect other states. The report shows tax systems as of July 1, 2024 (the beginning of Fiscal Year 2025).
Source: Tax Foundation, State Tax Competitiveness Index 2025

TRANSPORTATION

Means of Transportation to Work

Area	Car/Truck/Van		Public Transportation			Bicycle	Walked	Other Means	Worked at Home
	Drove Alone	Car-pooled	Bus	Subway	Railroad				
City	70.5	12.1	2.1	0.0	0.0	0.2	1.7	1.6	11.8
MSA[1]	71.5	10.9	1.3	0.0	0.0	0.2	1.5	1.5	13.0
U.S.	70.2	8.5	1.7	1.3	0.4	0.4	2.4	1.6	13.5

Note: Figures are percentages and cover workers 16 years of age and older; (1) Figures cover the San Antonio-New Braunfels, TX Metropolitan Statistical Area
Source: U.S. Census Bureau, 2019-2023 American Community Survey 5-Year Estimates

Travel Time to Work

Area	Less Than 10 Minutes	10 to 19 Minutes	20 to 29 Minutes	30 to 44 Minutes	45 to 59 Minutes	60 to 89 Minutes	90 Minutes or More
City	9.5	30.7	26.1	22.2	5.9	3.7	1.8
MSA[1]	9.5	27.1	24.0	23.8	8.3	5.1	2.3
U.S.	12.6	28.6	21.2	20.8	8.1	6.0	2.8

Note: Note: Figures are percentages and include workers 16 years old and over; (1) Figures cover the San Antonio-New Braunfels, TX Metropolitan Statistical Area
Source: U.S. Census Bureau, 2019-2023 American Community Survey 5-Year Estimates

Key Congestion Measures

Measure	2000	2010	2015	2020	2022
Annual Hours of Delay, Total (000)	38,579	54,651	66,862	44,999	64,395
Annual Hours of Delay, Per Auto Commuter	40	42	48	32	48
Annual Congestion Cost, Per Auto Commuter ($)	855	963	1,089	762	1,078

Note: Figures cover the San Antonio TX urban area
Source: Texas A&M Transportation Institute, 2023 Urban Mobility Report

Freeway Travel Time Index

Measure	1985	1990	1995	2000	2005	2010	2015	2020	2022
Urban Area Index[1]	1.11	1.12	1.19	1.22	1.24	1.23	1.23	1.12	1.21
Urban Area Rank[1,2]		25	35	23	24	27	28	29	10	33

Note: Freeway Travel Time Index—the ratio of travel time in the peak period to the travel time at free-flow conditions. For example, a value of 1.30 indicates a 20-minute free-flow trip takes 26 minutes in the peak (20 minutes x 1.30 = 26 minutes); (1) Covers the San Antonio TX urban area; (2) Rank is based on 101 larger urban areas (#1 = highest travel time index)
Source: Texas A&M Transportation Institute, 2023 Urban Mobility Report

Public Transportation

Agency Name / Mode of Transportation	Vehicles Operated in Maximum Service[1]	Annual Unlinked Passenger Trips[2] (in thous.)	Annual Passenger Miles[3] (in thous.)
VIA Metropolitan Transit (VIA)			
Bus (directly operated)	268	26,460.2	106,373.6
Demand Response (directly operated)	109	424.2	5,457.0
Demand Response (purchased transportation)	140	708.7	7,185.6
Demand Response - Taxi	17	8.3	92.4
Vanpool (purchased transportation)	134	363.9	18,302.9

Note: (1) Number of revenue vehicles operated by the given mode and type of service to meet the annual maximum service requirement. This is the revenue vehicle count during the peak season of the year; on the week and day that maximum service is provided. Vehicles operated in maximum service (VOMS) exclude atypical days and one-time special events; (2) Number of passengers who boarded public transportation vehicles. Passengers are counted each time they board a vehicle no matter how many vehicles they use to travel from their origin to their destination. (3) Sum of the distances ridden by all passengers during the entire fiscal year.
Source: Federal Transit Administration, National Transit Database, 2023

Air Transportation

Airport Name and Code / Type of Service	Passenger Airlines[1]	Passenger Enplanements	Freight Carriers[2]	Freight (lbs)
San Antonio International (SAT)				
Domestic service (U.S. carriers only)	24	5,109,821	17	93,145,181
International service (U.S. carriers only)	6	22,839	1	12,400,052

Note: (1) Includes all U.S.-based major, minor and commuter airlines that carried at least one passenger during the year; (2) Includes all U.S.-based airlines and freight carriers that transported at least one pound of freight during the year.
Source: Bureau of Transportation Statistics, The Intermodal Transportation Database, Air Carriers: T-100 Domestic Market (U.S. carriers only), 2024; Bureau of Transportation Statistics, The Intermodal Transportation Database, Air Carriers: T-100 International Market (U.S. carriers only), 2024

BUSINESSES

Major Business Headquarters

Company Name	Industry	Rankings	
		Fortune[1]	Forbes[2]
H-E-B Grocery Company	Food markets	-	5
United Services Automobile Assn.	Insurance: property and casualty (stock)	103	-
Valero Energy	Petroleum refining	29	-
Zachry Group	Construction	-	127

Note: (1) Companies that produce a 10-K are ranked 1 to 500 based on 2023 revenue; (2) All private companies with at least $2 billion in annual revenue through the end of their most current fiscal year are ranked 1 to 275; companies listed are headquartered in the city; dashes indicate no ranking
Source: Fortune, "Fortune 500," 2024; Forbes, "America's Largest Private Companies," 2024

Fastest-Growing Businesses

According to Deloitte, San Antonio is home to one of North America's 500 fastest-growing high-technology companies: **Stirista** (#399). Companies are ranked by percentage growth in revenue over a four-year period. Criteria for inclusion: company must be headquartered within North America; must own proprietary intellectual property or technology that is sold to customers in products that contributes to a significant portion of the company's operating revenue; must have been in business for a minumum of four years with 2020 operating revenues of at least $50,000 USD/CD and 2023 operating revenues of at least $5 million USD/CD. *Deloitte, 2024 Technology Fast 500™*

Living Environment

COST OF LIVING

Cost of Living Index

Composite Index	Groceries	Housing	Utilities	Trans-portation	Health Care	Misc. Goods/Services
91.2	94.5	79.0	81.8	94.3	111.3	98.5

Note: The Cost of Living Index measures regional differences in the cost of consumer goods and services, excluding taxes and non-consumer expenditures, for professional and managerial households in the top income quintile. It is based on more than 50,000 prices covering almost 60 different items for which prices are collected three times a year by chambers of commerce, economic development organizations or university applied economic centers in each participating urban area. The numbers shown should be read as a percentage above or below the national average of 100. For example, a value of 115.4 in the groceries column indicates that grocery prices are 15.4% higher than the national average. Small differences in the index numbers should not be interpreted as significant; Figures cover the San Antonio TX urban area.
Source: The Council for Community and Economic Research, Cost of Living Index, 2024

Grocery Prices

Area[1]	T-Bone Steak ($/pound)	Frying Chicken ($/pound)	Whole Milk ($/half gal.)	Eggs ($/dozen)	Orange Juice ($/64 oz.)	Coffee ($/11.5 oz.)
City[2]	14.53	1.33	4.57	2.98	4.25	5.05
Avg.	15.42	1.55	4.69	3.25	4.41	5.46
Min.	14.50	1.16	4.43	2.75	4.00	4.85
Max.	17.56	2.89	5.49	4.78	5.54	7.89

Note: (1) Values for the local area are compared with the average, minimum and maximum values for all 276 areas in the Cost of Living Index; (2) Figures cover the San Antonio TX urban area; **T-Bone Steak** (price per pound); **Frying Chicken** (price per pound, whole fryer); **Whole Milk** (half gallon carton); **Eggs** (price per dozen, Grade A, large); **Orange Juice** (64 oz. Tropicana or Florida Natural); **Coffee** (11.5 oz. can, vacuum-packed, Maxwell House, Hills Bros, or Folgers).
Source: The Council for Community and Economic Research, Cost of Living Index, 2024

Housing and Utility Costs

Area[1]	New Home Price ($)	Apartment Rent ($/month)	All Electric ($/month)	Part Electric ($/month)	Other Energy ($/month)	Telephone ($/month)
City[2]	357,072	1,521	-	105.82	36.26	202.34
Avg.	515,975	1,550	210.99	123.07	82.07	194.99
Min.	265,375	692	104.33	53.68	36.26	179.42
Max.	2,775,821	5,719	529.02	397.28	361.63	223.33

Note: (1) Values for the local area are compared with the average, minimum and maximum values for all 276 areas in the Cost of Living Index; (2) Figures cover the San Antonio TX urban area; **New Home Price** (2,400 sf living area, 8,000 sf lot, in urban area with full utilities); **Apartment Rent** (950 sf 2 bedroom/1.5 or 2 bath, unfurnished, excluding all utilities except water); **All Electric** (average monthly cost for an all-electric home); **Part Electric** (average monthly cost for a part-electric home); **Other Energy** (average monthly cost for natural gas, fuel oil, coal, wood, and any other forms of energy except electricity); **Telephone** (price includes the base monthly rate plus taxes and fees for three lines of mobile phone service).
Source: The Council for Community and Economic Research, Cost of Living Index, 2024

Health Care, Transportation, and Other Costs

Area[1]	Doctor ($/visit)	Dentist ($/visit)	Optometrist ($/visit)	Gasoline ($/gallon)	Beauty Salon ($/visit)	Men's Shirt ($)
City[2]	149.40	139.78	139.25	2.97	69.33	39.95
Avg.	143.77	117.51	129.23	3.32	48.57	38.14
Min.	36.74	58.67	67.33	2.80	24.00	13.41
Max.	270.44	216.82	307.33	5.28	94.00	63.89

Note: (1) Values for the local area are compared with the average, minimum and maximum values for all 276 areas in the Cost of Living Index; (2) Figures cover the San Antonio TX urban area; **Doctor** (general practitioners routine exam of an established patient); **Dentist** (adult teeth cleaning and periodic oral examination); **Optometrist** (full vision eye exam for established adult patient); **Gasoline** (one gallon regular unleaded, national brand, including all taxes, cash price at self-service pump if available); **Beauty Salon** (woman's shampoo, trim, and blow-dry); **Men's Shirt** (cotton/polyester dress shirt, pinpoint weave, long sleeves).
Source: The Council for Community and Economic Research, Cost of Living Index, 2024

HOUSING

Homeownership Rate

Area	2017 (%)	2018 (%)	2019 (%)	2020 (%)	2021 (%)	2022 (%)	2023 (%)	2024 (%)
MSA[1]	62.5	64.4	62.6	64.2	62.7	62.9	66.9	63.3
U.S.	63.9	64.4	64.6	66.6	65.5	65.8	65.9	65.6

Note: (1) Figures cover the San Antonio-New Braunfels, TX Metropolitan Statistical Area
Source: U.S. Census Bureau, Housing Vacancies and Homeownership Annual Statistics: 2017-2024

House Price Index (HPI)

Area	National Ranking[2]	Quarterly Change (%)	One-Year Change (%)	Five-Year Change (%)	Since 1991Q1 (%)
MSA[1]	228	4.07	1.99	49.58	357.13
U.S.[3]	—	1.43	4.51	57.13	327.82

Note: The HPI is a weighted repeat sales index. It measures average price changes in repeat sales or refinancings on the same properties. This information is obtained by reviewing repeat mortgage transactions on single-family properties whose mortgages have been purchased or securitized by Fannie Mae or Freddie Mac since January 1975; (1) Figures cover the San Antonio-New Braunfels, TX Metropolitan Statistical Area; (2) Rankings are based on annual percentage change for all metro areas containing at least 15,000 transactions over the last 10 years and ranges from 1 to 241; (3) figures based on a weighted average of Census Division estimates using a seasonally adjusted, purchase-only index; all figures are for the period ending December 31, 2024
Source: Federal Housing Finance Agency, Change in FHFA Metropolitan Area House Price Indexes, All Transactions Index, 2024Q4

Home Value

Area	Under $100,000	$100,000 -$199,999	$200,000 -$299,999	$300,000 -$399,999	$400,000 -$499,999	$500,000 -$999,999	$1,000,000 or more	Median ($)
City	13.7	29.8	29.2	14.1	6.3	5.9	1.0	219,700
MSA[1]	11.7	21.6	27.6	16.5	9.1	11.3	2.2	258,700
U.S.	12.1	17.8	19.5	14.4	10.5	19.1	6.5	303,400

Note: Figures are percentages except for median and cover owner-occupied housing units; (1) Figures cover the San Antonio-New Braunfels, TX Metropolitan Statistical Area
Source: U.S. Census Bureau, 2019-2023 American Community Survey 5-Year Estimates

Year Housing Structure Built

Area	2020 or Later	2010 -2019	2000 -2009	1990 -1999	1980 -1989	1970 -1979	1960 -1969	1950 -1959	1940 -1949	Before 1940	Median Year
City	1.6	11.9	15.2	11.3	16.2	13.8	10.1	9.5	5.2	5.2	1984
MSA[1]	3.0	18.3	18.5	12.4	13.9	11.8	7.6	6.7	3.7	4.0	1992
U.S.	1.2	8.9	13.6	12.8	13.0	14.4	10.0	9.7	4.5	11.9	1980

Note: Figures are percentages except for Median Year; Note: (1) Figures cover the San Antonio-New Braunfels, TX Metropolitan Statistical Area
Source: U.S. Census Bureau, 2019-2023 American Community Survey 5-Year Estimates

Gross Monthly Rent

Area	Under $500	$500 -$999	$1,000 -$1,499	$1,500 -$1,999	$2,000 -$2,499	$2,500 -$2,999	$3,000 and up	Median ($)
City	4.8	21.4	43.5	21.8	5.7	1.6	1.2	1,258
MSA[1]	4.4	19.8	41.8	22.8	7.7	2.0	1.4	1,299
U.S.	6.5	22.3	29.5	20.2	10.8	4.8	5.9	1,348

Note: Figures are percentages except for median; Gross rent is the contract rent plus the estimated average monthly cost of utilities (electricity, gas, and water and sewer) and fuels (oil, coal, kerosene, wood, etc.) if these are paid by the renter (or paid for the renter by someone else); (1) Figures cover the San Antonio-New Braunfels, TX Metropolitan Statistical Area
Source: U.S. Census Bureau, 2019-2023 American Community Survey 5-Year Estimates

HEALTH

Health Risk Factors

Category	MSA[1] (%)	U.S. (%)
Adults aged 18–64 who have any kind of health care coverage	86.4	90.8
Adults who reported being in good or better health	80.4	81.8
Adults who have been told they have high blood cholesterol	33.7	36.9
Adults who have been told they have high blood pressure	35.1	34.0
Adults who are current smokers	12.6	12.1
Adults who currently use e-cigarettes	7.8	7.7
Adults who currently use chewing tobacco, snuff, or snus	2.6	3.2
Adults who are heavy drinkers[2]	6.4	6.1
Adults who are binge drinkers[3]	18.4	15.2
Adults who are overweight (BMI 25.0 - 29.9)	35.4	34.4
Adults who are obese (BMI 30.0 - 99.8)	34.0	34.3
Adults who participated in any physical activities in the past month	73.1	75.8

Note: All figures are crude prevalence; (1) Figures cover the San Antonio-New Braunfels, TX Metropolitan Statistical Area; (2) Heavy drinkers are classified as adult men having more than 14 drinks per week and adult women having more than 7 drinks per week; (3) Binge drinkers are classified as males having five or more drinks on one occasion or females having four or more drinks on one occasion
Source: Centers for Disease Control and Prevention, Behavioral Risk Factor Surveillance System, SMART: Selected Metropolitan Area Risk Trends, 2023

Acute and Chronic Health Conditions

Category	MSA[1] (%)	U.S. (%)
Adults who have ever been told they had a heart attack	4.7	4.2
Adults who have ever been told they have angina or coronary heart disease	4.5	4.0
Adults who have ever been told they had a stroke	4.4	3.3
Adults who have ever been told they have asthma	12.3	15.7
Adults who have ever been told they have arthritis	24.6	26.3
Adults who have ever been told they have diabetes[2]	15.3	11.5
Adults who have ever been told they had skin cancer	4.3	5.6
Adults who have ever been told they had any other types of cancer	6.7	8.4
Adults who have ever been told they have COPD	4.6	6.4
Adults who have ever been told they have kidney disease	4.8	3.7
Adults who have ever been told they have a form of depression	20.5	22.0

Note: All figures are crude prevalence; (1) Figures cover the San Antonio-New Braunfels, TX Metropolitan Statistical Area; (2) Figures do not include pregnancy-related, borderline, or pre-diabetes
Source: Centers for Disease Control and Prevention, Behavioral Risk Factor Surveillance System, SMART: Selected Metropolitan Area Risk Trends, 2023

Health Screening and Vaccination Rates

Category	MSA[1] (%)	U.S. (%)
Adults who have ever been tested for HIV	42.1	37.5
Adults who have had their blood cholesterol checked within the last five years	85.9	87.0
Adults aged 65+ who have had flu shot within the past year	52.1	63.4
Adults aged 65+ who have ever had a pneumonia vaccination	66.1	71.9

Note: All figures are crude prevalence; (1) Figures cover the San Antonio-New Braunfels, TX Metropolitan Statistical Area.
Source: Centers for Disease Control and Prevention, Behavioral Risk Factor Surveillance System, SMART: Selected Metropolitan Area Risk Trends, 2023

Disability Status

Category	MSA[1] (%)	U.S. (%)
Adults who reported being deaf	6.0	7.4
Are you blind or have serious difficulty seeing, even when wearing glasses?	5.2	4.9
Do you have difficulty doing errands alone?	7.4	7.8
Do you have difficulty dressing or bathing?	4.7	3.6
Do you have serious difficulty concentrating/remembering/making decisions?	11.3	13.7
Do you have serious difficulty walking or climbing stairs?	13.2	13.2

Note: All figures are crude prevalence; (1) Figures cover the San Antonio-New Braunfels, TX Metropolitan Statistical Area.
Source: Centers for Disease Control and Prevention, Behavioral Risk Factor Surveillance System, SMART: Selected Metropolitan Area Risk Trends, 2023

Mortality Rates for the Top 10 Causes of Death in the U.S.

ICD-10[a] Sub-Chapter	ICD-10[a] Code	Crude Mortality Rate[2] per 100,000 population	
		County[3]	U.S.
Malignant neoplasms	C00-C97	136.1	182.7
Ischaemic heart diseases	I20-I25	83.7	109.6
Provisional assignment of new diseases of uncertain etiology[1]	U00-U49	74.9	65.3
Other forms of heart disease	I30-I51	55.3	65.1
Other degenerative diseases of the nervous system	G30-G31	67.0	52.4
Other external causes of accidental injury	W00-X59	37.6	52.3
Cerebrovascular diseases	I60-I69	43.8	49.1
Chronic lower respiratory diseases	J40-J47	27.1	43.5
Hypertensive diseases	I10-I15	31.4	38.9
Organic, including symptomatic, mental disorders	F01-F09	12.9	33.9

Note: (a) ICD-10 = International Classification of Diseases 10th Revision; (1) Includes COVID-19, adverse effects to COVID-19 vaccines, SARS, and vaping-related disorders; (2) Crude mortality rates are a three-year average covering 2021-2023; (3) Figures cover Bexar County.
Source: Centers for Disease Control and Prevention, National Center for Health Statistics. National Vital Statistics System, Mortality 2018-2023 on CDC WONDER Online Database

Mortality Rates for Selected Causes of Death

Cause of Death	ICD-10[a] Code	Crude Mortality Rate[1] per 100,000 population	
		County[2]	U.S.
Accidental poisoning and exposure to noxious substances	X40-X49	20.4	30.5
Alzheimer disease	G30	32.8	35.4
Assault	X85-Y09	10.0	7.3
COVID-19	U07.1	74.9	65.3
Diabetes mellitus	E10-E14	34.0	30.0
Diseases of the liver	K70-K76	26.3	20.8
Human immunodeficiency virus (HIV) disease	B20-B24	2.2	1.5
Influenza and pneumonia	J09-J18	8.7	13.4
Intentional self-harm	X60-X84	13.9	14.7
Malnutrition	E40-E46	7.4	6.0
Obesity and other hyperalimentation	E65-E68	2.5	3.1
Renal failure	N17-N19	16.3	16.4
Transport accidents	V01-V99	13.6	14.4

Note: (a) ICD-10 = International Classification of Diseases 10th Revision; (1) Crude mortality rates are a three-year average covering 2021-2023; (2) Figures cover Bexar County; Data are suppressed when the data meet the criteria for confidentiality constraints; Crude mortality rates are flagged as unreliable when the rate would be calculated with a numerator of 20 or less.
Source: Centers for Disease Control and Prevention, National Center for Health Statistics. National Vital Statistics System, Mortality 2018-2023 on CDC WONDER Online Database

Health Insurance Coverage

Area	With Health Insurance	With Private Health Insurance	With Public Health Insurance	Without Health Insurance	Population Under Age 19 Without Health Insurance
City	82.5	58.4	33.8	17.5	9.8
MSA[1]	85.0	64.6	31.8	15.0	9.1
U.S.	91.4	67.3	36.3	8.6	5.4

Note: Figures are percentages that cover the civilian noninstitutionalized population; (1) Figures cover the San Antonio-New Braunfels, TX Metropolitan Statistical Area
Source: U.S. Census Bureau, 2019-2023 American Community Survey 5-Year Estimates

Number of Medical Professionals

Area	MDs[3]	DOs[3,4]	Dentists	Podiatrists	Chiropractors	Optometrists
County[1] (number)	6,797	587	1,989	126	363	396
County[1] (rate[2])	330.0	28.5	95.3	6.0	17.4	19.0
U.S. (rate[2])	302.5	29.2	74.6	6.4	29.5	18.0

Note: Data as of 2023 unless noted; (1) Data covers Bexar County; (2) Number of medical professionals per 100,000 population; (3) Data as of 2022 and includes all active, non-federal physicians; (4) Doctor of Osteopathic Medicine
Source: U.S. Department of Health and Human Services, Health Resources and Services Administration, Bureau of Health Professions, Area Resource File (ARF) 2023-2024

EDUCATION

Public School District Statistics

District Name	Schls	Pupils	Pupil/ Teacher Ratio	Minority Pupils[1] (%)	Total Rev. per Pupil ($)	Total Exp. per Pupil ($)
Alamo Heights ISD	6	4,698	12.9	48.1	14,513	20,869
Basis Texas	14	6,266	16.5	85.8	10,972	9,186
Brooks Academies of Texas	4	2,817	19.6	93.1	13,722	11,668
Compass Rose Public Schools	8	3,600	17.5	85.3	15,489	13,804
East Central ISD	18	11,176	17.3	86.8	13,054	11,561
Edgewood ISD	26	7,930	14.9	99.1	15,843	15,020
Great Hearts Texas	13	12,019	20.8	63.3	11,602	9,902
Harlandale ISD	22	11,814	15.4	98.0	15,394	15,941
Harmony Science Academy (San Antonio)	9	4,855	14.8	95.8	14,577	12,995
Jubilee Academies	13	6,017	18.2	95.3	16,130	13,552
Judson ISD	34	23,848	14.5	87.7	14,109	12,560
North East ISD	75	57,374	13.8	77.7	13,783	12,524
Northside ISD	131	101,095	14.6	83.9	13,666	13,257
San Antonio ISD	98	44,670	14.8	96.8	17,756	17,992
School of Science and Technology	7	5,053	15.2	82.1	12,392	11,072
School of Science and Technology	9	5,967	14.5	86.9	11,874	10,485
South San Antonio ISD	15	7,429	14.7	96.6	15,929	14,591
Southside ISD	10	6,033	15.4	93.9	18,453	16,542
Southwest ISD	19	14,202	14.8	95.4	15,704	15,724

Note: Table includes school districts with 2,000 or more students; (1) Percentage of students that are not non-Hispanic white.
Source: U.S. Department of Education, National Center for Education Statistics, Common Core of Data, Local Education Agency (School District) Universe Survey: School Year 2023-2024; U.S. Department of Education, National Center for Education Statistics, Common Core of Data, School District Finance Survey (F-33): School Year 2021–22

Best High Schools

According to *U.S. News*, San Antonio is home to four of the top 500 high schools in the U.S.: **BASIS San Antonio- Shavano Campus** (#64); **Young Women's Leadership Academy** (#109); **IDEA Carver College Preparatory** (#131); **Health Careers High School** (#136). Nearly 25,000 public, magnet and charter schools were ranked based on their performance on state assessments and how well they prepare students for college. *U.S. News & World Report, "Best High Schools 2024"*

Highest Level of Education

Area	Less than H.S.	H.S. Diploma	Some College, No Deg.	Associate Degree	Bachelor's Degree	Master's Degree	Prof. School Degree	Doctorate Degree
City	15.7	25.6	21.8	8.2	17.7	7.7	2.1	1.3
MSA[1]	12.7	25.0	21.8	8.6	20.0	8.7	1.9	1.3
U.S.	10.6	26.2	19.4	8.8	21.3	9.8	2.3	1.6

Note: Figures cover persons age 25 and over; (1) Figures cover the San Antonio-New Braunfels, TX Metropolitan Statistical Area
Source: U.S. Census Bureau, 2019-2023 American Community Survey 5-Year Estimates

Educational Attainment by Race

Area	High School Graduate or Higher (%)					Bachelor's Degree or Higher (%)				
	Total	White	Black	Asian	Hisp.[2]	Total	White	Black	Asian	Hisp.[2]
City	84.3	88.4	91.0	85.7	78.0	28.7	33.7	25.0	56.5	19.4
MSA[1]	87.3	91.2	92.4	88.2	79.8	31.9	36.6	30.1	53.8	21.2
U.S.	89.4	92.9	88.1	88.0	72.5	35.0	37.7	24.7	57.0	19.9

Note: Figures shown cover persons 25 years old and over; (1) Figures cover the San Antonio-New Braunfels, TX Metropolitan Statistical Area; (2) People of Hispanic origin can be of any race
Source: U.S. Census Bureau, 2019-2023 American Community Survey 5-Year Estimates

School Enrollment by Grade and Control

Area	Preschool (%)		Kindergarten (%)		Grades 1 - 4 (%)		Grades 5 - 8 (%)		Grades 9 - 12 (%)	
	Public	Private	Public	Private	Public	Private	Public	Private	Public	Private
City	73.0	27.0	89.7	10.3	90.7	9.3	92.1	7.9	91.8	8.2
MSA[1]	65.5	34.5	87.7	12.3	89.4	10.6	90.3	9.7	90.5	9.5
U.S.	58.7	41.3	85.2	14.8	87.2	12.8	87.9	12.1	89.0	11.0

Note: Figures shown cover persons 3 years old and over; (1) Figures cover the San Antonio-New Braunfels, TX Metropolitan Statistical Area
Source: U.S. Census Bureau, 2019-2023 American Community Survey 5-Year Estimates

Higher Education

Four-Year Colleges			Two-Year Colleges			Medical Schools[1]	Law Schools[2]	Voc/ Tech[3]
Public	Private Non-profit	Private For-profit	Public	Private Non-profit	Private For-profit			
4	9	2	4	0	8	2	1	19

Note: Figures cover institutions located within the San Antonio-New Braunfels, TX Metropolitan Statistical Area and include main campuses only; (1) includes schools accredited by the Liaison Committee on Medical Education and the American Osteopathic Association's Commission on Osteopathic College Accreditation; (2) includes ABA-accredited schools, schools with provisional ABA accreditation, and state accredited schools; (3) includes all schools with programs that are less than 2 years.
Source: National Center for Education Statistics, Integrated Postsecondary Education System (IPEDS), 2023-24; Wikipedia, List of Medical Schools in the United States, accessed May 2, 2025; Wikipedia, List of Law Schools in the United States, accessed May 2, 2025

According to *U.S. News & World Report*, the San Antonio-New Braunfels, TX metro area is home to one of the top 100 liberal arts colleges in the U.S.: **Trinity University** (#40 tie). The indicators used to capture academic quality fall into a number of categories: assessment by administrators at peer institutions; retention of students; faculty resources; student selectivity; financial resources; alumni giving; high school counselor ratings of colleges; and graduation rate. *U.S. News & World Report*, "America's Best Colleges 2025"

According to *U.S. News & World Report*, the San Antonio-New Braunfels, TX metro area is home to one of the top medical schools for research in the U.S.: **University of Texas Health Science Center—San Antonio** (Tier 2). *U.S. News* placed medical and osteopathic schools into tiers based on their research productivity, faculty and admissions data. Each school's tier was derived from its overall score, calculated by summing the weighted normalized values generated across several factors of academic quality, outlined below. There are four tiers, with tier 1 medical schools as the highest-performing and tier 4 as the lowest-performing. Only tier 1 and 2 schools are shown. Because of the tier presentation, *U.S. News* calculated overall scores based on their percentile performance among all rated schools instead of dividing against the rescaled score of the No. 1-performing schools. Tier 1 included schools with overall scores of 85 to 99. The cutoffs for tiers 2 through 4 were schools scoring 50 to 84, 15 to 49 and 1 to 14, respectively. The rankings are based on a weighted average of the following measures of quality: total research activity; average research activity per faculty member; total NIH research grants at the medical school and its affiliated hospitals; average NIH research grants per faculty; median MCAT total score; median undergraduate GPA; acceptance rate; and faculty resources. *U.S. News & World Report*, "America's Best Graduate Schools, Medical, 2025"

According to *U.S. News & World Report*, the San Antonio-New Braunfels, TX metro area is home to one of the top medical schools for primary care in the U.S.: **University of Texas Health Science Center—San Antonio** (Tier 2). *U.S. News* placed medical and osteopathic schools into tiers based on their research productivity, faculty and admissions data. Each school's tier was derived from its overall score, calculated by summing the weighted normalized values generated across several factors of academic quality, outlined below. There are four tiers, with tier 1 medical schools as the highest-performing and tier 4 as the lowest-performing. Only tier 1 and 2 schools are shown. Because of the tier presentation, *U.S. News* calculated overall scores based on their percentile performance among all rated schools instead of dividing against the rescaled score of the No. 1-performing schools. Tier 1 included schools with overall scores of 85 to 99. The cutoffs for tiers 2 through 4 were schools scoring 50 to 84, 15 to 49 and 1 to 14, respectively. The rankings are based on a weighted average of the following measures of quality: graduates practicing in primary care specialties; graduates entering primary care residencies; median MCAT total score; median undergraduate GPA; acceptance rate; and faculty resources. *U.S. News & World Report*, "America's Best Graduate Schools, Medical, 2025"

EMPLOYERS

Major Employers

Company Name	Industry
AT&T	Phone, wireless & internet services
Baptist Health System	Healthcare services
Bill Miller BBQ	Restaurant chain
Christus Santa Rosa Health Care	Healthcare services
City of San Antonio	Municipal government
Clear Channel Communications	TV & radio stations, outdoor ads
CPS Energy	Utilities
Fort Sam Houston-U.S. Army	U.S. military
H-E-B	Super market chain
JPMorgan Chase	Financial services
Lackland Air Force Base	U.S. military
Methodist Healthcare System	Healthcare services
North East ISD	School districts
Northside ISD	School districts
Rackspace	IT managed hosting solutions
Randolph Air Force Base	U.S. military
San Antonio ISD	School districts
Toyota Motor Manufacturing	Manufacturing
USAA	Financial services & insurance
Wells Fargo	Financial services

Note: Companies shown are located within the San Antonio-New Braunfels, TX Metropolitan Statistical Area.
Source: Chambers of Commerce; State Departments of Labor; Wikipedia

Best Companies to Work For

NuStar Energy, headquartered in San Antonio, is among "Fortune's Best Workplaces for Parents." To pick the best companies, *Fortune* partnered with the Great Place to Work Institute. To be considered for the list, companies must be Great Place To Work-Certified and have at least 50 responses from parents in the US. The survey enables employees to share confidential quantitative and qualitative feedback about their organization's culture by responding to 60 statements on a 5-point scale and answering two open-ended questions. Collectively, these statements describe a great employee experience, defined by high levels of trust, respect, credibility, fairness, pride, and camaraderie. In addition, companies provide organizational data like size, location, industry, demographics, roles, and levels; and provide information about parental leave, adoption, flexible schedule, childcare and dependent health care benefits. *Fortune, "Best Workplaces for Parents," 2024*

USAA, headquartered in San Antonio, is among the "Best Places to Work in IT." To qualify, companies had to have a minimum of 100 total employees and five IT employees. The best places to work were selected based on DEI (diversity, equity, and inclusion) practices; IT turnover, promotions, and growth; IT retention and engagement programs; remote/hybrid working; benefits and perks (such as elder care and child care, flextime, and reimbursement for college tuition); and training and career development opportunities. *Computerworld, "Best Places to Work in IT," 2025*

PUBLIC SAFETY

Crime Rate

Area	Total Crime Rate	Violent Crime Rate				Property Crime Rate		
		Murder	Rape	Robbery	Aggrav. Assault	Burglary	Larceny-Theft	Motor Vehicle Theft
City	6,089.1	10.9	97.8	120.5	465.0	546.5	3,568.2	1,280.2
U.S.	2,290.9	5.7	38.0	66.5	264.1	250.7	1,347.2	318.7

Note: Figures are crimes per 100,000 population.
Source: FBI, Table 8, Offenses Known to Law Enforcement, by State by City, 2023

Hate Crimes

Area	Number of Quarters Reported	Number of Incidents per Bias Motivation					
		Race/Ethnicity/Ancestry	Religion	Sexual Orientation	Disability	Gender	Gender Identity
City[1]	4	27	6	10	1	0	2
U.S.	4	5,900	2,699	2,077	187	92	492

Note: (1) Figures include at least one incident reported with more than one bias motivation.
Source: Federal Bureau of Investigation, Hate Crime Statistics 2023

Identity Theft Consumer Reports

Area	Reports	Reports per 100,000 Population	Rank[2]
MSA[1]	7,889	302	65
U.S.	1,135,291	339	-

Note: (1) Figures cover the San Antonio-New Braunfels, TX Metropolitan Statistical Area; (2) Rank ranges from 1 to 401 where 1 indicates greatest number of identity theft reports per 100,000 population
Source: Federal Trade Commission, Consumer Sentinel Network Data Book 2024

Fraud and Other Consumer Reports

Area	Reports	Reports per 100,000 Population	Rank[2]
MSA[1]	36,765	1,407	74
U.S.	5,360,641	1,601	-

Note: (1) Figures cover the San Antonio-New Braunfels, TX Metropolitan Statistical Area; (2) Rank ranges from 1 to 401 where 1 indicates greatest number of fraud and other consumer reports per 100,000 population
Source: Federal Trade Commission, Consumer Sentinel Network Data Book 2024

POLITICS

2024 Presidential Election Results

Area	Trump (Rep.)	Harris (Dem.)	Stein (Green)	Kennedy (Ind.)	Oliver (Lib.)	Other
Bexar County	44.4	54.1	0.6	0.0	0.6	0.4
U.S.	49.7	48.2	0.6	0.5	0.4	0.6

Note: Results are percentages and may not add to 100% due to rounding
Source: Dave Leip's Atlas of U.S. Presidential Elections

SPORTS

Professional Sports Teams

Team Name	League	Year Established
San Antonio Spurs	National Basketball Association (NBA)	1973

Note: Includes teams located in the San Antonio-New Braunfels, TX Metropolitan Statistical Area.
Source: Wikipedia, Major Professional Sports Teams of the United States and Canada, May 1, 2025

CLIMATE

Average and Extreme Temperatures

Temperature	Jan	Feb	Mar	Apr	May	Jun	Jul	Aug	Sep	Oct	Nov	Dec	Yr.
Extreme High (°F)	89	97	100	100	103	105	106	108	103	98	94	90	108
Average High (°F)	62	66	74	80	86	92	95	95	90	82	71	64	80
Average Temp. (°F)	51	55	62	70	76	82	85	85	80	71	60	53	69
Average Low (°F)	39	43	50	58	66	72	74	74	69	59	49	41	58
Extreme Low (°F)	0	6	19	31	43	53	62	61	46	33	21	6	0

Note: Figures cover the years 1948-1990
Source: National Climatic Data Center, International Station Meteorological Climate Summary, 9/96

Average Precipitation/Snowfall/Humidity

Precip./Humidity	Jan	Feb	Mar	Apr	May	Jun	Jul	Aug	Sep	Oct	Nov	Dec	Yr.
Avg. Precip. (in.)	1.5	1.8	1.5	2.6	3.8	3.6	2.0	2.5	3.3	3.2	2.3	1.4	29.6
Avg. Snowfall (in.)	1	Tr	Tr	0	0	0	0	0	0	0	Tr	Tr	1
Avg. Rel. Hum. 6am (%)	79	80	79	82	87	87	87	86	85	83	81	79	83
Avg. Rel. Hum. 3pm (%)	51	48	45	48	51	48	43	42	47	46	48	49	47

Note: Figures cover the years 1948-1990; Tr = Trace amounts (<0.05 in. of rain; <0.5 in. of snow)
Source: National Climatic Data Center, International Station Meteorological Climate Summary, 9/96

Weather Conditions

Temperature			Daytime Sky			Precipitation		
32°F & below	45°F & below	90°F & above	Clear	Partly cloudy	Cloudy	0.01 inch or more precip.	0.1 inch or more snow/ice	Thunder-storms
23	91	112	97	153	115	81	1	36

Note: Figures are average number of days per year and cover the years 1948-1990
Source: National Climatic Data Center, International Station Meteorological Climate Summary, 9/96

HAZARDOUS WASTE

Superfund Sites

The San Antonio-New Braunfels, TX metro area is home to three sites on the EPA's Superfund National Priorities List (NPL) or Superfund Alternative Approach (SAA) list: **Bandera Road Ground Water Plume** (Final NPL); **Eldorado Chemical Co., Inc.** (Final NPL); **R & H Oil/Tropicana** (Proposed NPL). The Superfund alternative approach uses the same investigation and cleanup process and standards that are used for sites listed on the National Priorities List. The SAA is an alternative to listing a site on the NPL; it is not an alternative to Superfund or the Superfund process. There are a total

AIR QUALITY

Air Quality Trends: Ozone

	1990	1995	2000	2005	2010	2015	2020	2021	2022	2023
MSA[1]	0.090	0.095	0.078	0.084	0.072	0.079	0.069	0.070	0.076	0.074
U.S.	0.087	0.089	0.081	0.080	0.072	0.068	0.066	0.067	0.067	0.070

Note: (1) Data covers the San Antonio-New Braunfels, TX Metropolitan Statistical Area. The values shown are the composite ozone concentration averages among trend sites based on the highest fourth daily maximum 8-hour concentration in parts per million. These trends are based on sites having an adequate record of monitoring data during the trend period. Data from exceptional events are included.
Source: U.S. Environmental Protection Agency, Air Quality Monitoring Information, "Air Quality Trends by City, 1990-2023"

Air Quality Index

Area	Percent of Days when Air Quality was...[2]					AQI Statistics[2]	
	Good	Moderate	Unhealthy for Sensitive Groups	Unhealthy	Very Unhealthy	Maximum	Median
MSA[1]	41.6	55.1	2.7	0.3	0.0	309	53

Note: (1) Data covers the San Antonio-New Braunfels, TX Metropolitan Statistical Area; (2) Based on 365 days with AQI data in 2023. Air Quality Index (AQI) is an index for reporting daily air quality. EPA calculates the AQI for five major air pollutants regulated by the Clean Air Act: ground-level ozone, particle pollution (aka particulate matter), carbon monoxide, sulfur dioxide, and nitrogen dioxide. The AQI runs from 0 to 500. The higher the AQI value, the greater the level of air pollution and the greater the health concern. There are six AQI categories: "Good" AQI is between 0 and 50. Air quality is considered satisfactory; "Moderate" AQI is between 51 and 100. Air quality is acceptable; "Unhealthy for Sensitive Groups" When AQI values are between 101 and 150, members of sensitive groups may experience health effects; "Unhealthy" When AQI values are between 151 and 200 everyone may begin to experience health effects; "Very Unhealthy" AQI values between 201 and 300 trigger a health alert; "Hazardous" AQI values over 300 trigger warnings of emergency conditions (not shown).
Source: U.S. Environmental Protection Agency, Air Quality Index Report, 2023

Air Quality Index Pollutants

Area	Percent of Days when AQI Pollutant was...[2]					
	Carbon Monoxide	Nitrogen Dioxide	Ozone	Sulfur Dioxide	Particulate Matter 2.5	Particulate Matter 10
MSA[1]	0.0	0.3	37.5	(3)	62.2	0.0

Note: (1) Data covers the San Antonio-New Braunfels, TX Metropolitan Statistical Area; (2) Based on 365 days with AQI data in 2023. The Air Quality Index (AQI) is an index for reporting daily air quality. EPA calculates the AQI for five major air pollutants regulated by the Clean Air Act: ground-level ozone, particle pollution (also known as particulate matter), carbon monoxide, sulfur dioxide, and nitrogen dioxide. The AQI runs from 0 to 500. The higher the AQI value, the greater the level of air pollution and the greater the health concern; (3) Sulfur dioxide is no longer included in this table because SO_2 concentrations tend to be very localized and not necessarily representative of broad geographical areas like counties and CBSAs.
Source: U.S. Environmental Protection Agency, Air Quality Index Report, 2023

Maximum Air Pollutant Concentrations: Particulate Matter, Ozone, CO and Lead

	Particulate Matter 10 (ug/m³)	Particulate Matter 2.5 Wtd AM (ug/m³)	Particulate Matter 2.5 24-Hr (ug/m³)	Ozone (ppm)	Carbon Monoxide (ppm)	Lead (ug/m³)
MSA[1] Level	50	9	26	0.076	1	n/a
NAAQS[2]	150	15	35	0.075	9	0.15
Met NAAQS[2]	Yes	Yes	Yes	No	Yes	n/a

Note: (1) Data covers the San Antonio-New Braunfels, TX Metropolitan Statistical Area; Data from exceptional events are included; (2) National Ambient Air Quality Standards; ppm = parts per million; ug/m³ = micrograms per cubic meter; n/a not available.
Concentrations: Particulate Matter 10 (coarse particulate)—highest second maximum 24-hour concentration; Particulate Matter 2.5 Wtd AM (fine particulate)—highest weighted annual mean concentration; Particulate Matter 2.5 24-Hour (fine particulate)—highest 98th percentile 24-hour concentration; Ozone—highest fourth daily maximum 8-hour concentration; Carbon Monoxide—highest second maximum non-overlapping 8-hour concentration; Lead—maximum running 3-month average
Source: U.S. Environmental Protection Agency, Air Quality Monitoring Information, "Air Quality Statistics by City, 2023"

Maximum Air Pollutant Concentrations: Nitrogen Dioxide and Sulfur Dioxide

	Nitrogen Dioxide AM (ppb)	Nitrogen Dioxide 1-Hr (ppb)	Sulfur Dioxide AM (ppb)	Sulfur Dioxide 1-Hr (ppb)	Sulfur Dioxide 24-Hr (ppb)
MSA[1] Level	8	37	n/a	2	n/a
NAAQS[2]	53	100	30	75	140
Met NAAQS[2]	Yes	Yes	n/a	Yes	n/a

Note: (1) Data covers the San Antonio-New Braunfels, TX Metropolitan Statistical Area; Data from exceptional events are included; (2) National Ambient Air Quality Standards; ppm = parts per million; ug/m³ = micrograms per cubic meter; n/a not available.
Concentrations: Nitrogen Dioxide AM—highest arithmetic mean concentration; Nitrogen Dioxide 1-Hr—highest 98th percentile 1-hour daily maximum concentration; Sulfur Dioxide AM—highest annual mean concentration; Sulfur Dioxide 1-Hr—highest 99th percentile 1-hour daily maximum concentration; Sulfur Dioxide 24-Hr—highest second maximum 24-hour concentration
Source: U.S. Environmental Protection Agency, Air Quality Monitoring Information, "Air Quality Statistics by City, 2023"

Savannah, Georgia

Background

Savannah sits at the mouth of the Savannah River on the border between Georgia and South Carolina. It was established in 1733 when General James Oglethorpe landed with a group of settlers in the sailing vessel *Anne*, after a voyage of more than three months. City Hall now stands at the spot where Oglethorpe and his followers first camped on a small bluff overlooking the river.

Savannah was extensively planned while Oglethorpe was still in England, making it a unique American city. Each new settler was given a package of property, including a town lot, a garden space, and an outlying farm area. The town was sectioned in quadrants, the north and south for residences, and the east and west for public buildings.

The quadrant design was inspired in part by considerations of public defense, given the unsettled character of relations with Native Americans. In fact, an early treaty between the settlers and the Creek Native American Chief Tomochichi allowed Savannah to develop quite peacefully, with little of the hostility between Europeans and Native Americans that marred much of the development elsewhere in the colonies.

Savannah was taken by the British during the American Revolution and in the patriotic siege that followed many lives were lost. Savannah was eventually retaken in 1782 by the American Generals Nathaniel Greene and Anthony Wayne. In the post-Revolutionary period, Savannah grew dramatically, its economic strength being driven in large part by Eli Whitney's cotton gin. As the world's leader in the cotton trade, Savannah also hosted a great development in export activity, and the first American steamboat built in the United States to cross the Atlantic was launched in its busy port.

Savannah's physical structure had been saved from the worst ravages of war, but the destruction of the area's infrastructure slowed its further development for an extended period. In the long period of slow recovery that followed, the Girl Scouts was established in the city in 1912 by Juliette Gordon Low—a true Savannah success story.

In 1954, an extensive fire destroyed a large portion of the historic City Market, and the area was bulldozed to make room for a parking garage. The Historic Savannah Foundation has worked continuously since to maintain and improve Savannah's considerable architectural charms. As a result, Savannah's Historic District was designated a Registered National Historic Landmark, and the city has been a favored site for movie makers for decades. More than forty major movies have been filmed in Savannah including *Roots* (1976), *East of Eden* (1980), *Forrest Gump* (1994), *Midnight in the Garden of Good and Evil* (1997), *The Legend of Bagger Vance* (2000) *The Menu* (2022), and *Devotion* (2022).

The Port of Savannah, manufacturing, the military, and tourism are the city's major economic drivers in the twenty-first century. Its port facilities, operated by the Georgia Ports Authority, have seen notable growth in container tonnage in recent years. Garden City Terminal is the fourth largest container port in the United States, and the largest single-terminal operation in North America. In 2019, a second passenger airport, Paine Field, opened for business. Military installations in the area include Hunter Army Airfield and Fort Stewart military bases, employing nearly 50,000.

Museums include Juliette Gordon Low Museum, Flannery O'Connor Childhood Home/Museum, Telfair Museum of Art, and the Mighty 8th Air Force Museum. The Savannah Book Festival is a popular annual fair held on President's Day weekend. Football's XFL league resumed play in the city in 2022.

The city's beauty draws not just tourists, but conventioneers. The Savannah International Trade & Convention Center is a state-of-the-art facility with more than 100,000 square feet of exhibition space, accommodating nearly 10,000 people.

Colleges and universities in the city include the Savannah College of Art and Design, Savannah State University, and South University.

Savannah's climate is classified as humid subtropical. In the Deep South, this is characterized by long and almost tropical summers and short, mild winters. Savannah records few days of freezing temperatures each year and snowfall is rare. Due to its proximity to the Atlantic coast, Savannah rarely experiences temperatures as extreme as those in Georgia's interior. Seasonally, Savannah tends to have hot and humid summers with frequent, brief thunderstorms and sunny days are frequent. Winters are mild and sunny with November and December the driest months.

Savannah is at risk for hurricanes, particularly of the Cape Verde type of storms that take place during the peak of the season. Because of its location in the Georgia Bight (the arc of the Atlantic coastline in Georgia and northern Florida) as well as the tendency for hurricanes to re-curve up the coast, Savannah has a lower risk of hurricanes than some other coastal cities such as Charleston, South Carolina.

Rankings

General Rankings

- Savannah appeared on *Travel + Leisure's* list of "The 15 Best Cities in the United States." The city was ranked #3. Criteria: walkability; sights/landmarks; culture; food; friendliness; shopping; and overall value. *Travel + Leisure, "The World's Best Awards 2024" July 9, 2024*

- For its 37th annual "Readers' Choice Awards" survey, *Condé Nast Traveler* ranked its readers' favorite cities in the U.S. Whether it be a longed-for visit or the next big new thing, these are the places travelers loved best. The list was broken into large cities and cities under 250,000. Savannah ranked #6 in the small city category. *Condé Nast Traveler, Readers' Choice Awards 2024, "Best Small Cities in the U.S." October 1, 2024*

Business/Finance Rankings

- Savannah was cited as one of America's top metros for total major capital investment facility projects in 2024. The area ranked #3 in the Tier 2 (mid-sized) metro area category (population 200,000 to 1 million). *Site Selection, "Top Metros of 2024," March 2025*

- The Savannah metro area appeared on the Milken Institute "2025 Best Performing Cities" list. Rank: #42 out of 200 large metro areas (based on performance category). Criteria: job growth; wage growth; high-tech growth and impact; community resilience; housing affordability; household broadband access. *Milken Institute, "Best-Performing Cities 2025," January 14, 2025*

Culture/Performing Arts Rankings

- Savannah was selected as one of the ten best small North American cities and towns for moviemakers. Of cities with smaller populations, the area ranked #5. As with the 2025 list for bigger cities, film community and culture were highly factored in. Other criteria: access to equipment and facilities; affordability; tax incentives; and quality of life. *MovieMaker Magazine, "Best Places to Live and Work as a Moviemaker, 2025," January 29, 2025*

Education Rankings

- Personal finance website *WalletHub* analyzed the 150 largest U.S. metropolitan statistical areas to determine where the most educated Americans are putting their degrees to work. Criteria: education levels; percentage of workers with degrees; education quality and attainment gap; public school quality rankings; quality and enrollment of each metro area's universities. Savannah was ranked #88 (#1 = most educated city). *WalletHub.com, "Most & Least Educated Cities in America, 2025" July 2, 2024*

Seniors/Retirement Rankings

- Savannah made *Southern Living's* list of southern places—by the beach, in the mountains, or scenic city—to retire. From the incredible views and close knit communities, to the opportunities to put down new roots, and great places to eat and hike, these superb places are perfect for settling down. *Southern Living, "The Best Places to Retire in the South," March 9, 2024*

- Savannah made the 2024 *Forbes* list of "25 Best Places to Retire." Criteria, focused on overall affordability as well as quality of life indicators, include: housing/living costs compared to the national average and taxes; air quality; crime rates; median home prices; risk associated with climate-change/natural hazards; availability of medical care; bikeability; walkability; healthy living. *Forbes.com, "The Best Places to Retire in 2024: Las Cruces and Other Unexpected Hot Spots," May 10, 2024*

Miscellaneous Rankings

- In its roundup of St. Patrick's Day parades, *Gayot* listed the best festivals and parades of all things Irish. The festivities in Savannah as among the best in North America. *Gayot.com, "Best St. Patrick's Day Parades," March 2025*

- In *Condé Nast Traveler* magazine's 2024 Readers' Choice Survey, Savannah made the top ten list of friendliest American cities. Savannah ranked #6. *Condé Nast Traveler, "The Friendliest Cities in the U.S., According to Our Readers" October 28, 2024*

Business Environment

DEMOGRAPHICS

Population Growth

Area	1990 Census	2000 Census	2010 Census	2020 Census	2023 Estimate[2]	Population Growth 1990-2023 (%)
City	138,038	131,510	136,286	147,780	147,546	6.9
MSA[1]	258,060	293,000	347,611	404,798	412,089	59.7
U.S.	248,709,873	281,421,906	308,745,538	331,449,281	332,387,540	33.6

Note: (1) Figures cover the Savannah, GA Metropolitan Statistical Area; (2) 2019-2023 5-year ACS population estimate
Source: U.S. Census Bureau, 1990 Census, 2000 Census, 2010 Census, 2020 Census, 2019-2023 American Community Survey 5-Year Estimates

Race

Area	White Alone[2] (%)	Black Alone[2] (%)	Asian Alone[2] (%)	AIAN[3] Alone[2] (%)	NHOPI[4] Alone[2] (%)	Other Race Alone[2] (%)	Two or More Races (%)
City	37.2	52.2	2.9	0.2	0.2	2.0	5.4
MSA[1]	55.2	32.4	2.5	0.2	0.1	3.1	6.5
U.S.	63.4	12.4	5.8	0.9	0.2	6.6	10.7

Note: (1) Figures cover the Savannah, GA Metropolitan Statistical Area; (2) Alone is defined as not being in combination with one or more other races; (3) American Indian and Alaska Native; (4) Native Hawaiian and Other Pacific Islander
Source: U.S. Census Bureau, 2019-2023 American Community Survey 5-Year Estimates

Hispanic or Latino Origin

Area	Total (%)	Mexican (%)	Puerto Rican (%)	Cuban (%)	Other (%)
City	7.1	2.2	2.0	0.5	2.4
MSA[1]	7.7	2.9	1.9	0.5	2.4
U.S.	19.0	11.3	1.8	0.7	5.2

Note: Persons of Hispanic or Latino origin can be of any race; (1) Figures cover the Savannah, GA Metropolitan Statistical Area
Source: U.S. Census Bureau, 2019-2023 American Community Survey 5-Year Estimates

Age

Area	Under Age 5	Age 5–19	Age 20–34	Age 35–44	Age 45–54	Age 55–64	Age 65–74	Age 75–84	Age 85+	Median Age
City	6.1	18.1	28.1	11.9	10.3	11.4	8.1	4.5	1.4	33.7
MSA[1]	6.1	19.5	22.0	13.8	11.7	11.8	9.2	4.4	1.5	36.7
U.S.	5.7	19.1	20.2	13.1	12.3	12.8	10.0	4.9	1.9	38.7

Note: (1) Figures cover the Savannah, GA Metropolitan Statistical Area
Source: U.S. Census Bureau, 2019-2023 American Community Survey 5-Year Estimates

Disability by Age

Area	All Ages	Under 18 Years Old	18 to 64 Years Old	65 Years and Over
City	15.9	7.0	13.5	40.7
MSA[1]	14.5	5.3	12.8	35.7
U.S.	13.0	4.7	10.7	32.9

Note: Figures show percent of the civilian noninstitutionalized population that reported having a disability. Disability status is determined from six types of difficulty: vision, hearing, cognitive, ambulatory, self-care, and independent living. For children under 5 years old, hearing and vision difficulty are used to determine disability status. For children between the ages of 5 and 14, disability status is determined from hearing, vision, cognitive, ambulatory, and self-care difficulties. For people aged 15 years and older, they are considered to have a disability if they have difficulty with any one of the six difficulty types; Note: (1) Figures cover the Savannah, GA Metropolitan Statistical Area
Source: U.S. Census Bureau, 2019-2023 American Community Survey 5-Year Estimates

Ancestry

Area	German	Irish	English	American	Italian	Polish	French[2]	European	Scottish
City	6.6	7.3	6.3	3.8	3.2	1.1	1.3	0.8	1.4
MSA[1]	9.4	9.4	10.2	6.8	3.7	1.2	1.5	1.2	1.8
U.S.	12.6	9.4	9.1	5.5	4.9	2.6	2.0	1.6	1.6

Note: Figures are the percentage of the total population reporting a particular ancestry. The nine most commonly reported ancestries in the U.S. are shown. Figures include multiple ancestries (e.g. if a person reported being Irish and Italian, they were included in both columns); (1) Figures cover the Savannah, GA Metropolitan Statistical Area; (2) Excludes Basque
Source: U.S. Census Bureau, 2019-2023 American Community Survey 5-Year Estimates

Foreign-born Population

Area	Percent of Population Born in								
	Any Foreign Country	Asia	Mexico	Europe	Caribbean	Central America[2]	South America	Africa	Canada
City	6.7	2.6	0.8	0.8	0.9	0.7	0.5	0.4	0.2
MSA[1]	6.9	2.1	1.1	0.9	0.8	0.6	0.7	0.5	0.2
U.S.	13.9	4.3	3.3	1.4	1.4	1.2	1.2	0.8	0.2

Note: (1) Figures cover the Savannah, GA Metropolitan Statistical Area; (2) Excludes Mexico.
Source: U.S. Census Bureau, 2019-2023 American Community Survey 5-Year Estimates

Household Size

Area	Persons in Household (%)							Average Household Size
	One	Two	Three	Four	Five	Six	Seven or More	
City	35.4	34.5	14.8	9.4	3.7	1.1	1.1	2.35
MSA[1]	28.1	36.4	15.7	12.1	5.2	1.5	1.1	2.52
U.S.	28.5	33.8	15.4	12.7	5.9	2.3	1.4	2.54

Note: (1) Figures cover the Savannah, GA Metropolitan Statistical Area
Source: U.S. Census Bureau, 2019-2023 American Community Survey 5-Year Estimates

Household Relationships

Area	Householder	Opposite-sex Spouse	Same-sex Spouse	Opposite-sex Unmarried Partner	Same-sex Unmarried Partner	Child[2]	Grandchild	Other Relatives	Non-relatives
City	39.9	11.2	0.3	2.7	0.3	24.9	3.2	4.4	5.0
MSA[1]	38.7	16.6	0.2	2.4	0.2	28.0	2.8	4.1	3.4
U.S.	38.3	17.5	0.2	2.5	0.2	28.3	2.4	4.8	3.4

Note: Figures are percent of the total population; (1) Figures cover the Savannah, GA Metropolitan Statistical Area; (2) Includes biological, adopted, and stepchildren of the householder
Source: U.S. Census Bureau, 2020 Census

Gender

Area	Males	Females	Males per 100 Females
City	69,345	78,201	88.7
MSA[1]	200,060	212,029	94.4
U.S.	164,545,087	167,842,453	98.0

Note: (1) Figures cover the Savannah, GA Metropolitan Statistical Area
Source: U.S. Census Bureau, 2019-2023 American Community Survey 5-Year Estimates

Marital Status

Area	Never Married	Now Married[2]	Separated	Widowed	Divorced
City	48.6	31.4	2.6	5.4	12.0
MSA[1]	35.8	45.9	2.1	5.1	11.2
U.S.	34.1	47.9	1.7	5.6	10.7

Note: Figures are percentages and cover the population 15 years of age and older; (1) Figures cover the Savannah, GA Metropolitan Statistical Area; (2) Excludes separated
Source: U.S. Census Bureau, 2019-2023 American Community Survey 5-Year Estimates

Religious Groups by Family

Area	Catholic	Baptist	Methodist	LDS[2]	Pentecostal	Lutheran	Islam	Adventist	Other
MSA[1]	5.5	11.9	4.8	0.8	1.5	1.1	0.2	1.4	12.3
U.S.	18.7	7.3	3.0	2.0	1.8	1.7	1.3	1.3	11.6

Note: Figures are the number of adherents as a percentage of the total population and cover the eight largest religious groups in the U.S; (1) Figures cover the Savannah, GA Metropolitan Statistical Area; (2) Church of Jesus Christ of Latter-day Saints
Sources: 2020 U.S. Religion Census, Association of Statisticians of American Religious Bodies; The Association of Religion Data Archives (ARDA)

Religious Groups by Tradition

Area	Catholic	Evangelical Protestant	Mainline Protestant	Black Protestant	Islam	Judaism	Hinduism	Orthodox	Buddhism
MSA[1]	5.5	19.0	5.7	5.9	0.2	0.7	0.5	0.1	n/a
U.S.	18.7	16.5	5.2	2.3	1.3	0.6	0.4	0.4	0.3

Note: Figures are the number of adherents as a percentage of the total population; (1) Figures cover the Savannah, GA Metropolitan Statistical Area
Sources: 2020 U.S. Religion Census, Association of Statisticians of American Religious Bodies; The Association of Religion Data Archives (ARDA)

ECONOMY

Real Gross Domestic Product (GDP)

Area	2017	2018	2019	2020	2021	2022	2023	Rank[3]
MSA[1]	21.2	21.5	22.3	22.2	23.9	24.5	25.7	118
U.S.[2]	17,619.1	18,160.7	18,642.5	18,238.9	19,387.6	19,896.6	20,436.3	—

Note: Figures are in billions of chained 2017 dollars; (1) Figures cover the Savannah, GA Metropolitan Statistical Area; (2) Figures cover real GDP within metropolitan areas; (3) Rank is based on 2023 data and ranges from 1 to 384
Source: U.S. Bureau of Economic Analysis

Economic Growth

Area	2014	2015	2016	2017	2018	2019	2020	2021	2022	2023
MSA[1]	4.3	3.0	3.9	2.5	1.4	4.0	-0.5	7.7	2.6	4.9
U.S.[2]	2.6	3.2	2.0	2.7	3.1	2.7	-2.2	6.3	2.6	2.7

Note: Figures are real gross domestic product growth rates and represent percent change from preceding period; (1) Figures cover the Savannah, GA Metropolitan Statistical Area; (2) Figures are the average growth rates within metropolitan areas
Source: U.S. Bureau of Economic Analysis

Metropolitan Area Exports

Area	2018	2019	2020	2021	2022	2023	Rank[2]
MSA[1]	5,407.8	4,925.5	4,557.0	5,520.5	6,171.2	6,206.1	56
U.S.	1,664,056.1	1,645,173.7	1,431,406.6	1,753,941.4	2,062,937.4	2,019,160.5	—

Note: Figures are in millions of dollars; (1) Figures cover the Savannah, GA Metropolitan Statistical Area; (2) Rank is based on 2023 data and ranges from 1 to 386
Source: U.S. Department of Commerce, International Trade Administration, Office of Trade and Economic Analysis, Industry and Analysis, Exports by Metropolitan Area, data extracted April 2, 2025

Building Permits

Area	Single-Family			Multi-Family			Total		
	2023	2024	Pct. Chg.	2023	2024	Pct. Chg.	2023	2024	Pct. Chg.
City	589	565	-4.1	12	14	16.7	601	579	-3.7
MSA[1]	2,620	2,936	12.1	768	1,101	43.4	3,388	4,037	19.2
U.S.	920,000	981,900	6.7	591,100	496,100	-16.1	1,511,100	1,478,000	-2.2

Note: (1) Figures cover the Savannah, GA Metropolitan Statistical Area; Figures represent new, privately-owned housing units authorized (unadjusted data)
Source: U.S. Census Bureau, Building Permits Survey (BPS), 2023, 2024

Bankruptcy Filings

Area	Business Filings			Nonbusiness Filings		
	2023	2024	% Chg.	2023	2024	% Chg.
Chatham County	8	3	-62.5	732	695	-5.1
U.S.	18,926	23,107	22.1	434,064	494,201	13.9

Note: Business filings include Chapter 7, Chapter 9, Chapter 11, Chapter 12, Chapter 13, Chapter 15, and Section 304; Nonbusiness filings include Chapter 7, Chapter 11, and Chapter 13
Source: Administrative Office of the U.S. Courts, Business and Nonbusiness Bankruptcy, County Cases Commenced by Chapter of the Bankruptcy Code, During the 12-Month Period Ending December 31, 2023 and Business and Nonbusiness Bankruptcy, County Cases Commenced by Chapter of the Bankruptcy Code, During the 12-Month Period Ending December 31, 2024

Housing Vacancy Rates

Area	Gross Vacancy Rate[3] (%)			Year-Round Vacancy Rate[4] (%)			Rental Vacancy Rate[5] (%)			Homeowner Vacancy Rate[6] (%)		
	2022	2023	2024	2022	2023	2024	2022	2023	2024	2022	2023	2024
MSA[1]	n/a	n/a	n/a	n/a	n/a	n/a	n/a	n/a	n/a	n/a	n/a	n/a
U.S.[2]	9.1	9.0	9.1	7.5	7.5	7.6	5.7	6.5	6.8	0.8	0.8	1.0

Note: (1) Figures cover the Savannah, GA Metropolitan Statistical Area; (2) Figures cover the 75 largest Metropolitan Statistical Areas; (3) The percentage of the total housing inventory that is vacant; (4) The percentage of the housing inventory (excluding seasonal units) that is year-round vacant; (5) The percentage of rental inventory that is vacant for rent; (6) The percentage of homeowner inventory that is vacant for sale; n/a not available
Source: U.S. Census Bureau, Housing Vacancies and Homeownership Annual Statistics: 2022, 2023, 2024

INCOME

Income

Area	Per Capita ($)	Median Household ($)	Average Household ($)
City	32,004	56,782	77,786
MSA[1]	39,158	74,632	99,643
U.S.	43,289	78,538	110,491

Note: (1) Figures cover the Savannah, GA Metropolitan Statistical Area
Source: U.S. Census Bureau, 2019-2023 American Community Survey 5-Year Estimates

Household Income Distribution

Area	Percent of Households Earning							
	Under $15,000	$15,000 -$24,999	$25,000 -$34,999	$35,000 -$49,999	$50,000 -$74,999	$75,000 -$99,999	$100,000 -$149,999	$150,000 and up
City	13.4	8.3	9.8	13.0	18.8	11.7	13.9	11.2
MSA[1]	8.5	6.0	7.5	11.0	17.3	13.8	18.5	17.4
U.S.	8.5	6.6	6.8	10.4	15.7	12.7	17.4	21.9

Note: (1) Figures cover the Savannah, GA Metropolitan Statistical Area
Source: U.S. Census Bureau, 2019-2023 American Community Survey 5-Year Estimates

Poverty Rate

Area	All Ages	Under 18 Years Old	18 to 64 Years Old	65 Years and Over
City	19.5	28.9	17.6	14.0
MSA[1]	12.4	16.6	11.4	9.9
U.S.	12.4	16.3	11.6	10.4

Note: Figures are percentage of people whose income during the past 12 months was below the poverty level; (1) Figures cover the Savannah, GA Metropolitan Statistical Area
Source: U.S. Census Bureau, 2019-2023 American Community Survey 5-Year Estimates

EMPLOYMENT

Labor Force and Employment

Area	Civilian Labor Force			Workers Employed		
	Dec. 2023	Dec. 2024	% Chg.	Dec. 2023	Dec. 2024	% Chg.
City	69,925	69,887	-0.1	67,803	67,610	-0.3
MSA[1]	202,550	202,333	-0.1	197,273	196,748	-0.3
U.S.	166,661,000	167,746,000	0.7	160,754,000	161,294,000	0.3

Note: Data is not seasonally adjusted and covers workers 16 years of age and older; (1) Figures cover the Savannah, GA Metropolitan Statistical Area
Source: Bureau of Labor Statistics, Local Area Unemployment Statistics

Unemployment Rate

Area	2024											
	Jan.	Feb.	Mar.	Apr.	May	Jun.	Jul.	Aug.	Sep.	Oct.	Nov.	Dec.
City	3.5	3.5	3.5	3.0	3.6	4.1	4.0	4.2	3.5	3.6	3.4	3.3
MSA[1]	2.9	3.0	3.0	2.5	3.1	3.5	3.4	3.7	2.9	3.0	2.9	2.8
U.S.	4.1	4.2	3.9	3.5	3.7	4.3	4.5	4.4	3.9	3.9	4.0	3.8

Note: Data is not seasonally adjusted and covers workers 16 years of age and older; (1) Figures cover the Savannah, GA Metropolitan Statistical Area
Source: Bureau of Labor Statistics, Local Area Unemployment Statistics

Average Wages

Occupation	$/Hr.	Occupation	$/Hr.
Accountants and Auditors	40.41	Maintenance and Repair Workers	23.15
Automotive Mechanics	27.16	Marketing Managers	75.38
Bookkeepers	23.06	Network and Computer Systems Admin.	45.56
Carpenters	24.58	Nurses, Licensed Practical	27.56
Cashiers	13.64	Nurses, Registered	41.90
Computer Programmers	46.30	Nursing Assistants	17.49
Computer Systems Analysts	52.25	Office Clerks, General	19.60
Computer User Support Specialists	31.48	Physical Therapists	47.93
Construction Laborers	19.01	Physicians	140.56
Cooks, Restaurant	16.30	Plumbers, Pipefitters and Steamfitters	29.86
Customer Service Representatives	18.64	Police and Sheriff's Patrol Officers	30.08
Dentists	98.92	Postal Service Mail Carriers	28.40
Electricians	28.43	Real Estate Sales Agents	31.87
Engineers, Electrical	57.20	Retail Salespersons	15.49
Fast Food and Counter Workers	13.18	Sales Representatives, Technical/Scientific	43.92
Financial Managers	76.60	Secretaries, Exc. Legal/Medical/Executive	19.62
First-Line Supervisors of Office Workers	32.20	Security Guards	17.54
General and Operations Managers	55.21	Surgeons	n/a
Hairdressers/Cosmetologists	19.33	Teacher Assistants, Exc. Postsecondary[1]	13.88
Home Health and Personal Care Aides	14.47	Teachers, Secondary School, Exc. Sp. Ed.[1]	32.08
Janitors and Cleaners	15.78	Telemarketers	13.85
Landscaping/Groundskeeping Workers	17.56	Truck Drivers, Heavy/Tractor-Trailer	27.26
Lawyers	67.70	Truck Drivers, Light/Delivery Services	24.37
Maids and Housekeeping Cleaners	13.59	Waiters and Waitresses	13.65

Note: Wage data covers the Savannah, GA Metropolitan Statistical Area; (1) Hourly wages were calculated from annual wage data based on a 40 hour work week
Source: Bureau of Labor Statistics, Metro Area Occupational Employment & Wage Estimates, May 2024

Employment by Industry

Sector	MSA[1] Number of Employees	MSA[1] Percent of Total	U.S. Percent of Total
Construction, Mining, and Logging	10,000	4.8	5.5
Financial Activities	7,700	3.7	5.8
Government	25,700	12.3	14.9
Information	1,500	0.7	1.9
Leisure and Hospitality	27,500	13.1	10.4
Manufacturing	23,000	11.0	8.0
Other Services	8,500	4.1	3.7
Private Education and Health Services	29,700	14.2	16.9
Professional and Business Services	23,400	11.2	14.2
Retail Trade	24,100	11.5	10.0
Transportation, Warehousing, and Utilities	20,600	9.8	4.8
Wholesale Trade	7,800	3.7	3.9

Note: Figures are non-farm employment as of December 2024. Figures are not seasonally adjusted and include workers 16 years of age and older; (1) Figures cover the Savannah, GA Metropolitan Statistical Area
Source: Bureau of Labor Statistics, Current Employment Statistics, Employment, Hours, and Earnings

Employment by Occupation

Occupation Classification	City (%)	MSA[1] (%)	U.S. (%)
Management, Business, Science, and Arts	34.6	38.1	42.0
Natural Resources, Construction, and Maintenance	5.5	7.8	8.6
Production, Transportation, and Material Moving	15.2	15.4	13.0
Sales and Office	21.3	20.8	19.9
Service	23.4	18.0	16.5

Note: Figures cover employed civilians 16 years of age and older; (1) Figures cover the Savannah, GA Metropolitan Statistical Area
Source: U.S. Census Bureau, 2019-2023 American Community Survey 5-Year Estimates

Occupations with Greatest Projected Employment Growth: 2022 – 2032

Occupation[1]	2022 Employment	2032 Projected Employment	Numeric Employment Change	Percent Employment Change
Fast Food and Counter Workers	116,400	132,810	16,410	14.1
Laborers and Freight, Stock, and Material Movers, Hand	122,550	138,390	15,840	12.9
Stockers and Order Fillers	87,050	101,950	14,900	17.1
Cooks, Restaurant	41,200	56,070	14,870	36.1
Software Developers	46,900	60,700	13,800	29.4
General and Operations Managers	101,650	115,240	13,590	13.4
Retail Salespersons	137,730	150,700	12,970	9.4
Registered Nurses	81,800	94,310	12,510	15.3
Heavy and Tractor-Trailer Truck Drivers	78,240	90,230	11,990	15.3
Home Health and Personal Care Aides	36,890	46,020	9,130	24.7

Note: Projections cover Georgia; (1) Sorted by numeric employment change
Source: www.projectionscentral.org, State Occupational Projections, 2022–2032 Long-Term Projections

Fastest-Growing Occupations: 2022 – 2032

Occupation[1]	2022 Employment	2032 Projected Employment	Numeric Employment Change	Percent Employment Change
Nurse Practitioners	7,900	12,500	4,600	58.2
Data Scientists	5,340	7,680	2,340	43.8
Statisticians	520	720	200	38.5
Cooks, Restaurant	41,200	56,070	14,870	36.1
Recreational Vehicle Service Technicians	310	420	110	35.5
Medical and Health Services Managers	8,760	11,860	3,100	35.4
Entertainment Attendants and Related Workers, All Other	600	810	210	35.0
Rail Yard Engineers, Dinkey Operators, and Hostlers	230	310	80	34.8
Information Security Analysts (SOC 2018)	4,990	6,710	1,720	34.5
Actuaries	350	470	120	34.3

Note: Projections cover Georgia; (1) Sorted by percent employment change and excludes occupations with numeric employment change less than 50
Source: www.projectionscentral.org, State Occupational Projections, 2022–2032 Long-Term Projections

CITY FINANCES

City Government Finances

Component	2022 ($000)	2022 ($ per capita)
Total Revenues	578,030	4,024
Total Expenditures	581,097	4,046
Debt Outstanding	277,286	1,931

Source: U.S. Census Bureau, State & Local Government Finances 2022

City Government Revenue by Source

Source	2022 ($000)	2022 ($ per capita)	2022 (%)
General Revenue			
From Federal Government	60,697	423	10.5
From State Government	7,571	53	1.3
From Local Governments	92,052	641	15.9
Taxes			
Property	86,555	603	15.0
Sales and Gross Receipts	59,091	411	10.2
Personal Income	0	0	0.0
Corporate Income	0	0	0.0
Motor Vehicle License	0	0	0.0
Other Taxes	13,895	97	2.4
Current Charges	157,479	1,096	27.2
Liquor Store	0	0	0.0
Utility	19,050	133	3.3

Source: U.S. Census Bureau, State & Local Government Finances 2022

City Government Expenditures by Function

Function	2022 ($000)	2022 ($ per capita)	2022 (%)
General Direct Expenditures			
Air Transportation	43,761	304	7.5
Corrections	0	0	0.0
Education	0	0	0.0
Employment Security Administration	0	0	0.0
Financial Administration	5,897	41	1.0
Fire Protection	34,378	239	5.9
General Public Buildings	127,040	884	21.9
Governmental Administration, Other	21,159	147	3.6
Health	0	0	0.0
Highways	88,664	617	15.3
Hospitals	0	0	0.0
Housing and Community Development	0	0	0.0
Interest on General Debt	14,167	98	2.4
Judicial and Legal	5,681	39	1.0
Libraries	0	0	0.0
Parking	7,645	53	1.3
Parks and Recreation	25,876	180	4.5
Police Protection	61,825	430	10.6
Public Welfare	11,580	80	2.0
Sewerage	42,551	296	7.3
Solid Waste Management	30,235	210	5.2
Veterans' Services	0	0	0.0
Liquor Store	0	0	0.0
Utility	28,648	199	4.9

Source: U.S. Census Bureau, State & Local Government Finances 2022

TAXES

State Corporate Income Tax Rates

State	Tax Rate (%)	Income Brackets ($)	Num. of Brackets	Financial Institution Tax Rate (%)[a]	Federal Income Tax Ded.
Georgia	5.75 - 6.0	Flat rate	1	5.75	No

Note: Tax rates for tax year 2024; (a) Rates listed are the corporate income tax rate applied to financial institutions or excise taxes based on income. Some states have other taxes based upon the value of deposits or shares.
Source: Federation of Tax Administrators, State Corporate Income Tax Rates, January 1, 2025

State Individual Income Tax Rates

State	Tax Rate (%)	Income Brackets ($)	Personal Exemptions ($) Single	Married	Depend.	Standard Ded. ($) Single	Married
Georgia	5.5	Flat rate	—	—	—	12,000	18,500 (i)

Note: Tax rates for tax year 2024; Local- and county-level taxes are not included; Federal income tax is not deductible on state income tax returns; (i) GA moves to a flat tax rate regime, eliminates the personal exemption and increases the standard deduction amounts for single, HOH and married jointly filers.
Source: Federation of Tax Administrators, State Individual Income Tax Rates, January 1, 2025

Various State Sales and Excise Tax Rates

State	State Sales Tax (%)	Gasoline[1] ($/gal.)	Cigarette[2] ($/pack)	Spirits[3] ($/gal.)	Wine[4] ($/gal.)	Beer[5] ($/gal.)	Recreational Marijuana (%)
Georgia	4	0.34	0.37	3.79	1.51	0.48	Not legal

Note: All tax rates as of January 1, 2025; (1) The American Petroleum Institute has developed a methodology for determining the average tax rate on a gallon of fuel. Rates may include any of the following: excise taxes, environmental fees, storage tank fees, other fees or taxes, general sales tax, and local taxes; (2) The federal excise tax of $1.0066 per pack and local taxes are not included; (3) Rates are those applicable to off-premise sales of 40% alcohol by volume (a.b.v.) distilled spirits in 750ml containers. Local excise taxes are excluded; (4) Rates are those applicable to off-premise sales of 11% a.b.v. non-carbonated wine in 750ml containers; (5) Rates are those applicable to off-premise sales of 4.7% a.b.v. beer in 12 ounce containers.
Source: Tax Foundation, 2025 Facts & Figures: How Does Your State Compare?

State Tax Competitiveness Index

State	Overall Rank	Corporate Tax Rank	Individual Income Tax Rank	Sales Tax Rank	Property Tax Rank	Unemployment Insurance Tax Rank
Georgia	26	12	31	23	34	24

Note: The Tax Foundation's State Tax Competitiveness Index enables policymakers, taxpayers, and business leaders to gauge how their states' tax systems compare. A rank of 1 is best, 50 is worst. Rankings do not average to the total. States without a tax rank equally as 1. DC's scores and rankings do not affect other states. The report shows tax systems as of July 1, 2024 (the beginning of Fiscal Year 2025).
Source: Tax Foundation, State Tax Competitiveness Index 2025

TRANSPORTATION

Means of Transportation to Work

Area	Car/Truck/Van Drove Alone	Car-pooled	Public Transportation Bus	Subway	Railroad	Bicycle	Walked	Other Means	Worked at Home
City	70.4	10.3	2.5	0.1	0.0	1.5	3.8	1.4	10.1
MSA[1]	76.6	9.4	1.0	0.0	0.0	0.7	1.7	1.5	9.0
U.S.	70.2	8.5	1.7	1.3	0.4	0.4	2.4	1.6	13.5

Note: Figures are percentages and cover workers 16 years of age and older; (1) Figures cover the Savannah, GA Metropolitan Statistical Area
Source: U.S. Census Bureau, 2019-2023 American Community Survey 5-Year Estimates

Travel Time to Work

Area	Less Than 10 Minutes	10 to 19 Minutes	20 to 29 Minutes	30 to 44 Minutes	45 to 59 Minutes	60 to 89 Minutes	90 Minutes or More
City	14.0	40.1	23.5	14.7	4.4	2.3	1.0
MSA[1]	10.5	29.3	23.7	22.8	8.5	3.7	1.5
U.S.	12.6	28.6	21.2	20.8	8.1	6.0	2.8

Note: Note: Figures are percentages and include workers 16 years old and over; (1) Figures cover the Savannah, GA Metropolitan Statistical Area
Source: U.S. Census Bureau, 2019-2023 American Community Survey 5-Year Estimates

Key Congestion Measures

Measure	2000	2010	2015	2020	2022
Annual Hours of Delay, Total (000)	n/a	n/a	9,791	4,060	9,522
Annual Hours of Delay, Per Auto Commuter	n/a	n/a	34	14	34
Annual Congestion Cost, Per Auto Commuter ($)	n/a	n/a	787	358	777

Note: n/a not available
Source: Texas A&M Transportation Institute, 2023 Urban Mobility Report

Freeway Travel Time Index

Measure	1985	1990	1995	2000	2005	2010	2015	2020	2022
Urban Area Index[1]	n/a	n/a	n/a	n/a	n/a	n/a	1.11	1.06	1.12
Urban Area Rank[1,2]	n/a	n/a	n/a	n/a	n/a	n/a	n/a	n/a	n/a

Note: Freeway Travel Time Index—the ratio of travel time in the peak period to the travel time at free-flow conditions. For example, a value of 1.30 indicates a 20-minute free-flow trip takes 26 minutes in the peak (20 minutes x 1.30 = 26 minutes); (1) Covers the Savannah GA urban area; (2) Rank is based on 101 larger urban areas (#1 = highest travel time index); n/a not available
Source: Texas A&M Transportation Institute, 2023 Urban Mobility Report

Public Transportation

Agency Name / Mode of Transportation	Vehicles Operated in Maximum Service[1]	Annual Unlinked Passenger Trips[2] (in thous.)	Annual Passenger Miles[3] (in thous.)
Chatham Area Transit Authority (CAT)			
Bus (directly operated)	32	1,614.7	4,387.8
Demand Response (directly operated)	20	68.2	575.1
Demand Response (purchased transportation)	2	1.2	13.1
Ferryboat (directly operated)	2	602.0	210.7

Note: (1) Number of revenue vehicles operated by the given mode and type of service to meet the annual maximum service requirement. This is the revenue vehicle count during the peak season of the year; on the week and day that maximum service is provided. Vehicles operated in maximum service (VOMS) exclude atypical days and one-time special events; (2) Number of passengers who boarded public transportation vehicles. Passengers are counted each time they board a vehicle no matter how many vehicles they use to travel from their origin to their destination. (3) Sum of the distances ridden by all passengers during the entire fiscal year.
Source: Federal Transit Administration, National Transit Database, 2023

Air Transportation

Airport Name and Code / Type of Service	Passenger Airlines[1]	Passenger Enplanements	Freight Carriers[2]	Freight (lbs)
Savannah International (SAV)				
Domestic service (U.S. carriers only)	26	2,020,183	8	10,230,316
International service (U.S. carriers only)	3	176	0	0

Note: (1) Includes all U.S.-based major, minor and commuter airlines that carried at least one passenger during the year; (2) Includes all U.S.-based airlines and freight carriers that transported at least one pound of freight during the year.
Source: Bureau of Transportation Statistics, The Intermodal Transportation Database, Air Carriers: T-100 Domestic Market (U.S. carriers only), 2024; Bureau of Transportation Statistics, The Intermodal Transportation Database, Air Carriers: T-100 International Market (U.S. carriers only), 2024

BUSINESSES

Major Business Headquarters

Company Name	Industry	Rankings Fortune[1]	Rankings Forbes[2]
Colonial Group	Oil & gas operations	-	129

Note: (1) Companies that produce a 10-K are ranked 1 to 500 based on 2023 revenue; (2) All private companies with at least $2 billion in annual revenue through the end of their most current fiscal year are ranked 1 to 275; companies listed are headquartered in the city; dashes indicate no ranking
Source: Fortune, "Fortune 500," 2024; Forbes, "America's Largest Private Companies," 2024

Living Environment

COST OF LIVING

Cost of Living Index

Composite Index	Groceries	Housing	Utilities	Transportation	Health Care	Misc. Goods/Services
93.8	102.5	78.1	99.5	102.7	113.7	96.4

Note: The Cost of Living Index measures regional differences in the cost of consumer goods and services, excluding taxes and non-consumer expenditures, for professional and managerial households in the top income quintile. It is based on more than 50,000 prices covering almost 60 different items for which prices are collected three times a year by chambers of commerce, economic development organizations or university applied economic centers in each participating urban area. The numbers shown should be read as a percentage above or below the national average of 100. For example, a value of 115.4 in the groceries column indicates that grocery prices are 15.4% higher than the national average. Small differences in the index numbers should not be interpreted as significant; Figures cover the Savannah GA urban area.
Source: The Council for Community and Economic Research, Cost of Living Index, 2024

Grocery Prices

Area[1]	T-Bone Steak ($/pound)	Frying Chicken ($/pound)	Whole Milk ($/half gal.)	Eggs ($/dozen)	Orange Juice ($/64 oz.)	Coffee ($/11.5 oz.)
City[2]	15.52	1.43	4.72	3.53	4.53	5.62
Avg.	15.42	1.55	4.69	3.25	4.41	5.46
Min.	14.50	1.16	4.43	2.75	4.00	4.85
Max.	17.56	2.89	5.49	4.78	5.54	7.89

Note: (1) Values for the local area are compared with the average, minimum and maximum values for all 276 areas in the Cost of Living Index; (2) Figures cover the Savannah GA urban area; **T-Bone Steak** (price per pound); **Frying Chicken** (price per pound, whole fryer); **Whole Milk** (half gallon carton); **Eggs** (price per dozen, Grade A, large); **Orange Juice** (64 oz. Tropicana or Florida Natural); **Coffee** (11.5 oz. can, vacuum-packed, Maxwell House, Hills Bros, or Folgers).
Source: The Council for Community and Economic Research, Cost of Living Index, 2024

Housing and Utility Costs

Area[1]	New Home Price ($)	Apartment Rent ($/month)	All Electric ($/month)	Part Electric ($/month)	Other Energy ($/month)	Telephone ($/month)
City[2]	379,397	1,313	206.53	-	-	191.37
Avg.	515,975	1,550	210.99	123.07	82.07	194.99
Min.	265,375	692	104.33	53.68	36.26	179.42
Max.	2,775,821	5,719	529.02	397.28	361.63	223.33

Note: (1) Values for the local area are compared with the average, minimum and maximum values for all 276 areas in the Cost of Living Index; (2) Figures cover the Savannah GA urban area; **New Home Price** (2,400 sf living area, 8,000 sf lot, in urban area with full utilities); **Apartment Rent** (950 sf 2 bedroom/1.5 or 2 bath, unfurnished, excluding all utilities except water); **All Electric** (average monthly cost for an all-electric home); **Part Electric** (average monthly cost for a part-electric home); **Other Energy** (average monthly cost for natural gas, fuel oil, coal, wood, and any other forms of energy except electricity); **Telephone** (price includes the base monthly rate plus taxes and fees for three lines of mobile phone service).
Source: The Council for Community and Economic Research, Cost of Living Index, 2024

Health Care, Transportation, and Other Costs

Area[1]	Doctor ($/visit)	Dentist ($/visit)	Optometrist ($/visit)	Gasoline ($/gallon)	Beauty Salon ($/visit)	Men's Shirt ($)
City[2]	150.00	152.87	91.31	3.29	39.61	38.61
Avg.	143.77	117.51	129.23	3.32	48.57	38.14
Min.	36.74	58.67	67.33	2.80	24.00	13.41
Max.	270.44	216.82	307.33	5.28	94.00	63.89

Note: (1) Values for the local area are compared with the average, minimum and maximum values for all 276 areas in the Cost of Living Index; (2) Figures cover the Savannah GA urban area; **Doctor** (general practitioners routine exam of an established patient); **Dentist** (adult teeth cleaning and periodic oral examination); **Optometrist** (full vision eye exam for established adult patient); **Gasoline** (one gallon regular unleaded, national brand, including all taxes, cash price at self-service pump if available); **Beauty Salon** (woman's shampoo, trim, and blow-dry); **Men's Shirt** (cotton/polyester dress shirt, pinpoint weave, long sleeves).
Source: The Council for Community and Economic Research, Cost of Living Index, 2024

HOUSING

Homeownership Rate

Area	2017 (%)	2018 (%)	2019 (%)	2020 (%)	2021 (%)	2022 (%)	2023 (%)	2024 (%)
MSA[1]	n/a	n/a	n/a	n/a	n/a	n/a	n/a	n/a
U.S.	63.9	64.4	64.6	66.6	65.5	65.8	65.9	65.6

Note: (1) Figures cover the Savannah, GA Metropolitan Statistical Area; n/a not available
Source: U.S. Census Bureau, Housing Vacancies and Homeownership Annual Statistics: 2017-2024

House Price Index (HPI)

Area	National Ranking[2]	Quarterly Change (%)	One-Year Change (%)	Five-Year Change (%)	Since 1991Q1 (%)
MSA[1]	225	-1.45	2.18	77.13	438.29
U.S.[3]	–	1.43	4.51	57.13	327.82

Note: The HPI is a weighted repeat sales index. It measures average price changes in repeat sales or refinancings on the same properties. This information is obtained by reviewing repeat mortgage transactions on single-family properties whose mortgages have been purchased or securitized by Fannie Mae or Freddie Mac since January 1975; (1) Figures cover the Savannah, GA Metropolitan Statistical Area; (2) Rankings are based on annual percentage change for all metro areas containing at least 15,000 transactions over the last 10 years and ranges from 1 to 241; (3) figures based on a weighted average of Census Division estimates using a seasonally adjusted, purchase-only index; all figures are for the period ending December 31, 2024
Source: Federal Housing Finance Agency, Change in FHFA Metropolitan Area House Price Indexes, All Transactions Index, 2024Q4

Home Value

Area	Under $100,000	$100,000 -$199,999	$200,000 -$299,999	$300,000 -$399,999	$400,000 -$499,999	$500,000 -$999,999	$1,000,000 or more	Median ($)
City	12.1	29.9	27.2	12.5	6.6	9.4	2.4	225,200
MSA[1]	9.6	21.3	26.2	16.7	9.8	13.3	3.2	271,100
U.S.	12.1	17.8	19.5	14.4	10.5	19.1	6.5	303,400

Note: Figures are percentages except for median and cover owner-occupied housing units; (1) Figures cover the Savannah, GA Metropolitan Statistical Area
Source: U.S. Census Bureau, 2019-2023 American Community Survey 5-Year Estimates

Year Housing Structure Built

Area	2020 or Later	2010 -2019	2000 -2009	1990 -1999	1980 -1989	1970 -1979	1960 -1969	1950 -1959	1940 -1949	Before 1940	Median Year
City	1.3	11.9	9.0	6.3	11.5	11.7	10.7	13.9	6.9	16.7	1971
MSA[1]	2.2	15.8	19.4	13.1	12.7	11.0	6.7	7.5	3.8	7.7	1990
U.S.	1.2	8.9	13.6	12.8	13.0	14.4	10.0	9.7	4.5	11.9	1980

Note: Figures are percentages except for Median Year; Note: (1) Figures cover the Savannah, GA Metropolitan Statistical Area
Source: U.S. Census Bureau, 2019-2023 American Community Survey 5-Year Estimates

Gross Monthly Rent

Area	Under $500	$500 -$999	$1,000 -$1,499	$1,500 -$1,999	$2,000 -$2,499	$2,500 -$2,999	$3,000 and up	Median ($)
City	6.6	17.0	41.8	23.1	7.7	1.9	2.0	1,302
MSA[1]	4.2	17.2	38.3	28.2	8.4	1.9	1.8	1,370
U.S.	6.5	22.3	29.5	20.2	10.8	4.8	5.9	1,348

Note: Figures are percentages except for median; Gross rent is the contract rent plus the estimated average monthly cost of utilities (electricity, gas, and water and sewer) and fuels (oil, coal, kerosene, wood, etc.) if these are paid by the renter (or paid for the renter by someone else); (1) Figures cover the Savannah, GA Metropolitan Statistical Area
Source: U.S. Census Bureau, 2019-2023 American Community Survey 5-Year Estimates

HEALTH

Health Risk Factors

Category	MSA[1] (%)	U.S. (%)
Adults aged 18–64 who have any kind of health care coverage	n/a	90.8
Adults who reported being in good or better health	n/a	81.8
Adults who have been told they have high blood cholesterol	n/a	36.9
Adults who have been told they have high blood pressure	n/a	34.0
Adults who are current smokers	n/a	12.1
Adults who currently use e-cigarettes	n/a	7.7
Adults who currently use chewing tobacco, snuff, or snus	n/a	3.2
Adults who are heavy drinkers[2]	n/a	6.1
Adults who are binge drinkers[3]	n/a	15.2
Adults who are overweight (BMI 25.0 - 29.9)	n/a	34.4
Adults who are obese (BMI 30.0 - 99.8)	n/a	34.3
Adults who participated in any physical activities in the past month	n/a	75.8

Note: All figures are crude prevalence; (1) Figures for the Savannah, GA Metropolitan Statistical Area were not available.
(2) Heavy drinkers are classified as adult men having more than 14 drinks per week and adult women having more than 7 drinks per week; (3) Binge drinkers are classified as males having five or more drinks on one occasion or females having four or more drinks on one occasion
Source: Centers for Disease Control and Prevention, Behavioral Risk Factor Surveillance System, SMART: Selected Metropolitan Area Risk Trends, 2023

Acute and Chronic Health Conditions

Category	MSA[1] (%)	U.S. (%)
Adults who have ever been told they had a heart attack	n/a	4.2
Adults who have ever been told they have angina or coronary heart disease	n/a	4.0
Adults who have ever been told they had a stroke	n/a	3.3
Adults who have ever been told they have asthma	n/a	15.7
Adults who have ever been told they have arthritis	n/a	26.3
Adults who have ever been told they have diabetes[2]	n/a	11.5
Adults who have ever been told they had skin cancer	n/a	5.6
Adults who have ever been told they had any other types of cancer	n/a	8.4
Adults who have ever been told they have COPD	n/a	6.4
Adults who have ever been told they have kidney disease	n/a	3.7
Adults who have ever been told they have a form of depression	n/a	22.0

Note: All figures are crude prevalence; (1) Figures for the Savannah, GA Metropolitan Statistical Area were not available.
(2) Figures do not include pregnancy-related, borderline, or pre-diabetes
Source: Centers for Disease Control and Prevention, Behavioral Risk Factor Surveillance System, SMART: Selected Metropolitan Area Risk Trends, 2023

Health Screening and Vaccination Rates

Category	MSA[1] (%)	U.S. (%)
Adults who have ever been tested for HIV	n/a	37.5
Adults who have had their blood cholesterol checked within the last five years	n/a	87.0
Adults aged 65+ who have had flu shot within the past year	n/a	63.4
Adults aged 65+ who have ever had a pneumonia vaccination	n/a	71.9

Note: All figures are crude prevalence; (1) Figures for the Savannah, GA Metropolitan Statistical Area were not available.
Source: Centers for Disease Control and Prevention, Behavioral Risk Factor Surveillance System, SMART: Selected Metropolitan Area Risk Trends, 2023

Disability Status

Category	MSA[1] (%)	U.S. (%)
Adults who reported being deaf	n/a	7.4
Are you blind or have serious difficulty seeing, even when wearing glasses?	n/a	4.9
Do you have difficulty doing errands alone?	n/a	7.8
Do you have difficulty dressing or bathing?	n/a	3.6
Do you have serious difficulty concentrating/remembering/making decisions?	n/a	13.7
Do you have serious difficulty walking or climbing stairs?	n/a	13.2

Note: All figures are crude prevalence; (1) Figures for the Savannah, GA Metropolitan Statistical Area were not available.
Source: Centers for Disease Control and Prevention, Behavioral Risk Factor Surveillance System, SMART: Selected Metropolitan Area Risk Trends, 2023

Mortality Rates for the Top 10 Causes of Death in the U.S.

ICD-10[a] Sub-Chapter	ICD-10[a] Code	Crude Mortality Rate[2] per 100,000 population	
		County[3]	U.S.
Malignant neoplasms	C00-C97	173.5	182.7
Ischaemic heart diseases	I20-I25	81.2	109.6
Provisional assignment of new diseases of uncertain etiology[1]	U00-U49	67.6	65.3
Other forms of heart disease	I30-I51	68.6	65.1
Other degenerative diseases of the nervous system	G30-G31	62.5	52.4
Other external causes of accidental injury	W00-X59	45.7	52.3
Cerebrovascular diseases	I60-I69	53.4	49.1
Chronic lower respiratory diseases	J40-J47	54.7	43.5
Hypertensive diseases	I10-I15	60.5	38.9
Organic, including symptomatic, mental disorders	F01-F09	27.2	33.9

Note: (a) ICD-10 = International Classification of Diseases 10th Revision; (1) Includes COVID-19, adverse effects to COVID-19 vaccines, SARS, and vaping-related disorders; (2) Crude mortality rates are a three-year average covering 2021-2023; (3) Figures cover Chatham County.
Source: Centers for Disease Control and Prevention, National Center for Health Statistics. National Vital Statistics System, Mortality 2018-2023 on CDC WONDER Online Database

Mortality Rates for Selected Causes of Death

Cause of Death	ICD-10[a] Code	Crude Mortality Rate[1] per 100,000 population	
		County[2]	U.S.
Accidental poisoning and exposure to noxious substances	X40-X49	28.4	30.5
Alzheimer disease	G30	41.1	35.4
Assault	X85-Y09	12.4	7.3
COVID-19	U07.1	67.6	65.3
Diabetes mellitus	E10-E14	24.0	30.0
Diseases of the liver	K70-K76	24.1	20.8
Human immunodeficiency virus (HIV) disease	B20-B24	3.8	1.5
Influenza and pneumonia	J09-J18	13.9	13.4
Intentional self-harm	X60-X84	14.1	14.7
Malnutrition	E40-E46	9.8	6.0
Obesity and other hyperalimentation	E65-E68	2.6	3.1
Renal failure	N17-N19	17.9	16.4
Transport accidents	V01-V99	15.1	14.4

Note: (a) ICD-10 = International Classification of Diseases 10th Revision; (1) Crude mortality rates are a three-year average covering 2021-2023; (2) Figures cover Chatham County; Data are suppressed when the data meet the criteria for confidentiality constraints; Crude mortality rates are flagged as unreliable when the rate would be calculated with a numerator of 20 or less.
Source: Centers for Disease Control and Prevention, National Center for Health Statistics. National Vital Statistics System, Mortality 2018-2023 on CDC WONDER Online Database

Health Insurance Coverage

Area	With Health Insurance	With Private Health Insurance	With Public Health Insurance	Without Health Insurance	Population Under Age 19 Without Health Insurance
City	86.2	59.3	36.7	13.8	5.7
MSA[1]	88.0	67.8	32.8	12.0	6.6
U.S.	91.4	67.3	36.3	8.6	5.4

Note: Figures are percentages that cover the civilian noninstitutionalized population; (1) Figures cover the Savannah, GA Metropolitan Statistical Area
Source: U.S. Census Bureau, 2019-2023 American Community Survey 5-Year Estimates

Number of Medical Professionals

Area	MDs[3]	DOs[3,4]	Dentists	Podiatrists	Chiropractors	Optometrists
County[1] (number)	1,158	85	223	21	65	45
County[1] (rate[2])	384.6	28.2	73.4	6.9	21.4	14.8
U.S. (rate[2])	302.5	29.2	74.6	6.4	29.5	18.0

Note: Data as of 2023 unless noted; (1) Data covers Chatham County; (2) Number of medical professionals per 100,000 population; (3) Data as of 2022 and includes all active, non-federal physicians; (4) Doctor of Osteopathic Medicine
Source: U.S. Department of Health and Human Services, Health Resources and Services Administration, Bureau of Health Professions, Area Resource File (ARF) 2023-2024

EDUCATION

Public School District Statistics

District Name	Schls	Pupils	Pupil/ Teacher Ratio	Minority Pupils[1] (%)	Total Rev. per Pupil ($)	Total Exp. per Pupil ($)
Savannah-Chatham County	58	35,781	13.2	80.6	20,364	17,225

Note: Table includes school districts with 2,000 or more students; (1) Percentage of students that are not non-Hispanic white.
Source: U.S. Department of Education, National Center for Education Statistics, Common Core of Data, Local Education Agency (School District) Universe Survey: School Year 2023-2024; U.S. Department of Education, National Center for Education Statistics, Common Core of Data, School District Finance Survey (F-33): School Year 2021–22

Best High Schools

According to *U.S. News,* Savannah is home to one of the top 500 high schools in the U.S.: **Savannah Arts Academy** (#423). Nearly 25,000 public, magnet and charter schools were ranked based on their performance on state assessments and how well they prepare students for college. *U.S. News & World Report, "Best High Schools 2024"*

Highest Level of Education

Area	Less than H.S.	H.S. Diploma	Some College, No Deg.	Associate Degree	Bachelor's Degree	Master's Degree	Prof. School Degree	Doctorate Degree
City	10.1	27.0	23.7	7.2	20.6	8.1	2.0	1.3
MSA[1]	8.7	25.9	22.4	8.0	21.6	9.6	2.3	1.5
U.S.	10.6	26.2	19.4	8.8	21.3	9.8	2.3	1.6

Note: Figures cover persons age 25 and over; (1) Figures cover the Savannah, GA Metropolitan Statistical Area
Source: U.S. Census Bureau, 2019-2023 American Community Survey 5-Year Estimates

Educational Attainment by Race

Area	High School Graduate or Higher (%)					Bachelor's Degree or Higher (%)				
	Total	White	Black	Asian	Hisp.[2]	Total	White	Black	Asian	Hisp.[2]
City	89.9	95.3	86.3	81.6	86.9	32.0	47.8	17.9	46.9	32.4
MSA[1]	91.3	94.0	88.9	82.3	84.1	34.9	41.2	23.4	50.9	27.4
U.S.	89.4	92.9	88.1	88.0	72.5	35.0	37.7	24.7	57.0	19.9

Note: Figures shown cover persons 25 years old and over; (1) Figures cover the Savannah, GA Metropolitan Statistical Area; (2) People of Hispanic origin can be of any race
Source: U.S. Census Bureau, 2019-2023 American Community Survey 5-Year Estimates

School Enrollment by Grade and Control

Area	Preschool (%)		Kindergarten (%)		Grades 1 - 4 (%)		Grades 5 - 8 (%)		Grades 9 - 12 (%)	
	Public	Private	Public	Private	Public	Private	Public	Private	Public	Private
City	76.3	23.7	85.4	14.6	88.1	11.9	88.2	11.8	88.6	11.4
MSA[1]	57.5	42.5	79.1	20.9	84.4	15.6	84.9	15.1	85.2	14.8
U.S.	58.7	41.3	85.2	14.8	87.2	12.8	87.9	12.1	89.0	11.0

Note: Figures shown cover persons 3 years old and over; (1) Figures cover the Savannah, GA Metropolitan Statistical Area
Source: U.S. Census Bureau, 2019-2023 American Community Survey 5-Year Estimates

Higher Education

Four-Year Colleges			Two-Year Colleges			Medical Schools[1]	Law Schools[2]	Voc/ Tech[3]
Public	Private Non-profit	Private For-profit	Public	Private Non-profit	Private For-profit			
1	1	2	1	0	0	0	0	1

Note: Figures cover institutions located within the Savannah, GA Metropolitan Statistical Area and include main campuses only; (1) includes schools accredited by the Liaison Committee on Medical Education and the American Osteopathic Association's Commission on Osteopathic College Accreditation; (2) includes ABA-accredited schools, schools with provisional ABA accreditation, and state accredited schools; (3) includes all schools with programs that are less than 2 years.
Source: National Center for Education Statistics, Integrated Postsecondary Education System (IPEDS), 2023-24; Wikipedia, List of Medical Schools in the United States, accessed May 2, 2025; Wikipedia, List of Law Schools in the United States, accessed May 2, 2025

EMPLOYERS

Major Employers

Company Name	Industry
Ceres Marine Terminals	Marine cargo handling
Coastal Home Care	Medical care
Colonial Group	Petroleum products
CSX	Railroad
Dollar Tree	Retail
Effingham County Hospital Authority	Hospital
Georgia Power Company	Electric utility
Georgia Regional Hospital	Hospital
Goodwill Industries of the Coastal Empire	Adult vocational rehabilitation
Kroger Company	Retail food
Marine Terminals Corp.	Marine cargo handling
McDonalds	Restaurants
Memorial University Medical Center	Hospital
Publix Supermarkets	Retail grocery
SouthCoast Health	Healthcare services
SSA Cooper	Marine cargo handling
St. Joseph's/Candler	Hospital
The Landings Club	Private membership club
TMX Finance	Financial services
Wal-Mart Stores	Retail

Note: Companies shown are located within the Savannah, GA Metropolitan Statistical Area.
Source: Chambers of Commerce; State Departments of Labor; Wikipedia

PUBLIC SAFETY

Crime Rate

Area	Total Crime Rate	Violent Crime Rate				Property Crime Rate		
		Murder	Rape	Robbery	Aggrav. Assault	Burglary	Larceny-Theft	Motor Vehicle Theft
City	n/a	n/a	n/a	n/a	n/a	n/a	n/a	n/a
U.S.	2,290.9	5.7	38.0	66.5	264.1	250.7	1,347.2	318.7

Note: Figures are crimes per 100,000 population; n/a not available.
Source: FBI, Table 8, Offenses Known to Law Enforcement, by State by City, 2023

Hate Crimes

Area	Number of Quarters Reported	Number of Incidents per Bias Motivation					
		Race/Ethnicity/Ancestry	Religion	Sexual Orientation	Disability	Gender	Gender Identity
City	n/a	n/a	n/a	n/a	n/a	n/a	n/a
U.S.	4	5,900	2,699	2,077	187	92	492

Note: n/a not available.
Source: Federal Bureau of Investigation, Hate Crime Statistics 2023

Identity Theft Consumer Reports

Area	Reports	Reports per 100,000 Population	Rank[2]
MSA[1]	1,801	437	14
U.S.	1,135,291	339	-

Note: (1) Figures cover the Savannah, GA Metropolitan Statistical Area; (2) Rank ranges from 1 to 401 where 1 indicates greatest number of identity theft reports per 100,000 population
Source: Federal Trade Commission, Consumer Sentinel Network Data Book 2024

Fraud and Other Consumer Reports

Area	Reports	Reports per 100,000 Population	Rank[2]
MSA[1]	7,635	1,853	21
U.S.	5,360,641	1,601	-

Note: (1) Figures cover the Savannah, GA Metropolitan Statistical Area; (2) Rank ranges from 1 to 401 where 1 indicates greatest number of fraud and other consumer reports per 100,000 population
Source: Federal Trade Commission, Consumer Sentinel Network Data Book 2024

POLITICS

2024 Presidential Election Results

Area	Trump (Rep.)	Harris (Dem.)	Stein (Green)	Kennedy (Ind.)	Oliver (Lib.)	Other
Chatham County	40.4	58.3	0.3	0.0	0.4	0.7
U.S.	49.7	48.2	0.6	0.5	0.4	0.6

Note: Results are percentages and may not add to 100% due to rounding
Source: Dave Leip's Atlas of U.S. Presidential Elections

SPORTS

Professional Sports Teams

Team Name	League	Year Established

No teams are located in the metro area
Source: Wikipedia, Major Professional Sports Teams of the United States and Canada, May 1, 2025

CLIMATE

Average and Extreme Temperatures

Temperature	Jan	Feb	Mar	Apr	May	Jun	Jul	Aug	Sep	Oct	Nov	Dec	Yr.
Extreme High (°F)	84	86	91	95	100	104	105	104	98	97	89	83	105
Average High (°F)	60	64	70	78	84	89	92	90	86	78	70	62	77
Average Temp. (°F)	49	53	59	66	74	79	82	81	77	68	59	52	67
Average Low (°F)	38	41	48	54	62	69	72	72	68	57	47	40	56
Extreme Low (°F)	3	14	20	32	39	51	61	57	43	28	15	9	3

Note: Figures cover the years 1950-1995
Source: National Climatic Data Center, International Station Meteorological Climate Summary, 9/96

Average Precipitation/Snowfall/Humidity

Precip./Humidity	Jan	Feb	Mar	Apr	May	Jun	Jul	Aug	Sep	Oct	Nov	Dec	Yr.
Avg. Precip. (in.)	3.5	3.1	3.9	3.2	4.2	5.6	6.8	7.2	5.0	2.9	2.2	2.7	50.3
Avg. Snowfall (in.)	Tr	Tr	Tr	0	0	0	0	0	0	0	Tr	Tr	Tr
Avg. Rel. Hum. 7am (%)	83	82	83	84	85	87	88	91	91	88	86	83	86
Avg. Rel. Hum. 4pm (%)	53	50	49	48	52	58	61	63	62	55	53	54	55

Note: Figures cover the years 1950-1995; Tr = Trace amounts (<0.05 in. of rain; <0.5 in. of snow)
Source: National Climatic Data Center, International Station Meteorological Climate Summary, 9/96

Weather Conditions

Temperature			Daytime Sky			Precipitation		
10°F & below	32°F & below	90°F & above	Clear	Partly cloudy	Cloudy	0.01 inch or more precip.	0.1 inch or more snow/ice	Thunder-storms
<1	29	70	97	155	113	111	<1	63

Note: Figures are average number of days per year and cover the years 1950-1995
Source: National Climatic Data Center, International Station Meteorological Climate Summary, 9/96

HAZARDOUS WASTE

Superfund Sites

The Savannah, GA metro area has no sites on the EPA's Superfund Final National Priorities List (NPL) or Superfund Alternative Approach (SAA) list. The Superfund alternative approach uses the same investigation and cleanup process and standards that are used for sites listed on the National Priorities List. The SAA is an alternative to listing a site on the NPL; it is not an alternative to Superfund or the Superfund process. There are a total of 1,445 Superfund sites with a status of proposed or final on both lists in the United States. *U.S. Environmental Protection Agency, National Priorities List, May 1, 2025; U.S. Environmental Protection Agency, Superfund Alternative Approach Sites, May 1, 2025*

AIR QUALITY

Air Quality Trends: Ozone

	1990	1995	2000	2005	2010	2015	2020	2021	2022	2023
MSA[1]	n/a	n/a	n/a	n/a	n/a	n/a	n/a	n/a	n/a	n/a
U.S.	0.087	0.089	0.081	0.080	0.072	0.068	0.066	0.067	0.067	0.070

Note: (1) Data covers the Savannah, GA Metropolitan Statistical Area; n/a not available. The values shown are the composite ozone concentration averages among trend sites based on the highest fourth daily maximum 8-hour concentration in parts per million. These trends are based on sites having an adequate record of monitoring data during the trend period. Data from exceptional events are included.
Source: U.S. Environmental Protection Agency, Air Quality Monitoring Information, "Air Quality Trends by City, 1990-2023"

Air Quality Index

Area	Percent of Days when Air Quality was...[2]					AQI Statistics[2]	
	Good	Moderate	Unhealthy for Sensitive Groups	Unhealthy	Very Unhealthy	Maximum	Median
MSA[1]	56.0	43.5	0.6	0.0	0.0	108	48

Note: (1) Data covers the Savannah, GA Metropolitan Statistical Area; (2) Based on 352 days with AQI data in 2023. Air Quality Index (AQI) is an index for reporting daily air quality. EPA calculates the AQI for five major air pollutants regulated by the Clean Air Act: ground-level ozone, particle pollution (aka particulate matter), carbon monoxide, sulfur dioxide, and nitrogen dioxide. The AQI runs from 0 to 500. The higher the AQI value, the greater the level of air pollution and the greater the health concern. There are six AQI categories: "Good" AQI is between 0 and 50. Air quality is considered satisfactory; "Moderate" AQI is between 51 and 100. Air quality is acceptable; "Unhealthy for Sensitive Groups" When AQI values are between 101 and 150, members of sensitive groups may experience health effects; "Unhealthy" When AQI values are between 151 and 200 everyone may begin to experience health effects; "Very Unhealthy" AQI values between 201 and 300 trigger a health alert; "Hazardous" AQI values over 300 trigger warnings of emergency conditions (not shown).
Source: U.S. Environmental Protection Agency, Air Quality Index Report, 2023

Air Quality Index Pollutants

Area	Percent of Days when AQI Pollutant was...[2]					
	Carbon Monoxide	Nitrogen Dioxide	Ozone	Sulfur Dioxide	Particulate Matter 2.5	Particulate Matter 10
MSA[1]	0.0	0.0	14.8	(3)	85.2	0.0

Note: (1) Data covers the Savannah, GA Metropolitan Statistical Area; (2) Based on 352 days with AQI data in 2023. The Air Quality Index (AQI) is an index for reporting daily air quality. EPA calculates the AQI for five major air pollutants regulated by the Clean Air Act: ground-level ozone, particle pollution (also known as particulate matter), carbon monoxide, sulfur dioxide, and nitrogen dioxide. The AQI runs from 0 to 500. The higher the AQI value, the greater the level of air pollution and the greater the health concern; (3) Sulfur dioxide is no longer included in this table because SO_2 concentrations tend to be very localized and not necessarily representative of broad geographical areas like counties and CBSAs.
Source: U.S. Environmental Protection Agency, Air Quality Index Report, 2023

Maximum Air Pollutant Concentrations: Particulate Matter, Ozone, CO and Lead

	Particulate Matter 10 (ug/m^3)	Particulate Matter 2.5 Wtd AM (ug/m^3)	Particulate Matter 2.5 24-Hr (ug/m^3)	Ozone (ppm)	Carbon Monoxide (ppm)	Lead (ug/m^3)
MSA[1] Level	n/a	8.8	24	0.061	n/a	n/a
NAAQS[2]	150	15	35	0.075	9	0.15
Met NAAQS[2]	n/a	Yes	Yes	Yes	n/a	n/a

Note: (1) Data covers the Savannah, GA Metropolitan Statistical Area; Data from exceptional events are included; (2) National Ambient Air Quality Standards; ppm = parts per million; ug/m^3 = micrograms per cubic meter; n/a not available.
Concentrations: Particulate Matter 10 (coarse particulate)—highest second maximum 24-hour concentration; Particulate Matter 2.5 Wtd AM (fine particulate)—highest weighted annual mean concentration; Particulate Matter 2.5 24-Hour (fine particulate)—highest 98th percentile 24-hour concentration; Ozone—highest fourth daily maximum 8-hour concentration; Carbon Monoxide—highest second maximum non-overlapping 8-hour concentration; Lead—maximum running 3-month average
Source: U.S. Environmental Protection Agency, Air Quality Monitoring Information, "Air Quality Statistics by City, 2023"

Maximum Air Pollutant Concentrations: Nitrogen Dioxide and Sulfur Dioxide

	Nitrogen Dioxide AM (ppb)	Nitrogen Dioxide 1-Hr (ppb)	Sulfur Dioxide AM (ppb)	Sulfur Dioxide 1-Hr (ppb)	Sulfur Dioxide 24-Hr (ppb)
MSA[1] Level	n/a	n/a	n/a	44	n/a
NAAQS[2]	53	100	30	75	140
Met NAAQS[2]	n/a	n/a	n/a	Yes	n/a

Note: (1) Data covers the Savannah, GA Metropolitan Statistical Area; Data from exceptional events are included; (2) National Ambient Air Quality Standards; ppm = parts per million; ug/m^3 = micrograms per cubic meter; n/a not available.
Concentrations: Nitrogen Dioxide AM—highest arithmetic mean concentration; Nitrogen Dioxide 1-Hr—highest 98th percentile 1-hour daily maximum concentration; Sulfur Dioxide AM—highest annual mean concentration; Sulfur Dioxide 1-Hr—highest 99th percentile 1-hour daily maximum concentration; Sulfur Dioxide 24-Hr—highest second maximum 24-hour concentration
Source: U.S. Environmental Protection Agency, Air Quality Monitoring Information, "Air Quality Statistics by City, 2023"

Tampa, Florida

Background

Tampa sits about halfway up the Gulf Coast of Florida on the mouth of the Hillsborough River on Tampa Bay. It was visited by Spanish explorers, including Ponce de Leon and Hernando de Soto as early as 1521, but did not see significant growth until the mid-nineteenth century. Tampa was a fort during the Seminole War and captured by the Union Army during the Civil War. Later in the 19th century, Tampa prospered when the railroad transported tourists from up north to enjoy the warmth and sunshine of Florida.

Tampa distinguished itself from other Florida cities as a main port for American troops travelling to Cuba during the Spanish-American War in 1898. Colonel Theodore Roosevelt occupied a Tampa hotel as his military headquarters, and a cigar factory in nearby Ybor City played a part in the city's importance at this time when Jose Marti (the George Washington of Cuba) exhorted factory workers to take up arms against the tyranny of Spanish rule.

By 1900, Tampa was known as the Cigar Capital of the World. In the peak year of 1929, factories in Tampa and Ybor City hand rolled 500 million cigars. When machines pushed handmade production offshore, Tampa remained a major spot for machine-made cigars until 2009, when the last Hav-A-Tampa Jewel came off the machines. Today, the cigar legacy of Tampa lives on, and the city hosts The Tampa Cigar Week every year.

The city saw its share of organized crime, with crime family alliances in New York and Cuba, from the late nineteenth century to the 1950s. Rampant and open corruption ended with crime and the sensational misconduct of local officials.

Today, Tampa is the largest port in the state and host to many cruise ships. Major industries in and around Tampa include finance, retail, healthcare, insurance, shipping by air and sea, national defense, professional sports, and real estate. Like most of Florida, the city's economy is heavily based on tourism. Attractions include Tampa Riverwalk, Glazer Children's Museum, and Tampa Museum of Art.

Redeveloping Tampa's downtown continues. Water Street Tampa project recently completed new residential towers, an office tower, a new Publix GreenWise Market, and two hotels. More horizontal infrastructure, like pedestrian walkways, is expected to be complete by 2027.

Public transportation in the city includes Amtrak's Silver Star Line at Tampa Union Station and the TECO Line Streetcar System. Several sites have been designated historical landmarks. Tampa is also home to Big Cat Rescue, one of the largest accredited sanctuaries in the world dedicated entirely to abused and abandoned big cats, including lions, tigers, bobcats, and cougars.

Largest employers in the city include MacDill Air Force Base, BayCare Health, and Publix Super Markets. Tampa served as Wikipedia's primary data center until 2013, when it moved to Ashburn, Virginia, leaving Tampa as the online encyclopedia's back up center. There are 20 Fortune 500 companies located in Tampa.

The city boasts National Football's Tampa Bay Buccaneers, which won the Superbowl in 2022. The city also hosts Major League Baseball's Devil Rays baseball team, and National Hockey League's Lightning, which won the Stanley Cup in 2020. Other attractions include Florida's Latin Quarter known as Ybor City, Busch Gardens, and a Museum of Science and Industry. Two popular annual events are the MacDill Air Force Base air show, and the Gasparilla Pirate Festival, referred to as Tampa's "mardi gras."

Winters are mild, while summers are long, warm, and humid. Freezing temperatures occur on one or two mornings per year during November through March. Dramatic thunderstorms occur during the summer season, most during late afternoon, sometimes causing dramatic temperature drops. With an elevation of less than 15 feet above sea level, the city is vulnerable to tidal surges. Major hurricanes that have seriously threatened Tampa are Donna in 1960, Charley in 2004, Irma in 2017, and Milton in 2024.

Rankings

General Rankings

- To help military veterans find the best places in which to settle down, *WalletHub* compared the 100 largest U.S. cities across 19 key indicators of livability, affordability and veteran-friendliness. They range from the share of military skill-related jobs to veteran income growth to the availability of VA health facilities. Tampa ranked #4. *Wallethub.com, "Best & Worst Places for Veterans to Live (2025)," November 7, 2024*

- Tampa was selected as one of the best places to live in the United States by *Money* magazine. The city placed among the top 50. This year's list focused on cities built around community spirit, thoughtful policy and civic engagement. Instead of relying on a predetermined dataset, the cities and towns were grouped according to their strengths and chosen due their affordability, good schools and strong job markets. *Money, "The 50 Best Places to Live in the U.S., 2024" April 8, 2024*

- In their annual survey, Livability.com looked at data for more than 2,000 mid-sized U.S. cities to assign a "Livability Score" for each. The top 100 scoring cities make up Livability's "Top 100 Best Places to Live in the U.S." in 2025. Tampa was placed among the top 100 of the customizable list. Criteria: housing and economy; cost of living; environment; education; health care options; transportation; safety; and community amenities. *Livability.com, "Top 100 Best Places to Live in the U.S. in 2025" April 15, 2025*

Business/Finance Rankings

- Payscale.com ranked the 32 largest metro areas in terms of wage growth. The Tampa metro area ranked #18. Criteria: quarterly changes in private industry employee and education professional wage growth from the previous year. *PayScale, "Wage Trends by Metro Area-4th Quarter," February 4, 2025*

- The Tampa metro area appeared on the Milken Institute "2025 Best Performing Cities" list. Rank: #28 out of 200 large metro areas (based on performance category). Criteria: job growth; wage growth; high-tech growth and impact; community resilience; housing affordability; household broadband access. *Milken Institute, "Best-Performing Cities 2025," January 14, 2025*

Education Rankings

- Personal finance website *WalletHub* analyzed the 150 largest U.S. metropolitan statistical areas to determine where the most educated Americans are putting their degrees to work. Criteria: education levels; percentage of workers with degrees; education quality and attainment gap; public school quality rankings; quality and enrollment of each metro area's universities. Tampa was ranked #79 (#1 = most educated city). *WalletHub.com, "Most & Least Educated Cities in America, 2025" July 2, 2024*

Environmental Rankings

- Sperling's *BestPlaces* assessed the 50 largest metropolitan areas of the United States for the likelihood of dangerously extreme weather events or earthquakes. In general the Southeast and South-Central regions have the highest risk of weather extremes and earthquakes, while the Pacific Northwest enjoys the lowest risk. Of the most risky metropolitan areas, the Tampa metro area was ranked #8. *Bestplaces.net, "Avoid Natural Disasters: BestPlaces Reveals The Top 10 Safest Places to Live," October 25, 2017*

- The U.S. Environmental Protection Agency (EPA) released its list of U.S. metropolitan areas with the most ENERGY STAR certified buildings in 2023. The Tampa metro area was ranked #15 out of 25. *U.S. Environmental Protection Agency, "2024 Energy Star Top Cities," May 22, 2024*

Food/Drink Rankings

- WalletHub compared the 100 largest U.S. cities across 17 key indicators of vegan- and vegetarian-friendliness. Tampa was ranked #10. Cities were selected based on metrics such as the cost of groceries for vegetarians, the share of restaurants serving meatless options and the number of salad shops per capita. *WalletHub.com, "Best Cities for Vegans & Vegetarians (2025)," September 24, 2024*

Health/Fitness Rankings

- For each of the 100 largest cities in the United States, the American Fitness Index®, compiled in partnership between the American College of Sports Medicine and the Elevance Health Foundation, evaluated community infrastructure and more than 30 health behaviors including preventive health, levels of chronic disease conditions, food insecurity, pedestrian safety, air quality, and community/environment resources that support physical activity. Tampa ranked #45 for "community fitness." *americanfitnessindex.org, "2024 ACSM American Fitness Index Summary Report," July 23, 2024*

- The Tampa metro area was identified as one of the worst cities for bed bugs in America by pest control company Orkin. The area ranked #31 out of 50 based on the number of bed bug treatments Orkin performed from December 2022 to November 2023. *Orkin, "Chicago Joins Paris In Global Bed Bug Spotlight Ranking As The Worst City On Orkin's U.S. Bed Bug Cities List," January 22, 2024*

- Tampa was identified as a "2025 Allergy Capital." The area ranked #25 out of the nation's 100 largest metropolitan areas. Three groups of factors were used to identify the most challenging cities for people with allergies: annual tree, grass, and weed pollen scores; over the counter allergy medicine use; number of board-certified allergy specialists. *Asthma and Allergy Foundation of America, "2025 Allergy Capitals: The Most Challenging Places to Live with Allergies," March 18, 2025*

- Tampa was identified as a "2024 Asthma Capital." The area ranked #72 out of the nation's 100 largest metropolitan areas. Criteria: estimated asthma prevalence; asthma-related mortality; and ER visits due to asthma. Risk factors analyzed but not factored in the rankings: annual air quality including pollution and ozone levels; public smoking laws; indoor air quality; access to asthma specialists; rescue and controller medication use; uninsured rate; pollen allergy; poverty rate. *Asthma and Allergy Foundation of America, "Asthma Capitals 2024: The Most Challenging Places to Live With Asthma," September 10, 2024*

Pet Rankings

- Tampa appeared on *The Dogington Post* site as one of the top cities for dog lovers, ranking #10 out of 15. The real estate marketplace, Zillow®, and Rover, the largest pet sitter and dog walker network, introduced a new list of "Top Emerging Dog-Friendly Cities" for 2021. Criteria: number of new dog accounts on the Rover platform; and rentals and listings that mention features that attract dog owners (fenced-in yards, dog houses, dog door or proximity to a dog park). *Dogingtonpost.com, "15 Cities Emerging as Dog-Friendliest in 2021," May 11, 2021*

Real Estate Rankings

- *WalletHub* compared the most populated U.S. cities to determine which had the best markets for real estate agents. Tampa ranked #39 where demand was high and pay was the best. Criteria: sales per agent; annual median wage for real-estate agents; monthly average starting salary for real estate agents; real estate job density and competition; unemployment rate; home turnover rate; housing-market health index; and other relevant metrics. *WalletHub.com, "2021 Best Places to Be a Real Estate Agent," May 12, 2021*

- According to Penske Truck Rental, the Tampa metro area was named the #9 moving destination in 2023, based on one-way consumer truck rental reservations made through Penske's website, rental locations, and reservations call center. *gopenske.com, "Penske Truck Rental's 2023 Top Moving Destinations," May 7, 2024*

- The Tampa metro area was identified as one of the 20 worst housing markets in the U.S. in 2024. The area ranked #211 out of 226 markets. Criteria: year-over-year change of median sales price of existing single-family homes between the 4th quarter of 2023 and the 4th quarter of 2024. *National Association of Realtors®, Median Sales Price of Existing Single-Family Homes for Metropolitan Areas, 4th Quarter 2024*

- Tampa was ranked #136 out of 176 metro areas in terms of cost of housing in 2024 by the National Association of Home Builders (#1 = most affordable). Criteria: the portion of an average family's income necessary to pay the mortgage on a median-priced home. *National Association of Home Builders®, NAHB-Wells Fargo Cost of Housing Index, 4th Quarter 2024*

Safety Rankings

- Allstate ranked the 100 most populous cities in America in terms of driver safety. Tampa ranked #45. Criteria based on anonymized driving behavior data from Allstate's mobile app powered by Arity: high speed driving (over 80 mph), phone handling, and hard braking. The report helps increase the importance of safety and awareness behind the wheel. *Allstate, "16th Allstate America's Best Drivers Report®" July 11, 2024*

Women/Minorities Rankings

- Personal finance website *WalletHub* compared more than 180 U.S. cities across two key dimensions, "Hispanic Business-Friendliness" and "Hispanic Purchasing Power," to arrive at the most favorable conditions for Hispanic entrepreneurs. Tampa was ranked #11 out of 182. Criteria includes: share of Hispanic-Owned Businesses; average growth of Hispanic Business revenues; Small Business-Friendliness score; affordability; and number of Hispanics with at least a bachelor's degree. *WalletHub.com, "Best Cities for Hispanic Entrepreneurs," September 4, 2024*

Miscellaneous Rankings

- *MoveHub* ranked 446 hipster cities across 20 countries, using its new and improved alternative Hipster Index and Tampa came out as #11 among the top 50. Criteria: population over 150,000; number of vintage boutiques; density of tattoo parlors; vegan places to eat; coffee shops; and density of vinyl record stores. *MoveHub.com, "The Hipster Index: Brighton Pips Portland to Global Top Spot," July 28, 2021*

- *WalletHub* compared 148 of the most populated U.S. cities to determine their operating efficiency. A "Quality of Services" score was constructed for each city and then measured against the total budget per capita to reveal which were managed the best. Tampa ranked #82. Criteria: financial stability; economy; education; safety; health; infrastructure and pollution. *WalletHub.com, "2025's Best- & Worst-Run Cities in America," June 18, 2024*

Business Environment

DEMOGRAPHICS

Population Growth

Area	1990 Census	2000 Census	2010 Census	2020 Census	2023 Estimate[2]	Population Growth 1990-2023 (%)
City	279,960	303,447	335,709	384,959	393,389	40.5
MSA[1]	2,067,959	2,395,997	2,783,243	3,175,275	3,240,469	56.7
U.S.	248,709,873	281,421,906	308,745,538	331,449,281	332,387,540	33.6

Note: (1) Figures cover the Tampa-St. Petersburg-Clearwater, FL Metropolitan Statistical Area; (2) 2019-2023 5-year ACS population estimate
Source: U.S. Census Bureau, 1990 Census, 2000 Census, 2010 Census, 2020 Census, 2019-2023 American Community Survey 5-Year Estimates

Race

Area	White Alone[2] (%)	Black Alone[2] (%)	Asian Alone[2] (%)	AIAN[3] Alone[2] (%)	NHOPI[4] Alone[2] (%)	Other Race Alone[2] (%)	Two or More Races (%)
City	51.8	21.3	4.8	0.3	0.1	4.8	17.0
MSA[1]	66.0	11.8	3.8	0.3	0.1	4.8	13.2
U.S.	63.4	12.4	5.8	0.9	0.2	6.6	10.7

Note: (1) Figures cover the Tampa-St. Petersburg-Clearwater, FL Metropolitan Statistical Area; (2) Alone is defined as not being in combination with one or more other races; (3) American Indian and Alaska Native; (4) Native Hawaiian and Other Pacific Islander
Source: U.S. Census Bureau, 2019-2023 American Community Survey 5-Year Estimates

Hispanic or Latino Origin

Area	Total (%)	Mexican (%)	Puerto Rican (%)	Cuban (%)	Other (%)
City	26.2	3.2	6.1	7.8	9.1
MSA[1]	21.1	3.7	6.0	4.5	6.9
U.S.	19.0	11.3	1.8	0.7	5.2

Note: Persons of Hispanic or Latino origin can be of any race; (1) Figures cover the Tampa-St. Petersburg-Clearwater, FL Metropolitan Statistical Area
Source: U.S. Census Bureau, 2019-2023 American Community Survey 5-Year Estimates

Age

Area	Under Age 5	Age 5–19	Age 20–34	Age 35–44	Age 45–54	Age 55–64	Age 65–74	Age 75–84	Age 85+	Median Age
City	5.8	18.5	24.6	14.2	12.5	11.2	7.8	4.1	1.3	35.6
MSA[1]	5.0	16.7	18.7	12.9	12.8	13.7	11.4	6.4	2.4	42.2
U.S.	5.7	19.1	20.2	13.1	12.3	12.8	10.0	4.9	1.9	38.7

Note: (1) Figures cover the Tampa-St. Petersburg-Clearwater, FL Metropolitan Statistical Area
Source: U.S. Census Bureau, 2019-2023 American Community Survey 5-Year Estimates

Disability by Age

Area	All Ages	Under 18 Years Old	18 to 64 Years Old	65 Years and Over
City	11.9	4.1	9.3	38.0
MSA[1]	14.4	5.3	11.1	33.5
U.S.	13.0	4.7	10.7	32.9

Note: Figures show percent of the civilian noninstitutionalized population that reported having a disability. Disability status is determined from six types of difficulty: vision, hearing, cognitive, ambulatory, self-care, and independent living. For children under 5 years old, hearing and vision difficulty are used to determine disability status. For children between the ages of 5 and 14, disability status is determined from hearing, vision, cognitive, ambulatory, and self-care difficulties. For people aged 15 years and older, they are considered to have a disability if they have difficulty with any one of the six difficulty types; Note: (1) Figures cover the Tampa-St. Petersburg-Clearwater, FL Metropolitan Statistical Area
Source: U.S. Census Bureau, 2019-2023 American Community Survey 5-Year Estimates

Ancestry

Area	German	Irish	English	American	Italian	Polish	French[2]	European	Scottish
City	8.8	7.6	7.6	6.2	6.2	2.0	1.6	1.1	1.4
MSA[1]	11.3	9.8	9.2	8.6	7.2	2.8	2.1	1.3	1.6
U.S.	12.6	9.4	9.1	5.5	4.9	2.6	2.0	1.6	1.6

Note: Figures are the percentage of the total population reporting a particular ancestry. The nine most commonly reported ancestries in the U.S. are shown. Figures include multiple ancestries (e.g. if a person reported being Irish and Italian, they were included in both columns); (1) Figures cover the Tampa-St. Petersburg-Clearwater, FL Metropolitan Statistical Area; (2) Excludes Basque
Source: U.S. Census Bureau, 2019-2023 American Community Survey 5-Year Estimates

Foreign-born Population

Area	Percent of Population Born in								
	Any Foreign Country	Asia	Mexico	Europe	Caribbean	Central America[2]	South America	Africa	Canada
City	19.0	4.0	1.1	1.8	7.4	1.3	2.4	0.6	0.3
MSA[1]	15.0	2.9	1.2	2.2	4.3	0.8	2.4	0.5	0.6
U.S.	13.9	4.3	3.3	1.4	1.4	1.2	1.2	0.8	0.2

Note: (1) Figures cover the Tampa-St. Petersburg-Clearwater, FL Metropolitan Statistical Area; (2) Excludes Mexico.
Source: U.S. Census Bureau, 2019-2023 American Community Survey 5-Year Estimates

Household Size

Area	Persons in Household (%)							Average Household Size
	One	Two	Three	Four	Five	Six	Seven or More	
City	35.7	32.1	15.4	10.9	4.1	1.4	0.5	2.35
MSA[1]	30.8	36.3	15.0	10.9	4.6	1.6	0.8	2.44
U.S.	28.5	33.8	15.4	12.7	5.9	2.3	1.4	2.54

Note: (1) Figures cover the Tampa-St. Petersburg-Clearwater, FL Metropolitan Statistical Area
Source: U.S. Census Bureau, 2019-2023 American Community Survey 5-Year Estimates

Household Relationships

Area	Householder	Opposite-sex Spouse	Same-sex Spouse	Opposite-sex Unmarried Partner	Same-sex Unmarried Partner	Child[2]	Grandchild	Other Relatives	Non-relatives
City	40.9	13.8	0.3	3.2	0.3	25.8	2.3	4.9	4.5
MSA[1]	41.2	17.6	0.3	3.1	0.2	25.5	2.2	4.6	3.4
U.S.	38.3	17.5	0.2	2.5	0.2	28.3	2.4	4.8	3.4

Note: Figures are percent of the total population; (1) Figures cover the Tampa-St. Petersburg-Clearwater, FL Metropolitan Statistical Area; (2) Includes biological, adopted, and stepchildren of the householder
Source: U.S. Census Bureau, 2020 Census

Gender

Area	Males	Females	Males per 100 Females
City	197,565	195,824	100.9
MSA[1]	1,583,138	1,657,331	95.5
U.S.	164,545,087	167,842,453	98.0

Note: (1) Figures cover the Tampa-St. Petersburg-Clearwater, FL Metropolitan Statistical Area
Source: U.S. Census Bureau, 2019-2023 American Community Survey 5-Year Estimates

Marital Status

Area	Never Married	Now Married[2]	Separated	Widowed	Divorced
City	43.1	38.1	2.2	4.7	11.8
MSA[1]	32.1	46.3	1.8	6.8	13.1
U.S.	34.1	47.9	1.7	5.6	10.7

Note: Figures are percentages and cover the population 15 years of age and older; (1) Figures cover the Tampa-St. Petersburg-Clearwater, FL Metropolitan Statistical Area; (2) Excludes separated
Source: U.S. Census Bureau, 2019-2023 American Community Survey 5-Year Estimates

Religious Groups by Family

Area	Catholic	Baptist	Methodist	LDS[2]	Pentecostal	Lutheran	Islam	Adventist	Other
MSA[1]	23.1	6.3	2.9	0.5	1.9	0.6	0.7	1.8	12.1
U.S.	18.7	7.3	3.0	2.0	1.8	1.7	1.3	1.3	11.6

Note: Figures are the number of adherents as a percentage of the total population and cover the eight largest religious groups in the U.S; (1) Figures cover the Tampa-St. Petersburg-Clearwater, FL Metropolitan Statistical Area; (2) Church of Jesus Christ of Latter-day Saints
Sources: 2020 U.S. Religion Census, Association of Statisticians of American Religious Bodies; The Association of Religion Data Archives (ARDA)

Religious Groups by Tradition

Area	Catholic	Evangelical Protestant	Mainline Protestant	Black Protestant	Islam	Judaism	Hinduism	Orthodox	Buddhism
MSA[1]	23.1	16.9	3.8	1.7	0.7	0.4	0.3	0.8	0.4
U.S.	18.7	16.5	5.2	2.3	1.3	0.6	0.4	0.4	0.3

Note: Figures are the number of adherents as a percentage of the total population; (1) Figures cover the Tampa-St. Petersburg-Clearwater, FL Metropolitan Statistical Area
Sources: 2020 U.S. Religion Census, Association of Statisticians of American Religious Bodies; The Association of Religion Data Archives (ARDA)

ECONOMY

Real Gross Domestic Product (GDP)

Area	2017	2018	2019	2020	2021	2022	2023	Rank[3]
MSA[1]	152.7	158.0	163.9	165.5	180.0	190.7	198.9	23
U.S.[2]	17,619.1	18,160.7	18,642.5	18,238.9	19,387.6	19,896.6	20,436.3	—

Note: Figures are in billions of chained 2017 dollars; (1) Figures cover the Tampa-St. Petersburg-Clearwater, FL Metropolitan Statistical Area; (2) Figures cover real GDP within metropolitan areas; (3) Rank is based on 2023 data and ranges from 1 to 384
Source: U.S. Bureau of Economic Analysis

Economic Growth

Area	2014	2015	2016	2017	2018	2019	2020	2021	2022	2023
MSA[1]	2.0	4.2	3.3	2.1	3.5	3.7	1.0	8.8	5.9	4.3
U.S.[2]	2.6	3.2	2.0	2.7	3.1	2.7	-2.2	6.3	2.6	2.7

Note: Figures are real gross domestic product growth rates and represent percent change from preceding period; (1) Figures cover the Tampa-St. Petersburg-Clearwater, FL Metropolitan Statistical Area; (2) Figures are the average growth rates within metropolitan areas
Source: U.S. Bureau of Economic Analysis

Metropolitan Area Exports

Area	2018	2019	2020	2021	2022	2023	Rank[2]
MSA[1]	4,966.7	6,219.7	5,082.2	5,754.7	9,588.2	7,923.6	49
U.S.	1,664,056.1	1,645,173.7	1,431,406.6	1,753,941.4	2,062,937.4	2,019,160.5	—

Note: Figures are in millions of dollars; (1) Figures cover the Tampa-St. Petersburg-Clearwater, FL Metropolitan Statistical Area; (2) Rank is based on 2023 data and ranges from 1 to 386
Source: U.S. Department of Commerce, International Trade Administration, Office of Trade and Economic Analysis, Industry and Analysis, Exports by Metropolitan Area, data extracted April 2, 2025

Building Permits

Area	Single-Family			Multi-Family			Total		
	2023	2024	Pct. Chg.	2023	2024	Pct. Chg.	2023	2024	Pct. Chg.
City	738	912	23.6	2,415	1,634	-32.3	3,153	2,546	-19.3
MSA[1]	14,852	13,205	-11.1	10,534	7,745	-26.5	25,386	20,950	-17.5
U.S.	920,000	981,900	6.7	591,100	496,100	-16.1	1,511,100	1,478,000	-2.2

Note: (1) Figures cover the Tampa-St. Petersburg-Clearwater, FL Metropolitan Statistical Area; Figures represent new, privately-owned housing units authorized (unadjusted data)
Source: U.S. Census Bureau, Building Permits Survey (BPS), 2023, 2024

Bankruptcy Filings

Area	Business Filings			Nonbusiness Filings		
	2023	2024	% Chg.	2023	2024	% Chg.
Hillsborough County	121	158	30.6	1,822	2,440	33.9
U.S.	18,926	23,107	22.1	434,064	494,201	13.9

Note: Business filings include Chapter 7, Chapter 9, Chapter 11, Chapter 12, Chapter 13, Chapter 15, and Section 304; Nonbusiness filings include Chapter 7, Chapter 11, and Chapter 13
Source: Administrative Office of the U.S. Courts, Business and Nonbusiness Bankruptcy, County Cases Commenced by Chapter of the Bankruptcy Code, During the 12-Month Period Ending December 31, 2023 and Business and Nonbusiness Bankruptcy, County Cases Commenced by Chapter of the Bankruptcy Code, During the 12-Month Period Ending December 31, 2024

Housing Vacancy Rates

Area	Gross Vacancy Rate[3] (%)			Year-Round Vacancy Rate[4] (%)			Rental Vacancy Rate[5] (%)			Homeowner Vacancy Rate[6] (%)		
	2022	2023	2024	2022	2023	2024	2022	2023	2024	2022	2023	2024
MSA[1]	13.3	13.3	14.2	9.9	9.1	10.9	8.1	8.5	8.7	1.2	1.0	2.0
U.S.[2]	9.1	9.0	9.1	7.5	7.5	7.6	5.7	6.5	6.8	0.8	0.8	1.0

Note: (1) Figures cover the Tampa-St. Petersburg-Clearwater, FL Metropolitan Statistical Area; (2) Figures cover the 75 largest Metropolitan Statistical Areas; (3) The percentage of the total housing inventory that is vacant; (4) The percentage of the housing inventory (excluding seasonal units) that is year-round vacant; (5) The percentage of rental inventory that is vacant for rent; (6) The percentage of homeowner inventory that is vacant for sale
Source: U.S. Census Bureau, Housing Vacancies and Homeownership Annual Statistics: 2022, 2023, 2024

INCOME

Income

Area	Per Capita ($)	Median Household ($)	Average Household ($)
City	49,513	71,302	117,408
MSA[1]	42,023	71,254	100,901
U.S.	43,289	78,538	110,491

Note: (1) Figures cover the Tampa-St. Petersburg-Clearwater, FL Metropolitan Statistical Area
Source: U.S. Census Bureau, 2019-2023 American Community Survey 5-Year Estimates

Household Income Distribution

Area	Percent of Households Earning							
	Under $15,000	$15,000 -$24,999	$25,000 -$34,999	$35,000 -$49,999	$50,000 -$74,999	$75,000 -$99,999	$100,000 -$149,999	$150,000 and up
City	11.1	7.2	7.2	11.2	15.6	11.2	14.4	22.1
MSA[1]	8.6	6.9	7.6	11.6	17.6	12.8	16.6	18.3
U.S.	8.5	6.6	6.8	10.4	15.7	12.7	17.4	21.9

Note: (1) Figures cover the Tampa-St. Petersburg-Clearwater, FL Metropolitan Statistical Area
Source: U.S. Census Bureau, 2019-2023 American Community Survey 5-Year Estimates

Poverty Rate

Area	All Ages	Under 18 Years Old	18 to 64 Years Old	65 Years and Over
City	15.9	20.3	13.5	21.2
MSA[1]	12.2	15.5	11.3	11.9
U.S.	12.4	16.3	11.6	10.4

Note: Figures are percentage of people whose income during the past 12 months was below the poverty level; (1) Figures cover the Tampa-St. Petersburg-Clearwater, FL Metropolitan Statistical Area
Source: U.S. Census Bureau, 2019-2023 American Community Survey 5-Year Estimates

EMPLOYMENT

Labor Force and Employment

Area	Civilian Labor Force			Workers Employed		
	Dec. 2023	Dec. 2024	% Chg.	Dec. 2023	Dec. 2024	% Chg.
City	222,684	223,321	0.3	215,665	215,892	0.1
MD[1]	1,167,354	1,171,736	0.4	1,130,613	1,132,522	0.2
U.S.	166,661,000	167,746,000	0.7	160,754,000	161,294,000	0.3

Note: Data is not seasonally adjusted and covers workers 16 years of age and older; (1) Figures cover the Tampa, FL Metropolitan Division
Source: Bureau of Labor Statistics, Local Area Unemployment Statistics

Unemployment Rate

Area	2024											
	Jan.	Feb.	Mar.	Apr.	May	Jun.	Jul.	Aug.	Sep.	Oct.	Nov.	Dec.
City	3.5	3.3	3.4	3.1	3.3	3.8	3.9	4.0	3.6	3.7	3.8	3.3
MD[1]	3.5	3.4	3.3	3.1	3.3	3.8	4.0	4.0	3.7	3.7	3.8	3.3
U.S.	4.1	4.2	3.9	3.5	3.7	4.3	4.5	4.4	3.9	3.9	4.0	3.8

Note: Data is not seasonally adjusted and covers workers 16 years of age and older; (1) Figures cover the Tampa, FL Metropolitan Division
Source: Bureau of Labor Statistics, Local Area Unemployment Statistics

Average Wages

Occupation	$/Hr.	Occupation	$/Hr.
Accountants and Auditors	42.37	Maintenance and Repair Workers	22.66
Automotive Mechanics	25.41	Marketing Managers	73.93
Bookkeepers	25.17	Network and Computer Systems Admin.	48.19
Carpenters	24.57	Nurses, Licensed Practical	29.09
Cashiers	14.51	Nurses, Registered	43.40
Computer Programmers	46.54	Nursing Assistants	18.54
Computer Systems Analysts	53.50	Office Clerks, General	21.94
Computer User Support Specialists	29.29	Physical Therapists	47.43
Construction Laborers	21.37	Physicians	143.21
Cooks, Restaurant	17.47	Plumbers, Pipefitters and Steamfitters	26.24
Customer Service Representatives	20.59	Police and Sheriff's Patrol Officers	37.66
Dentists	112.24	Postal Service Mail Carriers	28.84
Electricians	26.80	Real Estate Sales Agents	34.03
Engineers, Electrical	55.02	Retail Salespersons	16.81
Fast Food and Counter Workers	14.40	Sales Representatives, Technical/Scientific	55.31
Financial Managers	81.07	Secretaries, Exc. Legal/Medical/Executive	22.08
First-Line Supervisors of Office Workers	32.48	Security Guards	18.32
General and Operations Managers	65.80	Surgeons	210.11
Hairdressers/Cosmetologists	18.35	Teacher Assistants, Exc. Postsecondary[1]	14.20
Home Health and Personal Care Aides	16.19	Teachers, Secondary School, Exc. Sp. Ed.[1]	30.50
Janitors and Cleaners	16.47	Telemarketers	17.64
Landscaping/Groundskeeping Workers	17.89	Truck Drivers, Heavy/Tractor-Trailer	25.87
Lawyers	67.66	Truck Drivers, Light/Delivery Services	21.83
Maids and Housekeeping Cleaners	16.79	Waiters and Waitresses	19.64

Note: Wage data covers the Tampa-St. Petersburg-Clearwater, FL Metropolitan Statistical Area; (1) Hourly wages were calculated from annual wage data based on a 40 hour work week
Source: Bureau of Labor Statistics, Metro Area Occupational Employment & Wage Estimates, May 2024

Employment by Industry

Sector	MD[1] Number of Employees	MD[1] Percent of Total	U.S. Percent of Total
Construction	71,300	6.6	5.1
Financial Activities	110,400	10.2	5.8
Government	112,400	10.4	14.9
Information	19,900	1.8	1.9
Leisure and Hospitality	111,500	10.3	10.4
Manufacturing	40,500	3.7	8.0
Mining and Logging	n/a	n/a	0.4
Other Services	35,400	3.3	3.7
Private Education and Health Services	172,400	16.0	16.9
Professional and Business Services	195,600	18.1	14.2
Retail Trade	118,100	10.9	10.0
Transportation, Warehousing, and Utilities	46,600	4.3	4.8
Wholesale Trade	46,100	4.3	3.9

Note: Figures are non-farm employment as of December 2024. Figures are not seasonally adjusted and include workers 16 years of age and older; (1) Figures cover the Tampa, FL Metropolitan Division; n/a not available
Source: Bureau of Labor Statistics, Current Employment Statistics, Employment, Hours, and Earnings

Employment by Occupation

Occupation Classification	City (%)	MSA[1] (%)	U.S. (%)
Management, Business, Science, and Arts	47.7	42.2	42.0
Natural Resources, Construction, and Maintenance	6.6	8.1	8.6
Production, Transportation, and Material Moving	9.4	10.0	13.0
Sales and Office	20.7	23.2	19.9
Service	15.5	16.5	16.5

Note: Figures cover employed civilians 16 years of age and older; (1) Figures cover the Tampa-St. Petersburg-Clearwater, FL Metropolitan Statistical Area
Source: U.S. Census Bureau, 2019-2023 American Community Survey 5-Year Estimates

Occupations with Greatest Projected Employment Growth: 2022 – 2032

Occupation[1]	2022 Employment	2032 Projected Employment	Numeric Employment Change	Percent Employment Change
Stockers and Order Fillers	236,990	274,060	37,070	15.6
Retail Salespersons	308,940	340,000	31,060	10.1
Waiters and Waitresses	195,320	223,820	28,500	14.6
Software Developers	75,620	101,940	26,320	34.8
General and Operations Managers	184,790	210,510	25,720	13.9
Registered Nurses	202,780	228,070	25,290	12.5
Fast Food and Counter Workers	185,000	209,460	24,460	13.2
Cooks, Restaurant	120,850	141,640	20,790	17.2
Landscaping and Groundskeeping Workers	112,240	129,030	16,790	15.0
Janitors and Cleaners, Except Maids and Housekeeping Cleaners	136,890	153,490	16,600	12.1

Note: Projections cover Florida; (1) Sorted by numeric employment change
Source: www.projectionscentral.org, State Occupational Projections, 2022–2032 Long-Term Projections

Fastest-Growing Occupations: 2022 – 2032

Occupation[1]	2022 Employment	2032 Projected Employment	Numeric Employment Change	Percent Employment Change
Nurse Practitioners	18,910	29,980	11,070	58.5
Data Scientists	8,470	12,450	3,980	47.0
Information Security Analysts (SOC 2018)	11,060	15,650	4,590	41.5
Statisticians	590	820	230	39.0
Solar Photovoltaic Installers	1,210	1,680	470	38.8
Computer and Information Research Scientists (SOC 2018)	3,160	4,380	1,220	38.6
Physician Assistants	8,830	12,180	3,350	37.9
Actuaries	1,640	2,260	620	37.8
Physical Therapist Assistants	7,430	10,230	2,800	37.7
Medical and Health Services Managers	34,490	47,200	12,710	36.9

Note: Projections cover Florida; (1) Sorted by percent employment change and excludes occupations with numeric employment change less than 50
Source: www.projectionscentral.org, State Occupational Projections, 2022–2032 Long-Term Projections

CITY FINANCES

City Government Finances

Component	2022 ($000)	2022 ($ per capita)
Total Revenues	1,114,835	2,735
Total Expenditures	1,436,710	3,525
Debt Outstanding	930,755	2,284

Source: U.S. Census Bureau, State & Local Government Finances 2022

City Government Revenue by Source

Source	2022 ($000)	2022 ($ per capita)	2022 (%)
General Revenue			
From Federal Government	64,815	159	5.8
From State Government	61,733	151	5.5
From Local Governments	31,298	77	2.8
Taxes			
Property	241,271	592	21.6
Sales and Gross Receipts	118,199	290	10.6
Personal Income	0	0	0.0
Corporate Income	0	0	0.0
Motor Vehicle License	0	0	0.0
Other Taxes	60,913	149	5.5
Current Charges	287,125	704	25.8
Liquor Store	0	0	0.0
Utility	147,370	362	13.2

Source: U.S. Census Bureau, State & Local Government Finances 2022

City Government Expenditures by Function

Function	2022 ($000)	2022 ($ per capita)	2022 (%)
General Direct Expenditures			
Air Transportation	0	0	0.0
Corrections	0	0	0.0
Education	0	0	0.0
Employment Security Administration	0	0	0.0
Financial Administration	283,102	694	19.7
Fire Protection	112,219	275	7.8
General Public Buildings	15,293	37	1.1
Governmental Administration, Other	4,141	10	0.3
Health	0	0	0.0
Highways	55,128	135	3.8
Hospitals	0	0	0.0
Housing and Community Development	44,137	108	3.1
Interest on General Debt	19,474	47	1.4
Judicial and Legal	5,670	13	0.4
Libraries	0	0	0.0
Parking	15,462	37	1.1
Parks and Recreation	72,878	178	5.1
Police Protection	176,247	432	12.3
Public Welfare	0	0	0.0
Sewerage	169,697	416	11.8
Solid Waste Management	102,127	250	7.1
Veterans' Services	0	0	0.0
Liquor Store	0	0	0.0
Utility	183,342	449	12.8

Source: U.S. Census Bureau, State & Local Government Finances 2022

TAXES

State Corporate Income Tax Rates

State	Tax Rate (%)	Income Brackets ($)	Num. of Brackets	Financial Institution Tax Rate (%)[a]	Federal Income Tax Ded.
Florida	5.5	Flat rate	1	5.5	No

Note: Tax rates for tax year 2024; (a) Rates listed are the corporate income tax rate applied to financial institutions or excise taxes based on income. Some states have other taxes based upon the value of deposits or shares.
Source: Federation of Tax Administrators, State Corporate Income Tax Rates, January 1, 2025

State Individual Income Tax Rates

State	Tax Rate (%)	Income Brackets ($)	Personal Exemptions ($)			Standard Ded. ($)	
			Single	Married	Depend.	Single	Married
Florida			– No state income tax –				

Note: Tax rates for tax year 2024; Local- and county-level taxes are not included
Source: Federation of Tax Administrators, State Individual Income Tax Rates, January 1, 2025

Various State Sales and Excise Tax Rates

State	State Sales Tax (%)	Gasoline[1] ($/gal.)	Cigarette[2] ($/pack)	Spirits[3] ($/gal.)	Wine[4] ($/gal.)	Beer[5] ($/gal.)	Recreational Marijuana (%)
Florida	6	0.39	1.34	6.50	2.25	0.48	Not legal

Note: All tax rates as of January 1, 2025; (1) The American Petroleum Institute has developed a methodology for determining the average tax rate on a gallon of fuel. Rates may include any of the following: excise taxes, environmental fees, storage tank fees, other fees or taxes, general sales tax, and local taxes; (2) The federal excise tax of $1.0066 per pack and local taxes are not included; (3) Rates are those applicable to off-premise sales of 40% alcohol by volume (a.b.v.) distilled spirits in 750ml containers. Local excise taxes are excluded; (4) Rates are those applicable to off-premise sales of 11% a.b.v. non-carbonated wine in 750ml containers; (5) Rates are those applicable to off-premise sales of 4.7% a.b.v. beer in 12 ounce containers.
Source: Tax Foundation, 2025 Facts & Figures: How Does Your State Compare?

State Tax Competitiveness Index

State	Overall Rank	Corporate Tax Rank	Individual Income Tax Rank	Sales Tax Rank	Property Tax Rank	Unemployment Insurance Tax Rank
Florida	4	16	1	14	21	10

Note: The Tax Foundation's State Tax Competitiveness Index enables policymakers, taxpayers, and business leaders to gauge how their states' tax systems compare. A rank of 1 is best, 50 is worst. Rankings do not average to the total. States without a tax rank equally as 1. DC's scores and rankings do not affect other states. The report shows tax systems as of July 1, 2024 (the beginning of Fiscal Year 2025).
Source: Tax Foundation, State Tax Competitiveness Index 2025

TRANSPORTATION

Means of Transportation to Work

Area	Car/Truck/Van		Public Transportation			Bicycle	Walked	Other Means	Worked at Home
	Drove Alone	Carpooled	Bus	Subway	Railroad				
City	66.1	8.2	1.3	0.0	0.0	0.8	2.3	2.1	19.3
MSA[1]	69.7	8.1	0.8	0.0	0.0	0.5	1.2	1.8	17.8
U.S.	70.2	8.5	1.7	1.3	0.4	0.4	2.4	1.6	13.5

Note: Figures are percentages and cover workers 16 years of age and older; (1) Figures cover the Tampa-St. Petersburg-Clearwater, FL Metropolitan Statistical Area
Source: U.S. Census Bureau, 2019-2023 American Community Survey 5-Year Estimates

Travel Time to Work

Area	Less Than 10 Minutes	10 to 19 Minutes	20 to 29 Minutes	30 to 44 Minutes	45 to 59 Minutes	60 to 89 Minutes	90 Minutes or More
City	10.8	31.4	22.8	22.5	6.5	4.2	1.8
MSA[1]	9.6	26.6	20.9	23.8	10.2	6.5	2.5
U.S.	12.6	28.6	21.2	20.8	8.1	6.0	2.8

Note: Note: Figures are percentages and include workers 16 years old and over; (1) Figures cover the Tampa-St. Petersburg-Clearwater, FL Metropolitan Statistical Area
Source: U.S. Census Bureau, 2019-2023 American Community Survey 5-Year Estimates

Key Congestion Measures

Measure	2000	2010	2015	2020	2022
Annual Hours of Delay, Total (000)	45,586	70,452	83,008	34,479	101,021
Annual Hours of Delay, Per Auto Commuter	36	42	47	18	57
Annual Congestion Cost, Per Auto Commuter ($)	843	1,035	1,115	448	1,285

Note: Figures cover the Tampa-St. Petersburg FL urban area
Source: Texas A&M Transportation Institute, 2023 Urban Mobility Report

Freeway Travel Time Index

Measure	1985	1990	1995	2000	2005	2010	2015	2020	2022
Urban Area Index[1]	1.12	1.15	1.18	1.19	1.22	1.21	1.22	1.08	1.24
Urban Area Rank[1,2]	21	22	26	32	33	34	34	44	22

Note: Freeway Travel Time Index—the ratio of travel time in the peak period to the travel time at free-flow conditions. For example, a value of 1.30 indicates a 20-minute free-flow trip takes 26 minutes in the peak (20 minutes x 1.30 = 26 minutes); (1) Covers the Tampa-St. Petersburg FL urban area; (2) Rank is based on 101 larger urban areas (#1 = highest travel time index)
Source: Texas A&M Transportation Institute, 2023 Urban Mobility Report

Public Transportation

Agency Name / Mode of Transportation	Vehicles Operated in Maximum Service[1]	Annual Unlinked Passenger Trips[2] (in thous.)	Annual Passenger Miles[3] (in thous.)
Hillsborough Area Regional Transit Authority (HART)			
Bus (directly operated)	99	11,062.4	49,514.0
Demand Response (directly operated)	45	202.0	2,132.5
Demand Response - Taxi	32	28.8	132.1
Streetcar Rail (directly operated)	5	1,281.4	1,713.3

Note: (1) Number of revenue vehicles operated by the given mode and type of service to meet the annual maximum service requirement. This is the revenue vehicle count during the peak season of the year; on the week and day that maximum service is provided. Vehicles operated in maximum service (VOMS) exclude atypical days and one-time special events; (2) Number of passengers who boarded public transportation vehicles. Passengers are counted each time they board a vehicle no matter how many vehicles they use to travel from their origin to their destination. (3) Sum of the distances ridden by all passengers during the entire fiscal year.
Source: Federal Transit Administration, National Transit Database, 2023

Air Transportation

Airport Name and Code / Type of Service	Passenger Airlines[1]	Passenger Enplanements	Freight Carriers[2]	Freight (lbs)
Tampa International (TPA)				
Domestic service (U.S. carriers only)	27	11,362,891	11	82,369,911
International service (U.S. carriers only)	14	167,424	1	264,759

Note: (1) Includes all U.S.-based major, minor and commuter airlines that carried at least one passenger during the year; (2) Includes all U.S.-based airlines and freight carriers that transported at least one pound of freight during the year.
Source: Bureau of Transportation Statistics, The Intermodal Transportation Database, Air Carriers: T-100 Domestic Market (U.S. carriers only), 2024; Bureau of Transportation Statistics, The Intermodal Transportation Database, Air Carriers: T-100 International Market (U.S. carriers only), 2024

BUSINESSES

Major Business Headquarters

Company Name	Industry	Rankings Fortune[1]	Rankings Forbes[2]
Coca-Cola Beverages Florida	Consumer durables	-	264
Crown Holdings	Packaging, containers	344	-
Mosaic	Chemicals	307	-

Note: (1) Companies that produce a 10-K are ranked 1 to 500 based on 2023 revenue; (2) All private companies with at least $2 billion in annual revenue through the end of their most current fiscal year are ranked 1 to 275; companies listed are headquartered in the city; dashes indicate no ranking
Source: Fortune, "Fortune 500," 2024; Forbes, "America's Largest Private Companies," 2024

Fastest-Growing Businesses

According to *Inc.*, Tampa is home to seven of America's 500 fastest-growing private companies: **KashKick** (#11); **Rise8** (#268); **Lawnline Marketing** (#306); **Greenlife Healthcare Staffing** (#331); **Ground Game Health** (#447); **Ridge IT Cyber** (#452); **Premier Metal Roof Manufacturing** (#474). Criteria: must be an independent, privately-held, for-profit, U.S. corporation, proprietorship or partnership as of December 31, 2023; revenues must be at least $100,000 in 2020 and $2 million in 2023; must have four-year operating/sales history. *Inc., "America's 500 Fastest-Growing Private Companies," 2024*

According to Deloitte, Tampa is home to one of North America's 500 fastest-growing high-technology companies: **Branch** (#223). Companies are ranked by percentage growth in revenue over a four-year period. Criteria for inclusion: company must be headquartered within North America; must own proprietary intellectual property or technology that is sold to customers in products that contributes to a significant portion of the company's operating revenue; must have been in business for a minumum of four years with 2020 operating revenues of at least $50,000 USD/CD and 2023 operating revenues of at least $5 million USD/CD. *Deloitte, 2024 Technology Fast 500™*

Living Environment

COST OF LIVING

Cost of Living Index

Composite Index	Groceries	Housing	Utilities	Transportation	Health Care	Misc. Goods/ Services
97.6	105.7	95.8	99.9	102.1	93.1	94.4

Note: The Cost of Living Index measures regional differences in the cost of consumer goods and services, excluding taxes and non-consumer expenditures, for professional and managerial households in the top income quintile. It is based on more than 50,000 prices covering almost 60 different items for which prices are collected three times a year by chambers of commerce, economic development organizations or university applied economic centers in each participating urban area. The numbers shown should be read as a percentage above or below the national average of 100. For example, a value of 115.4 in the groceries column indicates that grocery prices are 15.4% higher than the national average. Small differences in the index numbers should not be interpreted as significant; Figures cover the Tampa FL urban area.
Source: The Council for Community and Economic Research, Cost of Living Index, 2024

Grocery Prices

Area[1]	T-Bone Steak ($/pound)	Frying Chicken ($/pound)	Whole Milk ($/half gal.)	Eggs ($/dozen)	Orange Juice ($/64 oz.)	Coffee ($/11.5 oz.)
City[2]	15.52	1.46	4.73	3.60	4.59	5.56
Avg.	15.42	1.55	4.69	3.25	4.41	5.46
Min.	14.50	1.16	4.43	2.75	4.00	4.85
Max.	17.56	2.89	5.49	4.78	5.54	7.89

Note: (1) Values for the local area are compared with the average, minimum and maximum values for all 276 areas in the Cost of Living Index; (2) Figures cover the Tampa FL urban area; **T-Bone Steak** (price per pound); **Frying Chicken** (price per pound, whole fryer); **Whole Milk** (half gallon carton); **Eggs** (price per dozen, Grade A, large); **Orange Juice** (64 oz. Tropicana or Florida Natural); **Coffee** (11.5 oz. can, vacuum-packed, Maxwell House, Hills Bros, or Folgers).
Source: The Council for Community and Economic Research, Cost of Living Index, 2024

Housing and Utility Costs

Area[1]	New Home Price ($)	Apartment Rent ($/month)	All Electric ($/month)	Part Electric ($/month)	Other Energy ($/month)	Telephone ($/month)
City[2]	455,535	1,796	203.80	-	-	197.76
Avg.	515,975	1,550	210.99	123.07	82.07	194.99
Min.	265,375	692	104.33	53.68	36.26	179.42
Max.	2,775,821	5,719	529.02	397.28	361.63	223.33

Note: (1) Values for the local area are compared with the average, minimum and maximum values for all 276 areas in the Cost of Living Index; (2) Figures cover the Tampa FL urban area; **New Home Price** (2,400 sf living area, 8,000 sf lot, in urban area with full utilities); **Apartment Rent** (950 sf 2 bedroom/1.5 or 2 bath, unfurnished, excluding all utilities except water); **All Electric** (average monthly cost for an all-electric home); **Part Electric** (average monthly cost for a part-electric home); **Other Energy** (average monthly cost for natural gas, fuel oil, coal, wood, and any other forms of energy except electricity); **Telephone** (price includes the base monthly rate plus taxes and fees for three lines of mobile phone service).
Source: The Council for Community and Economic Research, Cost of Living Index, 2024

Health Care, Transportation, and Other Costs

Area[1]	Doctor ($/visit)	Dentist ($/visit)	Optometrist ($/visit)	Gasoline ($/gallon)	Beauty Salon ($/visit)	Men's Shirt ($)
City[2]	126.57	112.70	118.00	3.36	48.00	27.91
Avg.	143.77	117.51	129.23	3.32	48.57	38.14
Min.	36.74	58.67	67.33	2.80	24.00	13.41
Max.	270.44	216.82	307.33	5.28	94.00	63.89

Note: (1) Values for the local area are compared with the average, minimum and maximum values for all 276 areas in the Cost of Living Index; (2) Figures cover the Tampa FL urban area; **Doctor** (general practitioners routine exam of an established patient); **Dentist** (adult teeth cleaning and periodic oral examination); **Optometrist** (full vision eye exam for established adult patient); **Gasoline** (one gallon regular unleaded, national brand, including all taxes, cash price at self-service pump if available); **Beauty Salon** (woman's shampoo, trim, and blow-dry); **Men's Shirt** (cotton/polyester dress shirt, pinpoint weave, long sleeves).
Source: The Council for Community and Economic Research, Cost of Living Index, 2024

HOUSING

Homeownership Rate

Area	2017 (%)	2018 (%)	2019 (%)	2020 (%)	2021 (%)	2022 (%)	2023 (%)	2024 (%)
MSA[1]	60.4	64.9	68.0	72.2	68.3	68.4	66.9	68.9
U.S.	63.9	64.4	64.6	66.6	65.5	65.8	65.9	65.6

Note: (1) Figures cover the Tampa-St. Petersburg-Clearwater, FL Metropolitan Statistical Area
Source: U.S. Census Bureau, Housing Vacancies and Homeownership Annual Statistics: 2017-2024

House Price Index (HPI)

Area	National Ranking[2]	Quarterly Change (%)	One-Year Change (%)	Five-Year Change (%)	Since 1991Q1 (%)
MSA[1]	229	-0.90	1.88	77.61	480.18
U.S.[3]	–	1.43	4.51	57.13	327.82

Note: The HPI is a weighted repeat sales index. It measures average price changes in repeat sales or refinancings on the same properties. This information is obtained by reviewing repeat mortgage transactions on single-family properties whose mortgages have been purchased or securitized by Fannie Mae or Freddie Mac since January 1975; (1) Figures cover the Tampa-St. Petersburg-Clearwater, FL Metropolitan Statistical Area; (2) Rankings are based on annual percentage change for all metro areas containing at least 15,000 transactions over the last 10 years and ranges from 1 to 241; (3) figures based on a weighted average of Census Division estimates using a seasonally adjusted, purchase-only index; all figures are for the period ending December 31, 2024
Source: Federal Housing Finance Agency, Change in FHFA Metropolitan Area House Price Indexes, All Transactions Index, 2024Q4

Home Value

Area	Under $100,000	$100,000 -$199,999	$200,000 -$299,999	$300,000 -$399,999	$400,000 -$499,999	$500,000 -$999,999	$1,000,000 or more	Median ($)
City	4.8	12.4	20.8	16.0	12.1	24.0	10.0	375,300
MSA[1]	11.5	14.4	22.9	19.3	12.1	16.0	3.8	306,100
U.S.	12.1	17.8	19.5	14.4	10.5	19.1	6.5	303,400

Note: Figures are percentages except for median and cover owner-occupied housing units; (1) Figures cover the Tampa-St. Petersburg-Clearwater, FL Metropolitan Statistical Area
Source: U.S. Census Bureau, 2019-2023 American Community Survey 5-Year Estimates

Year Housing Structure Built

Area	2020 or Later	2010 -2019	2000 -2009	1990 -1999	1980 -1989	1970 -1979	1960 -1969	1950 -1959	1940 -1949	Before 1940	Median Year
City	1.8	13.8	16.5	10.7	11.7	10.3	9.1	12.9	4.9	8.3	1984
MSA[1]	1.6	10.2	15.4	13.0	19.8	18.9	8.7	7.9	1.9	2.5	1985
U.S.	1.2	8.9	13.6	12.8	13.0	14.4	10.0	9.7	4.5	11.9	1980

Note: Figures are percentages except for Median Year; Note: (1) Figures cover the Tampa-St. Petersburg-Clearwater, FL Metropolitan Statistical Area
Source: U.S. Census Bureau, 2019-2023 American Community Survey 5-Year Estimates

Gross Monthly Rent

Area	Under $500	$500 -$999	$1,000 -$1,499	$1,500 -$1,999	$2,000 -$2,499	$2,500 -$2,999	$3,000 and up	Median ($)
City	6.5	11.9	27.9	27.1	14.9	6.8	4.9	1,567
MSA[1]	3.2	13.0	34.1	27.7	13.7	4.8	3.5	1,497
U.S.	6.5	22.3	29.5	20.2	10.8	4.8	5.9	1,348

Note: Figures are percentages except for median; Gross rent is the contract rent plus the estimated average monthly cost of utilities (electricity, gas, and water and sewer) and fuels (oil, coal, kerosene, wood, etc.) if these are paid by the renter (or paid for the renter by someone else); (1) Figures cover the Tampa-St. Petersburg-Clearwater, FL Metropolitan Statistical Area
Source: U.S. Census Bureau, 2019-2023 American Community Survey 5-Year Estimates

HEALTH

Health Risk Factors

Category	MSA[1] (%)	U.S. (%)
Adults aged 18–64 who have any kind of health care coverage	85.4	90.8
Adults who reported being in good or better health	79.0	81.8
Adults who have been told they have high blood cholesterol	43.0	36.9
Adults who have been told they have high blood pressure	36.8	34.0
Adults who are current smokers	9.2	12.1
Adults who currently use e-cigarettes	8.9	7.7
Adults who currently use chewing tobacco, snuff, or snus	2.3	3.2
Adults who are heavy drinkers[2]	7.8	6.1
Adults who are binge drinkers[3]	16.8	15.2
Adults who are overweight (BMI 25.0 - 29.9)	35.5	34.4
Adults who are obese (BMI 30.0 - 99.8)	30.2	34.3
Adults who participated in any physical activities in the past month	75.4	75.8

Note: All figures are crude prevalence; (1) Figures cover the Tampa-St. Petersburg-Clearwater, FL Metropolitan Statistical Area; (2) Heavy drinkers are classified as adult men having more than 14 drinks per week and adult women having more than 7 drinks per week; (3) Binge drinkers are classified as males having five or more drinks on one occasion or females having four or more drinks on one occasion
Source: Centers for Disease Control and Prevention, Behavioral Risk Factor Surveillance System, SMART: Selected Metropolitan Area Risk Trends, 2023

Acute and Chronic Health Conditions

Category	MSA[1] (%)	U.S. (%)
Adults who have ever been told they had a heart attack	4.8	4.2
Adults who have ever been told they have angina or coronary heart disease	5.6	4.0
Adults who have ever been told they had a stroke	4.1	3.3
Adults who have ever been told they have asthma	15.8	15.7
Adults who have ever been told they have arthritis	28.1	26.3
Adults who have ever been told they have diabetes[2]	14.2	11.5
Adults who have ever been told they had skin cancer	9.8	5.6
Adults who have ever been told they had any other types of cancer	9.0	8.4
Adults who have ever been told they have COPD	7.6	6.4
Adults who have ever been told they have kidney disease	4.9	3.7
Adults who have ever been told they have a form of depression	20.4	22.0

Note: All figures are crude prevalence; (1) Figures cover the Tampa-St. Petersburg-Clearwater, FL Metropolitan Statistical Area; (2) Figures do not include pregnancy-related, borderline, or pre-diabetes
Source: Centers for Disease Control and Prevention, Behavioral Risk Factor Surveillance System, SMART: Selected Metropolitan Area Risk Trends, 2023

Health Screening and Vaccination Rates

Category	MSA[1] (%)	U.S. (%)
Adults who have ever been tested for HIV	41.8	37.5
Adults who have had their blood cholesterol checked within the last five years	88.9	87.0
Adults aged 65+ who have had flu shot within the past year	60.2	63.4
Adults aged 65+ who have ever had a pneumonia vaccination	65.6	71.9

Note: All figures are crude prevalence; (1) Figures cover the Tampa-St. Petersburg-Clearwater, FL Metropolitan Statistical Area.
Source: Centers for Disease Control and Prevention, Behavioral Risk Factor Surveillance System, SMART: Selected Metropolitan Area Risk Trends, 2023

Disability Status

Category	MSA[1] (%)	U.S. (%)
Adults who reported being deaf	8.4	7.4
Are you blind or have serious difficulty seeing, even when wearing glasses?	8.5	4.9
Do you have difficulty doing errands alone?	9.7	7.8
Do you have difficulty dressing or bathing?	5.2	3.6
Do you have serious difficulty concentrating/remembering/making decisions?	12.8	13.7
Do you have serious difficulty walking or climbing stairs?	17.8	13.2

Note: All figures are crude prevalence; (1) Figures cover the Tampa-St. Petersburg-Clearwater, FL Metropolitan Statistical Area.
Source: Centers for Disease Control and Prevention, Behavioral Risk Factor Surveillance System, SMART: Selected Metropolitan Area Risk Trends, 2023

Mortality Rates for the Top 10 Causes of Death in the U.S.

ICD-10[a] Sub-Chapter	ICD-10[a] Code	Crude Mortality Rate[2] per 100,000 population	
		County[3]	U.S.
Malignant neoplasms	C00-C97	158.3	182.7
Ischaemic heart diseases	I20-I25	98.1	109.6
Provisional assignment of new diseases of uncertain etiology[1]	U00-U49	57.1	65.3
Other forms of heart disease	I30-I51	41.9	65.1
Other degenerative diseases of the nervous system	G30-G31	52.4	52.4
Other external causes of accidental injury	W00-X59	57.2	52.3
Cerebrovascular diseases	I60-I69	41.7	49.1
Chronic lower respiratory diseases	J40-J47	32.8	43.5
Hypertensive diseases	I10-I15	41.5	38.9
Organic, including symptomatic, mental disorders	F01-F09	27.5	33.9

Note: (a) ICD-10 = International Classification of Diseases 10th Revision; (1) Includes COVID-19, adverse effects to COVID-19 vaccines, SARS, and vaping-related disorders; (2) Crude mortality rates are a three-year average covering 2021-2023; (3) Figures cover Hillsborough County.
Source: Centers for Disease Control and Prevention, National Center for Health Statistics. National Vital Statistics System, Mortality 2018-2023 on CDC WONDER Online Database

Mortality Rates for Selected Causes of Death

Cause of Death	ICD-10[a] Code	Crude Mortality Rate[1] per 100,000 population	
		County[2]	U.S.
Accidental poisoning and exposure to noxious substances	X40-X49	34.3	30.5
Alzheimer disease	G30	22.1	35.4
Assault	X85-Y09	6.5	7.3
COVID-19	U07.1	57.1	65.3
Diabetes mellitus	E10-E14	26.6	30.0
Diseases of the liver	K70-K76	16.7	20.8
Human immunodeficiency virus (HIV) disease	B20-B24	2.7	1.5
Influenza and pneumonia	J09-J18	13.1	13.4
Intentional self-harm	X60-X84	14.3	14.7
Malnutrition	E40-E46	2.8	6.0
Obesity and other hyperalimentation	E65-E68	2.3	3.1
Renal failure	N17-N19	12.1	16.4
Transport accidents	V01-V99	16.4	14.4

Note: (a) ICD-10 = International Classification of Diseases 10th Revision; (1) Crude mortality rates are a three-year average covering 2021-2023; (2) Figures cover Hillsborough County; Data are suppressed when the data meet the criteria for confidentiality constraints; Crude mortality rates are flagged as unreliable when the rate would be calculated with a numerator of 20 or less.
Source: Centers for Disease Control and Prevention, National Center for Health Statistics. National Vital Statistics System, Mortality 2018-2023 on CDC WONDER Online Database

Health Insurance Coverage

Area	With Health Insurance	With Private Health Insurance	With Public Health Insurance	Without Health Insurance	Population Under Age 19 Without Health Insurance
City	89.0	64.5	32.0	11.0	5.7
MSA[1]	88.9	64.2	36.5	11.1	6.0
U.S.	91.4	67.3	36.3	8.6	5.4

Note: Figures are percentages that cover the civilian noninstitutionalized population; (1) Figures cover the Tampa-St. Petersburg-Clearwater, FL Metropolitan Statistical Area
Source: U.S. Census Bureau, 2019-2023 American Community Survey 5-Year Estimates

Number of Medical Professionals

Area	MDs[3]	DOs[3,4]	Dentists	Podiatrists	Chiropractors	Optometrists
County[1] (number)	5,678	623	1,015	103	450	249
County[1] (rate[2])	375.2	41.2	66.1	6.7	29.3	16.2
U.S. (rate[2])	302.5	29.2	74.6	6.4	29.5	18.0

Note: Data as of 2023 unless noted; (1) Data covers Hillsborough County; (2) Number of medical professionals per 100,000 population; (3) Data as of 2022 and includes all active, non-federal physicians; (4) Doctor of Osteopathic Medicine
Source: U.S. Department of Health and Human Services, Health Resources and Services Administration, Bureau of Health Professions, Area Resource File (ARF) 2023-2024

Best Hospitals

According to *U.S. News,* the Tampa-St. Petersburg-Clearwater, FL metro area is home to three of the best hospitals in the U.S.: **Florida Orthopaedic Institute at Tampa General Hospital** (8 adult specialties); **H. Lee Moffitt Cancer Center and Research Institute** (1 adult specialty); **Tampa General Hospital** (8 adult specialties). The hospitals listed were nationally ranked in at least one of 15 adult or 11 pediatric specialties. The number of specialties shown cover the parent hospital. Only 160 U.S. hospitals performed well enough to be nationally ranked in one or more specialties. Twenty hospitals in the U.S. made the Honor Roll. The Best Hospitals Honor Roll takes both the national rankings and the procedure and condition ratings into account. Hospitals received points if they were nationally ranked in one of the 15 adult specialties—the higher they ranked, the more points they got—and how many ratings of "high performing" they earned in the 20 procedures and conditions. *U.S. News Online, "America's Best Hospitals 2024-25"*

According to *U.S. News,* the Tampa-St. Petersburg-Clearwater, FL metro area is home to one of the best children's hospitals in the U.S.: **Johns Hopkins All Children's Hospital** (6 pediatric specialties). The hospital listed was highly ranked in at least one of 11 pediatric specialties. One hundred five children's hospitals in the U.S. were nationally ranked in at least one specialty. Hospitals received points for being ranked in a specialty, and the 10 hospitals with the most points across the 11 specialties make up the Honor Roll. *U.S. News Online, "America's Best Children's Hospitals 2024-25"*

EDUCATION

Public School District Statistics

District Name	Schls	Pupils	Pupil/ Teacher Ratio	Minority Pupils[1] (%)	Total Rev. per Pupil ($)	Total Exp. per Pupil ($)
Hillsborough	305	224,152	18.3	70.3	12,612	11,744

Note: Table includes school districts with 2,000 or more students; (1) Percentage of students that are not non-Hispanic white.
Source: U.S. Department of Education, National Center for Education Statistics, Common Core of Data, Local Education Agency (School District) Universe Survey: School Year 2023-2024; U.S. Department of Education, National Center for Education Statistics, Common Core of Data, School District Finance Survey (F-33): School Year 2021–22

Best High Schools

According to *U.S. News,* Tampa is home to one of the top 500 high schools in the U.S.: **Plant High School** (#478). Nearly 25,000 public, magnet and charter schools were ranked based on their performance on state assessments and how well they prepare students for college. *U.S. News & World Report, "Best High Schools 2024"*

Highest Level of Education

Area	Less than H.S.	H.S. Diploma	Some College, No Deg.	Associate Degree	Bachelor's Degree	Master's Degree	Prof. School Degree	Doctorate Degree
City	10.2	22.5	14.7	8.0	26.3	11.7	4.4	2.2
MSA[1]	9.1	27.4	19.4	10.0	21.5	8.9	2.2	1.3
U.S.	10.6	26.2	19.4	8.8	21.3	9.8	2.3	1.6

Note: Figures cover persons age 25 and over; (1) Figures cover the Tampa-St. Petersburg-Clearwater, FL Metropolitan Statistical Area
Source: U.S. Census Bureau, 2019-2023 American Community Survey 5-Year Estimates

Educational Attainment by Race

Area	High School Graduate or Higher (%)					Bachelor's Degree or Higher (%)				
	Total	White	Black	Asian	Hisp.[2]	Total	White	Black	Asian	Hisp.[2]
City	89.8	94.4	85.6	90.4	80.9	44.6	56.0	20.5	68.9	29.4
MSA[1]	90.9	93.1	89.2	86.4	82.3	34.0	35.4	26.6	54.2	25.9
U.S.	89.4	92.9	88.1	88.0	72.5	35.0	37.7	24.7	57.0	19.9

Note: Figures shown cover persons 25 years old and over; (1) Figures cover the Tampa-St. Petersburg-Clearwater, FL Metropolitan Statistical Area; (2) People of Hispanic origin can be of any race
Source: U.S. Census Bureau, 2019-2023 American Community Survey 5-Year Estimates

School Enrollment by Grade and Control

Area	Preschool (%)		Kindergarten (%)		Grades 1 - 4 (%)		Grades 5 - 8 (%)		Grades 9 - 12 (%)	
	Public	Private	Public	Private	Public	Private	Public	Private	Public	Private
City	46.6	53.4	86.5	13.5	86.6	13.4	81.5	18.5	83.5	16.5
MSA[1]	54.3	45.7	82.4	17.6	84.7	15.3	84.3	15.7	86.4	13.6
U.S.	58.7	41.3	85.2	14.8	87.2	12.8	87.9	12.1	89.0	11.0

Note: Figures shown cover persons 3 years old and over; (1) Figures cover the Tampa-St. Petersburg-Clearwater, FL Metropolitan Statistical Area
Source: U.S. Census Bureau, 2019-2023 American Community Survey 5-Year Estimates

Higher Education

Four-Year Colleges			Two-Year Colleges			Medical Schools[1]	Law Schools[2]	Voc/ Tech[3]
Public	Private Non-profit	Private For-profit	Public	Private Non-profit	Private For-profit			
4	7	6	5	1	2	1	2	15

Note: Figures cover institutions located within the Tampa-St. Petersburg-Clearwater, FL Metropolitan Statistical Area and include main campuses only; (1) includes schools accredited by the Liaison Committee on Medical Education and the American Osteopathic Association's Commission on Osteopathic College Accreditation; (2) includes ABA-accredited schools, schools with provisional ABA accreditation, and state accredited schools; (3) includes all schools with programs that are less than 2 years.
Source: National Center for Education Statistics, Integrated Postsecondary Education System (IPEDS), 2023-24; Wikipedia, List of Medical Schools in the United States, accessed May 2, 2025; Wikipedia, List of Law Schools in the United States, accessed May 2, 2025

According to *U.S. News & World Report,* the Tampa-St. Petersburg-Clearwater, FL metro area is home to one of the top 200 national universities in the U.S.: **University of South Florida** (#91 tie). The indicators used to capture academic quality fall into a number of categories: assessment by administrators at peer institutions; retention of students; faculty resources; student selectivity; financial resources; alumni giving; high school counselor ratings of colleges; and graduation rate. *U.S. News & World Report, "America's Best Colleges 2025"*

According to *U.S. News & World Report,* the Tampa-St. Petersburg-Clearwater, FL metro area is home to one of the top 100 law schools in the U.S.: **Stetson University** (#99 tie). The rankings are based on a weighted average of 12 measures of quality: peer assessment score; assessment score by lawyers/judges; median LSAT scores; median undergrad GPA; acceptance rate; employment rates for graduates; placement success; bar passage rate; faculty resources; expenditures per student; student/faculty ratio; and library resources. *U.S. News & World Report, "America's Best Graduate Schools, Law, 2025"*

According to *U.S. News & World Report,* the Tampa-St. Petersburg-Clearwater, FL metro area is home to one of the top medical schools for research in the U.S.: **University of South Florida (Morsani)** (Tier 1). *U.S. News* placed medical and osteopathic schools into tiers based on their research productivity, faculty and admissions data. Each school's tier was derived from its overall score, calculated by summing the weighted normalized values generated across several factors of academic quality, outlined below. There are four tiers, with tier 1 medical schools as the highest-performing and tier 4 as the lowest-performing. Only tier 1 and 2 schools are shown. Because of the tier presentation, *U.S. News* calculated overall scores based on their percentile performance among all rated schools instead of dividing against the rescaled score of the No. 1-performing schools. Tier 1 included schools with overall scores of 85 to 99. The cutoffs for tiers 2 through 4 were schools scoring 50 to 84, 15 to 49 and 1 to 14, respectively. The rankings are based on a weighted average of the following measures of quality: total research activity; average research activity per faculty member; total NIH research grants at the medical school and its affiliated hospitals; average NIH research grants per faculty; median MCAT total score; median undergraduate GPA; acceptance rate; and faculty resources. *U.S. News & World Report, "America's Best Graduate Schools, Medical, 2025"*

EMPLOYERS

Major Employers

Company Name	Industry
Baycare Health System	General medical & surgical hospitals
Beall's	Manufacturing
Busch Gardens	Arts, entertainment & recreation
Caspers Company	Accommodation & food services
Citi	Finance & insurance
Florida Hospital	Healthcare & social assistance
Gerdau Ameristeel US	Manufacturing
HCA Healthcare	Healthcare & social assistance
Home Shopping Network	Information
JPMorgan Chase	Finance & insurance
MacDill Air Force Base	Public administration
Moffitt Cancer Center & Research Institute	Healthcare & social assistance
Progressive	Finance & insurance
Publix Supermarkets	Retail grocery
Raymond James Financial	Finance & insurance
Tampa General Hospital	Healthcare & social assistance
Tech Data Corp	Wholesale trade
University of South Florida	Educational services
Verizon	Information
WellCare	Finance & insurance

Note: Companies shown are located within the Tampa-St. Petersburg-Clearwater, FL Metropolitan Statistical Area.
Source: Chambers of Commerce; State Departments of Labor; Wikipedia

Best Companies to Work For

Schellman, headquartered in Tampa, is among "Fortune's Best Workplaces for Parents." To pick the best companies, *Fortune* partnered with the Great Place to Work Institute. To be considered for the list, companies must be Great Place To Work-Certified and have at least 50 responses from parents in the US. The survey enables employees to share confidential quantitative and qualitative feedback about their organization's culture by responding to 60 statements on a 5-point scale and answering two open-ended questions. Collectively, these statements describe a great employee experience, defined by high levels of trust, respect, credibility, fairness, pride, and camaraderie. In addition, companies provide organizational data like size, location, industry, demographics, roles, and levels; and provide information about parental leave, adoption, flexible schedule, childcare and dependent health care benefits. *Fortune, "Best Workplaces for Parents," 2024*

AnswerFirst Communications; Baldwin Risk Partners; Kforce, headquartered in Tampa, are among "Fortune's Best Workplaces for Women." To pick the best companies, *Fortune* partnered with the Great Place to Work Institute. To be considered for the list, companies must be Great Place To Work-Certified. Companies must also employ at least 50 women, at least 20% of their non-executive managers must be female, and at least one executive must be female. To determine the Best Workplaces for Women, Great Place To Work measured the differences in women's survey responses to those of their peers and assesses the impact of demographics and roles on the quality and consistency of women's experiences. Great Place To Work also analyzed the gender balance of each workplace, how it compared to each company's industry, and patterns in representation as women rise from front-line positions to the board of directors. *Fortune, "Best Workplaces for Women," 2024*

H. Lee Moffitt Cancer Center & Research Institute, headquartered in Tampa, is among the "Best Places to Work in IT." To qualify, companies had to have a minimum of 100 total employees and five IT employees. The best places to work were selected based on DEI (diversity, equity, and inclusion) practices; IT turnover, promotions, and growth; IT retention and engagement programs; remote/hybrid working; benefits and perks (such as elder care and child care, flextime, and reimbursement for college tuition); and training and career development opportunities. *Computerworld, "Best Places to Work in IT," 2025*

PUBLIC SAFETY

Crime Rate

Area	Total Crime Rate	Violent Crime Rate				Property Crime Rate		
		Murder	Rape	Robbery	Aggrav. Assault	Burglary	Larceny-Theft	Motor Vehicle Theft
City	2,115.0	10.2	42.4	65.4	341.8	194.1	1,272.2	188.9
U.S.	2,290.9	5.7	38.0	66.5	264.1	250.7	1,347.2	318.7

Note: Figures are crimes per 100,000 population.
Source: FBI, Table 8, Offenses Known to Law Enforcement, by State by City, 2023

Hate Crimes

Area	Number of Quarters Reported	Number of Incidents per Bias Motivation					
		Race/Ethnicity/Ancestry	Religion	Sexual Orientation	Disability	Gender	Gender Identity
City	4	1	2	0	0	0	0
U.S.	4	5,900	2,699	2,077	187	92	492

Source: Federal Bureau of Investigation, Hate Crime Statistics 2023

Identity Theft Consumer Reports

Area	Reports	Reports per 100,000 Population	Rank[2]
MSA[1]	13,953	431	17
U.S.	1,135,291	339	-

Note: (1) Figures cover the Tampa-St. Petersburg-Clearwater, FL Metropolitan Statistical Area; (2) Rank ranges from 1 to 401 where 1 indicates greatest number of identity theft reports per 100,000 population
Source: Federal Trade Commission, Consumer Sentinel Network Data Book 2024

Fraud and Other Consumer Reports

Area	Reports	Reports per 100,000 Population	Rank[2]
MSA[1]	66,454	2,051	9
U.S.	5,360,641	1,601	-

Note: (1) Figures cover the Tampa-St. Petersburg-Clearwater, FL Metropolitan Statistical Area; (2) Rank ranges from 1 to 401 where 1 indicates greatest number of fraud and other consumer reports per 100,000 population
Source: Federal Trade Commission, Consumer Sentinel Network Data Book 2024

POLITICS

2024 Presidential Election Results

Area	Trump (Rep.)	Harris (Dem.)	Stein (Green)	Kennedy (Ind.)	Oliver (Lib.)	Other
Hillsborough County	50.7	47.6	0.6	0.0	0.4	0.7
U.S.	49.7	48.2	0.6	0.5	0.4	0.6

Note: Results are percentages and may not add to 100% due to rounding
Source: Dave Leip's Atlas of U.S. Presidential Elections

SPORTS

Professional Sports Teams

Team Name	League	Year Established
Tampa Bay Buccaneers	National Football League (NFL)	1976
Tampa Bay Lightning	National Hockey League (NHL)	1993
Tampa Bay Rays	Major League Baseball (MLB)	1998

Note: Includes teams located in the Tampa-St. Petersburg-Clearwater, FL Metropolitan Statistical Area.
Source: Wikipedia, Major Professional Sports Teams of the United States and Canada, May 1, 2025

CLIMATE

Average and Extreme Temperatures

Temperature	Jan	Feb	Mar	Apr	May	Jun	Jul	Aug	Sep	Oct	Nov	Dec	Yr.
Extreme High (°F)	85	88	91	93	98	99	97	98	96	94	90	86	99
Average High (°F)	70	72	76	82	87	90	90	90	89	84	77	72	82
Average Temp. (°F)	60	62	67	72	78	81	82	83	81	75	68	62	73
Average Low (°F)	50	52	56	61	67	73	74	74	73	66	57	52	63
Extreme Low (°F)	21	24	29	40	49	53	63	67	57	40	23	18	18

Note: Figures cover the years 1948-1990
Source: National Climatic Data Center, International Station Meteorological Climate Summary, 9/96

Average Precipitation/Snowfall/Humidity

Precip./Humidity	Jan	Feb	Mar	Apr	May	Jun	Jul	Aug	Sep	Oct	Nov	Dec	Yr.
Avg. Precip. (in.)	2.1	2.8	3.5	1.8	3.0	5.6	7.3	7.9	6.5	2.3	1.8	2.1	46.7
Avg. Snowfall (in.)	Tr	Tr	Tr	0	0	0	0	0	0	0	0	Tr	Tr
Avg. Rel. Hum. 7am (%)	87	87	86	86	85	86	88	90	91	89	88	87	88
Avg. Rel. Hum. 4pm (%)	56	55	54	51	52	60	65	66	64	57	56	57	58

Note: Figures cover the years 1948-1990; Tr = Trace amounts (<0.05 in. of rain; <0.5 in. of snow)
Source: National Climatic Data Center, International Station Meteorological Climate Summary, 9/96

Weather Conditions

Temperature			Daytime Sky			Precipitation		
32°F & below	45°F & below	90°F & above	Clear	Partly cloudy	Cloudy	0.01 inch or more precip.	0.1 inch or more snow/ice	Thunderstorms
3	35	85	81	204	80	107	<1	87

Note: Figures are average number of days per year and cover the years 1948-1990
Source: National Climatic Data Center, International Station Meteorological Climate Summary, 9/96

HAZARDOUS WASTE

Superfund Sites

The Tampa, FL metro division is home to 14 sites on the EPA's Superfund National Priorities List (NPL) or Superfund Alternative Approach (SAA) list: **Alaric Area Gw Plume** (Final NPL); **Arkla Terra Property** (Final NPL); **Coronet Industries** (SAA); **Helena Chemical Co. (Tampa Plant)** (Final NPL); **JJ Seifert Machine** (Final NPL); **MRI Corp (Tampa)** (Final NPL); **Normandy Park Apartments** (Proposed NPL); **Peak Oil Co./Bay Drum Co.** (Final NPL); **Raleigh Street Dump** (Final NPL); **Reeves Southeastern Galvanizing Corp.** (Final NPL); **Southern Solvents, Inc.** (Final NPL); **Stauffer Chemical Co (Tampa)** (Final NPL); **Sydney Mine Sludge Ponds** (Final NPL); **Taylor Road Landfill** (Final NPL). The Superfund alternative approach uses the same investigation and cleanup process and standards that are used for sites listed on the National Priorities List. The SAA is an alternative to listing a site on the NPL; it is not an alternative to Superfund or the Superfund process. There are a total of 1,445 Superfund sites with a status of proposed or final on both lists in the United States. *U.S. Environmental Protection Agency, National Priorities List, May 1, 2025; U.S. Environmental Protection Agency, Superfund Alternative Approach Sites, May 1, 2025*

AIR QUALITY

Air Quality Trends: Ozone

	1990	1995	2000	2005	2010	2015	2020	2021	2022	2023
MSA[1]	0.080	0.075	0.081	0.075	0.067	0.062	0.063	0.060	0.061	0.066
U.S.	0.087	0.089	0.081	0.080	0.072	0.068	0.066	0.067	0.067	0.070

Note: (1) Data covers the Tampa-St. Petersburg-Clearwater, FL Metropolitan Statistical Area. The values shown are the composite ozone concentration averages among trend sites based on the highest fourth daily maximum 8-hour concentration in parts per million. These trends are based on sites having an adequate record of monitoring data during the trend period. Data from exceptional events are included.
Source: U.S. Environmental Protection Agency, Air Quality Monitoring Information, "Air Quality Trends by City, 1990-2023"

Air Quality Index

Area	Percent of Days when Air Quality was...[2]					AQI Statistics[2]	
	Good	Moderate	Unhealthy for Sensitive Groups	Unhealthy	Very Unhealthy	Maximum	Median
MSA[1]	39.5	59.2	1.4	0.0	0.0	114	52

Note: (1) Data covers the Tampa-St. Petersburg-Clearwater, FL Metropolitan Statistical Area; (2) Based on 365 days with AQI data in 2023. Air Quality Index (AQI) is an index for reporting daily air quality. EPA calculates the AQI for five major air pollutants regulated by the Clean Air Act: ground-level ozone, particle pollution (aka particulate matter), carbon monoxide, sulfur dioxide, and nitrogen dioxide. The AQI runs from 0 to 500. The higher the AQI value, the greater the level of air pollution and the greater the health concern. There are six AQI categories: "Good" AQI is between 0 and 50. Air quality is considered satisfactory; "Moderate" AQI is between 51 and 100. Air quality is acceptable; "Unhealthy for Sensitive Groups" When AQI values are between 101 and 150, members of sensitive groups may experience health effects; "Unhealthy" When AQI values are between 151 and 200 everyone may begin to experience health effects; "Very Unhealthy" AQI values between 201 and 300 trigger a health alert; "Hazardous" AQI values over 300 trigger warnings of emergency conditions (not shown).
Source: U.S. Environmental Protection Agency, Air Quality Index Report, 2023

Air Quality Index Pollutants

Area	Percent of Days when AQI Pollutant was...[2]					
	Carbon Monoxide	Nitrogen Dioxide	Ozone	Sulfur Dioxide	Particulate Matter 2.5	Particulate Matter 10
MSA[1]	0.0	0.0	27.7	(3)	71.5	0.8

Note: (1) Data covers the Tampa-St. Petersburg-Clearwater, FL Metropolitan Statistical Area; (2) Based on 365 days with AQI data in 2023. The Air Quality Index (AQI) is an index for reporting daily air quality. EPA calculates the AQI for five major air pollutants regulated by the Clean Air Act: ground-level ozone, particle pollution (also known as particulate matter), carbon monoxide, sulfur dioxide, and nitrogen dioxide. The AQI runs from 0 to 500. The higher the AQI value, the greater the level of air pollution and the greater the health concern; (3) Sulfur dioxide is no longer included in this table because SO_2 concentrations tend to be very localized and not necessarily representative of broad geographical areas like counties and CBSAs.
Source: U.S. Environmental Protection Agency, Air Quality Index Report, 2023

Maximum Air Pollutant Concentrations: Particulate Matter, Ozone, CO and Lead

	Particulate Matter 10 (ug/m³)	Particulate Matter 2.5 Wtd AM (ug/m³)	Particulate Matter 2.5 24-Hr (ug/m³)	Ozone (ppm)	Carbon Monoxide (ppm)	Lead (ug/m³)
MSA[1] Level	76	7.8	16	0.069	1	0.05
NAAQS[2]	150	15	35	0.075	9	0.15
Met NAAQS[2]	Yes	Yes	Yes	Yes	Yes	Yes

Note: (1) Data covers the Tampa-St. Petersburg-Clearwater, FL Metropolitan Statistical Area; Data from exceptional events are included; (2) National Ambient Air Quality Standards; ppm = parts per million; ug/m³ = micrograms per cubic meter; n/a not available.
Concentrations: Particulate Matter 10 (coarse particulate)—highest second maximum 24-hour concentration; Particulate Matter 2.5 Wtd AM (fine particulate)—highest weighted annual mean concentration; Particulate Matter 2.5 24-Hour (fine particulate)—highest 98th percentile 24-hour concentration; Ozone—highest fourth daily maximum 8-hour concentration; Carbon Monoxide—highest second maximum non-overlapping 8-hour concentration; Lead—maximum running 3-month average
Source: U.S. Environmental Protection Agency, Air Quality Monitoring Information, "Air Quality Statistics by City, 2023"

Maximum Air Pollutant Concentrations: Nitrogen Dioxide and Sulfur Dioxide

	Nitrogen Dioxide AM (ppb)	Nitrogen Dioxide 1-Hr (ppb)	Sulfur Dioxide AM (ppb)	Sulfur Dioxide 1-Hr (ppb)	Sulfur Dioxide 24-Hr (ppb)
MSA[1] Level	9	36	n/a	48	n/a
NAAQS[2]	53	100	30	75	140
Met NAAQS[2]	Yes	Yes	n/a	Yes	n/a

Note: (1) Data covers the Tampa-St. Petersburg-Clearwater, FL Metropolitan Statistical Area; Data from exceptional events are included; (2) National Ambient Air Quality Standards; ppm = parts per million; ug/m³ = micrograms per cubic meter; n/a not available.
Concentrations: Nitrogen Dioxide AM—highest arithmetic mean concentration; Nitrogen Dioxide 1-Hr—highest 98th percentile 1-hour daily maximum concentration; Sulfur Dioxide AM—highest annual mean concentration; Sulfur Dioxide 1-Hr—highest 99th percentile 1-hour daily maximum concentration; Sulfur Dioxide 24-Hr—highest second maximum 24-hour concentration
Source: U.S. Environmental Protection Agency, Air Quality Monitoring Information, "Air Quality Statistics by City, 2023"

Appendixes

Appendices

Appendix A: Comparative Statistics

Table of Contents

Demographics
- Population Growth: City........................... A-4
- Population Growth: Metro Area..................... A-6
- Male/Female Ratio: City........................... A-8
- Male/Female Ratio: Metro Area.................... A-10
- Race: City...................................... A-12
- Race: Metro Area................................ A-14
- Hispanic Origin: City............................ A-16
- Hispanic Origin: Metro Area...................... A-18
- Household Size: City............................. A-20
- Household Size: Metro Area....................... A-22
- Household Relationships: City.................... A-24
- Household Relationships: Metro Area.............. A-26
- Age: City....................................... A-28
- Age: Metro Area................................. A-30
- Ancestry: City.................................. A-32
- Ancestry: Metro Area............................ A-34
- Foreign-born Population: City.................... A-36
- Foreign-born Population: Metro Area.............. A-38
- Marital Status: City............................. A-40
- Marital Status: Metro Area....................... A-42
- Disability by Age: City.......................... A-44
- Disability by Age: Metro Area.................... A-46
- Religious Groups by Family....................... A-48
- Religious Groups by Tradition.................... A-50

Economy
- Gross Metropolitan Product....................... A-52
- Economic Growth................................. A-54
- Metropolitan Area Exports........................ A-56
- Building Permits: City........................... A-58
- Building Permits: Metro Area..................... A-60
- Housing Vacancy Rates............................ A-62
- Bankruptcy Filings............................... A-64

Income and Poverty
- Income: City.................................... A-66
- Income: Metro Area.............................. A-68
- Household Income Distribution: City.............. A-70
- Household Income Distribution: Metro Area........ A-72
- Poverty Rate: City............................... A-74
- Poverty Rate: Metro Area......................... A-76

Employment and Earnings
- Employment by Industry........................... A-78
- Labor Force, Employment and Job Growth: City..... A-80
- Labor Force, Employment and Job Growth: Metro Area.... A-82
- Unemployment Rate: City.......................... A-84
- Unemployment Rate: Metro Area.................... A-86
- Average Hourly Wages: Occupations A - C.......... A-88
- Average Hourly Wages: Occupations C - E.......... A-90
- Average Hourly Wages: Occupations F - J.......... A-92
- Average Hourly Wages: Occupations L - N.......... A-94
- Average Hourly Wages: Occupations N - P.......... A-96

- Average Hourly Wages: Occupations P - S.......... A-98
- Average Hourly Wages: Occupations T - W......... A-100
- Means of Transportation to Work: City........... A-102
- Means of Transportation to Work: Metro Area..... A-104
- Travel Time to Work: City....................... A-106
- Travel Time to Work: Metro Area................. A-108

Election Results
- 2020 Presidential Election Results.............. A-110

Housing
- House Price Index (HPI)......................... A-112
- Home Value: City................................ A-114
- Home Value: Metro Area.......................... A-116
- Homeownership Rate.............................. A-118
- Year Housing Structure Built: City.............. A-120
- Year Housing Structure Built: Metro Area........ A-122
- Gross Monthly Rent: City........................ A-124
- Gross Monthly Rent: Metro Area.................. A-126

Education
- Highest Level of Education: City................ A-128
- Highest Level of Education: Metro Area.......... A-130
- School Enrollment by Grade and Control: City.... A-132
- School Enrollment by Grade and Control: Metro Area.... A-134
- Educational Attainment by Race: City............ A-136
- Educational Attainment by Race: Metro Area...... A-138

Cost of Living
- Cost of Living Index............................ A-140
- Grocery Prices.................................. A-142
- Housing and Utility Costs....................... A-144
- Health Care, Transportation, and Other Costs.... A-146

Health Care
- Number of Medical Professionals................. A-148
- Health Insurance Coverage: City................. A-150
- Health Insurance Coverage: Metro Area........... A-152

Public Safety
- Crime Rate...................................... A-154

Climate
- Temperature & Precipitation: Yearly Averages and Extremes........................... A-156
- Weather Conditions.............................. A-158

Air Quality
- Air Quality Index............................... A-160
- Air Quality Index Pollutants.................... A-162
- Air Quality Trends: Ozone....................... A-164
- Maximum Air Pollutant Concentrations: Particulate Matter, Ozone, CO and Lead......... A-166
- Maximum Air Pollutant Concentrations: Nitrogen Dioxide and Sulfur Dioxide............ A-168

Population Growth: City

City	1990 Census	2000 Census	2010 Census	2020 Census	Current Estimate[1]	Population Growth 1990-2023 (%)
Albuquerque, NM	388,375	448,607	545,852	564,559	562,488	44.8
Anchorage, AK	226,338	260,283	291,826	291,247	289,069	27.7
Ann Arbor, MI	111,018	114,024	113,934	123,851	121,179	9.2
Athens, GA	86,561	100,266	115,452	127,315	126,987	46.7
Atlanta, GA	394,092	416,474	420,003	498,715	499,287	26.7
Austin, TX	499,053	656,562	790,390	961,855	967,862	93.9
Baltimore, MD	736,014	651,154	620,961	585,708	577,193	-21.6
Billings, MT	81,812	89,847	104,170	117,116	118,321	44.6
Boise City, ID	144,317	185,787	205,671	235,684	235,701	63.3
Boston, MA	574,283	589,141	617,594	675,647	663,972	15.6
Boulder, CO	87,737	94,673	97,385	108,250	106,274	21.1
Cape Coral, FL	75,507	102,286	154,305	194,016	206,387	173.3
Cedar Rapids, IA	110,829	120,758	126,326	137,710	136,859	23.5
Charleston, SC	96,102	96,650	120,083	150,227	152,014	58.2
Charlotte, NC	428,283	540,828	731,424	874,579	886,283	106.9
Chicago, IL	2,783,726	2,896,016	2,695,598	2,746,388	2,707,648	-2.7
Cincinnati, OH	363,974	331,285	296,943	309,317	309,595	-14.9
Clarksville, TN	78,569	103,455	132,929	166,722	171,897	118.8
Cleveland, OH	505,333	478,403	396,815	372,624	367,523	-27.3
College Station, TX	53,318	67,890	93,857	120,511	122,280	129.3
Colorado Springs, CO	283,798	360,890	416,427	478,961	483,099	70.2
Columbia, MO	71,069	84,531	108,500	126,254	127,200	79.0
Columbia, SC	115,475	116,278	129,272	136,632	138,019	19.5
Columbus, OH	648,656	711,470	787,033	905,748	906,480	39.7
Dallas, TX	1,006,971	1,188,580	1,197,816	1,304,379	1,299,553	29.1
Davenport, IA	95,705	98,359	99,685	101,724	101,083	5.6
Denver, CO	467,153	554,636	600,158	715,522	713,734	52.8
Des Moines, IA	193,569	198,682	203,433	214,133	212,464	9.8
Detroit, MI	1,027,974	951,270	713,777	639,111	636,644	-38.1
Durham, NC	151,737	187,035	228,330	283,506	288,465	90.1
El Paso, TX	515,541	563,662	649,121	678,815	678,147	31.5
Eugene, OR	118,073	137,893	156,185	176,654	177,520	50.3
Fargo, ND	74,372	90,599	105,549	125,990	129,064	73.5
Fort Collins, CO	89,555	118,652	143,986	169,810	169,705	89.5
Fort Wayne, IN	205,671	205,727	253,691	263,886	266,235	29.4
Fort Worth, TX	448,311	534,694	741,206	918,915	941,311	110.0
Gainesville, FL	90,519	95,447	124,354	141,085	143,611	58.7
Green Bay, WI	96,466	102,313	104,057	107,395	106,585	10.5
Greensboro, NC	193,389	223,891	269,666	299,035	298,564	54.4
Honolulu, HI	376,465	371,657	337,256	350,964	346,323	-8.0
Houston, TX	1,697,610	1,953,631	2,099,451	2,304,580	2,300,419	35.5
Huntsville, AL	161,842	158,216	180,105	215,006	218,814	35.2
Indianapolis, IN	730,993	781,870	820,445	887,642	882,043	20.7
Jacksonville, FL	635,221	735,617	821,784	949,611	961,739	51.4
Kansas City, MO	434,967	441,545	459,787	508,090	508,233	16.8
Lafayette, LA	104,735	110,257	120,623	121,374	121,537	16.0
Las Vegas, NV	261,374	478,434	583,756	641,903	650,873	149.0
Lexington, KY	225,366	260,512	295,803	322,570	321,122	42.5
Lincoln, NE	193,629	225,581	258,379	291,082	291,932	50.8
Little Rock, AR	177,519	183,133	193,524	202,591	202,739	14.2
Los Angeles, CA	3,487,671	3,694,820	3,792,621	3,898,747	3,857,897	10.6
Louisville, KY	269,160	256,231	597,337	386,884	627,210	133.0
Madison, WI	193,451	208,054	233,209	269,840	275,568	42.4
Manchester, NH	99,567	107,006	109,565	115,644	115,415	15.9
McAllen, TX	86,145	106,414	129,877	142,210	143,789	66.9

Table continued on following page.

City	1990 Census	2000 Census	2010 Census	2020 Census	Current Estimate[1]	Population Growth 1990-2023 (%)
Memphis, TN	660,536	650,100	646,889	633,104	629,063	-4.8
Miami, FL	358,843	362,470	399,457	442,241	446,663	24.5
Midland, TX	89,358	94,996	111,147	132,524	133,998	50.0
Milwaukee, WI	628,095	596,974	594,833	577,222	569,756	-9.3
Minneapolis, MN	368,383	382,618	382,578	429,954	426,845	15.9
Nashville, TN	488,364	545,524	601,222	689,447	684,298	40.1
New Orleans, LA	496,938	484,674	343,829	383,997	376,035	-24.3
New York, NY	7,322,552	8,008,278	8,175,133	8,804,190	8,516,202	16.3
Oklahoma City, OK	445,065	506,132	579,999	681,054	688,693	54.7
Omaha, NE	371,972	390,007	408,958	486,051	488,197	31.2
Orlando, FL	161,172	185,951	238,300	307,573	311,732	93.4
Philadelphia, PA	1,585,577	1,517,550	1,526,006	1,603,797	1,582,432	-0.2
Phoenix, AZ	989,873	1,321,045	1,445,632	1,608,139	1,624,832	64.1
Pittsburgh, PA	369,785	334,563	305,704	302,971	303,620	-17.9
Portland, OR	485,833	529,121	583,776	652,503	642,715	32.3
Providence, RI	160,734	173,618	178,042	190,934	190,214	18.3
Provo, UT	87,148	105,166	112,488	115,162	114,303	31.2
Raleigh, NC	226,841	276,093	403,892	467,665	470,763	107.5
Reno, NV	139,950	180,480	225,221	264,165	268,959	92.2
Richmond, VA	202,783	197,790	204,214	226,610	227,595	12.2
Rochester, MN	74,151	85,806	106,769	121,395	121,638	64.0
Sacramento, CA	368,923	407,018	466,488	524,943	524,802	42.3
Saint Louis, MO	396,685	348,189	319,294	301,578	293,109	-26.1
Saint Paul, MN	272,235	287,151	285,068	311,527	307,762	13.1
Salem, OR	112,046	136,924	154,637	175,535	176,666	57.7
Salt Lake City, UT	159,796	181,743	186,440	199,723	203,888	27.6
San Antonio, TX	997,258	1,144,646	1,327,407	1,434,625	1,458,954	46.3
San Diego, CA	1,111,048	1,223,400	1,307,402	1,386,932	1,385,061	24.7
San Francisco, CA	723,959	776,733	805,235	873,965	836,321	15.5
San Jose, CA	784,324	894,943	945,942	1,013,240	990,054	26.2
Santa Rosa, CA	123,297	147,595	167,815	178,127	177,216	43.7
Savannah, GA	138,038	131,510	136,286	147,780	147,546	6.9
Seattle, WA	516,262	563,374	608,660	737,015	741,440	43.6
Sioux Falls, SD	102,262	123,975	153,888	192,517	197,642	93.3
Tampa, FL	279,960	303,447	335,709	384,959	393,389	40.5
Tucson, AZ	417,942	486,699	520,116	542,629	543,348	30.0
Tulsa, OK	367,241	393,049	391,906	413,066	412,322	12.3
Virginia Beach, VA	393,069	425,257	437,994	459,470	457,066	16.3
Washington, DC	606,900	572,059	601,723	689,545	672,079	10.7
Wichita, KS	313,693	344,284	382,368	397,532	396,488	26.4
Wilmington, NC	64,609	75,838	106,476	115,451	118,578	83.5
Winston-Salem, NC	168,139	185,776	229,617	249,545	250,887	49.2
U.S.	248,709,873	281,421,906	308,745,538	331,449,281	332,387,540	33.6

Note: (1) 2019-2023 5-year estimated population
Source: U.S. Census Bureau: 1990 Census, Census 2000, Census 2010, Census 2020, 2019-2023 American Community Survey 5-Year Estimates

Appendix A: Comparative Statistics

Population Growth: Metro Area

Metro Area	1990 Census	2000 Census	2010 Census	2020 Census	Current Estimate[1]	Population Growth 1990-2023 (%)
Albuquerque, NM	599,416	729,649	887,077	916,528	918,567	53.2
Anchorage, AK	266,021	319,605	380,821	398,328	399,746	50.3
Ann Arbor, MI	282,937	322,895	344,791	372,258	368,394	30.2
Athens, GA	136,025	166,079	192,541	215,415	218,190	60.4
Atlanta, GA	3,069,411	4,247,981	5,268,860	6,089,815	6,176,937	101.2
Austin, TX	846,217	1,249,763	1,716,289	2,283,371	2,357,497	178.6
Baltimore, MD	2,382,172	2,552,994	2,710,489	2,844,510	2,839,409	19.2
Billings, MT	121,499	138,904	158,050	184,167	187,269	54.1
Boise City, ID	319,596	464,840	616,561	764,718	790,640	147.4
Boston, MA	4,133,895	4,391,344	4,552,402	4,941,632	4,917,661	19.0
Boulder, CO	208,898	269,758	294,567	330,758	328,317	57.2
Cape Coral, FL	335,113	440,888	618,754	760,822	792,692	136.5
Cedar Rapids, IA	210,640	237,230	257,940	276,520	275,960	31.0
Charleston, SC	506,875	549,033	664,607	799,636	817,756	61.3
Charlotte, NC	1,024,331	1,330,448	1,758,038	2,660,329	2,712,818	164.8
Chicago, IL	8,182,076	9,098,316	9,461,105	9,618,502	9,359,555	14.4
Cincinnati, OH	1,844,917	2,009,632	2,130,151	2,256,884	2,255,257	22.2
Clarksville, TN	189,277	232,000	273,949	320,535	328,626	73.6
Cleveland, OH	2,102,219	2,148,143	2,077,240	2,088,251	2,171,978	3.3
College Station, TX	150,998	184,885	228,660	268,248	273,280	81.0
Colorado Springs, CO	409,482	537,484	645,613	755,105	760,782	85.8
Columbia, MO	122,010	145,666	172,786	210,864	212,850	74.5
Columbia, SC	548,325	647,158	767,598	829,470	839,868	53.2
Columbus, OH	1,405,176	1,612,694	1,836,536	2,138,926	2,151,847	53.1
Dallas, TX	3,989,294	5,161,544	6,371,773	7,637,387	7,807,555	95.7
Davenport, IA	368,151	376,019	379,690	384,324	381,864	3.7
Denver, CO	1,666,935	2,179,296	2,543,482	2,963,821	2,977,085	78.6
Des Moines, IA	416,346	481,394	569,633	709,466	720,331	73.0
Detroit, MI	4,248,699	4,452,557	4,296,250	4,392,041	4,367,620	2.8
Durham, NC	344,646	426,493	504,357	649,903	594,291	72.4
El Paso, TX	591,610	679,622	800,647	868,859	869,606	47.0
Eugene, OR	282,912	322,959	351,715	382,971	382,628	35.2
Fargo, ND	153,296	174,367	208,777	249,843	254,914	66.3
Fort Collins, CO	186,136	251,494	299,630	359,066	363,561	95.3
Fort Wayne, IN	354,435	390,156	416,257	419,601	451,440	27.4
Fort Worth, TX	3,989,294	5,161,544	6,371,773	7,637,387	7,807,555	95.7
Gainesville, FL	191,263	232,392	264,275	339,247	344,521	80.1
Green Bay, WI	243,698	282,599	306,241	328,268	329,375	35.2
Greensboro, NC	540,257	643,430	723,801	776,566	779,894	44.4
Honolulu, HI	836,231	876,156	953,207	1,016,508	1,003,666	20.0
Houston, TX	3,767,335	4,715,407	5,946,800	7,122,240	7,274,714	93.1
Huntsville, AL	293,047	342,376	417,593	491,723	504,712	72.2
Indianapolis, IN	1,294,217	1,525,104	1,756,241	2,111,040	2,106,327	62.7
Jacksonville, FL	925,213	1,122,750	1,345,596	1,605,848	1,645,707	77.9
Kansas City, MO	1,636,528	1,836,038	2,035,334	2,192,035	2,202,006	34.6
Lafayette, LA	208,740	239,086	273,738	478,384	410,883	96.8
Las Vegas, NV	741,459	1,375,765	1,951,269	2,265,461	2,293,764	209.4
Lexington, KY	348,428	408,326	472,099	516,811	517,378	48.5
Lincoln, NE	229,091	266,787	302,157	340,217	341,309	49.0
Little Rock, AR	535,034	610,518	699,757	748,031	753,605	40.9
Los Angeles, CA	11,273,720	12,365,627	12,828,837	13,200,998	13,012,469	15.4
Louisville, KY	1,055,973	1,161,975	1,283,566	1,285,439	1,361,847	29.0
Madison, WI	432,323	501,774	568,593	680,796	683,967	58.2
Manchester, NH	336,073	380,841	400,721	422,937	424,732	26.4
McAllen, TX	383,545	569,463	774,769	870,781	880,921	129.7

Table continued on following page.

Metro Area	1990 Census	2000 Census	2010 Census	2020 Census	Current Estimate[1]	Population Growth 1990-2023 (%)
Memphis, TN	1,067,263	1,205,204	1,316,100	1,337,779	1,341,606	25.7
Miami, FL	4,056,100	5,007,564	5,564,635	6,138,333	6,138,876	51.3
Midland, TX	106,611	116,009	136,872	175,220	176,726	65.8
Milwaukee, WI	1,432,149	1,500,741	1,555,908	1,574,731	1,566,361	9.4
Minneapolis, MN	2,538,834	2,968,806	3,279,833	3,690,261	3,693,351	45.5
Nashville, TN	1,048,218	1,311,789	1,589,934	1,989,519	2,043,713	95.0
New Orleans, LA	1,264,391	1,316,510	1,167,764	1,271,845	988,763	-21.8
New York, NY	16,845,992	18,323,002	18,897,109	20,140,470	19,756,722	17.3
Oklahoma City, OK	971,042	1,095,421	1,252,987	1,425,695	1,445,122	48.8
Omaha, NE	685,797	767,041	865,350	967,604	972,840	41.9
Orlando, FL	1,224,852	1,644,561	2,134,411	2,673,376	2,721,022	122.2
Philadelphia, PA	5,435,470	5,687,147	5,965,343	6,245,051	6,241,882	14.8
Phoenix, AZ	2,238,480	3,251,876	4,192,887	4,845,832	4,941,206	120.7
Pittsburgh, PA	2,468,289	2,431,087	2,356,285	2,370,930	2,443,921	-1.0
Portland, OR	1,523,741	1,927,881	2,226,009	2,512,859	2,510,529	64.8
Providence, RI	1,509,789	1,582,997	1,600,852	1,676,579	1,673,807	10.9
Provo, UT	269,407	376,774	526,810	671,185	695,895	158.3
Raleigh, NC	541,081	797,071	1,130,490	1,413,982	1,449,594	167.9
Reno, NV	257,193	342,885	425,417	490,596	556,539	116.4
Richmond, VA	949,244	1,096,957	1,258,251	1,314,434	1,327,321	39.8
Rochester, MN	141,945	163,618	186,011	226,329	227,252	60.1
Sacramento, CA	1,481,126	1,796,857	2,149,127	2,397,382	2,406,563	62.5
Saint Louis, MO	2,580,897	2,698,687	2,812,896	2,820,253	2,809,414	8.9
Saint Paul, MN	2,538,834	2,968,806	3,279,833	3,690,261	3,693,351	45.5
Salem, OR	278,024	347,214	390,738	433,353	435,085	56.5
Salt Lake City, UT	768,075	968,858	1,124,197	1,257,936	1,261,337	64.2
San Antonio, TX	1,407,745	1,711,703	2,142,508	2,558,143	2,612,802	85.6
San Diego, CA	2,498,016	2,813,833	3,095,313	3,298,634	3,282,782	31.4
San Francisco, CA	3,686,592	4,123,740	4,335,391	4,749,008	4,653,593	26.2
San Jose, CA	1,534,280	1,735,819	1,836,911	2,000,468	1,969,353	28.4
Santa Rosa, CA	388,222	458,614	483,878	488,863	485,642	25.1
Savannah, GA	258,060	293,000	347,611	404,798	412,089	59.7
Seattle, WA	2,559,164	3,043,878	3,439,809	4,018,762	4,021,467	57.1
Sioux Falls, SD	153,500	187,093	228,261	276,730	293,107	90.9
Tampa, FL	2,067,959	2,395,997	2,783,243	3,175,275	3,240,469	56.7
Tucson, AZ	666,880	843,746	980,263	1,043,433	1,049,947	57.4
Tulsa, OK	761,019	859,532	937,478	1,015,331	1,026,209	34.8
Virginia Beach, VA	1,449,389	1,576,370	1,671,683	1,799,674	1,782,590	23.0
Washington, DC	4,122,914	4,796,183	5,582,170	6,385,162	6,263,796	51.9
Wichita, KS	511,111	571,166	623,061	647,610	648,935	27.0
Wilmington, NC	200,124	274,532	362,315	285,905	440,578	120.2
Winston-Salem, NC	361,091	421,961	477,717	675,966	683,637	89.3
U.S.	248,709,873	281,421,906	308,745,538	331,449,281	332,387,540	33.6

Note: (1) 2019-2023 5-year estimated population; Figures cover the Metropolitan Statistical Area (MSA)
Source: U.S. Census Bureau: 1990 Census, Census 2000, Census 2010, Census 2020, 2019-2023 American Community Survey 5-Year Estimates

Appendix A: Comparative Statistics

Male/Female Ratio: City

City	Males	Females	Males per 100 Females
Albuquerque, NM	275,413	287,075	95.9
Anchorage, AK	147,620	141,449	104.4
Ann Arbor, MI	60,397	60,782	99.4
Athens, GA	60,237	66,750	90.2
Atlanta, GA	242,994	256,293	94.8
Austin, TX	495,563	472,299	104.9
Baltimore, MD	268,932	308,261	87.2
Billings, MT	58,615	59,706	98.2
Boise City, ID	118,294	117,407	100.8
Boston, MA	319,182	344,790	92.6
Boulder, CO	55,022	51,252	107.4
Cape Coral, FL	103,313	103,074	100.2
Cedar Rapids, IA	67,551	69,308	97.5
Charleston, SC	72,280	79,734	90.7
Charlotte, NC	427,869	458,414	93.3
Chicago, IL	1,314,256	1,393,392	94.3
Cincinnati, OH	148,944	160,651	92.7
Clarksville, TN	86,129	85,768	100.4
Cleveland, OH	177,863	189,660	93.8
College Station, TX	62,870	59,410	105.8
Colorado Springs, CO	241,781	241,318	100.2
Columbia, MO	61,139	66,061	92.5
Columbia, SC	68,245	69,774	97.8
Columbus, OH	445,564	460,916	96.7
Dallas, TX	647,372	652,181	99.3
Davenport, IA	50,102	50,981	98.3
Denver, CO	359,969	353,765	101.8
Des Moines, IA	105,131	107,333	97.9
Detroit, MI	302,503	334,141	90.5
Durham, NC	136,368	152,097	89.7
El Paso, TX	333,802	344,345	96.9
Eugene, OR	87,095	90,425	96.3
Fargo, ND	65,129	63,935	101.9
Fort Collins, CO	84,686	85,019	99.6
Fort Wayne, IN	129,959	136,276	95.4
Fort Worth, TX	461,317	479,994	96.1
Gainesville, FL	68,593	75,018	91.4
Green Bay, WI	52,829	53,756	98.3
Greensboro, NC	138,079	160,485	86.0
Honolulu, HI	173,028	173,295	99.8
Houston, TX	1,138,504	1,161,915	98.0
Huntsville, AL	107,036	111,778	95.8
Indianapolis, IN	428,660	453,383	94.5
Jacksonville, FL	466,421	495,318	94.2
Kansas City, MO	245,780	262,453	93.6
Lafayette, LA	58,993	62,544	94.3
Las Vegas, NV	325,629	325,244	100.1
Lexington, KY	158,152	162,970	97.0
Lincoln, NE	146,855	145,077	101.2
Little Rock, AR	95,597	107,142	89.2
Los Angeles, CA	1,921,735	1,936,162	99.3
Louisville, KY	305,342	321,868	94.9
Madison, WI	137,655	137,913	99.8
Manchester, NH	57,084	58,331	97.9
McAllen, TX	71,212	72,577	98.1

Table continued on following page.

City	Males	Females	Males per 100 Females
Memphis, TN	298,855	330,208	90.5
Miami, FL	226,349	220,314	102.7
Midland, TX	68,527	65,471	104.7
Milwaukee, WI	275,637	294,119	93.7
Minneapolis, MN	218,753	208,092	105.1
Nashville, TN	331,646	352,652	94.0
New Orleans, LA	177,299	198,736	89.2
New York, NY	4,088,026	4,428,176	92.3
Oklahoma City, OK	340,327	348,366	97.7
Omaha, NE	242,508	245,689	98.7
Orlando, FL	153,714	158,018	97.3
Philadelphia, PA	749,410	833,022	90.0
Phoenix, AZ	815,308	809,524	100.7
Pittsburgh, PA	149,240	154,380	96.7
Portland, OR	319,454	323,261	98.8
Providence, RI	93,138	97,076	95.9
Provo, UT	56,107	58,196	96.4
Raleigh, NC	228,452	242,311	94.3
Reno, NV	136,341	132,618	102.8
Richmond, VA	108,090	119,505	90.4
Rochester, MN	59,099	62,539	94.5
Sacramento, CA	260,163	264,639	98.3
Saint Louis, MO	142,190	150,919	94.2
Saint Paul, MN	151,659	156,103	97.2
Salem, OR	89,295	87,371	102.2
Salt Lake City, UT	105,049	98,839	106.3
San Antonio, TX	722,875	736,079	98.2
San Diego, CA	703,091	681,970	103.1
San Francisco, CA	429,837	406,484	105.7
San Jose, CA	504,179	485,875	103.8
Santa Rosa, CA	86,188	91,028	94.7
Savannah, GA	69,345	78,201	88.7
Seattle, WA	378,278	363,162	104.2
Sioux Falls, SD	99,791	97,851	102.0
Tampa, FL	197,565	195,824	100.9
Tucson, AZ	270,198	273,150	98.9
Tulsa, OK	201,524	210,798	95.6
Virginia Beach, VA	224,463	232,603	96.5
Washington, DC	320,001	352,078	90.9
Wichita, KS	197,295	199,193	99.0
Wilmington, NC	55,595	62,983	88.3
Winston-Salem, NC	116,981	133,906	87.4
U.S.	164,545,087	167,842,453	98.0

Source: U.S. Census Bureau, 2019-2023 American Community Survey 5-Year Estimates

Appendix A: Comparative Statistics

Male/Female Ratio: Metro Area

Metro Area	Males	Females	Males per 100 Females
Albuquerque, NM	452,929	465,638	97.3
Anchorage, AK	205,511	194,235	105.8
Ann Arbor, MI	183,761	184,633	99.5
Athens, GA	105,119	113,071	93.0
Atlanta, GA	2,998,312	3,178,625	94.3
Austin, TX	1,190,277	1,167,220	102.0
Baltimore, MD	1,371,348	1,468,061	93.4
Billings, MT	92,957	94,312	98.6
Boise City, ID	397,370	393,270	101.0
Boston, MA	2,405,154	2,512,507	95.7
Boulder, CO	165,677	162,640	101.9
Cape Coral, FL	389,853	402,839	96.8
Cedar Rapids, IA	137,287	138,673	99.0
Charleston, SC	400,382	417,374	95.9
Charlotte, NC	1,323,612	1,389,206	95.3
Chicago, IL	4,607,366	4,752,189	97.0
Cincinnati, OH	1,113,237	1,142,020	97.5
Clarksville, TN	165,784	162,842	101.8
Cleveland, OH	1,057,990	1,113,988	95.0
College Station, TX	137,218	136,062	100.8
Colorado Springs, CO	386,799	373,983	103.4
Columbia, MO	103,590	109,260	94.8
Columbia, SC	407,291	432,577	94.2
Columbus, OH	1,066,090	1,085,757	98.2
Dallas, TX	3,864,152	3,943,403	98.0
Davenport, IA	189,025	192,839	98.0
Denver, CO	1,499,649	1,477,436	101.5
Des Moines, IA	359,219	361,112	99.5
Detroit, MI	2,140,962	2,226,658	96.2
Durham, NC	285,396	308,895	92.4
El Paso, TX	432,470	437,136	98.9
Eugene, OR	189,067	193,561	97.7
Fargo, ND	128,561	126,353	101.7
Fort Collins, CO	181,725	181,836	99.9
Fort Wayne, IN	222,504	228,936	97.2
Fort Worth, TX	3,864,152	3,943,403	98.0
Gainesville, FL	166,988	177,533	94.1
Green Bay, WI	165,274	164,101	100.7
Greensboro, NC	374,844	405,050	92.5
Honolulu, HI	507,355	496,311	102.2
Houston, TX	3,616,570	3,658,144	98.9
Huntsville, AL	249,354	255,358	97.6
Indianapolis, IN	1,034,791	1,071,536	96.6
Jacksonville, FL	804,019	841,688	95.5
Kansas City, MO	1,087,932	1,114,074	97.7
Lafayette, LA	200,575	210,308	95.4
Las Vegas, NV	1,148,112	1,145,652	100.2
Lexington, KY	254,019	263,359	96.5
Lincoln, NE	172,052	169,257	101.7
Little Rock, AR	365,071	388,534	94.0
Los Angeles, CA	6,447,486	6,564,983	98.2
Louisville, KY	669,908	691,939	96.8
Madison, WI	343,409	340,558	100.8
Manchester, NH	212,913	211,819	100.5
McAllen, TX	434,784	446,137	97.5

Table continued on following page.

Metro Area	Males	Females	Males per 100 Females
Memphis, TN	642,599	699,007	91.9
Miami, FL	3,005,200	3,133,676	95.9
Midland, TX	90,328	86,398	104.5
Milwaukee, WI	768,160	798,201	96.2
Minneapolis, MN	1,842,197	1,851,154	99.5
Nashville, TN	1,004,473	1,039,240	96.7
New Orleans, LA	476,985	511,778	93.2
New York, NY	9,622,708	10,134,014	95.0
Oklahoma City, OK	714,932	730,190	97.9
Omaha, NE	485,489	487,351	99.6
Orlando, FL	1,336,264	1,384,758	96.5
Philadelphia, PA	3,031,854	3,210,028	94.4
Phoenix, AZ	2,466,995	2,474,211	99.7
Pittsburgh, PA	1,200,522	1,243,399	96.6
Portland, OR	1,251,055	1,259,474	99.3
Providence, RI	819,607	854,200	96.0
Provo, UT	353,303	342,592	103.1
Raleigh, NC	711,279	738,315	96.3
Reno, NV	283,387	273,152	103.7
Richmond, VA	645,193	682,128	94.6
Rochester, MN	112,416	114,836	97.9
Sacramento, CA	1,184,908	1,221,655	97.0
Saint Louis, MO	1,370,976	1,438,438	95.3
Saint Paul, MN	1,842,197	1,851,154	99.5
Salem, OR	217,233	217,852	99.7
Salt Lake City, UT	637,671	623,666	102.2
San Antonio, TX	1,298,427	1,314,375	98.8
San Diego, CA	1,660,156	1,622,626	102.3
San Francisco, CA	2,318,841	2,334,752	99.3
San Jose, CA	1,003,282	966,071	103.9
Santa Rosa, CA	238,817	246,825	96.8
Savannah, GA	200,060	212,029	94.4
Seattle, WA	2,031,168	1,990,299	102.1
Sioux Falls, SD	148,246	144,861	102.3
Tampa, FL	1,583,138	1,657,331	95.5
Tucson, AZ	518,998	530,949	97.7
Tulsa, OK	506,779	519,430	97.6
Virginia Beach, VA	875,910	906,680	96.6
Washington, DC	3,081,518	3,182,278	96.8
Wichita, KS	323,191	325,744	99.2
Wilmington, NC	212,689	227,889	93.3
Winston-Salem, NC	330,177	353,460	93.4
U.S.	164,545,087	167,842,453	98.0

Note: Figures cover the Metropolitan Statistical Area (MSA)
Source: U.S. Census Bureau, 2019-2023 American Community Survey 5-Year Estimates

Race: City

City	White Alone[1] (%)	Black Alone[1] (%)	Asian Alone[1] (%)	AIAN[2] Alone[1] (%)	NHOPI[3] Alone[1] (%)	Other Race Alone[1] (%)	Two or More Races (%)
Albuquerque, NM	55.3	3.3	3.3	5.0	0.1	11.1	21.9
Anchorage, AK	58.3	5.3	9.8	7.3	3.1	3.1	13.1
Ann Arbor, MI	68.8	7.2	15.2	0.3	0.0	1.2	7.3
Athens, GA	57.6	26.2	4.3	0.4	0.0	3.4	8.1
Atlanta, GA	39.9	46.9	5.0	0.3	0.1	2.1	5.8
Austin, TX	59.9	7.5	8.6	0.7	0.1	7.7	15.5
Baltimore, MD	27.4	60.0	2.5	0.4	0.0	4.4	5.2
Billings, MT	86.3	1.0	0.9	4.4	0.1	1.4	6.1
Boise City, ID	83.6	1.4	3.3	0.7	0.3	3.0	7.6
Boston, MA	47.8	21.5	10.0	0.3	0.1	7.1	13.2
Boulder, CO	81.8	1.1	5.8	0.3	0.1	1.8	9.2
Cape Coral, FL	72.9	4.5	1.5	0.1	0.0	4.1	16.9
Cedar Rapids, IA	79.7	8.5	2.6	0.2	0.0	1.4	7.6
Charleston, SC	72.9	17.4	2.2	0.6	0.2	1.9	5.0
Charlotte, NC	41.5	34.1	6.4	0.4	0.0	8.8	8.9
Chicago, IL	39.0	28.4	7.1	0.9	0.1	12.4	12.0
Cincinnati, OH	49.4	38.7	2.8	0.1	0.0	2.0	7.0
Clarksville, TN	59.4	23.0	2.5	0.4	0.3	2.8	11.7
Cleveland, OH	36.7	46.8	2.3	0.4	0.0	4.6	9.2
College Station, TX	67.0	8.8	9.6	0.3	0.1	3.3	10.9
Colorado Springs, CO	72.3	5.8	3.0	1.0	0.2	4.9	12.8
Columbia, MO	74.3	12.1	6.1	0.1	0.1	1.2	6.1
Columbia, SC	49.9	39.5	2.7	0.2	0.2	1.7	5.9
Columbus, OH	53.3	29.0	5.8	0.3	0.0	3.4	8.2
Dallas, TX	41.9	23.7	3.7	0.8	0.1	12.5	17.3
Davenport, IA	75.9	11.2	2.0	0.3	0.1	2.1	8.5
Denver, CO	62.9	8.8	3.6	0.9	0.1	8.2	15.5
Des Moines, IA	66.9	12.0	6.2	0.5	0.0	5.2	9.1
Detroit, MI	11.7	76.8	1.6	0.4	0.0	4.6	4.8
Durham, NC	43.9	34.4	5.6	0.5	0.1	6.8	8.6
El Paso, TX	39.3	3.6	1.5	0.9	0.2	16.0	38.6
Eugene, OR	78.9	1.8	3.9	0.8	0.4	3.8	10.5
Fargo, ND	80.8	8.3	3.9	1.0	0.0	1.1	5.0
Fort Collins, CO	81.7	1.4	3.3	0.8	0.1	2.2	10.5
Fort Wayne, IN	66.4	14.6	5.8	0.4	0.0	4.3	8.4
Fort Worth, TX	47.7	19.5	5.2	0.6	0.1	10.4	16.4
Gainesville, FL	59.2	21.6	6.2	0.2	0.1	3.0	9.7
Green Bay, WI	69.9	3.8	4.1	3.3	0.0	7.1	11.8
Greensboro, NC	40.4	42.2	5.0	0.5	0.0	4.5	7.5
Honolulu, HI	17.0	1.8	52.9	0.2	8.5	1.2	18.4
Houston, TX	35.5	22.9	6.9	0.9	0.1	14.6	19.2
Huntsville, AL	58.4	29.7	2.0	0.6	0.1	2.9	6.2
Indianapolis, IN	53.6	28.1	4.1	0.5	0.0	5.7	8.0
Jacksonville, FL	51.2	30.1	4.9	0.2	0.1	3.9	9.6
Kansas City, MO	57.8	25.8	2.7	0.4	0.3	4.5	8.6
Lafayette, LA	59.1	28.6	2.1	0.1	0.1	1.2	8.8
Las Vegas, NV	49.2	11.9	6.9	1.1	0.8	13.9	16.2
Lexington, KY	69.9	14.4	4.2	0.2	0.0	3.5	7.8
Lincoln, NE	80.9	4.2	4.5	0.7	0.1	2.3	7.4
Little Rock, AR	46.3	39.4	3.0	0.3	0.1	4.2	6.6
Los Angeles, CA	37.3	8.5	12.0	1.2	0.1	25.1	15.7
Louisville, KY	63.1	23.7	2.6	0.1	0.0	2.1	8.4
Madison, WI	73.0	7.1	8.0	0.4	0.0	2.1	9.4
Manchester, NH	76.7	5.3	4.6	0.2	0.0	3.2	10.0

Table continued on following page.

City	White Alone[1] (%)	Black Alone[1] (%)	Asian Alone[1] (%)	AIAN[2] Alone[1] (%)	NHOPI[3] Alone[1] (%)	Other Race Alone[1] (%)	Two or More Races (%)
McAllen, TX	43.1	0.9	2.9	0.6	0.0	17.5	35.1
Memphis, TN	25.0	62.9	1.7	0.5	0.1	5.1	4.6
Miami, FL	34.2	13.7	1.6	0.4	0.0	7.5	42.6
Midland, TX	58.8	8.6	2.1	0.7	0.0	12.0	17.9
Milwaukee, WI	36.5	38.6	4.8	0.7	0.0	6.9	12.4
Minneapolis, MN	61.6	18.3	5.2	1.1	0.1	4.9	8.9
Nashville, TN	56.5	25.5	3.5	0.3	0.1	4.9	9.2
New Orleans, LA	31.6	55.2	2.8	0.3	0.0	2.8	7.3
New York, NY	35.9	22.7	14.6	0.7	0.1	15.5	10.5
Oklahoma City, OK	58.4	13.4	4.5	3.4	0.1	5.8	14.4
Omaha, NE	68.8	11.8	4.0	0.8	0.0	5.0	9.7
Orlando, FL	43.2	22.9	4.4	0.1	0.1	8.4	21.0
Philadelphia, PA	36.1	39.9	7.8	0.4	0.1	8.4	7.3
Phoenix, AZ	53.7	7.8	3.9	2.3	0.2	11.4	20.8
Pittsburgh, PA	63.7	22.5	5.8	0.2	0.0	1.6	6.2
Portland, OR	70.1	5.8	8.1	0.8	0.5	3.3	11.3
Providence, RI	40.7	13.3	5.9	1.0	0.1	20.4	18.7
Provo, UT	78.6	1.1	2.2	1.0	1.4	5.4	10.2
Raleigh, NC	53.8	27.5	4.7	0.4	0.0	5.5	8.0
Reno, NV	63.5	3.2	7.0	1.0	0.7	11.1	13.5
Richmond, VA	43.2	42.0	2.1	0.2	0.0	5.3	7.1
Rochester, MN	74.3	9.4	8.0	0.2	0.1	2.1	5.9
Sacramento, CA	36.8	12.4	19.7	1.0	1.7	13.4	15.0
Saint Louis, MO	45.7	43.1	3.4	0.2	0.0	1.6	5.9
Saint Paul, MN	53.2	16.2	17.9	0.7	0.0	3.5	8.4
Salem, OR	69.8	1.6	3.5	1.2	1.6	8.2	14.1
Salt Lake City, UT	70.5	2.7	5.4	1.2	1.4	9.2	9.6
San Antonio, TX	48.3	6.9	3.1	1.1	0.1	10.9	29.6
San Diego, CA	50.4	5.7	17.6	0.7	0.5	9.5	15.6
San Francisco, CA	40.5	5.1	35.0	0.7	0.4	7.7	10.7
San Jose, CA	29.0	2.9	38.6	1.0	0.5	13.6	14.4
Santa Rosa, CA	56.2	1.9	6.5	1.4	0.6	20.0	13.4
Savannah, GA	37.2	52.2	2.9	0.2	0.2	2.0	5.4
Seattle, WA	61.8	6.6	17.2	0.6	0.3	3.0	10.5
Sioux Falls, SD	79.9	7.0	2.3	1.9	0.0	2.0	7.0
Tampa, FL	51.8	21.3	4.8	0.3	0.1	4.8	17.0
Tucson, AZ	58.2	5.0	3.1	2.7	0.2	11.6	19.1
Tulsa, OK	57.0	14.2	3.5	4.3	0.2	5.9	14.9
Virginia Beach, VA	61.6	18.9	7.3	0.2	0.2	2.4	9.4
Washington, DC	39.1	43.3	4.1	0.3	0.1	4.8	8.4
Wichita, KS	66.6	9.7	4.9	0.9	0.0	5.5	12.4
Wilmington, NC	72.9	14.9	1.3	0.3	0.0	4.8	5.9
Winston-Salem, NC	48.7	32.4	2.3	0.5	0.0	7.3	8.8
U.S.	63.4	12.4	5.8	0.9	0.2	6.6	10.7

Note: (1) Alone is defined as not being in combination with one or more other races; (2) American Indian and Alaska Native; (3) Native Hawaiian and Other Pacific Islander
Source: U.S. Census Bureau, 2019-2023 American Community Survey 5-Year Estimates

Race: Metro Area

Metro Area	White Alone[1] (%)	Black Alone[1] (%)	Asian Alone[1] (%)	AIAN[2] Alone[1] (%)	NHOPI[3] Alone[1] (%)	Other Race Alone[1] (%)	Two or More Races (%)
Albuquerque, NM	55.2	2.7	2.5	6.2	0.1	10.9	22.3
Anchorage, AK	63.8	4.2	7.6	6.9	2.4	2.7	12.5
Ann Arbor, MI	69.9	11.6	8.9	0.3	0.0	1.6	7.7
Athens, GA	67.1	18.6	3.7	0.4	0.2	3.0	7.1
Atlanta, GA	46.3	34.0	6.4	0.4	0.1	4.9	7.9
Austin, TX	61.4	7.2	6.9	0.7	0.1	7.3	16.5
Baltimore, MD	54.8	29.0	5.8	0.3	0.0	3.6	6.4
Billings, MT	87.5	0.8	0.8	3.6	0.0	1.6	5.7
Boise City, ID	81.5	1.0	1.9	0.8	0.2	5.6	9.0
Boston, MA	69.2	7.5	8.5	0.2	0.0	5.5	9.1
Boulder, CO	80.7	0.8	4.7	0.3	0.1	2.9	10.6
Cape Coral, FL	70.5	8.0	1.7	0.6	0.0	4.3	15.0
Cedar Rapids, IA	86.2	5.0	2.0	0.3	0.0	1.1	5.5
Charleston, SC	64.6	23.9	2.0	0.4	0.2	3.3	5.7
Charlotte, NC	60.2	22.2	4.2	0.4	0.0	5.5	7.5
Chicago, IL	55.7	16.2	7.1	0.6	0.0	9.5	10.8
Cincinnati, OH	78.0	11.9	2.9	0.1	0.1	1.7	5.5
Clarksville, TN	67.3	18.5	2.1	0.3	0.3	2.2	9.5
Cleveland, OH	70.5	18.6	2.3	0.2	0.0	1.9	6.4
College Station, TX	66.6	11.4	5.1	0.6	0.1	4.4	11.8
Colorado Springs, CO	73.1	5.8	2.8	0.9	0.3	4.3	12.8
Columbia, MO	79.2	9.0	4.1	0.2	0.1	1.3	6.1
Columbia, SC	55.4	33.3	2.3	0.2	0.1	2.7	5.9
Columbus, OH	70.3	15.8	4.8	0.2	0.0	2.2	6.7
Dallas, TX	52.7	16.2	7.8	0.6	0.1	8.0	14.5
Davenport, IA	79.4	7.7	2.4	0.2	0.1	2.8	7.5
Denver, CO	69.1	5.6	4.3	0.9	0.2	6.4	13.6
Des Moines, IA	81.5	5.7	4.2	0.3	0.0	2.5	5.8
Detroit, MI	65.6	21.5	4.8	0.2	0.0	1.9	5.9
Durham, NC	56.6	24.0	5.1	0.5	0.0	5.9	7.8
El Paso, TX	39.2	3.3	1.3	0.9	0.2	16.3	38.9
Eugene, OR	82.0	1.2	2.6	1.0	0.2	3.6	9.5
Fargo, ND	84.2	6.1	2.7	0.9	0.1	0.9	5.1
Fort Collins, CO	84.1	1.0	2.1	0.6	0.1	2.6	9.5
Fort Wayne, IN	75.6	9.5	4.3	0.3	0.0	3.2	7.1
Fort Worth, TX	52.7	16.2	7.8	0.6	0.1	8.0	14.5
Gainesville, FL	66.6	17.1	4.9	0.2	0.0	2.5	8.7
Green Bay, WI	82.9	2.2	2.7	1.7	0.0	3.3	7.1
Greensboro, NC	57.7	26.9	3.8	0.4	0.0	4.3	6.9
Honolulu, HI	18.8	2.4	42.6	0.2	9.9	1.6	24.4
Houston, TX	45.3	17.3	8.2	0.7	0.1	10.7	17.8
Huntsville, AL	66.6	21.8	2.4	0.7	0.1	2.2	6.2
Indianapolis, IN	70.8	15.1	3.8	0.3	0.0	3.4	6.5
Jacksonville, FL	62.8	20.7	4.0	0.2	0.1	3.2	9.0
Kansas City, MO	73.0	11.9	2.9	0.4	0.2	3.7	7.8
Lafayette, LA	68.0	22.7	1.5	0.2	0.1	1.1	6.4
Las Vegas, NV	47.1	12.1	10.5	1.1	0.8	12.9	15.5
Lexington, KY	76.6	10.6	2.9	0.2	0.0	2.9	6.7
Lincoln, NE	83.0	3.6	3.9	0.7	0.1	2.0	6.8
Little Rock, AR	65.9	23.5	1.6	0.3	0.0	2.8	5.8
Los Angeles, CA	38.1	6.3	16.7	1.1	0.2	21.2	16.2
Louisville, KY	75.2	14.2	2.1	0.1	0.0	1.6	6.7
Madison, WI	81.4	4.5	5.0	0.3	0.1	1.7	7.1
Manchester, NH	83.3	2.6	4.2	0.1	0.0	2.1	7.7

Table continued on following page.

Metro Area	White Alone[1] (%)	Black Alone[1] (%)	Asian Alone[1] (%)	AIAN[2] Alone[1] (%)	NHOPI[3] Alone[1] (%)	Other Race Alone[1] (%)	Two or More Races (%)
McAllen, TX	39.5	0.7	1.0	0.4	0.0	10.8	47.6
Memphis, TN	42.5	46.8	2.2	0.3	0.1	3.4	4.7
Miami, FL	43.7	20.3	2.6	0.2	0.0	6.6	26.6
Midland, TX	60.4	7.1	2.1	0.6	0.0	12.8	17.1
Milwaukee, WI	67.4	16.1	4.0	0.4	0.0	3.8	8.3
Minneapolis, MN	73.8	8.9	6.9	0.5	0.0	3.0	6.8
Nashville, TN	71.6	14.3	2.9	0.2	0.1	3.4	7.6
New Orleans, LA	45.0	38.5	3.2	0.6	0.0	4.4	8.4
New York, NY	48.4	16.3	11.8	0.5	0.0	12.3	10.6
Oklahoma City, OK	66.5	9.8	3.3	3.6	0.1	3.9	12.8
Omaha, NE	77.1	7.4	3.2	0.6	0.1	3.7	7.9
Orlando, FL	52.5	16.0	4.5	0.3	0.1	9.5	17.2
Philadelphia, PA	61.4	20.2	6.3	0.2	0.0	4.9	6.9
Phoenix, AZ	63.2	5.7	4.1	2.2	0.2	8.4	16.1
Pittsburgh, PA	84.1	7.9	2.5	0.1	0.0	0.8	4.6
Portland, OR	73.0	3.0	7.0	0.8	0.5	4.5	11.2
Providence, RI	74.5	5.3	3.1	0.4	0.1	6.6	10.0
Provo, UT	83.9	0.7	1.4	0.6	0.8	4.0	8.6
Raleigh, NC	60.7	19.1	6.6	0.4	0.0	5.4	7.8
Reno, NV	66.9	2.3	5.1	1.4	0.6	10.0	13.7
Richmond, VA	56.8	28.5	4.1	0.3	0.1	4.0	6.2
Rochester, MN	83.0	5.4	4.7	0.2	0.1	1.7	4.9
Sacramento, CA	54.8	6.9	14.8	0.8	0.8	8.7	13.2
Saint Louis, MO	72.1	17.5	2.8	0.1	0.0	1.3	6.1
Saint Paul, MN	73.8	8.9	6.9	0.5	0.0	3.0	6.8
Salem, OR	71.3	1.1	2.0	1.4	1.0	9.3	14.0
Salt Lake City, UT	73.6	1.7	3.9	0.9	1.5	8.7	9.6
San Antonio, TX	53.5	7.0	2.8	0.9	0.1	9.5	26.2
San Diego, CA	53.0	4.7	12.2	0.9	0.4	10.6	18.1
San Francisco, CA	39.9	7.0	27.6	0.9	0.6	11.8	12.2
San Jose, CA	33.6	2.3	38.3	0.8	0.4	10.7	13.9
Santa Rosa, CA	64.5	1.6	4.4	1.3	0.4	14.1	13.7
Savannah, GA	55.2	32.4	2.5	0.2	0.1	3.1	6.5
Seattle, WA	60.9	6.1	15.4	0.8	0.9	4.6	11.4
Sioux Falls, SD	84.2	5.1	1.6	1.5	0.0	1.6	6.0
Tampa, FL	66.0	11.8	3.8	0.3	0.1	4.8	13.2
Tucson, AZ	63.2	3.6	3.0	3.1	0.2	9.9	17.0
Tulsa, OK	65.3	7.6	2.8	7.2	0.1	3.5	13.4
Virginia Beach, VA	55.0	29.7	4.1	0.3	0.1	2.4	8.4
Washington, DC	45.5	24.9	10.7	0.5	0.0	8.3	10.1
Wichita, KS	74.4	6.7	3.7	0.8	0.1	4.3	10.1
Wilmington, NC	78.8	10.4	1.0	0.3	0.0	3.5	5.9
Winston-Salem, NC	68.8	17.4	1.8	0.3	0.0	4.4	7.3
U.S.	63.4	12.4	5.8	0.9	0.2	6.6	10.7

Note: Figures cover the Metropolitan Statistical Area (MSA); (1) Alone is defined as not being in combination with one or more other races; (2) American Indian and Alaska Native; (3) Native Hawaiian & Other Pacific Islander
Source: U.S. Census Bureau, 2019-2023 American Community Survey 5-Year Estimates

Hispanic Origin: City

City	Hispanic or Latino (%)	Mexican (%)	Puerto Rican (%)	Cuban (%)	Other Hispanic or Latino (%)
Albuquerque, NM	47.9	28.9	0.7	0.5	17.9
Anchorage, AK	9.3	4.2	1.4	0.5	3.1
Ann Arbor, MI	5.4	2.3	0.7	0.2	2.3
Athens, GA	11.5	6.1	0.4	0.7	4.2
Atlanta, GA	6.3	2.0	0.9	0.3	3.0
Austin, TX	32.2	23.7	1.0	0.9	6.7
Baltimore, MD	7.9	1.6	1.0	0.4	4.8
Billings, MT	7.2	5.0	0.3	0.2	1.8
Boise City, ID	9.5	7.0	0.4	0.1	2.1
Boston, MA	18.9	1.2	4.4	0.4	13.0
Boulder, CO	11.2	6.6	0.3	0.5	3.8
Cape Coral, FL	25.0	1.9	4.9	10.7	7.5
Cedar Rapids, IA	5.1	3.5	0.4	0.1	1.2
Charleston, SC	5.9	2.6	0.7	0.2	2.4
Charlotte, NC	17.0	6.0	1.2	0.5	9.3
Chicago, IL	29.6	21.6	3.5	0.4	4.2
Cincinnati, OH	5.4	1.6	0.9	0.2	2.6
Clarksville, TN	12.5	6.0	3.0	0.3	3.2
Cleveland, OH	12.8	1.7	8.8	0.2	2.2
College Station, TX	18.4	12.9	0.7	0.5	4.3
Colorado Springs, CO	18.7	12.0	1.2	0.2	5.3
Columbia, MO	4.3	2.5	0.2	0.2	1.3
Columbia, SC	5.7	2.0	1.3	0.2	2.2
Columbus, OH	7.9	3.7	1.1	0.1	3.0
Dallas, TX	41.9	33.6	0.6	0.4	7.4
Davenport, IA	9.1	8.0	0.4	0.1	0.6
Denver, CO	27.9	20.9	0.7	0.3	6.1
Des Moines, IA	16.0	11.4	0.6	0.3	3.8
Detroit, MI	8.0	5.5	0.9	0.2	1.3
Durham, NC	14.7	6.6	0.9	0.5	6.7
El Paso, TX	81.3	76.1	1.1	0.2	3.9
Eugene, OR	11.4	8.0	0.4	0.2	2.8
Fargo, ND	3.7	2.2	0.6	0.0	0.8
Fort Collins, CO	12.3	8.2	0.7	0.2	3.3
Fort Wayne, IN	10.5	7.7	0.7	0.1	2.2
Fort Worth, TX	34.6	28.7	1.3	0.4	4.2
Gainesville, FL	13.4	1.3	2.9	2.9	6.3
Green Bay, WI	18.1	13.8	2.3	0.1	1.9
Greensboro, NC	10.5	4.5	1.7	0.2	4.1
Honolulu, HI	6.6	2.3	1.8	0.1	2.4
Houston, TX	44.1	28.5	0.8	0.8	14.0
Huntsville, AL	8.1	4.3	1.0	0.2	2.5
Indianapolis, IN	13.3	8.7	0.8	0.3	3.5
Jacksonville, FL	12.0	2.0	3.9	1.8	4.3
Kansas City, MO	12.3	8.3	0.6	0.4	3.0
Lafayette, LA	7.6	1.9	0.4	0.5	4.8
Las Vegas, NV	34.1	24.7	1.2	1.6	6.6
Lexington, KY	9.2	5.9	0.7	0.3	2.4
Lincoln, NE	8.8	5.7	0.4	0.2	2.5
Little Rock, AR	10.4	6.8	0.2	0.1	3.3
Los Angeles, CA	47.2	30.0	0.5	0.4	16.3
Louisville, KY	8.6	2.9	0.4	3.4	1.9
Madison, WI	9.3	5.7	0.7	0.2	2.8
Manchester, NH	13.4	1.5	4.4	0.1	7.4
McAllen, TX	86.5	81.1	0.5	0.1	4.8

Table continued on following page.

City	Hispanic or Latino (%)	Mexican (%)	Puerto Rican (%)	Cuban (%)	Other Hispanic or Latino (%)
Memphis, TN	10.2	5.7	0.3	0.2	3.9
Miami, FL	71.2	2.2	3.3	31.0	34.8
Midland, TX	44.3	38.1	0.6	1.3	4.3
Milwaukee, WI	20.7	13.7	4.9	0.1	1.9
Minneapolis, MN	10.5	5.9	0.4	0.2	4.0
Nashville, TN	13.8	6.8	0.7	0.6	5.7
New Orleans, LA	7.9	1.5	0.4	0.8	5.3
New York, NY	28.4	3.9	7.1	0.5	17.0
Oklahoma City, OK	21.7	17.3	0.5	0.1	3.8
Omaha, NE	15.6	11.4	0.5	0.2	3.5
Orlando, FL	35.6	2.0	15.2	2.6	15.8
Philadelphia, PA	15.2	1.4	8.4	0.2	5.2
Phoenix, AZ	41.8	36.7	0.7	0.4	4.0
Pittsburgh, PA	4.2	1.4	0.8	0.1	2.0
Portland, OR	11.3	7.6	0.5	0.4	2.8
Providence, RI	44.3	1.6	6.8	0.3	35.6
Provo, UT	18.9	11.4	0.7	0.2	6.6
Raleigh, NC	12.7	5.0	1.4	0.4	5.9
Reno, NV	24.6	17.9	0.7	0.3	5.7
Richmond, VA	10.3	2.1	1.1	0.3	6.8
Rochester, MN	6.2	3.9	0.4	0.1	1.8
Sacramento, CA	29.5	24.1	0.9	0.1	4.4
Saint Louis, MO	5.1	3.1	0.3	0.3	1.4
Saint Paul, MN	9.1	5.9	0.4	0.2	2.7
Salem, OR	23.4	20.0	0.4	0.1	2.9
Salt Lake City, UT	20.8	15.2	0.5	0.3	4.8
San Antonio, TX	64.4	54.1	1.4	0.4	8.6
San Diego, CA	29.6	24.9	0.8	0.3	3.6
San Francisco, CA	15.9	7.8	0.7	0.2	7.2
San Jose, CA	31.0	25.4	0.5	0.2	4.9
Santa Rosa, CA	35.8	30.3	0.5	0.1	4.9
Savannah, GA	7.1	2.2	2.0	0.5	2.4
Seattle, WA	8.2	4.8	0.4	0.2	2.8
Sioux Falls, SD	6.4	2.7	0.3	0.1	3.3
Tampa, FL	26.2	3.2	6.1	7.8	9.1
Tucson, AZ	42.7	38.1	0.8	0.3	3.5
Tulsa, OK	19.2	14.5	0.7	0.1	4.0
Virginia Beach, VA	8.9	2.8	2.5	0.3	3.3
Washington, DC	11.6	2.1	0.8	0.4	8.2
Wichita, KS	18.4	15.1	0.8	0.1	2.5
Wilmington, NC	8.9	3.6	1.4	0.4	3.5
Winston-Salem, NC	17.9	10.1	1.7	0.3	5.8
U.S.	19.0	11.3	1.8	0.7	5.2

Note: Persons of Hispanic or Latino origin can be of any race
Source: U.S. Census Bureau, 2019-2023 American Community Survey 5-Year Estimates

Hispanic Origin: Metro Area

Metro Area	Hispanic or Latino (%)	Mexican (%)	Puerto Rican (%)	Cuban (%)	Other Hispanic or Latino (%)
Albuquerque, NM	48.3	28.5	0.7	0.4	18.6
Anchorage, AK	8.2	3.8	1.2	0.4	2.8
Ann Arbor, MI	5.6	2.8	0.6	0.2	2.1
Athens, GA	9.3	5.1	0.4	0.5	3.3
Atlanta, GA	12.1	5.7	1.2	0.4	4.7
Austin, TX	32.0	24.8	1.0	0.6	5.6
Baltimore, MD	7.8	1.6	1.2	0.3	4.7
Billings, MT	6.1	4.4	0.2	0.1	1.3
Boise City, ID	14.7	11.8	0.4	0.1	2.4
Boston, MA	12.0	0.8	2.7	0.3	8.3
Boulder, CO	14.6	9.8	0.5	0.3	3.9
Cape Coral, FL	23.6	4.7	4.5	6.7	7.8
Cedar Rapids, IA	3.7	2.6	0.2	0.0	0.8
Charleston, SC	7.5	3.5	1.1	0.3	2.7
Charlotte, NC	12.0	4.9	1.1	0.4	5.6
Chicago, IL	23.8	18.3	2.3	0.3	2.9
Cincinnati, OH	4.3	1.8	0.5	0.2	1.9
Clarksville, TN	9.7	5.0	2.3	0.2	2.2
Cleveland, OH	6.5	1.5	3.6	0.1	1.3
College Station, TX	26.4	21.9	0.5	0.5	3.6
Colorado Springs, CO	18.0	10.8	1.5	0.3	5.3
Columbia, MO	4.1	2.7	0.2	0.1	1.0
Columbia, SC	6.8	3.2	1.1	0.3	2.3
Columbus, OH	5.3	2.5	0.8	0.1	2.0
Dallas, TX	29.4	23.1	0.9	0.4	5.1
Davenport, IA	9.5	8.3	0.4	0.1	0.8
Denver, CO	23.6	17.5	0.7	0.2	5.3
Des Moines, IA	8.4	5.7	0.4	0.1	2.2
Detroit, MI	5.1	3.4	0.6	0.1	1.0
Durham, NC	13.2	6.3	0.8	0.4	5.8
El Paso, TX	82.6	77.5	1.0	0.2	4.0
Eugene, OR	10.2	7.3	0.4	0.2	2.3
Fargo, ND	3.8	2.5	0.4	0.0	0.8
Fort Collins, CO	12.7	9.0	0.5	0.2	3.0
Fort Wayne, IN	8.0	5.7	0.6	0.1	1.7
Fort Worth, TX	29.4	23.1	0.9	0.4	5.1
Gainesville, FL	11.6	1.8	2.8	2.1	4.9
Green Bay, WI	8.7	6.2	1.0	0.1	1.3
Greensboro, NC	10.2	5.9	1.2	0.2	2.8
Honolulu, HI	9.3	3.1	3.1	0.2	3.0
Houston, TX	37.8	26.1	0.8	0.8	10.1
Huntsville, AL	6.7	3.6	0.9	0.2	1.9
Indianapolis, IN	8.6	5.4	0.6	0.2	2.4
Jacksonville, FL	10.6	1.8	3.3	1.5	4.0
Kansas City, MO	10.6	7.5	0.5	0.3	2.3
Lafayette, LA	5.3	1.9	0.2	0.2	3.0
Las Vegas, NV	31.4	22.7	1.1	1.5	6.1
Lexington, KY	7.8	4.9	0.5	0.3	2.0
Lincoln, NE	8.0	5.2	0.4	0.2	2.2
Little Rock, AR	7.1	4.6	0.3	0.1	2.1
Los Angeles, CA	44.8	33.8	0.5	0.4	10.2
Louisville, KY	6.5	2.7	0.5	1.8	1.5
Madison, WI	6.9	4.2	0.6	0.1	1.9
Manchester, NH	8.3	1.2	2.6	0.2	4.2
McAllen, TX	91.9	87.6	0.3	0.1	3.9

Table continued on following page.

Metro Area	Hispanic or Latino (%)	Mexican (%)	Puerto Rican (%)	Cuban (%)	Other Hispanic or Latino (%)
Memphis, TN	7.2	4.2	0.3	0.2	2.5
Miami, FL	46.0	2.5	3.7	18.4	21.5
Midland, TX	44.8	39.3	0.6	1.2	3.8
Milwaukee, WI	11.8	7.7	2.6	0.1	1.4
Minneapolis, MN	6.7	4.1	0.3	0.1	2.1
Nashville, TN	9.7	5.1	0.7	0.4	3.5
New Orleans, LA	12.6	2.0	0.7	0.9	9.1
New York, NY	25.4	3.0	5.6	0.8	16.0
Oklahoma City, OK	15.3	11.9	0.5	0.1	2.8
Omaha, NE	11.9	8.7	0.4	0.2	2.6
Orlando, FL	32.5	2.7	14.3	2.6	12.9
Philadelphia, PA	10.4	2.0	4.6	0.3	3.6
Phoenix, AZ	30.8	26.2	0.7	0.3	3.6
Pittsburgh, PA	2.3	0.8	0.5	0.1	0.9
Portland, OR	13.5	10.2	0.4	0.2	2.6
Providence, RI	14.6	1.0	4.3	0.2	9.1
Provo, UT	13.7	8.1	0.4	0.1	5.1
Raleigh, NC	12.1	6.0	1.4	0.4	4.4
Reno, NV	24.7	18.9	0.6	0.3	5.0
Richmond, VA	8.1	1.9	1.2	0.3	4.7
Rochester, MN	5.1	3.2	0.3	0.1	1.5
Sacramento, CA	22.6	17.9	0.7	0.2	3.8
Saint Louis, MO	3.8	2.3	0.3	0.1	1.1
Saint Paul, MN	6.7	4.1	0.3	0.1	2.1
Salem, OR	25.6	22.2	0.3	0.2	3.0
Salt Lake City, UT	19.6	13.7	0.4	0.1	5.3
San Antonio, TX	54.5	45.5	1.5	0.3	7.2
San Diego, CA	34.3	29.6	0.8	0.2	3.6
San Francisco, CA	23.0	14.5	0.7	0.2	7.6
San Jose, CA	26.3	21.2	0.4	0.2	4.5
Santa Rosa, CA	29.4	23.7	0.4	0.2	5.1
Savannah, GA	7.7	2.9	1.9	0.5	2.4
Seattle, WA	11.4	7.7	0.6	0.2	2.9
Sioux Falls, SD	5.3	2.4	0.2	0.1	2.6
Tampa, FL	21.1	3.7	6.0	4.5	6.9
Tucson, AZ	36.1	32.1	0.9	0.2	3.0
Tulsa, OK	12.0	8.9	0.5	0.1	2.5
Virginia Beach, VA	7.8	2.6	2.2	0.3	2.8
Washington, DC	17.6	2.5	1.2	0.3	13.6
Wichita, KS	14.5	11.8	0.6	0.1	2.0
Wilmington, NC	7.1	3.4	0.9	0.3	2.5
Winston-Salem, NC	11.8	7.0	1.1	0.3	3.4
U.S.	19.0	11.3	1.8	0.7	5.2

Note: Persons of Hispanic or Latino origin can be of any race; Figures cover the Metropolitan Statistical Area (MSA)
Source: U.S. Census Bureau, 2019-2023 American Community Survey 5-Year Estimates

Household Size: City

City	Persons in Household (%)							Average Household Size
	One	Two	Three	Four	Five	Six	Seven or More	
Albuquerque, NM	37.3	32.4	13.7	9.8	4.6	1.4	0.8	2.29
Anchorage, AK	28.5	33.7	14.8	13.5	5.4	2.3	1.8	2.61
Ann Arbor, MI	34.0	35.9	14.5	9.9	3.2	1.8	0.7	2.19
Athens, GA	33.6	35.1	15.3	10.6	4.0	0.9	0.6	2.18
Atlanta, GA	47.0	32.0	10.6	6.5	2.3	1.0	0.6	2.01
Austin, TX	36.9	34.0	13.4	10.0	3.4	1.5	0.7	2.14
Baltimore, MD	43.4	29.6	13.4	7.7	3.7	1.3	1.0	2.22
Billings, MT	34.0	35.0	13.2	10.8	4.7	1.2	1.1	2.29
Boise City, ID	30.1	37.7	15.0	10.9	4.2	1.5	0.7	2.30
Boston, MA	36.9	33.2	14.6	8.9	4.0	1.5	0.9	2.22
Boulder, CO	34.9	36.6	13.9	10.9	2.5	0.6	0.7	2.16
Cape Coral, FL	24.2	44.1	13.7	10.3	5.5	1.3	0.8	2.59
Cedar Rapids, IA	34.4	35.4	13.5	9.4	5.0	1.1	1.3	2.27
Charleston, SC	34.5	40.1	12.4	8.7	3.2	0.8	0.3	2.20
Charlotte, NC	35.1	31.7	14.8	11.2	4.7	1.5	1.0	2.42
Chicago, IL	39.2	29.4	13.1	9.9	4.8	2.1	1.5	2.32
Cincinnati, OH	44.9	30.5	10.7	8.5	3.0	1.4	1.0	2.07
Clarksville, TN	25.7	33.0	18.0	13.6	5.5	2.5	1.6	2.59
Cleveland, OH	46.4	28.4	11.9	7.4	3.4	1.7	0.9	2.11
College Station, TX	31.1	32.3	15.1	15.1	3.5	2.4	0.6	2.42
Colorado Springs, CO	28.2	36.1	15.4	11.8	5.3	2.2	1.0	2.39
Columbia, MO	34.5	33.8	13.4	12.2	4.6	1.0	0.5	2.29
Columbia, SC	39.3	33.0	14.2	8.3	3.7	1.2	0.3	2.16
Columbus, OH	36.5	32.2	13.4	9.7	4.9	2.0	1.3	2.29
Dallas, TX	37.1	29.7	12.7	10.1	6.1	2.6	1.6	2.43
Davenport, IA	34.9	35.3	13.1	9.5	5.1	1.4	0.7	2.25
Denver, CO	40.0	33.5	11.4	9.0	3.7	1.5	1.0	2.12
Des Moines, IA	37.1	30.7	13.2	10.3	4.8	2.1	1.8	2.30
Detroit, MI	42.5	25.3	13.8	8.9	4.8	2.7	1.9	2.47
Durham, NC	36.1	34.1	13.9	9.9	4.0	1.4	0.6	2.25
El Paso, TX	25.8	28.2	18.0	15.5	8.0	2.8	1.7	2.77
Eugene, OR	34.3	35.7	13.6	10.6	4.0	1.2	0.5	2.23
Fargo, ND	41.1	33.0	11.6	9.3	3.4	1.1	0.5	2.10
Fort Collins, CO	26.6	37.8	17.6	12.5	4.1	1.0	0.4	2.27
Fort Wayne, IN	33.5	33.1	13.3	10.7	5.4	2.5	1.4	2.39
Fort Worth, TX	27.7	29.8	15.6	14.1	7.6	3.1	2.0	2.76
Gainesville, FL	39.2	33.2	14.6	8.8	3.1	0.5	0.6	2.17
Green Bay, WI	35.7	32.4	12.0	11.7	4.8	2.0	1.3	2.35
Greensboro, NC	36.4	30.7	15.3	9.8	4.8	1.5	1.5	2.33
Honolulu, HI	35.0	31.1	14.6	9.7	4.5	2.1	3.0	2.47
Houston, TX	34.1	29.2	15.6	11.6	5.7	2.3	1.5	2.47
Huntsville, AL	36.9	35.6	13.6	8.6	3.8	1.2	0.4	2.21
Indianapolis, IN	36.6	31.9	13.1	9.8	5.4	1.9	1.3	2.41
Jacksonville, FL	32.2	33.3	16.2	10.6	5.0	1.8	0.9	2.44
Kansas City, MO	37.7	31.3	12.3	10.8	4.7	2.1	1.0	2.28
Lafayette, LA	33.8	36.5	13.4	9.1	5.0	1.4	0.9	2.25
Las Vegas, NV	30.3	31.2	15.8	11.9	6.3	2.7	1.9	2.63
Lexington, KY	34.8	33.4	14.3	10.8	4.0	1.7	0.9	2.24
Lincoln, NE	32.7	34.1	13.7	11.0	4.9	2.5	1.0	2.31
Little Rock, AR	39.4	31.1	13.5	9.1	4.3	1.4	1.1	2.28
Los Angeles, CA	31.5	28.9	15.5	12.5	6.4	2.6	2.5	2.64
Louisville, KY	34.5	32.8	15.3	10.3	4.6	1.7	0.9	2.34
Madison, WI	39.0	35.2	12.0	9.1	3.3	0.8	0.7	2.09
Manchester, NH	34.5	34.2	14.7	10.7	3.7	1.7	0.5	2.27

Table continued on following page.

City	Persons in Household (%)							Average Household Size
	One	Two	Three	Four	Five	Six	Seven or More	
McAllen, TX	21.4	28.2	18.3	16.3	10.9	2.4	2.5	2.96
Memphis, TN	38.9	29.6	14.5	9.4	4.3	1.8	1.5	2.42
Miami, FL	36.5	32.1	15.8	9.5	3.8	1.1	1.2	2.30
Midland, TX	29.9	27.2	15.3	16.3	7.6	2.6	1.1	2.51
Milwaukee, WI	38.7	29.0	13.7	9.4	5.6	2.1	1.6	2.40
Minneapolis, MN	42.0	30.8	11.5	9.2	3.5	1.5	1.4	2.16
Nashville, TN	36.9	33.0	13.6	9.2	4.6	1.5	1.2	2.19
New Orleans, LA	44.7	29.3	13.2	8.0	3.3	1.0	0.5	2.34
New York, NY	33.4	28.8	16.1	11.7	5.6	2.5	1.9	2.51
Oklahoma City, OK	31.6	31.7	15.5	11.5	6.3	2.3	1.1	2.46
Omaha, NE	34.5	31.5	13.1	10.7	6.0	2.5	1.7	2.39
Orlando, FL	32.4	33.5	15.9	11.2	4.5	1.4	1.1	2.44
Philadelphia, PA	37.6	29.9	14.9	9.6	4.8	1.7	1.4	2.29
Phoenix, AZ	28.3	30.6	15.2	12.8	7.3	3.3	2.5	2.66
Pittsburgh, PA	43.9	33.0	11.6	7.1	2.9	0.8	0.7	2.03
Portland, OR	36.4	34.8	13.8	9.9	3.2	1.1	0.7	2.18
Providence, RI	33.8	28.4	15.4	11.7	7.0	2.3	1.4	2.48
Provo, UT	14.0	36.9	17.7	14.4	7.6	6.5	3.0	2.98
Raleigh, NC	35.3	33.7	13.8	11.4	4.2	1.1	0.5	2.30
Reno, NV	31.9	34.1	14.9	12.1	4.5	1.3	1.2	2.35
Richmond, VA	42.9	32.7	12.2	7.7	2.6	1.2	0.6	2.13
Rochester, MN	31.6	34.6	13.4	12.5	5.0	1.8	1.1	2.35
Sacramento, CA	31.7	29.8	14.4	12.4	6.6	2.6	2.5	2.58
Saint Louis, MO	47.9	30.1	10.3	6.9	3.0	1.0	0.8	1.96
Saint Paul, MN	37.1	29.8	12.5	9.6	5.1	2.9	3.1	2.42
Salem, OR	29.2	33.2	15.5	11.5	5.8	3.0	1.8	2.51
Salt Lake City, UT	39.3	34.1	11.6	8.2	3.8	1.8	1.3	2.19
San Antonio, TX	31.3	29.4	15.5	12.5	6.7	2.8	1.8	2.62
San Diego, CA	28.8	34.2	15.5	12.8	5.4	2.0	1.4	2.55
San Francisco, CA	38.0	32.3	13.4	9.9	3.5	1.6	1.2	2.24
San Jose, CA	20.7	29.4	18.8	17.6	7.6	3.0	2.9	2.98
Santa Rosa, CA	28.0	33.1	16.1	13.7	5.7	2.2	1.2	2.54
Savannah, GA	35.4	34.5	14.8	9.4	3.7	1.1	1.1	2.35
Seattle, WA	41.3	35.4	11.2	8.5	2.5	0.7	0.5	2.03
Sioux Falls, SD	33.9	33.0	12.9	10.3	6.9	1.8	1.2	2.32
Tampa, FL	35.7	32.1	15.4	10.9	4.1	1.4	0.5	2.35
Tucson, AZ	36.3	31.0	13.7	10.7	5.2	2.0	1.1	2.30
Tulsa, OK	35.9	31.9	13.4	10.3	4.9	2.4	1.3	2.36
Virginia Beach, VA	26.1	35.6	17.3	12.7	5.9	1.7	0.8	2.50
Washington, DC	46.7	30.2	11.1	7.4	2.8	1.2	0.7	1.99
Wichita, KS	33.2	32.6	13.2	10.8	5.7	2.7	1.7	2.47
Wilmington, NC	38.5	38.5	12.3	6.8	2.8	0.8	0.3	2.06
Winston-Salem, NC	35.2	32.7	14.2	9.8	4.8	2.3	1.0	2.40
U.S.	28.5	33.8	15.4	12.7	5.9	2.3	1.4	2.54

U.S. Census Bureau, 2019-2023 American Community Survey 5-Year Estimates

Household Size: Metro Area

Metro Area	Persons in Household (%)							Average Household Size
	One	Two	Three	Four	Five	Six	Seven or More	
Albuquerque, NM	33.0	33.6	14.6	10.8	5.0	1.9	1.2	2.44
Anchorage, AK	27.2	33.9	14.5	13.6	6.1	2.7	2.1	2.64
Ann Arbor, MI	30.6	36.1	14.9	11.5	4.2	1.9	0.9	2.34
Athens, GA	28.1	35.1	16.5	12.8	5.1	1.7	0.7	2.43
Atlanta, GA	27.1	32.0	17.0	13.7	6.2	2.4	1.5	2.67
Austin, TX	28.7	33.8	15.6	13.2	5.3	2.3	1.1	2.44
Baltimore, MD	30.0	32.8	15.7	13.0	5.3	2.1	1.2	2.51
Billings, MT	31.0	36.9	13.2	11.3	4.8	1.5	1.3	2.36
Boise City, ID	23.2	36.6	15.4	13.4	6.5	3.3	1.7	2.62
Boston, MA	28.0	33.2	16.7	14.0	5.5	1.7	0.9	2.47
Boulder, CO	29.8	37.0	14.5	12.6	4.2	1.3	0.6	2.33
Cape Coral, FL	28.3	44.7	11.6	8.8	4.4	1.5	0.7	2.44
Cedar Rapids, IA	29.8	37.2	13.8	11.3	5.4	1.4	1.1	2.38
Charleston, SC	29.3	36.3	15.3	11.8	5.0	1.6	0.7	2.45
Charlotte, NC	28.0	34.2	15.9	13.2	5.6	1.9	1.1	2.55
Chicago, IL	29.9	31.0	15.4	13.5	6.4	2.3	1.5	2.55
Cincinnati, OH	29.7	34.2	14.5	12.8	5.6	2.1	1.2	2.46
Clarksville, TN	26.0	33.6	17.5	12.8	5.8	2.4	1.9	2.63
Cleveland, OH	35.3	33.7	13.6	10.5	4.4	1.6	0.9	2.29
College Station, TX	30.3	32.8	14.7	13.5	5.3	2.3	1.1	2.48
Colorado Springs, CO	24.8	36.1	16.2	13.0	6.1	2.4	1.4	2.51
Columbia, MO	31.1	36.1	13.7	12.2	5.0	1.2	0.8	2.37
Columbia, SC	30.6	34.0	15.5	11.9	5.2	1.9	0.9	2.42
Columbus, OH	29.4	33.6	15.1	12.7	5.8	2.2	1.2	2.46
Dallas, TX	25.9	30.9	16.4	14.7	7.5	2.9	1.7	2.73
Davenport, IA	31.5	35.8	13.6	11.3	5.3	1.8	0.8	2.32
Denver, CO	29.2	34.9	14.8	12.7	5.0	2.2	1.2	2.45
Des Moines, IA	29.6	33.9	14.0	12.8	6.4	2.1	1.1	2.44
Detroit, MI	31.9	32.8	15.0	11.9	5.3	1.9	1.2	2.46
Durham, NC	31.7	35.8	14.8	10.9	4.6	1.5	0.6	2.33
El Paso, TX	23.9	27.3	18.2	16.3	9.0	3.5	1.8	2.88
Eugene, OR	29.5	38.4	14.1	10.8	4.8	1.5	0.9	2.34
Fargo, ND	35.2	33.4	13.1	11.0	5.0	1.5	0.8	2.28
Fort Collins, CO	25.5	39.2	16.4	12.1	4.5	1.4	0.9	2.33
Fort Wayne, IN	29.7	34.7	13.4	11.7	6.1	2.7	1.6	2.48
Fort Worth, TX	25.9	30.9	16.4	14.7	7.5	2.9	1.7	2.73
Gainesville, FL	32.9	35.5	15.3	10.3	3.9	1.2	0.9	2.36
Green Bay, WI	29.3	37.6	13.1	12.1	5.2	1.8	0.8	2.38
Greensboro, NC	31.0	33.8	15.5	11.4	5.2	2.0	1.1	2.42
Honolulu, HI	24.9	30.8	16.7	13.1	6.8	3.5	4.1	2.88
Houston, TX	24.8	29.9	17.2	15.3	8.0	3.0	1.8	2.76
Huntsville, AL	29.4	36.4	15.1	12.1	4.8	1.5	0.6	2.42
Indianapolis, IN	29.6	33.8	14.7	12.7	6.1	1.9	1.1	2.50
Jacksonville, FL	27.8	35.6	16.4	11.8	5.5	1.9	1.0	2.51
Kansas City, MO	29.8	34.3	14.1	12.6	5.8	2.3	1.2	2.46
Lafayette, LA	29.1	33.5	16.1	12.4	5.4	2.1	1.2	2.49
Las Vegas, NV	28.0	32.7	15.8	12.3	6.8	2.8	1.8	2.68
Lexington, KY	31.6	34.5	15.2	11.6	4.3	1.9	0.9	2.35
Lincoln, NE	30.8	35.3	13.6	11.4	5.2	2.5	1.1	2.35
Little Rock, AR	31.7	34.1	15.2	11.0	5.3	1.7	1.0	2.41
Los Angeles, CA	25.1	29.0	17.0	15.1	7.7	3.2	2.8	2.86
Louisville, KY	30.6	34.4	15.5	11.8	5.1	1.8	0.9	2.43
Madison, WI	32.9	36.5	13.2	11.1	4.3	1.4	0.7	2.25
Manchester, NH	27.2	35.8	16.5	13.1	4.9	1.7	0.8	2.48

Table continued on following page.

Metro Area	Persons in Household (%)							Average Household Size
	One	Two	Three	Four	Five	Six	Seven or More	
McAllen, TX	18.5	25.1	16.9	17.1	12.2	5.6	4.5	3.30
Memphis, TN	31.2	31.7	16.4	11.7	5.5	2.0	1.5	2.55
Miami, FL	27.9	32.2	17.3	13.3	6.0	2.1	1.3	2.62
Midland, TX	28.9	27.1	15.8	16.0	8.2	2.7	1.4	2.53
Milwaukee, WI	33.0	34.4	13.7	11.3	5.1	1.7	0.9	2.37
Minneapolis, MN	28.9	34.2	14.3	13.3	5.8	2.1	1.4	2.49
Nashville, TN	28.0	34.5	16.1	12.7	5.7	1.9	1.1	2.49
New Orleans, LA	36.4	30.5	15.4	10.8	4.4	1.6	0.9	2.44
New York, NY	28.6	29.6	16.8	14.1	6.3	2.6	1.9	2.63
Oklahoma City, OK	29.0	33.1	15.7	12.4	6.3	2.3	1.2	2.51
Omaha, NE	29.6	33.1	14.3	12.3	6.6	2.5	1.5	2.49
Orlando, FL	24.5	34.1	17.0	14.3	6.5	2.2	1.3	2.71
Philadelphia, PA	29.7	32.3	16.0	13.2	5.7	1.9	1.1	2.49
Phoenix, AZ	26.0	34.8	14.8	12.6	6.7	3.0	2.1	2.62
Pittsburgh, PA	34.1	35.8	13.7	10.6	4.1	1.2	0.6	2.25
Portland, OR	27.6	35.7	15.6	12.8	5.2	1.9	1.2	2.47
Providence, RI	29.5	33.7	16.3	12.9	5.1	1.6	0.9	2.41
Provo, UT	12.3	29.0	16.2	16.6	12.5	8.1	5.3	3.40
Raleigh, NC	25.9	34.7	16.1	14.5	6.0	1.9	0.9	2.57
Reno, NV	27.5	35.2	15.5	12.9	5.6	2.1	1.3	2.49
Richmond, VA	29.5	34.7	15.8	12.2	5.1	1.8	1.0	2.47
Rochester, MN	27.9	36.9	13.2	13.3	5.9	1.8	1.1	2.42
Sacramento, CA	25.1	32.7	16.0	14.5	7.1	2.7	2.0	2.70
Saint Louis, MO	31.3	34.4	14.6	11.9	5.2	1.6	0.9	2.38
Saint Paul, MN	28.9	34.2	14.3	13.3	5.8	2.1	1.4	2.49
Salem, OR	25.5	33.8	15.8	12.5	6.7	3.3	2.3	2.67
Salt Lake City, UT	24.0	31.1	15.7	13.9	7.9	4.4	3.0	2.83
San Antonio, TX	26.8	31.1	16.3	13.8	7.3	2.8	1.9	2.71
San Diego, CA	24.5	33.0	16.7	14.6	6.7	2.6	1.8	2.74
San Francisco, CA	27.2	31.8	16.7	14.5	5.9	2.3	1.6	2.63
San Jose, CA	21.4	31.1	18.8	17.2	6.9	2.6	2.1	2.86
Santa Rosa, CA	27.5	35.1	15.1	13.5	5.5	2.0	1.2	2.50
Savannah, GA	28.1	36.4	15.7	12.1	5.2	1.5	1.1	2.52
Seattle, WA	28.0	34.0	15.8	13.6	5.4	1.9	1.3	2.49
Sioux Falls, SD	30.0	34.4	13.6	11.4	7.3	2.1	1.2	2.41
Tampa, FL	30.8	36.3	15.0	10.9	4.6	1.6	0.8	2.44
Tucson, AZ	31.8	35.4	13.2	11.1	5.1	2.3	1.2	2.37
Tulsa, OK	29.2	33.6	15.2	12.3	5.9	2.5	1.4	2.53
Virginia Beach, VA	28.6	34.6	16.5	12.2	5.5	1.9	0.9	2.46
Washington, DC	28.6	30.4	15.9	14.3	6.5	2.6	1.7	2.62
Wichita, KS	30.1	33.6	14.0	11.7	6.2	2.8	1.7	2.52
Wilmington, NC	29.9	42.0	14.0	8.9	3.6	1.2	0.4	2.26
Winston-Salem, NC	30.3	35.6	15.4	11.1	4.7	2.0	0.9	2.43
U.S.	28.5	33.8	15.4	12.7	5.9	2.3	1.4	2.54

Note: Figures cover the Metropolitan Statistical Area (MSA)
Source: U.S. Census Bureau, 2019-2023 American Community Survey 5-Year Estimates

Household Relationships: City

City	House-holder	Opposite-sex Spouse	Same-sex Spouse	Opposite-sex Unmarried Partner	Same-sex Unmarried Partner	Child[1]	Grand-child	Other Relatives	Non-relatives
Albuquerque, NM	42.1	15.1	0.3	3.4	0.3	27.0	2.5	4.6	3.2
Anchorage, AK	37.5	17.0	0.2	3.0	0.2	28.3	1.9	4.6	4.2
Ann Arbor, MI	40.3	13.3	0.3	2.4	0.2	17.1	0.5	1.6	11.5
Athens, GA	40.1	11.6	0.2	2.7	0.2	20.8	2.0	3.7	10.7
Atlanta, GA	45.7	10.4	0.5	3.1	0.6	20.7	2.1	3.9	5.9
Austin, TX	42.7	14.5	0.4	3.6	0.4	23.2	1.5	4.1	6.4
Baltimore, MD	42.9	9.6	0.3	3.3	0.3	24.9	3.7	5.8	6.1
Billings, MT	42.2	17.7	0.2	3.1	0.1	26.0	1.7	2.5	3.5
Boise City, ID	41.4	17.8	0.2	3.2	0.2	24.7	1.3	2.9	5.4
Boston, MA	41.4	10.4	0.5	3.1	0.4	20.6	1.7	5.3	9.7
Boulder, CO	40.2	13.0	0.3	3.1	0.2	16.4	0.3	1.6	12.3
Cape Coral, FL	39.5	21.2	0.3	3.2	0.1	25.5	2.1	4.8	2.8
Cedar Rapids, IA	42.2	16.7	0.2	3.5	0.2	26.8	1.3	2.9	3.4
Charleston, SC	45.0	17.0	0.3	3.1	0.2	21.8	1.4	2.7	5.3
Charlotte, NC	40.6	15.2	0.2	2.8	0.2	28.0	2.1	4.9	4.2
Chicago, IL	41.6	12.2	0.3	3.0	0.3	26.6	3.0	6.4	4.8
Cincinnati, OH	45.1	10.2	0.3	3.4	0.3	24.6	2.2	3.4	5.3
Clarksville, TN	36.6	16.9	0.2	2.5	0.1	31.2	2.4	3.9	3.5
Cleveland, OH	45.0	8.5	0.2	3.5	0.3	27.0	3.3	5.0	3.8
College Station, TX	35.2	11.2	0.2	1.8	0.1	19.7	0.7	2.7	13.7
Colorado Springs, CO	39.7	18.3	0.3	2.6	0.2	27.5	1.9	3.6	4.3
Columbia, MO	40.5	14.1	0.2	2.8	0.2	22.4	1.0	2.5	7.8
Columbia, SC	39.2	10.5	0.2	2.1	0.2	19.5	1.6	2.8	5.8
Columbus, OH	42.2	12.9	0.3	3.6	0.3	26.2	2.1	4.4	5.2
Dallas, TX	40.1	13.4	0.4	2.6	0.3	28.6	3.2	6.2	4.0
Davenport, IA	41.9	15.9	0.2	3.7	0.2	27.0	2.0	3.0	3.2
Denver, CO	44.4	14.0	0.5	4.1	0.4	22.3	1.9	4.4	5.9
Des Moines, IA	41.1	14.2	0.3	3.5	0.2	27.9	2.0	4.4	3.9
Detroit, MI	39.8	7.3	0.1	2.9	0.2	32.0	4.8	7.3	3.9
Durham, NC	42.0	14.8	0.4	2.9	0.3	24.6	1.8	4.4	4.6
El Paso, TX	35.9	15.8	0.2	1.8	0.1	32.7	3.9	6.4	2.0
Eugene, OR	41.6	14.7	0.3	3.8	0.3	20.7	1.1	2.7	8.3
Fargo, ND	44.5	15.5	0.1	3.6	0.2	23.5	0.7	2.5	5.0
Fort Collins, CO	39.9	16.0	0.2	3.3	0.2	22.1	0.9	2.4	9.0
Fort Wayne, IN	40.7	15.6	0.2	3.1	0.2	29.7	2.0	3.4	3.0
Fort Worth, TX	35.2	15.8	0.2	2.1	0.1	33.0	3.1	5.6	3.0
Gainesville, FL	41.0	9.4	0.3	3.0	0.3	17.0	1.5	3.4	12.5
Green Bay, WI	40.7	15.2	0.2	4.0	0.2	28.6	1.6	3.4	3.0
Greensboro, NC	40.9	13.6	0.2	2.6	0.2	26.4	2.0	4.1	3.6
Honolulu, HI	39.1	15.0	0.3	2.4	0.2	22.2	3.1	9.1	5.6
Houston, TX	38.9	14.0	0.3	2.4	0.2	29.5	2.9	6.5	3.6
Huntsville, AL	42.8	16.5	0.2	2.2	0.2	25.1	2.1	3.5	3.1
Indianapolis, IN	40.7	14.0	0.3	3.4	0.3	28.6	2.5	4.5	3.9
Jacksonville, FL	39.9	15.6	0.2	2.8	0.2	27.7	2.8	4.9	3.6
Kansas City, MO	42.6	14.5	0.3	3.3	0.3	27.2	2.3	4.0	3.8
Lafayette, LA	43.0	15.3	0.2	2.8	0.2	27.0	2.3	3.5	3.8
Las Vegas, NV	37.5	15.2	0.3	2.9	0.2	29.3	2.7	6.7	4.3
Lexington, KY	41.7	16.0	0.3	2.9	0.3	25.3	1.6	3.4	4.4
Lincoln, NE	40.1	16.9	0.2	2.8	0.1	26.6	1.1	2.7	4.6
Little Rock, AR	43.5	14.5	0.3	2.4	0.3	27.1	2.3	3.9	3.1
Los Angeles, CA	36.2	13.1	0.3	2.8	0.3	26.5	2.8	9.0	6.3
Louisville, KY	40.0	18.0	0.2	2.9	0.2	28.8	2.6	4.2	2.7
Madison, WI	44.8	14.5	0.4	3.8	0.3	19.7	0.7	2.4	8.2
Manchester, NH	42.5	14.9	0.3	4.3	0.2	24.3	1.6	4.3	4.7
McAllen, TX	34.3	16.0	0.1	1.7	0.1	34.6	3.5	6.8	2.0

Table continued on following page.

City	House-holder	Opposite-sex Spouse	Same-sex Spouse	Opposite-sex Unmarried Partner	Same-sex Unmarried Partner	Child[1]	Grand-child	Other Relatives	Non-relatives
Memphis, TN	40.4	10.9	0.2	2.7	0.2	29.7	4.3	6.1	3.7
Miami, FL	42.4	12.6	0.5	3.3	0.3	22.5	2.4	8.7	5.8
Midland, TX	36.4	18.5	0.1	2.1	0.1	31.9	3.0	4.2	2.5
Milwaukee, WI	40.8	10.2	0.2	3.6	0.2	30.2	2.7	4.9	4.4
Minneapolis, MN	43.7	12.0	0.6	3.9	0.5	22.1	1.1	3.5	8.0
Nashville, TN	42.1	14.3	0.3	3.0	0.3	24.0	1.9	4.7	5.7
New Orleans, LA	43.0	11.0	0.3	3.1	0.4	26.1	3.2	4.6	4.3
New York, NY	38.3	12.7	0.3	2.2	0.2	27.6	2.5	8.3	5.3
Oklahoma City, OK	39.4	16.6	0.2	2.6	0.2	29.4	2.3	4.3	3.1
Omaha, NE	39.8	16.0	0.2	2.8	0.2	29.6	1.8	3.7	3.6
Orlando, FL	41.7	13.7	0.5	3.5	0.4	26.1	2.0	5.9	5.0
Philadelphia, PA	41.0	10.9	0.3	3.1	0.3	26.8	3.6	5.9	5.2
Phoenix, AZ	36.3	14.4	0.3	3.1	0.3	30.2	2.9	6.6	4.2
Pittsburgh, PA	46.1	11.5	0.3	3.6	0.4	19.3	1.7	3.1	6.7
Portland, OR	43.2	14.9	0.7	4.4	0.6	21.2	1.1	3.7	7.2
Providence, RI	36.5	10.5	0.3	2.9	0.3	27.3	1.9	5.7	6.1
Provo, UT	29.6	15.9	0.1	0.6	0.0	25.7	1.6	4.0	12.7
Raleigh, NC	41.8	15.1	0.2	2.9	0.2	25.5	1.4	3.9	5.0
Reno, NV	41.1	15.2	0.3	3.8	0.2	24.8	1.7	4.7	5.7
Richmond, VA	45.2	10.4	0.4	4.0	0.4	20.8	2.1	4.3	7.4
Rochester, MN	41.1	18.5	0.2	2.8	0.1	27.8	0.9	2.8	3.3
Sacramento, CA	36.7	13.5	0.4	3.0	0.3	28.0	2.6	7.5	4.7
Saint Louis, MO	48.0	10.3	0.4	3.7	0.4	22.5	2.6	4.0	4.3
Saint Paul, MN	38.7	12.7	0.4	3.3	0.3	28.8	1.7	5.6	4.8
Salem, OR	36.6	16.0	0.2	3.1	0.2	28.1	1.9	4.6	4.2
Salt Lake City, UT	42.3	13.9	0.5	3.4	0.4	22.1	1.7	4.2	7.6
San Antonio, TX	37.5	14.7	0.3	2.7	0.2	30.3	3.8	5.5	3.2
San Diego, CA	37.2	15.7	0.4	2.6	0.3	25.0	2.0	6.2	6.1
San Francisco, CA	42.6	13.6	0.8	3.3	0.6	17.6	1.3	6.8	10.3
San Jose, CA	32.4	17.1	0.2	1.9	0.1	28.6	2.3	9.8	6.1
Santa Rosa, CA	37.6	16.2	0.4	3.0	0.2	27.3	1.8	6.2	5.5
Savannah, GA	39.9	11.2	0.3	2.7	0.3	24.9	3.2	4.4	5.0
Seattle, WA	46.9	15.2	0.8	4.3	0.6	17.5	0.7	2.8	7.3
Sioux Falls, SD	40.7	18.0	0.1	3.2	0.1	28.4	1.1	2.7	3.1
Tampa, FL	40.9	13.8	0.3	3.2	0.3	25.8	2.3	4.9	4.5
Tucson, AZ	41.1	13.3	0.3	3.3	0.3	25.4	2.8	4.8	4.5
Tulsa, OK	41.6	14.8	0.2	2.9	0.2	27.8	2.3	4.3	3.4
Virginia Beach, VA	38.8	18.6	0.2	2.4	0.1	28.7	2.2	4.0	3.5
Washington, DC	45.3	10.3	0.6	3.1	0.5	20.4	2.4	4.2	7.1
Wichita, KS	40.0	16.4	0.2	2.7	0.2	29.1	2.2	3.7	3.1
Wilmington, NC	45.7	14.9	0.3	3.4	0.3	21.2	1.5	3.0	5.9
Winston-Salem, NC	40.9	14.6	0.2	2.5	0.2	28.1	2.4	4.3	2.7
U.S.	38.3	17.5	0.2	2.5	0.2	28.3	2.4	4.8	3.4

Note: Figures are percent of the total population; (1) Includes biological, adopted, and stepchildren of the householder
Source: U.S. Census Bureau, 2020 Census

Household Relationships: Metro Area

Metro Area	House-holder	Opposite-sex Spouse	Same-sex Spouse	Opposite-sex Unmarried Partner	Same-sex Unmarried Partner	Child[1]	Grand-child	Other Relatives	Non-relatives
Albuquerque, NM	40.1	16.3	0.3	3.1	0.3	27.7	3.1	4.6	2.9
Anchorage, AK	37.1	17.6	0.2	2.9	0.1	29.1	1.9	4.2	4.0
Ann Arbor, MI	39.7	17.0	0.3	2.4	0.2	24.3	1.3	2.5	5.8
Athens, GA	38.6	15.6	0.2	2.3	0.2	25.1	2.3	3.7	7.3
Atlanta, GA	37.1	16.7	0.2	2.1	0.2	30.4	2.7	5.7	3.5
Austin, TX	38.6	17.3	0.3	2.7	0.3	27.8	1.9	4.4	4.6
Baltimore, MD	38.7	16.8	0.2	2.4	0.2	28.7	2.5	4.8	3.5
Billings, MT	41.3	19.5	0.1	2.8	0.1	26.5	1.8	2.5	3.1
Boise City, ID	36.6	19.5	0.2	2.5	0.1	29.7	1.9	3.5	3.8
Boston, MA	38.7	17.4	0.3	2.5	0.2	27.1	1.6	4.5	4.4
Boulder, CO	40.1	18.0	0.3	2.8	0.2	23.8	1.0	2.6	6.8
Cape Coral, FL	41.8	20.9	0.3	3.0	0.2	22.4	1.8	4.4	3.3
Cedar Rapids, IA	40.9	19.3	0.1	3.0	0.1	27.9	1.2	2.3	2.5
Charleston, SC	39.9	18.1	0.2	2.4	0.1	27.3	2.6	3.8	3.5
Charlotte, NC	38.9	18.3	0.2	2.4	0.2	29.2	2.4	4.2	2.8
Chicago, IL	38.2	17.1	0.2	2.3	0.1	30.3	2.4	5.1	2.8
Cincinnati, OH	39.5	18.1	0.2	2.7	0.1	28.9	2.3	3.2	2.9
Clarksville, TN	36.7	18.2	0.2	2.2	0.1	30.5	2.5	3.6	3.0
Cleveland, OH	42.5	17.1	0.1	2.7	0.1	27.7	2.1	3.3	2.3
College Station, TX	36.9	14.6	0.1	2.0	0.1	24.7	1.9	3.5	8.3
Colorado Springs, CO	37.5	19.3	0.2	2.2	0.1	28.5	2.0	3.6	3.8
Columbia, MO	39.8	16.5	0.2	2.8	0.2	24.9	1.4	2.5	5.7
Columbia, SC	39.9	17.0	0.2	2.1	0.2	27.5	2.7	3.8	3.0
Columbus, OH	39.4	17.4	0.2	2.9	0.2	28.5	2.0	3.5	3.3
Dallas, TX	36.2	17.6	0.2	2.0	0.2	31.7	2.7	5.5	2.9
Davenport, IA	41.4	18.8	0.2	2.9	0.1	27.9	1.8	2.5	2.2
Denver, CO	39.4	17.9	0.3	2.9	0.2	27.4	1.9	4.4	4.3
Des Moines, IA	39.6	19.2	0.2	2.7	0.1	29.6	1.3	2.8	2.6
Detroit, MI	40.1	17.2	0.1	2.5	0.1	30.1	2.3	4.2	2.4
Durham, NC	40.3	17.2	0.3	2.5	0.2	25.1	1.9	3.8	3.9
El Paso, TX	34.2	15.8	0.2	1.7	0.1	33.5	4.2	6.5	1.8
Eugene, OR	40.9	17.0	0.3	3.7	0.2	22.7	1.8	3.5	6.6
Fargo, ND	41.5	17.7	0.1	3.2	0.1	27.0	0.7	2.2	3.9
Fort Collins, CO	40.2	19.4	0.2	2.8	0.2	24.0	1.2	2.7	6.0
Fort Wayne, IN	39.5	18.0	0.2	2.7	0.1	30.5	1.9	2.9	2.5
Fort Worth, TX	36.2	17.6	0.2	2.0	0.2	31.7	2.7	5.5	2.9
Gainesville, FL	40.4	14.9	0.2	2.8	0.2	22.9	2.2	3.9	6.9
Green Bay, WI	40.5	19.8	0.1	3.3	0.1	28.1	1.2	2.2	2.2
Greensboro, NC	40.2	17.1	0.2	2.4	0.2	27.4	2.3	3.9	2.6
Honolulu, HI	33.1	16.3	0.2	1.9	0.1	26.2	4.5	9.2	4.9
Houston, TX	35.2	17.1	0.2	2.0	0.1	32.7	2.8	6.1	2.6
Huntsville, AL	40.1	19.3	0.1	1.9	0.1	27.8	2.3	3.4	2.3
Indianapolis, IN	39.2	17.9	0.2	2.8	0.2	29.6	2.1	3.5	2.8
Jacksonville, FL	39.1	17.9	0.2	2.6	0.2	28.0	2.6	4.3	3.2
Kansas City, MO	39.6	18.4	0.2	2.6	0.2	29.4	2.0	3.3	2.7
Lafayette, LA	39.5	17.1	0.2	2.7	0.2	30.4	2.9	3.5	2.5
Las Vegas, NV	37.3	15.5	0.3	3.0	0.2	28.7	2.6	7.0	4.4
Lexington, KY	40.5	17.4	0.2	2.8	0.2	26.5	2.0	3.4	3.7
Lincoln, NE	39.5	17.9	0.2	2.6	0.1	27.2	1.1	2.6	4.1
Little Rock, AR	40.8	17.7	0.2	2.3	0.2	27.9	2.6	3.6	2.7
Los Angeles, CA	34.0	15.2	0.2	2.3	0.2	29.0	3.0	9.1	5.1
Louisville, KY	40.5	17.7	0.2	2.8	0.2	27.6	2.5	3.6	2.9
Madison, WI	42.2	18.6	0.3	3.3	0.2	25.0	0.8	2.1	4.5
Manchester, NH	39.7	19.2	0.3	3.2	0.1	27.2	1.6	3.5	3.2
McAllen, TX	29.7	15.0	0.1	1.6	0.1	38.3	5.2	7.5	1.6

Table continued on following page.

Appendix A: Comparative Statistics

Metro Area	House-holder	Opposite-sex Spouse	Same-sex Spouse	Opposite-sex Unmarried Partner	Same-sex Unmarried Partner	Child[1]	Grand-child	Other Relatives	Non-relatives
Memphis, TN	38.6	15.1	0.1	2.2	0.1	30.4	3.9	5.2	2.7
Miami, FL	38.0	16.0	0.3	2.6	0.2	27.6	2.5	7.8	3.7
Midland, TX	35.8	18.6	0.1	2.0	0.1	32.3	3.2	4.4	2.6
Milwaukee, WI	41.3	17.5	0.2	2.9	0.2	28.7	1.6	3.1	2.7
Minneapolis, MN	38.9	18.7	0.2	2.8	0.2	29.4	1.2	3.3	3.3
Nashville, TN	38.8	18.2	0.2	2.4	0.2	28.1	2.2	4.1	3.8
New Orleans, LA	40.3	15.3	0.2	2.7	0.2	28.8	3.1	4.6	2.9
New York, NY	36.8	15.8	0.2	2.0	0.2	29.7	2.1	7.1	4.1
Oklahoma City, OK	38.8	17.7	0.2	2.4	0.2	29.0	2.3	3.8	3.1
Omaha, NE	38.8	18.4	0.2	2.6	0.1	30.6	1.6	3.1	2.8
Orlando, FL	37.0	17.0	0.3	2.7	0.2	28.4	2.4	6.0	4.2
Philadelphia, PA	38.7	16.9	0.2	2.5	0.2	29.2	2.5	4.4	3.0
Phoenix, AZ	36.9	17.2	0.2	2.8	0.2	29.0	2.5	5.4	3.7
Pittsburgh, PA	43.2	19.0	0.2	2.8	0.2	25.6	1.6	2.6	2.4
Portland, OR	39.0	18.1	0.4	3.2	0.3	26.7	1.6	4.2	4.9
Providence, RI	40.0	16.9	0.2	3.0	0.2	27.2	1.9	4.1	3.0
Provo, UT	28.0	18.8	0.1	0.7	0.0	39.0	2.1	4.0	4.8
Raleigh, NC	38.4	19.2	0.2	2.2	0.2	30.0	1.5	3.7	3.0
Reno, NV	39.5	17.2	0.2	3.4	0.2	26.1	2.1	5.0	4.9
Richmond, VA	39.5	17.3	0.2	2.5	0.2	27.7	2.4	4.0	3.3
Rochester, MN	40.1	20.5	0.1	2.7	0.1	28.9	1.0	2.2	2.5
Sacramento, CA	36.2	17.1	0.3	2.4	0.2	29.4	2.2	6.0	4.2
Saint Louis, MO	40.8	18.2	0.2	2.6	0.2	28.5	2.2	3.0	2.4
Saint Paul, MN	38.9	18.7	0.2	2.8	0.2	29.4	1.2	3.3	3.3
Salem, OR	35.7	17.6	0.2	2.7	0.1	29.3	2.3	5.0	4.1
Salt Lake City, UT	34.0	17.4	0.3	2.1	0.2	32.4	2.5	5.3	4.4
San Antonio, TX	36.2	16.9	0.2	2.3	0.2	31.0	3.5	5.1	2.8
San Diego, CA	35.1	16.9	0.3	2.3	0.2	27.8	2.3	6.6	5.1
San Francisco, CA	36.7	17.0	0.4	2.3	0.3	26.3	1.8	6.9	5.9
San Jose, CA	33.8	18.4	0.2	1.8	0.1	28.3	1.9	7.9	5.6
Santa Rosa, CA	38.4	17.6	0.4	2.9	0.2	26.1	1.9	5.2	5.5
Savannah, GA	38.7	16.6	0.2	2.4	0.2	28.0	2.8	4.1	3.4
Seattle, WA	38.9	18.3	0.3	2.9	0.2	26.7	1.5	4.6	4.7
Sioux Falls, SD	39.5	19.4	0.1	2.9	0.1	29.8	1.1	2.3	2.6
Tampa, FL	41.2	17.6	0.3	3.1	0.2	25.5	2.2	4.6	3.4
Tucson, AZ	40.9	17.2	0.3	2.9	0.2	25.5	2.6	4.4	3.4
Tulsa, OK	39.1	18.2	0.2	2.4	0.1	29.0	2.6	3.9	2.7
Virginia Beach, VA	39.0	17.4	0.2	2.3	0.1	27.7	2.5	4.0	3.3
Washington, DC	37.0	17.3	0.3	2.0	0.2	29.3	2.0	5.9	4.4
Wichita, KS	39.0	18.2	0.1	2.4	0.1	29.8	2.1	3.2	2.6
Wilmington, NC	42.3	18.7	0.2	2.9	0.2	24.4	1.9	3.1	3.9
Winston-Salem, NC	40.9	18.6	0.2	2.3	0.1	27.5	2.4	3.7	2.2
U.S.	38.3	17.5	0.2	2.5	0.2	28.3	2.4	4.8	3.4

Note: Figures are percent of the total population; Figures cover the Metropolitan Statistical Area (MSA); (1) Includes biological, adopted, and stepchildren of the householder
Source: U.S. Census Bureau, 2020 Census

Age: City

City	Percent of Population									Median Age
	Under Age 5	Age 5–19	Age 20–34	Age 35–44	Age 45–54	Age 55–64	Age 65–74	Age 75–84	Age 85+	
Albuquerque, NM	5.1	18.0	21.5	13.9	11.7	12.5	10.4	4.7	2.1	38.7
Anchorage, AK	6.5	19.6	24.0	14.2	11.6	11.6	8.2	3.4	0.9	34.9
Ann Arbor, MI	3.8	18.7	38.6	10.1	8.2	7.9	7.3	4.0	1.4	27.7
Athens, GA	4.8	19.9	33.9	11.5	9.1	8.9	7.4	3.5	1.1	29.2
Atlanta, GA	5.1	15.7	31.0	14.7	11.4	9.8	7.5	3.5	1.3	34.0
Austin, TX	5.4	15.7	29.9	17.3	12.0	9.6	6.4	2.6	1.1	34.5
Baltimore, MD	6.1	17.5	24.5	13.7	10.7	12.5	9.3	4.0	1.6	36.1
Billings, MT	5.9	18.9	21.1	14.0	10.2	11.6	10.3	5.4	2.6	38.1
Boise City, ID	4.4	17.8	23.2	14.2	12.6	12.5	9.2	4.6	1.6	38.2
Boston, MA	4.6	15.3	33.4	13.3	10.2	10.5	7.6	3.4	1.7	33.2
Boulder, CO	2.0	20.2	36.8	10.3	10.0	8.4	7.4	3.2	1.8	28.8
Cape Coral, FL	4.5	14.5	15.7	10.8	13.4	15.9	14.6	7.9	2.5	48.7
Cedar Rapids, IA	5.7	18.7	22.7	13.5	11.4	11.8	9.3	4.7	2.3	36.9
Charleston, SC	5.1	15.6	27.7	14.1	10.2	11.3	9.5	4.5	2.1	36.1
Charlotte, NC	6.5	19.1	25.5	14.8	12.8	10.7	6.7	2.8	1.2	34.4
Chicago, IL	5.6	16.6	26.7	14.6	11.8	11.2	8.1	3.9	1.7	35.7
Cincinnati, OH	6.3	18.7	28.1	12.5	10.0	11.1	8.2	3.4	1.7	33.0
Clarksville, TN	8.5	21.0	29.2	14.0	9.6	9.0	5.8	2.3	0.7	30.4
Cleveland, OH	5.6	18.2	24.4	12.2	11.2	13.4	9.3	4.1	1.6	36.3
College Station, TX	4.8	25.3	40.0	10.3	6.8	6.2	4.2	1.9	0.6	22.9
Colorado Springs, CO	5.9	18.5	24.7	13.7	11.2	11.2	8.7	4.3	1.7	35.6
Columbia, MO	5.4	20.7	32.4	12.5	8.9	8.8	6.4	3.3	1.6	29.2
Columbia, SC	5.4	21.9	32.9	10.9	9.5	8.4	6.8	3.2	1.0	28.7
Columbus, OH	6.7	18.6	28.6	13.8	10.9	10.5	6.9	2.9	1.2	33.0
Dallas, TX	7.0	19.5	26.0	13.8	11.6	10.7	7.0	3.1	1.3	33.4
Davenport, IA	6.1	17.9	22.1	13.4	11.1	12.9	9.8	4.6	2.2	37.8
Denver, CO	5.5	14.8	29.4	16.9	11.7	9.5	7.6	3.3	1.4	35.2
Des Moines, IA	6.8	19.2	24.7	13.0	11.8	11.9	7.7	3.3	1.5	34.6
Detroit, MI	6.8	20.8	22.2	11.8	11.8	11.8	9.0	4.1	1.7	35.1
Durham, NC	6.1	17.6	26.8	14.3	11.5	10.7	8.1	3.5	1.4	34.8
El Paso, TX	6.5	21.6	23.2	12.5	11.5	10.8	8.1	4.1	1.8	34.1
Eugene, OR	3.9	17.1	28.5	12.4	10.4	10.1	10.4	5.2	2.1	35.4
Fargo, ND	6.0	18.4	30.1	12.8	9.0	10.1	7.9	3.9	1.8	32.2
Fort Collins, CO	3.9	18.9	33.6	12.6	9.4	9.4	7.3	3.3	1.6	30.6
Fort Wayne, IN	7.0	20.0	22.9	12.5	11.4	11.3	8.8	4.1	2.0	35.0
Fort Worth, TX	7.3	22.1	23.3	14.4	12.0	10.3	6.5	2.9	1.0	33.4
Gainesville, FL	3.7	19.7	40.6	9.6	7.3	7.3	6.7	3.3	1.7	26.5
Green Bay, WI	6.5	20.5	21.8	13.5	11.6	12.2	8.3	3.7	1.7	35.7
Greensboro, NC	5.7	21.4	24.2	12.4	11.6	10.8	8.2	3.9	1.9	34.1
Honolulu, HI	4.5	13.9	20.6	13.8	12.8	12.7	11.5	6.5	3.6	42.9
Houston, TX	6.7	19.4	25.1	14.5	11.7	10.6	7.3	3.4	1.3	34.3
Huntsville, AL	5.6	17.5	24.7	12.3	10.9	12.5	9.2	5.2	2.1	36.4
Indianapolis, IN	7.0	20.5	23.8	13.2	11.2	11.4	8.1	3.3	1.5	34.1
Jacksonville, FL	6.5	18.7	22.6	13.4	11.8	12.5	9.0	4.1	1.6	36.4
Kansas City, MO	6.2	18.7	24.1	13.7	11.4	11.8	8.8	3.6	1.7	35.7
Lafayette, LA	6.1	18.0	22.9	12.8	10.2	12.9	10.9	4.5	1.8	37.1
Las Vegas, NV	5.8	19.1	20.4	13.7	13.0	12.4	9.3	4.8	1.5	38.5
Lexington, KY	5.7	18.8	25.1	13.1	11.6	11.2	8.8	4.2	1.4	35.2
Lincoln, NE	5.9	20.0	26.1	12.8	10.4	10.4	8.8	4.0	1.7	33.3
Little Rock, AR	6.7	19.9	21.8	13.4	12.1	11.0	9.2	4.0	2.0	36.4
Los Angeles, CA	5.2	16.8	24.8	14.8	13.0	11.6	8.1	3.8	1.9	36.9
Louisville, KY	6.2	18.8	21.1	13.1	12.1	12.8	9.9	4.5	1.6	37.7
Madison, WI	4.8	16.9	33.7	12.8	9.6	9.5	7.7	3.6	1.4	31.8
Manchester, NH	4.9	15.1	25.7	13.8	11.6	13.7	8.7	4.6	2.0	37.9

Table continued on following page.

City	Percent of Population									Median Age
	Under Age 5	Age 5–19	Age 20–34	Age 35–44	Age 45–54	Age 55–64	Age 65–74	Age 75–84	Age 85+	
McAllen, TX	7.0	23.3	21.2	13.3	12.4	9.4	8.1	3.8	1.5	34.0
Memphis, TN	7.2	20.2	23.7	12.1	11.1	11.6	8.9	3.9	1.3	34.3
Miami, FL	5.3	12.8	23.8	15.4	13.5	12.8	8.5	5.2	2.6	39.7
Midland, TX	8.8	22.6	24.9	14.7	9.6	8.9	6.0	2.9	1.6	31.6
Milwaukee, WI	6.9	22.2	25.1	13.0	10.6	10.4	7.4	3.0	1.4	32.2
Minneapolis, MN	5.7	17.1	30.9	14.9	10.7	9.9	7.0	2.7	1.1	33.0
Nashville, TN	6.6	16.9	27.6	14.5	11.2	10.8	7.9	3.4	1.2	34.4
New Orleans, LA	5.5	16.9	22.0	14.9	11.5	12.7	10.4	4.3	1.7	38.4
New York, NY	5.9	16.7	22.9	13.9	12.4	12.2	9.2	4.8	2.0	38.0
Oklahoma City, OK	6.8	20.5	22.6	14.2	11.4	11.1	8.3	3.8	1.2	35.0
Omaha, NE	6.8	20.5	22.4	13.6	11.2	11.4	8.7	3.9	1.5	35.3
Orlando, FL	6.2	16.8	26.7	16.5	12.4	10.2	6.6	3.2	1.3	35.1
Philadelphia, PA	6.1	18.4	25.5	13.4	10.9	11.6	8.6	4.1	1.6	35.1
Phoenix, AZ	6.1	20.7	23.4	14.1	12.5	11.2	7.4	3.2	1.2	34.8
Pittsburgh, PA	4.4	16.1	32.1	12.5	9.0	10.8	9.0	4.0	2.0	33.5
Portland, OR	4.3	14.5	24.5	18.0	13.8	10.7	8.8	3.9	1.5	38.6
Providence, RI	5.4	20.3	28.3	12.6	11.9	10.0	6.8	3.3	1.5	32.9
Provo, UT	5.8	20.1	48.3	8.2	5.7	5.3	3.7	1.9	0.9	23.7
Raleigh, NC	5.7	17.8	27.0	14.4	13.0	10.4	7.1	3.3	1.3	34.7
Reno, NV	5.3	17.2	23.9	13.8	11.0	12.3	10.1	4.6	1.6	37.3
Richmond, VA	5.9	15.4	29.6	13.5	10.1	11.9	8.7	3.5	1.4	34.5
Rochester, MN	6.8	18.9	22.4	14.1	10.3	11.5	8.8	4.9	2.3	36.4
Sacramento, CA	5.9	18.4	24.4	14.7	11.6	11.0	8.5	3.8	1.7	35.7
Saint Louis, MO	5.8	15.0	26.2	14.2	11.1	12.6	9.6	3.7	1.6	36.6
Saint Paul, MN	6.3	20.3	25.8	13.9	10.7	10.7	7.9	3.0	1.3	33.5
Salem, OR	5.9	20.2	22.9	13.6	11.4	10.8	8.9	4.7	1.7	35.7
Salt Lake City, UT	4.9	15.8	32.5	14.0	10.9	9.6	7.5	3.3	1.3	33.0
San Antonio, TX	6.3	20.5	23.7	13.8	11.8	10.7	7.9	3.7	1.6	34.6
San Diego, CA	5.3	16.6	26.4	14.7	12.0	10.9	8.2	4.3	1.7	36.0
San Francisco, CA	4.2	11.0	26.1	16.3	13.2	12.0	9.8	4.8	2.6	39.7
San Jose, CA	5.2	18.3	21.9	14.6	13.8	12.1	8.2	4.1	1.8	38.1
Santa Rosa, CA	4.9	17.9	19.3	14.1	12.9	12.1	11.2	5.1	2.4	40.5
Savannah, GA	6.1	18.1	28.1	11.9	10.3	11.4	8.1	4.5	1.4	33.7
Seattle, WA	4.2	12.2	32.7	16.3	12.2	9.7	7.7	3.4	1.6	35.5
Sioux Falls, SD	7.0	20.0	22.8	14.4	10.8	11.4	8.8	3.4	1.4	35.1
Tampa, FL	5.8	18.5	24.6	14.2	12.5	11.2	7.8	4.1	1.3	35.6
Tucson, AZ	5.3	18.5	26.7	12.2	10.4	11.0	9.0	4.8	2.0	34.6
Tulsa, OK	6.7	20.3	22.3	13.2	11.2	11.3	9.1	4.2	1.7	35.5
Virginia Beach, VA	6.0	18.3	22.1	14.1	11.7	12.6	9.2	4.5	1.6	37.4
Washington, DC	6.1	15.2	29.0	16.4	10.7	9.8	7.4	3.8	1.5	34.9
Wichita, KS	6.3	20.7	22.0	12.9	11.0	11.7	9.4	4.1	1.9	35.7
Wilmington, NC	4.3	17.0	25.9	11.7	10.8	12.6	10.2	5.3	2.3	37.5
Winston-Salem, NC	5.9	21.7	21.6	12.1	11.9	12.0	8.5	4.3	1.9	35.6
U.S.	5.7	19.1	20.2	13.1	12.3	12.8	10.0	4.9	1.9	38.7

Source: U.S. Census Bureau, 2019-2023 American Community Survey 5-Year Estimates

Age: Metro Area

Metro Area	Percent of Population									Median Age
	Under Age 5	Age 5–19	Age 20–34	Age 35–44	Age 45–54	Age 55–64	Age 65–74	Age 75–84	Age 85+	
Albuquerque, NM	5.0	18.5	20.0	13.4	11.8	12.9	11.1	5.1	2.0	39.6
Anchorage, AK	6.5	20.2	22.8	14.2	11.7	11.9	8.5	3.3	0.9	35.4
Ann Arbor, MI	4.6	19.1	26.4	11.9	11.3	11.3	9.2	4.5	1.5	34.8
Athens, GA	5.0	20.7	26.4	12.2	11.0	10.6	8.8	4.1	1.3	33.2
Atlanta, GA	5.9	20.6	20.5	13.9	13.7	12.2	8.2	3.7	1.2	37.0
Austin, TX	5.8	19.0	23.8	16.3	13.0	10.5	7.5	3.1	1.1	35.9
Baltimore, MD	5.8	18.8	19.8	13.5	12.3	13.4	9.7	4.7	1.9	38.9
Billings, MT	5.5	19.3	18.9	13.2	11.4	12.9	11.3	5.2	2.2	39.7
Boise City, ID	5.7	20.8	19.9	13.9	12.2	11.8	9.6	4.6	1.4	37.4
Boston, MA	5.1	17.2	21.6	13.2	12.6	13.5	9.8	4.7	2.1	39.3
Boulder, CO	4.0	19.1	23.8	12.6	12.6	12.2	9.8	4.2	1.8	37.5
Cape Coral, FL	4.5	14.9	15.7	10.6	11.3	14.2	15.4	10.2	3.3	49.3
Cedar Rapids, IA	5.8	19.3	19.1	13.2	12.1	13.1	10.1	5.1	2.2	39.3
Charleston, SC	5.9	18.2	21.0	14.1	12.0	12.6	10.0	4.5	1.6	38.1
Charlotte, NC	5.9	19.9	20.1	13.9	13.7	12.2	8.7	4.1	1.4	37.9
Chicago, IL	5.6	19.2	20.4	13.6	12.8	12.7	9.3	4.4	1.8	38.4
Cincinnati, OH	6.0	20.0	19.7	12.8	12.1	13.1	9.9	4.5	1.8	38.2
Clarksville, TN	8.1	21.2	25.9	13.1	10.3	10.0	7.1	3.3	1.1	31.9
Cleveland, OH	5.3	17.9	18.9	12.1	12.2	14.2	11.5	5.6	2.4	41.6
College Station, TX	5.6	22.3	30.9	11.6	9.2	9.0	6.9	3.0	1.4	28.4
Colorado Springs, CO	6.1	19.7	23.6	13.5	11.3	11.7	8.7	3.9	1.4	35.4
Columbia, MO	5.5	20.2	26.9	12.3	10.3	10.9	8.5	3.9	1.5	33.1
Columbia, SC	5.6	20.1	21.2	12.8	12.1	12.5	9.8	4.5	1.5	37.5
Columbus, OH	6.3	19.8	21.6	14.0	12.4	11.9	8.7	3.9	1.5	36.6
Dallas, TX	6.4	21.6	21.3	14.4	13.0	11.4	7.4	3.3	1.1	35.5
Davenport, IA	5.7	19.6	17.9	12.9	11.8	13.2	11.1	5.6	2.3	40.2
Denver, CO	5.5	18.2	22.7	15.4	12.8	11.6	8.6	3.8	1.4	37.2
Des Moines, IA	6.5	20.7	20.4	14.4	12.1	11.7	8.6	4.0	1.7	36.7
Detroit, MI	5.6	18.4	19.6	12.2	12.9	14.0	10.5	4.8	2.0	40.2
Durham, NC	5.3	18.5	22.6	13.0	12.2	12.1	10.0	4.7	1.7	37.6
El Paso, TX	6.8	22.6	23.1	12.8	11.4	10.4	7.6	3.7	1.6	33.3
Eugene, OR	4.4	16.8	22.2	12.5	11.2	12.5	12.5	5.8	2.2	40.2
Fargo, ND	6.5	20.6	26.1	13.8	10.0	9.9	7.7	3.6	1.7	33.0
Fort Collins, CO	4.5	18.2	24.9	12.9	11.0	11.7	10.5	4.5	1.8	36.6
Fort Wayne, IN	6.7	21.0	20.2	12.6	11.7	12.1	9.5	4.3	1.9	36.8
Fort Worth, TX	6.4	21.6	21.3	14.4	13.0	11.4	7.4	3.3	1.1	35.5
Gainesville, FL	4.9	18.6	27.4	11.4	10.1	11.2	9.9	4.7	2.0	34.3
Green Bay, WI	5.7	19.6	18.8	12.9	12.1	13.9	10.4	4.8	1.7	39.2
Greensboro, NC	5.6	20.1	19.7	12.0	12.9	13.0	9.9	4.8	1.9	38.9
Honolulu, HI	5.8	17.0	21.0	13.3	11.8	12.0	10.3	5.8	3.0	39.4
Houston, TX	6.7	22.0	20.8	14.5	12.8	11.1	7.7	3.3	1.1	35.3
Huntsville, AL	5.6	18.9	20.4	13.1	12.5	14.0	9.2	4.7	1.5	38.8
Indianapolis, IN	6.3	20.6	20.5	13.7	12.4	12.2	8.8	3.9	1.6	36.7
Jacksonville, FL	5.8	18.7	19.8	13.3	12.4	13.2	10.2	4.8	1.7	39.1
Kansas City, MO	6.1	20.1	19.9	13.7	12.2	12.6	9.4	4.4	1.8	37.8
Lafayette, LA	6.6	20.1	20.1	13.6	11.7	12.8	9.5	4.2	1.4	37.2
Las Vegas, NV	5.8	19.0	20.5	14.1	13.0	12.1	9.5	4.7	1.3	38.3
Lexington, KY	5.8	19.3	22.7	12.9	12.1	11.9	9.2	4.4	1.5	36.6
Lincoln, NE	5.9	20.6	24.1	12.8	10.7	10.9	9.3	4.0	1.7	34.4
Little Rock, AR	6.1	19.8	20.8	13.3	11.9	12.2	9.7	4.6	1.7	37.4
Los Angeles, CA	5.3	18.2	21.9	13.8	13.3	12.6	8.7	4.3	2.0	38.2
Louisville, KY	5.9	18.8	19.6	13.1	12.6	13.4	10.3	4.7	1.7	39.3
Madison, WI	5.2	18.3	23.8	13.6	11.6	12.0	9.6	4.2	1.7	36.9
Manchester, NH	5.1	17.1	20.1	12.9	13.2	15.0	10.1	4.8	1.8	41.0

Table continued on following page.

Metro Area	Percent of Population									Median Age
	Under Age 5	Age 5–19	Age 20–34	Age 35–44	Age 45–54	Age 55–64	Age 65–74	Age 75–84	Age 85+	
McAllen, TX	8.0	26.8	21.3	12.3	11.4	8.6	6.5	3.8	1.2	30.3
Memphis, TN	6.5	20.8	20.4	12.9	12.2	12.4	9.3	4.1	1.4	36.7
Miami, FL	5.4	16.9	18.5	13.2	13.6	13.4	10.2	6.1	2.7	41.9
Midland, TX	8.3	23.1	22.7	15.3	10.2	9.9	6.5	2.7	1.4	32.7
Milwaukee, WI	5.9	19.3	19.8	13.1	11.9	13.2	10.0	4.5	2.1	38.5
Minneapolis, MN	6.1	19.7	20.0	14.1	12.2	12.8	9.1	4.2	1.7	37.8
Nashville, TN	6.1	19.3	21.9	14.2	12.6	12.1	8.6	4.0	1.2	36.8
New Orleans, LA	5.9	18.1	20.2	13.9	11.8	13.3	10.5	4.5	1.9	38.9
New York, NY	5.8	17.9	20.4	13.3	12.9	13.2	9.6	4.9	2.1	39.4
Oklahoma City, OK	6.3	21.0	21.7	13.7	11.4	11.5	8.9	4.2	1.4	35.8
Omaha, NE	6.6	21.3	20.0	13.9	11.7	12.0	8.9	4.0	1.6	36.5
Orlando, FL	5.5	18.5	21.4	14.2	12.9	12.0	9.1	4.7	1.8	38.3
Philadelphia, PA	5.5	18.6	20.2	13.1	12.3	13.4	10.0	4.8	2.0	39.1
Phoenix, AZ	5.7	19.6	20.9	13.3	12.3	11.8	9.5	5.2	1.8	37.7
Pittsburgh, PA	4.9	16.6	18.7	12.4	12.0	14.5	12.4	5.9	2.8	42.8
Portland, OR	5.1	17.7	20.9	15.2	13.2	12.0	9.8	4.4	1.7	39.1
Providence, RI	5.0	17.6	20.1	12.6	12.6	14.2	10.6	5.2	2.2	40.6
Provo, UT	8.7	27.7	27.3	12.5	9.2	6.7	4.8	2.3	0.8	25.6
Raleigh, NC	5.9	20.4	20.2	14.8	14.1	11.9	8.0	3.6	1.3	37.5
Reno, NV	5.4	17.8	20.9	13.0	11.8	13.1	11.3	5.1	1.6	39.4
Richmond, VA	5.7	18.4	20.5	13.5	12.4	13.1	10.0	4.6	1.7	38.7
Rochester, MN	6.2	20.1	18.7	13.6	11.1	12.9	9.8	5.2	2.3	38.8
Sacramento, CA	5.6	19.3	20.3	13.8	12.2	12.3	9.7	4.6	2.0	38.3
Saint Louis, MO	5.6	18.8	19.2	13.2	12.0	13.8	10.5	4.9	2.0	39.8
Saint Paul, MN	6.1	19.7	20.0	14.1	12.2	12.8	9.1	4.2	1.7	37.8
Salem, OR	5.9	20.5	20.5	13.0	11.6	11.6	10.1	4.9	1.9	37.3
Salt Lake City, UT	6.6	22.3	23.3	14.9	11.7	9.9	7.2	3.1	1.2	33.7
San Antonio, TX	6.3	21.1	21.5	14.1	12.2	11.2	8.3	3.8	1.5	35.7
San Diego, CA	5.7	18.2	23.0	14.1	12.1	11.8	8.9	4.4	1.8	37.1
San Francisco, CA	5.1	16.5	20.6	15.0	13.5	12.7	9.6	4.8	2.1	40.0
San Jose, CA	5.4	18.3	22.1	14.4	13.4	12.1	8.1	4.3	2.0	37.8
Santa Rosa, CA	4.7	17.1	17.8	13.2	12.4	14.0	12.8	5.8	2.4	42.7
Savannah, GA	6.1	19.5	22.0	13.8	11.7	11.8	9.2	4.4	1.5	36.7
Seattle, WA	5.7	17.5	22.8	15.4	12.7	11.9	8.6	3.8	1.6	37.4
Sioux Falls, SD	6.9	21.1	20.4	14.3	11.2	11.8	9.1	3.7	1.5	36.1
Tampa, FL	5.0	16.7	18.7	12.9	12.8	13.7	11.4	6.4	2.4	42.2
Tucson, AZ	5.0	18.0	21.4	11.6	10.8	12.2	12.0	6.8	2.4	39.7
Tulsa, OK	6.3	20.7	19.9	13.1	11.9	12.2	9.6	4.7	1.7	37.3
Virginia Beach, VA	6.0	18.8	22.1	13.3	11.3	12.8	9.4	4.6	1.6	37.2
Washington, DC	6.1	19.2	20.3	14.8	13.4	12.3	8.3	4.0	1.5	37.9
Wichita, KS	6.3	21.5	20.2	12.8	11.2	12.3	9.6	4.3	2.0	36.6
Wilmington, NC	4.5	15.5	18.1	11.8	11.8	14.9	14.8	6.6	2.0	45.1
Winston-Salem, NC	5.5	19.2	18.7	11.8	13.0	13.8	10.7	5.4	2.0	40.6
U.S.	5.7	19.1	20.2	13.1	12.3	12.8	10.0	4.9	1.9	38.7

Note: Figures cover the Metropolitan Statistical Area (MSA)
Source: U.S. Census Bureau, 2019-2023 American Community Survey 5-Year Estimates

Ancestry: City

City	German	Irish	English	American	Italian	Polish	French[1]	European	Scottish
Albuquerque, NM	9.8	7.9	9.1	3.1	3.4	1.4	1.8	1.6	1.5
Anchorage, AK	13.5	9.0	9.9	3.6	3.1	1.9	1.9	2.1	1.8
Ann Arbor, MI	16.5	10.7	9.7	2.1	4.5	6.2	2.2	2.7	2.3
Athens, GA	9.0	8.9	12.2	3.9	3.1	1.8	1.6	2.7	2.7
Atlanta, GA	7.1	6.4	9.3	3.8	2.9	1.4	1.7	1.7	1.4
Austin, TX	11.5	8.7	10.2	2.8	3.2	1.9	2.4	2.4	2.2
Baltimore, MD	5.8	5.7	3.7	2.7	2.9	2.0	0.9	0.7	0.7
Billings, MT	27.7	13.2	13.3	3.7	3.1	1.7	2.6	2.0	2.8
Boise City, ID	18.2	11.5	17.8	3.9	4.2	1.7	2.4	3.7	3.1
Boston, MA	4.8	13.2	5.4	2.2	7.3	2.2	1.7	1.1	1.1
Boulder, CO	16.0	11.3	11.4	2.6	5.2	3.4	2.4	4.2	3.2
Cape Coral, FL	13.4	11.5	8.5	10.4	9.2	3.3	2.2	1.5	1.3
Cedar Rapids, IA	26.8	13.3	10.4	3.3	1.7	1.4	1.8	1.5	1.6
Charleston, SC	11.7	11.0	13.6	13.0	4.8	2.4	2.8	1.9	2.4
Charlotte, NC	7.4	6.7	7.7	4.7	3.5	1.5	1.2	1.1	1.6
Chicago, IL	7.4	7.2	3.2	2.0	3.8	5.0	0.9	0.9	0.7
Cincinnati, OH	17.5	9.8	6.9	3.0	3.7	1.4	1.2	1.2	1.0
Clarksville, TN	12.5	8.8	8.3	6.0	3.6	1.0	1.6	3.7	1.5
Cleveland, OH	9.4	8.4	3.5	2.5	4.4	3.7	0.8	0.5	0.7
College Station, TX	14.8	8.0	9.8	3.2	3.3	2.3	1.9	1.8	1.6
Colorado Springs, CO	17.8	11.4	12.8	4.2	4.7	2.6	2.4	2.9	2.6
Columbia, MO	24.0	12.1	13.5	5.1	3.4	1.6	1.9	2.2	2.3
Columbia, SC	9.0	7.2	8.8	5.3	3.0	1.1	1.7	1.9	2.0
Columbus, OH	14.9	10.0	8.0	3.4	4.6	2.1	1.3	1.5	1.6
Dallas, TX	5.4	4.4	6.0	3.8	1.7	0.8	1.2	1.2	1.1
Davenport, IA	28.1	14.7	8.7	3.0	2.6	1.9	1.3	1.1	1.8
Denver, CO	14.0	10.9	10.4	3.0	5.5	2.8	2.1	2.5	2.0
Des Moines, IA	19.1	12.4	9.2	3.1	3.5	1.0	1.4	1.5	1.3
Detroit, MI	1.8	1.6	1.1	4.4	0.8	1.1	0.5	0.2	0.3
Durham, NC	8.2	6.7	10.0	3.8	3.4	1.8	1.5	1.7	1.8
El Paso, TX	3.8	2.4	2.2	2.2	1.3	0.5	0.6	0.5	0.4
Eugene, OR	18.4	12.9	14.5	3.1	5.2	1.9	3.1	3.8	3.9
Fargo, ND	32.9	8.1	5.2	2.9	1.3	2.2	3.4	0.8	1.4
Fort Collins, CO	23.1	12.3	14.9	3.2	5.6	3.4	3.1	3.6	3.5
Fort Wayne, IN	22.5	9.0	9.2	5.0	2.1	1.9	2.4	2.3	1.9
Fort Worth, TX	7.1	6.0	7.4	3.7	1.8	0.8	1.3	1.4	1.5
Gainesville, FL	10.6	8.9	10.5	3.4	5.1	2.5	1.6	1.3	2.6
Green Bay, WI	26.6	8.2	4.6	3.6	2.0	7.2	3.0	1.6	1.0
Greensboro, NC	6.5	5.3	9.4	4.5	2.4	0.8	1.2	1.6	1.7
Honolulu, HI	4.5	3.4	3.6	1.4	1.3	0.9	1.0	0.5	0.7
Houston, TX	5.0	3.6	5.0	3.1	1.6	0.9	1.4	1.0	0.9
Huntsville, AL	9.2	8.5	13.0	10.2	2.4	1.3	1.8	2.2	2.1
Indianapolis, IN	12.8	7.9	8.0	4.5	2.0	1.4	1.4	1.4	1.5
Jacksonville, FL	7.8	7.7	7.6	6.3	3.6	1.4	1.4	2.2	1.6
Kansas City, MO	15.2	10.0	9.5	4.1	3.7	1.6	1.5	2.3	1.4
Lafayette, LA	9.2	5.6	6.7	5.2	3.8	0.5	16.7	0.7	1.1
Las Vegas, NV	8.0	7.2	7.2	2.9	4.9	1.8	1.5	1.6	1.3
Lexington, KY	12.7	10.8	13.8	7.7	2.7	1.4	1.6	2.4	2.4
Lincoln, NE	30.2	11.0	9.3	3.4	1.9	2.2	1.7	1.8	1.4
Little Rock, AR	7.5	6.5	10.4	4.6	1.2	0.7	1.3	1.7	1.7
Los Angeles, CA	3.9	3.7	3.5	3.8	2.7	1.3	1.1	1.3	0.7
Louisville, KY	14.8	11.3	10.8	5.8	2.5	1.1	1.5	1.6	1.6
Madison, WI	28.4	12.2	9.2	1.9	4.0	5.5	2.0	2.0	1.9
Manchester, NH	6.5	18.5	10.0	3.0	8.7	3.6	10.5	0.8	2.3
McAllen, TX	2.6	1.6	1.9	3.1	0.9	0.4	1.0	0.3	0.2
Memphis, TN	3.3	3.6	4.9	3.3	1.5	0.5	0.7	1.6	0.9

Table continued on following page.

City	German	Irish	English	American	Italian	Polish	French[1]	European	Scottish
Miami, FL	1.9	1.3	1.3	2.6	3.0	0.7	0.9	0.6	0.2
Midland, TX	6.6	6.1	7.8	4.6	0.9	0.4	1.3	1.1	1.5
Milwaukee, WI	15.1	5.4	2.2	1.4	2.4	5.5	1.2	1.0	0.5
Minneapolis, MN	21.0	10.7	7.4	1.7	2.6	3.9	2.7	2.0	1.4
Nashville, TN	8.7	7.9	10.2	5.9	2.7	1.4	1.5	1.7	1.9
New Orleans, LA	6.4	6.0	5.3	2.3	4.0	0.9	5.4	1.2	1.1
New York, NY	2.9	4.4	2.1	3.7	5.8	2.1	0.8	0.9	0.5
Oklahoma City, OK	10.1	7.8	9.5	5.3	1.5	0.7	1.2	1.9	1.7
Omaha, NE	24.8	12.8	8.4	2.7	3.7	3.3	1.9	1.6	1.8
Orlando, FL	6.4	5.4	5.9	6.1	4.5	1.6	1.5	0.8	0.9
Philadelphia, PA	7.0	9.6	3.2	2.2	6.7	3.0	0.7	0.7	0.7
Phoenix, AZ	9.6	7.4	6.8	2.7	3.9	1.8	1.4	1.5	1.3
Pittsburgh, PA	17.1	13.2	6.1	2.7	11.4	6.6	1.2	1.2	1.4
Portland, OR	15.2	11.6	12.9	4.3	4.5	2.4	2.6	4.4	3.1
Providence, RI	3.3	8.1	4.4	2.4	6.9	1.7	2.7	0.7	0.9
Provo, UT	10.4	4.9	28.2	2.2	2.2	0.7	1.3	4.0	3.6
Raleigh, NC	9.2	8.5	11.8	5.7	3.8	1.9	1.7	1.6	2.2
Reno, NV	12.3	11.0	11.1	4.4	5.9	1.6	2.2	2.6	2.0
Richmond, VA	8.2	7.9	9.9	3.9	3.8	1.4	1.5	1.3	1.8
Rochester, MN	28.8	9.8	7.1	2.6	1.8	2.6	1.8	1.6	1.4
Sacramento, CA	6.5	5.8	6.0	2.3	3.4	1.0	1.4	1.4	1.0
Saint Louis, MO	15.9	9.7	6.4	6.3	4.0	1.7	2.5	1.2	1.3
Saint Paul, MN	19.5	9.9	5.6	1.9	2.5	2.6	2.6	1.5	1.2
Salem, OR	16.3	8.2	12.7	4.1	2.9	1.2	2.3	4.2	2.5
Salt Lake City, UT	11.5	7.7	19.4	3.1	4.0	1.4	2.1	3.0	3.4
San Antonio, TX	7.2	4.6	4.7	3.4	2.0	0.9	1.2	0.8	0.9
San Diego, CA	8.7	7.3	7.0	2.3	4.2	1.8	1.7	1.7	1.3
San Francisco, CA	7.1	7.5	6.0	2.1	4.5	1.8	2.2	2.1	1.3
San Jose, CA	4.4	4.0	4.0	1.5	3.2	0.8	1.0	1.2	0.7
Santa Rosa, CA	11.1	10.1	10.4	2.2	6.3	1.6	2.4	2.4	1.9
Savannah, GA	6.6	7.3	6.3	3.8	3.2	1.1	1.3	0.8	1.4
Seattle, WA	14.0	10.8	12.2	2.4	4.7	2.6	2.8	3.9	2.7
Sioux Falls, SD	31.7	10.1	7.4	4.3	1.5	1.4	1.6	1.3	0.8
Tampa, FL	8.8	7.6	7.6	6.2	6.2	2.0	1.6	1.1	1.4
Tucson, AZ	11.5	8.4	8.0	2.9	3.7	1.9	1.8	1.5	1.7
Tulsa, OK	10.4	8.5	10.6	6.0	2.0	0.9	1.6	1.6	2.1
Virginia Beach, VA	11.2	10.5	11.3	7.5	5.5	2.3	1.9	1.6	2.2
Washington, DC	7.7	7.8	6.8	2.8	4.5	2.2	1.7	1.7	1.4
Wichita, KS	19.2	9.8	10.4	4.8	1.7	0.9	1.8	1.6	1.6
Wilmington, NC	10.8	10.8	13.8	4.7	5.6	2.2	2.1	2.3	2.7
Winston-Salem, NC	7.9	6.3	9.5	5.3	2.5	0.8	1.0	1.7	1.9
U.S.	12.6	9.4	9.1	5.5	4.9	2.6	2.0	1.6	1.6

Note: Figures are the percentage of the total population reporting a particular ancestry. The nine most commonly reported ancestries in the U.S. are shown. Figures include multiple ancestries (e.g. if a person reported being Irish and Italian, they were included in both columns); (1) Excludes Basque
Source: U.S. Census Bureau, 2019-2023 American Community Survey 5-Year Estimates

Ancestry: Metro Area

Metro Area	German	Irish	English	American	Italian	Polish	French[1]	European	Scottish
Albuquerque, NM	9.7	7.6	8.9	3.7	3.3	1.4	1.8	1.6	1.7
Anchorage, AK	14.5	9.7	10.1	4.2	2.9	1.9	1.9	2.1	1.9
Ann Arbor, MI	17.8	10.2	11.1	5.1	4.5	6.2	2.5	2.3	2.8
Athens, GA	8.8	10.4	13.5	6.1	2.8	1.4	1.5	2.4	2.5
Atlanta, GA	6.3	6.3	9.1	6.8	2.5	1.2	1.2	1.5	1.6
Austin, TX	12.4	8.3	10.4	3.6	2.9	1.7	2.3	2.4	2.2
Baltimore, MD	13.7	10.9	8.6	4.4	5.5	3.6	1.3	1.4	1.4
Billings, MT	29.0	13.1	12.6	4.2	3.2	1.5	2.6	2.1	2.6
Boise City, ID	17.0	10.2	18.2	4.8	3.5	1.4	2.4	3.1	3.1
Boston, MA	5.7	19.8	10.0	3.2	12.0	3.0	3.9	1.3	2.0
Boulder, CO	18.0	12.1	14.5	3.0	5.1	3.0	2.8	3.2	2.9
Cape Coral, FL	13.1	10.6	9.0	10.2	7.9	3.1	2.0	1.4	1.6
Cedar Rapids, IA	31.4	14.1	10.6	4.0	1.6	1.2	1.8	1.7	1.8
Charleston, SC	10.5	9.6	12.6	8.7	4.1	1.8	2.1	1.8	2.2
Charlotte, NC	10.2	8.4	10.3	8.3	3.9	1.7	1.4	1.5	2.0
Chicago, IL	12.9	10.2	4.8	2.5	6.1	8.0	1.2	1.2	0.9
Cincinnati, OH	25.7	12.9	11.4	5.6	3.9	1.6	1.6	1.6	1.8
Clarksville, TN	11.5	8.6	9.9	7.4	2.8	1.0	1.5	3.5	1.7
Cleveland, OH	18.5	13.3	8.6	4.1	9.1	6.9	1.4	1.1	1.5
College Station, TX	13.5	7.5	9.3	3.8	2.6	2.0	2.1	1.5	1.6
Colorado Springs, CO	17.6	11.0	12.3	4.5	4.5	2.4	2.3	3.0	2.7
Columbia, MO	24.4	11.8	13.9	6.4	2.8	1.4	1.9	2.2	2.1
Columbia, SC	9.5	7.3	9.5	6.5	2.5	1.3	1.5	1.6	1.9
Columbus, OH	20.0	12.4	11.1	5.3	5.1	2.2	1.6	1.8	2.1
Dallas, TX	8.1	6.4	8.7	5.3	2.2	1.0	1.4	1.4	1.5
Davenport, IA	25.2	13.0	9.4	3.8	2.5	1.9	1.5	1.5	1.5
Denver, CO	16.9	11.0	11.7	3.3	5.2	2.5	2.2	2.6	2.2
Des Moines, IA	25.8	13.5	11.3	3.8	3.1	1.2	1.6	2.3	1.7
Detroit, MI	14.3	9.1	7.9	4.0	5.8	8.9	2.8	1.5	2.0
Durham, NC	9.3	8.2	12.5	5.0	3.7	1.9	1.7	1.9	2.3
El Paso, TX	3.5	2.2	2.0	2.3	1.2	0.4	0.5	0.5	0.3
Eugene, OR	18.3	13.1	14.6	3.9	4.4	1.6	3.3	3.4	3.3
Fargo, ND	33.8	7.6	5.1	2.5	1.4	2.2	3.2	0.9	1.3
Fort Collins, CO	24.4	12.6	16.0	4.2	5.1	2.9	3.2	3.5	3.5
Fort Wayne, IN	26.1	9.0	9.8	5.8	2.2	2.0	2.8	2.6	1.8
Fort Worth, TX	8.1	6.4	8.7	5.3	2.2	1.0	1.4	1.4	1.5
Gainesville, FL	11.6	10.3	12.1	4.6	4.5	2.1	2.0	1.7	2.9
Green Bay, WI	33.7	9.3	4.9	4.0	2.2	9.4	3.5	1.6	0.7
Greensboro, NC	8.4	6.9	11.0	7.4	2.4	1.0	1.3	1.8	2.1
Honolulu, HI	5.2	4.0	4.1	1.3	1.8	0.8	1.0	0.6	0.7
Houston, TX	7.1	5.0	6.6	3.6	2.0	1.1	1.8	1.2	1.1
Huntsville, AL	9.4	9.3	13.8	11.4	2.3	1.2	1.5	2.2	2.1
Indianapolis, IN	16.6	9.4	10.9	7.3	2.5	1.7	1.5	1.7	1.8
Jacksonville, FL	9.6	9.6	10.2	7.5	4.5	1.8	1.8	2.1	2.0
Kansas City, MO	19.5	11.8	12.5	4.6	3.0	1.5	1.9	3.4	1.8
Lafayette, LA	7.1	4.5	5.3	6.2	3.0	0.6	17.1	0.7	0.7
Las Vegas, NV	7.9	6.8	7.0	2.9	4.7	1.7	1.4	1.3	1.2
Lexington, KY	12.3	11.3	14.6	10.4	2.5	1.3	1.5	2.3	2.3
Lincoln, NE	32.0	10.9	9.3	3.6	1.8	2.1	1.6	1.7	1.3
Little Rock, AR	8.5	8.4	11.7	6.6	1.4	0.8	1.4	1.6	1.8
Los Angeles, CA	5.1	4.3	4.5	3.5	2.8	1.1	1.1	1.2	0.8
Louisville, KY	16.6	12.4	12.6	7.6	2.6	1.1	1.7	1.7	1.9
Madison, WI	34.3	12.8	9.8	2.6	3.5	5.0	2.3	1.9	1.7
Manchester, NH	8.0	20.6	14.5	3.4	9.9	3.8	10.8	1.3	3.0
McAllen, TX	1.7	1.0	1.1	2.1	0.4	0.2	0.4	0.2	0.2
Memphis, TN	5.1	5.9	7.7	6.6	2.0	0.7	1.0	1.6	1.2

Table continued on following page.

Metro Area	German	Irish	English	American	Italian	Polish	French[1]	European	Scottish
Miami, FL	4.2	4.1	3.1	5.6	4.9	1.8	1.1	0.9	0.6
Midland, TX	7.0	5.8	7.6	5.2	0.9	0.3	1.3	1.0	1.4
Milwaukee, WI	31.6	9.3	5.0	2.4	4.3	9.8	2.1	1.4	0.9
Minneapolis, MN	27.4	10.7	6.9	3.1	2.5	4.0	2.9	2.0	1.2
Nashville, TN	9.6	8.9	12.9	10.5	2.6	1.2	1.6	2.3	2.2
New Orleans, LA	8.2	6.6	5.2	3.8	6.7	0.6	9.1	0.9	0.8
New York, NY	5.7	8.6	3.0	3.9	11.0	3.4	0.8	0.9	0.6
Oklahoma City, OK	11.8	9.0	11.2	6.2	1.7	0.8	1.5	2.0	1.9
Omaha, NE	27.8	12.9	9.7	3.5	3.7	3.5	1.8	1.7	1.6
Orlando, FL	8.2	7.2	7.1	9.1	5.0	1.7	1.6	1.1	1.2
Philadelphia, PA	13.7	16.9	7.8	3.2	12.2	4.6	1.2	1.0	1.2
Phoenix, AZ	12.6	8.7	9.5	4.2	4.5	2.2	1.8	1.8	1.6
Pittsburgh, PA	24.5	16.9	9.2	3.3	15.1	7.8	1.4	1.1	1.8
Portland, OR	16.0	10.5	12.8	4.4	3.5	1.7	2.4	3.8	2.8
Providence, RI	4.5	16.5	10.8	3.4	12.8	3.2	7.9	0.7	1.5
Provo, UT	10.0	4.9	32.1	4.1	2.1	0.5	1.4	4.8	4.1
Raleigh, NC	9.7	8.8	12.8	6.8	4.6	2.0	1.8	2.0	2.3
Reno, NV	12.7	10.9	11.6	4.0	6.0	1.6	2.3	3.5	2.0
Richmond, VA	9.1	8.2	12.7	6.6	3.7	1.5	1.4	1.7	1.8
Rochester, MN	32.8	10.3	7.3	3.6	1.5	2.5	1.7	1.8	1.3
Sacramento, CA	10.1	8.0	9.4	2.6	4.5	1.2	1.8	2.4	1.7
Saint Louis, MO	25.5	12.6	9.6	5.5	4.5	2.3	2.8	1.6	1.5
Saint Paul, MN	27.4	10.7	6.9	3.1	2.5	4.0	2.9	2.0	1.2
Salem, OR	16.6	8.4	12.1	3.9	2.6	1.4	2.3	3.6	2.6
Salt Lake City, UT	9.9	6.1	23.6	3.8	3.0	0.9	1.7	3.3	3.6
San Antonio, TX	10.0	5.8	6.6	3.8	2.2	1.4	1.5	1.1	1.3
San Diego, CA	9.0	7.5	7.6	2.6	4.1	1.6	1.8	1.9	1.5
San Francisco, CA	7.1	6.8	6.6	2.2	4.2	1.4	1.7	2.0	1.3
San Jose, CA	5.6	4.6	4.9	1.8	3.5	1.0	1.2	1.6	0.9
Santa Rosa, CA	12.4	12.2	11.8	2.4	7.9	1.8	2.9	3.7	2.5
Savannah, GA	9.4	9.4	10.2	6.8	3.7	1.2	1.5	1.2	1.8
Seattle, WA	13.2	9.0	10.9	2.9	3.4	1.7	2.4	3.2	2.3
Sioux Falls, SD	33.6	9.6	6.6	5.0	1.4	1.3	1.5	1.3	0.8
Tampa, FL	11.3	9.8	9.2	8.6	7.2	2.8	2.1	1.3	1.6
Tucson, AZ	13.2	9.0	10.1	3.5	4.1	2.2	2.1	1.7	2.0
Tulsa, OK	12.4	10.2	11.7	5.6	1.9	0.9	1.7	1.7	2.1
Virginia Beach, VA	9.4	8.6	10.8	8.0	4.1	1.7	1.7	1.6	1.8
Washington, DC	8.8	8.1	8.0	3.7	4.1	2.1	1.4	1.8	1.5
Wichita, KS	21.4	9.8	11.1	5.5	1.8	0.9	1.8	1.9	1.8
Wilmington, NC	12.2	12.4	14.8	5.9	5.9	2.4	2.1	1.8	2.8
Winston-Salem, NC	10.9	8.3	13.1	7.8	2.6	1.0	1.1	1.7	2.1
U.S.	12.6	9.4	9.1	5.5	4.9	2.6	2.0	1.6	1.6

Note: Figures are the percentage of the total population reporting a particular ancestry. The nine most commonly reported ancestries in the U.S. are shown. Figures include multiple ancestries (e.g. if a person reported being Irish and Italian, they were included in both columns); Figures cover the Metropolitan Statistical Area (MSA); (1) Excludes Basque
Source: U.S. Census Bureau, 2019-2023 American Community Survey 5-Year Estimates

Foreign-born Population: City

City	Percent of Population Born in							
	Any Foreign Country	Asia	Mexico	Europe	Caribbean	Central America[1]	South America	Africa	Canada
Albuquerque, NM	10.4	2.7	5.0	1.0	0.4	0.2	0.5	0.4	0.1
Anchorage, AK	10.9	6.0	0.6	1.2	0.5	0.2	0.6	0.5	0.4
Ann Arbor, MI	18.7	11.8	0.5	2.9	0.1	0.3	0.6	1.6	0.7
Athens, GA	9.8	3.2	2.3	0.9	0.4	1.3	0.8	0.7	0.2
Atlanta, GA	8.6	3.1	0.7	1.3	0.9	0.3	0.9	1.1	0.3
Austin, TX	18.1	6.2	5.2	1.6	0.8	2.0	0.9	1.0	0.3
Baltimore, MD	8.8	2.1	0.4	0.9	1.3	1.6	0.6	1.7	0.1
Billings, MT	2.0	0.7	0.2	0.6	0.0	0.0	0.1	0.0	0.3
Boise City, ID	7.2	3.0	1.3	1.3	0.1	0.1	0.3	0.6	0.5
Boston, MA	27.5	7.8	0.4	3.0	8.1	2.3	2.3	3.0	0.4
Boulder, CO	10.2	4.2	1.0	3.0	0.2	0.4	0.6	0.3	0.6
Cape Coral, FL	17.9	1.3	0.4	2.2	9.2	1.2	2.8	0.1	0.7
Cedar Rapids, IA	7.1	2.6	0.7	0.5	0.1	0.3	0.2	2.5	0.1
Charleston, SC	5.4	1.6	0.6	1.2	0.3	0.3	0.8	0.3	0.2
Charlotte, NC	18.1	4.9	2.7	1.5	1.2	3.8	1.7	2.1	0.2
Chicago, IL	20.7	5.2	8.2	3.3	0.4	0.9	1.4	1.1	0.2
Cincinnati, OH	7.1	2.1	0.3	0.7	0.2	1.0	0.3	2.2	0.1
Clarksville, TN	6.8	1.9	1.2	1.0	0.6	0.6	0.6	0.6	0.2
Cleveland, OH	6.1	2.3	0.4	1.1	0.5	0.5	0.3	0.9	0.1
College Station, TX	12.3	7.1	1.5	0.9	0.1	1.0	1.0	0.5	0.1
Colorado Springs, CO	7.4	2.0	1.7	1.5	0.2	0.6	0.4	0.5	0.3
Columbia, MO	8.1	4.9	0.6	0.4	0.3	0.2	0.5	1.1	0.0
Columbia, SC	5.1	2.0	0.2	0.7	0.8	0.3	0.5	0.4	0.1
Columbus, OH	14.4	4.7	1.3	0.8	0.7	0.9	0.7	5.1	0.1
Dallas, TX	23.4	2.9	12.8	0.8	0.4	3.3	1.0	2.0	0.1
Davenport, IA	4.6	1.5	1.5	0.5	0.0	0.1	0.0	0.6	0.2
Denver, CO	13.8	2.7	5.8	1.5	0.3	0.5	1.2	1.5	0.3
Des Moines, IA	14.0	4.4	3.6	0.8	0.2	1.6	0.1	3.2	0.1
Detroit, MI	6.0	2.4	1.7	0.2	0.3	0.5	0.1	0.5	0.2
Durham, NC	15.3	4.1	2.8	1.4	0.8	3.4	0.8	1.7	0.3
El Paso, TX	22.3	1.0	19.5	0.6	0.2	0.3	0.2	0.3	0.1
Eugene, OR	6.8	2.7	1.5	1.2	0.1	0.4	0.2	0.4	0.3
Fargo, ND	9.7	3.2	0.1	0.6	0.1	0.0	0.1	4.9	0.4
Fort Collins, CO	6.6	2.5	1.2	1.3	0.1	0.3	0.6	0.3	0.2
Fort Wayne, IN	9.0	4.4	2.1	0.5	0.2	1.0	0.2	0.5	0.2
Fort Worth, TX	17.0	4.1	8.9	0.5	0.3	0.8	0.6	1.6	0.1
Gainesville, FL	12.1	4.6	0.2	1.7	1.7	0.4	2.3	0.8	0.4
Green Bay, WI	8.8	2.1	4.5	0.4	0.2	0.5	0.3	0.6	0.2
Greensboro, NC	12.7	4.0	1.9	1.0	0.6	0.9	0.8	3.4	0.2
Honolulu, HI	27.8	22.9	0.2	1.0	0.1	0.1	0.3	0.2	0.2
Houston, TX	28.8	5.7	9.9	1.2	1.0	6.8	1.9	2.0	0.2
Huntsville, AL	6.6	1.7	1.6	0.8	0.7	0.5	0.3	0.5	0.2
Indianapolis, IN	11.6	3.1	3.2	0.5	0.7	1.3	0.6	2.2	0.1
Jacksonville, FL	12.2	4.1	0.5	1.7	2.5	0.8	1.7	0.8	0.1
Kansas City, MO	8.5	2.2	2.2	0.6	0.5	0.9	0.4	1.5	0.1
Lafayette, LA	6.6	2.1	0.5	0.4	0.2	1.8	0.8	0.4	0.1
Las Vegas, NV	20.9	5.3	8.5	1.6	1.3	2.2	1.0	0.4	0.4
Lexington, KY	11.0	3.8	2.3	1.0	0.4	0.8	0.5	2.0	0.2
Lincoln, NE	9.2	4.9	1.3	0.9	0.4	0.6	0.3	0.8	0.1
Little Rock, AR	7.9	2.7	2.1	0.6	0.1	1.6	0.3	0.4	0.1
Los Angeles, CA	35.8	11.2	11.2	2.4	0.3	8.3	1.2	0.7	0.4
Louisville, KY	9.8	2.5	1.0	0.8	2.8	0.6	0.4	1.6	0.1
Madison, WI	11.6	5.5	1.9	1.4	0.2	0.2	1.1	1.0	0.2
Manchester, NH	14.7	3.8	0.4	2.2	2.0	2.1	1.0	2.1	1.0

Table continued on following page.

City	Percent of Population Born in								
	Any Foreign Country	Asia	Mexico	Europe	Caribbean	Central America[1]	South America	Africa	Canada
McAllen, TX	25.7	2.2	22.0	0.2	0.3	0.5	0.4	0.1	0.0
Memphis, TN	7.4	1.3	2.3	0.3	0.3	1.9	0.5	0.7	0.1
Miami, FL	57.7	1.5	1.2	2.2	28.5	11.8	11.9	0.4	0.2
Midland, TX	13.7	2.0	7.1	0.4	1.0	0.5	1.1	1.0	0.6
Milwaukee, WI	10.8	2.8	5.1	0.6	0.3	0.4	0.3	1.0	0.1
Minneapolis, MN	14.1	3.2	1.8	1.0	0.2	0.3	1.5	5.7	0.3
Nashville, TN	15.1	3.6	3.1	0.8	0.6	3.1	0.6	2.9	0.3
New Orleans, LA	6.6	2.0	0.4	0.6	0.6	1.9	0.5	0.3	0.2
New York, NY	36.5	11.0	1.8	5.1	9.7	1.4	5.1	1.9	0.3
Oklahoma City, OK	12.0	3.1	5.4	0.5	0.2	1.3	0.5	0.7	0.2
Omaha, NE	11.0	3.3	3.4	0.6	0.2	1.5	0.3	1.5	0.2
Orlando, FL	24.1	3.0	0.8	1.8	6.5	1.2	10.1	0.5	0.2
Philadelphia, PA	14.6	5.6	0.5	2.2	2.8	0.7	1.0	1.7	0.1
Phoenix, AZ	19.0	3.1	11.3	1.3	0.4	0.9	0.4	1.1	0.3
Pittsburgh, PA	9.3	4.5	0.3	1.8	0.4	0.2	0.6	1.0	0.3
Portland, OR	12.4	5.5	2.0	2.3	0.2	0.4	0.3	0.8	0.5
Providence, RI	32.8	3.9	0.5	2.2	15.3	5.9	1.2	3.4	0.3
Provo, UT	12.2	1.6	3.8	0.7	0.4	1.0	3.3	0.5	0.4
Raleigh, NC	13.6	3.8	2.4	1.3	1.1	1.4	1.1	2.2	0.2
Reno, NV	16.1	5.4	5.3	1.4	0.3	2.2	0.4	0.5	0.3
Richmond, VA	8.6	1.5	0.9	0.8	0.7	3.5	0.4	0.6	0.1
Rochester, MN	14.1	5.9	1.0	1.2	0.1	0.3	0.4	4.9	0.2
Sacramento, CA	21.3	10.6	5.5	1.6	0.1	0.9	0.4	0.6	0.2
Saint Louis, MO	6.6	2.7	0.8	1.0	0.3	0.3	0.3	0.9	0.1
Saint Paul, MN	18.7	9.3	1.8	0.7	0.2	0.9	0.4	4.9	0.3
Salem, OR	12.2	2.5	6.2	1.0	0.0	0.8	0.2	0.4	0.2
Salt Lake City, UT	15.4	4.2	5.1	1.8	0.2	0.7	1.4	1.0	0.3
San Antonio, TX	14.3	2.6	8.8	0.6	0.3	1.0	0.6	0.4	0.1
San Diego, CA	24.8	11.8	7.5	2.3	0.2	0.5	0.9	1.0	0.4
San Francisco, CA	34.2	21.9	2.4	4.4	0.1	2.4	1.3	0.6	0.7
San Jose, CA	41.6	27.3	8.4	2.2	0.1	1.3	1.0	0.7	0.3
Santa Rosa, CA	20.8	4.7	11.5	1.5	0.1	1.4	0.3	0.6	0.3
Savannah, GA	6.7	2.6	0.8	0.8	0.9	0.7	0.5	0.4	0.2
Seattle, WA	19.9	11.4	1.4	2.5	0.2	0.4	0.7	2.1	1.1
Sioux Falls, SD	9.0	2.0	0.6	1.1	0.1	1.7	0.2	3.2	0.1
Tampa, FL	19.0	4.0	1.1	1.8	7.4	1.3	2.4	0.6	0.3
Tucson, AZ	13.7	2.4	8.3	1.0	0.1	0.4	0.3	0.8	0.2
Tulsa, OK	12.0	2.6	5.5	0.7	0.3	1.3	0.7	0.6	0.1
Virginia Beach, VA	9.1	5.0	0.3	1.4	0.5	0.4	0.8	0.5	0.2
Washington, DC	13.3	2.8	0.6	2.3	1.2	2.2	1.7	2.2	0.3
Wichita, KS	10.0	3.5	4.4	0.5	0.1	0.5	0.4	0.6	0.1
Wilmington, NC	5.7	1.2	1.5	1.0	0.2	0.8	0.7	0.2	0.1
Winston-Salem, NC	10.7	2.0	4.1	0.6	0.6	1.7	1.0	0.6	0.1
U.S.	13.9	4.3	3.3	1.4	1.4	1.2	1.2	0.8	0.2

Note: (1) Excludes Mexico
Source: U.S. Census Bureau, 2019-2023 American Community Survey 5-Year Estimates

Foreign-born Population: Metro Area

Metro Area	Any Foreign Country	Asia	Mexico	Europe	Caribbean	Central America[1]	South America	Africa	Canada
Albuquerque, NM	9.2	2.0	4.9	0.8	0.3	0.2	0.4	0.4	0.1
Anchorage, AK	8.7	4.6	0.5	1.2	0.4	0.2	0.5	0.4	0.3
Ann Arbor, MI	12.8	7.3	0.7	2.2	0.1	0.5	0.4	0.9	0.5
Athens, GA	8.0	2.7	1.7	0.7	0.2	1.1	0.5	0.7	0.2
Atlanta, GA	14.8	4.8	2.3	1.1	1.7	1.4	1.4	1.8	0.2
Austin, TX	15.5	5.1	5.1	1.3	0.5	1.4	0.8	0.8	0.3
Baltimore, MD	11.2	4.4	0.4	1.2	0.8	1.5	0.7	2.1	0.1
Billings, MT	1.8	0.5	0.2	0.5	0.0	0.0	0.1	0.1	0.2
Boise City, ID	6.6	1.5	2.6	1.1	0.0	0.3	0.3	0.3	0.3
Boston, MA	19.7	6.4	0.2	3.1	3.5	1.7	2.5	1.8	0.4
Boulder, CO	10.0	3.4	2.0	2.5	0.1	0.4	0.7	0.3	0.5
Cape Coral, FL	17.9	1.4	1.7	1.9	7.0	2.4	2.2	0.2	1.0
Cedar Rapids, IA	4.5	1.8	0.5	0.4	0.1	0.2	0.1	1.3	0.1
Charleston, SC	6.3	1.5	1.1	1.1	0.4	0.7	1.0	0.3	0.2
Charlotte, NC	11.4	3.2	2.0	1.2	0.7	1.8	1.2	1.0	0.2
Chicago, IL	18.3	5.4	6.5	3.7	0.3	0.6	0.8	0.7	0.2
Cincinnati, OH	5.7	2.3	0.5	0.7	0.2	0.6	0.2	0.9	0.2
Clarksville, TN	5.4	1.6	0.9	0.8	0.4	0.4	0.4	0.6	0.2
Cleveland, OH	5.8	2.2	0.3	2.0	0.2	0.2	0.3	0.5	0.2
College Station, TX	11.7	3.8	4.9	0.7	0.2	0.9	0.7	0.4	0.1
Colorado Springs, CO	6.7	1.8	1.5	1.4	0.3	0.5	0.4	0.4	0.3
Columbia, MO	5.8	3.4	0.6	0.4	0.2	0.1	0.3	0.7	0.0
Columbia, SC	5.6	1.8	1.0	0.7	0.5	0.7	0.5	0.3	0.1
Columbus, OH	9.5	3.8	0.8	0.7	0.4	0.5	0.4	2.7	0.1
Dallas, TX	19.0	6.0	7.4	0.8	0.3	1.7	0.8	1.7	0.2
Davenport, IA	5.4	1.8	1.7	0.4	0.1	0.1	0.1	1.1	0.1
Denver, CO	12.1	3.1	4.5	1.4	0.2	0.5	0.8	1.2	0.3
Des Moines, IA	8.6	3.1	1.6	1.0	0.1	0.8	0.3	1.6	0.1
Detroit, MI	10.3	6.0	0.8	1.9	0.2	0.2	0.2	0.4	0.5
Durham, NC	13.2	3.7	2.7	1.6	0.5	2.4	0.8	1.1	0.2
El Paso, TX	23.1	0.9	20.6	0.5	0.2	0.4	0.2	0.3	0.1
Eugene, OR	5.4	1.7	1.6	0.8	0.1	0.2	0.1	0.3	0.4
Fargo, ND	6.9	2.4	0.2	0.5	0.1	0.0	0.1	3.2	0.3
Fort Collins, CO	5.4	1.6	1.4	1.1	0.1	0.3	0.4	0.2	0.2
Fort Wayne, IN	6.9	3.3	1.4	0.5	0.1	0.7	0.2	0.4	0.2
Fort Worth, TX	19.0	6.0	7.4	0.8	0.3	1.7	0.8	1.7	0.2
Gainesville, FL	10.2	3.7	0.5	1.5	1.3	0.6	1.7	0.5	0.4
Green Bay, WI	4.8	1.5	1.9	0.5	0.1	0.3	0.2	0.2	0.1
Greensboro, NC	9.5	2.9	2.3	0.7	0.4	0.7	0.5	1.7	0.1
Honolulu, HI	19.6	15.7	0.2	0.7	0.1	0.1	0.2	0.1	0.3
Houston, TX	23.8	6.2	8.0	1.0	1.0	3.9	1.8	1.6	0.3
Huntsville, AL	5.4	1.8	1.1	0.8	0.4	0.4	0.3	0.3	0.2
Indianapolis, IN	8.4	2.8	1.8	0.6	0.4	0.7	0.5	1.5	0.1
Jacksonville, FL	10.0	3.2	0.5	1.7	1.8	0.6	1.4	0.5	0.2
Kansas City, MO	7.2	2.2	2.0	0.6	0.3	0.8	0.3	0.8	0.1
Lafayette, LA	3.8	1.2	0.5	0.2	0.2	1.0	0.4	0.1	0.0
Las Vegas, NV	21.7	7.4	7.3	1.6	1.3	1.8	0.9	0.9	0.4
Lexington, KY	8.2	2.6	1.8	0.9	0.3	0.7	0.4	1.3	0.2
Lincoln, NE	8.1	4.3	1.1	0.8	0.3	0.5	0.3	0.7	0.1
Little Rock, AR	4.6	1.3	1.4	0.4	0.1	0.9	0.2	0.2	0.1
Los Angeles, CA	32.5	13.0	11.1	1.7	0.3	4.3	1.0	0.6	0.3
Louisville, KY	6.7	1.9	0.9	0.6	1.5	0.4	0.3	1.0	0.1
Madison, WI	7.6	3.3	1.3	1.0	0.1	0.2	0.8	0.6	0.2
Manchester, NH	10.4	3.4	0.4	1.7	1.4	0.8	0.9	0.9	0.8

Table continued on following page.

Metro Area	Any Foreign Country	Asia	Mexico	Europe	Caribbean	Central America[1]	South America	Africa	Canada
McAllen, TX	26.0	0.8	24.1	0.1	0.1	0.5	0.2	0.1	0.1
Memphis, TN	6.1	1.7	1.6	0.4	0.2	1.0	0.4	0.6	0.1
Miami, FL	41.9	2.2	1.1	2.4	20.6	4.3	10.2	0.4	0.5
Midland, TX	13.0	1.9	7.2	0.3	0.9	0.4	0.9	0.8	0.5
Milwaukee, WI	7.6	2.7	2.4	1.1	0.2	0.2	0.3	0.6	0.1
Minneapolis, MN	10.7	4.0	1.2	1.0	0.2	0.4	0.6	3.1	0.2
Nashville, TN	9.4	2.4	2.1	0.7	0.4	1.6	0.5	1.4	0.3
New Orleans, LA	9.5	2.4	0.6	0.5	1.1	3.9	0.5	0.4	0.1
New York, NY	29.8	8.9	1.4	4.2	6.8	2.0	4.7	1.5	0.3
Oklahoma City, OK	8.2	2.3	3.4	0.5	0.1	0.8	0.4	0.5	0.2
Omaha, NE	7.9	2.6	2.4	0.6	0.2	0.9	0.3	1.0	0.1
Orlando, FL	20.3	3.1	0.9	1.6	5.9	1.2	6.8	0.6	0.3
Philadelphia, PA	11.5	4.7	0.8	1.8	1.5	0.5	0.8	1.2	0.2
Phoenix, AZ	13.9	3.3	6.6	1.3	0.3	0.6	0.4	0.7	0.6
Pittsburgh, PA	4.1	2.0	0.2	0.9	0.2	0.1	0.2	0.4	0.1
Portland, OR	12.5	5.0	3.0	2.3	0.2	0.5	0.4	0.6	0.4
Providence, RI	14.4	2.3	0.3	3.8	2.9	1.7	1.3	1.7	0.2
Provo, UT	7.7	1.0	2.5	0.5	0.2	0.6	2.0	0.3	0.3
Raleigh, NC	13.1	5.0	2.5	1.3	0.8	1.0	0.8	1.3	0.3
Reno, NV	13.4	3.6	5.5	1.1	0.2	1.6	0.4	0.3	0.3
Richmond, VA	8.7	3.2	0.7	1.0	0.5	1.8	0.7	0.8	0.1
Rochester, MN	8.8	3.5	0.8	0.9	0.1	0.2	0.4	2.7	0.2
Sacramento, CA	18.9	9.4	4.2	2.8	0.1	0.7	0.4	0.5	0.3
Saint Louis, MO	5.0	2.3	0.5	1.0	0.1	0.3	0.2	0.5	0.1
Saint Paul, MN	10.7	4.0	1.2	1.0	0.2	0.4	0.6	3.1	0.2
Salem, OR	12.0	1.5	7.4	1.0	0.1	0.8	0.2	0.3	0.2
Salt Lake City, UT	12.4	3.0	4.2	1.2	0.1	0.6	1.9	0.6	0.2
San Antonio, TX	11.8	2.2	6.8	0.6	0.3	0.8	0.5	0.4	0.1
San Diego, CA	22.5	8.9	9.1	1.9	0.2	0.6	0.7	0.6	0.4
San Francisco, CA	31.6	18.0	4.9	2.8	0.2	2.7	1.2	0.9	0.5
San Jose, CA	40.3	27.1	6.5	3.0	0.1	1.0	1.1	0.7	0.5
Santa Rosa, CA	16.6	3.1	9.1	1.8	0.1	1.0	0.5	0.4	0.4
Savannah, GA	6.9	2.1	1.1	0.9	0.8	0.6	0.7	0.5	0.2
Seattle, WA	20.4	11.0	2.4	2.8	0.2	0.6	0.7	1.7	0.7
Sioux Falls, SD	6.7	1.5	0.5	0.9	0.1	1.2	0.1	2.2	0.1
Tampa, FL	15.0	2.9	1.2	2.2	4.3	0.8	2.4	0.5	0.6
Tucson, AZ	11.9	2.3	6.6	1.3	0.2	0.3	0.3	0.6	0.3
Tulsa, OK	7.2	2.0	2.9	0.6	0.2	0.7	0.4	0.4	0.1
Virginia Beach, VA	6.8	2.9	0.4	1.1	0.6	0.6	0.4	0.5	0.2
Washington, DC	24.0	8.4	0.9	1.8	1.1	5.2	2.5	3.8	0.2
Wichita, KS	7.4	2.6	3.1	0.5	0.1	0.4	0.3	0.4	0.1
Wilmington, NC	4.9	0.9	1.2	1.0	0.1	0.7	0.7	0.2	0.2
Winston-Salem, NC	7.3	1.4	2.8	0.7	0.3	1.0	0.7	0.3	0.1
U.S.	13.9	4.3	3.3	1.4	1.4	1.2	1.2	0.8	0.2

Note: Figures cover the Metropolitan Statistical Area (MSA); (1) Excludes Mexico
Source: U.S. Census Bureau, 2019-2023 American Community Survey 5-Year Estimates

Marital Status: City

City	Never Married	Now Married[1]	Separated	Widowed	Divorced
Albuquerque, NM	38.6	39.4	1.5	5.5	15.1
Anchorage, AK	34.6	47.7	1.9	3.5	12.2
Ann Arbor, MI	55.4	35.4	0.6	2.3	6.3
Athens, GA	53.9	31.2	1.3	4.3	9.3
Atlanta, GA	55.0	28.9	1.5	4.1	10.5
Austin, TX	44.0	41.7	1.3	3.0	9.9
Baltimore, MD	52.7	27.1	2.9	5.9	11.4
Billings, MT	31.9	47.2	1.0	5.6	14.3
Boise City, ID	35.2	46.8	1.0	4.3	12.7
Boston, MA	55.7	31.0	2.2	3.8	7.4
Boulder, CO	57.8	30.4	0.5	2.2	9.0
Cape Coral, FL	24.7	52.6	1.5	7.8	13.4
Cedar Rapids, IA	36.8	44.3	1.5	5.0	12.3
Charleston, SC	39.4	44.3	1.6	4.8	10.0
Charlotte, NC	42.9	41.1	2.1	3.8	10.1
Chicago, IL	49.1	35.6	2.2	5.0	8.1
Cincinnati, OH	53.4	29.8	1.8	4.5	10.6
Clarksville, TN	30.0	50.9	2.2	4.2	12.7
Cleveland, OH	53.7	23.7	2.8	6.1	13.7
College Station, TX	60.3	31.2	1.2	2.4	5.0
Colorado Springs, CO	30.7	50.8	1.5	4.5	12.5
Columbia, MO	49.8	37.9	1.0	3.4	8.0
Columbia, SC	55.8	29.7	2.0	3.9	8.6
Columbus, OH	45.8	36.3	2.0	4.2	11.7
Dallas, TX	43.0	40.2	2.5	4.0	10.2
Davenport, IA	37.3	44.0	1.0	5.6	12.0
Denver, CO	44.4	39.3	1.3	3.4	11.5
Des Moines, IA	40.8	38.8	2.3	5.7	12.5
Detroit, MI	57.0	22.0	2.9	6.3	11.9
Durham, NC	44.1	40.5	1.8	3.7	9.8
El Paso, TX	35.5	44.8	3.3	5.6	10.9
Eugene, OR	44.6	37.5	1.3	4.2	12.4
Fargo, ND	44.3	41.2	1.0	3.8	9.6
Fort Collins, CO	46.5	41.1	0.7	3.0	8.8
Fort Wayne, IN	37.2	42.9	1.5	5.9	12.5
Fort Worth, TX	35.8	46.5	2.2	4.6	10.7
Gainesville, FL	62.8	24.3	1.3	2.9	8.8
Green Bay, WI	39.4	41.0	1.1	4.9	13.5
Greensboro, NC	45.1	36.4	2.4	5.8	10.3
Honolulu, HI	38.0	44.0	1.2	6.6	10.1
Houston, TX	42.2	40.5	2.8	4.4	10.0
Huntsville, AL	37.9	42.7	1.9	6.0	11.6
Indianapolis, IN	41.1	40.4	1.7	4.8	12.0
Jacksonville, FL	36.2	42.5	2.1	5.5	13.6
Kansas City, MO	39.5	40.6	1.9	4.8	13.2
Lafayette, LA	40.0	42.8	2.2	5.1	9.9
Las Vegas, NV	36.4	42.8	1.8	5.3	13.5
Lexington, KY	38.8	43.1	1.4	4.6	12.0
Lincoln, NE	39.6	45.4	0.8	4.2	10.0
Little Rock, AR	38.6	41.0	1.5	5.5	13.4
Los Angeles, CA	46.5	38.6	2.3	4.5	8.0
Louisville, KY	37.2	41.9	2.0	6.1	12.8
Madison, WI	50.7	37.5	0.8	3.0	8.0
Manchester, NH	39.0	39.6	1.6	5.5	14.3
McAllen, TX	35.1	48.8	2.1	5.6	8.4
Memphis, TN	48.1	30.9	3.3	5.9	11.7

Table continued on following page.

City	Never Married	Now Married[1]	Separated	Widowed	Divorced
Miami, FL	40.4	37.0	3.3	5.7	13.5
Midland, TX	29.3	54.5	1.9	4.8	9.6
Milwaukee, WI	54.7	29.2	1.9	4.3	9.9
Minneapolis, MN	52.0	33.9	1.2	2.9	9.9
Nashville, TN	41.6	41.4	1.7	4.3	11.0
New Orleans, LA	49.2	30.8	2.3	5.2	12.5
New York, NY	44.0	39.8	2.8	5.2	8.2
Oklahoma City, OK	34.2	46.4	2.1	5.2	12.2
Omaha, NE	37.9	45.3	1.2	4.7	11.0
Orlando, FL	42.9	38.6	2.4	3.7	12.5
Philadelphia, PA	50.7	31.9	2.8	5.5	9.1
Phoenix, AZ	40.2	42.0	1.9	4.0	11.9
Pittsburgh, PA	54.4	30.6	1.7	5.0	8.3
Portland, OR	42.9	39.8	1.3	3.5	12.6
Providence, RI	53.4	32.1	2.0	4.1	8.5
Provo, UT	49.3	43.5	0.7	2.2	4.3
Raleigh, NC	43.1	40.5	1.9	3.9	10.6
Reno, NV	37.7	41.7	1.5	4.9	14.2
Richmond, VA	51.4	30.0	2.7	4.6	11.2
Rochester, MN	34.2	51.3	0.9	4.8	8.8
Sacramento, CA	41.5	40.8	2.3	4.7	10.7
Saint Louis, MO	49.7	30.2	2.7	5.3	12.2
Saint Paul, MN	46.4	37.8	1.5	3.6	10.6
Salem, OR	35.6	44.6	1.4	5.3	13.1
Salt Lake City, UT	45.4	39.1	1.6	2.9	10.9
San Antonio, TX	39.1	40.8	2.9	5.3	12.0
San Diego, CA	40.5	44.7	1.6	3.9	9.2
San Francisco, CA	45.6	40.7	1.4	4.5	7.8
San Jose, CA	37.2	49.3	1.6	4.4	7.5
Santa Rosa, CA	34.6	45.9	2.0	5.6	12.0
Savannah, GA	48.6	31.4	2.6	5.4	12.0
Seattle, WA	46.1	40.3	1.1	3.0	9.5
Sioux Falls, SD	34.5	48.4	1.4	4.3	11.4
Tampa, FL	43.1	38.1	2.2	4.7	11.8
Tucson, AZ	42.9	36.0	1.8	5.2	14.1
Tulsa, OK	36.5	41.7	2.4	5.5	14.0
Virginia Beach, VA	31.2	50.6	2.0	5.0	11.2
Washington, DC	55.2	31.5	1.4	3.4	8.5
Wichita, KS	35.0	45.2	1.8	5.2	12.8
Wilmington, NC	42.2	38.8	2.3	5.3	11.4
Winston-Salem, NC	42.5	39.6	2.4	5.2	10.3
U.S.	34.1	47.9	1.7	5.6	10.7

Note: Figures are percentages and cover the population 15 years of age and older; (1) Excludes separated
Source: U.S. Census Bureau, 2019-2023 American Community Survey 5-Year Estimates

Marital Status: Metro Area

Metro Area	Never Married	Now Married[1]	Separated	Widowed	Divorced
Albuquerque, NM	36.1	43.1	1.4	5.4	13.9
Anchorage, AK	33.3	49.3	1.8	3.7	11.9
Ann Arbor, MI	42.3	44.6	0.9	3.8	8.4
Athens, GA	43.0	41.4	1.3	4.7	9.5
Atlanta, GA	36.2	47.1	1.7	4.4	10.6
Austin, TX	35.9	49.4	1.3	3.5	9.8
Baltimore, MD	36.4	46.2	1.8	5.7	9.9
Billings, MT	28.7	51.5	1.0	5.5	13.3
Boise City, ID	28.9	54.0	1.0	4.4	11.8
Boston, MA	37.5	47.6	1.5	4.9	8.6
Boulder, CO	39.2	45.4	0.7	3.7	11.1
Cape Coral, FL	26.5	51.8	1.5	7.8	12.3
Cedar Rapids, IA	30.9	51.1	1.3	5.2	11.5
Charleston, SC	33.2	48.9	2.0	5.4	10.5
Charlotte, NC	33.6	49.4	2.0	4.9	10.0
Chicago, IL	37.6	46.7	1.6	5.3	8.8
Cincinnati, OH	33.2	49.0	1.3	5.5	11.0
Clarksville, TN	29.2	51.6	1.9	5.2	12.0
Cleveland, OH	35.7	44.2	1.5	6.4	12.1
College Station, TX	46.7	39.5	1.6	4.3	7.9
Colorado Springs, CO	29.4	53.8	1.3	4.1	11.5
Columbia, MO	41.1	44.4	1.1	4.3	9.2
Columbia, SC	36.0	45.7	2.3	5.7	10.2
Columbus, OH	35.0	47.4	1.6	4.8	11.2
Dallas, TX	33.4	50.6	1.7	4.2	10.0
Davenport, IA	31.1	50.1	1.2	6.2	11.5
Denver, CO	34.5	49.4	1.3	3.7	11.0
Des Moines, IA	31.7	51.3	1.3	5.0	10.7
Detroit, MI	35.9	45.7	1.2	6.0	11.2
Durham, NC	38.3	46.2	1.7	4.5	9.3
El Paso, TX	35.5	45.7	3.2	5.4	10.2
Eugene, OR	35.8	44.3	1.3	5.4	13.2
Fargo, ND	38.8	47.3	0.9	3.9	9.1
Fort Collins, CO	35.3	50.3	0.8	3.9	9.7
Fort Wayne, IN	31.8	49.9	1.3	5.5	11.5
Fort Worth, TX	33.4	50.6	1.7	4.2	10.0
Gainesville, FL	43.5	39.6	1.3	5.1	10.4
Green Bay, WI	31.8	51.2	0.6	5.2	11.1
Greensboro, NC	35.2	45.3	2.3	6.2	11.0
Honolulu, HI	34.6	49.5	1.1	6.0	8.7
Houston, TX	34.3	50.1	2.1	4.3	9.2
Huntsville, AL	30.6	51.3	1.4	5.5	11.2
Indianapolis, IN	32.7	49.7	1.2	4.9	11.5
Jacksonville, FL	31.4	48.4	1.8	5.6	12.7
Kansas City, MO	31.3	50.3	1.5	5.1	11.8
Lafayette, LA	33.9	47.8	2.0	5.4	10.9
Las Vegas, NV	35.6	44.3	2.0	5.1	13.1
Lexington, KY	34.4	46.7	1.5	5.1	12.3
Lincoln, NE	37.2	48.2	0.8	4.2	9.6
Little Rock, AR	31.5	48.0	1.7	5.9	12.9
Los Angeles, CA	40.7	44.3	2.0	4.7	8.3
Louisville, KY	31.8	47.6	1.7	6.0	12.9
Madison, WI	37.6	48.1	0.7	4.1	9.5
Manchester, NH	32.0	49.8	1.1	5.2	11.8
McAllen, TX	36.7	47.8	3.0	4.9	7.6
Memphis, TN	38.5	42.0	2.5	5.9	11.1

Table continued on following page.

Metro Area	Never Married	Now Married[1]	Separated	Widowed	Divorced
Miami, FL	34.0	44.7	2.4	6.1	12.8
Midland, TX	28.6	55.2	1.6	4.9	9.8
Milwaukee, WI	37.7	45.9	1.2	5.1	10.1
Minneapolis, MN	34.1	50.7	0.9	4.3	10.0
Nashville, TN	32.8	50.3	1.4	4.9	10.6
New Orleans, LA	40.3	38.9	2.3	6.0	12.4
New York, NY	38.3	46.0	2.1	5.4	8.1
Oklahoma City, OK	32.3	48.6	1.8	5.5	11.9
Omaha, NE	32.4	51.2	1.1	4.6	10.8
Orlando, FL	35.1	47.0	1.8	4.9	11.2
Philadelphia, PA	37.7	45.7	1.8	5.6	9.1
Phoenix, AZ	34.3	47.9	1.4	4.9	11.5
Pittsburgh, PA	33.1	48.4	1.5	7.0	10.0
Portland, OR	33.7	48.9	1.3	4.3	11.8
Providence, RI	36.7	45.0	1.5	5.8	11.0
Provo, UT	33.4	57.7	0.8	2.6	5.5
Raleigh, NC	32.4	52.4	1.8	4.2	9.3
Reno, NV	32.6	47.1	1.4	5.1	13.8
Richmond, VA	35.0	47.0	2.0	5.5	10.4
Rochester, MN	29.3	55.9	0.7	4.9	9.1
Sacramento, CA	34.2	48.5	1.8	4.9	10.5
Saint Louis, MO	32.9	48.4	1.6	5.8	11.2
Saint Paul, MN	34.1	50.7	0.9	4.3	10.0
Salem, OR	32.4	48.5	1.6	5.4	12.1
Salt Lake City, UT	33.6	51.2	1.5	3.6	10.2
San Antonio, TX	34.3	47.2	2.3	5.1	11.1
San Diego, CA	36.3	48.1	1.6	4.4	9.6
San Francisco, CA	36.8	48.8	1.4	4.6	8.4
San Jose, CA	35.5	51.7	1.4	4.2	7.1
Santa Rosa, CA	32.7	48.5	1.4	5.2	12.2
Savannah, GA	35.8	45.9	2.1	5.1	11.2
Seattle, WA	33.8	50.4	1.3	4.0	10.5
Sioux Falls, SD	30.7	53.1	1.1	4.3	10.8
Tampa, FL	32.1	46.3	1.8	6.8	13.1
Tucson, AZ	35.1	44.8	1.5	5.8	12.9
Tulsa, OK	29.9	49.5	1.8	6.1	12.7
Virginia Beach, VA	33.7	47.7	2.2	5.5	10.8
Washington, DC	36.7	48.8	1.6	4.2	8.7
Wichita, KS	31.2	50.0	1.4	5.4	12.0
Wilmington, NC	28.5	52.5	1.9	6.2	10.9
Winston-Salem, NC	31.7	48.8	2.2	6.3	11.1
U.S.	34.1	47.9	1.7	5.6	10.7

Note: Figures are percentages and cover the population 15 years of age and older; Figures cover the Metropolitan Statistical Area (MSA); (1) Excludes separated
Source: U.S. Census Bureau, 2019-2023 American Community Survey 5-Year Estimates

Disability by Age: City

City	All Ages	Under 18 Years Old	18 to 64 Years Old	65 Years and Over
Albuquerque, NM	15.2	4.8	13.2	35.2
Anchorage, AK	12.2	4.9	10.7	33.7
Ann Arbor, MI	8.1	4.7	6.1	23.8
Athens, GA	12.2	5.9	10.1	34.0
Atlanta, GA	11.6	5.4	9.6	32.3
Austin, TX	9.5	3.8	8.4	28.3
Baltimore, MD	16.5	5.7	14.6	40.0
Billings, MT	14.5	4.4	11.8	36.3
Boise City, ID	12.1	5.3	10.2	29.4
Boston, MA	12.1	5.8	9.1	37.2
Boulder, CO	7.5	2.9	6.1	20.9
Cape Coral, FL	14.0	3.8	10.0	30.5
Cedar Rapids, IA	11.6	4.9	10.0	27.3
Charleston, SC	9.7	3.2	6.7	29.6
Charlotte, NC	8.3	2.8	7.0	28.3
Chicago, IL	11.9	3.8	9.6	35.4
Cincinnati, OH	13.6	6.0	12.6	31.7
Clarksville, TN	14.8	5.7	15.1	41.8
Cleveland, OH	19.9	9.8	18.5	40.7
College Station, TX	8.2	6.2	6.8	29.3
Colorado Springs, CO	13.2	5.7	11.9	30.1
Columbia, MO	11.9	5.4	10.5	32.2
Columbia, SC	12.7	3.9	10.7	38.0
Columbus, OH	12.2	5.3	10.9	34.7
Dallas, TX	11.4	4.7	9.8	34.9
Davenport, IA	13.9	5.5	11.8	33.3
Denver, CO	10.1	3.3	8.3	30.7
Des Moines, IA	14.3	5.8	13.4	35.2
Detroit, MI	19.6	6.0	19.7	42.6
Durham, NC	9.9	3.6	8.0	29.6
El Paso, TX	14.3	5.5	12.0	40.2
Eugene, OR	15.1	4.8	13.2	31.7
Fargo, ND	11.4	5.4	9.0	32.6
Fort Collins, CO	8.9	3.0	7.7	24.0
Fort Wayne, IN	13.6	5.3	12.5	32.5
Fort Worth, TX	10.2	3.7	9.0	34.4
Gainesville, FL	10.5	3.9	8.3	33.6
Green Bay, WI	15.0	7.1	13.9	34.3
Greensboro, NC	11.8	5.4	9.9	31.4
Honolulu, HI	12.5	3.9	7.9	32.1
Houston, TX	11.0	4.7	8.9	35.1
Huntsville, AL	14.3	5.4	11.8	34.8
Indianapolis, IN	13.5	5.1	12.6	34.6
Jacksonville, FL	13.5	5.0	11.8	34.1
Kansas City, MO	12.8	3.7	11.6	33.3
Lafayette, LA	12.9	3.5	10.3	33.9
Las Vegas, NV	13.3	4.5	11.3	34.2
Lexington, KY	12.8	4.9	11.0	32.4
Lincoln, NE	12.0	4.8	10.6	29.5
Little Rock, AR	13.9	6.8	12.0	33.8
Los Angeles, CA	11.1	3.5	8.3	36.3
Louisville, KY	14.7	5.3	13.3	34.1
Madison, WI	9.1	4.1	7.5	24.6
Manchester, NH	13.6	7.4	11.5	31.1
McAllen, TX	13.0	6.1	9.4	43.8

Table continued on following page.

City	All Ages	Under 18 Years Old	18 to 64 Years Old	65 Years and Over
Memphis, TN	13.6	4.6	12.5	34.6
Miami, FL	11.5	3.7	7.0	38.2
Midland, TX	10.4	3.4	8.7	40.3
Milwaukee, WI	13.2	4.8	12.5	35.3
Minneapolis, MN	11.6	4.8	10.7	30.5
Nashville, TN	11.0	4.5	8.8	33.8
New Orleans, LA	14.1	5.7	11.6	34.2
New York, NY	11.7	3.9	8.5	34.6
Oklahoma City, OK	13.9	5.6	12.5	36.6
Omaha, NE	11.1	3.8	9.8	30.2
Orlando, FL	10.3	5.2	8.3	33.4
Philadelphia, PA	17.4	7.7	15.6	40.8
Phoenix, AZ	11.5	4.6	10.2	32.5
Pittsburgh, PA	14.2	7.4	11.5	34.3
Portland, OR	13.2	4.9	10.9	34.3
Providence, RI	13.7	6.0	12.4	37.3
Provo, UT	10.2	4.2	8.9	42.2
Raleigh, NC	9.6	4.4	7.9	29.1
Reno, NV	12.1	4.0	9.8	31.2
Richmond, VA	14.0	7.0	12.0	33.1
Rochester, MN	10.1	3.8	7.8	28.9
Sacramento, CA	12.4	4.0	10.1	35.8
Saint Louis, MO	16.6	6.5	14.4	39.0
Saint Paul, MN	12.5	4.7	11.9	31.3
Salem, OR	15.4	5.9	13.7	36.8
Salt Lake City, UT	12.1	5.0	9.9	34.9
San Antonio, TX	15.5	6.7	13.5	41.8
San Diego, CA	10.0	3.4	7.3	31.2
San Francisco, CA	11.2	2.7	7.3	34.1
San Jose, CA	9.6	3.6	6.3	34.3
Santa Rosa, CA	12.7	4.3	10.3	30.0
Savannah, GA	15.9	7.0	13.5	40.7
Seattle, WA	10.0	2.8	8.0	30.3
Sioux Falls, SD	10.0	3.4	8.7	28.4
Tampa, FL	11.9	4.1	9.3	38.0
Tucson, AZ	15.5	6.1	13.2	36.8
Tulsa, OK	14.4	5.3	13.3	34.2
Virginia Beach, VA	11.7	4.4	10.1	28.7
Washington, DC	11.0	4.5	8.8	32.3
Wichita, KS	14.9	5.9	13.6	34.7
Wilmington, NC	12.9	3.7	10.4	31.1
Winston-Salem, NC	12.6	4.7	10.9	32.8
U.S.	13.0	4.7	10.7	32.9

Note: Figures show percent of the civilian noninstitutionalized population that reported having a disability. Disability status is determined from from six types of difficulty: vision, hearing, cognitive, ambulatory, self-care, and independent living. For children under 5 years old, hearing and vision difficulty are used to determine disability status. For children between the ages of 5 and 14, disability status is determined from hearing, vision, cognitive, ambulatory, and self-care difficulties. For people aged 15 years and older, they are considered to have a disability if they have difficulty with any one of the six difficulty types.
Source: U.S. Census Bureau, 2019-2023 American Community Survey 5-Year Estimates

Disability by Age: Metro Area

Metro Area	All Ages	Under 18 Years Old	18 to 64 Years Old	65 Years and Over
Albuquerque, NM	16.1	4.7	14.1	36.3
Anchorage, AK	12.6	4.8	11.3	34.0
Ann Arbor, MI	10.3	4.1	8.3	26.9
Athens, GA	12.8	4.9	11.0	32.7
Atlanta, GA	10.8	4.5	9.0	31.3
Austin, TX	10.0	4.3	8.5	29.1
Baltimore, MD	12.0	4.5	9.8	30.7
Billings, MT	14.3	4.4	11.6	35.1
Boise City, ID	12.7	4.9	11.0	31.0
Boston, MA	10.9	4.5	8.2	29.6
Boulder, CO	8.8	2.9	6.9	23.8
Cape Coral, FL	13.7	4.0	9.6	27.1
Cedar Rapids, IA	11.5	5.0	9.5	27.3
Charleston, SC	12.1	4.5	9.8	31.5
Charlotte, NC	10.6	3.4	8.7	31.0
Chicago, IL	10.7	3.6	8.4	30.2
Cincinnati, OH	12.7	5.1	10.8	31.5
Clarksville, TN	16.4	6.5	16.1	41.9
Cleveland, OH	14.6	5.6	12.2	32.1
College Station, TX	10.9	5.5	8.8	33.8
Colorado Springs, CO	12.5	5.4	11.3	29.7
Columbia, MO	13.0	5.3	11.5	31.9
Columbia, SC	14.3	5.1	12.3	35.3
Columbus, OH	12.1	5.0	10.4	32.3
Dallas, TX	10.1	4.0	8.5	32.0
Davenport, IA	13.5	5.7	10.9	30.9
Denver, CO	10.2	3.7	8.4	29.1
Des Moines, IA	10.8	3.8	9.3	29.8
Detroit, MI	14.0	4.6	11.9	33.5
Durham, NC	10.4	3.7	8.1	28.1
El Paso, TX	13.9	5.5	11.7	41.5
Eugene, OR	17.1	6.2	15.0	33.4
Fargo, ND	11.0	4.1	9.3	32.1
Fort Collins, CO	10.3	3.3	8.2	26.6
Fort Wayne, IN	12.4	4.7	11.1	30.4
Fort Worth, TX	10.1	4.0	8.5	32.0
Gainesville, FL	13.3	5.4	10.2	34.6
Green Bay, WI	12.0	4.4	10.6	27.3
Greensboro, NC	13.4	4.9	11.2	32.9
Honolulu, HI	12.2	3.6	8.5	32.8
Houston, TX	10.4	4.3	8.6	32.8
Huntsville, AL	13.5	4.5	11.5	34.9
Indianapolis, IN	12.4	5.0	10.9	32.1
Jacksonville, FL	13.1	4.8	11.1	31.8
Kansas City, MO	12.0	4.4	10.3	31.1
Lafayette, LA	14.5	4.7	12.9	37.2
Las Vegas, NV	13.0	4.4	10.7	34.3
Lexington, KY	13.9	5.4	12.2	33.8
Lincoln, NE	11.8	4.5	10.2	29.6
Little Rock, AR	15.5	5.7	13.6	37.4
Los Angeles, CA	10.5	3.5	7.7	32.8
Louisville, KY	14.4	5.0	12.5	34.4
Madison, WI	9.4	3.8	7.6	24.3
Manchester, NH	11.7	4.7	9.6	28.3
McAllen, TX	12.5	5.5	9.7	45.5

Table continued on following page.

Metro Area	All Ages	Under 18 Years Old	18 to 64 Years Old	65 Years and Over
Memphis, TN	13.5	5.0	12.1	34.6
Miami, FL	11.0	4.0	7.2	30.9
Midland, TX	10.9	3.5	9.3	40.7
Milwaukee, WI	11.3	4.0	9.4	28.9
Minneapolis, MN	10.4	4.0	8.6	27.9
Nashville, TN	11.4	4.2	9.4	32.9
New Orleans, LA	15.3	6.1	12.9	36.3
New York, NY	10.6	3.5	7.7	30.9
Oklahoma City, OK	14.7	5.2	13.0	38.3
Omaha, NE	11.2	3.8	9.7	31.0
Orlando, FL	12.3	5.6	9.5	33.1
Philadelphia, PA	13.2	5.5	11.0	31.5
Phoenix, AZ	12.3	4.9	10.1	31.1
Pittsburgh, PA	14.7	5.7	11.7	31.9
Portland, OR	12.9	4.5	10.8	32.6
Providence, RI	13.9	5.6	11.7	31.4
Provo, UT	8.7	3.9	8.3	31.3
Raleigh, NC	10.0	3.9	8.3	30.1
Reno, NV	13.0	4.7	10.4	31.7
Richmond, VA	12.8	5.3	10.7	30.4
Rochester, MN	10.1	3.6	7.8	27.2
Sacramento, CA	12.3	4.0	9.6	33.8
Saint Louis, MO	13.3	4.7	11.2	32.1
Saint Paul, MN	10.4	4.0	8.6	27.9
Salem, OR	15.8	5.8	13.8	36.9
Salt Lake City, UT	10.2	4.4	9.1	29.8
San Antonio, TX	14.6	6.3	12.6	39.1
San Diego, CA	10.7	3.6	8.2	31.3
San Francisco, CA	10.3	3.2	7.3	30.4
San Jose, CA	8.8	3.1	5.7	31.3
Santa Rosa, CA	12.1	4.0	9.1	28.2
Savannah, GA	14.5	5.3	12.8	35.7
Seattle, WA	11.4	4.2	9.2	32.6
Sioux Falls, SD	9.9	3.3	8.5	28.5
Tampa, FL	14.4	5.3	11.1	33.5
Tucson, AZ	15.1	5.6	12.2	32.3
Tulsa, OK	15.0	5.2	13.4	37.0
Virginia Beach, VA	13.6	5.4	11.6	32.5
Washington, DC	9.1	3.5	7.0	27.9
Wichita, KS	14.6	5.6	13.0	35.1
Wilmington, NC	13.5	5.5	10.7	26.6
Winston-Salem, NC	14.2	4.9	12.0	33.1
U.S.	13.0	4.7	10.7	32.9

Note: Figures show percent of the civilian noninstitutionalized population that reported having a disability. Disability status is determined from from six types of difficulty: vision, hearing, cognitive, ambulatory, self-care, and independent living. For children under 5 years old, hearing and vision difficulty are used to determine disability status. For children between the ages of 5 and 14, disability status is determined from hearing, vision, cognitive, ambulatory, and self-care difficulties. For people aged 15 years and older, they are considered to have a disability if they have difficulty with any one of the six difficulty types; Figures cover the Metropolitan Statistical Area (MSA)
Source: U.S. Census Bureau, 2019-2023 American Community Survey 5-Year Estimates

Religious Groups by Family

Metro Area	Catholic	Baptist	Methodist	LDS[1]	Pentecostal	Lutheran	Islam	Adventist	Other
Albuquerque, NM	32.6	3.2	0.9	2.7	1.7	0.4	0.7	1.5	10.8
Anchorage, AK	4.9	3.4	1.0	5.1	1.7	1.5	0.1	1.7	16.3
Ann Arbor, MI	9.7	2.0	2.4	0.8	1.5	2.3	2.2	0.9	10.0
Athens, GA	6.4	12.8	5.7	1.0	2.4	0.3	0.2	1.3	7.9
Atlanta, GA	10.7	14.7	6.7	0.8	2.0	0.4	1.9	1.9	12.4
Austin, TX	18.8	6.5	2.2	1.3	0.7	1.1	1.0	1.0	9.9
Baltimore, MD	12.4	3.2	4.4	0.6	1.2	1.4	3.3	1.2	11.7
Billings, MT	7.4	1.9	1.1	5.2	3.6	4.9	n/a	1.2	7.8
Boise City, ID	13.0	0.8	2.5	15.0	1.6	0.8	0.3	1.7	10.0
Boston, MA	37.0	1.0	0.7	0.5	0.7	0.2	2.2	0.9	7.1
Boulder, CO	16.0	0.3	0.7	0.7	0.5	1.7	0.4	0.9	15.2
Cape Coral, FL	18.8	2.5	1.7	0.6	3.0	0.7	0.2	2.0	12.2
Cedar Rapids, IA	16.8	1.0	5.3	1.0	1.3	8.1	1.3	0.6	9.6
Charleston, SC	11.5	7.7	8.0	0.8	1.9	0.7	0.2	1.0	12.8
Charlotte, NC	12.1	13.9	7.0	0.7	2.2	1.1	1.7	1.4	15.9
Chicago, IL	28.6	3.4	1.4	0.3	1.5	2.1	4.7	1.1	9.2
Cincinnati, OH	17.0	5.7	2.3	0.6	1.5	0.8	1.1	0.7	21.8
Clarksville, TN	4.6	23.2	4.4	1.4	3.2	0.5	0.1	0.8	12.4
Cleveland, OH	26.1	4.3	2.3	0.4	1.5	1.8	1.1	1.3	16.8
College Station, TX	17.2	10.6	4.3	1.7	0.5	1.1	0.6	0.5	6.8
Colorado Springs, CO	16.4	2.6	1.3	3.0	1.0	1.2	0.1	1.0	16.2
Columbia, MO	7.1	9.0	3.5	1.7	1.1	1.6	1.4	1.2	12.4
Columbia, SC	6.6	15.1	8.5	1.2	3.8	2.3	0.3	1.3	15.4
Columbus, OH	11.7	3.4	3.0	0.8	1.9	1.7	2.1	0.9	17.5
Dallas, TX	14.2	14.3	4.7	1.4	2.2	0.5	1.8	1.3	13.8
Davenport, IA	13.2	3.2	3.6	0.8	1.5	6.6	0.7	0.8	6.7
Denver, CO	16.1	1.5	1.0	2.1	0.6	1.4	0.3	1.1	10.4
Des Moines, IA	12.1	1.8	4.0	0.9	2.5	6.6	1.6	0.8	8.7
Detroit, MI	18.6	4.8	1.7	0.3	2.1	2.2	4.5	1.0	8.5
Durham, NC	8.5	12.3	6.5	0.9	1.3	0.3	1.5	1.1	13.7
El Paso, TX	47.9	2.5	0.4	1.2	1.1	0.2	0.1	2.1	6.9
Eugene, OR	5.6	0.7	0.5	2.8	2.5	0.8	<0.1	2.0	9.0
Fargo, ND	14.2	0.2	1.0	0.6	1.3	24.0	<0.1	0.6	8.1
Fort Collins, CO	9.9	1.2	1.3	4.0	2.7	2.5	<0.1	1.2	12.1
Fort Wayne, IN	13.1	8.1	3.9	0.4	1.1	7.1	1.0	0.9	17.6
Fort Worth, TX	14.2	14.3	4.7	1.4	2.2	0.5	1.8	1.3	13.8
Gainesville, FL	8.5	10.6	4.8	1.4	3.2	0.3	0.4	1.3	14.5
Green Bay, WI	31.8	0.3	1.4	0.5	1.1	10.8	0.4	0.9	7.0
Greensboro, NC	7.9	10.0	8.0	0.7	2.8	0.4	1.5	1.4	17.8
Honolulu, HI	18.0	1.4	0.5	4.1	2.6	0.2	<0.1	1.9	9.8
Houston, TX	18.3	13.1	3.7	1.2	1.6	0.7	1.7	1.5	13.1
Huntsville, AL	7.5	23.6	6.6	1.4	1.2	0.4	0.8	2.7	17.5
Indianapolis, IN	11.5	6.2	3.3	0.7	1.3	1.1	1.1	1.0	17.4
Jacksonville, FL	13.0	14.5	3.0	1.0	1.4	0.4	0.6	1.3	20.5
Kansas City, MO	11.3	9.1	5.0	1.6	2.7	1.7	1.0	1.0	12.1
Lafayette, LA	44.3	9.3	2.0	0.4	1.8	0.1	0.1	0.8	7.0
Las Vegas, NV	26.2	1.9	0.3	5.8	1.5	0.6	0.3	1.3	5.5
Lexington, KY	5.8	14.9	5.5	1.2	1.6	0.3	0.5	1.2	16.6
Lincoln, NE	13.2	1.0	5.7	1.2	3.1	9.1	0.1	1.8	10.0
Little Rock, AR	4.9	23.5	6.2	0.8	3.7	0.4	0.4	1.0	13.6
Los Angeles, CA	31.1	2.6	0.8	1.5	2.4	0.4	1.4	1.5	9.1
Louisville, KY	11.9	14.5	3.2	0.8	0.9	0.5	1.0	1.0	12.4
Madison, WI	14.4	0.5	2.0	0.7	0.2	9.2	1.2	0.7	8.4
Manchester, NH	16.3	0.6	0.6	0.6	0.3	0.3	0.1	0.8	8.1
McAllen, TX	46.6	2.2	0.8	1.2	1.0	0.3	0.2	3.2	6.0
Memphis, TN	4.8	26.6	6.0	0.7	5.1	0.3	1.3	1.3	18.4

Table continued on following page.

Metro Area	Catholic	Baptist	Methodist	LDS[1]	Pentecostal	Lutheran	Islam	Adventist	Other
Miami, FL	23.8	5.1	0.9	0.5	1.3	0.3	0.8	2.4	11.1
Midland, TX	15.4	25.5	2.5	2.0	1.2	0.3	0.4	1.3	16.5
Milwaukee, WI	24.5	3.0	1.0	0.4	2.8	9.1	2.8	0.9	10.7
Minneapolis, MN	19.8	0.8	1.4	0.5	2.5	10.7	2.9	0.7	7.4
Nashville, TN	6.2	16.4	4.8	0.9	1.6	0.4	0.8	1.3	19.4
New Orleans, LA	42.1	9.3	2.5	0.5	2.1	0.5	1.4	1.0	8.0
New York, NY	32.5	1.7	1.2	0.3	0.9	0.5	4.5	1.4	10.6
Oklahoma City, OK	10.0	16.6	6.2	1.3	3.9	0.6	0.6	0.9	21.4
Omaha, NE	19.9	2.8	2.8	1.6	1.0	6.1	0.2	1.0	9.0
Orlando, FL	17.6	5.7	2.1	0.9	2.7	0.6	1.3	2.8	14.6
Philadelphia, PA	26.8	3.3	2.4	0.3	1.0	1.2	2.6	1.0	10.5
Phoenix, AZ	22.9	1.7	0.6	6.2	1.5	1.0	1.9	1.5	9.3
Pittsburgh, PA	30.6	1.9	4.3	0.4	1.3	2.5	0.6	0.6	12.5
Portland, OR	11.8	0.8	0.6	3.3	1.4	1.1	0.2	2.0	14.4
Providence, RI	37.9	0.9	0.6	0.3	0.6	0.3	0.5	0.9	6.1
Provo, UT	4.9	0.1	<0.1	82.6	0.1	<0.1	0.3	0.3	0.4
Raleigh, NC	12.4	9.8	5.4	1.2	1.9	0.7	3.2	1.5	12.8
Reno, NV	24.4	1.4	0.5	4.0	0.9	0.5	0.3	1.4	5.3
Richmond, VA	12.3	14.2	4.8	0.9	3.2	0.5	2.1	1.2	14.8
Rochester, MN	15.6	0.4	2.8	1.5	1.9	19.3	1.0	0.7	10.1
Sacramento, CA	17.1	1.9	1.1	3.1	2.2	0.6	1.9	1.9	8.2
Saint Louis, MO	21.2	8.6	2.9	0.7	1.4	3.2	1.3	0.8	11.1
Saint Paul, MN	19.8	0.8	1.4	0.5	2.5	10.7	2.9	0.7	7.4
Salem, OR	19.5	0.5	0.6	3.8	2.9	1.2	n/a	2.5	10.7
Salt Lake City, UT	9.0	0.6	0.2	52.0	0.7	0.2	1.6	0.7	2.6
San Antonio, TX	27.3	6.4	2.1	1.4	1.6	1.1	0.5	1.5	11.0
San Diego, CA	22.9	1.5	0.6	2.1	1.0	0.6	1.5	1.9	9.4
San Francisco, CA	21.5	2.2	0.9	1.5	1.4	0.4	2.0	1.0	7.7
San Jose, CA	27.2	1.2	0.6	1.4	0.9	0.4	2.0	1.3	11.4
Santa Rosa, CA	23.5	1.1	0.5	1.4	0.5	0.5	0.2	1.8	6.9
Savannah, GA	5.5	11.9	4.8	0.8	1.5	1.1	0.2	1.4	12.3
Seattle, WA	11.0	1.0	0.7	2.6	2.8	1.2	0.6	1.4	19.8
Sioux Falls, SD	13.1	0.7	2.9	0.7	1.7	16.4	0.1	0.6	20.3
Tampa, FL	23.1	6.3	2.9	0.5	1.9	0.6	0.7	1.8	12.1
Tucson, AZ	18.9	1.9	0.6	2.8	1.3	1.1	1.0	1.4	9.7
Tulsa, OK	5.6	15.5	7.7	1.2	2.5	0.5	0.5	1.2	22.2
Virginia Beach, VA	8.3	9.5	4.8	0.7	2.0	0.5	1.0	0.9	16.1
Washington, DC	16.1	6.0	4.1	1.1	1.3	0.8	3.3	1.5	12.6
Wichita, KS	12.7	23.5	4.5	1.5	1.4	1.3	0.1	1.1	15.0
Wilmington, NC	13.2	9.9	8.1	1.0	1.0	0.7	0.7	1.4	12.6
Winston-Salem, NC	9.3	12.8	11.4	0.5	1.0	0.6	0.8	1.4	22.5
U.S.	18.7	7.3	3.0	2.0	1.8	1.7	1.3	1.3	11.6

Note: Figures are the number of adherents as a percentage of the total population; Figures cover the Metropolitan Statistical Area (MSA);
(1) Church of Jesus Christ of Latter-day Saints
Source: 2020 U.S. Religion Census, Association of Statisticians of American Religious Bodies; The Association of Religion Data Archives

Religious Groups by Tradition

Metro Area	Catholic	Evangelical Protestant	Mainline Protestant	Black Protestant	Islam	Judaism	Hinduism	Orthodox	Buddhism
Albuquerque, NM	32.6	13.4	2.2	0.5	0.7	0.2	0.2	0.1	0.6
Anchorage, AK	4.9	19.2	2.4	0.9	0.1	0.1	0.1	0.5	1.3
Ann Arbor, MI	9.7	8.1	5.6	2.5	2.2	0.8	0.5	0.4	0.3
Athens, GA	6.4	19.1	7.2	2.6	0.2	0.2	0.2	0.1	<0.1
Atlanta, GA	10.7	22.3	7.4	5.3	1.9	0.5	0.7	0.3	0.2
Austin, TX	18.8	13.5	4.0	1.7	1.0	0.2	0.6	0.2	0.3
Baltimore, MD	12.4	10.6	5.9	3.3	3.3	1.7	0.1	0.5	0.1
Billings, MT	7.4	13.9	5.2	0.1	n/a	n/a	n/a	0.1	n/a
Boise City, ID	13.0	11.9	3.9	<0.1	0.3	0.1	0.2	0.1	0.1
Boston, MA	37.0	3.4	3.2	0.3	2.2	1.1	0.3	0.9	0.4
Boulder, CO	16.0	12.7	3.4	n/a	0.4	0.7	0.5	0.2	1.0
Cape Coral, FL	18.8	16.4	3.0	0.6	0.2	0.2	0.2	0.1	0.1
Cedar Rapids, IA	16.8	11.9	12.2	0.4	1.3	0.1	0.7	0.1	<0.1
Charleston, SC	11.5	17.1	6.8	6.6	0.2	0.4	<0.1	0.2	n/a
Charlotte, NC	12.1	26.4	9.5	3.4	1.7	0.2	0.2	0.4	0.1
Chicago, IL	28.6	8.2	3.7	3.6	4.7	0.7	0.4	0.7	0.4
Cincinnati, OH	17.0	24.9	4.1	2.0	1.1	0.4	0.3	0.3	0.1
Clarksville, TN	4.6	35.7	4.8	3.4	0.1	n/a	n/a	0.1	n/a
Cleveland, OH	26.1	15.1	5.6	3.5	1.1	1.3	0.3	0.8	0.2
College Station, TX	17.2	16.1	5.3	1.8	0.6	n/a	0.1	0.1	n/a
Colorado Springs, CO	16.4	18.3	2.9	0.9	0.1	<0.1	<0.1	0.1	0.3
Columbia, MO	7.1	19.4	6.3	1.9	1.4	0.2	0.1	0.1	<0.1
Columbia, SC	6.6	27.9	10.7	5.6	0.3	0.2	0.4	0.1	0.3
Columbus, OH	11.7	18.1	6.8	1.5	2.1	0.4	0.4	0.5	0.2
Dallas, TX	14.2	25.4	5.9	3.3	1.8	0.3	0.5	0.3	0.2
Davenport, IA	13.2	8.5	10.6	1.9	0.7	0.1	0.2	0.1	n/a
Denver, CO	16.1	9.6	2.8	0.6	0.3	0.4	0.5	0.4	0.5
Des Moines, IA	12.1	10.3	12.2	1.0	1.6	<0.1	0.2	0.1	0.1
Detroit, MI	18.6	9.1	3.3	5.1	4.5	0.8	0.3	0.8	0.2
Durham, NC	8.5	20.0	8.8	4.3	1.5	0.5	0.1	0.3	0.1
El Paso, TX	47.9	9.9	0.6	0.4	0.1	0.2	<0.1	<0.1	0.2
Eugene, OR	5.6	10.3	2.3	0.1	<0.1	0.4	0.3	0.1	0.5
Fargo, ND	14.2	11.1	23.4	n/a	<0.1	<0.1	n/a	0.1	n/a
Fort Collins, CO	9.9	15.6	3.3	0.4	<0.1	n/a	0.1	0.1	0.1
Fort Wayne, IN	13.1	24.7	6.1	6.5	1.0	0.1	0.1	0.2	0.4
Fort Worth, TX	14.2	25.4	5.9	3.3	1.8	0.3	0.5	0.3	0.2
Gainesville, FL	8.5	25.3	5.4	2.0	0.4	0.3	0.3	<0.1	0.3
Green Bay, WI	31.8	14.6	6.2	<0.1	0.4	n/a	n/a	<0.1	<0.1
Greensboro, NC	7.9	24.9	10.1	3.5	1.5	0.3	0.3	0.1	0.1
Honolulu, HI	18.0	8.1	2.3	0.2	<0.1	0.1	0.2	<0.1	4.0
Houston, TX	18.3	23.8	4.7	2.3	1.7	0.3	0.7	0.3	0.3
Huntsville, AL	7.5	34.8	8.2	7.2	0.8	0.1	0.9	0.1	0.1
Indianapolis, IN	11.5	16.8	7.6	4.2	1.1	0.4	0.2	0.3	0.1
Jacksonville, FL	13.0	29.8	3.5	5.6	0.6	0.3	0.3	0.3	0.2
Kansas City, MO	11.3	19.1	7.1	3.6	1.0	0.3	0.4	0.1	0.2
Lafayette, LA	44.3	12.6	2.4	5.0	0.1	n/a	<0.1	<0.1	0.1
Las Vegas, NV	26.2	6.6	1.0	0.5	0.3	0.3	0.2	0.6	0.7
Lexington, KY	5.8	26.9	8.1	3.5	0.5	0.3	0.1	0.2	<0.1
Lincoln, NE	13.2	16.6	12.9	0.3	0.1	0.1	0.1	0.1	0.1
Little Rock, AR	4.9	32.1	6.6	8.5	0.4	0.1	<0.1	0.1	0.1
Los Angeles, CA	31.1	9.3	1.5	1.7	1.4	0.8	0.4	0.9	0.9
Louisville, KY	11.9	21.1	5.0	4.6	1.0	0.2	0.4	0.2	0.2
Madison, WI	14.4	8.0	10.6	0.2	1.2	0.4	0.1	0.1	0.9
Manchester, NH	16.3	5.8	2.7	n/a	0.1	0.3	<0.1	0.9	n/a
McAllen, TX	46.6	10.0	1.1	0.1	0.2	<0.1	<0.1	<0.1	n/a

Table continued on following page.

Metro Area	Catholic	Evangelical Protestant	Mainline Protestant	Black Protestant	Islam	Judaism	Hinduism	Orthodox	Buddhism
Memphis, TN	4.8	32.4	5.8	17.2	1.3	0.6	0.4	0.1	0.1
Miami, FL	23.8	13.7	1.6	2.2	0.8	1.2	0.3	0.2	0.3
Midland, TX	15.4	35.5	3.0	7.6	0.4	n/a	0.2	n/a	n/a
Milwaukee, WI	24.5	16.3	5.4	3.3	2.8	0.4	0.4	0.5	0.4
Minneapolis, MN	19.8	10.6	10.3	0.5	2.9	0.6	0.2	0.3	0.3
Nashville, TN	6.2	30.1	6.0	5.2	0.8	0.2	0.4	1.1	0.2
New Orleans, LA	42.1	13.5	3.0	4.9	1.4	0.4	0.3	0.1	0.3
New York, NY	32.5	4.4	3.0	1.5	4.5	4.4	1.0	0.8	0.3
Oklahoma City, OK	10.0	38.7	7.1	2.2	0.6	0.1	0.4	0.1	0.4
Omaha, NE	19.9	10.8	7.9	1.5	0.2	0.3	1.0	0.2	0.2
Orlando, FL	17.6	20.6	2.5	2.7	1.3	0.2	0.5	0.3	0.3
Philadelphia, PA	26.8	7.3	6.6	2.2	2.6	1.1	0.6	0.4	0.4
Phoenix, AZ	22.9	11.0	1.6	0.3	1.9	0.3	0.5	0.4	0.2
Pittsburgh, PA	30.6	8.8	10.1	1.3	0.6	0.6	1.2	0.6	0.1
Portland, OR	11.8	14.6	2.3	0.4	0.2	0.3	0.7	0.3	0.4
Providence, RI	37.9	4.0	3.2	0.1	0.5	0.6	0.1	0.5	0.2
Provo, UT	4.9	0.4	<0.1	n/a	0.3	n/a	0.1	n/a	n/a
Raleigh, NC	12.4	19.3	7.4	2.8	3.2	0.2	0.4	0.3	0.4
Reno, NV	24.4	6.8	1.3	0.2	0.3	0.1	0.1	0.1	0.2
Richmond, VA	12.3	23.1	9.3	3.1	2.1	0.3	1.3	0.4	0.2
Rochester, MN	15.6	15.0	19.1	n/a	1.0	0.1	0.1	0.2	0.2
Sacramento, CA	17.1	10.4	1.4	1.1	1.9	0.2	0.4	0.3	0.5
Saint Louis, MO	21.2	16.1	5.7	3.9	1.3	0.6	0.2	0.2	0.3
Saint Paul, MN	19.8	10.6	10.3	0.5	2.9	0.6	0.2	0.3	0.3
Salem, OR	19.5	14.4	2.0	0.2	n/a	0.1	<0.1	<0.1	<0.1
Salt Lake City, UT	9.0	2.4	0.7	0.1	1.6	0.1	0.3	0.4	0.3
San Antonio, TX	27.3	17.7	3.1	0.8	0.5	0.2	0.1	0.1	0.3
San Diego, CA	22.9	9.5	1.5	0.6	1.5	0.4	0.3	0.4	0.7
San Francisco, CA	21.5	5.2	2.2	1.8	2.0	0.7	1.1	0.7	1.1
San Jose, CA	27.2	8.4	1.4	0.3	2.0	0.6	2.4	0.6	1.2
Santa Rosa, CA	23.5	5.3	1.5	<0.1	0.2	0.4	0.3	0.4	1.7
Savannah, GA	5.5	19.0	5.7	5.9	0.2	0.7	0.5	0.1	n/a
Seattle, WA	11.0	19.5	2.7	0.6	0.6	0.4	0.4	0.6	1.6
Sioux Falls, SD	13.1	21.0	20.2	0.1	0.1	n/a	n/a	0.8	<0.1
Tampa, FL	23.1	16.9	3.8	1.7	0.7	0.4	0.3	0.8	0.4
Tucson, AZ	18.9	10.4	2.4	0.6	1.0	0.4	0.4	0.2	0.3
Tulsa, OK	5.6	37.8	8.6	1.7	0.5	0.2	0.1	0.1	<0.1
Virginia Beach, VA	8.3	21.3	6.9	3.7	1.0	0.3	0.2	0.3	0.3
Washington, DC	16.1	12.3	6.5	3.3	3.3	1.0	0.9	0.9	0.5
Wichita, KS	12.7	19.4	23.2	2.6	0.1	<0.1	0.1	0.2	0.5
Wilmington, NC	13.2	17.9	9.3	4.6	0.7	0.3	0.1	0.3	n/a
Winston-Salem, NC	9.3	31.4	13.6	3.4	0.8	n/a	<0.1	0.3	0.1
U.S.	18.7	16.5	5.2	2.3	1.3	0.6	0.4	0.4	0.3

Note: Figures are the number of adherents as a percentage of the total population; Figures cover the Metropolitan Statistical Area (MSA)
Source: 2020 U.S. Religion Census, Association of Statisticians of American Religious Bodies; The Association of Religion Data Archives

Real Gross Domestic Product (GDP)

Metro Area	2017	2018	2019	2020	2021	2022	2023	Rank[1]
Albuquerque, NM	41.9	42.7	43.9	43.3	45.7	47.4	48.6	70
Anchorage, AK	25.8	26.0	26.0	25.3	25.9	26.3	27.3	116
Ann Arbor, MI	24.0	24.6	25.6	25.0	26.3	27.0	27.8	114
Athens, GA	10.0	10.3	10.3	9.8	10.4	10.8	11.0	211
Atlanta, GA	398.2	413.0	429.7	416.6	444.7	462.0	471.7	10
Austin, TX	141.1	149.3	159.1	163.6	181.1	198.5	207.5	20
Baltimore, MD	198.3	200.4	201.6	194.8	204.8	210.2	213.5	19
Billings, MT	10.2	10.3	10.0	9.8	10.5	10.5	10.9	215
Boise City, ID	32.3	34.8	36.4	37.0	40.4	43.4	44.6	76
Boston, MA	433.8	451.3	467.4	463.3	495.9	507.8	515.4	8
Boulder, CO	26.3	27.2	29.7	29.1	31.3	31.9	32.9	100
Cape Coral, FL	31.3	32.6	33.3	33.2	36.0	38.8	40.4	84
Cedar Rapids, IA	18.3	18.7	18.3	18.0	19.2	19.0	18.8	155
Charleston, SC	41.7	43.4	45.5	44.2	46.6	49.6	52.1	65
Charlotte, NC	168.1	171.6	177.5	179.1	190.5	197.3	206.5	21
Chicago, IL	674.6	691.2	697.5	659.6	698.0	715.6	725.7	3
Cincinnati, OH	145.2	145.3	152.3	149.5	155.9	157.4	160.1	29
Clarksville, TN	12.3	12.4	12.7	12.9	13.6	13.9	14.2	189
Cleveland, OH	128.6	130.6	134.0	129.2	136.3	139.1	139.9	36
College Station, TX	12.5	13.0	13.6	13.5	14.2	14.7	15.8	171
Colorado Springs, CO	35.1	36.2	37.7	38.8	41.1	41.8	43.6	79
Columbia, MO	10.0	10.0	10.4	10.1	10.6	10.7	11.0	213
Columbia, SC	41.0	41.7	42.7	42.2	44.6	45.5	47.0	73
Columbus, OH	129.9	131.5	135.7	134.2	143.6	145.5	148.0	34
Dallas, TX	483.7	506.2	526.2	520.2	562.1	594.5	613.4	5
Davenport, IA	21.6	21.4	21.6	21.0	21.6	22.0	22.4	136
Denver, CO	202.2	211.2	222.5	222.8	239.1	250.3	259.0	18
Des Moines, IA	51.8	51.9	54.2	55.6	60.7	59.8	60.4	57
Detroit, MI	256.2	261.5	262.7	249.7	263.7	271.7	276.5	16
Durham, NC	46.4	48.7	50.1	51.5	55.1	57.0	59.0	58
El Paso, TX	30.4	31.4	33.1	32.9	35.3	35.9	38.1	87
Eugene, OR	15.9	16.3	16.4	16.3	17.4	17.7	18.1	157
Fargo, ND	15.0	15.1	15.4	14.9	15.7	15.8	16.3	167
Fort Collins, CO	18.6	19.5	20.3	20.2	21.3	21.7	22.0	139
Fort Wayne, IN	22.4	23.3	23.5	21.8	23.4	24.3	24.7	120
Fort Worth, TX	483.7	506.2	526.2	520.2	562.1	594.5	613.4	5
Gainesville, FL	14.5	15.0	15.4	15.4	16.4	17.0	17.7	159
Green Bay, WI	20.0	20.6	20.7	20.1	20.5	20.8	21.1	144
Greensboro, NC	41.2	41.4	41.0	39.5	41.1	42.2	42.5	80
Honolulu, HI	65.8	66.0	65.6	60.1	62.8	64.5	66.0	55
Houston, TX	470.7	491.2	486.9	478.0	501.2	522.6	550.8	7
Huntsville, AL	27.5	28.6	30.2	30.7	32.6	34.1	36.1	92
Indianapolis, IN	135.9	140.7	143.8	142.8	152.5	158.8	161.8	28
Jacksonville, FL	80.3	83.0	86.5	87.7	94.4	100.4	104.7	40
Kansas City, MO	133.8	136.4	139.5	136.8	141.7	148.9	152.8	32
Lafayette, LA	21.1	22.0	21.8	20.8	21.8	21.8	22.6	132
Las Vegas, NV	116.3	122.7	128.2	117.3	130.1	138.5	142.8	35
Lexington, KY	28.7	29.5	30.0	28.7	29.6	30.6	31.4	105
Lincoln, NE	19.6	19.9	20.3	20.2	21.1	22.1	22.8	130
Little Rock, AR	36.5	37.1	37.4	37.7	39.4	39.9	41.3	82
Los Angeles, CA	965.3	991.3	1,026.5	982.0	1,041.7	1,065.3	1,075.1	2
Louisville, KY	70.8	71.6	74.3	72.8	76.4	77.9	79.2	49
Madison, WI	47.4	49.3	50.6	49.4	52.3	53.4	55.1	59
Manchester, NH	26.0	26.5	27.2	27.0	29.5	30.0	30.5	108
McAllen, TX	20.7	21.2	22.0	21.5	22.7	23.1	24.0	124
Memphis, TN	75.3	76.0	76.6	75.7	79.9	79.7	81.2	47

Table continued on following page.

Metro Area	2017	2018	2019	2020	2021	2022	2023	Rank[1]
Miami, FL	347.0	359.9	367.6	353.8	391.4	415.2	431.9	12
Midland, TX	21.9	27.6	33.1	31.1	31.7	31.0	44.2	78
Milwaukee, WI	99.3	100.8	102.3	98.2	102.4	105.2	106.6	39
Minneapolis, MN	257.8	265.7	270.1	260.6	275.7	281.3	286.7	15
Nashville, TN	130.5	134.6	139.3	138.4	154.0	163.2	168.2	27
New Orleans, LA	78.2	78.1	79.8	73.4	76.8	75.7	79.6	48
New York, NY	1,714.1	1,766.3	1,801.1	1,744.7	1,834.5	1,875.1	1,905.2	1
Oklahoma City, OK	74.4	77.0	78.4	76.1	76.7	76.3	81.6	46
Omaha, NE	64.3	65.7	66.4	65.2	68.9	73.7	75.3	50
Orlando, FL	136.2	141.2	146.8	140.3	156.9	167.8	175.3	26
Philadelphia, PA	425.4	432.3	437.0	420.4	438.8	450.2	459.5	11
Phoenix, AZ	246.1	257.4	269.4	274.6	299.1	313.6	322.8	14
Pittsburgh, PA	150.7	154.3	155.9	147.7	153.2	155.0	159.6	30
Portland, OR	155.8	162.7	166.7	164.9	174.8	178.8	182.0	25
Providence, RI	84.6	84.7	86.8	84.2	88.5	89.3	90.4	45
Provo, UT	25.5	27.6	30.1	31.5	34.1	35.8	37.4	90
Raleigh, NC	84.9	89.5	92.3	92.4	101.0	105.8	110.6	38
Reno, NV	29.4	28.8	29.9	30.1	33.2	33.6	34.1	96
Richmond, VA	84.5	86.5	88.6	87.2	91.8	93.9	94.8	44
Rochester, MN	13.1	13.6	13.8	13.6	14.1	14.4	14.9	182
Sacramento, CA	131.2	136.9	141.9	138.9	147.4	150.4	153.8	31
Saint Louis, MO	164.4	166.6	169.5	165.7	175.8	180.2	184.8	24
Saint Paul, MN	257.8	265.7	270.1	260.6	275.7	281.3	286.7	15
Salem, OR	17.1	18.0	18.6	18.6	19.8	20.1	20.6	147
Salt Lake City, UT	92.0	97.2	103.0	102.5	111.3	114.3	118.0	37
San Antonio, TX	118.9	124.5	129.0	127.4	134.2	143.7	150.3	33
San Diego, CA	224.8	230.5	236.6	233.3	250.4	258.0	261.7	17
San Francisco, CA	526.6	560.6	594.3	596.5	662.4	659.3	681.9	4
San Jose, CA	282.7	304.6	319.4	339.4	381.6	379.7	392.5	13
Santa Rosa, CA	28.9	30.2	30.5	29.6	31.7	31.0	31.0	106
Savannah, GA	21.2	21.5	22.3	22.2	23.9	24.5	25.7	118
Seattle, WA	368.2	395.7	417.4	418.4	449.5	459.5	487.8	9
Sioux Falls, SD	22.2	21.9	22.8	22.0	23.2	22.8	23.2	128
Tampa, FL	152.7	158.0	163.9	165.5	180.0	190.7	198.9	23
Tucson, AZ	42.3	43.9	45.4	45.3	47.9	48.6	50.8	68
Tulsa, OK	51.6	53.1	52.0	49.2	51.1	51.6	53.9	61
Virginia Beach, VA	94.9	93.9	94.9	94.3	99.0	100.9	104.0	41
Washington, DC	528.9	542.4	551.9	543.4	571.1	584.2	600.2	6
Wichita, KS	35.9	35.8	35.8	34.7	35.7	36.7	37.7	89
Wilmington, NC	14.1	14.5	15.1	15.1	16.5	17.1	17.7	160
Winston-Salem, NC	34.9	34.2	34.7	32.6	34.8	35.7	36.1	91
U.S.[2]	17,619.1	18,160.7	18,642.5	18,238.9	19,387.6	19,896.6	20,436.3	—

Note: Figures are in billions of chained 2017 dollars; Figures cover the Metropolitan Statistical Area (MSA); (1) Rank is based on 2023 data and ranges from 1 to 384; (2) Figures cover real GDP within metropolitan areas
Source: U.S. Bureau of Economic Analysis

Economic Growth

Metro Area	2014	2015	2016	2017	2018	2019	2020	2021	2022	2023
Albuquerque, NM	2.0	1.2	1.7	0.4	1.9	2.9	-1.3	5.4	3.9	2.4
Anchorage, AK	0.3	4.3	1.2	-1.5	0.7	-0.3	-2.6	2.6	1.4	3.7
Ann Arbor, MI	1.7	3.7	2.2	3.3	2.5	4.0	-2.5	5.2	2.6	2.9
Athens, GA	2.4	4.3	2.2	5.7	3.5	-0.7	-4.3	5.7	4.5	1.5
Atlanta, GA	4.6	5.3	5.3	4.8	3.7	4.0	-3.0	6.7	3.9	2.1
Austin, TX	5.7	7.7	4.2	4.5	5.8	6.5	2.8	10.7	9.6	4.5
Baltimore, MD	1.6	2.0	3.4	2.1	1.0	0.6	-3.4	5.1	2.6	1.6
Billings, MT	5.4	4.6	-5.8	7.2	0.6	-2.4	-2.3	7.3	0.1	3.5
Boise City, ID	4.5	1.6	4.2	5.5	7.8	4.7	1.6	9.1	7.5	2.9
Boston, MA	2.1	4.0	1.7	2.3	4.0	3.6	-0.9	7.0	2.4	1.5
Boulder, CO	3.3	3.9	3.5	4.9	3.7	9.0	-1.9	7.5	1.9	3.4
Cape Coral, FL	5.0	6.1	7.5	0.6	4.1	2.4	-0.5	8.5	7.8	4.2
Cedar Rapids, IA	4.4	4.0	3.1	0.1	1.8	-1.9	-1.8	6.7	-1.0	-0.9
Charleston, SC	2.8	4.7	5.6	2.0	4.0	4.8	-2.7	5.4	6.4	5.2
Charlotte, NC	3.3	4.2	3.0	3.7	2.1	3.4	0.9	6.4	3.6	4.7
Chicago, IL	2.3	2.4	0.8	1.4	2.5	0.9	-5.4	5.8	2.5	1.4
Cincinnati, OH	3.6	2.9	3.7	3.1	0.0	4.8	-1.8	4.3	1.0	1.7
Clarksville, TN	-1.2	0.5	-1.0	0.0	1.1	2.0	1.4	5.9	2.1	1.9
Cleveland, OH	2.3	0.8	0.1	2.4	1.6	2.6	-3.6	5.5	2.1	0.6
College Station, TX	6.3	6.2	-0.3	1.7	4.3	4.5	-0.2	4.6	4.0	7.4
Colorado Springs, CO	0.9	1.1	2.0	4.2	3.3	4.2	2.9	5.8	1.7	4.4
Columbia, MO	0.4	2.1	0.4	2.4	0.6	4.0	-2.9	5.1	0.5	2.8
Columbia, SC	3.6	2.9	2.9	0.3	1.6	2.4	-1.0	5.6	2.0	3.4
Columbus, OH	3.6	2.1	2.1	4.4	1.2	3.2	-1.1	7.0	1.3	1.8
Dallas, TX	3.8	4.8	2.3	3.6	4.6	3.9	-1.1	8.1	5.8	3.2
Davenport, IA	0.4	-1.4	-0.7	1.0	-0.7	0.8	-2.4	2.8	1.6	2.1
Denver, CO	4.5	5.3	2.2	3.8	4.4	5.3	0.1	7.3	4.7	3.5
Des Moines, IA	12.6	8.5	3.8	-1.3	0.2	4.3	2.6	9.3	-1.5	1.0
Detroit, MI	1.4	1.7	1.9	0.9	2.1	0.4	-4.9	5.6	3.0	1.8
Durham, NC	-1.9	-1.7	-0.7	-0.5	4.9	2.8	2.8	7.0	3.4	3.5
El Paso, TX	-1.5	1.5	0.9	2.1	3.1	5.4	-0.5	7.2	1.9	6.1
Eugene, OR	1.5	5.0	3.0	3.8	2.7	0.4	-0.7	7.0	1.9	2.3
Fargo, ND	7.0	3.5	-0.3	3.3	0.7	2.5	-3.4	5.3	0.4	3.6
Fort Collins, CO	5.3	4.6	4.0	7.7	4.8	4.4	-0.9	5.8	1.9	1.3
Fort Wayne, IN	7.7	4.3	3.2	3.8	3.8	0.7	-7.1	7.2	4.2	1.4
Fort Worth, TX	3.8	4.8	2.3	3.6	4.6	3.9	-1.1	8.1	5.8	3.2
Gainesville, FL	3.2	1.9	2.1	3.8	3.3	2.9	0.1	6.5	3.4	4.5
Green Bay, WI	6.3	2.8	1.0	-0.2	3.2	0.4	-2.8	1.9	1.4	1.3
Greensboro, NC	-0.4	2.5	-1.1	0.5	0.5	-1.1	-3.6	4.0	2.8	0.5
Honolulu, HI	0.9	2.7	1.9	2.1	0.4	-0.6	-8.5	4.5	2.6	2.4
Houston, TX	1.7	5.5	-2.1	0.7	4.4	-0.9	-1.8	4.8	4.3	5.4
Huntsville, AL	0.3	1.8	3.1	3.8	3.9	5.7	1.6	6.0	4.6	6.0
Indianapolis, IN	2.1	-2.5	2.4	2.4	3.6	2.2	-0.7	6.8	4.1	1.9
Jacksonville, FL	2.4	4.2	3.8	4.5	3.3	4.3	1.3	7.7	6.3	4.3
Kansas City, MO	2.7	3.8	0.5	3.3	2.0	2.3	-1.9	3.6	5.0	2.7
Lafayette, LA	1.4	-7.6	-9.3	0.0	4.4	-1.0	-4.5	4.6	0.1	3.8
Las Vegas, NV	1.5	4.4	3.2	3.6	5.5	4.5	-8.5	10.9	6.4	3.2
Lexington, KY	2.6	3.9	2.2	1.2	2.8	1.9	-4.5	3.1	3.6	2.7
Lincoln, NE	4.9	3.5	1.7	5.3	2.0	1.9	-0.7	4.5	4.6	3.3
Little Rock, AR	1.1	1.4	1.1	-0.8	1.5	0.8	0.8	4.6	1.1	3.5
Los Angeles, CA	2.7	4.3	1.8	3.7	2.7	3.6	-4.3	6.1	2.3	0.9
Louisville, KY	1.3	2.6	1.9	1.7	1.2	3.8	-2.0	4.9	2.0	1.6
Madison, WI	5.0	3.7	3.3	1.5	3.9	2.7	-2.4	5.9	2.2	3.2
Manchester, NH	2.2	3.4	1.6	0.4	1.9	3.0	-0.9	9.3	1.7	1.6
McAllen, TX	1.7	1.1	-0.4	0.5	2.2	3.8	-2.1	5.4	1.9	3.8
Memphis, TN	-0.2	2.0	1.3	1.8	0.8	0.9	-1.2	5.5	-0.2	1.9

Table continued on following page.

Metro Area	2014	2015	2016	2017	2018	2019	2020	2021	2022	2023
Miami, FL	3.4	4.4	3.1	4.5	3.7	2.1	-3.7	10.6	6.1	4.0
Midland, TX	9.0	9.5	-1.7	14.0	25.9	20.3	-6.1	1.8	-2.3	42.9
Milwaukee, WI	0.6	1.2	0.5	1.5	1.6	1.5	-4.0	4.3	2.7	1.4
Minneapolis, MN	3.8	2.2	1.6	1.9	3.1	1.6	-3.5	5.8	2.0	2.0
Nashville, TN	4.6	6.7	3.7	4.6	3.1	3.6	-0.7	11.3	6.0	3.1
New Orleans, LA	1.2	0.3	0.8	5.8	-0.1	2.1	-8.0	4.6	-1.3	5.0
New York, NY	1.9	2.2	1.7	2.0	3.0	2.0	-3.1	5.1	2.2	1.6
Oklahoma City, OK	6.4	4.2	0.3	3.1	3.5	1.7	-2.8	0.7	-0.5	6.9
Omaha, NE	6.2	3.3	0.5	4.6	2.1	1.1	-1.8	5.6	7.0	2.2
Orlando, FL	3.8	5.5	3.8	5.5	3.7	4.0	-4.4	11.9	6.9	4.5
Philadelphia, PA	2.5	1.7	1.4	-0.3	1.6	1.1	-3.8	4.4	2.6	2.1
Phoenix, AZ	1.6	3.1	3.6	4.6	4.6	4.7	1.9	8.9	4.8	2.9
Pittsburgh, PA	1.8	3.1	0.2	4.4	2.4	1.0	-5.3	3.7	1.2	2.9
Portland, OR	3.4	5.7	4.7	5.7	4.4	2.5	-1.1	6.0	2.3	1.8
Providence, RI	1.6	2.5	0.2	0.5	0.1	2.4	-3.0	5.1	0.9	1.2
Provo, UT	4.7	8.2	7.0	6.8	8.3	9.1	4.6	8.3	4.9	4.4
Raleigh, NC	6.1	7.4	6.5	4.6	5.4	3.1	0.2	9.3	4.7	4.6
Reno, NV	0.4	7.7	4.1	7.1	-2.0	3.9	0.8	10.2	1.4	1.4
Richmond, VA	1.2	3.9	1.5	1.8	2.4	2.4	-1.6	5.3	2.3	1.0
Rochester, MN	1.6	2.9	1.4	3.6	3.5	2.0	-1.6	3.9	2.0	3.2
Sacramento, CA	2.8	4.3	2.1	2.9	4.4	3.6	-2.1	6.1	2.1	2.2
Saint Louis, MO	1.4	0.8	0.1	-0.4	1.3	1.7	-2.2	6.1	2.5	2.5
Saint Paul, MN	3.8	2.2	1.6	1.9	3.1	1.6	-3.5	5.8	2.0	2.0
Salem, OR	3.4	5.4	5.1	4.5	5.6	3.2	-0.3	6.4	1.7	2.6
Salt Lake City, UT	3.2	3.4	4.7	5.2	5.7	6.0	-0.5	8.6	2.7	3.2
San Antonio, TX	5.3	5.7	0.9	0.3	4.7	3.6	-1.3	5.4	7.1	4.6
San Diego, CA	3.1	3.3	1.3	3.7	2.6	2.7	-1.4	7.3	3.1	1.4
San Francisco, CA	6.1	6.0	5.7	9.3	6.5	6.0	0.4	11.0	-0.5	3.4
San Jose, CA	7.2	8.9	6.1	4.9	7.8	4.8	6.3	12.4	-0.5	3.4
Santa Rosa, CA	4.1	4.8	2.5	1.6	4.7	0.9	-3.0	7.0	-2.2	0.2
Savannah, GA	4.3	3.0	3.9	2.5	1.4	4.0	-0.5	7.7	2.6	4.9
Seattle, WA	4.9	4.6	4.1	8.2	7.5	5.5	0.2	7.4	2.2	6.2
Sioux Falls, SD	5.5	1.3	1.4	1.5	-1.2	4.3	-3.5	5.4	-2.0	2.0
Tampa, FL	2.0	4.2	3.3	2.1	3.5	3.7	1.0	8.8	5.9	4.3
Tucson, AZ	0.2	-0.5	3.4	3.5	3.7	3.5	-0.3	5.7	1.4	4.6
Tulsa, OK	5.4	1.7	-5.9	3.5	2.9	-2.1	-5.4	3.9	1.0	4.4
Virginia Beach, VA	-1.0	1.7	1.1	0.7	-1.2	1.2	-0.7	5.0	1.9	3.2
Washington, DC	1.2	2.1	2.5	2.4	2.5	1.8	-1.6	5.1	2.3	2.7
Wichita, KS	6.2	5.6	8.2	0.4	-0.1	-0.2	-2.9	2.8	2.9	2.8
Wilmington, NC	4.1	1.5	5.1	0.6	3.0	4.2	0.1	9.2	3.6	3.5
Winston-Salem, NC	2.6	1.0	1.4	2.6	-2.1	1.4	-6.0	6.9	2.5	1.3
U.S.[1]	2.6	3.2	2.0	2.7	3.1	2.7	-2.2	6.3	2.6	2.7

Note: Figures are real gross domestic product growth rates and represent percent change from preceding period; Figures cover the Metropolitan Statistical Area (MSA); (1) Figures are the average growth rates within metropolitan areas
Source: U.S. Bureau of Economic Analysis

Metropolitan Area Exports

Metro Area	2018	2019	2020	2021	2022	2023	Rank[1]
Albuquerque, NM	771.5	1,629.7	1,265.3	2,215.0	939.7	789.4	195
Anchorage, AK	1,510.8	1,348.0	990.9	n/a	n/a	n/a	n/a
Ann Arbor, MI	1,538.7	1,432.7	1,183.1	1,230.7	1,334.2	1,196.2	156
Athens, GA	378.1	442.1	338.7	448.1	489.9	533.9	217
Atlanta, GA	24,091.6	25,800.8	25,791.0	28,116.4	30,833.1	32,336.4	13
Austin, TX	12,929.9	12,509.0	13,041.5	15,621.9	17,290.7	17,251.5	27
Baltimore, MD	6,039.2	7,081.8	6,084.6	8,200.6	7,820.0	10,196.2	43
Billings, MT	114.3	141.9	116.0	173.8	156.0	119.2	349
Boise City, ID	2,771.7	2,062.8	1,632.9	1,937.1	2,156.7	1,922.6	121
Boston, MA	24,450.1	23,505.8	23,233.8	32,084.2	33,101.8	34,519.4	12
Boulder, CO	1,044.1	1,014.9	1,110.4	1,078.0	1,201.9	1,213.1	153
Cape Coral, FL	668.0	694.9	654.8	797.5	886.9	935.4	177
Cedar Rapids, IA	1,025.0	1,028.4	832.0	980.0	1,018.7	1,175.4	159
Charleston, SC	10,943.2	16,337.9	6,110.5	3,381.6	4,256.0	9,497.6	44
Charlotte, NC	14,083.2	13,892.4	8,225.6	10,554.3	12,223.1	11,470.3	34
Chicago, IL	47,287.8	42,438.8	41,279.4	54,498.1	63,374.6	56,656.6	5
Cincinnati, OH	27,396.3	28,778.3	21,002.2	23,198.7	29,285.0	31,216.2	14
Clarksville, TN	435.5	341.8	246.8	288.7	376.7	445.6	236
Cleveland, OH	9,382.9	8,829.9	7,415.8	8,560.4	9,561.2	10,206.2	42
College Station, TX	153.0	160.5	114.9	110.3	136.2	180.0	323
Colorado Springs, CO	850.6	864.2	979.2	866.9	1,209.5	1,425.7	137
Columbia, MO	238.6	291.4	256.2	335.4	368.7	474.1	230
Columbia, SC	2,083.8	2,184.6	2,058.8	2,100.2	2,351.3	2,160.3	112
Columbus, OH	7,529.5	7,296.6	6,304.8	6,557.9	7,597.3	8,418.9	47
Dallas, TX	36,260.9	39,474.0	35,642.0	43,189.0	50,632.9	51,863.7	6
Davenport, IA	6,761.9	6,066.3	5,097.5	6,341.0	8,173.6	6,050.0	57
Denver, CO	4,544.3	4,555.6	4,604.4	4,670.8	5,761.7	5,724.2	59
Des Moines, IA	1,293.7	1,437.8	1,414.0	1,706.6	1,706.8	2,175.7	110
Detroit, MI	44,131.4	41,070.4	30,715.1	35,433.2	40,395.3	45,591.4	7
Durham, NC	3,945.8	4,452.9	3,359.3	3,326.4	4,071.8	4,898.7	65
El Paso, TX	30,052.0	32,749.6	27,154.4	32,397.9	36,488.3	35,223.0	11
Eugene, OR	400.1	360.0	340.6	426.7	434.9	415.2	241
Fargo, ND	553.5	515.0	438.3	539.4	518.7	880.1	185
Fort Collins, CO	1,021.8	1,060.0	1,092.5	1,132.5	1,178.8	1,180.5	157
Fort Wayne, IN	1,593.3	1,438.5	1,144.6	1,592.7	1,787.5	2,032.1	115
Fort Worth, TX	36,260.9	39,474.0	35,642.0	43,189.0	50,632.9	51,863.7	6
Gainesville, FL	370.2	297.2	260.9	320.7	307.2	306.6	274
Green Bay, WI	1,044.3	928.2	736.4	765.6	855.1	835.1	190
Greensboro, NC	3,053.5	2,561.8	2,007.3	2,356.2	2,375.6	2,239.4	108
Honolulu, HI	438.9	308.6	169.0	164.3	258.8	450.6	234
Houston, TX	120,714.3	129,656.0	104,538.2	140,750.4	191,846.9	175,470.1	1
Huntsville, AL	1,608.7	1,534.2	1,263.0	1,579.5	1,558.7	1,762.1	125
Indianapolis, IN	11,069.9	11,148.7	11,100.4	12,740.4	14,671.5	23,080.6	20
Jacksonville, FL	2,406.7	2,975.5	2,473.3	2,683.7	3,007.8	2,730.8	92
Kansas City, MO	7,316.9	7,652.6	7,862.7	9,177.6	9,623.5	10,627.2	40
Lafayette, LA	1,001.7	1,086.2	946.2	895.7	911.8	836.2	189
Las Vegas, NV	2,240.6	2,430.8	1,705.9	1,866.2	2,116.3	2,762.3	91
Lexington, KY	2,148.0	2,093.8	1,586.3	1,880.0	2,677.2	3,343.3	81
Lincoln, NE	885.6	807.0	726.3	872.6	1,161.3	1,082.2	165
Little Rock, AR	1,607.4	1,642.5	n/a	1,370.6	1,373.7	1,464.0	134
Los Angeles, CA	64,814.6	61,041.1	50,185.4	58,588.4	60,979.7	59,561.6	4
Louisville, KY	8,987.0	9,105.5	8,360.3	10,262.8	10,618.7	11,072.0	37
Madison, WI	2,460.2	2,337.6	2,450.5	2,756.3	2,893.8	2,822.9	90
Manchester, NH	1,651.4	1,587.1	1,704.9	2,077.6	2,349.8	2,416.7	101
McAllen, TX	6,627.9	5,234.1	4,087.6	5,164.6	5,677.1	7,072.4	51
Memphis, TN	12,695.4	13,751.7	13,350.3	16,761.5	17,835.3	17,853.5	25

Table continued on following page.

Metro Area	2018	2019	2020	2021	2022	2023	Rank[1]
Miami, FL	35,650.2	35,498.9	29,112.1	36,011.3	41,517.8	44,256.4	8
Midland, TX	63.6	63.7	57.7	49.9	76.2	72.4	365
Milwaukee, WI	7,337.6	6,896.3	6,624.0	7,282.8	8,742.5	9,352.5	45
Minneapolis, MN	20,016.2	18,633.0	17,109.5	21,098.8	21,964.3	22,209.4	23
Nashville, TN	8,723.7	7,940.7	6,569.9	8,256.1	9,347.5	10,385.4	41
New Orleans, LA	36,570.4	34,109.6	31,088.4	35,773.5	52,912.9	38,978.6	9
New York, NY	97,692.4	87,365.7	75,745.4	103,930.9	120,643.7	106,209.0	2
Oklahoma City, OK	1,489.4	1,434.5	1,326.6	1,773.2	2,019.1	2,277.7	107
Omaha, NE	4,371.6	3,725.7	3,852.5	4,595.1	4,585.5	3,411.0	80
Orlando, FL	3,131.7	3,363.9	2,849.8	3,313.6	4,096.9	4,443.5	71
Philadelphia, PA	23,663.2	24,721.3	23,022.1	28,724.4	29,352.1	28,760.2	16
Phoenix, AZ	13,614.9	15,136.6	11,073.9	14,165.1	16,658.8	17,553.6	26
Pittsburgh, PA	9,824.2	9,672.9	7,545.1	9,469.6	11,188.3	11,538.4	33
Portland, OR	21,442.9	23,761.9	27,824.7	33,787.5	34,368.0	26,973.2	18
Providence, RI	6,236.6	7,424.8	6,685.2	6,708.2	7,179.7	6,517.8	53
Provo, UT	1,788.1	1,783.7	1,888.5	2,053.8	1,318.4	1,416.7	140
Raleigh, NC	3,193.2	3,546.8	3,372.0	3,962.7	4,714.1	5,965.8	58
Reno, NV	2,631.7	2,598.3	4,553.3	4,503.0	3,864.0	3,434.1	78
Richmond, VA	3,535.0	3,203.2	2,719.1	3,010.7	3,283.5	2,579.8	95
Rochester, MN	537.6	390.1	194.0	224.9	215.9	258.7	293
Sacramento, CA	6,222.8	5,449.2	4,980.9	5,682.3	5,716.7	7,586.6	50
Saint Louis, MO	10,866.8	10,711.1	9,089.4	10,486.1	14,215.6	13,817.0	30
Saint Paul, MN	20,016.2	18,633.0	17,109.5	21,098.8	21,964.3	22,209.4	23
Salem, OR	410.2	405.7	350.5	372.0	422.3	404.8	244
Salt Lake City, UT	9,748.6	13,273.9	13,565.5	13,469.1	12,340.1	12,775.2	32
San Antonio, TX	11,678.1	11,668.0	10,987.9	13,086.4	13,173.6	12,821.8	31
San Diego, CA	20,156.8	19,774.1	18,999.7	23,687.8	24,657.9	22,975.3	22
San Francisco, CA	27,417.0	28,003.8	23,864.5	29,972.0	30,649.0	24,253.0	19
San Jose, CA	22,224.2	20,909.4	19,534.5	22,293.6	24,342.2	22,985.4	21
Santa Rosa, CA	1,231.7	1,234.5	1,131.4	1,301.8	1,297.3	1,121.8	161
Savannah, GA	5,407.8	4,925.5	4,557.0	5,520.5	6,171.2	6,206.1	56
Seattle, WA	59,742.9	41,249.0	23,851.0	28,866.7	34,159.9	36,267.3	10
Sioux Falls, SD	400.0	431.5	524.9	547.3	371.3	510.9	224
Tampa, FL	4,966.7	6,219.7	5,082.2	5,754.7	9,588.2	7,923.6	49
Tucson, AZ	2,824.8	2,943.7	2,640.7	2,846.1	3,779.4	4,503.0	68
Tulsa, OK	3,351.7	3,399.2	2,567.8	3,064.8	3,379.2	3,234.5	84
Virginia Beach, VA	3,950.6	3,642.4	4,284.3	4,566.3	5,750.1	6,338.3	54
Washington, DC	13,602.7	14,563.8	13,537.3	12,210.8	14,001.9	14,758.9	29
Wichita, KS	3,817.0	3,494.7	2,882.1	3,615.3	4,550.4	4,475.1	69
Wilmington, NC	634.4	526.4	553.6	497.8	593.6	671.5	206
Winston-Salem, NC	1,107.5	1,209.1	913.1	918.2	1,012.1	1,071.1	166
U.S.	1,664,056.1	1,645,173.7	1,431,406.6	1,753,941.4	2,062,937.4	2,019,160.5	—

Note: Figures are in millions of dollars; Figures cover the Metropolitan Statistical Area (MSA); (1) Rank is based on 2023 data and ranges from 1 to 386
Source: U.S. Department of Commerce, International Trade Administration, Office of Trade and Economic Analysis, Industry and Analysis, Exports by Metropolitan Area, data extracted April 2, 2025

Building Permits: City

City	Single-Family			Multi-Family			Total		
	2023	2024	Pct. Chg.	2023	2024	Pct. Chg.	2023	2024	Pct. Chg.
Albuquerque, NM	587	525	-10.6	512	574	12.1	1,099	1,099	0.0
Anchorage, AK	271	161	-40.6	28	180	542.9	299	341	14.0
Ann Arbor, MI	161	28	-82.6	61	266	336.1	222	294	32.4
Athens, GA	168	212	26.2	238	960	303.4	406	1,172	188.7
Atlanta, GA	1,139	791	-30.6	6,482	7,318	12.9	7,621	8,109	6.4
Austin, TX	1,799	1,946	8.2	11,885	7,498	-36.9	13,684	9,444	-31.0
Baltimore, MD	92	165	79.3	1,751	1,108	-36.7	1,843	1,273	-30.9
Billings, MT	259	327	26.3	0	328	—	259	655	152.9
Boise City, ID	447	468	4.7	1,450	273	-81.2	1,897	741	-60.9
Boston, MA	108	72	-33.3	1,943	1,717	-11.6	2,051	1,789	-12.8
Boulder, CO	30	35	16.7	225	371	64.9	255	406	59.2
Cape Coral, FL	2,023	2,671	32.0	1,972	726	-63.2	3,995	3,397	-15.0
Cedar Rapids, IA	145	143	-1.4	229	465	103.1	374	608	62.6
Charleston, SC	891	878	-1.5	363	266	-26.7	1,254	1,144	-8.8
Charlotte, NC	n/a	n/a	n/a	n/a	n/a	n/a	n/a	n/a	n/a
Chicago, IL	290	325	12.1	3,326	4,046	21.6	3,616	4,371	20.9
Cincinnati, OH	117	110	-6.0	514	114	-77.8	631	224	-64.5
Clarksville, TN	805	1,366	69.7	1,455	703	-51.7	2,260	2,069	-8.5
Cleveland, OH	161	234	45.3	644	662	2.8	805	896	11.3
College Station, TX	448	650	45.1	293	462	57.7	741	1,112	50.1
Colorado Springs, CO	n/a	n/a	n/a	n/a	n/a	n/a	n/a	n/a	n/a
Columbia, MO	314	461	46.8	56	549	880.4	370	1,010	173.0
Columbia, SC	883	833	-5.7	718	1,315	83.1	1,601	2,148	34.2
Columbus, OH	943	828	-12.2	4,340	5,256	21.1	5,283	6,084	15.2
Dallas, TX	1,995	1,957	-1.9	4,429	4,081	-7.9	6,424	6,038	-6.0
Davenport, IA	94	149	58.5	121	162	33.9	215	311	44.7
Denver, CO	1,174	872	-25.7	4,551	3,122	-31.4	5,725	3,994	-30.2
Des Moines, IA	248	218	-12.1	321	400	24.6	569	618	8.6
Detroit, MI	397	483	21.7	828	1,436	73.4	1,225	1,919	56.7
Durham, NC	1,687	1,822	8.0	2,678	971	-63.7	4,365	2,793	-36.0
El Paso, TX	1,572	1,644	4.6	280	243	-13.2	1,852	1,887	1.9
Eugene, OR	171	309	80.7	422	693	64.2	593	1,002	69.0
Fargo, ND	292	241	-17.5	980	410	-58.2	1,272	651	-48.8
Fort Collins, CO	372	371	-0.3	631	314	-50.2	1,003	685	-31.7
Fort Wayne, IN	n/a	n/a	n/a	n/a	n/a	n/a	n/a	n/a	n/a
Fort Worth, TX	6,631	6,257	-5.6	3,429	6,891	101.0	10,060	13,148	30.7
Gainesville, FL	236	296	25.4	544	922	69.5	780	1,218	56.2
Green Bay, WI	37	42	13.5	0	434	—	37	476	1,186.5
Greensboro, NC	704	618	-12.2	1,063	1,336	25.7	1,767	1,954	10.6
Honolulu, HI	n/a	n/a	n/a	n/a	n/a	n/a	n/a	n/a	n/a
Houston, TX	6,609	6,808	3.0	9,821	5,090	-48.2	16,430	11,898	-27.6
Huntsville, AL	1,403	1,245	-11.3	1,197	240	-79.9	2,600	1,485	-42.9
Indianapolis, IN	896	1,170	30.6	1,517	653	-57.0	2,413	1,823	-24.5
Jacksonville, FL	4,223	5,037	19.3	5,485	1,361	-75.2	9,708	6,398	-34.1
Kansas City, MO	776	429	-44.7	458	2,449	434.7	1,234	2,878	133.2
Lafayette, LA	n/a	n/a	n/a	n/a	n/a	n/a	n/a	n/a	n/a
Las Vegas, NV	2,590	2,655	2.5	1,026	935	-8.9	3,616	3,590	-0.7
Lexington, KY	624	492	-21.2	774	544	-29.7	1,398	1,036	-25.9
Lincoln, NE	699	937	34.0	1,282	793	-38.1	1,981	1,730	-12.7
Little Rock, AR	703	468	-33.4	230	18	-92.2	933	486	-47.9
Los Angeles, CA	2,918	3,041	4.2	10,236	7,447	-27.2	13,154	10,488	-20.3
Louisville, KY	1,014	1,168	15.2	2,686	1,690	-37.1	3,700	2,858	-22.8
Madison, WI	332	250	-24.7	2,288	2,562	12.0	2,620	2,812	7.3
Manchester, NH	99	26	-73.7	280	167	-40.4	379	193	-49.1

Table continued on following page.

City	Single-Family			Multi-Family			Total		
	2023	2024	Pct. Chg.	2023	2024	Pct. Chg.	2023	2024	Pct. Chg.
McAllen, TX	428	669	56.3	753	1,053	39.8	1,181	1,722	45.8
Memphis, TN	n/a	n/a	n/a	n/a	n/a	n/a	n/a	n/a	n/a
Miami, FL	113	145	28.3	5,307	5,878	10.8	5,420	6,023	11.1
Midland, TX	805	1,504	86.8	0	0	0.0	805	1,504	86.8
Milwaukee, WI	61	72	18.0	36	164	355.6	97	236	143.3
Minneapolis, MN	70	65	-7.1	1,458	387	-73.5	1,528	452	-70.4
Nashville, TN	3,106	2,662	-14.3	8,052	4,137	-48.6	11,158	6,799	-39.1
New Orleans, LA	249	202	-18.9	818	508	-37.9	1,067	710	-33.5
New York, NY	232	197	-15.1	31,733	27,044	-14.8	31,965	27,241	-14.8
Oklahoma City, OK	3,339	3,460	3.6	805	938	16.5	4,144	4,398	6.1
Omaha, NE	1,294	1,692	30.8	1,756	2,668	51.9	3,050	4,360	43.0
Orlando, FL	887	914	3.0	1,514	1,056	-30.3	2,401	1,970	-18.0
Philadelphia, PA	405	539	33.1	3,458	2,423	-29.9	3,863	2,962	-23.3
Phoenix, AZ	4,200	4,062	-3.3	10,268	4,935	-51.9	14,468	8,997	-37.8
Pittsburgh, PA	229	229	0.0	2,283	1,435	-37.1	2,512	1,664	-33.8
Portland, OR	877	815	-7.1	2,212	885	-60.0	3,089	1,700	-45.0
Providence, RI	0	31	–	5	238	4,660.0	5	269	5,280.0
Provo, UT	147	133	-9.5	80	153	91.3	227	286	26.0
Raleigh, NC	1,762	1,653	-6.2	4,626	3,391	-26.7	6,388	5,044	-21.0
Reno, NV	1,059	1,087	2.6	2,176	1,636	-24.8	3,235	2,723	-15.8
Richmond, VA	387	380	-1.8	1,896	2,160	13.9	2,283	2,540	11.3
Rochester, MN	241	193	-19.9	551	925	67.9	792	1,118	41.2
Sacramento, CA	653	708	8.4	1,864	1,335	-28.4	2,517	2,043	-18.8
Saint Louis, MO	51	56	9.8	227	238	4.8	278	294	5.8
Saint Paul, MN	48	75	56.3	1,156	329	-71.5	1,204	404	-66.4
Salem, OR	360	392	8.9	326	513	57.4	686	905	31.9
Salt Lake City, UT	243	397	63.4	2,929	886	-69.8	3,172	1,283	-59.6
San Antonio, TX	4,299	5,000	16.3	4,860	1,258	-74.1	9,159	6,258	-31.7
San Diego, CA	516	775	50.2	5,249	5,840	11.3	5,765	6,615	14.7
San Francisco, CA	29	27	-6.9	1,107	743	-32.9	1,136	770	-32.2
San Jose, CA	581	642	10.5	2,069	1,356	-34.5	2,650	1,998	-24.6
Santa Rosa, CA	441	292	-33.8	905	0	-100.0	1,346	292	-78.3
Savannah, GA	589	565	-4.1	12	14	16.7	601	579	-3.7
Seattle, WA	473	405	-14.4	4,826	5,490	13.8	5,299	5,895	11.2
Sioux Falls, SD	750	880	17.3	1,986	1,239	-37.6	2,736	2,119	-22.6
Tampa, FL	738	912	23.6	2,415	1,634	-32.3	3,153	2,546	-19.3
Tucson, AZ	839	923	10.0	829	582	-29.8	1,668	1,505	-9.8
Tulsa, OK	524	424	-19.1	352	299	-15.1	876	723	-17.5
Virginia Beach, VA	201	319	58.7	341	347	1.8	542	666	22.9
Washington, DC	166	146	-12.0	2,854	1,591	-44.3	3,020	1,737	-42.5
Wichita, KS	605	558	-7.8	1,173	742	-36.7	1,778	1,300	-26.9
Wilmington, NC	n/a	n/a	n/a	n/a	n/a	n/a	n/a	n/a	n/a
Winston-Salem, NC	860	1,168	35.8	1,281	966	-24.6	2,141	2,134	-0.3
U.S.	920,000	981,900	6.7	591,100	496,100	-16.1	1,511,100	1,478,000	-2.2

Note: Figures represent new, privately-owned housing units authorized (unadjusted data)
Source: U.S. Census Bureau, Building Permits Survey (BPS), 2023, 2024

Building Permits: Metro Area

Metro Area	Single-Family 2023	Single-Family 2024	Pct. Chg.	Multi-Family 2023	Multi-Family 2024	Pct. Chg.	Total 2023	Total 2024	Pct. Chg.
Albuquerque, NM	2,057	2,064	0.3	777	812	4.5	2,834	2,876	1.5
Anchorage, AK	338	198	-41.4	119	228	91.6	457	426	-6.8
Ann Arbor, MI	485	557	14.8	1,112	636	-42.8	1,597	1,193	-25.3
Athens, GA	776	863	11.2	250	972	288.8	1,026	1,835	78.8
Atlanta, GA	24,022	25,773	7.3	14,617	14,914	2.0	38,639	40,687	5.3
Austin, TX	16,532	16,435	-0.6	22,241	15,859	-28.7	38,773	32,294	-16.7
Baltimore, MD	3,798	3,849	1.3	3,741	2,435	-34.9	7,539	6,284	-16.6
Billings, MT	343	896	161.2	6	629	10,383.3	349	1,525	337.0
Boise City, ID	6,508	8,252	26.8	3,383	811	-76.0	9,891	9,063	-8.4
Boston, MA	3,396	3,734	10.0	7,426	7,501	1.0	10,822	11,235	3.8
Boulder, CO	791	441	-44.2	851	1,239	45.6	1,642	1,680	2.3
Cape Coral, FL	8,654	10,554	22.0	4,902	4,857	-0.9	13,556	15,411	13.7
Cedar Rapids, IA	467	494	5.8	301	593	97.0	768	1,087	41.5
Charleston, SC	6,184	6,817	10.2	2,389	1,697	-29.0	8,573	8,514	-0.7
Charlotte, NC	19,146	18,954	-1.0	10,273	6,981	-32.0	29,419	25,935	-11.8
Chicago, IL	8,452	9,509	12.5	6,576	8,555	30.1	15,028	18,064	20.2
Cincinnati, OH	3,714	4,025	8.4	2,527	3,064	21.3	6,241	7,089	13.6
Clarksville, TN	1,385	1,975	42.6	1,554	823	-47.0	2,939	2,798	-4.8
Cleveland, OH	2,500	2,980	19.2	991	1,309	32.1	3,491	4,289	22.9
College Station, TX	1,155	1,482	28.3	307	839	173.3	1,462	2,321	58.8
Colorado Springs, CO	2,670	2,878	7.8	2,607	1,116	-57.2	5,277	3,994	-24.3
Columbia, MO	609	763	25.3	72	568	688.9	681	1,331	95.4
Columbia, SC	4,634	4,469	-3.6	831	1,423	71.2	5,465	5,892	7.8
Columbus, OH	5,364	6,094	13.6	6,076	7,868	29.5	11,440	13,962	22.0
Dallas, TX	44,366	46,440	4.7	23,663	25,348	7.1	68,029	71,788	5.5
Davenport, IA	366	401	9.6	248	564	127.4	614	965	57.2
Denver, CO	9,012	9,012	0.0	11,638	6,558	-43.7	20,650	15,570	-24.6
Des Moines, IA	3,689	3,717	0.8	1,311	1,347	2.7	5,000	5,064	1.3
Detroit, MI	4,541	4,878	7.4	2,193	2,826	28.9	6,734	7,704	14.4
Durham, NC	3,127	2,815	-10.0	4,083	1,043	-74.5	7,210	3,858	-46.5
El Paso, TX	1,967	2,077	5.6	280	243	-13.2	2,247	2,320	3.2
Eugene, OR	732	799	9.2	507	1,015	100.2	1,239	1,814	46.4
Fargo, ND	885	832	-6.0	1,204	660	-45.2	2,089	1,492	-28.6
Fort Collins, CO	1,289	1,370	6.3	1,397	416	-70.2	2,686	1,786	-33.5
Fort Wayne, IN	1,680	1,409	-16.1	756	625	-17.3	2,436	2,034	-16.5
Fort Worth, TX	44,366	46,440	4.7	23,663	25,348	7.1	68,029	71,788	5.5
Gainesville, FL	1,247	1,115	-10.6	698	928	33.0	1,945	2,043	5.0
Green Bay, WI	578	717	24.0	415	1,108	167.0	993	1,825	83.8
Greensboro, NC	2,368	2,337	-1.3	1,139	2,639	131.7	3,507	4,976	41.9
Honolulu, HI	657	706	7.5	1,194	932	-21.9	1,851	1,638	-11.5
Houston, TX	50,444	52,703	4.5	18,311	13,044	-28.8	68,755	65,747	-4.4
Huntsville, AL	3,908	3,972	1.6	2,032	1,234	-39.3	5,940	5,206	-12.4
Indianapolis, IN	7,252	9,168	26.4	5,302	2,620	-50.6	12,554	11,788	-6.1
Jacksonville, FL	12,479	12,936	3.7	7,847	2,066	-73.7	20,326	15,002	-26.2
Kansas City, MO	4,299	4,875	13.4	3,215	4,273	32.9	7,514	9,148	21.7
Lafayette, LA	2,008	2,001	-0.3	378	18	-95.2	2,386	2,019	-15.4
Las Vegas, NV	10,087	12,277	21.7	2,986	2,477	-17.0	13,073	14,754	12.9
Lexington, KY	1,319	1,392	5.5	1,123	809	-28.0	2,442	2,201	-9.9
Lincoln, NE	849	1,077	26.9	1,288	959	-25.5	2,137	2,036	-4.7
Little Rock, AR	1,932	2,055	6.4	732	551	-24.7	2,664	2,606	-2.2
Los Angeles, CA	12,035	11,777	-2.1	18,732	15,004	-19.9	30,767	26,781	-13.0
Louisville, KY	2,914	3,690	26.6	3,817	2,106	-44.8	6,731	5,796	-13.9
Madison, WI	1,534	1,679	9.5	3,827	4,159	8.7	5,361	5,838	8.9
Manchester, NH	532	427	-19.7	850	445	-47.6	1,382	872	-36.9

Table continued on following page.

Metro Area	Single-Family			Multi-Family			Total		
	2023	2024	Pct. Chg.	2023	2024	Pct. Chg.	2023	2024	Pct. Chg.
McAllen, TX	4,143	4,336	4.7	2,756	2,956	7.3	6,899	7,292	5.7
Memphis, TN	3,062	2,773	-9.4	996	1,467	47.3	4,058	4,240	4.5
Miami, FL	5,512	5,825	5.7	15,808	10,527	-33.4	21,320	16,352	-23.3
Midland, TX	810	1,505	85.8	8	4	-50.0	818	1,509	84.5
Milwaukee, WI	1,408	1,712	21.6	1,436	2,346	63.4	2,844	4,058	42.7
Minneapolis, MN	8,245	9,300	12.8	10,388	4,722	-54.5	18,633	14,022	-24.7
Nashville, TN	13,842	14,465	4.5	9,716	5,573	-42.6	23,558	20,038	-14.9
New Orleans, LA	1,865	1,007	-46.0	1,207	604	-50.0	3,072	1,611	-47.6
New York, NY	11,734	12,530	6.8	51,296	45,399	-11.5	63,030	57,929	-8.1
Oklahoma City, OK	5,573	6,014	7.9	1,163	1,693	45.6	6,736	7,707	14.4
Omaha, NE	2,763	3,505	26.9	1,956	3,692	88.8	4,719	7,197	52.5
Orlando, FL	17,049	15,364	-9.9	8,366	8,771	4.8	25,415	24,135	-5.0
Philadelphia, PA	6,255	8,324	33.1	5,764	5,890	2.2	12,019	14,214	18.3
Phoenix, AZ	24,708	30,277	22.5	20,908	15,607	-25.4	45,616	45,884	0.6
Pittsburgh, PA	3,332	3,530	5.9	2,962	1,882	-36.5	6,294	5,412	-14.0
Portland, OR	6,326	6,345	0.3	5,056	3,108	-38.5	11,382	9,453	-16.9
Providence, RI	1,255	1,339	6.7	675	1,281	89.8	1,930	2,620	35.8
Provo, UT	4,663	5,246	12.5	1,518	1,182	-22.1	6,181	6,428	4.0
Raleigh, NC	12,147	13,343	9.8	8,472	5,636	-33.5	20,619	18,979	-8.0
Reno, NV	1,992	2,474	24.2	2,279	1,917	-15.9	4,271	4,391	2.8
Richmond, VA	4,590	5,023	9.4	5,383	3,619	-32.8	9,973	8,642	-13.3
Rochester, MN	604	491	-18.7	570	993	74.2	1,174	1,484	26.4
Sacramento, CA	7,931	8,579	8.2	4,010	3,034	-24.3	11,941	11,613	-2.7
Saint Louis, MO	4,599	4,653	1.2	2,508	2,364	-5.7	7,107	7,017	-1.3
Saint Paul, MN	8,245	9,300	12.8	10,388	4,722	-54.5	18,633	14,022	-24.7
Salem, OR	826	994	20.3	1,140	865	-24.1	1,966	1,859	-5.4
Salt Lake City, UT	3,163	3,525	11.4	6,072	1,922	-68.3	9,235	5,447	-41.0
San Antonio, TX	8,718	10,999	26.2	7,767	3,858	-50.3	16,485	14,857	-9.9
San Diego, CA	3,049	3,377	10.8	8,420	8,195	-2.7	11,469	11,572	0.9
San Francisco, CA	3,015	2,776	-7.9	4,515	3,138	-30.5	7,530	5,914	-21.5
San Jose, CA	2,037	2,207	8.3	4,190	1,908	-54.5	6,227	4,115	-33.9
Santa Rosa, CA	1,020	832	-18.4	1,333	180	-86.5	2,353	1,012	-57.0
Savannah, GA	2,620	2,936	12.1	768	1,101	43.4	3,388	4,037	19.2
Seattle, WA	6,296	6,489	3.1	10,927	11,431	4.6	17,223	17,920	4.0
Sioux Falls, SD	1,155	1,270	10.0	2,284	1,532	-32.9	3,439	2,802	-18.5
Tampa, FL	14,852	13,205	-11.1	10,534	7,745	-26.5	25,386	20,950	-17.5
Tucson, AZ	3,688	4,150	12.5	1,567	1,100	-29.8	5,255	5,250	-0.1
Tulsa, OK	3,393	3,602	6.2	1,616	709	-56.1	5,009	4,311	-13.9
Virginia Beach, VA	3,393	3,544	4.5	2,721	862	-68.3	6,114	4,406	-27.9
Washington, DC	10,936	11,743	7.4	12,557	9,744	-22.4	23,493	21,487	-8.5
Wichita, KS	1,470	1,479	0.6	2,063	1,560	-24.4	3,533	3,039	-14.0
Wilmington, NC	2,228	7,263	226.0	1,737	2,355	35.6	3,965	9,618	142.6
Winston-Salem, NC	3,567	4,010	12.4	1,507	1,446	-4.0	5,074	5,456	7.5
U.S.	920,000	981,900	6.7	591,100	496,100	-16.1	1,511,100	1,478,000	-2.2

Note: Figures cover the Metropolitan Statistical Area (MSA); Figures represent new, privately-owned housing units authorized (unadjusted data)
Source: U.S. Census Bureau, Building Permits Survey (BPS), 2023, 2024

Housing Vacancy Rates

Metro Area	Gross Vacancy Rate[1] (%)			Year-Round Vacancy Rate[2] (%)			Rental Vacancy Rate[3] (%)			Homeowner Vacancy Rate[4] (%)		
	2022	2023	2024	2022	2023	2024	2022	2023	2024	2022	2023	2024
Albuquerque, NM	5.3	5.6	6.4	5.1	5.4	6.1	5.5	6.1	6.7	1.0	0.7	1.6
Anchorage, AK	n/a	n/a	n/a	n/a	n/a	n/a	n/a	n/a	n/a	n/a	n/a	n/a
Ann Arbor, MI	n/a	n/a	n/a	n/a	n/a	n/a	n/a	n/a	n/a	n/a	n/a	n/a
Athens, GA	n/a	n/a	n/a	n/a	n/a	n/a	n/a	n/a	n/a	n/a	n/a	n/a
Atlanta, GA	5.9	6.6	6.8	5.7	6.4	6.6	6.7	8.7	9.3	0.8	1.2	0.9
Austin, TX	5.5	8.5	8.6	4.9	8.2	8.3	5.6	9.0	8.2	0.6	1.3	1.7
Baltimore, MD	5.9	6.6	7.0	5.7	6.5	6.5	5.3	9.4	6.1	0.5	0.6	0.9
Billings, MT	n/a	n/a	n/a	n/a	n/a	n/a	n/a	n/a	n/a	n/a	n/a	n/a
Boise City, ID	n/a	n/a	n/a	n/a	n/a	n/a	n/a	n/a	n/a	n/a	n/a	n/a
Boston, MA	6.2	6.1	5.7	5.4	5.3	4.8	2.5	2.5	3.0	0.7	0.6	0.6
Boulder, CO	n/a	n/a	n/a	n/a	n/a	n/a	n/a	n/a	n/a	n/a	n/a	n/a
Cape Coral, FL	38.2	38.7	34.1	16.9	16.1	14.7	11.6	15.3	10.1	3.9	2.3	3.0
Cedar Rapids, IA	n/a	n/a	n/a	n/a	n/a	n/a	n/a	n/a	n/a	n/a	n/a	n/a
Charleston, SC	10.6	12.6	11.9	7.5	10.2	9.8	8.8	12.0	12.8	0.4	0.5	0.9
Charlotte, NC	7.4	7.6	8.1	7.0	7.4	7.7	5.9	6.6	6.7	0.7	0.4	0.9
Chicago, IL	7.3	6.0	5.8	7.1	5.8	5.6	6.1	5.6	5.1	1.1	0.5	0.6
Cincinnati, OH	6.8	5.4	5.8	6.3	5.2	5.5	6.3	7.2	6.1	0.3	0.2	0.8
Clarksville, TN	n/a	n/a	n/a	n/a	n/a	n/a	n/a	n/a	n/a	n/a	n/a	n/a
Cleveland, OH	7.0	7.6	7.5	6.8	7.2	7.4	3.2	4.7	5.8	1.0	0.5	0.4
College Station, TX	n/a	n/a	n/a	n/a	n/a	n/a	n/a	n/a	n/a	n/a	n/a	n/a
Colorado Springs, CO	n/a	n/a	n/a	n/a	n/a	n/a	n/a	n/a	n/a	n/a	n/a	n/a
Columbia, MO	n/a	n/a	n/a	n/a	n/a	n/a	n/a	n/a	n/a	n/a	n/a	n/a
Columbia, SC	12.0	12.7	8.8	12.0	12.6	8.8	6.1	8.5	6.8	0.6	1.0	0.5
Columbus, OH	5.6	6.6	7.4	5.4	6.5	7.3	3.8	5.8	7.3	0.8	0.8	0.3
Dallas, TX	6.6	7.6	7.9	6.3	7.2	7.6	6.8	8.4	8.9	0.7	0.8	1.3
Davenport, IA	n/a	n/a	n/a	n/a	n/a	n/a	n/a	n/a	n/a	n/a	n/a	n/a
Denver, CO	5.8	6.0	4.9	5.2	5.5	4.4	5.1	5.3	4.7	0.3	0.7	0.7
Des Moines, IA	n/a	n/a	n/a	n/a	n/a	n/a	n/a	n/a	n/a	n/a	n/a	n/a
Detroit, MI	7.1	9.0	9.4	6.6	8.7	9.3	4.5	9.3	8.7	0.9	1.0	1.1
Durham, NC	n/a	n/a	n/a	n/a	n/a	n/a	n/a	n/a	n/a	n/a	n/a	n/a
El Paso, TX	n/a	n/a	n/a	n/a	n/a	n/a	n/a	n/a	n/a	n/a	n/a	n/a
Eugene, OR	n/a	n/a	n/a	n/a	n/a	n/a	n/a	n/a	n/a	n/a	n/a	n/a
Fargo, ND	n/a	n/a	n/a	n/a	n/a	n/a	n/a	n/a	n/a	n/a	n/a	n/a
Fort Collins, CO	n/a	n/a	n/a	n/a	n/a	n/a	n/a	n/a	n/a	n/a	n/a	n/a
Fort Wayne, IN	n/a	n/a	n/a	n/a	n/a	n/a	n/a	n/a	n/a	n/a	n/a	n/a
Fort Worth, TX	6.6	7.6	7.9	6.3	7.2	7.6	6.8	8.4	8.9	0.7	0.8	1.3
Gainesville, FL	n/a	n/a	n/a	n/a	n/a	n/a	n/a	n/a	n/a	n/a	n/a	n/a
Green Bay, WI	n/a	n/a	n/a	n/a	n/a	n/a	n/a	n/a	n/a	n/a	n/a	n/a
Greensboro, NC	8.7	6.1	7.8	8.7	5.7	6.0	10.2	5.7	5.5	0.7	0.1	0.5
Honolulu, HI	10.6	11.5	11.9	10.0	10.7	11.1	5.7	6.8	6.2	0.6	0.5	0.9
Houston, TX	6.9	7.9	7.8	6.3	7.3	7.2	8.9	10.9	9.8	0.6	1.4	1.2
Huntsville, AL	n/a	n/a	n/a	n/a	n/a	n/a	n/a	n/a	n/a	n/a	n/a	n/a
Indianapolis, IN	7.7	6.2	6.7	7.2	5.6	5.8	11.0	8.8	9.2	1.0	0.8	0.8
Jacksonville, FL	8.9	8.6	9.2	7.7	7.8	8.5	6.2	9.4	8.8	1.7	0.7	1.0
Kansas City, MO	7.1	7.0	6.9	7.1	6.6	6.3	7.8	7.6	8.9	0.6	1.2	0.9
Lafayette, LA	n/a	n/a	n/a	n/a	n/a	n/a	n/a	n/a	n/a	n/a	n/a	n/a
Las Vegas, NV	9.2	9.6	9.7	8.3	8.8	9.3	5.7	7.2	8.3	0.9	1.1	1.1
Lexington, KY	n/a	n/a	n/a	n/a	n/a	n/a	n/a	n/a	n/a	n/a	n/a	n/a
Lincoln, NE	n/a	n/a	n/a	n/a	n/a	n/a	n/a	n/a	n/a	n/a	n/a	n/a
Little Rock, AR	9.4	10.1	10.7	9.2	9.8	9.9	11.4	10.8	11.7	0.7	0.9	0.6
Los Angeles, CA	5.9	5.8	6.2	5.5	5.7	6.1	4.1	4.0	4.8	0.5	0.6	0.7
Louisville, KY	5.7	6.3	6.7	5.7	6.2	6.5	5.3	3.6	7.1	0.5	0.4	1.2
Madison, WI	n/a	n/a	n/a	n/a	n/a	n/a	n/a	n/a	n/a	n/a	n/a	n/a
Manchester, NH	n/a	n/a	n/a	n/a	n/a	n/a	n/a	n/a	n/a	n/a	n/a	n/a

Table continued on following page.

Appendix A: Comparative Statistics   A-63

Metro Area	Gross Vacancy Rate[1] (%)			Year-Round Vacancy Rate[2] (%)			Rental Vacancy Rate[3] (%)			Homeowner Vacancy Rate[4] (%)		
	2022	2023	2024	2022	2023	2024	2022	2023	2024	2022	2023	2024
McAllen, TX	n/a	n/a	n/a	n/a	n/a	n/a	n/a	n/a	n/a	n/a	n/a	n/a
Memphis, TN	6.2	7.0	7.4	6.1	6.9	7.2	6.4	11.4	12.0	0.4	0.4	0.9
Miami, FL	12.6	14.7	14.8	7.5	8.9	9.3	6.3	8.4	9.5	1.1	0.9	1.4
Midland, TX	n/a	n/a	n/a	n/a	n/a	n/a	n/a	n/a	n/a	n/a	n/a	n/a
Milwaukee, WI	5.2	6.7	5.6	5.1	6.6	5.1	5.9	4.1	4.8	0.1	0.8	0.4
Minneapolis, MN	4.8	5.5	4.9	4.5	5.3	4.6	6.7	8.1	5.2	0.8	0.5	0.4
Nashville, TN	7.6	7.5	7.0	7.1	7.0	6.4	6.4	9.3	8.6	0.9	0.9	1.5
New Orleans, LA	13.4	10.9	11.9	11.5	9.8	10.8	6.6	9.2	9.1	1.6	1.6	1.4
New York, NY	8.2	7.8	8.3	7.0	6.7	7.4	3.5	3.9	4.7	1.0	0.9	1.0
Oklahoma City, OK	8.6	7.8	7.0	8.5	7.6	6.7	10.6	10.6	9.0	0.9	1.6	1.2
Omaha, NE	5.4	5.4	5.1	5.0	5.1	5.1	4.2	4.3	5.3	0.8	0.9	0.3
Orlando, FL	9.6	9.5	9.8	7.4	7.6	8.4	6.5	7.0	9.4	1.4	1.1	1.5
Philadelphia, PA	5.5	5.3	5.3	5.4	5.2	5.2	4.2	5.2	6.3	1.0	0.9	0.5
Phoenix, AZ	10.9	11.0	12.6	6.7	7.2	7.9	6.4	8.0	7.9	0.9	0.7	1.0
Pittsburgh, PA	11.5	10.0	10.5	11.0	9.2	9.7	8.3	6.3	8.9	0.7	0.9	0.8
Portland, OR	5.4	5.4	5.7	5.1	5.1	5.5	4.0	6.8	5.7	1.2	0.8	1.0
Providence, RI	9.5	9.4	8.5	7.6	7.6	6.8	4.5	3.7	3.2	0.4	0.3	0.4
Provo, UT	n/a	n/a	n/a	n/a	n/a	n/a	n/a	n/a	n/a	n/a	n/a	n/a
Raleigh, NC	7.4	6.7	6.3	7.3	6.6	6.2	7.1	8.8	8.8	0.5	0.5	0.7
Reno, NV	n/a	n/a	n/a	n/a	n/a	n/a	n/a	n/a	n/a	n/a	n/a	n/a
Richmond, VA	6.1	5.9	7.7	6.1	5.9	7.7	3.0	5.2	7.9	0.7	0.2	0.7
Rochester, MN	n/a	n/a	n/a	n/a	n/a	n/a	n/a	n/a	n/a	n/a	n/a	n/a
Sacramento, CA	6.3	6.4	8.0	6.1	6.2	7.6	2.3	4.2	3.9	0.6	0.6	0.9
Saint Louis, MO	7.2	7.4	7.7	7.1	7.3	7.6	6.8	7.8	7.9	1.4	0.6	0.9
Saint Paul, MN	4.8	5.5	4.9	4.5	5.3	4.6	6.7	8.1	5.2	0.8	0.5	0.4
Salem, OR	n/a	n/a	n/a	n/a	n/a	n/a	n/a	n/a	n/a	n/a	n/a	n/a
Salt Lake City, UT	5.1	6.1	10.1	4.5	5.0	5.8	4.6	6.2	6.1	0.6	0.6	0.7
San Antonio, TX	7.5	7.4	9.9	7.1	6.9	7.9	8.1	8.8	10.0	0.9	1.3	1.9
San Diego, CA	6.9	6.8	6.4	6.6	6.2	6.0	3.6	4.1	5.2	0.6	0.2	0.5
San Francisco, CA	7.9	8.1	8.3	7.7	8.0	8.1	5.4	6.6	6.3	1.3	0.5	0.7
San Jose, CA	5.8	4.5	4.7	5.8	4.5	4.7	4.7	3.3	3.3	0.4	0.3	1.0
Santa Rosa, CA	n/a	n/a	n/a	n/a	n/a	n/a	n/a	n/a	n/a	n/a	n/a	n/a
Savannah, GA	n/a	n/a	n/a	n/a	n/a	n/a	n/a	n/a	n/a	n/a	n/a	n/a
Seattle, WA	5.7	5.1	6.2	5.2	4.7	5.9	4.9	4.0	6.5	0.7	0.6	1.1
Sioux Falls, SD	n/a	n/a	n/a	n/a	n/a	n/a	n/a	n/a	n/a	n/a	n/a	n/a
Tampa, FL	13.3	13.3	14.2	9.9	9.1	10.9	8.1	8.5	8.7	1.2	1.0	2.0
Tucson, AZ	13.5	14.2	10.1	10.3	11.2	8.7	8.0	10.2	9.3	1.4	1.3	1.1
Tulsa, OK	8.9	8.3	7.5	8.5	7.9	6.8	5.6	6.7	7.2	0.7	0.8	0.7
Virginia Beach, VA	8.1	5.9	9.2	7.3	5.4	8.5	6.3	5.1	9.1	1.0	0.5	1.4
Washington, DC	5.2	5.1	5.5	5.0	5.0	5.4	5.3	5.5	4.7	0.6	0.3	0.4
Wichita, KS	n/a	n/a	n/a	n/a	n/a	n/a	n/a	n/a	n/a	n/a	n/a	n/a
Wilmington, NC	n/a	n/a	n/a	n/a	n/a	n/a	n/a	n/a	n/a	n/a	n/a	n/a
Winston-Salem, NC	n/a	n/a	n/a	n/a	n/a	n/a	n/a	n/a	n/a	n/a	n/a	n/a
U.S.[5]	9.1	9.0	9.1	7.5	7.5	7.6	5.7	6.5	6.8	0.8	0.8	1.0

Note: Figures cover the Metropolitan Statistical Area (MSA); (1) The percentage of the total housing inventory that is vacant; (2) The percentage of the housing inventory (excluding seasonal units) that is year-round vacant; (3) The percentage of rental inventory that is vacant for rent; (4) The percentage of homeowner inventory that is vacant for sale; (5) Figures cover the 75 largest Metropolitan Statistical Areas; n/a not available
Source: U.S. Census Bureau, Housing Vacancies and Homeownership Annual Statistics: 2022, 2023, 2024

Appendix A: Comparative Statistics

Bankruptcy Filings

City	Area Covered	Business Filings			Nonbusiness Filings		
		2023	2024	% Chg.	2023	2024	% Chg.
Albuquerque, NM	Bernalillo County	24	33	37.5	373	454	21.7
Anchorage, AK	Anchorage Borough	9	7	-22.2	113	90	-20.4
Ann Arbor, MI	Washtenaw County	7	8	14.3	396	404	2.0
Athens, GA	Clarke County	2	5	150.0	176	189	7.4
Atlanta, GA	Fulton County	318	251	-21.1	2,723	2,846	4.5
Austin, TX	Travis County	133	121	-9.0	408	619	51.7
Baltimore, MD	Baltimore City	35	43	22.9	1,502	1,656	10.3
Billings, MT	Yellowstone County	5	9	80.0	111	153	37.8
Boise City, ID	Ada County	18	26	44.4	350	466	33.1
Boston, MA	Suffolk County	53	63	18.9	233	316	35.6
Boulder, CO	Boulder County	25	35	40.0	228	247	8.3
Cape Coral, FL	Lee County	97	64	-34.0	860	1,216	41.4
Cedar Rapids, IA	Linn County	9	7	-22.2	224	278	24.1
Charleston, SC	Charleston County	7	13	85.7	195	215	10.3
Charlotte, NC	Mecklenburg County	69	60	-13.0	577	689	19.4
Chicago, IL	Cook County	361	479	32.7	12,419	13,840	11.4
Cincinnati, OH	Hamilton County	32	42	31.3	1,286	1,619	25.9
Clarksville, TN	Montgomery County	4	11	175.0	475	513	8.0
Cleveland, OH	Cuyahoga County	37	60	62.2	3,437	4,054	18.0
College Station, TX	Brazos County	5	7	40.0	65	80	23.1
Colorado Springs, CO	El Paso County	23	50	117.4	784	973	24.1
Columbia, MO	Boone County	3	5	66.7	191	201	5.2
Columbia, SC	Richland County	7	10	42.9	453	584	28.9
Columbus, OH	Franklin County	43	81	88.4	2,330	2,671	14.6
Dallas, TX	Dallas County	296	496	67.6	2,363	3,025	28.0
Davenport, IA	Scott County	9	4	-55.6	157	158	0.6
Denver, CO	Denver County	61	79	29.5	669	854	27.7
Des Moines, IA	Polk County	15	13	-13.3	566	594	4.9
Detroit, MI	Wayne County	43	58	34.9	6,087	6,501	6.8
Durham, NC	Durham County	14	42	200.0	162	195	20.4
El Paso, TX	El Paso County	65	72	10.8	1,351	1,512	11.9
Eugene, OR	Lane County	12	18	50.0	535	707	32.1
Fargo, ND	Cass County	5	14	180.0	129	132	2.3
Fort Collins, CO	Larimer County	21	28	33.3	347	417	20.2
Fort Wayne, IN	Allen County	17	17	0.0	924	959	3.8
Fort Worth, TX	Tarrant County	200	198	-1.0	2,934	3,513	19.7
Gainesville, FL	Alachua County	11	30	172.7	153	177	15.7
Green Bay, WI	Brown County	5	10	100.0	320	408	27.5
Greensboro, NC	Guilford County	11	16	45.5	375	473	26.1
Honolulu, HI	Honolulu County	36	38	5.6	757	840	11.0
Houston, TX	Harris County	356	426	19.7	3,285	3,853	17.3
Huntsville, AL	Madison County	20	35	75.0	902	946	4.9
Indianapolis, IN	Marion County	45	43	-4.4	2,601	3,166	21.7
Jacksonville, FL	Duval County	73	83	13.7	1,514	1,784	17.8
Kansas City, MO	Jackson County	22	27	22.7	1,186	1,166	-1.7
Lafayette, LA	Lafayette Parish	19	44	131.6	335	410	22.4
Las Vegas, NV	Clark County	194	178	-8.2	5,622	6,690	19.0
Lexington, KY	Fayette County	13	14	7.7	468	540	15.4
Lincoln, NE	Lancaster County	11	15	36.4	367	405	10.4
Little Rock, AR	Pulaski County	17	29	70.6	1,436	1,390	-3.2
Los Angeles, CA	Los Angeles County	815	977	19.9	10,059	12,169	21.0
Louisville, KY	Jefferson County	28	35	25.0	2,280	2,258	-1.0
Madison, WI	Dane County	25	21	-16.0	437	494	13.0
Manchester, NH	Hillsborough County	8	21	162.5	235	298	26.8
McAllen, TX	Hidalgo County	13	11	-15.4	263	274	4.2

Table continued on following page.

City	Area Covered	Business Filings			Nonbusiness Filings		
		2023	2024	% Chg.	2023	2024	% Chg.
Memphis, TN	Shelby County	48	45	-6.3	5,959	6,030	1.2
Miami, FL	Miami-Dade County	242	413	70.7	5,320	6,779	27.4
Midland, TX	Midland County	14	17	21.4	66	93	40.9
Milwaukee, WI	Milwaukee County	24	40	66.7	2,881	3,306	14.8
Minneapolis, MN	Hennepin County	64	77	20.3	1,473	1,952	32.5
Nashville, TN	Davidson County	303	123	-59.4	1,109	1,195	7.8
New Orleans, LA	Orleans Parish	28	35	25.0	388	446	14.9
New York, NY	Bronx County	25	44	76.0	1,071	1,319	23.2
New York, NY	Kings County	394	457	16.0	1,781	2,036	14.3
New York, NY	New York County	750	361	-51.9	684	793	15.9
New York, NY	Queens County	215	209	-2.8	1,921	2,120	10.4
New York, NY	Richmond County	23	29	26.1	490	494	0.8
Oklahoma City, OK	Oklahoma County	46	54	17.4	1,374	1,526	11.1
Omaha, NE	Douglas County	21	26	23.8	687	802	16.7
Orlando, FL	Orange County	152	231	52.0	1,832	2,279	24.4
Philadelphia, PA	Philadelphia County	227	131	-42.3	940	1,094	16.4
Phoenix, AZ	Maricopa County	252	355	40.9	6,085	7,026	15.5
Pittsburgh, PA	Allegheny County	59	111	88.1	1,217	1,424	17.0
Portland, OR	Multnomah County	35	61	74.3	938	1,078	14.9
Providence, RI	Providence County	13	22	69.2	520	581	11.7
Provo, UT	Utah County	33	36	9.1	925	1,070	15.7
Raleigh, NC	Wake County	51	76	49.0	653	830	27.1
Reno, NV	Washoe County	35	59	68.6	610	860	41.0
Richmond, VA	Richmond city	2	14	600.0	620	678	9.4
Rochester, MN	Olmsted County	8	6	-25.0	137	161	17.5
Sacramento, CA	Sacramento County	96	163	69.8	1,675	2,259	34.9
Saint Louis, MO	Saint Louis City	12	23	91.7	1,497	1,311	-12.4
Saint Paul, MN	Ramsey County	20	19	-5.0	694	840	21.0
Salem, OR	Marion County	10	11	10.0	599	674	12.5
Salt Lake City, UT	Salt Lake County	58	58	0.0	2,508	2,763	10.2
San Antonio, TX	Bexar County	126	169	34.1	1,270	1,813	42.8
San Diego, CA	San Diego County	214	267	24.8	3,866	4,558	17.9
San Francisco, CA	San Francisco County	68	140	105.9	348	417	19.8
San Jose, CA	Santa Clara County	86	105	22.1	782	1,008	28.9
Santa Rosa, CA	Sonoma County	17	56	229.4	338	378	11.8
Savannah, GA	Chatham County	8	3	-62.5	732	695	-5.1
Seattle, WA	King County	92	113	22.8	1,134	1,459	28.7
Sioux Falls, SD	Minnehaha County	10	8	-20.0	220	220	0.0
Tampa, FL	Hillsborough County	121	158	30.6	1,822	2,440	33.9
Tucson, AZ	Pima County	28	27	-3.6	1,402	1,638	16.8
Tulsa, OK	Tulsa County	46	44	-4.3	867	1,065	22.8
Virginia Beach, VA	Virginia Beach City	10	20	100.0	822	966	17.5
Washington, DC	District of Columbia	78	81	3.8	293	347	18.4
Wichita, KS	Sedgwick County	24	27	12.5	757	777	2.6
Wilmington, NC	New Hanover County	29	19	-34.5	145	183	26.2
Winston-Salem, NC	Forsyth County	7	18	157.1	263	330	25.5
U.S.	U.S.	18,926	23,107	22.1	434,064	494,201	13.9

Note: Business filings include Chapter 7, Chapter 9, Chapter 11, Chapter 12, Chapter 13, Chapter 15, and Section 304; Nonbusiness filings include Chapter 7, Chapter 11, and Chapter 13
Source: Administrative Office of the U.S. Courts, Business and Nonbusiness Bankruptcy, County Cases Commenced by Chapter of the Bankruptcy Code, During the 12-Month Period Ending December 31, 2023 and Business and Nonbusiness Bankruptcy, County Cases Commenced by Chapter of the Bankruptcy Code, During the 12-Month Period Ending December 31, 2024

Income: City

City	Per Capita ($)	Median Household ($)	Average Household ($)
Albuquerque, NM	39,117	65,604	88,262
Anchorage, AK	49,338	98,152	127,598
Ann Arbor, MI	54,604	81,089	121,561
Athens, GA	31,836	51,655	76,375
Atlanta, GA	64,063	81,938	135,218
Austin, TX	59,427	91,461	130,163
Baltimore, MD	39,195	59,623	87,339
Billings, MT	42,639	71,855	98,655
Boise City, ID	48,274	81,308	112,482
Boston, MA	60,001	94,755	140,807
Boulder, CO	59,450	85,364	140,662
Cape Coral, FL	39,603	76,062	97,070
Cedar Rapids, IA	39,824	67,859	91,040
Charleston, SC	58,583	90,038	129,666
Charlotte, NC	49,991	78,438	119,473
Chicago, IL	48,148	75,134	112,443
Cincinnati, OH	38,878	51,707	83,146
Clarksville, TN	31,266	66,786	79,769
Cleveland, OH	27,078	39,187	56,900
College Station, TX	32,123	51,776	84,849
Colorado Springs, CO	44,893	83,198	108,459
Columbia, MO	37,359	64,488	91,425
Columbia, SC	38,087	55,653	90,935
Columbus, OH	37,189	65,327	85,919
Dallas, TX	44,138	67,760	106,979
Davenport, IA	36,583	64,497	83,699
Denver, CO	61,202	91,681	131,349
Des Moines, IA	36,459	63,966	83,728
Detroit, MI	24,029	39,575	56,528
Durham, NC	47,246	79,234	108,538
El Paso, TX	28,942	58,734	78,842
Eugene, OR	41,035	63,836	94,063
Fargo, ND	42,212	66,029	91,129
Fort Collins, CO	46,341	83,598	110,629
Fort Wayne, IN	32,884	60,293	78,764
Fort Worth, TX	37,157	76,602	101,838
Gainesville, FL	30,282	45,611	71,640
Green Bay, WI	34,514	62,546	81,363
Greensboro, NC	35,858	58,884	85,861
Honolulu, HI	48,465	85,428	120,718
Houston, TX	41,142	62,894	101,848
Huntsville, AL	44,733	70,778	101,671
Indianapolis, IN	36,194	62,995	86,913
Jacksonville, FL	37,269	66,981	90,429
Kansas City, MO	40,112	67,449	91,703
Lafayette, LA	39,861	61,454	91,871
Las Vegas, NV	38,421	70,723	98,664
Lexington, KY	42,272	67,631	98,429
Lincoln, NE	39,187	69,991	94,181
Little Rock, AR	43,242	60,583	98,728
Los Angeles, CA	46,270	80,366	122,610
Louisville, KY	38,890	64,731	91,264
Madison, WI	48,557	76,983	104,969
Manchester, NH	44,220	77,415	100,102
McAllen, TX	29,406	60,165	86,175
Memphis, TN	32,314	51,211	77,102

Table continued on following page.

City	Per Capita ($)	Median Household ($)	Average Household ($)
Miami, FL	42,528	59,390	97,643
Midland, TX	49,327	91,169	126,317
Milwaukee, WI	29,679	51,888	70,559
Minneapolis, MN	50,605	80,269	112,607
Nashville, TN	46,820	75,197	106,483
New Orleans, LA	39,698	55,339	89,943
New York, NY	50,776	79,713	127,894
Oklahoma City, OK	37,109	66,702	91,131
Omaha, NE	42,515	72,708	103,010
Orlando, FL	41,985	69,268	100,135
Philadelphia, PA	37,669	60,698	88,307
Phoenix, AZ	40,309	77,041	106,845
Pittsburgh, PA	43,590	64,137	93,301
Portland, OR	55,312	88,792	122,267
Providence, RI	36,694	66,772	95,112
Provo, UT	26,755	62,800	86,072
Raleigh, NC	49,948	82,424	116,724
Reno, NV	45,180	78,448	107,386
Richmond, VA	44,249	62,671	94,647
Rochester, MN	49,727	87,767	119,510
Sacramento, CA	42,300	83,753	108,939
Saint Louis, MO	38,947	55,279	78,097
Saint Paul, MN	41,594	73,055	102,197
Salem, OR	36,477	71,900	94,087
Salt Lake City, UT	49,642	74,925	111,189
San Antonio, TX	32,983	62,917	85,107
San Diego, CA	54,678	104,321	139,707
San Francisco, CA	90,285	141,446	204,625
San Jose, CA	63,253	141,565	187,711
Santa Rosa, CA	50,520	97,410	129,680
Savannah, GA	32,004	56,782	77,786
Seattle, WA	82,508	121,984	170,038
Sioux Falls, SD	43,231	74,714	102,058
Tampa, FL	49,513	71,302	117,408
Tucson, AZ	31,152	54,546	73,528
Tulsa, OK	37,533	58,407	88,998
Virginia Beach, VA	47,372	90,685	118,081
Washington, DC	75,253	106,287	157,604
Wichita, KS	35,958	63,072	87,820
Wilmington, NC	46,062	63,900	98,401
Winston-Salem, NC	35,074	57,673	85,278
U.S.	43,289	78,538	110,491

Source: U.S. Census Bureau, 2019-2023 American Community Survey 5-Year Estimates

Income: Metro Area

Metro Area	Per Capita ($)	Median Household ($)	Average Household ($)
Albuquerque, NM	38,300	67,995	91,376
Anchorage, AK	47,015	95,918	123,232
Ann Arbor, MI	51,746	87,156	122,847
Athens, GA	36,105	62,897	91,841
Atlanta, GA	44,798	86,338	118,625
Austin, TX	53,550	97,638	132,189
Baltimore, MD	51,146	97,300	128,719
Billings, MT	43,176	74,599	102,275
Boise City, ID	41,793	82,694	110,044
Boston, MA	61,389	112,484	155,005
Boulder, CO	60,272	102,772	144,869
Cape Coral, FL	43,365	73,099	102,290
Cedar Rapids, IA	41,820	77,084	100,451
Charleston, SC	46,863	82,272	114,464
Charlotte, NC	44,995	80,201	113,387
Chicago, IL	48,107	88,850	122,980
Cincinnati, OH	43,371	79,490	107,457
Clarksville, TN	31,813	66,210	82,303
Cleveland, OH	41,791	68,507	96,273
College Station, TX	34,136	59,691	88,300
Colorado Springs, CO	44,315	87,180	112,662
Columbia, MO	37,799	69,463	93,435
Columbia, SC	37,159	66,146	90,520
Columbus, OH	43,665	79,847	108,257
Dallas, TX	44,447	87,155	120,397
Davenport, IA	39,357	71,925	93,006
Denver, CO	55,529	102,339	135,703
Des Moines, IA	44,796	84,209	109,864
Detroit, MI	42,145	75,123	102,705
Durham, NC	48,827	81,017	116,697
El Paso, TX	27,509	58,800	77,734
Eugene, OR	38,563	69,311	91,348
Fargo, ND	43,099	75,523	100,645
Fort Collins, CO	49,323	91,364	118,812
Fort Wayne, IN	36,444	69,378	90,705
Fort Worth, TX	44,447	87,155	120,397
Gainesville, FL	36,810	58,946	89,302
Green Bay, WI	40,606	77,459	98,052
Greensboro, NC	35,569	63,083	87,043
Honolulu, HI	46,361	104,264	133,753
Houston, TX	41,559	80,458	115,043
Huntsville, AL	45,250	83,529	110,607
Indianapolis, IN	42,522	77,065	106,219
Jacksonville, FL	41,987	77,013	104,828
Kansas City, MO	44,205	81,927	108,186
Lafayette, LA	34,845	60,910	86,057
Las Vegas, NV	38,654	73,845	101,010
Lexington, KY	41,230	70,717	99,405
Lincoln, NE	40,527	73,095	99,081
Little Rock, AR	37,678	65,309	90,691
Los Angeles, CA	46,385	93,525	132,022
Louisville, KY	40,019	71,737	97,103
Madison, WI	49,799	86,827	113,809
Manchester, NH	52,243	100,436	128,567
McAllen, TX	22,005	52,281	71,722
Memphis, TN	36,519	64,743	92,389

Table continued on following page.

Metro Area	Per Capita ($)	Median Household ($)	Average Household ($)
Miami, FL	42,369	73,481	109,356
Midland, TX	48,843	93,442	126,152
Milwaukee, WI	44,476	76,404	104,403
Minneapolis, MN	51,500	98,180	128,647
Nashville, TN	45,266	82,499	113,441
New Orleans, LA	37,547	62,271	90,627
New York, NY	54,510	97,334	144,032
Oklahoma City, OK	38,240	70,499	95,891
Omaha, NE	44,338	83,023	111,142
Orlando, FL	38,776	75,611	103,312
Philadelphia, PA	49,178	89,273	123,454
Phoenix, AZ	43,395	84,703	113,623
Pittsburgh, PA	44,726	73,942	101,289
Portland, OR	50,158	94,573	124,372
Providence, RI	45,170	85,646	111,377
Provo, UT	35,045	96,745	121,112
Raleigh, NC	49,462	96,066	126,566
Reno, NV	45,849	84,684	114,037
Richmond, VA	46,237	84,405	114,424
Rochester, MN	48,977	89,675	120,598
Sacramento, CA	45,964	93,986	123,767
Saint Louis, MO	44,689	78,225	107,013
Saint Paul, MN	51,500	98,180	128,647
Salem, OR	36,260	76,010	97,771
Salt Lake City, UT	43,026	95,045	121,478
San Antonio, TX	37,425	74,297	100,400
San Diego, CA	49,891	102,285	136,236
San Francisco, CA	72,306	133,780	190,258
San Jose, CA	75,895	157,444	217,226
Santa Rosa, CA	54,941	102,840	138,572
Savannah, GA	39,158	74,632	99,643
Seattle, WA	61,286	112,594	152,753
Sioux Falls, SD	43,434	81,418	106,253
Tampa, FL	42,023	71,254	100,901
Tucson, AZ	38,564	67,929	92,561
Tulsa, OK	37,865	67,823	94,114
Virginia Beach, VA	42,791	80,533	105,690
Washington, DC	62,026	123,896	162,905
Wichita, KS	36,529	68,930	91,559
Wilmington, NC	44,459	73,687	100,847
Winston-Salem, NC	35,829	64,282	87,020
U.S.	43,289	78,538	110,491

Note: Figures cover the Metropolitan Statistical Area (MSA)
Source: U.S. Census Bureau, 2019-2023 American Community Survey 5-Year Estimates

Household Income Distribution: City

City	Percent of Households Earning							
	Under $15,000	$15,000 -$24,999	$25,000 -$34,999	$35,000 -$49,999	$50,000 -$74,999	$75,000 -$99,999	$100,000 -$149,999	$150,000 and up
Albuquerque, NM	10.9	8.5	7.9	11.5	17.5	12.6	16.0	15.2
Anchorage, AK	5.2	4.6	4.4	8.3	14.6	13.7	19.5	29.7
Ann Arbor, MI	12.8	5.7	5.8	8.8	14.4	10.6	15.2	26.8
Athens, GA	15.5	10.4	10.3	12.4	16.1	10.9	12.9	11.6
Atlanta, GA	13.2	6.7	6.1	8.2	12.8	11.5	15.0	26.5
Austin, TX	7.8	4.6	4.9	9.3	15.1	12.4	17.2	28.7
Baltimore, MD	15.7	8.4	7.4	11.4	16.6	11.3	13.5	15.7
Billings, MT	7.2	7.0	7.4	12.6	18.1	13.0	17.9	16.9
Boise City, ID	5.7	6.0	6.3	11.2	16.6	15.1	17.4	21.6
Boston, MA	12.9	6.5	5.1	7.1	10.6	9.9	15.5	32.5
Boulder, CO	12.4	6.7	7.3	7.7	11.5	9.5	14.0	30.9
Cape Coral, FL	6.2	5.0	7.7	10.6	19.9	15.6	19.3	15.7
Cedar Rapids, IA	7.3	6.6	8.9	14.1	18.3	14.2	16.0	14.8
Charleston, SC	7.7	6.1	4.3	9.6	14.7	12.7	18.6	26.4
Charlotte, NC	7.0	5.6	6.2	11.6	17.6	12.7	16.9	22.5
Chicago, IL	12.1	7.2	6.9	9.8	14.0	11.7	16.0	22.4
Cincinnati, OH	16.9	10.2	8.7	12.9	15.0	10.3	11.8	14.2
Clarksville, TN	7.7	5.7	7.7	13.4	21.0	16.7	17.8	10.0
Cleveland, OH	22.1	12.6	10.7	14.2	16.0	9.2	8.9	6.4
College Station, TX	18.3	8.3	9.5	12.9	12.2	11.0	12.2	15.6
Colorado Springs, CO	6.2	5.3	5.8	10.4	17.7	13.6	19.8	21.3
Columbia, MO	12.4	8.3	8.5	10.8	17.1	11.8	14.3	17.0
Columbia, SC	16.5	8.6	8.2	11.7	16.7	10.7	11.7	15.8
Columbus, OH	10.0	7.1	7.4	13.3	18.5	13.5	16.6	13.5
Dallas, TX	10.2	6.8	7.7	12.3	17.9	12.5	13.7	18.8
Davenport, IA	10.8	7.0	8.8	11.5	19.0	13.5	17.4	12.0
Denver, CO	7.8	5.2	5.1	8.6	14.4	12.6	17.9	28.4
Des Moines, IA	8.8	7.7	7.2	14.3	19.3	15.4	15.2	12.1
Detroit, MI	22.8	12.2	10.2	15.2	15.1	9.5	9.2	5.8
Durham, NC	7.7	5.8	6.4	10.6	16.9	12.9	17.9	21.7
El Paso, TX	12.9	9.1	8.9	12.8	18.2	12.6	14.2	11.5
Eugene, OR	11.3	7.8	7.6	13.2	15.5	12.5	15.8	16.3
Fargo, ND	8.5	7.3	9.2	12.9	18.1	13.8	15.2	15.0
Fort Collins, CO	9.5	5.7	5.5	10.0	14.9	12.5	18.4	23.5
Fort Wayne, IN	9.3	7.9	9.6	14.5	19.5	14.1	15.2	9.9
Fort Worth, TX	7.4	5.9	6.9	11.1	17.3	13.7	18.1	19.4
Gainesville, FL	18.0	10.4	11.2	14.8	14.8	10.2	10.4	10.2
Green Bay, WI	9.5	8.6	7.4	13.6	19.7	14.6	16.2	10.4
Greensboro, NC	11.7	8.0	9.0	13.8	17.8	12.2	15.0	12.6
Honolulu, HI	8.8	5.7	5.1	9.4	15.2	12.7	17.4	25.7
Houston, TX	10.9	8.2	8.5	12.6	17.4	11.6	13.1	17.7
Huntsville, AL	9.2	8.0	8.7	11.3	15.0	12.6	15.6	19.6
Indianapolis, IN	10.7	7.5	8.2	13.5	18.7	12.5	15.0	13.8
Jacksonville, FL	10.0	7.3	7.5	12.7	17.9	13.3	16.9	14.5
Kansas City, MO	10.3	7.2	7.5	12.5	17.2	12.6	16.9	15.7
Lafayette, LA	13.8	8.8	8.0	11.5	14.6	12.8	14.9	15.6
Las Vegas, NV	10.0	6.7	7.5	11.4	17.3	12.9	16.8	17.4
Lexington, KY	9.8	7.2	8.6	11.9	16.8	11.9	15.7	18.1
Lincoln, NE	8.1	6.4	8.2	12.5	18.3	14.0	17.1	15.6
Little Rock, AR	10.7	8.2	9.9	13.9	15.6	11.3	13.1	17.2
Los Angeles, CA	10.8	6.7	6.5	9.4	14.0	11.5	16.0	25.1
Louisville, KY	10.6	7.6	8.2	12.7	17.2	12.8	15.9	15.0
Madison, WI	9.4	6.2	7.2	10.3	15.5	12.8	17.6	20.9
Manchester, NH	6.0	6.9	5.7	11.7	18.0	14.3	19.3	18.1

Table continued on following page.

City	Percent of Households Earning							
	Under $15,000	$15,000 -$24,999	$25,000 -$34,999	$35,000 -$49,999	$50,000 -$74,999	$75,000 -$99,999	$100,000 -$149,999	$150,000 and up
McAllen, TX	11.9	10.2	9.3	11.4	16.1	11.7	15.7	13.7
Memphis, TN	14.7	9.9	10.1	14.4	17.9	10.9	11.6	10.5
Miami, FL	14.4	9.3	8.1	11.9	15.7	10.2	13.1	17.4
Midland, TX	9.1	4.8	5.8	9.2	14.3	10.1	18.0	28.6
Milwaukee, WI	14.5	9.7	10.4	13.8	18.0	12.0	12.7	8.9
Minneapolis, MN	9.5	6.6	6.2	9.7	15.2	12.3	17.3	23.1
Nashville, TN	8.5	5.6	6.6	11.8	17.4	13.6	17.2	19.3
New Orleans, LA	18.7	9.7	7.7	10.8	14.8	9.6	12.8	15.8
New York, NY	12.3	7.0	6.3	8.9	13.3	10.8	15.3	26.1
Oklahoma City, OK	10.0	7.0	7.9	12.4	18.1	13.3	15.9	15.4
Omaha, NE	8.8	6.5	7.2	11.4	17.6	13.1	17.1	18.2
Orlando, FL	9.5	7.0	8.7	11.7	17.1	12.5	16.3	17.2
Philadelphia, PA	15.1	8.7	8.2	11.0	15.8	11.8	14.0	15.3
Phoenix, AZ	7.7	5.6	6.7	11.5	17.3	13.7	17.4	20.1
Pittsburgh, PA	14.2	8.1	7.4	11.0	16.6	11.4	14.6	16.8
Portland, OR	8.8	5.3	5.6	9.2	14.2	11.9	17.6	27.3
Providence, RI	13.7	8.4	6.6	10.7	16.0	11.7	15.8	17.1
Provo, UT	9.4	8.2	9.2	13.5	17.7	13.6	14.5	13.8
Raleigh, NC	7.0	5.6	6.0	11.2	15.9	13.0	17.2	24.1
Reno, NV	7.9	6.4	6.9	10.2	16.6	13.2	18.7	19.9
Richmond, VA	13.0	8.4	7.7	12.7	16.6	12.0	12.4	17.1
Rochester, MN	5.2	5.8	5.7	9.1	16.3	13.5	19.9	24.5
Sacramento, CA	9.1	6.1	5.2	9.5	15.1	13.6	18.7	22.7
Saint Louis, MO	15.5	8.8	9.1	12.5	17.5	11.3	13.1	12.4
Saint Paul, MN	9.0	6.6	6.9	10.4	18.4	13.2	16.1	19.4
Salem, OR	9.0	6.5	7.5	11.2	17.5	12.6	19.0	16.5
Salt Lake City, UT	9.0	6.7	6.5	11.1	16.8	13.5	15.9	20.5
San Antonio, TX	10.3	7.9	9.2	12.4	18.6	13.4	15.0	13.4
San Diego, CA	6.7	4.4	4.8	7.3	12.5	12.4	19.4	32.5
San Francisco, CA	8.5	4.8	3.9	5.2	8.1	8.4	13.4	47.7
San Jose, CA	4.9	3.6	3.5	5.5	9.2	9.3	16.6	47.3
Santa Rosa, CA	6.3	4.1	4.4	7.7	15.6	13.4	19.5	29.1
Savannah, GA	13.4	8.3	9.8	13.0	18.8	11.7	13.9	11.2
Seattle, WA	7.3	3.9	4.0	6.5	11.4	9.5	16.3	41.1
Sioux Falls, SD	6.0	5.5	7.5	12.3	18.8	14.3	18.6	16.9
Tampa, FL	11.1	7.2	7.2	11.2	15.6	11.2	14.4	22.1
Tucson, AZ	12.0	9.6	10.2	14.6	17.5	12.7	14.1	9.5
Tulsa, OK	11.9	7.6	10.1	13.5	17.8	11.5	13.4	14.2
Virginia Beach, VA	5.7	3.9	5.1	8.5	18.1	13.7	20.8	24.2
Washington, DC	10.5	4.6	3.8	6.8	11.4	10.4	15.7	36.9
Wichita, KS	9.5	7.6	9.6	13.0	18.1	13.3	15.6	13.3
Wilmington, NC	11.3	6.8	8.3	13.0	17.6	11.9	14.2	16.8
Winston-Salem, NC	11.3	8.9	10.0	13.2	17.2	12.5	13.8	13.0
U.S.	8.5	6.6	6.8	10.4	15.7	12.7	17.4	21.9

Source: U.S. Census Bureau, 2019-2023 American Community Survey 5-Year Estimates

Household Income Distribution: Metro Area

Metro Area	Percent of Households Earning							
	Under $15,000	$15,000 -$24,999	$25,000 -$34,999	$35,000 -$49,999	$50,000 -$74,999	$75,000 -$99,999	$100,000 -$149,999	$150,000 and up
Albuquerque, NM	10.3	7.9	7.6	11.2	17.5	12.8	16.6	16.0
Anchorage, AK	5.4	4.9	4.7	8.5	14.6	13.8	19.8	28.2
Ann Arbor, MI	8.8	5.3	5.8	9.3	14.9	11.8	17.5	26.6
Athens, GA	12.6	8.5	9.0	11.3	15.5	12.1	14.8	16.2
Atlanta, GA	6.9	5.4	6.0	9.8	15.4	13.4	18.3	24.8
Austin, TX	6.3	4.1	4.8	8.6	14.8	12.4	19.2	29.9
Baltimore, MD	7.6	4.9	5.0	8.3	13.3	12.0	18.8	30.1
Billings, MT	6.6	6.8	7.6	11.5	17.6	13.4	18.1	18.2
Boise City, ID	5.3	5.3	5.6	10.5	18.4	15.3	19.7	19.8
Boston, MA	7.2	4.9	4.5	6.7	11.2	10.5	17.7	37.2
Boulder, CO	7.5	5.3	5.2	7.4	12.4	11.1	17.3	33.9
Cape Coral, FL	7.9	6.2	7.5	11.7	18.0	14.2	17.3	17.2
Cedar Rapids, IA	6.1	6.2	7.2	12.0	17.3	14.5	18.2	18.5
Charleston, SC	7.2	6.1	6.1	10.0	16.8	13.0	19.2	21.6
Charlotte, NC	6.8	6.1	6.5	10.9	16.7	13.0	17.7	22.2
Chicago, IL	8.1	5.6	5.9	9.0	14.2	12.5	18.4	26.4
Cincinnati, OH	8.4	6.5	6.7	10.4	15.5	13.0	18.7	20.9
Clarksville, TN	9.1	6.6	8.1	12.3	20.0	15.2	17.1	11.5
Cleveland, OH	10.1	7.6	7.8	11.6	16.9	12.5	16.0	17.3
College Station, TX	14.7	7.7	8.7	12.5	14.6	12.2	14.2	15.4
Colorado Springs, CO	5.7	4.8	5.6	9.8	16.9	13.7	20.3	23.3
Columbia, MO	10.3	7.4	7.6	11.1	17.3	13.3	16.6	16.2
Columbia, SC	10.1	7.3	8.1	12.5	17.5	13.0	15.8	15.7
Columbus, OH	7.6	5.8	6.4	11.0	16.6	12.9	18.2	21.5
Dallas, TX	6.3	4.9	5.8	10.0	16.1	13.1	18.5	25.2
Davenport, IA	9.0	6.9	7.5	11.5	17.0	13.6	18.6	16.0
Denver, CO	5.7	4.1	4.5	7.9	14.0	12.8	19.7	31.4
Des Moines, IA	5.6	5.4	6.1	11.0	16.5	14.0	19.1	22.4
Detroit, MI	9.3	6.7	7.0	11.1	15.7	12.8	17.0	20.2
Durham, NC	7.8	6.2	6.4	10.3	16.0	12.0	17.3	23.9
El Paso, TX	12.8	8.9	8.9	12.8	18.6	12.6	14.4	11.1
Eugene, OR	10.0	7.3	7.5	12.5	16.2	14.2	17.8	14.6
Fargo, ND	7.8	6.5	7.5	11.4	16.5	13.8	18.0	18.5
Fort Collins, CO	7.2	5.1	5.3	8.9	14.9	13.5	19.9	25.2
Fort Wayne, IN	7.2	6.9	7.9	12.8	18.9	15.0	17.0	14.1
Fort Worth, TX	6.3	4.9	5.8	10.0	16.1	13.1	18.5	25.2
Gainesville, FL	13.2	8.5	9.1	12.6	16.2	11.1	14.0	15.2
Green Bay, WI	6.7	5.6	7.0	11.1	17.9	14.8	20.8	16.1
Greensboro, NC	10.1	8.0	8.3	13.7	17.6	12.6	16.3	13.5
Honolulu, HI	6.3	4.2	4.2	7.9	12.9	12.6	20.4	31.6
Houston, TX	7.7	6.2	6.7	10.5	15.9	12.5	16.9	23.6
Huntsville, AL	7.3	6.6	6.8	10.1	15.1	12.5	18.2	23.4
Indianapolis, IN	7.7	6.0	6.6	11.2	17.3	13.2	17.5	20.5
Jacksonville, FL	8.0	6.1	6.7	11.1	16.9	13.3	18.3	19.7
Kansas City, MO	6.9	5.7	6.4	10.4	16.6	13.3	19.1	21.3
Lafayette, LA	13.1	9.6	8.3	12.0	14.7	12.2	15.8	14.3
Las Vegas, NV	8.6	6.4	7.2	11.3	17.2	13.6	17.4	18.2
Lexington, KY	9.1	6.8	8.1	11.7	17.0	12.5	17.0	17.6
Lincoln, NE	7.4	6.1	7.7	12.0	17.9	13.8	18.0	17.1
Little Rock, AR	9.9	7.9	8.8	12.9	17.0	12.7	16.1	14.8
Los Angeles, CA	8.3	5.4	5.6	8.5	13.4	11.7	17.9	29.3
Louisville, KY	8.5	6.8	7.4	12.0	17.2	13.5	17.6	17.0
Madison, WI	6.5	5.2	6.1	9.4	16.1	13.5	19.4	23.8
Manchester, NH	4.5	4.5	4.6	8.8	14.6	12.8	19.9	30.3

Table continued on following page.

Metro Area	Percent of Households Earning							
	Under $15,000	$15,000 -$24,999	$25,000 -$34,999	$35,000 -$49,999	$50,000 -$74,999	$75,000 -$99,999	$100,000 -$149,999	$150,000 and up
McAllen, TX	14.0	11.7	10.0	12.6	16.7	11.7	13.8	9.5
Memphis, TN	10.9	8.0	8.2	12.2	16.7	12.1	16.0	15.9
Miami, FL	9.3	7.1	7.4	10.9	16.1	12.6	16.3	20.1
Midland, TX	8.0	4.3	5.9	9.4	13.7	11.6	18.6	28.4
Milwaukee, WI	8.5	6.5	7.4	10.4	16.3	13.1	17.8	20.0
Minneapolis, MN	5.5	4.5	4.9	8.5	14.5	13.0	20.3	28.9
Nashville, TN	6.6	5.5	5.8	10.7	16.8	13.9	19.0	21.7
New Orleans, LA	13.6	8.8	8.5	11.2	15.6	11.7	14.6	15.9
New York, NY	9.0	5.6	5.4	7.9	12.4	10.7	16.7	32.4
Oklahoma City, OK	8.9	6.7	7.8	11.9	17.6	13.5	17.0	16.6
Omaha, NE	6.9	5.6	6.3	10.1	16.6	13.2	19.6	21.7
Orlando, FL	7.3	6.3	7.3	11.1	17.7	13.5	18.0	18.9
Philadelphia, PA	8.4	5.8	6.0	8.9	14.0	11.9	17.9	27.1
Phoenix, AZ	6.6	5.0	5.9	10.1	16.6	13.9	19.3	22.5
Pittsburgh, PA	8.8	7.3	7.3	10.9	16.2	12.9	17.2	19.3
Portland, OR	6.4	4.7	5.1	8.8	14.6	13.1	19.7	27.6
Providence, RI	8.7	6.7	6.0	9.1	14.0	12.6	19.0	23.8
Provo, UT	4.4	4.1	4.6	8.5	15.1	15.0	22.7	25.6
Raleigh, NC	5.6	4.9	5.4	9.0	14.6	12.1	19.5	28.8
Reno, NV	6.9	5.4	6.0	9.9	16.4	13.4	20.5	21.6
Richmond, VA	7.2	5.6	5.9	10.0	16.3	12.7	18.9	23.4
Rochester, MN	5.2	5.4	5.6	9.0	16.3	13.4	20.4	24.7
Sacramento, CA	7.3	5.2	5.3	8.5	13.9	12.7	19.3	27.9
Saint Louis, MO	7.6	6.2	6.8	11.1	16.4	13.1	18.1	20.7
Saint Paul, MN	5.5	4.5	4.9	8.5	14.5	13.0	20.3	28.9
Salem, OR	7.7	6.4	6.9	11.0	17.3	13.4	19.7	17.5
Salt Lake City, UT	5.3	4.0	4.7	8.8	15.3	14.6	21.5	25.8
San Antonio, TX	8.2	6.5	7.5	10.9	17.2	13.3	17.4	18.9
San Diego, CA	6.3	4.7	5.0	7.8	13.1	12.1	19.1	31.9
San Francisco, CA	6.3	3.8	3.8	5.9	9.6	9.3	15.9	45.4
San Jose, CA	4.6	3.0	3.1	4.8	8.4	8.5	15.5	52.0
Santa Rosa, CA	5.9	4.1	4.7	7.8	13.4	12.7	19.3	32.2
Savannah, GA	8.5	6.0	7.5	11.0	17.3	13.8	18.5	17.4
Seattle, WA	5.6	3.8	4.2	7.0	12.6	11.5	19.2	36.1
Sioux Falls, SD	5.4	5.2	6.6	11.6	17.7	14.7	20.0	18.9
Tampa, FL	8.6	6.9	7.6	11.6	17.6	12.8	16.6	18.3
Tucson, AZ	9.3	7.6	8.5	12.3	16.7	12.8	16.7	16.0
Tulsa, OK	8.9	7.1	8.4	12.3	17.8	12.9	16.9	15.8
Virginia Beach, VA	7.5	5.5	6.6	10.0	17.3	13.3	19.2	20.7
Washington, DC	5.4	3.2	3.5	5.9	11.0	11.0	18.9	41.0
Wichita, KS	8.3	6.6	8.7	12.2	18.3	13.9	17.0	14.8
Wilmington, NC	8.2	6.4	6.8	11.5	18.0	13.4	17.6	18.0
Winston-Salem, NC	9.2	8.1	9.0	12.8	18.0	13.7	15.4	13.9
U.S.	8.5	6.6	6.8	10.4	15.7	12.7	17.4	21.9

Note: Figures cover the Metropolitan Statistical Area (MSA)
Source: U.S. Census Bureau, 2019-2023 American Community Survey 5-Year Estimates

Poverty Rate: City

City	All Ages	Under 18 Years Old	18 to 64 Years Old	65 Years and Over
Albuquerque, NM	16.0	20.8	15.3	12.6
Anchorage, AK	9.3	11.3	8.8	7.8
Ann Arbor, MI	23.0	13.5	27.9	6.0
Athens, GA	26.3	24.3	29.5	11.7
Atlanta, GA	17.9	25.9	15.6	18.7
Austin, TX	12.3	15.7	11.6	10.9
Baltimore, MD	20.1	26.4	17.8	20.9
Billings, MT	10.6	13.0	10.2	8.9
Boise City, ID	10.6	12.7	10.8	7.3
Boston, MA	16.9	21.8	15.0	21.0
Boulder, CO	21.8	9.7	26.8	6.2
Cape Coral, FL	9.8	13.1	9.1	9.2
Cedar Rapids, IA	11.8	14.3	11.9	7.8
Charleston, SC	12.0	15.4	12.2	7.3
Charlotte, NC	11.7	16.9	10.1	10.4
Chicago, IL	16.8	24.0	14.6	17.1
Cincinnati, OH	24.5	34.2	22.8	17.1
Clarksville, TN	12.8	16.8	11.8	7.7
Cleveland, OH	30.8	45.3	27.4	24.5
College Station, TX	28.6	14.8	34.5	5.8
Colorado Springs, CO	9.3	10.8	9.2	7.7
Columbia, MO	20.0	13.4	23.5	10.7
Columbia, SC	23.3	29.4	22.6	17.2
Columbus, OH	17.8	25.9	16.1	12.1
Dallas, TX	17.2	25.7	14.3	15.0
Davenport, IA	15.6	20.7	15.0	11.3
Denver, CO	11.2	14.9	10.2	11.5
Des Moines, IA	14.9	22.1	13.1	10.8
Detroit, MI	31.5	44.2	28.8	20.9
Durham, NC	12.2	16.9	11.5	8.2
El Paso, TX	18.4	24.8	15.4	20.0
Eugene, OR	18.2	15.1	21.4	9.4
Fargo, ND	12.8	14.6	13.7	6.0
Fort Collins, CO	16.0	9.2	19.1	8.0
Fort Wayne, IN	15.6	22.5	14.3	9.1
Fort Worth, TX	12.9	18.0	11.1	10.2
Gainesville, FL	28.0	18.0	32.8	11.4
Green Bay, WI	16.5	23.4	15.0	11.0
Greensboro, NC	18.4	26.0	16.5	14.2
Honolulu, HI	11.9	15.0	11.1	11.7
Houston, TX	19.7	29.9	16.6	16.0
Huntsville, AL	13.8	19.5	13.3	8.9
Indianapolis, IN	15.7	21.2	14.3	11.5
Jacksonville, FL	15.0	20.9	13.1	14.2
Kansas City, MO	14.6	20.5	12.9	12.4
Lafayette, LA	19.1	28.3	17.1	14.8
Las Vegas, NV	14.2	18.8	13.2	11.7
Lexington, KY	15.7	19.3	16.3	7.7
Lincoln, NE	12.6	13.0	13.6	8.0
Little Rock, AR	16.4	25.1	15.1	7.8
Los Angeles, CA	16.5	22.1	14.8	16.9
Louisville, KY	16.1	23.2	14.9	10.8
Madison, WI	16.2	13.1	18.7	7.0
Manchester, NH	10.7	17.2	9.3	9.5
McAllen, TX	20.2	27.2	17.6	17.0

Table continued on following page.

City	All Ages	Under 18 Years Old	18 to 64 Years Old	65 Years and Over
Memphis, TN	22.5	34.7	18.9	16.4
Miami, FL	19.2	23.4	15.3	31.4
Midland, TX	11.7	14.0	10.6	11.5
Milwaukee, WI	23.3	32.5	20.7	16.7
Minneapolis, MN	16.4	19.8	15.7	14.2
Nashville, TN	14.1	21.2	12.5	11.2
New Orleans, LA	22.6	32.2	20.1	20.7
New York, NY	17.4	23.2	15.1	18.9
Oklahoma City, OK	15.2	20.6	14.2	9.4
Omaha, NE	12.8	15.9	12.3	9.3
Orlando, FL	15.5	23.0	12.9	16.8
Philadelphia, PA	22.0	30.1	19.5	21.1
Phoenix, AZ	14.3	20.3	12.5	11.7
Pittsburgh, PA	19.5	29.5	18.4	14.1
Portland, OR	12.8	14.5	12.5	11.8
Providence, RI	20.1	26.0	18.2	19.9
Provo, UT	22.3	12.8	26.3	9.4
Raleigh, NC	11.4	14.6	10.9	9.1
Reno, NV	12.5	13.9	12.2	11.8
Richmond, VA	18.8	28.3	17.2	14.6
Rochester, MN	9.1	9.0	9.4	7.6
Sacramento, CA	14.4	17.9	13.5	12.8
Saint Louis, MO	19.8	26.9	18.2	17.8
Saint Paul, MN	15.7	22.9	13.8	11.7
Salem, OR	14.7	17.2	14.4	11.8
Salt Lake City, UT	13.4	12.3	14.1	11.0
San Antonio, TX	17.1	24.8	14.8	14.2
San Diego, CA	11.1	12.3	11.0	10.2
San Francisco, CA	10.6	8.2	9.6	16.4
San Jose, CA	7.8	7.6	7.4	10.5
Santa Rosa, CA	9.5	10.8	9.1	9.5
Savannah, GA	19.5	28.9	17.6	14.0
Seattle, WA	9.9	8.6	9.7	12.3
Sioux Falls, SD	9.6	12.3	9.1	7.1
Tampa, FL	15.9	20.3	13.5	21.2
Tucson, AZ	18.8	24.3	18.7	12.5
Tulsa, OK	18.6	27.0	17.3	10.4
Virginia Beach, VA	8.4	11.2	8.0	5.9
Washington, DC	14.5	20.4	12.9	14.6
Wichita, KS	15.9	21.6	15.0	10.3
Wilmington, NC	16.3	18.1	17.3	11.0
Winston-Salem, NC	17.9	27.1	16.0	10.7
U.S.	12.4	16.3	11.6	10.4

Note: Figures are percentage of people whose income during the past 12 months was below the poverty level
Source: U.S. Census Bureau, 2019-2023 American Community Survey 5-Year Estimates

Poverty Rate: Metro Area

Metro Area	All Ages	Under 18 Years Old	18 to 64 Years Old	65 Years and Over
Albuquerque, NM	15.1	19.6	14.5	12.0
Anchorage, AK	9.6	11.6	9.1	7.9
Ann Arbor, MI	13.8	12.5	16.2	5.9
Athens, GA	19.7	19.0	22.1	10.1
Atlanta, GA	11.0	15.0	9.7	9.3
Austin, TX	9.9	11.5	9.6	8.7
Baltimore, MD	9.9	12.0	9.0	10.2
Billings, MT	10.0	12.0	9.9	8.2
Boise City, ID	9.1	10.7	8.9	7.7
Boston, MA	8.9	9.7	8.3	10.3
Boulder, CO	11.4	7.5	13.7	7.1
Cape Coral, FL	11.7	17.1	11.2	9.5
Cedar Rapids, IA	9.7	11.5	9.7	7.5
Charleston, SC	11.2	15.6	10.3	9.0
Charlotte, NC	10.5	14.2	9.4	9.3
Chicago, IL	11.1	14.8	10.0	10.2
Cincinnati, OH	11.6	14.7	11.1	9.2
Clarksville, TN	13.2	16.4	12.3	10.5
Cleveland, OH	13.6	19.3	12.6	10.6
College Station, TX	22.6	19.9	26.0	8.5
Colorado Springs, CO	8.5	10.2	8.2	6.9
Columbia, MO	16.5	14.6	18.8	9.0
Columbia, SC	14.7	19.8	13.9	10.6
Columbus, OH	12.2	16.5	11.4	8.7
Dallas, TX	10.5	14.5	9.2	9.3
Davenport, IA	12.4	16.9	12.0	8.3
Denver, CO	8.2	10.3	7.6	7.6
Des Moines, IA	8.9	11.0	8.5	7.1
Detroit, MI	13.2	19.1	12.0	10.2
Durham, NC	12.3	16.2	12.2	7.9
El Paso, TX	18.9	25.1	15.8	20.6
Eugene, OR	15.3	14.3	17.4	9.7
Fargo, ND	11.4	11.8	12.2	6.7
Fort Collins, CO	11.1	8.5	12.9	7.1
Fort Wayne, IN	11.8	16.1	11.1	7.3
Fort Worth, TX	10.5	14.5	9.2	9.3
Gainesville, FL	18.9	16.3	21.8	10.7
Green Bay, WI	9.5	11.6	9.3	7.5
Greensboro, NC	15.3	21.4	14.1	11.6
Honolulu, HI	9.1	11.4	8.5	8.7
Houston, TX	13.6	19.1	11.7	11.3
Huntsville, AL	10.4	13.1	9.8	9.1
Indianapolis, IN	10.5	13.6	9.8	8.3
Jacksonville, FL	12.1	16.9	10.9	10.2
Kansas City, MO	10.0	13.2	9.2	8.5
Lafayette, LA	18.5	25.0	16.8	14.8
Las Vegas, NV	13.2	18.1	12.1	10.6
Lexington, KY	14.0	17.4	14.1	8.6
Lincoln, NE	11.4	11.3	12.5	7.6
Little Rock, AR	14.2	19.7	13.5	8.7
Los Angeles, CA	12.6	16.0	11.4	13.1
Louisville, KY	12.3	17.0	11.4	9.2
Madison, WI	10.0	8.5	11.4	6.1
Manchester, NH	6.5	8.1	6.0	6.7
McAllen, TX	27.2	37.1	22.6	22.9

Table continued on following page.

Metro Area	All Ages	Under 18 Years Old	18 to 64 Years Old	65 Years and Over
Memphis, TN	16.3	24.2	14.0	12.2
Miami, FL	13.1	16.9	11.0	15.9
Midland, TX	10.6	12.7	9.3	11.6
Milwaukee, WI	12.4	17.0	11.2	10.3
Minneapolis, MN	8.2	9.6	7.7	7.7
Nashville, TN	10.4	13.6	9.5	8.9
New Orleans, LA	18.3	25.6	16.5	14.9
New York, NY	12.4	16.4	10.9	13.0
Oklahoma City, OK	13.9	18.3	13.3	8.8
Omaha, NE	9.5	11.2	9.1	8.1
Orlando, FL	11.8	15.0	11.0	10.5
Philadelphia, PA	11.7	15.7	10.6	10.3
Phoenix, AZ	11.2	15.1	10.3	9.2
Pittsburgh, PA	10.9	14.4	10.5	8.9
Portland, OR	9.5	10.5	9.4	9.0
Providence, RI	11.2	14.2	10.3	10.6
Provo, UT	8.7	7.2	10.0	5.5
Raleigh, NC	8.6	10.3	8.0	7.9
Reno, NV	10.7	12.1	10.3	10.3
Richmond, VA	10.0	13.4	9.3	8.0
Rochester, MN	7.8	8.3	7.8	7.1
Sacramento, CA	11.6	13.6	11.4	9.3
Saint Louis, MO	10.3	13.3	9.7	8.7
Saint Paul, MN	8.2	9.6	7.7	7.7
Salem, OR	12.9	16.0	12.5	10.2
Salt Lake City, UT	8.1	8.8	8.0	7.5
San Antonio, TX	13.4	18.5	11.9	11.4
San Diego, CA	10.4	12.0	10.0	9.4
San Francisco, CA	8.7	8.8	8.2	10.4
San Jose, CA	6.9	6.6	6.5	9.0
Santa Rosa, CA	8.6	9.3	8.4	8.4
Savannah, GA	12.4	16.6	11.4	9.9
Seattle, WA	8.4	9.5	7.9	8.8
Sioux Falls, SD	8.1	9.7	7.7	6.8
Tampa, FL	12.2	15.5	11.3	11.9
Tucson, AZ	14.4	18.7	14.9	8.9
Tulsa, OK	13.7	18.9	12.9	8.9
Virginia Beach, VA	10.9	15.4	9.9	8.4
Washington, DC	7.9	9.8	7.2	7.6
Wichita, KS	13.1	17.4	12.4	8.8
Wilmington, NC	11.1	13.9	11.9	7.0
Winston-Salem, NC	13.9	21.2	12.5	9.7
U.S.	12.4	16.3	11.6	10.4

Note: Figures are percentage of people whose income during the past 12 months was below the poverty level;
Figures cover the Metropolitan Statistical Area (MSA)
Source: U.S. Census Bureau, 2019-2023 American Community Survey 5-Year Estimates

Employment by Industry

Metro Area	(A)	(B)	(C)	(D)	(E)	(F)	(G)	(H)	(I)	(J)	(K)	(L)	(M)	(N)
Albuquerque, NM	6.6	n/a	4.6	19.8	1.3	10.4	4.0	n/a	3.1	17.3	16.0	10.3	3.9	2.7
Anchorage, AK	7.3	6.2	4.0	19.3	1.7	10.9	1.3	1.1	3.7	19.1	11.0	10.9	8.0	2.8
Ann Arbor, MI	2.2	n/a	2.9	37.3	2.5	7.1	5.1	n/a	2.8	15.0	12.4	7.3	2.2	3.1
Athens, GA	3.9	n/a	3.3	28.7	0.7	11.4	6.7	n/a	3.6	16.0	8.8	11.1	1.8	4.0
Atlanta, GA[1]	4.2	4.1	7.0	11.9	3.8	9.7	5.3	0.1	3.6	14.6	18.3	9.4	7.1	5.1
Austin, TX	6.5	n/a	6.5	15.3	3.6	10.7	5.3	n/a	3.9	12.0	20.5	9.0	2.7	4.1
Baltimore, MD	5.4	n/a	5.3	16.6	1.1	8.4	3.9	n/a	3.7	20.0	17.5	9.0	5.3	3.7
Billings, MT	8.0	n/a	5.4	11.1	0.9	14.6	4.3	n/a	4.2	18.0	9.8	12.6	5.0	6.0
Boise City, ID	9.1	n/a	5.8	13.3	1.1	10.0	7.6	n/a	3.5	15.4	14.6	10.0	4.6	4.7
Boston, MA[1]	4.1	n/a	9.6	12.2	2.6	10.5	2.8	n/a	3.6	24.6	16.3	7.8	3.4	2.5
Boulder, CO	2.7	n/a	3.3	19.7	4.0	9.6	10.0	n/a	4.3	13.2	20.1	8.2	1.1	3.7
Cape Coral, FL	13.6	n/a	4.9	15.3	1.1	13.0	2.6	n/a	4.0	11.5	14.2	14.3	2.5	3.0
Cedar Rapids, IA	6.3	n/a	6.6	11.9	2.0	8.4	14.2	n/a	3.6	16.3	11.1	10.4	5.1	4.1
Charleston, SC	5.7	n/a	5.1	16.7	1.8	12.4	8.1	n/a	3.9	11.9	15.8	10.9	4.7	3.0
Charlotte, NC	5.9	n/a	8.8	12.9	1.9	10.9	7.7	n/a	4.0	11.1	16.2	10.0	6.1	4.7
Chicago, IL[1]	3.4	3.4	7.2	11.2	1.8	9.8	7.3	<0.1	4.1	17.0	18.0	8.7	6.5	4.9
Cincinnati, OH	4.6	n/a	6.8	11.6	1.1	10.6	10.4	n/a	3.6	15.9	15.3	9.0	5.8	5.3
Clarksville, TN	4.5	n/a	3.8	20.6	1.3	12.1	12.9	n/a	3.3	13.1	8.4	13.2	4.5	2.3
Cleveland, OH	3.7	n/a	6.5	12.5	1.3	9.5	11.6	n/a	3.5	19.7	13.9	9.1	3.8	4.9
College Station, TX	5.3	n/a	3.3	35.1	1.1	14.4	4.2	n/a	2.8	10.9	9.8	9.1	1.9	2.2
Colorado Springs, CO	5.4	n/a	5.8	17.9	1.5	12.4	3.6	n/a	7.0	14.6	16.0	10.2	3.8	2.0
Columbia, MO	3.6	3.5	7.6	31.5	1.1	10.6	4.7	0.1	2.8	13.9	9.1	10.1	2.6	2.5
Columbia, SC	4.3	n/a	8.3	19.4	1.1	9.4	7.4	n/a	4.2	13.9	13.6	10.5	4.2	3.7
Columbus, OH	4.5	n/a	6.9	16.6	1.5	9.1	6.5	n/a	3.8	15.5	16.3	9.2	6.7	3.6
Dallas, TX[1]	5.4	n/a	10.0	11.3	2.5	9.4	6.6	n/a	3.1	11.5	20.2	9.0	5.4	5.6
Davenport, IA	5.7	n/a	4.1	14.4	0.8	9.7	12.8	n/a	3.7	15.0	11.3	11.7	4.2	6.5
Denver, CO	6.9	n/a	7.1	13.7	3.0	10.4	4.0	n/a	4.2	12.9	19.4	8.5	5.3	4.7
Des Moines, IA	5.9	n/a	13.6	12.8	1.5	8.8	5.4	n/a	3.3	15.2	13.4	10.6	4.8	4.8
Detroit, MI[1]	4.0	n/a	6.2	9.6	1.4	9.1	12.1	n/a	3.8	16.2	18.4	9.9	5.2	4.1
Durham, NC	3.1	n/a	4.8	19.3	1.6	7.8	7.9	n/a	3.7	21.8	17.8	6.9	2.4	2.8
El Paso, TX	4.5	n/a	4.1	20.8	1.8	11.6	4.8	n/a	2.8	15.5	12.6	11.4	6.0	4.0
Eugene, OR	5.0	4.4	5.2	19.8	1.2	10.1	8.5	0.6	3.1	18.6	10.9	11.7	2.3	3.5
Fargo, ND	6.0	n/a	7.1	14.0	1.5	9.6	8.0	n/a	3.3	19.6	9.5	10.3	5.2	5.9
Fort Collins, CO	6.0	n/a	3.8	26.3	1.3	12.1	8.0	n/a	3.6	11.3	11.6	10.5	2.5	3.2
Fort Wayne, IN	5.5	n/a	5.1	9.6	0.8	8.8	15.8	n/a	5.6	19.2	9.6	10.4	5.0	4.6
Fort Worth, TX[1]	7.1	n/a	6.4	11.7	1.0	11.1	8.9	n/a	3.5	12.9	12.8	10.9	8.7	5.0
Gainesville, FL	4.3	n/a	4.0	28.7	1.2	10.5	3.1	n/a	3.0	19.7	10.7	10.0	2.8	2.1
Green Bay, WI	4.8	n/a	4.7	11.8	0.9	9.8	18.1	n/a	4.4	15.8	10.5	9.5	4.8	4.9
Greensboro, NC	5.3	n/a	4.3	12.6	1.0	9.9	12.8	n/a	3.7	14.9	12.6	11.3	5.7	5.8
Honolulu, HI	6.0	n/a	4.5	21.0	1.5	15.8	2.1	n/a	4.4	14.9	12.1	9.3	5.5	2.9
Houston, TX	9.0	6.7	5.2	13.4	0.9	10.4	6.9	2.3	3.9	13.3	16.4	9.6	5.8	5.2
Huntsville, AL	4.0	n/a	3.1	20.8	1.0	8.4	12.4	n/a	3.3	9.0	23.6	9.9	2.2	2.5
Indianapolis, IN	5.5	5.5	6.3	12.6	1.0	9.1	8.1	0.1	4.1	15.8	15.7	8.8	8.3	4.7
Jacksonville, FL	6.6	6.6	9.0	10.1	1.8	11.3	4.5	<0.1	3.6	16.3	14.9	11.0	7.3	3.7
Kansas City, MO	5.3	5.2	6.9	13.4	1.5	9.6	7.9	0.1	3.7	15.3	16.0	9.9	6.0	4.6
Lafayette, LA	9.6	5.5	4.7	12.6	0.8	11.1	7.7	4.1	3.6	18.3	11.3	12.6	3.3	4.4
Las Vegas, NV	6.8	6.8	5.3	10.7	1.3	25.8	2.6	<0.1	3.0	11.4	14.3	9.8	6.7	2.3
Lexington, KY	4.9	n/a	4.0	19.6	1.0	10.7	10.5	n/a	4.8	13.2	13.5	9.6	4.2	3.9
Lincoln, NE	5.4	n/a	5.4	21.8	2.0	9.7	7.4	n/a	4.3	17.0	10.3	9.3	5.3	2.2
Little Rock, AR	5.4	n/a	7.1	17.8	1.3	8.5	5.4	n/a	4.8	16.9	12.4	10.0	6.0	4.6
Los Angeles, CA[1]	3.2	3.2	4.5	12.9	4.1	11.6	6.5	<0.1	3.4	21.4	14.4	8.9	4.9	4.2
Louisville, KY	5.1	n/a	6.4	10.6	1.1	9.6	11.8	n/a	3.8	15.4	12.2	9.5	9.8	4.7
Madison, WI	4.6	n/a	5.5	22.4	5.0	8.4	8.7	n/a	5.0	13.1	12.2	9.1	2.5	3.6
Manchester, NH	4.3	n/a	5.6	10.8	2.4	9.0	12.0	n/a	3.8	20.1	14.1	12.5	2.4	3.1
McAllen, TX	3.0	n/a	3.3	20.3	1.0	9.8	2.3	n/a	2.2	30.1	8.9	12.7	3.3	3.1
Memphis, TN	3.8	n/a	4.5	13.2	0.8	9.3	6.1	n/a	4.2	15.2	13.5	9.4	14.1	5.8

Table continued on following page.

Appendix A: Comparative Statistics

Metro Area	(A)	(B)	(C)	(D)	(E)	(F)	(G)	(H)	(I)	(J)	(K)	(L)	(M)	(N)
Miami, FL[1]	4.5	4.5	7.1	10.6	1.7	11.4	3.5	<0.1	3.7	16.6	15.7	11.2	7.8	6.2
Midland, TX	33.1	n/a	5.0	8.7	0.8	9.2	3.7	n/a	3.4	7.7	9.5	7.9	5.2	5.8
Milwaukee, WI	4.3	4.2	5.5	9.6	1.3	9.2	12.8	0.1	5.1	20.8	14.0	9.0	4.0	4.5
Minneapolis, MN	4.3	n/a	7.2	13.2	1.4	8.9	10.0	n/a	3.9	19.0	14.4	9.2	4.4	4.2
Nashville, TN	5.5	n/a	6.8	11.2	2.7	11.2	7.4	n/a	4.2	15.1	16.1	9.2	6.4	4.2
New Orleans, LA	6.0	5.6	5.0	11.6	1.4	14.5	5.5	0.4	4.3	20.3	12.9	9.3	5.6	3.6
New York, NY[1]	3.3	n/a	9.8	12.5	4.0	9.0	2.1	n/a	3.8	25.2	16.1	7.3	3.7	3.3
Oklahoma City, OK	6.5	5.0	5.2	19.0	0.9	11.4	4.9	1.4	4.3	16.7	12.7	10.2	4.7	3.5
Omaha, NE	6.2	n/a	7.7	13.5	1.7	10.7	6.9	n/a	3.5	17.6	13.6	10.2	5.2	3.2
Orlando, FL	6.3	6.3	6.1	8.9	1.8	19.2	3.5	<0.1	3.7	12.9	19.1	10.5	4.5	3.5
Philadelphia, PA[1]	2.4	n/a	6.1	13.0	1.8	9.3	3.1	n/a	4.2	32.9	14.4	6.7	3.9	2.2
Phoenix, AZ	7.3	7.2	8.5	10.5	1.6	10.7	6.0	0.1	3.2	16.9	15.6	10.3	5.3	4.1
Pittsburgh, PA	5.3	4.7	6.5	9.9	1.7	9.8	7.1	0.7	4.1	22.2	15.4	10.0	4.5	3.5
Portland, OR	6.4	6.3	5.8	12.9	2.1	9.4	9.6	0.1	3.5	16.6	15.5	9.3	4.3	4.6
Providence, RI	4.5	4.5	5.5	13.3	1.0	10.7	8.5	<0.1	4.2	21.6	12.1	11.0	3.6	3.8
Provo, UT	9.5	n/a	4.0	11.9	3.9	9.1	7.8	n/a	2.3	22.1	14.4	10.8	2.0	2.2
Raleigh, NC	7.0	n/a	5.5	14.4	3.3	10.5	4.5	n/a	4.4	13.8	19.4	10.1	3.5	3.8
Reno, NV	8.8	8.5	4.2	12.8	1.4	14.2	10.6	0.3	2.7	11.6	12.1	9.4	8.8	3.5
Richmond, VA	5.9	n/a	7.9	15.7	0.9	9.3	4.4	n/a	4.6	15.3	17.0	9.2	6.0	3.8
Rochester, MN	4.1	n/a	2.2	10.5	0.8	8.2	6.9	n/a	3.0	45.2	5.3	9.6	2.1	2.1
Sacramento, CA	6.9	6.8	4.2	24.0	0.9	10.1	3.6	<0.1	3.5	18.7	12.2	9.2	4.0	2.6
Saint Louis, MO	5.4	n/a	6.7	11.2	2.0	9.7	8.2	n/a	3.6	19.5	14.9	9.6	4.8	4.6
Saint Paul, MN	4.3	n/a	7.2	13.2	1.4	8.9	10.0	n/a	3.9	19.0	14.4	9.2	4.4	4.2
Salem, OR	7.4	7.1	3.2	24.5	1.0	8.5	6.2	0.3	3.0	19.9	10.0	10.1	3.9	2.2
Salt Lake City, UT	7.2	n/a	7.7	14.3	2.8	8.3	7.7	n/a	2.7	12.2	17.1	9.2	6.0	4.9
San Antonio, TX	6.3	5.7	8.5	16.1	1.6	12.2	5.2	0.6	3.5	15.2	13.3	10.7	4.0	3.2
San Diego, CA	5.8	5.7	4.5	16.6	1.3	12.9	7.0	<0.1	3.6	16.6	17.0	9.1	2.9	2.7
San Francisco, CA[1]	3.4	3.3	6.7	12.4	9.7	10.6	2.6	<0.1	3.3	14.3	25.1	5.5	4.4	2.0
San Jose, CA	4.6	4.5	3.1	8.8	8.1	9.0	10.6	<0.1	2.4	18.4	24.6	6.5	1.5	2.5
Santa Rosa, CA	8.0	7.9	3.3	13.9	1.3	12.4	10.5	0.1	3.8	18.6	11.5	11.2	2.3	3.2
Savannah, GA	4.8	n/a	3.7	12.3	0.7	13.1	11.0	n/a	4.1	14.2	11.2	11.5	9.8	3.7
Seattle, WA[1]	4.8	4.8	4.9	12.8	8.7	9.3	6.2	<0.1	3.2	13.7	20.9	7.2	4.5	4.0
Sioux Falls, SD	6.8	n/a	8.2	9.5	1.5	9.1	8.7	n/a	3.7	21.6	9.7	11.4	4.6	5.2
Tampa, FL[1]	n/a	6.6	10.2	10.4	1.8	10.3	3.7	n/a	3.3	16.0	18.1	10.9	4.3	4.3
Tucson, AZ	5.7	5.0	4.3	19.9	1.3	11.2	7.0	0.6	3.7	17.9	11.1	10.9	5.1	2.0
Tulsa, OK	6.4	5.7	5.1	13.2	1.0	9.9	11.1	0.7	4.5	17.0	13.2	10.3	4.6	3.7
Virginia Beach, VA	5.0	n/a	4.9	20.1	1.0	11.1	7.0	n/a	4.3	15.4	14.8	10.0	3.9	2.4
Washington, DC[1]	4.2	n/a	3.3	30.2	1.8	9.9	0.8	n/a	6.7	14.8	19.4	5.6	1.9	1.4
Wichita, KS	5.5	n/a	4.1	14.0	1.1	10.2	16.7	n/a	4.0	15.9	10.8	10.1	4.4	3.2
Wilmington, NC	7.3	n/a	4.9	12.9	1.6	15.5	4.5	n/a	4.6	16.9	12.2	13.3	3.6	2.8
Winston-Salem, NC	4.7	n/a	4.5	12.3	0.7	10.7	11.7	n/a	3.9	21.5	11.9	11.4	3.6	3.2
U.S.	5.5	5.1	5.8	14.9	1.9	10.4	8.0	0.4	3.7	16.9	14.2	10.0	4.8	3.9

Note: All figures are percentages covering non-farm employment as of December 2024 and are not seasonally adjusted; Figures cover the Metropolitan Statistical Area (MSA) except where noted; (1) Metropolitan Division; (A) Construction, Mining, and Logging (some areas report Construction separate from Mining and Logging); (B) Construction; (C) Financial Activities; (D) Government; (E) Information; (F) Leisure and Hospitality; (G) Manufacturing; (H) Mining and Logging; (I) Other Services; (J) Private Education and Health Services; (K) Professional and Business Services; (L) Retail Trade; (M) Transportation and Utilities; (N) Wholesale Trade; n/a not available
Source: Bureau of Labor Statistics, Current Employment Statistics, Employment, Hours, and Earnings, December 2024

Appendix A: Comparative Statistics

Labor Force, Employment and Job Growth: City

City	Civilian Labor Force			Workers Employed		
	Dec. 2023	Dec. 2024	% Chg.	Dec. 2023	Dec. 2024	% Chg.
Albuquerque, NM	295,286	297,348	0.7	286,112	286,738	0.2
Anchorage, AK	153,020	155,068	1.3	147,538	149,604	1.4
Ann Arbor, MI	66,518	68,304	2.6	64,986	66,059	1.6
Athens, GA	61,309	61,837	0.8	59,338	59,852	0.8
Atlanta, GA	278,364	279,245	0.3	268,161	267,879	-0.1
Austin, TX	692,732	711,010	2.6	671,863	690,459	2.7
Baltimore, MD	276,136	279,771	1.3	267,011	268,805	0.6
Billings, MT	59,483	58,785	-1.1	57,662	57,121	-0.9
Boise City, ID	146,113	151,831	3.9	142,029	147,110	3.5
Boston, MA	403,771	411,958	2.0	390,365	395,765	1.3
Boulder, CO	68,299	68,728	0.6	66,297	66,171	-0.1
Cape Coral, FL	100,486	101,752	1.2	97,397	98,477	1.1
Cedar Rapids, IA	70,086	70,636	0.7	67,783	68,276	0.7
Charleston, SC	81,443	83,687	2.7	79,209	80,914	2.1
Charlotte, NC	531,420	537,158	1.0	513,465	519,577	1.1
Chicago, IL	1,391,216	1,432,019	2.9	1,330,946	1,363,159	2.4
Cincinnati, OH	150,446	153,060	1.7	145,104	146,196	0.7
Clarksville, TN	65,211	66,900	2.5	62,910	64,067	1.8
Cleveland, OH	154,882	158,055	2.0	148,680	151,454	1.8
College Station, TX	70,826	73,610	3.9	68,915	71,605	3.9
Colorado Springs, CO	254,636	258,951	1.6	245,377	247,188	0.7
Columbia, MO	69,206	70,699	2.1	67,566	68,998	2.1
Columbia, SC	59,838	60,914	1.8	57,599	58,055	0.7
Columbus, OH	490,638	493,589	0.6	474,627	473,223	-0.3
Dallas, TX	753,950	773,828	2.6	727,021	746,370	2.6
Davenport, IA	49,490	49,873	0.7	47,766	47,656	-0.2
Denver, CO	439,297	444,521	1.1	421,359	422,120	0.1
Des Moines, IA	113,506	113,721	0.1	109,944	109,495	-0.4
Detroit, MI	252,407	254,935	1.0	235,064	230,371	-2.0
Durham, NC	161,695	163,549	1.1	156,943	158,778	1.1
El Paso, TX	321,869	330,289	2.6	309,686	317,905	2.6
Eugene, OR	86,438	87,547	1.2	82,952	83,877	1.1
Fargo, ND	75,385	76,672	1.7	73,971	74,762	1.0
Fort Collins, CO	104,877	106,076	1.1	101,643	102,156	0.5
Fort Wayne, IN	130,643	133,106	1.8	126,751	127,554	0.6
Fort Worth, TX	492,810	506,338	2.7	474,900	487,778	2.7
Gainesville, FL	71,265	72,407	1.6	68,797	69,722	1.3
Green Bay, WI	53,842	54,171	0.6	52,558	52,661	0.2
Greensboro, NC	145,300	143,645	-1.1	139,667	137,971	-1.2
Honolulu, HI	458,516	467,102	1.8	447,781	454,669	1.5
Houston, TX	1,221,575	1,251,524	2.4	1,168,408	1,201,001	2.7
Huntsville, AL	110,121	113,202	2.8	107,585	109,886	2.1
Indianapolis, IN	468,727	483,276	3.1	453,754	464,036	2.2
Jacksonville, FL	491,737	495,209	0.7	476,373	479,227	0.6
Kansas City, MO	261,274	264,629	1.2	252,452	255,316	1.1
Lafayette, LA	59,760	59,993	0.3	57,644	57,720	0.1
Las Vegas, NV	330,736	337,672	2.1	312,658	317,296	1.4
Lexington, KY	178,351	182,353	2.2	172,195	175,041	1.6
Lincoln, NE	164,857	168,647	2.3	161,204	164,571	2.0
Little Rock, AR	100,778	102,786	1.9	97,463	99,326	1.9
Los Angeles, CA	2,074,549	2,094,633	0.9	1,964,638	1,972,226	0.3
Louisville, KY	394,849	401,525	1.6	379,511	382,789	0.8
Madison, WI	167,700	168,775	0.6	164,752	165,214	0.2
Manchester, NH	64,039	66,140	3.2	62,588	64,103	2.4
McAllen, TX	72,499	74,052	2.1	69,572	71,063	2.1

Table continued on following page.

City	Civilian Labor Force			Workers Employed		
	Dec. 2023	Dec. 2024	% Chg.	Dec. 2023	Dec. 2024	% Chg.
Memphis, TN	283,933	286,196	0.8	271,779	271,426	-0.1
Miami, FL	247,114	249,197	0.8	242,276	243,343	0.4
Midland, TX	93,937	96,111	2.3	91,915	93,872	2.1
Milwaukee, WI	273,443	274,723	0.4	264,071	263,797	-0.1
Minneapolis, MN	244,672	245,657	0.4	238,965	239,886	0.3
Nashville, TN	421,198	426,189	1.1	411,304	413,569	0.5
New Orleans, LA	173,294	173,800	0.2	165,506	165,809	0.1
New York, NY	4,197,201	4,289,830	2.2	4,004,371	4,065,287	1.5
Oklahoma City, OK	352,331	357,109	1.3	341,478	346,634	1.5
Omaha, NE	251,851	256,156	1.7	245,154	248,481	1.3
Orlando, FL	181,418	181,948	0.2	176,377	176,719	0.1
Philadelphia, PA	750,976	745,485	-0.7	719,837	713,546	-0.8
Phoenix, AZ	913,817	927,572	1.5	887,451	898,365	1.2
Pittsburgh, PA	152,654	151,757	-0.5	148,435	147,774	-0.4
Portland, OR	386,871	388,825	0.5	372,067	372,849	0.2
Providence, RI	90,820	92,307	1.6	86,757	87,271	0.5
Provo, UT	73,763	74,411	0.8	72,156	72,484	0.4
Raleigh, NC	276,576	277,882	0.4	267,801	269,378	0.5
Reno, NV	144,664	147,939	2.2	138,887	141,134	1.6
Richmond, VA	123,724	126,447	2.2	120,027	122,541	2.0
Rochester, MN	68,874	73,886	7.2	67,640	72,557	7.2
Sacramento, CA	246,247	248,837	1.0	234,662	236,718	0.8
Saint Louis, MO	150,472	152,715	1.4	144,679	146,505	1.2
Saint Paul, MN	156,382	157,144	0.4	152,569	153,219	0.4
Salem, OR	86,857	88,580	1.9	83,316	84,776	1.7
Salt Lake City, UT	128,957	131,406	1.9	125,261	127,540	1.8
San Antonio, TX	780,314	813,666	4.2	753,069	786,995	4.5
San Diego, CA	730,171	734,863	0.6	701,246	703,991	0.3
San Francisco, CA	564,822	561,032	-0.6	545,573	541,446	-0.7
San Jose, CA	550,266	551,509	0.2	528,718	529,659	0.1
Santa Rosa, CA	87,410	88,152	0.8	84,056	84,516	0.5
Savannah, GA	69,925	69,887	0.0	67,803	67,610	-0.2
Seattle, WA	511,941	526,448	2.8	495,245	511,570	3.3
Sioux Falls, SD	113,602	115,243	1.4	111,615	112,947	1.1
Tampa, FL	222,684	223,321	0.2	215,665	215,892	0.1
Tucson, AZ	263,211	266,440	1.2	254,477	256,864	0.9
Tulsa, OK	206,897	209,496	1.2	199,811	203,133	1.6
Virginia Beach, VA	237,550	239,534	0.8	231,972	233,678	0.7
Washington, DC	411,135	417,094	1.4	391,912	396,492	1.1
Wichita, KS	194,170	197,795	1.8	188,497	190,038	0.8
Wilmington, NC	69,827	69,943	0.1	67,604	67,846	0.3
Winston-Salem, NC	118,508	118,217	-0.2	114,267	114,055	-0.1
U.S.	166,661,000	167,746,000	0.7	160,754,000	161,294,000	0.3

Note: Data is not seasonally adjusted and covers workers 16 years of age and older
Source: Bureau of Labor Statistics, Local Area Unemployment Statistics

Labor Force, Employment and Job Growth: Metro Area

Metro Area	Civilian Labor Force			Workers Employed		
	Dec. 2023	Dec. 2024	% Chg.	Dec. 2023	Dec. 2024	% Chg.
Albuquerque, NM	459,168	462,519	0.7	444,472	445,570	0.2
Anchorage, AK	203,512	206,186	1.3	195,498	198,110	1.3
Ann Arbor, MI	201,644	207,512	2.9	195,986	199,223	1.6
Athens, GA	103,836	104,775	0.9	100,776	101,698	0.9
Atlanta, GA[1]	2,520,105	2,525,607	0.2	2,441,223	2,439,016	0.0
Austin, TX	1,480,563	1,521,172	2.7	1,434,717	1,474,387	2.7
Baltimore, MD	1,496,175	1,509,109	0.8	1,460,563	1,468,370	0.5
Billings, MT	99,307	98,165	-1.1	96,370	95,349	-1.0
Boise City, ID	432,273	448,781	3.8	418,731	433,330	3.4
Boston, MA[1]	1,158,650	1,182,153	2.0	1,119,472	1,135,105	1.4
Boulder, CO	204,348	205,677	0.6	197,756	197,382	-0.1
Cape Coral, FL	376,769	381,593	1.2	365,271	369,323	1.1
Cedar Rapids, IA	141,248	142,473	0.8	136,873	137,885	0.7
Charleston, SC	433,190	445,523	2.8	421,406	430,483	2.1
Charlotte, NC	1,472,294	1,492,625	1.3	1,424,686	1,443,425	1.3
Chicago, IL[1]	3,780,647	3,890,015	2.8	3,630,697	3,719,159	2.4
Cincinnati, OH	1,154,630	1,170,746	1.4	1,116,229	1,123,236	0.6
Clarksville, TN	126,537	129,924	2.6	121,844	124,244	1.9
Cleveland, OH	1,067,052	1,088,179	1.9	1,033,451	1,051,761	1.7
College Station, TX	154,708	160,796	3.9	150,546	156,418	3.9
Colorado Springs, CO	380,947	387,217	1.6	366,679	369,336	0.7
Columbia, MO	113,118	115,648	2.2	110,484	112,817	2.1
Columbia, SC	419,770	426,736	1.6	406,945	410,354	0.8
Columbus, OH	1,134,646	1,141,335	0.5	1,099,340	1,096,249	-0.2
Dallas, TX[1]	3,019,102	3,099,037	2.6	2,914,521	2,992,023	2.6
Davenport, IA	184,725	184,714	0.0	177,254	176,542	-0.4
Denver, CO	1,731,722	1,751,255	1.1	1,667,215	1,670,077	0.1
Des Moines, IA	394,185	394,876	0.1	384,347	382,847	-0.3
Detroit, MI[1]	816,930	814,679	-0.2	784,713	769,048	-2.0
Durham, NC	323,131	326,577	1.0	313,852	317,268	1.0
El Paso, TX	388,422	398,643	2.6	372,959	382,859	2.6
Eugene, OR	184,890	187,239	1.2	177,117	179,091	1.1
Fargo, ND	149,293	152,175	1.9	146,516	148,732	1.5
Fort Collins, CO	216,529	219,305	1.2	209,634	210,691	0.5
Fort Wayne, IN	220,472	224,223	1.7	214,223	215,591	0.6
Fort Worth, TX[1]	1,397,596	1,435,889	2.7	1,349,809	1,386,446	2.7
Gainesville, FL	168,667	171,235	1.5	163,355	165,582	1.3
Green Bay, WI	174,722	175,808	0.6	170,734	171,226	0.2
Greensboro, NC	366,503	362,230	-1.1	353,122	348,882	-1.2
Honolulu, HI	458,516	467,102	1.8	447,781	454,669	1.5
Houston, TX	3,704,314	3,811,882	2.9	3,557,779	3,657,192	2.7
Huntsville, AL	257,532	264,722	2.7	252,062	257,486	2.1
Indianapolis, IN	1,114,296	1,147,341	2.9	1,082,623	1,106,085	2.1
Jacksonville, FL	845,904	852,367	0.7	820,842	825,781	0.6
Kansas City, MO	1,160,004	1,182,211	1.9	1,127,092	1,144,249	1.5
Lafayette, LA	185,004	185,747	0.4	178,352	178,532	0.1
Las Vegas, NV	1,199,294	1,224,775	2.1	1,135,389	1,152,230	1.4
Lexington, KY	278,181	284,384	2.2	268,513	272,804	1.6
Lincoln, NE	191,591	195,942	2.2	187,422	191,304	2.0
Little Rock, AR	371,026	378,813	2.1	359,838	366,941	1.9
Los Angeles, CA[1]	5,037,643	5,091,130	1.0	4,782,176	4,800,645	0.3
Louisville, KY	691,184	703,358	1.7	666,258	672,517	0.9
Madison, WI	410,987	413,894	0.7	403,502	404,881	0.3
Manchester, NH	238,986	245,151	2.5	233,791	237,759	1.7
McAllen, TX	385,693	394,540	2.2	362,243	370,007	2.1

Table continued on following page.

Metro Area	Civilian Labor Force			Workers Employed		
	Dec. 2023	Dec. 2024	% Chg.	Dec. 2023	Dec. 2024	% Chg.
Memphis, TN	620,716	627,549	1.1	598,585	600,246	0.2
Miami, FL[1]	1,433,283	1,445,779	0.8	1,404,765	1,410,954	0.4
Midland, TX	116,721	119,415	2.3	114,162	116,595	2.1
Milwaukee, WI	822,104	825,110	0.3	800,656	800,116	0.0
Minneapolis, MN	2,005,284	2,015,070	0.4	1,956,084	1,964,999	0.4
Nashville, TN	1,150,386	1,163,681	1.1	1,123,659	1,129,538	0.5
New Orleans, LA	461,088	463,007	0.4	442,552	443,450	0.2
New York, NY[1]	6,077,969	6,169,474	1.5	5,813,964	5,874,694	1.0
Oklahoma City, OK	752,168	762,662	1.4	729,908	740,966	1.5
Omaha, NE	505,378	514,350	1.7	492,693	499,953	1.4
Orlando, FL	1,476,354	1,481,986	0.3	1,432,973	1,435,926	0.2
Philadelphia, PA[1]	1,055,097	1,047,116	-0.7	1,014,794	1,006,018	-0.8
Phoenix, AZ	2,660,126	2,699,326	1.4	2,583,768	2,614,930	1.2
Pittsburgh, PA	1,218,768	1,213,214	-0.4	1,179,001	1,172,526	-0.5
Portland, OR	1,358,801	1,358,994	0.0	1,305,393	1,301,850	-0.2
Providence, RI	887,464	901,729	1.6	854,672	862,458	0.9
Provo, UT	363,569	366,874	0.9	354,453	356,068	0.4
Raleigh, NC	799,354	803,302	0.4	775,484	780,100	0.6
Reno, NV	291,520	298,309	2.3	279,599	284,384	1.7
Richmond, VA	703,806	718,292	2.0	685,441	699,371	2.0
Rochester, MN	128,702	138,168	7.3	126,091	135,339	7.3
Sacramento, CA	1,144,784	1,156,797	1.0	1,094,502	1,103,633	0.8
Saint Louis, MO	1,476,468	1,495,860	1.3	1,428,392	1,447,762	1.3
Saint Paul, MN	2,005,284	2,015,070	0.4	1,956,084	1,964,999	0.4
Salem, OR	215,316	219,611	1.9	206,688	210,311	1.7
Salt Lake City, UT	738,638	754,401	2.1	719,094	732,202	1.8
San Antonio, TX	1,308,187	1,349,973	3.1	1,265,057	1,304,101	3.0
San Diego, CA	1,608,713	1,619,332	0.6	1,543,490	1,549,532	0.3
San Francisco, CA[1]	1,011,370	1,004,815	-0.6	978,032	970,469	-0.7
San Jose, CA	1,075,900	1,078,520	0.2	1,034,963	1,036,708	0.1
Santa Rosa, CA	249,694	251,825	0.8	240,531	241,848	0.5
Savannah, GA	202,550	202,333	-0.1	197,273	196,748	-0.2
Seattle, WA[1]	1,366,721	1,405,582	2.8	1,318,947	1,362,424	3.3
Sioux Falls, SD	171,226	173,604	1.3	168,466	170,431	1.1
Tampa, FL[1]	1,167,354	1,171,736	0.3	1,130,613	1,132,522	0.1
Tucson, AZ	493,139	499,226	1.2	477,781	482,263	0.9
Tulsa, OK	510,676	517,614	1.3	494,038	502,372	1.6
Virginia Beach, VA	883,468	890,934	0.8	860,628	866,842	0.7
Washington, DC[1]	1,000,003	1,013,650	1.3	966,020	974,957	0.9
Wichita, KS	320,952	326,697	1.7	311,687	314,280	0.8
Wilmington, NC	222,997	222,642	-0.1	215,630	215,604	0.0
Winston-Salem, NC	329,205	328,631	-0.1	318,577	317,977	-0.1
U.S.	166,661,000	167,746,000	0.7	160,754,000	161,294,000	0.3

Note: Data is not seasonally adjusted and covers workers 16 years of age and older; Figures cover the Metropolitan Statistical Area (MSA) except where noted; (1) Metropolitan Division
Source: Bureau of Labor Statistics, Local Area Unemployment Statistics

Unemployment Rate: City

City	2024											
	Jan.	Feb.	Mar.	Apr.	May	Jun.	Jul.	Aug.	Sep.	Oct.	Nov.	Dec.
Albuquerque, NM	3.5	3.4	3.1	3.1	3.5	4.4	4.9	4.3	3.8	3.9	3.9	3.6
Anchorage, AK	4.0	4.2	3.8	3.7	3.6	4.2	3.8	3.5	3.5	3.6	3.8	3.5
Ann Arbor, MI	2.5	2.7	2.8	2.6	3.2	3.8	4.2	3.7	3.2	3.1	3.2	3.3
Athens, GA	3.7	3.5	3.6	2.8	3.7	4.6	4.5	4.5	3.8	4.0	3.3	3.2
Atlanta, GA	3.9	3.9	3.8	3.6	4.0	4.5	4.5	4.6	4.1	4.2	4.2	4.1
Austin, TX	3.3	3.5	3.2	2.9	3.1	3.5	3.5	3.5	3.3	3.2	3.2	2.9
Baltimore, MD	4.2	4.2	4.0	3.6	3.8	4.5	4.8	4.8	4.0	4.3	4.2	3.9
Billings, MT	3.5	3.3	3.0	2.6	2.6	3.2	3.1	3.0	2.5	2.5	2.6	2.8
Boise City, ID	3.3	3.4	3.3	2.9	3.0	3.3	3.5	3.3	3.1	3.1	3.3	3.1
Boston, MA	3.7	3.7	3.5	3.2	3.8	4.3	4.6	4.4	3.8	3.9	3.9	3.9
Boulder, CO	3.3	3.5	3.4	3.2	4.0	4.5	4.5	4.5	4.1	4.1	4.4	3.7
Cape Coral, FL	3.4	3.2	3.2	3.0	3.2	3.8	3.9	3.9	3.6	3.5	3.6	3.2
Cedar Rapids, IA	3.9	4.3	3.2	2.7	3.6	4.5	4.2	4.0	3.3	3.5	3.6	3.3
Charleston, SC	3.0	3.3	3.0	2.7	3.2	3.9	4.0	4.1	3.5	3.7	3.6	3.3
Charlotte, NC	3.8	3.9	3.6	3.2	3.4	3.8	4.1	3.9	3.2	3.3	3.5	3.3
Chicago, IL	5.0	5.5	5.1	5.1	5.6	6.9	6.7	6.4	5.8	5.8	5.4	4.8
Cincinnati, OH	4.3	4.4	4.3	4.1	4.5	5.2	5.3	5.0	4.6	4.3	4.6	4.5
Clarksville, TN	4.0	3.7	3.8	3.3	3.5	4.6	4.6	4.4	4.2	4.2	4.3	4.2
Cleveland, OH	5.0	5.8	5.2	4.7	5.0	5.5	5.5	4.7	4.1	3.8	4.0	4.2
College Station, TX	3.4	3.6	3.0	2.5	3.0	3.7	3.8	3.7	3.3	3.2	3.1	2.7
Colorado Springs, CO	4.1	4.2	3.8	3.7	3.9	4.4	4.7	4.6	4.3	4.4	4.7	4.5
Columbia, MO	3.1	2.9	3.2	2.7	3.3	3.6	3.8	3.4	2.4	2.7	2.8	2.4
Columbia, SC	4.1	4.4	4.1	3.8	5.0	5.8	6.1	5.8	4.9	5.7	5.3	4.7
Columbus, OH	4.0	4.0	4.0	3.8	4.0	4.5	4.5	4.3	4.2	3.9	4.2	4.1
Dallas, TX	4.0	4.1	3.9	3.5	3.7	4.3	4.3	4.3	4.0	4.0	4.0	3.5
Davenport, IA	4.2	3.6	3.5	3.0	3.8	4.5	4.8	4.9	5.1	4.9	4.9	4.4
Denver, CO	4.5	4.5	4.0	4.1	4.1	4.5	4.9	4.9	4.6	4.8	5.0	5.0
Des Moines, IA	4.3	3.8	3.5	2.6	3.1	3.6	4.1	4.4	3.5	3.7	3.9	3.7
Detroit, MI	8.3	8.3	8.1	7.4	8.6	10.0	12.7	9.7	9.6	10.8	10.6	9.6
Durham, NC	3.3	3.3	3.2	2.8	3.1	3.4	3.6	3.5	2.9	2.9	3.1	2.9
El Paso, TX	4.3	4.5	4.1	3.7	3.9	4.5	4.5	4.5	4.2	4.2	4.2	3.7
Eugene, OR	4.6	4.5	4.2	3.6	3.6	4.1	4.5	4.4	4.0	3.9	3.8	4.2
Fargo, ND	2.5	2.6	2.7	2.3	2.0	2.5	2.2	2.3	1.9	1.9	2.2	2.5
Fort Collins, CO	3.5	3.6	3.3	3.1	3.5	3.9	4.1	4.1	3.8	3.7	4.1	3.7
Fort Wayne, IN	3.9	4.3	4.1	3.4	3.9	4.4	6.0	4.4	4.0	4.1	4.4	4.2
Fort Worth, TX	4.1	4.3	4.1	3.6	3.9	4.6	4.6	4.4	4.1	4.1	4.1	3.7
Gainesville, FL	3.8	3.6	4.0	3.4	3.8	4.6	4.4	4.6	3.9	4.2	4.4	3.7
Green Bay, WI	2.7	3.2	3.3	2.8	2.8	3.3	3.1	2.8	2.5	2.5	2.6	2.8
Greensboro, NC	4.4	4.4	4.3	3.7	4.0	4.8	5.2	4.9	4.0	3.9	4.2	4.0
Honolulu, HI	2.5	2.5	2.4	2.4	2.3	3.2	3.0	3.1	3.1	2.9	3.0	2.7
Houston, TX	4.4	4.4	4.2	3.8	4.0	4.7	5.1	4.9	4.5	4.4	4.5	4.0
Huntsville, AL	2.8	2.8	2.6	2.1	2.1	2.9	3.1	3.1	2.7	2.8	2.9	2.9
Indianapolis, IN	3.9	4.3	4.2	3.6	4.0	4.4	4.7	4.5	4.1	4.0	4.2	4.0
Jacksonville, FL	3.5	3.4	3.3	3.1	3.3	3.9	4.1	4.0	3.6	3.6	3.5	3.2
Kansas City, MO	3.9	4.1	4.1	3.5	4.0	4.1	4.6	4.2	3.3	3.6	3.6	3.5
Lafayette, LA	4.0	3.9	3.8	3.4	3.6	4.5	4.4	4.4	4.3	4.3	4.1	3.8
Las Vegas, NV	5.7	5.8	5.7	5.5	5.6	6.2	6.5	6.3	5.9	6.0	6.1	6.0
Lexington, KY	3.9	4.3	4.2	3.5	3.9	4.5	4.7	4.4	4.1	4.0	4.1	4.0
Lincoln, NE	2.5	2.7	2.5	2.2	2.5	3.0	2.7	2.8	2.4	2.6	2.6	2.4
Little Rock, AR	3.8	3.8	3.6	3.3	3.4	3.8	4.0	3.6	3.3	3.3	3.4	3.4
Los Angeles, CA	5.8	5.5	5.4	5.1	5.5	6.2	6.8	6.8	6.1	6.1	6.1	5.8
Louisville, KY	4.5	4.9	4.7	4.2	4.3	4.9	5.9	4.9	4.6	4.7	4.7	4.7
Madison, WI	1.9	2.2	2.4	2.2	2.3	2.8	2.6	2.3	2.2	2.1	2.1	2.1
Manchester, NH	2.8	3.1	2.9	2.5	2.4	2.7	3.0	2.9	2.5	2.6	3.2	3.1
McAllen, TX	4.5	4.6	4.3	4.0	4.2	4.9	4.9	4.8	4.3	4.2	4.3	4.0

Table continued on following page.

City	2024											
	Jan.	Feb.	Mar.	Apr.	May	Jun.	Jul.	Aug.	Sep.	Oct.	Nov.	Dec.
Memphis, TN	4.9	4.5	4.7	4.2	4.4	5.8	6.2	5.8	5.3	5.4	5.3	5.2
Miami, FL	1.8	2.0	2.2	2.2	2.2	2.4	2.8	2.8	2.4	2.4	2.3	2.3
Midland, TX	2.6	2.8	2.4	2.2	2.4	2.8	2.8	2.9	2.6	2.7	2.7	2.3
Milwaukee, WI	3.9	4.5	4.6	4.2	4.0	4.9	4.9	4.8	3.8	3.9	4.1	4.0
Minneapolis, MN	2.8	3.0	2.8	2.6	2.5	3.3	3.4	3.4	2.9	2.7	2.5	2.3
Nashville, TN	2.6	2.5	2.6	2.4	2.5	3.1	3.2	3.1	2.9	3.0	3.1	3.0
New Orleans, LA	5.3	4.8	4.7	4.3	4.4	5.7	5.8	5.5	5.2	5.3	4.9	4.6
New York, NY	4.8	5.1	4.8	4.6	4.9	5.4	6.1	6.1	5.3	5.5	5.5	5.2
Oklahoma City, OK	3.4	3.4	3.1	2.7	3.2	3.4	3.4	3.3	3.1	3.1	3.1	2.9
Omaha, NE	3.2	3.5	3.2	3.1	3.1	3.5	3.6	3.3	3.0	3.2	3.0	3.0
Orlando, FL	3.0	2.8	2.7	2.7	2.9	3.3	3.5	3.5	3.2	3.1	3.1	2.9
Philadelphia, PA	4.7	4.9	4.4	4.0	4.4	4.9	5.5	5.7	4.4	4.6	4.5	4.3
Phoenix, AZ	3.0	3.0	2.7	2.5	2.9	3.5	3.8	3.7	3.4	3.4	3.4	3.1
Pittsburgh, PA	3.2	3.2	3.1	2.5	3.0	3.5	3.7	4.0	2.8	3.0	2.9	2.6
Portland, OR	4.5	4.4	4.3	3.6	3.6	4.0	4.4	4.3	3.9	3.9	4.0	4.1
Providence, RI	5.7	6.4	5.6	4.7	5.4	5.4	6.3	6.7	5.2	5.3	5.8	5.5
Provo, UT	2.6	2.6	2.4	2.4	3.2	3.8	3.2	3.4	2.9	2.6	2.8	2.6
Raleigh, NC	3.5	3.6	3.5	3.0	3.2	3.6	3.8	3.6	3.0	3.0	3.3	3.1
Reno, NV	4.5	4.6	4.6	4.4	4.6	4.9	5.1	4.9	4.4	4.6	4.5	4.6
Richmond, VA	3.4	3.4	3.4	3.0	3.4	3.6	3.8	3.9	3.5	3.4	3.4	3.1
Rochester, MN	2.2	2.5	2.1	2.0	1.9	2.6	2.6	2.5	2.0	1.9	1.9	1.8
Sacramento, CA	5.2	5.2	4.9	4.5	4.3	5.1	5.5	5.6	5.0	5.1	5.2	4.9
Saint Louis, MO	4.4	4.8	4.6	3.9	4.3	4.6	4.9	4.8	3.8	4.0	4.0	4.1
Saint Paul, MN	3.0	3.3	3.1	2.8	2.7	3.6	3.7	3.7	3.1	2.8	2.6	2.5
Salem, OR	4.7	4.6	4.5	3.8	3.7	4.2	4.6	4.5	4.0	4.0	4.1	4.3
Salt Lake City, UT	3.0	3.4	3.2	3.0	3.0	3.3	3.5	3.5	3.0	3.1	3.1	2.9
San Antonio, TX	3.9	4.1	3.6	3.4	3.4	4.5	4.3	4.2	3.8	3.8	4.0	3.3
San Diego, CA	4.4	4.4	4.2	3.8	3.7	4.4	4.8	4.9	4.3	4.4	4.5	4.2
San Francisco, CA	3.8	3.6	3.5	3.3	3.1	3.7	4.0	4.1	3.6	3.7	3.7	3.5
San Jose, CA	4.3	4.2	4.1	3.8	3.6	4.4	4.7	4.7	4.2	4.3	4.3	4.0
Santa Rosa, CA	4.5	4.3	4.2	3.8	3.6	4.3	4.7	4.7	4.1	4.3	4.4	4.1
Savannah, GA	3.5	3.5	3.5	3.0	3.6	4.1	4.0	4.2	3.5	3.6	3.4	3.3
Seattle, WA	4.0	3.6	3.5	3.5	3.7	4.5	4.2	4.1	3.9	3.7	3.4	2.8
Sioux Falls, SD	1.9	2.2	1.7	1.7	1.6	1.8	1.6	1.8	1.4	1.6	1.6	2.0
Tampa, FL	3.5	3.3	3.4	3.1	3.3	3.8	3.9	4.0	3.6	3.7	3.8	3.3
Tucson, AZ	3.5	3.4	3.1	2.9	3.4	4.2	4.4	4.3	3.9	3.8	3.9	3.6
Tulsa, OK	4.0	4.0	3.3	3.0	3.5	3.7	3.7	3.6	3.2	3.3	3.3	3.0
Virginia Beach, VA	2.6	2.7	2.5	2.3	2.7	2.9	3.0	3.1	2.8	2.7	2.8	2.4
Washington, DC	5.1	5.3	5.0	4.5	5.0	5.7	6.0	6.0	5.2	5.2	5.0	4.9
Wichita, KS	3.7	4.1	3.9	3.5	3.9	4.4	5.1	4.7	3.9	4.4	4.5	3.9
Wilmington, NC	3.6	3.5	3.3	2.8	3.1	3.5	3.7	3.5	2.9	2.9	3.2	3.0
Winston-Salem, NC	4.0	4.0	4.0	3.4	3.8	4.3	4.6	4.4	3.5	3.6	3.8	3.5
U.S.	4.1	4.2	3.9	3.5	3.7	4.3	4.5	4.4	3.9	3.9	4.0	3.8

Note: Data is not seasonally adjusted and covers workers 16 years of age and older; All figures are percentages
Source: Bureau of Labor Statistics, Local Area Unemployment Statistics

Unemployment Rate: Metro Area

Metro Area	2024											
	Jan.	Feb.	Mar.	Apr.	May	Jun.	Jul.	Aug.	Sep.	Oct.	Nov.	Dec.
Albuquerque, NM	3.6	3.5	3.2	3.3	3.6	4.6	5.1	4.4	3.9	4.0	4.1	3.7
Anchorage, AK	4.4	4.6	4.2	4.0	3.9	4.5	4.1	3.7	3.7	3.9	4.2	3.9
Ann Arbor, MI	3.1	3.3	3.4	3.2	3.9	4.6	5.1	4.5	3.9	3.8	3.8	4.0
Athens, GA	3.4	3.2	3.3	2.6	3.4	4.1	4.0	4.1	3.4	3.6	3.1	2.9
Atlanta, GA[1]	3.4	3.4	3.4	3.1	3.5	4.0	3.9	4.0	3.5	3.6	3.6	3.4
Austin, TX	3.5	3.6	3.4	3.0	3.2	3.7	3.7	3.7	3.5	3.4	3.4	3.1
Baltimore, MD	3.0	3.1	2.9	2.5	2.7	3.4	3.5	3.5	2.9	3.1	3.0	2.7
Billings, MT	3.3	3.3	2.9	2.6	2.5	3.1	3.0	2.9	2.4	2.3	2.4	2.9
Boise City, ID	3.8	3.9	3.7	3.2	3.3	3.6	3.8	3.7	3.3	3.4	3.6	3.4
Boston, MA[1]	3.9	4.0	3.7	3.2	3.8	4.2	4.5	4.3	3.7	3.9	3.9	4.0
Boulder, CO	3.6	3.7	3.4	3.3	3.7	4.2	4.4	4.3	4.0	4.1	4.3	4.0
Cape Coral, FL	3.4	3.3	3.2	3.0	3.2	3.7	4.0	3.9	3.7	3.6	3.6	3.2
Cedar Rapids, IA	3.9	4.0	3.2	2.5	3.2	3.8	3.8	3.7	3.0	3.3	3.4	3.2
Charleston, SC	3.1	3.4	3.1	2.7	3.3	4.0	4.2	4.3	3.6	3.8	3.6	3.4
Charlotte, NC	3.6	3.8	3.5	3.1	3.4	3.8	4.0	3.9	3.3	3.4	3.5	3.3
Chicago, IL[1]	4.7	5.2	4.8	4.6	5.1	6.2	6.0	5.7	5.1	5.1	4.8	4.4
Cincinnati, OH	4.1	4.2	4.2	3.8	4.0	4.6	4.6	4.3	4.1	3.9	4.1	4.1
Clarksville, TN	4.2	4.1	4.1	3.6	3.8	4.8	4.9	4.6	4.4	4.4	4.5	4.4
Cleveland, OH	4.0	4.7	4.2	3.6	3.9	4.4	4.4	3.7	3.3	3.0	3.2	3.3
College Station, TX	3.3	3.4	3.0	2.6	3.0	3.6	3.7	3.6	3.2	3.1	3.1	2.7
Colorado Springs, CO	4.2	4.3	3.9	3.8	4.0	4.5	4.8	4.8	4.4	4.5	4.8	4.6
Columbia, MO	3.2	3.0	3.2	2.7	3.2	3.5	3.7	3.3	2.4	2.7	2.7	2.4
Columbia, SC	3.5	3.7	3.5	3.1	3.8	4.5	4.7	4.8	4.1	4.3	4.1	3.8
Columbus, OH	3.9	3.9	3.9	3.6	3.8	4.3	4.3	4.1	4.0	3.7	4.0	4.0
Dallas, TX[1]	3.9	4.0	3.8	3.4	3.6	4.2	4.2	4.2	3.9	3.8	3.8	3.5
Davenport, IA	5.2	4.8	4.5	4.0	4.2	4.7	4.8	4.9	5.2	5.0	4.8	4.4
Denver, CO	4.1	4.2	3.8	3.8	3.9	4.4	4.6	4.7	4.3	4.5	4.7	4.6
Des Moines, IA	3.3	2.9	2.7	2.1	2.6	3.1	3.5	3.6	3.0	3.1	3.2	3.0
Detroit, MI[1]	4.8	4.8	4.7	4.3	5.0	5.8	7.5	5.6	5.6	6.3	6.2	5.6
Durham, NC	3.2	3.2	3.2	2.8	3.0	3.4	3.6	3.4	2.8	2.9	3.1	2.9
El Paso, TX	4.5	4.7	4.3	3.9	4.1	4.8	4.8	4.7	4.4	4.4	4.4	4.0
Eugene, OR	4.9	4.7	4.4	3.8	3.8	4.2	4.7	4.6	4.1	4.1	4.1	4.4
Fargo, ND	2.5	2.7	2.7	2.2	2.0	2.6	2.3	2.3	1.8	1.8	2.0	2.3
Fort Collins, CO	3.6	3.8	3.4	3.3	3.5	3.9	4.1	4.2	3.8	3.9	4.2	3.9
Fort Wayne, IN	3.8	4.1	3.9	3.2	3.7	4.2	5.8	4.1	3.7	3.8	4.1	3.8
Fort Worth, TX[1]	3.9	4.1	3.8	3.4	3.6	4.2	4.3	4.2	3.9	3.9	3.9	3.4
Gainesville, FL	3.5	3.3	3.5	3.1	3.4	4.0	4.0	4.0	3.5	3.7	3.8	3.3
Green Bay, WI	2.6	3.1	3.1	2.6	2.6	3.0	2.9	2.6	2.3	2.3	2.4	2.6
Greensboro, NC	4.2	4.2	4.0	3.5	3.9	4.5	4.8	4.5	3.7	3.7	4.0	3.7
Honolulu, HI	2.5	2.5	2.4	2.4	2.3	3.2	3.0	3.1	3.1	2.9	3.0	2.7
Houston, TX	4.4	4.5	4.1	3.8	4.0	4.7	5.0	4.8	4.5	4.4	4.4	4.1
Huntsville, AL	2.6	2.7	2.4	2.0	2.0	2.7	2.9	3.0	2.6	2.7	2.8	2.7
Indianapolis, IN	3.6	3.9	3.9	3.2	3.6	4.0	4.3	4.0	3.6	3.6	3.9	3.6
Jacksonville, FL	3.3	3.2	3.2	2.9	3.1	3.7	3.9	3.8	3.4	3.4	3.5	3.1
Kansas City, MO	3.5	3.8	3.8	3.2	3.6	3.8	4.2	3.9	3.2	3.5	3.3	3.2
Lafayette, LA	4.1	4.0	3.8	3.4	3.6	4.5	4.4	4.4	4.3	4.3	4.2	3.9
Las Vegas, NV	5.6	5.6	5.5	5.4	5.5	6.1	6.4	6.2	5.8	5.9	6.0	5.9
Lexington, KY	4.0	4.4	4.2	3.5	3.9	4.6	4.7	4.5	4.1	4.1	4.2	4.1
Lincoln, NE	2.4	2.6	2.4	2.2	2.5	3.0	2.6	2.7	2.4	2.6	2.5	2.4
Little Rock, AR	3.5	3.5	3.2	2.9	3.1	3.5	3.7	3.3	3.0	2.9	3.0	3.1
Los Angeles, CA[1]	5.6	5.3	5.3	5.0	5.4	6.1	6.7	6.7	6.0	6.0	6.0	5.7
Louisville, KY	4.3	4.7	4.4	3.9	4.1	4.7	5.6	4.6	4.3	4.4	4.5	4.4
Madison, WI	2.1	2.5	2.5	2.2	2.3	2.7	2.6	2.3	2.1	2.1	2.2	2.2
Manchester, NH	2.7	3.0	2.9	2.4	2.3	2.6	3.0	2.9	2.5	2.6	3.1	3.0
McAllen, TX	6.5	6.0	5.8	5.4	5.7	6.9	6.9	6.5	5.9	5.4	6.0	6.2

Table continued on following page.

Metro Area	2024											
	Jan.	Feb.	Mar.	Apr.	May	Jun.	Jul.	Aug.	Sep.	Oct.	Nov.	Dec.
Memphis, TN	4.0	3.7	3.8	3.4	3.7	4.9	5.0	4.8	4.4	4.5	4.5	4.4
Miami, FL[1]	1.9	2.0	2.3	2.3	2.3	2.6	2.8	2.9	2.4	2.4	2.4	2.4
Midland, TX	2.6	2.8	2.5	2.2	2.5	2.8	2.9	2.9	2.7	2.7	2.7	2.4
Milwaukee, WI	3.0	3.5	3.6	3.2	3.1	3.8	3.7	3.4	2.9	2.9	3.1	3.0
Minneapolis, MN	3.1	3.3	3.1	2.7	2.6	3.5	3.4	3.4	2.7	2.4	2.4	2.5
Nashville, TN	2.6	2.5	2.5	2.3	2.4	3.1	3.2	3.1	2.9	3.0	3.0	2.9
New Orleans, LA	4.6	4.3	4.2	3.8	3.9	5.0	5.0	4.9	4.7	4.7	4.5	4.2
New York, NY[1]	4.6	4.9	4.6	4.3	4.6	5.1	5.7	5.6	4.8	5.0	5.0	4.8
Oklahoma City, OK	3.3	3.4	3.0	2.6	3.0	3.3	3.3	3.2	3.0	3.0	3.0	2.8
Omaha, NE	3.1	3.2	2.9	2.7	2.9	3.3	3.4	3.1	2.8	3.0	2.9	2.8
Orlando, FL	3.2	3.1	3.1	2.9	3.1	3.6	3.8	3.8	3.4	3.4	3.5	3.1
Philadelphia, PA[1]	4.3	4.6	4.1	3.7	4.1	4.5	5.1	5.3	4.1	4.2	4.2	3.9
Phoenix, AZ	3.0	3.0	2.7	2.6	3.0	3.5	3.8	3.6	3.4	3.4	3.3	3.1
Pittsburgh, PA	3.9	4.1	3.6	3.1	3.3	3.9	4.2	4.4	3.1	3.4	3.3	3.4
Portland, OR	4.4	4.5	4.2	3.6	3.7	3.9	4.4	4.3	3.9	3.9	4.0	4.2
Providence, RI	4.8	5.2	4.5	3.8	4.1	4.3	4.9	5.0	4.0	4.2	4.4	4.4
Provo, UT	3.0	3.2	3.0	2.9	3.2	3.7	3.6	3.7	3.1	3.0	3.1	2.9
Raleigh, NC	3.3	3.4	3.2	2.9	3.1	3.4	3.6	3.5	2.9	2.9	3.1	2.9
Reno, NV	4.7	4.8	4.7	4.5	4.6	5.0	5.1	4.9	4.5	4.6	4.6	4.7
Richmond, VA	3.0	3.0	2.9	2.6	2.9	3.2	3.3	3.4	3.0	2.9	3.0	2.6
Rochester, MN	2.8	3.0	2.6	2.2	2.2	2.8	2.7	2.6	2.0	1.8	1.9	2.0
Sacramento, CA	4.9	4.9	4.7	4.2	4.0	4.8	5.1	5.2	4.6	4.7	4.8	4.6
Saint Louis, MO	3.9	4.1	3.9	3.4	3.7	4.0	4.2	3.9	3.2	3.3	3.3	3.2
Saint Paul, MN	3.1	3.3	3.1	2.7	2.6	3.5	3.4	3.4	2.7	2.4	2.4	2.5
Salem, OR	4.7	4.6	4.3	3.6	3.6	4.0	4.6	4.4	3.9	3.9	4.0	4.2
Salt Lake City, UT	3.0	3.4	3.2	3.0	3.1	3.5	3.5	3.6	3.0	3.1	3.0	2.9
San Antonio, TX	3.8	4.0	3.6	3.3	3.5	4.1	4.2	4.1	3.8	3.8	3.8	3.4
San Diego, CA	4.5	4.5	4.2	3.9	3.7	4.6	4.9	5.0	4.5	4.6	4.6	4.3
San Francisco, CA[1]	3.7	3.6	3.4	3.2	3.1	3.6	3.9	4.0	3.5	3.6	3.7	3.4
San Jose, CA	4.2	4.2	4.0	3.7	3.6	4.2	4.5	4.5	4.1	4.1	4.1	3.9
Santa Rosa, CA	4.3	4.2	4.0	3.6	3.4	4.1	4.4	4.5	3.9	4.1	4.2	4.0
Savannah, GA	2.9	3.0	3.0	2.5	3.1	3.5	3.4	3.7	2.9	3.0	2.9	2.8
Seattle, WA[1]	4.2	3.8	3.7	3.7	3.8	4.7	4.4	4.2	4.1	4.0	3.7	3.1
Sioux Falls, SD	1.8	2.1	1.6	1.6	1.6	1.8	1.5	1.8	1.3	1.5	1.5	1.8
Tampa, FL[1]	3.5	3.4	3.3	3.1	3.3	3.8	4.0	4.0	3.7	3.7	3.8	3.3
Tucson, AZ	3.3	3.3	3.0	2.8	3.3	4.0	4.3	4.0	3.7	3.7	3.6	3.4
Tulsa, OK	3.8	3.8	3.2	2.8	3.3	3.6	3.5	3.4	3.1	3.2	3.2	2.9
Virginia Beach, VA	3.0	3.0	2.9	2.6	3.0	3.2	3.4	3.4	3.1	3.0	3.1	2.7
Washington, DC[1]	3.9	4.1	3.9	3.4	3.7	4.4	4.6	4.7	4.0	4.1	4.1	3.8
Wichita, KS	3.6	3.8	3.7	3.4	3.7	4.2	5.0	4.6	3.8	4.2	4.3	3.8
Wilmington, NC	3.8	3.8	3.4	3.0	3.3	3.6	3.7	3.7	3.1	3.2	3.4	3.2
Winston-Salem, NC	3.6	3.7	3.6	3.1	3.4	3.9	4.1	4.0	3.3	3.3	3.6	3.2
U.S.	4.1	4.2	3.9	3.5	3.7	4.3	4.5	4.4	3.9	3.9	4.0	3.8

Note: Data is not seasonally adjusted and covers workers 16 years of age and older; All figures are percentages; (1) Figures cover the Metropolitan Statistical Area (MSA) except where noted; (1) Metropolitan Division
Source: Bureau of Labor Statistics, Local Area Unemployment Statistics

Average Hourly Wages: Occupations A – C

Metro Area	Accountants/ Auditors	Automotive Mechanics	Book-keepers	Carpenters	Cashiers	Computer Programmers	Computer Systems Analysts
Albuquerque, NM	40.90	25.69	23.51	26.42	14.93	43.80	46.83
Anchorage, AK	42.24	31.29	26.96	36.09	17.64	44.68	45.88
Ann Arbor, MI	41.19	27.70	24.68	30.96	15.32	39.67	53.91
Athens, GA	39.24	25.81	21.79	22.39	12.95	36.03	36.11
Atlanta, GA	46.20	28.17	24.88	24.84	13.99	49.60	53.95
Austin, TX	44.19	27.17	26.04	24.84	15.10	45.82	53.57
Baltimore, MD	44.96	27.65	26.87	28.13	16.18	52.85	56.04
Billings, MT	39.29	28.20	22.49	27.02	14.91	48.63	46.01
Boise City, ID	35.88	24.94	23.92	24.55	15.24	43.27	44.48
Boston, MA	49.79	29.49	28.51	38.40	17.37	57.83	60.98
Boulder, CO[2]	46.39	28.81	26.63	29.94	17.71	71.62	67.66
Cape Coral, FL	39.76	25.28	24.21	23.36	14.53	43.02	46.99
Cedar Rapids, IA	39.80	26.02	24.03	27.03	14.47	39.50	44.19
Charleston, SC	44.26	24.26	23.80	25.54	13.77	53.17	52.43
Charlotte, NC	47.13	27.27	24.68	25.51	14.02	44.72	57.50
Chicago, IL	44.28	28.71	25.75	38.11	16.33	46.08	48.09
Cincinnati, OH	41.81	24.64	24.76	27.72	14.23	56.17	52.48
Clarksville, TN	35.41	23.62	22.04	24.61	13.04	n/a	39.08
Cleveland, OH	41.49	26.14	24.08	29.35	14.16	44.94	47.53
College Station, TX	36.32	24.82	21.78	22.38	13.30	39.46	42.81
Colorado Springs, CO[2]	41.44	26.83	23.32	26.46	16.36	53.50	54.60
Columbia, MO	35.97	23.99	23.55	26.93	14.42	n/a	44.38
Columbia, SC	34.91	23.93	22.33	24.28	12.66	54.49	41.80
Columbus, OH	44.22	27.22	24.48	29.44	14.46	48.11	49.66
Dallas, TX	45.03	27.86	25.94	24.01	14.32	47.68	57.86
Davenport, IA	39.77	25.81	23.07	28.79	14.78	38.43	42.15
Denver, CO[2]	46.80	28.10	26.85	27.44	17.46	54.01	56.16
Des Moines, IA	40.26	26.59	24.64	28.46	14.74	45.02	47.37
Detroit, MI	43.77	27.01	25.39	31.70	14.88	39.07	50.95
Durham, NC	46.33	26.94	26.20	24.03	14.15	51.55	54.64
El Paso, TX	35.86	22.04	20.35	20.00	12.41	34.05	44.84
Eugene, OR	40.17	26.31	23.97	29.35	16.41	44.82	51.80
Fargo, ND	36.22	26.79	24.09	29.49	15.21	43.27	50.62
Fort Collins, CO[2]	43.11	27.93	24.64	26.93	16.61	54.48	53.23
Fort Wayne, IN	38.36	24.39	22.76	27.40	13.68	39.45	44.73
Fort Worth, TX	45.03	27.86	25.94	24.01	14.32	47.68	57.86
Gainesville, FL	38.54	24.87	23.70	23.37	14.25	44.12	41.84
Green Bay, WI	40.76	27.11	23.58	30.80	14.24	45.19	48.58
Greensboro, NC	41.27	25.40	22.80	21.70	13.29	43.91	50.14
Honolulu, HI	36.77	27.01	23.29	42.67	17.05	50.07	44.25
Houston, TX	45.33	27.12	24.69	24.93	14.10	n/a	56.46
Huntsville, AL	41.06	25.69	22.10	23.65	13.43	52.24	59.51
Indianapolis, IN	41.42	25.35	23.97	30.07	13.91	47.00	50.67
Jacksonville, FL	41.72	25.10	23.66	24.55	14.62	50.71	50.41
Kansas City, MO	41.41	26.51	24.38	31.38	15.02	46.73	48.94
Lafayette, LA	35.63	23.75	20.97	22.46	11.84	40.56	49.57
Las Vegas, NV	39.57	25.88	24.90	32.87	14.94	44.52	47.58
Lexington, KY	36.98	22.15	23.60	25.79	13.44	52.20	41.98
Lincoln, NE	34.67	25.66	22.74	25.07	14.50	43.25	40.47
Little Rock, AR	36.16	23.85	22.54	23.06	13.71	45.30	29.95
Los Angeles, CA	48.45	30.20	28.58	36.97	18.47	50.36	59.72
Louisville, KY	39.40	23.99	24.07	26.54	14.14	52.89	45.74
Madison, WI	41.87	28.99	25.40	32.44	15.63	42.40	46.04
Manchester, NH	42.84	28.99	25.41	28.98	14.89	41.19	52.98
McAllen, TX	33.75	22.30	19.81	18.97	12.40	38.07	37.09

Table continued on following page.

Metro Area	Accountants/ Auditors	Automotive Mechanics	Book-keepers	Carpenters	Cashiers	Computer Programmers	Computer Systems Analysts
Memphis, TN	39.28	25.26	23.48	25.20	13.30	43.86	48.38
Miami, FL	43.02	26.45	24.75	24.57	14.99	57.85	54.87
Midland, TX	47.51	26.20	25.44	24.81	14.69	42.10	57.62
Milwaukee, WI	43.31	28.74	24.38	32.43	14.53	43.19	50.52
Minneapolis, MN	45.40	29.52	26.89	35.62	16.35	50.83	53.62
Nashville, TN	41.77	26.05	24.43	25.67	14.57	n/a	42.96
New Orleans, LA	40.08	24.79	22.70	25.98	13.04	39.98	48.21
New York, NY	58.64	29.75	29.11	37.32	17.91	58.71	61.28
Oklahoma City, OK	41.96	23.62	22.88	25.29	13.24	57.04	47.08
Omaha, NE	37.98	26.58	24.02	26.11	14.93	46.38	46.14
Orlando, FL	42.38	25.24	23.73	24.25	15.21	46.42	49.67
Philadelphia, PA	46.34	27.57	26.12	32.62	15.31	46.77	51.52
Phoenix, AZ	42.29	28.52	25.59	28.74	16.53	40.51	51.41
Pittsburgh, PA	39.21	24.59	23.05	31.17	14.11	42.07	47.00
Portland, OR	44.95	29.63	26.60	35.28	17.91	57.44	60.32
Providence, RI	46.37	26.05	26.20	32.98	16.12	49.33	57.45
Provo, UT	38.12	23.63	23.58	25.60	15.11	43.63	48.54
Raleigh, NC	44.26	26.71	24.19	23.43	13.98	41.74	52.76
Reno, NV	41.47	27.04	25.86	32.80	15.27	49.79	47.77
Richmond, VA	42.37	27.70	24.33	24.90	15.01	46.29	51.27
Rochester, MN	46.22	27.15	27.32	32.24	15.88	n/a	n/a
Sacramento, CA	45.29	31.97	28.08	37.87	18.42	56.85	57.48
Saint Louis, MO	40.41	25.56	25.12	33.56	15.63	48.91	46.89
Saint Paul, MN	45.40	29.52	26.89	35.62	16.35	50.83	53.62
Salem, OR	42.14	27.01	26.35	27.76	16.54	52.83	53.95
Salt Lake City, UT	41.61	25.97	24.91	27.86	15.51	46.78	45.51
San Antonio, TX	41.41	25.74	23.19	23.06	14.39	62.03	51.53
San Diego, CA	50.36	29.84	28.01	36.37	18.50	60.74	57.81
San Francisco, CA	57.63	35.20	32.85	41.44	20.07	62.74	71.92
San Jose, CA	61.89	39.24	32.88	41.63	20.75	76.50	77.64
Santa Rosa, CA	47.74	31.99	29.51	40.36	19.48	48.16	55.29
Savannah, GA	40.41	27.16	23.06	24.58	13.64	46.30	52.25
Seattle, WA	51.01	30.63	28.45	39.76	20.63	80.47	66.53
Sioux Falls, SD	40.80	28.20	21.98	23.96	14.91	n/a	48.25
Tampa, FL	42.37	25.41	25.17	24.57	14.51	46.54	53.50
Tucson, AZ	39.27	26.22	24.08	25.46	15.74	46.55	51.81
Tulsa, OK	40.70	24.36	23.49	24.64	13.45	47.67	55.21
Virginia Beach, VA	41.24	26.43	23.13	24.88	14.28	50.07	50.99
Washington, DC	52.24	31.94	28.25	30.71	17.17	54.17	62.36
Wichita, KS	37.74	24.13	21.79	25.64	13.10	50.82	48.92
Wilmington, NC	37.67	23.96	22.76	24.06	13.23	37.74	46.73
Winston-Salem, NC	40.27	25.20	22.66	23.60	13.15	44.83	50.74

Notes: Figures cover the Metropolitan Statistical Area (MSA); (1) Data is from 2023 due to data quality issues in the state of Colorado and its substate areas in 2024; n/a not available
Source: Bureau of Labor Statistics, Metro Area Occupational Employment and Wage Estimates, May 2024

Average Hourly Wages: Occupations C – E

Metro Area	Comp. User Support Specialists	Construction Laborers	Cooks, Restaurant	Customer Service Reps.	Dentists	Electricians	Engineers, Electrical
Albuquerque, NM	24.18	20.58	16.62	20.23	92.52	28.48	71.65
Anchorage, AK	30.11	30.31	19.67	22.30	96.63	38.60	57.20
Ann Arbor, MI	27.63	24.45	18.17	20.90	n/a	37.90	52.52
Athens, GA	24.25	19.20	15.36	17.62	86.37	28.38	52.45
Atlanta, GA	31.11	20.30	16.66	21.35	102.19	30.62	56.08
Austin, TX	29.47	20.17	17.40	20.72	105.18	28.24	67.90
Baltimore, MD	33.50	22.42	18.38	21.60	108.70	33.58	59.60
Billings, MT	26.60	24.46	18.09	21.17	118.06	34.75	51.14
Boise City, ID	26.79	22.50	16.50	21.14	85.60	29.13	65.01
Boston, MA	37.62	33.95	21.98	25.48	n/a	40.10	64.82
Boulder, CO[1]	36.17	22.30	20.42	22.82	85.12	31.85	63.49
Cape Coral, FL	28.07	21.08	17.88	19.48	132.27	25.82	49.73
Cedar Rapids, IA	28.20	23.76	16.74	21.95	76.51	26.89	53.76
Charleston, SC	28.38	21.91	17.47	20.80	78.30	28.18	56.11
Charlotte, NC	30.08	21.52	17.64	21.55	106.87	27.55	58.48
Chicago, IL	30.31	34.99	18.66	23.30	89.54	44.39	57.06
Cincinnati, OH	28.23	26.28	15.92	21.20	103.59	30.46	51.81
Clarksville, TN	25.48	20.62	15.08	18.84	87.66	28.77	45.74
Cleveland, OH	28.26	27.82	17.24	22.13	81.41	32.62	49.77
College Station, TX	24.10	17.72	14.89	17.74	103.68	25.02	50.62
Colorado Springs, CO[1]	30.73	21.28	19.05	20.87	88.76	28.83	56.23
Columbia, MO	27.69	28.79	16.00	20.94	105.42	30.08	n/a
Columbia, SC	27.54	21.14	16.57	19.31	120.35	29.62	51.67
Columbus, OH	30.19	27.99	16.81	22.27	78.07	31.75	49.68
Dallas, TX	29.72	19.90	17.09	21.47	96.90	28.56	56.38
Davenport, IA	27.46	27.61	16.58	20.62	95.43	34.34	54.36
Denver, CO[1]	36.27	22.62	20.14	22.82	64.29	30.65	55.39
Des Moines, IA	29.14	24.89	17.75	24.02	93.83	32.28	69.53
Detroit, MI	29.25	26.26	18.06	22.70	93.92	36.41	53.76
Durham, NC	32.70	22.51	17.45	22.07	96.79	29.52	58.62
El Paso, TX	22.07	17.25	14.12	17.31	101.96	23.92	44.54
Eugene, OR	30.29	24.26	18.28	21.66	107.76	40.45	54.89
Fargo, ND	30.52	25.14	17.42	21.49	100.00	33.30	50.36
Fort Collins, CO[1]	32.68	21.53	18.75	20.21	100.41	29.77	55.88
Fort Wayne, IN	26.58	23.81	15.90	21.57	98.97	31.08	49.63
Fort Worth, TX	29.72	19.90	17.09	21.47	96.90	28.56	56.38
Gainesville, FL	25.88	19.68	16.92	19.63	98.53	25.55	51.00
Green Bay, WI	28.66	26.49	17.71	22.50	81.11	33.62	47.47
Greensboro, NC	26.94	20.44	16.19	20.71	85.23	26.42	53.13
Honolulu, HI	28.29	33.27	21.30	21.38	65.12	42.47	50.66
Houston, TX	29.02	20.13	15.99	20.40	115.55	28.39	57.48
Huntsville, AL	25.12	18.37	16.05	19.29	n/a	27.47	63.59
Indianapolis, IN	29.12	25.60	16.96	22.07	89.99	32.56	53.74
Jacksonville, FL	28.60	20.35	16.89	20.86	86.80	27.03	52.71
Kansas City, MO	28.37	26.74	18.07	21.64	89.46	35.72	51.97
Lafayette, LA	30.51	20.27	13.44	18.01	82.38	26.35	47.69
Las Vegas, NV	27.07	24.69	19.59	19.65	69.07	34.73	51.25
Lexington, KY	27.96	21.98	15.85	20.23	86.12	27.82	50.32
Lincoln, NE	28.07	21.86	17.81	19.65	85.28	29.82	47.88
Little Rock, AR	26.42	18.42	15.24	19.85	92.76	24.62	51.32
Los Angeles, CA	35.73	31.23	21.28	25.04	83.74	39.39	65.77
Louisville, KY	27.34	23.10	16.46	20.93	90.25	30.65	47.48
Madison, WI	29.81	27.12	18.70	23.53	98.38	36.51	51.89
Manchester, NH	34.06	22.66	18.60	23.92	77.22	30.59	70.89
McAllen, TX	21.73	15.75	13.57	17.73	106.72	21.99	46.39

Table continued on following page.

Metro Area	Comp. User Support Specialists	Construction Laborers	Cooks, Restaurant	Customer Service Reps.	Dentists	Electricians	Engineers, Electrical
Memphis, TN	28.25	22.21	16.20	21.10	91.70	27.81	53.37
Miami, FL	32.66	21.69	17.30	20.41	89.88	27.58	53.23
Midland, TX	27.70	20.63	16.62	20.78	n/a	28.92	61.86
Milwaukee, WI	30.47	28.30	18.61	23.48	97.31	35.83	50.13
Minneapolis, MN	33.76	30.67	20.11	24.54	108.57	41.70	54.81
Nashville, TN	29.95	22.45	18.35	21.72	97.05	29.83	55.61
New Orleans, LA	28.92	21.90	15.42	19.43	97.54	29.41	56.07
New York, NY	35.37	34.43	20.82	25.80	89.32	41.08	60.31
Oklahoma City, OK	26.99	20.63	17.14	20.02	112.93	30.47	53.72
Omaha, NE	29.50	23.84	18.03	21.38	103.65	31.36	48.89
Orlando, FL	28.57	21.13	18.25	19.99	85.11	26.17	56.13
Philadelphia, PA	31.66	28.19	17.84	23.03	87.74	38.14	61.83
Phoenix, AZ	32.43	23.17	19.56	22.50	98.52	29.58	59.00
Pittsburgh, PA	29.05	25.52	15.76	21.46	78.26	34.21	53.62
Portland, OR	31.89	27.95	20.13	23.78	94.71	46.08	57.53
Providence, RI	30.62	30.51	19.97	22.77	n/a	34.24	54.44
Provo, UT	28.65	22.38	17.58	19.85	66.32	29.16	60.54
Raleigh, NC	29.83	22.02	17.14	21.36	104.78	26.83	65.68
Reno, NV	28.19	27.64	18.27	20.68	74.31	32.97	57.15
Richmond, VA	29.64	19.84	17.56	20.92	103.90	29.24	56.26
Rochester, MN	33.24	28.42	18.68	23.08	122.85	39.75	50.77
Sacramento, CA	47.62	31.16	20.88	24.98	89.82	39.30	65.09
Saint Louis, MO	29.80	31.00	18.07	22.36	n/a	36.65	56.55
Saint Paul, MN	33.76	30.67	20.11	24.54	108.57	41.70	54.81
Salem, OR	31.51	25.90	18.91	22.72	104.28	40.07	55.99
Salt Lake City, UT	32.60	23.53	18.51	21.44	80.35	31.02	55.43
San Antonio, TX	27.32	19.44	15.83	20.34	78.33	26.69	55.23
San Diego, CA	35.01	30.44	21.15	24.53	87.88	39.61	65.99
San Francisco, CA	43.40	36.32	22.87	29.30	109.18	50.12	77.50
San Jose, CA	43.29	35.06	24.13	30.67	90.06	49.71	90.89
Santa Rosa, CA	37.08	32.20	21.98	25.04	82.86	42.00	63.20
Savannah, GA	31.48	19.01	16.30	18.64	98.92	28.43	57.20
Seattle, WA	37.28	31.08	22.67	27.52	97.55	48.19	67.55
Sioux Falls, SD	23.81	20.75	17.44	21.01	89.53	28.14	48.75
Tampa, FL	29.29	21.37	17.47	20.59	112.24	26.80	55.02
Tucson, AZ	28.35	21.11	17.71	19.74	92.54	28.60	62.08
Tulsa, OK	27.43	21.54	16.20	19.80	97.17	30.23	53.92
Virginia Beach, VA	29.01	19.76	17.15	19.47	87.77	29.26	53.55
Washington, DC	38.26	23.15	20.33	23.55	109.72	37.78	67.24
Wichita, KS	24.62	20.29	15.63	19.26	82.76	31.51	46.39
Wilmington, NC	28.36	21.81	16.50	19.57	104.98	26.12	54.21
Winston-Salem, NC	27.29	21.31	15.89	19.29	77.83	26.05	42.46

Notes: Figures cover the Metropolitan Statistical Area (MSA); (1) Data is from 2023 due to data quality issues in the state of Colorado and its substate areas in 2024; n/a not available
Source: Bureau of Labor Statistics, Metro Area Occupational Employment and Wage Estimates, May 2024

Average Hourly Wages: Occupations F – J

Metro Area	Fast Food and Counter Workers	Financial Managers	First-Line Supervisors/ of Office Workers	General and Operations Managers	Hair- dressers/ Cosme- tologists	Home Health and Personal Care Aides	Janitors/ Cleaners
Albuquerque, NM	14.78	67.06	31.40	59.24	18.37	14.44	16.27
Anchorage, AK	16.07	66.10	34.12	67.82	n/a	18.20	19.57
Ann Arbor, MI	15.01	78.28	33.10	66.91	21.16	17.05	18.60
Athens, GA	12.25	70.43	29.73	48.33	20.63	13.58	14.96
Atlanta, GA	13.55	92.61	34.57	65.51	22.26	14.69	16.89
Austin, TX	14.09	89.92	36.88	68.18	20.93	13.82	16.90
Baltimore, MD	15.89	80.29	35.89	61.48	20.61	18.43	18.03
Billings, MT	14.42	73.01	31.75	52.57	21.23	16.16	18.70
Boise City, ID	13.54	68.45	30.86	47.05	15.23	16.17	16.90
Boston, MA	17.43	100.73	38.59	78.73	24.97	19.58	21.75
Boulder, CO[1]	17.78	93.87	36.12	81.98	25.46	19.56	19.68
Cape Coral, FL	14.23	82.00	32.80	57.19	17.77	16.30	16.54
Cedar Rapids, IA	13.79	67.28	31.58	49.70	22.37	17.35	17.85
Charleston, SC	13.83	72.75	33.77	59.32	18.76	15.46	15.59
Charlotte, NC	14.27	91.39	33.22	66.57	20.12	15.34	16.27
Chicago, IL	16.05	88.31	35.22	68.58	20.23	17.79	19.25
Cincinnati, OH	14.06	77.39	32.81	58.30	20.06	15.99	17.45
Clarksville, TN	12.79	65.73	29.27	48.25	16.23	15.17	15.39
Cleveland, OH	14.06	76.95	33.00	57.91	17.62	15.55	17.41
College Station, TX	12.43	70.24	29.93	51.36	16.38	12.18	15.33
Colorado Springs, CO[1]	15.91	84.63	32.60	70.11	22.98	17.68	17.57
Columbia, MO	14.25	67.68	31.10	46.12	20.40	17.18	16.98
Columbia, SC	12.71	64.62	33.15	54.00	16.41	14.20	15.80
Columbus, OH	14.24	75.71	33.43	60.59	18.45	15.89	17.74
Dallas, TX	13.48	83.96	36.12	67.98	17.46	13.45	16.43
Davenport, IA	14.11	69.21	30.67	52.32	21.43	16.37	17.91
Denver, CO[1]	16.95	93.78	36.61	79.34	23.38	18.27	18.56
Des Moines, IA	14.21	77.18	33.94	54.24	22.00	17.30	17.35
Detroit, MI	14.34	77.60	33.92	65.30	21.26	15.95	17.41
Durham, NC	14.66	87.22	34.76	68.52	24.56	15.58	17.12
El Paso, TX	11.61	67.83	27.70	46.07	15.79	11.14	13.49
Eugene, OR	16.00	72.01	33.88	52.88	21.53	19.39	18.09
Fargo, ND	14.66	75.72	33.25	56.75	20.05	18.76	18.02
Fort Collins, CO[1]	16.21	90.82	32.90	67.45	28.72	18.19	18.27
Fort Wayne, IN	13.24	65.40	33.46	64.53	16.40	15.55	16.97
Fort Worth, TX	13.48	83.96	36.12	67.98	17.46	13.45	16.43
Gainesville, FL	14.25	67.20	30.71	55.75	15.92	15.70	16.07
Green Bay, WI	13.45	72.06	32.86	64.79	18.07	15.70	16.94
Greensboro, NC	13.39	82.48	31.23	58.89	18.93	14.32	15.59
Honolulu, HI	16.01	67.37	32.34	60.89	24.25	17.39	18.20
Houston, TX	12.78	88.07	35.05	66.82	19.05	12.11	15.20
Huntsville, AL	13.10	78.84	31.88	74.54	15.09	13.34	15.09
Indianapolis, IN	14.01	75.66	36.11	72.23	17.77	15.78	16.98
Jacksonville, FL	13.94	80.15	33.12	59.57	17.54	15.94	16.39
Kansas City, MO	14.34	76.99	34.02	53.13	20.28	15.65	17.70
Lafayette, LA	12.06	57.76	27.80	57.89	12.82	10.36	13.40
Las Vegas, NV	14.78	68.81	30.93	60.08	16.64	14.71	18.25
Lexington, KY	13.35	70.52	31.52	48.11	21.66	16.98	16.37
Lincoln, NE	14.42	68.94	30.73	50.12	17.48	16.47	16.83
Little Rock, AR	13.24	60.66	28.31	42.89	14.46	13.31	15.15
Los Angeles, CA	18.75	96.29	37.23	81.25	27.74	17.43	19.78
Louisville, KY	13.57	71.03	33.66	51.34	24.77	17.39	16.81
Madison, WI	14.40	77.53	36.80	69.40	17.58	17.03	18.27
Manchester, NH	14.45	76.66	37.63	74.48	18.36	18.05	18.24

Table continued on following page.

Metro Area	Fast Food and Counter Workers	Financial Managers	First-Line Supervisors/ of Office Workers	General and Operations Managers	Hair-dressers/ Cosme-tologists	Home Health and Personal Care Aides	Janitors/ Cleaners
McAllen, TX	11.81	63.80	28.02	44.25	14.51	11.34	14.44
Memphis, TN	13.12	76.07	34.04	61.94	17.10	15.01	15.76
Miami, FL	14.62	85.42	34.06	64.93	18.78	16.09	15.94
Midland, TX	13.82	87.54	36.53	69.94	n/a	12.83	16.27
Milwaukee, WI	13.86	78.61	35.29	68.07	19.57	15.84	17.69
Minneapolis, MN	16.17	85.12	37.88	59.75	22.01	17.88	19.66
Nashville, TN	14.12	79.15	35.70	66.64	20.68	16.69	17.04
New Orleans, LA	13.66	67.51	30.04	62.93	14.33	11.68	14.73
New York, NY	17.50	119.16	39.92	89.97	24.83	19.02	21.61
Oklahoma City, OK	12.18	71.53	32.48	52.56	18.80	13.47	15.40
Omaha, NE	14.83	75.03	31.66	51.15	21.52	17.13	17.41
Orlando, FL	14.19	78.11	32.58	58.33	17.70	16.03	16.19
Philadelphia, PA	15.05	85.35	35.52	66.76	19.65	15.40	18.54
Phoenix, AZ	16.50	75.51	33.09	59.06	19.33	17.28	18.02
Pittsburgh, PA	13.48	73.83	32.42	57.41	17.44	14.92	17.29
Portland, OR	17.61	86.12	36.29	70.26	25.82	21.37	20.22
Providence, RI	15.96	82.12	36.46	63.72	19.74	19.36	19.58
Provo, UT	13.85	75.16	33.39	54.43	18.78	17.59	15.34
Raleigh, NC	14.64	85.21	31.78	66.79	22.26	15.48	16.07
Reno, NV	15.29	67.77	32.24	59.24	23.92	16.38	17.04
Richmond, VA	14.48	88.63	33.36	63.23	25.31	14.98	16.42
Rochester, MN	15.53	77.53	34.14	50.21	22.80	17.71	20.40
Sacramento, CA	19.02	82.16	37.86	67.60	20.39	16.89	20.72
Saint Louis, MO	15.19	76.57	34.31	53.75	20.57	15.72	17.54
Saint Paul, MN	16.17	85.12	37.88	59.75	22.01	17.88	19.66
Salem, OR	16.51	80.64	34.43	56.23	22.06	20.60	19.35
Salt Lake City, UT	13.99	78.19	35.75	60.12	21.89	18.64	16.02
San Antonio, TX	13.32	77.30	32.68	57.15	16.98	12.52	15.75
San Diego, CA	18.39	92.64	36.65	n/a	22.37	17.55	19.51
San Francisco, CA	20.67	117.20	43.48	85.95	23.49	18.28	23.06
San Jose, CA	20.83	142.60	46.77	94.44	21.94	18.62	21.80
Santa Rosa, CA	19.46	82.80	36.40	66.12	22.13	18.18	21.32
Savannah, GA	13.18	76.60	32.20	55.21	19.33	14.47	15.78
Seattle, WA	19.74	96.69	42.38	82.62	33.56	23.17	22.62
Sioux Falls, SD	15.01	86.95	31.03	76.69	23.12	18.16	16.68
Tampa, FL	14.40	81.07	32.48	65.80	18.35	16.19	16.47
Tucson, AZ	15.89	66.97	29.60	57.34	19.10	16.54	17.29
Tulsa, OK	12.63	71.47	31.71	53.60	17.42	13.24	15.65
Virginia Beach, VA	14.30	78.26	32.80	57.87	23.44	14.33	16.05
Washington, DC	16.65	93.22	38.57	77.26	25.20	18.26	18.52
Wichita, KS	12.56	75.40	30.36	48.65	17.46	14.72	15.77
Wilmington, NC	13.68	73.03	29.78	55.43	19.37	14.82	16.04
Winston-Salem, NC	13.91	77.03	30.59	59.42	18.68	14.44	15.37

Notes: Figures cover the Metropolitan Statistical Area (MSA); (1) Data is from 2023 due to data quality issues in the state of Colorado and its substate areas in 2024; n/a not available
Source: Bureau of Labor Statistics, Metro Area Occupational Employment and Wage Estimates, May 2024

Average Hourly Wages: Occupations L – N

Metro Area	Landscapers	Lawyers	Maids/House-keepers	Maintenance/Repairers	Marketing Managers	Network Admin.	Nurses, Licensed Practical
Albuquerque, NM	18.15	67.75	15.65	23.82	62.50	44.51	26.25
Anchorage, AK	21.86	65.58	18.49	27.18	60.07	45.18	37.16
Ann Arbor, MI	19.91	80.54	17.03	24.12	70.18	46.70	33.06
Athens, GA	17.53	49.61	13.10	20.51	72.47	40.57	27.62
Atlanta, GA	18.84	98.50	15.44	25.02	82.69	48.68	29.80
Austin, TX	18.93	83.20	15.47	24.12	79.43	50.49	30.98
Baltimore, MD	19.36	76.50	16.48	25.58	76.43	60.34	34.04
Billings, MT	19.81	52.20	17.08	22.86	66.97	39.58	26.99
Boise City, ID	20.23	67.91	16.90	24.14	62.17	49.66	30.70
Boston, MA	24.09	109.06	21.01	28.49	98.23	53.85	37.85
Boulder, CO[1]	23.16	120.91	18.76	28.09	89.78	53.52	32.93
Cape Coral, FL	17.78	72.21	16.09	23.30	65.95	46.21	29.34
Cedar Rapids, IA	18.72	61.80	15.71	26.12	66.98	41.23	29.02
Charleston, SC	18.21	62.85	15.15	23.84	66.50	46.44	29.19
Charlotte, NC	18.72	89.69	16.06	25.50	77.80	48.36	30.80
Chicago, IL	21.26	89.56	19.33	27.90	78.03	49.76	34.69
Cincinnati, OH	18.59	69.29	15.43	26.32	72.86	48.96	29.78
Clarksville, TN	17.20	67.51	13.62	22.72	56.80	57.61	26.97
Cleveland, OH	18.91	71.42	15.21	25.41	67.80	46.55	30.00
College Station, TX	16.48	67.99	13.30	20.21	61.86	38.10	26.76
Colorado Springs, CO[1]	20.66	69.39	16.92	23.63	81.56	49.17	30.52
Columbia, MO	17.79	71.41	15.77	22.42	59.28	43.70	28.34
Columbia, SC	17.37	65.86	13.97	23.42	63.36	43.01	28.97
Columbus, OH	19.22	72.24	15.53	25.88	70.72	48.31	30.09
Dallas, TX	18.42	85.71	15.45	24.02	74.76	50.61	30.36
Davenport, IA	18.79	67.21	15.51	25.55	69.88	40.45	28.99
Denver, CO[1]	21.35	95.55	18.17	26.82	89.00	51.25	31.94
Des Moines, IA	19.53	64.42	15.83	25.62	70.53	44.92	30.46
Detroit, MI	19.93	69.97	16.33	24.30	72.83	48.72	32.31
Durham, NC	19.05	73.55	17.00	25.50	82.71	53.21	30.26
El Paso, TX	15.24	61.03	12.61	19.68	55.59	39.84	27.06
Eugene, OR	19.74	68.79	17.08	24.77	64.41	45.54	35.15
Fargo, ND	20.93	60.13	16.65	25.20	66.41	40.53	28.38
Fort Collins, CO[1]	20.58	104.22	17.22	24.61	88.03	47.68	30.10
Fort Wayne, IN	17.85	65.81	14.93	25.25	n/a	39.62	29.69
Fort Worth, TX	18.42	85.71	15.45	24.02	74.76	50.61	30.36
Gainesville, FL	17.73	53.79	15.37	23.13	64.71	41.00	27.62
Green Bay, WI	19.50	69.46	16.12	25.64	75.74	41.79	28.26
Greensboro, NC	17.87	68.03	14.93	23.70	80.15	41.61	30.11
Honolulu, HI	20.46	58.87	25.07	27.07	63.78	48.37	32.75
Houston, TX	17.42	78.80	14.99	23.29	75.23	48.11	30.16
Huntsville, AL	17.69	69.83	13.23	22.69	67.44	48.12	25.96
Indianapolis, IN	18.81	82.32	15.57	25.58	64.61	43.51	30.93
Jacksonville, FL	17.93	62.65	15.49	23.93	69.06	44.92	28.41
Kansas City, MO	20.15	84.26	16.32	25.52	69.71	44.91	30.67
Lafayette, LA	15.75	66.98	12.04	19.43	52.19	45.64	24.52
Las Vegas, NV	19.84	n/a	20.07	26.40	59.85	49.09	34.18
Lexington, KY	18.10	57.22	14.59	22.68	59.96	41.66	28.18
Lincoln, NE	18.75	54.48	15.57	24.63	54.33	42.93	28.51
Little Rock, AR	16.67	65.50	13.80	22.43	55.96	40.49	26.10
Los Angeles, CA	21.42	130.10	21.39	27.74	87.09	53.71	37.14
Louisville, KY	18.54	58.69	15.46	25.41	68.75	43.31	29.46
Madison, WI	21.04	69.54	16.72	26.12	67.95	41.94	30.71
Manchester, NH	21.01	90.60	16.93	26.41	79.04	50.29	34.71
McAllen, TX	14.92	57.98	12.70	17.79	54.38	37.41	24.78

Table continued on following page.

Metro Area	Landscapers	Lawyers	Maids/House-keepers	Maintenance/Repairers	Marketing Managers	Network Admin.	Nurses, Licensed Practical
Memphis, TN	18.30	71.60	15.17	23.77	70.27	43.88	25.70
Miami, FL	18.25	78.54	16.01	23.66	69.64	47.57	30.32
Midland, TX	18.44	95.87	14.15	23.89	73.71	47.24	30.11
Milwaukee, WI	19.82	86.63	17.09	26.01	71.02	46.35	30.73
Minneapolis, MN	22.32	79.57	19.15	28.72	85.36	48.14	30.75
Nashville, TN	19.47	80.00	15.97	24.27	70.23	54.49	28.30
New Orleans, LA	16.51	66.68	14.95	22.29	60.16	47.36	28.31
New York, NY	21.91	103.90	24.09	28.95	96.08	57.33	34.69
Oklahoma City, OK	17.06	59.75	13.86	21.81	69.08	41.11	26.98
Omaha, NE	20.04	68.96	16.54	25.08	63.75	45.55	29.24
Orlando, FL	17.82	68.56	16.98	23.02	75.25	45.79	28.81
Philadelphia, PA	19.86	82.76	16.94	26.00	81.62	49.02	32.87
Phoenix, AZ	19.42	81.05	17.66	25.41	74.34	46.72	35.33
Pittsburgh, PA	18.69	72.59	15.75	24.30	63.96	44.03	28.96
Portland, OR	21.90	76.99	19.20	28.31	81.04	50.92	38.94
Providence, RI	21.36	73.53	17.71	25.96	82.62	50.61	35.27
Provo, UT	20.19	70.82	16.07	24.23	70.63	46.73	28.85
Raleigh, NC	19.00	71.98	15.98	24.47	81.03	50.43	30.60
Reno, NV	21.79	96.52	18.19	25.86	73.52	48.59	35.06
Richmond, VA	18.50	80.01	15.53	25.46	84.07	49.36	30.78
Rochester, MN	21.83	65.23	18.18	26.25	80.62	52.13	29.80
Sacramento, CA	22.37	97.12	21.69	27.33	84.16	52.73	39.66
Saint Louis, MO	19.80	73.53	16.55	26.56	66.03	43.67	30.72
Saint Paul, MN	22.32	79.57	19.15	28.72	85.36	48.14	30.75
Salem, OR	20.37	76.23	19.11	25.44	64.66	52.82	35.99
Salt Lake City, UT	20.01	76.47	17.31	25.87	72.64	49.94	31.60
San Antonio, TX	17.39	73.65	14.28	22.06	67.10	43.87	29.23
San Diego, CA	21.52	93.11	20.83	27.48	93.41	50.55	37.47
San Francisco, CA	25.75	132.29	25.07	33.69	109.71	64.21	43.56
San Jose, CA	25.28	151.17	27.28	33.50	137.00	63.55	44.06
Santa Rosa, CA	23.68	124.30	22.21	28.52	80.50	50.04	41.93
Savannah, GA	17.56	67.70	13.59	23.15	75.38	45.56	27.56
Seattle, WA	24.35	88.39	20.95	30.02	94.44	55.61	39.88
Sioux Falls, SD	17.48	64.81	15.77	23.21	78.00	37.26	24.52
Tampa, FL	17.89	67.66	16.79	22.66	73.93	48.19	29.09
Tucson, AZ	18.04	67.35	16.29	22.70	65.42	44.42	34.81
Tulsa, OK	17.01	57.59	13.86	22.39	70.25	51.21	27.71
Virginia Beach, VA	17.88	71.39	15.26	24.23	77.38	47.60	29.68
Washington, DC	20.84	105.48	18.53	27.76	91.27	60.06	34.17
Wichita, KS	18.31	60.10	14.70	22.57	67.18	39.93	27.76
Wilmington, NC	17.61	60.44	14.71	22.36	72.18	42.11	29.97
Winston-Salem, NC	17.78	83.92	15.70	24.06	74.45	43.84	28.98

Notes: Figures cover the Metropolitan Statistical Area (MSA); (1) Data is from 2023 due to data quality issues in the state of Colorado and its substate areas in 2024; n/a not available
Source: Bureau of Labor Statistics, Metro Area Occupational Employment and Wage Estimates, May 2024

Average Hourly Wages: Occupations N – P

Metro Area	Nurses, Registered	Nursing Assistants	Office Clerks	Physical Therapists	Physicians	Plumbers	Police Officers
Albuquerque, NM	45.99	18.59	18.52	48.32	146.53	30.61	33.46
Anchorage, AK	54.49	22.44	25.42	54.28	n/a	40.27	52.82
Ann Arbor, MI	46.65	19.82	21.46	47.54	117.60	35.47	37.47
Athens, GA	40.42	17.28	20.80	45.86	148.79	26.20	28.56
Atlanta, GA	46.46	18.72	20.88	50.04	128.59	29.64	30.37
Austin, TX	44.74	18.68	21.24	50.22	140.23	30.87	40.67
Baltimore, MD	46.70	20.15	22.45	50.65	111.79	32.84	38.57
Billings, MT	43.06	20.43	21.25	46.45	n/a	37.35	35.12
Boise City, ID	44.68	18.92	21.13	46.02	150.09	28.71	36.96
Boston, MA	55.63	22.73	25.39	49.54	104.76	42.81	39.16
Boulder, CO[1]	47.77	22.19	27.23	47.73	157.65	33.25	43.85
Cape Coral, FL	41.84	18.75	22.60	46.75	178.53	25.11	36.26
Cedar Rapids, IA	37.78	19.56	21.03	42.76	148.31	33.30	35.70
Charleston, SC	42.57	18.63	20.56	47.07	142.06	26.91	30.52
Charlotte, NC	42.86	19.15	20.94	48.26	150.06	27.07	32.47
Chicago, IL	45.47	21.85	23.22	52.46	109.22	44.43	47.28
Cincinnati, OH	41.93	19.66	21.56	48.99	137.38	32.13	38.17
Clarksville, TN	37.88	17.59	18.67	45.46	154.95	31.80	26.37
Cleveland, OH	43.24	19.22	22.21	48.56	117.07	33.28	37.16
College Station, TX	40.15	16.34	n/a	49.86	118.72	26.89	36.08
Colorado Springs, CO[1]	41.57	20.55	25.08	47.11	145.41	29.44	40.85
Columbia, MO	39.72	18.73	20.78	43.86	149.57	30.64	28.96
Columbia, SC	40.80	17.13	19.07	45.02	172.10	25.12	32.54
Columbus, OH	42.87	19.72	22.35	47.24	129.01	32.38	42.38
Dallas, TX	46.50	18.80	21.12	52.68	105.52	30.24	41.90
Davenport, IA	36.47	18.90	20.19	45.91	133.88	34.59	34.22
Denver, CO[1]	44.80	21.50	27.01	47.63	148.66	32.33	44.76
Des Moines, IA	38.30	20.34	21.64	46.36	117.95	32.51	39.83
Detroit, MI	44.56	19.58	22.38	47.96	79.84	36.88	36.19
Durham, NC	n/a	19.70	21.79	44.30	69.93	28.13	30.46
El Paso, TX	42.08	16.41	16.95	46.74	120.70	25.72	36.19
Eugene, OR	54.25	23.01	22.54	47.48	165.85	40.25	42.81
Fargo, ND	39.76	19.70	24.78	43.52	165.27	31.67	36.83
Fort Collins, CO[1]	43.16	20.38	25.12	44.64	119.01	30.07	44.59
Fort Wayne, IN	39.85	18.10	21.10	46.11	144.14	35.26	36.57
Fort Worth, TX	46.50	18.80	21.12	52.68	105.52	30.24	41.90
Gainesville, FL	42.66	18.80	21.26	46.21	130.80	24.73	29.02
Green Bay, WI	41.77	19.98	21.47	47.00	196.56	39.90	39.06
Greensboro, NC	41.93	18.27	19.68	44.25	144.60	25.64	30.89
Honolulu, HI	60.17	21.81	21.33	48.19	152.85	40.69	45.53
Houston, TX	46.51	18.77	19.64	53.94	123.51	29.30	35.97
Huntsville, AL	35.22	16.31	16.03	47.20	140.44	26.63	30.79
Indianapolis, IN	42.93	18.85	22.26	47.40	154.93	33.46	38.34
Jacksonville, FL	41.31	18.27	21.57	46.05	130.38	26.34	33.29
Kansas City, MO	41.12	20.02	22.34	46.79	76.04	36.37	33.12
Lafayette, LA	38.87	14.75	15.09	45.77	127.73	26.64	26.21
Las Vegas, NV	49.23	21.32	21.50	55.52	108.49	31.52	41.22
Lexington, KY	40.98	19.39	19.89	44.65	134.53	31.89	32.13
Lincoln, NE	39.04	19.33	18.58	44.86	136.23	30.39	40.64
Little Rock, AR	39.00	16.82	19.51	45.58	113.68	25.08	28.58
Los Angeles, CA	66.35	23.03	23.99	56.57	82.19	37.49	52.17
Louisville, KY	42.06	19.38	18.96	44.32	137.23	33.07	31.32
Madison, WI	46.09	21.62	21.81	47.86	156.17	42.99	38.38
Manchester, NH	44.26	22.36	24.15	44.89	148.76	31.71	36.87
McAllen, TX	36.77	15.66	16.04	50.03	144.98	22.61	29.67

Table continued on following page.

Metro Area	Nurses, Registered	Nursing Assistants	Office Clerks	Physical Therapists	Physicians	Plumbers	Police Officers
Memphis, TN	40.79	17.76	19.17	48.19	143.52	28.45	32.26
Miami, FL	44.26	19.01	22.54	42.79	117.21	27.27	50.84
Midland, TX	42.82	18.39	23.20	54.19	n/a	27.83	40.49
Milwaukee, WI	43.77	21.00	21.09	48.16	115.37	41.81	41.03
Minneapolis, MN	49.42	22.60	24.20	47.65	159.99	42.95	42.99
Nashville, TN	42.71	19.32	20.60	47.86	134.22	29.46	30.96
New Orleans, LA	43.12	16.45	16.23	51.00	147.27	29.90	27.76
New York, NY	55.60	23.60	24.07	52.54	125.08	43.78	44.53
Oklahoma City, OK	41.29	17.28	19.03	48.05	113.07	27.59	35.39
Omaha, NE	40.84	20.08	19.65	45.26	132.45	34.64	39.22
Orlando, FL	41.57	17.96	21.36	47.77	152.34	26.02	32.01
Philadelphia, PA	46.88	20.72	22.87	50.29	103.98	38.73	41.45
Phoenix, AZ	46.26	21.03	24.26	50.72	101.37	33.45	42.24
Pittsburgh, PA	41.36	19.62	21.43	45.46	106.62	34.88	39.89
Portland, OR	59.41	24.32	24.99	51.26	145.16	46.10	45.23
Providence, RI	47.85	20.93	23.21	47.81	115.77	36.48	37.31
Provo, UT	40.74	18.10	20.61	47.91	138.71	27.75	34.98
Raleigh, NC	43.18	18.76	20.44	45.60	140.88	27.06	31.94
Reno, NV	49.60	21.66	22.82	51.17	119.36	34.61	40.69
Richmond, VA	43.52	19.49	22.18	49.10	124.83	28.27	33.25
Rochester, MN	50.31	21.62	23.84	46.20	142.26	41.69	38.02
Sacramento, CA	78.37	23.25	25.08	60.12	165.05	35.78	53.46
Saint Louis, MO	40.74	19.04	21.94	46.78	n/a	37.26	34.71
Saint Paul, MN	49.42	22.60	24.20	47.65	159.99	42.95	42.99
Salem, OR	58.70	24.31	23.22	46.55	156.96	38.33	41.55
Salt Lake City, UT	44.02	19.66	22.49	47.44	112.68	32.12	40.23
San Antonio, TX	42.93	17.50	19.72	48.60	148.25	28.13	33.62
San Diego, CA	67.00	23.07	23.88	52.74	133.58	36.03	53.06
San Francisco, CA	85.79	27.59	27.96	65.53	127.97	41.48	61.75
San Jose, CA	91.29	27.97	28.51	68.75	89.33	49.42	69.86
Santa Rosa, CA	82.45	23.29	26.18	62.99	96.04	38.02	53.85
Savannah, GA	41.90	17.49	19.60	47.93	140.56	29.86	30.08
Seattle, WA	57.82	25.24	26.95	50.63	142.83	45.49	53.76
Sioux Falls, SD	34.16	18.18	18.51	42.66	n/a	27.31	37.35
Tampa, FL	43.40	18.54	21.94	47.43	143.21	26.24	37.66
Tucson, AZ	44.18	20.24	22.28	47.48	134.43	27.72	37.95
Tulsa, OK	43.20	17.41	19.08	46.55	83.29	28.27	31.70
Virginia Beach, VA	42.13	18.43	21.17	48.12	125.27	27.83	32.02
Washington, DC	49.29	20.85	26.37	53.25	100.51	34.13	41.76
Wichita, KS	36.06	17.82	16.54	46.81	100.27	29.54	28.31
Wilmington, NC	39.17	18.20	18.96	41.99	129.60	25.08	26.40
Winston-Salem, NC	42.11	18.13	19.25	47.50	n/a	25.08	27.78

Notes: Figures cover the Metropolitan Statistical Area (MSA); (1) Data is from 2023 due to data quality issues in the state of Colorado and its substate areas in 2024; n/a not available
Source: Bureau of Labor Statistics, Metro Area Occupational Employment and Wage Estimates, May 2024

Appendix A: Comparative Statistics

Average Hourly Wages: Occupations P – S

Metro Area	Postal Mail Carriers	R.E. Sales Agents	Retail Salespersons	Sales Reps., Technical/ Scientific	Secretaries, Exc. Leg./ Med./Exec.	Security Guards	Surgeons
Albuquerque, NM	28.74	40.95	16.73	41.73	21.86	21.72	219.96
Anchorage, AK	27.61	43.45	19.57	40.10	21.78	26.71	n/a
Ann Arbor, MI	28.15	31.11	18.46	105.25	24.23	21.89	n/a
Athens, GA	28.08	27.38	14.88	n/a	17.77	21.83	n/a
Atlanta, GA	28.20	34.66	16.55	55.13	20.91	19.64	216.10
Austin, TX	29.21	41.46	17.04	45.57	22.22	19.26	n/a
Baltimore, MD	28.82	27.82	17.59	44.15	23.24	20.69	171.05
Billings, MT	28.52	37.77	17.80	49.31	21.21	19.51	n/a
Boise City, ID	28.72	n/a	18.06	59.59	20.77	20.32	n/a
Boston, MA	29.71	46.11	19.71	54.45	27.63	22.25	161.25
Boulder, CO[1]	29.62	37.36	20.20	68.73	23.54	25.69	n/a
Cape Coral, FL	29.05	37.59	16.92	57.39	20.71	17.45	n/a
Cedar Rapids, IA	28.91	21.00	16.36	49.65	21.59	19.04	n/a
Charleston, SC	29.37	n/a	16.45	50.27	21.83	18.35	n/a
Charlotte, NC	29.03	30.17	16.65	63.70	20.49	19.12	248.26
Chicago, IL	29.11	29.28	18.67	58.57	25.84	21.16	161.04
Cincinnati, OH	29.19	24.40	17.19	57.27	23.98	19.14	n/a
Clarksville, TN	27.83	25.11	16.33	34.76	19.85	19.00	n/a
Cleveland, OH	28.67	23.45	17.25	47.42	22.52	19.46	n/a
College Station, TX	27.95	29.01	15.01	41.37	19.66	16.89	n/a
Colorado Springs, CO[1]	27.18	33.25	18.80	53.78	21.04	19.20	n/a
Columbia, MO	28.47	24.50	16.22	46.86	20.78	18.70	n/a
Columbia, SC	27.58	25.47	15.69	55.80	20.60	16.75	n/a
Columbus, OH	29.11	25.57	17.40	54.37	23.47	19.81	n/a
Dallas, TX	29.14	35.39	16.85	49.39	22.33	19.16	172.43
Davenport, IA	28.67	31.72	16.82	46.92	21.95	19.78	n/a
Denver, CO[1]	29.38	n/a	20.04	57.52	23.31	22.24	n/a
Des Moines, IA	30.06	20.22	17.08	60.11	22.86	19.84	207.59
Detroit, MI	28.48	32.41	19.31	68.16	23.38	19.17	n/a
Durham, NC	29.34	28.62	16.63	57.68	23.09	21.40	n/a
El Paso, TX	28.75	31.06	14.45	41.79	18.76	14.38	n/a
Eugene, OR	27.06	26.12	18.58	52.14	23.51	19.91	186.25
Fargo, ND	30.03	34.07	18.57	54.80	21.50	20.01	n/a
Fort Collins, CO[1]	28.36	32.17	18.87	52.65	21.68	19.32	n/a
Fort Wayne, IN	28.41	37.39	16.08	52.60	20.58	20.23	n/a
Fort Worth, TX	29.14	35.39	16.85	49.39	22.33	19.16	172.43
Gainesville, FL	28.67	29.50	16.05	48.82	21.09	17.73	n/a
Green Bay, WI	29.14	28.56	17.47	31.64	22.49	20.67	n/a
Greensboro, NC	29.19	31.36	15.70	47.29	21.42	17.81	n/a
Honolulu, HI	27.98	33.03	19.06	58.17	25.07	20.40	n/a
Houston, TX	28.58	36.58	16.26	50.66	22.14	18.23	n/a
Huntsville, AL	27.93	22.98	16.48	52.53	21.47	19.04	n/a
Indianapolis, IN	29.29	36.12	16.89	55.71	21.53	21.17	222.23
Jacksonville, FL	29.28	35.39	16.85	47.51	21.36	17.65	n/a
Kansas City, MO	29.08	40.62	17.76	57.49	21.49	22.78	n/a
Lafayette, LA	28.33	20.17	14.62	53.76	19.61	15.29	n/a
Las Vegas, NV	28.67	32.12	17.32	51.43	22.21	19.00	n/a
Lexington, KY	28.80	31.80	16.41	45.46	21.53	17.37	n/a
Lincoln, NE	30.57	27.17	16.38	40.00	22.03	20.05	n/a
Little Rock, AR	29.24	n/a	15.97	38.95	19.79	18.85	n/a
Los Angeles, CA	29.11	36.15	20.52	56.19	26.51	21.76	181.61
Louisville, KY	28.87	25.01	16.47	51.44	22.05	18.78	n/a
Madison, WI	29.38	32.13	17.90	43.29	24.50	21.74	n/a
Manchester, NH	29.69	25.56	18.32	57.21	22.59	22.02	n/a
McAllen, TX	30.28	28.28	14.03	39.87	18.47	13.98	n/a

Table continued on following page.

Metro Area	Postal Mail Carriers	R.E. Sales Agents	Retail Salespersons	Sales Reps., Technical/ Scientific	Secretaries, Exc. Leg./ Med./Exec.	Security Guards	Surgeons
Memphis, TN	28.14	27.09	16.86	48.33	21.52	18.00	n/a
Miami, FL	28.58	35.78	17.72	72.39	22.74	19.47	n/a
Midland, TX	27.68	57.72	17.23	n/a	22.14	23.02	n/a
Milwaukee, WI	28.92	36.71	17.62	43.52	23.21	21.24	n/a
Minneapolis, MN	29.62	34.01	18.56	50.40	25.28	24.99	180.26
Nashville, TN	29.67	24.17	17.69	49.18	22.79	20.23	n/a
New Orleans, LA	28.47	24.83	15.83	70.24	20.08	17.58	n/a
New York, NY	28.97	50.92	21.03	71.17	25.44	21.96	153.50
Oklahoma City, OK	28.83	n/a	16.29	44.00	19.75	20.95	n/a
Omaha, NE	29.45	23.46	16.96	41.73	22.46	21.05	165.50
Orlando, FL	28.68	33.44	16.93	50.60	21.59	18.05	n/a
Philadelphia, PA	28.61	31.43	17.58	57.13	23.47	20.88	n/a
Phoenix, AZ	29.45	33.31	18.61	47.67	23.90	20.06	201.58
Pittsburgh, PA	28.52	31.38	16.07	51.43	20.70	18.83	n/a
Portland, OR	28.58	33.65	20.03	60.80	26.92	23.38	n/a
Providence, RI	29.03	31.86	18.21	51.21	24.94	19.43	n/a
Provo, UT	29.07	24.11	17.69	38.31	20.88	20.05	n/a
Raleigh, NC	29.38	33.92	16.98	55.52	22.71	20.01	n/a
Reno, NV	28.83	27.04	18.04	54.60	23.35	20.48	n/a
Richmond, VA	29.19	34.95	17.09	54.94	22.38	21.69	n/a
Rochester, MN	30.26	32.82	18.61	63.87	25.11	23.45	n/a
Sacramento, CA	29.98	35.09	20.50	56.67	26.05	21.11	n/a
Saint Louis, MO	28.63	22.92	17.47	49.86	21.95	21.78	n/a
Saint Paul, MN	29.62	34.01	18.56	50.40	25.28	24.99	180.26
Salem, OR	28.32	31.93	18.59	51.43	25.45	21.67	n/a
Salt Lake City, UT	29.32	31.26	19.37	49.93	22.46	21.09	n/a
San Antonio, TX	28.61	27.84	16.14	48.30	21.21	17.26	n/a
San Diego, CA	28.81	33.54	20.16	56.30	26.29	21.29	215.16
San Francisco, CA	29.93	39.65	22.87	70.21	31.24	24.81	n/a
San Jose, CA	29.61	49.32	23.09	78.15	31.07	24.80	n/a
Santa Rosa, CA	28.63	39.71	21.77	56.13	27.28	22.66	n/a
Savannah, GA	28.40	31.87	15.49	43.92	19.62	17.54	n/a
Seattle, WA	29.52	40.04	21.76	71.82	28.37	25.48	164.19
Sioux Falls, SD	29.60	44.83	20.29	72.14	19.77	19.11	n/a
Tampa, FL	28.84	34.03	16.81	55.31	22.08	18.32	210.11
Tucson, AZ	29.27	30.47	18.32	47.81	21.86	18.88	n/a
Tulsa, OK	29.17	29.25	16.41	43.73	19.75	19.04	n/a
Virginia Beach, VA	28.31	31.93	16.44	52.97	21.87	20.46	n/a
Washington, DC	29.66	34.90	18.96	54.33	26.32	26.46	178.95
Wichita, KS	28.32	n/a	16.72	58.23	19.03	18.73	n/a
Wilmington, NC	29.33	24.73	16.08	51.06	21.11	21.00	n/a
Winston-Salem, NC	28.87	23.59	15.88	51.83	21.50	20.24	n/a

Notes: Figures cover the Metropolitan Statistical Area (MSA); (1) Data is from 2023 due to data quality issues in the state of Colorado and its substate areas in 2024; n/a not available
Source: Bureau of Labor Statistics, Metro Area Occupational Employment and Wage Estimates, May 2024

Average Hourly Wages: Occupations T – W

Metro Area	Teacher Assistants[2]	Teachers, Secondary School[2]	Telemarketers	Truck Drivers, Heavy	Truck Drivers, Light	Waiters/ Waitresses
Albuquerque, NM	15.58	32.70	33.59	25.68	20.59	18.83
Anchorage, AK	16.43	39.21	n/a	31.27	29.20	20.08
Ann Arbor, MI	16.34	35.96	n/a	28.12	23.79	20.05
Athens, GA	12.66	31.86	n/a	26.99	22.11	12.40
Atlanta, GA	14.65	35.49	16.14	28.06	23.97	13.74
Austin, TX	15.99	29.94	16.65	28.00	23.95	17.05
Baltimore, MD	18.88	36.16	16.80	28.16	23.74	19.68
Billings, MT	15.66	31.64	n/a	29.65	24.41	14.05
Boise City, ID	15.78	32.07	18.37	27.48	27.08	16.87
Boston, MA	20.03	42.74	18.61	29.10	25.46	22.07
Boulder, CO[1]	19.34	37.59	n/a	28.09	24.74	22.52
Cape Coral, FL	17.30	27.48	17.59	24.75	21.61	18.95
Cedar Rapids, IA	14.24	28.68	15.78	29.58	24.80	14.45
Charleston, SC	13.41	31.47	n/a	27.48	22.40	12.20
Charlotte, NC	14.49	27.70	19.21	27.14	21.73	16.65
Chicago, IL	18.41	42.55	17.05	31.25	25.40	16.76
Cincinnati, OH	17.09	33.20	16.50	30.56	24.16	18.39
Clarksville, TN	15.35	26.88	n/a	26.20	18.98	13.57
Cleveland, OH	17.13	37.67	15.51	28.14	21.75	18.81
College Station, TX	14.65	28.00	n/a	24.31	25.81	15.16
Colorado Springs, CO[1]	16.56	28.08	25.27	26.24	21.53	21.16
Columbia, MO	15.25	26.79	n/a	26.84	22.33	15.03
Columbia, SC	14.58	28.10	13.70	26.77	22.11	11.85
Columbus, OH	16.73	38.26	15.60	30.84	23.64	19.12
Dallas, TX	14.37	31.75	17.73	28.88	23.68	15.52
Davenport, IA	15.98	32.25	15.38	26.97	22.49	14.76
Denver, CO[1]	18.20	34.07	24.12	29.22	24.04	18.83
Des Moines, IA	15.17	29.25	15.86	29.34	22.55	15.00
Detroit, MI	15.96	34.65	16.11	27.01	21.91	19.88
Durham, NC	14.99	27.78	17.39	26.62	21.88	16.09
El Paso, TX	13.36	29.30	n/a	25.51	19.26	13.84
Eugene, OR	18.52	38.08	n/a	28.02	23.03	18.82
Fargo, ND	18.13	29.54	n/a	27.21	24.35	16.96
Fort Collins, CO[1]	17.53	31.75	n/a	26.38	22.67	21.70
Fort Wayne, IN	15.68	30.99	n/a	28.99	21.73	14.84
Fort Worth, TX	14.37	31.75	17.73	28.88	23.68	15.52
Gainesville, FL	15.81	33.04	n/a	24.90	21.27	18.15
Green Bay, WI	17.43	29.58	n/a	27.16	22.51	14.93
Greensboro, NC	13.56	25.65	16.15	26.84	21.55	15.80
Honolulu, HI	17.06	30.19	n/a	27.42	23.32	25.96
Houston, TX	14.01	31.15	18.64	27.49	23.30	15.23
Huntsville, AL	11.76	30.28	n/a	27.09	22.62	12.42
Indianapolis, IN	16.14	32.97	18.55	30.71	24.66	15.51
Jacksonville, FL	16.11	33.35	17.68	27.47	22.53	18.38
Kansas City, MO	15.24	29.47	18.48	28.62	23.71	17.04
Lafayette, LA	12.65	24.74	n/a	26.47	19.63	11.17
Las Vegas, NV	15.55	31.27	16.68	28.15	22.31	15.55
Lexington, KY	17.74	30.50	n/a	29.78	22.45	14.52
Lincoln, NE	13.52	29.94	14.12	38.54	22.72	19.50
Little Rock, AR	15.65	27.84	n/a	28.31	21.58	14.13
Los Angeles, CA	21.70	49.74	19.37	28.59	24.21	20.65
Louisville, KY	16.51	31.82	n/a	30.63	24.78	14.86
Madison, WI	18.13	30.40	17.61	27.62	23.52	17.52
Manchester, NH	18.04	34.04	15.89	27.49	22.94	21.07
McAllen, TX	13.28	30.53	n/a	24.00	19.17	13.40

Table continued on following page.

Metro Area	Teacher Assistants[2]	Teachers, Secondary School[2]	Telemarketers	Truck Drivers, Heavy	Truck Drivers, Light	Waiters/ Waitresses
Memphis, TN	14.32	28.90	13.76	29.58	29.29	13.80
Miami, FL	15.86	28.86	18.31	26.65	23.18	18.71
Midland, TX	15.30	31.99	n/a	28.32	23.98	15.93
Milwaukee, WI	17.98	34.09	17.30	28.14	22.92	16.18
Minneapolis, MN	20.05	35.70	22.16	31.39	25.01	13.95
Nashville, TN	14.83	29.56	15.16	28.95	23.69	15.99
New Orleans, LA	14.58	28.89	n/a	25.97	22.33	12.40
New York, NY	19.26	48.38	19.76	33.26	25.01	25.65
Oklahoma City, OK	14.11	27.06	16.04	27.43	20.70	14.43
Omaha, NE	14.60	29.23	14.96	27.64	23.61	19.47
Orlando, FL	15.02	27.08	17.71	26.28	22.34	18.62
Philadelphia, PA	16.42	37.57	18.66	29.70	23.32	19.57
Phoenix, AZ	17.41	33.10	25.15	27.04	25.25	23.73
Pittsburgh, PA	15.48	37.69	18.78	27.85	20.24	16.99
Portland, OR	19.63	42.02	19.64	31.98	24.55	22.74
Providence, RI	17.96	39.10	18.03	28.07	23.04	20.77
Provo, UT	15.72	32.55	19.36	27.39	21.30	16.73
Raleigh, NC	15.69	26.95	n/a	26.45	20.95	16.07
Reno, NV	17.00	36.97	16.27	31.35	24.02	13.93
Richmond, VA	16.87	30.92	n/a	29.88	21.77	19.74
Rochester, MN	18.97	34.45	n/a	30.88	23.86	12.89
Sacramento, CA	21.20	45.34	19.22	29.27	24.31	21.77
Saint Louis, MO	16.42	31.39	15.91	27.24	23.38	15.95
Saint Paul, MN	20.05	35.70	22.16	31.39	25.01	13.95
Salem, OR	18.55	36.88	n/a	29.67	22.75	20.45
Salt Lake City, UT	15.41	35.90	17.54	29.38	23.05	16.60
San Antonio, TX	12.78	29.49	16.58	25.47	21.43	15.16
San Diego, CA	20.95	54.30	19.47	28.38	23.68	22.56
San Francisco, CA	24.02	55.15	23.72	32.89	27.39	22.18
San Jose, CA	24.13	52.38	23.11	33.44	26.28	24.41
Santa Rosa, CA	22.92	47.05	n/a	29.46	25.70	21.12
Savannah, GA	13.88	32.08	13.85	27.26	24.37	13.65
Seattle, WA	24.88	47.37	21.66	33.99	26.42	27.97
Sioux Falls, SD	13.44	24.78	n/a	28.36	21.88	15.30
Tampa, FL	14.20	30.50	17.64	25.87	21.83	19.64
Tucson, AZ	16.88	25.54	n/a	25.42	23.43	20.95
Tulsa, OK	13.50	28.84	16.76	27.89	20.63	14.21
Virginia Beach, VA	18.39	34.95	20.17	24.69	20.85	19.88
Washington, DC	20.42	38.87	19.03	29.14	24.85	22.84
Wichita, KS	14.38	28.72	n/a	26.88	19.57	17.67
Wilmington, NC	14.70	25.61	16.58	24.77	19.92	14.23
Winston-Salem, NC	13.12	26.41	n/a	25.99	20.43	14.25

Notes: Figures cover the Metropolitan Statistical Area (MSA); (1) Data is from 2023 due to data quality issues in the state of Colorado and its substate areas in 2024; (2) Hourly wages were calculated from annual wage data based on a 40 hour work week; n/a not available
Source: Bureau of Labor Statistics, Metro Area Occupational Employment and Wage Estimates, May 2024

Means of Transportation to Work: City

City	Car/Truck/Van		Public Transportation			Bicycle	Walked	Other Means	Worked at Home
	Drove Alone	Car-pooled	Bus	Subway	Railroad				
Albuquerque, NM	73.2	8.8	1.2	0.0	0.1	0.9	1.9	1.2	12.8
Anchorage, AK	71.0	12.4	1.3	0.0	0.0	0.6	2.6	2.5	9.6
Ann Arbor, MI	45.6	5.0	7.3	0.1	0.0	2.4	13.1	0.5	26.2
Athens, GA	72.0	7.8	2.1	0.0	0.0	0.9	4.5	0.8	11.9
Atlanta, GA	55.2	4.6	3.6	2.5	0.1	0.7	4.2	2.4	26.6
Austin, TX	58.8	6.9	1.9	0.0	0.0	0.8	2.4	1.6	27.5
Baltimore, MD	56.8	6.9	9.3	1.0	0.8	0.6	5.6	3.1	15.9
Billings, MT	78.5	9.1	1.0	0.0	0.0	0.7	2.0	1.0	7.6
Boise City, ID	68.6	7.6	0.5	0.0	0.0	2.3	3.4	1.6	15.8
Boston, MA	34.1	5.4	8.6	13.6	1.2	2.1	13.8	2.4	18.8
Boulder, CO	41.9	3.6	5.8	0.0	0.0	7.6	8.6	0.9	31.6
Cape Coral, FL	76.0	8.1	0.2	0.0	0.0	0.1	1.0	1.4	13.1
Cedar Rapids, IA	77.0	6.5	0.6	0.0	0.0	0.3	2.2	0.8	12.6
Charleston, SC	68.1	6.5	0.9	0.0	0.0	1.5	4.1	1.2	17.6
Charlotte, NC	61.0	8.1	1.4	0.1	0.0	0.2	1.7	2.0	25.5
Chicago, IL	46.0	7.4	9.5	8.5	1.2	1.4	5.7	2.1	18.3
Cincinnati, OH	66.2	7.5	5.7	0.0	0.0	0.3	5.3	1.8	13.2
Clarksville, TN	81.0	8.7	0.5	0.0	0.0	0.0	1.2	1.5	7.1
Cleveland, OH	65.4	10.0	6.3	0.4	0.0	0.5	5.3	1.9	10.1
College Station, TX	70.8	8.0	2.3	0.0	0.0	1.9	3.9	1.1	12.1
Colorado Springs, CO	71.1	9.0	0.4	0.0	0.0	0.5	1.8	1.1	16.1
Columbia, MO	74.1	7.6	1.1	0.0	0.0	1.0	5.6	0.9	9.6
Columbia, SC	62.9	6.9	1.4	0.0	0.0	0.3	16.4	2.2	9.8
Columbus, OH	70.1	7.5	2.1	0.0	0.0	0.4	2.6	1.2	16.1
Dallas, TX	68.5	11.4	1.7	0.2	0.1	0.2	2.2	1.7	14.0
Davenport, IA	78.8	7.3	0.8	0.0	0.1	0.2	2.7	1.1	8.9
Denver, CO	57.7	6.5	2.8	0.3	0.1	1.6	3.9	2.7	24.4
Des Moines, IA	72.3	11.2	1.1	0.0	0.0	0.4	2.2	1.3	11.4
Detroit, MI	66.3	11.0	5.9	0.0	0.0	0.5	3.1	3.1	10.1
Durham, NC	65.2	8.0	2.2	0.0	0.0	0.5	2.3	1.4	20.6
El Paso, TX	76.5	11.1	1.0	0.0	0.0	0.1	1.1	2.3	7.8
Eugene, OR	63.0	7.9	2.6	0.0	0.0	4.7	5.3	1.1	15.3
Fargo, ND	78.7	6.6	0.7	0.0	0.1	0.3	3.5	2.0	8.1
Fort Collins, CO	63.3	5.6	1.4	0.0	0.0	4.2	4.2	1.0	20.2
Fort Wayne, IN	78.1	9.9	1.1	0.0	0.0	0.3	1.5	0.8	8.2
Fort Worth, TX	72.9	10.9	0.4	0.0	0.1	0.2	1.2	1.5	12.9
Gainesville, FL	62.9	9.0	4.9	0.0	0.0	3.5	5.0	2.3	12.4
Green Bay, WI	75.9	10.7	1.0	0.0	0.0	0.4	2.3	1.1	8.5
Greensboro, NC	73.7	8.2	2.4	0.0	0.0	0.2	2.3	1.4	11.8
Honolulu, HI	55.7	14.2	7.9	0.0	0.0	1.8	7.7	3.7	8.9
Houston, TX	69.7	10.1	2.9	0.1	0.0	0.4	1.9	3.1	11.7
Huntsville, AL	77.5	6.8	0.3	0.0	0.0	0.0	1.3	1.0	13.1
Indianapolis, IN	73.7	9.6	1.4	0.0	0.0	0.4	1.8	0.9	12.3
Jacksonville, FL	72.8	9.0	1.2	0.0	0.0	0.4	1.2	2.0	13.5
Kansas City, MO	72.7	7.4	1.9	0.0	0.0	0.2	1.5	1.5	14.8
Lafayette, LA	80.4	5.6	0.6	0.0	0.0	0.5	2.2	1.2	9.5
Las Vegas, NV	72.6	10.0	2.4	0.0	0.0	0.3	1.3	2.9	10.5
Lexington, KY	74.8	8.4	1.3	0.0	0.0	0.5	3.0	1.0	10.9
Lincoln, NE	75.7	8.6	0.9	0.0	0.0	0.9	3.2	0.8	10.0
Little Rock, AR	76.5	8.9	1.0	0.0	0.0	0.2	1.8	0.9	10.8
Los Angeles, CA	61.4	8.8	5.7	0.6	0.1	0.7	3.1	2.3	17.3
Louisville, KY	73.5	8.7	2.2	0.0	0.0	0.3	2.0	1.7	11.6
Madison, WI	57.6	5.9	5.6	0.0	0.1	3.1	8.2	1.3	18.2
Manchester, NH	74.2	9.1	0.4	0.1	0.0	0.3	2.4	1.5	12.1

Table continued on following page.

City	Car/Truck/Van		Public Transportation			Bicycle	Walked	Other Means	Worked at Home
	Drove Alone	Car-pooled	Bus	Subway	Railroad				
McAllen, TX	72.2	10.4	0.4	0.0	0.0	0.3	0.9	4.3	11.5
Memphis, TN	77.8	10.0	0.8	0.0	0.0	0.2	1.7	1.5	8.0
Miami, FL	61.7	7.9	5.4	1.1	0.1	0.8	5.4	3.5	14.2
Midland, TX	79.9	12.2	0.4	0.0	0.0	0.2	0.7	1.0	5.6
Milwaukee, WI	67.8	10.0	5.3	0.0	0.0	0.5	4.0	1.2	11.2
Minneapolis, MN	53.4	5.9	6.3	0.2	0.0	2.3	6.0	2.5	23.3
Nashville, TN	68.1	8.3	1.6	0.0	0.0	0.3	1.9	1.5	18.3
New Orleans, LA	63.2	8.7	3.8	0.1	0.0	1.9	5.6	3.0	13.7
New York, NY	21.9	4.3	9.8	34.4	1.0	1.5	9.4	2.7	15.0
Oklahoma City, OK	77.0	9.6	0.4	0.0	0.0	0.2	1.4	1.6	9.8
Omaha, NE	73.3	8.7	1.1	0.0	0.0	0.2	1.8	1.3	13.6
Orlando, FL	69.5	8.9	1.8	0.0	0.0	0.5	1.6	2.5	15.1
Philadelphia, PA	46.7	7.6	10.9	4.7	1.6	1.9	7.5	2.8	16.4
Phoenix, AZ	66.1	10.9	1.8	0.0	0.0	0.4	1.6	2.2	16.9
Pittsburgh, PA	48.2	6.2	11.6	0.3	0.0	1.1	9.8	2.3	20.4
Portland, OR	50.5	7.0	5.4	0.2	0.1	3.7	4.8	3.0	25.3
Providence, RI	62.6	9.8	3.1	0.0	1.1	0.8	7.3	2.6	12.7
Provo, UT	57.4	10.4	4.3	0.1	0.9	1.4	10.3	1.1	14.2
Raleigh, NC	65.1	6.6	1.3	0.0	0.0	0.4	1.6	1.6	23.4
Reno, NV	67.6	12.6	2.4	0.0	0.0	0.6	3.2	2.8	10.8
Richmond, VA	64.9	7.8	3.6	0.0	0.0	1.1	4.2	1.5	16.9
Rochester, MN	65.5	11.1	4.1	0.0	0.0	0.8	4.3	1.3	12.9
Sacramento, CA	65.5	9.0	1.0	0.2	0.1	1.4	2.7	2.4	17.7
Saint Louis, MO	66.6	6.7	4.4	0.4	0.1	0.9	4.0	1.9	15.0
Saint Paul, MN	59.3	10.0	5.0	0.1	0.0	0.8	3.7	2.7	18.3
Salem, OR	68.4	10.4	1.8	0.0	0.0	1.1	3.0	1.4	14.0
Salt Lake City, UT	60.2	8.1	3.1	0.3	0.3	1.6	4.8	2.9	18.5
San Antonio, TX	70.5	12.1	2.1	0.0	0.0	0.2	1.7	1.6	11.8
San Diego, CA	64.2	7.8	2.3	0.1	0.1	0.7	3.4	2.2	19.2
San Francisco, CA	28.6	6.0	14.1	4.8	1.1	3.3	10.0	4.5	27.5
San Jose, CA	64.6	10.5	1.6	0.2	0.5	0.5	1.8	1.7	18.5
Santa Rosa, CA	73.1	11.1	0.9	0.0	0.2	0.6	2.3	1.3	10.5
Savannah, GA	70.4	10.3	2.5	0.1	0.0	1.5	3.8	1.4	10.1
Seattle, WA	37.6	5.1	11.2	0.5	0.0	2.5	8.3	3.5	31.3
Sioux Falls, SD	79.4	7.7	0.7	0.0	0.0	0.2	1.9	0.9	9.4
Tampa, FL	66.1	8.2	1.3	0.0	0.0	0.8	2.3	2.1	19.3
Tucson, AZ	69.5	9.9	2.3	0.0	0.0	1.6	2.7	1.6	12.4
Tulsa, OK	75.4	10.2	0.5	0.0	0.0	0.3	1.7	1.8	10.1
Virginia Beach, VA	75.3	7.5	0.8	0.0	0.0	0.4	1.8	1.6	12.7
Washington, DC	28.2	4.3	8.1	13.8	0.3	3.3	10.0	2.7	29.4
Wichita, KS	80.0	9.6	0.6	0.0	0.0	0.4	0.9	1.5	6.9
Wilmington, NC	70.9	7.0	0.4	0.0	0.0	0.8	2.2	1.0	17.7
Winston-Salem, NC	73.2	9.5	1.1	0.0	0.0	0.3	2.0	1.6	12.3
U.S.	70.2	8.5	1.7	1.3	0.4	0.4	2.4	1.6	13.5

Note: Figures are percentages and cover workers 16 years of age and older
Source: U.S. Census Bureau, 2019-2023 American Community Survey 5-Year Estimates

Means of Transportation to Work: Metro Area

Metro Area	Car/Truck/Van		Public Transportation			Bicycle	Walked	Other Means	Worked at Home
	Drove Alone	Carpooled	Bus	Subway	Railroad				
Albuquerque, NM	73.5	9.1	0.8	0.0	0.1	0.6	1.6	1.3	12.9
Anchorage, AK	71.3	11.7	1.1	0.0	0.0	0.5	2.4	3.1	9.8
Ann Arbor, MI	61.9	6.3	3.7	0.0	0.0	1.0	5.8	0.8	20.3
Athens, GA	74.7	7.3	1.3	0.0	0.0	0.6	3.3	0.9	12.1
Atlanta, GA	68.0	8.7	1.2	0.5	0.1	0.1	1.2	1.8	18.5
Austin, TX	63.4	7.7	1.0	0.0	0.0	0.4	1.8	1.4	24.2
Baltimore, MD	69.2	6.9	2.7	0.5	0.5	0.2	2.2	1.6	16.1
Billings, MT	76.5	10.5	1.0	0.0	0.0	0.5	2.3	1.0	8.2
Boise City, ID	71.7	8.3	0.3	0.0	0.0	1.1	2.2	1.4	15.1
Boston, MA	58.6	6.3	2.6	4.6	1.4	1.0	4.7	2.0	18.7
Boulder, CO	55.6	5.7	3.1	0.0	0.0	3.0	3.8	0.9	27.9
Cape Coral, FL	72.7	9.4	0.4	0.0	0.0	0.6	1.1	1.8	13.8
Cedar Rapids, IA	76.8	6.5	0.5	0.0	0.0	0.2	1.9	0.8	13.3
Charleston, SC	75.3	7.8	0.6	0.0	0.0	0.5	1.7	1.2	12.9
Charlotte, NC	69.3	8.1	0.7	0.1	0.0	0.1	1.2	1.5	19.0
Chicago, IL	63.6	7.8	3.3	2.9	2.0	0.6	2.8	1.6	15.6
Cincinnati, OH	75.0	7.7	1.3	0.0	0.0	0.2	1.8	1.1	12.9
Clarksville, TN	79.6	9.5	0.4	0.0	0.0	0.2	2.4	1.5	6.5
Cleveland, OH	74.3	7.4	1.9	0.1	0.0	0.2	2.1	1.3	12.6
College Station, TX	75.1	9.5	1.3	0.0	0.0	1.0	2.1	1.3	9.7
Colorado Springs, CO	70.5	9.0	0.3	0.0	0.0	0.4	3.3	1.1	15.4
Columbia, MO	76.0	8.8	0.7	0.0	0.0	0.7	3.8	1.0	8.9
Columbia, SC	76.2	8.1	0.5	0.0	0.0	0.1	3.5	1.7	9.9
Columbus, OH	72.2	6.8	1.1	0.0	0.0	0.2	1.9	1.1	16.6
Dallas, TX	71.2	9.4	0.5	0.1	0.1	0.1	1.2	1.5	15.9
Davenport, IA	80.1	7.2	0.8	0.0	0.0	0.1	2.4	0.9	8.4
Denver, CO	65.0	7.3	1.6	0.1	0.1	0.7	2.0	2.0	21.2
Des Moines, IA	74.3	7.9	0.4	0.0	0.0	0.2	1.6	1.2	14.3
Detroit, MI	74.8	7.6	1.0	0.0	0.0	0.2	1.3	1.2	13.8
Durham, NC	65.1	7.4	2.2	0.0	0.0	0.7	2.5	1.5	20.6
El Paso, TX	76.3	11.4	0.9	0.0	0.0	0.1	1.5	2.0	7.8
Eugene, OR	67.4	8.9	1.9	0.0	0.0	2.8	4.1	1.1	13.9
Fargo, ND	78.5	6.8	0.7	0.0	0.0	0.3	2.8	1.6	9.3
Fort Collins, CO	68.4	5.6	0.9	0.0	0.0	2.4	2.8	1.1	18.9
Fort Wayne, IN	79.9	9.1	0.7	0.0	0.0	0.3	1.2	0.7	8.1
Fort Worth, TX	71.2	9.4	0.5	0.1	0.1	0.1	1.2	1.5	15.9
Gainesville, FL	71.5	8.8	2.4	0.0	0.0	1.6	2.9	1.5	11.2
Green Bay, WI	78.7	7.8	0.4	0.0	0.0	0.2	1.7	0.9	10.4
Greensboro, NC	76.6	8.9	1.0	0.0	0.0	0.1	1.6	1.6	10.3
Honolulu, HI	64.0	13.7	5.2	0.0	0.0	1.0	5.0	2.6	8.4
Houston, TX	73.5	9.7	1.4	0.0	0.0	0.2	1.2	2.0	11.9
Huntsville, AL	78.3	6.8	0.2	0.0	0.0	0.0	0.8	1.1	12.7
Indianapolis, IN	74.5	8.4	0.6	0.0	0.0	0.3	1.3	0.9	14.0
Jacksonville, FL	72.1	8.2	0.7	0.0	0.0	0.4	1.1	1.8	15.6
Kansas City, MO	75.0	6.9	0.6	0.0	0.0	0.1	1.1	1.1	15.2
Lafayette, LA	82.4	6.3	0.3	0.0	0.0	0.3	1.8	1.3	7.7
Las Vegas, NV	72.6	10.3	2.3	0.0	0.0	0.2	1.2	2.6	10.7
Lexington, KY	76.1	8.6	0.9	0.0	0.0	0.4	2.5	0.8	10.7
Lincoln, NE	76.3	8.5	0.8	0.0	0.0	0.8	3.0	0.7	9.9
Little Rock, AR	79.2	8.8	0.5	0.0	0.0	0.1	1.2	1.0	9.1
Los Angeles, CA	67.1	9.2	2.9	0.3	0.1	0.6	2.3	1.9	15.5
Louisville, KY	76.0	8.4	1.1	0.0	0.0	0.2	1.5	1.2	11.6
Madison, WI	67.3	5.9	2.6	0.0	0.0	1.6	4.8	1.1	16.7
Manchester, NH	72.9	7.4	0.4	0.1	0.1	0.2	1.7	1.1	16.1

Table continued on following page.

Metro Area	Car/Truck/Van		Public Transportation			Bicycle	Walked	Other Means	Worked at Home
	Drove Alone	Car-pooled	Bus	Subway	Railroad				
McAllen, TX	75.8	10.3	0.2	0.0	0.0	0.1	1.2	3.7	8.6
Memphis, TN	79.5	9.2	0.4	0.0	0.0	0.1	1.0	1.1	8.6
Miami, FL	71.3	9.2	2.0	0.2	0.1	0.4	1.6	2.3	12.9
Midland, TX	79.8	12.0	0.3	0.0	0.0	0.2	1.1	1.3	5.2
Milwaukee, WI	73.8	7.1	2.1	0.0	0.0	0.3	2.2	0.9	13.5
Minneapolis, MN	67.7	7.1	2.2	0.0	0.0	0.5	2.0	1.4	19.0
Nashville, TN	72.4	8.2	0.7	0.0	0.0	0.1	1.1	1.2	16.3
New Orleans, LA	73.0	9.7	1.8	0.0	0.0	0.9	3.1	1.9	9.6
New York, NY	45.5	6.1	6.4	15.6	2.6	0.8	5.4	2.7	14.9
Oklahoma City, OK	78.1	9.0	0.3	0.0	0.0	0.2	1.6	1.3	9.5
Omaha, NE	75.8	7.8	0.6	0.0	0.0	0.1	1.5	1.1	13.0
Orlando, FL	70.8	9.2	1.0	0.0	0.1	0.3	1.2	1.8	15.6
Philadelphia, PA	64.4	7.0	3.4	1.5	1.3	0.6	3.2	1.7	16.8
Phoenix, AZ	66.9	9.7	1.0	0.0	0.0	0.5	1.4	2.0	18.5
Pittsburgh, PA	69.9	6.9	3.2	0.2	0.0	0.2	2.9	1.4	15.4
Portland, OR	62.7	7.7	2.6	0.2	0.1	1.4	3.1	2.0	20.4
Providence, RI	74.9	8.1	1.1	0.1	0.7	0.3	2.6	1.5	10.9
Provo, UT	66.7	10.1	1.2	0.0	0.6	0.5	2.9	1.0	17.1
Raleigh, NC	67.0	6.5	0.5	0.0	0.0	0.2	1.1	1.3	23.4
Reno, NV	70.2	12.5	1.8	0.0	0.0	0.4	2.2	2.1	10.8
Richmond, VA	71.6	7.3	1.0	0.0	0.1	0.3	1.7	1.2	16.7
Rochester, MN	69.6	9.9	2.4	0.0	0.0	0.6	3.5	1.1	12.8
Sacramento, CA	67.7	8.6	0.8	0.1	0.1	1.1	1.8	1.9	17.9
Saint Louis, MO	75.6	6.6	1.1	0.1	0.0	0.2	1.5	1.1	13.8
Saint Paul, MN	67.7	7.1	2.2	0.0	0.0	0.5	2.0	1.4	19.0
Salem, OR	70.9	11.0	1.1	0.0	0.0	0.7	2.4	1.3	12.6
Salt Lake City, UT	67.0	10.0	1.2	0.2	0.2	0.5	1.7	1.7	17.5
San Antonio, TX	71.5	10.9	1.3	0.0	0.0	0.2	1.5	1.5	13.0
San Diego, CA	67.6	8.2	1.6	0.1	0.1	0.5	3.1	2.0	16.9
San Francisco, CA	50.9	8.2	4.7	3.9	1.1	1.5	3.9	2.6	23.2
San Jose, CA	62.1	9.0	1.5	0.2	0.6	1.3	2.0	1.7	21.5
Santa Rosa, CA	71.0	9.2	0.7	0.1	0.2	0.7	2.4	1.4	14.4
Savannah, GA	76.6	9.4	1.0	0.0	0.0	0.7	1.7	1.5	9.0
Seattle, WA	59.1	8.2	4.7	0.1	0.3	0.8	3.3	1.8	21.6
Sioux Falls, SD	79.3	7.2	0.5	0.0	0.0	0.1	2.0	0.8	10.1
Tampa, FL	69.7	8.1	0.8	0.0	0.0	0.5	1.2	1.8	17.8
Tucson, AZ	70.7	9.6	1.5	0.0	0.0	1.0	1.9	1.5	13.8
Tulsa, OK	78.2	9.0	0.3	0.0	0.0	0.2	1.2	1.2	9.8
Virginia Beach, VA	75.8	8.2	1.0	0.0	0.0	0.3	2.4	1.6	10.7
Washington, DC	56.4	8.0	2.9	4.4	0.4	0.7	2.7	1.9	22.6
Wichita, KS	80.6	8.6	0.4	0.0	0.0	0.3	1.4	1.3	7.3
Wilmington, NC	73.9	7.8	0.2	0.0	0.0	0.3	1.2	1.1	15.5
Winston-Salem, NC	77.9	8.7	0.5	0.0	0.0	0.1	1.2	1.1	10.6
U.S.	70.2	8.5	1.7	1.3	0.4	0.4	2.4	1.6	13.5

Note: Figures are percentages and cover workers 16 years of age and older; Figures cover the Metropolitan Statistical Area (MSA)
Source: U.S. Census Bureau, 2019-2023 American Community Survey 5-Year Estimates

Travel Time to Work: City

City	Less Than 10 Minutes	10 to 19 Minutes	20 to 29 Minutes	30 to 44 Minutes	45 to 59 Minutes	60 to 89 Minutes	90 Minutes or More
Albuquerque, NM	11.7	36.0	27.6	17.3	3.0	2.5	1.9
Anchorage, AK	15.6	44.8	23.3	11.1	2.3	1.4	1.5
Ann Arbor, MI	12.9	45.8	18.9	13.6	5.8	2.3	0.7
Athens, GA	17.2	45.0	17.6	10.5	3.8	3.6	2.3
Atlanta, GA	7.8	29.8	25.5	22.5	6.3	5.1	3.0
Austin, TX	9.6	33.4	24.5	21.5	6.1	3.5	1.4
Baltimore, MD	7.2	24.8	24.3	24.3	8.5	6.9	4.0
Billings, MT	19.3	51.9	18.3	6.8	1.2	1.2	1.2
Boise City, ID	14.3	44.2	25.5	11.5	1.7	1.6	1.2
Boston, MA	6.9	21.3	20.7	28.8	11.4	8.6	2.3
Boulder, CO	20.2	44.2	16.9	9.4	5.0	2.9	1.3
Cape Coral, FL	7.8	24.9	22.7	24.9	10.5	6.5	2.7
Cedar Rapids, IA	19.8	47.9	17.9	8.7	1.8	2.5	1.4
Charleston, SC	11.8	32.8	24.8	19.0	7.2	2.5	1.8
Charlotte, NC	9.1	29.7	27.1	23.2	6.1	3.0	1.9
Chicago, IL	5.2	17.2	19.2	29.8	14.6	10.9	3.0
Cincinnati, OH	11.2	34.5	26.3	19.1	3.8	2.8	2.2
Clarksville, TN	10.5	32.6	25.9	13.1	7.3	8.3	2.3
Cleveland, OH	10.5	35.0	27.3	19.4	3.3	2.6	1.9
College Station, TX	17.5	54.7	15.3	7.9	1.4	1.8	1.5
Colorado Springs, CO	11.6	35.7	27.6	16.9	3.0	3.0	2.1
Columbia, MO	19.5	54.4	14.3	7.2	2.1	1.2	1.3
Columbia, SC	27.7	37.4	19.1	10.0	2.7	1.2	1.8
Columbus, OH	10.3	35.1	31.0	17.2	3.1	2.1	1.3
Dallas, TX	8.8	28.5	23.6	24.7	7.4	5.6	1.5
Davenport, IA	15.3	45.9	24.3	8.4	2.9	2.0	1.1
Denver, CO	8.6	28.3	25.3	25.9	6.5	3.9	1.5
Des Moines, IA	14.1	43.0	25.7	11.9	2.0	1.9	1.5
Detroit, MI	8.1	30.2	27.0	22.3	6.0	4.0	2.3
Durham, NC	10.2	37.8	25.1	17.8	4.8	2.6	1.6
El Paso, TX	9.3	33.5	28.5	20.1	4.3	2.4	1.9
Eugene, OR	16.3	50.9	19.5	7.2	2.2	2.1	1.9
Fargo, ND	20.1	56.1	15.1	4.6	1.5	1.7	0.9
Fort Collins, CO	15.6	45.7	19.3	10.1	4.6	3.3	1.4
Fort Wayne, IN	13.1	38.1	27.8	13.7	2.9	2.2	2.2
Fort Worth, TX	7.4	29.2	23.5	23.5	8.9	5.7	1.8
Gainesville, FL	16.1	43.8	23.4	11.6	2.6	1.6	0.9
Green Bay, WI	18.1	47.5	18.0	9.1	3.9	1.9	1.5
Greensboro, NC	13.4	40.9	22.3	14.6	3.5	3.0	2.4
Honolulu, HI	9.0	39.2	22.3	20.5	4.5	3.4	1.2
Houston, TX	7.5	25.3	23.6	27.7	8.6	5.5	1.8
Huntsville, AL	13.9	39.8	27.2	14.9	2.2	1.2	0.7
Indianapolis, IN	9.8	29.6	28.6	23.1	4.5	2.5	2.0
Jacksonville, FL	8.7	29.0	28.0	24.9	5.6	2.5	1.3
Kansas City, MO	11.7	35.0	28.3	18.3	3.5	1.8	1.4
Lafayette, LA	16.4	44.8	19.9	11.5	2.3	3.6	1.6
Las Vegas, NV	7.3	24.0	30.9	27.3	6.0	2.6	1.9
Lexington, KY	13.0	40.1	26.4	13.7	2.7	2.3	1.9
Lincoln, NE	16.8	46.0	22.5	8.9	2.9	2.1	1.0
Little Rock, AR	15.3	46.6	22.6	10.7	2.2	1.7	0.9
Los Angeles, CA	6.3	22.2	19.9	28.5	10.4	9.4	3.3
Louisville, KY	10.1	31.8	31.9	19.1	3.6	2.0	1.4
Madison, WI	14.4	40.3	25.5	14.3	3.2	1.7	0.6
Manchester, NH	12.9	35.1	23.0	16.0	6.2	5.1	1.9
McAllen, TX	14.6	39.5	23.9	15.2	2.9	2.1	1.7

Table continued on following page.

City	Less Than 10 Minutes	10 to 19 Minutes	20 to 29 Minutes	30 to 44 Minutes	45 to 59 Minutes	60 to 89 Minutes	90 Minutes or More
Memphis, TN	11.2	31.8	33.7	18.2	2.7	1.5	1.0
Miami, FL	6.4	24.1	25.7	27.6	8.7	6.0	1.5
Midland, TX	16.2	45.2	18.6	11.9	4.0	2.3	1.9
Milwaukee, WI	10.6	36.2	26.5	18.9	3.4	2.9	1.6
Minneapolis, MN	8.3	36.1	28.8	19.2	4.2	2.4	1.0
Nashville, TN	9.2	28.7	26.8	23.2	7.0	3.8	1.3
New Orleans, LA	11.9	35.1	24.3	18.7	5.2	3.1	1.7
New York, NY	4.4	12.7	14.0	27.0	16.1	18.7	7.1
Oklahoma City, OK	10.4	35.0	28.8	19.2	3.6	1.5	1.6
Omaha, NE	14.6	41.3	26.4	12.4	2.3	1.8	1.2
Orlando, FL	7.5	26.1	27.4	26.5	6.4	3.9	2.2
Philadelphia, PA	6.7	19.7	20.8	28.1	12.0	9.2	3.5
Phoenix, AZ	9.0	26.7	26.8	24.6	7.1	4.2	1.6
Pittsburgh, PA	10.3	34.0	26.0	20.5	4.6	3.2	1.5
Portland, OR	9.3	29.9	27.1	22.5	6.1	3.7	1.5
Providence, RI	11.0	36.1	20.6	16.8	6.7	6.1	2.7
Provo, UT	20.5	44.9	16.6	10.2	4.4	2.3	1.1
Raleigh, NC	10.3	33.4	26.8	19.9	5.4	2.5	1.7
Reno, NV	15.1	39.7	23.5	13.2	4.9	2.4	1.2
Richmond, VA	11.4	37.4	27.0	16.8	2.9	2.8	1.7
Rochester, MN	18.3	54.5	14.7	6.1	2.8	2.7	0.9
Sacramento, CA	8.9	32.2	25.8	21.3	5.1	3.5	3.2
Saint Louis, MO	9.9	36.2	27.2	19.5	3.2	2.5	1.6
Saint Paul, MN	10.5	35.0	27.6	19.0	4.4	2.1	1.4
Salem, OR	14.6	41.5	18.2	12.3	5.5	6.3	1.6
Salt Lake City, UT	14.6	45.2	20.6	12.7	3.5	2.1	1.3
San Antonio, TX	9.5	30.7	26.1	22.2	5.9	3.7	1.8
San Diego, CA	8.2	33.2	27.9	20.4	5.4	3.3	1.7
San Francisco, CA	5.3	21.2	22.1	28.8	10.6	8.9	3.1
San Jose, CA	5.9	26.5	25.5	25.0	8.6	5.7	2.7
Santa Rosa, CA	13.1	42.1	19.4	14.4	4.5	3.6	2.9
Savannah, GA	14.0	40.1	23.5	14.7	4.4	2.3	1.0
Seattle, WA	8.0	26.0	24.5	26.4	9.2	4.4	1.4
Sioux Falls, SD	15.9	52.2	22.0	6.2	1.5	1.0	1.2
Tampa, FL	10.8	31.4	22.8	22.5	6.5	4.2	1.8
Tucson, AZ	12.3	34.4	25.8	19.3	4.6	2.1	1.4
Tulsa, OK	14.0	46.0	25.7	9.8	1.8	1.4	1.3
Virginia Beach, VA	10.2	31.3	27.8	21.8	5.4	2.1	1.4
Washington, DC	5.2	19.2	22.5	33.1	11.8	6.3	1.9
Wichita, KS	14.0	46.0	25.9	9.5	1.8	1.4	1.4
Wilmington, NC	16.7	46.7	20.7	10.2	2.9	1.2	1.6
Winston-Salem, NC	14.4	39.6	23.0	14.0	4.1	2.9	2.0
U.S.	12.6	28.6	21.2	20.8	8.1	6.0	2.8

Note: Figures are percentages and include workers 16 years old and over
Source: U.S. Census Bureau, 2019-2023 American Community Survey 5-Year Estimates

Travel Time to Work: Metro Area

Metro Area	Less Than 10 Minutes	10 to 19 Minutes	20 to 29 Minutes	30 to 44 Minutes	45 to 59 Minutes	60 to 89 Minutes	90 Minutes or More
Albuquerque, NM	11.5	31.1	25.0	20.6	5.8	3.8	2.3
Anchorage, AK	14.7	40.5	21.8	11.4	5.1	4.0	2.6
Ann Arbor, MI	11.2	33.3	25.2	18.5	7.2	3.5	1.2
Athens, GA	13.4	38.2	22.3	13.7	5.2	4.1	3.0
Atlanta, GA	7.3	22.7	20.1	25.5	12.0	9.0	3.3
Austin, TX	9.5	27.1	21.8	24.0	9.7	6.0	1.9
Baltimore, MD	8.2	24.1	21.7	24.6	10.7	7.5	3.1
Billings, MT	18.7	42.7	20.8	11.0	2.7	2.1	2.0
Boise City, ID	13.4	31.8	25.2	19.9	5.8	2.3	1.5
Boston, MA	9.4	22.9	19.3	24.4	11.2	9.6	3.1
Boulder, CO	15.0	34.3	20.7	17.0	6.9	4.4	1.6
Cape Coral, FL	8.8	24.5	22.6	25.2	10.2	6.3	2.4
Cedar Rapids, IA	19.1	39.1	20.6	13.0	4.3	2.6	1.3
Charleston, SC	9.1	26.3	23.3	24.0	9.9	5.4	2.1
Charlotte, NC	9.8	27.9	22.9	23.4	9.2	4.9	2.0
Chicago, IL	8.9	22.3	19.5	25.3	11.9	9.3	2.9
Cincinnati, OH	10.7	28.7	25.2	23.3	6.9	3.4	1.7
Clarksville, TN	14.1	30.9	22.8	15.1	7.2	6.9	3.0
Cleveland, OH	12.0	28.7	25.7	22.7	6.4	2.8	1.7
College Station, TX	16.2	48.4	17.1	11.0	3.2	2.3	1.9
Colorado Springs, CO	12.1	32.3	26.6	19.0	4.3	3.5	2.2
Columbia, MO	17.1	44.0	20.2	11.8	3.4	1.7	1.8
Columbia, SC	12.7	28.9	23.6	22.0	7.3	3.2	2.3
Columbus, OH	11.7	29.8	27.5	20.7	5.8	3.1	1.5
Dallas, TX	8.8	25.5	21.7	25.3	10.2	6.5	2.0
Davenport, IA	18.0	35.9	26.0	12.4	3.7	2.6	1.4
Denver, CO	8.8	25.1	23.7	26.4	9.0	5.1	1.9
Des Moines, IA	15.2	35.6	26.7	15.6	3.8	1.7	1.3
Detroit, MI	10.0	27.0	23.7	24.2	8.5	4.8	1.7
Durham, NC	10.6	32.7	25.3	20.0	6.2	3.8	1.5
El Paso, TX	9.7	32.0	27.4	21.6	4.9	2.4	2.0
Eugene, OR	16.0	43.1	21.9	11.6	3.0	2.6	1.8
Fargo, ND	17.7	51.4	18.0	7.1	2.4	1.9	1.5
Fort Collins, CO	13.9	36.1	21.5	15.8	6.0	4.6	2.1
Fort Wayne, IN	13.8	34.9	28.2	15.9	3.4	1.9	2.0
Fort Worth, TX	8.8	25.5	21.7	25.3	10.2	6.5	2.0
Gainesville, FL	12.2	32.8	25.2	19.2	5.7	3.2	1.7
Green Bay, WI	16.8	39.6	22.4	13.1	4.3	2.1	1.7
Greensboro, NC	13.3	34.4	23.7	18.1	5.0	3.2	2.2
Honolulu, HI	9.9	27.1	20.0	25.2	9.1	6.5	2.1
Houston, TX	7.7	22.9	20.7	26.9	11.5	7.9	2.5
Huntsville, AL	10.8	30.8	28.1	22.2	4.9	1.9	1.2
Indianapolis, IN	11.3	27.6	24.2	24.6	7.2	3.3	1.9
Jacksonville, FL	9.2	26.2	24.8	26.0	8.2	3.9	1.7
Kansas City, MO	12.4	30.9	26.3	20.9	5.7	2.4	1.4
Lafayette, LA	13.7	32.9	21.8	19.4	5.2	3.8	3.2
Las Vegas, NV	7.9	27.2	29.2	25.9	5.3	2.6	2.0
Lexington, KY	14.4	35.7	24.4	16.8	4.4	2.5	1.8
Lincoln, NE	17.0	42.8	23.2	10.6	3.2	2.3	1.0
Little Rock, AR	13.2	32.4	22.2	21.1	6.6	3.1	1.5
Los Angeles, CA	7.3	25.0	20.8	25.4	9.7	8.5	3.3
Louisville, KY	10.6	29.6	28.4	20.9	6.1	2.9	1.5
Madison, WI	15.8	32.4	25.5	17.6	5.0	2.5	1.1
Manchester, NH	11.5	29.3	21.6	19.8	8.2	6.9	2.8
McAllen, TX	15.4	33.5	24.2	18.6	3.8	2.4	2.2

Table continued on following page.

Metro Area	Less Than 10 Minutes	10 to 19 Minutes	20 to 29 Minutes	30 to 44 Minutes	45 to 59 Minutes	60 to 89 Minutes	90 Minutes or More
Memphis, TN	11.0	26.8	27.9	23.6	6.6	2.6	1.4
Miami, FL	6.8	23.2	23.1	27.1	9.9	7.2	2.6
Midland, TX	15.7	40.3	20.4	14.4	4.2	2.3	2.7
Milwaukee, WI	12.3	32.4	26.0	20.7	4.7	2.5	1.4
Minneapolis, MN	11.1	29.6	25.3	22.3	6.9	3.5	1.4
Nashville, TN	9.6	26.0	21.1	24.2	10.7	6.6	1.8
New Orleans, LA	11.4	31.5	22.9	21.7	6.6	3.9	2.0
New York, NY	7.3	19.0	16.6	23.9	12.6	14.2	6.4
Oklahoma City, OK	12.2	31.4	25.4	21.2	5.6	2.6	1.7
Omaha, NE	14.0	36.2	27.4	15.9	3.5	1.8	1.2
Orlando, FL	7.1	23.4	22.2	27.8	10.6	6.3	2.5
Philadelphia, PA	10.0	24.4	20.8	24.1	10.6	7.3	2.8
Phoenix, AZ	10.2	26.0	24.3	23.7	8.7	5.3	1.8
Pittsburgh, PA	12.3	27.5	21.7	22.5	8.7	5.3	2.0
Portland, OR	11.5	29.0	23.7	21.7	7.7	4.5	1.8
Providence, RI	11.7	30.0	21.3	20.3	7.9	6.1	2.9
Provo, UT	17.2	34.7	19.9	17.0	6.2	3.7	1.3
Raleigh, NC	9.0	26.8	23.5	24.3	9.6	5.0	1.8
Reno, NV	12.8	34.1	24.2	17.6	6.0	3.6	1.6
Richmond, VA	9.7	28.3	26.8	23.2	6.5	3.2	2.2
Rochester, MN	18.1	41.6	18.7	12.5	4.6	2.9	1.6
Sacramento, CA	10.3	28.8	22.7	22.9	7.1	4.4	3.8
Saint Louis, MO	11.3	28.2	24.6	23.4	7.3	3.5	1.6
Saint Paul, MN	11.1	29.6	25.3	22.3	6.9	3.5	1.4
Salem, OR	15.0	32.4	19.8	17.1	7.4	6.5	1.8
Salt Lake City, UT	11.1	33.7	26.6	19.0	5.5	2.9	1.3
San Antonio, TX	9.5	27.1	24.0	23.8	8.3	5.1	2.3
San Diego, CA	8.5	29.3	25.1	23.4	7.1	4.5	2.1
San Francisco, CA	7.5	24.2	18.7	23.7	11.0	10.8	4.1
San Jose, CA	7.5	28.4	24.3	23.1	8.2	5.8	2.7
Santa Rosa, CA	14.0	34.1	19.3	17.3	6.3	5.6	3.4
Savannah, GA	10.5	29.3	23.7	22.8	8.5	3.7	1.5
Seattle, WA	8.7	23.7	21.6	24.7	10.5	7.8	3.0
Sioux Falls, SD	17.3	43.1	23.9	10.5	2.5	1.3	1.3
Tampa, FL	9.6	26.6	20.9	23.8	10.2	6.5	2.5
Tucson, AZ	11.0	29.4	25.2	23.2	6.8	2.6	1.7
Tulsa, OK	13.4	34.0	26.6	17.7	4.7	2.2	1.5
Virginia Beach, VA	10.5	31.2	24.1	21.7	6.9	3.9	1.8
Washington, DC	6.5	20.1	19.2	26.3	13.2	11.0	3.6
Wichita, KS	15.7	38.0	25.6	14.9	2.8	1.6	1.4
Wilmington, NC	12.4	35.0	23.4	18.2	5.8	3.0	2.3
Winston-Salem, NC	12.5	32.1	24.5	19.3	5.8	3.5	2.2
U.S.	12.6	28.6	21.2	20.8	8.1	6.0	2.8

Note: Figures are percentages and include workers 16 years old and over; Figures cover the Metropolitan Statistical Area (MSA)
Source: U.S. Census Bureau, 2019-2023 American Community Survey 5-Year Estimates

2024 Presidential Election Results

City	Area Covered	Trump (Rep.)	Harris (Dem.)	Stein (Green)	Kennedy (Ind.)	Oliver (Lib.)	Other
Albuquerque, NM	Bernalillo County	38.2	59.2	0.7	1.0	0.5	0.5
Anchorage, AK	State of Alaska	54.5	41.4	0.7	1.7	0.9	0.8
Ann Arbor, MI	Washtenaw County	26.5	70.7	1.3	0.4	0.4	0.7
Athens, GA	Clarke County	30.2	68.3	0.5	0.0	0.6	0.4
Atlanta, GA	Fulton County	26.8	71.3	0.6	0.0	0.5	0.8
Austin, TX	Travis County	29.2	68.3	1.0	0.0	0.8	0.6
Baltimore, MD	Baltimore City	12.1	84.6	1.4	0.8	0.4	0.7
Billings, MT	Yellowstone County	62.0	34.9	0.4	1.9	0.8	0.0
Boise City, ID	Ada County	53.8	43.4	0.4	1.3	0.6	0.5
Boston, MA	Suffolk County	22.2	74.3	1.1	0.0	0.4	2.0
Boulder, CO	Boulder County	20.8	76.5	0.8	0.9	0.6	0.4
Cape Coral, FL	Lee County	63.6	35.3	0.2	0.0	0.2	0.6
Cedar Rapids, IA	Linn County	44.1	54.0	0.0	0.8	0.5	0.6
Charleston, SC	Charleston County	46.3	51.9	0.5	0.0	0.8	0.6
Charlotte, NC	Mecklenburg County	32.5	65.2	0.7	0.0	0.5	1.1
Chicago, IL	Cook County	28.1	69.6	0.9	1.2	0.1	0.2
Cincinnati, OH	Hamilton County	41.7	56.5	0.4	0.0	0.6	0.8
Clarksville, TN	Montgomery County	58.3	39.9	0.3	0.8	0.0	0.7
Cleveland, OH	Cuyahoga County	33.6	64.7	0.5	0.0	0.4	0.8
College Station, TX	Brazos County	61.6	36.8	0.6	0.0	0.9	0.1
Colorado Springs, CO	El Paso County	53.5	43.7	0.5	1.1	0.8	0.4
Columbia, MO	Boone County	43.9	53.6	0.9	0.0	1.1	0.4
Columbia, SC	Richland County	31.8	66.4	0.4	0.0	0.5	0.9
Columbus, OH	Franklin County	34.9	63.0	0.6	0.0	0.6	0.9
Dallas, TX	Dallas County	37.8	59.9	1.1	0.0	0.7	0.5
Davenport, IA	Scott County	51.0	47.1	0.0	0.8	0.5	0.6
Denver, CO	Denver County	20.6	76.6	0.9	0.8	0.6	0.5
Des Moines, IA	Polk County	43.7	54.5	0.0	0.6	0.5	0.7
Detroit, MI	Wayne County	33.6	62.5	2.4	0.4	0.3	0.8
Durham, NC	Durham County	18.2	79.8	0.7	0.0	0.4	0.8
El Paso, TX	El Paso County	41.7	56.8	0.6	0.0	0.6	0.3
Eugene, OR	Lane County	36.6	59.5	0.9	1.5	0.4	1.1
Fargo, ND	Cass County	52.7	44.4	0.0	0.0	1.8	1.1
Fort Collins, CO	Larimer County	39.7	57.3	0.5	1.2	0.8	0.5
Fort Wayne, IN	Allen County	55.2	42.7	0.0	0.9	0.8	0.4
Fort Worth, TX	Tarrant County	51.8	46.7	0.7	0.0	0.7	0.1
Gainesville, FL	Alachua County	38.6	59.4	0.6	0.0	0.5	0.9
Green Bay, WI	Brown County	53.0	45.5	0.2	0.5	0.3	0.5
Greensboro, NC	Guilford County	38.3	60.0	0.5	0.0	0.4	0.8
Honolulu, HI	Honolulu County	38.3	59.9	0.7	0.0	0.5	0.5
Houston, TX	Harris County	46.4	51.9	1.0	0.0	0.6	0.1
Huntsville, AL	Madison County	53.4	44.4	0.3	0.8	0.5	0.6
Indianapolis, IN	Marion County	35.1	62.6	0.0	0.9	0.8	0.7
Jacksonville, FL	Duval County	49.9	48.5	0.5	0.0	0.4	0.7
Kansas City, MO	Jackson County	39.3	58.5	0.8	0.0	0.8	0.6
Lafayette, LA	Lafayette Parish	64.8	33.5	0.4	0.4	0.4	0.5
Las Vegas, NV	Clark County	47.8	50.4	0.0	0.0	0.4	1.4
Lexington, KY	Fayette County	39.8	57.9	0.7	0.9	0.5	0.2
Lincoln, NE	Lancaster County	46.8	51.0	0.4	0.0	0.8	1.1
Little Rock, AR	Pulaski County	37.7	59.8	0.6	1.1	0.5	0.3
Los Angeles, CA	Los Angeles County	31.9	64.8	1.1	1.2	0.3	0.6
Louisville, KY	Jefferson County	40.6	57.1	0.6	0.7	0.3	0.6
Madison, WI	Dane County	23.4	74.9	0.5	0.4	0.3	0.6
Manchester, NH	Hillsborough County	47.8	50.7	0.5	0.0	0.5	0.5
McAllen, TX	Hidalgo County	51.0	48.1	0.5	0.0	0.4	0.0

Table continued on following page.

City	Area Covered	Trump (Rep.)	Harris (Dem.)	Stein (Green)	Kennedy (Ind.)	Oliver (Lib.)	Other
Memphis, TN	Shelby County	36.2	61.5	0.6	0.8	0.0	1.0
Miami, FL	Miami-Dade County	55.2	43.8	0.3	0.0	0.2	0.5
Midland, TX	Midland County	79.6	19.2	0.2	0.0	0.6	0.3
Milwaukee, WI	Milwaukee County	29.7	68.2	0.7	0.4	0.2	0.7
Minneapolis, MN	Hennepin County	27.4	69.8	0.8	0.6	0.5	1.0
Nashville, TN	Davidson County	35.0	62.2	0.6	0.9	0.0	1.2
New Orleans, LA	Orleans Parish	15.2	82.2	0.9	0.3	0.5	1.0
New York, NY	New York City	30.0	68.1	0.9	0.0	0.0	1.0
New York, NY	Bronx County	27.0	71.9	0.6	0.0	0.0	0.5
New York, NY	Kings County	27.4	70.4	1.1	0.0	0.0	1.1
New York, NY	New York County	17.2	80.8	0.7	0.0	0.0	1.3
New York, NY	Queens County	37.0	61.1	1.2	0.0	0.0	0.7
New York, NY	Richmond County	63.9	34.6	0.9	0.0	0.0	0.6
Oklahoma City, OK	Oklahoma County	49.7	48.0	0.0	1.1	0.8	0.4
Omaha, NE	Douglas County	43.9	54.1	0.4	0.0	0.6	1.0
Orlando, FL	Orange County	42.4	55.9	0.7	0.0	0.3	0.7
Philadelphia, PA	Philadelphia County	19.9	78.6	0.9	0.0	0.3	0.3
Phoenix, AZ	Maricopa County	51.0	47.5	0.6	0.0	0.5	0.4
Pittsburgh, PA	Allegheny County	39.2	59.4	0.5	0.0	0.5	0.5
Portland, OR	Multnomah County	17.1	78.7	1.5	1.0	0.3	1.4
Providence, RI	Providence County	41.7	55.7	0.6	0.9	0.3	0.8
Provo, UT	Utah County	66.7	27.8	0.5	0.0	1.4	3.6
Raleigh, NC	Wake County	36.2	61.7	0.8	0.0	0.5	0.8
Reno, NV	Washoe County	48.3	49.3	0.0	0.0	0.5	1.8
Richmond, VA	Richmond City	64.7	34.5	0.2	0.0	0.2	0.3
Rochester, MN	Olmsted County	43.4	54.0	0.6	0.8	0.5	0.7
Sacramento, CA	Sacramento County	38.4	58.1	1.2	1.4	0.5	0.5
Saint Louis, MO	St. Louis City	16.5	80.7	1.2	0.0	0.7	0.8
Saint Paul, MN	Ramsey County	27.1	70.2	0.8	0.5	0.5	0.9
Salem, OR	Marion County	49.2	47.2	0.6	1.7	0.4	0.9
Salt Lake City, UT	Salt Lake County	42.9	52.9	0.7	0.0	1.0	2.5
San Antonio, TX	Bexar County	44.4	54.1	0.6	0.0	0.6	0.4
San Diego, CA	San Diego County	40.1	56.9	1.0	1.1	0.5	0.4
San Francisco, CA	San Francisco County	15.5	80.3	1.7	1.1	0.5	0.9
San Jose, CA	Santa Clara County	28.1	68.0	1.6	1.2	0.5	0.5
Santa Rosa, CA	Sonoma County	25.2	71.4	0.9	1.5	0.4	0.4
Savannah, GA	Chatham County	40.4	58.3	0.3	0.0	0.4	0.7
Seattle, WA	King County	22.3	73.6	1.2	1.0	0.4	1.4
Sioux Falls, SD	Minnehaha County	55.2	42.5	0.0	1.6	0.7	0.0
Tampa, FL	Hillsborough County	50.7	47.6	0.6	0.0	0.4	0.7
Tucson, AZ	Pima County	41.7	56.8	0.6	0.0	0.6	0.4
Tulsa, OK	Tulsa County	56.5	41.3	0.0	1.1	0.7	0.4
Virginia Beach, VA	Virginia Beach City	47.8	50.4	0.4	0.0	0.5	0.9
Washington, DC	District of Columbia	6.5	90.3	0.0	0.9	0.0	2.4
Wichita, KS	Sedgwick County	55.7	42.0	0.1	1.1	0.6	0.5
Wilmington, NC	New Hanover County	49.0	49.6	0.4	0.0	0.4	0.6
Winston-Salem, NC	Forsyth County	42.6	55.8	0.4	0.0	0.4	0.8
U.S.	U.S.	49.7	48.2	0.6	0.5	0.4	0.6

Note: Results are percentages and may not add to 100% due to rounding
Source: Dave Leip's Atlas of U.S. Presidential Elections

House Price Index (HPI)

Metro Area	National Ranking[2]	Quarterly Change (%)	One-Year Change (%)	Five-Year Change (%)	Since 1991Q1 (%)
Albuquerque, NM	152	0.28	4.68	60.38	291.99
Anchorage, AK	120	-2.19	5.44	38.20	272.70
Ann Arbor, MI	111	0.79	5.63	45.12	265.98
Athens, GA	145	0.95	4.82	77.54	363.29
Atlanta, GA	169	-0.09	4.19	66.19	310.49
Austin, TX	237	-1.06	-0.80	47.35	579.98
Baltimore, MD	113	0.13	5.59	41.90	246.61
Billings, MT	211	-0.95	2.58	54.45	434.47
Boise City, ID	156	0.77	4.58	63.16	546.52
Boston, MA[1]	123	0.36	5.29	50.28	365.78
Boulder, CO	218	0.54	2.49	40.60	618.40
Cape Coral, FL	240	-0.39	-2.44	67.84	353.01
Cedar Rapids, IA	204	-0.20	3.04	39.04	206.71
Charleston, SC	84	2.18	6.43	77.86	536.36
Charlotte, NC	175	0.39	4.07	71.74	349.74
Chicago, IL[1]	70	0.05	6.77	43.67	208.59
Cincinnati, OH	93	0.82	6.08	61.42	247.18
Clarksville, TN	(a)	n/a	3.55	67.67	n/a
Cleveland, OH	71	0.34	6.77	57.08	194.72
College Station, TX	(a)	n/a	1.96	50.70	n/a
Colorado Springs, CO	196	-0.38	3.24	49.58	453.42
Columbia, MO	24	0.09	8.46	58.84	279.40
Columbia, SC	61	0.87	6.97	64.02	248.40
Columbus, OH	63	1.20	6.96	61.81	293.84
Dallas, TX[1]	181	0.68	3.91	56.27	350.14
Davenport, IA	143	-0.86	4.87	39.11	236.99
Denver, CO	193	0.30	3.30	43.23	580.34
Des Moines, IA	174	-0.70	4.10	43.67	253.81
Detroit, MI[1]	40	0.25	7.71	52.17	227.11
Durham, NC	150	0.26	4.76	67.43	344.03
El Paso, TX	67	1.00	6.86	63.01	237.09
Eugene, OR	220	-1.37	2.45	48.27	459.38
Fargo, ND	214	-1.86	2.52	33.66	292.25
Fort Collins, CO	215	-0.72	2.52	44.72	544.83
Fort Wayne, IN	32	1.26	7.98	72.59	239.64
Fort Worth, TX[1]	194	0.54	3.30	53.69	324.24
Gainesville, FL	(a)	n/a	5.55	65.26	n/a
Green Bay, WI	103	-1.16	5.89	63.68	299.15
Greensboro, NC	65	0.24	6.92	68.92	226.57
Honolulu, HI	183	-0.33	3.85	35.89	242.48
Houston, TX	195	0.35	3.29	44.19	326.50
Huntsville, AL	76	-1.12	6.65	66.60	239.11
Indianapolis, IN	136	1.08	4.99	59.79	247.41
Jacksonville, FL	168	-0.18	4.19	65.48	401.54
Kansas City, MO	149	-0.76	4.78	56.68	300.63
Lafayette, LA	132	3.26	5.15	25.86	238.79
Las Vegas, NV	44	1.27	7.43	58.90	295.91
Lexington, KY	147	-0.02	4.79	58.94	282.27
Lincoln, NE	60	0.91	6.97	52.28	300.89
Little Rock, AR	197	-1.14	3.23	47.11	222.55
Los Angeles, CA[1]	114	0.65	5.59	48.41	341.40
Louisville, KY	81	0.59	6.45	50.59	291.73
Madison, WI	118	0.61	5.50	54.87	369.35
Manchester, NH	25	-0.15	8.25	67.31	310.83
McAllen, TX	(a)	n/a	8.58	59.26	n/a

Table continued on following page.

Metro Area	National Ranking[2]	Quarterly Change (%)	One-Year Change (%)	Five-Year Change (%)	Since 1991Q1 (%)
Memphis, TN	206	-0.64	2.99	49.80	207.31
Miami, FL[1]	19	2.12	8.69	89.36	668.91
Midland, TX	(a)	n/a	1.09	21.00	n/a
Milwaukee, WI	49	0.11	7.27	55.07	296.31
Minneapolis, MN	153	0.20	4.68	37.75	302.55
Nashville, TN	164	-0.12	4.28	65.94	467.10
New Orleans, LA	233	0.13	0.85	25.47	285.27
New York, NY[1]	34	0.62	7.86	43.82	309.75
Oklahoma City, OK	129	-0.57	5.22	50.62	294.07
Omaha, NE	154	0.12	4.63	51.76	295.39
Orlando, FL	56	2.87	7.06	70.73	377.10
Philadelphia, PA[1]	110	0.84	5.64	41.74	286.32
Phoenix, AZ	200	0.13	3.14	69.09	488.41
Pittsburgh, PA	104	0.17	5.87	45.46	262.85
Portland, OR	182	0.32	3.88	37.41	518.30
Providence, RI	41	0.25	7.70	64.34	289.70
Provo, UT	139	-1.41	4.94	59.50	545.94
Raleigh, NC	185	0.14	3.78	65.05	335.12
Reno, NV	121	0.31	5.40	49.95	361.77
Richmond, VA	98	0.07	5.98	59.60	306.38
Rochester, MN	160	-1.25	4.39	42.16	268.82
Sacramento, CA	198	0.32	3.19	42.05	255.25
Saint Louis, MO	92	1.02	6.12	48.75	237.26
Saint Paul, MN	153	0.20	4.68	37.75	302.55
Salem, OR	209	0.85	2.90	48.54	494.72
Salt Lake City, UT	115	0.53	5.58	59.66	644.94
San Antonio, TX	228	4.07	1.99	49.58	357.13
San Diego, CA	102	1.05	5.91	61.16	410.00
San Francisco, CA[1]	191	0.32	3.50	15.70	376.10
San Jose, CA	221	-0.52	2.35	36.42	433.00
Santa Rosa, CA	192	-0.37	3.47	28.24	304.85
Savannah, GA	225	-1.45	2.18	77.13	438.29
Seattle, WA[1]	91	-0.16	6.14	47.96	484.10
Sioux Falls, SD	224	0.06	2.21	52.27	347.79
Tampa, FL	229	-0.90	1.88	77.61	480.18
Tucson, AZ	223	-1.32	2.30	65.72	364.15
Tulsa, OK	116	1.84	5.52	56.84	272.73
Virginia Beach, VA	64	1.54	6.94	53.57	289.47
Washington, DC[1]	106	-0.50	5.79	38.73	288.38
Wichita, KS	170	-0.42	4.15	57.02	241.93
Wilmington, NC	137	0.32	4.98	74.07	421.24
Winston-Salem, NC	33	1.41	7.91	70.24	245.21
U.S.[3]	—	1.43	4.51	57.13	327.82

Note: The HPI is a weighted repeat sales index. It measures average price changes in repeat sales or refinancings on the same properties. This information is obtained by reviewing repeat mortgage transactions on single-family properties whose mortgages have been purchased or securitized by Fannie Mae or Freddie Mac since January 1975; all figures are for the period ended December 31, 2024; Figures cover the Metropolitan Statistical Area (MSA) unless noted otherwise; (1) Metropolitan Division; (2) Rankings are based on annual percentage change, for all MSAs containing at least 15,000 transactions over the last 10 years and ranges from 1 to 241; (3) Figures based on a weighted division average; (a) Not ranked because of increased index variability due to smaller sample size; n/a not available
Source: Federal Housing Finance Agency, Change in FHFA Metropolitan Area House Price Indexes, All Transactions Index, 2024Q4

Home Value: City

City	Under $100,000	$100,000 -$199,999	$200,000 -$299,999	$300,000 -$399,999	$400,000 -$499,999	$500,000 -$999,999	$1,000,000 or more	Median ($)
Albuquerque, NM	6.9	18.8	34.6	19.9	10.2	8.7	0.9	266,700
Anchorage, AK	5.3	7.4	17.7	25.8	19.8	21.8	2.2	375,900
Ann Arbor, MI	1.8	5.6	14.3	20.1	23.3	29.4	5.4	435,100
Athens, GA	8.3	18.2	31.4	20.3	9.1	11.0	1.8	271,800
Atlanta, GA	4.8	10.7	17.8	14.5	11.2	27.8	13.3	420,600
Austin, TX	2.9	2.8	11.0	14.7	17.1	39.2	12.2	512,700
Baltimore, MD	15.5	28.6	26.5	13.5	6.5	7.8	1.5	219,300
Billings, MT	6.6	10.2	30.1	25.7	15.5	10.6	1.3	311,800
Boise City, ID	4.2	3.9	12.0	18.2	21.0	33.8	6.9	456,000
Boston, MA	3.4	0.7	3.2	5.8	9.4	53.3	24.2	710,400
Boulder, CO	4.3	2.6	2.6	3.9	4.0	33.9	48.6	982,600
Cape Coral, FL	3.1	8.9	28.1	25.5	15.2	16.3	3.0	339,200
Cedar Rapids, IA	12.5	47.4	24.5	8.5	3.9	2.7	0.5	177,100
Charleston, SC	2.0	3.6	12.8	18.9	18.2	31.3	13.1	469,100
Charlotte, NC	4.4	13.0	22.8	19.2	12.6	20.8	7.2	351,500
Chicago, IL	6.6	16.0	24.7	17.7	11.1	18.1	5.8	315,200
Cincinnati, OH	14.9	31.5	20.8	12.4	7.1	10.7	2.6	215,300
Clarksville, TN	7.4	25.5	40.9	15.0	6.3	4.1	0.7	236,100
Cleveland, OH	53.4	31.8	8.1	3.0	1.6	1.7	0.5	94,100
College Station, TX	2.4	7.5	32.9	27.0	15.6	12.5	2.1	326,500
Colorado Springs, CO	4.1	3.5	14.0	23.8	22.3	29.5	2.8	420,700
Columbia, MO	6.6	23.2	30.2	18.4	10.8	10.1	0.8	268,300
Columbia, SC	12.4	26.0	23.5	11.7	8.3	14.7	3.5	243,500
Columbus, OH	11.3	27.4	31.0	18.0	6.6	4.9	0.8	234,500
Dallas, TX	9.9	20.3	20.7	12.2	8.8	19.9	8.2	295,300
Davenport, IA	18.4	45.7	19.6	9.4	3.8	2.8	0.3	162,900
Denver, CO	2.3	2.1	6.6	11.4	17.3	44.6	15.7	586,700
Des Moines, IA	13.7	44.2	27.4	8.7	2.6	2.7	0.7	183,700
Detroit, MI	63.8	21.8	7.7	3.4	1.3	1.6	0.4	76,800
Durham, NC	3.1	10.7	22.2	25.3	16.4	20.2	2.1	355,300
El Paso, TX	14.2	47.6	24.4	7.7	2.7	2.8	0.7	171,700
Eugene, OR	6.5	3.0	11.6	20.1	24.6	31.0	3.0	435,400
Fargo, ND	6.0	16.7	36.1	22.1	9.0	8.7	1.4	269,800
Fort Collins, CO	3.7	1.7	4.2	9.6	22.7	52.5	5.6	548,400
Fort Wayne, IN	19.8	42.0	25.3	7.7	2.8	2.0	0.3	169,700
Fort Worth, TX	8.5	18.0	31.0	21.0	10.5	8.9	2.0	277,300
Gainesville, FL	7.9	27.4	35.1	16.9	5.7	6.3	0.7	235,000
Green Bay, WI	8.5	46.2	29.0	8.4	4.0	3.6	0.3	191,500
Greensboro, NC	10.1	33.8	25.7	14.3	6.6	8.2	1.4	221,300
Honolulu, HI	2.1	1.6	3.1	8.6	10.6	35.0	39.0	834,100
Houston, TX	11.1	24.9	22.9	12.3	8.6	14.1	6.1	253,400
Huntsville, AL	11.8	23.6	22.4	17.3	9.3	12.8	2.7	263,100
Indianapolis, IN	14.2	33.3	28.5	11.6	5.2	6.1	1.1	207,000
Jacksonville, FL	11.0	20.4	27.6	19.5	10.1	9.1	2.2	266,100
Kansas City, MO	16.8	25.8	25.2	14.7	8.5	7.8	1.2	227,000
Lafayette, LA	11.2	23.8	28.6	14.9	9.3	10.0	2.2	251,300
Las Vegas, NV	3.9	4.5	17.2	25.6	19.7	24.9	4.2	395,300
Lexington, KY	5.4	22.4	29.2	18.8	10.0	11.8	2.4	272,100
Lincoln, NE	5.9	26.1	34.7	18.1	7.5	6.6	1.1	248,200
Little Rock, AR	15.5	28.7	22.6	12.2	8.1	10.2	2.6	221,200
Los Angeles, CA	2.5	1.2	1.2	2.5	5.7	47.7	39.2	879,500
Louisville, KY	11.8	32.0	25.5	13.2	7.6	8.4	1.5	221,500
Madison, WI	2.9	9.1	25.1	27.7	16.5	17.0	1.8	346,900
Manchester, NH	3.9	10.2	24.0	32.7	19.8	8.6	0.7	336,300
McAllen, TX	20.0	40.0	22.5	10.6	3.3	3.0	0.8	173,800

Table continued on following page.

City	Under $100,000	$100,000 -$199,999	$200,000 -$299,999	$300,000 -$399,999	$400,000 -$499,999	$500,000 -$999,999	$1,000,000 or more	Median ($)
Memphis, TN	31.7	28.3	18.4	8.8	4.5	6.3	1.9	157,100
Miami, FL	2.9	5.9	12.9	14.6	18.1	31.4	14.1	475,200
Midland, TX	7.8	12.9	29.7	24.9	10.4	11.8	2.5	298,600
Milwaukee, WI	19.7	43.3	25.1	5.9	2.6	2.6	0.8	172,000
Minneapolis, MN	2.9	10.4	25.0	25.6	14.0	18.1	4.0	345,600
Nashville, TN	3.4	6.6	21.4	22.5	16.9	22.1	7.1	383,100
New Orleans, LA	6.4	21.2	23.1	13.8	9.7	19.4	6.4	296,400
New York, NY	4.7	2.9	4.7	5.6	7.1	44.9	30.1	751,700
Oklahoma City, OK	14.8	30.5	27.8	13.1	5.7	6.6	1.6	215,100
Omaha, NE	9.8	29.2	31.6	14.2	7.4	6.7	1.2	230,100
Orlando, FL	3.5	15.0	19.9	19.6	14.5	22.0	5.4	359,000
Philadelphia, PA	14.0	26.4	26.8	14.6	6.6	9.5	2.0	232,400
Phoenix, AZ	5.7	6.6	20.5	21.1	16.0	24.9	5.2	381,900
Pittsburgh, PA	22.7	29.2	19.5	10.3	5.6	10.3	2.2	193,200
Portland, OR	2.5	1.5	4.8	11.9	21.2	50.0	8.1	557,600
Providence, RI	4.1	9.3	30.8	25.2	11.6	14.5	4.4	322,800
Provo, UT	5.1	1.8	10.4	24.4	22.4	31.3	4.6	437,100
Raleigh, NC	3.1	7.7	22.7	21.2	15.2	24.4	5.7	377,800
Reno, NV	6.1	3.0	6.9	14.9	19.3	42.7	7.1	498,600
Richmond, VA	4.9	17.9	22.4	17.1	13.0	19.0	5.7	328,100
Rochester, MN	4.4	16.0	33.6	19.2	12.2	13.4	1.1	287,500
Sacramento, CA	4.3	2.4	7.6	17.7	21.3	41.5	5.2	484,600
Saint Louis, MO	22.9	31.6	22.8	11.1	5.1	5.2	1.2	185,100
Saint Paul, MN	3.5	15.9	37.6	19.5	9.9	11.4	2.0	280,300
Salem, OR	6.8	5.2	14.1	29.1	22.7	21.4	0.8	382,400
Salt Lake City, UT	4.1	3.4	11.3	15.5	16.4	37.9	11.4	495,700
San Antonio, TX	13.7	29.8	29.2	14.1	6.3	5.9	1.0	219,700
San Diego, CA	2.6	1.2	1.5	3.4	7.1	48.7	35.6	848,500
San Francisco, CA	1.5	1.2	0.7	1.3	1.6	16.0	77.8	1,380,500
San Jose, CA	2.2	2.2	2.3	1.5	1.3	22.4	68.0	1,187,800
Santa Rosa, CA	3.7	2.8	2.7	3.8	7.2	65.4	14.3	685,000
Savannah, GA	12.1	29.9	27.2	12.5	6.6	9.4	2.4	225,200
Seattle, WA	1.1	0.6	1.2	3.6	5.2	47.4	40.8	912,100
Sioux Falls, SD	7.9	18.0	32.8	18.7	10.0	10.5	2.2	271,400
Tampa, FL	4.8	12.4	20.8	16.0	12.1	24.0	10.0	375,300
Tucson, AZ	12.9	21.2	34.4	17.5	7.6	5.4	1.1	242,200
Tulsa, OK	20.0	33.1	20.0	10.7	5.6	8.3	2.3	189,600
Virginia Beach, VA	3.1	7.5	23.9	23.4	16.1	21.5	4.5	366,300
Washington, DC	1.4	1.8	4.6	9.1	11.2	41.8	30.1	724,600
Wichita, KS	21.6	34.9	24.3	9.6	4.5	4.2	0.9	179,500
Wilmington, NC	3.3	13.2	23.0	21.1	14.2	19.1	6.2	350,300
Winston-Salem, NC	12.9	34.6	25.9	12.1	4.6	8.3	1.7	208,200
U.S.	12.1	17.8	19.5	14.4	10.5	19.1	6.5	303,400

Note: Figures are percentages except for median and cover owner-occupied housing units.
Source: U.S. Census Bureau, 2019-2023 American Community Survey 5-Year Estimates

Home Value: Metro Area

Metro Area	Under $100,000	$100,000 -$199,999	$200,000 -$299,999	$300,000 -$399,999	$400,000 -$499,999	$500,000 -$999,999	$1,000,000 or more	Median ($)
Albuquerque, NM	9.6	19.3	31.5	17.9	9.9	10.1	1.6	263,500
Anchorage, AK	5.4	8.2	21.3	25.5	18.1	19.7	1.8	358,900
Ann Arbor, MI	7.1	11.0	21.8	19.2	16.2	21.4	3.4	353,000
Athens, GA	10.5	18.0	26.3	18.0	10.1	14.3	2.8	280,900
Atlanta, GA	5.5	13.6	23.9	19.8	13.6	19.9	3.6	335,100
Austin, TX	5.1	5.2	15.7	18.2	16.6	30.5	8.6	434,800
Baltimore, MD	5.5	10.2	19.7	19.9	15.1	25.5	4.1	373,300
Billings, MT	8.9	10.1	25.9	22.6	14.8	15.5	2.2	322,700
Boise City, ID	5.0	4.9	13.8	19.8	19.1	31.9	5.6	434,400
Boston, MA	2.6	1.9	5.8	10.4	15.0	48.7	15.6	610,900
Boulder, CO	3.9	1.2	2.5	6.2	10.6	49.6	25.9	713,900
Cape Coral, FL	8.7	12.9	23.1	19.9	12.6	17.6	5.1	326,300
Cedar Rapids, IA	11.7	37.7	25.8	12.6	6.1	5.0	1.0	202,100
Charleston, SC	8.4	11.0	22.2	18.2	12.1	19.8	8.1	345,400
Charlotte, NC	8.7	15.9	21.8	18.3	12.5	18.3	4.4	319,400
Chicago, IL	6.2	16.9	26.5	19.9	12.0	15.0	3.5	301,900
Cincinnati, OH	10.2	28.0	26.6	15.7	8.7	9.3	1.5	240,200
Clarksville, TN	13.8	25.6	31.2	14.6	7.2	6.3	1.2	229,400
Cleveland, OH	16.6	33.1	23.9	12.6	6.4	6.4	1.0	201,000
College Station, TX	15.0	18.5	26.1	17.3	9.5	11.2	2.3	261,900
Colorado Springs, CO	4.0	3.9	13.2	22.2	21.5	31.2	4.1	431,600
Columbia, MO	11.1	26.8	26.5	15.4	9.6	9.0	1.6	242,500
Columbia, SC	15.7	30.4	25.4	12.9	6.5	7.4	1.7	213,400
Columbus, OH	9.2	20.9	26.3	18.4	10.8	12.8	1.6	274,300
Dallas, TX	6.8	13.3	23.8	20.1	13.1	18.8	4.1	330,300
Davenport, IA	20.4	38.7	21.3	9.7	5.0	4.2	0.7	170,000
Denver, CO	3.2	1.7	5.1	11.3	18.6	49.8	10.3	570,300
Des Moines, IA	8.7	25.7	28.2	18.3	9.0	9.0	1.1	252,400
Detroit, MI	16.3	23.8	24.2	15.1	9.2	9.8	1.5	237,100
Durham, NC	6.8	12.7	19.0	19.3	14.3	23.7	4.1	359,400
El Paso, TX	17.9	45.6	23.7	7.1	2.7	2.4	0.6	167,000
Eugene, OR	7.7	4.1	16.6	22.5	19.7	25.8	3.5	395,800
Fargo, ND	6.0	16.9	33.8	21.7	10.4	9.8	1.5	276,600
Fort Collins, CO	4.8	1.6	4.6	11.8	22.6	47.6	6.9	532,200
Fort Wayne, IN	16.3	35.8	25.6	11.4	5.1	5.0	0.7	194,000
Fort Worth, TX	6.8	13.3	23.8	20.1	13.1	18.8	4.1	330,300
Gainesville, FL	13.9	23.8	25.3	16.2	9.0	10.1	1.6	245,800
Green Bay, WI	7.8	29.2	31.1	15.7	8.0	7.3	0.9	238,700
Greensboro, NC	15.0	33.0	23.9	13.1	6.3	7.9	1.0	207,600
Honolulu, HI	2.2	1.5	2.2	5.1	7.6	43.9	37.6	873,000
Houston, TX	9.2	18.8	28.6	17.5	10.0	12.4	3.6	275,200
Huntsville, AL	10.6	22.2	26.0	17.6	10.3	11.7	1.6	265,000
Indianapolis, IN	10.9	25.6	27.2	15.9	8.9	9.9	1.7	244,000
Jacksonville, FL	8.7	15.7	24.0	19.1	12.4	16.2	4.0	308,900
Kansas City, MO	10.8	22.1	25.5	17.5	10.4	11.8	1.8	265,400
Lafayette, LA	22.9	24.9	27.1	12.6	6.3	5.2	1.0	206,900
Las Vegas, NV	4.7	4.8	15.2	25.2	21.6	24.5	4.1	400,800
Lexington, KY	6.9	24.4	28.6	17.8	9.1	10.7	2.5	258,900
Lincoln, NE	5.8	24.3	32.7	18.0	8.9	8.9	1.3	257,500
Little Rock, AR	17.5	32.8	24.9	11.9	5.4	6.1	1.5	199,300
Los Angeles, CA	3.2	1.7	1.8	3.2	6.3	50.5	33.3	825,300
Louisville, KY	10.5	28.4	27.1	15.9	8.1	8.6	1.3	236,400
Madison, WI	3.7	11.6	24.1	23.9	16.0	18.4	2.3	344,600
Manchester, NH	3.8	6.2	18.2	25.4	21.4	23.3	1.5	385,500
McAllen, TX	39.7	34.5	16.0	5.7	2.2	1.6	0.4	124,000

Table continued on following page.

Metro Area	Under $100,000	$100,000 -$199,999	$200,000 -$299,999	$300,000 -$399,999	$400,000 -$499,999	$500,000 -$999,999	$1,000,000 or more	Median ($)
Memphis, TN	18.7	24.3	22.8	15.3	8.1	9.3	1.6	228,100
Miami, FL	6.3	9.6	15.7	17.5	16.5	26.1	8.3	405,600
Midland, TX	12.7	13.2	26.8	21.6	10.8	12.6	2.4	290,300
Milwaukee, WI	7.4	19.6	27.2	19.0	11.7	13.0	2.1	283,800
Minneapolis, MN	4.0	7.4	24.9	25.1	16.1	19.6	2.9	354,400
Nashville, TN	4.8	8.7	20.9	20.4	15.0	23.6	6.7	376,800
New Orleans, LA	8.9	25.9	28.3	15.3	7.8	10.8	3.0	248,000
New York, NY	3.6	3.3	7.3	11.1	14.3	44.4	16.0	587,400
Oklahoma City, OK	14.4	31.1	26.8	12.7	6.2	7.1	1.7	214,700
Omaha, NE	8.7	25.0	29.9	16.9	9.6	8.7	1.3	248,100
Orlando, FL	7.9	10.2	22.8	23.6	15.2	17.1	3.2	338,500
Philadelphia, PA	7.1	14.6	23.2	19.2	13.4	19.5	3.0	326,700
Phoenix, AZ	6.7	5.9	16.8	20.3	17.5	26.9	5.9	401,400
Pittsburgh, PA	19.2	29.5	23.7	12.0	6.6	7.6	1.3	204,500
Portland, OR	3.9	2.2	5.4	12.8	22.0	46.6	7.0	526,500
Providence, RI	3.3	4.7	20.9	24.5	18.9	24.2	3.4	385,900
Provo, UT	3.5	1.6	7.4	18.5	22.0	41.2	6.0	487,200
Raleigh, NC	5.3	9.2	19.3	20.0	16.2	26.2	3.9	381,000
Reno, NV	5.5	4.0	9.4	17.0	18.9	36.5	8.6	474,000
Richmond, VA	4.9	12.5	26.9	22.4	13.5	17.3	2.6	325,800
Rochester, MN	6.7	18.1	29.5	17.4	11.9	14.4	2.0	284,600
Sacramento, CA	4.1	2.1	5.1	12.0	18.3	49.6	8.8	559,000
Saint Louis, MO	14.9	26.3	25.0	14.9	8.2	8.9	1.8	232,100
Saint Paul, MN	4.0	7.4	24.9	25.1	16.1	19.6	2.9	354,400
Salem, OR	7.5	5.1	14.2	25.9	20.5	24.2	2.7	389,800
Salt Lake City, UT	4.0	2.6	9.9	17.6	20.3	38.7	6.9	478,200
San Antonio, TX	11.7	21.6	27.6	16.5	9.1	11.3	2.2	258,700
San Diego, CA	3.7	1.9	2.1	3.4	6.8	52.6	29.5	791,600
San Francisco, CA	2.1	1.4	1.3	1.7	3.4	31.8	58.4	1,113,800
San Jose, CA	2.1	1.7	1.8	1.3	1.2	19.3	72.6	1,342,700
Santa Rosa, CA	3.3	3.1	2.4	2.7	5.4	57.0	26.2	779,000
Savannah, GA	9.6	21.3	26.2	16.7	9.8	13.3	3.2	271,100
Seattle, WA	3.2	1.7	3.9	8.3	12.9	46.7	23.2	673,500
Sioux Falls, SD	8.4	18.3	30.7	18.5	10.4	11.8	1.9	274,800
Tampa, FL	11.5	14.4	22.9	19.3	12.1	16.0	3.8	306,100
Tucson, AZ	11.2	15.2	26.9	19.0	11.6	13.4	2.6	286,900
Tulsa, OK	17.5	31.2	25.4	12.1	5.9	6.5	1.4	204,400
Virginia Beach, VA	5.2	13.4	27.6	21.5	14.3	15.6	2.5	318,000
Washington, DC	2.5	2.4	8.4	14.5	16.2	42.5	13.4	553,000
Wichita, KS	20.1	33.8	25.4	10.2	4.8	4.9	0.8	188,200
Wilmington, NC	7.5	14.3	22.8	19.4	13.3	19.0	3.8	328,000
Winston-Salem, NC	14.0	32.0	26.0	13.0	6.5	7.3	1.2	213,300
U.S.	12.1	17.8	19.5	14.4	10.5	19.1	6.5	303,400

Note: Figures are percentages except for median and cover owner-occupied housing units; Figures cover the Metropolitan Statistical Area (MSA)
Source: U.S. Census Bureau, 2019-2023 American Community Survey 5-Year Estimates

Homeownership Rate

Metro Area	2017	2018	2019	2020	2021	2022	2023	2024
Albuquerque, NM	67.0	67.9	70.0	69.5	66.5	67.3	69.1	71.8
Anchorage, AK	n/a	n/a	n/a	n/a	n/a	n/a	n/a	n/a
Ann Arbor, MI	n/a	n/a	n/a	n/a	n/a	n/a	n/a	n/a
Athens, GA	n/a	n/a	n/a	n/a	n/a	n/a	n/a	n/a
Atlanta, GA	62.4	64.0	64.2	66.4	64.2	64.4	67.5	67.5
Austin, TX	55.6	56.1	59.0	65.4	62.2	62.4	60.3	56.2
Baltimore, MD	67.5	63.5	66.5	70.7	67.5	70.4	72.9	70.0
Billings, MT	n/a	n/a	n/a	n/a	n/a	n/a	n/a	n/a
Boise City, ID	n/a	n/a	n/a	n/a	n/a	n/a	n/a	n/a
Boston, MA	58.8	61.0	60.9	61.2	60.7	59.4	59.9	60.7
Boulder, CO	n/a	n/a	n/a	n/a	n/a	n/a	n/a	n/a
Cape Coral, FL	65.5	75.1	72.0	77.4	76.1	70.8	78.5	77.1
Cedar Rapids, IA	n/a	n/a	n/a	n/a	n/a	n/a	n/a	n/a
Charleston, SC	67.7	68.8	70.7	75.5	73.2	71.9	69.6	68.1
Charlotte, NC	64.6	67.9	72.3	73.3	70.0	68.7	64.8	62.7
Chicago, IL	64.1	64.6	63.4	66.0	67.5	66.8	67.3	68.0
Cincinnati, OH	65.7	67.3	67.4	71.1	72.1	67.1	69.6	72.3
Clarksville, TN	n/a	n/a	n/a	n/a	n/a	n/a	n/a	n/a
Cleveland, OH	66.6	66.7	64.4	66.3	64.7	63.0	63.1	65.6
College Station, TX	n/a	n/a	n/a	n/a	n/a	n/a	n/a	n/a
Colorado Springs, CO	n/a	n/a	n/a	n/a	n/a	n/a	n/a	n/a
Columbia, MO	n/a	n/a	n/a	n/a	n/a	n/a	n/a	n/a
Columbia, SC	70.7	69.3	65.9	69.7	69.4	70.9	69.2	73.4
Columbus, OH	57.9	64.8	65.7	65.6	64.6	61.5	58.6	61.5
Dallas, TX	61.8	62.0	60.6	64.7	61.8	60.4	61.7	61.1
Davenport, IA	n/a	n/a	n/a	n/a	n/a	n/a	n/a	n/a
Denver, CO	59.3	60.1	63.5	62.9	62.8	64.6	65.9	61.6
Des Moines, IA	n/a	n/a	n/a	n/a	n/a	n/a	n/a	n/a
Detroit, MI	70.2	70.9	70.2	71.8	71.6	71.9	73.5	72.0
Durham, NC	n/a	n/a	n/a	n/a	n/a	n/a	n/a	n/a
El Paso, TX	n/a	n/a	n/a	n/a	n/a	n/a	n/a	n/a
Eugene, OR	n/a	n/a	n/a	n/a	n/a	n/a	n/a	n/a
Fargo, ND	n/a	n/a	n/a	n/a	n/a	n/a	n/a	n/a
Fort Collins, CO	n/a	n/a	n/a	n/a	n/a	n/a	n/a	n/a
Fort Wayne, IN	n/a	n/a	n/a	n/a	n/a	n/a	n/a	n/a
Fort Worth, TX	61.8	62.0	60.6	64.7	61.8	60.4	61.7	61.1
Gainesville, FL	n/a	n/a	n/a	n/a	n/a	n/a	n/a	n/a
Green Bay, WI	n/a	n/a	n/a	n/a	n/a	n/a	n/a	n/a
Greensboro, NC	61.9	63.2	61.7	65.8	61.9	70.0	69.4	67.0
Honolulu, HI	53.8	57.7	59.0	56.9	55.9	57.7	60.4	58.5
Houston, TX	58.9	60.1	61.3	65.3	64.1	63.7	61.8	61.6
Huntsville, AL	n/a	n/a	n/a	n/a	n/a	n/a	n/a	n/a
Indianapolis, IN	63.9	64.3	66.2	70.0	70.1	68.8	70.2	69.6
Jacksonville, FL	65.2	61.4	63.1	64.8	68.1	70.6	72.9	67.0
Kansas City, MO	62.4	64.3	65.0	66.7	63.8	63.8	64.1	65.3
Lafayette, LA	n/a	n/a	n/a	n/a	n/a	n/a	n/a	n/a
Las Vegas, NV	54.4	58.1	56.0	57.3	57.7	58.7	58.9	58.5
Lexington, KY	n/a	n/a	n/a	n/a	n/a	n/a	n/a	n/a
Lincoln, NE	n/a	n/a	n/a	n/a	n/a	n/a	n/a	n/a
Little Rock, AR	61.0	62.2	65.0	67.7	64.6	64.4	62.6	61.7
Los Angeles, CA	49.1	49.5	48.2	48.5	47.9	48.3	48.0	48.3
Louisville, KY	71.7	67.9	64.9	69.3	71.4	71.7	68.3	67.0
Madison, WI	n/a	n/a	n/a	n/a	n/a	n/a	n/a	n/a
Manchester, NH	n/a	n/a	n/a	n/a	n/a	n/a	n/a	n/a
McAllen, TX	n/a	n/a	n/a	n/a	n/a	n/a	n/a	n/a
Memphis, TN	62.4	63.5	63.7	62.5	60.7	59.7	63.2	60.1

Table continued on following page.

Metro Area	2017	2018	2019	2020	2021	2022	2023	2024
Miami, FL	57.9	59.9	60.4	60.6	59.4	58.3	58.6	60.8
Midland, TX	n/a	n/a	n/a	n/a	n/a	n/a	n/a	n/a
Milwaukee, WI	63.9	62.3	56.9	58.5	56.8	57.3	60.0	62.7
Minneapolis, MN	70.1	67.8	70.2	73.0	75.0	73.0	72.0	67.8
Nashville, TN	69.4	68.3	69.8	69.8	65.7	70.4	70.7	71.6
New Orleans, LA	61.7	62.6	61.1	66.3	66.2	66.3	63.2	63.2
New York, NY	49.9	49.7	50.4	50.9	50.7	50.5	50.2	49.4
Oklahoma City, OK	64.7	64.6	64.3	68.3	61.9	64.8	68.1	65.0
Omaha, NE	65.5	67.8	66.9	68.6	68.6	67.9	67.0	67.4
Orlando, FL	59.5	58.5	56.1	64.2	63.0	62.1	61.9	62.6
Philadelphia, PA	65.6	67.4	67.4	69.2	69.8	68.2	67.4	69.6
Phoenix, AZ	64.0	65.3	65.9	67.9	65.2	68.0	69.7	69.4
Pittsburgh, PA	72.7	71.7	71.5	69.8	69.1	72.7	72.4	71.7
Portland, OR	61.1	59.2	60.0	62.5	64.1	65.2	65.6	61.1
Providence, RI	58.6	61.3	63.5	64.8	64.1	66.3	65.4	63.2
Provo, UT	n/a	n/a	n/a	n/a	n/a	n/a	n/a	n/a
Raleigh, NC	68.2	64.9	63.0	68.2	62.7	65.1	68.8	65.0
Reno, NV	n/a	n/a	n/a	n/a	n/a	n/a	n/a	n/a
Richmond, VA	63.1	62.9	66.4	66.5	64.9	66.3	64.9	65.4
Rochester, MN	n/a	n/a	n/a	n/a	n/a	n/a	n/a	n/a
Sacramento, CA	60.1	64.1	61.6	63.4	63.2	63.5	64.4	63.0
Saint Louis, MO	65.6	65.8	68.1	71.1	73.8	69.9	69.4	68.2
Saint Paul, MN	70.1	67.8	70.2	73.0	75.0	73.0	72.0	67.8
Salem, OR	n/a	n/a	n/a	n/a	n/a	n/a	n/a	n/a
Salt Lake City, UT	68.1	69.5	69.2	68.0	64.1	66.6	62.9	61.0
San Antonio, TX	62.5	64.4	62.6	64.2	62.7	62.9	66.9	63.3
San Diego, CA	56.0	56.1	56.7	57.8	52.6	51.6	54.5	51.4
San Francisco, CA	55.7	55.6	52.8	53.0	54.7	56.4	55.0	56.4
San Jose, CA	50.4	50.4	52.4	52.6	48.4	53.1	53.5	52.3
Santa Rosa, CA	n/a	n/a	n/a	n/a	n/a	n/a	n/a	n/a
Savannah, GA	n/a	n/a	n/a	n/a	n/a	n/a	n/a	n/a
Seattle, WA	59.5	62.5	61.5	59.4	58.0	62.7	62.7	61.1
Sioux Falls, SD	n/a	n/a	n/a	n/a	n/a	n/a	n/a	n/a
Tampa, FL	60.4	64.9	68.0	72.2	68.3	68.4	66.9	68.9
Tucson, AZ	60.1	63.8	60.1	67.1	63.5	71.6	73.3	66.4
Tulsa, OK	66.8	68.3	70.5	70.1	63.8	63.7	62.8	65.3
Virginia Beach, VA	65.3	62.8	63.0	65.8	64.4	61.4	67.8	69.8
Washington, DC	63.3	62.9	64.7	67.9	65.8	66.2	65.1	64.0
Wichita, KS	n/a	n/a	n/a	n/a	n/a	n/a	n/a	n/a
Wilmington, NC	n/a	n/a	n/a	n/a	n/a	n/a	n/a	n/a
Winston-Salem, NC	n/a	n/a	n/a	n/a	n/a	n/a	n/a	n/a
U.S.	63.9	64.4	64.6	66.6	65.5	65.8	65.9	65.6

Note: Figures are percentages and cover the Metropolitan Statistical Area (MSA); n/a not available
Source: U.S. Census Bureau, Housing Vacancies and Homeownership Annual Statistics: 2017-2024

Year Housing Structure Built: City

City	2020 or Later	2010-2019	2000-2009	1990-1999	1980-1989	1970-1979	1960-1969	1950-1959	1940-1949	Before 1940	Median Year
Albuquerque, NM	0.7	6.9	16.2	14.2	14.1	19.2	9.5	12.3	3.9	3.0	1982
Anchorage, AK	0.2	6.6	12.1	11.6	24.8	27.5	9.7	5.8	0.9	0.8	1982
Ann Arbor, MI	1.3	6.5	6.8	11.2	9.9	16.0	17.9	10.6	4.8	15.2	1971
Athens, GA	1.6	8.9	19.0	16.3	14.5	14.3	12.0	5.8	2.7	4.9	1987
Atlanta, GA	2.3	15.8	21.0	8.9	7.8	7.8	10.2	8.8	5.3	12.1	1987
Austin, TX	2.5	20.7	17.2	13.0	17.3	13.7	7.2	4.1	2.0	2.3	1993
Baltimore, MD	0.3	4.3	4.1	4.1	4.6	5.8	8.6	15.3	11.6	41.1	1948
Billings, MT	2.3	12.7	10.6	11.9	11.3	16.3	9.0	13.1	5.5	7.4	1979
Boise City, ID	1.3	10.8	11.4	19.6	14.4	17.8	7.8	7.2	3.7	6.3	1985
Boston, MA	0.9	9.2	6.5	4.3	5.6	7.6	7.2	7.1	4.9	46.8	1947
Boulder, CO	0.5	8.5	8.8	12.4	15.5	19.8	16.2	9.0	1.5	7.7	1978
Cape Coral, FL	2.0	11.6	34.3	15.2	21.1	10.3	4.5	0.8	0.3	0.0	1999
Cedar Rapids, IA	0.8	9.6	11.3	10.9	7.5	14.7	13.9	12.4	4.3	14.7	1973
Charleston, SC	2.6	22.7	19.1	10.1	10.5	7.5	8.2	5.6	3.0	10.8	1994
Charlotte, NC	1.8	16.9	20.9	17.3	13.9	10.2	8.2	5.8	2.4	2.6	1994
Chicago, IL	0.4	5.1	8.2	4.9	5.0	7.9	9.7	11.6	8.2	39.1	1952
Cincinnati, OH	0.5	4.4	4.1	4.0	6.3	9.3	12.0	10.9	8.3	40.3	1951
Clarksville, TN	3.3	18.0	21.2	18.8	12.9	11.3	6.2	4.2	2.3	1.7	1996
Cleveland, OH	0.6	3.8	3.8	2.9	3.0	5.6	7.8	12.1	10.8	49.6	1940
College Station, TX	2.4	23.2	20.3	16.5	18.5	12.2	3.9	1.7	0.5	0.7	1998
Colorado Springs, CO	1.9	11.6	14.9	14.2	17.5	16.8	9.3	7.0	1.7	5.3	1986
Columbia, MO	0.8	17.5	20.3	17.0	12.3	9.9	10.3	4.5	2.4	5.0	1993
Columbia, SC	1.0	12.9	14.8	9.8	9.6	9.6	10.1	13.3	8.9	10.1	1978
Columbus, OH	1.0	9.6	11.8	13.7	13.3	14.4	10.7	9.6	4.0	12.0	1980
Dallas, TX	1.0	12.0	11.0	10.0	16.3	15.0	12.0	12.7	4.6	5.2	1980
Davenport, IA	0.6	4.8	9.1	8.4	6.9	15.3	12.8	11.8	6.0	24.2	1966
Denver, CO	2.3	15.5	10.9	6.6	7.4	12.0	9.9	13.0	5.2	17.2	1974
Des Moines, IA	0.6	6.9	7.3	6.8	6.4	12.8	9.5	14.6	7.3	27.8	1960
Detroit, MI	0.1	1.5	2.7	2.3	3.2	4.9	7.8	21.8	20.4	35.2	1947
Durham, NC	2.6	21.5	17.1	14.2	14.0	9.6	7.1	5.3	3.4	5.2	1994
El Paso, TX	0.9	14.1	13.5	11.7	14.9	15.9	10.2	10.9	3.2	4.7	1983
Eugene, OR	0.7	10.2	13.3	15.0	9.2	19.9	11.7	8.5	5.5	6.0	1979
Fargo, ND	1.3	20.3	14.9	14.5	11.5	13.7	5.8	7.7	2.5	7.9	1991
Fort Collins, CO	1.5	15.0	18.9	19.0	14.5	15.7	6.5	3.0	1.3	4.5	1992
Fort Wayne, IN	0.5	3.4	7.4	12.9	11.3	16.9	15.5	12.0	5.7	14.4	1971
Fort Worth, TX	2.4	17.7	20.8	11.1	13.2	8.7	6.9	9.3	4.5	5.6	1992
Gainesville, FL	1.3	6.5	14.0	14.2	19.5	20.2	11.8	7.0	2.7	2.9	1983
Green Bay, WI	0.4	3.2	7.3	9.8	12.5	17.9	12.6	16.1	5.9	14.4	1971
Greensboro, NC	0.8	9.8	14.7	14.5	15.6	13.9	11.0	10.1	3.8	5.7	1983
Honolulu, HI	0.5	7.5	6.7	7.8	10.5	25.9	19.6	11.6	5.1	4.8	1973
Houston, TX	1.4	14.0	13.0	9.3	14.1	19.0	12.1	9.4	3.7	4.1	1981
Huntsville, AL	2.3	15.6	12.4	10.8	14.8	11.9	20.1	7.8	1.8	2.6	1984
Indianapolis, IN	0.6	6.5	9.9	12.0	11.2	12.1	13.4	12.1	6.0	16.1	1972
Jacksonville, FL	2.4	10.6	17.4	13.1	15.9	11.9	9.3	10.3	4.1	5.0	1986
Kansas City, MO	1.0	8.2	10.1	8.5	8.6	11.4	12.0	13.2	5.5	21.6	1968
Lafayette, LA	0.8	12.4	11.5	9.3	18.6	21.5	12.8	8.7	2.7	1.6	1981
Las Vegas, NV	1.4	8.8	21.4	29.3	16.3	10.2	7.0	4.1	1.0	0.5	1994
Lexington, KY	1.1	10.0	14.5	15.6	13.0	14.5	13.4	8.5	2.7	6.7	1983
Lincoln, NE	1.0	11.9	14.2	13.6	10.1	14.5	8.7	10.3	3.2	12.4	1981
Little Rock, AR	0.4	9.7	11.7	11.8	13.1	17.9	14.7	8.5	4.9	7.2	1978
Los Angeles, CA	0.8	6.1	5.6	5.7	10.8	13.4	13.2	16.2	9.1	19.2	1964
Louisville, KY	0.8	7.7	11.8	10.4	6.9	13.0	12.7	14.2	6.6	15.9	1970
Madison, WI	0.9	11.8	14.3	11.8	9.5	12.8	11.9	9.2	4.3	13.4	1979
Manchester, NH	0.5	3.5	6.5	7.7	15.5	11.5	8.1	10.7	6.6	29.4	1964
McAllen, TX	1.2	13.0	24.8	16.8	18.5	15.3	5.0	2.3	1.2	1.9	1993

Table continued on following page.

City	2020 or Later	2010-2019	2000-2009	1990-1999	1980-1989	1970-1979	1960-1969	1950-1959	1940-1949	Before 1940	Median Year
Memphis, TN	0.5	3.6	6.5	9.7	12.4	17.3	14.6	20.0	7.7	7.7	1970
Miami, FL	1.8	15.4	17.0	6.0	7.4	11.9	10.0	13.5	9.1	7.9	1978
Midland, TX	2.2	21.9	10.1	9.7	17.3	10.9	7.7	16.6	2.5	1.1	1986
Milwaukee, WI	0.3	3.5	3.7	3.5	3.8	9.2	11.6	18.8	10.9	34.7	1952
Minneapolis, MN	1.0	8.8	6.2	4.2	6.8	8.2	6.8	8.2	6.2	43.6	1950
Nashville, TN	3.2	15.4	13.9	11.0	14.2	12.8	10.9	9.0	3.4	6.2	1985
New Orleans, LA	0.4	5.7	7.6	3.0	7.8	13.9	10.2	12.0	7.1	32.1	1959
New York, NY	0.4	5.5	5.5	3.7	5.0	7.0	12.2	12.8	9.4	38.4	1952
Oklahoma City, OK	1.6	13.7	13.3	9.3	13.4	15.6	11.3	9.2	5.0	7.4	1981
Omaha, NE	0.4	6.4	8.7	11.9	10.8	15.1	13.9	10.5	4.2	18.1	1972
Orlando, FL	1.3	16.1	21.0	13.1	15.1	12.7	7.2	8.4	2.6	2.6	1991
Philadelphia, PA	0.6	4.8	3.2	2.7	4.5	7.8	10.9	15.0	10.7	39.9	1949
Phoenix, AZ	1.1	8.6	16.4	14.3	17.3	18.9	9.5	9.6	2.4	1.9	1984
Pittsburgh, PA	0.5	4.8	3.7	3.4	4.2	6.5	7.9	13.0	7.6	48.4	1942
Portland, OR	0.9	11.0	10.1	7.3	6.4	10.5	8.4	11.0	7.2	27.1	1966
Providence, RI	0.4	2.2	4.9	4.5	5.6	7.8	5.4	7.5	6.3	55.6	1938
Provo, UT	1.1	7.6	11.6	18.7	14.7	17.7	9.7	7.3	5.0	6.6	1982
Raleigh, NC	1.6	17.5	23.5	17.1	16.0	9.6	6.8	3.7	1.3	2.9	1996
Reno, NV	3.0	11.6	19.1	15.0	13.3	17.7	8.5	5.7	3.1	2.9	1989
Richmond, VA	1.1	8.6	5.9	5.7	7.3	8.7	11.1	14.1	9.0	28.6	1959
Rochester, MN	1.2	12.9	18.5	14.1	11.1	12.4	9.9	9.0	3.7	7.2	1987
Sacramento, CA	0.9	6.3	15.0	7.8	15.2	13.3	11.3	11.9	7.2	11.0	1976
Saint Louis, MO	0.2	3.2	4.0	3.0	3.7	4.3	6.1	9.7	7.6	58.3	1938
Saint Paul, MN	0.7	4.5	5.1	3.5	7.3	9.8	9.4	11.7	6.7	41.2	1952
Salem, OR	1.8	9.1	13.5	15.9	9.5	18.5	9.3	9.3	4.5	8.6	1980
Salt Lake City, UT	1.8	10.6	6.8	5.5	7.4	11.4	9.8	12.2	8.2	26.3	1963
San Antonio, TX	1.6	11.9	15.2	11.3	16.2	13.8	10.1	9.5	5.2	5.2	1984
San Diego, CA	0.8	7.1	10.2	10.6	17.7	20.2	12.2	11.0	3.7	6.6	1978
San Francisco, CA	0.7	6.4	6.5	4.0	5.3	7.1	8.1	7.9	8.7	45.4	1945
San Jose, CA	0.6	7.3	9.6	9.6	12.1	23.6	18.5	10.9	2.7	5.2	1975
Santa Rosa, CA	1.0	6.2	12.3	12.5	17.9	20.9	11.9	8.1	4.4	4.9	1980
Savannah, GA	1.3	11.9	9.0	6.3	11.5	11.7	10.7	13.9	6.9	16.7	1971
Seattle, WA	1.2	17.6	12.0	7.4	7.5	7.2	7.7	8.4	7.4	23.4	1974
Sioux Falls, SD	2.0	19.1	18.4	13.3	10.6	10.4	6.5	8.0	3.0	8.6	1992
Tampa, FL	1.8	13.8	16.5	10.7	11.7	10.3	9.1	12.9	4.9	8.3	1984
Tucson, AZ	0.7	4.6	13.0	12.7	16.5	20.2	11.0	13.4	4.8	3.2	1979
Tulsa, OK	0.4	6.0	6.5	8.2	13.8	20.0	14.5	15.5	6.2	8.9	1972
Virginia Beach, VA	0.4	8.2	10.9	13.1	27.2	19.7	12.3	5.7	1.3	1.1	1984
Washington, DC	1.7	12.5	7.7	3.0	4.7	6.7	9.9	11.6	10.3	31.7	1957
Wichita, KS	0.7	6.9	10.1	11.2	12.8	13.3	9.1	18.0	7.7	10.3	1974
Wilmington, NC	2.3	13.1	14.9	16.2	15.2	11.1	6.2	6.3	5.7	9.1	1988
Winston-Salem, NC	1.1	8.6	13.2	12.5	15.0	14.4	11.0	12.2	4.1	7.7	1980
U.S.	1.2	8.9	13.6	12.8	13.0	14.4	10.0	9.7	4.5	11.9	1980

Note: Figures are percentages except for median year
Source: U.S. Census Bureau, 2019-2023 American Community Survey 5-Year Estimates

Year Housing Structure Built: Metro Area

Metro Area	2020 or Later	2010-2019	2000-2009	1990-1999	1980-1989	1970-1979	1960-1969	1950-1959	1940-1949	Before 1940	Median Year
Albuquerque, NM	0.9	7.5	17.4	16.2	15.7	17.7	8.6	9.5	3.3	3.2	1985
Anchorage, AK	0.5	9.5	16.8	12.5	23.9	22.9	7.8	4.6	0.8	0.7	1986
Ann Arbor, MI	1.2	6.4	13.0	16.0	10.5	15.4	12.3	9.1	4.3	11.8	1978
Athens, GA	1.8	10.2	19.4	18.1	15.0	14.1	9.5	4.6	2.2	5.1	1990
Atlanta, GA	1.7	11.8	23.5	19.3	16.7	11.5	6.8	4.2	1.7	2.8	1993
Austin, TX	4.0	25.5	21.4	14.6	14.3	9.7	4.5	2.8	1.3	2.0	2000
Baltimore, MD	0.6	7.2	9.6	13.0	13.4	12.8	10.3	12.4	6.0	14.6	1975
Billings, MT	2.1	12.3	12.8	12.9	11.6	16.7	7.7	10.1	4.8	9.1	1981
Boise City, ID	3.5	17.3	22.2	17.7	8.9	13.4	4.7	4.2	2.8	5.2	1996
Boston, MA	0.8	7.1	7.5	7.1	10.5	10.6	9.8	10.4	4.8	31.5	1963
Boulder, CO	1.5	11.2	12.5	18.7	14.7	19.1	9.9	5.0	1.4	6.2	1986
Cape Coral, FL	1.9	11.4	29.2	16.2	20.5	12.9	5.0	1.8	0.4	0.6	1995
Cedar Rapids, IA	0.9	10.2	13.2	12.8	7.4	13.6	11.6	10.2	3.6	16.6	1976
Charleston, SC	2.9	19.5	20.3	14.1	14.6	11.3	7.2	4.5	2.2	3.4	1995
Charlotte, NC	2.2	16.8	21.6	17.2	12.3	10.0	7.2	5.8	2.9	4.1	1994
Chicago, IL	0.5	4.6	11.5	10.7	9.2	13.9	11.6	12.4	5.5	20.1	1970
Cincinnati, OH	0.9	6.6	12.1	13.5	10.7	13.4	10.4	11.3	4.7	16.5	1975
Clarksville, TN	2.6	16.3	19.0	18.9	12.1	12.6	7.3	5.5	2.6	3.0	1994
Cleveland, OH	0.5	4.0	7.0	8.8	7.1	12.5	13.3	17.0	7.3	22.6	1962
College Station, TX	2.6	20.0	19.0	15.1	17.1	12.3	5.7	3.9	2.1	2.2	1994
Colorado Springs, CO	1.9	12.9	17.5	15.2	16.4	15.8	8.0	5.9	1.4	4.9	1988
Columbia, MO	1.0	14.0	17.9	16.8	13.2	13.1	9.7	4.6	2.4	7.3	1990
Columbia, SC	1.6	13.8	18.3	16.7	13.5	14.1	8.8	6.7	2.8	3.7	1990
Columbus, OH	1.4	9.5	14.1	14.9	11.5	13.7	10.1	9.2	3.5	12.1	1981
Dallas, TX	2.6	16.9	18.6	14.3	16.5	12.2	7.6	6.6	2.2	2.5	1992
Davenport, IA	0.6	5.3	8.4	7.9	7.0	16.0	13.7	12.1	6.9	22.1	1966
Denver, CO	1.9	13.0	15.6	13.8	13.5	16.4	8.7	8.4	2.4	6.3	1986
Des Moines, IA	2.2	15.6	15.3	12.1	7.8	12.5	7.5	8.3	3.5	15.3	1984
Detroit, MI	0.5	4.0	8.7	11.1	9.0	14.5	12.4	18.3	8.8	12.8	1968
Durham, NC	2.3	17.4	17.1	16.3	14.5	11.4	7.5	5.9	2.9	4.7	1992
El Paso, TX	1.4	16.4	15.2	12.8	14.7	14.6	8.7	9.3	2.8	4.1	1987
Eugene, OR	0.8	7.5	12.2	14.5	9.1	21.0	13.2	8.5	6.7	6.4	1977
Fargo, ND	1.9	19.2	17.1	13.2	9.8	14.3	6.5	7.4	2.2	8.2	1991
Fort Collins, CO	2.2	16.8	18.4	17.5	12.3	16.7	5.8	3.2	1.8	5.3	1993
Fort Wayne, IN	1.0	7.6	11.5	13.5	10.2	14.7	12.3	9.9	4.7	14.5	1976
Fort Worth, TX	2.6	16.9	18.6	14.3	16.5	12.2	7.6	6.6	2.2	2.5	1992
Gainesville, FL	1.8	9.8	17.7	17.7	18.9	16.6	8.4	4.7	1.9	2.5	1988
Green Bay, WI	1.0	8.5	13.4	15.1	11.6	15.5	9.9	9.3	4.0	11.7	1980
Greensboro, NC	0.9	9.0	15.8	16.5	14.4	14.3	10.1	8.9	4.1	6.0	1985
Honolulu, HI	0.6	7.7	9.6	11.4	12.8	23.9	17.3	10.0	3.8	3.0	1977
Houston, TX	2.3	18.1	19.6	12.8	14.7	15.1	7.6	5.4	2.1	2.3	1992
Huntsville, AL	2.9	16.7	18.5	15.2	14.9	9.8	12.7	5.5	1.4	2.3	1992
Indianapolis, IN	1.4	10.4	14.9	15.5	9.9	11.7	10.3	9.4	4.3	12.2	1982
Jacksonville, FL	3.2	13.5	20.2	14.3	16.1	11.4	7.3	7.2	2.9	3.8	1991
Kansas City, MO	1.2	8.8	13.5	13.3	12.0	14.1	11.2	10.6	4.0	11.4	1979
Lafayette, LA	1.4	15.7	15.9	12.0	15.0	15.9	9.4	8.3	3.2	3.4	1987
Las Vegas, NV	1.9	12.3	28.8	25.5	13.7	10.1	4.7	2.0	0.6	0.4	1997
Lexington, KY	1.2	10.3	15.9	16.7	13.1	14.2	10.8	7.5	2.8	7.5	1985
Lincoln, NE	1.1	11.9	14.3	13.5	9.6	14.7	8.9	9.5	3.2	13.1	1981
Little Rock, AR	1.3	13.5	17.7	15.3	13.9	15.3	9.9	6.3	3.2	3.7	1988
Los Angeles, CA	0.6	5.3	6.3	7.4	12.6	15.9	15.0	17.6	7.8	11.5	1969
Louisville, KY	1.1	8.4	13.5	13.4	9.3	14.8	11.1	11.7	5.1	11.6	1977
Madison, WI	1.2	11.5	15.9	14.2	10.4	13.6	9.2	7.5	3.3	13.1	1983
Manchester, NH	0.5	5.4	9.6	10.5	20.2	15.3	9.2	7.3	3.6	18.6	1977
McAllen, TX	1.6	18.0	27.8	19.0	15.8	9.7	3.9	2.1	1.1	1.1	1999

Table continued on following page.

Appendix A: Comparative Statistics   A-123

Metro Area	2020 or Later	2010 -2019	2000 -2009	1990 -1999	1980 -1989	1970 -1979	1960 -1969	1950 -1959	1940 -1949	Before 1940	Median Year
Memphis, TN	0.9	7.4	15.0	16.1	13.3	15.3	10.5	11.7	4.8	4.9	1982
Miami, FL	1.0	7.4	12.8	13.8	19.0	20.4	11.5	9.6	2.6	2.0	1982
Midland, TX	2.4	24.0	11.8	9.7	17.4	10.3	6.8	13.7	2.4	1.3	1989
Milwaukee, WI	0.7	5.5	8.2	10.4	7.6	13.1	11.6	15.3	7.0	20.7	1966
Minneapolis, MN	1.3	8.6	13.3	13.4	13.8	13.9	9.3	9.1	3.6	13.6	1980
Nashville, TN	3.1	17.7	18.1	15.3	13.0	11.9	8.2	6.0	2.5	4.3	1993
New Orleans, LA	0.4	5.1	9.9	6.8	13.1	19.6	13.9	10.8	5.1	15.2	1973
New York, NY	0.5	5.3	6.6	5.9	7.8	9.6	13.3	15.3	8.3	27.3	1959
Oklahoma City, OK	1.7	13.5	14.4	10.3	13.8	16.5	11.2	8.6	4.3	5.6	1983
Omaha, NE	1.3	10.7	14.3	11.8	9.6	13.9	11.2	8.2	3.4	15.6	1978
Orlando, FL	2.1	15.3	21.5	17.9	18.5	11.6	5.5	4.9	1.1	1.5	1994
Philadelphia, PA	0.7	5.3	7.9	8.9	9.9	12.2	11.7	14.9	7.0	21.5	1966
Phoenix, AZ	1.9	12.2	23.7	17.9	16.2	14.9	6.3	4.8	1.1	0.9	1993
Pittsburgh, PA	0.6	4.6	6.4	7.3	7.7	11.8	11.3	16.3	8.2	25.8	1960
Portland, OR	1.4	11.1	14.0	16.3	10.9	16.0	8.0	6.7	4.2	11.3	1983
Providence, RI	0.4	3.6	6.3	7.6	11.6	11.9	10.3	11.6	5.9	30.8	1962
Provo, UT	3.7	22.3	22.9	16.1	8.5	11.7	4.3	4.2	2.6	3.9	1999
Raleigh, NC	2.9	20.7	23.7	19.4	13.7	8.2	4.8	3.0	1.2	2.5	1999
Reno, NV	2.3	10.8	21.1	16.9	14.2	17.6	7.9	4.6	2.3	2.3	1991
Richmond, VA	1.3	10.3	14.2	14.3	15.3	13.7	9.3	8.5	4.2	8.8	1984
Rochester, MN	1.2	10.4	18.3	13.5	10.5	13.0	8.9	7.5	3.4	13.3	1984
Sacramento, CA	1.2	6.8	17.1	14.0	16.3	17.3	10.4	9.3	3.3	4.2	1983
Saint Louis, MO	0.8	6.3	11.4	11.6	11.1	12.8	12.2	12.3	5.4	16.1	1973
Saint Paul, MN	1.3	8.6	13.3	13.4	13.8	13.9	9.3	9.1	3.6	13.6	1980
Salem, OR	1.6	8.1	14.1	16.7	9.7	21.1	9.8	7.1	3.9	7.9	1980
Salt Lake City, UT	1.9	14.7	14.4	14.0	11.3	16.8	8.3	8.1	3.2	7.2	1986
San Antonio, TX	3.0	18.3	18.5	12.4	13.9	11.8	7.6	6.7	3.7	4.0	1992
San Diego, CA	0.8	6.5	12.0	11.5	18.6	21.7	11.6	10.1	3.1	4.1	1980
San Francisco, CA	0.7	5.6	7.7	7.8	10.6	14.2	12.8	13.4	7.7	19.5	1967
San Jose, CA	0.9	8.8	9.2	9.6	11.7	20.4	17.4	13.7	3.4	4.8	1975
Santa Rosa, CA	1.0	5.3	10.1	13.2	18.0	19.8	11.8	8.5	4.2	8.0	1979
Savannah, GA	2.2	15.8	19.4	13.1	12.7	11.0	6.7	7.5	3.8	7.7	1990
Seattle, WA	1.3	12.4	14.7	14.0	13.7	12.9	10.5	6.8	3.9	9.7	1985
Sioux Falls, SD	1.9	17.3	17.9	13.6	9.2	11.2	6.3	7.4	3.1	12.2	1990
Tampa, FL	1.6	10.2	15.4	13.0	19.8	18.9	8.7	7.9	1.9	2.5	1985
Tucson, AZ	1.2	7.5	18.2	16.5	17.1	18.6	8.3	7.9	2.8	1.9	1986
Tulsa, OK	1.2	11.0	13.9	11.1	13.9	18.2	10.3	9.8	4.1	6.7	1981
Virginia Beach, VA	1.0	9.6	12.6	14.0	18.1	14.3	11.5	9.1	4.2	5.6	1983
Washington, DC	1.2	10.7	14.1	12.9	15.2	13.0	11.5	8.7	4.7	8.1	1983
Wichita, KS	0.9	7.8	12.0	12.8	12.5	13.0	8.1	15.9	6.1	10.7	1977
Wilmington, NC	2.7	17.1	23.5	18.8	14.4	9.9	4.4	3.2	2.4	3.6	1996
Winston-Salem, NC	1.0	8.7	15.6	15.9	14.5	15.5	10.1	9.0	3.7	6.1	1984
U.S.	1.2	8.9	13.6	12.8	13.0	14.4	10.0	9.7	4.5	11.9	1980

Note: Figures are percentages except for median year; Figures cover the Metropolitan Statistical Area (MSA)
Source: U.S. Census Bureau, 2019-2023 American Community Survey 5-Year Estimates

Gross Monthly Rent: City

City	Under $500	$500 -$999	$1,000 -$1,499	$1,500 -$1,999	$2,000 -$2,499	$2,500 -$2,999	$3,000 and up	Median ($)
Albuquerque, NM	5.3	37.7	35.1	16.1	3.9	0.8	1.1	1,085
Anchorage, AK	3.5	14.0	35.7	25.6	12.6	5.5	3.0	1,453
Ann Arbor, MI	3.0	11.6	32.6	26.6	14.6	4.9	6.7	1,552
Athens, GA	3.8	33.4	37.8	17.1	5.0	1.5	1.3	1,162
Atlanta, GA	9.7	10.8	22.9	28.6	16.1	6.4	5.6	1,617
Austin, TX	2.5	4.7	32.4	33.5	15.4	6.4	5.0	1,655
Baltimore, MD	13.0	15.9	35.9	21.5	8.9	2.8	2.0	1,290
Billings, MT	7.9	34.2	37.7	14.4	3.3	0.7	1.7	1,097
Boise City, ID	4.1	15.0	41.7	26.5	9.3	1.9	1.6	1,359
Boston, MA	12.2	9.1	9.8	15.4	18.7	13.2	21.6	2,093
Boulder, CO	2.9	4.3	17.5	29.8	18.2	10.7	16.5	1,924
Cape Coral, FL	0.8	4.6	24.6	39.7	20.2	6.3	3.7	1,751
Cedar Rapids, IA	7.5	49.3	31.3	8.7	0.9	0.3	2.0	925
Charleston, SC	4.4	7.5	29.8	31.4	16.4	4.4	6.1	1,632
Charlotte, NC	2.7	10.1	36.9	33.9	10.9	3.2	2.3	1,504
Chicago, IL	7.2	17.6	32.2	20.1	11.6	5.4	5.9	1,380
Cincinnati, OH	11.8	43.6	26.9	11.1	3.9	1.5	1.3	953
Clarksville, TN	2.4	26.4	43.4	20.7	6.1	0.8	0.3	1,215
Cleveland, OH	17.2	43.0	26.0	9.4	2.6	0.9	0.8	894
College Station, TX	2.3	31.8	36.6	18.4	6.6	3.1	1.1	1,168
Colorado Springs, CO	2.7	10.7	32.8	30.0	15.9	4.3	3.6	1,562
Columbia, MO	4.0	39.3	38.9	9.8	5.8	1.4	0.8	1,067
Columbia, SC	8.4	26.7	42.3	16.5	5.4	0.5	0.2	1,158
Columbus, OH	4.5	22.1	46.5	19.4	5.3	1.2	0.9	1,224
Dallas, TX	3.1	12.2	42.5	25.9	9.5	3.4	3.4	1,403
Davenport, IA	7.1	52.5	29.5	6.8	1.6	0.1	2.4	930
Denver, CO	5.7	6.3	22.4	28.8	19.9	9.0	7.9	1,770
Des Moines, IA	5.4	39.0	40.2	12.9	2.0	0.2	0.3	1,054
Detroit, MI	11.7	35.1	39.5	10.0	2.5	0.8	0.4	1,034
Durham, NC	4.9	15.5	37.1	29.7	8.9	2.1	1.8	1,412
El Paso, TX	8.8	37.4	37.3	12.4	3.1	0.6	0.5	1,041
Eugene, OR	4.5	22.0	34.3	25.4	8.7	2.5	2.6	1,347
Fargo, ND	4.3	56.5	27.7	8.1	1.6	0.7	1.1	916
Fort Collins, CO	2.5	10.8	26.1	33.0	19.7	6.0	1.9	1,661
Fort Wayne, IN	6.7	48.7	37.3	5.3	1.4	0.4	0.3	959
Fort Worth, TX	2.6	13.5	40.6	25.3	12.3	3.4	2.2	1,412
Gainesville, FL	3.6	27.6	37.8	20.0	7.3	2.2	1.6	1,214
Green Bay, WI	6.7	55.0	31.7	5.1	0.7	0.1	0.6	904
Greensboro, NC	4.8	31.8	45.3	12.5	3.2	0.8	1.5	1,114
Honolulu, HI	5.7	7.6	21.8	26.2	16.6	7.5	14.5	1,783
Houston, TX	2.7	21.1	39.5	23.4	8.1	2.6	2.7	1,313
Huntsville, AL	4.8	38.7	37.7	14.0	2.9	0.5	1.3	1,078
Indianapolis, IN	4.8	32.8	43.9	13.7	3.2	1.0	0.6	1,112
Jacksonville, FL	4.9	16.1	38.9	26.9	9.7	2.3	1.2	1,375
Kansas City, MO	6.7	25.9	41.6	18.6	4.6	1.5	1.2	1,186
Lafayette, LA	6.5	37.0	39.7	13.7	2.6	0.2	0.4	1,065
Las Vegas, NV	3.1	14.4	35.9	29.4	11.7	3.5	1.9	1,456
Lexington, KY	4.4	36.0	40.3	13.9	3.8	1.2	0.5	1,101
Lincoln, NE	4.7	41.3	37.3	12.0	3.0	0.5	1.4	1,045
Little Rock, AR	5.2	38.1	39.8	12.0	2.8	0.8	1.2	1,067
Los Angeles, CA	4.6	7.2	20.1	23.9	18.3	10.6	15.3	1,879
Louisville, KY	9.7	34.0	39.6	12.5	2.8	0.7	0.7	1,069
Madison, WI	3.6	15.5	41.6	26.0	8.2	2.4	2.7	1,364
Manchester, NH	5.5	12.8	34.2	31.7	12.5	1.9	1.3	1,465
McAllen, TX	8.3	40.3	37.2	11.2	2.0	0.9	0.0	1,017

Table continued on following page.

City	Under $500	$500 -$999	$1,000 -$1,499	$1,500 -$1,999	$2,000 -$2,499	$2,500 -$2,999	$3,000 and up	Median ($)
Memphis, TN	4.9	32.5	43.3	15.2	2.8	0.7	0.6	1,123
Miami, FL	8.4	9.2	25.4	22.3	16.1	8.1	10.5	1,657
Midland, TX	3.2	15.5	38.6	24.4	11.7	4.2	2.3	1,407
Milwaukee, WI	7.0	39.6	38.2	10.7	2.4	1.0	1.1	1,033
Minneapolis, MN	8.7	16.4	35.0	22.5	10.8	3.3	3.3	1,329
Nashville, TN	6.2	10.7	34.1	28.4	12.8	4.5	3.3	1,486
New Orleans, LA	10.0	21.7	38.2	19.5	6.2	2.7	1.7	1,211
New York, NY	8.3	10.0	19.2	22.4	16.2	8.5	15.4	1,779
Oklahoma City, OK	5.3	36.3	40.4	13.3	2.8	1.1	0.7	1,083
Omaha, NE	4.4	29.7	43.5	16.1	4.3	0.8	1.3	1,150
Orlando, FL	3.1	6.0	30.0	36.5	17.1	4.7	2.6	1,650
Philadelphia, PA	8.5	18.1	35.8	22.6	8.7	3.1	3.2	1,323
Phoenix, AZ	3.5	13.5	36.2	29.1	12.0	3.7	2.0	1,458
Pittsburgh, PA	10.6	21.9	35.1	18.4	8.3	3.3	2.4	1,221
Portland, OR	4.6	9.6	30.1	29.6	15.0	6.3	4.8	1,596
Providence, RI	16.9	11.3	33.2	22.3	10.5	3.4	2.4	1,333
Provo, UT	5.6	28.6	40.3	16.6	6.4	1.9	0.5	1,152
Raleigh, NC	2.5	9.3	41.1	33.8	8.8	2.7	1.8	1,468
Reno, NV	4.9	15.0	33.3	26.7	13.4	4.0	2.7	1,453
Richmond, VA	9.4	14.9	41.0	24.1	7.9	1.9	0.8	1,314
Rochester, MN	6.3	23.1	32.8	23.3	8.8	1.7	4.0	1,316
Sacramento, CA	4.4	10.1	23.1	31.7	19.4	7.9	3.3	1,694
Saint Louis, MO	9.1	43.5	33.0	9.9	3.0	0.9	0.7	978
Saint Paul, MN	9.5	16.7	41.4	20.1	9.0	1.6	1.7	1,248
Salem, OR	5.6	16.1	43.1	24.0	8.2	1.8	1.2	1,323
Salt Lake City, UT	6.7	16.6	37.5	23.0	10.1	3.7	2.5	1,343
San Antonio, TX	4.8	21.4	43.5	21.8	5.7	1.6	1.2	1,258
San Diego, CA	2.3	3.9	11.3	22.8	21.9	16.0	21.8	2,223
San Francisco, CA	7.8	8.1	11.1	11.9	13.2	10.9	36.9	2,419
San Jose, CA	3.7	4.7	6.6	12.7	18.3	17.6	36.5	2,617
Santa Rosa, CA	4.1	5.1	12.9	24.0	23.2	15.4	15.3	2,084
Savannah, GA	6.6	17.0	41.8	23.1	7.7	1.9	2.0	1,302
Seattle, WA	5.0	4.2	15.6	25.4	21.5	13.0	15.5	1,998
Sioux Falls, SD	4.5	46.5	36.9	8.1	2.4	0.3	1.2	993
Tampa, FL	6.5	11.9	27.9	27.1	14.9	6.8	4.9	1,567
Tucson, AZ	4.5	38.5	36.3	15.0	3.5	0.8	1.3	1,079
Tulsa, OK	7.3	42.9	36.4	9.1	2.1	1.0	1.2	998
Virginia Beach, VA	1.9	5.3	31.3	38.7	14.9	3.9	4.0	1,649
Washington, DC	7.4	7.8	17.8	21.2	16.8	11.4	17.6	1,900
Wichita, KS	4.8	50.2	34.2	7.8	2.1	0.3	0.7	960
Wilmington, NC	6.3	17.3	40.7	25.1	7.1	1.9	1.5	1,311
Winston-Salem, NC	6.7	40.1	36.5	11.4	3.5	0.8	1.0	1,033
U.S.	6.5	22.3	29.5	20.2	10.8	4.8	5.9	1,348

Note: Figures are percentages except for Median; Gross rent is the contract rent plus the estimated average monthly cost of utilities (electricity, gas, and water and sewer) and fuels (oil, coal, kerosene, wood, etc.) if these are paid by the renter (or paid for the renter by someone else).
Source: U.S. Census Bureau, 2019-2023 American Community Survey 5-Year Estimates

Gross Monthly Rent: Metro Area

Metro Area	Under $500	$500 -$999	$1,000 -$1,499	$1,500 -$1,999	$2,000 -$2,499	$2,500 -2,999	$3,000 and up	Median ($)
Albuquerque, NM	5.5	36.2	35.3	16.7	4.3	0.9	1.1	1,102
Anchorage, AK	3.9	15.2	36.0	25.1	12.2	4.8	2.7	1,422
Ann Arbor, MI	4.3	14.9	39.0	23.1	10.3	3.5	4.7	1,400
Athens, GA	4.0	34.6	36.7	16.4	4.9	2.0	1.4	1,144
Atlanta, GA	3.5	10.4	31.9	33.0	14.4	4.1	2.7	1,563
Austin, TX	2.2	6.5	32.0	32.0	16.4	6.3	4.6	1,646
Baltimore, MD	6.9	10.5	29.1	28.1	15.8	5.6	3.9	1,562
Billings, MT	8.5	35.8	36.1	14.7	2.8	0.7	1.4	1,072
Boise City, ID	4.7	16.9	37.0	26.4	10.2	2.7	2.2	1,383
Boston, MA	9.4	8.3	13.6	21.1	19.8	12.2	15.5	1,940
Boulder, CO	3.0	4.7	17.7	31.3	20.8	10.0	12.5	1,893
Cape Coral, FL	2.9	8.6	31.7	34.5	14.0	4.2	4.1	1,597
Cedar Rapids, IA	7.8	50.9	29.5	8.0	1.3	0.3	2.2	899
Charleston, SC	3.1	11.1	36.7	27.9	13.4	4.0	3.8	1,488
Charlotte, NC	3.8	18.7	36.7	27.1	9.1	2.5	2.0	1,377
Chicago, IL	5.8	16.7	35.4	21.8	11.0	4.6	4.6	1,378
Cincinnati, OH	8.2	37.8	34.1	12.7	4.4	1.5	1.4	1,047
Clarksville, TN	4.4	33.0	39.4	17.7	4.4	0.6	0.5	1,141
Cleveland, OH	9.8	40.6	34.0	10.8	2.6	0.9	1.3	996
College Station, TX	4.0	32.0	38.0	16.6	5.7	2.2	1.4	1,146
Colorado Springs, CO	2.7	10.6	30.1	29.6	18.6	5.0	3.4	1,611
Columbia, MO	4.7	41.2	38.4	9.2	4.6	1.1	0.8	1,041
Columbia, SC	5.2	31.0	41.5	15.6	5.0	0.9	0.9	1,145
Columbus, OH	5.1	24.3	43.9	18.5	5.5	1.4	1.2	1,208
Dallas, TX	2.1	9.7	37.7	28.7	13.8	4.7	3.3	1,509
Davenport, IA	11.1	50.2	27.2	7.3	1.5	0.8	1.9	899
Denver, CO	3.6	5.3	21.2	32.6	21.1	9.5	6.7	1,805
Des Moines, IA	4.6	33.5	42.0	15.1	3.4	0.5	0.9	1,113
Detroit, MI	7.5	26.8	41.4	16.4	4.7	1.3	1.8	1,162
Durham, NC	5.0	18.6	36.6	26.5	8.7	2.4	2.3	1,374
El Paso, TX	8.7	37.2	37.0	13.0	3.1	0.5	0.4	1,045
Eugene, OR	5.4	23.6	36.5	23.0	7.6	1.9	1.9	1,287
Fargo, ND	4.7	52.7	29.3	9.2	2.5	0.8	0.9	940
Fort Collins, CO	2.6	10.0	25.7	33.1	18.9	6.6	3.1	1,677
Fort Wayne, IN	6.6	48.2	36.5	6.1	1.7	0.5	0.4	963
Fort Worth, TX	2.1	9.7	37.7	28.7	13.8	4.7	3.3	1,509
Gainesville, FL	3.9	27.5	36.4	20.0	7.2	2.6	2.3	1,219
Green Bay, WI	4.8	50.7	35.3	6.6	1.4	0.4	0.8	959
Greensboro, NC	7.6	37.7	39.7	10.5	2.6	0.7	1.2	1,045
Honolulu, HI	4.7	6.3	16.7	20.6	15.8	11.3	24.6	2,054
Houston, TX	2.6	17.5	39.1	24.9	10.1	3.2	2.6	1,378
Huntsville, AL	4.8	37.6	36.8	14.6	4.3	0.6	1.2	1,091
Indianapolis, IN	4.8	30.7	41.9	15.6	4.7	1.4	0.9	1,142
Jacksonville, FL	4.3	15.8	36.2	27.0	11.0	2.9	2.7	1,416
Kansas City, MO	5.4	25.3	41.7	18.9	5.6	1.4	1.6	1,201
Lafayette, LA	11.3	44.1	33.2	9.1	1.7	0.3	0.2	954
Las Vegas, NV	1.8	12.2	34.8	31.6	13.6	3.7	2.2	1,518
Lexington, KY	5.5	38.0	38.7	13.0	3.1	1.1	0.5	1,070
Lincoln, NE	4.8	41.4	37.2	11.8	2.9	0.5	1.4	1,043
Little Rock, AR	6.2	43.2	37.0	10.4	1.7	0.6	0.9	1,007
Los Angeles, CA	3.5	5.8	16.8	24.5	21.1	12.0	16.3	1,987
Louisville, KY	9.1	34.6	40.1	12.2	2.6	0.7	0.8	1,064
Madison, WI	3.9	19.6	41.6	23.8	6.9	1.9	2.2	1,300
Manchester, NH	5.5	11.2	31.2	31.7	14.5	3.8	2.0	1,532
McAllen, TX	11.1	48.5	30.9	7.4	1.4	0.5	0.2	925

Table continued on following page.

Metro Area	Under $500	$500 -$999	$1,000 -$1,499	$1,500 -$1,999	$2,000 -$2,499	$2,500 -2,999	$3,000 and up	Median ($)
Memphis, TN	4.9	30.4	42.2	16.0	4.3	1.2	1.0	1,153
Miami, FL	3.9	6.5	23.2	30.3	19.3	8.6	8.2	1,770
Midland, TX	3.7	17.8	38.4	23.7	10.7	3.8	2.0	1,377
Milwaukee, WI	6.0	33.5	39.6	14.3	3.8	1.5	1.3	1,105
Minneapolis, MN	6.6	14.0	36.6	25.6	10.8	3.3	3.2	1,396
Nashville, TN	5.4	15.0	34.3	27.1	11.6	3.7	2.8	1,434
New Orleans, LA	7.3	24.9	41.7	18.2	5.0	1.7	1.1	1,182
New York, NY	7.3	9.0	20.0	24.4	16.9	8.6	13.8	1,780
Oklahoma City, OK	5.3	36.8	39.1	13.4	3.1	1.1	1.1	1,081
Omaha, NE	5.0	29.1	42.6	16.6	4.3	0.9	1.5	1,152
Orlando, FL	2.1	8.2	28.7	34.6	18.0	5.3	3.0	1,659
Philadelphia, PA	6.4	14.6	35.3	25.2	11.2	3.7	3.7	1,413
Phoenix, AZ	2.7	10.8	31.5	30.9	15.3	5.2	3.5	1,581
Pittsburgh, PA	11.8	37.3	32.0	11.5	4.4	1.5	1.6	1,011
Portland, OR	3.4	7.7	28.4	33.9	16.2	6.3	4.1	1,654
Providence, RI	12.9	18.9	35.1	20.9	7.8	2.5	1.9	1,236
Provo, UT	3.1	16.5	34.5	27.9	12.6	3.7	1.8	1,434
Raleigh, NC	3.4	13.4	36.5	31.2	10.0	3.4	2.1	1,459
Reno, NV	4.2	14.7	31.6	27.3	14.8	4.0	3.4	1,491
Richmond, VA	5.5	14.0	39.6	27.9	9.1	1.8	2.0	1,388
Rochester, MN	7.9	29.2	31.6	19.9	7.1	1.3	3.0	1,195
Sacramento, CA	3.6	8.3	24.6	29.4	19.8	8.6	5.7	1,729
Saint Louis, MO	6.4	36.8	37.9	12.7	3.4	1.2	1.8	1,073
Saint Paul, MN	6.6	14.0	36.6	25.6	10.8	3.3	3.2	1,396
Salem, OR	4.9	16.5	43.8	24.6	7.3	1.8	1.1	1,324
Salt Lake City, UT	3.9	11.4	35.8	29.9	13.2	3.6	2.2	1,486
San Antonio, TX	4.4	19.8	41.8	22.8	7.7	2.0	1.4	1,299
San Diego, CA	2.2	4.0	12.0	24.8	22.5	14.8	19.6	2,154
San Francisco, CA	5.1	5.6	9.5	14.1	18.4	15.0	32.3	2,426
San Jose, CA	2.7	3.7	5.4	10.8	16.8	17.8	42.7	2,794
Santa Rosa, CA	4.1	6.8	13.4	21.5	22.3	14.4	17.4	2,093
Savannah, GA	4.2	17.2	38.3	28.2	8.4	1.9	1.8	1,370
Seattle, WA	4.0	4.8	16.7	28.3	22.6	11.5	12.2	1,932
Sioux Falls, SD	5.6	46.3	36.0	8.1	2.6	0.3	1.1	987
Tampa, FL	3.2	13.0	34.1	27.7	13.7	4.8	3.5	1,497
Tucson, AZ	4.3	32.8	35.8	18.7	4.9	1.4	2.1	1,154
Tulsa, OK	7.1	39.7	37.8	10.4	2.9	1.0	1.1	1,034
Virginia Beach, VA	5.0	13.8	37.7	28.0	10.3	2.6	2.7	1,416
Washington, DC	3.7	4.7	14.3	28.7	23.5	12.3	12.9	1,975
Wichita, KS	5.7	48.1	34.1	8.5	2.5	0.5	0.6	969
Wilmington, NC	5.1	19.5	40.4	23.1	7.7	2.0	2.3	1,313
Winston-Salem, NC	7.6	45.5	32.7	10.3	2.5	0.7	0.6	973
U.S.	6.5	22.3	29.5	20.2	10.8	4.8	5.9	1,348

Note: Figures are percentages except for Median; Gross rent is the contract rent plus the estimated average monthly cost of utilities (electricity, gas, and water and sewer) and fuels (oil, coal, kerosene, wood, etc.) if these are paid by the renter (or paid for the renter by someone else); Figures cover the Metropolitan Statistical Area (MSA)
Source: U.S. Census Bureau, 2019-2023 American Community Survey 5-Year Estimates

Highest Level of Education: City

City	Less than H.S.	H.S. Diploma	Some College, No Deg.	Associate Degree	Bachelors Degree	Masters Degree	Profess. School Degree	Doctorate Degree
Albuquerque, NM	9.1	21.6	21.2	9.5	20.9	12.0	2.8	2.9
Anchorage, AK	6.0	24.5	23.2	8.6	23.4	9.9	2.7	1.7
Ann Arbor, MI	2.4	7.0	8.9	4.0	30.5	26.4	8.7	12.1
Athens, GA	10.1	17.7	16.5	7.0	24.3	15.3	2.9	6.2
Atlanta, GA	7.0	16.0	13.6	5.0	32.8	16.8	5.7	3.0
Austin, TX	8.4	13.2	14.8	5.4	36.2	15.9	3.6	2.5
Baltimore, MD	12.8	27.9	18.4	5.5	18.1	11.7	3.1	2.5
Billings, MT	4.5	27.6	22.5	8.3	25.0	7.7	2.6	1.7
Boise City, ID	5.2	19.3	21.5	7.3	29.2	12.0	3.1	2.2
Boston, MA	11.1	18.3	11.6	4.9	28.5	16.4	5.2	3.9
Boulder, CO	3.1	6.4	10.2	3.5	36.9	25.7	5.1	9.1
Cape Coral, FL	6.8	35.3	22.6	9.5	16.7	6.0	1.7	1.3
Cedar Rapids, IA	5.9	25.9	22.4	12.9	22.2	7.8	2.1	0.8
Charleston, SC	4.1	15.4	16.0	6.8	35.5	13.8	5.2	3.2
Charlotte, NC	10.4	16.6	17.5	8.0	30.4	12.8	2.9	1.3
Chicago, IL	13.2	21.3	16.4	5.8	24.9	12.8	3.6	2.0
Cincinnati, OH	10.3	24.1	17.0	7.3	23.2	11.7	3.8	2.5
Clarksville, TN	5.8	27.4	24.2	12.0	18.9	9.4	1.2	1.1
Cleveland, OH	16.5	33.5	21.6	7.1	12.5	5.8	2.2	0.9
College Station, TX	5.4	14.4	16.9	6.2	29.5	16.1	2.0	9.5
Colorado Springs, CO	5.4	19.2	23.0	10.6	25.2	12.8	2.1	1.9
Columbia, MO	4.7	16.9	15.7	6.2	30.1	15.7	4.8	5.9
Columbia, SC	9.1	19.2	18.2	7.4	25.2	12.7	5.0	3.1
Columbus, OH	10.2	25.2	19.2	7.2	24.1	10.2	2.1	1.8
Dallas, TX	19.2	21.5	16.7	5.1	22.9	9.7	3.4	1.4
Davenport, IA	7.4	28.8	22.1	11.7	18.9	8.2	1.8	1.1
Denver, CO	8.6	14.8	15.7	5.3	33.8	15.0	4.7	2.2
Des Moines, IA	12.7	29.1	20.0	9.1	19.9	6.3	1.8	0.9
Detroit, MI	16.6	33.2	25.4	7.2	10.5	5.4	1.0	0.7
Durham, NC	8.6	15.4	13.7	6.6	28.8	16.9	4.5	5.5
El Paso, TX	18.1	24.4	21.3	8.8	18.3	6.7	1.4	1.0
Eugene, OR	5.2	17.4	24.3	8.8	23.7	13.5	3.6	3.5
Fargo, ND	4.7	18.7	20.7	12.7	29.0	9.9	2.0	2.3
Fort Collins, CO	2.4	13.5	16.1	8.2	34.3	18.9	2.8	3.9
Fort Wayne, IN	11.1	28.7	21.8	9.9	19.4	7.2	1.1	0.9
Fort Worth, TX	15.7	24.7	20.5	7.4	20.6	8.4	1.6	1.1
Gainesville, FL	5.7	17.7	14.9	10.0	25.7	15.1	4.2	6.8
Green Bay, WI	11.0	31.4	20.4	11.7	18.4	5.3	1.2	0.7
Greensboro, NC	9.9	21.5	20.1	8.7	24.2	11.3	2.3	2.1
Honolulu, HI	9.1	22.8	17.2	10.1	25.2	9.9	3.4	2.2
Houston, TX	19.7	21.5	16.6	6.2	21.3	9.6	3.2	1.9
Huntsville, AL	8.4	17.3	20.8	7.3	26.7	14.8	2.3	2.3
Indianapolis, IN	12.5	26.8	18.9	7.7	21.7	8.8	2.3	1.4
Jacksonville, FL	9.2	28.2	20.7	10.0	21.6	7.4	1.7	1.1
Kansas City, MO	8.2	25.0	21.6	7.4	23.8	10.1	2.7	1.2
Lafayette, LA	9.1	25.3	18.9	6.0	27.1	7.7	4.0	1.9
Las Vegas, NV	14.2	26.7	23.7	8.1	17.3	6.9	2.1	1.0
Lexington, KY	7.6	19.0	18.5	7.6	26.5	12.9	4.3	3.6
Lincoln, NE	7.0	20.4	20.3	11.4	26.4	9.8	2.3	2.5
Little Rock, AR	7.7	21.2	20.7	6.5	25.0	11.7	4.7	2.6
Los Angeles, CA	20.7	18.5	16.6	6.3	24.5	8.7	3.1	1.6
Louisville, KY	9.5	27.7	21.0	8.4	19.9	9.6	2.4	1.5
Madison, WI	4.3	14.6	14.4	7.5	33.5	16.0	3.7	6.0
Manchester, NH	11.3	29.1	18.1	8.0	22.5	8.8	1.3	0.9
McAllen, TX	20.1	20.7	20.6	6.5	20.3	7.6	2.9	1.2

Table continued on following page.

City	Less than H.S.	H.S. Diploma	Some College, No Deg.	Associate Degree	Bachelors Degree	Masters Degree	Profess. School Degree	Doctorate Degree
Memphis, TN	12.6	30.6	22.5	6.1	16.9	7.9	2.0	1.4
Miami, FL	20.0	25.2	11.6	7.5	21.5	8.8	4.1	1.3
Midland, TX	13.5	22.5	22.4	8.0	23.9	7.4	1.4	1.0
Milwaukee, WI	14.5	30.8	20.9	7.3	17.2	7.0	1.4	1.0
Minneapolis, MN	8.9	13.8	15.7	7.2	32.7	14.8	4.1	2.9
Nashville, TN	9.8	20.2	17.0	6.0	29.1	11.7	3.4	2.7
New Orleans, LA	10.9	21.3	20.7	5.2	22.5	12.0	4.8	2.6
New York, NY	16.3	23.0	13.2	6.5	23.6	12.4	3.3	1.7
Oklahoma City, OK	12.2	24.5	21.3	8.0	21.5	8.5	2.6	1.3
Omaha, NE	9.5	21.3	21.3	7.7	25.6	9.7	3.2	1.8
Orlando, FL	8.1	23.1	15.7	10.9	26.1	11.2	3.2	1.8
Philadelphia, PA	12.6	29.8	16.4	6.5	19.4	10.2	3.0	2.1
Phoenix, AZ	15.6	23.1	21.1	7.9	19.9	8.9	2.3	1.3
Pittsburgh, PA	5.7	23.7	14.7	8.0	24.6	14.1	4.5	4.6
Portland, OR	6.7	14.7	18.5	6.7	32.1	14.2	4.5	2.7
Providence, RI	18.1	27.5	14.8	4.9	18.3	9.7	3.5	3.3
Provo, UT	7.5	14.4	24.4	8.7	31.1	9.5	1.7	2.6
Raleigh, NC	7.5	15.9	16.2	7.4	32.5	14.3	3.5	2.6
Reno, NV	10.7	22.8	22.6	8.3	21.4	9.4	2.8	2.2
Richmond, VA	10.7	21.2	18.8	5.3	26.0	12.3	3.5	2.2
Rochester, MN	5.5	18.9	14.9	10.6	27.7	13.2	5.2	3.9
Sacramento, CA	13.1	20.5	21.6	8.4	22.9	8.7	3.3	1.6
Saint Louis, MO	9.5	24.5	19.7	6.1	22.0	12.1	3.4	2.7
Saint Paul, MN	11.1	20.8	16.9	7.7	25.2	12.3	3.3	2.8
Salem, OR	11.3	22.4	25.4	9.3	19.3	8.6	2.1	1.5
Salt Lake City, UT	8.4	17.1	16.9	6.7	28.9	13.6	4.7	3.7
San Antonio, TX	15.7	25.6	21.8	8.2	17.7	7.7	2.1	1.3
San Diego, CA	9.8	15.0	17.8	7.5	28.8	13.6	3.6	3.8
San Francisco, CA	11.2	11.3	12.0	5.3	35.1	16.7	4.9	3.4
San Jose, CA	14.5	16.4	15.5	7.1	26.2	15.1	2.1	3.1
Santa Rosa, CA	14.5	19.2	21.9	9.7	21.3	9.0	3.2	1.2
Savannah, GA	10.1	27.0	23.7	7.2	20.6	8.1	2.0	1.3
Seattle, WA	4.3	9.5	12.9	5.8	37.6	20.5	5.3	4.2
Sioux Falls, SD	6.9	24.3	20.1	11.2	25.4	8.2	2.5	1.3
Tampa, FL	10.2	22.5	14.7	8.0	26.3	11.7	4.4	2.2
Tucson, AZ	12.7	23.0	25.2	9.0	17.7	9.0	1.6	1.9
Tulsa, OK	12.4	25.0	21.2	8.2	20.8	8.0	3.0	1.5
Virginia Beach, VA	5.3	21.3	22.4	10.5	25.0	11.4	2.3	1.8
Washington, DC	7.2	14.5	11.8	2.9	26.1	22.7	10.3	4.6
Wichita, KS	12.0	26.0	23.0	8.1	19.7	8.5	1.6	1.1
Wilmington, NC	6.5	18.0	18.9	10.8	29.2	11.1	3.3	2.3
Winston-Salem, NC	11.6	23.7	19.5	7.9	21.6	10.2	2.8	2.6
U.S.	10.6	26.2	19.4	8.8	21.3	9.8	2.3	1.6

Note: Figures cover persons age 25 and over
Source: U.S. Census Bureau, 2019-2023 American Community Survey 5-Year Estimates

Highest Level of Education: Metro Area

Metro Area	Less than H.S.	H.S. Diploma	Some College, No Deg.	Associate Degree	Bachelors Degree	Masters Degree	Profess. School Degree	Doctorate Degree
Albuquerque, NM	9.7	23.6	22.0	9.7	19.2	11.0	2.4	2.5
Anchorage, AK	5.9	27.1	23.6	9.4	21.3	9.0	2.3	1.4
Ann Arbor, MI	4.2	14.2	16.8	6.7	27.1	19.4	5.1	6.5
Athens, GA	10.2	21.4	17.5	7.5	21.9	13.4	3.3	4.9
Atlanta, GA	9.2	23.0	18.4	7.9	25.4	11.7	2.6	1.8
Austin, TX	8.4	17.1	18.0	6.6	31.6	13.6	2.7	2.1
Baltimore, MD	7.9	23.6	18.2	7.0	23.4	14.4	3.1	2.5
Billings, MT	4.8	30.1	22.7	9.0	22.8	7.0	2.2	1.5
Boise City, ID	7.5	23.3	24.0	8.6	24.3	8.8	2.1	1.4
Boston, MA	7.7	20.8	13.3	7.0	27.5	16.4	3.6	3.7
Boulder, CO	4.5	11.0	14.5	6.1	34.5	20.0	3.8	5.6
Cape Coral, FL	9.6	30.0	19.8	9.8	18.8	8.2	2.3	1.4
Cedar Rapids, IA	4.8	27.8	20.7	13.9	22.2	8.0	1.7	0.9
Charleston, SC	8.1	22.9	19.8	9.3	24.9	10.7	2.8	1.6
Charlotte, NC	9.6	22.6	19.4	9.5	25.4	10.4	2.1	1.1
Chicago, IL	10.3	23.2	18.4	7.3	24.4	12.1	2.8	1.6
Cincinnati, OH	7.7	28.8	18.0	8.6	22.7	10.4	2.2	1.6
Clarksville, TN	7.7	29.5	23.6	11.2	17.4	8.2	1.3	1.1
Cleveland, OH	8.3	29.0	20.4	8.8	20.0	9.6	2.5	1.4
College Station, TX	11.7	23.8	18.7	6.8	22.2	10.2	1.7	5.0
Colorado Springs, CO	4.9	19.7	23.4	11.0	24.9	12.6	1.8	1.7
Columbia, MO	6.0	22.6	16.6	7.3	26.7	13.0	3.5	4.2
Columbia, SC	8.9	25.3	21.2	9.6	20.8	10.2	2.2	1.8
Columbus, OH	7.9	26.7	18.4	7.5	24.4	10.8	2.5	1.7
Dallas, TX	12.7	21.7	19.7	7.4	24.5	10.7	2.0	1.3
Davenport, IA	7.6	29.3	22.7	11.1	18.6	8.2	1.5	1.1
Denver, CO	7.7	18.4	18.2	7.3	30.3	13.3	2.9	1.9
Des Moines, IA	6.5	25.0	19.0	10.4	26.4	9.0	2.1	1.5
Detroit, MI	8.8	26.0	22.0	9.2	20.4	10.3	2.2	1.1
Durham, NC	8.9	17.0	14.3	7.5	26.3	15.5	4.8	5.6
El Paso, TX	19.4	24.9	21.1	9.2	17.1	6.1	1.2	0.9
Eugene, OR	6.9	22.8	27.0	9.9	19.7	9.4	2.3	2.1
Fargo, ND	4.4	19.1	20.8	13.5	28.4	9.7	1.9	2.3
Fort Collins, CO	3.4	16.8	19.3	8.8	31.0	14.9	2.7	3.1
Fort Wayne, IN	9.3	29.7	20.7	10.6	20.0	7.3	1.5	0.9
Fort Worth, TX	12.7	21.7	19.7	7.4	24.5	10.7	2.0	1.3
Gainesville, FL	7.3	24.2	16.4	11.1	20.3	11.8	4.0	4.8
Green Bay, WI	6.7	31.3	19.1	13.0	21.0	6.8	1.3	0.8
Greensboro, NC	11.7	26.5	20.8	9.6	20.0	8.5	1.5	1.4
Honolulu, HI	7.1	25.2	19.0	11.0	23.7	9.4	2.8	1.8
Houston, TX	14.9	22.7	19.5	7.5	22.1	9.3	2.3	1.7
Huntsville, AL	8.5	20.7	20.4	8.0	25.3	13.5	1.7	1.9
Indianapolis, IN	8.9	26.7	18.4	8.1	24.1	9.9	2.4	1.5
Jacksonville, FL	7.9	26.4	20.5	10.0	23.0	8.9	2.0	1.3
Kansas City, MO	6.9	24.9	21.1	7.9	24.4	11.0	2.5	1.3
Lafayette, LA	13.0	34.8	17.9	7.3	19.0	5.3	1.8	0.9
Las Vegas, NV	13.2	27.6	23.4	8.5	18.0	6.6	1.7	1.0
Lexington, KY	8.1	23.5	19.2	8.1	23.4	11.4	3.5	2.8
Lincoln, NE	6.4	20.9	20.1	11.9	26.2	9.8	2.1	2.4
Little Rock, AR	7.9	29.1	21.7	8.4	20.3	8.8	2.4	1.4
Los Angeles, CA	17.8	19.5	18.1	7.1	23.9	9.2	2.8	1.6
Louisville, KY	8.7	29.4	20.8	8.9	19.5	9.2	2.2	1.3
Madison, WI	4.1	20.2	16.6	9.7	29.9	12.7	2.9	3.8
Manchester, NH	7.0	25.6	17.2	9.6	25.4	12.1	1.6	1.5
McAllen, TX	30.7	25.2	18.3	5.6	13.9	4.8	1.0	0.6

Table continued on following page.

Metro Area	Less than H.S.	H.S. Diploma	Some College, No Deg.	Associate Degree	Bachelors Degree	Masters Degree	Profess. School Degree	Doctorate Degree
Memphis, TN	10.5	29.1	22.1	7.6	18.5	8.9	2.0	1.4
Miami, FL	13.1	25.7	16.0	9.5	21.8	9.0	3.4	1.4
Midland, TX	13.8	24.0	23.3	8.2	20.9	7.4	1.4	0.8
Milwaukee, WI	7.3	25.6	19.3	9.0	25.2	9.8	2.2	1.5
Minneapolis, MN	5.8	20.2	18.7	10.5	29.1	11.3	2.7	1.9
Nashville, TN	8.5	25.7	18.7	7.3	25.6	10.0	2.4	1.9
New Orleans, LA	12.5	26.2	21.5	6.7	19.6	8.7	3.1	1.6
New York, NY	12.4	23.2	14.0	6.8	24.9	13.3	3.5	1.8
Oklahoma City, OK	10.1	26.2	22.3	8.0	21.3	8.4	2.2	1.5
Omaha, NE	7.3	22.5	21.7	9.4	24.9	10.2	2.5	1.5
Orlando, FL	9.3	25.1	18.5	11.2	23.2	9.2	2.1	1.3
Philadelphia, PA	7.9	27.0	16.1	7.5	24.1	12.2	3.0	2.2
Phoenix, AZ	10.5	22.7	23.0	9.2	21.6	9.4	2.1	1.4
Pittsburgh, PA	5.1	31.4	15.5	10.6	22.6	10.6	2.3	1.9
Portland, OR	7.2	19.8	22.1	8.8	26.0	11.1	2.8	2.1
Providence, RI	11.6	27.8	17.2	8.4	21.3	9.9	2.1	1.7
Provo, UT	4.7	17.1	24.8	10.1	30.1	9.9	1.7	1.6
Raleigh, NC	7.1	17.3	16.6	8.8	30.8	14.4	2.6	2.4
Reno, NV	11.4	24.4	24.0	8.8	19.2	8.4	2.2	1.6
Richmond, VA	8.1	24.4	19.5	7.8	24.4	11.7	2.5	1.7
Rochester, MN	5.2	23.0	17.1	12.5	24.7	10.8	4.1	2.7
Sacramento, CA	9.9	20.6	23.3	9.9	23.0	8.7	3.0	1.6
Saint Louis, MO	6.7	25.5	21.0	9.3	22.3	11.2	2.3	1.7
Saint Paul, MN	5.8	20.2	18.7	10.5	29.1	11.3	2.7	1.9
Salem, OR	12.8	24.9	25.6	9.8	17.4	6.9	1.6	1.0
Salt Lake City, UT	8.2	22.7	22.1	9.2	24.1	9.7	2.3	1.7
San Antonio, TX	12.7	25.0	21.8	8.6	20.0	8.7	1.9	1.3
San Diego, CA	11.0	17.9	20.6	8.3	25.6	11.0	2.9	2.6
San Francisco, CA	10.5	15.0	15.5	6.6	30.0	15.1	3.9	3.4
San Jose, CA	10.9	13.9	13.9	6.5	27.8	19.3	2.9	4.8
Santa Rosa, CA	11.1	18.6	23.0	9.4	23.5	9.4	3.4	1.5
Savannah, GA	8.7	25.9	22.4	8.0	21.6	9.6	2.3	1.5
Seattle, WA	6.7	18.8	19.2	9.1	27.8	13.5	2.8	2.2
Sioux Falls, SD	6.3	25.7	19.7	12.6	24.8	7.7	2.0	1.2
Tampa, FL	9.1	27.4	19.4	10.0	21.5	8.9	2.2	1.3
Tucson, AZ	10.1	21.2	23.9	9.0	20.4	10.7	2.4	2.4
Tulsa, OK	9.9	28.6	22.4	9.4	19.7	7.0	1.9	1.1
Virginia Beach, VA	7.2	25.1	22.8	9.8	21.2	10.4	1.9	1.6
Washington, DC	8.5	17.3	14.6	5.8	27.0	18.7	4.7	3.4
Wichita, KS	9.7	26.4	23.4	9.0	20.2	8.8	1.5	1.0
Wilmington, NC	6.9	22.3	20.8	11.4	24.9	9.7	2.5	1.4
Winston-Salem, NC	10.8	28.4	21.4	9.8	18.9	7.3	1.9	1.5
U.S.	10.6	26.2	19.4	8.8	21.3	9.8	2.3	1.6

Note: Figures cover persons age 25 and over; Figures cover the Metropolitan Statistical Area (MSA)
Source: U.S. Census Bureau, 2019-2023 American Community Survey 5-Year Estimates

School Enrollment by Grade and Control: City

City	Preschool (%)		Kindergarten (%)		Grades 1 - 4 (%)		Grades 5 - 8 (%)		Grades 9 - 12 (%)	
	Public	Private	Public	Private	Public	Private	Public	Private	Public	Private
Albuquerque, NM	51.7	48.3	85.1	14.9	87.2	12.8	89.7	10.3	91.4	8.6
Anchorage, AK	53.5	46.5	89.2	10.8	84.1	15.9	87.8	12.2	91.8	8.2
Ann Arbor, MI	44.3	55.7	86.7	13.3	89.6	10.4	87.0	13.0	91.2	8.8
Athens, GA	65.1	34.9	95.8	4.2	88.4	11.6	86.4	13.6	89.2	10.8
Atlanta, GA	44.5	55.5	67.2	32.8	82.9	17.1	77.0	23.0	78.1	21.9
Austin, TX	51.1	48.9	85.1	14.9	87.7	12.3	86.7	13.3	90.3	9.7
Baltimore, MD	65.6	34.4	85.0	15.0	83.9	16.1	85.1	14.9	85.3	14.7
Billings, MT	39.2	60.8	80.1	19.9	84.7	15.3	84.3	15.7	86.1	13.9
Boise City, ID	34.8	65.2	80.0	20.0	85.7	14.3	89.3	10.7	86.4	13.6
Boston, MA	46.4	53.6	83.7	16.3	86.5	13.5	85.2	14.8	85.4	14.6
Boulder, CO	43.0	57.0	93.0	7.0	86.9	13.1	92.7	7.3	90.7	9.3
Cape Coral, FL	65.1	34.9	94.7	5.3	84.1	15.9	91.1	8.9	88.5	11.5
Cedar Rapids, IA	73.1	26.9	85.9	14.1	88.2	11.8	87.2	12.8	86.4	13.6
Charleston, SC	55.1	44.9	79.8	20.2	86.0	14.0	85.5	14.5	80.9	19.1
Charlotte, NC	50.8	49.2	86.8	13.2	88.6	11.4	87.4	12.6	88.8	11.2
Chicago, IL	56.4	43.6	81.6	18.4	82.8	17.2	83.6	16.4	85.2	14.8
Cincinnati, OH	60.9	39.1	77.2	22.8	78.5	21.5	78.9	21.1	81.8	18.2
Clarksville, TN	65.2	34.8	88.2	11.8	93.2	6.8	91.6	8.4	88.3	11.7
Cleveland, OH	68.9	31.1	68.7	31.3	78.2	21.8	77.9	22.1	77.6	22.4
College Station, TX	57.7	42.3	82.6	17.4	90.0	10.0	87.4	12.6	86.2	13.8
Colorado Springs, CO	64.6	35.4	88.0	12.0	87.3	12.7	88.4	11.6	90.7	9.3
Columbia, MO	49.7	50.3	85.6	14.4	87.0	13.0	89.5	10.5	91.0	9.0
Columbia, SC	33.0	67.0	81.8	18.2	76.7	23.3	85.6	14.4	84.0	16.0
Columbus, OH	64.5	35.5	79.2	20.8	84.3	15.7	85.7	14.3	87.2	12.8
Dallas, TX	69.0	31.0	88.5	11.5	89.5	10.5	91.1	8.9	89.8	10.2
Davenport, IA	52.6	47.4	86.2	13.8	79.3	20.7	86.4	13.6	92.5	7.5
Denver, CO	56.0	44.0	85.1	14.9	89.4	10.6	88.2	11.8	92.7	7.3
Des Moines, IA	76.4	23.6	88.0	12.0	90.8	9.2	91.8	8.2	93.8	6.2
Detroit, MI	81.6	18.4	91.8	8.2	93.4	6.6	92.1	7.9	92.4	7.6
Durham, NC	51.3	48.7	86.2	13.8	86.0	14.0	85.2	14.8	87.8	12.2
El Paso, TX	87.0	13.0	91.9	8.1	92.8	7.2	94.1	5.9	95.7	4.3
Eugene, OR	52.8	47.2	85.1	14.9	88.6	11.4	89.0	11.0	93.6	6.4
Fargo, ND	46.4	53.6	89.8	10.2	91.9	8.1	92.1	7.9	94.3	5.7
Fort Collins, CO	48.1	51.9	87.7	12.3	89.2	10.8	92.4	7.6	94.5	5.5
Fort Wayne, IN	45.6	54.4	70.8	29.2	78.5	21.5	82.0	18.0	79.2	20.8
Fort Worth, TX	61.4	38.6	86.8	13.2	90.9	9.1	91.0	9.0	91.3	8.7
Gainesville, FL	61.4	38.6	70.4	29.6	82.4	17.6	88.7	11.3	92.3	7.7
Green Bay, WI	71.0	29.0	86.2	13.8	87.3	12.7	89.8	10.2	90.4	9.6
Greensboro, NC	56.8	43.2	89.0	11.0	88.9	11.1	89.3	10.7	88.6	11.4
Honolulu, HI	36.4	63.6	74.0	26.0	79.9	20.1	76.4	23.6	69.1	30.9
Houston, TX	65.2	34.8	87.6	12.4	91.1	8.9	91.5	8.5	91.7	8.3
Huntsville, AL	63.7	36.3	80.9	19.1	81.8	18.2	78.2	21.8	84.2	15.8
Indianapolis, IN	61.1	38.9	85.4	14.6	82.9	17.1	83.7	16.3	85.2	14.8
Jacksonville, FL	56.5	43.5	83.5	16.5	83.4	16.6	80.0	20.0	83.7	16.3
Kansas City, MO	61.2	38.8	86.8	13.2	85.4	14.6	87.0	13.0	83.4	16.6
Lafayette, LA	55.1	44.9	71.4	28.6	76.8	23.2	72.2	27.8	78.4	21.6
Las Vegas, NV	68.6	31.4	91.1	8.9	87.6	12.4	89.3	10.7	91.2	8.8
Lexington, KY	29.5	70.5	81.0	19.0	82.3	17.7	85.7	14.3	85.4	14.6
Lincoln, NE	53.4	46.6	79.0	21.0	82.6	17.4	84.2	15.8	90.3	9.7
Little Rock, AR	66.2	33.8	86.5	13.5	78.2	21.8	76.0	24.0	77.5	22.5
Los Angeles, CA	55.2	44.8	85.7	14.3	87.7	12.3	87.5	12.5	88.0	12.0
Louisville, KY	50.3	49.7	77.2	22.8	81.9	18.1	81.0	19.0	78.2	21.8
Madison, WI	47.1	52.9	87.9	12.1	88.1	11.9	89.4	10.6	89.8	10.2
Manchester, NH	51.8	48.2	85.9	14.1	88.1	11.9	92.7	7.3	92.2	7.8
McAllen, TX	81.6	18.4	90.0	10.0	94.4	5.6	96.7	3.3	98.3	1.7

Table continued on following page.

City	Preschool (%)		Kindergarten (%)		Grades 1 - 4 (%)		Grades 5 - 8 (%)		Grades 9 - 12 (%)	
	Public	Private	Public	Private	Public	Private	Public	Private	Public	Private
Memphis, TN	60.2	39.8	87.7	12.3	88.1	11.9	88.5	11.5	85.6	14.4
Miami, FL	61.1	38.9	80.7	19.3	85.9	14.1	86.9	13.1	91.6	8.4
Midland, TX	57.2	42.8	67.9	32.1	78.9	21.1	76.4	23.6	84.3	15.7
Milwaukee, WI	77.0	23.0	73.9	26.1	75.5	24.5	73.9	26.1	79.9	20.1
Minneapolis, MN	53.1	46.9	86.3	13.7	86.2	13.8	87.0	13.0	88.8	11.2
Nashville, TN	51.0	49.0	82.7	17.3	82.9	17.1	78.2	21.8	81.2	18.8
New Orleans, LA	42.8	57.2	76.0	24.0	75.5	24.5	80.0	20.0	78.6	21.4
New York, NY	67.6	32.4	78.2	21.8	80.9	19.1	80.6	19.4	80.3	19.7
Oklahoma City, OK	69.7	30.3	86.9	13.1	87.9	12.1	86.4	13.6	86.9	13.1
Omaha, NE	54.5	45.5	79.9	20.1	82.7	17.3	82.7	17.3	83.3	16.7
Orlando, FL	60.7	39.3	81.8	18.2	85.9	14.1	90.0	10.0	88.0	12.0
Philadelphia, PA	54.5	45.5	78.0	22.0	79.4	20.6	79.1	20.9	77.6	22.4
Phoenix, AZ	62.6	37.4	86.7	13.3	88.9	11.1	91.5	8.5	92.2	7.8
Pittsburgh, PA	53.9	46.1	71.0	29.0	75.1	24.9	79.8	20.2	79.1	20.9
Portland, OR	36.8	63.2	84.3	15.7	87.0	13.0	86.9	13.1	85.7	14.3
Providence, RI	58.9	41.1	80.8	19.2	89.3	10.7	86.2	13.8	90.1	9.9
Provo, UT	64.9	35.1	88.2	11.8	91.6	8.4	95.6	4.4	91.6	8.4
Raleigh, NC	33.6	66.4	86.9	13.1	85.2	14.8	87.2	12.8	86.8	13.2
Reno, NV	54.6	45.4	96.7	3.3	89.2	10.8	88.3	11.7	93.6	6.4
Richmond, VA	53.2	46.8	90.2	9.8	87.7	12.3	84.7	15.3	82.7	17.3
Rochester, MN	43.6	56.4	90.6	9.4	86.3	13.7	84.5	15.5	90.2	9.8
Sacramento, CA	56.9	43.1	92.4	7.6	91.3	8.7	92.3	7.7	89.5	10.5
Saint Louis, MO	56.5	43.5	85.1	14.9	83.3	16.7	82.7	17.3	84.0	16.0
Saint Paul, MN	64.7	35.3	82.1	17.9	89.2	10.8	87.3	12.7	90.7	9.3
Salem, OR	70.2	29.8	88.8	11.2	88.5	11.5	91.6	8.4	97.2	2.8
Salt Lake City, UT	52.1	47.9	81.8	18.2	85.6	14.4	90.6	9.4	93.7	6.3
San Antonio, TX	73.0	27.0	89.7	10.3	90.7	9.3	92.1	7.9	91.8	8.2
San Diego, CA	47.0	53.0	84.6	15.4	88.6	11.4	91.3	8.7	90.8	9.2
San Francisco, CA	25.0	75.0	67.5	32.5	69.1	30.9	68.5	31.5	72.8	27.2
San Jose, CA	43.5	56.5	83.1	16.9	86.1	13.9	87.4	12.6	87.1	12.9
Santa Rosa, CA	55.2	44.8	90.3	9.7	92.4	7.6	88.6	11.4	92.8	7.2
Savannah, GA	76.3	23.7	85.4	14.6	88.1	11.9	88.2	11.8	88.6	11.4
Seattle, WA	35.0	65.0	76.0	24.0	77.9	22.1	74.8	25.2	78.3	21.7
Sioux Falls, SD	59.5	40.5	86.0	14.0	85.9	14.1	86.2	13.8	86.7	13.3
Tampa, FL	46.6	53.4	86.5	13.5	86.6	13.4	81.5	18.5	83.5	16.5
Tucson, AZ	71.7	28.3	90.3	9.7	88.2	11.8	88.1	11.9	91.9	8.1
Tulsa, OK	65.1	34.9	83.2	16.8	82.9	17.1	82.2	17.8	82.6	17.4
Virginia Beach, VA	39.5	60.5	77.6	22.4	88.8	11.2	88.5	11.5	91.2	8.8
Washington, DC	74.8	25.2	90.5	9.5	85.6	14.4	83.0	17.0	79.9	20.1
Wichita, KS	61.8	38.2	82.0	18.0	84.6	15.4	84.4	15.6	86.3	13.7
Wilmington, NC	55.8	44.2	84.8	15.2	79.3	20.7	75.6	24.4	87.1	12.9
Winston-Salem, NC	60.4	39.6	88.7	11.3	88.2	11.8	90.5	9.5	90.4	9.6
U.S.	58.7	41.3	85.2	14.8	87.2	12.8	87.9	12.1	89.0	11.0

Note: Figures shown cover persons 3 years old and over
Source: U.S. Census Bureau, 2019-2023 American Community Survey 5-Year Estimates

School Enrollment by Grade and Control: Metro Area

Metro Area	Preschool (%)		Kindergarten (%)		Grades 1 - 4 (%)		Grades 5 - 8 (%)		Grades 9 - 12 (%)	
	Public	Private	Public	Private	Public	Private	Public	Private	Public	Private
Albuquerque, NM	60.4	39.6	84.3	15.7	86.3	13.7	88.4	11.6	90.3	9.7
Anchorage, AK	51.9	48.1	87.7	12.3	83.6	16.4	86.9	13.1	89.7	10.3
Ann Arbor, MI	53.0	47.0	89.6	10.4	85.0	15.0	84.6	15.4	91.8	8.2
Athens, GA	63.8	36.2	93.2	6.8	88.2	11.8	87.2	12.8	88.5	11.5
Atlanta, GA	56.1	43.9	84.1	15.9	88.3	11.7	87.2	12.8	88.5	11.5
Austin, TX	49.6	50.4	87.0	13.0	90.0	10.0	89.2	10.8	91.1	8.9
Baltimore, MD	47.0	53.0	82.9	17.1	84.6	15.4	84.0	16.0	84.2	15.8
Billings, MT	41.5	58.5	84.1	15.9	87.0	13.0	87.1	12.9	88.2	11.8
Boise City, ID	40.0	60.0	86.5	13.5	85.6	14.4	88.0	12.0	88.4	11.6
Boston, MA	45.6	54.4	87.8	12.2	90.3	9.7	89.1	10.9	85.9	14.1
Boulder, CO	48.1	51.9	87.6	12.4	88.7	11.3	91.5	8.5	93.0	7.0
Cape Coral, FL	61.4	38.6	86.9	13.1	88.2	11.8	88.7	11.3	90.3	9.7
Cedar Rapids, IA	74.7	25.3	87.6	12.4	88.4	11.6	88.3	11.7	89.7	10.3
Charleston, SC	47.5	52.5	82.7	17.3	86.5	13.5	87.9	12.1	87.7	12.3
Charlotte, NC	50.5	49.5	86.2	13.8	87.8	12.2	87.3	12.7	88.6	11.4
Chicago, IL	56.8	43.2	84.8	15.2	87.6	12.4	88.1	11.9	90.0	10.0
Cincinnati, OH	50.7	49.3	79.1	20.9	81.9	18.1	82.2	17.8	83.0	17.0
Clarksville, TN	62.8	37.2	85.3	14.7	86.8	13.2	86.0	14.0	87.6	12.4
Cleveland, OH	53.0	47.0	75.5	24.5	80.6	19.4	80.7	19.3	82.4	17.6
College Station, TX	61.4	38.6	87.5	12.5	90.5	9.5	87.7	12.3	90.5	9.5
Colorado Springs, CO	66.9	33.1	86.3	13.7	87.4	12.6	88.5	11.5	89.8	10.2
Columbia, MO	55.0	45.0	87.6	12.4	84.6	15.4	90.4	9.6	90.7	9.3
Columbia, SC	51.6	48.4	88.3	11.7	87.8	12.2	90.4	9.6	91.7	8.3
Columbus, OH	56.4	43.6	81.4	18.6	87.0	13.0	88.1	11.9	88.9	11.1
Dallas, TX	57.4	42.6	88.0	12.0	90.4	9.6	91.4	8.6	91.5	8.5
Davenport, IA	65.1	34.9	87.2	12.8	87.0	13.0	91.2	8.8	92.2	7.8
Denver, CO	58.5	41.5	86.4	13.6	89.3	10.7	89.9	10.1	91.6	8.4
Des Moines, IA	68.1	31.9	87.6	12.4	91.2	8.8	89.9	10.1	91.5	8.5
Detroit, MI	62.5	37.5	86.9	13.1	88.7	11.3	89.8	10.2	89.9	10.1
Durham, NC	43.5	56.5	80.2	19.8	85.4	14.6	85.0	15.0	89.7	10.3
El Paso, TX	87.0	13.0	94.1	5.9	93.1	6.9	94.4	5.6	96.2	3.8
Eugene, OR	54.2	45.8	84.1	15.9	87.0	13.0	89.6	10.4	91.4	8.6
Fargo, ND	65.0	35.0	90.0	10.0	89.1	10.9	90.7	9.3	91.7	8.3
Fort Collins, CO	52.8	47.2	85.7	14.3	85.4	14.6	86.7	13.3	88.2	11.8
Fort Wayne, IN	44.1	55.9	73.2	26.8	75.7	24.3	76.8	23.2	81.3	18.7
Fort Worth, TX	57.4	42.6	88.0	12.0	90.4	9.6	91.4	8.6	91.5	8.5
Gainesville, FL	53.9	46.1	72.0	28.0	76.7	23.3	78.1	21.9	86.5	13.5
Green Bay, WI	68.0	32.0	84.2	15.8	86.1	13.9	87.0	13.0	90.5	9.5
Greensboro, NC	56.8	43.2	86.7	13.3	85.9	14.1	85.7	14.3	87.9	12.1
Honolulu, HI	34.7	65.3	79.0	21.0	79.9	20.1	78.2	21.8	74.9	25.1
Houston, TX	57.2	42.8	88.1	11.9	90.9	9.1	92.0	8.0	91.7	8.3
Huntsville, AL	56.0	44.0	79.7	20.3	82.9	17.1	82.3	17.7	83.1	16.9
Indianapolis, IN	53.8	46.2	84.3	15.7	85.1	14.9	85.7	14.3	87.4	12.6
Jacksonville, FL	56.0	44.0	85.4	14.6	84.0	16.0	82.8	17.2	85.6	14.4
Kansas City, MO	60.8	39.2	86.2	13.8	87.9	12.1	88.5	11.5	88.5	11.5
Lafayette, LA	56.7	43.3	78.8	21.2	77.7	22.3	77.9	22.1	79.1	20.9
Las Vegas, NV	64.0	36.0	87.1	12.9	88.8	11.2	90.1	9.9	91.8	8.2
Lexington, KY	40.9	59.1	82.4	17.6	83.7	16.3	84.8	15.2	85.9	14.1
Lincoln, NE	54.3	45.7	79.6	20.4	81.9	18.1	84.4	15.6	90.5	9.5
Little Rock, AR	69.9	30.1	86.8	13.2	86.2	13.8	85.4	14.6	87.1	12.9
Los Angeles, CA	54.7	45.3	86.6	13.4	89.1	10.9	89.9	10.1	90.6	9.4
Louisville, KY	53.0	47.0	79.7	20.3	81.8	18.2	82.4	17.6	81.0	19.0
Madison, WI	64.6	35.4	89.5	10.5	88.4	11.6	90.8	9.2	93.5	6.5
Manchester, NH	45.6	54.4	81.4	18.6	85.2	14.8	87.5	12.5	89.8	10.2
McAllen, TX	93.3	6.7	96.4	3.6	97.7	2.3	98.1	1.9	98.7	1.3

Table continued on following page.

Metro Area	Preschool (%)		Kindergarten (%)		Grades 1 - 4 (%)		Grades 5 - 8 (%)		Grades 9 - 12 (%)	
	Public	Private	Public	Private	Public	Private	Public	Private	Public	Private
Memphis, TN	59.8	40.2	87.5	12.5	86.3	13.7	87.0	13.0	84.8	15.2
Miami, FL	50.2	49.8	80.4	19.6	84.2	15.8	85.0	15.0	85.7	14.3
Midland, TX	65.0	35.0	65.8	34.2	80.9	19.1	78.8	21.2	83.9	16.1
Milwaukee, WI	59.4	40.6	75.9	24.1	78.5	21.5	78.7	21.3	84.9	15.1
Minneapolis, MN	60.7	39.3	85.8	14.2	88.3	11.7	88.7	11.3	91.5	8.5
Nashville, TN	50.1	49.9	82.5	17.5	84.8	15.2	83.3	16.7	83.0	17.0
New Orleans, LA	50.8	49.2	76.7	23.3	76.5	23.5	78.6	21.4	75.1	24.9
New York, NY	58.7	41.3	80.9	19.1	83.9	16.1	84.6	15.4	83.7	16.3
Oklahoma City, OK	70.9	29.1	86.9	13.1	87.7	12.3	87.4	12.6	87.8	12.2
Omaha, NE	58.9	41.1	81.9	18.1	84.5	15.5	85.7	14.3	85.5	14.5
Orlando, FL	48.9	51.1	79.8	20.2	82.1	17.9	85.3	14.7	87.0	13.0
Philadelphia, PA	47.4	52.6	81.4	18.6	85.0	15.0	84.4	15.6	83.6	16.4
Phoenix, AZ	60.3	39.7	85.5	14.5	88.1	11.9	90.4	9.6	91.9	8.1
Pittsburgh, PA	52.6	47.4	81.9	18.1	87.4	12.6	89.1	10.9	89.6	10.4
Portland, OR	40.0	60.0	83.8	16.2	85.8	14.2	88.1	11.9	89.6	10.4
Providence, RI	57.9	42.1	85.5	14.5	89.4	10.6	88.9	11.1	88.7	11.3
Provo, UT	55.5	44.5	87.9	12.1	90.3	9.7	92.6	7.4	94.0	6.0
Raleigh, NC	33.6	66.4	82.6	17.4	85.2	14.8	85.7	14.3	87.6	12.4
Reno, NV	51.8	48.2	90.8	9.2	90.9	9.1	89.7	10.3	92.1	7.9
Richmond, VA	44.4	55.6	86.4	13.6	87.5	12.5	89.1	10.9	90.0	10.0
Rochester, MN	61.3	38.7	91.0	9.0	88.1	11.9	87.9	12.1	91.8	8.2
Sacramento, CA	55.0	45.0	87.3	12.7	89.8	10.2	90.5	9.5	90.7	9.3
Saint Louis, MO	53.9	46.1	82.1	17.9	82.1	17.9	83.2	16.8	84.7	15.3
Saint Paul, MN	60.7	39.3	85.8	14.2	88.3	11.7	88.7	11.3	91.5	8.5
Salem, OR	59.8	40.2	86.8	13.2	86.0	14.0	90.3	9.7	92.4	7.6
Salt Lake City, UT	57.4	42.6	84.7	15.3	89.9	10.1	93.4	6.6	93.9	6.1
San Antonio, TX	65.5	34.5	87.7	12.3	89.4	10.6	90.3	9.7	90.5	9.5
San Diego, CA	50.7	49.3	86.1	13.9	89.3	10.7	90.8	9.2	91.9	8.1
San Francisco, CA	38.9	61.1	81.4	18.6	84.7	15.3	83.8	16.2	85.8	14.2
San Jose, CA	36.2	63.8	80.1	19.9	84.7	15.3	85.9	14.1	86.5	13.5
Santa Rosa, CA	53.1	46.9	91.2	8.8	92.9	7.1	89.9	10.1	91.1	8.9
Savannah, GA	57.5	42.5	79.1	20.9	84.4	15.6	84.9	15.1	85.2	14.8
Seattle, WA	40.8	59.2	79.5	20.5	85.6	14.4	86.7	13.3	90.0	10.0
Sioux Falls, SD	64.5	35.5	86.8	13.2	86.8	13.2	87.8	12.2	87.7	12.3
Tampa, FL	54.3	45.7	82.4	17.6	84.7	15.3	84.3	15.7	86.4	13.6
Tucson, AZ	71.3	28.7	88.0	12.0	87.2	12.8	87.8	12.2	89.8	10.2
Tulsa, OK	67.2	32.8	84.6	15.4	84.2	15.8	85.3	14.7	85.5	14.5
Virginia Beach, VA	50.5	49.5	80.8	19.2	87.9	12.1	88.8	11.2	89.9	10.1
Washington, DC	45.5	54.5	82.8	17.2	86.8	13.2	87.5	12.5	88.2	11.8
Wichita, KS	63.2	36.8	80.5	19.5	85.1	14.9	86.3	13.7	87.5	12.5
Wilmington, NC	52.1	47.9	83.4	16.6	83.8	16.2	84.3	15.7	88.3	11.7
Winston-Salem, NC	48.5	51.5	85.5	14.5	87.3	12.7	89.0	11.0	86.7	13.3
U.S.	58.7	41.3	85.2	14.8	87.2	12.8	87.9	12.1	89.0	11.0

Note: Figures shown cover persons 3 years old and over; Figures cover the Metropolitan Statistical Area (MSA)
Source: U.S. Census Bureau, 2019-2023 American Community Survey 5-Year Estimates

Educational Attainment by Race: City

City	High School Graduate or Higher (%)					Bachelor's Degree or Higher (%)				
	Total	White	Black	Asian	Hisp.[1]	Total	White	Black	Asian	Hisp.[1]
Albuquerque, NM	90.9	94.6	94.0	88.3	84.4	38.7	45.2	38.8	51.0	25.4
Anchorage, AK	94.0	96.7	91.7	86.6	86.6	37.7	45.2	23.6	30.5	23.8
Ann Arbor, MI	97.6	98.6	92.7	97.2	92.8	77.7	79.7	44.8	85.2	75.5
Athens, GA	89.9	96.9	82.5	88.5	66.8	48.7	62.8	22.6	67.8	31.7
Atlanta, GA	93.0	98.5	87.9	97.7	86.1	58.4	81.2	34.6	86.7	50.5
Austin, TX	91.6	95.1	90.6	93.6	78.3	58.2	63.9	36.7	78.4	35.6
Baltimore, MD	87.2	92.9	85.7	92.2	70.0	35.4	62.2	20.0	73.3	31.3
Billings, MT	95.5	96.2	98.6	89.9	85.1	37.0	38.3	35.8	56.4	14.6
Boise City, ID	94.8	96.2	73.7	89.9	80.6	46.6	47.4	24.4	60.1	30.3
Boston, MA	88.9	96.4	86.4	80.9	72.8	54.1	72.5	26.7	57.4	26.6
Boulder, CO	96.9	98.3	95.0	95.1	78.4	76.8	79.1	43.7	79.9	48.6
Cape Coral, FL	93.2	94.9	87.7	90.2	87.3	25.7	26.8	21.3	50.2	18.9
Cedar Rapids, IA	94.1	95.5	81.1	88.4	90.0	32.9	33.6	15.5	55.7	25.0
Charleston, SC	95.9	98.3	86.7	92.1	87.9	57.7	65.3	22.9	67.6	39.8
Charlotte, NC	89.6	95.9	91.6	85.3	60.5	47.4	63.1	33.3	61.3	20.5
Chicago, IL	86.8	93.4	87.4	88.3	71.9	43.3	61.9	25.2	65.0	20.4
Cincinnati, OH	89.7	94.6	83.8	93.1	81.1	41.3	57.9	16.2	80.1	36.2
Clarksville, TN	94.2	95.8	95.2	84.5	84.8	30.6	33.8	27.3	27.8	19.9
Cleveland, OH	83.5	87.5	82.3	78.8	70.9	21.3	31.8	12.7	55.6	10.6
College Station, TX	94.6	97.4	88.7	95.6	83.0	57.1	60.8	24.5	79.1	40.4
Colorado Springs, CO	94.6	96.4	94.1	89.0	84.6	41.9	45.3	32.1	43.8	21.6
Columbia, MO	95.3	96.4	92.0	94.2	86.7	56.5	59.4	33.9	72.5	48.5
Columbia, SC	90.9	96.0	85.2	89.9	85.6	46.1	62.6	25.4	73.0	39.5
Columbus, OH	89.8	93.6	86.6	82.8	71.2	38.2	45.8	21.1	57.8	25.2
Dallas, TX	80.8	87.6	89.0	89.3	58.2	37.4	53.6	23.6	68.5	15.3
Davenport, IA	92.6	94.7	87.4	84.3	78.3	30.0	31.7	16.8	59.3	15.0
Denver, CO	91.4	96.4	91.5	87.1	72.5	55.6	66.7	31.4	58.1	23.3
Des Moines, IA	87.3	93.7	79.3	61.3	60.1	29.0	33.5	15.8	23.0	10.8
Detroit, MI	83.4	84.3	85.3	75.5	56.8	17.6	37.4	14.1	43.5	11.6
Durham, NC	91.4	96.1	91.7	92.8	59.7	55.7	70.7	39.4	76.8	22.1
El Paso, TX	81.9	87.0	94.8	88.4	78.7	27.5	31.5	30.8	52.7	23.9
Eugene, OR	94.8	95.7	98.0	92.9	86.2	44.2	44.8	37.2	59.1	33.3
Fargo, ND	95.3	96.6	82.3	87.0	95.2	43.2	44.3	20.1	69.9	31.7
Fort Collins, CO	97.6	98.4	87.7	95.1	91.1	59.9	62.0	34.6	76.2	37.0
Fort Wayne, IN	88.9	94.1	87.7	49.2	65.7	28.5	33.1	13.9	19.7	15.4
Fort Worth, TX	84.3	91.2	90.0	82.7	64.6	31.7	41.0	23.0	46.0	14.7
Gainesville, FL	94.3	96.5	87.4	96.9	94.7	51.7	57.0	28.8	77.5	61.4
Green Bay, WI	89.0	92.6	69.5	84.3	65.8	25.5	27.8	16.2	32.8	11.5
Greensboro, NC	90.1	95.2	89.5	75.7	70.2	39.9	52.3	28.0	46.5	19.4
Honolulu, HI	90.9	97.6	91.5	88.1	93.6	40.8	54.6	32.5	40.7	30.5
Houston, TX	80.3	88.5	89.9	86.6	60.7	36.0	50.8	27.4	61.7	16.7
Huntsville, AL	91.6	94.8	86.8	91.0	77.4	46.2	54.1	30.1	57.6	29.7
Indianapolis, IN	87.5	91.3	87.9	70.4	64.5	34.2	41.0	22.1	41.0	18.6
Jacksonville, FL	90.8	93.0	88.6	88.9	84.8	31.8	35.1	22.6	52.6	28.1
Kansas City, MO	91.8	94.9	89.8	89.9	73.9	37.8	47.4	17.5	49.5	20.7
Lafayette, LA	90.9	95.4	81.2	91.6	83.8	40.6	50.4	17.4	55.0	36.6
Las Vegas, NV	85.8	91.7	88.5	91.7	66.8	27.3	32.2	19.5	44.8	12.5
Lexington, KY	92.4	95.3	90.4	89.9	65.1	47.3	51.9	27.1	72.2	25.3
Lincoln, NE	93.0	95.2	86.6	81.2	70.7	41.0	42.7	25.0	43.3	21.1
Little Rock, AR	92.3	96.3	91.5	92.7	63.7	44.0	58.0	26.6	73.5	13.5
Los Angeles, CA	79.3	89.6	90.1	91.1	59.4	37.8	51.6	31.9	57.6	15.1
Louisville, KY	90.5	92.9	87.6	83.3	78.7	33.4	37.4	20.2	56.1	27.5
Madison, WI	95.7	97.7	91.9	92.5	78.5	59.2	62.9	25.6	70.4	37.4
Manchester, NH	88.7	91.3	75.7	81.2	68.7	33.5	35.4	22.8	35.6	13.5
McAllen, TX	79.9	85.7	99.5	89.7	77.2	32.0	35.4	31.6	64.7	28.6

Table continued on following page.

City	High School Graduate or Higher (%)					Bachelor's Degree or Higher (%)				
	Total	White	Black	Asian	Hisp.[1]	Total	White	Black	Asian	Hisp.[1]
Memphis, TN	87.4	93.9	87.8	86.8	52.0	28.2	49.9	17.9	60.0	17.8
Miami, FL	80.0	82.6	78.1	95.4	76.7	35.6	44.7	17.5	69.4	31.3
Midland, TX	86.5	91.9	90.5	70.2	74.6	33.7	40.3	20.1	39.1	22.1
Milwaukee, WI	85.5	92.8	86.0	74.3	64.6	26.6	41.0	13.7	32.7	12.0
Minneapolis, MN	91.1	97.2	74.9	86.3	71.6	54.5	65.6	19.1	62.7	31.0
Nashville, TN	90.2	93.9	89.5	83.4	61.8	46.9	56.0	29.8	55.1	20.5
New Orleans, LA	89.1	96.8	85.9	77.4	79.1	42.0	68.0	24.1	50.4	42.2
New York, NY	83.7	92.5	85.1	77.3	71.7	41.0	59.2	26.7	45.2	21.5
Oklahoma City, OK	87.8	91.4	90.7	81.6	61.7	34.0	38.4	26.1	48.0	12.8
Omaha, NE	90.5	95.1	86.9	71.7	61.9	40.3	45.7	18.6	50.2	15.0
Orlando, FL	91.9	95.6	84.1	93.4	90.9	42.2	53.5	21.7	59.3	33.9
Philadelphia, PA	87.4	93.5	88.1	74.3	72.6	34.6	51.0	20.4	42.0	19.5
Phoenix, AZ	84.4	91.2	89.2	89.2	66.9	32.3	38.9	27.3	62.6	13.6
Pittsburgh, PA	94.3	95.7	90.6	92.3	87.4	47.8	53.2	20.3	82.0	55.8
Portland, OR	93.3	96.2	88.6	81.7	80.0	53.5	58.1	29.8	47.3	35.7
Providence, RI	81.9	89.9	87.0	87.7	69.5	34.7	51.7	23.6	58.3	12.9
Provo, UT	92.5	95.3	99.6	84.9	75.2	45.0	49.0	29.9	52.7	20.8
Raleigh, NC	92.5	96.8	92.0	90.0	67.3	52.9	66.4	32.5	62.5	23.7
Reno, NV	89.3	94.9	91.5	90.5	65.3	35.7	39.9	26.6	49.2	15.2
Richmond, VA	89.3	96.6	85.0	90.3	61.4	44.1	70.1	16.1	64.9	25.2
Rochester, MN	94.5	97.2	73.9	86.1	78.6	50.1	51.6	25.7	61.6	34.9
Sacramento, CA	86.9	93.0	91.4	82.5	76.4	36.4	45.2	24.4	38.9	23.7
Saint Louis, MO	90.5	95.0	85.7	86.9	81.7	40.2	56.0	18.1	63.5	35.3
Saint Paul, MN	88.9	96.6	81.4	67.4	73.7	43.5	55.6	21.2	23.6	24.2
Salem, OR	88.7	93.5	94.1	86.4	63.7	31.4	35.1	27.7	46.3	12.8
Salt Lake City, UT	91.6	95.7	86.1	85.3	72.5	50.9	56.2	30.7	62.6	24.5
San Antonio, TX	84.3	88.4	91.0	85.7	78.0	28.7	33.7	25.0	56.5	19.4
San Diego, CA	90.2	95.2	90.0	90.2	76.2	49.9	57.6	31.3	57.3	25.4
San Francisco, CA	88.8	97.5	88.8	80.8	80.1	60.1	76.3	30.9	51.0	40.1
San Jose, CA	85.5	93.1	90.1	88.3	69.6	46.5	51.5	37.5	59.7	17.5
Santa Rosa, CA	85.5	94.7	85.7	83.6	63.0	34.8	42.5	21.8	45.8	14.6
Savannah, GA	89.9	95.3	86.3	81.6	86.9	32.0	47.8	17.9	46.9	32.4
Seattle, WA	95.7	98.4	89.9	91.2	87.8	67.5	72.6	33.8	69.8	49.3
Sioux Falls, SD	93.1	95.7	83.0	76.0	64.7	37.4	40.0	21.0	42.2	14.8
Tampa, FL	89.8	94.4	85.6	90.4	80.9	44.6	56.0	20.5	68.9	29.4
Tucson, AZ	87.3	91.8	87.3	88.4	76.7	30.2	35.6	17.5	51.9	17.3
Tulsa, OK	87.6	92.1	90.0	77.0	59.5	33.3	39.7	19.7	38.0	12.4
Virginia Beach, VA	94.7	96.4	92.7	89.4	89.9	40.4	44.2	27.9	46.6	32.5
Washington, DC	92.8	99.1	88.5	95.8	81.3	63.6	92.0	33.3	84.7	56.7
Wichita, KS	88.0	92.3	87.4	74.0	63.9	30.9	34.8	19.0	31.6	14.7
Wilmington, NC	93.5	96.4	84.9	87.8	77.5	45.8	51.7	23.0	61.8	30.2
Winston-Salem, NC	88.4	91.9	89.4	96.1	61.1	37.2	47.5	24.1	70.3	16.3
U.S.	89.4	92.9	88.1	88.0	72.5	35.0	37.7	24.7	57.0	19.9

Note: Figures shown cover persons 25 years old and over; (1) People of Hispanic origin can be of any race
Source: U.S. Census Bureau, 2019-2023 American Community Survey 5-Year Estimates

Educational Attainment by Race: Metro Area

Metro Area	High School Graduate or Higher (%)					Bachelor's Degree or Higher (%)				
	Total	White	Black	Asian	Hisp.[1]	Total	White	Black	Asian	Hisp.[1]
Albuquerque, NM	90.3	94.2	93.1	88.8	84.0	35.0	41.5	38.7	52.7	22.6
Anchorage, AK	94.1	96.2	91.7	86.6	87.7	34.0	38.9	23.5	29.7	23.9
Ann Arbor, MI	95.8	97.1	90.9	95.6	85.8	58.1	60.0	31.5	82.0	47.3
Athens, GA	89.8	94.2	82.4	85.0	66.0	43.5	49.5	21.4	64.9	30.8
Atlanta, GA	90.8	93.8	91.9	87.8	69.6	41.5	46.4	34.0	61.2	24.7
Austin, TX	91.6	94.9	93.3	93.8	78.2	49.9	54.2	36.5	76.1	29.0
Baltimore, MD	92.1	94.7	90.2	89.3	77.0	43.3	48.4	30.1	64.0	32.9
Billings, MT	95.2	95.8	99.0	87.5	84.4	33.5	34.3	31.1	47.3	15.7
Boise City, ID	92.5	94.9	80.7	90.9	72.9	36.6	38.2	24.7	55.8	19.1
Boston, MA	92.3	95.8	87.4	87.0	74.8	51.2	54.8	31.8	65.0	26.6
Boulder, CO	95.5	97.6	93.4	92.4	76.4	63.9	67.0	40.6	70.1	30.8
Cape Coral, FL	90.4	94.0	82.6	89.5	75.7	30.8	34.0	16.7	50.3	17.1
Cedar Rapids, IA	95.2	96.1	83.2	90.9	85.2	32.8	33.3	16.5	53.6	24.3
Charleston, SC	91.9	95.4	86.5	90.2	72.3	40.0	47.6	20.1	51.7	25.5
Charlotte, NC	90.4	93.4	90.6	88.0	67.0	39.0	42.6	30.0	61.9	21.4
Chicago, IL	89.7	94.4	89.4	91.3	71.8	40.9	47.4	25.8	67.0	18.6
Cincinnati, OH	92.3	93.5	87.9	88.6	76.7	36.9	38.1	22.8	63.4	31.1
Clarksville, TN	92.3	92.8	93.3	87.6	84.0	28.0	29.3	25.3	35.5	20.5
Cleveland, OH	91.7	93.6	87.0	87.8	78.0	33.4	36.9	18.3	63.6	19.0
College Station, TX	88.3	91.8	87.1	96.0	69.9	39.1	43.4	15.1	77.8	18.7
Colorado Springs, CO	95.1	96.6	95.2	90.1	86.4	41.0	43.8	32.5	44.9	23.2
Columbia, MO	94.0	94.6	91.5	92.8	87.6	47.5	48.9	28.5	71.0	38.4
Columbia, SC	91.1	93.5	88.9	91.0	75.3	35.0	39.2	27.3	64.1	22.7
Columbus, OH	92.1	94.2	87.4	86.3	75.0	39.4	41.8	23.9	62.6	27.7
Dallas, TX	87.3	92.0	92.2	90.0	66.3	38.5	42.8	31.6	65.4	17.8
Davenport, IA	92.4	94.5	83.5	82.5	77.4	29.4	30.4	14.2	61.6	16.8
Denver, CO	92.3	96.0	90.8	86.3	75.5	48.4	54.4	30.3	55.4	21.7
Des Moines, IA	93.5	96.3	82.0	73.9	69.3	39.1	40.8	20.1	44.7	17.4
Detroit, MI	91.2	92.9	88.4	89.5	76.9	34.1	36.5	19.4	66.4	26.5
Durham, NC	91.1	95.0	90.1	92.2	59.9	52.3	60.5	35.3	77.4	23.4
El Paso, TX	80.6	85.8	95.3	88.8	77.4	25.3	29.4	32.0	50.5	21.9
Eugene, OR	93.1	94.1	96.1	90.4	81.3	33.4	33.6	33.2	53.7	25.3
Fargo, ND	95.6	96.6	84.7	88.7	89.2	42.2	43.0	24.6	67.9	30.1
Fort Collins, CO	96.6	97.7	91.5	95.6	85.2	51.7	53.4	37.7	69.3	29.5
Fort Wayne, IN	90.7	93.8	88.5	59.3	68.5	29.7	32.0	15.8	29.2	16.9
Fort Worth, TX	87.3	92.0	92.2	90.0	66.3	38.5	42.8	31.6	65.4	17.8
Gainesville, FL	92.7	93.9	87.4	94.6	89.8	40.9	41.6	24.2	73.6	49.6
Green Bay, WI	93.3	95.2	74.2	85.9	69.6	29.9	30.8	18.3	44.5	15.5
Greensboro, NC	88.3	91.1	88.5	78.6	63.3	31.4	34.4	24.7	49.1	16.3
Honolulu, HI	92.9	97.2	95.8	90.6	94.5	37.7	51.2	32.8	39.2	29.2
Houston, TX	85.1	90.6	92.3	87.6	67.9	35.4	40.8	32.1	58.0	17.8
Huntsville, AL	91.5	93.3	88.5	91.9	77.4	42.4	45.2	33.2	63.5	30.7
Indianapolis, IN	91.1	93.5	88.2	81.4	70.5	37.8	40.4	24.9	54.4	24.0
Jacksonville, FL	92.1	93.8	88.5	89.6	87.1	35.1	37.9	23.6	52.4	30.2
Kansas City, MO	93.1	95.0	90.9	89.1	75.0	39.2	42.6	21.9	56.7	20.9
Lafayette, LA	87.0	90.1	79.6	72.7	76.8	27.0	30.1	15.1	36.6	27.1
Las Vegas, NV	86.8	91.8	90.6	90.6	69.6	27.3	31.1	21.2	42.9	12.7
Lexington, KY	91.9	93.9	90.6	89.7	65.7	41.1	43.4	25.4	67.8	23.0
Lincoln, NE	93.6	95.4	86.4	81.1	71.1	40.6	42.0	24.8	43.2	20.9
Little Rock, AR	92.1	93.9	91.4	89.9	68.2	32.9	35.4	25.8	55.9	17.4
Los Angeles, CA	82.2	90.4	91.1	89.2	65.7	37.4	46.4	31.8	55.5	16.2
Louisville, KY	91.3	92.7	87.7	86.4	77.4	32.1	33.7	20.6	60.2	25.4
Madison, WI	95.9	97.1	91.4	92.5	78.5	49.3	50.1	25.9	69.7	33.2
Manchester, NH	93.0	94.3	83.0	90.5	74.3	40.6	41.1	26.8	60.6	20.1
McAllen, TX	69.3	76.0	84.4	92.3	66.7	20.3	22.9	23.5	67.0	18.2

Table continued on following page.

Metro Area	High School Graduate or Higher (%)					Bachelor's Degree or Higher (%)				
	Total	White	Black	Asian	Hisp.[1]	Total	White	Black	Asian	Hisp.[1]
Memphis, TN	89.5	93.3	88.5	88.2	57.9	30.7	39.1	21.4	64.8	19.0
Miami, FL	86.9	90.6	84.2	88.6	81.7	35.6	42.4	22.4	56.3	31.2
Midland, TX	86.2	91.5	91.3	74.8	74.3	30.6	35.7	20.6	48.7	19.3
Milwaukee, WI	92.7	96.2	86.7	86.3	72.7	38.8	44.4	15.3	53.9	18.1
Minneapolis, MN	94.2	97.0	84.0	83.5	76.4	44.9	47.7	25.1	47.6	27.2
Nashville, TN	91.5	93.4	90.4	85.7	68.4	39.9	42.0	30.5	56.8	22.2
New Orleans, LA	87.5	92.2	85.3	80.0	74.8	33.0	41.2	22.5	47.7	25.0
New York, NY	87.6	93.7	86.9	84.4	74.1	43.5	52.7	28.4	57.0	22.8
Oklahoma City, OK	89.9	92.3	91.0	83.8	65.5	33.4	36.0	25.3	50.9	14.8
Omaha, NE	92.7	95.6	88.8	74.3	68.3	39.1	41.8	21.4	48.0	18.5
Orlando, FL	90.7	93.5	85.8	90.2	86.5	35.8	39.4	25.0	54.9	28.8
Philadelphia, PA	92.1	95.3	89.7	85.5	74.5	41.5	46.8	24.3	59.2	22.5
Phoenix, AZ	89.5	93.7	91.6	90.3	73.5	34.6	38.2	29.8	60.9	16.4
Pittsburgh, PA	94.9	95.4	91.7	87.5	86.9	37.4	37.8	21.5	69.8	39.9
Portland, OR	92.8	95.2	90.7	88.4	74.5	42.1	43.3	31.8	55.8	23.6
Providence, RI	88.4	90.8	85.6	88.6	72.1	35.0	37.5	25.4	56.3	16.8
Provo, UT	95.3	96.5	97.2	94.6	83.1	43.4	44.7	38.3	62.7	26.4
Raleigh, NC	92.9	96.0	92.2	93.3	69.1	50.2	55.5	33.9	76.2	22.7
Reno, NV	88.6	93.5	90.2	90.5	65.8	31.4	34.6	21.8	45.8	14.4
Richmond, VA	91.9	95.0	89.7	90.1	71.2	40.2	47.4	24.6	63.9	22.8
Rochester, MN	94.8	96.5	74.4	85.8	79.8	42.3	42.2	25.1	60.4	33.9
Sacramento, CA	90.1	94.4	91.4	85.1	78.1	36.3	39.2	26.0	45.0	22.0
Saint Louis, MO	93.3	94.7	88.8	90.9	82.6	37.6	40.1	22.0	68.6	31.0
Saint Paul, MN	94.2	97.0	84.0	83.5	76.4	44.9	47.7	25.1	47.6	27.2
Salem, OR	87.2	92.5	91.1	85.4	62.2	26.9	30.0	28.2	43.5	11.0
Salt Lake City, UT	91.8	95.2	84.3	86.9	74.6	37.8	40.9	25.4	52.0	18.6
San Antonio, TX	87.3	91.2	92.4	88.2	79.8	31.9	36.6	30.1	53.8	21.2
San Diego, CA	89.0	93.8	91.0	91.1	75.0	42.1	48.0	29.6	55.2	21.5
San Francisco, CA	89.5	96.2	91.4	88.4	73.3	52.4	61.6	32.3	59.9	25.1
San Jose, CA	89.1	94.7	92.0	91.9	72.1	54.8	57.5	42.1	69.5	20.2
Santa Rosa, CA	88.9	95.8	88.8	86.2	66.2	37.8	44.2	29.4	46.1	16.0
Savannah, GA	91.3	94.0	88.9	82.3	84.1	34.9	41.2	23.4	50.9	27.4
Seattle, WA	93.3	96.0	90.4	91.0	77.4	46.3	47.0	28.6	61.7	27.5
Sioux Falls, SD	93.7	95.6	83.4	76.1	66.5	35.7	37.4	20.1	40.3	16.0
Tampa, FL	90.9	93.1	89.2	86.4	82.3	34.0	35.4	26.6	54.2	25.9
Tucson, AZ	89.9	93.9	89.2	89.8	78.6	35.9	41.0	25.7	56.3	19.7
Tulsa, OK	90.1	92.7	90.7	77.9	66.0	29.8	32.6	21.1	33.6	15.1
Virginia Beach, VA	92.8	95.3	89.6	88.9	86.0	35.1	39.9	24.9	47.4	29.2
Washington, DC	91.5	96.2	92.8	91.8	70.7	53.8	64.4	39.1	67.2	29.3
Wichita, KS	90.3	93.5	87.6	75.1	67.1	31.5	34.2	19.0	32.5	16.4
Wilmington, NC	93.1	95.0	86.8	85.4	75.6	38.5	41.1	23.8	56.4	25.1
Winston-Salem, NC	89.2	91.0	90.0	88.5	63.8	29.6	31.4	24.6	54.1	14.7
U.S.	89.4	92.9	88.1	88.0	72.5	35.0	37.7	24.7	57.0	19.9

Note: Figures shown cover persons 25 years old and over; Figures cover the Metropolitan Statistical Area (MSA); (1) People of Hispanic origin can be of any race
Source: U.S. Census Bureau, 2019-2023 American Community Survey 5-Year Estimates

Cost of Living Index

Urban Area	Composite	Groceries	Housing	Utilities	Transp.	Health	Misc.
Albuquerque, NM	94.9	97.4	89.1	87.3	85.9	102.0	101.8
Anchorage, AK	122.8	126.5	133.1	112.4	113.6	147.1	114.1
Ann Arbor, MI	n/a	n/a	n/a	n/a	n/a	n/a	n/a
Athens, GA	98.9	100.4	97.3	99.4	95.0	96.7	100.8
Atlanta, GA	96.0	100.9	86.9	99.7	100.2	107.9	97.6
Austin, TX	97.3	96.6	104.1	98.6	94.9	98.6	92.2
Baltimore, MD	100.5	102.8	86.5	110.6	104.2	94.2	108.4
Billings, MT	99.8	103.5	95.3	82.7	120.0	114.8	98.9
Boise City, ID	102.1	103.7	101.0	77.8	109.9	98.2	106.6
Boston, MA	145.9	104.4	218.9	149.7	109.8	125.3	115.2
Boulder, CO	n/a	n/a	n/a	n/a	n/a	n/a	n/a
Cape Coral, FL	104.9	104.0	105.1	106.5	105.9	111.8	103.5
Cedar Rapids, IA	n/a	n/a	n/a	n/a	n/a	n/a	n/a
Charleston, SC	101.9	102.1	103.8	113.9	94.9	85.7	101.2
Charlotte, NC	98.9	101.1	84.8	101.3	94.4	99.6	110.0
Chicago, IL	115.1	103.9	140.1	96.7	107.3	107.9	107.0
Cincinnati, OH	96.0	100.7	87.3	99.6	96.2	94.8	100.4
Clarksville, TN	n/a	n/a	n/a	n/a	n/a	n/a	n/a
Cleveland, OH	91.4	99.8	81.2	85.5	96.7	92.2	96.1
College Station, TX	n/a	n/a	n/a	n/a	n/a	n/a	n/a
Colorado Springs, CO	101.9	101.9	110.2	75.7	95.1	95.5	104.0
Columbia, MO	90.0	96.2	79.7	96.8	84.8	98.8	94.3
Columbia, SC	89.2	99.1	69.2	117.6	80.6	75.6	98.3
Columbus, OH	95.3	100.6	96.5	104.2	87.5	82.3	93.6
Dallas, TX	101.7	98.9	95.1	115.6	91.2	104.5	107.4
Davenport, IA	90.1	97.4	76.8	83.2	105.1	97.3	94.6
Denver, CO	108.6	101.3	123.4	89.3	94.7	109.6	107.7
Des Moines, IA	85.8	99.6	66.1	80.8	93.2	87.2	94.9
Detroit, MI	103.3	101.0	106.0	100.6	103.7	107.0	102.0
Durham, NC	98.5	102.0	101.6	93.4	93.8	103.8	96.2
El Paso, TX	88.1	96.7	70.7	91.5	101.2	88.7	94.3
Eugene, OR	107.3	105.2	120.6	92.5	110.3	108.2	100.0
Fargo, ND	97.3	97.9	85.1	80.1	98.8	118.1	108.0
Fort Collins, CO	n/a	n/a	n/a	n/a	n/a	n/a	n/a
Fort Wayne, IN	90.3	99.0	77.5	91.0	100.4	97.4	93.1
Fort Worth, TX	96.0	99.3	85.8	116.7	94.7	105.7	97.0
Gainesville, FL	n/a	n/a	n/a	n/a	n/a	n/a	n/a
Green Bay, WI	90.5	97.9	80.9	82.0	102.8	95.1	93.4
Greensboro, NC	n/a	n/a	n/a	n/a	n/a	n/a	n/a
Honolulu, HI	186.8	130.4	310.0	197.6	133.6	120.8	130.4
Houston, TX	94.1	99.3	79.2	92.4	94.0	97.5	104.1
Huntsville, AL	90.8	100.2	72.3	88.7	96.5	92.5	100.7
Indianapolis, IN	88.8	98.0	76.9	88.4	98.0	86.9	92.5
Jacksonville, FL	92.9	104.0	87.1	89.7	87.2	85.2	96.0
Kansas City, MO	91.1	97.3	87.5	105.6	89.3	83.8	89.1
Lafayette, LA	87.2	97.1	64.5	84.1	97.9	80.7	100.5
Las Vegas, NV	98.5	103.7	104.6	113.8	115.0	85.2	85.1
Lexington, KY	91.9	100.5	77.2	84.4	97.3	97.6	99.7
Lincoln, NE	94.3	99.3	77.6	92.2	99.5	105.4	103.5
Little Rock, AR	93.4	97.3	77.6	84.2	94.5	84.6	107.8
Los Angeles, CA	149.4	109.3	232.5	107.2	136.1	101.1	118.9
Louisville, KY	94.1	99.1	80.1	83.2	96.7	114.9	102.4
Madison, WI	104.7	98.8	106.4	98.8	98.3	113.2	107.8
Manchester, NH	112.6	99.9	117.6	112.2	105.9	103.9	117.0
McAllen, TX	85.1	93.4	60.2	119.6	94.1	79.2	92.1
Memphis, TN	89.8	98.8	86.2	80.9	88.8	86.0	91.7

Table continued on following page.

Urban Area	Composite	Groceries	Housing	Utilities	Transp.	Health	Misc.
Miami, FL	120.9	110.8	157.4	104.9	100.6	98.1	107.4
Midland, TX	96.4	96.2	83.8	100.9	94.3	87.6	107.5
Milwaukee, WI	100.5	100.8	104.2	94.0	102.7	105.0	97.7
Minneapolis, MN	93.6	102.6	82.9	96.6	96.4	96.0	96.5
Nashville, TN	98.7	99.5	101.4	98.2	90.8	95.5	98.7
New Orleans, LA	112.4	99.2	148.7	71.6	95.6	102.6	104.0
New York, NY[2]	161.1	113.0	276.5	115.1	114.9	128.1	114.9
Oklahoma City, OK	82.2	94.9	60.1	96.8	91.3	103.9	86.0
Omaha, NE	91.9	99.1	82.5	84.2	94.4	94.0	97.5
Orlando, FL	96.4	104.7	91.7	103.7	97.4	91.9	95.2
Philadelphia, PA	103.2	104.1	99.2	105.5	105.3	96.2	106.0
Phoenix, AZ	106.3	102.8	115.6	106.6	105.4	91.6	102.2
Pittsburgh, PA	98.1	97.8	94.9	119.9	107.2	99.2	93.2
Portland, OR	116.6	107.2	146.0	86.6	127.4	110.5	101.9
Providence, RI	112.2	102.0	113.4	139.7	96.5	104.4	114.1
Provo, UT	102.5	96.7	111.3	93.2	107.4	89.9	100.5
Raleigh, NC	97.2	100.6	91.9	89.8	92.1	112.2	101.0
Reno, NV	104.0	102.9	110.9	93.4	123.5	88.5	98.6
Richmond, VA	94.2	99.9	84.6	96.2	95.3	91.1	99.2
Rochester, MN	n/a	n/a	n/a	n/a	n/a	n/a	n/a
Sacramento, CA	128.8	106.9	139.2	174.4	152.0	99.7	116.9
Saint Louis, MO	89.1	98.8	78.0	97.9	93.3	87.6	90.9
Saint Paul, MN	94.0	105.2	81.3	95.6	96.0	96.7	98.1
Salem, OR	n/a	n/a	n/a	n/a	n/a	n/a	n/a
Salt Lake City, UT	109.0	98.1	128.7	95.4	111.4	88.5	103.0
San Antonio, TX	91.2	94.5	79.0	81.8	94.3	111.3	98.5
San Diego, CA	145.3	111.1	212.1	139.4	140.9	102.2	113.9
San Francisco, CA	166.8	123.6	263.3	160.1	143.6	127.6	119.3
San Jose, CA	180.6	115.0	321.1	158.6	140.7	120.1	117.9
Santa Rosa, CA	n/a	n/a	n/a	n/a	n/a	n/a	n/a
Savannah, GA	93.8	102.5	78.1	99.5	102.7	113.7	96.4
Seattle, WA	145.1	110.3	212.2	101.4	128.4	128.5	122.4
Sioux Falls, SD	91.0	96.4	88.5	91.3	89.9	92.6	90.7
Tampa, FL	97.6	105.7	95.8	99.9	102.1	93.1	94.4
Tucson, AZ	n/a	n/a	n/a	n/a	n/a	n/a	n/a
Tulsa, OK	84.7	95.9	65.1	98.3	88.4	93.5	90.3
Virginia Beach, VA[3]	94.0	98.5	82.4	104.2	96.0	110.6	96.4
Washington, DC	141.9	105.9	222.4	102.4	107.9	117.0	113.2
Wichita, KS	88.8	94.9	65.9	98.2	97.5	94.3	99.6
Wilmington, NC	n/a	n/a	n/a	n/a	n/a	n/a	n/a
Winston-Salem, NC	93.4	97.0	77.5	101.7	92.1	105.8	101.5
U.S.	100.0	100.0	100.0	100.0	100.0	100.0	100.0

Note: The Cost of Living Index measures regional differences in the cost of consumer goods and services, excluding taxes and non-consumer expenditures, for professional and managerial households in the top income quintile. It is based on more than 50,000 prices covering almost 60 different items for which prices are collected three times a year by chambers of commerce, economic development organizations or university applied economic centers in each participating urban area. The numbers shown should be read as a percentage above or below the national average of 100. For example, a value of 115.4 in the groceries column indicates that grocery prices are 15.4% higher than the national average. Small differences in the index numbers should not be interpreted as significant. In cases where data is not available for the city, data for the metro area or for a neighboring city has been provided and noted as follows: (2) Brooklyn, NY; (3) Hampton Roads-SE Virginia
Source: The Council for Community and Economic Research, Cost of Living Index, 2024

Grocery Prices

Urban Area	T-Bone Steak ($/pound)	Frying Chicken ($/pound)	Whole Milk ($/half gal.)	Eggs ($/dozen)	Orange Juice ($/64 oz.)	Coffee ($/11.5 oz.)
Albuquerque, NM	14.86	1.51	4.61	3.01	4.27	5.45
Anchorage, AK	17.56	2.89	5.34	4.09	5.40	7.86
Ann Arbor, MI	n/a	n/a	n/a	n/a	n/a	n/a
Athens, GA	15.55	1.45	4.70	3.57	4.49	5.28
Atlanta, GA	15.52	1.44	4.67	3.38	4.47	5.59
Austin, TX	14.52	1.37	4.62	3.05	4.27	5.19
Baltimore, MD	15.52	1.44	4.64	3.35	4.34	5.56
Billings, MT	15.52	1.47	4.72	3.46	4.19	6.92
Boise City, ID	15.52	1.52	4.75	3.63	4.45	6.38
Boston, MA	15.52	1.51	4.76	3.03	4.54	5.39
Boulder, CO	n/a	n/a	n/a	n/a	n/a	n/a
Cape Coral, FL	15.51	1.46	4.69	3.46	4.51	5.45
Cedar Rapids, IA	n/a	n/a	n/a	n/a	n/a	n/a
Charleston, SC	15.51	1.64	4.54	3.41	4.43	5.46
Charlotte, NC	15.53	1.61	4.69	3.30	4.33	5.36
Chicago, IL	15.52	1.45	4.88	3.50	4.50	5.80
Cincinnati, OH	15.52	1.74	4.74	3.73	4.36	5.67
Clarksville, TN	n/a	n/a	n/a	n/a	n/a	n/a
Cleveland, OH	15.51	1.42	4.58	3.24	4.44	5.24
College Station, TX	n/a	n/a	n/a	n/a	n/a	n/a
Colorado Springs, CO	15.53	1.46	4.60	2.91	4.42	6.03
Columbia, MO	15.51	1.47	4.69	3.41	4.45	5.17
Columbia, SC	15.51	1.66	4.62	3.28	4.38	5.27
Columbus, OH	15.51	1.72	4.72	3.39	4.39	5.52
Dallas, TX	14.56	1.54	4.61	3.13	4.31	5.41
Davenport, IA	15.52	1.43	4.92	3.35	4.44	5.02
Denver, CO	15.52	1.45	4.62	2.98	4.42	6.16
Des Moines, IA	15.52	1.44	4.76	3.47	4.47	4.94
Detroit, MI	15.53	1.73	4.80	3.37	4.41	5.64
Durham, NC	15.53	1.48	4.61	3.25	4.39	5.40
El Paso, TX	14.86	1.41	4.63	2.97	4.27	5.42
Eugene, OR	15.53	1.92	4.92	3.47	4.49	6.40
Fargo, ND	15.51	1.46	4.85	3.12	4.28	5.46
Fort Collins, CO	n/a	n/a	n/a	n/a	n/a	n/a
Fort Wayne, IN	15.51	1.66	4.69	3.49	4.36	5.41
Fort Worth, TX	14.52	1.56	4.61	3.13	4.28	5.46
Gainesville, FL	n/a	n/a	n/a	n/a	n/a	n/a
Green Bay, WI	15.51	1.42	4.70	3.25	4.43	5.29
Greensboro, NC	n/a	n/a	n/a	n/a	n/a	n/a
Honolulu, HI	16.57	2.86	5.49	3.98	5.19	7.89
Houston, TX	14.53	1.62	4.64	3.18	4.33	5.40
Huntsville, AL	15.52	1.41	4.54	3.35	4.41	5.49
Indianapolis, IN	15.51	1.63	4.67	3.40	4.33	5.39
Jacksonville, FL	15.52	1.42	4.72	3.41	4.53	5.38
Kansas City, MO	15.52	1.45	4.70	3.17	4.38	5.06
Lafayette, LA	15.29	1.41	4.60	3.05	4.38	5.07
Las Vegas, NV	15.54	1.74	4.78	3.08	4.43	6.31
Lexington, KY	15.52	1.44	4.69	3.40	4.30	5.70
Lincoln, NE	15.51	1.44	4.68	3.13	4.43	5.17
Little Rock, AR	14.86	1.43	4.62	3.40	4.31	5.24
Los Angeles, CA	15.55	2.45	5.00	3.14	4.55	6.68
Louisville, KY	15.51	1.48	4.71	3.39	4.37	5.37
Madison, WI	15.51	1.43	4.77	3.34	4.44	5.60
Manchester, NH	15.51	1.42	4.71	2.98	4.42	5.31
McAllen, TX	14.52	1.28	4.54	2.96	4.22	5.08

Table continued on following page.

Urban Area	T-Bone Steak ($/pound)	Frying Chicken ($/pound)	Whole Milk ($/half gal.)	Eggs ($/dozen)	Orange Juice ($/64 oz.)	Coffee ($/11.5 oz.)
Memphis, TN	15.53	1.31	4.67	3.47	4.35	5.24
Miami, FL	15.52	1.45	4.80	3.77	4.78	5.91
Midland, TX	14.53	1.41	4.61	3.04	4.30	4.99
Milwaukee, WI	15.50	1.43	4.80	3.34	4.45	5.96
Minneapolis, MN	15.53	1.44	4.66	3.56	4.49	5.23
Nashville, TN	15.51	1.43	4.63	3.32	4.40	5.35
New Orleans, LA	15.51	1.36	4.66	3.19	4.38	4.94
New York, NY[2]	15.52	1.56	5.14	3.63	4.79	5.93
Oklahoma City, OK	15.34	1.46	4.55	2.97	4.28	5.16
Omaha, NE	15.51	1.44	4.87	3.22	4.43	5.50
Orlando, FL	15.52	1.45	4.63	3.47	4.53	5.53
Philadelphia, PA	15.46	1.52	4.70	3.48	4.41	5.43
Phoenix, AZ	15.53	1.77	4.76	2.95	4.40	6.24
Pittsburgh, PA	15.52	1.43	4.52	3.27	4.44	5.15
Portland, OR	15.52	1.89	4.93	3.57	4.49	6.85
Providence, RI	15.51	1.68	4.70	3.55	4.43	4.91
Provo, UT	15.52	1.54	4.57	2.91	4.17	5.79
Raleigh, NC	15.51	1.45	4.58	3.33	4.31	5.44
Reno, NV	15.53	2.26	4.66	2.91	4.36	5.88
Richmond, VA	15.51	1.43	4.65	3.38	4.37	5.55
Rochester, MN	n/a	n/a	n/a	n/a	n/a	n/a
Sacramento, CA	15.53	2.13	5.01	2.90	4.40	6.44
Saint Louis, MO	15.51	1.44	4.67	3.37	4.43	5.05
Saint Paul, MN	15.52	1.44	4.64	3.81	4.58	5.13
Salem, OR	n/a	n/a	n/a	n/a	n/a	n/a
Salt Lake City, UT	15.51	1.53	4.62	3.03	4.19	6.11
San Antonio, TX	14.53	1.33	4.57	2.98	4.25	5.05
San Diego, CA	15.56	2.40	5.07	3.17	4.63	6.78
San Francisco, CA	15.55	2.66	5.03	3.35	4.86	7.53
San Jose, CA	15.54	2.57	5.09	3.10	4.64	6.92
Santa Rosa, CA	n/a	n/a	n/a	n/a	n/a	n/a
Savannah, GA	15.52	1.43	4.72	3.53	4.53	5.62
Seattle, WA	15.51	1.98	4.94	3.87	4.58	7.06
Sioux Falls, SD	15.53	1.49	4.52	3.10	4.37	5.10
Tampa, FL	15.52	1.46	4.73	3.60	4.59	5.56
Tucson, AZ	n/a	n/a	n/a	n/a	n/a	n/a
Tulsa, OK	15.52	1.45	4.59	2.97	4.32	5.06
Virginia Beach, VA[3]	15.52	1.46	4.58	3.35	4.34	5.34
Washington, DC	15.51	1.42	4.62	3.47	4.44	5.77
Wichita, KS	15.50	1.43	4.66	3.16	4.30	5.36
Wilmington, NC	n/a	n/a	n/a	n/a	n/a	n/a
Winston-Salem, NC	15.51	1.46	4.60	3.19	4.30	5.15
Average[1]	15.42	1.55	4.69	3.25	4.41	5.46
Minimum[1]	14.50	1.16	4.43	2.75	4.00	4.85
Maximum[1]	17.56	2.89	5.49	4.78	5.54	7.89

*Note: **T-Bone Steak** (price per pound); **Frying Chicken** (price per pound, whole fryer); **Whole Milk** (half gallon carton); **Eggs** (price per dozen, Grade A, large); **Orange Juice** (64 oz. Tropicana or Florida Natural); **Coffee** (11.5 oz. can, vacuum-packed, Maxwell House, Hills Bros, or Folgers); (1) Average, minimum, and maximum values for all 276 areas in the Cost of Living Index report; n/a not available; In cases where data is not available for the city, data for the metro area or for a neighboring city has been provided and noted as follows: (2) Brooklyn, NY; (3) Hampton Roads-SE Virginia*
Source: The Council for Community and Economic Research, Cost of Living Index, 2024

Housing and Utility Costs

Urban Area	New Home Price ($)	Apartment Rent ($/month)	All Electric ($/month)	Part Electric ($/month)	Other Energy ($/month)	Telephone ($/month)
Albuquerque, NM	424,687	1,574	-	115.74	50.09	192.92
Anchorage, AK	758,772	1,670	-	108.68	138.69	193.41
Ann Arbor, MI	n/a	n/a	n/a	n/a	n/a	n/a
Athens, GA	483,427	1,622	-	113.87	91.54	192.87
Atlanta, GA	428,946	1,464	-	113.87	91.54	194.22
Austin, TX	500,842	1,849	-	137.02	59.06	203.47
Baltimore, MD	390,678	1,695	-	134.88	101.43	201.97
Billings, MT	517,409	1,317	-	94.77	60.66	185.25
Boise City, ID	514,076	1,611	-	83.70	59.41	179.42
Boston, MA	1,039,939	3,993	-	190.85	180.18	190.24
Boulder, CO	n/a	n/a	n/a	n/a	n/a	n/a
Cape Coral, FL	509,774	1,897	225.95	-	-	197.01
Cedar Rapids, IA	n/a	n/a	n/a	n/a	n/a	n/a
Charleston, SC	526,080	1,748	249.82	-	-	197.48
Charlotte, NC	398,825	1,562	213.43	-	-	189.47
Chicago, IL	566,384	3,240	-	113.94	70.31	212.43
Cincinnati, OH	443,467	1,416	-	116.95	90.88	189.55
Clarksville, TN	n/a	n/a	n/a	n/a	n/a	n/a
Cleveland, OH	391,639	1,431	-	83.27	78.55	189.85
College Station, TX	n/a	n/a	n/a	n/a	n/a	n/a
Colorado Springs, CO	557,240	1,828	-	86.01	42.49	192.15
Columbia, MO	451,668	1,041	-	114.12	78.36	199.61
Columbia, SC	328,383	1,205	-	119.24	143.41	195.98
Columbus, OH	482,718	1,613	-	146.60	76.69	189.10
Dallas, TX	477,656	1,572	-	171.06	80.72	203.47
Davenport, IA	387,652	1,218	-	85.51	62.12	200.43
Denver, CO	650,555	1,899	-	93.55	76.25	197.22
Des Moines, IA	359,756	846	-	84.52	63.10	188.12
Detroit, MI	568,077	1,560	-	134.21	78.36	187.38
Durham, NC	521,333	1,650	187.89	-	-	189.44
El Paso, TX	354,072	1,146	-	111.01	62.07	203.47
Eugene, OR	666,539	1,654	-	89.38	96.37	187.81
Fargo, ND	390,066	1,596	-	81.39	58.17	197.46
Fort Collins, CO	n/a	n/a	n/a	n/a	n/a	n/a
Fort Wayne, IN	364,871	1,370	-	109.31	68.72	192.42
Fort Worth, TX	422,585	1,470	-	170.29	80.72	210.13
Gainesville, FL	n/a	n/a	n/a	n/a	n/a	n/a
Green Bay, WI	447,400	1,055	-	90.06	61.14	188.34
Greensboro, NC	n/a	n/a	n/a	n/a	n/a	n/a
Honolulu, HI	1,681,170	4,424	529.02	-	-	187.39
Houston, TX	388,197	1,322	-	124.12	48.31	209.27
Huntsville, AL	361,221	1,123	172.74	-	-	189.28
Indianapolis, IN	360,369	1,336	-	99.46	70.12	192.42
Jacksonville, FL	391,862	1,714	170.55	-	-	197.76
Kansas City, MO	429,449	1,506	-	103.82	115.85	202.40
Lafayette, LA	306,872	1,150	-	96.15	60.82	190.09
Las Vegas, NV	554,723	1,576	-	160.52	94.44	188.64
Lexington, KY	380,651	1,239	-	82.51	72.69	194.48
Lincoln, NE	390,814	1,216	-	90.57	84.28	204.27
Little Rock, AR	407,536	1,155	-	76.85	69.20	208.40
Los Angeles, CA	1,311,286	2,988	-	163.45	65.93	194.86
Louisville, KY	388,161	1,369	-	82.51	72.69	188.14
Madison, WI	622,141	1,233	-	126.81	79.79	187.45
Manchester, NH	552,244	2,205	-	135.10	114.30	189.12
McAllen, TX	291,921	981	-	176.13	88.49	203.47

Table continued on following page.

Urban Area	New Home Price ($)	Apartment Rent ($/month)	All Electric ($/month)	Part Electric ($/month)	Other Energy ($/month)	Telephone ($/month)
Memphis, TN	404,407	1,598	-	105.22	38.46	195.12
Miami, FL	711,025	3,211	220.47	-	-	197.31
Midland, TX	400,707	1,483	-	150.59	53.85	202.34
Milwaukee, WI	541,477	1,627	-	123.28	67.66	187.62
Minneapolis, MN	405,152	1,419	-	98.70	98.25	191.53
Nashville, TN	519,432	1,670	-	105.42	77.00	223.33
New Orleans, LA	812,851	2,128	-	68.38	47.92	190.09
New York, NY[2]	1,411,780	3,995	-	157.71	92.60	203.07
Oklahoma City, OK	320,395	811	-	115.46	78.66	197.38
Omaha, NE	385,889	1,500	-	93.49	55.47	203.73
Orlando, FL	441,765	1,690	216.79	-	-	197.01
Philadelphia, PA	470,985	1,851	-	138.01	81.94	201.51
Phoenix, AZ	609,926	1,792	232.03	-	-	187.62
Pittsburgh, PA	478,461	1,602	-	137.23	130.44	200.01
Portland, OR	723,737	2,574	-	70.81	96.37	186.81
Providence, RI	474,141	2,453	-	171.99	161.54	198.12
Provo, UT	612,973	1,544	-	77.11	106.23	195.59
Raleigh, NC	466,683	1,514	-	107.05	69.13	189.30
Reno, NV	596,654	1,646	-	129.17	59.21	188.64
Richmond, VA	418,775	1,466	-	117.64	80.21	187.77
Rochester, MN	n/a	n/a	n/a	n/a	n/a	n/a
Sacramento, CA	718,604	2,241	-	397.28	53.75	191.51
Saint Louis, MO	427,558	1,128	-	100.98	92.58	203.68
Saint Paul, MN	404,109	1,358	-	92.16	101.15	192.06
Salem, OR	n/a	n/a	n/a	n/a	n/a	n/a
Salt Lake City, UT	717,422	1,758	-	96.56	93.13	196.83
San Antonio, TX	357,072	1,521	-	105.82	36.26	202.34
San Diego, CA	1,113,702	3,153	-	255.41	87.52	181.36
San Francisco, CA	1,383,739	3,749	-	264.12	131.73	205.06
San Jose, CA	1,860,932	3,311	-	267.58	131.25	192.30
Santa Rosa, CA	n/a	n/a	n/a	n/a	n/a	n/a
Savannah, GA	379,397	1,313	206.53	-	-	191.37
Seattle, WA	1,093,157	3,259	204.50	-	-	204.74
Sioux Falls, SD	509,371	977	-	103.68	71.55	198.68
Tampa, FL	455,535	1,796	203.80	-	-	197.76
Tucson, AZ	n/a	n/a	n/a	n/a	n/a	n/a
Tulsa, OK	339,822	935	-	118.37	80.52	197.22
Virginia Beach, VA[3]	389,841	1,484	-	120.02	103.90	187.93
Washington, DC	1,149,206	3,212	-	122.00	92.52	193.65
Wichita, KS	334,425	1,007	-	113.92	81.43	202.42
Wilmington, NC	n/a	n/a	n/a	n/a	n/a	n/a
Winston-Salem, NC	383,928	1,301	214.90	-	-	189.30
Average[1]	515,975	1,550	210.99	123.07	82.07	194.99
Minimum[1]	265,375	692	104.33	53.68	36.26	179.42
Maximum[1]	2,775,821	5,719	529.02	397.28	361.63	223.33

Note: **New Home Price** *(2,400 sf living area, 8,000 sf lot, in urban area with full utilities)*; **Apartment Rent** *(950 sf 2 bedroom/1.5 or 2 bath, unfurnished, excluding all utilities except water)*; **All Electric** *(average monthly cost for an all-electric home)*; **Part Electric** *(average monthly cost for a part-electric home)*; **Other Energy** *(average monthly cost for natural gas, fuel oil, coal, wood, and any other forms of energy except electricity)*; **Telephone** *(price includes the base monthly rate plus taxes and fees for three lines of mobile phone service)*; (1) Average, minimum, and maximum values for all 276 areas in the Cost of Living Index report; n/a not available; In cases where data is not available for the city, data for the metro area or for a neighboring city has been provided and noted as follows: (2) Brooklyn, NY; (3) Hampton Roads-SE Virginia

Source: The Council for Community and Economic Research, Cost of Living Index, 2024

Health Care, Transportation, and Other Costs

Urban Area	Doctor ($/visit)	Dentist ($/visit)	Optometrist ($/visit)	Gasoline ($/gallon)	Beauty Salon ($/visit)	Men's Shirt ($)
Albuquerque, NM	133.41	115.32	145.00	3.10	47.25	37.35
Anchorage, AK	243.83	173.17	265.00	3.68	50.00	45.44
Ann Arbor, MI	n/a	n/a	n/a	n/a	n/a	n/a
Athens, GA	123.75	128.33	97.63	3.12	56.40	40.51
Atlanta, GA	132.58	142.21	130.44	3.22	56.70	30.32
Austin, TX	109.05	135.58	126.98	2.98	67.39	27.11
Baltimore, MD	135.14	116.91	119.20	3.41	61.43	41.00
Billings, MT	215.23	110.57	164.07	3.33	38.78	36.85
Boise City, ID	169.88	102.77	145.10	3.61	52.55	48.06
Boston, MA	222.77	144.00	161.33	3.33	66.76	39.88
Boulder, CO	n/a	n/a	n/a	n/a	n/a	n/a
Cape Coral, FL	178.39	133.21	101.13	3.36	54.67	30.93
Cedar Rapids, IA	n/a	n/a	n/a	n/a	n/a	n/a
Charleston, SC	123.53	99.17	82.86	3.03	56.00	24.77
Charlotte, NC	157.61	120.57	92.08	3.12	79.44	57.64
Chicago, IL	179.67	126.00	113.83	3.55	62.23	34.52
Cincinnati, OH	158.21	98.92	97.57	3.18	39.43	41.70
Clarksville, TN	n/a	n/a	n/a	n/a	n/a	n/a
Cleveland, OH	117.00	111.33	110.47	3.21	40.20	39.79
College Station, TX	n/a	n/a	n/a	n/a	n/a	n/a
Colorado Springs, CO	134.99	106.17	132.00	3.04	50.14	30.58
Columbia, MO	182.67	95.67	138.50	3.10	45.42	37.14
Columbia, SC	150.00	58.67	67.33	3.12	38.83	34.56
Columbus, OH	115.70	94.35	93.20	3.19	49.51	36.47
Dallas, TX	138.26	133.49	135.65	3.07	72.78	43.45
Davenport, IA	167.17	105.92	108.62	3.41	39.87	34.38
Denver, CO	134.18	140.57	122.31	3.05	50.44	22.71
Des Moines, IA	119.38	101.96	128.70	3.15	42.46	37.61
Detroit, MI	183.09	126.33	95.64	3.42	60.83	52.14
Durham, NC	179.33	112.78	133.40	3.38	54.35	30.66
El Paso, TX	129.11	95.03	101.95	3.23	33.64	34.89
Eugene, OR	196.75	117.67	126.00	3.83	40.19	36.32
Fargo, ND	230.71	124.67	113.44	3.12	40.47	44.83
Fort Collins, CO	n/a	n/a	n/a	n/a	n/a	n/a
Fort Wayne, IN	137.75	106.33	122.67	3.32	33.28	39.34
Fort Worth, TX	138.71	136.11	137.89	3.03	52.39	37.44
Gainesville, FL	n/a	n/a	n/a	n/a	n/a	n/a
Green Bay, WI	167.58	112.11	84.28	3.14	30.42	26.22
Greensboro, NC	n/a	n/a	n/a	n/a	n/a	n/a
Honolulu, HI	201.94	127.00	258.67	4.58	75.33	58.48
Houston, TX	97.07	129.17	137.54	2.98	73.30	50.68
Huntsville, AL	121.00	115.28	99.56	3.04	58.56	30.30
Indianapolis, IN	112.66	105.53	77.80	3.35	39.07	43.61
Jacksonville, FL	106.53	98.40	97.76	3.34	79.67	30.27
Kansas City, MO	95.79	108.20	95.10	3.06	34.80	29.79
Lafayette, LA	95.33	95.87	120.20	3.01	40.73	44.86
Las Vegas, NV	110.44	99.25	100.78	4.13	48.86	25.05
Lexington, KY	144.23	113.73	92.42	3.19	60.23	44.97
Lincoln, NE	183.29	113.07	119.17	3.25	42.20	52.31
Little Rock, AR	133.00	83.67	105.53	2.95	52.55	47.99
Los Angeles, CA	130.00	133.17	127.53	4.85	94.00	38.64
Louisville, KY	152.10	159.00	107.05	3.21	43.89	48.00
Madison, WI	236.64	124.37	72.86	3.27	76.22	41.80
Manchester, NH	183.83	108.17	116.33	3.24	56.33	42.69
McAllen, TX	91.69	88.11	100.21	2.96	47.50	32.95

Table continued on following page.

Urban Area	Doctor ($/visit)	Dentist ($/visit)	Optometrist ($/visit)	Gasoline ($/gallon)	Beauty Salon ($/visit)	Men's Shirt ($)
Memphis, TN	112.80	97.80	83.95	3.00	46.92	27.44
Miami, FL	134.75	118.47	110.39	3.43	87.63	28.46
Midland, TX	97.50	108.17	132.67	3.13	69.08	43.45
Milwaukee, WI	174.22	122.03	86.17	3.30	44.20	32.41
Minneapolis, MN	170.09	100.86	120.48	3.16	40.96	41.19
Nashville, TN	122.71	110.37	114.45	3.08	48.65	32.66
New Orleans, LA	161.78	121.36	115.44	3.11	48.33	49.00
New York, NY[2]	192.84	171.93	152.60	3.43	68.80	44.04
Oklahoma City, OK	149.53	124.67	99.96	3.02	51.40	22.45
Omaha, NE	151.64	90.62	117.00	3.08	33.92	35.09
Orlando, FL	123.06	110.00	97.28	3.34	53.19	32.49
Philadelphia, PA	148.84	111.61	125.00	3.33	67.25	36.90
Phoenix, AZ	99.00	127.08	103.50	3.64	55.36	22.95
Pittsburgh, PA	96.56	128.63	105.71	3.67	44.32	28.77
Portland, OR	218.48	116.33	147.50	4.17	60.17	35.98
Providence, RI	168.33	117.58	111.08	3.28	50.22	31.37
Provo, UT	113.66	105.45	127.59	3.41	51.34	49.04
Raleigh, NC	146.67	153.61	109.33	3.23	55.17	32.17
Reno, NV	115.00	105.00	118.17	4.35	49.17	27.27
Richmond, VA	120.19	104.13	133.02	3.24	48.38	20.26
Rochester, MN	n/a	n/a	n/a	n/a	n/a	n/a
Sacramento, CA	151.58	121.82	173.55	5.28	71.49	36.48
Saint Louis, MO	92.32	115.88	95.55	3.38	41.97	28.19
Saint Paul, MN	169.08	101.40	118.46	3.16	41.44	42.25
Salem, OR	n/a	n/a	n/a	n/a	n/a	n/a
Salt Lake City, UT	129.02	100.40	125.47	3.38	56.68	44.66
San Antonio, TX	149.40	139.78	139.25	2.97	69.33	39.95
San Diego, CA	139.44	126.00	143.70	4.93	67.95	39.49
San Francisco, CA	183.65	160.37	168.34	5.07	86.22	48.81
San Jose, CA	212.00	131.83	166.92	5.00	65.28	32.93
Santa Rosa, CA	n/a	n/a	n/a	n/a	n/a	n/a
Savannah, GA	150.00	152.87	91.31	3.29	39.61	38.61
Seattle, WA	208.77	157.05	179.39	4.49	85.33	49.17
Sioux Falls, SD	116.42	116.32	140.94	3.04	40.11	30.74
Tampa, FL	126.57	112.70	118.00	3.36	48.00	27.91
Tucson, AZ	n/a	n/a	n/a	n/a	n/a	n/a
Tulsa, OK	109.57	109.83	111.11	2.95	35.40	29.28
Virginia Beach, VA[3]	144.92	148.93	69.03	3.20	42.70	32.71
Washington, DC	177.67	151.33	125.50	3.36	78.76	37.95
Wichita, KS	111.32	102.90	144.60	3.09	48.13	54.27
Wilmington, NC	n/a	n/a	n/a	n/a	n/a	n/a
Winston-Salem, NC	152.89	120.67	145.61	3.15	50.94	38.49
Average[1]	143.77	117.51	129.23	3.32	48.57	38.14
Minimum[1]	36.74	58.67	67.33	2.80	24.00	13.41
Maximum[1]	270.44	216.82	307.33	5.28	94.00	63.89

Note: **Doctor** *(general practitioners routine exam of an established patient);* **Dentist** *(adult teeth cleaning and periodic oral examination);* **Optometrist** *(full vision eye exam for established adult patient);* **Gasoline** *(one gallon regular unleaded, national brand, including all taxes, cash price at self-service pump if available);* **Beauty Salon** *(woman's shampoo, trim, and blow-dry);* **Men's Shirt** *(cotton/polyester dress shirt, pinpoint weave, long sleeves); (1) Average, minimum, and maximum values for all 276 areas in the Cost of Living Index report; n/a not available; In cases where data is not available for the city, data for the metro area or for a neighboring city has been provided and noted as follows: (2) Brooklyn, NY; (3) Hampton Roads-SE Virginia*
Source: The Council for Community and Economic Research, Cost of Living Index, 2024

Number of Medical Professionals

City	Area Covered	MDs[1]	DOs[1,2]	Dentists	Podiatrists	Chiropractors	Optometrists
Albuquerque, NM	Bernalillo County	503.5	30.6	87.4	9.4	24.9	17.7
Anchorage, AK	Anchorage Borough	384.5	55.4	134.9	5.9	65.7	31.5
Ann Arbor, MI	Washtenaw County	1,420.9	52.7	208.7	9.0	26.5	19.4
Athens, GA	Clarke County	392.7	17.7	50.0	3.8	21.5	16.2
Atlanta, GA	Fulton County	548.6	18.3	76.9	5.1	60.5	21.3
Austin, TX	Travis County	332.0	21.9	76.9	4.4	36.6	18.8
Baltimore, MD	Baltimore City	1,247.2	36.1	88.5	8.0	16.8	16.6
Billings, MT	Yellowstone County	379.2	40.0	101.3	9.4	38.6	26.9
Boise City, ID	Ada County	286.2	40.1	83.7	4.6	54.9	23.1
Boston, MA	Suffolk County	1,797.9	24.3	251.7	9.0	16.9	39.0
Boulder, CO	Boulder County	365.5	34.2	116.9	6.4	84.4	30.0
Cape Coral, FL	Lee County	198.8	29.9	56.1	7.9	28.8	13.3
Cedar Rapids, IA	Linn County	181.2	25.3	77.7	8.7	62.5	17.9
Charleston, SC	Charleston County	881.5	45.6	117.8	5.7	54.7	25.9
Charlotte, NC	Mecklenburg County	352.8	20.9	72.1	3.7	37.2	14.5
Chicago, IL	Cook County	472.9	34.3	100.5	12.9	30.1	22.5
Cincinnati, OH	Hamilton County	662.9	36.0	77.1	10.4	21.6	23.3
Clarksville, TN	Montgomery County	91.4	16.6	45.0	2.9	12.9	10.4
Cleveland, OH	Cuyahoga County	799.3	74.0	110.6	18.8	20.5	18.2
College Station, TX	Brazos County	254.5	20.2	58.0	3.3	19.6	18.0
Colorado Springs, CO	El Paso County	214.0	37.9	107.1	5.4	47.7	25.7
Columbia, MO	Boone County	864.2	95.9	78.6	5.8	41.2	28.0
Columbia, SC	Richland County	358.7	21.6	93.1	6.8	22.8	18.8
Columbus, OH	Franklin County	473.2	78.8	99.2	8.0	26.5	29.9
Dallas, TX	Dallas County	380.9	24.6	96.6	4.5	40.3	15.6
Davenport, IA	Scott County	256.4	56.3	85.5	5.2	190.5	16.6
Denver, CO	Denver County	610.0	36.3	84.8	6.8	40.6	17.3
Des Moines, IA	Polk County	221.1	118.9	80.8	12.3	63.7	21.2
Detroit, MI	Wayne County	348.3	61.0	80.1	9.8	19.1	12.4
Durham, NC	Durham County	1,206.3	21.9	77.2	4.2	21.1	13.7
El Paso, TX	El Paso County	231.2	22.1	49.5	4.7	9.2	10.8
Eugene, OR	Lane County	250.6	16.5	75.6	5.2	29.4	17.3
Fargo, ND	Cass County	401.6	26.5	78.4	5.1	75.9	33.6
Fort Collins, CO	Larimer County	251.9	39.3	85.2	6.5	57.4	21.3
Fort Wayne, IN	Allen County	272.1	33.5	72.7	5.6	23.8	26.6
Fort Worth, TX	Tarrant County	197.7	39.4	64.9	4.5	30.4	17.3
Gainesville, FL	Alachua County	1,059.4	68.3	193.4	5.6	26.9	19.2
Green Bay, WI	Brown County	265.5	25.6	80.7	3.3	50.5	19.9
Greensboro, NC	Guilford County	262.2	18.9	62.9	4.7	15.1	10.2
Honolulu, HI	Honolulu County	357.2	23.8	103.9	3.9	22.6	25.8
Houston, TX	Harris County	363.6	16.0	75.3	5.0	24.0	21.6
Huntsville, AL	Madison County	275.3	16.1	53.3	2.9	23.0	20.1
Indianapolis, IN	Marion County	475.0	31.6	95.4	6.9	17.5	22.1
Jacksonville, FL	Duval County	369.2	38.0	77.4	6.9	27.6	16.4
Kansas City, MO	Jackson County	343.6	110.1	94.5	7.1	49.3	20.2
Lafayette, LA	Lafayette Parish	383.7	17.3	71.3	4.0	33.6	14.4
Las Vegas, NV	Clark County	188.3	42.2	69.1	4.7	21.1	14.8
Lexington, KY	Fayette County	844.1	66.5	149.6	8.1	25.9	29.4
Lincoln, NE	Lancaster County	215.9	16.9	109.0	5.5	49.9	20.5
Little Rock, AR	Pulaski County	822.8	30.3	80.2	5.2	24.0	22.7
Los Angeles, CA	Los Angeles County	336.3	17.6	99.4	6.9	32.1	20.8
Louisville, KY	Jefferson County	506.3	25.2	107.8	8.5	28.2	17.9
Madison, WI	Dane County	669.0	28.0	77.3	5.2	45.9	21.9
Manchester, NH	Hillsborough County	235.1	26.7	85.2	6.6	26.9	22.5
McAllen, TX	Hidalgo County	145.8	4.7	31.4	1.6	8.0	7.2
Memphis, TN	Shelby County	429.3	17.8	78.8	4.0	15.5	33.0

Table continued on following page.

Appendix A: Comparative Statistics   A-149

City	Area Covered	MDs[1]	DOs[1,2]	Dentists	Podiatrists	Chiropractors	Optometrists
Miami, FL	Miami-Dade County	415.2	27.2	81.5	10.0	20.1	16.3
Midland, TX	Midland County	154.1	6.4	60.4	2.3	14.1	11.9
Milwaukee, WI	Milwaukee County	431.6	36.6	92.8	7.1	22.0	12.1
Minneapolis, MN	Hennepin County	570.7	32.9	106.5	5.7	80.2	23.3
Nashville, TN	Davidson County	698.9	19.2	84.9	5.3	29.8	17.8
New Orleans, LA	Orleans Parish	1,005.0	33.8	86.5	4.9	10.2	8.8
New York, NY	New York City	545.5	24.3	90.9	13.8	16.8	19.8
Oklahoma City, OK	Oklahoma County	432.6	52.2	111.5	4.8	29.7	21.3
Omaha, NE	Douglas County	600.0	44.3	105.5	5.4	44.4	23.6
Orlando, FL	Orange County	349.3	28.9	54.1	4.1	29.8	14.1
Philadelphia, PA	Philadelphia County	663.2	66.9	86.4	16.3	15.6	20.8
Phoenix, AZ	Maricopa County	258.2	37.8	73.7	7.4	34.3	17.5
Pittsburgh, PA	Allegheny County	677.7	59.4	99.5	9.3	44.9	21.1
Portland, OR	Multnomah County	687.2	44.4	105.1	5.1	80.2	26.2
Providence, RI	Providence County	526.4	19.5	59.8	10.1	21.2	22.4
Provo, UT	Utah County	115.9	24.3	60.3	4.7	26.7	11.4
Raleigh, NC	Wake County	293.0	15.8	75.8	3.8	29.7	16.6
Reno, NV	Washoe County	310.2	25.2	72.1	4.4	30.7	23.7
Richmond, VA	Richmond City	822.6	63.6	155.7	13.5	7.4	15.7
Rochester, MN	Olmsted County	2,670.4	71.3	137.1	7.3	45.5	24.9
Sacramento, CA	Sacramento County	344.7	20.3	84.3	4.5	22.0	19.4
Saint Louis, MO	St. Louis City	1,491.0	56.9	71.0	4.3	23.4	21.7
Saint Paul, MN	Ramsey County	379.6	17.2	95.7	5.8	71.4	14.7
Salem, OR	Marion County	180.0	18.7	88.3	6.6	35.5	16.7
Salt Lake City, UT	Salt Lake County	422.6	23.4	83.1	6.6	29.7	15.1
San Antonio, TX	Bexar County	330.0	28.5	95.3	6.0	17.4	19.0
San Diego, CA	San Diego County	364.2	22.2	100.8	5.0	36.4	21.2
San Francisco, CA	San Francisco County	942.4	16.7	175.9	11.4	44.0	34.6
San Jose, CA	Santa Clara County	483.8	14.5	129.4	7.4	47.0	30.7
Santa Rosa, CA	Sonoma County	289.0	21.3	99.6	6.8	44.8	18.9
Savannah, GA	Chatham County	384.6	28.2	73.4	6.9	21.4	14.8
Seattle, WA	King County	521.6	19.0	118.3	6.4	48.4	24.3
Sioux Falls, SD	Minnehaha County	395.6	31.4	56.1	5.8	57.5	18.4
Tampa, FL	Hillsborough County	375.2	41.2	66.1	6.7	29.3	16.2
Tucson, AZ	Pima County	387.9	35.6	67.8	5.6	19.4	17.6
Tulsa, OK	Tulsa County	265.4	153.1	71.8	4.2	40.1	25.0
Virginia Beach, VA	Virginia Beach City	263.4	14.9	82.0	7.5	26.7	16.3
Washington, DC	District of Columbia	928.4	29.2	130.5	9.3	11.2	15.2
Wichita, KS	Sedgwick County	266.0	42.1	71.3	1.9	43.9	29.0
Wilmington, NC	New Hanover County	367.8	37.9	82.9	8.4	36.0	24.3
Winston-Salem, NC	Forsyth County	716.2	41.1	64.9	6.9	19.1	18.6
U.S.	U.S.	302.5	29.2	74.6	6.4	29.5	18.0

Note: All figures are the number of medical professionals per 100,000 population; Data as of 2023 unless noted; (1) Data as of 2022 and includes all active, non-federal physicians; (2) Doctor of Osteopathic Medicine
Source: U.S. Department of Health and Human Services, Health Resources and Services Administration, Bureau of Health Professions, Area Resource File (ARF) 2023-2024

Health Insurance Coverage: City

City	With Health Insurance	With Private Health Insurance	With Public Health Insurance	Without Health Insurance	Population Under Age 19 Without Health Insurance
Albuquerque, NM	91.7	60.1	45.1	8.3	5.0
Anchorage, AK	90.0	70.0	34.0	10.0	7.4
Ann Arbor, MI	97.2	86.7	20.9	2.8	2.1
Athens, GA	88.8	72.8	25.0	11.2	8.1
Atlanta, GA	89.5	70.4	27.2	10.5	6.2
Austin, TX	87.6	74.8	20.6	12.4	9.2
Baltimore, MD	94.2	58.5	46.8	5.8	3.8
Billings, MT	93.1	67.1	39.9	6.9	4.8
Boise City, ID	92.3	74.4	29.4	7.7	4.9
Boston, MA	97.0	69.9	35.8	3.0	1.9
Boulder, CO	96.5	83.8	21.0	3.5	1.0
Cape Coral, FL	88.4	65.5	38.4	11.6	10.1
Cedar Rapids, IA	95.5	71.1	36.8	4.5	1.6
Charleston, SC	93.6	79.0	27.0	6.4	2.0
Charlotte, NC	87.1	67.8	26.5	12.9	8.3
Chicago, IL	90.2	61.6	35.8	9.8	4.0
Cincinnati, OH	92.4	61.1	40.3	7.6	5.7
Clarksville, TN	90.7	72.1	34.3	9.3	4.3
Cleveland, OH	92.3	43.8	57.2	7.7	3.7
College Station, TX	91.9	83.0	16.5	8.1	4.7
Colorado Springs, CO	92.3	69.8	36.4	7.7	4.7
Columbia, MO	93.6	79.1	23.3	6.4	4.7
Columbia, SC	91.9	71.0	31.4	8.1	3.2
Columbus, OH	90.2	62.3	35.5	9.8	5.8
Dallas, TX	77.0	54.1	29.3	23.0	15.7
Davenport, IA	92.8	65.0	41.1	7.2	4.7
Denver, CO	91.2	68.3	30.8	8.8	5.3
Des Moines, IA	93.3	62.0	42.7	6.7	2.2
Detroit, MI	92.5	41.8	62.6	7.5	2.7
Durham, NC	88.4	70.6	27.4	11.6	8.6
El Paso, TX	79.0	53.1	34.9	21.0	11.9
Eugene, OR	94.5	68.2	39.0	5.5	2.3
Fargo, ND	93.9	79.5	26.0	6.1	4.5
Fort Collins, CO	94.4	78.3	25.0	5.6	4.8
Fort Wayne, IN	90.6	62.9	38.1	9.4	6.7
Fort Worth, TX	81.4	61.7	26.4	18.6	12.7
Gainesville, FL	91.8	76.6	23.8	8.2	5.0
Green Bay, WI	91.6	59.8	40.9	8.4	4.9
Greensboro, NC	90.9	65.5	35.7	9.1	4.1
Honolulu, HI	96.2	75.5	38.3	3.8	2.4
Houston, TX	76.0	52.1	30.3	24.0	16.0
Huntsville, AL	90.6	73.2	32.5	9.4	3.2
Indianapolis, IN	91.0	62.3	38.6	9.0	5.7
Jacksonville, FL	88.3	64.4	34.4	11.7	7.1
Kansas City, MO	88.7	68.3	29.8	11.3	7.4
Lafayette, LA	90.5	60.7	41.3	9.5	4.4
Las Vegas, NV	86.8	60.3	36.5	13.2	8.8
Lexington, KY	93.2	69.8	34.5	6.8	2.9
Lincoln, NE	93.3	76.3	28.6	6.7	3.9
Little Rock, AR	90.0	62.0	39.1	10.0	7.0
Los Angeles, CA	90.0	55.2	41.9	10.0	3.6
Louisville, KY	94.2	64.2	43.1	5.8	3.8
Madison, WI	95.7	81.9	24.1	4.3	2.9
Manchester, NH	91.2	66.6	35.0	8.8	4.9
McAllen, TX	74.2	48.4	32.3	25.8	14.9

Table continued on following page.

City	With Health Insurance	With Private Health Insurance	With Public Health Insurance	Without Health Insurance	Population Under Age 19 Without Health Insurance
Memphis, TN	85.2	55.1	41.3	14.8	8.6
Miami, FL	82.4	52.6	33.5	17.6	8.8
Midland, TX	85.2	72.0	21.3	14.8	11.7
Milwaukee, WI	90.9	52.2	46.7	9.1	3.6
Minneapolis, MN	94.1	69.5	32.8	5.9	2.8
Nashville, TN	87.4	69.0	29.0	12.6	9.0
New Orleans, LA	91.6	55.4	45.3	8.4	5.4
New York, NY	93.6	58.2	45.3	6.4	2.3
Oklahoma City, OK	86.0	63.0	34.4	14.0	7.6
Omaha, NE	90.3	69.2	31.0	9.7	6.9
Orlando, FL	86.1	64.6	27.6	13.9	8.0
Philadelphia, PA	92.8	58.8	45.9	7.2	4.5
Phoenix, AZ	85.5	58.6	34.6	14.5	9.8
Pittsburgh, PA	94.8	72.9	33.5	5.2	3.8
Portland, OR	94.5	71.5	33.1	5.5	2.1
Providence, RI	92.6	57.0	44.1	7.4	5.1
Provo, UT	90.6	78.6	17.5	9.4	9.8
Raleigh, NC	89.9	73.5	26.0	10.1	6.0
Reno, NV	89.5	67.9	31.5	10.5	7.0
Richmond, VA	90.2	63.3	36.9	9.8	7.2
Rochester, MN	95.7	79.7	30.5	4.3	3.7
Sacramento, CA	94.5	65.3	40.5	5.5	3.2
Saint Louis, MO	90.7	63.5	35.7	9.3	3.7
Saint Paul, MN	93.6	62.5	41.0	6.4	4.5
Salem, OR	92.6	63.9	41.9	7.4	1.9
Salt Lake City, UT	89.0	73.9	22.8	11.0	10.2
San Antonio, TX	82.5	58.4	33.8	17.5	9.8
San Diego, CA	93.7	71.9	31.7	6.3	3.6
San Francisco, CA	96.5	75.8	30.7	3.5	2.0
San Jose, CA	95.1	72.5	30.6	4.9	1.8
Santa Rosa, CA	93.6	67.8	39.1	6.4	3.9
Savannah, GA	86.2	59.3	36.7	13.8	5.7
Seattle, WA	95.6	80.5	23.5	4.4	1.8
Sioux Falls, SD	92.2	77.7	25.8	7.8	5.6
Tampa, FL	89.0	64.5	32.0	11.0	5.7
Tucson, AZ	89.0	57.0	42.7	11.0	7.4
Tulsa, OK	83.5	56.6	37.7	16.5	8.4
Virginia Beach, VA	93.5	78.0	30.8	6.5	3.8
Washington, DC	96.6	72.4	34.2	3.4	2.7
Wichita, KS	87.6	65.3	34.1	12.4	6.1
Wilmington, NC	88.4	69.5	32.5	11.6	8.0
Winston-Salem, NC	88.1	61.8	37.5	11.9	4.7
U.S.	91.4	67.3	36.3	8.6	5.4

Note: Figures are percentages that cover the civilian noninstitutionalized population
Source: U.S. Census Bureau, 2019-2023 American Community Survey 5-Year Estimates

Health Insurance Coverage: Metro Area

Metro Area	With Health Insurance	With Private Health Insurance	With Public Health Insurance	Without Health Insurance	Population Under Age 19 Without Health Insurance
Albuquerque, NM	91.9	59.2	47.2	8.1	5.0
Anchorage, AK	89.4	68.4	35.1	10.6	8.2
Ann Arbor, MI	96.7	81.5	28.7	3.3	2.0
Athens, GA	89.0	71.4	27.8	11.0	7.2
Atlanta, GA	87.8	69.1	28.2	12.2	7.2
Austin, TX	87.9	75.2	21.9	12.1	9.0
Baltimore, MD	95.1	74.5	34.4	4.9	3.6
Billings, MT	93.2	68.2	39.6	6.8	5.2
Boise City, ID	91.4	72.1	31.8	8.6	6.2
Boston, MA	97.2	76.4	33.5	2.8	1.6
Boulder, CO	95.6	79.6	26.6	4.4	2.0
Cape Coral, FL	87.5	62.0	43.6	12.5	9.7
Cedar Rapids, IA	96.3	74.8	35.1	3.7	1.4
Charleston, SC	90.3	71.9	32.2	9.7	6.8
Charlotte, NC	89.9	70.0	29.9	10.1	5.9
Chicago, IL	92.4	69.8	32.5	7.6	3.5
Cincinnati, OH	94.5	72.3	33.5	5.5	3.8
Clarksville, TN	90.7	69.7	36.3	9.3	6.7
Cleveland, OH	94.4	67.4	40.0	5.6	3.9
College Station, TX	88.1	73.2	24.7	11.9	7.6
Colorado Springs, CO	92.9	71.5	35.9	7.1	4.6
Columbia, MO	93.4	77.7	26.6	6.6	4.4
Columbia, SC	91.0	69.6	36.0	9.0	5.2
Columbus, OH	92.6	70.0	32.5	7.4	4.5
Dallas, TX	83.7	66.7	24.5	16.3	11.8
Davenport, IA	94.5	71.3	38.0	5.5	3.7
Denver, CO	92.2	72.2	29.4	7.8	5.0
Des Moines, IA	95.5	75.1	32.5	4.5	2.3
Detroit, MI	95.1	70.0	40.0	4.9	2.6
Durham, NC	90.2	72.6	29.5	9.8	6.1
El Paso, TX	78.1	52.1	34.3	21.9	12.9
Eugene, OR	94.1	63.9	44.5	5.9	2.9
Fargo, ND	94.8	80.6	25.8	5.2	4.2
Fort Collins, CO	94.3	74.9	31.0	5.7	3.8
Fort Wayne, IN	92.0	68.5	34.5	8.0	6.3
Fort Worth, TX	83.7	66.7	24.5	16.3	11.8
Gainesville, FL	90.9	71.2	30.8	9.1	5.2
Green Bay, WI	94.8	72.2	34.1	5.2	3.4
Greensboro, NC	90.2	64.1	37.2	9.8	4.2
Honolulu, HI	96.6	78.2	36.3	3.4	2.6
Houston, TX	81.3	61.4	27.1	18.7	12.6
Huntsville, AL	92.2	77.5	29.4	7.8	2.8
Indianapolis, IN	93.0	70.9	32.9	7.0	4.6
Jacksonville, FL	90.1	69.3	33.4	9.9	6.3
Kansas City, MO	91.1	74.1	27.9	8.9	5.6
Lafayette, LA	92.3	60.4	42.4	7.7	3.2
Las Vegas, NV	87.9	62.5	35.9	12.1	8.3
Lexington, KY	93.9	69.8	36.2	6.1	3.2
Lincoln, NE	93.7	77.6	28.1	6.3	3.8
Little Rock, AR	91.7	65.3	39.2	8.3	5.1
Los Angeles, CA	91.8	60.8	38.8	8.2	3.5
Louisville, KY	94.7	69.5	38.9	5.3	3.6
Madison, WI	96.3	82.6	26.5	3.7	2.8
Manchester, NH	94.0	77.1	29.3	6.0	4.0
McAllen, TX	70.3	37.7	37.5	29.7	15.7

Table continued on following page.

Metro Area	With Health Insurance	With Private Health Insurance	With Public Health Insurance	Without Health Insurance	Population Under Age 19 Without Health Insurance
Memphis, TN	88.9	64.1	36.1	11.1	6.4
Miami, FL	86.3	60.5	33.6	13.7	8.2
Midland, TX	84.7	70.7	21.7	15.3	12.1
Milwaukee, WI	94.6	70.6	35.5	5.4	2.8
Minneapolis, MN	95.7	77.3	30.9	4.3	2.7
Nashville, TN	90.6	72.8	28.6	9.4	5.8
New Orleans, LA	90.8	55.9	45.1	9.2	5.6
New York, NY	93.5	66.6	37.8	6.5	3.1
Oklahoma City, OK	87.7	66.8	33.5	12.3	7.3
Omaha, NE	92.9	74.5	29.2	7.1	4.7
Orlando, FL	88.7	66.6	31.4	11.3	6.3
Philadelphia, PA	94.7	72.5	35.5	5.3	3.4
Phoenix, AZ	89.3	66.2	34.1	10.7	8.6
Pittsburgh, PA	96.2	74.5	37.9	3.8	2.4
Portland, OR	94.2	72.3	34.0	5.8	3.2
Providence, RI	96.1	70.1	39.7	3.9	2.4
Provo, UT	92.3	82.1	17.4	7.7	6.0
Raleigh, NC	91.3	76.0	25.6	8.7	5.0
Reno, NV	90.4	69.0	32.8	9.6	6.8
Richmond, VA	93.2	73.3	33.5	6.8	5.0
Rochester, MN	95.6	79.5	31.1	4.4	4.0
Sacramento, CA	95.3	70.1	38.7	4.7	2.7
Saint Louis, MO	94.0	73.7	31.5	6.0	3.5
Saint Paul, MN	95.7	77.3	30.9	4.3	2.7
Salem, OR	92.0	63.0	42.6	8.0	3.3
Salt Lake City, UT	90.6	77.4	20.8	9.4	7.7
San Antonio, TX	85.0	64.6	31.8	15.0	9.1
San Diego, CA	93.2	69.6	34.3	6.8	3.8
San Francisco, CA	95.9	75.5	31.5	4.1	2.4
San Jose, CA	95.9	77.1	27.4	4.1	1.8
Santa Rosa, CA	94.6	71.3	38.3	5.4	3.2
Savannah, GA	88.0	67.8	32.8	12.0	6.6
Seattle, WA	94.4	75.5	29.6	5.6	2.7
Sioux Falls, SD	93.1	79.1	25.6	6.9	4.8
Tampa, FL	88.9	64.2	36.5	11.1	6.0
Tucson, AZ	91.1	62.8	42.8	8.9	7.0
Tulsa, OK	86.8	63.7	35.3	13.2	7.6
Virginia Beach, VA	93.3	73.2	35.8	6.7	4.0
Washington, DC	92.6	76.7	27.8	7.4	4.9
Wichita, KS	89.7	69.9	32.5	10.3	5.3
Wilmington, NC	90.4	71.3	38.0	9.6	6.8
Winston-Salem, NC	89.6	64.5	37.6	10.4	4.6
U.S.	91.4	67.3	36.3	8.6	5.4

Note: Figures are percentages that cover the civilian noninstitutionalized population; Figures cover the Metropolitan Statistical Area (MSA)
Source: U.S. Census Bureau, 2019-2023 American Community Survey 5-Year Estimates

Crime Rate: City

City	Total Crime	Violent Crime Rate				Property Crime Rate		
		Murder	Rape	Robbery	Aggrav. Assault	Burglary	Larceny-Theft	Motor Vehicle Theft
Albuquerque, NM	6,021.7	19.3	54.2	175.5	1,068.0	671.8	3,003.1	1,029.9
Anchorage, AK	3,953.3	7.7	150.2	161.7	742.0	334.0	2,132.4	425.2
Ann Arbor, MI	2,058.1	3.4	37.3	39.0	232.1	171.1	1,438.1	137.2
Athens, GA	2,950.7	3.9	60.2	61.7	305.6	238.4	2,063.4	217.6
Atlanta, GA	4,599.8	26.4	23.2	120.3	537.4	346.9	2,500.1	1,045.6
Austin, TX	3,804.7	6.7	50.3	93.3	348.8	468.0	2,125.2	712.4
Baltimore, MD	5,850.2	41.2	45.1	577.9	908.2	445.5	1,987.6	1,844.7
Billings, MT	4,487.3	7.4	83.2	123.6	674.0	346.1	2,723.2	529.8
Boise City, ID	1,512.1	2.1	67.9	21.9	177.7	131.7	971.9	138.8
Boston, MA	2,571.3	5.3	32.5	136.6	452.5	180.9	1,589.2	174.2
Boulder, CO	3,414.5	2.9	38.4	36.5	279.2	457.6	2,276.7	323.3
Cape Coral, FL	n/a	n/a	n/a	n/a	n/a	n/a	n/a	n/a
Cedar Rapids, IA	3,184.6	5.9	8.1	30.2	255.6	345.4	2,281.7	257.8
Charleston, SC	2,379.5	6.4	28.4	52.8	314.5	164.3	1,501.0	311.9
Charlotte, NC	4,562.0	9.4	25.4	128.4	563.0	430.0	2,578.2	827.7
Chicago, IL	4,038.7	19.0	47.3	412.3	128.1	280.1	2,145.0	1,006.8
Cincinnati, OH	4,956.6	22.0	71.4	208.4	426.2	617.2	2,416.3	1,195.2
Clarksville, TN	2,193.3	6.0	57.7	29.7	373.8	214.9	1,285.8	225.4
Cleveland, OH	6,515.8	38.8	119.5	448.1	1,096.8	894.3	2,475.2	1,443.0
College Station, TX	1,493.6	3.2	49.2	17.4	88.8	141.9	1,086.9	106.2
Colorado Springs, CO	4,386.7	4.9	104.2	76.4	506.5	521.6	2,354.6	818.4
Columbia, MO	2,897.3	7.7	59.4	33.2	285.5	307.1	1,859.5	344.9
Columbia, SC	4,223.4	7.8	45.2	107.4	596.5	455.8	2,537.2	473.5
Columbus, OH	3,089.1	10.5	115.3	117.5	141.8	412.2	1,553.0	738.9
Dallas, TX	4,701.5	18.5	36.8	157.8	458.4	470.3	2,126.6	1,433.1
Davenport, IA	4,501.0	9.0	102.1	91.1	488.4	688.6	2,601.3	520.5
Denver, CO	6,772.3	11.9	93.2	175.8	740.8	716.9	3,284.7	1,749.0
Des Moines, IA	4,056.1	4.3	69.2	90.6	542.8	451.2	2,271.3	626.7
Detroit, MI	6,785.7	40.6	109.3	225.5	1,676.7	756.9	2,485.8	1,490.8
Durham, NC	4,397.4	15.2	53.4	168.4	399.3	497.0	2,574.8	689.3
El Paso, TX	1,955.2	5.0	40.9	48.0	242.2	157.2	1,116.4	345.4
Eugene, OR	3,545.1	3.4	56.7	77.4	210.4	497.8	2,306.5	392.8
Fargo, ND	4,394.2	1.5	71.5	75.2	367.2	768.6	2,690.1	420.1
Fort Collins, CO	2,736.2	0.6	29.0	36.7	229.7	273.6	1,958.1	208.4
Fort Wayne, IN	2,623.8	9.6	43.7	64.9	153.1	251.0	1,800.3	301.0
Fort Worth, TX	3,135.9	8.7	69.1	71.2	340.8	391.4	1,763.5	491.2
Gainesville, FL	3,608.3	10.9	100.9	119.3	507.7	286.2	2,572.5	10.9
Green Bay, WI	1,915.3	5.7	66.3	31.3	283.4	215.1	1,029.2	284.3
Greensboro, NC	4,560.5	24.7	24.4	164.9	612.1	555.0	2,682.7	496.6
Honolulu, HI	2,128.6	0.6	28.0	51.7	105.8	193.1	1,377.3	372.0
Houston, TX	5,599.2	14.9	61.1	295.7	720.0	606.3	3,034.5	866.7
Huntsville, AL	834.6	2.7	15.1	17.4	94.8	101.9	521.4	81.4
Indianapolis, IN	4,653.4	18.9	55.9	174.2	782.0	615.8	2,229.9	776.8
Jacksonville, FL	n/a	n/a	n/a	n/a	n/a	n/a	n/a	n/a
Kansas City, MO	6,436.1	35.5	78.5	241.2	1,122.5	549.6	2,633.3	1,775.6
Lafayette, LA	5,421.0	23.1	24.7	98.1	672.4	1,017.6	3,291.8	293.3
Las Vegas, NV	3,551.8	8.0	49.8	77.6	334.6	524.7	1,681.3	875.9
Lexington, KY	3,004.7	4.4	56.6	76.9	115.9	337.8	2,022.9	390.3
Lincoln, NE	3,052.3	2.4	90.4	52.9	220.4	252.4	2,106.4	327.5
Little Rock, AR	7,228.6	30.5	122.2	223.2	1,425.2	925.7	4,003.7	498.1
Los Angeles, CA	3,666.8	8.6	51.4	230.1	530.0	406.4	1,764.3	676.0
Louisville, KY	4,385.4	22.9	32.7	148.2	561.8	498.8	2,104.4	1,016.8
Madison, WI	2,636.1	3.6	27.7	44.5	225.4	280.4	1,859.0	195.5
Manchester, NH	2,061.5	7.0	59.1	87.9	229.6	147.9	1,342.2	187.9

Table continued on following page.

		Violent Crime Rate				Property Crime Rate		
City	Total Crime	Murder	Rape	Robbery	Aggrav. Assault	Burglary	Larceny-Theft	Motor Vehicle Theft
McAllen, TX	2,092.9	4.8	35.7	24.0	79.6	111.2	1,774.4	63.2
Memphis, TN	11,214.8	57.0	73.4	451.1	2,030.5	1,110.9	4,942.0	2,549.9
Miami, FL	3,436.7	7.1	28.3	109.7	346.9	254.1	2,223.1	467.6
Midland, TX	2,321.6	5.2	63.6	33.3	328.3	274.3	1,354.5	262.5
Milwaukee, WI	4,136.0	31.0	74.3	284.4	1,048.0	418.1	1,278.7	1,001.6
Minneapolis, MN	6,384.2	17.0	86.7	339.8	688.1	605.7	2,806.3	1,840.7
Nashville, TN	5,533.6	14.5	59.1	163.4	892.0	401.7	3,232.8	770.2
New Orleans, LA	6,450.6	53.0	187.0	180.1	941.0	478.3	2,770.8	1,840.5
New York, NY	3,066.4	4.2	25.3	200.0	438.8	167.2	2,006.8	224.2
Oklahoma City, OK	3,571.8	9.0	68.9	88.0	471.6	566.1	1,965.4	402.7
Omaha, NE[1]	4,029.5	6.0	61.6	69.5	424.0	259.6	2,514.4	694.4
Orlando, FL[1]	4,864.3	10.3	72.7	137.1	615.7	449.9	3,173.7	404.9
Philadelphia, PA	6,039.7	26.0	46.6	336.1	574.4	363.9	3,161.8	1,530.9
Phoenix, AZ	3,268.6	11.5	65.6	168.8	538.9	342.6	1,577.4	563.9
Pittsburgh, PA	n/a	n/a	n/a	n/a	n/a	n/a	n/a	n/a
Portland, OR	6,575.8	11.8	51.1	193.1	459.2	792.8	3,756.6	1,311.2
Providence, RI	2,215.3	5.8	34.3	59.6	209.9	157.2	1,482.7	265.8
Provo, UT	1,531.8	0.0	60.3	16.0	98.5	110.0	1,149.5	97.6
Raleigh, NC	3,117.6	5.4	32.1	87.2	403.4	306.3	1,891.3	391.8
Reno, NV	3,234.8	6.8	102.2	111.6	375.1	381.9	1,838.8	418.3
Richmond, VA	4,078.2	26.9	29.5	97.1	204.1	287.3	2,899.2	534.3
Rochester, MN	1,754.4	0.8	36.1	22.9	102.4	182.7	1,283.2	126.2
Sacramento, CA	3,692.9	7.7	32.1	225.3	535.6	520.1	1,672.4	699.8
Saint Louis, MO	7,844.8	56.4	70.3	260.3	1,058.2	751.1	3,434.0	2,214.5
Saint Paul, MN	3,714.1	9.0	67.3	126.8	420.8	434.5	1,962.9	692.8
Salem, OR	3,650.5	5.0	15.1	98.7	328.7	384.2	2,312.7	506.0
Salt Lake City, UT	6,514.5	7.7	159.7	175.6	524.9	555.4	4,504.8	586.4
San Antonio, TX	6,089.1	10.9	97.8	120.5	465.0	546.5	3,568.2	1,280.2
San Diego, CA	2,229.6	2.9	21.5	87.4	306.1	201.5	1,118.7	491.6
San Francisco, CA	6,422.7	6.6	37.3	349.7	316.5	720.8	4,135.3	856.4
San Jose, CA[1]	3,178.2	3.7	93.4	132.1	298.2	405.9	1,568.7	676.1
Santa Rosa, CA	1,799.8	5.7	65.0	63.9	196.2	257.8	1,004.2	206.9
Savannah, GA	n/a	n/a	n/a	n/a	n/a	n/a	n/a	n/a
Seattle, WA	5,789.3	9.0	36.2	221.7	510.2	1,126.3	2,662.2	1,223.7
Sioux Falls, SD	2,864.1	0.5	16.9	32.4	385.4	287.6	1,635.4	505.9
Tampa, FL	2,115.0	10.2	42.4	65.4	341.8	194.1	1,272.2	188.9
Tucson, AZ	n/a	n/a	n/a	n/a	n/a	n/a	n/a	n/a
Tulsa, OK	4,850.8	8.8	101.5	100.0	702.2	878.8	2,486.1	573.5
Virginia Beach, VA	1,751.8	3.7	22.0	29.5	40.1	86.6	1,431.3	138.5
Washington, DC	5,205.1	38.9	38.4	558.0	412.1	245.1	2,905.0	1,007.6
Wichita, KS	5,864.8	9.9	87.8	104.7	930.0	548.2	3,662.4	521.9
Wilmington, NC	3,995.9	8.2	31.0	99.4	348.9	455.7	2,763.4	289.4
Winston-Salem, NC	3,897.6	16.7	34.9	97.2	737.7	629.4	1,994.6	387.1
U.S.	2,290.9	5.7	38.0	66.5	264.1	250.7	1,347.2	318.7

Note: Figures are crimes per 100,000 population in 2023 except where noted; (1) 2022 data; n/a not available.
Source: FBI, Table 8, Offenses Known to Law Enforcement, by State by City, 2022, 2023

Temperature & Precipitation: Yearly Averages and Extremes

City	Extreme Low (°F)	Average Low (°F)	Average Temp. (°F)	Average High (°F)	Extreme High (°F)	Average Precip. (in.)	Average Snow (in.)
Albuquerque, NM	-17	43	57	70	105	8.5	11
Anchorage, AK	-34	29	36	43	85	15.7	71
Ann Arbor, MI	-21	39	49	58	104	32.4	41
Athens, GA	-8	52	62	72	105	49.8	2
Atlanta, GA	-8	52	62	72	105	49.8	2
Austin, TX	-2	58	69	79	109	31.1	1
Baltimore, MD	-7	45	56	65	105	41.2	21
Billings, MT	-32	36	47	59	105	14.6	59
Boise City, ID	-25	39	51	63	111	11.8	22
Boston, MA	-12	44	52	59	102	42.9	41
Boulder, CO	-25	37	51	64	103	15.5	63
Cape Coral, FL	26	65	75	84	103	53.9	0
Cedar Rapids, IA	-34	36	47	57	105	34.4	33
Charleston, SC	6	55	66	76	104	52.1	1
Charlotte, NC	-5	50	61	71	104	42.8	6
Chicago, IL	-27	40	49	59	104	35.4	39
Cincinnati, OH	-25	44	54	64	103	40.9	23
Clarksville, TN	-17	49	60	70	107	47.4	11
Cleveland, OH	-19	41	50	59	104	37.1	55
College Station, TX	-2	58	69	79	109	31.1	1
Colorado Springs, CO	-24	36	49	62	99	17.0	48
Columbia, MO	-20	44	54	64	111	40.6	25
Columbia, SC	-1	51	64	75	107	48.3	2
Columbus, OH	-19	42	52	62	104	37.9	28
Dallas, TX	-2	56	67	77	112	33.9	3
Davenport, IA	-24	40	50	60	108	31.8	33
Denver, CO	-25	37	51	64	103	15.5	63
Des Moines, IA	-24	40	50	60	108	31.8	33
Detroit, MI	-21	39	49	58	104	32.4	41
Durham, NC	-9	48	60	71	105	42.0	8
El Paso, TX	-8	50	64	78	114	8.6	6
Eugene, OR	-12	42	53	63	108	47.3	7
Fargo, ND	-36	31	41	52	106	19.6	40
Fort Collins, CO	-25	37	51	64	103	15.5	63
Fort Wayne, IN	-22	40	50	60	106	35.9	33
Fort Worth, TX	-1	55	66	76	113	32.3	3
Gainesville, FL	10	58	69	79	102	50.9	Trace
Green Bay, WI	-31	34	44	54	99	28.3	46
Greensboro, NC	-8	47	58	69	103	42.5	10
Honolulu, HI	52	70	77	84	94	22.4	0
Houston, TX	7	58	69	79	107	46.9	Trace
Huntsville, AL	-11	50	61	71	104	56.8	4
Indianapolis, IN	-23	42	53	62	104	40.2	25
Jacksonville, FL	7	58	69	79	103	52.0	0
Kansas City, MO	-23	44	54	64	109	38.1	21
Lafayette, LA	8	57	68	78	103	58.5	Trace
Las Vegas, NV	8	53	67	80	116	4.0	1
Lexington, KY	-21	45	55	65	103	45.1	17
Lincoln, NE	-33	39	51	62	108	29.1	27
Little Rock, AR	-5	51	62	73	112	50.7	5
Los Angeles, CA	27	55	63	70	110	11.3	Trace
Louisville, KY	-20	46	57	67	105	43.9	17
Madison, WI	-37	35	46	57	104	31.1	42
Manchester, NH	-33	34	46	57	102	36.9	63
McAllen, TX	16	65	74	83	106	25.8	Trace

Table continued on following page.

City	Extreme Low (°F)	Average Low (°F)	Average Temp. (°F)	Average High (°F)	Extreme High (°F)	Average Precip. (in.)	Average Snow (in.)
Memphis, TN	0	52	65	77	107	54.8	1
Miami, FL	30	69	76	83	98	57.1	0
Midland, TX	-11	50	64	77	116	14.6	4
Milwaukee, WI	-26	38	47	55	103	32.0	49
Minneapolis, MN	-34	35	45	54	105	27.1	52
Nashville, TN	-17	49	60	70	107	47.4	11
New Orleans, LA	11	59	69	78	102	60.6	Trace
New York, NY	-2	47	55	62	104	47.0	23
Oklahoma City, OK	-8	49	60	71	110	32.8	10
Omaha, NE	-23	40	51	62	110	30.1	29
Orlando, FL	19	62	72	82	100	47.7	Trace
Philadelphia, PA	-7	45	55	64	104	41.4	22
Phoenix, AZ	17	59	72	86	122	7.3	Trace
Pittsburgh, PA	-18	41	51	60	103	37.1	43
Portland, OR	-3	45	54	62	107	37.5	7
Providence, RI	-13	42	51	60	104	45.3	35
Provo, UT	-22	40	52	64	107	15.6	63
Raleigh, NC	-9	48	60	71	105	42.0	8
Reno, NV	-16	33	50	67	105	7.2	24
Richmond, VA	-8	48	58	69	105	43.0	13
Rochester, MN	-40	34	44	54	102	29.4	47
Sacramento, CA	18	48	61	73	115	17.3	Trace
Saint Louis, MO	-18	46	56	66	115	36.8	20
Saint Paul, MN	-34	35	45	54	105	27.1	52
Salem, OR	-12	41	52	63	108	40.2	7
Salt Lake City, UT	-22	40	52	64	107	15.6	63
San Antonio, TX	0	58	69	80	108	29.6	1
San Diego, CA	29	57	64	71	111	9.5	Trace
San Francisco, CA	24	49	57	65	106	19.3	Trace
San Jose, CA	21	50	59	68	105	13.5	Trace
Santa Rosa, CA	23	42	57	71	109	29.0	n/a
Savannah, GA	3	56	67	77	105	50.3	Trace
Seattle, WA	0	44	52	59	99	38.4	13
Sioux Falls, SD	-36	35	46	57	110	24.6	38
Tampa, FL	18	63	73	82	99	46.7	Trace
Tucson, AZ	16	55	69	82	117	11.6	2
Tulsa, OK	-8	50	61	71	112	38.9	10
Virginia Beach, VA	-3	51	60	69	104	44.8	8
Washington, DC	-5	49	58	67	104	39.5	18
Wichita, KS	-21	45	57	68	113	29.3	17
Wilmington, NC	0	53	64	74	104	55.0	2
Winston-Salem, NC	-8	47	58	69	103	42.5	10

Source: National Climatic Data Center, International Station Meteorological Climate Summary, 9/96; NOAA

Weather Conditions

City	Temperature			Daytime Sky			Precipitation		Thunder-storms
	10°F & below	32°F & below	90°F & above	Clear	Partly cloudy	Cloudy	0.01 inch or more precip.	1.0 inch or more snow/ice	
Albuquerque, NM	4	114	65	140	161	64	60	9	38
Anchorage, AK	n/a	194	n/a	50	115	200	113	49	2
Ann Arbor, MI	n/a	136	12	74	134	157	135	38	32
Athens, GA	1	49	38	98	147	120	116	3	48
Atlanta, GA	1	49	38	98	147	120	116	3	48
Austin, TX	<1	20	111	105	148	112	83	1	41
Baltimore, MD	6	97	31	91	143	131	113	13	27
Billings, MT	n/a	149	29	75	163	127	97	41	27
Boise City, ID	n/a	124	45	106	133	126	91	22	14
Boston, MA	n/a	97	12	88	127	150	253	48	18
Boulder, CO	24	155	33	99	177	89	90	38	39
Cape Coral, FL	n/a	n/a	115	93	220	52	110	0	92
Cedar Rapids, IA	n/a	156	16	89	132	144	109	28	42
Charleston, SC	<1	33	53	89	162	114	114	1	59
Charlotte, NC	1	65	44	98	142	125	113	3	41
Chicago, IL	n/a	132	17	83	136	146	125	31	38
Cincinnati, OH	14	107	23	80	126	159	127	25	39
Clarksville, TN	5	76	51	98	135	132	119	8	54
Cleveland, OH	n/a	123	12	63	127	175	157	48	34
College Station, TX	<1	20	111	105	148	112	83	1	41
Colorado Springs, CO	21	161	18	108	157	100	98	33	49
Columbia, MO	17	108	36	99	127	139	110	17	52
Columbia, SC	<1	58	77	97	149	119	110	1	53
Columbus, OH	n/a	118	19	72	137	156	136	29	40
Dallas, TX	1	34	102	108	160	97	78	2	49
Davenport, IA	n/a	137	26	99	129	137	106	25	46
Denver, CO	24	155	33	99	177	89	90	38	39
Des Moines, IA	n/a	137	26	99	129	137	106	25	46
Detroit, MI	n/a	136	12	74	134	157	135	38	32
Durham, NC	n/a	n/a	39	98	143	124	110	3	42
El Paso, TX	1	59	106	147	164	54	49	3	35
Eugene, OR	n/a	n/a	15	75	115	175	136	4	3
Fargo, ND	n/a	180	15	81	145	139	100	38	31
Fort Collins, CO	24	155	33	99	177	89	90	38	39
Fort Wayne, IN	n/a	131	16	75	140	150	131	31	39
Fort Worth, TX	1	40	100	123	136	106	79	3	47
Gainesville, FL	n/a	n/a	77	88	196	81	119	0	78
Green Bay, WI	n/a	163	7	86	125	154	120	40	33
Greensboro, NC	3	85	32	94	143	128	113	5	43
Honolulu, HI	n/a	n/a	23	25	286	54	98	0	7
Houston, TX	n/a	n/a	96	83	168	114	101	1	62
Huntsville, AL	2	66	49	70	118	177	116	2	54
Indianapolis, IN	19	119	19	83	128	154	127	24	43
Jacksonville, FL	<1	16	83	86	181	98	114	1	65
Kansas City, MO	22	110	39	112	134	119	103	17	51
Lafayette, LA	<1	21	86	99	150	116	113	<1	73
Las Vegas, NV	<1	37	134	185	132	48	27	2	13
Lexington, KY	11	96	22	86	136	143	129	17	44
Lincoln, NE	n/a	145	40	108	135	122	94	19	46
Little Rock, AR	1	57	73	110	142	113	104	4	57
Los Angeles, CA	0	<1	5	131	125	109	34	0	1
Louisville, KY	8	90	35	82	143	140	125	15	45
Madison, WI	n/a	161	14	88	119	158	118	38	40
Manchester, NH	n/a	171	12	87	131	147	125	32	19

Table continued on following page.

City	Temperature			Daytime Sky			Precipitation		Thunder-storms
	10°F & below	32°F & below	90°F & above	Clear	Partly cloudy	Cloudy	0.01 inch or more precip.	1.0 inch or more snow/ice	
McAllen, TX	n/a	n/a	116	86	180	99	72	0	27
Memphis, TN	1	53	86	101	152	112	104	2	59
Miami, FL	n/a	n/a	55	48	263	54	128	0	74
Midland, TX	1	62	102	144	138	83	52	3	38
Milwaukee, WI	n/a	141	10	90	118	157	126	38	35
Minneapolis, MN	n/a	156	16	93	125	147	113	41	37
Nashville, TN	5	76	51	98	135	132	119	8	54
New Orleans, LA	0	13	70	90	169	106	114	1	69
New York, NY	n/a	n/a	18	85	166	114	120	11	20
Oklahoma City, OK	5	79	70	124	131	110	80	8	50
Omaha, NE	n/a	139	35	100	142	123	97	20	46
Orlando, FL	n/a	n/a	90	76	208	81	115	0	80
Philadelphia, PA	5	94	23	81	146	138	117	14	27
Phoenix, AZ	0	10	167	186	125	54	37	<1	23
Pittsburgh, PA	n/a	121	8	62	137	166	154	42	35
Portland, OR	n/a	37	11	67	116	182	152	4	7
Providence, RI	n/a	117	9	85	134	146	123	21	21
Provo, UT	n/a	128	56	94	152	119	92	38	38
Raleigh, NC	n/a	n/a	39	98	143	124	110	3	42
Reno, NV	14	178	50	143	139	83	50	17	14
Richmond, VA	3	79	41	90	147	128	115	7	43
Rochester, MN	n/a	165	9	87	126	152	114	40	41
Sacramento, CA	0	21	73	175	111	79	58	<1	2
Saint Louis, MO	13	100	43	97	138	130	109	14	46
Saint Paul, MN	n/a	156	16	93	125	147	113	41	37
Salem, OR	n/a	66	16	78	118	169	146	6	5
Salt Lake City, UT	n/a	128	56	94	152	119	92	38	38
San Antonio, TX	n/a	n/a	112	97	153	115	81	1	36
San Diego, CA	0	<1	4	115	126	124	40	0	5
San Francisco, CA	0	6	4	136	130	99	63	<1	5
San Jose, CA	0	5	5	106	180	79	57	<1	6
Santa Rosa, CA	n/a	43	30	n/a	365	n/a	n/a	n/a	2
Savannah, GA	<1	29	70	97	155	113	111	<1	63
Seattle, WA	n/a	38	3	57	121	187	157	8	8
Sioux Falls, SD	n/a	n/a	n/a	95	136	134	n/a	n/a	n/a
Tampa, FL	n/a	n/a	85	81	204	80	107	<1	87
Tucson, AZ	0	18	140	177	119	69	54	2	42
Tulsa, OK	6	78	74	117	141	107	88	8	50
Virginia Beach, VA	<1	53	33	89	149	127	115	5	38
Washington, DC	2	71	34	84	144	137	112	9	30
Wichita, KS	13	110	63	117	132	116	87	13	54
Wilmington, NC	<1	42	46	96	150	119	115	1	47
Winston-Salem, NC	3	85	32	94	143	128	113	5	43

Note: Figures are average number of days per year
Source: National Climatic Data Center, International Station Meteorological Climate Summary, 9/96; NOAA

Air Quality Index

Metro Area (Days[1])	Percent of Days when Air Quality was...					AQI Statistics	
	Good	Moderate	Unhealthy for Sensitive Groups	Unhealthy	Very Unhealthy	Maximum	Median
Albuquerque, NM (365)	26.6	72.3	0.8	0.0	0.3	207	60
Anchorage, AK (365)	81.1	18.6	0.3	0.0	0.0	102	25
Ann Arbor, MI (365)	46.0	50.4	2.5	0.5	0.5	218	52
Athens, GA (365)	47.4	51.8	0.8	0.0	0.0	147	52
Atlanta, GA (365)	26.6	67.7	4.9	0.8	0.0	172	57
Austin, TX (365)	40.3	56.7	3.0	0.0	0.0	122	54
Baltimore, MD (365)	55.1	40.3	3.6	0.8	0.3	205	49
Billings, MT (357)	85.7	13.2	0.8	0.3	0.0	191	29
Boise City, ID (365)	49.3	49.9	0.8	0.0	0.0	120	51
Boston, MA (365)	52.1	46.0	1.9	0.0	0.0	136	50
Boulder, CO (365)	52.6	45.8	1.1	0.5	0.0	181	50
Cape Coral, FL (363)	94.5	5.2	0.3	0.0	0.0	101	35
Cedar Rapids, IA (365)	35.6	59.5	3.8	0.8	0.3	207	54
Charleston, SC (365)	57.8	41.6	0.5	0.0	0.0	105	47
Charlotte, NC (365)	39.7	58.1	2.2	0.0	0.0	150	53
Chicago, IL (365)	20.8	67.4	9.0	2.2	0.5	246	60
Cincinnati, OH (365)	25.2	68.2	5.2	1.4	0.0	197	57
Clarksville, TN (365)	56.2	42.5	1.4	0.0	0.0	117	47
Cleveland, OH (365)	31.5	64.1	3.0	1.1	0.3	285	57
College Station, TX (348)	67.0	33.0	0.0	0.0	0.0	79	39
Colorado Springs, CO (365)	65.8	33.7	0.3	0.3	0.0	154	47
Columbia, MO (244)	79.9	18.0	2.0	0.0	0.0	143	42
Columbia, SC (365)	54.5	44.4	1.1	0.0	0.0	123	48
Columbus, OH (365)	37.0	59.5	2.5	0.8	0.3	210	54
Dallas, TX (365)	20.5	64.9	12.1	2.5	0.0	177	60
Davenport, IA (365)	37.3	56.4	5.2	0.8	0.3	232	54
Denver, CO (365)	19.7	72.3	7.4	0.5	0.0	179	64
Des Moines, IA (365)	46.0	49.9	3.3	0.8	0.0	166	52
Detroit, MI (365)	18.6	74.0	6.3	0.8	0.3	226	61
Durham, NC (361)	69.5	29.4	1.1	0.0	0.0	121	44
El Paso, TX (365)	18.9	75.9	4.9	0.3	0.0	155	64
Eugene, OR (365)	52.1	43.6	2.5	1.6	0.3	211	49
Fargo, ND (358)	50.3	46.4	2.8	0.6	0.0	175	50
Fort Collins, CO (365)	47.9	50.7	1.1	0.3	0.0	156	51
Fort Wayne, IN (365)	45.2	52.1	1.9	0.5	0.3	223	52
Fort Worth, TX (365)	20.5	64.9	12.1	2.5	0.0	177	60
Gainesville, FL (365)	74.0	25.8	0.3	0.0	0.0	104	40
Green Bay, WI (365)	57.0	38.1	3.3	1.6	0.0	182	46
Greensboro, NC (365)	50.1	48.8	1.1	0.0	0.0	131	50
Honolulu, HI (365)	92.3	7.4	0.3	0.0	0.0	117	31
Houston, TX (365)	9.9	74.5	12.3	3.0	0.3	205	65
Huntsville, AL (364)	56.0	43.1	0.8	0.0	0.0	135	49
Indianapolis, IN (365)	21.9	71.5	5.5	0.5	0.5	259	60
Jacksonville, FL (365)	41.6	57.8	0.5	0.0	0.0	124	52
Kansas City, MO (365)	34.0	58.1	6.8	1.1	0.0	166	55
Lafayette, LA (365)	56.7	43.0	0.3	0.0	0.0	112	47
Las Vegas, NV (365)	29.0	63.8	6.8	0.3	0.0	197	61
Lexington, KY (365)	63.3	35.9	0.5	0.3	0.0	167	45
Lincoln, NE (283)	69.6	29.3	0.7	0.4	0.0	160	42
Little Rock, AR (365)	33.4	65.2	1.1	0.3	0.0	174	55
Los Angeles, CA (365)	11.2	64.9	14.2	8.8	0.8	210	67
Louisville, KY (365)	32.1	62.2	5.5	0.3	0.0	182	55
Madison, WI (365)	49.6	43.6	5.5	0.5	0.8	268	51
Manchester, NH (365)	83.6	15.1	1.4	0.0	0.0	119	39

Table continued on following page.

Metro Area (Days[1])	Percent of Days when Air Quality was...					AQI Statistics	
	Good	Moderate	Unhealthy for Sensitive Groups	Unhealthy	Very Unhealthy	Maximum	Median
McAllen, TX (357)	57.7	42.3	0.0	0.0	0.0	95	44
Memphis, TN (365)	28.5	67.4	4.1	0.0	0.0	140	55
Miami, FL (365)	37.3	61.6	0.3	0.8	0.0	170	53
Midland, TX (n/a)	n/a	n/a	n/a	n/a	n/a	n/a	n/a
Milwaukee, WI (365)	43.6	48.8	6.6	0.3	0.8	270	53
Minneapolis, MN (365)	36.7	55.1	6.6	1.6	0.0	190	55
Nashville, TN (365)	34.8	62.5	2.7	0.0	0.0	133	54
New Orleans, LA (365)	38.1	59.2	2.7	0.0	0.0	126	53
New York, NY (365)	29.3	64.1	4.7	1.6	0.3	278	56
Oklahoma City, OK (365)	35.1	60.8	4.1	0.0	0.0	143	54
Omaha, NE (365)	50.4	42.7	6.3	0.5	0.0	169	50
Orlando, FL (365)	71.0	28.2	0.8	0.0	0.0	115	44
Philadelphia, PA (365)	17.8	75.3	5.2	1.1	0.3	331	59
Phoenix, AZ (365)	8.5	67.9	20.3	2.7	0.3	709	78
Pittsburgh, PA (365)	26.8	66.6	5.5	0.5	0.5	237	58
Portland, OR (365)	60.0	38.4	1.1	0.5	0.0	153	43
Providence, RI (365)	54.8	42.2	3.0	0.0	0.0	140	48
Provo, UT (365)	55.1	44.7	0.3	0.0	0.0	104	48
Raleigh, NC (365)	50.4	48.2	1.4	0.0	0.0	130	50
Reno, NV (365)	52.3	47.7	0.0	0.0	0.0	97	50
Richmond, VA (365)	55.9	42.7	0.5	0.8	0.0	159	48
Rochester, MN (365)	51.8	44.1	3.8	0.3	0.0	167	49
Sacramento, CA (365)	35.3	60.8	3.8	0.0	0.0	143	58
Saint Louis, MO (365)	14.0	79.5	5.8	0.8	0.0	185	60
Saint Paul, MN (365)	36.7	55.1	6.6	1.6	0.0	190	55
Salem, OR (365)	73.4	25.5	1.1	0.0	0.0	128	38
Salt Lake City, UT (365)	40.5	55.1	4.1	0.3	0.0	154	54
San Antonio, TX (365)	41.6	55.1	2.7	0.3	0.0	309	53
San Diego, CA (365)	16.7	71.2	12.1	0.0	0.0	150	67
San Francisco, CA (365)	34.0	62.5	3.6	0.0	0.0	130	54
San Jose, CA (365)	61.6	37.3	1.1	0.0	0.0	134	45
Santa Rosa, CA (365)	88.5	11.0	0.5	0.0	0.0	117	33
Savannah, GA (352)	56.0	43.5	0.6	0.0	0.0	108	48
Seattle, WA (365)	51.0	47.1	1.1	0.8	0.0	195	50
Sioux Falls, SD (365)	64.4	28.2	6.3	1.1	0.0	181	44
Tampa, FL (365)	39.5	59.2	1.4	0.0	0.0	114	52
Tucson, AZ (365)	33.7	64.4	1.9	0.0	0.0	147	54
Tulsa, OK (365)	37.8	56.7	4.9	0.5	0.0	197	53
Virginia Beach, VA (365)	62.7	36.4	0.5	0.3	0.0	174	44
Washington, DC (365)	43.3	51.2	4.4	0.8	0.3	222	52
Wichita, KS (365)	44.7	54.0	1.1	0.3	0.0	157	52
Wilmington, NC (362)	65.5	34.3	0.3	0.0	0.0	142	44
Winston-Salem, NC (365)	40.3	57.8	1.6	0.3	0.0	154	53

Note: The Air Quality Index (AQI) is an index for reporting daily air quality. EPA calculates the AQI for five major air pollutants regulated by the Clean Air Act: ground-level ozone, particle pollution (also known as particulate matter), carbon monoxide, sulfur dioxide, and nitrogen dioxide. The AQI runs from 0 to 500. The higher the AQI value, the greater the level of air pollution and the greater the health concern. There are six AQI categories: "Good" The AQI is between 0 and 50. Air quality is considered satisfactory; "Moderate" The AQI is between 51 and 100. Air quality is acceptable; "Unhealthy for Sensitive Groups" When AQI values are between 101 and 150, members of sensitive groups may experience health effects; "Unhealthy" When AQI values are between 151 and 200 everyone may begin to experience health effects; "Very Unhealthy" AQI values between 201 and 300 trigger a health alert; "Hazardous" AQI values over 300 trigger health warnings of emergency conditions; Figures cover the Metropolitan Statistical Area (MSA); (1) Number of days with AQI data in 2023
Source: U.S. Environmental Protection Agency, Air Quality Index Report, 2023

Air Quality Index Pollutants

Metro Area (Days)[1]	Percent of Days when AQI Pollutant was...					
	Carbon Monoxide	Nitrogen Dioxide	Ozone	Sulfur Dioxide[2]	Particulate Matter 2.5	Particulate Matter 10
Albuquerque, NM (365)	0.0	0.3	53.2	–	23.8	22.7
Anchorage, AK (365)	0.8	0.0	0.0	–	70.1	29.0
Ann Arbor, MI (365)	0.0	0.0	33.2	–	66.8	0.0
Athens, GA (365)	0.0	0.0	26.8	–	73.2	0.0
Atlanta, GA (365)	0.0	0.8	31.5	–	67.7	0.0
Austin, TX (365)	0.0	1.1	29.3	–	69.6	0.0
Baltimore, MD (365)	0.0	1.1	54.5	–	44.4	0.0
Billings, MT (357)	0.0	0.0	0.0	–	100.0	0.0
Boise City, ID (365)	0.0	0.3	44.9	–	54.0	0.8
Boston, MA (365)	0.0	0.5	36.7	–	62.7	0.0
Boulder, CO (365)	0.0	0.0	74.5	–	25.5	0.0
Cape Coral, FL (363)	0.0	0.0	100.0	–	0.0	0.0
Cedar Rapids, IA (365)	0.0	0.0	23.6	–	76.4	0.0
Charleston, SC (365)	0.0	0.0	24.4	–	75.1	0.5
Charlotte, NC (365)	0.0	0.0	45.8	–	54.2	0.0
Chicago, IL (365)	0.0	1.6	27.1	–	67.7	3.6
Cincinnati, OH (365)	0.0	0.5	25.5	–	72.1	1.9
Clarksville, TN (365)	0.0	0.0	23.3	–	76.7	0.0
Cleveland, OH (365)	0.5	0.0	27.1	–	71.2	1.1
College Station, TX (348)	0.0	0.0	0.0	–	100.0	0.0
Colorado Springs, CO (365)	0.0	0.0	91.5	–	8.5	0.0
Columbia, MO (244)	0.0	0.0	100.0	–	0.0	0.0
Columbia, SC (365)	0.0	0.3	32.9	–	66.8	0.0
Columbus, OH (365)	0.0	0.0	26.6	–	71.2	2.2
Dallas, TX (365)	0.0	0.5	40.5	–	58.4	0.5
Davenport, IA (365)	0.0	0.0	30.4	–	62.2	7.4
Denver, CO (365)	0.0	5.5	66.6	–	23.3	4.7
Des Moines, IA (365)	0.0	0.8	22.2	–	77.0	0.0
Detroit, MI (365)	0.0	0.5	11.5	–	87.9	0.0
Durham, NC (361)	0.0	0.0	45.2	–	52.4	2.5
El Paso, TX (365)	0.0	1.4	29.9	–	56.4	12.3
Eugene, OR (365)	0.0	0.0	21.4	–	78.6	0.0
Fargo, ND (358)	0.0	0.3	31.3	–	68.4	0.0
Fort Collins, CO (365)	0.0	0.0	83.3	–	16.7	0.0
Fort Wayne, IN (365)	0.0	0.0	38.9	–	61.1	0.0
Fort Worth, TX (365)	0.0	0.5	40.5	–	58.4	0.5
Gainesville, FL (365)	0.0	0.0	38.1	–	61.9	0.0
Green Bay, WI (365)	0.0	0.0	35.9	–	64.1	0.0
Greensboro, NC (365)	0.0	0.0	31.8	–	66.8	1.4
Honolulu, HI (365)	0.0	0.0	47.7	–	51.2	1.1
Houston, TX (365)	0.0	0.3	31.5	–	62.7	5.5
Huntsville, AL (364)	0.0	0.0	25.3	–	74.7	0.0
Indianapolis, IN (365)	0.0	0.0	19.2	–	80.8	0.0
Jacksonville, FL (365)	0.0	0.0	17.0	–	83.0	0.0
Kansas City, MO (365)	0.0	1.4	39.5	–	55.6	3.6
Lafayette, LA (365)	0.0	0.0	54.8	–	44.7	0.5
Las Vegas, NV (365)	0.0	0.3	67.7	–	27.7	4.4
Lexington, KY (365)	0.0	1.1	40.0	–	58.9	0.0
Lincoln, NE (283)	0.0	0.0	74.9	–	25.1	0.0
Little Rock, AR (365)	0.0	0.0	16.4	–	83.6	0.0
Los Angeles, CA (365)	0.0	1.4	41.1	–	55.6	1.9
Louisville, KY (365)	0.0	0.5	28.2	–	71.2	0.0
Madison, WI (365)	0.0	0.0	31.5	–	68.5	0.0
Manchester, NH (365)	0.8	0.0	80.3	–	18.9	0.0

Table continued on following page.

Metro Area (Days[1])	Percent of Days when AQI Pollutant was...					
	Carbon Monoxide	Nitrogen Dioxide	Ozone	Sulfur Dioxide[2]	Particulate Matter 2.5	Particulate Matter 10
McAllen, TX (357)	0.0	0.0	5.3	–	94.7	0.0
Memphis, TN (365)	0.0	0.0	34.2	–	65.8	0.0
Miami, FL (365)	0.0	3.6	13.7	–	82.7	0.0
Midland, TX (n/a)	n/a	n/a	n/a	–	n/a	n/a
Milwaukee, WI (365)	0.0	1.4	31.5	–	67.1	0.0
Minneapolis, MN (365)	0.3	0.8	33.4	–	61.1	4.4
Nashville, TN (365)	0.0	0.5	26.0	–	73.4	0.0
New Orleans, LA (365)	0.0	0.3	37.5	–	62.2	0.0
New York, NY (365)	0.0	4.1	27.7	–	68.2	0.0
Oklahoma City, OK (365)	0.0	2.2	42.7	–	54.2	0.8
Omaha, NE (365)	0.0	0.0	48.2	–	47.4	4.4
Orlando, FL (365)	0.0	0.5	55.1	–	44.4	0.0
Philadelphia, PA (365)	0.0	0.3	22.5	–	77.3	0.0
Phoenix, AZ (365)	0.0	0.0	41.9	–	24.1	34.0
Pittsburgh, PA (365)	0.0	0.0	19.7	–	80.3	0.0
Portland, OR (365)	0.0	1.1	42.7	–	56.2	0.0
Providence, RI (365)	0.0	0.3	41.9	–	57.8	0.0
Provo, UT (365)	0.0	0.3	63.3	–	36.2	0.3
Raleigh, NC (365)	0.0	0.3	32.1	–	67.7	0.0
Reno, NV (365)	0.0	1.1	67.9	–	30.7	0.3
Richmond, VA (365)	0.0	4.4	34.8	–	60.8	0.0
Rochester, MN (365)	0.0	0.0	32.6	–	67.4	0.0
Sacramento, CA (365)	0.0	0.0	60.5	–	39.5	0.0
Saint Louis, MO (365)	0.0	0.0	27.7	–	67.4	4.9
Saint Paul, MN (365)	0.3	0.8	33.4	–	61.1	4.4
Salem, OR (365)	0.0	0.0	35.6	–	64.4	0.0
Salt Lake City, UT (365)	0.0	5.5	60.0	–	32.3	2.2
San Antonio, TX (365)	0.0	0.3	37.5	–	62.2	0.0
San Diego, CA (365)	0.0	0.3	50.7	–	41.4	7.7
San Francisco, CA (365)	0.3	4.4	17.8	–	77.5	0.0
San Jose, CA (365)	0.0	0.0	57.5	–	41.9	0.5
Santa Rosa, CA (365)	0.3	0.0	64.9	–	34.5	0.3
Savannah, GA (352)	0.0	0.0	14.8	–	85.2	0.0
Seattle, WA (365)	0.0	0.8	32.9	–	66.3	0.0
Sioux Falls, SD (365)	0.0	1.6	69.6	–	26.3	2.5
Tampa, FL (365)	0.0	0.0	27.7	–	71.5	0.8
Tucson, AZ (365)	0.0	0.0	49.0	–	33.7	17.3
Tulsa, OK (365)	0.0	0.0	45.2	–	52.9	1.9
Virginia Beach, VA (365)	0.0	1.6	33.7	–	64.7	0.0
Washington, DC (365)	0.0	1.4	44.1	–	54.2	0.3
Wichita, KS (365)	0.0	0.5	45.2	–	51.2	3.0
Wilmington, NC (362)	0.0	0.0	25.1	–	74.9	0.0
Winston-Salem, NC (365)	0.0	0.0	27.7	–	72.3	0.0

Note: The Air Quality Index (AQI) is an index for reporting daily air quality. EPA calculates the AQI for five major air pollutants regulated by the Clean Air Act: ground-level ozone, particle pollution (also known as particulate matter), carbon monoxide, sulfur dioxide, and nitrogen dioxide. The AQI runs from 0 to 500. The higher the AQI value, the greater the level of air pollution and the greater the health concern; Figures cover the Metropolitan Statistical Area (MSA); (1) Number of days with AQI data in 2023; (2) Sulfur dioxide is no longer included in this table because SO_2 concentrations tend to be very localized and not necessarily representative of broad geographical areas like counties and CBSAs
Source: U.S. Environmental Protection Agency, Air Quality Index Report, 2023

Air Quality Trends: Ozone

Metro Area	1990	1995	2000	2005	2010	2015	2020	2021	2022	2023
Albuquerque, NM	0.072	0.070	0.072	0.073	0.066	0.066	0.071	0.071	0.071	0.067
Anchorage, AK	n/a	n/a	n/a	n/a	n/a	n/a	n/a	n/a	n/a	n/a
Ann Arbor, MI	0.025	0.034	0.035	0.023	0.034	0.064	0.067	0.063	0.066	0.072
Athens, GA	n/a	n/a	n/a	n/a	n/a	n/a	n/a	n/a	n/a	n/a
Atlanta, GA	0.088	0.089	0.089	0.077	0.067	0.069	0.059	0.064	0.063	0.072
Austin, TX	0.088	0.089	0.088	0.082	0.074	0.073	0.066	0.066	0.073	0.074
Baltimore, MD	0.100	0.103	0.088	0.089	0.084	0.073	0.064	0.071	0.066	0.073
Billings, MT	n/a	n/a	n/a	n/a	n/a	n/a	n/a	n/a	n/a	n/a
Boise City, ID	n/a	n/a	n/a	n/a	n/a	n/a	n/a	n/a	n/a	n/a
Boston, MA	0.078	0.085	0.067	0.075	0.066	0.065	0.053	0.059	0.066	0.060
Boulder, CO	n/a	n/a	n/a	n/a	n/a	n/a	n/a	n/a	n/a	n/a
Cape Coral, FL	0.069	0.066	0.073	0.071	0.065	0.058	0.061	0.055	0.058	0.064
Cedar Rapids, IA	n/a	n/a	n/a	n/a	n/a	n/a	n/a	n/a	n/a	n/a
Charleston, SC	0.059	0.075	0.076	0.077	0.068	0.054	0.053	0.059	0.059	0.056
Charlotte, NC	0.094	0.091	0.099	0.089	0.082	0.071	0.060	0.067	0.068	0.072
Chicago, IL	0.074	0.094	0.073	0.084	0.070	0.066	0.076	0.071	0.070	0.081
Cincinnati, OH	0.083	0.082	0.074	0.075	0.069	0.069	0.067	0.065	0.068	0.072
Clarksville, TN	n/a	n/a	n/a	n/a	n/a	n/a	n/a	n/a	n/a	n/a
Cleveland, OH	0.084	0.090	0.079	0.084	0.074	0.069	0.069	0.066	0.068	0.071
College Station, TX	n/a	n/a	n/a	n/a	n/a	n/a	n/a	n/a	n/a	n/a
Colorado Springs, CO	n/a	n/a	n/a	n/a	n/a	n/a	n/a	n/a	n/a	n/a
Columbia, MO	n/a	n/a	n/a	n/a	n/a	n/a	n/a	n/a	n/a	n/a
Columbia, SC	0.091	0.079	0.089	0.082	0.069	0.058	0.053	0.061	0.061	0.064
Columbus, OH	0.090	0.091	0.085	0.084	0.073	0.066	0.062	0.061	0.061	0.066
Dallas, TX	0.094	0.103	0.096	0.096	0.079	0.078	0.070	0.076	0.072	0.081
Davenport, IA	0.065	0.072	0.064	0.065	0.057	0.060	0.063	0.066	0.061	0.079
Denver, CO	0.076	0.070	0.069	0.077	0.069	0.072	0.081	0.082	0.074	0.073
Des Moines, IA	n/a	n/a	n/a	n/a	n/a	n/a	n/a	n/a	n/a	n/a
Detroit, MI	0.083	0.088	0.076	0.083	0.074	0.068	0.072	0.069	0.068	0.074
Durham, NC	0.078	0.080	0.082	0.079	0.074	0.061	0.051	0.063	0.058	0.066
El Paso, TX	0.080	0.078	0.082	0.074	0.072	0.071	0.076	0.071	0.071	0.071
Eugene, OR	0.068	0.062	0.056	0.068	0.058	0.070	0.054	0.061	0.058	0.060
Fargo, ND	n/a	n/a	n/a	n/a	n/a	n/a	n/a	n/a	n/a	n/a
Fort Collins, CO	0.066	0.072	0.074	0.075	0.072	0.070	0.070	0.077	0.070	0.067
Fort Wayne, IN	0.086	0.094	0.086	0.081	0.067	0.061	0.064	0.062	0.064	0.067
Fort Worth, TX	0.094	0.103	0.096	0.096	0.079	0.078	0.070	0.076	0.072	0.081
Gainesville, FL	n/a	n/a	n/a	n/a	n/a	n/a	n/a	n/a	n/a	n/a
Green Bay, WI	n/a	n/a	n/a	n/a	n/a	n/a	n/a	n/a	n/a	n/a
Greensboro, NC	0.097	0.089	0.089	0.082	0.076	0.064	0.057	0.066	0.063	0.067
Honolulu, HI	0.034	0.049	0.044	0.042	0.046	0.048	0.044	0.045	0.044	0.046
Houston, TX	0.119	0.114	0.102	0.087	0.079	0.083	0.067	0.072	0.068	0.079
Huntsville, AL	0.079	0.080	0.088	0.075	0.071	0.063	0.057	0.061	0.065	0.064
Indianapolis, IN	0.085	0.095	0.081	0.081	0.070	0.065	0.065	0.067	0.070	0.073
Jacksonville, FL	0.080	0.068	0.072	0.076	0.068	0.060	0.057	0.061	0.062	0.060
Kansas City, MO	0.075	0.095	0.087	0.082	0.067	0.063	0.064	0.067	0.066	0.074
Lafayette, LA	n/a	n/a	n/a	n/a	n/a	n/a	n/a	n/a	n/a	n/a
Las Vegas, NV	n/a	n/a	n/a	n/a	n/a	n/a	n/a	n/a	n/a	n/a
Lexington, KY	0.078	0.088	0.077	0.078	0.070	0.069	0.060	0.064	0.065	0.070
Lincoln, NE	0.057	0.060	0.057	0.056	0.050	0.061	0.054	0.059	0.055	0.068
Little Rock, AR	0.080	0.086	0.090	0.083	0.072	0.063	0.062	0.066	0.063	0.067
Los Angeles, CA	0.128	0.109	0.090	0.086	0.074	0.082	0.096	0.076	0.077	0.081
Louisville, KY	0.082	0.091	0.087	0.083	0.076	0.071	0.063	0.064	0.063	0.072
Madison, WI	0.077	0.084	0.072	0.079	0.062	0.064	0.070	0.066	0.062	0.082
Manchester, NH	0.085	0.088	0.070	0.082	0.067	0.061	0.055	0.061	0.058	0.065
McAllen, TX	n/a	n/a	n/a	n/a	n/a	n/a	n/a	n/a	n/a	n/a
Memphis, TN	0.088	0.095	0.092	0.086	0.076	0.065	0.063	0.067	0.071	0.071

Table continued on following page.

Metro Area	1990	1995	2000	2005	2010	2015	2020	2021	2022	2023
Miami, FL	0.068	0.072	0.075	0.065	0.064	0.061	0.058	0.057	0.063	0.061
Midland, TX	n/a	n/a	n/a	n/a	n/a	n/a	n/a	n/a	n/a	n/a
Milwaukee, WI	0.095	0.106	0.082	0.092	0.079	0.069	0.074	0.072	0.073	0.077
Minneapolis, MN	0.068	0.084	0.065	0.074	0.066	0.061	0.060	0.067	0.057	0.077
Nashville, TN	0.089	0.092	0.084	0.078	0.073	0.065	0.061	0.064	0.065	0.071
New Orleans, LA	0.082	0.088	0.091	0.079	0.074	0.067	0.061	0.060	0.061	0.068
New York, NY	0.101	0.105	0.089	0.090	0.080	0.074	0.064	0.069	0.067	0.071
Oklahoma City, OK	0.080	0.087	0.083	0.077	0.071	0.067	0.066	0.068	0.071	0.072
Omaha, NE	n/a	n/a	n/a	n/a	n/a	n/a	n/a	n/a	n/a	n/a
Orlando, FL	0.081	0.075	0.080	0.083	0.069	0.060	0.059	0.061	0.062	0.066
Philadelphia, PA	0.102	0.109	0.099	0.091	0.083	0.074	0.065	0.069	0.067	0.071
Phoenix, AZ	0.080	0.086	0.082	0.077	0.075	0.072	0.079	0.079	0.074	0.077
Pittsburgh, PA	0.080	0.100	0.084	0.083	0.077	0.070	0.066	0.066	0.064	0.067
Portland, OR	0.081	0.065	0.059	0.059	0.056	0.064	0.058	0.058	0.059	0.062
Providence, RI	0.106	0.107	0.087	0.090	0.072	0.070	0.065	0.067	0.060	0.066
Provo, UT	n/a	n/a	n/a	n/a	n/a	n/a	n/a	n/a	n/a	n/a
Raleigh, NC	0.093	0.081	0.087	0.082	0.071	0.065	0.054	0.062	0.064	0.064
Reno, NV	0.074	0.069	0.067	0.069	0.068	0.071	0.073	0.078	0.064	0.065
Richmond, VA	0.083	0.089	0.080	0.082	0.079	0.062	0.054	0.061	0.060	0.063
Rochester, MN	n/a	n/a	n/a	n/a	n/a	n/a	n/a	n/a	n/a	n/a
Sacramento, CA	0.087	0.092	0.085	0.084	0.072	0.073	0.072	0.072	0.067	0.069
Saint Louis, MO	0.077	0.084	0.074	0.078	0.069	0.067	0.066	0.067	0.070	0.077
Saint Paul, MN	0.068	0.084	0.065	0.074	0.066	0.061	0.060	0.067	0.057	0.077
Salem, OR	n/a	n/a	n/a	n/a	n/a	n/a	n/a	n/a	n/a	n/a
Salt Lake City, UT	n/a	n/a	n/a	n/a	n/a	n/a	n/a	n/a	n/a	n/a
San Antonio, TX	0.090	0.095	0.078	0.084	0.072	0.079	0.069	0.070	0.076	0.074
San Diego, CA	0.110	0.085	0.079	0.074	0.073	0.068	0.078	0.068	0.067	0.072
San Francisco, CA	0.062	0.077	0.060	0.060	0.063	0.064	0.062	0.064	0.057	0.053
San Jose, CA	0.078	0.084	0.065	0.063	0.072	0.067	0.066	0.067	0.062	0.057
Santa Rosa, CA	n/a	n/a	n/a	n/a	n/a	n/a	n/a	n/a	n/a	n/a
Savannah, GA	n/a	n/a	n/a	n/a	n/a	n/a	n/a	n/a	n/a	n/a
Seattle, WA	0.082	0.062	0.056	0.053	0.053	0.059	0.056	0.061	0.065	0.056
Sioux Falls, SD	n/a	n/a	n/a	n/a	n/a	n/a	n/a	n/a	n/a	n/a
Tampa, FL	0.080	0.075	0.081	0.075	0.067	0.062	0.063	0.060	0.061	0.066
Tucson, AZ	0.073	0.078	0.074	0.075	0.068	0.065	0.070	0.068	0.069	0.069
Tulsa, OK	0.086	0.091	0.081	0.072	0.069	0.061	0.061	0.063	0.070	0.072
Virginia Beach, VA	0.085	0.084	0.083	0.078	0.074	0.061	0.053	0.057	0.057	0.059
Washington, DC	0.075	0.083	0.073	0.069	0.069	0.067	0.057	0.066	0.061	0.069
Wichita, KS	0.077	0.069	0.080	0.074	0.075	0.064	0.059	0.061	0.072	0.066
Wilmington, NC	0.082	0.079	0.080	0.075	0.062	0.057	0.054	0.062	0.058	0.067
Winston-Salem, NC	0.084	0.086	0.089	0.080	0.078	0.065	0.058	0.062	0.057	0.066
U.S.	0.087	0.089	0.081	0.080	0.072	0.068	0.066	0.067	0.067	0.070

Note: Figures cover the Metropolitan Statistical Area (MSA); n/a not available. The values shown are the composite ozone concentration averages among trend sites based on the highest fourth daily maximum 8-hour concentration in parts per million. These trends are based on sites having an adequate record of monitoring data during the trend period. Data from exceptional events are included.
Source: U.S. Environmental Protection Agency, Air Quality Monitoring Information, "Air Quality Trends by City, 1990-2023"

Maximum Air Pollutant Concentrations: Particulate Matter, Ozone, CO and Lead

Metro Area	PM 10 (ug/m³)	PM 2.5 Wtd AM (ug/m³)	PM 2.5 24-Hr (ug/m³)	Ozone (ppm)	Carbon Monoxide (ppm)	Lead (ug/m³)
Albuquerque, NM	182	7.5	23	0.069	2	n/a
Anchorage, AK	130	4.2	18	n/a	2	n/a
Ann Arbor, MI	n/a	10.6	33	0.073	n/a	n/a
Athens, GA	n/a	9.3	26	0.068	n/a	n/a
Atlanta, GA	60	10.6	28	0.077	2	n/a
Austin, TX	53	10.4	25	0.074	2	n/a
Baltimore, MD	42	10.1	32	0.075	1	n/a
Billings, MT	n/a	6.7	29	n/a	n/a	n/a
Boise City, ID	84	n/a	n/a	0.066	1	n/a
Boston, MA	47	7.8	22	0.071	1	n/a
Boulder, CO	39	6.8	19	0.071	n/a	n/a
Cape Coral, FL	n/a	n/a	n/a	0.064	n/a	n/a
Cedar Rapids, IA	68	9.9	25	0.08	n/a	n/a
Charleston, SC	70	8.1	20	0.062	n/a	n/a
Charlotte, NC	51	10	26	0.073	2	n/a
Chicago, IL	137	11.2	31	0.086	1	0.1
Cincinnati, OH	111	12.2	44	0.077	1	n/a
Clarksville, TN	n/a	8.6	22	0.07	n/a	n/a
Cleveland, OH	147	12.8	40	0.075	5	0.04
College Station, TX	n/a	8	20	n/a	n/a	n/a
Colorado Springs, CO	32	5.4	13	0.069	1	n/a
Columbia, MO	n/a	n/a	n/a	0.072	n/a	n/a
Columbia, SC	44	8.2	22	0.069	1	n/a
Columbus, OH	97	10.9	36	0.069	1	0
Dallas, TX	70	10.7	23	0.084	2	0.07
Davenport, IA	109	10.4	28	0.08	1	n/a
Denver, CO	89	8.7	24	0.077	2	n/a
Des Moines, IA	56	10.2	31	0.077	n/a	n/a
Detroit, MI	161	14.7	46	0.079	2	0.03
Durham, NC	42	8	24	0.066	n/a	n/a
El Paso, TX	180	8.6	23	0.074	2	n/a
Eugene, OR	118	10.1	46	0.06	n/a	n/a
Fargo, ND	n/a	11.5	39	0.07	n/a	n/a
Fort Collins, CO	n/a	n/a	n/a	0.071	1	n/a
Fort Wayne, IN	n/a	10	33	0.075	n/a	n/a
Fort Worth, TX	70	10.7	23	0.084	2	0.07
Gainesville, FL	n/a	6.3	17	0.058	n/a	n/a
Green Bay, WI	n/a	9.5	38	0.075	n/a	n/a
Greensboro, NC	39	9.8	25	0.067	n/a	n/a
Honolulu, HI	46	4.1	10	0.046	0	n/a
Houston, TX	161	13.1	28	0.09	2	n/a
Huntsville, AL	61	8.6	21	0.067	n/a	n/a
Indianapolis, IN	147	13.7	44	0.077	2	n/a
Jacksonville, FL	55	7.9	20	0.062	1	n/a
Kansas City, MO	256	9.6	27	0.077	1	n/a
Lafayette, LA	48	8.2	15	0.068	n/a	n/a
Las Vegas, NV	209	8.2	27	0.074	2	n/a
Lexington, KY	28	8.3	27	0.07	n/a	n/a
Lincoln, NE	n/a	n/a	n/a	0.068	n/a	n/a
Little Rock, AR	39	10.8	23	0.07	1	n/a
Los Angeles, CA	124	11.1	28	0.103	3	0.02
Louisville, KY	96	10.7	32	0.075	2	n/a
Madison, WI	208	10.7	39	0.082	n/a	n/a
Manchester, NH	n/a	4.5	20	0.067	1	n/a
McAllen, TX	47	n/a	n/a	0.051	n/a	n/a

Table continued on following page.

Metro Area	PM 10 (ug/m³)	PM 2.5 Wtd AM (ug/m³)	PM 2.5 24-Hr (ug/m³)	Ozone (ppm)	Carbon Monoxide (ppm)	Lead (ug/m³)
Memphis, TN	67	10.6	27	0.074	1	n/a
Miami, FL	65	9.4	24	0.066	2	n/a
Midland, TX	n/a	n/a	n/a	n/a	n/a	n/a
Milwaukee, WI	209	11	39	0.08	1	n/a
Minneapolis, MN	118	10.6	41	0.079	4	0.46
Nashville, TN	57	10.2	25	0.076	2	n/a
New Orleans, LA	49	9.4	19	0.071	2	0.02
New York, NY	41	10.5	40	0.076	2	n/a
Oklahoma City, OK	89	9.2	21	0.074	1	n/a
Omaha, NE	79	9.7	33	0.082	1	0.06
Orlando, FL	54	6.8	16	0.069	1	n/a
Philadelphia, PA	174	13.3	37	0.074	1	0
Phoenix, AZ	387	9.8	32	0.083	2	n/a
Pittsburgh, PA	168	12	36	0.071	3	0
Portland, OR	27	6.5	25	0.068	1	n/a
Providence, RI	29	8.2	29	0.075	2	n/a
Provo, UT	76	6.8	21	0.066	1	n/a
Raleigh, NC	60	9.2	31	0.064	1	n/a
Reno, NV	63	7.2	18	0.067	2	n/a
Richmond, VA	65	8.7	28	0.067	1	n/a
Rochester, MN	n/a	9.6	33	0.074	n/a	n/a
Sacramento, CA	57	9.4	28	0.077	n/a	n/a
Saint Louis, MO	160	11.3	26	0.082	2	0.1
Saint Paul, MN	118	10.6	41	0.079	4	0.46
Salem, OR	n/a	n/a	n/a	0.064	n/a	n/a
Salt Lake City, UT	79	8.6	31	0.076	1	n/a
San Antonio, TX	50	9	26	0.076	1	n/a
San Diego, CA	142	12.5	24	0.08	1	0.02
San Francisco, CA	48	9.9	23	0.069	4	n/a
San Jose, CA	59	8.2	25	0.067	1	0.02
Santa Rosa, CA	48	5	17	0.046	1	n/a
Savannah, GA	n/a	8.8	24	0.061	n/a	n/a
Seattle, WA	17	8.5	29	0.068	1	n/a
Sioux Falls, SD	80	n/a	n/a	0.082	n/a	n/a
Tampa, FL	76	7.8	16	0.069	1	0.05
Tucson, AZ	201	7.8	16	0.07	1	n/a
Tulsa, OK	101	9.3	20	0.078	1	n/a
Virginia Beach, VA	62	8.1	28	0.066	1	n/a
Washington, DC	142	9.7	33	0.076	2	n/a
Wichita, KS	99	n/a	n/a	0.068	n/a	n/a
Wilmington, NC	45	6.8	19	0.067	n/a	n/a
Winston-Salem, NC	72	9.5	31	0.069	n/a	n/a
NAAQS[1]	150	15.0	35	0.075	9	0.15

Note: Data from exceptional events are included; Figures cover the Metropolitan Statistical Area (MSA); (1) National Ambient Air Quality Standards; ppm = parts per million; ug/m³ = micrograms per cubic meter; n/a not available
Concentrations: Particulate Matter 10 (coarse particulate)—highest second maximum 24-hour concentration; Particulate Matter 2.5 Wtd AM (fine particulate)—highest weighted annual mean concentration; Particulate Matter 2.5 24-Hour (fine particulate)—highest 98th percentile 24-hour concentration; Ozone—highest fourth daily maximum 8-hour concentration; Carbon Monoxide—highest second maximum non-overlapping 8-hour concentration; Lead—maximum running 3-month average
Source: U.S. Environmental Protection Agency, Air Quality Monitoring Information, "Air Quality Statistics by City, 2023"

Maximum Air Pollutant Concentrations: Nitrogen Dioxide and Sulfur Dioxide

Metro Area	Nitrogen Dioxide AM (ppb)	Nitrogen Dioxide 1-Hr (ppb)	Sulfur Dioxide AM (ppb)	Sulfur Dioxide 1-Hr (ppb)	Sulfur Dioxide 24-Hr (ppb)
Albuquerque, NM	8	43	n/a	n/a	n/a
Anchorage, AK	n/a	n/a	n/a	n/a	n/a
Ann Arbor, MI	n/a	n/a	n/a	n/a	n/a
Athens, GA	n/a	n/a	n/a	n/a	n/a
Atlanta, GA	15	48	n/a	5	n/a
Austin, TX	13	n/a	n/a	n/a	n/a
Baltimore, MD	15	45	n/a	4	n/a
Billings, MT	n/a	n/a	n/a	19	n/a
Boise City, ID	8	38	n/a	3	n/a
Boston, MA	11	45	n/a	5	n/a
Boulder, CO	n/a	n/a	n/a	n/a	n/a
Cape Coral, FL	n/a	n/a	n/a	n/a	n/a
Cedar Rapids, IA	n/a	n/a	n/a	10	n/a
Charleston, SC	7	n/a	n/a	6	n/a
Charlotte, NC	11	37	n/a	2	n/a
Chicago, IL	17	54	n/a	79	n/a
Cincinnati, OH	18	49	n/a	21	n/a
Clarksville, TN	n/a	n/a	n/a	n/a	n/a
Cleveland, OH	9	44	n/a	27	n/a
College Station, TX	n/a	n/a	n/a	29	n/a
Colorado Springs, CO	n/a	n/a	n/a	5	n/a
Columbia, MO	n/a	n/a	n/a	n/a	n/a
Columbia, SC	3	28	n/a	2	n/a
Columbus, OH	9	43	n/a	4	n/a
Dallas, TX	14	46	n/a	17	n/a
Davenport, IA	n/a	n/a	n/a	4	n/a
Denver, CO	24	65	n/a	6	n/a
Des Moines, IA	n/a	n/a	n/a	n/a	n/a
Detroit, MI	14	50	n/a	55	n/a
Durham, NC	n/a	n/a	n/a	3	n/a
El Paso, TX	15	57	n/a	6	n/a
Eugene, OR	n/a	n/a	n/a	n/a	n/a
Fargo, ND	4	n/a	n/a	3	n/a
Fort Collins, CO	n/a	n/a	n/a	n/a	n/a
Fort Wayne, IN	n/a	n/a	n/a	n/a	n/a
Fort Worth, TX	14	46	n/a	17	n/a
Gainesville, FL	n/a	n/a	n/a	n/a	n/a
Green Bay, WI	n/a	n/a	n/a	n/a	n/a
Greensboro, NC	n/a	n/a	n/a	4	n/a
Honolulu, HI	3	23	n/a	60	n/a
Houston, TX	18	60	n/a	13	n/a
Huntsville, AL	n/a	n/a	n/a	n/a	n/a
Indianapolis, IN	13	44	n/a	3	n/a
Jacksonville, FL	10	40	n/a	40	n/a
Kansas City, MO	11	45	n/a	6	n/a
Lafayette, LA	n/a	n/a	n/a	n/a	n/a
Las Vegas, NV	20	52	n/a	5	n/a
Lexington, KY	6	39	n/a	7	n/a
Lincoln, NE	n/a	n/a	n/a	n/a	n/a
Little Rock, AR	3	13	n/a	4	n/a
Los Angeles, CA	21	61	n/a	8	n/a
Louisville, KY	13	47	n/a	13	n/a
Madison, WI	n/a	n/a	n/a	n/a	n/a
Manchester, NH	n/a	n/a	n/a	1	n/a
McAllen, TX	n/a	n/a	n/a	n/a	n/a

Table continued on following page.

Metro Area	Nitrogen Dioxide AM (ppb)	Nitrogen Dioxide 1-Hr (ppb)	Sulfur Dioxide AM (ppb)	Sulfur Dioxide 1-Hr (ppb)	Sulfur Dioxide 24-Hr (ppb)
Memphis, TN	9	38	n/a	2	n/a
Miami, FL	15	53	n/a	2	n/a
Midland, TX	n/a	n/a	n/a	n/a	n/a
Milwaukee, WI	11	46	n/a	3	n/a
Minneapolis, MN	12	45	n/a	14	n/a
Nashville, TN	13	52	n/a	6	n/a
New Orleans, LA	8	39	n/a	52	n/a
New York, NY	19	60	n/a	5	n/a
Oklahoma City, OK	12	29	n/a	1	n/a
Omaha, NE	n/a	n/a	n/a	39	n/a
Orlando, FL	n/a	n/a	n/a	4	n/a
Philadelphia, PA	15	48	n/a	5	n/a
Phoenix, AZ	24	58	n/a	4	n/a
Pittsburgh, PA	9	38	n/a	65	n/a
Portland, OR	9	29	n/a	n/a	n/a
Providence, RI	13	35	n/a	3	n/a
Provo, UT	8	39	n/a	n/a	n/a
Raleigh, NC	9	36	n/a	2	n/a
Reno, NV	11	49	n/a	3	n/a
Richmond, VA	13	47	n/a	3	n/a
Rochester, MN	n/a	n/a	n/a	n/a	n/a
Sacramento, CA	9	33	n/a	2	n/a
Saint Louis, MO	10	43	n/a	38	n/a
Saint Paul, MN	12	45	n/a	14	n/a
Salem, OR	n/a	n/a	n/a	n/a	n/a
Salt Lake City, UT	16	57	n/a	5	n/a
San Antonio, TX	8	37	n/a	2	n/a
San Diego, CA	14	49	n/a	n/a	n/a
San Francisco, CA	11	102	n/a	18	n/a
San Jose, CA	13	44	n/a	2	n/a
Santa Rosa, CA	3	25	n/a	n/a	n/a
Savannah, GA	n/a	n/a	n/a	44	n/a
Seattle, WA	15	50	n/a	3	n/a
Sioux Falls, SD	5	40	n/a	1	n/a
Tampa, FL	9	36	n/a	48	n/a
Tucson, AZ	13	39	n/a	1	n/a
Tulsa, OK	6	33	n/a	3	n/a
Virginia Beach, VA	8	37	n/a	3	n/a
Washington, DC	16	47	n/a	3	n/a
Wichita, KS	6	23	n/a	2	n/a
Wilmington, NC	n/a	n/a	n/a	n/a	n/a
Winston-Salem, NC	7	40	n/a	2	n/a
NAAQS[1]	53	100	30	75	140

Note: Data from exceptional events are included; Figures cover the Metropolitan Statistical Area (MSA); (1) National Ambient Air Quality Standards; ppb = parts per billion; n/a not available
Concentrations: Nitrogen Dioxide AM—highest arithmetic mean concentration; Nitrogen Dioxide 1-Hr—highest 98th percentile 1-hour daily maximum concentration; Sulfur Dioxide AM—highest annual mean concentration; Sulfur Dioxide 1-Hr—highest 99th percentile 1-hour daily maximum concentration; Sulfur Dioxide 24-Hr—highest second maximum 24-hour concentration
Source: U.S. Environmental Protection Agency, Air Quality Monitoring Information, "Air Quality Statistics by City, 2023"

Appendix B: Metropolitan Area Definitions

Includes Metropolitan Statistical Areas (MSA) and Metropolitan Divisions (MD) referenced in this book.

Note: On July 21, 2023, the Office of Management and Budget (OMB) announced changes to metropolitan and micropolitan statistical area definitions. The current definitions are shown below.

Albuquerque, NM MSA
Bernalillo, Sandoval, Torrance, and Valencia Counties

Anchorage, AK MSA
Anchorage Municipality and Matanuska-Susitna Borough

Ann Arbor, MI MSA
Washtenaw County

Athens-Clarke County, GA MSA
Clarke, Madison, Oconee, and Oglethorpe Counties

Atlanta, GA

Atlanta-Sandy Springs-Roswell, GA MSA
Barrow, Bartow, Butts, Carroll, Cherokee, Clayton, Cobb, Coweta, Dawson, DeKalb, Douglas, Fayette, Forsyth, Fulton, Gwinnett, Haralson, Heard, Henry, Jasper, Lumpkin, Meriwether, Morgan, Newton, Paulding, Pickens, Pike, Rockdale, Spalding, and Walton Counties

Atlanta-Sandy Springs-Roswell, GA MD
Barrow, Butts, Carroll, Clayton, Coweta, Dawson, DeKalb, Douglas, Fayette, Forsyth, Fulton, Gwinnett, Heard, Henry, Jasper, Lumpkin, Meriwether, Morgan, Newton, Pickens, Pike, Rockdale, Spalding, and Walton Counties

Austin-Round Rock-San Marcos, TX MSA
Bastrop, Caldwell, Hays, Travis, and Williamson Counties

Baltimore-Columbia-Towson, MD MSA
Baltimore city; Anne Arundel, Baltimore, Carroll, Harford, Howard, and Queen Anne's Counties

Billings, MT MSA
Carbon, Stillwater, and Yellowstone Counties

Boise City, ID MSA
Previously Boise City-Nampa, ID MSA
Ada, Boise, Canyon, Gem, and Owyhee Counties

Boston, MA

Boston-Cambridge-Newton, MA-NH MSA
Essex, Middlesex, Norfolk, Plymouth, and Suffolk Counties, MA; Rockingham and Strafford Counties, NH

Boston, MA MD
Norfolk, Plymouth, and Suffolk Counties

Boulder, CO MSA
Boulder County

Cape Coral-Fort Myers, FL MSA
Lee County

Cedar Rapids, IA, MSA
Benton, Jones, and Linn Counties

Charleston-North Charleston, SC MSA
Berkeley, Charleston, and Dorchester Counties

Charlotte-Concord-Gastonia, NC-SC MSA
Anson, Cabarrus, Gaston, Iredell, Lincoln, Mecklenburg, Rowan, and Union Counties, NC; Chester, Lancaster, and York Counties, SC

Chicago, IL

Chicago-Naperville-Elgin, IL-IN MSA
Cook, DeKalb, DuPage, Grundy, Kane, Kendall, Lake, McHenry, and Will Counties, IL; Jasper, Lake, Newton, and Porter Counties, IN

Chicago-Naperville-Schaumburg, IL MD
Cook, DuPage, Grundy, McHenry, and Will Counties

Cincinnati, OH-KY-IN MSA
Brown, Butler, Clermont, Hamilton, and Warren Counties, OH; Boone, Bracken, Campbell, Gallatin, Grant, Kenton, and Pendleton County, KY; Dearborn, Franklin, and Ohio Counties, IN

Clarksville, TN-KY MSA
Montgomery and Stewart Counties, TN; Christian and Trigg Counties, KY

Cleveland, OH MSA
Ashtabula, Cuyahoga, Geauga, Lake, Lorain, and Medina Counties

College Station-Bryan, TX MSA
Brazos, Burleson, and Robertson Counties

Colorado Springs, CO MSA
El Paso and Teller Counties

Columbia, MO MSA
Boone, Cooper, and Howard Counties

Columbia, SC MSA
Calhoun, Fairfield, Kershaw, Lexington, Richland, and Saluda Counties

Columbus, OH MSA
Delaware, Fairfield, Franklin, Hocking, Licking, Madison, Morrow, Perry, Pickaway, and Union Counties

Dallas, TX

Dallas-Fort Worth-Arlington, TX MSA
Collin, Dallas, Denton, Ellis, Hunt, Johnson, Kaufman, Parker, Rockwall, Tarrant, and Wise Counties

Dallas-Plano-Irving, TX MD
Collin, Dallas, Denton, Ellis, Hunt, Kaufman, and Rockwall Counties

Davenport-Moline-Rock Island, IA-IL MSA
Scott County, IA; Henry, Mercer, and Rock Island Counties, IL

Denver-Aurora-Centennial, CO MSA
Adams, Arapahoe, Broomfield, Clear Creek, Denver, Douglas, Elbert, Gilpin, Jefferson, and Park Counties

Des Moines-West Des Moines, IA MSA
Dallas, Guthrie, Jasper, Madison, Polk, and Warren Counties

Detroit, MI

Detroit-Warren-Dearborn, MI MSA
Lapeer, Livingston, Macomb, Oakland, St. Clair, and Wayne Counties

Detroit-Dearborn-Livonia, MI MD
Wayne County

Durham-Chapel Hill, NC MSA
Chatham, Durham, Orange, and Person Counties

El Paso, TX MSA
El Paso and Hudspeth Counties

Eugene-Springfield, OR MSA
Lane County

Fargo, ND-MN MSA
Cass County, ND; Clay County, MN

Fort Collins-Loveland, CO MSA
Larimer County

Fort Wayne, IN MSA
Allen, Wells, and Whitley Counties

Fort Worth, TX

Dallas-Fort Worth-Arlington, TX MSA
Collin, Dallas, Denton, Ellis, Hunt, Johnson, Kaufman, Parker, Rockwall, Tarrant, and Wise Counties

Fort Worth-Arlington-Grapevine, TX MD
Johnson, Parker, Tarrant, and Wise Counties

Gainesville, FL MSA
Alachua, Gilchrist, and Levy Counties

Green Bay, WI MSA
Brown, Kewaunee, and Oconto Counties

Greensboro-High Point, NC MSA
Guilford, Randolph, and Rockingham Counties

Honolulu, HI
See Urban Honolulu, HI

Houston-Pasadena-The Woodlands, TX MSA
Austin, Brazoria, Chambers, Fort Bend, Galveston, Harris, Liberty, Montgomery, San Jacinto, and Waller Counties

Huntsville, AL MSA
Limestone and Madison Counties

Indianapolis-Carmel-Greenwood, IN MSA
Boone, Brown, Hamilton, Hancock, Hendricks, Johnson, Madison, Marion, Morgan, Shelby, and Tipton Counties

Jacksonville, FL MSA
Baker, Clay, Duval, Nassau, and St. Johns Counties

Kansas City, MO-KS MSA
Johnson, Leavenworth, Linn, Miami, and Wyandotte Counties, KS; Bates, Caldwell, Cass, Clay, Clinton, Jackson, Lafayette, Platte, and Ray Counties, MO

Lafayette, LA MSA
Acadia, Lafayette, St. Martin, and Vermilion Parishes

Las Vegas-Henderson-North Las Vegas, NV MSA
Clark County

Lexington-Fayette, KY MSA
Bourbon, Clark, Fayette, Jessamine, Scott, and Woodford Counties

Lincoln, NE MSA
Lancaster and Seward Counties

Little Rock-North Little Rock-Conway, AR MSA
Faulkner, Grant, Lonoke, Perry, Pulaski, and Saline Counties

Los Angeles, CA

Los Angeles-Long Beach-Anaheim, CA MSA
Los Angeles and Orange Counties

Los Angeles-Long Beach-Glendale, CA MD
Los Angeles County

Louisville/Jefferson County, KY-IN MSA
Clark, Floyd, Harrison, and Washington Counties, IN; Bullitt, Henry, Jefferson, Meade, Nelson, Oldham, Shelby, and Spencer Counties, KY

Madison, WI MSA
Columbia, Dane, Green, and Iowa Counties

Manchester-Nashua, NH MSA
Hillsborough County

McAllen-Edinburg-Mission, TX
Hidalgo County

Memphis, TN-AR-MS MSA
Fayette, Shelby and Tipton Counties, TN; Crittenden County, AR; Benton, DeSoto, Marshall, Tate and Tunica Counties, MS

Miami, FL

Miami-Fort Lauderdale-West Palm Beach, FL MSA
Broward, Miami-Dade, and Palm Beach Counties

Miami-Miami Beach-Kendall, FL MD
Miami-Dade County

Midland, TX MSA
Martin and Midland Counties

Milwaukee-Waukesha, WI MSA
Milwaukee, Ozaukee, Washington, and Waukesha Counties

Minneapolis-St. Paul-Bloomington, MN-WI MSA
Anoka, Carver, Chisago, Dakota, Hennepin, Isanti, Le Sueur, Mille Lacs, Ramsey, Scott, Sherburne, Washington, and Wright Counties, MN; Pierce and St. Croix Counties, WI

Nashville-Davidson–Murfreesboro–Franklin, TN MSA
Cannon, Cheatham, Davidson, Dickson, Hickman, Macon, Maury, Robertson, Rutherford, Smith, Sumner, Trousdale, Williamson, and Wilson Counties

New Orleans-Metarie, LA MSA
Jefferson, Orleans, Plaquemines, St. Bernard, St. Charles, St. James, and St. John the Baptist Parishes

New York, NY

New York-Newark-Jersey City, NY-NJ MSA
Bergen, Essex, Hudson, Hunterdon, Middlesex, Monmouth, Morris, Ocean, Passaic, Somerset, Sussex, and Union Counties, NJ; Bronx, Kings, Nassau, New York, Putnam, Queens, Richmond, Rockland, Suffolk, and Westchester Counties, NY

New York-Jersey City-White Plains, NY-NJ MD
Bergen, Hudson, and Passaic Counties, NJ; Bronx, Kings, New York, Putnam, Queens, Richmond, Rockland, and Westchester Counties, NY

Oklahoma City, OK MSA
Canadian, Cleveland, Grady, Lincoln, Logan, McClain, and Oklahoma Counties

Omaha, NE-IA MSA
Harrison, Mills, and Pottawattamie Counties, IA; Cass, Douglas, Sarpy, Saunders, and Washington Counties, NE

Orlando-Kissimmee-Sanford, FL MSA
Lake, Orange, Osceola, and Seminole Counties

Philadelphia, PA

Philadelphia-Camden-Wilmington, PA-NJ-DE-MD MSA
New Castle County, DE; Cecil County, MD; Burlington, Camden, Gloucester, and Salem Counties, NJ; Bucks, Chester, Delaware, Montgomery, and Philadelphia Counties, PA

Philadelphia, PA MD
Delaware and Philadelphia Counties

Phoenix-Mesa-Chandler, AZ MSA
Maricopa and Pinal Counties

Pittsburgh, PA MSA
Allegheny, Armstrong, Beaver, Butler, Fayette, Lawrence, Washington, and Westmoreland Counties

Portland-Vancouver-Hillsboro, OR-WA MSA
Clackamas, Columbia, Multnomah, Washington, and Yamhill Counties, OR; Clark and Skamania Counties, WA

Providence-Warwick, RI MSA
Bristol County, MA; Bristol, Kent, Newport, Providence, and Washington Counties, RI

Provo-Orem-Lehi, UT MSA
Juab and Utah Counties

Raleigh-Cary, NC MSA
Franklin, Johnston, and Wake Counties

Reno, NV MSA
Lyon, Storey, and Washoe Counties

Richmond, VA MSA
Amelia, Charles City, Chesterfield, Dinwiddie, Goochland, Hanover, Henrico, King and Queen, King William, New Kent, Powhatan, Prince George, and Sussex Counties; Colonial Heights, Hopewell, Petersburg, and Richmond Cities

Rochester, MN MSA
Dodge, Fillmore, Olmsted, and Wabasha Counties

Sacramento-Roseville-Folsom, CA MSA
El Dorado, Placer, Sacramento, and Yolo Counties

Saint Louis, MO-IL MSA
Bond, Calhoun, Clinton, Jersey, Macoupin, Madison, Monroe, and St. Clair Counties, IL; St. Louis city; Crawford (part–Sullivan city), Franklin, Jefferson, Lincoln, St. Charles, St. Louis, and Warren Counties, MO

Saint Paul, MN
See Minneapolis-St. Paul-Bloomington, MN-WI MSA

Salem, OR MSA
Marion and Polk Counties

Salt Lake City-Murray, UT MSA
Salt Lake and Tooele Counties

San Antonio-New Braunfels, TX MSA
Atascosa, Bandera, Bexar, Comal, Guadalupe, Kendall, Medina, and Wilson Counties

San Diego-Chula Vista-Carlsbad, CA MSA
San Diego County

San Francisco, CA

San Francisco-Oakland-Fremont, CA MSA
Alameda, Contra Costa, Marin, San Francisco, and San Mateo Counties

San Francisco-San Mateo-Redwood City, CA MD
San Francisco and San Mateo Counties

San Jose-Sunnyvale-Santa Clara, CA MSA
San Benito and Santa Clara Counties

Santa Rosa-Petaluma, CA MSA
Sonoma County

Savannah, GA MSA
Bryan, Chatham, and Effingham Counties

Seattle, WA

Seattle-Tacoma-Bellevue, WA MSA
King, Pierce, and Snohomish Counties

Seattle-Bellevue-Kent, WA MD
King County

Sioux Falls, SD-MN MSA
Lincoln, McCook, Minnehaha, and Turner Counties, SD; Rock County, MN

Tampa, FL

Tampa-St. Petersburg-Clearwater, FL MSA
Hernando, Hillsborough, Pasco, and Pinellas Counties

Tampa, FL MD
Hernando, Hillsborough, and Pasco Counties

Tucson, AZ MSA
Pima County

Tulsa, OK MSA
Creek, Okmulgee, Osage, Pawnee, Rogers, Tulsa, and Wagoner Counties

Urban Honolulu, HI MSA
Honolulu County

Virginia Beach-Chesapeake-Norfolk, VA-NC MSA
Camden, Currituck, and Gates Counties, NC; Chesapeake, Hampton, Newport News, Norfolk, Poquoson, Portsmouth, Suffolk, Virginia Beach and Williamsburg cities, VA; Gloucester, Isle of Wight, James City, Mathews, Surry, and York Counties, VA

Washington, DC

Washington-Arlington-Alexandria, DC-VA-MD-WV MSA
District of Columbia; Calvert, Charles, Frederick, Montgomery, and Prince George's Counties, MD; Alexandria, Fairfax, Falls Church, Fredericksburg, Manassas, and Manassas Park cities, VA; Arlington, Clarke, Culpepper, Fairfax, Fauquier, Loudoun, Prince William, Rappahannock, Spotsylvania, Stafford, and Warren Counties, VA; Jefferson County, WV

Washington, DC-MD MD
District of Columbia; Charles and Prince George's Counties, MD

Wichita, KS MSA
Butler, Harvey, Sedgwick, and Sumner Counties

Wilmington, NC MSA
Brunswick, New Hanover and Pender Counties

Winston-Salem, NC MSA
Davidson, Davie, Forsyth, Stokes, and Yadkin Counties

Appendix C: Government Type and Primary County

This appendix includes the government structure of each place included in this book. It also includes the county or county equivalent in which each place is located. If a place spans more than one county, the county in which the majority of the population resides is shown.

Albuquerque, NM
Government Type: City
County: Bernalillo

Anchorage, AK
Government Type: Municipality
Borough: Anchorage

Ann Arbor, MI
Government Type: City
County: Washtenaw

Athens, GA
Government Type: Consolidated city-county
County: Clarke

Atlanta, GA
Government Type: City
County: Fulton

Austin, TX
Government Type: City
County: Travis

Baltimore, MD
Government Type: Independent city

Baton Rouge, LA
Government Type: Consolidated city-parish
Parish: East Baton Rouge

Billings, MT
Government Type: City
County: Yellowstone

Boise City, ID
Government Type: City
County: Ada

Boston, MA
Government Type: City
County: Suffolk

Boulder, CO
Government Type: City
County: Boulder

Cape Coral, FL
Government Type: City
County: Lee

Cedar Rapids, IA
Government Type: City
County: Linn

Charleston, SC
Government Type: City
County: Charleston

Charlotte, NC
Government Type: City
County: Mecklenburg

Chicago, IL
Government Type: City
County: Cook

Cincinnati, OH
Government Type: City
County: Hamilton

Clarksville, TN
Government Type: City
County: Montgomery

Cleveland, OH
Government Type: City
County: Cuyahoga

College Station, TX
Government Type: City
County: Brazos

Colorado Springs, CO
Government Type: City
County: El Paso

Columbia, MO
Government Type: City
County: Boone

Columbia, SC
Government Type: City
County: Richland

Columbus, OH
Government Type: City
County: Franklin

Dallas, TX
Government Type: City
County: Dallas

Davenport, IA
Government Type: City
County: Scott

Denver, CO
Government Type: City
County: Denver

Des Moines, IA
Government Type: City
County: Polk

Detroit, MI
Government Type: City
County: Wayne

Durham, NC
Government Type: City
County: Durham

El Paso, TX
Government Type: City
County: El Paso

Eugene, OR
Government Type: City
County: Lane

Fargo, ND
Government Type: City
County: Cass

Fort Collins, CO
Government Type: City
County: Larimer

Fort Wayne, IN
Government Type: City
County: Allen

Fort Worth, TX
Government Type: City
County: Tarrant

Gainesville, FL
Government Type: City
County: Alachua

Green Bay, WI
Government Type: City
County: Brown

Greensboro, NC
Government Type: City
County: Guilford

Honolulu, HI
Government Type: Census Designated Place (CDP)
County: Honolulu

Houston, TX
Government Type: City
County: Harris

Huntsville, AL
Government Type: City
County: Madison

Indianapolis, IN
Government Type: City
County: Marion

Jacksonville, FL
Government Type: City
County: Duval

Kansas City, MO
Government Type: City
County: Jackson

Lafayette, LA
Government Type: City
Parish: Lafayette

Las Vegas, NV
Government Type: City
County: Clark

Lexington, KY
Government Type: Consolidated city-county
County: Fayette

Lincoln, NE
Government Type: City
County: Lancaster

Little Rock, AR
Government Type: City
County: Pulaski

Los Angeles, CA
Government Type: City
County: Los Angeles

Louisville, KY
Government Type: Consolidated city-county
County: Jefferson

Madison, WI
Government Type: City
County: Dane

Manchester, NH
Government Type: City
County: Hillsborough

McAllen, TX
Government Type: City
County: Hidalgo

Memphis, TN
Government Type: City
County: Shelby

Miami, FL
Government Type: City
County: Miami-Dade

Midland, TX
Government Type: City
County: Midland

Milwaukee, WI
Government Type: City
County: Milwaukee

Minneapolis, MN
Government Type: City
County: Hennepin

Nashville, TN
Government Type: Consolidated city-county
County: Davidson

New Orleans, LA
Government Type: City
Parish: Orleans

New York, NY
Government Type: City
Counties: Bronx; Kings; New York; Queens; Staten Island

Oklahoma City, OK
Government Type: City
County: Oklahoma

Omaha, NE
Government Type: City
County: Douglas

Orlando, FL
Government Type: City
County: Orange

Philadelphia, PA
Government Type: City
County: Philadelphia

Phoenix, AZ
Government Type: City
County: Maricopa

Pittsburgh, PA
Government Type: City
County: Allegheny

Portland, OR
Government Type: City
County: Multnomah

Providence, RI
Government Type: City
County: Providence

Provo, UT
Government Type: City
County: Utah

Raleigh, NC
Government Type: City
County: Wake

Reno, NV
Government Type: City
County: Washoe

Richmond, VA
Government Type: Independent city

Riverside, CA
Government Type: City
County: Riverside

Rochester, MN
Government Type: City
County: Olmsted

Rochester, NY
Government Type: City
County: Monroe

Sacramento, CA
Government Type: City
County: Sacramento

Saint Louis, MO
Government Type: Independent city

Saint Paul, MN
Government Type: City
County: Ramsey

Salem, OR
Government Type: City
County: Marion

Salt Lake City, UT
Government Type: City
County: Salt Lake

San Antonio, TX
Government Type: City
County: Bexar

San Diego, CA
Government Type: City
County: San Diego

San Francisco, CA
Government Type: City
County: San Francisco

San Jose, CA
Government Type: City
County: Santa Clara

Santa Rosa, CA
Government Type: City
County: Sonoma

Savannah, GA
Government Type: City
County: Chatham

Seattle, WA
Government Type: City
County: King

Sioux Falls, SD
Government Type: City
County: Minnehaha

Tampa, FL
Government Type: City
County: Hillsborough

Tucson, AZ
Government Type: City
County: Pima

Tulsa, OK
Government Type: City
County: Tulsa

Virginia Beach, VA
Government Type: Independent city

Washington, DC
Government Type: City
County: District of Columbia

Wichita, KS
Government Type: City
County: Sedgwick

Wilmington, NC
Government Type: City
County: New Hanover

Winston-Salem, NC
Government Type: City
County: Forsyth

Appendix D: Chambers of Commerce

Albuquerque, NM
Albuquerque Chamber of Commerce
P.O. Box 25100
Albuquerque, NM 87125
Phone: (505) 764-3700
Fax: (505) 764-3714
www.abqchamber.com

Albuquerque Economic Development Dept
851 University Blvd SE, Suite 203
Albuquerque, NM 87106
Phone: (505) 246-6200
Fax: (505) 246-6219
www.cabq.gov/econdev

Anchorage, AK
Anchorage Chamber of Commerce
1016 W Sixth Avenue, Suite 303
Anchorage, AK 99501
Phone: (907) 272-2401
Fax: (907) 272-4117
www.anchoragechamber.org

Anchorage Economic Development Department
900 W 5th Avenue, Suite 300
Anchorage, AK 99501
Phone: (907) 258-3700
Fax: (907) 258-6646
aedcweb.com

Ann Arbor, MI
Ann Arbor Area Chamber of Commerce
115 West Huron, 3rd Floor
Ann Arbor, MI 48104
Phone: (734) 665-4433
Fax: (734) 665-4191
www.annarborchamber.org

Ann Arbor Economic Development Department
201 S Division, Suite 430
Ann Arbor, MI 48104
Phone: (734) 761-9317
www.annarborspark.org

Athens, GA
Athens Area Chamber of Commerce
246 W Hancock Avenue
Athens, GA 30601
Phone: (706) 549-6800
Fax: (706) 549-5636
www.aacoc.org

Athens-Clarke County Economic Development Department
246 W. Hancock Avenue
Athens, GA 30601
Phone: (706) 613-3233
Fax: (706) 613-3812
www.athensbusiness.org

Atlanta, GA
Metro Atlanta Chamber of Commerce
235 Andrew Young International Blvd NW
Atlanta, GA 30303
Phone: (404) 880-9000
Fax: (404) 586-8464
www.metroatlantachamber.com

Austin, TX
Greater Austin Chamber of Commerce
210 Barton Springs Road, Suite 400
Austin, TX 78704
Phone: (512) 478-9383
Fax: (512) 478-6389
www.austin-chamber.org

Baltimore, MD
Baltimore City Chamber of Commerce
P.O. Box 43121
Baltimore, MD 21236
443-860-2020
baltimorecitychamber.org

Baltimore County Chamber of Commerce
102 W. Pennsylvania Avenue, Suite 305
Towson, MD, 21204
Phone: (410) 825-6200
Fax: (410) 821-9901
www.baltcountychamber.com

Billings, MT
Billings Chamber of Commerce
815 S. 27th St
Billings, MT 59101
Phone: (406) 245-4111
Fax: (406) 245-7333
www.billingschamber.com

Boise City, ID
Boise Metro Chamber of Commerce
250 S. 5th Street, Suite 800
Boise City, ID 83701
Phone: (208) 472-5200
Fax: (208) 472-5201
www.boisechamber.org

Boston, MA
Greater Boston Chamber of Commerce
265 Franklin Street, 12th Floor
Boston, MA 02110
Phone: (617) 227-4500
Fax: (617) 227-7505
www.bostonchamber.com

Boulder, CO
Boulder Chamber of Commerce
2440 Pearl Street
Boulder, CO 80302
Phone: (303) 442-1044
Fax: (303) 938-8837
www.boulderchamber.com

Cape Coral, FL
Chamber of Commerce of Cape Coral
2051 Cape Coral Parkway East
Cape Coral, FL 33904
Phone: (239) 549-6900
www.capecoralchamber.com

Cedar Rapids, IA
Cedar Rapids Chamber of Commerce
424 First Avenue NE
Cedar Rapids, IA 52401
Phone: (319) 398-5317
Fax: (319) 398-5228
www.cedarrapids.org

Cedar Rapids Economic Development
50 Second Avenue Bridge, Sixth Floor
Cedar Rapids, IA 52401-1256
Phone: (319) 286-5041
Fax: (319) 286-5141
www.cedar-rapids.org

Charleston, SC
Charleston Metro Chamber of Commerce
P.O. Box 975
Charleston, SC 29402
Phone: (843) 577-2510
www.charlestonchamber.net

Charlotte, NC
Charlotte Chamber of Commerce
330 S Tryon Street
P.O. Box 32785
Charlotte, NC 28232
Phone: (704) 378-1300
Fax: (704) 374-1903
www.charlottechamber.com

Charlotte Regional Partnership
1001 Morehead Square Drive, Suite 200
Charlotte, NC 28203
Phone: (704) 347-8942
Fax: (704) 347-8981
www.charlotteusa.com

Chicago, IL
Chicagoland Chamber of Commerce
200 E Randolph Street, Suite 2200
Chicago, IL 60601-6436
Phone: (312) 494-6700
Fax: (312) 861-0660
www.chicagolandchamber.org

City of Chicago Department of Planning and Development
City Hall, Room 1000
121 North La Salle Street
Chicago, IL 60602
Phone: (312) 744-4190
Fax: (312) 744-2271
www.cityofchicago.org/city/en/depts/dcd.html

Cincinnati, OH
Cincinnati USA Regional Chamber
3 East 4th Street, Suite 200
Cincinnati, Ohio 45202
Phone: (513) 579-3111
www.cincinnatichamber.com

Clarksville, TN
Clarksville Area Chamber of Commerce
25 Jefferson Street, Suite 300
Clarksville, TN 37040
Phone: (931) 647-2331
www.clarksvillechamber.com

Cleveland, OH
Greater Cleveland Partnership
1240 Huron Rd. E, Suite 300
Cleveland, OH 44115
Phone: (216) 621-3300
www.gcpartnership.com

Appendix D: Chambers of Commerce

College Station, TX
Bryan-College Station Chamber of Commerce
4001 East 29th St, Suite 175
Bryan, TX 77802
Phone: (979) 260-5200
www.bcschamber.org

Colorado Springs, CO
Colorado Springs Chamber and EDC
102 South Tejon Street, Suite 430
Colorado Springs, CO 80903
Phone: (719) 471-8183
coloradospringschamberedc.com

Columbia, MO
Columbia Chamber of Commerce
300 South Providence Rd.
P.O. Box 1016
Columbia, MO 65205-1016
Phone: (573) 874-1132
Fax: (573) 443-3986
www.columbiamochamber.com

Columbia, SC
The Columbia Chamber
930 Richland Street
Columbia, SC 29201
Phone: (803) 733-1110
Fax: (803) 733-1113
www.columbiachamber.com

Columbus, OH
Greater Columbus Chamber
37 North High Street
Columbus, OH 43215
Phone: (614) 221-1321
Fax: (614) 221-1408
www.columbus.org

Dallas, TX
City of Dallas Economic Development Department
1500 Marilla Street, 5C South
Dallas, TX 75201
Phone: (214) 670-1685
Fax: (214) 670-0158
www.dallas-edd.org

Greater Dallas Chamber of Commerce
700 North Pearl Street, Suite1200
Dallas, TX 75201
Phone: (214) 746-6600
Fax: (214) 746-6799
www.dallaschamber.org

Davenport, IA
Quad Cities Chamber
331 W. 3rd Street, Suite 100
Davenport, IA 52801
Phone: (563) 322-1706
quadcitieschamber.com

Denver, CO
Denver Metro Chamber of Commerce
1445 Market Street
Denver, CO 80202
Phone: (303) 534-8500
Fax: (303) 534-3200
www.denverchamber.org

Downtown Denver Partnership
511 16th Street, Suite 200
Denver, CO 80202
Phone: (303) 534-6161
Fax: (303) 534-2803
www.downtowndenver.com

Des Moines, IA
Des Moines Downtown Chamber
301 Grand Ave
Des Moines, IA 50309
Phone: (515) 309-3229
desmoinesdowntownchamber.com

Greater Des Moines Partnership
700 Locust Street, Suite 100
Des Moines, IA 50309
Phone: (515) 286-4950
Fax: (515) 286-4974
www.desmoinesmetro.com

Durham, NC
Durham Chamber of Commerce
P.O. Box 3829
Durham, NC 27702
Phone: (919) 682-2133
Fax: (919) 688-8351
www.durhamchamber.org

North Carolina Institute of Minority Economic Development
114 W Parish Street
Durham, NC 27701
Phone: (919) 956-8889
Fax: (919) 688-7668
www.ncimed.com

El Paso, TX
City of El Paso Department of Economic Development
2 Civic Center Plaza
El Paso, TX 79901
Phone: (915) 541-4000
Fax: (915) 541-1316
www.elpasotexas.gov

Greater El Paso Chamber of Commerce
10 Civic Center Plaza
El Paso, TX 79901
Phone: (915) 534-0500
Fax: (915) 534-0510
www.elpaso.org

Eugene, OR
Eugene Area Chamber of Commerce
1401 Williamette Street
Eugene, OR 97401
Phone: (541) 484-1314
Fax: (541) 484-4942
www.eugenechamber.com

Fargo, ND
Chamber of Commerce of Fargo Moorhead
202 First Avenue North
Fargo, ND 56560
Phone: (218) 233-1100
Fax: (218) 233-1200
www.fmchamber.com

Greater Fargo-Moorhead Economic Development Corporation
51 Broadway, Suite 500
Fargo, ND 58102
Phone: (701) 364-1900
Fax: (701) 293-7819
www.gfmedc.com

Fort Collins, CO
Fort Collins Chamber of Commerce
225 South Meldrum
Fort Collins, CO 80521
Phone: (970) 482-3746
Fax: (970) 482-3774
fortcollinschamber.com

Fort Wayne, IN
City of Fort Wayne Economic Development
1 Main Street
Fort Wayne, IN 46802
Phone: (260) 427-1111
Fax: (260) 427-1375
www.cityoffortwayne.org

Greater Fort Wayne Chamber of Commerce
826 Ewing Street
Fort Wayne, IN 46802
Phone: (260) 424-1435
Fax: (260) 426-7232
www.fwchamber.org

Fort Worth, TX
Fort Worth Chamber of Commerce
777 Taylor Street, Suite 900
Fort Worth, TX 76102-4997
Phone: (817) 336-2491
Fax: (817) 877-4034
www.fortworthchamber.com

City of Fort Worth Economic Development
City Hall
900 Monroe Street, Suite 301
Fort Worth, TX 76102
Phone: (817) 392-6103
Fax: (817) 392-2431
www.fortworthgov.org

Gainesville, FL
Greater Gainesville Chamber
300 East University Avenue, Suite 100
Gainesville, FL 32601
Phone: (352) 334-7100
Fax: (352) 334-7141
www.gainesvillechamber.com

Green Bay, WI
Greater Green Bay Chamber
300 N. Broadway, Suite 3A
Green Bay, WI 54303
Phone: (920) 593-3400
www.greatergbc.org

Greensboro, NC
Greensboro Chamber of Commerce
111 W. February One Place
Greensboro, NC 27401
Phone: (336) 387-8301
greensboro.org

Honolulu, HI
The Chamber of Commerce of Hawaii
1132 Bishop Street, Suite 402
Honolulu, HI 96813
Phone: (808) 545-4300
Fax: (808) 545-4369
www.cochawaii.com

Houston, TX
Greater Houston Partnership
1200 Smith Street, Suite 700
Houston, TX 77002-4400
Phone: (713) 844-3600
Fax: (713) 844-0200
www.houston.org

Huntsville, AL
Chamber of Commerce of
Huntsville/Madison County
225 Church Street
Huntsville, AL 35801
Phone: (256) 535-2000
www.huntsvillealabamausa.com

Indianapolis, IN
Greater Indianapolis Chamber of Commerce
111 Monument Circle, Suite 1950
Indianapolis, IN 46204
Phone: (317) 464-2222
Fax: (317) 464-2217
www.indychamber.com

Jacksonville, FL
Jacksonville Chamber of Commerce
3 Independent Drive
Jacksonville, FL 32202
Phone: (904) 366-6600
Fax: (904) 632-0617
www.myjaxchamber.com

Kansas City, MO
Greater Kansas City Chamber of Commerce
2600 Commerce Tower
911 Main Street
Kansas City, MO 64105
Phone: (816) 221-2424
Fax: (816) 221-7440
www.kcchamber.com

Kansas City Area Development Council
2600 Commerce Tower
911 Main Street
Kansas City, MO 64105
Phone: (816) 221-2121
www.thinkkc.com

Lafayette, LA
Greater Lafayette Chamber of Commerce
804 East Saint Mary Blvd.
Lafayette, LA 70503
Phone: (337) 233-2705
Fax: (337) 234-8671
www.lafchamber.org

Las Vegas, NV
Las Vegas Chamber of Commerce
6671 Las Vegas Blvd South, Suite 300
Las Vegas, NV 89119
Phone: (702) 735-1616
Fax: (702) 735-0406
www.lvchamber.org

Las Vegas Office of Business Development
400 Stewart Avenue
City Hall
Las Vegas, NV 89101
Phone: (702) 229-6011
Fax: (702) 385-3128
www.lasvegasnevada.gov

Lexington, KY
Greater Lexington Chamber of Commerce
330 East Main Street, Suite 100
Lexington, KY 40507
Phone: (859) 254-4447
Fax: (859) 233-3304
www.commercelexington.com

Lexington Downtown Development
Authority
101 East Vine Street, Suite 500
Lexington, KY 40507
Phone: (859) 425-2296
Fax: (859) 425-2292
www.lexingtondda.com

Lincoln, NE
Lincoln Chamber of Commerce
1135 M Street, Suite 200
Lincoln, NE 68508
Phone: (402) 436-2350
www.lcoc.com

Little Rock, AR
Little Rock Regional Chamber
One Chamber Plaza
Little Rock, AR 72201
Phone: (501) 374-2001
Fax: (501) 374-6018
www.littlerockchamber.com

Los Angeles, CA
Los Angeles Area Chamber of Commerce
350 South Bixel Street
Los Angeles, CA 90017
Phone: (213) 580-7500
Fax: (213) 580-7511
www.lachamber.org

Los Angeles County Economic
Development Corporation
444 South Flower Street, 34th Floor
Los Angeles, CA 90071
Phone: (213) 622-4300
Fax: (213) 622-7100
www.laedc.org

Louisville, KY
The Greater Louisville Chamber of
Commerce
614 West Main Street, Suite 6000
Louisville, KY 40202
Phone: (502) 625-0000
Fax: (502) 625-0010
www.greaterlouisville.com

Madison, WI
Greater Madison Chamber of Commerce
615 East Washington Avenue
P.O. Box 71
Madison, WI 53701-0071
Phone: (608) 256-8348
Fax: (608) 256-0333
www.greatermadisonchamber.com

Manchester, NH
Greater Manchester Chamber of Commerce
889 Elm Street
Manchester, NH 03101
Phone: (603) 666-6600
Fax: (603) 626-0910
www.manchester-chamber.org

Manchester Economic Development Office
One City Hall Plaza
Manchester, NH 03101
Phone: (603) 624-6505
Fax: (603) 624-6308
www.yourmanchesternh.com

McAllen, TX
McAllen Chamber of Commerce
1200 Ash Avenue
McAllen, TX 78501
Phone: (956) 682-2871
Fax: (956) 687-2917
mcallenchamber.com

Memphis, TN
Greater Memphis Chamber
22 North Front Street, Suite 200
Memphis, TN 38103-2100
Phone: (901) 543-3500
memphischamber.com

Miami, FL
Greater Miami Chamber of Commerce
1601 Biscayne Boulevard
Miami, FL 33132-1260
Phone: (305) 350-7700
Fax: (305) 374-6902
www.miamichamber.com

The Beacon Council
80 Southwest 8th Street, Suite 2400
Miami, FL 33130
Phone: (305) 579-1300
Fax: (305) 375-0271
www.beaconcouncil.com

Midland, TX
Midland Chamber of Commerce
303 W. Wall Street, Suite 200
Midland, TX 79701
Phone: (432) 683-3381
www.midlandtxchamber.com

Milwaukee, WI
Greater Milwaukee Chamber of Commerce
6815 W. Capitol Drive, Suite 300
Milwaukee, WI 53216
Phone: (414) 465-2422
www.gmcofc.org

Minneapolis, MN
Minneapolis Regional Chamber
81 South Ninth Street, Suite 200
Minneapolis, MN 55402
Phone: (612) 370-9100
Fax: (612) 370-9195
www.minneapolischamber.org

Minneapolis Community Development
Agency
Crown Roller Mill
105 5th Avenue South, Suite 200
Minneapolis, MN 55401
Phone: (612) 673-5095
Fax: (612) 673-5100
www.ci.minneapolis.mn.us

Nashville, TN
Nashville Area Chamber of Commerce
211 Commerce Street, Suite 100
Nashville, TN 37201
Phone: (615) 743-3000
Fax: (615) 256-3074
www.nashvillechamber.com

TVA Economic Development
400 West Summit Hill Drive
Knoxville TN 37902
Phone: (865) 632-2101
www.tvaed.com

New Orleans, LA
New Orleans Chamber of Commerce
1515 Poydras Street, Suite 1010
New Orleans, LA 70112
Phone: (504) 799-4260
Fax: (504) 799-4259
www.neworleanschamber.org

New York, NY
New York City Economic Development
Corporation
110 William Street
New York, NY 10038
Phone: (212) 619-5000
www.nycedc.com

The Partnership for New York City
One Battery Park Plaza
5th Floor
New York, NY 10004
Phone: (212) 493-7400
Fax: (212) 344-3344
www.pfnyc.org

Oklahoma City, OK
Greater Oklahoma City Chamber of
Commerce
123 Park Avenue
Oklahoma City, OK 73102
Phone: (405) 297-8900
Fax: (405) 297-8916
www.okcchamber.com

Omaha, NE
Omaha Chamber of Commerce
1301 Harney Street
Omaha, NE 68102
Phone: (402) 346-5000
Fax: (402) 346-7050
www.omahachamber.org

Orlando, FL
Metro Orlando Economic Development
Commission of Mid-Florida
East Pine Street, Suite 900
FL 32801
(07) 422-7159
425.6428
edc.com

Orlando Regional Chamber of Commerce
75 South Ivanhoe Boulevard
P.O. Box 1234
Orlando, FL 32802
Phone: (407) 425-1234
Fax: (407) 839-5020
www.orlando.org

Philadelphia, PA
Greater Philadelphia Chamber of
Commerce
200 South Broad Street, Suite 700
Philadelphia, PA 19102
Phone: (215) 545-1234
Fax: (215) 790-3600
www.greaterphilachamber.com

Phoenix, AZ
Greater Phoenix Chamber of Commerce
201 North Central Avenue, 27th Floor
Phoenix, AZ 85073
Phone: (602) 495-2195
Fax: (602) 495-8913
www.phoenixchamber.com

Greater Phoenix Economic Council
2 North Central Avenue, Suite 2500
Phoenix, AZ 85004
Phone: (602) 256-7700
Fax: (602) 256-7744
www.gpec.org

Pittsburgh, PA
Allegheny County Industrial Development
Authority
425 6th Avenue, Suite 800
Pittsburgh, PA 15219
Phone: (412) 350-1067
Fax: (412) 642-2217
www.alleghenycounty.us

Greater Pittsburgh Chamber of Commerce
425 6th Avenue, 12th Floor
Pittsburgh, PA 15219
Phone: (412) 392-4500
Fax: (412) 392-4520
www.alleghenyconference.org

Portland, OR
Portland Business Alliance
200 SW Market Street, Suite 1770
Portland, OR 97201
Phone: (503) 224-8684
Fax: (503) 323-9186
www.portlandalliance.com

Providence, RI
Greater Providence Chamber of Commerce
30 Exchange Terrace, Fourth Floor
Providence, RI 02903
Phone: (401) 521-5000
Fax: (401) 351-2090
www.provchamber.com

Rhode Island Economic Development
Corporation
Providence City Hall
25 Dorrance Street
Providence, RI 02903
Phone: (401) 421-7740
Fax: (401) 751-0203
www.providenceri.com

Provo, UT
Provo-Orem Chamber of Commerce
51 South University Avenue, Suite 215
Provo, UT 84601
Phone: (801) 851-2555
Fax: (801) 851-2557
www.thechamber.org

Raleigh, NC
Greater Raleigh Chamber of Commerce
800 South Salisbury Street
Raleigh, NC 27601-2978
Phone: (919) 664-7000
Fax: (919) 664-7099
www.raleighchamber.org

Reno, NV
Reno + Sparks Chamber of Commerce
449 S. Virginia Street, 2nd Floor
Reno, NV 89501
Phone: (775) 636-9550
www.thechambernv.org

Richmond, VA
Greater Richmond Chamber
600 East Main Street, Suite 700
Richmond, VA 23219
Phone: (804) 648-1234
www.grcc.com

Greater Richmond Partnership
901 East Byrd Street, Suite 801
Richmond, VA 23219-4070
Phone: (804) 643-3227
Fax: (804) 343-7167
www.grpva.com

Rochester, MN
Rochester Area Chamber of Commerce
220 South Broadway, Suite 100
Rochester, MN 55904
Phone: (507) 288-1122
www.rochestermnchamber.com

Sacramento, CA
Sacramento Metro Chamber
One Capitol Mall, Suite 700
Sacramento, CA 95814
Phone: (916) 552-6800
metrochamber.org

Saint Louis, MO
St. Louis Regional Chamber
One Metropolitan Square, Suite 1300
St. Louis, MO 63102
Phone: (314) 231-5555
www.stlregionalchamber.com

Saint Paul, OR
St. Paul Area Chamber
401 Robert Street N, Suite 150
St. Paul, MN 55101
Phone: (651) 223-5000
www.stpaulchamber.com

Salem, OR
Salem Area Chamber of Commerce
1110 Commercial Street NE
Salem, OR 97301
Phone: (503) 581-1466
www.salemchamber.org

Salt Lake City, UT
Salt Lake Chamber
175 E. University Blvd. (400 S), Suite 600
Salt Lake City, UT 84111
Phone: (801) 364-3631
www.slchamber.com

San Antonio, TX
The Greater San Antonio Chamber of Commerce
602 E. Commerce Street
San Antonio, TX 78205
Phone: (210) 229-2100
Fax: (210) 229-1600
www.sachamber.org

San Antonio Economic Development Department
P.O. Box 839966
San Antonio, TX 78283-3966
Phone: (210) 207-8080
Fax: (210) 207-8151
www.sanantonio.gov/edd

San Diego, CA
San Diego Economic Development Corp.
401 B Street, Suite 1100
San Diego, CA 92101
Phone: (619) 234-8484
Fax: (619) 234-1935
www.sandiegobusiness.org

San Diego Regional Chamber of Commerce
402 West Broadway, Suite 1000
San Diego, CA 92101-3585
Phone: (619) 544-1300
Fax: (619) 744-7481
www.sdchamber.org

San Francisco, CA
San Francisco Chamber of Commerce
235 Montgomery Street, 12th Floor
San Francisco, CA 94104
Phone: (415) 392-4520
Fax: (415) 392-0485
www.sfchamber.com

San Jose, CA
Office of Economic Development
60 South Market Street, Suite 470
San Jose, CA 95113
Phone: (408) 277-5880
Fax: (408) 277-3615
www.sba.gov

The Silicon Valley Organization
101 W Santa Clara Street
San Jose, CA 95113
Phone: (408) 291-5250
www.thesvo.com

Santa Rosa, CA
Santa Rosa Chamber of Commerce
1260 North Dutton Avenue, Suite 272
Santa Rosa, CA 95401
Phone: (707) 545-1414
www.santarosachamber.com

Savannah, GA
Savannah Chamber of Commerce
101 E. Bay Street
Savannah, GA 31402
Phone: (912) 644-6400
Fax: (912) 644-6499
www.savannahchamber.com

Seattle, WA
Greater Seattle Chamber of Commerce
1301 Fifth Avenue, Suite 2500
Seattle, WA 98101
Phone: (206) 389-7200
Fax: (206) 389-7288
www.seattlechamber.com

Sioux Falls, SD
Sioux Falls Area Chamber of Commerce
200 N. Phillips Avenue, Suite 102
Sioux Falls, SD 57104
Phone: (605) 336-1620
Fax: (605) 336-6499
www.siouxfallschamber.com

Tampa, FL
Greater Tampa Chamber of Commerce
P.O. Box 420
Tampa, FL 33601-0420
Phone: (813) 276-9401
Fax: (813) 229-7855
www.tampachamber.com

Tucson, AZ
Tucson Metro Chamber
212 E. Broadway Blvd
Tucson, AZ 85701
Phone: (520) 792-1212
tucsonchamber.org

Tulsa, OK
Tulsa Regional Chamber
One West Third Street, Suite 100
Tulsa, OK 74103
Phone: (918) 585-1201
www.tulsachamber.com

Virginia Beach, VA
Hampton Roads Chamber of Commerce
500 East Main Street, Suite 700
Virginia Beach, VA 23510
Phone: (757) 664-2531
www.hamptonroadschamber.com

Washington, DC
District of Columbia Chamber of Commerce
1213 K Street NW
Washington, DC 20005
Phone: (202) 347-7201
Fax: (202) 638-6762
www.dcchamber.org

District of Columbia Office of Planning and Economic Development
J.A. Wilson Building
1350 Pennsylvania Ave NW, Suite 317
Washington, DC 20004
Phone: (202) 727-6365
Fax: (202) 727-6703
www.dcbiz.dc.gov

Wichita, KS
Wichita Regional Chamber of Commerce
350 W Douglas Avennue
Wichita, KS 67202
Phone: (316) 265-7771
www.wichitachamber.org

Wilmington, NC
Wilmington Chamber of Commerce
One Estell Lee Place
Wilmington, NC 28401
Phone: (910) 762-2611
www.wilmingtonchamber.org

Winston-Salem, NC
Winston-Salem Chamber of Commerce
411 West Fourth Street, Suite 211
Winston-Salem, NC 27101
Phone: (336) 728-9200
www.winstonsalem.com

Appendix E: State Departments of Labor

Alabama
Alabama Department of Labor
P.O. Box 303500
Montgomery, AL 36130-3500
Phone: (334) 242-3072
adol.alabama.gov

Alaska
Dept of Labor and Workforce Development
P.O. Box 11149
Juneau, AK 99822-2249
Phone: (907) 465-2700
www.labor.state.ak.us

Arizona
Industrial Commission or Arizona
800 West Washington Street
Phoenix, AZ 85007
Phone: (602) 542-4661
www.azica.gov

Arkansas
Department of Labor
10421 West Markham
Little Rock, AR 72205
Phone: (501) 682-4500
www.labor.ar.gov

California
Labor and Workforce Development
445 Golden Gate Ave., 10th Floor
San Francisco, CA 94102
Phone: (916) 263-1811
www.labor.ca.gov

Colorado
Dept of Labor and Employment
633 17th St., 2nd Floor
Denver, CO 80202-3660
Phone: (888) 390-7936
cdle.colorado.gov

Connecticut
Department of Labor
200 Folly Brook Blvd.
Wethersfield, CT 06109-1114
Phone: (860) 263-6000
www.ctdol.state.ct.us

Delaware
Department of Labor
4425 N. Market St., 4th Floor
Wilmington, DE 19802
Phone: (302) 451-3423
dol.delaware.gov

District of Columbia
Department of Employment Services
614 New York Ave., NE, Suite 300
Washington, DC 20002
Phone: (202) 671-1900
does.dc.gov

Florida
Florida Department of Economic Opportunity
The Caldwell Building
107 East Madison St. Suite 100
Tallahassee, FL 32399-4120
Phone: (800) 342-3450
www.floridajobs.org

Georgia
Department of Labor
Sussex Place, Room 600
148 Andrew Young Intl Blvd., NE
Atlanta, GA 30303
Phone: (404) 656-3011
dol.georgia.gov

Hawaii
Dept of Labor & Industrial Relations
830 Punchbowl Street
Honolulu, HI 96813
Phone: (808) 586-8842
labor.hawaii.gov

Idaho
Department of Labor
317 W. Main St.
Boise, ID 83735-0001
Phone: (208) 332-3579
www.labor.idaho.gov

Illinois
Department of Labor
160 N. LaSalle Street, 13th Floor
Suite C-1300
Chicago, IL 60601
Phone: (312) 793-2800
www.illinois.gov/idol

Indiana
Indiana Department of Labor
402 West Washington Street, Room W195
Indianapolis, IN 46204
Phone: (317) 232-2655
www.in.gov/dol

Iowa
Iowa Workforce Development
1000 East Grand Avenue
Des Moines, IA 50319-0209
Phone: (515) 242-5870
www.iowadivisionoflabor.gov

Kansas
Department of Labor
401 S.W. Topeka Blvd.
Topeka, KS 66603-3182
Phone: (785) 296-5000
www.dol.ks.gov

Kentucky
Department of Labor
1047 U.S. Hwy 127 South, Suite 4
Frankfort, KY 40601-4381
Phone: (502) 564-3070
www.labor.ky.gov

Louisiana
Louisiana Workforce Commission
1001 N. 23rd Street
Baton Rouge, LA 70804-9094
Phone: (225) 342-3111
www.laworks.net

Maine
Department of Labor
45 Commerce Street
Augusta, ME 04330
Phone: (207) 623-7900
www.state.me.us/labor

Maryland
Department of Labor, Licensing & Regulation
500 N. Calvert Street
Suite 401
Baltimore, MD 21202
Phone: (410) 767-2357
www.dllr.state.md.us

Massachusetts
Dept of Labor & Workforce Development
One Ashburton Place
Room 2112
Boston, MA 02108
Phone: (617) 626-7100
www.mass.gov/lwd

Michigan
Department of Licensing and Regulatory Affairs
611 W. Ottawa
P.O. Box 30004
Lansing, MI 48909
Phone: (517) 373-1820
www.michigan.gov/lara

Minnesota
Dept of Labor and Industry
443 Lafayette Road North
Saint Paul, MN 55155
Phone: (651) 284-5070
www.doli.state.mn.us

Mississippi
Dept of Employment Security
P.O. Box 1699
Jackson, MS 39215-1699
Phone: (601) 321-6000
www.mdes.ms.gov

Missouri
Labor and Industrial Relations
P.O. Box 599
3315 W. Truman Boulevard
Jefferson City, MO 65102-0599
Phone: (573) 751-7500
labor.mo.gov

Montana
Dept of Labor and Industry
P.O. Box 1728
Helena, MT 59624-1728
Phone: (406) 444-9091
www.dli.mt.gov

Appendix E: State Departments of Labor

Nebraska
Department of Labor
550 S 16th Street
Lincoln, NE 68508
Phone: (402) 471-9000
dol.nebraska.gov

Nevada
Dept of Business and Industry
3300 W. Sahara Ave, Suite 425
Las Vegas, NV 89102
Phone: (702) 486-2750
business.nv.gov

New Hampshire
Department of Labor
State Office Park South
95 Pleasant Street
Concord, NH 03301
Phone: (603) 271-3176
www.nh.gov/labor

New Jersey
Department of Labor & Workforce Devel.
John Fitch Plaza, 13th Floor, Suite D
Trenton, NJ 08625-0110
Phone: (609) 777-3200
lwd.dol.state.nj.us/labor

New Mexico
Department of Workforce Solutions
401 Broadway, NE
Albuquerque, NM 87103-1928
Phone: (505) 841-8450
www.dws.state.nm.us

New York
Department of Labor
State Office Bldg. # 12
W.A. Harriman Campus
Albany, NY 12240
Phone: (518) 457-9000
www.labor.ny.gov

North Carolina
Department of Labor
4 West Edenton Street
Raleigh, NC 27601-1092
Phone: (919) 733-7166
www.labor.nc.gov

North Dakota
North Dakota Department of Labor and
Human Rights
State Capitol Building
600 East Boulevard, Dept 406
Bismark, ND 58505-0340
Phone: (701) 328-2660
www.nd.gov/labor

Ohio
Department of Commerce
77 South High Street, 22nd Floor
Columbus, OH 43215
Phone: (614) 644-2239
www.com.state.oh.us

Oklahoma
Department of Labor
4001 N. Lincoln Blvd.
Oklahoma City, OK 73105-5212
Phone: (405) 528-1500
www.ok.gov/odol

Oregon
Bureau of Labor and Industries
800 NE Oregon St., #32
Portland, OR 97232
Phone: (971) 673-0761
www.oregon.gov/boli

Pennsylvania
Dept of Labor and Industry
1700 Labor and Industry Bldg
7th and Forster Streets
Harrisburg, PA 17120
Phone: (717) 787-5279
www.dli.pa.gov

Rhode Island
Department of Labor and Training
1511 Pontiac Avenue
Cranston, RI 02920
Phone: (401) 462-8000
www.dlt.state.ri.us

South Carolina
Dept of Labor, Licensing & Regulations
P.O. Box 11329
Columbia, SC 29211-1329
Phone: (803) 896-4300
www.llr.state.sc.us

South Dakota
Department of Labor & Regulation
700 Governors Drive
Pierre, SD 57501-2291
Phone: (605) 773-3682
dlr.sd.gov

Tennessee
Dept of Labor & Workforce Development
Andrew Johnson Tower
710 James Robertson Pkwy
Nashville, TN 37243-0655
Phone: (615) 741-6642
www.tn.gov/workforce

Texas
Texas Workforce Commission
101 East 15th St.
Austin, TX 78778
Phone: (512) 475-2670
www.twc.state.tx.us

Utah
Utah Labor Commission
160 East 300 South, 3rd Floor
Salt Lake City, UT 84114-6600
Phone: (801) 530-6800
laborcommission.utah.gov

Vermont
Department of Labor
5 Green Mountain Drive
P.O. Box 488
Montpelier, VT 05601-0488
Phone: (802) 828-4000
labor.vermont.gov

Virginia
Dept of Labor and Industry
Powers-Taylor Building
13 S. 13th Street
Richmond, VA 23219
Phone: (804) 371-2327
www.doli.virginia.gov

Washington
Dept of Labor and Industries
P.O. Box 44001
Olympia, WA 98504-4001
Phone: (360) 902-4200
www.lni.wa.gov

West Virginia
Division of Labor
749 B Building 6
Capitol Complex
Charleston, WV 25305
Phone: (304) 558-7890
labor.wv.gov

Wisconsin
Dept of Workforce Development
201 E. Washington Ave., #A400
P.O. Box 7946
Madison, WI 53707-7946
Phone: (608) 266-6861
dwd.wisconsin.gov

Wyoming
Department of Workforce Services
1510 East Pershing Blvd.
Cheyenne, WY 82002
Phone: (307) 777-7261
www.wyomingworkforce.org

Titles from Grey House

Visit www.GreyHouse.com for Product Information, Table of Contents, and Sample Pages.

Opinions Throughout History

Opinions Throughout History: Church & State
Opinions Throughout History: Conspiracy Theories
Opinions Throughout History: The Death Penalty
Opinions Throughout History: Diseases & Epidemics
Opinions Throughout History: Domestic Terrorism
Opinions Throughout History: Drug Use & Abuse
Opinions Throughout History: The Environment
Opinions Throughout History: Fame & Celebrity in America
Opinions Throughout History: Free Speech & Censorship
Opinions Throughout History: Gender: Roles & Rights
Opinions Throughout History: Globalization
Opinions Throughout History: Guns in America
Opinions Throughout History: Immigration
Opinions Throughout History: Law Enforcement in America
Opinions Throughout History: LGBTQ+ Rights
Opinions Throughout History: Mental Health
Opinions Throughout History: Nat'l Security vs. Civil & Privacy Rights
Opinions Throughout History: Presidential Authority
Opinions Throughout History: Refugees & Asylum Seekers
Opinions Throughout History: Robotics & Artificial Intelligence
Opinions Throughout History: Social Media Issues
Opinions Throughout History: Spies & Espionage
Opinions Throughout History: The Supreme Court
Opinions Throughout History: Truth & Lies in the Media
Opinions Throughout History: Voters' Rights
Opinions Throughout History: War & the Military
Opinions Throughout History: Workers Rights & Wages

General Reference

American Environmental Leaders
Constitutional Amendments
Encyclopedia of African-American Writing
Encyclopedia of Invasions & Conquests
Encyclopedia of Prisoners of War & Internment
Encyclopedia of the Continental Congresses
Encyclopedia of the United States Cabinet
Encyclopedia of War Journalism
The Environmental Debate
Environmental Sustainability: Skills & Strategies
Financial Literacy Starter Kit
From Suffrage to the Senate
The Gun Debate: Gun Rights & Gun Control in the U.S.
Historical Warrior Peoples & Modern Fighting Groups
Human Rights and the United States
Political Corruption in America
Privacy Rights in the Digital Age
The Religious Right and American Politics
Speakers of the House of Representatives, 1789-2021
US Land & Natural Resources Policy
The Value of a Dollar 1600-1865 Colonial to Civil War
The Value of a Dollar 1860-2024

This is Who We Were

This is Who We Were: Colonial America (1492-1775)
This is Who We Were: Civil War & Reconstruction
This is Who We Were: 1880-1899
This is Who We Were: In the 1900s
This is Who We Were: In the 1910s
This is Who We Were: In the 1920s
This is Who We Were: A Companion to the 1940 Census
This is Who We Were: In the 1940s (1940-1949)
This is Who We Were: In the 1950s
This is Who We Were: In the 1960s
This is Who We Were: In the 1970s
This is Who We Were: In the 1980s
This is Who We Were: In the 1990s
This is Who We Were: In the 2000s
This is Who We Were: In the 2010s

Working Americans

Working Americans—Vol. 1: The Working Class
Working Americans—Vol. 2: The Middle Class
Working Americans—Vol. 3: The Upper Class
Working Americans—Vol. 4: Children
Working Americans—Vol. 5: At War
Working Americans—Vol. 6: Working Women
Working Americans—Vol. 7: Social Movements
Working Americans—Vol. 8: Immigrants
Working Americans—Vol. 9: Revolutionary War to the Civil War
Working Americans—Vol. 10: Sports & Recreation
Working Americans—Vol. 11: Inventors & Entrepreneurs
Working Americans—Vol. 12: Our History through Music
Working Americans—Vol. 13: Education & Educators
Working Americans—Vol. 14: African Americans
Working Americans—Vol. 15: Politics & Politicians
Working Americans—Vol. 16: Farming & Ranching
Working Americans—Vol. 17: Teens in America
Working Americans—Vol. 18: Health Care Workers
Working Americans—Vol. 19: The Performing Arts

Grey House Health & Wellness Guides

Addiction Handbook & Resource Guide
Adolescent Mental Health Handbook & Resource Guide
Anxiety & Stress Handbook & Resource Guide
Attention Disorders Handbook & Resource Guide
The Autism Spectrum Handbook & Resource Guide
Autoimmune Disorders Handbook & Resource Guide
Breast Cancer Handbook & Resource Guide
Cardiovascular Disease Handbook & Resource Guide
Chronic Pain Handbook & Resource Guide
Dementia Handbook & Resource Guide
Depression Handbook & Resource Guide
Diabetes Handbook & Resource Guide
Nutrition, Obesity & Eating Disorders Handbook & Resource Guide

Consumer Health

Complete Mental Health Resource Guide
Complete Resource Guide for Pediatric Disorders
Complete Resource Guide for People with Chronic Illness
Complete Resource Guide for People with Disabilities
Older Americans Information Resource
Parenting: Styles & Strategies
Social Media & Your Mental Health
Teens: Growing Up, Skills & Strategies

Guide to Venture Capital & Private Equity Firms
Hudson's Washington News Media Contacts Guide
New York State Directory
Sports Market Place

Grey House Publishing | Salem Press | H.W. Wilson | 4919 Route 22, PO Box 56, Amenia NY 12501-0056

Grey House Imprints

Visit www.GreyHouse.com for Product Information, Table of Contents, and Sample Pages.

Grey House Titles, continued

Business Information
Business Information Resources
Complete Broadcasting Industry Guide: TV, Radio, Cable & Streaming
Directory of Mail Order Catalogs
Environmental Resource Handbook
Food & Beverage Market Place
Guide to Healthcare Group Purchasing Organizations
Guide to U.S. HMOs and PPOs

Education
Complete Learning Disabilities Resource Guide
Digital Literacy: Skills & Strategies

Statistics & Demographics
America's Top-Rated Cities
America's Top-Rated Smaller Cities
Profiles of California
Profiles of Florida
Profiles of Illinois
Profiles of Indiana
Profiles of Massachusetts
Profiles of Michigan
Profiles of New Jersey
Profiles of New York
Profiles of North Carolina & South Carolina
Profiles of Ohio
Profiles of Pennsylvania
Profiles of Texas
Profiles of Virginia
Profiles of Wisconsin

Canadian Resources
Associations Canada
Canadian Almanac & Directory
Canadian Environmental Resource Guide
Canadian Parliamentary Guide
Canadian Venture Capital & Private Equity Firms
Canadian Who's Who
Cannabis Canada
Careers & Employment Canada
Financial Post: Directory of Directors
Financial Services Canada
FP Bonds: Corporate
FP Bonds: Government
FP Equities: Preferreds & Derivatives
FP Survey: Industrials
FP Survey: Mines & Energy
FP Survey: Predecessor & Defunct
Health Guide Canada
Indigenous History & Culture in Canada
Libraries Canada
Major Canadian Cities: 50 Cities Compared, Ranked & Profiled

Books in Print Series
American Book Publishing Record® Annual
American Book Publishing Record® Monthly
Books In Print®
Books In Print® Supplement
Books Out Loud™
Bowker's Complete Video Directory™
Children's Books In Print®
El-Hi Textbooks & Serials In Print®
Forthcoming Books®
Law Books & Serials In Print™
Medical & Health Care Books In Print™
Publishers, Distributors & Wholesalers of the US™
Subject Guide to Books In Print®
Subject Guide to Children's Books In Print®

Weiss Financial Ratings
Financial Literacy Basics
Financial Literacy: How to Become an Investor
Financial Literacy: Planning for the Future
Weiss Ratings Consumer Guides
Weiss Ratings Guide to Banks
Weiss Ratings Guide to Credit Unions
Weiss Ratings Guide to Health Insurers
Weiss Ratings Guide to Life & Annuity Insurers
Weiss Ratings Guide to Property & Casualty Insurers
Weiss Ratings Investment Research Guide to Bond & Money Market Mutual Funds
Weiss Ratings Investment Research Guide to Exchange-Traded Funds
Weiss Ratings Investment Research Guide to Stock Mutual Funds
Weiss Ratings Investment Research Guide to Stocks

Grey House Publishing | Salem Press | H.W. Wilson | 4919 Route 22, PO Box 56, Amenia NY 12501-0056

Titles from Salem Press

Visit www.SalemPress.com for Product Information, Table of Contents, and Sample Pages.

LITERATURE
Critical Insights: Authors
Louisa May Alcott
Sherman Alexie
Dante Alighieri
Isabel Allende
Maya Angelou
Isaac Asimov
Margaret Atwood
Jane Austen
James Baldwin
Saul Bellow
Roberto Bolano
Ray Bradbury
The Brontë Sisters
Gwendolyn Brooks
Albert Camus
Raymond Carver
Willa Cather
Geoffrey Chaucer
John Cheever
Kate Chopin
Joseph Conrad
Charles Dickens
Emily Dickinson
Frederick Douglass
T. S. Eliot
George Eliot
Harlan Ellison
Ralph Waldo Emerson
Louise Erdrich
William Faulkner
F. Scott Fitzgerald
Gustave Flaubert
Horton Foote
Benjamin Franklin
Robert Frost
Neil Gaiman
Gabriel Garcia Marquez
Thomas Hardy
Nathaniel Hawthorne
Robert A. Heinlein
Lillian Hellman
Ernest Hemingway
Langston Hughes
Zora Neale Hurston
Henry James
Thomas Jefferson
James Joyce
Jamaica Kincaid
Stephen King
Martin Luther King, Jr.
Barbara Kingsolver
Abraham Lincoln
C.S. Lewis
Mario Vargas Llosa
Jack London
James McBride
Cormac McCarthy
Herman Melville
Arthur Miller
Toni Morrison
Alice Munro
Tim O'Brien
Flannery O'Connor
Eugene O'Neill
George Orwell
Sylvia Plath
Edgar Allan Poe
Philip Roth
Salman Rushdie
J.D. Salinger
Mary Shelley
John Steinbeck
Amy Tan
Leo Tolstoy
Mark Twain
John Updike
Kurt Vonnegut
Alice Walker
David Foster Wallace
H. G. Wells
Edith Wharton
Walt Whitman
Oscar Wilde
Tennessee Williams
Virginia Woolf
Richard Wright
Malcolm X

Critical Insights: Works
Absalom, Absalom!
Adventures of Huckleberry Finn
The Adventures of Tom Sawyer
Aeneid
All Quiet on the Western Front
All the Pretty Horses
Animal Farm
Anna Karenina
As You Like It
The Awakening
The Bell Jar
Beloved
Billy Budd, Sailor
The Bluest Eye
The Book Thief
Brave New World
The Canterbury Tales
Catch-22
The Catcher in the Rye
The Color Purple
Crime and Punishment
The Crucible
Death of a Salesman
The Diary of a Young Girl
Dracula
Fahrenheit 451
A Farewell to Arms
Frankenstein; or, The Modern Prometheus
The Grapes of Wrath
Great Expectations
The Great Gatsby
Hamlet
The Handmaid's Tale
Harry Potter Series
Heart of Darkness
The Hobbit
The House on Mango Street
How the Garcia Girls Lost Their Accents
The Hunger Games Trilogy
I Know Why the Caged Bird Sings
In Cold Blood
The Inferno
Invisible Man
Jane Eyre
The Joy Luck Club
Julius Caesar
King Lear
The Kite Runner
Life of Pi
Little Women
Lolita
Lord of the Flies
The Lord of the Rings
Macbeth
The Merchant of Venice
The Metamorphosis
Midnight's Children
A Midsummer Night's Dream
Moby-Dick
Mrs. Dalloway
Native Son
Nineteen Eighty-Four
The Odyssey
Of Mice and Men
The Old Man and the Sea
On the Road
One Flew Over the Cuckoo's Nest
One Hundred Years of Solitude
Othello
The Outsiders
Paradise Lost
The Pearl
The Plague
The Poetry of Baudelaire
The Poetry of Edgar Allan Poe
A Portrait of the Artist as a Young Man
Pride and Prejudice
A Raisin in the Sun
The Red Badge of Courage
Romeo and Juliet
The Scarlet Letter
Sense and Sensibility
Short Fiction of Flannery O'Connor
Slaughterhouse-Five
The Sound and the Fury
A Streetcar Named Desire
The Sun Also Rises
A Tale of Two Cities
The Tales of Edgar Allan Poe
Their Eyes Were Watching God
Things Fall Apart
To Kill a Mockingbird
Twelfth Night, or What You Will
Twelve Years a Slave
War and Peace
The Woman Warrior
Wuthering Heights

Grey House Publishing | Salem Press | H.W. Wilson | 4919 Route 22, PO Box 56, Amenia NY 12501-0056

Titles from Salem Press

Visit www.SalemPress.com for Product Information, Table of Contents, and Sample Pages.

Critical Insights: Themes
The American Comic Book
American Creative Non-Fiction
The American Dream
American Multicultural Identity
American Road Literature
American Short Story
American Sports Fiction
The American Thriller
American Writers in Exile
Censored & Banned Literature
Civil Rights Literature, Past & Present
Coming of Age
Conspiracies
Contemporary Canadian Fiction
Contemporary Immigrant Short Fiction
Contemporary Latin American Fiction
Contemporary Speculative Fiction
Crime and Detective Fiction
Crisis of Faith
Cultural Encounters
Dystopia
Family
The Fantastic
Feminism Flash Fiction
Friendship
Gender, Sex and Sexuality
Going Into the Woods
Good & Evil
The Graphic Novel
Greed
Harlem Renaissance
The Hero's Quest
Historical Fiction
Holocaust Literature
The Immigrant Experience
Inequality
LGBTQ Literature
Literature in Times of Crisis
Literature of Protest
Love
Magical Realism
Midwestern Literature
Modern Japanese Literature
Nature & the Environment
Paranoia, Fear & Alienation
Patriotism
Political Fiction
Postcolonial Literature
Power & Corruption
Pulp Fiction of the '20s and '30s
Rebellion
Russia's Golden Age
Satire
Slave Narrative
Social Justice and American Literature
Southern Gothic Literature
Western Literature
Supernatural
& Humanity
Truth & Lies
Violence in Literature
Virginia Woolf & 20th Century Women Writers
War

Critical Insights: Film
Bonnie & Clyde
Casablanca
Alfred Hitchcock
Stanley Kubrick

Critical Approaches to Literature
Critical Approaches to Literature: Feminist
Critical Approaches to Literature: Moral
Critical Approaches to Literature: Multicultural
Critical Approaches to Literature: Psychological

Literary Classics
Recommended Reading: 600 Classics Reviewed

Novels into Film
Novels into Film: Adaptations & Interpretation
Novels into Film: Adaptations & Interpretation, Volume 2

Critical Surveys of Literature
Critical Survey of American Literature
Critical Survey of Drama
Critical Survey of Long Fiction
Critical Survey of Mystery and Detective Fiction
Critical Survey of Poetry
Critical Survey of Poetry: Contemporary Poets
Critical Survey of Science Fiction & Fantasy Literature
Critical Survey of Shakespeare's Film Adaptations
Critical Survey of Shakespeare's Plays
Critical Survey of Shakespeare's Sonnets
Critical Survey of Short Fiction
Critical Survey of World Literature
Critical Survey of Young Adult Literature

Critical Surveys of Graphic Novels
Heroes & Superheroes
History, Theme, and Technique
Independents & Underground Classics
Manga

Critical Surveys of Mythology & Folklore
Creation Myths
Deadly Battles & Warring Enemies
Gods & Goddesses
Heroes and Heroines
Legendary Creatures
Love, Sexuality, and Desire
World Mythology

Cyclopedia of Literary Characters & Places
Cyclopedia of Literary Characters
Cyclopedia of Literary Places

Grey House Publishing | Salem Press | H.W. Wilson | 4919 Route 22, PO Box 56, Amenia NY 12501-0056

Titles from Salem Press

Visit www.SalemPress.com for Product Information, Table of Contents, and Sample Pages.

Introduction to Literary Context
American Poetry of the 20th Century
American Post-Modernist Novels
American Short Fiction
English Literature
Plays
World Literature

Magill's Literary Annual
Magill's Literary Annual, Annual Editions 1977-2024

Masterplots
Masterplots, Fourth Edition
Masterplots, 2010-2018 Supplement

Notable Writers
Notable African American Writers
Notable American Women Writers
Notable Horror Fiction Writers
Notable Mystery & Detective Fiction Writers
Notable Writers of the American West & the Native American Experience
Notable Writers of LGBTQ+ Literature

HISTORY
The Decades
The 1900s in America
The 1910s in America
The Twenties in America
The Thirties in America
The Forties in America
The Fifties in America
The Sixties in America
The Seventies in America
The Eighties in America
The Nineties in America
The 2000s in America
The 2010s in America

Defining Documents in American History
Defining Documents: The 1900s
Defining Documents: The 1910s
Defining Documents: The 1920s
Defining Documents: The 1930s
Defining Documents: The 1950s
Defining Documents: The 1960s
Defining Documents: The 1970s
Defining Documents: The 1980s
Defining Documents: American Citizenship
Defining Documents: The American Economy
Defining Documents: The American Revolution
Defining Documents: The American West
Defining Documents: Business Ethics
Defining Documents: Capital Punishment
Defining Documents: Censorship
Defining Documents: Civil Rights
Defining Documents: Civil War
Defining Documents: Conservatism
Defining Documents: The Constitution
Defining Documents: The Cold War
Defining Documents: Dissent & Protest
Defining Documents: Domestic Terrorism & Extremism
Defining Documents: Drug Policy
Defining Documents: The Emergence of Modern America
Defining Documents: Environment & Conservation
Defining Documents: Espionage & Intrigue
Defining Documents: Exploration and Colonial America
Defining Documents: The First Amendment
Defining Documents: The Free Press
Defining Documents: The Great Depression
Defining Documents: The Great Migration
Defining Documents: The Gun Debate
Defining Documents: Immigration & Immigrant Communities
Defining Documents: The Legacy of 9/11
Defining Documents: LGBTQ+
Defining Documents: Liberalism
Defining Documents: Manifest Destiny and the New Nation
Defining Documents: Native Americans
Defining Documents: Political Campaigns, Candidates & Discourse
Defining Documents: Postwar 1940s
Defining Documents: Prison Reform
Defining Documents: The Salem Witch Trials
Defining Documents: Secrets, Leaks & Scandals
Defining Documents: Slavery
Defining Documents: Supreme Court Decisions
Defining Documents: Reconstruction Era
Defining Documents: The Vietnam War
Defining Documents: The Underground Railroad
Defining Documents: U.S. Involvement in the Middle East
Defining Documents: Voters' Rights
Defining Documents: Watergate
Defining Documents: Workers' Rights
Defining Documents: World War I
Defining Documents: World War II

Defining Documents in World History
Defining Documents: The 17th Century
Defining Documents: The 18th Century
Defining Documents: The 19th Century
Defining Documents: The 20th Century (1900-1950)
Defining Documents: The Ancient World
Defining Documents: Asia
Defining Documents: Genocide & the Holocaust
Defining Documents: Human Rights
Defining Documents: The Middle Ages
Defining Documents: The Middle East
Defining Documents: Nationalism & Populism
Defining Documents: The Nuclear Age
Defining Documents: Pandemics, Plagues & Public Health
Defining Documents: Religious Freedom & Religious Persecution
Defining Documents: Renaissance & Early Modern Era
Defining Documents: Revolutions
Defining Documents: The Rise & Fall of the Soviet Union
Defining Documents: Treason
Defining Documents: Women's Rights

Grey House Publishing | Salem Press | H.W. Wilson | 4919 Route 22, PO Box 56, Amenia NY 12501-0056

Titles from Salem Press

Visit www.SalemPress.com for Product Information, Table of Contents, and Sample Pages.

Great Events from History
Great Events from History: American History, Exploration to the Colonial Era, 1492-1775
Great Events from History: American History, Forging a New Nation, 1775-1850
Great Events from History: American History, War, Peace & Growth, 1850-1918
Great Events from History: The Ancient World
Great Events from History: The Middle Ages
Great Events from History: The Renaissance & Early Modern Era
Great Events from History: The 17th Century
Great Events from History: The 18th Century
Great Events from History: The 19th Century
Great Events from History: The 20th Century, 1901-1940
Great Events from History: The 20th Century, 1941-1970
Great Events from History: The 20th Century, 1971-2000
Great Events from History: Modern Scandals
Great Events from History: African American History
Great Events from History: The 21st Century, 2000-2016
Great Events from History: LGBTQ Events
Great Events from History: Human Rights
Great Events from History: Women's History

Great Lives from History
Great Athletes
Great Athletes of the Twenty-First Century
Great Lives from History: The 17th Century
Great Lives from History: The 18th Century
Great Lives from History: The 19th Century
Great Lives from History: The 20th Century
Great Lives from History: The 21st Century, 2000-2017
Great Lives from History: African Americans
Great Lives from History: The Ancient World
Great Lives from History: American Heroes
Great Lives from History: American Women
Great Lives from History: Asian and Pacific Islander Americans
Great Lives from History: Autocrats & Dictators
Great Lives from History: The Incredibly Wealthy
Great Lives from History: Inventors & Inventions
Great Lives from History: Jewish Americans
Great Lives from History: Latinos
Great Lives from History: LGBTQ+
Great Lives from History: The Middle Ages
Great Lives from History: The Renaissance & Early Modern Era
Great Lives from History: Scientists and Science

History & Government
American First Ladies
American Presidents
The 50 States
The Ancient World: Extraordinary People in Extraordinary Societies
The Bill of Rights
The Criminal Justice System
 S. Court Cases
 U.S. Supreme Court

SOCIAL SCIENCES
Civil Rights Movements: Past & Present
Countries, Peoples and Cultures
Countries: Their Wars & Conflicts: A World Survey
Education Today: Issues, Policies & Practices
Encyclopedia of American Immigration
Ethics: Questions & Morality of Human Actions
Issues in U.S. Immigration
Principles of Sociology: Group Relationships & Behavior
Principles of Sociology: Personal Relationships & Behavior
Principles of Sociology: Societal Issues & Behavior
Racial & Ethnic Relations in America
Weapons, Warfare & Military Technology
World Geography

HEALTH
Addictions, Substance Abuse & Alcoholism
Adolescent Health & Wellness
Aging
Cancer
Community & Family Health Issues
Integrative, Alternative & Complementary Medicine
Genetics and Inherited Conditions
Infectious Diseases and Conditions
Magill's Medical Guide
Men's Health
Nutrition
Parenting: Styles & Strategies
Psychology & Behavioral Health
Social Media & Your Mental Health
Teens: Growing Up, Skills & Strategies
Women's Health

Principles of Health
Principles of Health: Allergies & Immune Disorders
Principles of Health: Anxiety & Stress
Principles of Health: Depression
Principles of Health: Diabetes
Principles of Health: Hypertension
Principles of Health: Nursing
Principles of Health: Obesity
Principles of Health: Occupational Therapy & Physical Therapy
Principles of Health: Pain Management
Principles of Health: Prescription Drug Abuse
Principles of Health: Whole Body Wellness

BUSINESS
Principles of Business: Accounting
Principles of Business: Economics
Principles of Business: Entrepreneurship
Principles of Business: Finance
Principles of Business: Globalization
Principles of Business: Leadership
Principles of Business: Management
Principles of Business: Marketing

Grey House Publishing | Salem Press | H.W. Wilson | 4919 Route 22, PO Box 56, Amenia NY 12501-0056

Titles from Salem Press

Visit www.SalemPress.com for Product Information, Table of Contents, and Sample Pages.

SCIENCE
Ancient Creatures
Applied Science
Applied Science: Engineering & Mathematics
Applied Science: Science & Medicine
Applied Science: Technology
Biomes and Ecosystems
Digital Literacy: Skills & Strategies
Earth Science: Earth Materials and Resources
Earth Science: Earth's Surface and History
Earth Science: Earth's Weather, Water and Atmosphere
Earth Science: Physics and Chemistry of the Earth
Encyclopedia of Climate Change
Encyclopedia of Energy
Encyclopedia of Environmental Issues
Encyclopedia of Global Resources
Encyclopedia of Mathematics and Society
Environmental Sustainability: Skills & Strategies
Forensic Science
Notable Natural Disasters
The Solar System
USA in Space

Principles of Science
Principles of Aeronautics
Principles of Anatomy
Principles of Archaeology
Principles of Architecture
Principles of Astronomy
Principles of Behavioral Science
Principles of Biology
Principles of Biotechnology
Principles of Botany
Principles of Chemistry
Principles of Climatology
Principles of Computer-aided Design
Principles of Computer Science
Principles of Cybersecurity
Principles of Digital Arts & Multimedia
Principles of Ecology
Principles of Energy
Principles of Environmental Engineering
Principles of Fire Science
Principles of Food Science
Principles of Forestry & Conservation
Principles of Geology
Principles of Graphic Design & Typography
Principles of Information Technology
Principles of Marine Science
Principles of Mass Communication
Principles of Mathematics
Principles of Mechanics
Principles of Microbiology
Principles of Modern Agriculture
Principles of Pharmacology
Principles of Physical Science
Principles of Physics
Principles of Probability & Statistics
Principles of Programming & Coding
Principles of Robotics & Artificial Intelligence
Principles of Scientific Research
Principles of Sports Medicine & Exercise Science
Principles of Sustainability
Principles of Zoology

CAREERS
Careers: Paths to Entrepreneurship
Careers in Archaeology & Museum Services
Careers in Artificial Intelligence
Careers in the Arts: Fine, Performing & Visual
Careers in the Automotive Industry
Careers in Biology
Careers in Biotechnology
Careers in Building Construction
Careers in Business
Careers in Chemistry
Careers in Communications & Media
Careers in Criminal Justice
Careers in Culinary Arts
Careers in Cybersecurity
Careers in Earth Science
Careers in Education & Training
Careers in Engineering
Careers in Environment & Conservation
Careers in Financial Services
Careers in Fish & Wildlife
Careers in Forensic Science
Careers in Gaming
Careers in Green Energy
Careers in Healthcare
Careers in Heavy Equipment Operation, Maintenance & Repair
Careers in Hospitality & Tourism
Careers in Human Services
Careers in Illustration & Animation
Careers in Information Technology
Careers in Intelligence & National Security
Careers in Law, Criminal Justice & Emergency Services
Careers in Mass Communication
Careers in the Music Industry
Careers in Manufacturing & Production
Careers in Medical Technology
Careers in Nursing
Careers in Physics
Careers in Protective Services
Careers in Psychology & Behavioral Health
Careers in Public Administration
Careers in Sales, Insurance & Real Estate
Careers in Science & Engineering
Careers in Social Media
Careers in Sports & Fitness
Careers in Sports Medicine & Training
Careers in Technical Services & Equipment Repair
Careers in Transportation
Careers in Travel & Adventure
Careers in Writing & Editing
Careers Outdoors
Careers Overseas
Careers Working with Infants & Children
Careers Working with Animals

Grey House Publishing | Salem Press | H.W. Wilson | 4919 Route 22, PO Box 56, Amenia NY 12501-0056

Titles from H.W. Wilson

Visit www.HWWilsonInPrint.com for Product Information, Table of Contents, and Sample Pages.

The Reference Shelf
Affordable Housing
Aging in America
Alternative Facts, Post-Truth and the Information War
The American Dream
Artificial Intelligence
Book Bans & Censorship
The Business of Food
Campaign Trends & Election Law
College Sports
Democracy Evolving
The Digital Age
Embracing New Paradigms in Education
Food Insecurity & Hunger in the United States
Future of U.S. Economic Relations: Mexico, Cuba, & Venezuela
Gene Editing & Genetic Engineering
Global Climate Change
Guns in America
Hacktivism
Hate Crimes
Health Conspiracies
Immigration & Border Control in the 21st Century
Income Inequality
Internet Abuses & Privacy Rights
Internet Law
Labor Unions
LGBTQ in the 21st Century
Marijuana Reform
Mental Health Awareness
Money in Politics
National Debate Topic 2020/2021: Criminal Justice Reform
National Debate Topic 2021/2022: Water Resources
National Debate Topic 2022/2023: Emerging Technologies & International Security
National Debate Topic 2023/2024: Economic Inequality
National Debate Topic 2024/2025: Intellectual Property Rights
National Debate Topic 2025/2026: The Arctic
New Developments in Artificial Intelligence
New Frontiers in Space
Policing in 2020
Pollution
Prescription Drug Abuse
Propaganda and Misinformation
Racial Tension in a Postracial Age
Reality Television
Renewable Energy
Representative American Speeches, Annual Editions
Reproductive Rights
Rethinking Work
Revisiting Gender
Russia & Ukraine
The South China Sea Conflict
Space Exploration
Sports in America
The Supreme Court
The Transformation of American Cities
 Two Koreas
 s
   ations
     Rights
       wers

Core Collections
Children's Core Collection
Fiction Core Collection
Graphic Novels Core Collection
Middle & Junior High School Core
Public Library Core Collection: Nonfiction
Senior High Core Collection
Young Adult Fiction Core Collection

Current Biography
Current Biography Cumulative Index 1946-2025
Current Biography Magazine
Current Biography Yearbook

Readers' Guide to Periodical Literature
Abridged Readers' Guide to Periodical Literature
Readers' Guide to Periodical Literature

Indexes
Index to Legal Periodicals & Books
Short Story Index

Sears List
Sears List of Subject Headings
Sears List of Subject Headings, Online Database

History
American Game Changers: Invention, Innovation & Transformation
American Reformers
Speeches of the American Presidents

Facts About Series
Facts About the 20th Century
Facts About American Immigration
Facts About China
Facts About the Presidents
Facts About the World's Languages

Nobel Prize Winners
Nobel Prize Winners: 1901-1986
Nobel Prize Winners: 1987-1991
Nobel Prize Winners: 1992-1996
Nobel Prize Winners: 1997-2001
Nobel Prize Winners: 2002-2018

Famous First Facts
Famous First Facts
Famous First Facts About American Politics
Famous First Facts About Sports
Famous First Facts About the Environment
Famous First Facts: International Edition

American Book of Days
The American Book of Days
The International Book of Days

Grey House Publishing | Salem Press | H.W. Wilson | 4919 Route 22, PO Box 56, Amenia NY 12501-0056